# Emma Goldman

For Gloria Eire
~ with appreciation
and solidarity!
It is an honor to know
that you are drawn
to honoring the memory
of your parents
in our Emma Goldman
collection

~~wishes you well

See ~ "791, 786

Candace Falk
22 May 2022
Emma Goldman Papers
Public history
project

Berkeley CA

**EMMA GOLDMAN**
A DOCUMENTARY HISTORY
OF THE AMERICAN YEARS

Candace Falk, EDITOR
Barry Pateman, ASSOCIATE EDITOR
Susan Wengraf, ILLUSTRATIONS EDITOR
Robert Cohen, CONSULTING EDITOR

1. *Made for America, 1890–1901*
2. *Making Speech Free, 1902–1909*
3. *Light and Shadows, 1910–1916*

# Emma Goldman

## A DOCUMENTARY HISTORY OF THE AMERICAN YEARS

VOLUME THREE

## Light and Shadows, 1910–1916

CANDACE FALK • EDITOR

BARRY PATEMAN • ASSOCIATE EDITOR

SUSAN WENGRAF • ILLUSTRATIONS EDITOR

ROBERT COHEN • CONSULTING EDITOR

STANFORD UNIVERSITY PRESS

*Stanford, California*

FRONTISPIECE

Emma Goldman, ca. 1910. Gerhard Sisters Studio (International Institute for Social History)

Stanford University Press
Stanford, California

This book has been published with the assistance of the National Historical
Publications and Records Commission.

Library of Congress Cataloging-in-Publication Data

Emma Goldman: a documentary history of the American years / Candace
Falk, editor; Barry Pateman, associate editor
   p.    cm.
   Includes bibliographical references and index.
   ISBN 978-0-8047-7854-1 (v.3: alk.paper).

   1. Goldman, Emma, 1869–1940.   2. Anarchists—United States—
Biography.   3. Anarchism—United States—History—Sources.
4. Freedom of Speech—United States—History —Sources.   I. Title.—
Documentary history of the American years.   II. Goldman, Emma, 1869–
1940.   III. Falk, Candace, 1947–   IV. Pateman, Barry 1952–
   HX843.7G65 E427   2012
   335'.83'092—dc22

Printed in the United States of America on acid-free, archival-quality paper.

Typeset by BookMatters in 9.5/14 Scala Pro.

We dedicate our book with love and gratitude to Lois Blum Feinblatt,
passionate advocate of social justice,
a woman who affirms the life force of the myriads in her midst
dear friend, anchor, and inspiration

## SPONSORS

*The Emma Goldman Papers thanks all of our supporters, including these sustaining sponsors for the volumes, for helping to keep history alive through their generous contributions.*

National Historical Publications and Records Commission

University of California, Berkeley, Office of the Vice Chancellor for Research: Joseph Cerny, Vice Chancellor for Research and Graduate Dean (1994–2000); Linda Fabbri, Assistant Vice Chancellor for Research; SusanHirano, Budget Director

University of California, Berkeley, Department of International and Area Studies: John Lie, Dean of International and Area Studies; Joan Kask, Associate Dean of International and Area Studies; Charlene Nicholas, Mary Lewis, and Susan Meyers, Budget and Personnel Officers

Leon F. Litwack, Alexander F. and May T. Morrison Professor of American History

Edwin M. Epstein, Former Chair of Peace and Conflict Studies

Lois Blum Feinblatt, Irving and Lois BlumFoundation

Furthermore: A Project of the J.M. Kaplan Fund

Milken Family Foundation

National Endowment for the Humanities (2002–2003), (2010–2012), & (2012–2014)

Samuel Rubin Foundation

Stephen M. Silberstein

Judith Taylor

Anonymous

---

Alice Merner Agogino

Harriet Alonso

Carol Amyx

Elizabeth Anderson and the late Henry Mayer

Eric Berg

Sheila Biddle

Carolyn Patty Blum and Harry Chotiner

The late Art and Libera Bortolotti

Ben and Ida Capes family: Susan Chasson, David and Judith Capes, Bonnie Capes Tabatznik, and Albert and Marlene Chasson

Mecca Reitman Carpenter

Yvette Chalom and Paul Fogel

Mariam Chamberlain

The late Marcus Cohn

Patrick Coughlin

Tom Debley and Mary Jane Holmes

Barbara Dobkin

Martin Duberman

# CONTENTS

# ILLUSTRATIONS

Lunching in Paris with Emma Goldman, Theodore Dreiser pleaded with her, "You must write the story of your life, E.G.; it is the richest of any woman's of our century." It had not been the first time a friend had suggested that she chronicle her life. With the assistance of her comrades, she heeded the advice, collected the necessary funds, and began to write her remarkable autobiography, *Living My Life*. Goldman wanted very much to share her life, thoughts, and struggles with the people she had sought to influence and change, and she hoped the publisher, Alfred A. Knopf, would charge a minimal sum for the book. "I am anxious to reach the mass of the American reading public," she wrote a friend, "not so much because of the royalties, but because I have always worked for the mass."

Emma Goldman succeeded in a variety of ways in reaching "the mass," both a reading and listening audience. *Living My Life* went through several editions, her life has been portrayed on film and in song as well as on stage, and numerous biographies have been written. None of these, however, is as critical as the publication of the four volumes of selected letters, speeches, government documents, and commentaries from the Emma Goldman Papers Project, making that vast and invaluable resource available to scholars, students, and a reading public throughout the world.

This is a truly remarkable achievement, the culmination of several decades of collaborative work, including an international search for documents, the identification of correspondents, and the preparation of biographical, historical, and bibliographical guides. To appreciate the magnitude of this task is to know that Goldman's papers were as scattered as her scores of correspondents, in private collections and archives here and abroad, even in places like the Department of Justice, whose agents had seized a portion of her papers before ordering her deportation. Only the commitment of many friends and comrades over many decades, and the untiring efforts of librarians, scholars, and archivists, have made these volumes possible.

In closing her autobiography, Emma Goldman reflected over her tumultuous years on this earth: "My life—I had lived in its heights and its depths, in bitter sorrow and ecstatic joy, in black despair and fervent hope. I had drunk the cup to the last drop. I had lived my life. Would I had the gift to paint the life I had lived!" It will now be left to scores of scholars, students, artists, and dramatists to use this extensive collection to enrich their accounts of an extraordinary career. This is more, however, than material for future biographers; it is an indispensable collection for studying the history of American social movements. That is clear from the moment one scans the list of Goldman correspondents and finds the names of some of the leading cultural and political figures of her time, alongside the names of less known but no less important men and women who shared—and did not share—her commitments.

Emma Goldman came out of a unique and expressive subculture that flourished in America in the late nineteenth and early twentieth centuries. The participants included some of the nation's most creative and iconoclastic artists, writers, and intellectuals, most of them libertarians, some of them revolutionaries. What drew them together was their rejection of the inequities of capitalism and the absurdities of bourgeois culture and politics. That led them to embrace such causes as the labor movement, sexual and reproductive freedom, feminism, atheism, anarchism, and socialism. They represented everything that was irreverent and blasphemous in American culture. In their lives and in their work, they dedicated themselves to the vision of a free society of liberated individuals. They were too undisciplined, too free-spirited to adapt to any system or bureaucratic structure that rested on the suppression of free thought, whether in Woodrow Wilson's United States or in Vladimir Lenin's Soviet Russia. "All I want is freedom," Emma Goldman declared, "perfect, unrestricted liberty for myself and others."

The economic depression of the 1890s introduced Americans to scenes that contradicted the dominant success creed—unemployment, poverty, labor violence, urban ghettos, and, in 1894, an army of the unemployed marching on the nation's capital. In that spirit, Emma Goldman engaged herself in these struggles, employing her oratorical powers to stir audiences and awaken them to the perils of capitalism and the violence of poverty. According to newspaper accounts of her address in 1893 to a crowd of unemployed workers in New York City's Union Square, Goldman implored them, "Demonstrate before the palaces of the rich, demand work. If they do not give you work, demand bread. If they deny you both, take bread. It is your sacred right." That statement was Goldman at her oratorical best, and it did not go unnoticed. For her exhortation she was arrested, convicted, and sentenced to a year's imprisonment. It would be only one of many arrests, whether for lecturing on anarchism, circulating birth control information, advocating workers' and women's rights, or opposing war and the military draft.

The life of Emma Goldman is a forcible reminder that the right to free expression in America has always been precarious. Intellectual inquiry and dissent have been perceived—often for good reason—as subversive activities, and they have, in fact, been known to topple institutions and discredit beliefs of long standing. To be identified as public enemies, to be hounded as disturbers of the peace, was the price Goldman and her comrades paid for their intellectual curiosity, expression, and agitation. During her lifetime, Emma Goldman was denounced for godlessness, debauchery, free thinking, subversion, and for exposing people within the sound of her voice to radical and unconventional ideas. Her life provides a unique perspective on the varieties of anarchist and feminist thought, radical and socialist movements in the late nineteenth and early twentieth centuries and the causes championed, the position of women in American society (and within radical organizations), and the political repression that followed the outbreak of World War I and the imprisonment and political exile of dissenters. In 1919, Goldman was deported to Soviet Russia, where she found something less than a revolutionary utopia. Her stay in Moscow provides an intimate glimpse of both the promise of the Russian Revolution to American radicals and their subsequent disillusionment with its betrayal. Her exile continued in Germany, France, Britain, and Canada, bringing her finally into the Spanish Civil War and still another chapter in the turbulent history of radicalism in the twentieth century.

Since the birth of the United States, Americans have struggled to define the meaning of freedom. That has often been a difficult and perilous struggle. For Emma Goldman, freedom required individuals to shake off the "shackles and restraints of government." The price of freedom, she came to recognize, was eternal vigilance, a wariness of those who in the name of protecting freedom would diminish freedom, and resistance to rules, codes, regulations, and censorship (no matter how well intended) that would mock free expression by restricting or penalizing it. Free speech meant not only the right to dissent but more importantly the active exercise of that right in the face of attempts to suppress it. And, perhaps most important of all, it insisted on the right of others to speak out on behalf of what the majority believed to be wrong, freedom for the most offensive and disturbing speech. That was the true test of freedom of speech. "Free speech," Goldman declared, "means either the unlimited right of expression, or nothing at all. The moment any man or set of men can limit speech, it is no longer free."

What Emma Goldman said provoked controversy, both within and outside the radical movement, and not all radicals were enamored with her political positions. Margaret Anderson, a radical editor and literary modernist, appreciated Goldman's sheer presence more than her ideological commitments: "Emma Goldman's genius is not so much that she is a great thinker as that she is a great woman." But whatever one might think of Emma Goldman's political views, actions, blind spots, and vision, few individuals in American society so exemplify the tradition of dissent and nonconformity. Few brought more passion, intensity, exuberance, perseverance, and self-sacrifice to the causes she espoused. Even when she failed to convert people to her positions, she compelled many of them to reexamine their assumptions and to question the accepted wisdom and elected leadership.

For much of her life in America, Emma Goldman defined the limits of political dissent. True loyalty to a nation, she believed, often demanded disloyalty to its pretenses and policies and a willingness to unmask its leaders. To Goldman, liberty was more than an ideology, it was a passion, to be lived and breathed each day. "Liberty was always her theme," said Harry Weinberger, her lawyer and close friend: "liberty was always her dream; liberty was always her goal . . . liberty was more important than life itself." And, as he went on to suggest, free expression has always led a precarious existence. "She spoke out in this country against war and conscription, and went to jail. She spoke out for political prisoners, and was deported. She spoke out in Russia against the despotism of Communism, and again became a fugitive on the face of the earth. She spoke out against Nazism and the combination of Nazism and Communism and there was hardly a place where she could live."

It must be said, however, that Goldman did not speak out with equal fervor about the most repressive and violent denial of human rights in her lifetime. She identified with the struggles of oppressed workers, and the New Declaration of Independence she issued in 1909 proclaimed that "all human beings, irrespective of race, color, or sex, are born with the equal right to share at the table of life." But in a time of racist terror and severe racial subjugation (political, social, and economic), far more severe than any of the violations of civil liberties she so courageously deplored and fought, Emma Goldman avoided the South and mostly ignored the struggle for black rights and racial equality, a struggle that involved not only black Americans but a coterie of progressive white allies. Perhaps she was trying to appease the racism pervading the labor and socialist movements. More likely, she was unconscious of this contradiction in her life's commitment to "the wretched of the earth." Whatever her personal feelings about these matters, they would occupy little space in her writings or speeches, and hence are mostly absent from these volumes.

The Emma Goldman Papers Project at the University of California at Berkeley, in selecting, editing, and annotating the documents for this valuable series under the direction of Candace Falk, has brought into our historical consciousness a most extraordinary woman, whose passion, spiritual qualities, and commitments illuminate a certain time in our history, even as the lesson she taught remains timeless: that social and economic inequities are neither unintentional nor inevitable but reflect the assumptions, beliefs, and policies of certain people who command enormous power over lives. Her life forces us to think more deeply and more reflectively about those men and women in our history—from the abolitionists of the 1830s to the labor organizers of the 1890s and 1930s to the civil rights activists of the 1960s—who, individually and collectively, tried to flesh out and give meaning to abstract notions of liberty, independence, and freedom, and for whom a personal commitment to social justice became a moral imperative. No better epitaph might be written for Emma Goldman than the one composed in 1917 by A. S. Embree, an organizer for the Industrial Workers of the World imprisoned in Tombstone, Arizona: "The end in view is well worth striving for, but in the struggle itself lies the happiness of the fighter."

LEON LITWACK,
MORRISON PROFESSOR
OF AMERICAN HISTORY,
BERKELEY, CALIFORNIA

*The following introductory essay attempts to re-create the experience of being immersed in a documentary archive where themes and variations surface and resurface to create a textural weave where those who are little known are valued no less than those who are well known in the assembling of a flesh-and-blood portrait of one woman's life. As in volumes 1 and 2 of* **Emma Goldman: A Documentary History of the American Years,** *each of the sections—1. The Arc of Her Story, 2. A Historical Context, 3. Chronological Narrative Weaving Through the Texts: Year by Year, and 4. A Long View: Light Defining Shadows—of the introductory essay stands alone and begins anew, allowing the reader to become familiar with the stories within the stories, as they are told and retold.*

## 1. THE ARC OF HER STORY

Emma Goldman could not have known at the time that the years from 1910 to 1916 would be her most prolific, perhaps the most celebrated period of her entire life.[1] Reveling in love and in anarchy, immersed in visions of social harmony, dissent against injustice, and interest in the new, Goldman blossomed as a political theorist, writer, and orator. The circles of her influence radiated away from the predominantly immigrant radical culture of New York City's Lower East Side and moved across town just a few blocks west to the milieu of the bohemians and radical intellectuals of Greenwich Village. The setting was, in some ways, reminiscent of her youth in St. Petersburg, where she read revolutionary novels that prefigured new ways of living, loving, and theorizing, and where militants plotted the assassination of the tsar. Goldman, a cultural hybrid, strove to create an American counterpart to the vanguard intelligentsia of Russia, one grounded in the free flow of ideas, a sense of imminent change, and an indefatigable quest for justice. In the process she attempted to forge a place in the American consciousness that

---

1. See Candace Falk, "Let Icons Be Bygones!—Emma Goldman, the Grand Expositor," in *Feminist Interpretations of Emma Goldman*, eds. P. Weiss and L. Kinzinger (University Park: Penn State University Press, 2008), especially pp. 43–44.

tapped her remarkable ability to articulate the wrongs of the time and to offer an almost unfathomable, but nonetheless appealing, vision of how to right them.

She traveled across her adopted country, speaking in cities and towns in an effort to dispel preconceptions of anarchism as dangerous and foreign and instead promote the idea that anarchism was indigenous to the American spirit of individual liberty and its national pledge to freedom and justice for all. In so doing, Goldman often temporarily succeeded in convincing her audiences that she was neither fearsome nor dangerous.

Anarchism was a cause widely misunderstood. Although anarchist ideas were intended to be a catalyst for the realization of a more harmonious world, many of its adherents, anxious for a more immediate reversal of injustice, resorted to violent tactics to instill terror in the hearts of those who abused their power. Stories of assassination attempts on the tsar remained etched into Goldman's soul, the shadowy edges of ever-present violence regardless of how brilliant the light of her glorious vision. She was well aware of the dangers that accompanied her commitment to anarchism—arrest, imprisonment, expulsion, or even death—and seemed unfazed by the improbabilities of its realization in her lifetime. Like most visionaries, however, she sometimes experienced the melancholy chasm between what was and what could be—and wondered, in a country that strives to guarantee life, liberty, and the pursuit of happiness—"Who can boast of happyness?"[2]

## BRUTALITY AND BENEVOLENCE IN AN ERA OF PROGRESSIVE REFORM

Whatever one's interpretation of the actual intent and impact of the Progressive era, at its best it signaled a world of new possibility to liberals, who were moving into the White House, Congress, and both state and city governments and enacting historic reform legislation. Earnest reformers tried to implement good government laws and practices, and women experienced new freedoms and the promise of fuller participation in the public sphere.[3] Social welfare reforms like improved sanitation, transportation, and access to education could be felt across a large spectrum of the population.

It was also the heyday of muckraking—with sensational exposés of the underside of industrial capitalism a consistent feature in the daily news. People were shaken by tragic events across the country. Among the most horrific was the fire that broke out in 1911 in the Triangle Shirtwaist Company's factory on the top floors of New York's Asch Building, where 146 mostly immigrant women garment workers, locked in by their bosses, died in the fire or jumped from factory windows to their deaths. The fire's cause,

2. EG to Max Nettlau, 17 October 1907, see vol. 2, *Making Speech Free*, pp. 250–51 (also in Max Nettlau Archive, IISH and *EGP*, reel 2); see also Candace Falk, *Love, Anarchy and Emma Goldman*, rev. ed. (New Brunswick, N.J.: Rutgers University Press, 1999), chap. 3, p. 43 (abbreviated hereafter as *LA&EG*).

3. See section 2 of this introduction for background on the variety of issues and trends critical to an understanding of the changing conditions and attitudes of the time.

according to Goldman,[4] was "economic and social pressure—the squeezing of souls into dollars. The slave-driving employer squeezes his sweatshop employees into coin, but he likewise wrings his own soul from his body in that ever-lasting greed. It is this which permits him to erect ten-story sweatshops, where 100 helpless girls can lose their lives in less than half an hour." Reported widely in the city's newspapers, the event shook many middle-class readers out of their complacency to the plight of industrial workers. Existing laws mandating safer working conditions and barring child labor were enforced with a new sense of urgency. Workplace battles for unionization spread across the country like a prairie fire.

At the same time, however, the era was marked by rampant industrial violence and the frequent presence of company-hired agents of the Pinkerton Detective Agency and Burns Detective Agency, working in tandem with federal troops to suppress and defuse countless strikes. Unequal access to work was affected by many factors. Segregation, with its purported separate-but-equal ideology, limited rights and possibilities of African Americans, especially in the South where conditions were predominantly separate-because-unequal.[5] Anti-immigrant laws, too, created uncertainty among those who encountered prejudice in a country that had been upheld as the land of opportunity. Their tenuous status was well understood by African Americans, who, unlike many of the European immigrants, could never blend into the culture of white privilege, even if they had achieved economic or intellectual status within their own race. Class differences cut across the lines of race, leaving the poor vulnerable to unsafe workplaces and widespread disease, while the privileged enjoyed lives of relative security.

These countervailing and inconsistent tendencies created the dynamic tension that characterized this era of change, with its mixture of inclusion and exclusion, of benevolence and brutality, of community and alienation, of hope and despair.

### THE ANARCHIST TAUNT: CAPITALISM EXPOSED

As an anarchist Goldman was convinced that the practice of gradualism diminished the possibility of lasting constructive change; it masked the destructive dynamic of unrelenting, seemingly ever-adaptive profit-driven capitalism. She was certain that no significant economic or political transformation was possible without a grand-scale social and cultural shift embodied in individual enlightenment. Like many of her anarchist

---

4. "Emma Goldman Blames Greed for Holocaust," *Omaha World Herald*, 27 March 1911, Emma Goldman Papers, office newsclipping files.

5. In the context of the African American experience the gradualism of reform, while generally benefiting sanitation, transportation, and other areas, was also deemed to be too slow moving by many African American radical reformers. In many cases loopholes in the laws allowed for the exclusion of African Americans. Separate reform groups emerged from within the black community to address the problems often disregarded by white reformers. See, for example, Dorothy Schneider and Carl J. Schneider, "Black Women on the Move," in *American Women in the Progressive Era, 1900–1920* (New York: FactsOnFile, 1993), pp. 115–26. See also the Bibliography for other sources.

comrades, she feared that reforms would ameliorate underlying problems (including inherent income gaps), resulting in short-term improvement with little long-term effect.

To Goldman, compromise in the name of pragmatism seemed to be the fatal flaw common to even the most well-meaning politicians, liberal reformers, and socialists. Most liberal reformers not only dismissed the anarchist's blanket rejection of the state as unrealistic and essentially impossible (even if they acknowledged the worthiness of its intent), but also resented the disparaging critique of their hard-won pragmatic changes. With the government more open to reform, even the socialists whose credo included an eventual withering away of the state participated in party politics. From Goldman's critical perspective the leadership hierarchies of the Socialist Party and most union organizations mimicked the prevailing corporate structure that ultimately would undermine the spirit of cooperation.

Yet it was the spirit of reform that set the stage for Goldman to speak to those beyond the relatively small clusters of anarchists in the United States and other parts of the world who were engaged in the politics of change. With charisma and eloquence she voiced that which underlies the impetus for reform. Her ability to articulate despair and offer hope, and to expose the corrupting influences of capitalism, affecting almost every realm of personal life, was inspiring. She spoke of longings for love, for community, for freedom from constraint, feelings that echoed her audience's experience and encouraged them to challenge the authority of existing social and political norms.

The times provided inquisitive audiences, many from the radicalized American middle class. These were people Goldman hoped would become a vanguard of intellectuals who would inspire a revolution in values to transform the social order. In tandem with the comrades on her magazine, *Mother Earth*,[6] she would reach the "intellectual proletariat"[7] and satisfy her own need to be taken seriously as a thinker. Although Goldman's sharp critique of the limitations of many reform efforts may have alienated some, she did succeed in galvanizing a remarkable number of people to imagine alternative ways of living and to adopt the habits of critical thinking. And even though anarchists, socialists, and liberal reformers differed in ideology, organizational configuration, and tactics, their desires to fight against injustice often were remarkably similar.

## GRADUALISM—SHUNNED IN POLITICS, EMBRACED IN PERSONAL LIFE

Although Goldman rejected gradualism in politics, as a lecturer and writer she expressed her belief in each person's evolving capacity for change, for opening the mind to criti-

---

6. Most notably close among the editors was Alexander Berkman, who shared her sense of being part of the vanguard of change and the importance of directing their message to the middle class, though his constituency of choice was primarily the unemployed poor and the working class. While he had organizational patience with militant intent, she had the capacity to elicit and sustain the interest of a wider audience across the nation.
7. See Emma Goldman, "Intellectual Proletarians," *Mother Earth*, February 1914.

cal thinking and developing the ability to question the authority of established beliefs and ideas. It was in the interpersonal realm that Goldman inadvertently bore witness to the positive aspects of gradualism as a daily affirmation of individual control inextricable from the transformation of society as a whole—the way in which small shifts in attitudes and behavior were important building blocks of change. While she never hesitated to condemn gradualism in government, capitalism, and even labor union reform in the realm of the individual, she affirmed the power of incremental effort to embody the values wished for in the world.

She never expected people to immediately abandon the familiar or cast off the long-standing institution of marriage. Instead, she offered critical tools with which to judge its constraints, to imagine love in complete freedom. Her critique of the family and advocacy of birth control were based not on a belief that the dissolution of the family was imminent but rather on her belief in a woman's right to control her own destiny, especially on the issue of choosing when or whether to have a child. In her talks on "The Tragedy of Women's Emancipation" she was not assuming that suffragists would give up fighting for the vote; instead, she spoke of the limitations of voting itself, the false expectations of the complete transformation it was purported to bring. And so it was with many of the issues she addressed, including anarchism itself. She consistently strove to break the boundaries of convention, to encourage people to see beyond the immediacy of their situations, to recognize the inadequacy of even the most well-meaning reforms and aspire toward a vision of freedom and cooperation, whether or not it was within reach.

### THE TIGHTROPE OF PERSONAL FREEDOM: RELINQUISHING THE SAFETY NET OF SOCIAL CONVENTION

The times shaped the challenges Goldman chose to address and were the underpinnings of her victories and defeats. The highs and lows of her life seemed to follow the contours of the political world around her. Although never a mass movement in the United States, anarchism nonetheless struck a resonant chord in the American imagination. Goldman lectured on changing social conventions, on sexuality and marriage at a time when the divorce rate and the number of women who chose not to marry were increasing. In her lectures on modern drama she focused on plays that wrestled with the angst of bourgeois family life as it reflected the corrosive effects of the existing social order.[8]

The suffrage movement was taking hold.[9] After decades of organizing, the swell of support made it clear that national enfranchisement of women was within reach. It would

8. For example, Ibsen's *A Doll's House* dramatizes the frustrations of a woman trapped in the constrictive limits of wife and keeper of the home until she finally slams the door and leaves to reclaim her own will and freedom.

9. By 1916 eleven states and the Alaska Territory had granted women full voting rights (Wyoming, 1869; Colorado, 1893; Utah, 1895; Idaho, 1896; Washington, 1910; California, 1911; Oregon, Arizona, Kansas, 1912; Alaska Territory, 1913; Montana and Nevada, 1914).

be among the greatest victories of the twentieth century for women. Goldman, the anarchist who on principle did not advocate the vote as a palliative to political ills, nonetheless rode the wave of interest the struggle represented. Rather than obstructing the suffrage movement's progress, she hoped to redirect it: "I do not see why women shouldn't have the vote if she wants to, neither can I see why she has anything to gain by the ballot. Women's sphere is the whole world, and there is no moral reason for denying it to her."[10] She challenged women to acknowledge that complete freedom could never take place in a polling booth before it had taken root in a woman's soul. Goldman empowered her audiences with her assertion that personal and political change were inextricably intertwined.

With the growth of urban centers and the influx of women into the work force, more and more Americans were prepared to take their chances on the tightrope of personal freedom from which the social constraints of the past had been withdrawn.[11] The work terrain had shifted as individuals who once had their place in agricultural communities now more easily lost their moorings in the anonymity of the urban landscape. Many middle-class liberals took an interest in the unifying potential of anarchism and socialism as alternatives to the inadequacy of existing social and political organization. They were curious, not only about the ideas but also about the strong personalities who espoused the various political ideologies. Lectures and debates on the differences between anarchism and socialism could draw up to 3,000 listeners.[12] Those who came to hear Goldman also found themselves inspired by her ideas on a variety of challenging, often taboo subjects—free love, homosexuality, and even political violence.

Women were especially drawn to those talks that addressed issues of independence in love and motherhood. Often lectures on cultural, feminist topics were deemed more dangerous than direct expositions on anarchist theory and practice. (For example, one could get arrested more frequently for distributing practical pamphlets on birth control than for publishing accolades about those who bombed a nonunion company or assassinated a president.) Negative consequences for challenging the status quo were sporadically encountered in contrast to the years before.[13] Many (though not all) relished the stimulation of being able to engage in free speech in America—at a time when social critiques and proposals for improvement went hand in hand.

Excited by the new personal and economic freedoms in this time of transition that accompanied their entry into the work force, women no longer felt limited to a life defined by the security of a husband and family; self-reliance laid the groundwork for new configurations of intimacy. Women were drawn to the topics of birth control and

---

10. "Emma Goldman and Ben Reitman Here," *Omaha World Herald*, 26 March 1910.
11. See, for instance, Nancy Cott, *Public Vows: A History of Marriage and the Nation* (Cambridge, Mass.: Harvard University Press, 2000).
12. For example, her debate with the socialist Arthur Lewis on "Direct Action Versus Political Action" took place in Chicago on 3 March 1912.
13. See vol. 1, *Made for America* and vol. 2, *Making Speech Free*.

the relatively new dilemma of choosing between monogamy and "varietism" (multiple intimate involvements), of shifting gender roles, and of the novelty of changing attitudes about sexual orientation and marriage. Among her lectures, those on "Love and Marriage," on "Jealousy: Its Cause and Possible Cure," and on "The Tragedy of Women's Emancipation" attracted large crowds and reached an even wider audience in print.

## RECASTING THE IMMIGRANT LIFE

Although the working poor, especially immigrant radicals, found her critique of marriage and love intriguing, usually it was those with more privilege and economic advantage who had the luxury of being able to envision a more fulfilling life. Goldman, who had been born into the middle class, who gravitated toward German high culture with its masterpieces of literature and philosophy,[14] spent her formative teenage years in the intellectual and political swirl of St. Petersburg and gained a vision of life beyond mere subsistence. Thus, she never completely identified with the manual work that, by necessity, she had to perform. It was the anti-Semitism of tsarist Russia that forced her family into relative poverty, but the family never changed its self-perception as part of the educated middle class. In her early years in America, Goldman had little choice but to live in the world of newly arrived immigrants; her direct experience of the oppressive conditions of garment factory life shaped her long-standing relationship to the workers' movement.[15] As time went on, Goldman expanded her horizons; she became more acculturated, having succeeded in mastering the language and assessing the political conditions of her adopted country, and she educated herself in what was considered the best of European literature and the basic tracts of American politics. She attained skills that gave her some degree of independence, which allowed her to shed some of her immigrant stigma and gradually become recognized as a leading proponent of radical ideas.

In lectures and in print Goldman emerged as a powerful voice for anarchism in America. Her magazine, *Mother Earth* (published March 1906–August 1917), with its original emphasis on social science and literature, was part of a trend in publishing. It was one of many little magazines and books on subjects deemed outside mainstream interests. These publications reflected an intense excitement for the new and satisfied a growing readership hungry for information about literature, politics, art, and culture. However, the intellectuals, bohemians, and new urbanites who gravitated to emergent avant-garde literature found only a handful of magazines that, like *Mother Earth*, directly addressed labor issues.[16]

14. See *LML*, pp. 39–40, on Königsberg teacher initiating EG to German culture at the age of ten; and see Introduction, vol. 1, *Made for America*, p. 46.
15. See *LML*, pp. 15–18.
16. Besides *Mother Earth*, see *International Socialist Review* (1907–1918) and the *Masses* (1911–1917; continued as the *Liberator*, 1918–1924). However, many foreign-language newspapers also avidly followed labor issues, especially as they affected their immigrant constituencies; see Directory of Periodicals.

Still, Goldman was a far more talented orator than writer. Some consider her theoretical contribution more a tour de force of accessibly integrating complex philosophical and literary works than of originating novel ideas—a position only partially true and generally advanced by those unfamiliar with the breadth of Goldman's published and unpublished writings, the nuances of her thinking, and a common lack of appreciation for the breakthrough feminist, anarchist, and internationalist discoveries that continue to emerge in close analyses of her work. Nevertheless, *Mother Earth* and the two books she published during this period, *Anarchism and Other Essays* (1910) and *The Social Significance of the Modern Drama* (1914), enhanced her influence on American radical politics, thereby expanding the general readership for anarchist ideas, and on a personal level elevated Goldman's class and social position. Similarly, the international reach of the journal, the exchange of ideas and updates on the state of anarchism across national boundaries, educated American readers and extended the magazine's (and Goldman's) spheres of interest outside the country.

### LISTENING TO THE VOICE OF LABOR

The turn-of-the-century boom that had brought so many people into the cities from the countryside and the influx of immigrants, especially to the Northeast, created a sense of possibility as well as disappointment. Pitched labor battles for shorter hours, fair pay, and safe workplace conditions persisted. Business competition among manufacturers, garment factories, big oil companies, and mining enterprises, combined with the rapid mechanization of industry, catalyzed a wave of drastic pay cuts and widespread unemployment. In an era before transnational outsourcing, costs were minimized and wages slashed as profits increased, all in the gaze of the nation's work force. Violent clashes between big business and militant labor provoked the handshakes necessary for winning significant union reforms or losing them all, arrangements that required significant compromises on both sides. Strikes were a constant across the country, especially in mining, the steel industry, and clothing manufacturing. In response to the force and brutality against striking workers, meaningful labor reforms were sometimes implemented and militants' tactic of fighting fire with fire emboldened.[17]

Although Goldman raised funds for strike committees and for legal challenges, her relationship to unions and to the labor movement itself was ambivalent. She distrusted union hierarchical structures and the tendency of union members to cede their will to the leadership, as well as the predominantly socialist leanings of both rank-and-file members and officials. She believed that the unions' attempts to build bridges to government and industry would backfire and could potentially quell labor justice agitation, co-opt the strength of militant unions, and weaken the burgeoning Socialist Party. Some

---

17. Each incident provided an observation point for those critics of capitalism who genuinely considered the possibility for a reorganization of the relations of production and the redistribution of wealth.

unions were reluctant to be associated with the open use of violence as part of their effort to attract a larger constituency, although it was not unusual for militant sectors of the unions to employ such methods themselves clandestinely. Rather than organizing the workers, Goldman served the cause by spreading awareness, raising financial support, and evoking sympathy from the middle classes for the laboring classes and their struggles. Goldman identified with labor but, unlike many immigrants, never played an integral role in the labor movement.

Immigrant labor itself was a complex issue, permeated by insidious racism in most unions, including the American Federation of Labor.[18] Scab labor often included the otherwise excluded Asian and Mexican immigrants in the West, and African Americans in the Midwest, Northeast, and Southwest. The pervasive exploitation of African Americans in the South heightened racial tensions among the working poor.

"Progressive" impulses—that is, the desire to address the inequities and injustices of a fast-growing industrial society—spread throughout the nation. Labor struggles for decent wages and working hours were accompanied by the fear of being weakened by the huge influx of low-wage immigrant workers.[19]

In the public sphere immigrants had become a vital and challenging component of the work force; yet some natural-born American citizens believed immigrants spread disease, lacked moral standing, drained municipal resources, and were the primary participants in militant labor activity. Impoverished immigrants were a central concern for reformers. Goldman, an immigrant and former garment worker, believed such interest in the welfare of poor immigrants actually created a more efficient means of control through the amelioration of the worst excesses of the system.

From 1910 to 1916 Goldman shifted, though not completely, to addressing these and other concerns of the English-speaking public with the intention of not only speaking on behalf of, but also reaching beyond, her earlier audience of primarily Yiddish-, German-, and Italian-speaking immigrants.[20]

## HEAVEN AND EARTH

Religious institutions often were safe gathering places for communities with shared concerns. In times of unpredictable change the apprehensive tend to grasp tightly to the norms of the past while the intrepid often are enlivened with excitement for the unknown. Although Goldman regularly worked with religious liberals who were sym-

---

18. Generally, AFL members had to apprentice in a trade, something that for most immigrants and African Americans would never have been possible. Also, Olav Tveitmoe, friend of EG and AB and a militant labor leader based in San Francisco, for example, was president of the Asian Exclusion League.
19. See Introduction, vol. 1, *Made for America*, for a discussion of foreign labor; and Introduction, vol. 2, *Making Speech Free*, pp. 17–18, for a discussion of newly enacted immigration laws. The person credited with bringing the issue of white slave traffic into public consciousness was George Kibbe Turner.
20. See Chronology, vols. 1 and 2, for examples of the variety of audiences EG addressed.

pathetic to her humanitarian message, most religious communities, composed as they were of social and political conservatives, were scornful of her critique. Goldman, an atheist, rejected even the slightest hint of positive social and ethical cohesion created under the mantle of religious belief. She shared Marx's position that religion is the opiate of the people.[21] Yet in an effort to separate ethical values from the institution of religion, she appropriated Jesus as a rebel and revolutionary,[22] claiming that his opposition to Roman rule, his belief in the people, and his ethic of kindness identified him as an anarchist. Equally provocative to those who identified with her own Jewish heritage was Goldman's criticism of the double standard of the "chosen people" and the ethical superiority the term implied, mocking those who became small-time capitalists in their frantic efforts to assimilate into a greedy American culture that essentially spurned them.[23]

In spite of her firm anti-religious conviction, Goldman's practice of anarchism had a certain similarity to the religious orthodoxy of her youth: a global ideology, almost Talmudic disputes, and a consistent set of values meant to guide one's personal and public life. She had grown up in a community that, on the surface, seemed to encourage openness to reflection and debate, while at the same time neglecting a fundamental contradiction—the underlying belief in the existence of an all-controlling wrathful god.[24]

## BRIDGING THE CULTURAL DIVIDE

Goldman prided herself as a woman whose acquired cosmopolitanism enabled her to bridge the divide between English speakers and German- and Yiddish-speaking audiences.[25] Though completely nonreligious, disdainful of orthodoxy of any kind, and boastful of no "nationalist tendencies," she still felt close to "her people" and considered her personal resilience to be an inherited cultural trait: "[T]he perseverance which I inherited from my race . . . the indomitable will to persevere is peculiarly characteristic of the Jews . . . [and] helped them to survive centuries of persecution."[26] She believed that they "owe their survival only to the capacity of sticking together."[27]

---

21. See Karl Marx, "Contribution to a Critique of Hegel's 'Philosophy of Right,'" *Deutsch-Französische Jahrbücher*, 1844.
22. See the poem "The First Anarchist" by Victor Hugo. Many anarchists similarly assessed Jesus.
23. Goldman too had assimilated into American culture, pulling away from a primary identification with her Jewish roots, but she prided herself with having rejected the country's dominant economic structure.
24. For more discussion on EG's relationship to her Jewish roots see Introduction, vol. 1, *Made for America*, p. 46; and on the emotional resilience of the Jewish race see Introduction, vol. 2, *Making Speech Free*, pp. 9, 15. And see Candace Falk, "Emma Goldman—Jewish Spokeswoman for Freedom," *Encyclopedia of Jewish History*, eds. S. Norwood and E. Pollack (Santa Barbara: ABC-CLIO, 2008), pp. 310–13.
25. Her accent was waning, except for her rolling *r*'s.
26. EG to W. S. Van Valkenburgh, 14 April 1915, *EGP*, reel 8.
27. EG to BR, 24 September [1914], *EGP*, reel 8. In this letter EG also criticized BR's judgmental attitudes, accusing him, playfully, of being anti-Semitic.

Proficient but not fluent in Yiddish, Goldman felt more comfortable lecturing in German, her native language, which was easily understood by her Yiddish-speaking audiences. And although she looked down on those Jews who cared only for "their own," she was grateful for her few Yiddish meetings and the Jewish comrades who hosted her along the way. She felt compelled to warn away those "nationalistic Jews to expect anything from the tsar or any government privileges" in her lecture "The Tsar and 'My Jews.'"[28] Her attempt to adopt a more universal identity often fell short. Newspapers, and even her beloved new American middle-class friends, considered her somewhat exotic. Still, Goldman was adept at piercing through the comfort zone of sameness; she had genuine friendships across cultures. Although she never denied her own culture, she chose not to be limited by it. Yet her cosmopolitanism was coupled with unshakable feelings of displacement. Her desire to bring unity to the world around her also may have been an expression of her own yearning for a sense of belonging.

She selected themes from the public discourse and appropriated whatever she considered meaningful (and useful) for the eventual realization of anarchism, which she envisioned as a social and economic order based on free will, mutual aid, and cooperation. In spite of bitter differences with socialists, capitalists, reformers, and religious congregants, anarchists shared the conviction that their work served the betterment of humankind.

### TOPPLING THE HOLY TRINITY OF GOD, THE STATE, AND THE FAMILY

Goldman's challenges to true believers of every stripe added to her reputation as a woman who dared to question the most sacred embodiments of authority. She challenged the "three forces which have held men in bondage—religion, capitalism, and government,"[29] as well as marriage as it was practiced, which she considered a legalistic variant of property rights.

With virulence she stood against the tide of fundamentalism and never hesitated to take on the tripod of social stability, the "Holy Trinity of God, the State, and the Family."[30] In its place she urged her audiences to imagine harmonious self-regulating communities free of coercion, no punitive hand of the law, and no dread of eternal punishment in the hereafter. Her visions of order without government or without the rule

---

28. Ibid.
29. "Doctrine of Anarchists," *Duluth Herald,* 17 March 1911.
30. A fierce anti-religious atheism had long been part of the theory and practice of anarchism. See, for example, "For my part I say that the first duty of the thinking free man is ceaselessly to banish the idea from his mind and consciousness. . . . Each stop in our progress represents one more victory in which we annihilate the Deity." Pierre Joseph Proudhon, *System of Economical Contradictions, or, the Philosophy of Misery* (Boston: Benjamin R. Tucker, 1888). And again: "The idea of God implies the abdication of human reason and justice; it is the most decisive negation of human liberty and necessarily ends in the enslavement of mankind, both in theory and practice." Michael Bakunin, *God and the State* (Boston: Benjamin R. Tucker, 1883), p. 15.

of law were perceived by the public at large as misguided, impossible, and the precursor to bedlam and destruction. Even a whisper of advocacy for a people without God and religion would have been considered not only blasphemous but grave enough to boot the offender into eternal hell.

Not only were such critiques considered a threat to traditional religious doctrine, but they also represented a direct counterpoint to stability, to societal well-being, and even to eventual freedom. The God-fearing were terrified by the anarchist rejection of belief in an omnipresent "higher law"; the word "anarchy" was perceived as a portent of unbridled chaos and escalating political violence. Such assumptions were not unreasonable, considering the number of violent acts associated with anarchists. Ordinary people were often as terrified of such attacks as those in power who were targeted by them; they considered civil violence an inexcusable offense, whether or not it was inspired by a glorious vision.

Although Goldman's ideas about violence were considered threatening by many, her critique of the traditional family seemed even more terrifying to others. At a time of widespread fear about the disintegration of the institution of marriage Goldman's interpretation of the meaning of freedom from constraint in personal life included support for universal access to birth control, advocacy of free love, acceptance of the varieties of sexual expression, and the promotion of sex education for children. Although Goldman's theories of complete freedom in all spheres of life were too difficult for most people to live by, some liberals considered her anarchist challenge to the holy trinity of God, the family, and the State thought provoking, engaging, and even vicariously liberating.[31]

Fear of anarchism itself, especially by those who equated the term with chaos—or a lack of order in the public and private domain—was allayed by stringent laws against anarchists.[32] These laws often resulted in the arrest and imprisonment of those who advocated or acted on anarchism's principles. Still, dissent, whether anarchist, socialist, labor, or liberal, could not be repressed entirely; nor could the government contain the aggression of those who perceived themselves to be the victims of officially sanctioned attacks. Consequences of such political dissent never matched the horrifying impact of racial prejudice especially in the South—with lynching the most graphic and egregious expression of racist terrorism in the country (a subject Goldman alluded to but never chose as the focus of her general critique).[33]

---

31. This margin of openness in the culture, especially among those inspired to imagine and "demand the impossible," was, and continues to be, fertile ground for Goldman's appeal.
32. See, for example, New York State's Criminal Anarchy Act and New Jersey's Criminal Anarchy Act, both passed in 1902. In March 1903 the Immigration Act was passed by Congress. The act barred those who claimed to be anarchists from immigration and naturalization in the United States.
33. See vol. 4, *The War Years*, for examples of the gradations of Goldman's attunement to the complexity of race and of race relations, forthcoming.

## UP AGAINST THE "POLITICAL CLAPTRAP"

In 1910 an electoral race for the House of Representatives was in full swing. Even though anarchists never advocated voting, in part because they didn't believe in ceding control to anyone, Goldman was reinvigorated by the general public's temporary focus on political issues. However, her attempts to tap into and redirect the attention lavished on electoral candidates were largely unsuccessful, and attendance at anarchist lectures dropped significantly during election cycles.

Various public officials, including Theodore Roosevelt, who is remembered as being among the earliest proponents of progressive reform, considered anarchists to be a public enemy of the first order. This attitude is no surprise, since Roosevelt had succeeded President McKinley following his assassination in 1901, an act attributed to an anarchist.[34] During his presidency Roosevelt had done his utmost to suppress anarchists' ideas, which he considered seductive to impoverished immigrants vulnerable to their anti-government messages.[35] Succeeding presidents William Howard Taft (1909–1913) and Woodrow Wilson (1913–1921) also considered anarchists (and many outspoken socialists) a threat to the stability of the nation.[36] Taft often tried to neutralize the clashing forces by claiming that "the interests of the wealthiest capitalist and of the humblest laborer are exactly the same."[37] Anarchists, and most socialists, completely rejected his rationale, believing that democratic ideals were antithetical to the built-in avarice of capitalism; combining "the common man" and "the capitalist" under the rubric of "the people" obscured the genuine clash of class interests.[38]

Nonetheless, Goldman was dedicated to the task of forging links between disparate groups,[39] to elicit and promote empathy as the foundation for eventual social harmony.

34. See vol. 1, *Made for America*, pp. 460–78, for details of the shockwaves following the McKinley assassination.
35. For example, Theodore Roosevelt said, "The anarchist, and especially the anarchist in the United States, is merely one type of criminal, more dangerous than any other because he represents the same depravity in a greater degree." He also said, "No man or body of men preaching anarchist doctrines should be allowed at large any more than if preaching the murder of some specified private individual. Anarchistic speeches, writings, and meetings are essentially seditious and treasonable." First Annual Message to Congress, *Messages and Papers of the Presidents*, vol. 14, 1 December 1901.
36. By 1917, in the face of direct attacks on U.S. ships, President Wilson reversed his initial platform promise to avoid entering the war raging in Europe; later he signed deportation orders for many immigrant anarchists and socialists deemed disloyal to a country at war and, years after the war was over, refused to pardon Eugene Debs from prison for his stance against military recruitment and U.S. entry into the First World War.
37. William Taft lecture on "Labor and Capital," Cooper Union, New York, 10 January 1908, in Oscar Davis, *William Howard Taft, the Man of the Hour* (Philadelphia: P. W .Ziegler, 1908), p. 343. "Until men are perfect beings of this kind, socialism must either constitute a tyranny so rigid as to destroy not only the right of liberty and to interfere with the pursuit of happiness, or it must be a failure." *New York Times*, 9 June 1914.
38. See Shelton Stromquist, *Reinventing the People* (Urbana: University of Illinois Press, 2006) for a refutation of the misleading, though compelling, concept of "the people" as it was used to support the creation of unified goals during the Progressive era.
39. In the tradition of the Russian intellectual vanguard the educated, often middle- and upper-class

The basis for the realization of this premise was a context suitable for the nurturance of a person's creative abilities and critical thinking skills.

Whereas on the one hand she denigrated use of "the masses" as a concept that assumed too much uniformity, on the other hand she rejected the notion of Max Stirner, the theorist of anarchist egoism, that "individual will" took precedence over the consensus of any group. Goldman also never subscribed to the notion of irreparable class divisions even as she defended the cause of labor. Though idiosyncratic, her ideas were embedded firmly in the ethos of a time that sought the betterment of "the people." Yet in spite of her best intentions she continued to be labeled by many "an enemy of the people."

President Taft's attempts to obscure the lines between labor and capital were interpreted by anarchists and socialists as an indication of their growing power; they welcomed the fight.[40] Goldman dismissed the power of the increasing ranks of Socialists, sure that the government could never truly be reformed from within. She scorned the socialist impetus to compete in the electoral process, even if their intended end point was the overthrow of capitalism. Still, she often was linked to Eugene V. Debs, the charismatic socialist whose popularity was growing, and who shared many of the same interests, as exemplified by his early admission that he considered himself an anarchist in spirit.[41] Despite their similarities they parted ways on many critical issues beyond his participation in the electoral system.[42] Goldman, for example, never rallied around Debs's successes as the Socialist Party of America (SPA) challenger to the two-party system. She was not particularly impressed by his cross-country "Red Special" railway campaign, or by his popularity as evidenced by the remarkable number of votes he received in the presidential elections of 1904, 1908, and 1912, or even by his bid for the presidency while imprisoned in 1920.[43] The SPA held a conference in May 1912 at the height of its influence with a membership of 150,000. Goldman was nevertheless incensed by the Socialist Party's decision that year to reverse its earlier support for the use and advocacy of sabotage, a position the Party suddenly deemed harmful to its desire for popular support.[44]

---

revolutionaries played a critical role in strategizing and carrying out the tactics that succeeded in bringing about the Russian Revolution.

40. "Socialism the Issue—Taft," *Appeal to Reason,* June 1910.

41. *LML,* p. 220.

42. See vol. 1, *Made for America,* p. 311. She describes Debs as "frightened out of his wits by Gompers." After Debs was arrested for protesting the war, however, Goldman would find herself sympathetic to his plight.

43. For more detail see Ron Radosh, *Debs* (Engelwood, N.J.: Prentice Hall, 1971); Nick Salvatore, *Eugene V. Debs: Citizen and Socialist* (Urbana: University of Illinois Press, 1982). See also Ernst Freeberg, *Democracy's Prisoner* (Cambridge, Mass.: Harvard University Press, 2008).

44. "But unless a Socialist continues to be under the influence of bourgeois morality—a morality which enables the few to monopolize the earth at the expense of the many—he can not consistently maintain that capitalist property is inviolate. Sabotage undermines this form of criminal possession, can it therefore be considered criminal? On the contrary, it is ethical in the best sense, since it helps

Debs too had shifted away from any formal association with retaliatory labor violence, though he never failed to do what he could to help the accused. In 1906, Debs had written the essay "Arouse Ye Slaves"[45] as a call to spur the working class to take militant actions to free Moyer, Pettibone, and Haywood, the men accused of the murder of the Idaho governor Frank Steunenberg in 1905. When Debs later changed his public position on labor cases involving political violence, Goldman interpreted his withdrawal from the McNamara case once the defendants pleaded guilty as a sign that the boldness of his earlier socialist platform had been compromised by political ambition. From an anarchist perspective she considered this reversal evidence of his underlying cowardice.[46] Debs, however, chose to frame the issue of labor militancy as part of his wide-ranging effort to rise above the factional fighting among radicals, including refusing to involve himself in the internal disputes of the Socialist Party of America. Regardless of Goldman's assessment of his character flaws, Debs was considered the most influential figure on the left at the time. His popularity and appeal came from his courageous political stands and his ability to address the problems of the nation, his choices of whom to support along the way notwithstanding.

## ADDRESSING THE CROWD—APPEALING TO WOMEN

The field of political action expanded with a powerful surge in the culture at large of interest in issues of gender, sexuality, and the family. These concerns crossed classes and political divisions and were championed by many women in the Socialist Party, the dominant party on the left, and in the women's trade unions.[47] As women entered the work force, Goldman questioned whether they had traded one form of subservience in the household for another and whether they had substituted devotion to their newfound professional lives for love. Preferring independence to the dependence of marriage, she also warned women against the false assurances of security in this State-sanctioned legal arrangement. She warned naïve lovers to prepare for the erosion of any semblance of independence in the signing of its contract. For Goldman, the State and religion had no place in matters of the heart; love could neither be legislated nor sealed by a deity or the State.[48]

In what often seemed like a heartless world, local interest groups satisfied a common yearning for belonging to a community of caring. They joined forces to implement change on a multitude of issues, including unionization, suffrage, and prohibi-

---

society to get rid of its worst foe, the most detrimental factor of social life." Emma Goldman, *Syndicalism: Its Theory and Practice* (New York: Mother Earth Publishing Association); and article in *Mother Earth*, February 1913.

45. Debs's article appeared in *Appeal to Reason*, 10 March 1906.

46. See Emma Goldman, "Letters from a Tour," vol. 1, *Made for America*, p. 300.

47. Among those prominent women were Women's Trade Union League activist and theorist of socialism Charlotte Perkins Gilman. While many took up the cause of working-class women, they still fell prey to dominant attitudes about race exclusion, especially in relation to unions.

48. *Cupid's Yokes* was both a critique of marriage and an affirmation of free love.

tion. Goldman acted as a gadfly, voicing the contradictory aspects of their positions, and she especially enjoyed needling the temperance women as "immoral." Goldman's lectures on the subjects of marriage and the family often deviated from ideas about sexuality among even the most progressive of the groups. Yet prudes joined free lovers to come to her defense; often when she faced locks on lecture hall entry doors, arrests, and even short stints in jail, a sizable community of free speech advocates rallied around her.

Unified efforts for social change, even among urban cosmopolitans attracted to the transformative possibilities of the New Woman and the New Negro, were marred by intense racial segregation. Only occasionally would there be persons of color in Goldman's audience, although parallel figures across—and sometimes crossing—the color line were engaged with similar issues. For example, Hubert Harrison, an African American political scholar who taught at the Ferrer School, was influenced by anarchism, though the debate in which he participated with Berkman and others focused primarily on issues related to socialism rather than race.[49] He was also a member of the Sunrise Club, the freethought organization that was also a venue for Goldman's lectures. Still, she rarely discussed racial issues other than in passing references to lynching in the South as an example of the enormous cruelties tolerated in America. Although she often identified John Brown's rebellion as part of both the American and anarchist traditions, anarchism had few, if any, followers among African Americans.[50] Goldman later explained that she had never spoken in the South, in part because anarchist comrades had forewarned her "never to touch on the Negro question," fearing that raising the issue of racism would jeopardize her safety there. Equivocating that because she "couldn't compromise on that point," she "never reached the part of America that . . . [she] wanted very much to know from personal contact and experience."[51] African Americans in the North also generally gravitated toward separate race-based groups focused on more immediate concerns, and like Goldman rarely breached those unspoken racial boundaries.

Among diverse immigrant groups in the West, Goldman's appeal was more fluid. Many Asian American anarchists flocked to her lectures and covered her talks in local Japanese- and Chinese-language radical newspapers intent on countering Hearst's anti-Asian campaign—a prejudice that seeped into most union workplaces as well. Mexicans and Mexican Americans appreciated her fund-raising efforts and propaganda work on behalf of Enrique and Ricardo Flores Magón, the Mexican revolutionaries who were incarcerated in California.[52]

49. Jeffrey B. Perry, *Hubert Harrison: The Voice of Harlem Radicalism, 1883–1918* (New York: Columbia University Press, 2008), pp. 116–17, 234–36.

50. For EG's relationship with African Americans when she was on Blackwell's Island in 1893, see vol. 1, *Made for America*, pp. 194–202. For advocates of racial justice, see p. 722 and vol. 2, *Making Speech Free*, p. 419n4.

51. Emma Goldman to Leonardo Andrea, Edgefield, South Carolina, 29 December 1931, *EGP*, reel 25.

52. Colin MacLachlan, *Anarchism and the Mexican Revolution* (Berkeley: University of California Press, 1991), p. 62; originally published as "Brave Voices from Prison," *The Blast*, 15 March 1916, p. 4.

Women from across an array of ethnic and class lines were also attracted to Goldman's lectures. Young mothers with baby carriages braved the crowds, anxious to hear Goldman's challenging critique and alternative vision of intimacy. Her lectures were precursors to the trend toward companionate marriage, the desire for equal partnership in love instead of the power relations inherent in an economic nuptial pact. Many women went to her talks for more practical advice. Controlling family size was an issue of immediate importance to the poor, but dispensing information about sexuality and family limitation was punishable under the anti-obscenity Comstock Act.[53] In 1915 and 1916, Goldman dared to venture into this perilous terrain, surreptitiously distributing how-to educational material that addressed the principles behind birth control,[54] for which she was more than willing to go to jail.

Ultimately, Goldman believed that freedom, whether in the workplace or in the family, was a step toward a more equitable society in which each individual's happiness was integral to the well-being of all. She never failed to incorporate an explanation of the links between the principles of anarchism and the topical issues she addressed. Tapping into the ethos of the New Woman, Goldman addressed women in their multiple roles—as workers, mothers, union organizers, educated professionals, literati, and as participants in movements for social change. More than any other topics that she talked about and worked for, birth control and women's independence extended her sphere of influence beyond the radical left.

### "MY BOOK MUST SPEAK FOR ITSELF"

Audiences were drawn to Goldman's personal charisma, her ability to connect and titillate them with challenging ideas that touched both their emotions and their intellects in a manner that was as playful as it was deeply serious. Although many claimed that her eloquent critique and beautiful vision changed the course of their lives, Goldman began to feel that her impact was too timebound and ephemeral.

The constant struggle to gather and entertain an audience, combined with her frustration with the impermanence of the spoken word, provoked a change in her political work. In 1910, her twentieth year of cross-country lecture tours, Goldman began to feel

---

Regarding EG's help for Ricardo and Enrique Flores Magón, "Deeds speak louder than words. This is not the first time that Emma has come to the rescue at the critical moment. Our readers are familiar with her solidarity in this direction." *Regeneración*, no. 254, 24 February 1916.

53. See vols. 1 and 2 for EG's various encounters with the Comstock Act, and this volume for various letters, including "Emma Goldman Is Fined $100," *Oregon Journal*, 8 August 1915. Also, for earlier resistance to the Comstock laws see Hal Sears, *The Sex Radicals: Free Love in High Victorian America* (Lawrence: Regents Press of Kansas, 1977); and Joanne Passet, *Sex Radicals and the Quest for Women's Equality* (Urbana: University of Illinois Press, 2003).

54. Ben Reitman's 1915 pamphlet, *Why and How the Poor Should Not Have Children*, the authorship of which was claimed by birth control advocate and eugenicist William J. Robinson, was essentially an instruction manual on contraception; it argued that "poor people should have as few children as possible [until] society is prepared to offer every child that is born proper food, shelter and care."

restless and dissatisfied. It was not only the seemingly random interruptions and arrests but also the transient rewards of the lecturer's life and the stress of publishing, support- ing, and disseminating a monthly magazine that depleted her energies.

She was determined to bring her ideas to open-minded readers who, away from noisy lecture halls, could thoughtfully consider taking part in the creation of a more equita- ble world. "I prefer to reach the few who really want to learn, rather than the many who come to be amused."[55] A book seemed a much more permanent medium than a peri- odical; its format might extend her reach to those outside her usual political circles, to touch them with a vision she believed was universal and timeless.

Thus, Goldman embarked on an extensive foray into the world of print. She chose to refine her earlier lectures, repeating themes that had long been part of her repertoire,[56] adding insights of both contemporary and universal significance for a forthcoming book of essays, rather than writing completely new pieces. The written word, however, could never capture the subtlety of her inflection or the immediacy of an encounter with her political performance, or the enjoyment of watching her spar with the police—or even socialists and liberals—who came to her talks ready for a fight. A visionary critique that might have pierced one's soul in a lecture hall, when read as part of a series of essays, might seem stiffly predictable. Yet, her consistent brilliance was evident in the ways in which a complex analysis could be delivered as common sense. The publication of her book was the grand opportunity that she not only aspired to but desperately needed.

With radical books on the rise, her volume would give her an entrée into a league of thinkers whose print presence had bolstered their influence.[57] Feeling somewhat depressed and exhausted, she was ever more convinced that although oral propaganda shook people from their lethargy, "it leaves no lasting impression."[58] When no outside publisher would pay for the production costs,[59] Goldman and her colleagues expanded the Mother Earth Publishing Association's mission to include publishing her book. The

---

55. Emma Goldman, *Anarchism and Other Essays*, p. 49.
56. First appearances of these talks had variant titles: 1897, "What Is Anarchism"; 1897, "Prostitution, Its causes and Cure"; 1897, "Free Love"; 1898, "The New Woman"; 1898, "The Absurdity of Non-Resistance to Evil"; 1900, "What Will Lessen Vice"; 1904, "The Tragedy of Women's Emancipation"; 1907, "The Revolutionary Spirit of the Modern Drama"; 1907, "The Education of Children"; 1908, "The Menace of Patriotism"; 1908, "Marriage and Love"; 1909, "Puritanism: The Greatest Obstacle to Liberty," "The Psychology of Political Violence." See titles in *Anarchism and Other Essays*, as well as the Chronology in vols. 1, 2, and 3.
57. Christine Stansell, "Emma Goldman and the American Public," in *American Moderns: Bohemian New York and the Creation of a New Century* (New York: Metropolitan Books, 2000).
58. Emma Goldman, Preface to *Anarchism and Other Essays*, p. 42. See also Letter to Max Nettlau, vol. 1, *Made for America*, pp. 412–13.
59. Emma Goldman approached several publishers with extracts from the manuscript of *Anarchism and Other Essays*, including Bobbs-Merrill, Indianapolis. All declined. Eventually the book was published by Mother Earth Publishing Association and printed by Goldman Printers (not EG), which also printed *Mother Earth* magazine. The initial print run for the book was 2,000, delivered 17 December 1910.

1911 second edition confirmed interest in anarchism and in Goldman, not only as a propagandist, but also as a thinker.[60]

### ANARCHISM AND OTHER ESSAYS

In the preface to *Anarchism and Other Essays*, in what she assumed would be a surprising aspect of the book, Goldman confronted readers seeking a blueprint for an anarchist society. She asserted that each generation would have to create its own strategic plan for an equitable society that would be tempered by the particular ethos and conditions of its times; no quick solution to immediate problems was possible because it would take time to change the mind-set that had thwarted such action thus far. She then assured her readers that various theories of anarchist social and economic organization were unified by principles that supported freedom and responsibility in all aspects of life.

Goldman assumed that the second most surprising aspect of her book would be her controversial warning to both anarchist and socialist readers to reject the notion of serving "the will of the masses" in favor of heeding the guidance of "intelligent minorities." Her essay "Majorities and Minorities" dispelled reliance on "the virtues of the majority, because their very scheme of life means the perpetuation of power. . . . As a mass its aim has always been to make life uniform, gray, and monotonous as the desert. As a mass it will always be the annihilator of individuality, of free initiative, of originality."[61] She aimed to reach the intelligent minority, a group open to change, sophisticated in their thinking, and ready to take action as they were able.[62]

The third surprise was her attempt to exorcise perhaps the most threatening misconception about anarchism: the fear of its violent edge. Goldman addressed this issue in her essay on the psychology of political violence, adopting the role of interpreter of the intent behind acts she believed spoke louder than words. In this essay she chose not to address the violence of war, labor, or lynching but focused exclusively on individual acts of political violence. She countered the prevailing notion that any hint of public sympathy with the *Attentäter* left one vulnerable to accusations of being an accomplice. She

60. Thus far, Goldman has had more influence on the American political and intellectual tradition in the sociocultural realm, sexual freedom and free speech, and among some as a symbol of principled anti-consumerist and anti-capitalist sentiment, and as a proponent of anarchism as a non-hierarchical form of political organization. Reprints of Goldman's books, over a hundred years later, are evidence of the long-term appeal of her ideas and eloquence, and of her relevance to many in generations beyond her own. For an intriguing study of Goldman as political theorist, see Kathy E. Ferguson, *Emma Goldman: Political Thinking in the Streets* (Lanham, MD: Rowman and Littlefield, 2011), a counterpoint to those who maximize their portrayal of Goldman's activism and minimize the theoretical component of her work.

61. Emma Goldman, "Minorities Versus Majorities," in *Anarchism and Other Essays*, p. 78.

62. See V. I. Lenin, *What Is to Be Done?* Goldman, too, was inspired by Chernyshevsky's novel *What Is to Be Done?* and firmly believed in the transformative powers of revolutionary Russia's intellectual vanguard.

insisted that compassion for human suffering was critical to understanding political violence and martyrdom.

*Mother Earth* regularly published a definition of "direct action": "conscious, individual or collective effort to protest against or remedy social conditions through the systematic assertion of the economic power of the workers."[63] This strategy was often linked to sabotage, a tactic organized by workers against the bosses and including strikes, worker slow-downs, and intentional property damage,[64] thus differentiating itself from standard political action. It was Goldman's willingness to publicly support direct action and sabotage that separated her as an anarchist even from those in the Socialist Party and the labor movement who privately did not hesitate to resort to such methods but often feared that public advocacy of direct action, especially violence, might alienate those who had begun to support their cause.[65] Goldman included essays that clarified and explained the tactics of retaliatory violence as a necessary component of any overview of the theory and practice of anarchism (see "The Psychology of Political Violence," Essay in *Mother Earth*, 1911). Yet "The Psychology of Political Violence," as clear as it seems to be, has an element of obfuscation that was perhaps her own way of being pragmatic—a somewhat disingenuous holding on to a wider audience as the interpreter rather than the covert supporter of the person who commits an act of political violence. During these years she never spoke of her own involvement in hiding or facilitating acts of violence—to protect both herself (and others) from the law and, in some ways, from her rejection by a growing circle of public enthusiasts.

Most of the essays in her book, however, focus not on violence but on social institutions and attitudes that she believed either thwarted or promoted true individual and social freedom. Most of the essays are selections from a broader array of lectures, transcribed almost verbatim, edited mostly for style but with some deletions for time-bound references. *Anarchism and Other Essays* includes the following (where indicated, see the essays in this volume): "Prisons: A Social Crime and Failure"; "Patriotism: A Menace to Liberty"; "Ferrer and the Modern School"; "The Hypocrisy of Puritanism" (see *Victims of Morality*, *Mother Earth* pamphlet, March 1913; and "The Failure of Christianity," *Mother Earth*, April 1913); "The Traffic in Women" (see "White Slave Traffic," *Mother Earth*, January 1910); "Woman Suffrage" (see "Woman Suffrage" in the *Woman Rebel*, June 1914); "The Tragedy of Women's Emancipation"; "Marriage and Love" (see essay published by Mother Earth Publishing Association, 1911); and "The Drama: A Powerful Dissemina-

63. See *Mother Earth* 9, no. 3 (May 1914), p. 79.
64. Sabotage was an essential part of the IWW strategy—although it was not adopted as an official policy until 1914. For discussion of the topic from IWW members see William E. Trautmann, *Direct Action and Sabotage* (1912); Walker C. Smith, *Sabotage* (1913); and Elizabeth Gurley Flynn, *Sabotage* (1916). All three pamphlets were reprinted together in Salvatore Salerno, ed., *Direct Action and Sabotage* (Chicago: Charles H. Kerr, 1977).
65. See Fund Appeals in *Mother Earth* in this volume. See premise of Graham Adams Jr., *Age of Industrial Violence 1910–1915* (New York and London: Columbia University Press, 1966).

tor of Radical Thought" (see "Foreword" to the *Social Significance of the Modern Drama*, 1914). What all of these—including the first three essays, "Anarchism: What It Really Means" (see "Anarchism: What It Really Stands For," essay published by Mother Earth Publishing Association, 1911); "Minorities Versus Majorities"; and "The Psychology of Political Violence"—share is a critique of laws and the state, of religion, of social mores, and of capitalism as the underlying driving force of competition and greed.

The lead essay, "Anarchism: What It Really Stands For," provided a platform for Goldman to dispel misconceptions about anarchism, especially about violence, and the fear of chaos without government. She argued that anarchism "brings to man the consciousness of himself." Human nature, outside the prison of capitalism, could be changed; there would be no conflict between individual instincts and social instincts. Of the many existing theories of anarchism, Goldman's vision of social harmony was based on the combined forces of individual liberty and economic equality.

The writings and lectures that addressed cultural and social topics like marriage, free love, and education were often considered more acceptable to those excited by progressive and radical ideas.[66] Her overtly cultural and political messages overlapped but were perceived differently depending upon the general ideological orientation of the audience. Goldman defied any simple classification; elusive and striving to be all-encompassing, she tapped into the urge toward freedom. Thus, her critique of marriage could be received selectively, although it included a scathing commentary on capitalism as well. It was easy to identify with the pieces of her exposition that one found most appealing and to grasp the essential pattern of the whole, without having to accept that which one found objectionable.[67] The advocacy of violence was there too, but one didn't have to define her, or identify her, with it because there were so many other issues she addressed with such piercing eloquence:

> As to the protection of the woman,—therein lies the curse of marriage. Not that it really protects her, but the very idea is so revolting, such an outrage and an insult on life, so degrading to human dignity, as to forever condemn this parasitic institution.
>
> It is like that other paternal arrangement—capitalism. It robs man of his birthright, stunts his growth, poisons his body, keeps him in ignorance, in poverty and dependence, and then institutes charities that thrive on the last vestige of man's self-respect.[68]

66. For example, a lecture on "Marriage and Love" is in some ways as challenging as her lectures on "The Psychology of Political Violence" or on "The Failure of Christianity." When the U.S. government built its case for Goldman's deportation in 1919 her rejection of marriage and family as moral compasses intensified the fear of her advocacy, however reticent, of retaliatory violence and of those who practiced it to reach that aim.

67. This selectivity was especially apparent in the outpouring of support for the legal defense of anarchists from those who advocated the right to a fair trial system of justice, without regard to the particulars of the crime or the politics of the defendant.

68. Emma Goldman, "Marriage and Love," *Anarchism and Other Essays*, p. 241.

Building on decades of riveting talks, Goldman transformed her lecture notes and eventually published two books of essays, as well as an array of *Mother Earth* pamphlets.[69] Although they were hardly best sellers as she had hoped, the publication of *Anarchism and Other Essays* (1910), and to a lesser extent *The Social Significance of the Modern Drama* (1914), allowed her to take on the role of author and public intellectual, as an internationally respected theorist of anarchism, and as one of anarchism's most compelling spokeswomen.

Always cognizant of the range of her audience and her readers' knowledge of anarchism, Goldman was determined to educate rather than alienate, to share information with others who may not have had the access or the time or the inclination to do the same. Goldman was a voracious reader who found traces of anarchist ideals in almost everything. She integrated the works of the most sophisticated anarchist thinkers including Kropotkin, Bakunin, Stirner, and Proudhon with philosophers and literary figures including Nietzsche, Ibsen, and Strindberg. Although one could trace the intellectual roots of the ideas that constituted the base of Goldman's theoretical work, her works were distinguished from most of her male counterparts by her combined empathy and intelligence, her fusion of the heart and mind,[70] a wide range of ideas— and, in large part, the source of her oratorical powers.

Close examination of the multiple drafts of her wide-ranging lectures can serve to track Goldman's evolution as a popular theorist, and to demonstrate the ways in which she continually integrated and added her own flair to the emergent ideas of her time.[71] *Anarchism and Other Essays* reached future generations in ways that she hoped for, but to an extent she could not have imagined.[72]

*Anarchism and Other Essays* received mixed appraisals in her own circles. The Italian-language anarchist paper *Nuova Era* predicted that her book would be read only by those who attended her lectures. Yet its relatively positive reception by others demonstrated her ability to advance ideas that were marginal, or left of center, into the liberal discourse.

By the book's second printing, its back cover reviews included *Life* magazine's laudatory though condescending misogynist suggestion that "it ought to be read by all so-called respectable women. . . . [and] adopted as a textbook by women's clubs throughout the country. . . . Repudiating as she does practically every tenet of what the modern State holds good, she stands for some of the noblest traits in human nature." Close friends

---

69. See Publications of Mother Earth Publishing Association, 1910–1916, in this volume; see also vol. 2, *Making Speech Free*, p. 573.

70. For example, she asserted in "The Tragedy of Woman's Emancipation" that women's freedom cannot be won at the polling place but must first be found in a woman's soul.

71. See section 2 of the Introduction below. Note that Goldman often minimized (or neglected) attributions to the sources of the works she integrated into her lectures and essays.

72. The Dover publication of *Anarchism and Other Essays* has been in print constantly since the 1960s, with a consistent readership for over forty years.

added their reviews to the mix. Leonard Abbott, the associate editor of *Current Literature*, not only praised the book and Goldman herself but also noted that "[i]t appears at a time when Anarchist ideas are undoubtedly in the ascendant throughout the world." Author and social critic Hutchins Hapgood, also a friend,[73] reiterated these sentiments in *Bookman*, asserting not only that "[e]very thoughtful person ought to read the volume" but astutely noting that "[i]t will help the public to understand a group of serious-minded and morally strenuous individuals and also to feel the spirit that underlies the most radical tendencies of the great labor movement of our day."[74]

## DARK SHADOWS, HIDDEN LIAISONS

Goldman's book, as well as the documentation of her life in letters, newspaper clippings, and trial and government records, reveals a telling patchwork of the attitudes and aspirations of her era. The wealth of written material from this period belies the presence of that which by necessity was unwritten—the tracings of a clandestine web of comrades intent on countering force with force. Although her cross-country lecture tours generated support and interest in anarchist ideas, she no doubt took advantage of this mobility to convey secret information to those in hiding who were more directly engaged in acts of political violence. Goldman kept her fingers on the pulse of both worlds. The veiled side of her crusade was deliberately hidden from the gaze of those who most likely would not have understood or approved of the use of violence.[75]

As a result, she left her public with lingering questions, the answers to which might have been perplexing. Could the same woman who had become the rage of feature pages of newspapers across America—a woman who had the ear and sympathy of a swelling group of those who both welcomed progressive reform and identified with the "lyrical left"[76]—also be a supporter and confidante of militant labor and anarchist bombers of the time? Had they been aware of the spectrum of Goldman's beliefs, would her audience have chosen to aid and abet reactive terror, to advocate the destruction of the old as a means to make way for the new?[77]

The erudite Goldman encouraged her listeners to ask themselves how, as progressive reformers, they could tolerate the impending mass slaughter of men and women as

---

73. See Hutchins Hapgood in Directory of Individuals.
74. *Bookman* (New York) 32, no. 4 (February 1911).
75. See, for example, Introduction, vol. 2, *Making Speech Free*, pp. 3–6.
76. The lyrical left was a constellation of people who "offered a trans-political, redemptive vision of personal freedom and social liberation." Edward Abrams, *The Lyrical Left: Randolph Bourne, Alfred Stieglitz, and the Origins of Cultural Radicalism in America* (Charlottesville: University Press of Virginia, 1986).
77. Much of her audience was made up of burgeoning groups of idealists, middle-class sympathizers with those who cast off materialism, appreciated new forms of artistic expression, heralded the principle of free speech, and strove for lasting change within the current system of government.

the United States edged into war in Europe. Her anti-war stance had the dual intent of illustrating the parallels between State-sanctioned violence as defense against foreign aggressors and of political or labor violence as collective self-defense.

## "VARIETY OR MONOGAMY, WHICH?"

Goldman faced both crowded and sparsely populated lecture halls. In each case she was asked the same questions about her attitude toward violence and questions about free love. At her side Goldman had the man who was both her paramour and road manager. In love and work, passion permeated their lives. She came to rely on Ben Reitman's meticulous advance work promoting her lecture tours—setting up speaking venues and newspaper interviews, hawking *Mother Earth* magazine and literature at every event. His efforts increased her public presence as well as recognition of the "Emma Goldman" name.

A veteran of politics and love, Goldman, almost thirty-nine in 1908 when they met, was wrapped up in the most erotic and turbulent affair of her life. The force of Reitman's seemingly insatiable sexual drive prompted recurrent bouts of jealousy that plagued their relationship. She complained, "[Y]our escapades, your promiscuity, tears my very vital, fills me with gall and horror and twists my whole being into something foreign to myself."[78] Goldman's public call for free love made her disenchantment with her own relationship an insidious double bind. She felt powerless in the face of what she considered base sentiments like possessiveness (which she linked to the false entitlement in the culture of capitalism), but she could not exorcise those sentiments from her own life. Although she strove for complete consistency, the difficulties she faced in her intimate life were painful and visceral reminders of the profound challenges that accompanied most efforts at transforming social relations. Her lectures on the subject—including "The False Fundamentals of Free Love," "Variety or Monogamy, Which?" and, addressing her own dilemma, "Jealousy, Its Cause and Possible Cure"—were, in part, exhortations to her lover. Goldman's own attempts to practice what she preached were a major source of her bouts of self-doubt. "Love is beginning to be a mockery to me. . . . I shiver at the thought of putting down on paper, my foolish exalted conception of love which does not exist in reality."[79] In private she confessed that she felt "condemned before the bar of my own reason."[80]

Although she was not without detractors and skeptics, even among those in her own ranks, Goldman was known for holding to a high personal standard of what she considered anarchist conduct—living by her ideals—and looked to as "the great example."[81] In spite of the pain they caused her, however, Goldman's personal trials and tribulations

78. EG to BR, 28 July [1911], *EGP*, reel 5. See also *LA&EG*, p. 96.
79. EG to BR, 28 July 1910, *EGP*, reel 4; *LA&EG*, p. 136.
80. See EG to BR, June 1908, *EGP*, reel 2.
81. See letter from Mollie Steimer to Candace Falk, January 1978, in context in *LA&EG*, pbk., p. xv.

in the realm of love might have been the experiences that sharpened her attunement to the political dimensions of sexual desire.

## BEYOND EQUALITY OF THE SEXES

Female audiences, especially those primed by the New Woman movement of the 1890s and by the burgeoning suffrage activism,[82] attended talks that addressed both dilemmas and possibilities associated with their new privileges. Goldman's lecture topics mirrored these concerns.

She challenged those involved in legal reforms to rethink the premise and limits of their approach to the attainment of women's emancipation.[83] For Goldman, true freedom was based in equality rather than differentiation of the sexes by convention or law. Goldman asserted that "thousands of women do not want to vote, although the privilege should not be denied to them. Sex emancipation must come through thinking— through knowledge of herself and her relation to man."[84] Thus, she pushed back at those who still identified with the vestiges of the New Woman movement, asserting that real change would rely on the cooperative efforts of the New Man and a system that was grounded not in oppression but in openness to the new. The disconnection between marriage and love, even linking marriage to prostitution when the issue of the sex trade was in the spotlight, served as a provocative leitmotif in her discourse, and a general theme among anarchists.[85]

Somewhat surprisingly, authorities often felt less threatened by Goldman's pronouncements on political violence[86] than by the more popular appeal of her lectures on sex and gender issues. Huge receptive crowds attracted to topics related to sex and birth control seemed to threaten the traditional family and present a more immediate threat to a cornerstone of national stability. Goldman cited the high divorce rate as proof that love and marriage were diametrically opposed, compounded by the diminished status and

82. Some define the New Woman movement as a group of forward-looking women representing the radical shift of women's primary role from the private to the public sphere. These primarily middle- and upper-class women participated in social and literary clubs, reform and suffrage groups, as well as breaking open the employment market. As the women's colleges established in the 1870s and 1880s flourished, women began to pursue careers as teachers, social reformers, health experts, writers, artists, and physicians.

83. This refers to partiality based on gender assumptions and protectionism—special laws to accommodate those who, as a category, are deemed weaker, that is, women and children, as in *Muller v. Oregon* (1903), which allowed for shorter working hours for women to accommodate their reproductive responsibility.

84. "Emma Goldman Lectures on 'Love and Marriage' and 'Anarchy': Woman Who Has Aroused the World by Expressions of Radical Sentiments and Beliefs Talks to Reno People—Carried No Bombs in Her Pockets," *Reno Evening Gazette*, 18 April 1910.

85. See also Voltairine de Cleyre, "Those Who Marry Do Ill," in *Selected Works of Voltairine de Cleyre* (New York: Mother Earth Publishing Association, 1914).

86. These pronouncements on political violence, however, would later be used in court to imprison and deport Goldman.

capacity of women who tithed themselves to their husbands and families.[87] According to Goldman, the institution of marriage held a weak guarantee of security for women and children, asserting that emotional bonds were always stronger than legal bonds; she contended that if love was to last "not marriage, but love, will be the parent."[88] The inclusion of such ideas in her lectures, and in essays about the myths and realities of the conventions of personal life, continued to broaden her audiences and extended her readership.

Boldly, she addressed the subject of "the intermediate sex" at a time when homosexuality was relatively concealed,[89] and she broached the equally charged subject of birth control when information on conception was outlawed. As usual, Goldman challenged the drumbeat for women's suffrage as a panacea for all political ills, and with her lifelong interest in education she urged schools to cast off their time-worn emphasis on rote learning by encouraging creativity as well as critical thinking. Lively debates on electoral politics between Goldman and revolutionary socialists piqued popular interest at a time when the Socialist Party was gaining influence. The range of topics for her lectures drew large crowds[90] and sparked stimulating (and controversial) newspaper interviews that reached social reformers, among others, who might never have attended her lectures otherwise.

Her lectures (and reports in the press about them) attracted a diverse following. Goldman's excitement over new developments in European and Russian theater facilitated the integration of her European, Russian, and American sensibilities.

## STAGE SETTINGS: THE TRANSFORMATIVE POWER OF MODERN DRAMA

When introducing the social significance of modern drama to the American public (as few of the plays had been performed in the United States), Goldman recounted each plot line as a platform from which to address general themes integral to the transformation of society—most notably the encouragement of personal integrity and individual courage against the backdrop of hypocrisy, greed, and stifling social mores.

Goldman's appreciation of the dramatic arts and identification with stage performers also enhanced her performance on the lecture platform. Her variant of political theater,

---

87. Others, most notably socialist Charlotte Perkins Gilman, in *Women and Economics* (Boston: Small, Maynard, 1899), had addressed the issue of socialized housework as a possible solution to the insularity and slavishness of conventional responsibilities in the home.
88. Concluding commentary in EG's essay "Marriage and Love," in *Anarchism and Other Essays*.
89. Edward Carpenter, in his essay "The Intermediate Sex," first published in *Love's Coming of Age* (London: Swann Sonnenschein, 1906) and later in the United States as *The Immediate Sex* (Michell Kennerley, 1911), argues for the recognition of homosexuality, identifying it as an emotional as well as a sexual reality. Those in the intermediate sex were considered both masculine and feminine. For further discussion on EG's attitude, experience, and contribution to an expansive acceptance of sexual expression, see pp. 118–119, 124–125, 152–153.
90. See Chronology.

with her humorous audience repartee, was so lively that she was once solicited for (but quickly rejected) a chance to participate in vaudeville.[91]

Enthralled with serious theater, committed to its advancement in America, and convinced of its crucial role in the political awakening of the country, she not only incorporated modern drama into her lecture series but encouraged the training of young performers. In 1914 Goldman endorsed dramatist Maurice Browne's ideas about the creation of little theaters in each town and city along her lecture tour across the country. Companies would produce modern plays with socially significant themes performed by many otherwise unknown actors and actresses, rather than relying on the "one star" system, inspired in part by English stage societies and the musical talent spawned by an association of music teachers in Los Angeles.[92]

Frustrated with the abstract rhetoric of her political colleagues who relied on Marxist terms like "economic determinism" and "class consciousness" to move the masses,[93] Goldman frequently alluded to the politics of daily life, addressed so naturally in the contemporary plays of Europe. She believed that a play could reach people more effectively than the "wildest harangue of the soapbox orator."[94] Especially for those whose lives were relatively untouched by poverty and persecution, a forceful dramatic production on the subject could evoke, with disarming authenticity, sympathy for the poor. Through lectures delivered with a theatrical flair, she aspired to "embrac[e] the entire gamut of human emotions."[95]

Drawn to the ways in which the theater was so firmly embedded in the emotional details of life and the subtleties of human interaction, the way in which it linked personal courage to political ideals and made political action an everyday, common opportunity for all, Goldman used theater as a bridge. She considered modern drama to be the medium that revealed "the complex struggle of life," which was "at once the reflex and the inspiration of mankind in its eternal seeking for things higher and better."[96] Using the metaphor of drama was not only a winning strategy to avert the gaze of censors but also a means by which to tap into a shared humanity with her audience. To reiterate, she was especially effective in her ability to evoke empathy in comfortable intellectuals, spurring them into a growing awareness of the life of common people. Goldman also

---

91. See Candace Falk, "Emma Goldman: Passion, Politics, and the Theatrics of Free Expression," *Women's History Review* 2, no. 1 (2002). See also *LML*, vol. 2, p. 526.

92. See Falk, "Emma Goldman: Passion, Politics." See also "'Anarchist Queen' with Ambitious Dream," Article in the *Butte Miner*, 29 August 1913, in this volume.

93. Emma Goldman, *The Social Significance of the Modern Drama* (Boston: R. G. Badger 1914), p. 4.

94. Ibid., p. 5.

95. Ibid., p. 6

96. Ibid., p. 6.

became a voice for those "thrown in prison . . . mobbed, tarred, and deported."[97] She recognized the urgency of building links between intellectuals and labor.[98] Capitalizing on her access to those who had the resources to contribute and the openness to the ideas she introduced, Goldman also raised funds for *Mother Earth* and for the legal support for fair trials for many accused of political crimes.

In her 1914 book, *The Social Significance of the Modern Drama*, Goldman identified theater as "the dynamite which undermines superstition, shakes the social pillars and prepares men and women for the reconstruction,"[99] a role that she herself hoped to play in the grand theater of history.

She integrated her interests as a political performance artist, a proponent of the modern drama, and an occasional drama critic for the press.[100] Her various drama series included informal classes and individual lectures, extended her contact with the same group several times and thus provided an opportunity to make lasting friends and gather new supporters.[101] In Denver in 1912 and 1913 her Woman's Club lectures focused on Russian, German, French, and English drama and presented news of international trends in the theater. She appreciated the flexibility and range of topics she could address in her drama series, particularly because of increasing government repression. Unencumbered by censoring town officials or the presence of surveillance stenographers, she employed literary and dramatic allegory to circulate her politically challenging ideas.

Throughout her career Goldman continued to hold the modern drama firmly within the boundaries of her conception of political activism. In the 1950s literary historian Van Wyck Brooks remarked, "No one did more to spread the new ideas of literary Europe that influenced so many young people in the West as elsewhere—at least the ideas of the dramatists on the continent and in England—than the Russian-American Emma Goldman who established in New York, in 1906, the anarchist magazine *Mother Earth*."[102] [103]

97. Ibid., p. 7.
98. In Europe intellectuals and laborers had stronger bonds, were more effective as a movement, and had recently been subjects of severely repressive laws.
99. See Goldman, *The Social Significance of the Modern Drama*, p. 8.
100. EG reviewed a local production of Edmund Rostand's *Chantecler*: "Fair production which mystifies society—some wonder what it's about—more interested in themselves than symbolism," *Denver Post*, 23 April 1912.
101. In 1910 Goldman reworked her lecture as "The Drama as a Revolutionary Agency," variants of which were delivered through 1916. See Chronology for dates and places.
102. See Van Wyck Brooks, *The Confident Years* (New York: E. P. Dutton 1955), p. 375.
103. During her twenty years in exile she continued to lecture on modern drama, focusing on Russian playwrights, though she had failed in her attempt to publish a manuscript based on her lectures on the social and personal roots of their art. See Emma Goldman, "Foremost Russian Dramatists: Their Life and Work" (unpublished manuscript, 1926), *EGP*, reel 50.

Her lectures became the basis for published essays that, along with her later autobiography, would cement her commitment to imparting ideas through the stories of human interaction. Both the essays and the autobiography shaped her historical legacy and extended the reach of her own audience.

## BERKMAN'S PRISON MEMOIR: STORIES OF ISOLATION, CRUELTY, AND LOVE

Writing and editing require intense periods of concentration. The person with whom Goldman shared the intellectual foundation of her work was her "chum of a lifetime," Alexander "Sasha" Berkman. For Berkman it was a time of personal agony, acute observation, and intense contemplation. Still plagued in 1906 by the trauma of long periods in solitary confinement, Berkman found ordinary life often too difficult to bear. Goldman intermittently jumped in to protect him—sometimes even from himself.[104] In 1910 she and their comrade Voltairine de Cleyre (who had broached the subject as early as 1907)[105] encouraged him to write the memoir. Taking a break from the daily editorial duties he had assumed at the *Mother Earth* office, Sasha set off with Emma to her country retreat in Ossining, New York.[106] The task was emotionally and intellectually arduous.[107] Goldman was sure that his *Prison Memoirs of an Anarchist* (1912) would document details rarely recorded from the inside—the horror as well as the homoerotic love between prisoners. As they concentrated on the process of writing, they hoped, but could not know, that the book would have lasting influence.

Upon publication, Berkman's book was considered a literary masterpiece—an articulate exposé of his years in the penitentiary. The magazine *Coming Nation* predicted that his book "for generations will be one of the greatest counts in the indictment against our present system of punishing prisoners."[108] His eloquent prose and depiction of the graphic torment of prison life were compared to writings of Dostoevsky, Turgenev, and Tolstoy. Bayard Boyesen's review in *Mother Earth*[109] stated that from an anarchist point of view Berkman's book was one of "rare power and beauty, majestic in its structure, filled with the truth of imagination and the truth of actuality, emphatic in its declarations

---

104. See *LML*, pp. 387–90.
105. See Voltairine de Cleyre in Directory of Individuals in vol. 2, *Making Speech Free*, pp. 518–19.
106. The Ossining, New York, retreat had been given to Goldman by a dear friend and supporter, the single-taxer Bolton Hall. For background see Bolton Hall in Directory of Individuals, vol. 2, *Making Speech Free.*
107. "Yes, his book is truly great, but who will ever guess what it has cost me, what I have endured, what pains and struggles and tears, to make it possible. Why dear, it was worse than nursing an incurable sufferer back to life, for Berk. is such a difficult case to deal with. I am all worn out mentally and psychically. But I do not regret, because the value of the book makes up for all." EG to Nunia Seldes, 24 October 1912, *EGP*, reel 6.
108. *Mother Earth*, March 1913; *Coming Nation*, January 1913.
109. See *Mother Earth*, February 1913, pp. 422–24.

and noble in its reach." Writing his story played an important role in freeing Berkman from his past and enabled him to engage more fully in the present and to imagine his future unbound.

## BERKMAN UNFETTERED

Berkman's desire to strike out on his own in late 1914 was related to the fluid and ever-changing intimacies in their inner anarchist circle, with its inevitable jealousies and differences of opinion. He had long since broken his sexual ties to Emma,[110] who had evolved into his confidante, comrade, and defender. Among his many subsequent lovers was the young Becky Edelsohn, a militant who, along with many other young anarchist women, shared his loathing of John D. Rockefeller Jr.'s brutal role in squelching labor organizing in Ludlow, Colorado, and who was willing to protest and wage a hunger strike, with little care about personal consequences.[111]

Eventually, the red-headed, hard-working M. Eleanor Fitzgerald, affectionately called "Fitzi" or "Lioness," joined their group as an office assistant and also kindled Sasha's desires (in spite of the fact that she was a former lover of Emma's manager, Ben).[112] The necessary interactions at the *Mother Earth* office among them all became a serious source of tension, especially given Sasha's disdain of Ben and Emma's initial jealousy of Fitzi.

In the October 1914 issue of *Mother Earth* Sasha wrote an article entitled "My Resurrection Jubilee" in which he announced his upcoming tour to Pittsburgh and "further West." Originally he had intended to leave on 18 May 1914, "the eighth anniversary of my release from prison,"[113] but the events in Colorado called for immediate protest in Tarrytown. He felt compelled to aid Caplan and Schmidt, the men who had recently been arrested for involvement in the bombing of the building of the anti-union *Los Angeles Times* many years before (in October 1910). Motivated by this and a renewed sense of his own power, Sasha was headed for the lecture trail by November 1914. He traveled with Fitzi to Pittsburgh, Homestead, Wilkinsburg, and New Kensington, then on to Cleveland, Elyria, Detroit, Chicago, Minneapolis, and finally Los Angeles to work directly with the Caplan-Schmidt Defense Fund. Caveats by some Los Angeles trade unionists, who feared that any ties to anarchism would limit the broader support for the cause may have influenced Berkman's decision to take to the road again. His tour from Los Angeles to New York from July to September 1915 included talks related to his

---

110. His "sailor girl," Goldman had been his lover before his prison stay 1892–1906. After that their tie evolved into a deep, nonsexual, friendship.

111. Becky Edelsohn was his "Spitfire." See Directory of Individuals.

112. In this discussion of personal life I've chosen to address Goldman, Berkman, Reitman, and Fitzgerald as Emma, Sasha, Ben, and Fitzi, to evoke a more familiar, intimate rendition of the closeness of their circle.

113. Alexander Berkman, "An Innocent Abroad," *Mother Earth*, January 1915.

*Prison Memoirs* but were primarily intended to draw audiences and to make the case for contributing to the Caplan-Schmidt defense.

Not long after Sasha and Fitzi returned to New York, they again set off for the West. San Francisco, a place with a strong militant labor base,[114] seemed like the perfect revolutionary locale to fulfill his longtime dream of publishing an anarchist weekly: "We live in a psychologic moment,[115] especially as far as the West is concerned."[116] January 1916 marked the publication of the first edition of *The Blast*.[117] The reportage was immediate and action-oriented, while its articles kept some of the literary and theoretical qualities of *Mother Earth*. Although not averse to Goldman's monthly, Sasha believed his anarchist labor weekly could fill a critical gap in the movement.[118]

On the surface, given the titles *The Blast* and *Mother Earth* as well as the style of presentation, Berkman's magazine with its fiery language might seem less cautious than Goldman's in its presentation of violent anarchist actions. His anarchist militancy never wavered, nor did his support of direct-action tactics.[119] Their overarching vision, however, remained unchanged.[120]

Committed as they both were to a shared anarchist approach to the betterment of humanity, and as devoted to their mutual friends and comrades, each found the other difficult to live with. A physical separation allowed for a new kind of blossoming and individuation. Yet no matter where they were, their friendship, camaraderie, shared history, and daily commitment to their ideal bonded them for life.

The two had become adept at the art of publishing periodicals for a relatively small targeted readership. Berkman was determined to broaden the base with *The Blast*, while

114. Including Eric Morton and Anton Johannsen.
115. *Psychologic moment* was often used as an expression of readiness for militant political action—strikes, sabotage, or targeted acts of retaliatory violence.
116. AB to Anna Strunsky Walling, 31 December 1915. Emma Goldman Papers, third party correspondence file.
117. See introduction to "Down with the Anarchists," *The Blast*, 15 August 1916.
118. Most labor-oriented papers were not in English. "At its peak in the 1910s, the number of ethnic non-English periodicals in the United States (weeklies, dailies, monthlies) reached more than 1300 different titles." Dirk Hoerder, ed., *The Immigrant Labor Press in North America, 1840s–1970s* (New York: Greenwood Press, 1987). The English-language labor-oriented periodicals were primarily socialist: the *International Socialist Review* appealed to those on the left of the SPA and the IWW and had a large circulation. See Directory of Periodicals.
119. William E. Trautmann, *Direct Action and Sabotage* (Pittsburgh: Socialist News Company, 1912).
120. Still, there was an important distinction between a magazine and an agitational newspaper. For example, although *The Blast*, like *Mother Earth*, covered some birth control arrests as well as EG's trial in 1916, once the Preparedness Day explosion came to dominate the news in San Francisco, the paper focused primarily on issues of "class war"—and actively came to Tom Mooney and Warren Billings's defense after their arrest. And although *Mother Earth*'s Observations and Comments section (most likely written by Max Baginski and, later, Alexander Berkman) and essays like EG's "Self-Defense for Labor" represented a stance that was as militant as that of *The Blast*, *Mother Earth*'s cultural and political commentary offered readers the choice to select articles that matched their particular interest, though after 1912 *Mother Earth* abandoned much of its literary aspiration.

Goldman expanded hers mostly through cross-country lecture tours. The output of the magazine was consistent, despite its new configuration. The Mother Earth Publishing Association remained an anchor, however precarious the operation, and continued to provide a secure emotional and political grounding for Emma's work. Her ties with Sasha and Fitzi, however strained, remained strong and, perhaps with distance, became more solid than ever.

## ANARCHISM AND THE AVANT-GARDE

Goldman had always taken an interest in the relationship between politics and art. As previously described, years of following the developments in modern European drama gave her a creative topic through which to counteract suppression of subjects that, if spoken of directly, would be considered dangerous. Her interest in bringing European drama to wider audiences in America served as a connection to the arts that solidified Goldman's identification with the international avant-garde movement and with local Greenwich Village bohemian intellectuals.

Among the bohemian avant-garde of Greenwich Village, Goldman made a place for herself as a spokeswoman for anarchism. She felt at home with others who shunned materialism and considered themselves "moderns" by shedding conventionality and believing themselves part of a new movement that would shape the future.[121] Goldman smoked and drank with European comrades and Village bohemians and addressed new audiences hungry for change. She socialized with several members of the Heterodoxy Club,[122] many of whom identified with the New Woman movement and recognized the political dimensions of personal life; some even opened themselves to her anarchist ideas about unrestricted sexual freedom.[123]

## WAR IN EUROPE, REPRESSION IN AMERICA

In 1914 the atmosphere of burgeoning possibilities for Goldman, political and personal, was clouded by an abrupt turn of world events. The Great War raged through Europe. President Wilson had been reelected by a small margin in 1916 as the peace candidate, promising to keep America out of the war. Yet by April 1917, as battles on the sea were

---

121. See Stansell, *American Moderns.*
122. The Heterodoxy Club was a group of independent women thinkers, mostly professional and educated in universities or by their experiences in radical and bohemian circles. See Judith Schwarz, *Radical Feminists of Heterodoxy: Greenwich Village, 1912–1940* (Lebanon, N.H.: New Victoria Publishers, 1986).
123. At the same time, Goldman's own sexuality broke with tradition to include open amorous involvements with both women and men. Thus, her belief in the expansiveness of love acquired an added nuance. An example of the complex nature of her bisexuality during these years was that although EG obviously was more drawn to Ben than to Almeda Sperry, and Ben was more drawn to Emma than to Hutchins Hapgood, with whom he may have had a homosexual liaison, crossing sexual convention was clearly part of their modus vivendi. See *LA&EG*, p. 105.

encroaching and a national preparedness campaign was building, he reluctantly shifted toward the position that the risk of losing the war was too high; henceforth, joining the war effort was considered a critical step toward making the world safe for democracy.[124]

By mid-1916, the United States was preparing to defend itself should the Great War spread. Much of the country had entered a preparedness mode, edging toward a war footing. Government surveillance agencies readied themselves to take action against those who would eventually be deemed threats to the stability of a country preparing for war. As in the past, when the protection of civil liberties and the right of dissent eroded, so too did the arc of Goldman's life take a downward curve.

In this time of heightened awareness of child mortality rates among the poor, there was a widespread clampdown on discussions about birth control and women's freedom to determine the size of their own families. The renewed stringency of such laws cast the actions of Goldman and others who offered women information about reproductive choice as unpatriotic attempts to control the bearers of the next generation of soldiers and workers.[125] Signaling the upcoming weakening of individual rights, State interven-

124. Background for the war footing included a National Security League (NSL) formed in New York in 1914, followed by a call for a Council of National Defense. Responding in part to fears that America might not be capable of defending itself in an attack, large daily newspapers reported on the need for, and in most cases supported, the expansion of the army and navy—and a national preparedness campaign. Neither President Wilson nor organized labor signed on until after the sinking of the British ship *Lusitania* in May 1915, with the loss of over a hundred American lives. In June the National Security League hosted a conference on peace and preparedness attended by 3,000 delegates from twenty-five states. By November there were seventy branches of the NSL across the country. Early in 1916, while Congress debated military legislation, cities all over the United States began staging preparedness parades. In May the National Defense Act passed, increasing the military and national guard and mobilizing industrial support. In August Samuel Gompers, president of the American Federation of Labor, was brought in by Wilson to the new Council of National Defense, a think tank for simultaneously maintaining economic productivity and preparing for war.

125. Birth control arrests: In 1915 William Sanger, for distributing birth control information. On 20 April 1916 EG sentenced to fifteen days in Queens County Jail after refusing to pay a $100 fine, having been convicted for speaking on birth control at Star Casino, New York City, on 8 February 1916. On 27 April 1916 BR arrested for distributing birth control pamphlets at a meeting in the Harlem Masonic Temple on 23 April 1916; on 8 May 1916 he was sentenced to sixty days in the workhouse, Queens County Jail. On 20 May 1916, New York meeting at Union Square to protest BR's imprisonment, Ida Rauh Eastman, Bolton Hall, Jessie Ashley were arrested for distributing birth control leaflets. On 30 June 1916 in Portland, Oregon, Margaret Sanger and others were arrested for distributing "Family Limitation" (three union men had been arrested on 19 June for a similar offense; all were tried on 1 July, found guilty, and fined $10). In July 1916 in Boston Van Kleek Allison (editor of radical paper the *Flame*) was arrested for distributing birth control literature; he was sentenced to three years' imprisonment. On 20 October 1916 Bolton Hall was acquitted on charge of distributing birth control literature at the 20 May 1916 meeting in Union Square; EG was arrested on same charge when she appeared to testify on Hall's behalf. On 12 December 1916 in Cleveland BR was arrested at a meeting on birth control "for calling for volunteers to distribute birth control literature"; he was released on $1,000 bail. On 15 December 1916 in Rochester BR was arrested at a meeting for distributing birth control literature. Sanger's birth control clinic, Brownsville, Brooklyn, opened 16 October 1916 and was closed down by police

tion in the private domain escalated. Suddenly in 1915 and 1916 the same birth control talks Goldman had delivered for years were monitored more intensely by law enforcement officials. Birth control literature surreptitiously distributed to the audience landed Goldman (and Reitman) in jail, sometimes overnight and sometimes for weeks or even months.[126] Suppression of almost anything that challenged the status quo, especially on issues of sexuality, may have served as a testing ground to gauge public toleration of the suppression of free speech in anticipation of the enactment of more restrictive measures that would accompany entry into the war.

In July 1916 Goldman traveled to San Francisco with the intention of lecturing on "Preparedness: The Road to Universal Slaughter." She had the misfortune to arrive in the city just days before a bomb exploded on 22 July amid a group of Spanish-American War veterans waiting to join the Preparedness Day parade. She witnessed the police roundup and arrest of local labor activists. Militants within the San Francisco labor movement were prime suspects. The anti-preparedness movement not only defended young working-class men who were sure to be drafted into military service for the First World War but served as a shield for unions that also feared that an armaments industry would break the strength of the city's renowned closed shop. Berkman was among the group suspected in the bombing but not detained. His weekly paper, *The Blast*, as well as other papers, wholeheartedly defended the accused prime suspects—Thomas Mooney and Warren Billings.[127] Initially, *The Blast* was the only paper to voice support. Given the panic and outrage following the bombings, to speak out in defense of the accused took considerable courage.[128]

While others hesitated, unsure about associating with the act and fearful of reprisals, Berkman enlisted a first-rate lawyer, Bourke Cochran, on the case. Berkman and Goldman left San Francisco to mount a campaign on both the East and West coasts to raise funds and support from unions for the arrested suspects in the Preparedness Day bombing. By August they had revived the International Workers' Defense League, and in December 1916 Goldman addressed a large crowd on the subject at a rally in New York City's Carnegie Hall, sponsored and generously supported by the United Hebrew Trades (UHT). Berkman's close association with the militant San Francisco unionists was why

---

26 October 1916; Margaret Sanger, Ethel Byrne (her sister), and Fani Mindell were arrested; the clinic reopened 13 November 1916, and Sanger was arrested on 14 November 1916 on charges of maintaining a public nuisance, and police were stationed at clinic to ensure it remained closed.

126. They were charged, separately and together, with surreptitious distribution of illegal information on birth control when they were arrested in Portland in 1915 (where they were tried by "a very remarkable Judge . . . the first man on the bench who deprecates the fact that people are entirely too prudish." EG to W. S. Van Valkenburgh, 18 August 1915, *EGP*, reel 9). Another arrest took place in New York in 1916.

127. See *The Blast*, 1 September 1916.

128. When it became clear that the threat of Berkman's direct implication in the crime might be imminent, he and Fitzi closed the office of *The Blast* in March 1917 and returned to New York.

he was named as a suspect in the bombing and threatened with extradition from New York to face trial. The UHT joined a support committee and not only published the pamphlet *They Want to Hang Alexander Berkman* but also donated over $1,000 to his defense.[129] The immediacy of the case took precedence over all other commitments.

## LOVE AND WAR

Within a few months of Goldman's return to New York her personal world shattered, compounded by her anxiety about Berkman's extradition. Ben Reitman, the love of her life, had succumbed to what he considered an ordinary man's desire for a wife and family and settled down with Anna Martindale, a labor activist he'd met at the *Mother Earth* office in 1912.[130] Five years his junior, and fifteen years younger than Emma, she devoted herself to Ben. In Cleveland in 1916, during his two-month prison sentence for distributing birth control pamphlets,[131] Anna provided the emotional support he craved. Within a year Anna Martindale was pregnant with their child.[132] All of Emma's previous efforts to live collectively with Ben, including integrating his mother into their busy political household, had failed miserably. Ultimately, her devotion to "the cause" trumped all attempts to create a lasting intimate relationship—conduct both self-protective and experienced as true to the essence of her highest self.

Upon receiving news of her many anarchist comrades in Europe languishing behind bars as victims of wartime repression, Goldman had a strong inkling that the worst was yet to come.

## 2. A HISTORICAL CONTEXT

Just as Goldman viewed history from the perspective of one who had been inspired to political action by the hanging of the Haymarket anarchists, so too each generation fil-

---

129. However, in Chicago, the UHT refused to host Berkman, prompting a split in the organization, at which point a break-off group set up its own organization and speaking venue to support his campaign to raise funds for the defense of Mooney and Billings—countering claims of undivided UHT support. Samuel Holland, oral history, shared with EGP by Thomas Busch.

130. "I began to dream of a home with my mother, my wife and baby and steady practice . . . visions of teaching in a medical college, of being a reformer to outcasts and an active worker in the church." BR, "Following the Monkey" (unpublished autobiography), UI-C, p. 358, cited in *LA&EG*, p. 259.

131. The birth control pamphlets contained information about the use of vinegar and makeshift condoms, as well as open discussions of the rhythm method and of female physiology.

132. For more on Anna Martindale, and an excellent discussion of her relationship with Reitman, see Mecca Reitman Carpenter, *No Regrets—Dr. Ben Reitman and the Women Who Loved Him* (Lexington, Mass.: Southside Press, 1999), pp. 45–48; see also, Roger A. Bruns, *The Damndest Radical* (Urbana: University of Illinois Press, 1987), p. 177.

ters the past through the sensibilities of its own times. A historian's work is to recapture that past with minimal distortion, while recognizing that the telling of history is also bound by time.[133]

Goldman reframed the central issues of her time, one by one, through her own lens. Addressing topics very much in the public consciousness, she attempted to expose the social price of political compromise—while inviting her audiences to imagine the excitement of living in a world in which social harmony was contingent on unharnessed freedom.[134] Though many considered her anarchist outlook wildly unrealistic, distorted, and blind to the value of incremental change, they nonetheless recognized the truth of her fundamental critique and assessment of what was lacking. She addressed what she considered to be the double-standard morality of laws to control prostitution and birth control, the hypocrisy of religion, the limitations of the traditional family, the inadequacy of prison reform, and the unrealistic expectations for change that would accompany woman's suffrage. She attempted to challenge the inflated claims of progressive reform, and the hierarchical framework underlying the burgeoning socialist and labor union movements. As her interest grew in how children learn, she helped initiate Modern Schools that cultivated creativity and fostered individuality, believing that "every child is an anarchist at heart."[135] As a spokeswoman for anarchism, she clarified the difference between anarchism and socialism to those who often confused the two ideologies, and she attempted to unravel the complex weave of violence. Though never uniformly acclaimed for her ideas, Goldman had a dramatic, eloquent presence as a propagandist making her much sought after and a spectacle to behold.

## DISCRIMINATING WHITE FROM BLACK: PUBLIC OUTRAGE AND THE BURGEONING SEX TRADE

The third volume opens with Goldman's powerful essay "The White Slave Traffic" (see Essay in *Mother Earth*, January 1910).[136] In it she addressed issues raised by the

133. No doubt my own trajectory as one influenced by the collaborative, egalitarian aspects of feminism and political activism of the 1970s framed my initial interest in Emma Goldman; gradually, as the editor/director of the Emma Goldman Papers for over thirty years my insights into Goldman, her vision, and the forces that influenced her life and ideas have evolved, thus broadening my own temporal and historical awareness of "time-boundedness." For a fuller discussion see Candace Falk, "Let Icons Be Bygones! Emma Goldman: The Grand Expositor," in *Feminist Interpretations of Emma Goldman*, eds. Penny A. Weiss and Loretta Kinzinger (University Park: Penn State University Press, 2007).

134. "Some Civitas Members Wanted to Be 'Thrilled,' So Goldman Was Asked to Address Them," interview in *Brooklyn Eagle*, 16 January 1916, *EGP*, reel 48.

135. "A new day is dawning when the school will serve life in all its phases and reverently lift each human child to its appropriate place in common life of beneficent social efficiency, whose motto will be not uniformity and discipline but freedom, expansion, good will and joy for each and all." "The Social Importance of the Modern School" (draft, unpublished manuscript), *EGP*, reel 55.

136. A revised version was published, with some significant changes, as "The Traffic in Women," in her book *Anarchism and Other Essays* (1910; 2nd ed., 1911; 3rd ed., 1917).

recent passage of the Mann Act,[137] a law intended as a legal tool for policing the sex trade that focused on abductions of young women across state lines for immoral purposes. Goldman, ever the naysayer to the panacea of legal fixes, suggested that although the degradation and exploitation of these women clearly was unjust, the law diverted attention away from the socioeconomic conditions that forced poor women into prostitution. Although many newspapers and journals published articles on the general topic without interference, the postal delivery of the January 1910 issue of Goldman's monthly magazine was delayed, ostensibly because it included her essay "The White Slave Traffic."

Perhaps the attempts to censor Goldman were related to her view that reports of middle-class girls being coerced into the trade by unscrupulous men were justified but that the act purporting to protect those forced into prostitution also provided an opportunity to victimize poor working women "on the streets"—those who might choose prostitution over "working for a few shillings a week in scullery, eighteen hours a day."[138] The law could not in itself alleviate the poverty limiting the work options for women, thus leaving them vulnerable to both industrial and sexual abuse. She considered the efforts of well-meaning protectionist reformers to be a veiled form of a generalized prejudice against the immigrant women in the flourishing sex trade. She was familiar with the lure of young immigrant women to American men, based on the mix of attraction and repulsion with which she had been received by many who saw her only as an immigrant woman. She spoke as one who was no longer a greenhorn—a newly arrived clueless immigrant—but as someone who was protective of those easily exploited, because they lacked both resources and knowledge about the harsh side of the New World.

When the Mann Act was passed in 1910, public discussion was less about racism than it was about curbing a rampant development that had arisen in two of the oldest professions—prostitution and pimping—in which individuals were captured for the economic advancement of their masters.[139] Years before the law's passage, the term coined to refer to the sexual trafficking of women, "white slave traffic,"[140] conjured up images of the injustice of the black slavery, or chattel slavery, that was recalled by a nation just a few generations removed from the Civil War—a nation still plagued by racism and lynching. Thus, the designation "white slavery" was merely a distinction from "black slavery" before the Civil War. Much of the outrage, however, was a response to the notion that white women (especially those in the lower middle class) were being trafficked as sexual

---

137. The Mann Act was passed in June 1910, six months after "The White Slave Traffic" was written.
138. Referring to George Bernard Shaw's *Mrs. Warren's Profession* in essay cited above, "The White Slave Traffic."
139. This is not to imply that black slaves were not also coerced into sexual liaisons with their masters.
140. See George Kibbe Turner, "The City of Chicago: A Study of the Great Immoralities," *McClure's Magazine* 28 (April 1907).

slaves. The racial and ethnic underside of the Mann Act's focus on white slave traffic was evident in the predominance of white male frequenters of ethnic immigrant brothels, as well as in the relative tolerance of coercion and even rape of black women by white men at a time when consensual relations between black men and white women was not only a social taboo but, in most instances, punishable by law.

Thus, in the case of white slave traffic, "whiteness" as opposed to "blackness" encompassed women from many ethnic backgrounds who were often discriminated against for their "racial" difference.[141] Frequenting brothels was a fixed element of male culture, but the preponderance of Jewish and Italian women and their "cadets" in the trade was seen as foreign corruption of native moral values, whether or not that assumption was statistically correct.[142]

The pervasiveness of the sex trade was also perceived as a menace to the institution of marriage and even a possible contaminant leading to the spread of infectious diseases. "Women adrift" frequented new urban centers, places in which leisure activities—including saloons and dance halls—enticed single women with the pleasures of post-poning the responsibilities of marriage and children. In fact, family size dropped significantly with the rise of birth control and increasing numbers of professional middle-class women.[143] Years before, Teddy Roosevelt had warned that this phenomenon was a sign of impending "race suicide."[144] From another vantage point, however twisted the logic may seem, the existence of the thriving business of prostitution, with its clientele of pre-

141. That is, the Jewish and Italian "races." For an excellent group of essays on the issue of race and ethnicity in the Progressive era, see Charlotte J. Rich, *Transcending the New Woman: Multi-ethnic Narratives in the Progressive Era* (Columbia: University of Missouri Press, 2009).

142. Cadets (otherwise known as "pimps") are men who procure customers for prostitutes, exact a commission, and often brutally control the lives of the sex workers they consider under their employ. For an intriguing study of prostitution and specifics of the history of white slavery see Ruth Rosen, *The Lost Sisterhood: Prostitution in America, 1900–1918* (Baltimore: John Hopkins University Press, 1982).

143. A. Maurice Low, "Lower Birth Rate and Higher Prices Signs of Progress; A. Maurice Low Says That When They Are World-Wide They Cease to Be Unnatural Phenomena and Become the Natural Order of Things—What Has Caused Them in Modern Times," *New York Times*, 4 May 1913. Also according to the Thirteenth Census of the United States from 1900 to 1910 the number of women in professional services increased. And the Fourteenth Census, covering the years between 1910 and 1920, ascertained that the number of working women in professional services rose from 733,891 to 1,016,498, and that the percentage of all working women in professional services in the population of female wage earners increased from 9.1 percent to 11.9 percent.

144. "If the men of the nation are not anxious to work in many different ways, with all their might and strength, and ready and able to fight at need, and anxious to be fathers of families, and if the women do not recognize that the greatest thing for any woman is to be a good wife and mother, why, that nation has cause to be alarmed about its future." Theodore Roosevelt, prefatory letter to *The Woman Who Toils* by Mrs. John Van Vorst and Marie Van Vorst, http://www.gutenberg.org/files/15218/15218-h/15218-h.htm.

dominantly native-born men, actually might have stabilized the middle-class family as an institution for the containment of male sexual desire. Prostitution, with all its dangers, nonetheless also provided a relatively lucrative option for the working woman to support herself, and perhaps her family, when other jobs were unavailable.

Instead, public concern about harm to women and the threat to moral standards prompted legislation to criminalize prostitution, forcing it to become another secret, illicit activity. While Goldman agreed that forced prostitution was a transgression on every level, she objected to the moral stigmas attached to women who sold sex. She believed that each person must be in command of her or his own body.[145] "Woman is a human being first, and her sex should be a secondary consideration."[146] Goldman linked her position on the subject of prostitution to her anarchist principles of complete sexual autonomy. It should be up to the woman to determine how many and which lovers to choose and to decide when or whether to join the ranks of motherhood. In fact, she proposed that marriage, in its present form, was economic and physical prostitution.[147]

Goldman discussed the class and gender disparity between access to contraception and knowledge about sexuality, the double standard on the sexual practices of men and women,[148] and the pitifully few work options open to poor immigrant women whose economic survival was tenuous. Most of all, she spoke out against punishing the victims rather than the perpetrators of an unequal system.

Goldman's critique of capitalism's dependence on the working poor distinguished her from those who sought legal remedies to ameliorate the plight of prostitutes and who considered stricter protective regulations for women in the trade evidence of progressive change. Goldman judged the mediating effect of a patchwork of progressive laws ultimately doomed to failure.[149] However sympathetic Goldman was to the exploitation of and prejudice against the women who worked as prostitutes and to those who were kidnapped and forced into the sex trade, she nonetheless characterized those who were preoccupied with the issue of white slavery as middle-class moralists whose economic self-interest eclipsed their ability to come to terms with the underlying problem of wage

---

145. C. L. James to EG, ca. January 1911, *EGP*, reel 4.

146. "Talks of Free Love," *Wyoming Tribune*, 8 April 1910, Emma Goldman Papers, office newspaper files.

147. See "Marriage," Essay in the *Firebrand*, vol. 1, *Made for America*, pp. 269–73.

148. "Talks of Free Love," *Wyoming Tribune*, 8 April 1910, Emma Goldman Papers, office third party newspaper files. See also illustration on cover of *The Blast*, 12 February 1916, addressing the class discrepancy in access to birth control, p. 000 in this volume.

149. See, for example, Susan Lehrer, *Origins of Protective Labor Legislation for Women 1905–1925* (Albany: State University of New York Press, 1987), which also includes an excellent bibliography. See also Julie Novkov, *Constituting Workers, Protecting Women: Gender, Law, and Labor in the Progressive Era and New Deal Years* (Ann Arbor: University of Michigan Press, 2001–2004), especially "Cases Cited," pp. 297–305.

slavery. The post office's hesitation about, and then release of, the issue of *Mother Earth* that included her essay "The White Slave Traffic" is an example of sexual and political censorship, steeped in unspoken racial prejudice.

In many ways, the unpredictable pattern of suppression and arrests increased the effectiveness of instilling fear as a means for controlling dissent. Such intimidation generally meant that only those few who were unafraid of arrest dared to speak out. Although Goldman found such roadblocks obstructing her talks and publications frustrating and annoying, she also seized these brief periods of intense public attention as opportunities to articulate anarchist ideas. The intermittent repression she, and others, faced in this time of liberalism was not a coordinated effort but one tied rather to the specifics of who was in charge as well as the time and place. Goldman was a moving target in a country that had yet to centralize its police and surveillance capabilities, where more often than not she was able to evade censorship and arrest.

## MUTED ON RACISM

Racism and repression went hand in hand. The country's protracted history of racial inequality upheld the hierarchies of white-skin privilege. Even the Mann Act, written in response to the problem of white slave traffic, with its focus on the plight of Jews, Italians, Filipinas, and women of mixed race, approached them all as "other" in spite of their formal classification as "white." The long-standing sexual abuse of black women never elicited the same outrage. And, it was not long before the Mann Act would be turned against African Americans.[150]

In this time of rampant racism, African American journalist Ida B. Wells, among other black activists, had publicized the egregious practice of lynching.[151] Chicago papers published news of race riots that had erupted in the city Goldman often visited. Yet when confronted with these horrors, Goldman was uncharacteristically brief.[152]

Why did Goldman not devote more time and energy to analyzing and battling racial hatred toward African Americans? Perhaps both anarchists and advocates for racial jus-

---

150. For example, the Mann Act was used against Jack Johnson, who on the Fourth of July 1910 became the first African American World Heavyweight Champion. His opponent, Jim Jeffries, was dubbed "The Great White Hope" and set out to prove "that a white man is better than a Negro." Johnson's smashing victory was rumored to have been reported in the *San Francisco Chronicle* the next day as "a calamity worse than the San Francisco earthquake." In 1913, within a year of Johnson's marriage to a white former prostitute, he was accused of violating the Mann Act, based on a broad interpretation of interstate commerce for immoral purposes. According to the presiding judge, Johnson's ultimate crime was the misfortune to be the foremost example of the evil in permitting the intermarriage of whites and blacks.

151. Ida B. Wells-Barnett, *A Red Record: Tabulated Statistics and Alleged Causes of Lynching in the United States, 1892–1893–1894, Respectfully Submitted to the Nineteenth Century Civilization in the "Land of the Free and the Home of the Brave"* (Chicago: Donohue and Henneberry, 1895).

152. Later, in her 1917 "Address to the Jury," Goldman would discuss lynching parallels. See vol. 4, *The War Years* (forthcoming).

tice—black and white—thought mixing the fight against racism with the challenge of anarchism would dilute their struggles. In her 1912 lecture "Are We Really Advancing?" she did note that "the same well-dressed, howling, hooting, blood-thirsty mob" was targeting "Anarchists instead of Abolitionists" with a sharp difference—"the mob didn't have a rope." She then extended the analogy: "It is today a[s] great [a] crime to work for the emancipation of the White Slave as it had been [in the time of William Lloyd Garrison and Wendell Phillips] to espouse the cause of the Black Slave."[153] Goldman felt ill-equipped to take on the cause, feeling unwelcome in a divided nation in which her anarchist politics, however all-encompassing and universal its ideals, most likely represented too much of a stretch for African Americans attempting to counter the immediate impact of racism. As a Russian Jewish immigrant who identified with other eastern European immigrants, she too experienced racial prejudice, but never with the same intensity as African Americans in the United States. For Goldman, just reaching an audience of natural-born citizens took tremendous powers of persuasion, but did not excuse her oblivion to the racism against others.

Later in her life she would reflect on her relationship to the South and the race issue in America and regret this gap in her lifelong advocacy of freedom.[154] Yet a serious failing of Goldman and much of the white left of her time was that they were too urban, northern, and Eurocentric to connect with the South—and fearful of the backlash.

Her closest contact with African Americans was in prison.[155] A hallmark of Goldman's character was independence of thought; she was not afraid to speak her truth about fairness and oppression, even if it raised the possibility of being misunderstood or thought insensitive on the issue of race. In her 1931 autobiography Goldman shared her observations on the double-edged sword of racism as she experienced it in prison for almost a year in 1893:

> I was gradually given entire charge of the hospital ward, part of my duties being to divide the special rations allowed the sick prisoners. . . . They consisted of a quart of milk, a cup of beef tea, two eggs, two crackers, and two lumps of sugar for each invalid. On several occasions milk and tea were missing and I reported the matter. . . . [A] head matron said that it did not matter. . . . I had had considerable opportunity to study this head matron, who felt a violent dislike of everyone not Anglo-Saxon. Her special targets were the Irish and the Jews, against whom she discriminated habitually. . . .
>
> . . . [T]he missing portions had been given by this head matron to two husky Negro prison-

153. Emma Goldman, "Are We Really Advancing?" (unpublished manuscript, ca. June 1912), *EGP*, reel 47.
154. EG to Leonardo Andrea, Edgefield, South Carolina, 29 December 1931, *EGP*, reel 25.
155. Later, during her years of exile in London, she developed a deep and mutually adoring friendship with Eslanda and Paul Robeson, as expressed in their letters from 1930–1938. For Paul Robeson, see *EGP*, reel 35; for Eslanda, see reels 22, 23, 26, 35, 36, 42. And see Robeson's tribute to Goldman: Paul Robeson, "A Vote of Thanks," in "An Anarchist Looks at Life," Foyle's Twenty-Ninth Literary Luncheon, 1 March 1933, *EGP*, reel 52.

ers. . . . I knew she had a special fondness for the coloured inmates. She rarely punished them and often gave them unusual privileges. In return her favourites would spy on the other prisoners, even on those of their own colour who were too decent to be bribed. I myself never had any prejudice against coloured people; in fact, I felt deeply for them because they were being treated like slaves in America. But I hated discrimination. The idea that sick people, white or coloured should be robbed of their rations to feed healthy persons outraged my sense of justice, but I was powerless to do anything in the matter.

Journalist John Swinton read Goldman's observations on race when this excerpt was published in the *New York World* and reacted in print. She responded,

John Swinton was grieved to see that Emma Goldman had "the white man's prejudice against the coloured race." . . . I pointed out the discrimination practiced between sick starved women and Negro favourites. I should have protested as much had coloured women been robbed of their rations. . . . [To which] Swinton replied, "still, you should not have emphasized the partiality. We white people have committed so many crimes against the Negro that no amount of extra kindness can atone for them. The matron is no doubt a beast, but I forgive her much for her sympathy with the poor Negro prisoners." I [Goldman] protested, "she was kind because she could use them in every despicable way."

Swinton was not convinced. He had been closely allied with the most active abolitionists, he had fought and been wounded in the Civil War; it was apparent that his feelings for the coloured race had made him partial.[156]

Goldman's letters and lectures testify that her commitment to anarchism and anarchists was the unifying principle through which she made sense of, interacted with, and inhabited the world.[157] She believed that she was indispensable to the anarchist cause, though she knew there were many others who were willing and able to attend to many equally vital struggles.

Perhaps more importantly with regard to the issue of race, she saw little evidence of interest among African American radicals in associating with anarchists, anarchism, or Emma Goldman. She had met W. E. B. Du Bois, who was among the most prominent Negro intellectuals of the time, but she considered his socialism an impediment to their working together. Even though she was sympathetic to the plight of those affected by racial prejudice, Goldman was so focused on her role as a proponent of anarchism that

156. *LML*, p. 138, on EG's discussion of racial bias in the prison hospital, and pp. 154–55 on EG's article and Swinton's response.

157. This predisposition for anarchist causes was especially pronounced later in her life in her choice to work for the Spanish anarchists from 1936 to 1938 more directly than for European Jews as Hitler gained but had not yet taken power. With great foresight, she sent out an early warning linking Hitler's Nazism to Stalin's Communism and Franco's Fascism. Just before World War II, she wrote extensively about the importance of Jewish culture to German culture. See EG, "Collapse of German Culture," fragment of unpublished manuscript, *EGP*, reel 55.

she rarely crossed ideological lines. Still, when reporting to international anarchist congresses about the situation in America, she expounded on the horrors of lynching and the pervasiveness of racial prejudice.[158]

## EVADING CENSORSHIP: DISCREPANCIES IN LAWS GOVERNING SPOKEN AND WRITTEN EXPRESSION

Freedom of speech was rarely synonymous with print freedom; in the prewar period the motivation for honoring or suppressing free expression continued to fluctuate.

In some places crowds could gather to hear impassioned speakers discuss the reorganization of labor, birth control, even homosexuality with relatively few repercussions. Yet, at the same time, IWW demonstrators in the West were systematically arrested for their attempts to assert the right to speak (and organize labor) in public spaces.

Information about birth control and sexual practices that was transmitted through the mails was subject to censorship laws enforced by Anthony Comstock, a man for whom Goldman and comrades made no secret of their disdain. A memorable joke in *Mother Earth* refers to Comstock's birth: "Judging from his exploits of forty years what a moral terror it must be to this he-angel to look back to the day he made his first appearance on this planet devoid of the conventional frock coat and long trousers and exposing his unclothed anatomy to the vulgar gaze of doctor and nurse."[159] Comstock was a social conservative and a post office official who flexed his power over what was at the time the principal means of personal and political communication. He had broadly interpreted anti-obscenity laws to legitimatize censorship by banning from the mails material that he construed as obscene—and took it upon himself to be the arbiter of moral purity.

He exercised his power by halting the mail delivery of periodicals that included arti-

158. "Sad and deplorable in the extreme is the position of the American negro. Rivers of blood have been shed to free the black man from slavery; yet, after almost half a century of so-called freedom, the negro question is more acute than ever. The persecution, suffering and injustice to which this much-hated race is being constantly subjected can be compared only to the brutal treatment of the Jews in Russia. Hardly a day passes without a negro being lynched in some part of the country. It is no uncommon occurrence for a whole town to turn out to witness the no less brutalizing than brutal spectacle of so-called 'mob justice': the hanging or burning of a colored man. Nor are these terrible atrocities perpetrated in the South only. Though in a lesser degree, the North is guilty as well. Nowhere in the country does the negro enjoy equal opportunity with the white man—socially, politically or economically—notwithstanding his alleged constitutional rights. Legally and theoretically, black slavery has been abolished; in reality, however, the negro is as much a slave now as in ante-bellum days, and even more ostracized socially and exploited economically. . . . [However,] persecution [is] not limited to the negro. . . . Only recently Japanese residents were made the victims of the curse." Emma Goldman, "The Situation in America," Report to the International Anarchist Conference, Amsterdam, *Mother Earth*, October 1907.
159. Van Valkenburgh, "In Book of Anthony," *Mother Earth*, August 1915.

cles on human reproduction and literature touching on sexual themes.[160] *Mother Earth*, with its cautiously chosen material, enjoyed a consistent print run from 1906 to 1917 (in 1917 periodicals that included antiwar material were officially suppressed); only the January 1910 "White Slave Traffic" issue was held up in the mails.

Comstock's actions were widely championed by well-financed puritanical morality societies[161] that pressed for the banning of books with explicitly erotic content.[162] Comstock believed that the crusade to suppress such works was consistent with other progressive reform agendas and was merely an extension of the child protection laws that had already been written to shield the children from what were considered immoral influences.[163] Harassment cases and other legal cases filled the courts.[164]

Similarly, Goldman's arrests during this period were generally connected to distributing printed matter on methods of birth control. Interestingly, she faced more restrictions from law enforcers on the subject matter of her talks than on the content of her magazine. The emphasis on suppressing print or speech was fluid and determined by the particular circumstances of the time. In the period from 1910 to 1916 the monitoring of radical publications was inconsistent, and the influence on readership difficult to measure—especially in the case of an anarchist periodical with a relatively small circulation. However, Goldman's persuasive powers over a large and diverse crowd on issues of sexuality were in the public gaze, and reactions were visceral; raucous applause from her audiences in response to her challenging pronouncements was bound to provoke the ire of conservative officials who feared the destabilizing impact of women's sexual freedom on male privilege and the traditional family. Police and government agents were assigned to witness and control such unruly spectacles, but they could never completely restrain the free flow of challenging ideas.

Although Goldman was becoming more acculturated, as an immigrant anarchist with precarious citizenship rights, her lectures and articles attest to her adeptness at averting arrest and suppression—whenever possible. Attuned to the realities of censor-

160. Examples included *Physical Culture, Hearst's Magazine,* and the *Woman Rebel.*
161. Vice squads like the American Protective League prefigured "private citizens'" pro-war and intensely patriotic groups in 1917. See, for example, Joan M. Jensen, *The Price of Vigilance* (Chicago: Rand McNally, 1968).
162. Elinor Glyn's novel *Three Weeks* (New York: Macaulay, 1909), for example, caused an uproar for its suggestive descriptions of love making; for some, this provoked a stampede to buy the book; for others, a race to ban it. However, much of the "purification" of print culture may actually have been accomplished through intimidation, with many works never even submitted for publication. Some groups, like the radical free lovers, rarely backed down; for years they had been prime targets for "Comstockery"—sometimes resulting in years of prison time for such print offenses.
163. See Introduction and opening chapters in Paul S. Boyer, *Purity in Print: Book Censorship in America from the Gilded Age to the Computer Age,* 2nd ed. (Madison: University of Wisconsin Press, 2002).
164. For early free speech obscenity contestations, see Janice Ruth Wood, *The Struggle for Free Speech in the United States, 1872–1915: Edward Bliss Foote, Edward Bond Foote, and Anti-Comstock Operations* (New York: Routledge, 2007).

ship and surveillance, she warned the general population (including natural-born citizens) that free expression, the hallmark of American freedom, seemed to be eroding—especially in 1916 as preparedness for war was in the air. Yet her view of the ominous state of free expression was not completely accurate: the unpredictability of official censorship actually allowed for intermittent flourishing of radical cultural and political discourse as witnessed by the consistent monthly press run of *Mother Earth* 1906–1917.[165] From the country's beginnings protection of free speech against governmental abridgments was affirmed by federal and most state constitutional guarantees. Still, freedom of speech and freedom of the press were not yet uniformly protected. Generally state and/or local laws prevailed. Thus, while traveling Goldman really never knew whether she'd be met with a warm welcome or a locked lecture hall. Location played a role, not only in the ability to lecture without being censored, but also in the freedom to print and distribute political tracts without risking imprisonment. She gravitated toward cities and towns where anarchism had a stronghold, however small, in both English- and Yiddish-speaking audiences.[166]

To avoid police harassment and arrests for talks considered by authorities to be culturally or politically incendiary, she tried to map her lecture tours through cities and towns known for their permissive, liberal public officials. Given the conflict between the burgeoning Socialist Party and the anarchists, who were associated with violence and who shunned participation in electoral politics, Goldman often found herself equally unwelcome in towns with socialist mayors as in those with conservative ones. Of course, there were some exceptions. Often it was the liberals and single-taxers who were most open and committed to the principle of free speech. But there were some areas she simply could not enter. For example, as previously mentioned, she steered clear of the South; it was there that fundamentalism, racism, and Christian temperance campaigns were prevalent, and few people had ever encountered a Jewish immigrant anarchist woman, let alone on a lecture platform. Although she avoided districts perceived as hostile to "her kind," Goldman lectured in a remarkable number of places across the country, especially those known for comunities open to radical ideas.[167]

Even when it seemed to those who challenged social conventions that civil liberties were eroding, the constitutional right to free speech continued to be heralded as a privilege intrinsic to America.[168] In her lifetime of activism the political pendulum seemed to swing toward openness. With time, the trauma of the 1901 assassination of President McKinley dissipated, and to a certain extent, by 1909, repression against political agita-

---

165. See Introduction, vol. 2, *Making Speech Free*, pp. 40–47.
166. See Ben Reitman, "Emma Goldman Welcomed in Chicago," *Mother Earth*, May 1914.
167. See Chronology for a list of cities and towns on Goldman's lecture tours.
168. See, for example, Eric Foner, *The Story of American Freedom* (New York: W. W. Norton, 1999), which is among many fine books on the subject of free speech in the United States.

tors like Goldman had lifted as well.[169] In comparison to the years before and after, in the period between 1910 and 1916 Goldman and many others were able to reach out to audiences on cultural and social issues with relative freedom (albeit at the discretion of authorities). Lecture halls were streaming with police who made intermittent arrests and there was always a backdrop of violent repression of militant labor strikes. Historian Paul Murphy in his book *World War I and the Origin of Civil Liberties in the United States* added a caveat, astutely observing the narrowed conditions upon which free speech was assured:

> The attitude of a majority of public and private leaders of the late nineteenth and early twentieth centuries toward civil liberties held that such liberties were only to be protected for those citizens who had demonstrated, both by their attitudes and their behavior, that they were prepared to utilize those freedoms in positive and constructive ways. The decision as to whether a citizen deserved to have his civil liberties formally protected was to be made by those responsible elements within the society that were knowledgeable in the proper use of personal freedom. Liberty, in short, was a condition conferred by the community at its discretion, usually only to "good people" who had earned their prerogatives. Blacks, Indians, Orientals, aliens—particularly those from Eastern Europe—women, or people espousing radical and destructive economic and political theories, clearly were not ready for the full utilization of their constitutional liberties.[170]

### UNIONS ON THE FIRING LINE

Labor's right to organize, with its direct economic consequences to owners of factories and mills, remained dangerous and contested. IWW free speech fights shifted to direct confrontations at the workplace, and bloody battles ensued. Violent labor strife had become commonplace, with death tolls mounting on both sides. Publishing pro-union and anti-corporate opinions in a company town had especially severe consequences and was considered an incitement to violence.[171] The strike at the Westing gun factory might have been especially threatening as early industrial support for and profits from the war in Europe began to take hold.[172]

169. See vol. 2, *Making Speech Free.*
170. Paul Murphy, *World War 1 and the Origin of Civil Liberties in the United States* (New York: W. W. Norton, 1979), pp. 40–41.
171. Although certainly without the extreme violence and beatings the IWW endured, this phenomenon resonated with Goldman's experience earlier when in 1893 she addressed a demonstration of the unemployed, urging them to demonstrate before the palaces of the rich and demand bread, and, if denied, to take it, as their "sacred right"—for which she was arrested and imprisoned for almost one year. See vol. 1, *Made for America*, pp. 151–89.
172. Ronald R. Kline and Thomas C. Lassman, "Competing Research Traditions in American Industry: Uncertain Alliances Between Engineering and Science at Westinghouse Electric, 1886–1935," *Enterprise & Society* 6, no. 4 (December 2005), pp. 601–45. Sales at Westinghouse jumped 50 percent, from $33 million in 1915 to $50 million in 1916, driven primarily by orders of munitions (artillery shells and rifles for Britain). Sales billed in 1917 soared again, to $89 million, for

Goldman's relationship to labor was complex.[173] When a strike occurred, she packed her lectures with reports on atrocities at the site and raised funds for militant strikers on the line and in court. Many unions fought for change through negotiations as well as force, enlisting militant tactics to reinforce the immediacy of otherwise gradualist demands.[174]

Her support was conditional. Goldman criticized union hierarchies, the relative hegemony of socialist control, and the disincentive for factory worker solidarity inherent in the creation of separate unions for skilled and unskilled workers; many of the skilled workers in the American Federation of Labor (AFL), for example, had to train as apprentices, a difficult program to enter and one that was racially exclusive as well. Even if the employer was race blind, many employees were not. Racism and immigration played out in the more established unions—to the detriment of the more transcendent cause of labor organization. Unskilled laborers gravitated to or were recruited by unions such as the Industrial Workers of the World, which, unlike its counterparts (including the AFL), welcomed workers of all skill levels and races. Goldman's attitude toward both the IWW and the AFL was complex and situational. Although Goldman had few official affiliations to unions, she did have the respect and cooperation of many in the union ranks. She never acted as a spokeswoman for a particular union, but throughout her life she remained, despite her many reservations, a rallying voice for the cause of labor.

Nonetheless, worried about laborers giving up their autonomy to the union or to a political party, Goldman rejected the concept of the will of the masses. With a certain insensitivity to the immediate needs of workers,[175] especially in her earliest talks, she critiqued their focus on fighting for a living wage, warning that it would only further labor's dependence. She proposed, and continued to stand by, her belief in an overall restructuring of the power relationship between bosses and workers. Although many of her fund appeals dealt directly with practical issues, her anarchist vision, while attractive, could not sufficiently satisfy most workers' immediate needs for reasonable hours and wages, for safe workplaces, and for the mediating promise of collective bargaining.

the same reason. Net income rose sharply, quadrupling to $9.6 million in 1916 and then nearly doubling to $18 million the following year.

173. See Candace Falk, essay on Emma Goldman in *Encyclopedia of U.S. Labor and Working Class History* (New York: Routledge, 2007) for a succinct summary of Goldman's complex relationship to labor.

174. A reading of the Fund Appeals in *Mother Earth*, along with the documents that track Goldman's collections at meetings, reveals an impressive range of labor defense funds: the Aberdeen Free Speech Fund (1911), the Alexander Aldamas Defense Fund (1912–1913), the Wheatland Case (1913), Suhr and Ford Cases (1914), the (Colorado) War Fund (a 1914 collection to purchase arms for striking workers in and around Ludlow), the Free Speech Fight (Everett, Washington, 1916), and the Ingar Defense Committee (March 1916).

175. See Introduction, vol. 1, *Made for America*, p. 37. See also *LML*, p. 46, for her critique of the eight-hour movement.

## GOLDMAN'S WRITINGS: TIME-BOUND AND TIMELESS

Even as Goldman challenged the specifics of the organization of the workplace or of family norms, the underlying themes of freedom, autonomy, and cooperation remained constant. Although most of Goldman's published and unpublished lectures were inspired by the events and concerns of her day,[176] the particulars served as springboards for addressing basic universal issues meant to be relevant to audiences and readers across time. As Goldman prepared the manuscript of her first book, *Anarchism and Other Essays*, she modified some, though not all, of the date- and location-specific material in her lectures with the intention of reaching an international, mostly anarchist-leaning, readership. This pattern continued throughout her career as a public speaker. Thus, for example, "Preparedness, the Road to Universal Slaughter" (Essay in *Mother Earth*, December 1915), her caveat to a nation poised to enter the First World War, was written as a template of ideas applicable to almost any country on the verge of war.[177] Goldman's published essays appeared in bookstores in London, Paris, Madrid, Milan, Vienna, Berlin, Buenos Aires, and Tokyo, among other cities. Exchanges with the London publication *Freedom* and other papers,[178] as well as with American readers of *Mother Earth*, secured a wider distribution of ideas and provided mutual support for those on trial for acts of resistance around the world. In the process Goldman's international stature as a formidable anarchist propagandist and theorist grew.[179]

Goldman's popular essay "The Psychology of Political Violence" piqued the interest of many readers, including those who were deeply conflicted on the subject and sought to understand what moved people to participate in violence. It was, perhaps, her clearest, most succinct exposition on this issue. Other essays that attracted a readership outside anarchist circles were those that focused on issues of morality: religion, including "The Philosophy of Atheism" (see Essay in *Mother Earth*, February 1916); birth control, including "The Social Aspects of Birth Control" (see Essay in *Mother Earth*, April 1916); women's suffrage, including "Woman Suffrage" (see Essay in *Anarchism and Other Essays*, 1910, and excerpted in the *Woman Rebel*, June 1914).[180]

Goldman's critique of the suffrage movement followed much of the same reasoning in her essays on other topics concerning electoral politics and the law. She believed that enfranchisement for women could not guarantee their freedom because of the limita-

---

176. Perhaps assuming that there would be a second volume of *Anarchism and Other Essays*, Goldman did not publish essay versions of all of her lectures. To read those extant unpublished lectures—like "Socialism: Caught in a Political Trap"—as well as newspaper excerpts from others that have been lost, see *EGP*, reel 55 and *EGP*, reels 47–53.

177. As she had written before in her essay "The Effect of War on Workers," Transcript of Address in *Freedom*, 20 February 1900. See vol. 1, *Made for America*, pp. 384–88.

178. See issues of *Mother Earth* for lists of papers received.

179. For EG's lectures in England, see vol. 1, *Made for America*, p. 61, and *LML*, pp. 255–57.

180. See also Goldman, *Anarchism and Other Essays*, for additional examples.

tions, corruption, and compromise inherent in electoral politics. Vanquishing long-held habits of subservience was not a matter of law (see "Woman Suffrage," in *Anarchism and Other Essays*, 1910, and excerpted in the *Woman Rebel*, June 1914). She warned that women were prisoners of the internal tyrant of conformity, and, with or without the vote, they alone had the capability to realize their freedom.[181] Goldman's expositions on the issue of inner and outer freedom especially appealed to women outside the limited states.

Translations of Goldman's controversial works were published in Japanese, German, Yiddish, Italian, Spanish, and Russian. Had these essays been written by local authors, the personal consequences as well as public censorship might have been extraordinarily severe.

## MODERN DRAMA: SUBVERSIVE "DYNAMITE"

Official censorship was not an unfamiliar concept to Goldman, who was sometimes forced by circumstance and restrictive laws to circumvent official arbiters of morality.

Her book *The Social Significance of the Modern Drama* (1914) featured edited transcripts from her drama lecture series from 1904 to 1914. The plays she chose offered an opportunity to examine the issues of social injustice, sexual and religious hypocrisy, corrupting compromises of bourgeois life, and the stifling of women's creativity and independence, as well as the ills of capitalism and the underlying problem of class conflict.[182] Goldman commented on the works of Strindberg, Ibsen, Shaw, Galsworthy, Rostand, Suderman, Chekhov, Wedekind, and contemporary Irish, Russian, and Yiddish theater circles, familiarizing an uninitiated audience with the European theater, which was artfully engaged in the projection of a political message.

To prepare for her lectures, Goldman read about European theater, especially in *Current Literature*, hoping to bring news and eventual performances to theaters in the United States.[183] Goldman's lecture-essays were often narrative summaries of the plot line of each play, highlighting the dilemmas that plagued its characters. Her approach differed from her French anarchist comrade Augustin Hamon, whose book on the Irish playwright George Bernard Shaw focused primarily on technique, the nuance and meaning communicated through his comic art form.[184] Her volume seems to have

---

181. Simultaneous challenges to internal and external barriers to freedom were the consistent philosophical template from which Goldman addressed the question of how to effect lasting positive change.

182. Bernard Smith, *Forces in American Criticism: A Study in the History of American Literary Thought* (New York: Harcourt, Brace, 1939), pp. 291–94.

183. For example, there were no productions of Ibsen's plays in America from 1911 to 1915, although they were being performed and appreciated in avant-garde circles in Europe.

184. Augustin Hamon, *The Technique of Bernard Shaw's Plays*, trans. Frank Maurice (London: C. W. Daniel, 1912).

been influenced in form by her friend and drama critic J. G. Huneker's *Iconoclasts: A Book of Dramatists*,[185] which includes biographical information on playwrights and synopses of several of their emblematic plays along with Huneker's opinions about the relative political importance of each. Although Goldman gained a reputation for bringing European drama to America, she was relatively isolated within the larger context of theater circles. Goldman's polemical approach was not uniformly accepted by the public—in fact, it did not take long for her book to be remaindered.

Nonetheless, at least three times, while lecturing on the drama in Denver, she complied with a newspaper request to write in the style of a drama critic—to comment on both the form and content of shows.[186] Her forte, as previously noted, was in the retelling of messages of plays she regarded as compelling and universal. This idea-oriented commentary on the theater distinguished her from other critics of the time who published in the *Bookman*, *Current Literature* (which morphed into *Current Opinion*), and in most newspapers.[187]

In hindsight, a decade later, she would judge her earlier work to be less mature, rarely engaging with the literary structure of the play or the performance itself.[188] An example of her later work, a 1926 unpublished essay on Galsworthy's *Escape*, noted, "it is not a great work in point of construction—indeed the author has himself described it as 'episodic,'" and then proceeded to describe some reactions to the play by the London audience. She jotted on her rough draft that her next step would be to compare this play to a novel on a similar subject.[189]

Later, her essays, especially those on "Foremost Russian Dramatists," included more psychobiographical material on the playwrights, as a basis for understanding why certain themes were compelling, not only politically but also in relation to their own lives. This approach expanded her earlier focus on the narrative message and was intended as a means by which to foster a closer connection between the playwright, the play, and the reader.

185. For EG's relationship to Huneker, see vol. 2, *Making Speech Free*, p. 165. See J. G. Huneker, *Iconoclasts: A Book of Dramatists: Ibsen, Strindberg, Becque, Hauptmann, Suderman, Herviu, Gorky, Duse, and Dannunzio, Maeterlinck and Bernard Shaw* (New York: Charles Scribner's Sons, 1905).

186. *Denver Post*, 23 April 1912.

187. See, for example, excerpts from reviews in the *New York Sun Critic, New York Evening Post, New York World* in: "'Justice'—Galsworthy's Intense Prison Drama Has Startled New York Playgoers: A Composite Review Published," *Current Opinion* 60, no. 5 (May 1916).

188. EG, "Galsworthy's *Escape*" (unpublished manuscript), *EGP*, reel 54.

189. See EG on Galsworthy, unpublished manuscript 1928, *EGP*, reel 54 (also in IISH). EG's notation next to her commentary on Galsworthy's *Escape* referred to a novel, favorably reviewed by AB in *Mother Earth: 9009* by James Hopper and Frederick Bechdolt (New York: McClure, 1908) similarly focused on the horrors of prison life. EG's self-reflections on the limitations of her early drama criticism appears in "Foremost Russian Dramatists: Their Life and Work" (unpublished manuscript, 1926), *EGP*, reels 50–51.

So convinced was she of the political power of modern European drama to overcome class and ethnic divides that Goldman once delivered the same lecture to a women's drama club in the evening and to coal miners in a mineshaft during their lunch break the next day.[190] The primary audience for her drama lectures, however, was the educated middle class—"people of culture."[191]

Goldman recognized the social role played by those whose relative leisure allowed for participation in movements for political change, whose vision was not clouded by hunger and the grinding pace of factory work. She genuinely appreciated the generosity and friendship of her upper- and middle-class bohemian donors. However, in her essay "Intellectual Proletarians" she warned about the downside of the habits of privilege: the late nights and lost mornings that diminished the potential of individuals, and a false sense of immunity to the system's injustices.[192]

Although she enjoyed the opportunity to reach middle-class audiences, she realized that they were unlikely to attend talks in working-class halls, assuming that the topics addressed there were sure to be far from their own concerns, and often knowing that the halls would be far from home. Her drama talks, no matter where they were held, rarely attracted large crowds; this was true even in Denver and New York, where she generally had a solid following.

Her successes often were quantifiable—not necessarily by the number of people in her audiences but rather by the amount of money she raised. At literally every speaking event Goldman solicited donations to help support legal defense funds for anarchists and striking workers. She considered these appeals critical to the movement,[193] and integral to her work. These efforts were appreciated by those who had little access to funds necessary for a fair trial and by others who welcomed the opportunity to contribute to the cause of economic and social justice.

*Mother Earth* too reaped extra funds for its operations through the sale of reprints of more than one hundred scripts of plays,[194] hawked at her talks or ordered through the mail. Although she applauded the burgeoning of little theaters around the country and interest in the dramatic form, it would take some years for the American drama to fully develop in a manner that her circles would embrace. Goldman became a friend and fan of the Provincetown Players, a repertory group that performed controversial and sometimes-censored plays. Perhaps its most talented playwright was Eugene O'Neill, whose

---

190. *LML*, p. 493.
191. "Emma Goldman, the Talented Anarchist," *Chicago Daily Tribune*, 15 November 1914.
192. And the sense of being eternally protected, even from the harmful physical consequences of their excesses. See "Educating the Educated: Awakening the Late-Night Intellectual Proletarian" in the Introduction below.
193. See Fund Appeals in *Mother Earth*.
194. For example, the December 1912 *Mother Earth* advertised the complete works of Gerhart Hauptmann for sale.

works included characters modeled on many of the anarchists, including Goldman.[195] Goldman's niece Stella Comyn Ballantine was married to one of the players, Teddy Ballantine. Goldman, Reitman, and Berkman followed the group's evolution, and Fitzi eventually became part of its inner workings. The Provincetown Players was an incubator of a transformation in American theater away from a reputation for being light and airy.[196] Goldman included American dramatists like Butler Davenport in *The Social Significance of the Modern Drama* as representatives of this new direction in the national theater. In the contemporary debate between those who favored art for art's sake and those who viewed art as a vehicle to promote the social good, her volume underscored "the social significance which differentiates modern dramatic art—from art for art's sake."

## ART AND REVOLUTION

Goldman's interest in the social and political significance of art did not stop at the theater. The anarchist credo is one of complete freedom of expression, of a movement that includes all aspects of life, one that breaks from tradition to create ever new vistas of aesthetics and culture. To Goldman "life in all its variety and color, in all its fullness and wealth is art, the highest art."[197] Her lecture "Art and Revolution" was regularly included in her speaking tours. Drawing in part from Oscar Wilde's *The Soul of Man Under Socialism*,[198] she promoted works that challenged the public's ability to appreciate and enhance life with beauty. The anarchists' openness to new art forms attracted artists to the recently established Ferrer Modern School;[199] there they taught art classes that encouraged experimentation, gave lectures, and found camaraderie in the company of other creative rebels. Among those who participated, in the audiences or in classes, were the artists George Bellows and John Sloan (of the Ashcan School), as well as Man Ray, Abraham Walkowitz, Robert Minor, and Moses Soyer. The French anarchist-syndicalist artist Jules-Félix Grandjouan contributed cover illustrations to *Mother Earth,* along with Man Ray and Robert Minor.[200] Robert Henri enjoyed several sittings with Emma Goldman as he painted her portrait. Photographer Alfred Stieglitz also considered himself and his gallery, 291, on the front lines of American modernism

195. See, for example, Leona Rust Egan, *Provincetown as a Stage* (Orleans, Mass.: Parnassus Imprints, 1994). See also Eugene O'Neill's *The Iceman Cometh.*

196. "The Essential Difference Between an American Play and a European Play," *Current Opinion* 58, no. 2 (February 1915).

197. Emma Goldman, "Life as Art," *Mother Earth,* March 1910

198. Oscar Wilde, *The Soul of Man Under Socialism* (London: privately printed, 1904).

199. See Ferrer Modern School in Directory of Organizations.

200. For a summary of the use and description of illustrated covers in *Mother Earth,* see Peter Glassgold, *Anarchy! An Anthology of Emma Goldman's* Mother Earth (Washington, D.C.: Counterpoint, 2001), pp. xvi–xvii.

and often displayed announcements of Goldman's upcoming lectures in the window of his shop.[201] Despite resistance to modernism by traditional artists trained in Europe, the international exhibition of modern art at the Armory Show of 1913 drew more than 300,000 people.[202] The art establishment's fear of the combination of art and politics spilled over to the government. By 1917 surveillance agents would be scanning audiences to note who had applauded most enthusiastically for Isadora Duncan's red-veil dance to the "La Marseillaise."[203]

Goldman also reveled in the visceral freedom of the dance,[204] mocked temperance advocates' fear of gathering places with easy-flowing alcohol, and defied their attempts to close down dance halls. Despite her passion for dance, her artistic medium ultimately was the spoken and written word. Her attraction to the new linked her to the modernist movement and to the "light and shadows in the life of the avant-guard."[205] She believed that "in the life of the avant-guard each little event plays a part in the great struggle."[206] For Goldman, however, art was to be distinguished from beauty, which she considered essential to human experience. She described "the tragedy of the masses: they have no taste or desire for beautiful things, therefore they make no attempt to get out of the drabness of life."[207] When her dear friend W. S. Van Valkenburgh countered her argument, insisting that the masses never have a chance or an incentive to appreciate the beautiful, she claimed

> a sense of beauty is innate rather than acquired. Because if material means and opportunity would teach one to appreciate beauty, the middle-class ought to be the greatest sponsors of art: but, as a matter of fact, it is not. It is the greatest stumbling-block to real art. . . . I do not believe that physical hunger alone suffices to arouse people. It is the ideal which counts. Without the ideal there can be no revolutionary change.[208]

---

201. See Allan Antliff, *Anarchist Modernism* (Chicago: University of Chicago Press, 2001) for an excellent study of anarchist artists and their influence on early modernist painting, among other forms of art.

202. Milton Brown, *The Story of the Armory Show* (New York: Abbeville, 1988); and Munson-Williams-Proctor Institute, *The Armory Show—50th Anniversary Exhibition* (Utica, N.Y.: Munson-Williams-Proctor Institute, 1968).

203. See Agent P. J. Barry to Captain Hayes, 2 July 1917, National Archives Record Group 165, GS, MID 10110–551, *EGP*, reel 57. For more detail on surveillance at this time, see vol. 4, *The War Years* (forthcoming).

204. On her love of dancing, see, for example, *LML*, p. 56.

205. EG chose the title "Light and Shadows in the Life of an Avant-Guard," for her *Mother Earth* reports from the road from February to June 1910. She called the column that covered the last stops on a six-month tour "The End of the Odyssey." After that the reports from the road included the titles "En Route" and "Ups and Downs in the Life of an Agitator."

206. *Mother Earth*, July 1910.

207. EG to W. S. Van Valkenburgh, 18 May 1915, *EGP*, reel 9.

208. Ibid.

In her many attempts to define anarchism she was consistent in her belief that the solution to economic evil "can be brought about only through the consideration of *every phase* of life—individual, as well as the collective; the internal, as well as the external phases."[209] In what was, in part, an homage to alcohol, she proclaimed, "Every stimulus which quickens the imagination and raises the spirits is as necessary to our life as air. . . . Without [it] creative work is impossible."[210]

In an attempt to pin down Goldman's likes and dislikes the bohemian literary editor of Chicago's *Little Review*, Margaret Anderson, in her autobiography, *My Thirty Years' War*, poked fun at Goldman:

> Although she gives the impression of being able to stand anything, there are any number of things she can't stand. She can't stand wearing a fur coat—the thought of the murdered animal would suffocate her. She can't stand food that has been cooked by inexpert hands—she would rather go hungry than eat it. She can't stand small handkerchiefs, certain colors, many perfumes, flowers in a room at night. She can't stand reporters' questions. She can't stand references to money. I once addressed affectionately as our "angel" a man who helped to bring out a number of the L.R. [*Little Review*]. She was deeply shocked, found it vulgar. Of course the things she *can* stand needn't be entered into here.
>
> I made a joke for her: If the world only knew what a prima donna Emma Goldman is! She laughed—but she couldn't quite stand that either.[211]

## "SOCIAL ARTISTS"

Margaret Anderson was taken with Emma Goldman's "certain something."[212] She extolled Goldman's greatness in the pages of the *Little Review*, hoping that those drawn to the magazine for literature, drama, music, and art would welcome an introduction to "the Immutable" agitator.[213] Goldman felt understood and inspired, never before having made the acquaintance of so many strong and accepting American women in the bohemian community. Observing Margaret Anderson and Jane Heap's courage to live openly as lesbians, she distinguished them from the bourgeois intellectuals she had sparred with in New York City.

One of the readers of the magazine linked Emma Goldman to two other great women of the era:

209. Emma Goldman, "Anarchism: What It Really Stands For," in *Anarchism and Other Essays*, p. 56.

210. *EG*, "The Hypocrisy of Puritanism," in *Anarchism and Other Essays*, p. 182.

211. Margaret Anderson, *My Thirty Years' War* (New York: Covici, Friede, 1930).

212. Margaret Anderson, "The Challenge of Emma Goldman," *Little Review*, May 1914.

213. See, for example, vol. 2, *Making Speech Free*, p. 161. See also Margaret Anderson, "The Immutable," *Little Review*, November 1914, pp. 19–22. "The Immutable" was also Berkman's affectionate moniker for Goldman, as written in his *Prison Memoirs of an Anarchist*.

Mother Jones, Emma Goldman, and Elizabeth Gurley Flynn are social artists, working in different directions, yet in the same direction, now seeming to exclude each other entirely, and now, no doubt, sustaining each other in spirit across the separating gaps in the common purpose just as old age, middle age, and youth do sometimes in life, or just as three mountains may have separate and distinct characters and yet be a part of the same range.... Emma Goldman stands alone as far as organizations are concerned, like so many great artists in other fields, always an isolated figure of heroic beauty, always the creator, lifting the world in spite of itself.[214]

Other readers complained bitterly about such grandiose descriptions of Goldman, believing that Anderson and others were carried away by a personality to the approval of a social program.

[They felt it was] proof . . . that belief in anarchism is a product of the artistic temperament rather than the result of an intelligent attempt to criticize and remould society. . . . [I]t annoys me so much . . . just the sort of shoddy thinking that justifies conservatives in dismissing social theorists with a sneer and imprisoning them when they get dangerous. . . . Emma Goldman could preach until she lost her voice without producing an appreciable effect. . . . There would be something finally tragic about the waste of such a personality as hers unless there were a better way to accomplish her object. . . . [N]inety nine percent of Americans regard her as a sort of Carrie Nation.[215] The more we long for her success, the more we appreciate her personality, the more keenly we must criticize her method. . . . Now that I've spoken honestly, don't think I have joined the ranks of irascible conservatives. . . . No one realizes more than I the necessity of greater emotion, or more sweeping vision. But let's not make our vision sweeping by the simple process of cutting off our view![216]

The Reader Critic section of the magazine fostered such conversation and debate among the editors, writers, and readers. The *Little Review* prided itself on its openness to a plurality of voices and perspectives.[217]

The critique was consistent in many ways with those voiced by progressive intellectuals who cared about progress and tangible results in a time when the alleviation of poverty, improved sanitation, modernization of schools, and the lessening of child labor, though meaningful immediate advances, were minuscule in relation to the larger problems of economic and social inequities that needed to be addressed. Progressives

214. F. Guy Davis, Chicago, "Three Women," in the Reader Critic section of *Little Review* 2 (May 1915).
215. Carry Nation (1846–1911), temperance reformer remembered for her violent attacks on saloons with a hatchet, a tactic she justified as a "response to women's sufferings from the operation of the liquor traffic." Jack S. Blocker, "Nation, Carry," in *American National Biography Online*, article published February 2000, http://www.anb.org/articles/15/15–00504.html.
216. S. H. G., New York, The Reader Critic, *Little Review* 1 (January 1915).
217. Catherine Hollis, "Do Not Eat the *Little Review*!" (conference paper, Modernist Studies Association, October 2004).

faulted Goldman for lack of an exact road map to change. Vague, yes; hers was an ode to individual will in interaction with the particular historical conditions as the only way to guarantee a gratifying and sustainable future—the form of which cannot be predicted. Margaret Anderson lauded Goldman's prescience against critics who considered her ideas unrealizable:

> Ten years ago she was preaching, under the most absurd persecution, ideas which thinking people accept as a matter of course today. Now the ignorant public still shudders at her name; the intellectuals, especially those of the Greenwich Village radical types, dismiss her casually as a sort of good Christian—one not to be taken too seriously: there are so many more daring revolutionists among their own ranks that they can't understand why Emma Goldman should make such a stir and get all the credit; . . . her Anarchism is a metaphysical hodge-podge, the outburst of an artistic rather than scientific temperament. . . . They all miss the real issue . . . that the chief business of a prophet is to usher in those new times which often appear in direct opposition to scientific prediction, and—this above all—that life in her has a great grandeur.[218]

Anderson continued to publish articles and letters written by Goldman and about her, and to advertise her lectures and publications.

Goldman shared page space with James Joyce and the Dada performance artist Elsa von Freytag-Loringhoven—a representation of the crossover between avant-garde art, politics, performance, and culture. Although in 1915 and 1916 the magazine was regionally American in its artistic and political concerns, it would soon transition to trans-Atlantic interest and adopt the masthead "Making No Compromise with the Public Taste."[219]

The debates about Goldman in Anderson's *Little Review*, a magazine with limited circulation and influence, nonetheless captured the essence of the attitudes of educated avant-garde radicals. While Goldman's eloquence on the political dimensions of personal life drew wide interest, many considered her association with anarchism as reason enough to characterize her as either a dreamer or a terrorist—and to dismiss her ideas.

### BOHEMIAN CIRCLES

Although the Greenwich Village bohemian milieu suited her temperament and political bent, she had a love-hate relationship with most people outside her immediate anarchist circle. She was welcomed into the parlor of Mabel Dodge but alienated some of the guests by the somewhat patronizing force of her anarchist stance on almost every issue discussed throughout the evening. Dodge was impressed with "Goldman and her bunch," and "wanted these people to think well of [her]," but always feared that they were

---

218. Margaret Anderson, "The Immutable," p. 20. Among passages omitted: "the Socialists concede her a personality and condone her failure to attach herself to that line of evolutionary progress which is sure to establish itself. 'Unscientific' is their damning judgment of her."
219. Hollis, "Do Not Eat the *Little Review!*"

planning "for the day when blood would flow in the streets of New York"[220]—the eruption of a violent social war between the rich and poor. Many activists harbored the same fears; the editors and contributors to the socialist magazine the *Masses,* Max Eastman and Floyd Dell, kept Goldman, the editor of the anarchist magazine *Mother Earth,* at a distance while maintaining just enough contact with each other to act jointly on issues of mutual concern.

Other circles in which Goldman moved included the Heterodoxy Club. Her niece Stella Comyn Ballantine, a member of the association, was often accompanied by her "Tante Emma." The club was composed of independent women thinkers, mostly professional and educated in universities or by their experiences in radical and bohemian circles. They did not wait for the vote to participate in civic life, nor did they see themselves as moral custodians of the home and nation. Even with their many common interests, Goldman, the immigrant autodidact, had an uneasy alliance with these women. She delighted in the intellectual and political discussion and enjoyed the contact with women of privilege who were equally committed to the birth control movement and who often lived independently without submitting to the constraints of conventional marriage and family. With some women, like Rose Pastor Stokes, Henrietta Rodman, and Jessie Ashley, Goldman had true supportive friendships. In general, however, Goldman's anarchism—as well as her sometimes acerbic personal style—was a dividing line. Many of the women with whom she came into contact at the club were socialists, suffragists, and open lesbians, although some were none of these. Even though her political arena of choice was very different, Goldman enjoyed the company of intelligent, forward-thinking women.

Interestingly, while some considered Goldman too radical, others like Elizabeth Gurley Flynn, whose major focus was labor organizing, later (after the Russian Revolution and upon joining the Communist Party) viewed Goldman's ties to the middle class as compromising not only her politics but her talents as well. Early on, Flynn had been completely impressed: "Emma Goldman spoke to poor people in the small hall with sawdust on the floor—there was an agitational vibrancy in her speeches." Flynn's disenchantment came during the years when Goldman "blossomed as a lecturer, the idol of middle class liberals," when she "lost the dynamic quality as an agitator . . . and became quite prosaic"[221]—a position shared by younger, more militant anarchists as well. These varying reactions attest to how Goldman's cultural iconoclasm allowed her to cross class lines in a way that more conventional radicals (like Flynn) could neither understand nor emulate, nor necessarily want to.

The New York Liberal Club, another essentially middle-class radical intellectual orga-

220. Mabel Dodge Luhan, *Intimate Memories* (New York: Harcourt, Brace, 1933–1937), in 1936, pp. 115–17.
221. Elizabeth Gurley Flynn, *I Speak My Own Piece: Autobiography of "The Rebel Girl"* (New York: International Publishers, 1973), p. 50.

nization, included men and women (some of whom were also in the Heterodoxy Club)[222] who were eager to make friends and hear one another's points of view on a range of topics. Many in the group—including John Reed, Theodore Dreiser, Upton Sinclair, Eugene O'Neill, Edna St. Vincent Millay, Neith Boyce, Anna Strunsky Walling, Ida Rauh, and Louise Bryant—became Goldman's lifelong friends and political acquaintances. Here freethinkers, socialists, anarchists, liberal reformers, suffragists and birth control advocates could exchange ideas and mute their animosities. Goldman's closest ally in the Liberal Club group was Hutchins Hapgood, the author of *The Spirit of the Ghetto*, who was enchanted by Lower East Side Jews and radicals. Gradually, he became a transitional figure between the Village intelligentsia and its immigrant radicals, as well as between anarchist-oriented bohemian artists and political agitators, many of whom frequented the variety of clubs proliferating there. Margaret Sanger was loosely affiliated with the group, though she was disappointed at its lack of support for her at her birth control trial.

Margaret Sanger got her earliest recognition as a lecturer at the Ferrer Center, which also published her early birth control pamphlets. She appreciated the informal friendships that developed and the sense of belonging nurtured through their frequent meetings and open format, recognizing also that she could advance the cause of birth control in groups other than those focused on women's advocacy.

The Ferrer Modern School doubled as a haunt for militant anarchist labor radicals, providing a relatively safe cover for clandestine meetings.[223] The radicals came to discuss politics, deepen their camaraderie, and sometimes plot their next action—rumors of which sparked intensified surveillance by agents of U.S. Military Intelligence.[224]

## FROM SALOONS TO SALONS

In her earlier years in America, Goldman frequented meeting places in saloons, some of which were known for their gatherings of mostly immigrant radicals. There they argued and drank, sang and laughed, in many languages at all hours of the day and night. In the 1890s Goldman preferred the old Schwab's saloon, a place she patronized so often that reporters sometimes went there to interview her. Each saloon had its own ambience and constituency and functioned like a home away from home. Although the saloons were much less exclusive than the Greenwich Village clubs and salons, the language barrier itself would discourage bourgeois Americans' participation, though many came at Goldman's invitation.

---

222. See Stansell, *American Moderns*, for more detail, and for an interesting exposition of the Greenwich Village "moderns," especially the ambiance of the radical intelligentsia and women's role in the actual and mythological changes it inspired.

223. See Paul Avrich, *The Modern School Movement* (Princeton, N.J.: Princeton University Press, 1967).

224. E. W. Powell, "Ferrer School in New Jersey," *New York Sun*, 13 February 1916, microfilm files of U.S. Military Intelligence, National Archives (also in Emma Goldman Papers, third-party government documents collection).

At the turn of the century various saloons provided readers and editors of immigrant radical publications a place to discuss, in their own languages, articles published or about to be included in their journals.[225] After Justus Schwab's death in 1900 his saloon no longer served as Goldman's public meeting place. Anarchists and socialists, progressive men and women, African Americans, natural-born citizens, and immigrants from different townships in the old country were already forming social clubs to create new friendships and cement old ones; expand their impact; improve access to public health, business, and education; and, together, counter injustice.

## CREATIVITY AND CRITICAL INQUIRY

Anarchists, who believed in the primacy of individual development and critical-thinking skills, were among the early U.S. proponents of the Modern School movement, which was intended to prepare each child to live in freedom and in harmony with others. As opponents of coercion in any form, many anarchists found the art of learning and teaching both a political and a creative act in the service of their ideal. The Ferrer Center also served as a place for adult development and the promotion of the creative interplay of skills and ideas. Writers, including Upton Sinclair, and artists taught classes, gave public lectures, and assembled cutting-edge exhibitions.

Experimental learning centers for children sprang up in Europe, especially in England, France, and Spain. The French Beehive, established by Sébastien Faure, was an experimental school devoted to rational (i.e., nonreligious) education with no fixed curriculum.[226] Similarly, the Spanish Modern Schools set up by Francisco Ferrer were intended as havens for critical inquiry outside the religious institutional influence that had permeated the educational system in Spain. The separation of Church and State in such matters was considered heresy, a crime for which Ferrer was a constant suspect. Accused of organizing a general strike in Barcelona in 1909, Ferrer was jailed, tortured, and shot; his death was mourned throughout the world by those who shared his belief in the independence from the authority of the Church.[227]

Goldman was part of the group of anarchists—Harry Kelly, Leonard Abbott, and Alexander Berkman, joined later by educators and artists—who established the first Ferrer Modern School in the United States. The movement grew and spread across the nation, from New York City to Detroit, San Francisco, and Los Angeles. The schools fostered creativity and attracted artists and free spirits.

Much of the philosophical base and practice of the Modern Schools echoed John Dewey's commitment to continuity and familiarity as critical to a child's psychologi-

---

225. For a lurid sample of anarchist saloon life see "Anarchy's Den," Interview in the *New York World*, in vol. 1, *Made for America*, pp. 111–15.
226. See Emma Goldman, "La Ruche" (The Beehive), *Mother Earth*, November 1907.
227. See vol. 2, *Making Speech Free*, pp. 61, 520–21. See also J. Romero Maura, "Terrorism in Barcelona and Its Impact on Spanish Politics, 1904–1909," *Past and Present*, December 1968.

cal ability to grasp abstraction as well as to his belief in the importance of learning by doing.[228] Modern Schools, however, rejected the mainstream progressives' application of techniques aimed at improving efficiency (an approach that Dewey rejected as well). Modern School teachers believed that the provision of a flexible environment conducive to each child's unique form of expression was crucial to personal empowerment. Those who fostered innovative approaches to childhood education enjoyed their largest following initially in urban industrial centers, where they also strove to improve the life of the community and to foster a sense of belonging.

### *MOTHER EARTH* MAGAZINE AND
### THE CIRCULATION OF ANARCHIST IDEAS

Education and uplift movements took many forms. The reading public, inspired by the challenges of promoting social justice, gobbled up novels, exposés, magazines, newspapers, and official reports in an effort to comprehend the complex and changing world around them.

Although Goldman was proficient at oral recitation, at debating and lecturing in salons, saloons, public halls, city squares, private homes, and even in exclusive clubs, she wanted to extend her reach. She downplayed her power as an orator at a time when excitement for print was taking hold.

*Mother Earth* magazine was the product of the collective efforts of a talented group of editors who were responsible for most of the content and editing.[229] Along with Alexander Berkman, the writers and editors were primarily Max Baginski, erudite in politics and culture (writing in German, translated by Berkman and Goldman); Hippolyte Havel, an eccentric, temperamental, hard-drinking, yet well-read and talented Czech anarchist; and Harry Kelly, anarchist printer, editor, lecturer, and loyal friend of Goldman.[230] The magazine's office staff included Ben Reitman; M. Eleanor "Fitzi" Fitzgerald, a former lover of Reitman's who served as an all-around assistant and participant at *Mother Earth*; Anna Baron, a correspondence and mailing secretary; and, intermittently, Fanya Baron,[231] among others. Goldman spent six months of each year lecturing on behalf of the magazine and thus remained its most consistent public voice.

Although the magazine was intended as a venue for social science and literature, a

228. For Dewey's involvement in the Modern School see Avrich, *The Modern School Movement*. The book also covers the day-to-day free flow of the schools and their individual characteristics, some more structured than others. See also E. W. Powell, "Ferrer School in New Jersey."

229. See Peter Glassgold, *Anarchy! An Anthology of Emma Goldman's* Mother Earth (Washington, D.C.: Counterpoint, 2001), the best book to date on the character and substance of the magazine.

230. See "Our Sixth Birthday," Editorial in *Mother Earth*, March 1911.

231. Later, Fanya Baron, EG, and AB, would share experiences in Bolshevik Russia that contributed to their disillusionment with the restrictive course of the revolution, especially on issues of freedom of speech and association, as well as the increasingly harsh measures against those deemed a

place for the avant-garde of social ideas and art to meet, its emphasis would become primarily political. By default the magazine had chosen this road with its special issue honoring the memory of Czolgosz, the assassin of President McKinley; readers' responses ranged from appreciation to alienation. Gradually, the focus of the magazine shifted; it became more of an organizing tool, raising funds and heightening awareness of various trials, reporting on international anarchist developments, and musing about the character of towns and cities she visited across the United States of America. Many of the essays published in its pages addressed topics and challenges of the time. The magazine garnered a steady 3,000 subscribers over its twelve years in circulation—the longest-standing anarchist monthly of its time.[232]

Readers of *Mother Earth* followed Goldman across the country through her regular column, the title of which often changed: "The Joys of Touring," "On the Road," "En Route," "Adventures in the Desert of American Liberty," "On the Trail," "The Power of the Ideal," "The Ups and Downs of an Anarchist Propagandist," and "Stray Thoughts." Among her series of reports from the road was "Light and Shadows of the Avant-Guard," a term common to bohemian "moderns" of the time.[233] Goldman clearly identified with the bohemians, who considered themselves the cutting edge of a new era of freedom and creativity in the United States.[234]

Goldman's column also functioned as a vehicle by which she could share her perceptions and general political critique. In person and in print, she focused on her mission, which was always twofold: to apply and to spread her anarchist analysis to the key social and political issues of the time, and to raise support for needy comrades, not only in the United States but also in Japan, Mexico, Germany, and Russia.[235] Lectures and a monthly magazine proved to be relatively effective formats for the dissemination of opinions and of news that was ignored or sensationalized in the mainstream press.

Her columns also chronicled her tours, attributing her success to particular people and criticizing others for organizing meetings that were less than packed. Mostly, however, they were appreciated for the retelling of her adventures, which offered vicarious thrills, especially to those immigrant readers confined to the ghetto, curious about the many faces of America as she experienced it; she believed that "cities, like human

---

threat to the new regime, including anarchists who had been integral to deposing the tsar. Baron was subsequently executed.

232. See Introduction, vol. 2, *Making Speech Free*, pp. 40–45, for a fuller background and explication of the themes running through *Mother Earth* magazine, as well as a list of those who participated in its editorial and publishing group.

233. See Stansell, *American Moderns*. N.B. Goldman's spelling of "avant-garde."

234. Goldman also drew from the European anarchists, echoing the spirit of the French anarchist publication *L'Avant Garde* and the intellectual vanguard of Russian revolutionaries.

235. International affairs were often covered in the regular column "Observation and Comments" of *Mother Earth*.

beings, have a particular psychology."[236] White American-born readers who rarely crossed the race barrier, too, felt all the more cosmopolitan with insider access to her narrative. Goldman identified with those who took risks and—intent on empowering readers with her tales of the "light and shadows of an avant-guard" (see Article in *Mother Earth*, February 1910)—chastised those bound to old ways.

## SURRENDERING TO LOVE—LIKE "ALL GREAT THINGS MERELY IN THE IDEAL"

Her tour manager Ben Reitman's advance work allowed her the necessary time to concentrate on preparing a lecture, then walk into an event and shine. He planned her tours, enticed news reporters, and solicited halls and audiences in small towns and big cities across the country. With Reitman in the wings keeping the crowds rolling in and selling literature on the side, she delivered talks not only for the general public but also for the road companion who affirmed and applauded her "woman nature" as well.[237] By 1910 Goldman had surrendered to the intoxicating Reitman, a man who promoted her work more effectively than anyone had ever done before. The combination was irresistible. Goldman was in love.

Dr. Ben Reitman, who grew up around hoboes, riding the rails and sleeping in boxcars at the edges of cities, was known for his advocacy of itinerant workers and the unemployed, especially in his hometown of Chicago. Accordingly, he applied his medical skills to underserved outcasts.[238]

In his intimate life his familiarity with gynecology gave him an edge over other men who lacked his detailed knowledge of female sexual anatomy. Goldman credited him with having "opened the gates of her womanhood,"[239] releasing all the passion that had been pent up for so many years. Orgasmic release, which Goldman compartmentalized as part of what she called her "primitive" nature, eclipsed any "civilized" rational response to his behavior. During their ten-year affair, Reitman was unable to control his sexual desire and would sometimes glance over Goldman's audience, catch a woman's eye, and leave the hall for a brief liaison.

The woman who preached free love and the pitfalls of possessiveness, who advised others to cure jealousy by devoting themselves to complete freedom in love and in motherhood, found that she was wracked with distrust and insecurity that turned her into something "foreign to [her]self."[240] Thus, it was no wonder that she chose to lecture

---

236. Emma Goldman, "On the Trail," *Mother Earth*, September 1914.
237. EG to Max Nettlau, 17 October 1907, IISH (also in *LA&EG*, p. 43).
238. Later in his life, Reitman was said to have been the on-call doctor for Chicago's gangsters. See Roger Bruns, *The Damndest Radical* (Urbana and Chicago: University of Illinois Press, 1987), pp. 221–22.
239. See EG to BR, 27 September 1908, *EGP*, reel 2 (also in *LA&EG*, p. 4).
240. See EG to BR, 28 July 1908, *EGP*, reel 2 (also in *LA&EG*, p. 4).

on the fine distinctions of the concept and practice of free love. Women and men flocked to her lectures on "Variety or Monogamy, Which?" and "Jealousy, Its Cause and Possible Cure." Yet she had become so emotionally and sexually entwined with Reitman, finding him ever more indispensable to her work and to the success of the *Mother Earth* office, that she persevered in their relationship with the hope of eventually reforming her "wayward boy." Other comrades and friends in her circles (especially Berkman, who found Reitman crude)[241] recognized that Goldman was smitten, and though they disliked him, realized that they all benefited from his talent as a political organizer.

For Goldman, who hoped to live and love in complete consistency with her ideal of anarchism, the challenge of Reitman's "transgressions" and her inability to exorcise her feelings of jealousy, sent her into a downward spiral. Although she felt certain about her critiques against the capitalist state and the system of oppression, her personal relationship with Reitman made her feel like a fraud. The gap between her beautiful vision and her ugly experience elicited a complex array of feelings. The genuine grievances expressed in her letters to Reitman were magnified by Goldman's propensity for the high drama of self-righteousness coupled with chronic disappointment: "I'd rather do without reality if my ideal is forever to be abused, insulted, spate upon, dragged through the mud" (see Letter to Ben Reitman, 22 June 1910). Defensive, Reitman matched her undercurrent of blame with a lament about the challenge of holding up his part of the relationship: "You are such a powerful creature, it is difficult to be a simple lover to you" (see Letter from Ben Reitman, 2 January 1911).

Despite their turbulent relationship, their work sustained and moved them forward; lessening Goldman's angst and Reitman's feeling of inadequacy (see Letter to Ben Reitman, ca. 25 September 1912). Although lecture tours were demanding, they also served as brief vacations from the daily routine, allowing Reitman and Goldman to be alone, even amid the crowds that gathered around them. As traveling partners, they were often at their best.[242] When apart, they communicated through letters that combined passion and immediate practicalities; thus, Goldman would write of her longing, her sexual fantasies, her emotional anguish, and then end with a shopping list for the household, an accounting of books and pamphlets given and received, or some details about arrangements for their next lecture tour.

241. See, for example, a description of Reitman's escapades in Philadelphia, where he evaded the police trailing him, making sure a reporter was observing, dashing in and out of "department stores, saloons, grocery stores, corset shops, and beauty parlors," something that EG did not find funny when she read about it in the papers. In Bruns, *The Damndest Radical*, pp. 104–5. An equally distasteful incident from EG's perspective was BR's public allusions to the scars of San Diego on his rear in his nervous retelling of the trauma, in part to release the pain with bawdy humor. Ibid., pp. 124–25.
242. See *LA&EG*. And see Bruns, *The Damndest Radical*.

## BACK ON THE LECTURE TRAIL

This was a time when public lectures were a source of news otherwise unreported and of entertainment outside the home, in the company of others. Whatever the personal circumstance, speakers often feel let down after their performance. The contrasting experiences of emoting to a crowd and unwinding alone were unsettling features of the life Goldman had chosen—though perhaps her lingering loneliness factored into her remarkable ability to elicit an intimate connection with her audience.

Intelligent and articulate, Goldman developed a reputation as a formidable speaker. Her prepared talk on a current topic would always be followed by a lively exchange with her listeners. Provocative comments, often directed at the uniformed police and under-cover spies,[243] sparked bellowing laughter for her audacity and her willingness to confront law and convention. She was also admired for her ability to break through language and cultural barriers in the name of justice.

Straddling the fence between political propagandist and public intellectual, Goldman challenged her audiences to question authority, social convention, and even their own assumptions. Often people showed up on a dare and felt a kind of pride for having subjected themselves to her dangerous harangues. Many memoirists who knew her—including Margaret Anderson of the *Little Review* and Roger Baldwin, co-founder of the American Civil Liberties Union—attested that hearing Goldman speak had changed their lives.[244]

Goldman was not the only speaker on the lecture trail. Eugene Debs inspired his audiences on an even wider scale. Suffragists, too, took to the lecture trail to speak for enfranchisement. Mother Jones, Elizabeth Gurley Flynn, and Lucy Parsons, among others, were powerful advocates for labor (although many men did not want them in their unions). Progressive reformers, on the other hand, preferred to hear experts and law-makers speak about child labor laws, prison reform, settlement houses, and peace.[245] Accordingly, the size of Goldman's audience varied according to the topic, the language, the degree of publicity and of censorship, and whether or not other speakers were in town.

To calm her nerves and quiet her mind on those long train rides from one town to the next, Goldman caught up on her correspondence and her reading. Among the many novels Goldman read and reread was *Comrade Yetta*.[246] The book, written by a friend in

---

243. See vol. 4, *The War Years* (forthcoming).

244. See Margaret Anderson, *My Thirty Years' War* (1930; repr., Westport, Conn: Greenwood Press, 1971), pp. 67–69, 72–73, 531; Margaret Anderson, "Emma Goldman in Chicago," *Mother Earth*, December 1914, pp. 320–24; see also *LA&EG*, pp. 9–10, 129–30. Roger Baldwin, "Recollections of a Life in Civil Liberties," *Civil Liberties Review* 2, no. 2 (1975), pp. 43–45.

245. See publications of various papers projects for details: papers of Jane Addams, Margaret Sanger, Eugene V. Debs, and for the earlier suffrage movement, Elizabeth Cady Stanton–Susan B. Anthony papers.

246. Arthur Bullard, *Comrade Yetta* (New York: Macmillan, 1913).

socialist circles, Arthur Bullard, presented a tale of a young immigrant girl swept out of misery by the interweaving of love and work for the cause of social justice. For Goldman, Yetta was a fictional heroine who had risen from the depths through a powerful combination of intimacy and loyalty to a cause. The novel, though didactic, reflected for Goldman the transitional immigrant world in which she lived.

The finale of *Comrade Yetta*—"I'd die if I wasn't doing things! Love isn't enough by itself. I'd starve. I'm hungry to get back to work. That's the Real Thing, we got. . . . It makes our Love worth while. Our Work"[247]—may have confirmed that her relationship to Reitman, which had all the elements of the love and work combination of her dreams, was worth the effort. Inviting his mother to leave her lonely Chicago world behind to join their cooperative household in New York turned out to be disastrous (see Letter to Ben Reitman, 20 September 1913) in terms of the many near breakups it fueled (see Letter from Ben Reitman, January 1914; Letter to Ben Reitman, 21 February 1914). Goldman and Reitman, however, managed to sustain their bond through mutual devotion to *Mother Earth* magazine (see Letter to Ben Reitman, 25 September 1914), which cemented the tortured interdependence from which neither of them could easily escape.

## SHAKEN BY MOB VIOLENCE, REITMAN RETREATS

The letters reveal that the most intense threats to their relationship were external and came in the form of trauma. In 1912, for example, Reitman suddenly found himself the target of a premeditated assault by vigilantes in San Diego. The California city had become a volatile site for the roaming IWW free speech campaign. The Wobblies crowded into public squares and stood on street corners to demand the right to speak openly about any and all ideas. One participant was arrested for reading from the Bible. Although this strategy, jamming the jails beyond capacity to create chaos in response to overzealous attempts to enforce law and order, had worked elsewhere over the past several years, it floundered in San Diego. Vigilantes responded with mob violence.

Reitman, who had always remained in the shadows, bore the brunt of the vigilantes' wrath against the radical takeover of their town. A twisted sense of gender decorum shielded Goldman, a white woman, from any immediate physical harm. Reitman, in contrast, was whisked away from their hotel, dragged into the desert, stripped naked, tarred and sage-brushed, his rear penetrated with a cane, with a lit cigar branded with the letters *IWW*, and forced to kneel before a flag and sing "The Star-Spangled Banner" (see "The Outrage of San Diego," Article in *Mother Earth*, June 1912; see also "Emma Goldman and Ben Reitman Tell of San Diego Experience," Interview in the *Industrial Worker*, 6 June 1912). An insistent police escort ordered a panic-stricken Goldman out of town, though she was loath to leave Reitman behind. After the San Diego incident she tried to understand (see "Emma Goldman Lauds the Hobo," Article in the *Seattle Post-*

247. Ibid., p. 448.

*Intelligencer*, 12 August 1913) but could not fathom the depth of Reitman's depression nor the posttraumatic impact of the terror of that event in his life. Worse yet, the violence Reitman had experienced was not unique.[248]

Upon his return from the abuse he suffered in the desert, he sobbed, nervously joked, and ultimately retreated into the arms of his mother. In an act of sheer exhibitionism and defiance, however, he chose to describe the scars on his buttocks in great detail at a protest meeting planned by Goldman on his behalf and on behalf of others who had been tormented by vigilantes in San Diego's free speech fight.[249] Goldman was shocked and embarrassed, a response that Reitman interpreted as characteristic insensitivity and a surprising lack of caring.

He could not control his emotional distress and anger. Shortly after this episode, he broke down in tears after one of Goldman's debate opponents had given her an especially hard time and subsequently congratulated her adversary.[250] Returning home to Chicago, he basked in the regressive joy of having his mother wash his hair, prepare his meals, and protect him from the political world that was more threatening than he had ever imagined it would be.[251] Before he met Goldman, he had been beaten by the police at a demonstration of the unemployed,[252] but he had never been the isolated object of hatred, attacked by an angry sadistic crowd of "respected citizens."[253]

Goldman's apparent lack of compassion, and the timing of the newly published *Prison Memoirs of an Anarchist*, which renewed her adoration for Berkman's bravery, distanced Reitman even further. It was no wonder that within a few years, during his birth control tour with Goldman, he would end up in the arms of another woman. He had met Anna Martindale at the *Mother Earth* office, and by the time of the tour, she was already pregnant with his child.[254] The prospect of a new life—a baby on its way—gave him the courage to sever the bond between Goldman and himself. The beating and humiliation Reitman had endured at the hands of the San Diego vigilantes in 1912, coupled with his sixty-day prison sentence for distributing birth control leaflets in 1916, altered his sense of

---

248. Such horrors and worse had been the fate of untold numbers of African Americans in the South during this time. The number of lynchings of men, women, and children was equivalent to one every three days, not only in the South but in the North as well. Neither Goldman nor Reitman had ever faced such vicious, concentrated physical antagonism. The Wobblies, however, were consistently beaten, hosed, and tarred and feathered, especially in the Pacific Northwest, where many died in violent labor conflicts.

249. See Bruns, *The Damndest Radical*, chap. 12, pp. 118–32 (also in *LA&EG*, chap. 6, pp. 99–116).

250. See Ben Reitman, "Following the Monkey," IU-C, Reitman's reminiscence of childhood, an unpublished autobiography, ca. 1925. *LA&EG*, pp. 115–16. Miriam Alan de Ford, *Up-Hill All the Way: The Life of Maynard Shipley* (Yellow Springs, Ohio: Antioch Press, 1956), pp. 143–144, 147–148.

251. *LML*, p. 520.

252. See vol. 2, *Making Speech Free*, p. 540.

253. Goldman had returned to San Diego with Reitman a year later, but they were immediately escorted out of town. Then, in 1915, she returned with Berkman, not Reitman, without incident.

254. For BR and Anna Martindale's relationship, see Bruns, *The Damndest Radical*.

just how much risk he was willing to take and where he could best use his talents for bettering humankind. The harsh undertone of labor violence that had swept the country and the use of incarceration to quell opposition were unnerving to Reitman, as were the aftershocks of those experiences that destabilized his resolve. He could reminisce about his late-night soirees, his drinking with Hapgood and Havel, his making love to "the Queen of Anarchy," but he sensed that harder times were coming. Association with anarchist militants was laced with danger that no longer seemed exciting. He had already taken the risk of harboring Matthew Schmidt,[255] as well as Nestor Dondoglio, a Galleanist who went by the name of Jean Crones and was accused of attempting to poison the archbishop of Chicago and his guests at a dinner in 1916. At the same time, however, Reitman's desire for a wife and family and the comfort of a home was overwhelming. To Goldman, excitement and risk for what she perceived as a higher cause was an elixir for her soul.

## VIOLENCE INCITES VIOLENCE

Goldman and most other anarchists publicly reiterated that they opposed personal invasion by institutional authorities and that violence was never their strategy of choice.[256] She acknowledged that their sanction of violence, however reluctant, was often a wedge between anarchists, social reformers, and socialists. The subtleties of her position, however, took many seemingly conflicting forms of expression. For example, she sometimes welcomed the backlash against violence that accompanied such acts as an opportunity to explain and elicit interest in anarchism among those with little knowledge of the broad spectrum of anarchist ideas and tactics.[257] While addressing the confusion and fear that followed political violence and the resulting erosion of civil liberties through restrictive laws and heavy surveillance, she seized the opportunity to create a bridge between liberals and radicals. By engaging those who championed free expression to stretch their support of this right to those who voiced opinions that they themselves did not hold, she helped to secure the right to voice opposition, advocating well-being for all,[258] consistent with her conviction that "all human beings, irrespective of race, color, or sex, are born with the equal right to share at the table of life."[259]

The struggle for an equal share of the bounties of life was brutal. Labor violence had become a constant wherever there was a mine, a mill, or an agricultural colony controlled by employers. Almost 40,000 work stoppages, mostly strikes and lockouts,

255. Schmidt was an anarchist and friend of EG and AB. Together with David Caplan (another of their friends), he was accused of involvement in the *Los Angeles Times* bombing. See Directory of Individuals.

256. "Conditions drive a man to Violence and . . . every real revolutionary change necessitates the use of Violence. . . . We do insist . . . [V]iolence is only the last medium of individual and social redress." EG to BR, 26 August 1910, *EGP*, reel 4 (also in Ben Reitman Collection, IU-U).

257. See Introduction, vol. 1, *Made for America*.

258. See Introduction, vol. 2, *Making Speech Free*, pp. 3 and 77–80.

259. Emma Goldman, "A New Declaration of Independence," *Mother Earth*, July 1909.

occurred from 1881 to 1905,[260] and more than 6 million laborers went on strike. The following years between 1911 and 1916, however, were among the most violent in American history.[261] Even the term "labor unrest" was an understatement. With each side blaming the other the "class war" descriptor was not an overstatement. Among the most pressing issues were the right to a closed shop that would put labor on a more equal footing with employers and the urgent need for improvements in health and safety in the workplace. With the power to stop production, labor unions expected to gain the right to resolve grievances about working conditions, hours and pay, and the constant surveillance by company spies. But poverty pitched scab laborers against union strikers: for example, African Americans and Chinese immigrants against eastern European immigrants and native-born factory and mine workers, as well as agricultural laborers. Collusion among employers, local and sometimes federal officials, and even the courts, combined with the brute force of hired guards and detective agencies in the service of "law and order," actually fueled counterviolence. The tug-of-war between strikes and lockouts slowed the wheels of industry. A solution to this battle became an issue of urgent concern to the government as well as the general public, who were seeking answers to why and who attacked first, questions considered essential to the stability of the nation.

At this time labor unions in Los Angeles—bolstered by the involvement of union militants from San Francisco—were actively organizing. Years of tension between labor and management in Los Angeles, a city in which both sides were ready to fight to the end, culminated in a blast in the building that housed the *Los Angeles Times*.[262] Twenty-one people were killed, and one hundred people were injured in what the paper's owner dubbed "the crime of the century." The American Federation of Labor's leadership, while not openly in agreement with the tactics, considered the newspaper "the most unfair, unscrupulous enemy of organized labor in America"; they argued that the arrested men had been set up in a grand attempt to break up a militant union. The union claimed the cause was gas explosion rather than a bomb. Fear of escalating violence reinforced the shared interests of manufacturers and lawmakers in the passage of anti-union laws, including an ordinance against picketing. Bombings on the same day that the newspaper building exploded targeted the anti-union Llewellyn Iron Works, the home of the secretary of the Merchants and Manufacturers Association, and the home of Harrison Gray Otis, the anti-union publisher of the *Los Angeles Times*. Management blamed the unions, while the unions, claiming they were innocent, garnered public support. Two

260. See *Annual Report of the Commissioner of Labor: Strikes and Lockouts*, vol. 21, 1906.

261. Hugh Davis Graham and Ted Robert Gurr, eds., *The History of Violence in America: Historical and Comparative Perspectives* (New York: Frederick A. Praeger, 1969), p. 320.

262. See Graham Adams Jr., *Age of Industrial Violence, 1910–1915: The Activities and Findings of the United States Commission on Industrial Relations* (New York and London: Columbia University Press, 1968), pp. 10–18, for an excellent discussion of the McNamara case and many others that marked this period and that form the basis for reportage in this volume.

men, John J. McNamara, secretary of the union, and his brother James, who in the past had engineered numerous bombings of bridges and other key targets on behalf of the union, now fell victim to what appeared to be a company frame-up.[263] Funds for their trial poured in, especially from unions across the nation. Portending a political shift toward respect for the dignity of labor, a victory was predicted for the socialist mayoral candidate in Los Angeles, Job Harriman.

Popular support for the McNamara brothers abruptly disintegrated as a consequence of the deal brokered by their lawyer, Clarence Darrow, with the help of Lincoln Steffens. In a calculated effort to avert a possible death sentence and to protect others who may have been involved in the conspiracy, Darrow urged the two men to plead guilty.[264] Emma Goldman and other anarchists were unshaken by the news. Nonetheless, the result was shocking to many who had presumed the innocence of the McNamaras and had rallied to their cause. With the McNamara brothers no longer identified as victims, the widespread impression of nonviolent union hegemony faded. Following this, public support shifted away from militant unions, from anarchists, and from Los Angeles' hitherto popular socialist mayoral candidate to a mainstream contender.

## PRO-LABOR FINDINGS: FRANK WALSH AND THE U.S. COMMISSION ON INDUSTRIAL RELATIONS

Spurred on by the 1910 bombing of the building that housed the *Los Angeles Times*, President Taft proposed the creation of the U.S. Commission on Industrial Relations, which would be charged with determining the causes of labor violence and finding solutions to them. President Wilson established the commission and chose as its director Frank Walsh, a liberal labor supporter and socialist reformer. The five-year report of the committee found that the worst offenses, the most sensational outbreaks, were rooted in the "1) unjust distribution of wealth and income; 2) unemployment and denial of an opportunity to earn a living; 3) denial of justice in the creation, in the adjudication, and in the administration of law; 4) denial of the right and opportunity to form effective organizations."[265]

Among the many incidents studied was the 1913 strike of the Paterson, New Jersey, silk workers. This action was led primarily by the Industrial Workers of the World (also known as the Wobblies), and it became the basis for the arrest of some key IWW leaders. Their trial attracted more than 5,000 spectators. A "pageant" performance was organized by John Reed and took place in New York City's Madison Square Garden. It

---

263. The men were seized by agents of the Burns Detective Agency and extradited from the Midwest to California to face trial.
264. Later, Darrow was charged with two counts of attempting to bribe jurors. After Darrow was acquitted in his first trial and got a hung jury in the next, the district attorney agreed not to try the case again on the condition that Darrow promise never to practice law again in California. Darrow left the state and went home to Chicago.
265. *Final Report of the U.S. Commission on Industrial Relations* (Washington, D.C., 1915), p. 23.

was intended to dramatize the situation and elicit sympathy from many people in New York's middle class, who had never experienced the squalid conditions of the silk workers or the violence of the company's hired thugs.

The commission uncovered facts about labor battles of clothing workers in New York. It found disagreements among unions in the needle trades, activism of women, and attempts and failures to mediate the situation—all against the backdrop of the 1911 Triangle Shirtwaist Company fire, (as discussed above in Brutality and Benevolence in an Era of Progressive Reform), which was among the most horrific examples of workers' lives at risk.

The commission also examined working conditions and demands in the West and Midwest. Militant strikers on the Illinois Central Railroad protested against the use of dangerous run-down trains and long, exhausting schedules, and they boldly countered the company's attempt to sabotage their work stoppage by ambushing and attacking railroad cars bearing scabs.

The most horrendous of all such labor battles took place in Ludlow, Colorado, in 1914. It marked the culmination of many other struggles in Colorado over the years, including battles between strikers and government militias, as well as targeted arrests of labor organizers coming into town (including the eighty-year-old Mother Jones).[266] Ludlow coal workers cared about exerting control over their lives in the feudal coal colony as well as adequate wages and shorter working hours. To live in a company town meant that literally every part of a laborer's existence was determined by the boss. Their strike was intended to address grievances about these conditions, the consequences of which included the threat of prompt dismissal, which would leave families with no housing, food, school, or medical care; squalid and inadequate, those amenities were provided at a company-determined price. To avoid paying rent to the company and in an effort to protect their women and children during the strike, workers erected a tent colony at the edge of, and away from, the company town, digging trenches underground where their children could be protected from harm. Militiamen and national guardsmen were stationed near the tent colony ready to attack. Once the first shot was fired, both sides exchanged fire. But the greatest tragedy came when the tents burst into flames and women and children who were trapped in the pits under them burned to death. Newspapers across the nation reported on the horror of the Ludlow Massacre, and violence broke out between the workers and the state and company troops. Not until the federal government intervened was a tentative peace brokered in Colorado.

The Commission on Industrial Relations was in the midst of its investigations of the causes of the country's intense labor violence. Even before the Ludlow incident, an investigative committee determined that the militia, not the union, was responsible for

266. George P. West, *U.S. Commission on Industrial Relations: Report on the Colorado Strike* (Washington, D.C., 1915), p. 122; Adams, *Age of Industrial Violence*, p. 155.

the tent colony fire. In the wake of the horror and bad press, the company made some significant conciliatory cleanups of their town, but the image of women and children in flames could not be erased from the memory of the workers or from those who read about the massacre.

John Lawson, who was at Ludlow on the day of the battle and a member of the executive board of the United Mine Workers of America, was sentenced by a judge, who had been an attorney for the Colorado Fuel and Iron Company, to life imprisonment and hard labor for the death of a company guard. The report on the Colorado strike blamed the incidents on the "perverted and debauched" government collusion with the "selfish private interests" of the company. It asserted that it was "anarchism stripped of every pretense of even that chimerical idealism that fires the unbalanced mind of the bomb thrower. It is anarchism for profits and revenge, and it menaces the security and integrity of American institutions as they seldom have been menaced before."[267] This statement is an interesting example of how a reformer can appropriate the word *anarchism*, and conflate it with selfish brute force to describe company-sponsored terror.

John D. Rockefeller Jr., whose family members were the largest stockholders of the Ludlow Colorado Fuel and Iron Company, refused to apologize for the tent colony deaths and became a symbol of the cruel indifference of corporate capitalism. A year after the Ludlow Massacre, in an effort to clear his name, Rockefeller testified before the Commission on Industrial Relations. He countered the virulent antilabor stance attributed to him as "so abhorrent to me personally and so contrary to the spirit of my whole purpose and training that I cannot allow these allegations to pass unnoticed without at least outlining my responsibilities as I have viewed them and my obligations as I have sought to discharge them."[268] He then proceeded to explain his belief that the interests of the company, its stockholders, directors, officers, and employees, were not only intertwined but essentially the same—each relying on the success and well-being of the other. He concluded his talk by voicing what seemed to be the genuine motivation for his work: "to contribute toward the well-being of my fellow men, through the lessening of injustice and the alleviation of human suffering, I shall feel that it has been possible to realize the highest purpose of my life."[269] His statement confused the public, eliciting some appreciation for the man, who in apparent sincerity had overcome the overwhelmingly critical appraisal of his character.

It was not long before Walsh, a skilled trial lawyer, was able to reveal Rockefeller's true stance. Confidential letters he had procured between Rockefeller and the company operator, among others, proved without a doubt not only his absolute disdain for unions and his consistent refusal to meet with them but also his long-time complicity in the

---

267. West, *U.S. Commission on Industrial Relations*, p. 23.
268. John D. Rockefeller Jr., *Statement of John D. Rockefeller, Jr. Before United States Commission on Industrial Relations*, 25 January 1915, p. 3.
269. Ibid., p. 11.

abhorrent actions of the company, the guards, the state militia, the judicial system, and the secretary of labor. Rockefeller even wrote a letter to the president, submitted under another name, urging him to quell the strength of the union by any means possible. Although Walsh's relentless examination of the "plutocrat" made some cringe, it was mild compared to those who were angry and believed that the situation demanded—at the very least—a public apology from the young heir to the Rockefeller fortune.

The "Supplemental Statement of Chairman Frank P. Walsh" in the *Final Report of the U.S. Commission on Industrial Relations* was the clearest indictment of the system of exploitation as a whole. It made a plea that the "evils which threaten to defeat American ideals and to destroy the well-being of the Nation may be generally recognized and effectively attacked":

> WE FIND THE BASIC CAUSE OF INDUSTRIAL DISSATISFACTION TO BE LOW WAGES; OR, STATED IN ANOTHER WAY, THE FACT THAT THE WORKERS OF THE NATION, THROUGH COMPULSORY AND OPPRESSIVE METHODS, LEGAL AND ILLEGAL, ARE DENIED THE FULL PRODUCT OF THEIR TOIL.
>
> . . . Citizens numbering millions smart under a sense of injustice and of oppression, born of the conviction that the opportunity is denied them to acquire for themselves and their families that degree of economic well-being necessary for the enjoyment of those material and spiritual satisfactions which alone make life worth living.
>
> . . . By thwarting the human passion for liberty . . . modern industry has kindled a spirit in these dissatisfied millions that lies deeper and springs from nobler impulses than physical need and human selfishness.
>
> Among these millions and their leaders we have encountered a spirit religious in its fervor and in its willingness to sacrifice for a cause held sacred. And we earnestly submit that only in the light of this spirit can the aggressive propaganda of the discontented be understood and judged.
>
> The extent and depth of industrial unrest can hardly be exaggerated. State and national conventions of labor organizations, numbering many thousands of members, have cheered the names of leaders imprisoned for participation in a campaign of violence, conducted as one phase of a conflict with organized employers. Thirty thousand workers in a single strike have followed the leadership of men who denounced government and called for relentless warfare on organized society. Employers from coast to coast have created and maintained small private armies of armed men and have used these forces to intimidate and suppress their striking employees by deporting, imprisoning, assaulting or killing their leaders. . . . Prison records for labor leaders have become badges of honor in the eyes of many of their people, and great mass meetings throughout the Nation, cheer denunciations of courts and court decisions.
>
> To the support of the militant and aggressive propaganda of organized labor has come, within recent years, a small but rapidly increasing host of ministers of the gospel, college professors, writers, journalists and others of the professional classes, distinguished in many instance by exceptional talent which they devote to agitation, with no hope of material reward. . . . [W]e call upon our citizenship, regardless of politics or economic conditions, to use every means of agitation, all avenues of education, and every department and function of

the Government, to eliminate the injustices exposed by the Commission, to the end that each laborer may "secure the whole product of his labor."[270]

Walsh's statements and the conclusions of his committee's investigative report humiliated industrial magnates like Rockefeller and J. P. Morgan. Although some members of the committee might have preferred a more measured appraisal of the forces that fueled labor unrest, according to the *Masses*,[271] their report was "probably the most interesting and significant investigation that the world has ever made." In fact, its statements were so bold that the *New York Herald* dubbed Walsh a "Mother Jones in trousers."[272]

Did the commission's findings change the course of labor-management relations? Did the report eliminate company violence against striking workers? Was it dismissed for its presumed liberal bias? Certainly bitter battles continued and even escalated in some places—especially in the Pacific Northwest, California, Arizona, and Montana, where the IWW tried desperately to hold its own, as did the AFL.

Years before, in 1911, Walsh (considered to be on the outside of anarchist circles and closer to the liberal establishment) had been solicited by Reitman, on behalf of Goldman, to help those fighting for Mexican freedom. His private position on armed struggle was clear in his response:

> If a machine gun does not cost too much, I will be glad to contribute that to the revolution. By too much, I mean beyond the amount which I have on hand at present. In case I do not feel able to make such a contribution I will accept your suggestion and do something along the line of education. In the circumstances I believe, of course, in the power of brute force as well as education. Sometimes education works too slowly. Then of course, there is no alternative except the former. I wish they would establish a co-operative commonwealth in Mexico....
> Please convey my kindest regards to Miss Goldman and accept the same for yourself.[273]

Later, in light of his political and material support for the Mexican Revolution, Goldman approached Walsh after the Preparedness Day bombing, hoping he would become counsel for the Mooney-Billings trial.[274] Although he was too busy to take the case, he (along with many others) expressed his support in an address to a crowd gathered on their behalf at Union Square. But Walsh had also thrown himself into the campaign to reelect Wilson, whom he saw as the only candidate who could keep the United

270. "Supplemental Statement of Chairman Frank P. Walsh," in *The U.S. Commission on Industrial Relations—Final Report* (Washington, D.C., 1915), pp. 297–302.
271. Inez Haynes Gilmore, "Shadows of Revolt," *Masses*, July 1915.
272. *New York Herald*, 30 May 1915.
273. Frank Walsh to Ben Reitman, 6 June 1911, in Emma Goldman Papers, third party correspondence file (also in Goldman Collection, IISH).
274. As an aside and in the same vein, in 1914 Goldman approached Walsh to take the case of a prisoner at Jefferson City with whom she corresponded and to whom she had sent money. Jesse Clyde Rumsey to EG, 18 December 1914, *EGP*, reel 8 (also in Astor, Lenox and Tilden Foundations, Frank P. Walsh Papers, NYPL).

States out of the war. He even asked Goldman to persuade other anarchists to drop their aversion to electoral politics in order to maintain the peace. In response, Goldman related this exchange in her autobiography as an example of the "political blindness and social muddle-headedness of American liberals."[275]

In many ways, the Goldman-Walsh relationship demonstrates the complexities of the progressive versus radical propensities of the time. Although she considered those who participated in government as complicit in a system of injustice, she maintained a qualified respect for Walsh. His report can be seen as a reflection of the period covered in this volume and as a liberal appraisal of the conditions that bred the social war.

## ADJUSTING THE HISTORICAL LENS: INDUSTRIAL VIOLENCE, REFORM, AND WIDE-ANGLE VISIONS OF RADICAL TRANSFORMATION

Historians of the Progressive era and Gilded Age differ in their interpretations of the turbulence and excitement of the time. Whether class divisions played a formative role in this era of reform has been a point of contention. Some considered it a time of unification, of reciprocal rewards, marked by the transcendence of differences for "the common good." Others perceived the passage of "progressive laws" as part of a master strategy to control the outbreak of violent strikes across the nation. New perspectives and interpretative works on the period have expanded over the years. The U.S. Commission on Industrial Relations' study of "industrial unrest" between 1913 and 1915 concluded that its root causes were the ghastly conditions of work and of those whose economic survival was subject to the ever-expanding greed of government-protected industrialists. Reforming the laws to improve the lives of workers held the promise of containment as well as of genuine change. Whether this approach was perceived as a tactic to obliterate class differences, or, conversely, to acknowledge and ameliorate them,[276] depended on one's vantage point. However, it is fair to say that most reformers of the day—on the left and right of the spectrum of progressive activists—viewed their work not as conspiratorial but rather as a step toward a more equitable society in which the disparities of the system were being addressed with a patchwork of new laws and provisions for the needy.[277]

Some historians approach the problems that sparked industrial violence by identifying, integrating, and distinguishing among the many spokes of the wheel propelling reform—incorporating women's social and industrial work, child labor laws, health and educational reform, as well as voluntary organizations. As the debate shifts—either to

275. *LML*, p. 586.
276. See, for example, Sheldon Stromquist, *Reinventing "The People": The Progressive Movement, the Class Problem, and the Origins of Modern Liberalism* (Urbana: University of Illinois Press, 2006). The approach might have served to undercut challenges to racial inequities as well.
277. See, for example, Review Forum, "Re-class-ifying the Progressive Movement," Stromquist response to Nancy Cohen in Review 1: "The Progressives' Disappearing Act: Modern Liberalism's Retreat from Class," *Journal of Gilded Age and Progressive Era* 6, no. 4 (October 2007).

regional differences, the particulars of the consolidation of government control, party politics,[278] or the evolution of capitalism—so too does the interpretation. Similarly, when scholars evaluate the intersection of these and other findings from the perspective of gender, race, and ethnicity,[279] intricate and important layers of meaning discourage them from forming sweeping generalizations without acknowledging the underside of the assumption that this was a time of rapid change and a transition phase in the road to modernity[280] (though that too remains a point of contention).[281]

Whether one considers it a time of progressive reform, an age of industrial violence, or something else, it is clear that Emma Goldman, forever the political gadfly, bridged a vast range of issues, adding her voice to the public discourse of her era. Intellectuals had already jumped into the fray, searching for a genuine role as agents of social change—with more or less success.[282] "Public intellectuals,"[283] thinkers whose focus was outside the academic community, reframed America's democratic vision, bridging the gap between the rich and the poor. At a time of displacement and uncertainty, many middle-class intellectuals attempted to understand and articulate the commonalities of the two classes.[284] Although radical progressivism in the United States differed from the model

278. See, for example, Robert W. Cherny, *American Politics in the Gilded Age, 1868–1900*, American History Series (Wheeling, Ill.: Harlan Davidson, 1997); Robert H. Wiebe, *The Search for Order, 1877–1920* (New York: Hill and Wang, 1967).

279. See, for example, Charlotte Rich, *Transcending the New Woman: Multi-ethnic Narratives in the Progressive Era* (Columbia and London: University of Missouri Press, 2009).

280. See, for example, Maureen Flanagan, *America Reformed: Progressives and Progressivisms* (New York: Oxford University Press, 2007), which includes an excellent bibliography in footnote form, including works on race, gender, ethnicity, by progressivism's diverse travelers; John Whiteclay Chambers II, *The Tyranny of Change: America in the Progressive Era, 1890–1920*, 2nd ed. (New Jersey: Rutgers University Press, 2000), including a supplementary bibliography.

281. Early studies include Richard Schneirov, "Thoughts on Periodizing the Gilded Age: Capital Accumulation, Society, and Politics, 1873–1898," *Journal of Gilded Age and Progressive Era* 5, no. 3, including fine bibliography of "the early classics" in the field, such as Robert H. Wiebe, *Search for Order*; Richard Hofstadter, *Age of Reform* (New York: Knopf, 1955); Samuel P. Hays, "The New Organizational Society," in *Building the Organizational Society: Essays on Association Activities in Modern America*, ed. Jerry Israel (New York: Free Press, 1972); James Weinstein, *The Corporate Ideal and the Liberal State, 1900–1918* (Boston: Beacon Press, 1968); James Livingston, *Origins of the Federal Reserve System: Money, Class, and Corporate Capitalism, 1890–1913* (Ithaca, N.Y.: Cornell University Press, 1986); Martin J. Sklar, *The Corporate Reconstruction of American Capitalism 1890–1916: The Market, the Law, and Politics* (Cambridge: Cambridge University Press, 1988). These are just a sampling of the abundant research and publications that make up the study of the Gilded Age and Progressive era.

282. Leon Fink, *Progressive Intellectuals and the Dilemmas of Democratic Commitment* (Cambridge, Mass.: Harvard University Press, 1997). See also "Supplemental Statement of Chairman Frank P. Walsh" in *The U.S. Commission on Industrial Relations—Final Report* (Washington, D.C., 1915).

283. Russell Jacoby, *The Last Intellectuals: American Culture in the Age of Academe* (New York: Basic Books, 1987).

284. The Women's Trade Union League, established in 1909, was an example of middle-class women allying themselves with working-class women: they funded strikes, hosted "tea parties" to "uplift" and Americanize immigrant workers, and they provided child care, food, and money to families of strikers. Although organizing was an important part of the life of a woman worker,

of the Russian revolutionary intelligentsia as the vanguard of the working class, the ethos was strong enough for Goldman to turn the issue around: she urged intellectuals to first recognize their own oppression as solid ground for camaraderie with those considered less privileged.[285]

What she considered most important, however, was to bring the intellectual class closer to the struggle of the working classes, to encourage them to see the similarities as well as the obvious differences in their forms of servitude. Goldman never dismissed their capacity to be genuine allies. She acted as an interpreter of acts of violence, an interrogator of complacency, an instigator of change, a protector (and fund-raiser) for those who risked their lives for the cause of freedom.

## UNION MILITANTS, TACTICAL EXTREMES

Goldman presented the accused, whether the actual perpetrators or not, as victims of a country that thrived on scapegoats and that needed an "alien" enemy to control its fears.

The country was wracked with social unrest. The fight to organize at the workplace and in open-air meetings in the streets was framed by the IWW as a fight for free speech, though after 1912 the union's direct labor struggles took precedence. The IWW fought back with industrial sabotage and force, when necessary, in its effort to win control of the workplace. (See "So-Called IWW Raids Really Hatched by Schoolboys," Interview in the *New York Times Sunday Magazine*, 29 March 1914.) The American Federation of Labor, although ostensibly committed to negotiation, sometimes surreptitiously utilized the skills of workers proficient in the use of dynamite to tip the scales. The cycle of violence also extended to government forces and private citizens who joined together against such militant union actions but were rarely punished themselves by the law for their brutality against the strikers and activists; labor violence, albeit sensational and terrorizing, became commonplace (see "Self-Defense for Labor," Article in *Mother Earth*, January 1914).

Although many people associate anarchists and anarchism with the Industrial Workers of the World, in part because of its militant tactics, Goldman's relationship to the IWW was far from unreservedly enthusiastic.[286] Goldman cared about the fate of striking workers and tended to focus her attention on those situations that directly affected anarchists, especially those that involved violence and armed action.

---

in this period women workers were caught between the poles of class and gender. The American Federation of Labor generally did not include women workers, and only those skilled women workers who had waged successful strikes were even eligible for the privileges and protection of membership in the union.

285. See Emma Goldman, "The Intellectual Proletarians," *Mother Earth*, February 1914.
286. The IWW began as a predominantly socialist union in 1905, and although Goldman adhered to its advocacy of the inclusion of all workers, she often considered the IWW a front for socialists engaged in a factional fight to gain power, and during this period, sometimes mocked them in *Mother Earth*. See Directory of Organizations in vol. 2 and this volume and Introduction in vol. 2, pp. 55–56.

Affirming the importance of a fair trial, Goldman raised funds for legal defense on behalf of militants in her support of the Caplan-Schmidt Defense Fund[287] (see Letter to Jacob Margolis, 6 April 1916).[288] She had been similarly supportive of those associated with the Lexington Avenue bombing, and of the "Italian boys,"[289] whose plot included an attempt to bomb St. Patrick's Cathedral and other churches in New York that had denied unemployed demonstrators a sanctuary of food and shelter, whose leader, Frank Tannenbaum, was arrested at the church in March 1914. The bomb, set at the cathedral on 13 October 1914, was intended to commemorate the anniversary of Ferrer's execution. Similarly, on the anniversary of the hanging of the Haymarket anarchists, 11 November 1914, explosives were found at the Tombs Police Court. Police agent provocateurs infiltrated anarchist groups, trapped the "Italian boys," and also kept a watch on the Ferrer Center. Anarchists, even those who were American born, were easy prey for marginalization as the threatening "other."

Intended as a mirror to reflect on conditions and gather support for resistance to injustice in the world, *Mother Earth* reported on turmoil at a time when the Great War was brewing in Europe,[290] and when labor violence was erupting in the United States.[291] The editors offered discreet and relatively safe expositions on sub rosa tactics in the anarchist movement. Goldman, who never denied her support of those who engaged in violent direct action as a necessary evil, nonetheless calibrated her public and private views on the subject with great care. She was certain that the success of the anarchist movement and of her magazine depended on curbing any reckless disregard of the law on controversial issues, including the advocacy of violence and the publication of sexually explicit material.[292]

In 1913 and 1914, during a period of massive unemployment centered primarily in New York, Berkman divided his time between editing *Mother Earth* and organizing mil-

287. Matthew Schmidt, who had pleaded not guilty, was sentenced in January 1916 to life imprisonment for murder in the first degree. David Caplan's first trial, in April 1916, ended with a hung jury. The next trial began in October, and by December, having pleaded guilty, Caplan was sentenced to ten years in prison on the charge of voluntary manslaughter.

288. Many such incidents that required legal support were planned at the Ferrer Modern School, which also served as an organizing institution for many militant actions. For the McNamara brothers, Mooney and Billings, Caplan and Schmidt, see Letter to the *Spur*, 16 October 1915. See also reference to Donald Vose in Letter to Leon Malmed, 11 November 1915. *EGP*, reel 9. See also Fund Appeals in *Mother Earth*.

289. See EG to Leon Malmed, 13 April [1915], *EGP*, reel 8. Regarding the frame-up and trial of the boys, and the guilty verdict, the judge acknowledged the role of the agents provocateurs, asserting that "if the police plant a bomb in his official duty . . . he is not guilty, because he does these things to protect society and not with criminal intent." In her article "Legendizing the Martyrs of Revolution," *Mother Earth*, May 1915, EG writes that the judge informed the jury that "an officer may commit any crime; so long as he does it out of duty he can not be responsible."

290. European antiwar activity in 1914 and 1915 foreshadowed the protests that occurred later in the United States.

291. See Fund Appeals in *Mother Earth*.

292. The magazine did print more articles that addressed the issue of violence than of sexuality.

itant anarchists and the unemployed. He had become a magnet for young anarchists, who honored his past "deed" and respected his skills as an organizer adept at fostering cooperation among disparate militant groups. The young anarchists joined his campaign to bring about a revolution and barely related to the older, seemingly more distant, Goldman.[293] His planning meetings were held in public places at first, but by necessity the meetings moved to clandestine locales, usually on the Lower East Side of New York City, some at the Ferrer Modern School.

In July 1914 a group of anarchists, furious with John D. Rockefeller Jr. for his arrogant refusal to apologize for the atrocities at Ludlow, retaliated against him.[294] Rockefeller ignored the silent vigil of mourners who marched by his Tarrytown home. Among those arrested and incarcerated for the action was Becky Edelsohn, who continued her protest in her jail cell when she initiated the first hunger strike in America. Injustice fed the desire for revenge. Shortly after the vigil, a bomb, intended for deployment at Rockefeller's estate in Tarrytown, blew up as it was being prepared; three anarchists died in this New York townhouse explosion. Some suggested that the act had been planned at a meeting at the Ferrer Center. The editors of *Mother Earth*, with Berkman playing a key role, honored the dead as martyrs to the cause.[295] Ten thousand people, still seething at the atrocities of Ludlow, gathered in Union Square, and many of them joined the procession to the *Mother Earth* office to view the urns filled with ashes of the deceased.

Goldman's sympathy was matched by her fury. In private she was critical that preparations had taken place in a townhouse where innocent people were harmed. She mourned the death of a girl unrelated to the plot, as well as the deaths of the three anarchists. Goldman had no problem with the sentiment that provoked the action and the intended act itself, or the right of those involved to carry it out. However, she thought it was not politically prudent to be so explicit as to put *Mother Earth* magazine and the Mother Earth Publishing Association, which published books and pamphlets, in danger of being shut down. In her 1931 autobiography her support of the act was less than wholehearted. She remembered having a flashback to 1892, when she too had collaborated with Berkman in a failed attempt to make a bomb in a tenement apartment in New York.[296] In her memoir she wrote, "[T]hough my sympathies were for the man who

293. Even the burgeoning anarchist-feminist youth movement in New York between 1912 and 1914 had little to do with Emma Goldman. See Goldman's reaction to the younger anarchists, EG to AB, 14 May 1929, *EGP*, reel 21, as a woman in her forties who by that time appealed more to an older set.

294. It wasn't until 1915 that Rockefeller appeared before the Walsh committee with a persuasive but disingenuous statement, after the fact, about his desire to do his best for the workers.

295. This issue of the magazine, as well as the issues that included the 1911 "The Psychology of Political Violence," "The Tragedy at Buffalo" (referring to the 1901 McKinley assassination), and other earlier articles, were cited as evidence against them and would later confirm the government's perception of EG's and AB's support of violent actions, which led to their deportation.

296. The bomb was intended to retaliate for Frick's role in the shooting of the Homestead locked-out workers.

resorted to such measures, I nevertheless felt now that I could never again participate in or approve of methods that jeopardized human lives."[297]

The ethics of defending those whose actions took the lives of others was generally blurred by the distinction between targeting individuals or property—the latter of which often included unintended injuries or even death.

Yet Goldman's life was rooted in the world of militant anarchists, with its codes of secrecy, risks of danger, and the bonds of loyalty and devotion to a cause. Once on the inside, one could not turn back. Even the slightest hint of betrayal threatened to put the entire community at risk. Every dollar collected for a militant was experienced as an assertion of the power of solidarity.

## PRISONS—"A SOCIAL CRIME AND FAILURE"

Goldman had long dreamed of a future anarchist society where there would be no need for prisons. Nonetheless, especially given the number of comrades who had been imprisoned, she joined the ongoing dialogue on prison reform.

Although progressives hoped to improve conditions for prisoners, Goldman considered the prison system itself "a social crime and a failure."[298] Most reformers agreed that punishment was counterproductive, but they also assumed that it was possible to isolate socioenvironmental and biological ills and to rehabilitate prisoners with new scientific and humane practices.[299] Goldman took the position that crime was primarily caused by poverty and tremendous gaps in wealth.[300] Others considered psychological and environment/family issues central.

Architects worked on the structural design of prisons to maximize light, diminish crowding, and improve poor sanitation facilities. Rehabilitation of prisoners became the responsibility of professionals in social work, counseling, and criminology. A wider use of indeterminate sentences, probation, parole, and even job placement assistance was encouraged. Supervised freedom rather than incarceration fit the progressive concept

---

297. *LML*, vol. 2, p. 536.

298. Emma Goldman, "Prisons: A Social Crime and Failure," in *Anarchism and Other Essays*, pp. 109–26.

299. See Larry E. Sullivan, *The Prison Reform Movement: Forlorn Hope* (Boston: Twayne Publishers, 1990), the source of this interpretation.

300. Goldman was a powerful speaker on the issue of jails and crime: newspapers reported her assertion that "we can never remove [crimes of poverty] until we remove poverty." The article "Doctrine of Anarchists—Emma Goldman Outlines It to an Intensely Interested Audience.—Religion, Capitalism and Government Hold Men in Bondage," *Duluth Herald,* 17 March 1911, described her talk on prisons, among other issues, in a manner that revealed how she and her ideas were perceived: "More than 200 people from nearly as many walks of life, sat for nearly two hours in the Owls' hall last evening, while a very short, very stout, and very earnest woman harangued in a high pitched, nervous, and harsh toned voice. The speaker was Emma Goldman, and her subject was anarchy. . . . Miss Goldman's talk was forceful, logical and intensely interesting. She did not rant or rave and she kept away from the shop worn expressions of the ordinary social propaganda. A slight accent added to the effectiveness of her voice."

of community uplift. This was an idea that reformers were willing to support in spite of objections waged by those who feared that "coddling" of prisoners threatened to compromise standards of public safety.[301]

A complex set of standards was used to determine eligibility for parole. It was assumed that those who committed crimes were impaired mentally or physically, and psychological tests were used to determine whether the prisoners' intelligence and mental balance were sufficient to allow them to reenter society. Among the many contradictions within the medical model was the general acceptance of the principles of eugenics to justify sterilization, life sentences, or release only after reproduction was impossible.[302] (Although Goldman disagreed with the eugenicists, she often found herself on the same platform with them in her fight for access to birth control. She never openly opposed or challenged their godlike assumptions about who should live and who should die, preferring to advance her own, very different, position relating to the impact of poverty on the underclass.)

Rehabilitation included work—presumably of mutual benefit to the prisoner and to the coffers of the prison institution. Prison labor compensation undercut the fight for union wages and was an increasingly bitter source of contention, even for private businesses lacking the prison-industrial competitive advantage.[303] For Goldman the business of prison labor was proof that reforms were shadowed by the sinister and unremitting pursuit of profit.

In her attempt to synthesize contemporary writings on criminal tendencies, the issue of slave labor, and of the harsh punishment of prisoners, she credited, selectively quoted, and misquoted Havelock Ellis and Edward Carpenter to support her own premises.[304] In the end she concluded that the extravagant expenditure of funds by the government to improve prisons was misdirected. More than statistics, direct observation (and reading W. C. Owen's work on the subject)[305] and her interest in the efforts of the Los Angeles Prison Reform League confirmed her beliefs.

301. Sullivan, *The Prison Reform Movement*, pp. 27–30.
302. For prisoners with "germ plasm"—a term used when the theory of heredity was relatively new, attributed to August Weismann (in 1883 and published in 1893), who thought that independent germ cells (egg and sperm) contain material that is passed from one generation to another. Many prisons adopted the belief that dangerous criminal behavior can be inherited. See Nicole Hahn Rafter and Debra L. Stanley, *Prisons in America: A Reference Handbook* (Santa Barbara, Cal.: ABC-CLIO, 1999), pp. 10–12.
303. See, for example, Rebecca M. McLennan, *The Crisis of Imprisonment: Protest, Politics, and the Making of the American Penal State, 1776–1941*, Cambridge History of American Law (Cambridge: Cambridge University Press, March 2008).
304. For direct comparisons with Emma Goldman, "Prisons: A Social Crime and Failure," in *Anarchism and Other Essays* (New York: Mother Earth Publishing Association, 1910) see Havelock Ellis, *The Criminal* (New York: Charles Scribner's and Sons, 1890) and Edward Carpenter, *Prisons, Police, and Punishment* (London: Arthur C. Fifield, 1905).
305. See Prison Reform League, *Crime and Criminals* (Los Angeles: Prison Reform League, 1910).

Insights into prison life at the time came not only from her own relatively brief experiences behind bars, but also from her connection to Alexander Berkman, for whom the deep scars and trauma of a long imprisonment could not be healed by freedom alone.

## INTERNATIONAL SOLIDARITY

Anarchists and revolutionaries around the world regularly risked imprisonment. Often repressive regimes, intolerant of dissent in their own countries, responded to protests of unfair treatment waged by the international community. Outside pressure groups sometimes succeeded in softening sentences, raising public interest and funds for the trials, and offering gestures of solidarity that could not be expressed for fear of reprisals, including imprisonment.

A commitment to the welfare of humanity and to nations without borders spun a network of support for those anarchist revolutionaries perceived to be in the dangerous hold of the state. Thus, in 1910 and 1911 when a group of Japanese anarchists, including Kōtoku Shūsui, was accused of attempting to kill the emperor and faced the prospect of execution, Goldman and others came to their aid (see "Japanese Radicals Condemned to Die," Article in *New York Call*, 12 November 1910; Letter to Lillian Wald, 29 November 1910; and Letter to Jack and Charmian London, 30 November 1910). When the Magón brothers fled from Mexico, and were later imprisoned in the course of attempting to influence the course of the Mexican Revolution from the United States, Goldman and her comrades came to their support (see Exchange of Letters between Ricardo Flores Magón and Emma Goldman in *Regeneración*, 22 April 1911); and when Rangel (who was associated with the PLM) and Cline (who was associated with the IWW) were arrested for smuggling guns to the PLM in Mexico (including the accusation of killing a deputy who pursued them), she joined others in coming to their defense. In her column "On the Trail," Goldman, the great orator, felt inadequate: "I wish I had the eloquence of a Camille Desmoulin, or the pen of Marat, that I could convey the spirit and the devotion which animates the heroic efforts of the Mexican rebels. . . . [W]hatever the beginning of the Revolution or its end, it has gone beyond all political consideration, straight to the goal of economic emancipation—Land and Liberty!"[306]

306. Emma Goldman, "On the Trail," *Mother Earth*, June 1911. For concurrent activities with regard to Mexico, the McNamara case, and IWW strategy of filling the jails see "Emma Goldman Comes to Preach Anarchism to IWW's," Article in *Fresno Morning Republican*, 14 May 1911; Letter to the International Mexican Meeting, 23 June 1911; for query on his position on the Mexican Revolution see Letter to Peter Kropotkin, 29 May 1911. When Francisco Ferrer was executed in Spain—accused of having fomented an insurrection in Barcelona—Goldman and her comrades initiated Ferrer Modern Schools across the country to carry on his tradition of promoting education devoid of the influence and domination of the Church. See vol 2, *Made for America*, p. 521. Others, like "the Italian boys," planned a series of bombings in New York City churches as a militant commemoration of Ferrer's death and to protest the lack of support of the Catholic Church for New York City's unemployed.

In the United States noncitizens had few guaranteed rights, and those who took part in radical activities were more vulnerable than the natural born to imprisonment or even deportation. Among the immigrant anarchists and radicals in Goldman's circles, many had been imprisoned or managed to escape imprisonment in their repressive home countries, were on the run, and had changed their names to continue the fight in the United States. If they had been caught, they would have found themselves in jail, treated as second-class citizens.

### INTERNAL CONFLICTS: ANARCHISTS AND THE GREAT WAR

With the eruption of the First World War in Europe in 1914, internationalism and a sense of solidarity on the left began to break down. The Second International had expelled the anarchists in 1896, distancing themselves from direct action tactics, and choosing instead to pursue a socialist electoral challenge. Anarchists struggled with the issue of war itself and worked together to create a unified manifesto on the subject (see "International Anarchist Manifesto on the War," Manifesto in *Mother Earth*, May 1915). Always mindful of the importance of noncoercion, the various factions argued their cases initially in the pages of *Freedom*.

Yet by 1917 when the war in Europe had escalated and the momentum of the preparedness movement in the United States moved easily onto a war footing, only the *Freie Arbeiter Stimme* of the established anarchist newspapers supported the war.[307] There were definitely some in Goldman's circles who supported the war as well, including Harry Kelly and W. C. Owen. The revered anarchist Peter Kropotkin in 1914 came out on the side of war as a way to support a world without exploitation. Kropotkin believed that "the causes of war must be attacked at the root" and that there was hope that the conflict would "open the eyes of the masses of workers" so that they could "see the part that Capital and State have played in bringing about the armed conflict between nations."[308] He also maintained that war was necessary to protect France, home of the 1789 revolution and the 1869 Paris Commune, to keep them from being overrun by Prussian-German tyranny. In 1915 Goldman crystallized her position on the relationship between war, militarism, imperialism, and the importance of standing against the impending bloodshed, as consistent with her interpretation of anarchist values, in "Preparedness, the Road to Universal Slaughter" (see Essay in *Mother Earth*, December 1915), affirming her advocacy of social wars over wars between nations.

### WINNING HEARTS AND MINDS

Even in 1916, as the clouds of war ominously hovered over America with many in government office challenged by fears of an inadequate military defense, the bursting explosion

---

307. At first, its editor, Saul Yanovsky, was against the war, but he later changed his mind.
308. Peter Kropotkin, "Kropotkin on the Present War," *Mother Earth*, November, 1914.

of creativity about the promise of a new era, a new woman, and a new social order had yet to be overshadowed. As the federal government strengthened and consolidated, progressive reformers crafted legislation on behalf of the poor, suffragists fought for the right to vote, and unions won significant organizing victories that improved the conditions of workers. Little magazines published political critiques and spread avant-garde art and ideas. It was fertile ground for a commentator like Goldman to enter the fray, to insert an anarchist voice into the clamor of those who believed that change was possible and imminent. The escalating efforts to stifle the birth control movement and the tensions over preparedness perhaps signaled the government's fear of losing potential soldiers and factory workers and, in Goldman's case, reinvigorated distrust of immigrant radicals.

## INSIGHT AND EXPERIENCE, COUNTERING RELIGIOUS DETERMINISM

Literally every topic Goldman addressed contained insights borne of her own experience. As a follower and disseminator of the ideas of Charles Darwin and T. H. Huxley on evolution, she rejected writings fixed on variants of the Adam and Eve story, which she believed undermined reason and individual will and reinforced an authoritarian mindset and submission to authority. During this period of a strong religious revival and fundamentalist movement in America, she spoke on the hypocrisy of Christianity and countered religious practice with an exposition on atheism (see "The Philosophy of Atheism," Essay in *Mother Earth*, February 1916)—lectures that attracted allies among the antireligious movement, a few of whom were freethinkers whose critique extended beyond the Church.[309] She also vehemently attacked the popular revivalist Billy Sunday,[310] whose appeal was primarily directed to those who feared change not only in the outside world but also within religious ranks. Liberal interpretations of religion reflecting the spirit of the times, with an emphasis on helping the poor rather than close study of the Bible, threatened those in Billy Sunday's grasp, who were hell-bent on holding on to traditional concepts of good and evil. Religious fundamentalists, who followed what they considered strict adherence to the ethics of the original doctrine, believed that the new freedoms led to "loose morals"—such as the frequenting of urban dance halls, saloons,

309. She was equally forceful in her critique of what she considered Jewish dogmatic religious practice. See essays by Candace Falk on Emma Goldman in *Encyclopedia of Jewish History; Jewish Women in America,* Paula Hyman, Deborah Dash Moore, eds. (American Jewish Historical Society, 1998); *Jewish History: A Research Guide to Biography and Criticism*, Joseph Adler, ed. (Checkmark Books, 1986). Also, Candace Falk, "To Dream of Becoming a Judith: The Jewish Roots of EG's Anarchism" (unpublished manuscript).
310. See *Mother Earth* cover, May 1915, "Billy Sunday Tango," illustrated by Robert Minor, and various references to Sunday's hypocrisy. EG also refers to Billy Sunday in her article "The Philosophy of Atheism," *Mother Earth,* February 1916. For excellent contextual information on Sunday and others as they appear in the magazine see Peter Glassgold, editor and commentator for *Anarchy! An Anthology of Emma Goldman's* Mother Earth (Washington, D.C.: Counterpoint Press); see also Roger A. Bruns, *Preacher: Billy Sunday and Big Time American Evangelism* (New York: W. W. Norton, 1992).

and red-light districts—and signified the demise of the world as they had known it. Revivalists strove to save themselves from sin and cast aspersions on those who in their eyes had forsaken "God's law."[311]

In response, Goldman traveled to Paterson, New Jersey, in 1915 to hold an anti–Billy Sunday meeting that attracted 1,000 attendees while Sunday spoke to a gathering of 9,000; dual meetings of even greater numbers followed. Goldman and Sunday each expressed animosity toward the other to their respective audiences. He dismissed her as part of a cohort of "reds" and intellectuals whose corrupting, out-of-touch pronouncements were destroying the country, which was reason enough to send them straight to hell. She considered him a "frothing, howling huckster"—a sentiment echoed by Eugene Debs, who looked upon Billy Sunday as "a vulgar harlequin, a ranting mountebank who, in the pay of the plutocracy, prostitutes religion to perpetuate hell on earth."[312]

Goldman equated religious fundamentalism with blind patriotism that sometimes justified the most horrendous forms of domination and control.

There are some, however, who might see traces of religiosity in Goldman's staunch commitment to anarchism's ethical codes and overarching beliefs. Yet her homage was to free will—in concert with other people—here on earth, with no rewards save the knowledge of having moved the world closer to freedom of the individual and freedom from want. She said, to "bring about peace on earth and good will toward men is to concede the superiority of the individual, as the unit of social life, to the organized force known as the State . . . to emancipate the masses from economic and social slavery. In other words, to teach man the value of himself and his right to take the things he has produced. That alone will establish peace on earth and good will toward man."[313] She also stated that, "It may be true that the vast majority of people are not yet 'good' enough to be Anarchists (personally, I do not believe it is a matter of good or bad), but I do not see how they are ever going to become good enough, if they do not make the first step."[314]

Her ideas resonated with atheist political philosophers popular at the time, notably Nietzsche and to a lesser extent Stirner. Goldman incorporated into her lectures and essays Nietzsche's concept of transvaluation as integral to social and political transformation—the belief in the possibility of complete internal and external transformation disentangled from the antisocial values and predominant power relations of the time. Later, she would explain it this way:

311. See Bruns, *Preacher: Billy Sunday.*
312. Ibid., particularly chapter 8, "Emma Goldman et al.," for a fuller depiction of Billy Sunday's life, work, and place within the times.
313. See also Emma Goldman, "Peace on Earth and Good Will Towards Men," *Mother Earth*, January 1915.
314. EG to [Edwin A. R.] Rumball, 17 December 1909, *EGP*, reel 3.

Revolution is the negation of the existing, . . . the destroyer of dominant values upon which a complex system of injustice, oppression, and wrong has been built up by ignorance and brutality. It is the herald of NEW VALUES, ushering in a transformation of the basic relations of man to man, and of man to society. It is not a mere reformer, patching up some social evils; not a mere changer of forms and institutions; not only a re-distributor of social well-being. It is all that, yet more. . . . It is . . . the TRANSVALUATOR, the bearer of *new* values. It is the great TEACHER of the NEW ETHICS, inspiring man with a new concept of life and its manifestations in social relationships. It is the mental and spiritual regenerator.[315]

She was intrigued also by Stirner's assertion of the centrality of the individual, including a rejection of universal concepts—the Hegelian notion of "mankind," the Christian belief in the "spirit," or what for the ancients constituted "the world." "The only truth is what the individual can appropriate for himself without becoming estranged from himself."[316] For Stirner, "The divine is God's concern; the human, man's. My concern is neither the divine nor the human, not the true, good, just, free, etc., but solely what is *mine*, and is not a general one, but is—*unique*, as I am unique. 'Nothing is more to me than myself!'"[317] In the preface to *Anarchism and Other Essays* Goldman writes, "That Stirner's individualism contains the greatest social possibilities is utterly ignored. Yet, it is nevertheless true that if society is ever to become free, it will be so through liberated individuals, whose free efforts make societies."[318] His influence is evident in Goldman's essay "Minorities Versus Majorities," in which she dares to express her distrust of the masses—and their blindly followed leaders. In "The Psychology of Political Violence" Goldman includes Stirner's distinction between revolution (the creation of a new social order) and a continuous state of rebellion (of permanent insurrection on the part of the individual) by sympathizing with those, like Czolgosz, who through individual acts of violence attempted to embody the revolution. Her ideas about religion and the State and conventional schooling were influenced by Stirner's classic work *The Ego and Its Own*.[319] To Stirner, belief in the necessity of institutional authority over the individual—no matter how grand its intent—was misguided, any claims for a fixed truth impossible.[320] A new world could be realized only through the cooperation of strong individuals, free

315. Emma Goldman, *My Further Disillusionment with Russia* (Garden City, N.Y.: Doubleday, Page, 1924).
316. Karl Lowith, *From Hegel to Nietzsche: The Revolution in Nineteenth-Century Thought* (New York: Holt, Rinehart, and Winston, 1964), p. 357. See also R. W. K. Paterson, *The Nihilistic Egoist Max Stirner* (London: Oxford University Press, 1971); and James Carroll, *Break-Out from the Crystal Palace: The Anarcho-Psychological Critique: Stirner, Nietzsche, Dostoevsky* (London: Routledge and Kegan Paul, 1974).
317. Max Stirner, *The Ego and Its Own*, trans. Steven Byington (New York: Benjamin Tucker, 1907). Emphasis in original.
318. Goldman, preface to *Anarchism and Other Essays*, p. 50.
319. Stirner, *The Ego and Its Own*. Ibid.
320. His ideas, and Nietsche's, also influenced modern dramatists, including Ibsen and Strindberg.

from all constraints. Goldman incorporated Stirner's ideas about individual freedom in her essay "Anarchism: What It Really Means" along with Kropotkin's emphasis on mutual aid as she created a synthesis of her own.

## FORBIDDEN ACTS: SEXUALITY AND THE DISSEMINATION OF BIRTH CONTROL

The struggle for sexual freedom and individual autonomy were intertwined. Perhaps the fiercest crusade of the evangelists, among other moral purists, was the attempt to tame sexual desire. Abstinence was considered the only acceptable form of birth control. And although marriage and the family were encouraged, education about sexuality and reproduction was forbidden.

The movement for the reversal of the attitudes behind the laws forbidding the dissemination of birth control information appealed to women (and men) across class lines.[321] Goldman, who had long been associated with both the neo-Malthusian and the eugenics movements,[322] a complex mix, never abandoned her focus on the impoverished conditions that often determined a woman's decision of whether to have a child or not—a position she shared with William J. Robinson as well as Peter Kropotkin (who opposed the sterilization of criminals). She warned her single-issue activists of the pitfalls of turning one's back on larger, underlying conditions. In her discussion of birth control she alerted listeners about the consequences of fighting for birth control without an equally strong demand for the alleviation of poverty, a circumstance that affected women who needed help the most, women who often put their lives in danger with back-alley abortions rather than jeopardize the precarious stability of their families (see "The Social Aspects of Birth Control," Essay in *Mother Earth*, April 1916; "En Route," Article in *Mother Earth*, June 1914; Letter to Margaret Sanger, 26 May 1914). Reformers too sought solutions to the link between poverty and high infant mortality rates;[323] one such attempt was to station public health nurses in poor communities to educate women in pre- and postnatal care.

Both Goldman and Margaret Sanger,[324] the renowned birth control advocate, understood the role of poverty and the importance of a woman's freedom to choose whether

321. "Birth strike" was a common term among early anarchists like Moses Harmon and interchangeable in many later contexts with the demand for birth control, especially among the poor.
322. For a definition and more detail on EG's relationship to the neo-Malthusian and eugenics movements see pp. 89, 418n11. EG attended the Neo-Malthusian Congress, August 4–8, 1900. See Chronology in vol. 1, *Made for America*, p. 509.
323. The Sheppard-Towner Maternity and Infancy Protection Act was passed in 1921 to provide federal matching funds to states for prenatal and child health care centers.
324. For the best study of Margaret Sanger see the Margaret Sanger Papers, microfilm, book, and website: E. Katz, ed., *Selected Papers of Margaret Sanger, vol. 1, The Woman Rebel 1900–1928* (Urbana: University of Illinois Press, 2003); *The Margaret Sanger Papers Microfilm Edition* (University Publications of America, 1997); and ww.nyu.edu/projects/sanger/index.html.

or not she wanted, or could provide for, a child—and the critical need for public support. Early in her career, Sanger took advice and direction from Goldman, who at the time was a far more experienced propagandist. The masthead subtitle of Sanger's magazine, the *Woman Rebel,* read "No Gods, No Masters"—taken from an IWW banner—expressed her rebellion against the authority of the Church and State for forbidding women's access to birth control, which she considered a class issue. Reflecting Sanger's strong early militancy, the magazine even ran an article titled "A Defense of Assassination."[325] However, the combination of that contentious article with birth control content in the March and May 1914 issues of the magazine caused Sanger to be indicted.[326] In a letter to the editor of *Mother Earth* Sanger thanked those who rallied to her cause and made no excuses for the inclusion of the article, asserting that "if free speech and free press means anything . . . an opinion on a question which at that time was the cause of throwing all of Europe into a state of war . . . he has the right to express his opinion." Sanger ended her note with an appeal for funds and expressed her disappointment at the silence of *Mother Earth* on the post office's censorship of the *Woman Rebel,* an omission Goldman, who claimed never to have faltered in her solidarity for her "brave friend," attributed to Sanger's failure "to keep *Mother Earth* posted on the status of her case."[327] The August 1914 issue of the *Woman Rebel* was banned although there were no apparent differences in its birth control information and messages from those in other issues of the magazine. Arraigned on 24 August, Sanger requested and was granted a postponement of her trial by the presiding judge as well as the assistant district attorney for the Southern District of New York, Harold Content,[328] but she chose not to appear for her 20 October court date. At the end of the month Sanger left the country to avoid prosecution, and the *Woman Rebel* ceased publication. In Europe she expanded her circle of comrades and lovers and continued her work in freedom, principally through the Neo-Malthusian League.[329] By December her husband, William Sanger, had become the target of a Comstock sting, in which an agent of the New York Society for the Suppression of Vice who pretended to need birth control information caught William Sanger in the act of distributing such pamphlets from his home. The Free Speech League came to his aid with funds and an attorney, but after many postponements Gilbert Roe pleaded the case. The trial was also a big news event, attended by many New York City free speech advocates and radicals, including Alexander Berkman, Elizabeth Gurley Flynn,

---

325. See Herbert A. Thorpe, "A Defense of Assassination," *Woman Rebel,* July 1914.
326. Sanger was indicted twice under Section 211 of the U.S. Criminal Code for the March and May 1914 issues of the *Woman Rebel,* and under Section 480 of the Postal Code the August 1914 issue was banned from the mails.
327. Margaret Sanger to Emma Goldman, *Mother Earth,* April 1915.
328. Harold Content would later indict Goldman for her anti-conscription activities.
329. See description of the Neo-Malthusian League in Letter to Margaret Sanger, 26 May 1914, note 2.

Leonard Abbot, and Carlo Tresca. Sanger was sentenced and jailed from 10 September to 9 October 1915.

Margaret Sanger, whose many lovers included Alexander Berkman and sexologist Havelock Ellis, returned to the United States just a few days before William Sanger's release, with the intention of finalizing papers for their divorce.[330] In the midst of all this, their five-year-old daughter—who was placed in the care of the Modern School—died of pneumonia. Bereft and confused, Sanger forged on, trying to decide whether or not to plead guilty. Goldman's condolence note was more an exhortation to action than an expression of sympathy. Goldman and Berkman urged her to make a public fight by pleading not guilty and to take the opportunity of having the attention of the nation to speak out about the legitimacy of birth control. Others, including Leonard Abbott, feared that the consequence of such a strategy would be a prolonged jail sentence. After many postponements, Attorney General Harold Content, who had also sent Sanger a letter of condolence, requested that the charges be dropped. Although this dispensation was a relief to the still-mourning Sanger, *Mother Earth* reported that "as far as the stupid laws are concerned, absolutely nothing was gained," implicitly criticizing Sanger's refusal to fight.[331]

Yet Sanger was a pragmatic and persistent fighter. She opened the nation's first birth control clinic in the Brownsville section of Brooklyn on 16 October 1916; it was shut down ten days later. She was arrested along with Fania Mindell and Ethel Byrne (Sanger's sister), and they were released on bail; by 13 November 1916 she had reopened the clinic, only to be arrested again the next day.[332] In spite of Goldman's original advice to wait until she was better known, Sanger began publishing *Birth Control Review,* a new magazine, in 1917 (see Letter to Margaret Sanger, 22 June 1914; see also Letter to W. S. Van Valkenburgh, 21 February 1916).

Sanger's commitment to the poor, expressed solely in relation to the issue of birth control, won the support of middle-class women, who joined the protest activities but

---

330. See also Phyllis Chesler, *Woman of Valor: Margaret Sanger and the Birth Control Movement in America* (New York: Simon and Schuster, 1992), especially for Ellis, pp. 110–25, and for Berkman, pp. 142–43, and reference on p. 501 to letter from AB to Sanger, 9 December 1915: "I would hold you in my arms again." See also *The Selected Papers of Margaret Sanger*, vol. 1, *The Woman Rebel 1900–1928.*

331. Goldman, "Observations and Comments," *Mother Earth*, March 1916. In a letter to EG (14 March 1916), William Sanger confronted Goldman for being "condescending" and for the "contention that [Margaret's] was the first case to be tried in a state court on the proposition of Birth Control." He asserted that "Margaret's work stands out clear cut and revolutionary. . . . She was the first one, to my mind, to attack the statutes *involving long terms of imprisonment.* Your arrests have only been based on misdemeanors and disorderly conduct." He recalled Goldman dissuading Sanger from birth control work "until she was better known. . . . [I]t is only when the pioneers have done their work and when results are achieved that others come in for applause."

332. On 2 February 1917 Margaret Sanger began serving thirty days for opening the clinic.

rarely were subject to arrest. Many liberal activists, too, found that the battle for repro-ductive rights was less threatening than tackling economic conditions.

Because women's suffrage was a privilege that had been won only in some states, women who identified as progressives took a more gradualist approach to change; anar-chists like Goldman, however, had little faith in the effectiveness of piecemeal change, even when they addressed the same issues. Eugenicists and neo-Malthusians[333] were among the birth control supporters in a movement that represented a bewildering cross-section of political and personal biases.[334] Advocates of birth control drew their commit-ment from very different philosophies: one to assert the rights of women to control their own bodies, the other to encourage the development of the "master race" with abortions for the disabled and for those seen as unfit to raise children.

Eugenicists also represented attitudes toward the family that were outside the main-stream. Those on the radical end of the spectrum supported the right to have sex-ual experiences outside of reproductive constraints; others, whose perspectives were more conservative, hailed eugenics as a means to stabilize marriage and the family as it always had been. Still, their points of commonality brought them together and drew an audience. It would be a while before the mass birth control movement overturned Comstock's legacy of labeling dissemination of birth control information "obscene."

The ebbs and flows of government efforts to control women's bodies could easily be transposed as a map on the template of the period of fear and constraint soon to follow. Goldman was imprisoned for the same lecture on birth control she had delivered "in at least 50 cities throughout the country always in the presence of detectives,"[335] signaling the coming of a more insidious form of repression (see "Emma Goldman Is Put Under Arrest," Article in the *Oregonian*, 7 August 1915; "Emma Goldman Is Fined $100 in City Court," Article in the *Oregonian*, 8 August 1915; Press Circular, 15 February 1916). Repression later came in the guise of patriotism and preparedness for war and dealt a blow to those, including Emma Goldman, who were perceived by the government as seriously threatening the nation's stability.

No longer identified primarily as an immigrant anarchist, Goldman had won the hearts and minds of some civil libertarians who considered her one of their own. To a liberal audience, advocacy of the right of free expression was the most appealing among

---

333. Neo-Malthusians advocated population limitation and supported birth control or abortion. Some among them were eugenicists whose primary interest was the improvement of the "race stock." The International Neo-Malthusian Bureau of Correspondence and Defence was founded at the Third International Neo-Malthusian Conference in the Hague in July 1910 to alert and elicit support for those facing legal charges for advocacy of family limitation intervention.

334. See Linda Gordon, *Woman's Body, Woman's Right: Birth Control in America* (New York: Pen-guin Books, 1977) for an excellent overview of the history and movement for birth control rights in America.

335. Emma Goldman, "Emma Goldman's Defense: Birth Control," *Masses*, June 1916.

Goldman's many causes. Her lectures and essays on sexuality, birth control, marriage and the family, education, religious and labor movements, and the modern drama raised challenging questions debated in the culture at large. Access to birth control information was a rallying point across a wide political spectrum. Although eventually diminished by impending war and repression of dissent, the light of the avant-garde, the spirit of the new, remained strong in the period from 1910 to 1916, and the vigilant struggle for dignity and justice against the darkness of industrial and social violence, racism, hunger, and unemployment would not wane.

## 3. CHRONOLOGICAL NARRATIVE WEAVING THROUGH THE TEXTS: YEAR BY YEAR

Free speech, the pride of the nation, was for Goldman a matter of practical politics as well as egalitarian principle. The issue unified a disparate array of people across a broad political spectrum and often functioned as a lightning rod for anarchist ideas and financial support for the many causes and legal cases she championed. Goldman's success and impact as a public speaker and anarchist thinker was grounded in free expression, which she considered "the greatest and only safety in a sane society."[336]

### 1910

The year 1910 marked relative openness to new ideas; in spite of a rebuff from officials in Detroit and Buffalo, Goldman got an official Chicago police permit to lecture, in contrast to her 1908 tour in Chicago and in New York, where she had been met with police clubs and locked halls. Yet given the unpredictability of official attitudes about political dissent, even in times when more liberals and socialists than ever before held public office, she still never knew what to expect.

Among those who rallied around Goldman's Philadelphia 1909 free speech fight was Joseph Fels, a prominent single-taxer and businessman who publicly admonished his city for its disrespectful treatment of her.[337] But the trust Emma Goldman inspired often did not extend to her associate Ben Reitman. When she tried to get Fels to support her request "to head a fund to be collected for the successful enforcement of free speech," he declined, citing not only lack of time but also lack of confidence in Goldman's prime organizer, Ben Reitman, whose shady reputation recently had come to his attention (see

---

336. "The free expression of the hopes and the aspirations of a people is the greatest and only safety in a sane society," statement by EG at her federal hearing on her deportation, 27 October 1919.

337. See Letter to the *Philadelphia Ledger*, in vol. 2, *Making Speech Free*, pp. 454–56. See Joseph Fels in Directory of Individuals.

Letter to Josephs Fels, 12 January 1910). Fels's negative feelings for Reitman were typical. The *Denver Post* fanned the flames in a sensationalized article headlined "Dynamite Doctor Would Have a Blood Red Revolt—Ben Reitman Absorbs a Highball and Foretells Doom of the Press and Explains Why Girls Leave Home," documenting Reitman's careless advocacy of violence. The article damned and racialized him further, noting that "there is not a shadow of sincerity in his voice; his eyes, gloomy as they are with race tragedy. . . . But that very lyric quality of presence and utterance that captivates one's curiosity makes followers, believers, hypnotized subjects for the man, and according to their number and ignorance is he to be reckoned as a factor of danger to law and order and decency."[338] Reitman was a man whose flamboyant exhibitionism was often a source of embarrassment, and many in her circle of liberal supporters (like Ellen Kennan) grappled with the seeming incongruity of Reitman's centrality in Goldman's life.

## "OH BEN, BEN": PASSION AND POLITICS ON THE LECTURE TRAIL

With Reitman at her side, in his broad-brimmed black hat, silk cravat, and dramatic cape, Goldman felt emboldened. On lecture tours on behalf of *Mother Earth*, they crisscrossed the country together. She chronicled her adventures through travel reports, four of which were titled "Light and Shadows in the Life of an Avant-Guard" (see Article in *Mother Earth*, February 1910, among others).[339] Goldman voiced her conviction in the language of Nietzsche that anarchism was a "social theory that has undertaken to transvalue all values."[340] Goldman and many of the bohemians—writers, artists, and musicians of her time—linked the transformative force of her politics to the spirit of "the life of the avant-guard, that, with all its shadows, can never lose its light, its rich warm light."

Ben Reitman also sent travel notes. He reported with great enthusiasm in the March 1910 issue on the free speech fight, in which he vowed that his "life's work . . . will always be with Emma Goldman and the great cause of human liberty" (see "The Free Speech Fight," Article in *Mother Earth*, March 1910). He compared 1908 with 1910, recounting police violence at the Chicago 1908 march of the unemployed. This was followed by a description of the "attack" by Lazarus Averbuch on a police chief. Because Averbuch was identified by Chicago police authorities with anarchism, the act prompted a quick closure of all halls in the city slated for a Goldman lecture.[341] Reitman recalled offering his

---

338. *Denver Post*, 3 April 1910.
339. Instances of "Light and Shadows": *Mother Earth* 5 (March to July 1910), pp. 16, 32 (table of contents), 45 (title), 46 (heading), 48 (heading), 50 (says, "shall it be light or shadow for the avant-guard?"), 64 (table of contents), 87 (title), 88 (heading), 90 (heading), 113 (table of contents), 124 (title), 126 (heading), 128 (heading), 130 (says, "Dear brave comrade, if not for such as you the shadows in the life of the avant-guard would shut out the light completely"), 159.
340. See F. W. Nietzsche, *Will to Power, an Attempted Transvaluation of All Values*, trans. Anthony M. Ludovici (New York: Macmillan, 1914) for a discussion of the concept of transvaluation.
341. See vol. 2, *Making Speech Free*, pp. 281–83.

Hobo Hall as the first step in his long journey with Goldman.[342] Recording the victories they had won in town after town, he boasted of expanding the public political conversation to include a serious consideration of anarchism. He reveled in tales of overcoming arrest in places like San Francisco, where he and Goldman were charged by police with "being Anarchists and denouncing the government as being unnecessary"—an accusation the court refused to consider. Reitman reassured the readers in *Mother Earth* that: "whether in Detroit, or Buffalo, or Indianapolis, New York, or Burlington, the Free Speech Committee takes up the fight. It circulates free speech literature and tries to create public sentiment." Reitman, like Goldman, pointed out that, regrettably, socialists were often the first to censor anarchists. Free speech advocates, less sectarian and more universal in their defense of free expression, were ultimately the best allies of the anarchists, whether or not they agreed with the anarchist perspective.

Interest in socialism and in the Socialist Party was growing.[343] The membership expanded across the country as socialist candidates for public office became more common. Even though some of Goldman's associates were staunch socialists,[344] many in the Socialist Party believed that anarchists and socialists had little in common. In fact, most socialists chose to distance themselves from anarchists as part of their public disavowal of violence and of the political methodology of those who espoused violence. Anarchists did not ascribe to Marxist ideas and economic determinism and the primacy of the working class to revoutionary change; most considered electoral politics futile. Marxists and Socialists considered anarchism impractical. As far back as 1896 anarchists had been expelled from the socialist Second International. Perhaps, then, it was no surprise that Goldman received a chilly reception from some (not all) socialist mayors and a blackout or harsh critique in local and party newspapers. However, in Goldman's opinion Ben Reitman could work miracles to overcome those and other obstacles. In 1910 his talents made for an extraordinarily successful lecture tour. Thus, in spite of the snub by the authorities and "the wretched Chicago weather," more than 4,000 people paid admission, a feat nearly matched in Milwaukee and in Madison. In *Mother Earth*, Goldman reported on events, notable political organizations, and individuals in each town—including being hosted by the Milwaukee Socialist Students' Club and Professor Ross, among others, in Madison at the University of Wisconsin. After her talk at this taxpayer-supported state institution, an angry backlash ensued—one that prompted the university president to fire Goldman's host professor. Faculty and student strikes culminated with a reinstatement that would set a precedent, inoculat-

---

342. For details of this incident see Introduction, vol. 2, p. 73; and Roger A. Bruns, *The Damndest Radical*, pp. 62–63.
343. James Weinstein, *The Corporate Ideal in the Liberal State, 1900–1918* (Boston: Beacon Press, 1969).
344. Socialists included Rose and Anna Strunsky and William English Walling of the SPA.

ing the campus for years to come from threats of suppression of free speech or denial of academic inquiry.[345]

Such reports in *Mother Earth* were interspersed with personal details, from complaints about physical discomfort, such as sniffles and falls, to experiences like a Wisconsin sleigh ride reminiscent of the Russian troika and an array of festivities and camaraderie—to add authenticity and color to the rendering of her tours.

But her peripatetic life on the road called out for a counterbalance. Her espousal of free love did not preclude being drawn into the fantasy of sharing her life with Ben.[346] She even pledged to move away from the tight quarters of "210," the *Mother Earth* home and office space, to find an apartment of her own and a proper office (see Letter to Ben Reitman, 2 July 1910). To assuage Ben's wanderlust before they settled down together, and to ensure him a secure place in the anarchist movement, Emma even arranged for him to travel to London to meet (and perhaps convey messages not meant to be revealed in writing) Peter Kropotkin, Errico Malatesta, and Guy Aldred.[347] She sent a formal letter of introduction to Kropotkin to establish Ben's credentials not only as one who had "completely abandoned himself to our propaganda" but also as one who had sustained "a very severe and brutal attack" by Chicago police in a demonstration of the unemployed (see Letter to Peter Kropotkin, 19 July 1910).

His time abroad was also an opportunity for her to spend time alone reworking her lectures for *Anarchism and Other Essays*. Commenting on her essays, she wrote to Ben before she left for "the farm" that of the three manuscripts (on the psychology of political violence, on Ferrer, and on marriage), "the one on Marriage & Love, is the most brilliant I suppose because I have so little of it. Well, are not all great things merely in the ideal[?] Thus my ideal of love will die with me, never realized." The articulation of her anarchist vision was consoling, even as she lamented her personal situation.

345. See the archives at the State Historical Society of Wisconsin for fuller coverage of the incident. According to the late Professor Norman Jacobson a controversial bronze plaque dedicated to academic freedom, prompted by both the Ely and Ross incidents and given to the university by the class of 1910, was the site of demonstrations during 1950s McCarthyism to protest the trend of targeting those deemed communist sympathizers and un-American. See also "Emma Goldman Incident: State Aghast at University Reds—Sponsors for Emma Goldman's Visit to Madison Have Brought a Storm of Protest About Their Heads—Citizens Believe It Time for Housecleaning at the University," *Beloit Daily Free Press*, 31 January 1910, Theodore Herfurth Papers, State Historical Society of Wisconsin (Herfurth was instrumental in securing the public display of the bronze plaque).

346. Thus, Goldman refused to give in to the ways in which she felt that Ben's promiscuous behavior distorted her vision of anarchism and of the possibility of a love that was truly free. Instead, she wrote that she'd rather "do without reality" if her ideal was constantly "abused, insulted, spate upon, dragged through the mud" (see Letter to BR, 22 June 1910). Where others might have been resigned to the stance that "what has to be must be," her rejection of the baser realities of the world around her, the ways in which she "resisted it, fought it, defied it" with a more exalted vision of social harmony was her hallmark and a beacon in dark times—not only in the political realm but also in love.

347. See Errico Malatesta in Directory of Individuals. For Guy Aldred, see Letter to the *Spur*, 16 October 1915; and Letter to Ben Reitman, 26 August 1910, note 7.

Feelings of abandonment, perhaps stirred by Ben's record of infidelity, merged with her childhood traumas of feeling abandoned when her parents sent her away to live with physically and emotionally abusive relatives.[348] When she broke her kneecap and was hospitalized,[349] the loneliness and the pain of her early neglect were restimulated and redirected at Ben for his absence in times of need.

During this first long stretch of time away from Reitman she also pined for the sexual pleasures so integral to their love. They wrote in code: her "m" (mountains) and her "tb" (treasure box) a reference to her breasts and her treasure box of intimacy. She channeled her sexual longings into focused concentration on her writing. (See Letter to BR, 1 August 1910.)

## BEN'S CARELESS ADVOCACY OF VIOLENCE

Goldman's loneliness mixed with longing for Ben turned to disappointment and anger upon hearing reports from London about the ways in which he had bandied about ideas related to the tactic of violence. Ben had alienated most of the guests at a special event there by preaching an extreme version of the doctrine of force as the prerequisite for social change. Such pronouncements were reminiscent of his April interview, "highball" in hand, with a Denver reporter, who labeled him the "Dynamite Doctor."[350] Goldman was furious then and now about his carelessness and reminded him that anarchism ultimately means "non-invasion." She asserted that "[v]iolence is only the last medium of individual and social redress." While she did not deny her own militancy, she emphasized the nuances: "[C]onditions drive a man to Violence and . . . every real revolutionary change necessitates the use of Violence. . . . [I]f no other method is left, violence is not only justifiable, but imperative, not because anarchism teaches it, but because human nature does and must resist repression."

She warned Ben that his new obsession with simplistic edicts on the topic was "playing with fire" and would land him "into prison for absolutely nothing." Goldman prided herself on reaching beyond their anarchist circles and for the many positive newspaper features reporting with playful relief that "she carried no bombs in her pocket."[351] Goldman hectored Reitman to respect that most people know themselves, and understand what they accept and what they reject. Her letter to Reitman challenges his careless advocacy and offers a clear exposition of her perception of violence as a provocative strategy that required thoughtful intelligence in its practice.

---

348. See *LML*, pp. 66–69.
349. She wrote in her autobiography that she was treated by the same doctor who had tended to President McKinley's fatal gunshot wound. See *LML*, p. 472. The doctor's name, however, does not appear in the official list of doctors who treated the president.
350. Frances Wayne, "Dynamite Doctor Would Have a Blood Red Revolt," *Denver Post*, 3 April 1910.
351. Leslie Curtis, "Emma Goldman Lectures on 'Marriage and Love' and 'Anarchy,'" *Reno Evening Gazette*, 17 May 1910.

So long as I resist every convention and law imposed upon me I am a Revolutionist. As to the method I employ, that depends too not on anarchism but on the time, place and condition. Intelligent Violence. Why the very idea of it, implys discretion judgment as to the time and place, do you ever exercise it? You go about like a steer smashing blindly everything before you and when people resented you are surprised!

If as she hoped, Ben would eventually become a force in the anarchist movement, he would have to become more discerning about public discourse on the subject of violence, especially with anti-anarchist laws in force. Most likely also because she was aware of clandestine actions in the making, she chose not to address the *when* and *where* of violent tactics in her forthcoming book, or in her formal lectures and essays. Instead she chose to explain the *why* of those who dared to take them. Her letter to Ben, filled with political advice and ambiguous maternal eroticism, ended with her customary parting words "Your Mommy always" (see Letter to Ben Reitman, 26 August 1910).

## FREE SPEECH FRAMED

Most of the correspondence with Goldman during her hospital convalescence (from her knee injury) was from well-wishers eager for her to return to the road. Adeline Champney, anarchist and member of the Cleveland Freethought Society, was one of many anarchists and free-spirited women across the country who drew political sustenance from the unifying impact of *Mother Earth* magazine. Champney enjoyed the national community it fostered and was emboldened as a woman in an era in which the political terrain was still largely dominated by men. Although eventually Champney attempted a slight distancing from her association with Goldman (as expressed in Champney's essay "Congratulations—Plus" in the tenth-anniversary issue of *Mother Earth*, March 1915, in which she railed against violence and criticized both the personal animosity expressed in the pages of the magazine and the magazine's doctrinaire interpretations of events), their early correspondence evinced the initial closeness between them. In a chatty letter to Goldman, Champney reported on meetings, pamphlet distribution, and editorial decisions. She even included reports of daily annoyances like visitors who smoked in her house (see Letter from Adeline Champney, 4 September 1910).

In spite of the many friends and comrades she met along the way, Goldman's tours had not been easy. Meeting with opposition at almost every turn, she often countered her detractors by employing the techniques of a political performance artist to dramatize the absurdity of censorship. In November 1910 she had an opportunity to speak directly to Anthony Comstock, the post office inspector who banned mail that included sex education in his vague definition of obscenity.[352] Goldman and Reitman

---

352. For the effects of the Comstock law on freedom of speech in America, see vol. 1, *Made for America*, and vol. 2, *Making Speech Free*, and *The Selected Papers of Margaret Sanger*, vol. 1, *The Woman Rebel (1900–1928)*.

planted themselves in the audience to heckle and taunt him. Reitman accused him of being responsible for sending "1,000 people to jail . . . for spreading information about sex . . . and [driving] as many to suicide." Comstock defended himself as one who "acted only according to the rules of law." Goldman then charged Comstock with using "perjured testimony," followed by Comstock's characterization of her remarks as "indecent and uncalled for." Within seconds of his attack, the audience spontaneously applauded the daring Goldman, and the floor was hers. The entertainment had only just begun. Comstock threatened to use his privilege as "a peace officer of this country" to take Reitman "into custody . . . [for] disorderly conduct," specifically for shouting derogatory comments without being recognized by the chair. A roar of laughter followed when Goldman asked Comstock how he had maintained his purity and his ability to keep his will under subjection by obeying laws of God and morality while spending forty years inspecting obscene literature. Others in the audience chimed in, "Isn't prudery the chief cause of immorality?" Comstock's retort: these questions were "too absurd to be answered," asserting that "it would be shameful" to describe publicly what made him deem a book obscene. When a respondent queried whether "it was right to place in the hands of a child the Bible," Comstock unilaterally defended "the Word of God." The battle for sex education and for the right to political speech continued to be an area of the law necessitating constant vigilance, while religious freedom, the inspiration for the Pilgrims' migration to North America, was now used to suppress free speech (see "Comstock Heckled at Labor Temple," Article in the *New York Times*, 2 November 1910).

## INTERNATIONAL SOLIDARITY

In June 1910 Japanese police discovered four anarchists with a stock of bomb-making material, and several Japanese socialists and anarchists, some of whom were writers, were charged with conspiracy to kill the emperor of Japan,[353] a crime punishable by death. American anarchists, some of whom had come in contact with Kōtoku in 1906, believed that the accused were subjects of trumped-up charges, proof of the Japanese imperial family's fear of dissent and willingness to go to extremes to prevent its spread.[354] Their trial ran from 10 December through 24 December. In the interim Goldman and the *Mother Earth* group joined the international protest "in the name of humanity" against the planned executions. Many engaged in their defense likened their fate to that of the Haymarket anarchists—the judicial hangings on scant evidence that in 1887 had sent warning signals around the world. Kanno Suga and eight others were definitely involved in the plot, and Kōtoku Shūsui had acted as their inspiration and gatherer of informa-

---

353. A list of other charges compounded those related to the assassination plot.
354. Kōtoku and Sakai Tashiko published the first Japanese translation of Marx and Engels's *Communist Manifesto* in 1904. Kōtoku and others finished translating Kropotkin's *Conquest of Bread* in 1909. Translations of Marx, Kropotkin, and even Tolstoy were considered a threat.

tion for preparing the bomb.[355] Goldman rallied others against the "barbarous method against intellectuals." She was part of an international effort to embarrass and pressure the Japanese ambassador to rescind the sentence against Kōtoku, ex-companion Kanno, and twenty-four comrades (see "Japanese Radicals Condemned to Die," Article in *New York Call*, 12 November 1910).

The isolationist imperial order in Japan was bombarded with criticism from abroad. Goldman sent as many letters as she could to influential friends and associates urging them to join the campaign against political barbarism, assuring them of the innocence of the accused. Among those on her list was Lillian Wald, who had become a prominent leader in the early social work movement. Goldman's intent was in part to appeal to Wald, as a woman, to defend Kanno Suga, "the first woman Japan held for a political offence."[356] Goldman believed in the efficacy of international human rights campaigns: "such a protest . . . saved Babushka and Tchaikovsky from death."[357] On Goldman's urging, based on principle, Wald added her name to the list of prominent international spokespeople for social justice who opposed the sentence against Kōtoku, Kanno, and their comrades (see Letter to Lillian Wald, 29 November 1910). Goldman also approached the writer Jack London and his wife, Charmian, for help, suggesting that a few lines from London could "help to save the 26 lives" (see Letter to Jack and Charmian London, 30 November 1910).

She confided to Ben, the "madness complete. It would take hours to tell you all I did to day and I am so tired I can hardly sit up." Along with the outreach letters for the Japanese cause were others directed more specifically to her anarchist circle, including pleas for funds to keep an old anarchist and his sick wife from being evicted from their home. Mundane day-to-day planning for upcoming meetings was reserved for Ben. By autumn she was anxious to get away to the house in Ossining, New York, to rest as well as work away from the city. She went off to "the farm" to finish preparing next season's lecture notes and to transform some lectures into written essays.

Being away from the city and from her "great companion in work and struggle" prompted a series of passionate letters to Ben, each filled with an array of coded titillations: "I love you awfully much, so do the m and the t-b and every inch of me. Come close to me dearest, and let me rest, I is so tired. Good night. Hobo's Mommy" (see Letter to Ben Reitman, 29 November 1910).

---

355. For confirmation of Kanno's guilt see extracts from her letters in Mikiso Hane, *Reflections on the Way to the Gallows* (Berkeley: University of California Press, 1988), pp. 51–75. For Kōtoku's involvement see John Crump, *The Origins of Socialist Thought in Japan* (London, 1983), pp. 291–322.

356. Goldman also used her letter to ask whether Wald would be willing to exert her influence and investigate the case of a poor young nurse wrongfully held in an insane asylum for disclosing information about "the cruel conditions at a nursing home."

357. Catherine Breshkovskaya Babuska and Nikolai Chaikovsky, members of the PSR (Socialist Revolutionary Party), were tried as revolutionaries in March 1910. Chaikovsky pleaded not guilty and was acquitted. Breshkovskaya, who described herself as a "revolutionary propagandist," was found guilty of advocating terror and agrarian disorder and plotting assassinations, and sentenced to perpetual exile in Siberia.

In the public domain, Reitman's ability to find welcoming lecture halls was also a tremendous asset. However, other lecturers, like Voltairine de Cleyre in an article in *Mother Earth*, were critical of Goldman's preference for "respectable halls" that catered to the privileged; de Cleyre expressed equal disdain for what she characterized as Reitman's crude "Barnum and Bailey" circus style. Goldman was sure that bringing anarchist propaganda to middle-class audiences, along with Ben's theatrical flair, was as important as Voltairine's primary focus on the poor. Goldman saw the potential of those in the middle class who suffered in their own ways from the alienation inherent in a system of greed and hypocrisy. She defended her preference for "clean halls," in neighborhoods that matched the demographics of her audience, whether from the middle or working classes.[358] Her inclination was also symptomatic of the racial separation of her times. Goldman rejected halls in the "nigger district," where "American [white and ethnic] workers would not attend."[359] De Cleyre, on the other hand, chose to speak to the impoverished, wherever and whoever they were. Goldman compared herself to de Cleyre in her ability to reach white and ethnic working people, to cross class and ethnic divides (though not racial divides as they are now defined) because of her own experience as a factory worker. She criticized the self-righteousness of her sister anarchist de Cleyre, who as a woman born into relative privilege lived in dire poverty and identified primarily with the poor, as if she had no choice.

Goldman, with great eloquence, referred to her own past in Russia, heralding the intellectual as the vanguard of the revolution: "The pioneers of every new thought rarely come from the ranks of workers. Possibly because the economic whip gives the latter little opportunity to easily grasp a truth. Besides, it is an undisputed fact that those who have but their chains to lose cling tenaciously to them." Thus, she cited several cases in which the workers turned upon one another.

Lenin had situated the Russian Social Democratic Labor Party in the tradition of

358. Goldman added complexity to her stance on the issue in an interview about her experience as a speaker to a privileged women's civic club. "Some Civitas Members Wanted to be 'Thrilled,' So Emma Goldman Was Asked to Address Them—'Red' Leader Claims That Invitation to Appear Before This Exclusive Club Was an Exemplification of the Principles of Anarchy. Prefers to Talk to Working Class—Wealthy Women Too Reluctant to Adopt New Ideas. Score the 'Uplifter,'" *Brooklyn Eagle*, 16 January 1916, *EGP*, reel 48.

359. See David Roediger, *The Wages of Whiteness: Race and the Making of the American Working Class*, rev. ed. (New York: Verso, 1999, 2007), for an excellent overview of the way whiteness was constructed by laborers, as a form of self-definition and exclusion, which by implication sheds light on Goldman's complex relationship to her immigrant roots, to her white audiences, and her own implicit racism in relation to "the color line." This is one of many books on the subject written in recent years. See also David W. Southern, *The Progressive Era and Race: Reaction and Reform 1900–1917* (Wheeling, Ill.: Harlan Davidson, 2005), which also includes excellent bibliographic essays.

Chernyshevsky and Narodnaya Volya in his 1902 essay *What Is to Be Done?*[360] In it he argued that left to themselves the working class would, at best, develop only trade union consciousness rather than take part in revolutionary change. Thus, an educated cadre of professional revolutionaries was a necessary catalyst. Both Goldman and Berkman recognized the importance of a radical middle class.[361] Although Berkman began to concentrate primarily on the development of a militant labor elite, the two were mutually supportive. That Goldman saw the possibilities for, and the strength of, the European syndicalist movement (of complete worker rule) was an interesting departure from her own role as part of an intellectual vanguard. She hoped that its influence might spread to the American working class and usher in a more cooperative and militant form of labor organizing than had hitherto existed in the United States.

Tracing the similarities in Russia, Germany, England, and even America, Goldman lauded the bravery of "the so-called respectable classes. . . . Unlike other social theories, Anarchism builds not on classes, but on men and women. . . . Anarchism calls to battle all libertarian elements as against authority. . . . [S]piritual hunger and unrest are often the most lasting incentives."

Thus, she answered de Cleyre's critique of Goldman's preferences for addressing the middle class with the assertion that there was room for both of them, "for every one who earnestly desires to work for the overthrow of authority, physical as well as mental" (see "A Rejoinder," Article in *Mother Earth*, December 1910). This inclusive breadth of vision played a large part in Goldman's ability to reach beyond her anarchist circles.

Roger Baldwin, a Harvard-educated St. Louis social worker, was one of the people who shepherded Goldman through the technicalities of locating just the right "clean hall" at the right price in his town. They gradually built a friendship based on their mutual commitment to free expression that would last for years (see Letter to Roger Baldwin, 7 December 1910).[362] As he looked back on his life, he named Emma Goldman as the inspiration for his founding of the American Civil Liberties Union.[363]

## A BOOK IS BORN

Goldman made a last grand push to refine, edit, and proofread the manuscript for *Anarchism and Other Essays*. A book was in keeping with her desire to educate as well as agitate, to reach beyond the limits of the lecture hall. Anarchism, however marginal,

---

360. For a sense of the influence of Chernyshevsky and Narodnaya Volya on EG and others, see Introduction, vol. 1, *Made for America*, p. 14.

361. See Letter from AB, in vol. 2, *Making Speech Free*, pp. 150–54.

362. Baldwin first heard EG speak in 1908 when he was working in St. Louis. See vol. 2, *Making Speech Free*, pp. 3, 453, and 510.

363. Roger Baldwin, "Recollections of My Life in Civil Liberties," *Civil Liberties Review* 2, no. 2 (1975): 41–45. See also *LA&EG*, p. 9.

was a political philosophy that matched the daring experimental élan that accompanied both the turbulence and creativity of her era.[364]

The book began with a biographical introduction by her friend and comrade Hippolyte Havel; this would be the first time she had authorized anyone to write the story of her life. Differences between the narrative of the same events in Goldman's later autobiography primarily relate to details of her childhood—the age at which she was sent away to live with her grandmother in Königsberg (when she was thirteen in Havel's biographical sketch, and eight in *Living My Life*) and, perhaps more significantly, the identification of those who had been cruel to her during that vulnerable time (her aunts in the first account, and her uncle in her autobiography). Havel's biographical sketch in *Anarchism and other Essays* closed with Voltairine de Cleyre's 1893 homage to Goldman's spirit as "the only one which will emancipate the slave from his slavery the tyrant from his tyranny—the spirit which is willing to dare and suffer."

"Unnerved from the strain," of having endured the labor pains of writer's angst (not evidently the suffering de Cleyre celebrated), Emma sent a telegram to Ben announcing the birth of her book: "Baby arrived three pm has beautiful body hope soul is worth while" to its "wayward but precious father." Ben greeted the newborn with roses in New York and "brought cheer to Mommy Mickey" (see Letter to Ben Reitman, 17–18 December 1910). By anthropomorphizing her book even further, Emma, who had a complex history and relationship to child bearing, publicly claimed motherhood of her new volume, envisioning a transformative role for her offspring.[365]

Among the first to receive her "precious" book was a young organizer of the Industrial Workers of the World, Elizabeth Gurley Flynn. Goldman's inscription honored her as "The first American woman rebel," with the hope that the essays might "help her onward ever onward towards our great ideal" (Book Inscription, 18 December 1910).

### 1911

### DISARMING TERROR

In 1911 Goldman published "The Psychology of Political Violence," the third essay in her book, in pamphlet form. Of all her essays, it was considered among the most sensitive and important, both difficult *and* frightening to some: "If such acts are treated with understanding, one is immediately accused of eulogizing them. If, on the other hand, human sympathy is expressed for the *Attentäter,* one risks being considered a possible accomplice. Yet it is only intelligence and sympathy that can bring us closer to the source

364. Among the many other books and articles citing the spirit of reform, however inconsistent, during what is known as the Progressive era see Kevin Mattson, *Creating a Democratic Public: The Struggle for Urban Participatory Democracy During the Progressive Era* (University Park: Penn State University Press, 1998).

365. For more on the issue of Goldman and motherhood, see Introduction, vol. 2, *Making Speech Free,* pp. 31–33 and Candace Falk, essay, "Mother Liberty," (forthcoming).

of human suffering, and teach us the ultimate way out of it." Goldman attempted to heighten awareness of "the indignity of our social wrongs; one's very being must throb with the despair millions of people are daily made to endure." Rather than cast aside the perpetrator of violence as "a wild beast, a cruel, heartless monster," she urged her readers to adopt the stance of "the social student, of the man that knows that beyond every violent act there is a vital cause." Quoting from others, including Bjørnson, Coppée, Zola, Hamon, and Sanborn,[366] she underscored their sense that "homicidal outrages have, from time immemorial, been the reply of goaded and desperate classes . . . and individuals, to the wrongs of their fellow-men." In recounting instances of terror across the globe, Goldman tipped the scales of blame, claiming that "all were driven by desperate circumstances to this terrible form of revolt." Violent tactics, though not exclusively employed by anarchists, were nevertheless closely associated with their movement, and were often seen as an easy cover for those in power to shift the blame away from their own abuses.

To Goldman, however, the people who resorted to violence were brave soldiers in a social war for the new against the old.[367] Insisting that "resistance to tyranny is man's highest ideal," she also wrote that "so long as tyranny exists, in whatever form, man's deepest aspiration must resist it as inevitably as man must breathe." She further surmised that "[c]ompared to wholesale violence of capital and government, political acts of violence are but a drop in the ocean." In the end, she asserted that it was not a social theory that prompted violence so much as it was the visceral witnessing of "slain women and infants" that overrode "any spoken word, ever so eloquent [that] could burn into a human soul with such white heat as the life blood trickling drop by drop from those dying forms." Some, however, like her comrade Alexander Berkman, "actively responded to the outrage at Homestead . . . because it was the only force that made the discord between his spiritual longing and the world without at all bearable." "Anarchism, or any other social theory, making man a conscious social unit, will act as a leaven for rebellion." Goldman offered examples of testimony before the courts in the United States as well as from England, France, Italy, Germany, Africa, India, and Spain, where outrageous events precipitated acts of violence in retribution. She ended her essay with homage to the memory of martyrs of the cause: "Untuned ears hear nothing but discord. But those who feel the agonized cry understand its harmony; they hear in it the fulfillment of the most compelling moment of human nature" (see "Psychology of Political Violence," Essay published by Mother Earth Publishing Association, 1911). Thus, with great respect for the perpetrator, Goldman defused the issue of violence and of the murder that had

366. For more on Bjørnson, Coppée, Zola, Hamon, and Sanborn see notes, "Psychology of Political Violence," Essay published by Mother Earth Publishing Association, 1911, in this volume.
367. She herself had been falsely accused of instigating the act of the man who, in 1901, shot President McKinley. The assassin called himself an anarchist, although some in the anarchist movement questioned the authenticity of his claim. Goldman believed he had suffered the consequences of a social consciousness that had become "too sensitive."

been committed by shifting to a psychological and political exploration of what might propel someone to commit such an act.

## DEFINING ANARCHISM

Goldman's book was also an opportunity for her to create her own template from the wealth of writings in anarchist theory. The book delivered the message of anarchism as an overarching theory of freedom and community. She was pleased to stimulate discussion among her comrades and newcomers to anarchism and anarchist ideas.

Although Goldman believed it would take volumes to provide a thorough study of anarchism, she carefully outlined what she believed were its main ideas. She linked resistance to anarchism to the age-old struggle of the new against the old:

> Anarchism could not hope to escape the fate of all other ideas of innovation. Indeed, as the most revolutionary and uncompromising innovator, Anarchism must needs meet with the combined ignorance and venom of the world it aims to reconstruct. . . .
>
> Anarchism urges man to think, to investigate, to analyze every proposition; but that the brain capacity of the average reader be taxed too much, I also shall begin with a definition, and then elaborate on the latter.
>
> Anarchism:—The philosophy of a new social order based on liberty unrestricted by man-made law; the theory that all forms of government rest on violence, and are therefore wrong and harmful, as well as unnecessary. The new social order rests, of course, on the materialistic basis of life; but while all Anarchists agree that the main evil today is an economic one, they maintain that the solution of that evil can be brought about only through the consideration of every phase of life,—individual, as well as the collective; the internal, as well as the external phases. . . .
>
> Freedom, expansion, opportunity, and, above all, peace and repose, alone can teach us the real dominant factors of human nature and all its wonderful possibilities.
>
> Anarchism, then, really stands for the liberation of the human mind from the dominion of religion; the liberation of the human body from the dominion of property; liberation from the shackles and restraint of government. Anarchism stands for a social order based on the free grouping of individuals for the purpose of producing real social wealth; an order that will guarantee to every human being free access to the earth and full enjoyment of the necessities of life, according to individual desires, tastes, and inclinations. . . .
>
> . . . It is the philosophy of the sovereignty of the individual. It is the theory of social harmony. It is the great, surging, living truth that is reconstructing the world, and that will usher in the Dawn. (See "Anarchism: What It Really Stands For," Essay published by Mother Earth Publishing Association, 1911.)

C. L. James, anarchist historian, predicted that Goldman's book would appeal to "the most intelligent of our comrades and some bourgeois of inquiring mind." He commented on her essay on white slave traffic, adding to and extending her critique by suggesting that prostitution was the root of sex slavery, which was the stem upon which all forms of marriage—"polyandrous, polygamous, and monogamous"—grew (see Letter from C. L. James, January 1911). Her commentary about the underlying power relationships in the realm of sexuality and marriage attracted crowds to her lectures and upon publication drew a broad readership, thereby extending the impact of her ideas.

Ben Reitman took charge of the distribution of her book and was largely responsible for its relative success. Because no mainstream company took an interest in publishing the book, Goldman's Mother Earth Publishing Association decided to take responsibility for its printing and distribution. Ben sold copies at lectures, sent them to sympathetic bookstores, and advertised price "specials" in *Mother Earth*. His letters to Emma included lists of books and pamphlets to bring on their road trips. They sold and distributed material with their own imprint, including Ferrer's *Modern School*, Kropotkin's *Modern Science and Anarchism*, and Owen's *Anarchy Versus Socialism*. They also distributed Kropotkin's *The Great French Revolution*, Wilde's *Ballad of Reading Gaol*, Harris's *The Bomb*, Lucy Parsons's collection *The Famous Speeches of the Haymarket Martyrs*, James's *History of the French Revolution*, and plays by Brieux and Shaw.

Their interest in preserving anarchist history had become essential to a movement constantly on the run. Anarchist history was nearly obliterated by repressive laws and dismissive commentators and historians. Reitman constantly reminded Goldman, "Be sure and put away one of all the pamphlet the M.E. publishes" (see Letter from Ben Reitman, ca. 1 January to 4 April 1911); and "Also please . . . make up a new scrap book of all the reviews get every line good or bad . . . so when we publish your autobiography or any new book we will have these reviews to show the publishers" (see Letter from Ben Reitman, 2 January 1911). He kept meticulous records of each book sold or given away, including lists of free copies given to their mailman, the elevator man, the stenographer, and to family members. Outreach included gifts to public libraries and consignment arrangements with bookstores. Ben reminded both Emma and Sasha to include a brief definition of anarchism in all their literature. Emma believed that all anarchists are socialists, but not all socialists are anarchists,[368] a distinction most people found confusing. Ben tried to convince Emma to transcribe her debates on the differences between the two theories, but her lecture "Socialism, Caught in the Political Trap" was never published.

Meanwhile, in spite of all his work, he was barraged by Emma's bitter complaints about his neglect of her; Ben defended himself against her perennial dissatisfaction and affirmed the binding force of their love.

> You are such a powerful creature it is difficult to be a simple lover to you. Your passion is so strong so glorious that fate provide that I never can have enough. Oh love I come to you full of hope and life. Full of burning desire for the big lovely mountains . . . for the sweet tasting treasure box. I come to you full of love for you. I come as your admirer your lover your manager. . . . Willie is starved and waiting.[369] Mommy I love you Hobo. (See Letter from Ben Reitman, 2 January 1911.)

---

368. Emma Goldman, "Anarchism and Socialism," *Herald of Revolt* 1, no. 5 (April 1911).
369. "W" or "Willie" refers to Ben's penis.

Reitman did not share Goldman's ambition, nor did he seek her power and public influence. He brought in the audiences, but it was she who would rally many key figures around the movement to support their anarchist cause, sometimes even imploring them to sell tickets to her lectures (see Letter to Floyd Dell, 23 January 1911; Letter to Roger Baldwin, 24 January 1911). And it was often she was the one who curried the favor of reviewers.

## HUTCHINS HAPGOOD: SOUL MATE IN BOHEMIA

Hutchins Hapgood's flattering review of her book reinvigorated their ties, their shared "World Wide reputation for getting sweethearts." Still, she lamented that it was "harder to live down one's reputation than it was to live up to it" (see Letter to Hutchins Hapgood, 31 January 1911). As soul mates in bohemia they influenced each other's ideas. Hutch had a distinctive, almost journalistic writing style, a mix of fact and fiction that lent itself to dramatic renderings of the anarchist milieu; the style was especially evident in his books *Spirit of Labor* (1907) and *An Anarchist Woman* (1909).[370] They exchanged confidences, not only about their mutual attraction to each other *and* to Ben (as well as her attraction to Hutch's brother Tom) but also about the difficulties of holding to a vision of love and politics that did not diminish each one's freedom or sense of self.

Hapgood was embroiled in a turbulent open marriage with his wife, the author Neith Boyce, who was constantly on the verge of ending the relationship.[371] Emma was equally conflicted, not only about Ben's promiscuity but about her ability to endure the harsh realities of a political life. Often she felt that she could not go on and confided to Hutch: "I have grown so damnably sensitive to all kinds of impressions, as if my soul were covered with tissue paper. Fate, or the devil must have entered into some conspiracy when I was thrust into the public arena. I realize more and more how deficient I am for that. And yet I am not much fit for a private life." Imagining a life of "love and flowers" in contrast to "standing in ugly dirty Hall[s] facing dull people, with your soul inside out for everyone to stick a dirty thumb into it," she fantasized about "scattering everything to the winds and just drink[ing] from the cup of life." Each revealed the depth of depression and self-hatred that shadowed their glorious vision. In her "wretched moods," she wrote that "I too do not like myself, still less do I like life, or that which we call life," and "It's only fortunate my friends do not know me, or I would be lonelier than I am now" (see Letter to Hutchins Hapgood, 23 February 1911). To her friend Nunia Seldes, one of Goldman's few women confidantes, she described the mad pace, the compulsion to forge on, to face the difficulties, and crowd out the constant restlessness in her soul:

> We have been racing from place to place always busy, always in anxiety. . . . [S]omehow we do
> not get ahead. The reasons? . . . absolute silence on the part of the press in most Cities, . . . poor

370. N.B. Hapgood's book *An Anarchist Woman* was despised by Voltairine de Cleyre.
371. See Neith Boyce, *The Modern World of Neith Boyce: Autobiography and Diaries*, ed. Carol De Boer-Langworthy (Albuquerque: University of New Mexico Press, 2003).

Halls bad weather and considerable opposition on the part of my dear comrades. . . . And yet you see, I go on, I can not help otherwise. Everything in me rebels against the idea of submitting to things. Indeed the greater the obstacles the more I am driven on, driven by some uncontrollable force within me which will not let me rest. (See Letter to Nunia Seldes, 23 February 1911).

At the age of forty-two she surmised that perhaps her increasing "unfortunate sensitiveness" could be attributed to getting old, relatively certain that she "never knew the agony of soul in former years."

## DESPAIR IN JAPAN

On 18 January 1911, only three weeks after it began, the Kōtoku case came to a fatal resolution. Goldman was bereft. Of the twenty-four sentenced to death, twelve had their sentences commuted to life, while the remaining twelve, including Kōtoku and Kanno Suga, were hung. Their executions sent ripples of despair and anger around the world, especially among anarchists and radicals. Goldman had thrown herself into the campaign to prove the innocence of the twelve accused of plotting to kill the Japanese emperor. *Mother Earth* had published their pleas and reported on the progress of the defense and international support. Goldman was especially stricken at the thought of Kōtoku's companion, Kanno, facing the gallows, and accentuated her vulnerability in a stereotypical portrayal of the delicate Asian woman: "Somehow our Russian heroines seem of sturdier stuff, therefore their death never effected me so terribly. But this delicate flower tender and yielding as Japanese women are, what glorious courage, what simple faith to die, as she has died" (see Letter to Nunia Seldes, 23 February 1911). For Goldman, Kanno's death became part of the legacy of women martyrs—a fate she imagined that she, too, might face some day. Her sense of foreboding was heightened by the deaths of many anarchist comrades abroad and the shadow cast by the hanging of the Haymarket anarchists in America.

After the news of the executions, a bright spot in the winter 1911 tour was Goldman's visit with William Buwalda in Grand Rapids, Michigan. She had seen him only infrequently since the dramatic day in San Francisco in 1908 when, in military uniform, he rose to shake her hand after her lecture on patriotism.[372] The military's disproportionate punishment prompted him to turn in his war medals to protest doubts that his patriotism could be questioned for merely opening his mind to the opinion of others. Goldman looked back, three years later, and boasted, "I am prouder of having made Buwalda think, than of anything I have accomplished through my public work" (see Letter to Nunia Seldes, 23 February 1911).

## SOMETHING TO CELEBRATE

*Mother Earth* was also a source of satisfaction and a vehicle for encouraging critical inquiry. Goldman and fellow editor Alexander Berkman evaluated the journal on its

372. See vol. 2, *Making Speech Free*, p. 513.

sixth birthday, musing about whether "the magazine justified the expectations that gave it life." Its financial base was precarious and its readership small; it never represented the full spectrum of anarchist ideas, "nor does the magazine satisfy even some of our own comrades." They nonetheless prided themselves in having created "a leaven of thought," "a medium for the free expression of our ideas . . . that . . . neither friend nor foe has been able to gag." *Mother Earth* succeeded in becoming "a gathering point," and a vehicle for "an American Anarchist propaganda literature," including book publishing and distribution. The journal (and anarchism as it was practiced) was far from perfect; Goldman and Berkman prompted their readers (and perhaps themselves) to find satisfaction in the process: "[I]t is the striving for, rather than the attainment of, perfection which is the essence of all effort, of life itself. The struggle is ever before us" (see "Our Sixth Birthday," Editorial in *Mother Earth*, March 1911).

## THE ANARCHIST SPECTRUM

The magazine published letters that aired differences among its readers. In the wake of the movement's efforts during the Kōtoku trial, the April 1911 issue published an exchange between Goldman and Bolton Hall. Hall was a prominent single-taxer and financial contributor to *Mother Earth* who identified himself as a "philosophical anarchist," a term that some anarchists considered an impossible contradiction. Hall was convinced that the most pressing task in the Kōtoku case was "to save those persons who under pretext of conspiracy are being punished for the expression of their opinions." Thus, he feared that any association with the word "anarchist" so often erroneously conflated with "terrorist," "is practically to stab them in the back . . . [and] would only prejudice the Japanese officials against the prisoners." In retrospect he regretted having lent his name to a protest meeting in which the call to action identified the accused as "anarchists and socialists," labels he believed harmed rather than helped them as they stood trial. Instead, he preferred to identify the twelve Japanese as anti-imperialists or at most "philosophical anarchists," and early on cautioned Emma and the *Mother Earth* circle not to prejudice the case.

Goldman disagreed, and although the magazine had been the beneficiary of Hall's friendship and material generosity, she did not hesitate to correct him. First, she clarified that the protest meeting was organized collaboratively and "represented all shades of radicalism," and then chastised him for his inappropriate use of the term "philosophical" to distinguish among anarchists. To her the difference in their ranks was more precisely based on "economic arrangements under Anarchism," and thus she accepted the descriptive terms "individualist-anarchist"[373] and "anarcho-communist" and sharply rejected the distinction between "philosophics and terrorists." She clarified her posi-

---

373. By far the most thorough and perceptive account of anarchist individualism in the American tradition remains James J. Martin, *Men Against the State* (DeKalb, Ill: Adrian Allen Associates, 1953).

tion in the pages of the magazine, asserting that anarchism was never a political discourse that preached violence, only the right "to resist oppression," and that "the term 'anarchist' is quite broad enough to cover whatever concept we have of a society based on individual freedom and economic opportunity." Goldman believed that the use of the word "philosophical" would create what she considered to be a false polarization.

As to Bolton Hall's accusation (which in this case may have been correct) that linking the term "anarchist" to those charged with conspiracy in Japan weakened their case for international support, Goldman made sure to convey that Kōtoku was known as a "Kropotkinist" for translating Kropotkin's works, an action that in fact provoked bitter attacks by Marxian socialists.[374]

Hall was upset by the intensity of their misunderstanding, insisting that his disagreement pertained to methods, not to the principles, about which he believed they were in complete accord. In the spirit of creating a popular front, he intentionally used the term "philosophical anarchist" to better describe and attract the public to what he considered his primary work as a single-taxer.[375]

### MEXICAN REVOLUTIONARIES: ENRIQUE AND RICARDO FLORES MAGÓN

Similar debates about whether the use of anarchist terminology would help or harm comrades in need of international support were echoed in *Regeneración,* the Mexican journal of the Partido Liberal Mexicano (PLM),[376] which avoided describing itself as anarchist, even though the anarchist W. C. Owen edited its English-language pages. The magazine included debates on an array of topics as an expression of the editors' desire to "wage a campaign of education." In 1911, for example, they published letters from Ricardo Flores Magón, exiled leader of the junta of the PLM. The PLM hoped to gather support from recognized leaders of radical thought in the United States, including labor leader Samuel Gompers, socialist Eugene Debs, and anarchist Emma Goldman. Debs, in *Appeal to Reason* (19 August 1911), challenged the PLM to openly identify itself as an anarchist organization. In 1912, frustrated on many levels, the Socialist Party of America supported Madero instead of Enrique and Ricardo Flores Magón. Goldman, moved by the vision represented by the Magóns, raised awareness and money for the Mexican comrades. Her support differed from that of Gompers, who expressed his public sympathy with the PLM but did not include financial support.

To Goldman the Mexican cause transcended "the special cause of Socialists, Anarchists, Single Taxers, Trades Unionists, or other individual wings of the great army of discontent." She considered the situation in Mexico "the most brutal instance on record of absolutely heartless expropriation by that money power which worships the dol-

---

374. See EG to Bolton Hall, 11 February 1911, *Mother Earth,* April 1911, *EGP,* reel 5.
375. See Bolton Hall to EG, 13 February 1911, *Mother Earth,* April 1911, *EGP,* reel 5. For more on single tax see vol. 1, pp. 574–75.
376. See Directory of Organizations for more about the PLM.

lar alone, and is deaf, dumb and blind to the claims of human life. No question of 'isms'
is involved. This is a plain call to universal duty." In that spirit, she signed her letter
"Yours for human liberty and a life worth living" and proceeded to reproduce copies of
her exchange with Magón in pamphlet format and distribute them to all attendees of her
1911 tour of the western United States (see Exchange of Letters Between Ricardo Flores
Magón and EG in *Regeneración*, 22 April 1911). She did her best to educate audiences—
many of whom knew nothing other than mainstream newspaper fear-mongering and
were unaware of the urgency of the situation—and even predicted a revolution similar
to that going on in Mexico in the United States. A true believer in the powers of persuasion, Goldman lamented to the readers of *Mother Earth* how inadequate she felt to the
sublime task of supporting "the greatest uprising of our time." She harkened back to
those whose writing helped inspire the French Revolution: "I wish I had the eloquence
of a Camille Desmoulin, or the pen of a Marat, that I could convey the spirit and the
devotion which animates the heroic efforts of the Mexican rebels. I am sure no one could
then fail to realize that, whatever the beginning of the Revolution or its end, it has gone
beyond all political consideration, straight to the goal of economic emancipation,—Land
and Liberty!"[377]

Goldman was responding to the urgency of Magón's plea on behalf of the displaced
and chattelled Mexican farmers, those who were quickly losing land as President Díaz's
land laws facilitated the transfer of their land to foreign owners. Official land transfers
to copper companies in the United States rattled reformers and created sympathy for
the Mexican Revolution—thereby backing Madero's bold challenge to Díaz's reelection.
Many socialists believed that Madero had the ability to create an updated capitalist industrial economy in Mexico that that could catalyze a transition to socialism. Anarchists
who sided with Magón, on the other hand, were energized at the possibility of a land-
based anarchist revolution just across the border. Most anarchists, however, were indifferent and assumed, as Goldman lamented, that Latin American power politics was a
ruse "merely to displace one Dictator for another."

But the U.S. government knew otherwise. Alarmed by the threats to U.S. propertied
interests in Mexico, it stationed troops on the U.S.-Mexican border to prevent the flow
of arms to Mexican rebels. In the heat of battle rebel leaders often escaped across the
border, hoping to strategize in relative safety. But the Magóns, arrested with two others
in June 1911, were charged with "hiring persons in the United States to enter service of
a foreign people as soldiers."

They were found guilty in June 1912 and sentenced to one year and eleven months in
the McNeil Island federal penitentiary in Washington State. In January 1914, with four
months off for good behavior, the Magóns were released, but in February they were

377. Emma Goldman, "On the Trail," *Mother Earth* June 1911.

charged, along with W. C. Owen, with violating Section 211 of the U.S. Criminal Code of 1910, for printing information in *Regeneración* considered "vile and filthy substance in language." Owen escaped arrest. The Magóns were eventually found guilty, and Enrique was sentenced to nine years, Ricardo to three years and three months (because of his ill health) for violating U.S. neutrality laws. The case was appealed, and Goldman raised their bail while visiting Los Angeles.

From their U.S. prison cells, earlier on, the Magóns continued their resistance through communiqués with constituents and appeals for help (see Exchange of Letters Between Ricardo Flores Magón and EG in *Regeneración*, 22 April 1911).

Despite local exceptions, as an organization the IWW had taken part in the PLM invasion of Baja California in 1911, offering men, money, and weapons. The shared hope was that Baja would serve as a model of a revolution that would go beyond the land redistribution that Madero had planned and would have the power to spread across Mexico. Initially the invading forces, almost half of them non-Mexicans and including an IWW group that took part in the capture of Tijuana, had some success. But when Díaz resigned in May, Madero became president. The campaign of the PLM fell into disarray, weakened by in-fighting among factions of the IWW, the PLM, and anarchists.

Newspapers including the *Los Angeles Times* reported on the IWW and the PLM as though they were composed of only adventurers and bandits. Most U.S. socialist periodicals supported Madero after his victory rather than the PLM. The revolutionaries' invasion of Baja California collapsed in June 1911, an action witnessed by, among others, several Galleanistas from the East Coast and, perhaps, Joe Hill.[378] The *New York Call* criticized Magón's failure to lead the invasion force (a criticism echoed by the French anarchist newspaper *Les Temps Nouveaux*). Furthermore, financial irregularities discredited the PLM. By 1912 Mother Jones was also speaking out against the PLM, and even Eugene Debs began to refer to them as bandits. Goldman, however, did not falter in her support for the Magón brothers. As they languished in jail, her loyalty, as well as her successful fund-raising on their behalf, was especially appreciated.

## GUILTY OR INNOCENT: STEADFAST SUPPORT FOR THE MCNAMARA BROTHERS

Goldman also remained steadfast in her support of the McNamara brothers, the men accused of the October 1910 bombing of the building of the anti-union *Los Angeles Times*. Initially, their case attracted significant popular support. They were portrayed as victims of a government frame-up, and labor groups, especially their own AFL, came to their aid, more or less unconditionally. General sympathy fell away in 1911 when the brothers confessed to the crime in which—however unintentionally—twenty-one innocent

---

378. Lowell Blaisdell, *The Desert Revolution: Baja California, 1911* (Madison: University of Wisconsin Press, 1962).

people were killed and one hundred injured. Goldman, among the first to come to their defense, reframed the discussion by focusing on the intent rather than the act itself. Raising funds for their legal defense was not an easy task, but as always she would not abandon those who took direct action. Asserting that "America is the worst country in the world for the laboring class," she said that the men were driven to action by the steel trust, who sought to destroy their union. "I do not believe the McNamaras wanted to take the lives of people . . . but their crime, if it was such, was no worse than what the Steel Trust and the Erectors' Association is doing every day. The laboring men with whom the McNamara's were associated were being denied the right to live and naturally they rebelled."[379]

## HER MASCULINE AFFABILITY

Predictably, a woman with affinity for militancy was the subject of prurient curiosity. In one particularly biting sexist evaluation of Goldman that appeared in the *Fresno Morning Republican*, her face was described as "masculine rather than coarse, of the stern type of the battler against heavy odds." Awed by her personal and political range, the male reporter found himself both taken with her "affability" and confused by her ability to "excuse a man for blowing up his fellow workers, while destroying a bitter opponent's property." Playing both sides, she shifted the focus of her talks to a very different controversy—that marriage and love were incompatible (see "Emma Goldman Comes to Preach Anarchism to the I.W.W.'s," *Fresno Morning Republican*, 14 May 1911).

## STIRRING INTEREST IN ANARCHISM

Provocation was essential to Goldman's ability to engage her audiences. As she trekked through the West, she updated anarchist writer Peter Kropotkin in London about the general state of anarchism in the United States. Although they agreed that the "'starting point,' the people, is correct," she worried that "it is the most difficult thing on earth to get them." Without any form of organization, most people seemed apathetic and uninterested in ideas; but with organization, she complained "they become like automatons, moving at the dictates of their leaders." She wrote to Kropotkin about the growth of working-class support for the McNamara brothers: "[T]he first time in my public career" that such an awakening aroused "a spark of interest in our ideas." It was a rarity because, in her opinion, "opposition to anarchism, in this country, at any rate, is much stronger among the working-people than it is in the ranks of the intellectuals."

Kropotkin's response included a general wariness of intellectuals as unreliable crusaders for their cause. Goldman defended her interest in the potential of the intellectual class. Her enthusiasm for the workers in the garment industry and the mines waned, and she resigned herself to the belief that anarchism had "failed to strike root

379. "Emma Goldman Sees Only Gloom," *St. Louis Republican,* 28 February 1911.

in the ranks of the workers, except in an indirect way." Kropotkin and Goldman discussed their differences on the subject. In the United States, receptivity to anarchism differed greatly from that of eastern and western Europe, where syndicalism and anarchist workers' associations were on the rise: labor had established strongholds, and syndicalism in particular had gained popularity. She valued these interchanges as an opportunity to reflect on how well the movement was going—and to share new work. She thanked Kropotkin for his praise of her recent book, *Anarchism and Other Essays*, and her magazine, *Mother Earth*, but distinguished her activism from his writing: "One who stands in the fight has little time for theorizing" (see Letter to Peter Kropotkin, 29 May 1911).

## THE PEN AND THE SWORD

Goldman was nonetheless ambivalent about her relationship to the theory versus action debate. In her letters to Charmian London, the wife of Jack London, Goldman begrudged those who fought "in safety" while she was "fighting under fire." Charmian recoiled from what she experienced as Emma's judgmental condescension. Once Goldman realized that she had offended the London family, she backtracked and solicitously recast but did not withdraw her original statement. "To tell the truth I am inclined to think that the writer does more effective work than the speaker. I have infinite faith in the written word, but that does not do away with the fact that whereas, one in Jack's position can get some recreation, can enjoy the country's beauty or arrange his life in harmony with himself, one in my position cannot" (see Letter to Charmian London, 23 June 1911).

Although Goldman was in fact always on call and responsive to the exigencies of the day, she nonetheless did manage to pull away from her busy life to spend time in the country long enough to revise, edit, and publish her lectures. Although she might have wished for more acclaim for her literary and philosophical efforts, she was appropriately modest in her exchange on the subject with Kropotkin. As a political propagandist, she said that her intention was to write that which "would be simple and apply to the American economic struggle. Never for one moment did I make myself believe that it is going to fill the place in the theoretical discourses of our ideas" (see Letter to Peter Kropotkin, 29 May 1911). Instead, she strove to weave new ideas together—by bridging social class and ethnic divides—to create thought-provoking syntheses and concepts of her own.

## J'ACCUSE: SUSPECTED OF POLICE COMPLICITY

The spotlight inevitably cast its shadows. Goldman's critics came from inside and outside anarchist circles and quite often from the ranks of the socialists. The editors of *Justice*, the London publication of the Social Democratic Party, asked, "how it is that this female firebrand should carry on her propaganda of violence with such impunity." They questioned Goldman's integrity, based on a rumor that she was employed by the police like "nine cases out of ten of those 'prominent' Anarchists who only kill with their mouths, who are never on hand when an outrage occurs and who manage to escape so mysteriously when their associates are arrested."[380] On the surface she appeared to take the accusation of being a police spy in stride; she viewed it as a battle scar akin to what the great anarchist Bakunin had suffered from Marx.[381] This was not the first time she had been suspected of wrongdoing.[382] Still, she hoped for a groundswell of opposition to the accusation; she solicited rebuttals from renowned socialist figures like Jack London (see Letter to Charmian London, 23 June 1911). Whether her close escapes could be attributed to state and city criminal codes that were subject to prosecutorial discretion, to varying perceptions of the link between incitement and practice, or to her own caution and gender advantage, she believed that her willingness to take risks had proven her steadfast loyalty. Backbiting between the socialists and the anarchists weakened the possibility of solidarity. A movement that incorporated violence relied on the loyalty of its participants to avert imprisonment or even death. With such high stakes, anarchists were often vulnerable to paranoia, from inside and outside the ranks. Anarchists were often targeted for entrapment by agents provocateurs, an increasingly active component of surveillance tactics of the period.[383] Thus, it was not surprising that in the process of airing disparate opinions under the rubric of noncensorship in many journals of the political left, including the socialist *Justice*, an opportunity arose to express disdain—for police and government abuses and for vituperative critiques of various strains of anarchism and socialism[384]—and even to incite vendettas against select comrades.

## FROM THE PARIS COMMUNE TO THE MEXICAN UPRISING

Ever resilient, Goldman redirected her focus away from responding to personal attacks on her integrity to address the recent developments in the Mexican Revolution. She sent

380. *Justice*, 13 May 1911, p. 7; see also Letter to Peter Kropotkin, 29 May 1911, note 7. Many anarchists escaped, though many others did not.

381. In July 1848 the newspaper *Neue Rheinische Zeitung*, edited by Marx and Engels, printed an article suggesting that Bakunin was a police spy. This claim would occur regularly in the Marxist press over the next thirty years. See Mark Leier, *Bakunin: The Creative Passion* (New York: Thomas Dunne Books, 2006).

382. See Introduction, vol. 1, *Made for America*, p. 40; regarding the misappropriation of legal funds collected during Berkman's imprisonment, see "The Berkman Fund Again," *Firebrand* 5 (August 1896).

383. The spy accusation against EG in *Justice* was reported in *Der Anarchist*, 15 August 1911, and submitted for inclusion in EG's German police file. On police entrapment see Emma Goldman, "The Barnum and Bailey Staging of the 'Anarchist Plot,'" *Mother Earth*, April 1915. On agents provocateurs see the role of spies in the Ferrer Center in Avrich, *The Modern School Movement*; Military Intelligence files included a *New York Sun* article on the Ferrer Modern School's move to New Jersey, 16 February 1916, and another one, E. W. Powell, "Ferrer School in New Jersey," *New York Sun*, 13 February 1916. On surveillance tactics see Candace Falk, "Archival Code-Breaking: The Editor's Dilemma," *Documentary Editing* 27, no. 1 (spring 2005), especially p. 2 regarding double-agent Sullivan.

384. See Emma Goldman, "Socialism, Caught in the Political Trap," *EGP*, reel 55.

Kropotkin background reading and elicited his opinion on what she considered to be "the most genuine uprising of the people since the Paris commune" (see Letter to Peter Kropotkin, 29 May 1911). She also relayed an enthusiastic message about the historic significance of their struggle to the New York Mexican Revolution Conference assembled in Cooper Union: "[T]he Mexican revolution is . . . more sublime than the great uprising in Russia" because those who fought for "emancipation of the Russian masses" were "from the higher station in society," and had "the sympathy and approval of the whole civilized world." In contrast, Goldman saw the isolation of the "outraged humanity in Mexico" who "without much preparation has risen like a mighty giant." Comparing them to anarchist martyrs, she believed its lone rebels were viciously misrepresented as "bandits," not only by conservatives but also by competing socialist activists in both Mexico and the United States. Never fully understanding the history of the Mexican uprising, Goldman overestimated the support of the PLM within Mexico. Nonetheless, she appealed for money and drummed up support for the PLM rebels, most of whom were anarchists who refrained from identifying themselves as such (see "Letter to the International Mexican Meeting," 23 June 1911).

With the help of Reitman, she and the *Mother Earth* group prepared the ground for a large follow-up meeting in Union Square.[385] They canvassed unions for contributions to the Mexican cause, arranged for a series of lectures accompanied by a stereopticon, and even considered taking their message to Chautauqua gatherings.[386] Their sense of urgency was prompted in part by a letter from W. C. Owen of *Regeneración* about the desperation of the Magón brothers and the dire conditions of those who had taken part in the PLM revolt.[387]

### "STRUGGLE IS LIFE"—AND LOVE

A longtime advocate of free love, Goldman found herself torn between fury at her lover's infidelities and her own inability to shed her possessiveness. Reitman's uncontrolled promiscuity, especially in Chicago, infuriated her. Yet she hung on to the passion that her young lover had awakened. "As to my lover, he is still in the embrio. Will he ever be born into radiant maturity? To strive for it is worth the struggle, because struggle is life."

The younger Emma had always been critical of weakness in women, and especially intolerant of the contradiction between Mary Wollstonecraft's articulation of women's freedom and her "humiliating love life with Imlay."[388] She never suspected that later in life her own struggles with Ben would resonate with Wollstonecraft's, as she identi-

---

385. These meetings did not take place as quickly as Goldman had planned. Reitman decided to postpone his trip to New York, also causing an unfortunate delay of his "operation" on Berkman's lover Becky Edelsohn, who was sick and going through the early weeks of an unwanted pregnancy.

386. Chautauqua was an adult education movement, highly popular at that time, with its focus and leanings in the mainstream.

387. See W. C. Owen in Directory of Individuals and in vol. 1, *Made for America*, pp. 548–49.

388. Emma Goldman, "Mary Wollstonecraft, Her Tragic Life and Her Passionate Struggle for Freedom," *EGP*, reel 54.

fied with her as a prominent spokeswoman for women's independence thwarted by her infatuation with a man:

> Mary Wollstonecraft the most daring woman of her time, the freest and boldest exponent of liberty, of free love the slave of her passion for Imlay. How could anyone forgive such weakness?
>
> Thus I reasoned many years ago. Today? EG the Wollstonecraft of the 20th Century even like her great sister, is weak and dependent, clinging to the man, no matter how worthless and faithless he is. What an irony of fate. (See Letter to Ben L. Reitman, 26 July 1911.)

Goldman, who had always prided herself on her consistency and courage, suddenly felt adrift.

> I am indeed strange lover dear. . . . I do not even recognize myself. 38½ years I walked through life serenely sure of myself in all conditions and circumstances. I dared Lucifer himself never knew weakness, never failed to live up to what seemed right to me.
>
> Then, a great element of nature came along, a Cyclone that swept across the plane of my existence tearing me root and all from my usual sure position. It twisted my soul and turned my brain until all was gone. Only one thing remained, the elemental force, it is in my very blood now, the master power of my thought and actions. It is my love for you my Hobo and nothing else counts.

Obsessed, she wished to "cling . . . until we are glewed into one."

The painful contrast between her transcendent message about love and her humiliating experience of it was something she worked hard to hide from the public. In a letter to Ben, she once again bemoaned her fate and mused: "If ever our correspondence should be published, the World would stand aghast. That I, EG, the 'strong revolutionist, the dare devil, the one who has defied laws and convention,' should have been as helpless as a shipwrecked crew on the foaming ocean. It is indeed the irony of fate" (Letter to Ben L. Reitman, 29 July 1911).

### "BOORISH" BEHAVIOR

Some of her dearest friends—even those who had facilitated her talks, shielded her from police, published her works, and supported her magazine—felt alienated from and neglected by Goldman. Among them was Joseph Labadie, a Detroit comrade who was insulted by Goldman's "boorish, discourteous, and unjust" assumption that he harbored enmity against her. Quick to correct the record, he also resented the derogatory characterization of the Detroit comrades she printed in *Mother Earth*,[389] especially against "those who have gone gray in the movement . . . have stood faithfully by their guns, even long before you knew there was a social movement." Intolerant of "invective or abuse"

---

389. See Emma Goldman, "Light and Shadows in the Life of an Avant-Guard," *Mother Earth*, February 1910; and Emma Goldman, "On the Trail," *Mother Earth*, March 1911.

of anyone who propagated anarchism, Labadie nonetheless made it clear to Goldman that his criticism of her conduct—her occasional propensity to publicly lash out against those whom she believed had let her down or betrayed her or the movement—did not diminish his recognition of her remarkable unmatched talents (expressed with an air of sarcasm), nor of the shortcomings of their comrades:

> It goes without argument that none of us have the wonderful gifts of oratory, keenness of perception, wide and varied and abstruse knowledge, unbounded courage and limitless moral rectitude of never flinching in the face of fire as has our own peerless Emma. Nature does not make a marvelous man or woman every day, and we are willing to grant these splendid virtues to you, but why you should find it necessary to emphasize the difference between us poor mortals and yourself we cannot for the life of us understand. (See Letter from Joseph A. Labadie, 3 August 1911.)

Goldman also attacked Carl Nold, who had played a supportive role to Berkman before and after Berkman's *Attentat* against Henry Clay Frick, a man they held responsible for the shooting of locked-out workers at the Homestead Steel plant in 1892.[390] A letter Carl Nold sent to Max Metzkow revealed that the tensions between Emma and himself had clearly been building over time. Nold expressed his annoyance with Goldman's accusations about his "mental atrophy," remembering that it was he who had actively intervened with the Detroit police on her behalf, an act he believed was largely responsible for her successful lecture series. Unfortunately, however, an anti-Semitic barb followed his remarks: "I'll be frank with you. Emma's not about propaganda anymore, it's all dollars and cents. The Jew in her, which she'd suppressed for years, is now suddenly, with Reitman's help, coming to the fore again."[391]

Goldman, a woman and a Jew, did challenge the purist Protestant norms for a celebrated figure in the world of radical public engagement. Anarchists who thought her habits excessive and different from theirs were not immune to the anti-Semitic prejudices of the culture at large, despite their genuine intentions to transcend them. Some, like the Italian anarchist Ludovico Caminita, felt personally wounded by the disparity between what appeared to be Goldman's extravagant lifestyle in comparison to his, and in comparison to others' dire poverty. Nor was Goldman able to control her judgmental remarks in *Mother Earth* about comrades who did not rise to her standard of constant political activism—a criticism that fed on her somewhat overblown sense of herself. She expected those in her orbit to follow her example and respond selflessly to her every call, and although many did, others decidedly did not. Jack London, for example, at Goldman's request wrote a protest letter to the editors of *Justice*, when they accused her of being a police spy. Her next request of him, however, was met with a mixed response. She addressed London as "the only revo-

---

390. See vol. 1, *Made for America*, pp. 106–7.
391. Carl Nold to Max Metzkow, 14 February 1911, Joseph Ishill Papers, MH-H; also in EGP Third Party Files.

lutionary American writer" when she asked him a favor: to write the preface to Alexander Berkman's manuscript for what she considered "the first revolutionary literary American book, dealing with the American economic struggle, as viewed through one, who spent 14 years, as a 'political' in an American prison" (see Letter to Jack London, 26 September 1911). London's preface praised the book but was critical of anarchism and disclaimed any association with anarchism. Both Goldman and Berkman promptly rejected it.[392]

### CRIME AND PUNISHMENT: REFLECTIONS ON CZOLGOSZ'S EXECUTION

The October 1911 issue of *Mother Earth* included reflections on, and remembrances of, the tenth anniversary of Leon Czolgosz's execution. Goldman blamed the press and the "so-called radicals" for defiling his name. She considered the assassination of President McKinley to be of noble intent, believing that had radicals come to Czolgosz's defense, "his last moment would not have been agonized by the consciousness of being deserted, betrayed, forsaken by his own brothers, even like Christ." She recounted the story of his brutal treatment by "a fury-drunk mob and the police . . . [and] forced to go through a thousand Golgothas." Then, "in the name of 'a merciful God' and a 'just law' he was done to death."[393] Just before his execution, Czolgosz asserted: "I did it for the good of the people." Goldman's *Mother Earth* tribute to Czolgosz cast his death as "solitary and sublime," as the death of a man who believed that President McKinley was an enemy of the workers (see "October Twenty-Ninth, 1901," Essay in *Mother Earth*, October 1911).

### THE MCNAMARA BROTHERS ON TRIAL

In part, the tribute to Czolgosz was intended to arouse support for the McNamara brothers and impede the government from executing them for their alleged bombing of the building of the anti-union *Los Angeles Times*. They had been kidnapped by the Burns Detective Agency and transported across state lines, and their trial was set for 11 October 1911. In an interview with the *New York Globe and Commercial Advertiser*, Goldman predicted that "should the forces of capitalism which seem determined to execute these two brothers succeed . . . their deaths will be quickly avenged," not only by militant laborers but also by their kinsmen, the Irish. Predicting "a mighty social upheaval" based on observations from her recent tour, she remarked that the tolerance for militant (or violent) tactics against injustice could not be squelched by fear of reprisals: "[T]he temper of the people [is] very different from the days of the Chicago anarchists." Although in her experience the tenor of the times had certainly changed, and the hangings of the

---

392. See Letter to Jack London, 26 September 1911, note 6. For more background on this interchange see also Earle Lobor and Robert Leitz III, "Jack London on Alexander Berkman: An Unpublished Introduction," in *American Literature* 61 (1984), pp. 447–56.

393. She contrasted that sham defense to the dignified legal battle on behalf of Francisco Ferrer in the autocratic Spanish courts by a lawyer who pleaded his case "as if for his own life" in spite of "his antagonism to his client." See "October Twenty-Ninth, 1901," Essay in *Mother Earth*, October 1911.

accused in the Haymarket affair seemed quite distant, violent labor clashes continued to erupt, and lynching remained a terrorizing component of American race politics. The reporter shifted quickly from his hyperbolic labeling of Goldman as "Labor's Seeress," the editor of "one of the most radical monthlies in the world and which has subscribers in practically every country," to the appearance of the "soft-spoken" Goldman. She was described in detail (a common aspect of reportage in a time before photographs appeared daily) that revealed more about the reporter's attitudes about women than the woman herself: "Now passing her forty-second year, of moderate blonde type, with the clear healthy complexion of a girl of fifteen, strong features and wearing glasses, rather short and just a little stout, she looks very much like a school teacher" (see Interview in the *New York Globe and Commercial Advertiser,* 9 October 1911).

## 1912

Goldman was, in fact, a dedicated teacher; her school was the world around her, and her lessons were intended as a basis for social and economic transformation. Words were her most potent public weapon against injustice. Her comrade Alexander Berkman, though far more dedicated to local organizing, was also remarkably articulate and a meticulous editor for *Mother Earth.* Goldman worked closely with him as he wrote about the horrors of prison life, shared in the framing of the book's dedication, and hoped his words would be a beacon "[to] all who struggle against bondage" (see Letter to Alexander Berkman, New York, ca. 1912). He later modified the dedication in the opening pages of *Prison Memoirs of an Anarchist:* "To all those who in and out of prison fight against their bondage."

## COUNTERING REPRESSION

Whether in relation to words or deeds, repression was rampant. The range is best illustrated by the fact that Jay Fox was indicted for advocating nude swimming at Home Colony, Washington, and the McNamara brothers faced possible execution for the bombing of the building of the *Los Angeles Times.* Reitman assessed that it was only a matter of time before "the hounds will spring at our throats," but Goldman reframed his apprehension as proof of their success at forcing the established power structure into a defensive posture. She asserted, somewhat naïvely, that in fact it was a sign that "the people are beginning to realize the significance and wide import of Anarchism."

They remained focused on strengthening *Mother Earth.* Reitman scolded Goldman for not contributing enough written material for the magazine: "If you are willing to struggle to raise money I don't see why you are not willing to write an article every month," lobbying her for "a 'great number' every issue. . . . I hate to see any thing less than your best."[394]

---

394. His letters, though far less articulate than hers, evinced the flavor of their particular mix of work and passion. Each in his or her own way pulled the other closer with memories and promises

A reference to target practice (a skill that may have been integral to their belief in self-defense should that ever become necessary) was inserted into Ben's whimsical note, along with a flirtatious invitation to join him in a romp in the snow together—while he went rabbit hunting—"to get a little target practice that I need. . . . Wish me and Mommy could go to gether and be free for a . . . week and shoot bugs and grass hoppers and do it" (see Letter from Ben Reitman, 14 January 1912).

## AWAKENING THE FEMINIST MIND

Interviewed by a reporter on their spring 1912 tour, Goldman boasted that she had tapped into "the slow but sure awakening of the feminine mind," with lectures "on sex subjects ten years ago . . . thought to be lewd . . . immoral." She noted the contrast; her talks on "broad subjects of economics are very poorly attended." The Denver newspaper headline read: "Sex Problem Talks Fill Hall to Doors, Says Emma Goldman."

The reporter, Alice Rohe, was sympathetic to the new wave of women who expanded their horizons, and she described Goldman as a woman who was both ahead of her time and "recognized by the dispassionate as one of the greatest intellectual forces of the day."[395] Goldman and the reporter agreed that "the greatest upheaval of the present day . . . [was] the woman movement." She called the present condition "the strike of the sex" and believed that "the emancipation of the race is absolutely interwoven with sex enslavement. Economic conditions must be solved, along with the woman question. . . . [I]ndividual emancipation is the forerunner, of course, of a more universal emancipation." Like those who advocated birth control, Goldman believed that sexuality was a natural human pleasure not necessarily tied to nuptial vows and reproduction: "Motherhood should be a desired event in a woman's life. She should not be forced to bear children against her will because she wears a gold band on her left hand." While advocating choice, Goldman glorified motherhood, in a manner that made her ideas more acceptable to a wide audience.

Goldman's separation of sexuality as pleasure from procreation distinguished her from many who fought for birth control primarily for practical reasons. Although she shared Freud's recognition of the centrality of sexuality, she disagreed with his notion that creativity and repressed sexuality went hand in hand and that creativity was rooted in the repression of sexual desire—an idea that coincided with the belief that civilization

---

of intimate moments and challenging projects in service of the cause of anarchism. Ben even proposed extending their reach to include Pavel Orlenev and his Russian theater group, taking them on tour with them, and having Emma translate the troupes' sketches into English.

395. Alice Rohe noted the similarity of ideas but discrepancy in reception between Goldman and Karin Michaelis and Ellen Key, whose avant-garde literary works celebrating free love and exploring the emotional complexities of the modern woman were taken far more seriously in most literary feminist circles. Seemingly unfazed by the long haul toward progress and acceptance, Goldman claimed to be "content to announce the coming of the new dawn."

necessitated the control of such elemental forces, linking sexuality with aggression.[396] In Goldman's opinion sexual expression was a key element in creative work and in the normal healthy and contented maturation of a child.

Alice Rohe enjoyed their interchange, describing it as "[a] quiet, bomb-throwing less, bloodless conversation with Emma Goldman, a woman who has read beyond the belief of the busy worker's ideas, a thinker who has, through her insistence upon telling the truth, expressed her ideas regardless of conventions" (see "Sex Problem Fill Hall to Doors, Says Emma Goldman," Article in *Denver Daily News,* 17 April 1912).

Goldman was quick to point out the hypocrisy of "the woman movement" as well. The *Denver Post* reported her reactions to the sinking of the *Titanic* and the horrific deaths of those left aboard the sinking luxury ship. She criticized those who privileged women as the frailer sex, willing to be rescued as "weaker and dependent"—ladies first.[397] She voiced the same complaint about those who assumed that their class privilege entitled them to lifeboats unavailable to the ship's working crew. In contrast, as always, those who choose voluntary sacrifice in times of peril represented something far different to Goldman. Such acts were the expression of "deep social kinship" and hope for "still greater possibilities for the future, when man shall no longer his brother maim!" (see "Suffrage Dealt Blow by Women of Titanic," Article in *Denver Post*, 21 April 1912).

## THE OUTRAGE OF SAN DIEGO

Goldman knew that she could be in imminent danger, but she and Reitman, who lived by the belief in kinship and cooperation, had no idea that upon their arrival in San Diego, Reitman would be dragged from his hotel room into the desert, stripped naked, branded, tarred and sage-brushed, and forced to kiss the flag and sing "The Star Spangled Banner." Local and national newspapers would pick up the story, although as Goldman pointed out, hundreds of previous mob victims, "half-starved, obscure beings" were ignored; few papers would credit what they had to say (see Letter to Fred G. Bonfils, *Denver Post,* 16 May 1912). Goldman wrote to Charles Erskine Scott Wood, a Portland lawyer and friend, that although she certainly had seen her share of "police and brutality . . . the conditions in San Diego are beyond anything I have ever experienced."

Once again her instinctual response was to turn up the heat: "If only the workers would learn the use of direct action from their enemies, matters might come to a break soon. As it is, the Industrial Workers and other victims have practiced passive resistance while the good Christians and patriotic citizens are exercising direct action." In the end, however, she tempered her sweeping generalizations about the revolutionary potential

---

396. See Sigmund Freud, *Three Essays on Sexuality* (1905); his ideas on sexual repression and social order and control were developed further in *Civilization and Its Discontents* (New York: J. Cape and H. Smith, 1930).

397. This ladies-first stance was used by some women suffragists who claimed their right to vote first as educated women over uneducated African American men.

of educated professionals as compared to the laboring masses and shared her conviction that "professional people . . . need education much more than working people do" (see Letter to C. E. S. Wood, 21 May 1912).

Over time she spread news of the events in San Diego to influential friends, many of whom had worked previously with her in the Free Speech League, and, as always, she reached out to the press. She told them about the man who had gone "in the unrestricted quarter and quoted a passage of the Bible. For that he was most brutally kicked about and finally arrested." Goldman sent E. B. Foote Jr. a draft of her *Mother Earth* article on the subject. She also solicited Theodore Schroeder, who was a key figure in the Free Speech League, to help link issues of free expression to the right to organize to the San Diego free speech fight. Although Schroeder was more than sympathetic and in fact had written "The Story of the Free Speech Fight" in the *New York Call*,[398] it was difficult to arouse the interest of East Coast free speech advocates, an indication of a pervasive disconnect between the two coasts (see Letter to Theodore Schroeder, 29 May 1912).

Through *Mother Earth* Goldman reached a small national readership on the importance of "the outrage of San Diego." She likened the intensity of her time there to the transformative experience of "America's greatest orator," Wendell Phillips, who had witnessed a well-dressed mob dragging the abolitionist William Lloyd Garrison, editor of the anti-slavery paper the *Liberator*, through the streets of Boston in an effort to hang him for the persuasive eloquence of his abolitionist stance. She considered the struggle for free expression in the workplace an extension of earlier emancipation efforts. Goldman was sure that these parallels between the "blood thirsty mob" of anti-abolitionists and anti–trade unionists would alert the public to the relationship of race and class injustice—"chattel slavery" and wage slavery. To the vigilantes "it is to-day as great a crime to work for the emancipation of the white slave as it was to work for the cause of the black slave fifty years ago." In speaking about the violence against the IWW she referred to the horrors of lynching and the similarity between the two forms of vicious mob brutality.

Blow by blow, incident by incident, the story of Goldman's and Reitman's terrifying encounters in San Diego was recounted in *Mother Earth*. With novelistic flair Goldman described their afternoon arrival: "the mob outbreak," "cars full of vigilantes in mad pursuit, screaming, yelling, and cursing the chauffeur [of the bus to their hotel]," "as if the entire city had turned into an insane asylum." By "7:30 P.M . . . [f]ive thousand people, preceded by a hundred autos, with fashionably-dressed women and men as their occupants, with American flags, their riot-whistles creating a deafening noise, surrounded the hotel. Five hundred of these maniacs, led by a good Christian and American patriot . . . reporter on the *San Diego Union*, entered the hotel lobby, unfurled the American flag, compelled everybody to sing the 'Star Spangled Banner' as

398. Schroeder's history of the San Diego free speech fight was serialized in the *New York Call* magazine, 15, 22, 29 March and 5 April 1914.

an inspiration for their heroic work." When Goldman refused police protection, suggesting that the police chief revoke the City ordinance, "the ordinance which has made it a felony to gather in the business districts of the city and for which three hundred IWW men had been beaten, clubbed, arrested, and subjected to every cruelty and indignation imaginable," he refused on grounds that "the mob had outgrown his power." Although Goldman insisted that "if I had to die, I was just as willing to die at the hands of the mob as at the hands of the police," Reitman was the one who almost lost his life to the mob. He was driven to the Escondido desert outside of the city, abused, and left naked and alone. Goldman, in danger, was rushed into a train heading to Los Angeles, while the angry mob hurled vile insults and attempted to bang down the doors of the train until it left the station. Eventually, Reitman dragged himself aboard a train, fortunate to have enough money for his ticket and to have people waiting to take him to a safe place and attend to his wounds. The experience left both Goldman and Reitman physically and psychologically traumatized. For Goldman it evoked the nightmarish days when she had to disguise her identity to avoid vicious mob attacks after her wrongful implication in the assassination of President McKinley. For Reitman the vigilante attack might have stimulated the memory of the beating by the Chicago police he had suffered in the 1908 demonstration of the unemployed. Some of the trauma was alleviated just in the telling. Ben's version of the San Diego story was published, alongside Emma's, in *Mother Earth*.

Goldman also made sure to distinguish the "San Diego outrage" from the other times her rights had been interfered with. She reported that the practice and lack of free speech protection in "American cities . . . [which] . . . depends entirely on the whims and arbitrary will of ignorant police officials," as exemplified by the manner in which San Diego suppressed the right of free speech and assemblage, which "would have put to shame the Spanish Inquisition." She sent out a warning that regardless of whether the IWW was right or wrong, "violence inevitably gives birth to violence. If San Diego is justified in violence, why not its victims?" Her celebrity status encouraged the mainstream press to follow the plight of the hundreds of others who had been caught in the horrors of San Diego. She threatened apathetic citizens with more forceful national retaliation if they refused to exert pressure on the vigilantes (see "The Outrage of San Diego," Article in *Mother Earth*, June 1912).

### DIRECT ACTION

As the news about the incident in San Diego spread across and beyond the country, especially in anarchist publications, the events took on a certain kind of bravado. Goldman wrote to her Austrian comrade, Rudolf Grossman, a veteran of the Paterson, New Jersey, silk workers' strike in 1902.[399] She compared the massive influx of the IWW in sup-

---

399. Grossman had various aliases well before the strike, which began in April 1902. The pen name, Pierre Ramus, was the one that he used most often.

port of free speech in San Diego with the direct action tactics of Lawrence mill workers, who had recently (and successfully) protested wage cuts: with the support of farmers "providing the workers with food supplies during the strikes, or taking care of the strikers' children . . . practical solidarity has for the first time been tried in this country during the Lawrence strike, with inspiring results."[400] Direct action was her tactic of choice, one she shared with the IWW organizers of the textile workers.[401] Divisions still existed, especially because many of the union's members did not strictly adhere to the organization's revised policy to sever formal ties to electoral politics (see Letter to Rudolf Grossman, 4 June 1912).

Her tendency toward sectarianism on labor issues was muted, and in many ways countered by responsibilities to her magazine, which was created, in part, to offer a space for information and support of movements that meshed with her anarchist principles and strategies for change. Thus, while she voiced her support for the IWW free speech fights in San Diego, Goldman also opened the pages of *Mother Earth* to an article about the Butte, Montana, labor struggles by William Z. Foster, who was then associated with the short-lived Syndicalist League of North America. This group (which included the anarchists Jay Fox and Lucy Parsons, and even Tom Mooney, who left the IWW with the intention of radicalizing the AFL from the inside), practiced the French tactic of working within the existing union structure. They identified themselves as a militant minority within the AFL and adhered to the strategy of "boring from within" rather working in separate unions like the IWW. But Goldman herself, who never engaged with the microfactions within the unions, also began to express a comradely loyalty to the IWW, perhaps because it was becoming clear that the government had redirected much of its suspicion and violence away from anarchists toward the Wobblies. This targeting by the government, symbolized later by the murder of Joe Hill, was a travesty of justice to which she added her voice in a chorus of outrage and continued to support both IWW-led strikes and their retaliatory actions.[402]

Interchanges with anarchists like Rudolf Grossman also revealed differences among comrades about what constituted anarchist activities. He published an article in his paper, *Wohlstand für Alle* (Wealth for All; 1907–1914), covering the free speech fights, aware that Goldman had been teaching a course in Denver on modern drama shortly after the San Diego incident. In this article he included a defense of Goldman, asking readers not to begrudge her not "devoting herself entirely to agitation on behalf of

---

400. A mass walkout of the 3,500 mill workers prompted thousands of others, in solidarity, to engage in a sympathy strike. Emma Goldman, "Syndicalism," Essay in *Mother Earth*, February 1913.

401. *Mother Earth*'s definition for "direct action": "Conscious individual or collective effort to protest against, or remedy, social conditions through the systematic assertion of the economic power of the workers." *Mother Earth*, May 1914.

402. For EG's reaction to Hill's death, and the internal pressures he faced before he died, see EG to W. S. Van Valkenburgh, 21 November [1915], *EGP*, reel 9. Goldman also noted that she hadn't had the time to write something about him for *Mother Earth*.

anarchism." As one who believed that she lived and breathed devotion to anarchism, Goldman was irate, convinced that many anarchists had a narrow view of what she considered was in fact all encompassing.[403] Rather than straying from the cause, she believed she was expanding its reach (see Letter to Rudolf Grossman, 23 August 1912).

## "MY AGITATION" WITH WOMEN'S SUBORDINATION

At times, Goldman brazenly took all the credit for the advances of the anarchist movement: "I do not believe that is an exaggeration to say that everything that is known in America about anarchism is due to my agitation." Modern drama was for Goldman a perfect medium for inserting anarchist ideas into the social narrative and applying the values championed on stage to everyday life; she saw drama as a vehicle for her implicit critiques of capitalism and capitalist morality —despite the wariness of some comrades.

In her exchange with Rudolf Grossman (aka Pierre Ramus) she confronted the undercurrent of sexist attitudes of some anarchists that often colored their reactions to her ideas and practice. For example, from his many letters to her over the years Grossman conveyed his stereotypical idealization of her sister anarchist Voltairine de Cleyre as one who, he assumed, loved children. Goldman quickly, and rather coarsely, pointed out that Voltairine "can not stand children and has . . . repudiated her own child. . . ."[404] She was not at all a hypocrite, and she didn't feign maternal love any more than she did any other, and it was in this where her merit lay," an interchange perhaps also hinting at Goldman's complex relationship to the subject of maternity.[405] Accustomed to over-riding gender slights, Goldman countered Grossman's assumptions without skipping a beat as they exchanged ideas about their shared devotion to anarchism (see Letter to Rudolf Grossman, 23 August 1912).

Goldman, who was always cognizant of the subordination of women, nevertheless took it as a duty to critique her sisters' political shortcomings. She was especially forthcoming on these and other issues with the reporter Caroline Nelson,[406] a member of the IWW whose commentary and interview appeared in the *Industrial Worker*. Goldman nipped at the reformist socialist women as "a lot of geese, that confine themselves to cackling about uplifting the workers, and sprawl before upper class or professional women who will condescend to grace their meeting to hand them out a little respectability." Nelson's article, which playfully dubbed Goldman "the most disreputable woman in America," included examples of "'cultured' women who hooted [at Goldman] . . . 'Give up that anarchist, we will strip her naked; we will tear out her guts,'" followed by descrip-

---

403. See Letter to Rudolf Grossman, 23 August 1912, in EGP, reel 6.
404. In 1932 when Goldman again wrote about Voltairine de Cleyre, she included an apology to Voltairine's son, who had alerted her to an erroneous statement she had made in a later essay about his mother's repudiation and which she introduces here.
405. See Introduction, vol. 2, *Making Speech Free*, pp. 30–33.
406. For Caroline Nelson, see Interview in the *Industrial Worker*, 6 June 1912, note 2.

tions of Ben's travails in San Diego—the tearing off of his clothes, branding him with the letters "IWW" on his back with a lighted cigar, and, most horrific, one of the "doctors, lawyers, real estate and business men" putting a cane up Ben's rectum. She attributed spreading of the news of their "torture and humiliation" through the mainstream press to a rising general interest in the IWW and a renewed consciousness of the raging class struggle. It was a time when the IWW was assessing the effectiveness of civil disobedience as a tactic. Nelson used her article about Goldman and San Diego as a call to "revolution"—unlike those of other reporters who feigned a journalistic distance and objectivity—and warned the readers of the IWW paper, in accordance with Goldman's call, that "[p]eace and submission is our greatest enemy at this stage of the game" (see Caroline Nelson, Interview in the *Industrial Worker,* 6 June 1912).

## DRAMA

Politically sympathetic articles in the mainstream press, however, were the exception rather than the rule. Usually Goldman and Reitman had to court newspaper coverage, but in Denver in 1912 the editor of the *Denver Post* lured her with the promise of a three-part series of drama reviews (her first foray into theater criticism), only to counter her impact by minimizing the paper's reporting of her activities in the city.

Emma detailed her visit to Denver in a letter to Ben, writing of her entourage of drama lecture devotees, new friends, and supporters, as well as her mix of envy and revulsion at the crowds that gathered while she was there to hear the educator G. Stanley Hall discuss, as she characterized it, "[s]ex instruction, to preserve Chastity, Morality and Religion. And a lot such other rot, it was awful."[407]

Goldman firmly believed "that there was too much self-control in the world and this was fostered by Christianity."[408] In defiance, and as part of her general flirtation with Ben, she ended her letter with "[t]he T.B. and M. are starved so you had better prepare plenty of W. wine and other things that go with it. I want a real feast, as in the old long ago, when Hobo first met me. . . . I loves you very much, Mommy." Lurking in the same note was an even more suggestive hidden code warning him of the dangers of recklessness: "be cautious with your Monday morning visitor"; any slip would be "impardonable," indicating the likely possibility that clandestine meetings were combined with public lectures like her drama series in Denver and even during Ben's visit home in Chicago (see Letter to Ben Reitman, 13 July 1912).

## LOVE BETWEEN WOMEN WHO LOVE MEN

Ben was Emma's lover and road manager, but he was not the only one to share her erotic affections. Almeda Sperry, a Pennsylvania socialist activist and self-described prostitute,

---

407. For G. S. Hall see Letter to Ben Reitman, 13 July 1912, note 5.
408. "Emma Goldman Sees Only Gloom," *St. Louis Republican,* 2 February 1911.

involved in a turbulent relationship with a socialist man, was among Goldman's amorous admirers. Almeda wrote of her appreciation for "expressions of endearment" from a woman who was "a tower of strength . . . purged from all superstition," as she firmed up her plans to come up to New York City to spend the night (see Letter from Almeda Sperry, 24 August 1912). After their visit, Almeda wrote a poem to her "rock of indifference": "Greedily do I lick / Thy substance / with the shafts / of my light. / I possess you and compel you to / Love me / causing your dissolution."[409] Bisexuality, so forcefully affirmed by polyamorous anarchists of the day, was nonetheless relatively hidden, and although Goldman's inner circle was aware of her intimacies, she chose not to share them with her already wary public. Yet Goldman's cautiously intimate relationships with women throughout her life was overridden by her profound sexual and emotional longings for men—Reitman more than any other. After a particularly close encounter she wrote to Ben, "My great and wonderful lover . . . why can you not disclose the beauty of your soul to me more often?" Still, she was thankful for the "occasional glimpse, . . . so rich and soothing and passionate," and was hungry for his "passionate burning W on the T.B it is ecstatic and maddening."

Equally passionate about her work, she seamlessly shifted the focus of her letter to Ben to an account of writing her lectures, especially on "Anarchism and Vice," rehearsing them with friends "to get the thought thoroughly into my mind." She hoped to receive objective feedback on their content and delivery. As always, she engaged Ben in thinking through the finances of the *Mother Earth* office. The magazine was reaching its sixth year of publication, and he, the fourth year of his role as her manager. Protective of the livelihood of those in the circle around the magazine—Sasha, Max Baginski,[410] Ben's mother, and Ben and Emma themselves—she puzzled about "how we might simplify our lives and reduce expences so we can free our work from commercialism"— which was a seemingly never-ending struggle (see Letter to BR, ca. 25 September 1912).

## BERKMAN'S PRISON MEMOIR

In Ossining, away from the turmoil and immediate worries of the *Mother Earth* office and Reitman's gaze, Goldman faced the next challenge: writing her lectures and being supportive to Berkman as he finished *Prison Memoirs of an Anarchist*. She described to her dear friend Nunia Seldes the process of helping him through the agony of writing about the harrowing experiences of his past as "worse than nursing an incurable sufferer back to life. . . . I am worn out mentally and psychically. But I do not regret, because the value of the book makes up for all."[411]

Berkman's book was truly a pathbreaking exposé of prison life and was labeled a

---

409. Almeda Sperry to EG, ca. 5 September–30 September 1912, in *EGP*, reel 6.
410. See Max Baginski in Directory of Individuals.
411. EG to Nunia Seldes, 24 October [1912], in *EGP*, reel 6, a letter also asking for Nunia's help in organizing a lecture date for Berkman close to the Allegheny State Prison.

masterpiece.[412] It was positively received by their comrades. Few books about the emotional and physical realities of prison life had ever been written by former prisoners with such eloquence.[413] Believing in the importance of the book for posterity, Goldman shifted her allegiances and energies from her work with Reitman to gathering a readership for Berkman's book. After reading it elder anarchist William T. Holmes, who had been close to those involved in the Haymarket affair, remarked that Berkman's book brought back the memory of Haymarket anarchist Albert Parsons, of so many of his old acquaintances, of the risks they took, of the lasting impression they made; he only wished the book "could be placed in the hands of every humane prison official in the country." Addressing Goldman directly, Holmes wrote: "I have grieved over your misfortunes and rejoiced over your successes. After long arduous service such as you have given to the Cause should come peace and rest. That these blessings may fall to your lot is the earnest wish of Your far away Comrade" (see Letter from William T. Holmes, 8 November 1912). With the book's broad appeal, Berkman had broken out of the anarchist ghetto. In recounting the harrowing experience of prison with tenderness and humanity, he had engaged in a political act.

### KROPOTKIN, "TENDEREST FRIEND OF THE OPPRESSED"

Among the books and essays central to many anarchists were those of the writer Peter Kropotkin. The editors of *Mother Earth* took the occasion of his seventieth birthday to devote the issue to "the most uncompromising enemy of all social injustice; the deepest and tenderest friend of oppressed and outraged mankind: old in years, yet aglow with the eternal spirit of youth and the undying faith in the final triumph of liberty and equality." Goldman's tribute lauded Kropotkin for his contribution to theories of mutual aid, his remarkable disavowal of royal "princely" ties in favor of solidarity with the workers and peasants, his instinctive opposition to oppression and tyranny, and his support of and refusal to abandon those who engaged in political acts of violence. As a young man in Russia, Kropotkin had been imprisoned for his association with the militant Chaikovsky Circle (a group that included Berkman's uncle—the driver of Kropotkin's escape carriage); he fled to and settled in England, where he began to develop the concept of anarchist communism and mutual aid. Later his ideas, articulated in books and essays, were widely circulated among anarchists and political theorists. Goldman valued his friendship, and her letters to him often served as a vehicle by which to convey her assessments of the evolution of anarchism in America (see "Peter Kropotkin," Tribute in *Mother Earth*, December 1912).

---

412. *Coming Nation*, January 1913.
413. "Berkman's book is the work of a genius. It has made me realize above all else, the sincerity of a true revolutionary . . . as near to absolute truth as is possible in a universe in which all things are relative." Almeda Sperry to EG, November 1912, *EGP*, reel 6 (previously hidden by EG's office assistant, Anna Baron, whose papers are housed in the Boston University Libraries).

**1913**

INTERNATIONAL SYNDICALISM

When Goldman shared her experiences on the road with the readers of *Mother Earth,* she often compared U.S. and European political trends. She wrote about syndicalism and the strikes in France, Italy, and Spain, emphasizing the prevalence of direct action tactics such as sabotage and general strikes, in contrast to the increasing emphasis in the United States on negotiations between unions and management (sometimes to the extent of announcing the date and time of intended strikes). Although syndicalist practice in the United States was strongly associated with the IWW, the union's socialist majority (from 1905 to 1907) and hierarchical organization prompted Goldman to distance herself from the group. By 1912, with the creation of the Syndicalist League of North America, many anarchists chose to leave the IWW and instead joined the AFL as a small, militant minority.[414] In a sense, the IWW competed for members and influence with the mainstream labor movement, and thus a move to—or even dual membership in—the AFL and IWW seemed practical and promising.

Goldman separated herself from "a sad chaos in the radical movement, a sort of intellectual hash, which has neither taste nor character" and criticized the recent "faddish interest" among American academics in syndicalism. Goldman denounced those who claimed syndicalism's tactical breakthroughs as their own but who had little understanding that such a movement was "born in the actual struggle and experience of the workers themselves—not in universities, colleges, libraries, or in the brain of some scientists. The revolutionary philosophy of labor—that is the true and vital meaning of Syndicalism."

To Goldman, "[t]he fundamental difference between Syndicalism and the old trade union is this: while the old trade unions, without exception, move within the wage system and capitalism, recognizing the latter as inevitable, Syndicalism repudiates and condemns present industrial arrangements as unjust and criminal, and holds out no hope to the worker for lasting results from the system."

As socialists saw the possibility of electing members into official local and federal government positions, they began to denounce their earlier support for confrontational tactics. An amendment was passed at the 1912 convention of the SPA to expel from its membership any party member who opposed political action or advocated sabotage or violence as a weapon of the working class. Thus, Bill Haywood relinquished his position in the SPA; his resignation as well as the expulsion of several hundred IWW members split the labor movement and, at least on paper, separated union gradualists from militants. Goldman believed that the positive impact of the interest in syndicalism was the hope it represented for restructuring society, for "nurturing the seeds of the new within

---

414. For more on the Syndicalist League of North America, see James Barrett, *William Z. Foster and the Tragedy of American Radicalism* (Urbana: University of Illinois Press, 1999).

the shell of the old."[415] For her, nothing short of "the complete overthrow of the wage system," and the establishment of a "free, federated grouping of the workers along lines of economic and social liberty" would constitute "the economic expression of Anarchism." Spontaneity therefore "takes the enemy unawares, hence compels him to a speedy settlement or causes him great loss."

In contrast, she attributed the failures of the labor movement to its "large union treasury . . . as corrupting an element in the ranks of labor as it is in those of capitalism. . . . [Large treasuries] create class distinctions and jealousies within the ranks of labor, so detrimental to the spirit of solidarity." An advocate of direct action, she also supported sabotage—suggesting that workers break packages that say "handle with care"—as a tactical "weapon of defense in the industrial warfare, which is more effective, because it touches capitalism in its most vital spot, the pocket." She equated syndicalism at its best to true mutual aid among workers, "applied education" in preparation for an active role in a free society. Control of production and distribution, she wrote, "can exist only through voluntary association" (see "Syndicalism: Its Theory and Practice," Essay in *Mother Earth,* January–February 1913). Thus, she defined and explained what she considered labor's closest affinity to anarchist practice. In the process she turned away from her usual revolutionary vanguard approach to an incorporation of the syndicalist vision of complete worker control.

### RELIGION: THE GOSPEL OF NONRESISTANCE

Goldman linked her critique of gradualist union organization to the controversial topic of religion. She claimed that because workers strove for justice, they were susceptible to the notion of a "higher" justice, and thus "the subtleness of Christian teachings is more powerful protection against rebellion and discontent than the club or the gun." Without denying "some good in Christianity 'itself,'" she focused on the superstructure of religion rather than on those who adhered to its principles.[416] Thus, she identified "the gospel of Christ" with the "gospel of non-resistance [which] contains nothing dangerous to the regime of authority and wealth; [rather,] it stands for self-denial and self-abnegation, for penance and regret." Goldman rejected the Christian concept of the opposing duality of body and soul: "[T]he body as something evil, the flesh as the tempter to everything that is sinful . . . has mutilated [man's] being in the vain attempt to keep his soul pure, while his body rotted away from the injuries and tortures inflicted upon it." Christianity's self-denial as "its test of human worth, its passport to the entry into heaven," left it "indifferent to the horrors of the earth."

Self-sacrifice, on the other hand, had a special appeal to anarchists, who glorified

---

415. Rudolf Rocker would later discuss this idea in his book *Anarcho-Syndicalism* (London: Secker and Warburg, 1938).
416. Goldman offers a parallel analysis of government.

martyrs and who sometimes took another's life and sacrificed their own. However, she distinguished anarchist martyrs, and even Socrates, who asked nothing in return, from Christ, for whom "the whole human family . . . unto all eternity" was expected to repent for he who "hath died for them." She observed that especially "the poor . . . cling to the promise of the Christian heaven, as the home for old age, the sanitarium for crippled bodies and weak minds. They endure and submit, they suffer and wait, until every bit of self-respect has been knocked out of them."[417]

She questioned the very notion of repentance: "Why repent, why regret, in the face of something that was supposed to bring deliverance? . . . Take the Sermon on the Mount, . . . a eulogy on submission to fate, to the inevitability of things? 'Blessed are the poor in spirit, for theirs is the Kingdom of Heaven.' Heaven must be an awfully dull place if the poor in spirit live there. How can anything creative, anything vital, useful and beautiful come from the poor in spirit? . . . Meekness has been the whip, which capitalism and governments have used to force man into dependency. . . . The most faithful servants of the State, of wealth, of special privilege, could not preach a more convenient gospel than did Christ." She expanded her analysis with an interpretation of "Render to Caesar the things that are Caesar's, and to God the things that are God's" as a compromise that acts as "a fearful lash and relentless tax-gatherer, to the impoverishment . . . [and] degradation of the very people for whom Christ is supposed to have died." Instead, Goldman asserted that righteousness does not come from the stars, or because Christ willed it so. Righteousness grows out of liberty, out of social and economic opportunity and equality. But how can the meek, the poor in spirit, ever establish such a state of affairs?"

Thus, Goldman taunted her audience and readers with her contention that "[t]he reward in heaven is the perpetual bait. . . . [S]in and penance, heaven and hell . . . have been the stumbling-block in the world's work." If the workers knew the cause of their misery, "the make-up of our iniquitous social and industrial system, [they could] do more for [themselves] . . . than Christ and the followers of Christ have ever done for humanity; certainly more than meek patience, ignorance, and submission have done."

Ultimately, she believed that Christ's legacy was as a reformer rather than revolutionary, a man who did not expose the systemic source of poverty but rather promised rewards in the hereafter. To Goldman, "the whole history of the State, Capitalism, and the Church" was perpetuated because of Jesus's assertion "I come not to destroy the law," which allowed "poverty and evil [and fear of punishment to] continue to rule the world."

417. She even speculated "that the Jews might have rejected Jesus as their redeemer from Roman dominion" when, "according to the gospels . . . they turned him over to the cross . . . bitterly disappointed," because his interests were not for "the poor and disinherited of his time" instead his "sentimental mysticism . . . promised joy and bliss in another world, while the people were starving, suffering . . . before his very eyes." The Romans, she mused, "strong and unflinching as they were, must have laughed in their sleeves over the man who talked repentance and patience, instead of calling to arms against the despoilers and oppressors of his people."

In her "oppos[ition] to every religion," she did not hesitate to criticize the hypocrisy of her own people who practiced Judaism as the chosen people. Yet her critique of Christianity was more forceful than her critique of other religions because "[r]edemption through the Cross [unto all eternity] is worse than damnation." She challenged progressive thinkers who practiced Christianity under "New Liberalism, Spiritualism, Christian Science, New Thought," and what Goldman judged as "a thousand and one other forms of hysteria and neurasthenia." Her lecture "The Failure of Christianity," was published in *Mother Earth* as a response to the growth of fundamentalist Christianity and was thus read by many Christian-born anarchists, Jews, and others who in this time of the rise of new religions joined forces, and accepted Goldman's critique as their own (see "The Failure of Christianity," Essay in *Mother Earth*, April 1913).

### LOATHING BEN

As Goldman traveled across the country, the prejudice she encountered was not always based on an aversion to her ideas on religion, the State, and the family as much as it was antipathy for her traveling companion, Ben Reitman.[418] Many of her friends and associates expressed their acute distaste for her talented but vulgar road manager and lover. In 1913, disapproval of Ben was especially high. He was held in contempt by Emma's friend and lecture series organizer in Denver, Ellen Kennan (who was busy arranging the details of Goldman's 1913 planned course on Nietzsche). Kennan and many in the Women's Drama Club already had been offended by Ben's overbearing zealousness. Goldman was sure that in spite of the aversion of the women's club, "he can take care of himself" and even defended him from what she may have attributed to their intolerance: "It merely occurs to me that people who start with prejudice may not get much out of Nietzsche who fought prejudice as no other man has" (see Letter to Ellen Kennan, 1 April 1913). In this way she stood both by her man and by her principles.

### RUSSIAN SOULS

One of the men Goldman most respected, whose articulation of anarchist principles remained central to her own thinking, was the anarchist communist writer Peter Kropotkin. As deep as their commitment to anarchism was, they shared equally deep rootedness to Russia. Goldman wrote, "While my whole life is rapt up in the American struggle, almost as if I had been born here, still my soul is in Russia, and probably will never be anywhere else." She reminisced about the times that she considered leaving America during the years 1904 and 1905, "when the struggle was so intense in Russia." Yet she feared that her anarchism might be met with disapproval by her Social Revolutionary Party comrades "should I come before court in Russia. That is, whether I

418. See Letter to Joseph Fels, 12 January 1910.

would say 'I am an Anarchist.'" They might not have defended her—precisely because she was an anarchist, rather than a social democrat.[419] Thus, "for good or evil," and as hard as it was to be far from the action, Goldman remained in the United States (see Letter to Peter Kropotkin, 5 May 1913). She continued her participation from afar and acted as a liaison, as she did in 1905—serendipitously raising funds for smuggling guns to support the revolution in Russia.

## POST-ELECTION BLUES

Goldman's 1913 lecture tour did not go well. The post-election malady was described in *Mother Earth* in Elisée Reclus's essay "Why Anarchists Don't Vote": "Electors do certainly believe in the honesty of the candidates and this is to a certain extent existing while the fervor and the heat of the contest remains. But every day has its tomorrow. As soon as the conditions alter, likewise do men change. To-day your candidate bows humbly before your presence; tomorrow he will say 'pish' to you. From a cadger of votes he has turned to be a master of yours."[420]

Goldman attributed the disappointing turnout for her lectures to "the usual reaction from the political tension which follows every Presidential election in the United States. . . . [The people] concentrate all their hopes and expectations on their political candidate, and when the election is over, a mental apathy and spiritual indifference sets in, which nothing will overcome. . . . [E]verybody outside of the Anarchists perpetuate the political spook, even the I.W.W . . . the Socialist Party. . . . [H]ow very much alone we stand and how difficult and trying is our position."

The context had changed over the past fifteen years, however (in spite of the brutalities of San Diego): "[O]n the whole we do get a hearing and we are treated with great respect." Berkman's prison memoir was "favorably reviewed," though, perhaps predictably, it did not sell well; and yet she wrote to Kropotkin, "even if it only reaches the few, it will continue to live among them, and that is all one may hope for a great work" (see Letter to Peter Kropotkin, 5 May 1913).

When she and Reitman reached the West Coast, her luck began to change, but not without a price. When they returned to San Diego, the mob shouted for their lives, and the police forcibly escorted them out of town. Humiliated, Goldman became "more resolute than ever to go back to San Diego if it takes me the rest of my life until I have established free speech." But for Ben, the return to San Diego recalled the terror of his earlier experience there. The frustrated and unempathic Goldman was adamant in her resolve that next time she would go alone. The sensationalist press coverage that accom-

---

419. For background on the Social Revolutionary Party, see Introduction, vol. 2, *Making Speech Free*, pp. 24–26; see also Letter to Lillian Wald, 29 November 1910, note 5.
420. Élyseé Reclus, "Why Anarchists Don't Vote," Essay in *Mother Earth* July 1913.

panied Goldman's foiled attempt to return to San Diego sparked interest and packed meetings in Los Angeles and San Francisco, even at her drama courses (see Letter to Ellen Kennan, 22 May 1913).

## THE MCNAMARA CASE AND CLARENCE DARROW'S ILL-FATED PLEA BARGAIN

Goldman's focus on drama during this 1913 lecture series in Los Angeles was in part a strategy to discuss ideas and questions that had arisen about difficult current legal proceedings in the McNamara brothers' case. The brothers were known labor organizers—steelworkers with experience blowing up bridges—recruited for bombing the headquarters of the anti-union *Los Angeles Times*. In 1911 (as discussed in section "From Saloons to Salons"), they had been tried for conspiracy, and their lawyer, Clarence Darrow, plea-bargained: he suggested that the brothers plead guilty in exchange for protecting other labor union organizers associated with the case, as well as to secure shorter sentences. However, in 1913 the government broke its promise and prosecuted thirty-eight union officials for "aiding and abetting the transportation of explosives."[421] Goldman, in retrospect, considered Darrow's ill-fated plea bargain to have been influenced by Lincoln Steffens, the notorious muckraking political journalist,[422] and saw it as a sign of Darrow's "weakness and compromise" and another example of the pitfalls of the progressive mentality (see Letter to T. Perceval Gerson, 28 May 1913).[423]

Such reminders of the inherent compromises and conventions of the courtroom and the polling booth reinforced Goldman's anarchist convictions.

## HUNGRY FOR INSPIRATION

Anarchists, and radical thinkers in "the provinces" looked forward to Goldman's traveling lecture tours. In New Kensington, Pennsylvania, Almeda Sperry maintained an infatuation with Goldman that changed her life. New to anarchism, and with a growing appreciation for Nietzsche and Kropotkin's works, she and her husband suddenly found themselves at odds with the Pittsburgh socialist newspaper for which they worked. Sperry, as previously described, was an unusual mix of street prostitute, married bisexual, and political activist. She wrote to Goldman for support. Evidently, as long as the two of them "gave the capitalists hell," all was fine on the paper, but as soon as they "exposed some of the socialist owners of the Free Press" they found themselves reined

---

421. Although Clarence Darrow, the attorney who tried the case and was responsible for the plea bargain, was viewed by some as a legal hero of the laboring classes, in 1912 he was indicted and tried for tampering with and bribing the jury, although the charges were eventually dropped.
422. See Lincoln Steffens in Directory of Individuals.
423. As with most decisions, others played a role, and Goldman, Berkman, and Reitman remained bitter toward Steffens and his role influencing Darrow and the McNamara case. See Letter from Ben Reitman, 14 January 1912, note 7.

in. "Socialists are even meaner than Christians," Sperry complained. But "the vanguard of revolution in small towns are to be commended for their firmness for surely such people know what isolation means. . . . [with] no atmosphere, so sordid, so mean, so stagnant [as] the atmosphere enveloping American provincials."[424]

In contrast, some cities, like Seattle, were havens of open-mindedness. In August 1913 two hundred people paid admission to hear Emma Goldman speak about workers' alienation from the product of their labor in a "society [that] rushes in a mad chase after vulgar wealth, and the poor hang to the coat-tails of the rich and think they may get what they desire if they vote, pray and work long enough." With Reitman at her side, in her talks she sometimes included praise for hoboes (like him) for their perseverance and culture of cooperation. Yet no matter what the subject of her lecture was, the public posed the same questions about anarchists and violence; Goldman turned around their concerns, insisting that what she was "preaching [was] education against violence which is epitomized in our modern society in war, capital punishment, prisons, capitalism and plutocracy." Even so, she never denied that "anarchy advocated direct action," as a tactic of last resort against exploitation (see "Emma Goldman Lauds the Hobo," Article in the *Seattle Post-Intelligencer*, 12 August 1913).

## THEATER AND THEATRICS FOR THE PEOPLE

Goldman's commitment to bringing the message of modern theater to people of all classes was a counterpoint to the notion that only the rich can impart "civilization." She equated the phenomenon with the settlement house movement: "They have their charities, their pro-cathedrals, their settlements. Yes their settlements have done one good thing. They went down to the people to teach them to eat with a fork instead of a knife, and the people taught them that with what they had to eat they might as well eat with a knife."[425]

Still, in spite of her intent to overthrow the "one star" system, Goldman herself was perhaps the consummate "one star" of political road theater. Offering her audience a spectacle to remember, she dramatized the suppression of free speech, sometimes sitting with a handkerchief stuffed in her mouth in front of the stage from which she was barred from speaking.[426] In one instance she chained herself to the podium while a comrade threw the chain out the window and another roped it to an iron fence outside—all to prevent the police from easily dragging her off the stage before she had finished making

---

424. See Almeda Sperry to EG, 14 July [1913?], *EGP*, reel 7.
425. Quoted in Frances Jolliffe, "Emma Goldman Outlines Plan for Free Theater—Incidentally, She Says, the Rich Are So Ignorant They Don't Know What the People Want," *San Francisco Bulletin*, 30 April 1910, Emma Goldman Papers, third-party newsclipping file.
426. See vol. 4, *The War Years* (forthcoming).

her political point.[427] More regularly, the audience could expect Goldman to be hurling biting insults at the police and exposing the hypocrisy of not only conventional culture but of bohemian intellectuals as well.[428] It was no surprise that the great stage performers, as well as playwrights and drama patrons, attracted her interest.[429]

She was thoroughly convinced of the positive power of entertainment and of dramatic performance to arouse empathy and thereby reach a more profound level of understanding across class and racial barriers. Therefore, she announced that her next task would be arranging for the publication of a new book, *The Social and Revolutionary Significance of the Modern Drama*. She believed that "the stage today is the most important place for putting before the people the great pressing social and economical questions" (see "'Anarchist Queen' with Ambitious Dream," Article in the *Butte Miner*, 29 August 1913).

Hyperbolically displaying the equal credence she placed on the efficacy of violence, she opened *The Social Significance of the Modern Drama* with the assertion that theater is as volatile and effective as dynamite, with a power that "undermines superstition, shakes the social pillars, and prepares men and women for the reconstruction" (see Foreword to *The Social Significance of the Modern Drama*, 1914). She was convinced that a well-crafted story involved and motivated readers more than even the most incriminating facts about social injustice. Ben Reitman, the primary distributor of literature at Goldman's talks, agreed: "[I]f I hand a man one of Hauptmann's plays, and he learns about the bitter conflict between labor and capital, I have done more for him than if I had influenced him to join a movement. And I feel that if I call a man's attention to William Morris's 'News from Nowhere,' he will have a clearer vision and a greater ideal than if I had sold him a dozen pamphlets on 'How We Are Exploited.'"[430]

## LOVE "MORE MADLY":
## CREATING A HAVEN OF LOVE AND WORK

Much of the emotional drama in Goldman's personal life was centered on Reitman: "my inspiration, my impetus, my great urging power in work . . . lover mine." It was he who

427. Joseph Cohen, *Di Yiddish-Anarkhistishe Bavegung in America* [The Jewish Anarchist Movement in America] (Philadelphia, 1945), pp. 374–75. The event took place in 1914 at the Philadelphia Radical Library, after she was prevented from entering the Labor Lyceum. The police never showed up!

428. Margaret Anderson in *My Thirty Years' War*, p. 71, boasted that she did not fall into Goldman's category of hypocritical bohemian intellectuals: "She [EG] was by this time entirely reassured as to my unbourgeois nature, and eager to see the empty apartment"; and see *LML*, p. 531: "A few hours with her entirely changed my first impression and made me realize that underneath her apparent lightness was depth and strength of character to pursue whatever aim in life she might choose. . . . Strongly individualized, they [Margaret Anderson and Harriet Dean] had broken the shackles of their middle-class homes to find release from family bondage and bourgeois tradition."

429. Candace Falk, "Emma Goldman: Passion, Politics, and the Theatrics of Free Expression," *Women's History Review* 11, no. 1, pp. 11–28.

430. Ben Reitman, "The End of the Tour and a Peep at the Next One," *Mother Earth*, September 1913.

recognized her as "also a woman, not only the agitator." Whenever they were apart, she longed for him—"for tenderness, for affection, for the thousand and one things, that make love worth having . . . not from other men, but you, you alone . . . my big, wild, black haired savage lover. Hobo, darling . . . I love you madly and want you still more madly." The letters are templates of shifting volatile swings of love and reproach. By 1913 Goldman proposed that their work and love life would greatly improve if they could live together. She found a house uptown in Manhattan on West 119th Street that was large enough to accommodate the *Mother Earth* office and provide living quarters for the circle of people responsible for the magazine's production, even including a separate area for Ben's mother.[431] With this new arrangement Goldman imagined that all would "be well and harmounious at our new house. . . . I want my lover, my darling comrade, co-worker, friend and sweetheart, I want you more than everything else in the World and I want our work." Ben's concerns were less about his relationship with Emma and more about how the group would hold together, given his complaints about Sasha's temperamental behavior, Havel's alcoholism, and Max's lack of organizational ability. Emma defended them, citing as most important their loyalty and trustworthiness "in time of police trouble"—a crucial quality even overriding their talents on the magazine. In part to ease Ben's discomfort with the group she suggested that Ben's former lover, the efficient Fitzi, join them. In effect, Goldman had created the extended work/love family of her dreams, a variant on Chernyshevsky's imagined cooperative in *What Is to Be Done?*,[432] a book that had long been an inspiration (see Letter to Ben Reitman, 20 September 1913).

## IN SEARCH OF "GOOD MALE DANCERS"

Goldman's new household became a place large enough for a party to usher in the New Year. She sent word to women friends like Edna Kenton, a suffragist member of the Greenwich Village Heterodoxy Club, "more fortunate than I." Goldman then began a search for good male dancers, lamenting, "I know so few good males on general principles. . . . If you know of such miracles, bring them along, but not too many at a time" (see Letter to Edna Kenton, 18 December 1913). Theodore Dreiser, the author of *Sister Carrie*, was among those "male miracles" invited to "kick out the old year and meet the new" (see Letter to Theodore Dreiser, 27 December 1913).

To gather an audience for her lectures, she reached out to her bohemian circle in Greenwich Village, and even uptown New York. She called on journalist John Reed's

---

431. EG wrote that his mother-craving was symptomatic of the child in him; although she could not fulfill the mother's doting role, Goldman asserts that she had done more, having given him an "Ideal with the desire to do big things" at the expense of her friends' repudiation, and yet in spite of "all the pain and hurts you have often caused me, I love you." EG to BR, 29 Oct [1913?], *EGP*, reel 7.

432. For discussion of Chernyshevsky's *What Is to Be Done?* see Introduction, vol. 1, *Made for America*, pp. 13 and 14.

companion, the fashionable Mabel Dodge, who was known for bringing diverse combinations of people together, to distribute "a package of cards announcing my Sunday lectures." She hoped they would attend her Thursday talk on "The Intellectual Proletarians," which was intended to raise awareness of the commonalities between intellectuals and common laborers.

Goldman also enjoyed hosting visits from and arranging lectures for European anarchists and syndicalists. In 1913 she especially wanted people in the United States to meet the syndicalist Tom Mann.[433] He spoke about syndicalists in the British and French labor movements who believed, contrary to the belief of the IWW, that militant labor activists ought to join with and influence the dominant labor union in the United States: the American Federation of Labor, which in fact was already under way.

## 1914

It was a brutal time for labor in America. Goldman commiserated with her Denver friend Ellen Kennan over violent attacks on strikers at the mines in Colorado. Yet in spite of the horrors of the coal miners' strike and the arrest of visiting organizer and socialist agitator Mother Jones, Goldman misread the situation and was unusually dismissive of union tactics. She railed against the self-importance of Colorado as the first state to grant women suffrage.[434] She then displayed her ignorance of the actual struggles of the miners in Colorado: "After all, the mine owners could not act as they do, if the workers were not such cringing slaves, and their leaders such lickspittals. I must say I am disgusted."[435] Citing the weakening effect of internal union and party conflicts, she continued her harangue against the miners, who had turned their backs on Bill Haywood.[436]

On internal strife within the movement, she said that "[i]t takes an iron constitution to survive the struggle with your enemies and even more than that to survive the misunderstanding of your friends." Here she was referring to the accusations thrown at her over the years, but also realizing that anarchists were vulnerable to the shortcomings of

---

433. Goldman also enjoyed hosting visits from European anarchists and syndicalists. In 1913 she was especially pleased at the ease of access for British syndicalist Tom Mann's U.S. tour, in contrast to that of John Turner. Turner was a British anarchist, lecturer, and founder of the Shop Assistants' Union; he played an important role in her challenge to the 1903 Anti-Anarchist Immigration Act. See Introduction, vol. 2, *Making Speech Free*, pp. 19–24 and 545.

434. She claimed that although "the privilege should not be denied to them," suffrage in Colorado "had brought about no reforms." Leslie Curtis, "Emma Goldman Lectures on 'Love and Marriage' and 'Anarchy': Woman Who Has Aroused the World by Expressions of Her Radical Sentiments and Beliefs Talks to Reno People—Carried No Bombs in Her Pockets," *Reno Evening Gazette*, 18 April 1910, Emma Goldman Papers, third-party newsclipping collection.

435. The Ludlow miners were an organized and united presence against which the company resorted to brutality, not only against the miners but against the women and children as well.

436. Haywood was a prominent organizer of the Paterson, New Jersey, silk workers' strike.

sectarianism. This in-fighting was in part the reasoning behind her belief that in the end, one must "break lose from all party lines and start out on his own hook. That is the only way to serve the cause of freedom." Yet her ferocious independence was also isolating. Goldman's broad vision was not easily translatable into action. A certain contradictory rigidity often emerged as she stood against the crowd. For solace and companionship, she depended on a few close friends and confidantes (see Letter to Ellen Kennan, 26 January 1914).

Goldman also longed for the kind of labor solidarity and "more effective [militant] means of self-defense" that she believed might have prevented "the numberless brutalities and cold-blooded outrages perpetrated against labor." She was both critical of and outraged by the plight of labor: "Investigations [into the carnage alone] . . . only tend to distract the attention of the people from the real issue, which is that the workers in this country are absolutely at the mercy of their masters." Goldman recited "the horrors enacted in West Virginia, . . . in the hop fields of Wheatland, Calif., in the mines in Trinidad, Colorado, and Calumet, Michigan.[437] In all these places the police, the militia, and armed gangs of citizen thugs are carrying on a reign of terror that would put to shame the Black Hundreds of Russia. . . . The law winks its eye, and not a single thug is apprehended or punished. On the contrary, it is the strikers who are dragged before the bar of justice" (see "Self-Defense for Labor," Article in *Mother Earth*, January 1914). Goldman was unaware of the extent of radical union resistance or that the Colorado union had purchased arms for its striking workers. Such recourse may have been more prevalent than previously recorded in labor records or academic histories.

### BREAKING THE FETTERS OF THIS ERA OF NEW SLAVERY

In 1914, with war raging in Europe, Goldman felt compelled to warn of the dangers the war presented in America. Among her most powerful talks on impending war was one in which she used the Reverend I. N. Ross's address to his congregation of African Americans, for whom slavery was a harrowing part of their collective memory. She incorporated Ross's words more formally into an essay in *Mother Earth*, thus evincing her familiarity with the scant newspaper reportage relating to the African American community. Reverend Ross "called upon his hearers to fight for their political, social, and industrial rights. 'To prepare for war in times of peace is the policy of this nation,' he argued. 'It should be your policy, if you wish to free yourself from the oppression and break the fetters of this era of new slavery.'" Applauding the militancy of his pronouncement, Goldman noted, "It is not often that an Anarchist can agree with a Christian gentleman; but I heartily concur in this case, except that I feel that [it] is not only the negro who must learn to fight against the oppression, the fetters of the era of the new slavery,

---

437. See "Self-Defense for Labor," Article in *Mother Earth*, January 1914, notes 2–5.

but also the white man, the workers at large. They owe it to themselves, to the cause of labor, and above all to their own self-respect and dignity that they should no longer submit meekly to the indignity, injustice and crimes heaped upon them" (see "Self-Defense for Labor," Article in *Mother Earth,* January 1914).

Here she used the militancy of the "negro" who fights against oppression as a model for the predominantly white and ethnic minority laborers to recognize their form of slavery as well. Given the bloody strikes erupting across the country, the issue of union gradualism versus labor militancy clearly had not been settled. And black-white divisions seemed to run so deep that the same people who took risks for economic and political justice often distanced themselves from the brutal lynching in the South—as did others, excluded on the basis of their race, distance themselves from union-based labor struggles.

### DRAMA: "BEYOND THE STAGE OF PATCHING UP"

In Goldman's book on drama, published in 1914, she refined her stated intention to act as a mediator and an educator and to extend human experience as fully as possible. Goldman highlighted the plight of the "'common' people . . . who are thrown into prison; . . . who are persecuted and mobbed, tarred and deported" and thought that a medium was needed "to arouse the intellectuals of this country, to make them realize their relation to the people, to the social unrest permeating the atmosphere." To create this solidarity she used her skills to reach the intellectual onlookers through the protected medium of modern drama, which had the power to show "each and all caught in the throes of the tremendous changes going on, and forced either to become part of the process or be left behind." She believed that "dramatists . . . know that society has gone beyond the stage of patching up, and that man must throw off the dead weight of the past, with all its ghosts and spooks, if he is to go foot free to meet the future" (see Foreword to *The Social Significance of the Modern Drama*, 1914).[438]

Goldman's Sunday night drama lecture series in New York City from January to March 1914 was, as expected, not well attended. Yet in the intimate atmosphere created by the small audiences, it was easier for Goldman to establish lasting relationships and gather loyal contributors. She continued to solicit *Mother Earth* subscribers across the country for support, not only for her drama book but also for little theaters that were cropping up around the country.[439]

438. For example, in Goldman's favorite play, Henrik Ibsen's *Ghosts* (1881), Mrs. Alving ponders that "we are all ghosts, . . . not only what we have inherited from our fathers and mothers that exists again in us, but all sorts of dead ideas and . . . dead beliefs . . . dormant . . . ghosts all over the world. . . . [W]e are so miserably afraid of the light" (p. 43). See also Emma Goldman, "The Ups and Downs of an Anarchist Propagandist," *Mother Earth,* August 1913.

439. See EG to Maurice Browne, 4 May 1914, *EGP*, reel 8.

## EDUCATING THE EDUCATED:
## AWAKENING LATE-NIGHT INTELLECTUAL PROLETARIANS

Speaking in an upbeat, rhetorical code for revolution, Goldman reached out to the privileged class in a subtle reference to their stake in the fate of those who bore the direct brunt of economic and political inequality.

This solidarity included a redefinition of the term "workers" to include "intellectual proletarians." Goldman asserted, "The proletarization of our time reaches far beyond the field of manual labor; indeed, in the larger sense all those who work for their living, whether with hand or brain, all those who must sell their skill, knowledge, experience and ability, are proletarians." Goldman believed that intellectuals were not exempt from this classification "inasmuch as they are slavishly dependent" upon employers "and, above all, upon a stupid and vulgar public opinion." Without dismissing the obvious differences in income and social position, she surmised, "From this point of view . . . our entire system, excepting a very limited class, has been proletarianized."

She further asserted that the intellectual's position is "more degrading than the position of the worker in any trade. . . . [T]hose who are engaged in intellectual occupations, no matter how sensitive they might have been in the beginning, grow callous, cynical and indifferent to their degradation. . . . Their dream is to 'arrive,' no matter at what cost. . . . [P]ity the unfortunate victim . . . [whose] 'arrival' is synonymous with mediocrity." The intellectual "haves" are distinguished from "those who work in the shops or mines," because they have less freedom," "less mobility," and "cannot put on overalls, and ride the bumpers to the next town in search of a job."

Goldman also observed that intellectuals develop a slavishness to ingrained habits of appropriate clothes, acceptable neighborhoods, and the effect of late-night coffee and conversation that leaves them "unfitted for the next day's work," whereas the manual laborer has stamina to "meet the hardships of the road." Still, she wrote, intellectuals "consider themselves superior, better, and more fortunate than their fellow-comrades in the ranks of labor." Taking her argument even further, she addressed the plight of professional women, who "grow weary and faint with the search for employment," never realizing that they are as economically dependent as "the girl of the red light district." Her lecture, primarily directed at middle-class radicals and liberal intellectuals, was a plea to the educated class to "come down from their lofty pedestal and realize how closely related they are to the people!" She spurned the efforts of society women in furs who joined striking garment workers, who passively watched their less fortunate sisters when "scores of girls were manhandled and brutally hustled into the patrol wagons, [while] the well-dressed pickets were treated with deference and allowed to go home." Thus, she minimized the contribution of society women, sure they had their excitement at the expense of the cause of labor.

Journalists and muckrakers too came under Goldman's fire. She considered them providers of titillation in newspapers without truly challenging the ruling class, in part because of their attachment to the professional accolades and reputation gleaned from uncovering wrongs against others. Similarly, she berated the intellectuals in the United States who distanced themselves from the militants of the IWW and from those accused of bombing the anti-union *Los Angeles Times* building, but whose feigned sympathy for the exploited workers is "never strong enough to establish a bond, a solidarity between him and the disinherited. It is the sympathy of aloofness, of experiment."

She suggested that the intellectuals and bohemian "avant-gardists" in the United States might learn from Europeans, who "made common cause with the struggling masses . . . and [gave] to the world a real culture." She cited the Russian revolutionary intellectuals of the Narodnaya Volya (People's Will) as the ultimate model; they early on identified the peasantry as the source of revolutionary change, went to live among them to learn, teach, share their skills, and together they developed tactics, including terrorism, to overthrow the tsar. She saw the potential of writers, artists, intellectuals in America to "give themselves to the new completely and unreservedly . . . [to] become a forceful factor in the life of the people. [These intellectuals] repudiated wealth and station. . . . They went among the people not to lift them up but themselves to be lifted up, to be instructed." Among those whom Goldman believed had the capacity for reconciling and solidifying class division in America and for breaking down the conventions of puritanism and narrow moral ties were strong and proudly defiant women, whose full power was yet to emerge (see "Intellectual Proletarians," Essay in *Mother Earth*, February 1914).

### LOVER'S FAREWELL

On the home front Goldman was shaken to the core. Ben began to resent Emma's rejection of his mother; both had been banished from the communal household. He felt that he had been living between two strong female forces that could never mix. His anger increased, leading to a tirade of self-deprecation mixed with outward fury and an internal compulsion to run away from responsibilities, to escape the harsh judgments of their anarchist circle, to reassess his life. He was about to turn thirty-five.

In a letter Ben vented his anger, threatened to leave, then admitted that he might come crawling back to Emma. He warned her not to respond to his letter with the same old self-righteous refrain: "I know you are always right—At least I have never heard you [admit] you were wrong or unjust or unkind since I have been with you" (see Letter from Ben Reitman, ca. January 1914).

Goldman ignored Reitman's wishes. She lashed back with counteraccusations that he lacked appreciation for the intensity of her love. "It is true that I can not submerge myself in you, as your mother has but I have been able to do what she has not, imbue you with an ideal with a desire to do big things. And if I have been critical of you at times it was because, I did not want you to waste yourself on sensations, on love and trying things. Because I wanted you to do deep and thorough work. I have succeeded on that so I need not complain, . . . Deeply and intensely your Mommy."[440] Although she had hoped that her love and kindness would overcome his bitterness, eventually she did acknowledge the discomfort inherent in his position within her anarchist circle. Yet she also believed that the kind of secure relationship he craved, and had with his mother, was something she could never deliver. Goldman believed that her life "of necessity must remain insecure always," a state being freely chosen: "Security means stagnation. I hope I shall never get to that." In fact, "[b]eing in the movement all one's life, is like being married all one's life, it incapacitates one for other things." In her farewell letter to him she assured him that he was "wise to get away from [the anarchist movement], before it's too much in your blood."

She also attributed his disaffection and disillusionment as Goldman's advance man "to the fact that you were my manager first & always and incidentally my lover. . . . EG work was your aim and EG was the means to that aim. Not for yourself but . . . because you were infatuated with the work" (see Letter to Ben Reitman, 21 February 1914). For Goldman, however, the two were more completely intertwined. It was not long before Ben did in fact come back, but never again did he include his mother in the *Mother Earth* community. In September Goldman moved out of their collective household into a small furnished room, as she had "25 years ago when I came to NY. . . . I have gotten back to the starting point." Negotiating with Reitman about the terms of his return to the office, she insisted that his work could not be done long-distance from Chicago and that it was necessary for him to return to New York, even though he did not relish it. She claimed to be worn out from "7 incessant years of talking," and was determined to tour and speak only enough to pay her debts and instead to more fully devote herself to the success of the magazine (see Letter to Ben Reitman, 25 September 1914).

## DEMONSTRATIONS OF THE UNEMPLOYED

Goldman believed that *Mother Earth*'s critique was especially important at a time, from 1913 into 1914, when New York's unemployment crisis continued to worsen, catapulting the city into a deep depression. Starvation was rampant. Various organizations coordinated demonstrations of the unemployed: the Labor Defense Committee founded by Elizabeth Gurley Flynn, Carlo Tresca, Bill Haywood, and others; the New York IWW union local; and the Conference of the Unemployed.[441] Although mass demonstrations of the unemployed were generally attributed less to the anarchists and more to the IWW, groups often worked together because of their shared direct action tactics. According to historian Paul Avrich, "If the movement had an overall strategist it was Alexander

---

440. EG to BR, 29 October [1913], *EGP*, reel 7.
441. The Conference of the Unemployed was formed at the Ferrer Center. Its secretary was Joseph Cohen.

Berkman, who moved from center to center providing guidance, inspiration, and organizational talent."[442]

Charles Willis Thompson, an astute writer for the *New York Times Sunday Magazine*, reported direct anarchist involvement in many of the most militant marches. He traced their organizers to the Ferrer Modern School,[443] where many classes were taught by prominent radical intellectuals, poets, and artists who encouraged a revolt against injustice and fostered free-spirited creativity. The reporter noted that much of the planning of the city's demonstrations of the unemployed originated with a group of young men at the Ferrer Modern School. The journalist warned his readers that the unrest they were witnessing in 1913 and 1914 mirrored conditions of 1886 and 1887 all too closely and might spark Haymarket-like demonstrations, bombings, and even executions of anarchists.[444]

Yet the reporter contrasted Goldman's 1893 talk inciting the hungry to "take bread" (which landed her in jail for a year) with her 1914 address in Union Square to the mass meeting of the Conference of the Unemployed. The latter was preceded by a relatively similar parade of the unemployed up Fifth Avenue, for which she was not arrested. He attributed this difference in the local practice of free speech protection to a general awareness of and tolerance for the plight of the unemployed (and fear of reprisals). And although Goldman was by no means the leader of the unemployed movement, she had brought attention to "the change of the intellectual class toward the condition of labor. . . . There is a tremendous contingent of professional men and women everywhere who are proletarians. . . . They have to walk around looking for jobs." She posited that "the danger to present-day society is greater from these intellectual proletarians than from the unemployed, because they have tasted the good things of life and know what they are missing."

Thus, what Goldman considered a positive alliance between intellectuals and laborers was perceived as a double-edged threat by Thompson, whose article was intended as a caveat to the *New York Times*'s educated readership. He described those who had taken part in the event as "men of education and culture . . . writers, poets, artists,"[445] including fifty anarchist women who along with other rebels "led, inspired, and guided" the unemployed and even had money that Emma Goldman had raised for their cause. The detail in his article also served as an introductory profile of the key activists, stating that Goldman's role was peripheral to the actions. His account also humanized the march-

---

442. Avrich, *The Modern School*, p. 188.
443. For more on the Ferrer Modern School, see *Directory of Individuals* and *Directory of Organizations*; also in vol. 2, *Made for America*.
444. See Introduction, vol. 1, *Made for America*, pp. 6–7.
445. In February and March 1914 IWW members occupied churches as night shelters, an action intended to dramatize the situation of the unemployed. While Protestant churches acquiesced, the same strategy failed at the Catholic Church of St. Alphonsus on West Broadway. Among those arrested and sentenced to a year in prison was Frank Tannenbaum (who would later become a prominent scholar of Latin America). His $500 bail was raised by the Labor Defense Committee, the Ferrer Center, and the *Freie Arbeiter Stimme*.

ers passing Mount Sinai Hospital in silence so as not to disturb the sick, and in its own way created sympathy with those associated with the newsworthy Emma Goldman (see "So-Called I.W.W. Raids Really Hatched by Schoolboys," Interview in the *New York Times Sunday Magazine*, 29 March 1914).

Such sympathy, however, was sorely lacking when in the second rally, organized in part by Berkman, two weeks later on 4 April 1914, many of its participants were beaten in a confrontation with the New York police force. Demonstrators arrested for disorderly conduct, like Joe O'Carroll and Arthur Caron,[446] bore such obvious physical signs of police brutality that the magistrate dismissed the case because he was appalled and for fear of fueling an even more virulent backlash by the unemployed.

## ACCESS TO BIRTH CONTROL: MARGARET SANGER AND EMMA GOLDMAN

Among the most valiant crusaders against poverty in 1914 was Margaret Sanger, the young birth control advocate whom Emma Goldman had taken under her wing. Although Sanger later gained support among educated, forward-thinking bourgeois women, she hoped to reach the poor who bore the brunt of ignorance about reproduction. Her pamphlets were inspired by a vision of changing the conditions of hunger and deprivation as well as providing practical birth control information.

Postal obscenity laws made it difficult and sometimes even impossible to distribute Sanger's magazine, the *Woman Rebel*.[447] Thus, to spread the word lectures and friendships with those who had access to a broad public were ever more important. The letters between Sanger and Goldman offer a rare glimpse into the lives of two women beset by police and sometimes angry mobs, on the one hand, and greeted by enthusiastic female crowds anxious to take control of their reproductive lives, on the other.

In an effort to subvert the ban on distribution of *Woman Rebel* through the mails, Goldman took Sanger's magazine to sell at her cross-country lecture tours. Sanger complained in a letter to Goldman that ordinary citizens and even her neighbors sometimes seemed more vicious than law enforcement.[448] Goldman replied with disgust: "[T]he people themselves are so dense[449] that they are capable of greater outrage than even the police. The best proof of that is the lynching in the south and the horrors committed by the vigilantes in San Diego and other cities. Of course the people help, but mob brutality, which is the result of ignorance, is by far more terrible than police brutality which

---

446. See Caron (of the townhouse bombing) in Directory of Individuals. For O'Carroll see "So-Called I. W. W. Raids Really Hatched by Schoolboys," Article in *New York Times Sunday Magazine*, 29 March 1914, note 11.

447. Much earlier, the one issue of the magazine that was completely banned from distribution actually had an article advocating assassination.

448. She also observed with some irony that law enforcers often contributed to the attention given to the issue of birth control they intended to silence.

449. See Emma Goldman, "Minorities Versus Majorities," in *Anarchism and Other Essays*, for a fuller exposition on this point.

might be reasoned with occasionally." She reinforced Sanger's confidence, asserting that her paper was "a very brave attempt and the first commenced by a woman in this country." She was less optimistic about its success if, in fact, it could not be sent through the mails (see Letter to Margaret Sanger, 14 April 1914).

In this early phase of Sanger's political activism Goldman mentored and encouraged her, commenting that "[n]ot one of my lectures brings out such . . . crowds as the one on the birth strike and it is the same with the W.R. [*Woman Rebel*]. It sells better than anything we have" (see Letter to Margaret Sanger, 26 May 1914). The March and May issues of the magazine had been cited for violations of Section 211 of the U.S. Criminal Code. "If only the authorities were not so stupid, they would realize that they are doing you more good by holding up the paper than any amount of money could do. 'The Woman Rebel' is the best seller of anything we've got, just because it is known that the paper has been held up. But then, the authorities will die stupid" (see Letter to Margaret Sanger, 22 June 1914). "If you could arrange, my suggestion would be that you make a tour, talk about prevention, organize leagues and take the paper with you. I am inclined to think you'd have a tremendous success. . . . [Y]ou have no idea what the personal element means in reaching people."

But even though she had dissuaded Sanger from organizing neo-Malthusian leagues in the open rather than in secret,[450] she objected to the idea of conducting clandestine birth control work. "I do not believe the American psychology is fit for conspiratory work, too many [detective] agents of J. J. Burns about who would only cause mischief." As to the regulation of free speech, which was a critical link in raising support for their meetings, Goldman hoped that speaking openly might also "help to break the Comstock control, besides I don't think there is a law dealing with that question" (see Letter to Margaret Sanger, 26 May 1914). "The stupid postal law will be broken only when there is enough intelligent determined opinion against it. . . . [If] you will have readers interested enough in making a fight in case you go to prison, it is worth while going there; but not otherwise" (see Letter to Margaret Sanger, 22 June 1914).[451]

Goldman also contributed a short excerpt from her lecture "Woman Suffrage" to the *Woman Rebel*. It included her message to suffragists, reminding them that ultimately women must rely on themselves for both inner and outer emancipation: "First, by asserting herself as a personality and not as a sex commodity. Second, by refusing the right to anyone over her body; by refusing to bear children, unless she wants them; by refusing to be a servant to God, the State, society, the husband, the family, etc., by making her life simpler, but deeper and richer . . . freeing herself from the fear of public opinion and public condemnation. Only that, and not the ballot, will set woman free, will make

---

450. Neo-Malthusian leagues were birth control organizations, as distinguished from Malthusian population-control organizations.
451. For earlier discussion of Comstock laws and censorship of the mails see p. 17.

her a force hitherto unknown in the world . . . a force of divine fire, of life giving; a creator of free men and women."[452]

Expanding her message to women about living a full life, Goldman enjoyed discussing what she called her "woman nature." In a whimsical interview with a female newspaper reporter in Des Moines, Iowa, she linked her ideas about women's freedom to fashion, defending "women's love of dress." The journalist described Goldman as a "Bohemian . . . modishly dressed," and described every item of clothing she wore, as well as the "stays or girdles" she chose not to wear. She selected for inclusion in her article Goldman's comments on a woman's "right to dare to choose what she wore irrespective of the opinion of any man," concluding her article with a provocative statement by Goldman: "Clothing is physical covering, not a part of a person. I am more concerned about the brain of woman than about her dress. Every time I see a woman who has dared to be independent in dress—even if she is extremely dressed—I am glad of it. I know she has brains and has dared to prove it" (see "Emma Goldman in Defense of Modern Women's Fashions," Interview in the *Des Moines Register and Leader*, 26 April 1914).

## A DISAPPOINTING TOUR

Playful press coverage that exposed the nuances of Goldman's personality as it converged with her challenging ideas was a counterpoint to the dismal state of the economy and to the rise of labor unrest.[453] With rising unemployment, 1914 was not a good year for those who derived income from their lectures. In general, attendance at her meetings was disappointing because of "the results of the unemployment of last winter and the radical movement [afflicted] by a sort of a mental apathy. That applies to every shade of opinion. Most of the I.W.W. and others, including the Anarchists, haven't enough spirit to kill a fly, let alone offer resistance to the increased reactionary tendencies infesting the country. Perhaps it is the quiet before the storm." The despair she often complained of—over "the uselessness of it all," attributed "to getting old, or perhaps worn out"[454]—in response to what she perceived as hopelessly submissive workers revealed how removed she was from the action. Once again, Goldman had not incorporated the recent and ongoing labor turmoil in New York or in Ludlow, Paterson, Lawrence, Trinidad, or Wheatland in her critique of the passivity of the working class—and she consistently misread the situation.

She considered her generally popular lecture on birth control an inroad into ending the cycle of poverty. Sanger and Goldman reinforced each other, equally committed to

---

452. Article in the *Woman Rebel*, June 1914.
453. For example, "The Real Emma Goldman—A Self-Possessed, Quiet Woman of Intelligence—Calls Tolstoy an Anarchist," *Evening Sun* (Baltimore), 24 November 1910, described EG's "refined and very soft laughter" upon hearing the description "Yiddish evangelist." Emma Goldman Papers, office newsclipping files.
454. EG to Nunia Seldes, 4 October [1912?], *EGP*, reel 6.

the cause, regardless of the current "hell" they were confronted with: "[W]e must go on to the very end" (see EG to Margaret Sanger, 22 June 1914). Still, the two women eventually parted ways. Within a few months the August issue of the *Woman Rebel* resulted in Sanger's arraignment for violating Section 211 of the U.S. Criminal Code; she then left for Europe to evade her trial and prosecution. When Sanger returned, the charges were dropped. Goldman, however, was facing arrest for the distribution of birth control information. By then, with each bruised in some way by the other, each with distinct strategies and constituencies, the two women had little connection, nor did they actively support each other.

## UNEMPLOYMENT, ANTI-MILITARISM, AND FREE SPEECH

In her column "En Route," Goldman shared her experiences and perceptions of the state of the country with the readers of *Mother Earth*. She believed that the "paralyzing effect" of unemployment, which was always felt most acutely by the poor, was finally being acknowledged by "even by the most stupid upholders of present conditions. . . . Even the horrors of Ludlow did not wake [Denver] up for very long, though there was a slight ripple. Most people are so wrapped up in their own little lives, especially when material distress is added to poor health . . . that their interest in the murder of women and children was only a passing moment." Instead, they "threw the responsibility on the government," as its violence, especially against the children of the striking workers in Colorado, soon faded from consciousness. The report of the U.S. Commission of Industrial Relations, especially the Report on the Colorado Strike, may serve as the document of official proof that she was correct in her general assessment of the vicious social war being waged across the country.

The Anti-Militarist League was founded in 1914 at the Ferrer Center by many in Goldman's circle, including Becky Edelsohn, Leonard Abbott, Alexander Berkman, and M. Eleanor Fitzgerald, along with many anarchist and socialist members of the Conference of the Unemployed. Anti-Militarism was not pacifism. The league was organized not only to fight against war and militarism, especially the threat of war with Mexico, but also to foment domestic insurrection, armed if necessary, to counter the violence of private company armies and detective agencies used against labor. Goldman shared her enthusiasm at a Denver anti-militarist meeting where in a gathering of 2,000 people a young high school student gave an impassioned speech. She marveled at the young man, who stood in stark contrast to others of his age "who joined the militia and became a party to the crimes in Ludlow."

She also marveled at the organizing skills exhibited by Reitman, who formed a free speech fight on behalf of the Industrial Workers of the World. He brought attention to the almost sixty people in jail for open-air meetings; some were arrested for reading the Declaration of Independence and had had no publicity until Goldman and Reitman's arrival. Goldman threatened to start street speaking, as well. She secured the help of radical lawyers and succeeded "in bringing the gross brutality of the police to the notice of the public," proclaiming it an unequivocal victory: "Two days before we closed our course, thirty of the boys were discharged and the original twenty-seven released from jail." Reitman, who loved a spectacle, took the opportunity to celebrate their release with a gala event, marching them from jail, "singing, through the street, into the nearest restaurant for a general feed." In spite of their clear victory, sectarianism seemed inescapable. Goldman complained that although the Denver IWW cheerfully accepted the assistance and solidarity of the anarchists, the IWW local officials proceeded to cast them aside and refused to allow their members to sell *Mother Earth* or handle any anarchist literature. In response she hurled what she considered the gravest insult: "What a pity that the I.W.W. must imitate the politicians."

During these difficult times, old friends provided comfort and support wherever she went. The trip from Denver to Salt Lake City, and on into Los Angeles and San Francisco, was just one of many such examples of the hospitality that countered hostilities she faced on the road. Her readers, too, became her vicarious, cross-country travel partners; and those who helped her along the way took pride in Goldman's acknowledgment of their efforts on her behalf in the pages of *Mother Earth* (see "En Route," Article in *Mother Earth*, June 1914).

## PROTESTING THE LUDLOW MASSACRE

While Goldman was out west, a storm was brewing in the East. Protests were held in Tarrytown, New York, near the Rockefeller estate, to publicly condemn John D. Rockefeller Jr. for his failure to apologize and accept responsibility for his role as president of Standard Oil in the Ludlow Massacre. These protests ended in brutal beatings, head bashings, and jail sentences for many caught trespassing, blocking traffic, or holding a street meeting without a permit. The young anarchist Rebecca Edelsohn landed in jail, where she waged a hunger strike.

Goldman raised money for their defense. She wrote her friend and supporter Perceval Gerson that her anarchism was inspired not by the hostile environment of her youth in Russia but by the harsh tactics of Ludlow, in "the land of freedom and promise" (see Letter to T. Perceval Gerson, 12 August 1914).

In haste, Berkman sent a telegram to Goldman (see Letter from Alexander Berkman, 27 July 1914), keeping her informed and thanking her for sending money. As she traveled, Goldman worked to raise funds and public awareness. She wrote to friends, sharing the details of the trial and arrests, linking the Rockefeller Mourners' Campaign (also known as the Free Silence Movement) to the fear of labor unrest in the mines and to her sense that the war industry was gaining strength. Becky Edelsohn's prison hunger strike, the first of its kind in the United States, was intended to draw attention to the case. Goldman protested the treatment received by Edelsohn and the others with a letter-writing campaign to the commissioner of corrections, a woman known as a social reformer and member of Heterodoxy, but who nonetheless allegedly treated radical prisoners harshly.

Goldman was completely supportive of the protests against the Colorado Fuel and Iron Company, which was the largest coal operator in the western United States and was controlled by the unrepentant John D. Rockefeller Jr., who was largely responsible for the Ludlow Massacre. She was taken aback, nonetheless, when a bomb intended for Rockefeller exploded in a townhouse on Lexington Avenue in Manhattan in July 1914 and killed the anarchists engaged in its preparation. She had not known about the action, but once she learned of it she and Berkman privately disagreed. In spite of what Goldman thought about the Lexington Avenue explosion, Berkman claimed, somewhat disingenuously, that his role as "an actor in it, is only incidental," but at the same time he boldly stated: "It simply happened to be a psychologic moment & I think it did a lot of propaganda" (see Letter from Alexander Berkman, September 1914).

Political fissures had already split their large household apart. Reitman and his mother had gone back to Chicago; Berkman, who had been intimately involved first with Becky Edelsohn and then with Eleanor "Fitzi" Fitzgerald, all living under one roof, gradually became more focused on the movement for the unemployed; he was less engaged with the birth control battleground that occupied much of Goldman's public work, although he wholeheartedly believed in the cause.[455] The shift in political emphasis was not the only reason for the splintering of the group. Berkman resented Goldman's coolness toward his two young anarchist lovers—a pattern he had observed before in her dealings with other young women in the movement.

Within a month of the townhouse bombing incident Goldman rented a furnished room. With contention about the Lexington Avenue explosion in the air she engaged in a dispute with Reitman. He argued against what appeared to be senseless violence, in part agreeing with Goldman's initial criticism of the event. She insisted that "my position is not against violence and never will be unless I become weak minded." Her opposition to Lexington was because "the place was ill and stupidly chosen." She continued, "[E]ven if I did not approve . . . I should still be on the side of the actionists because I hold that if society makes no provision for the individual, society must take the consequences."[456] Countering Ben's emotionalism on the subject, she underscored her belief in the efficacy of violent tactics, asserting: "[M]y ideas have been derived through years of thought, study, struggle suffering and persecution, they are bred in my blood and until I am proven otherwise, no one shall change my attitude." With an air of mystery and perhaps a slight reversal she chose not to lock herself into the belief in the inevitability of violence. On the one hand she asserted, "[N]ever mind what Jesus said. . . . [M]y place is on the side of the social outcast, has and will be." On the other hand she claimed, "I do

455. Later, in 1916, *The Blast*, Berkman's magazine directed to militant workers, would include large sections on birth control.
456. EG to BR, 24 September [1914], *EGP*, reel 8.

not know what attitude I will take to violence in time to come but at present I believe in the right of workers to resist whether in Colorado Butte or elsewhere. . . . Do I approve of the Lexingt business? Certainly not Because it is unpardonable to endanger the lives of innocent people, also for other reasons I can not discuss here."[457] Regardless of their differences on the subject of violence, her political agenda was much broader and more all-encompassing. She continued to rely on Reitman to plan the details of her *Mother Earth* speaking tours, signing a letter to him, "I love you but I am weary with the World, with people, with myself. I shall be cheerful soon have patience dear. Your Mommy" (see Letter to Ben Reitman, 25 September 1914).

## 1915

### A MANIFESTO AGAINST THE WAR

As 1915 approached, Europe was engulfed in war, "twelve million men engaged in the most frightful butchery that history has ever recorded," as Goldman put it. As the First World War raged, so too did the debate about it. Even the international anarchist movement split between those like anarchist writer Peter Kropotkin, who supported France and England against what was perceived as German aggression, and those who opposed all war on principle, except class war. The nuances of Kropotkin's views were articulated in his article in *Mother Earth*: "The causes of war must be attacked at the root. And we have great hope that the present war will open the eyes of the masses of workers and of numbers of men amid the educated middle classes. They will see the part that Capital and State have played in bringing about the armed conflicts between nations."[458] Berkman replied that "war is the game of the masters, always at the expense of the duped workers. The workers have nothing to gain by the victory of one or the other of the contending sides."[459] Goldman was part of the group that authored and signed the 1915 International Anarchist Manifesto on the War. The group voiced the position that war was "permanently fostered by the present social system. Armed conflict, restricted or wide-spread, colonial or European, is the . . . inevitable and fatal outcome of a society that is founded on the exploitation of the workers, rests on the savage struggle of the classes, and compels Labor to submit to the domination of a minority of parasites who hold both political and economic power." Thus, she and the anarchist framers of the manifesto made no distinction "between offensive and defensive wars," citing examples of each country's use of force and coercion to subdue revolt. As anarchists, they proclaimed their resolute rejection of "all wars between peoples," affirming instead their support for wars of liberation "waged by the oppressed against the oppressors, by the exploited against the exploiters."

Until such wars took place they vowed to cultivate the spirit of revolt and to remind

457. See also EG to BR, 16 September [1914], *EGP*, reel 8; Ibid.
458. Peter Kropotkin, "Peter Kropotkin on the Present War," *Mother Earth*, November 1914.
459. Alexander Berkman, "In Reply to Peter Kropotkin," *Mother Earth*, November 1914.

the "workers in factory and mine . . . that the rifles they now have in their hands have been used against them in the days of strike and of revolt, and that later on they will be again used against them in order to compel them to undergo and endure capitalist exploitation." Their proclamation was an appeal to soldiers, to workers in factories, mines, farms and fields, to all outcasts, and to mothers, wives, and daughters—those who they hoped would build a movement against war and militarism through social justice and the abolition of the State (see "International Anarchist Manifesto on the War," Manifesto in *Mother Earth*, May 1915).[460]

The Anarchist Manifesto on the War was published in *Mother Earth* and drew many signatures, with the notable absence of some prominent anarchists who chose to support the war. As war swept rapidly across national borders, Goldman's magazine became part of the heated discourse to clarify and promote their anarchist critique of the situation. In the magazine she noted the class differences between the poor immigrant women and children who died in Ludlow and the privileged passengers aboard the *Lusitania*: "The pathos of it all is that the America which is to be protected by a large military force is not the America of the people, but that of the privileged class; the class which robs their lives from cradle to the grave. No less pathetic is that so few people realize that preparedness never leads to peace, but that it is indeed the road to universal slaughter."[461]

## PERSONAL AND POLITICAL LONGINGS

With patriotic zeal building in the United States, even Goldman's family ties were affected. Her young nephew, David Hochstein, the talented violinist, would enlist in the army in 1917, perhaps in part as an act of separation from his notorious Aunt Emma. In 1915 Goldman was among his biggest fans. At her urging friends and associates, including the photographer Alfred Stieglitz, eagerly attended his recitals (see Letter to Alfred Stieglitz, 5 January 1915).

Along with the invitation to the concert, she sent announcements of her upcoming lectures for Steiglitz to post in his gallery. Added to the topics she planned to address in 1915 was a talk on homosexuality (which she, like Edward Carpenter, referred to as "the intermediate sex") directed to the homosexual community in New York City and elsewhere.[462] Homosexuality was, at that time, rarely openly discussed. Goldman spoke about the courage and creativity of the lesbian, gay, bisexual, and transgender com-

460. Signs of the disintegration of the anti-militarist movement were already apparent, amid the gradual growth in the weapons industry for the war in Europe and the precariousness of the labor and economic situation in the United States.
461. Emma Goldman, "Preparedness, the Road to Universal Slaughter," *Mother Earth*, December 1915.
462. See G. Chauncey, *Gay New York* (New York: Basic Books, 1994), pp. 230–31, for a more complete contextual history of the nuanced overlapping of homosexual and bohemian characteristics. See Sheila Rowbotham, *Edward Carpenter: A Life of Liberty and Love* (London: Verso, 2008), pp. 282–85.

munity and chose to approach homosexuality as a physiological topic. She valued her friendships with bohemian lesbians like the writer Margaret Anderson in Chicago and, possibly, Ellen Kennan in Denver, both of whom helped her gather audiences to these and other talks.

More than 7,000 advertisement cards were distributed, in batches of 200, for friends, including Kennan, to pass along to arouse local interest and to draw in the press. Goldman's letter to Kennan included a rather mocking response to Kennan's recounting of how earnestly a friend of hers was working to contest a medical bill; Goldman linked such faith in the system to the "political bug," which she considered "a more dangerous germ than the religious bug." She commented disparagingly, "I notice that the most advanced people still cling to the ragged edges of the ballot." She felt that they thus retained a knee-jerk aversion to anarchism as synonymous with chaos and violence, however complex and varied its political theory and practice (see Letter to Ellen Kennan, 6 May 1915).

## CAPLAN AND SCHMIDT: BETRAYED AND ARRESTED

Caplan and Schmidt, anarchists accused of supplying dynamite for the 1910 bombing of the *Los Angeles Times* building, had been at large for several years. Because the McNamara brothers had pleaded guilty to the charge and were serving time in prison, many assumed that the case was essentially over, although Goldman, Berkman, and others forged on, organizing support wherever they could. But in 1915 Caplan and Schmidt were found and arrested through the surveillance efforts of a spy close to the anarchist community—and perhaps even through carelessness on the part of Goldman and her circle.[463] Schmidt had been visiting and briefly hiding out in her apartment when Donald Vose, a paid spy who was the son of Goldman's friend Gertie Vose, dropped by. He then tipped off the Burns agency about Schmidt's whereabouts, which also led them to Caplan. Upon the arrest of Caplan and Schmidt, Goldman quickly organized their defense, undeterred by Charles Erskine Scott Wood's refusal to represent them. Later, attorney Jacob Margolis accepted the case (see Letter to Jacob Margolis, 6 April 1916).[464] Audiences flocked to the trial to hear the details, and many of them offered to help with legal expenses. Eugene O'Neill would later dramatize aspects of the betrayal in his play *The Iceman Cometh*.[465]

After this incident Goldman deduced that she too would be stalked by the surveil-

---

463. Goldman was careless in her trust of the son of her friend and comrade Gertie Vose. Donald Vose had spent time in the apartment, had drunk with Hapgood and others, and befriended them all. He visited EG's apartment when Schmidt, while in hiding, also visited her and he drank with Schmidt, who also trusted him with information that Vose then reported to government surveillance agents.

464. See Jacob Margolis in Directory of Individuals.

465. In *The Iceman Cometh* Goldman is conflated with longtime anarchist Gertie Vose, the mother of Donald Vose.

lance arms of various government and corporate entities including the Burns agency, which had kidnapped McNamara and hunted down Caplan and Schmidt.[466] Although the omnipresence of spies closely tracking her activities was an intimidation tactic, her boldness was reinforced by the warm circles of comrades who hosted her and loosely bound anarchist enclaves along her cross-country lecture tours, cushioning her from the disappointment of a near-empty hall or the unpredictable reception of hostile policemen or solicitous newspaper reporters.

## GOLDMAN AND REITMAN: ARRESTED IN PORTLAND

But repression was in the air. While Goldman was on tour in Portland, the mayor heard allegations that a birth control flyer had been distributed at one of her previous lectures, an act considered a violation of the city ordinance against the distribution of "improper literature" (see "Emma Goldman Is Put Under Arrest," Article in the *Oregonian*, 7 August 1915). Within minutes of C. E. S. Wood's introduction to her talk on "Nietzsche: The Intellectual Storm Center of Europe," she and Reitman were charged and arrested for distributing literature on birth control. Acting as her lawyer, C. E. S. Wood demanded that the police officer read the warrant for Goldman's arrest for distributing the birth control pamphlet *Why and How the Poor Should Not Have Many Children*.[467] Shouts, hooting, and general pandemonium followed. Her trial attracted crowds of onlookers to the official courtroom display of prudishness and censorship of the most essential information about human reproduction. C. E. S. Wood considered the ordeal a "disgrace" and "a prostitution of justice." Several members of the audience had received the forbidden birth control handouts from Reitman, discreetly slipped—possibly unbeknownst to Goldman—into copies of *Mother Earth*, pamphlets, and books he was selling. Standing trial for this offense, the two atheists refused to be sworn in but did "affirm" the truth of their testimony, a practice common to nonbelievers. They assured the judge that "the circular was not posted" or "generally distributed among the spectators."

Upon her release from the court on bail set on the condition that she refrain from speaking in the city, the chief of police discovered, much to his dismay, that he had failed to issue his conditional release with formal complaint and warrant; thus, she resumed her controversial lecture series on the subject of birth control but came at the subject more indirectly, first with "The Intermediate Sex," then with "Variety or Monogamy,

466. Whereas each government department, such as Labor and Justice, had its own surveillance unit, gradually these were brought under a central bureau that would eventually become the Federal Bureau of Investigation. It was during this time that the consolidation was beginning to take form.

467. Reitman assumed credit for writing this pamphlet in 1913 and notes in his unpublished autobiography, "Following the Monkey," "that the pamphlet was translated into Jewish, German, Italian, and many other languages," and it was distributed free to hundreds of thousands. Reitman Archive, IU-U. Most scholars, however, attribute the writing of this pamphlet to William J. Robinson (see Directory of Individuals).

Which?" (see "Emma Goldman Is Fined $100 in City Court," Article in *Oregon Journal*, 8 August 1915). Goldman's boldness attracted the attention and support not only of birth control advocates but also of those who, regardless of the issue, firmly believed in the right of free speech. Within the week her case was dismissed by a circuit court judge, who complained, "There is too much tendency to prudery nowadays. We are shocked to hear things uttered that we are familiar with in our every-day life."[468]

In response to the dismissal Goldman sent an enthusiastic report to the *Spur* in London about the "Birth Control movement . . . gaining ground and [requiring] constant attention." She also referred to Berkman's success among various trade unions in raising support for the defense of Caplan and Schmidt. But gradually war preparedness became the concern that overshadowed all else. Goldman took on the issues of conscription and the war itself, causes for which her anarchist comrades abroad were then being imprisoned. Her lecture series as she traveled from New York to Chicago and many cities in between was intended to counter the overzealous patriotism of a nation moving to a war footing. In the process she spoke out against those anarchists who supported the war.[469] Her lectures also served to inform her audiences that the IWW no longer attracted the same kind of membership or support and was "losing what little ground they gained in the past." Such concerns were rarely covered in the mainstream press. Goldman's tours and distribution of *Mother Earth* served as a means of holding the anarchist movement together; they were united (for the most part) by their view of war as a vehicle for the promotion of capitalism and patriotism. As expressed in *Mother Earth,* in war "man must be set against man . . . divided into opposing nationalities, each taught to despise and hate the other, the earth broken up by artificial boundary lines, each little spot breathing blood-thirsty patriotism of accidental birthplace."[470]

## PATRIOTISM AND WAR PREPAREDNESS

Support for war preparedness was driven by a mix of interests—the unemployed, those who feared the growing labor militancy at home, and those who would benefit from the economic opportunities afforded by the incipient war industry. Workers were conflicted on the subject. Some unionists supported the war, while others believed that preparedness was an excuse for breaking labor agreements and ending the proliferation of closed (union-dominated) shops along with skirting union wage, health, and safety mandates.

---

468. Goldman was arrested 6 August 1915, and her case was dismissed by Judge Gatens on 13 August. EG was defended by C. E. S. Wood. Goldman commended the judge in a letter to W. S. Van Valkenburgh, 13 August 1915: "to my knowledge, he is the first man on the bench who deprecates the fact that people are entirely too prudish. . . . I am asking all my friends to write to him and compliment him on his splendid stand." *EGP*, reel 9.

469. This split among the anarchists was paralleled by the split in the Second Socialist International when in 1917 only the SPA stood against the war, and German, English, and French socialists, among others, supported it.

470. Emma Goldman, "Observations and Comments," *Mother Earth*, June 1914.

Goldman was proud of the success of many of her antiwar meetings, especially one where "in front of one of the largest canon factories, the Westing house, we got several thousand workers to listen on Preparedness" (see Letter to Leon Malmed, 11 November 1915). As war industries strengthened, Goldman's crowd-drawing talk on "Preparedness, the Road to Universal Slaughter" was perceived by the government as a significant threat not only to the war effort but also to the economic interests of the United States.

With talk of war seemingly everywhere, Goldman surmised that "our entire culture is concentrated in the mad demand for the most perfected weapons of slaughter. . . . Just like cattle, panic-stricken in the face of fire, throw themselves into the very flames, so all of the European people have fallen over each other into the devouring flames of the furies of war, and America, pushed to the very brink by unscrupulous politicians, by ranting demagogues, and by military sharks, is preparing for the same terrible feat." She warned her audiences: "In the face of this approaching disaster, it behooves men and women not yet overcome by the war madness to raise their voice of protest, to call the attention of the people to the crime and outrage which are about to be perpetrated upon them."

Goldman was quick to call attention to the class interests that fueled the war. "The pathos of it all is that the America which is to be protected by a huge military force is not the America of the people, but that of the privileged class; the class which robs and exploits the masses and controls their lives from the cradle to the grave. . . . [T]he institutions which drain the blood of the native as well as the foreigner . . . rob the alien of any originality he brings with him and in return gives him cheap Americanism, whose glory consists in mediocrity and arrogance."[471] Boldly, she countered the belief that the country's preparedness efforts would guarantee the peace: "[I]n reality it will be the cause of war. It always has been thus—all through blood-stained history, and it will continue until nation will refuse to fight against nation, and until the people of the world will stop preparing for slaughter. . . . [T]o prepare for peace means to invite war."

As to the economic well-being and advancement of the country itself, she called attention to an age-old problem of national priorities: "Almost nothing is spent on education, art, literature and science compared with the amount devoted to militarism in times of peace, while in times of war everything else is set at naught; . . . the very sweat and blood of the masses are used to feed this insatiable monster—militarism." Goldman blamed "the international war supply trust who cares not a hang for patriotism or for love of the people, but who uses both to incite war and to pocket millions of profits out of the terrible bargain" (see "Preparedness, the Road to Universal Slaughter," Article in *Mother Earth*, December 1915). She feared for those who would soon "wade [in] oceans of blood and heap up mountains of human sacrifice." Although these powerful warnings drew sizeable crowds, the drumbeat of war continued.

471. "Preparedness, the Road to Universal Slaughter," *Mother Earth*, December 1915.

Government repression of dissent was widespread. Goldman received a letter from birth control advocate Margaret Sanger, who had left the country to avoid imprisonment and was being encouraged by her lawyers to plead guilty to obscenity law violations as a plea bargain if she ever wanted to return to the United States. Ever the purist, Goldman tried to dissuade her, claiming, "That would be too awful. Just kill the movement you have helped to advance in 50 years." She urged her instead to "be as brave as you have so far" (see Letter to Margaret Sanger, 8 December 1915). As it turned out, federal prosecutors dropped the charges, partly in response to the tragic death of Sanger's young daughter. They also feared a backlash, and were determined to avoid making a martyr of Sanger; the prosecutors also recognized the absurdity of punishing her for charges placed so long ago. At this time of readiness for war the government hoped to rally rather than lose public support, especially among liberals.

## 1916

### "PHILOSOPHY OF ATHEISM"

The year 1916 would test the limits of both resistance and reaction. The February 1916 issue of *Mother Earth* extended Goldman's critique to the subject of religion. In the summer of 1915 in San Francisco she lectured on the "Philosophy of Atheism," which stirred controversy everywhere, especially during the meeting of the Congress of Religious Philosophy. The issue seemed more immediate than ever. Revivalists like Billy Sunday gathered huge numbers of war supporters, making the Church an active agent of conservative government, patriotism, the restoration of traditional values, and the primacy of the Bible.

Goldman advanced her own view to the readers of her magazine—especially to the "godless, free-loving anarchists" among them. Although her claim that "the God idea is growing more impersonal and nebulous in proportion as the human mind is learning to understand natural phenomena and in the degree that science progressively correlates human and social events" had obvious opponents, others were deeply grateful to Goldman for countering the overbearing hegemony of religious belief. She believed that "the idea of God implies the abdication of human reason and justice; it is the most decisive negation of human liberty, and necessarily ends in the enslavement of mankind, both in theory and practice. . . . How far man will be able to find his relation to his fellows will depend entirely upon how much he can outgrow his dependence upon God." Goldman surmised that "only after the triumph of the Atheistic philosophy . . . will freedom and beauty be realized. . . . [J]ustice, truth, and fidelity are not conditioned in heaven, but . . . interwoven with the tremendous changes going on in the social and material life of the human race; not fixed and eternal, but fluctuating, even as life itself" (see "Philosophy of Atheism," *Mother Earth*, February 1916).

As for spirituality, Goldman was sure that anarchism would nurture the essence of the spiritual in beauty. She considered beauty an integral part of life, along with food, shelter, work, and camaraderie. She wanted "freedom, the right to self-expression, every-body's right to beautiful radiant things,"[472] longings she considered universal, resonant with the ever-widening political spectrum of her audiences. She loved books, opera, beautiful scarves and earrings, buggy rides in the country, a neat home, and well-prepared food. She enjoyed the sensory experience of a flower, a fragrance, a cup of freshly ground morning coffee. (Goldman's blend was described by her friends to be dark as night, strong as the revolution, and sweet as love.)

### POVERTY AND REPRODUCTION: "THE CHILD'S RIGHT NOT TO BE BORN"

An advocate of living life to its fullest, Goldman linked reproductive rights to poverty and believed in "the child's right not to be born"[473] if it was condemned to squalor and deprivation. Helen Keller, the socialist activist and advocate for the blind and deaf, also extended the connection between the fight against poverty and for access to birth control with the potential power of workers' strikes against war industries—a strategy at home to raise the cost of war and potentially promote peace abroad. Goldman wrote to Keller hoping to educate her about anarchist philosophy and to ask that they find time in their busy lives to talk someday (Goldman was lecturing six times a week in and out of New York). Goldman's admiration for Keller contrasted with her characteristic condescension toward other women who she believed allowed themselves to be trapped and weakened by convention: "[F]or twenty-five years I have been searching, searching diligently to find one truly big, brave American woman. Unfortunately I have not discovered very many. You are among the very few" (see Letter to Helen Keller, 8 February 1916).

### OBSCENITY LAWS AND BIRTH CONTROL

On 9 February 1916, just a day after she had written to Keller, Goldman was arrested unexpectedly just as she was about to speak on the "Philosophy of Atheism." She was charged not with religious blasphemy but rather with having violated the obscenity law during her previous lecture on birth control. This was the same birth control lecture she had been delivering for several years, but times had changed and surveillance escalated; distribution of birth control leaflets was, as always, cause for arrest. She was searched "in a vulgar manner," then locked up and released on $500 bail. Goldman took this as proof that the death, in 1915, of Anthony Comstock, the architect of the obscenity law, had not yet diminished his impact.

Her arrest did not diminish the numbers of people clamoring for birth control information; each meeting was larger than the next. Her announcement that she fully intended to go to jail to "add my might to the importance of birth control and the wip-

472. *LML*, p. 56
473. Lectures on this topic and birth control were delivered several times in 1916. See Chronology.

ing off our antiquated law upon the statute" sparked the interest of newspaper reporters. Goldman asked the press to report her case fairly and set aside their prejudice against anarchism; her press circular was also intended to remind them that that they too shared her empathy and responsibility for "the desperate condition among the masses of workers and even professional people, when they cannot meet the demands of numerous children." She campaigned against the obscenity law, especially as it applied to the dissemination of birth control information, which "has outgrown time and necessity . . . [and] must go" (see Press Circular, 15 February 1916).

A "Jubilee" meeting was called by the National Birth Control League to celebrate the dropping of charges against Margaret Sanger.[474] Little support was forthcoming for Goldman, who was facing charges for the distribution of birth control information. This kind of sectarianism—which also represented a split between liberal socialists and anarchists—angered Goldman, who assumed it was primarily middle-class "respectable" people who chose not to risk much in their fight for birth control. They allied themselves with Sanger but feared association with Goldman. Many other women, like socialist Rose Pastor Stokes, were loyal to Goldman to the end. Yet, over and over, Goldman saw a similar pattern, as was the case with anarchist support for William Sanger, who had been tricked and arrested in 1915 for offering birth control pamphlets to an agent who solicited his help:[475] "[T]he anarchists are merely used to fetch the chestnuts out of the fire and . . . when they are in trouble they need not hope for any support from those who pose as liberals and radicals." Although Goldman was generally adept at forging ties with liberal reformers, the alliance seemed to be waning. Nonetheless, she never hesitated to go it alone. Her stated aim was to attract "attention to birth control rather than to myself," to argue her own case the next week, and in preparation she organized a group of radicals to speak out at Carnegie Hall on the subject. In fact, her call for funds for legal assistance for her upcoming trial was as successful as her work to raise public awareness about the case for the decriminalization of the dissemination of birth control information (see Letter to W. S. Van Valkenburgh, 21 February 1916). Still, the betrayal by some liberal reformers in her birth control campaign increased her disdain for reformers who in the end always played it safe and allowed others to forge the way at some significant risk.

Goldman boasted of having been the lightning rod for the "first time in the history of New York and in fact in America, [when] the issue of Birth Control will be frankly

474. For National Birth Control League (NBCL) see Directory of Organizations. Tensions existed between NBCL and Sanger; after Sanger declined a position on their executive board the NBCL refused to raise funds for her defense.

475. His trial took place on 10 September 1915 and was attended by Berkman, Flynn, Abbott, Tresca, and others. See "Biographical Sketch," Margaret Sanger Papers Project, http://www.nyu .edu/projects/sanger/secure/aboutms/index.html.

thrashed out in such a place as Carnegie Hall by radical men and women. That in itself is worth having been arrested for." She worked around the clock—preparing the evening's event, preparing for the trial the following week, raising funds, laying the groundwork for the continued functioning of *Mother Earth*—because she feared that a prison sentence would interrupt the flow of their publishing schedule. She began feeling as if her brain "would burst." To regain her balance during this frantic period Goldman "took the bus and rode downtown looking at every silly shop window in order to distract my mind from the thousand and one things I am doing" (see Letter to Ellen Kennan, 1 March 1916).

As successful as it was, the birth control movement proved to be a perfect example of what she considered to be the limitations of compromise. In the clamor for results, gradualism and piecemeal reform "has made every radical movement bloodless . . . [and] led to no results whatever." Birth control "has been propagated for 50 odd years yet it came to the fore only when the law was defied not before." Conservatives and radicals differed on the level of importance they placed on birth control, as well as their reasons for supporting it. Advocates like William Robinson began to fear that association with Goldman, with anarchism, or both might antagonize other doctors. Free speech champions like Theodore Schroeder understood her plight and often advised her on the importance of resisting the suppression of free expression while weighing possible legal implications of speaking openly (see Letter to Theodore Schroeder, 19 March 1916).[476] Some, like San Francisco anarchist Rebekah Raney, assumed that all radicals believed in birth control, and therefore it was unnecessary to devote an issue of *Mother Earth* to the topic, especially with larger social issues threatening to rip apart the very fiber of life. But Goldman asserted the importance of birth control, if only because it was a taboo subject, and because of the persecution of those who advocated it, underscoring that the issue represented "the immediate question of life and death to the masses of people." She rallied organized opposition to the trial through letters, protest meetings, and strong resolutions sent to the district attorney prosecuting her case. She tapped into the wave of interest in birth control when Sanger's publication was forced to cease publication. She raised funds for their ongoing work at a time when she was also concerned about the dwindling sales of *Mother Earth*, which was "not self supporting and would discontinue if I should stop lecturing" (see "An Urgent Appeal to My Friends," Appeal in *Mother Earth*, April 1916).

Goldman also wrote an essay on birth control for *Mother Earth*. In the essay, she articulated her belief that as a group, women "will no longer be a party to the crime of bringing hapless children into the world only to be ground into dust by the wheel of capitalism and to be torn into shreds in trenches and battle fields." She believed that women

476. For example, whether or not to distribute "Women's Worst Enemy Is Women" at her meetings. EG to BR, 15–16 August [1910], *EGP*, reel 4.

would no longer tolerate the lack of control over whether to bear children and how many children they should bear. She also believed that men had a direct interest in matching these decisions to their situations and to the mutual desires of companions free enough to share equally in the challenges of family and community. Goldman asserted: "From whatever angle, then, the question of Birth Control may be considered, it is the most dominant issue of modern times and as such it cannot be driven back by persecution, imprisonment or a conspiracy of silence."

The suppression of free speech on grounds of obscenity prompted Goldman to bring attention to the ironic fact that she could not read aloud the indictment upon which she was arrested for fear of incurring yet another punishable offense; nor could the prosecutor but whisper it to the judge "as at the confessional in a Catholic Church" out of fear of offending the women present in the court.

Goldman considered the free motherhood movement "vital enough to defy all the laws upon the statute-books." She found it especially important to support "the right of medical science to experiment with contracepts as it has in the treatment of tuberculosis and any other disease." Her plea reached a dramatic crescendo: "I may be arrested, I may be tried and thrown into jail, but I never will be silent; I never will acquiesce or submit to authority, nor will I make peace with a system which degrades woman to a mere incubator and which fattens on her innocent victims. I now and here declare war upon this system and shall not rest until the path has been cleared for a free motherhood, and a healthy, joyous and happy childhood" (see "The Social Aspects of Birth Control," Essay in *Mother Earth*, April 1916). Goldman's defense before the jury echoed the words of her essay and was published in the *Masses*, which gave the issue as she framed it a much broader readership.[477]

Goldman objected to the hypocrisy of the glorification of motherhood. Women were often compelled to work to support their children but were barred from the teaching profession if they dared to become mothers. Facing such a double bind, poor pregnant women often had to resort to back-alley abortions.[478] Rather than accuse women of shirking responsibility by limiting childbirth, Goldman believed that birth control was a woman's way of regaining her dignity and taking full responsibility for the life of the child she brought into the world.

Goldman's choice to reject the prospect of motherhood was rooted in her belief that nurturing a child would be a hindrance to her absolute devotion to anarchism. She needed to be ready to face danger, to risk her life. Although she coveted her freedom and wasn't particularly fond of children, Goldman presented her sacrifice as a form of martyrdom unique to women.[479]

---

477. Emma Goldman, "Emma Goldman's Defense," *Masses*, June 1916.
478. Among Ben Reitman's services to the birth control movement was his capacity as a doctor to perform safe (and secret) abortions.
479. See Introduction, vol. 2, *Making Speech Free*, pp. 30–33; Candace Falk, "Mother Liberty" (forthcoming article).

## JAILED, YET RESOLUTE:
### "WOMEN NEED NOT ALWAYS KEEP THEIR MOUTHS SHUT AND THEIR WOMBS OPEN"

It was not long before Emma Goldman was back behind bars. Her role in the distribution of birth control pamphlets resulted in a fourteen-day jail sentence.[480] Her offense was best summed up by her friend Margaret Anderson, editor of the *Little Review*: "In 1916, Emma Goldman was sent to prison for advocating that 'women need not always keep their mouths shut and their wombs open.'"[481]

From Queens County Jail Goldman wrote a letter to Anderson, which Anderson shared with the readers of the *Little Review*. For Goldman imprisonment provided a unique political education: "It would be well if every rebel were sent to prison for a time; it would fan his smoldering flame of hate of the things that make prisons possible." She perceived the outpouring of "love and devotion and adulation," for her willingness to go to jail for the cause of birth control to be disproportionate to the act, which was "infinitesimal compared with the truly heroic deeds of the great souls." Still, she shared her reflections on the horrors of prison life, describing the pace, the food, the punishment, and even some rewards. Her cell felt cleaner than that of her 1893 incarceration, and the matrons actually seemed interested in her work. The days were bearable, but the fifteen-hour lockdown of the nights was "ghastly": "They lie like stone upon your heart. The thoughts, the sobs, the moans that emerge like pale shadows from every human soul. It is stifling. Yet people talk of hell. There is no more threatening thing in all the world than the hell of jailed nights" (see "Letters from Prison," Letters in the *Little Review*, April 1916).

To her friend Van Valkenburgh she commented jokingly about how odd it was to be in prison at Easter time and Passover, reporting that she had "turned into a good Jewish" and even requested matzos for an observance she admitted might also "protect my stomach," especially as she wasn't going to be there long enough "to get used to the bread," as well as "reducing my fat."

Her mind wandered back to savoring the dinner held at the Brevoort Hotel in her honor and to the assemblage of artists, writers, and social activists she considered to be of the highest order, including Robert Henri, George Bellows, Robert Minor, and John Sloan. At the event, left-wing socialist and future member of the Communist Party Rose Pastor Stokes dared to reveal the hypocrisy and class bias of the New York law against speaking about birth control by delivering a talk and circulating material on the subject; not surprisingly, no charges were filed. Goldman boasted to her inmates, and to her friends in her letters from prison, that on every level her send-off was a great success. The trial attracted "fully a thousand people gathered in the Court room, Court corridors

---

480. For details on imprisonment and charges see Press Circular, 15 February 1916.
481. Margaret Anderson, *The Little Review Anthology* (New York: Hermitage House, 1953).

and around the building. It was a great demonstration." But what she felt most proud of was how in her defense she was "able to bring out the social and economic side of the movement as was never done in a NY Court"—something she was sure could never have been done by a lawyer. Fourteen days in jail seemed a small price to pay, and she mused that perhaps it was given just "to save the face of the Prosecution." Her next public event would be a grand celebration of her release at Carnegie Hall. Years of political savvy had taught her the value of "forging the fire while it's hot" (see Letter to W. S. Van Valkenburgh, 23 April 1916).

Reports reached her about rallies and petitions circulated on her behalf, including one petition by forty women of San Francisco who pledged to distribute contraceptive information in defiance of the law. Small victories like these reinforced Goldman's sense that her stay at New York City's Queens County Jail, as well as the eventual sentencing of Ben Reitman who was next in line for a trial on similar charges,[482] had done the movement for the advancement of birth control in the United States more good than she ever imagined, as "even conservative women came to the fore" (see Letter to Sara Bard Field, 28 April 1916).

She responded to the hundreds who had written to her in jail with a circular published in *Mother Earth* after her release. It spoke of how her imprisonment reached "thousands of men and women to whom Birth Control information has become a necessity and who are with us in our fight to break down the conspiracy of silence." It also conveyed the importance of keeping in "touch with the social victims, whom society first drives into crime and then hides behind closed bars in order to appease its conscience." Giving example after example, Goldman shared stories of people she met behind bars, stories that underscored the direct relationship between poverty and crime. She believed that their plight, both in and out of jail, the weakening of body and mind, accounted for recidivism, especially of drug-addicted prisoners who were "undernourished and indifferently left to fight out the mad craving which they have neither the strength nor vitality to overcome. When their time is up . . . their will, never too strong, is completely broken. They cannot sustain their existence unless they have some stimulant, so they go back to their habit."

Goldman was sure that the authorities—the police, the courts, the district attorneys—"thrive upon those whom poverty and ignorance drive into crime . . . and then hypocritically pretend they are saving the system from the criminal." To make matters worse, because work and opportunity were generally unavailable to prisoners upon release, they had no incentive to serve the society that excluded them: "[T]heir prison experience . . . make[s] them hate society more." But for "criminals like myself, . . . [it]

---

482. BR wrote a detailed description of his equally rambunctious trial and the conditions of his imprisonment; see "Following the Monkey" (unpublished autobiography), IU-U (also in Emma Goldman Papers, Third Party Reminiscences File).

intensified my devotion to our cause." Boasting of the thousands who clamored for birth control information at her last meeting in Union Square on 20 May, she determined to take her message on the road out west and return to "continue until a free motherhood and a glorious childhood will be established" (see "To My Friends, Old and New," Letter in *Mother Earth,* June 1916). Her eloquence and compassion made her that much more appealing to female audiences who otherwise might have distanced themselves from the challenge posed by her political beliefs.

## BUILDING SUPPORT FOR BIRTH CONTROL

Thrown off schedule, with more to do than she anticipated, she continued her lecture tours, and she kept up her correspondence. In a letter from the road, a response to a letter from her friend Helen Keller about the direct action protests that had taken place since her birth control arrest, she shared her enthusiasm about the many society women who had "distributed over 20,000 birth control circulars" at the recent Union Square demonstration. Keller mused about the perceived danger to those who engage in "direct action against frightfulness of the industrial conflict." Goldman, who had been labeled the most dangerous woman in America,[483] concurred, stating that "if the time should come when I am no longer considered by the authorities 'dangerous,' I hope my friends will disown me." She went even a step further: "I hope I shall never live to see Anarchism become thoroughly respectable, for then I shall have to look for a new ideal"[484] (see Letter to Helen Keller, 4 June 1916).

Goldman's lectures on "Free or Enforced Motherhood—the Necessity for Birth Control," attracted steady crowds by the hundreds and gave her an opportunity to raise support for those facing charges for distributing birth control literature. A letter to the district attorney of New York sent from "the men and women of Los Angeles" in response to Goldman's lecture there encouraged national protest in defense of two of the New York birth control detainees who "bravely stand the brunt in behalf of a healthier and better race." The letter proved successful as a public pressure tactic for the dismissal of legal charges (see Letter to Anna Strunsky Walling, 8 July 1916).

## REACHING ACROSS THE BORDER:
## EXTENDING HER HAND TO THE REVOLUTION IN MEXICO

Understanding the importance of outside support, Goldman tried to rescue the Mexican revolutionaries Enrique and Ricardo Flores Magón, who had been "languishing in that

---

483. For example, the headline upon Goldman's arrival in Beloit, Wisconsin, "Most Dangerous Woman in America," *Beloit Daily Free Press,* 31 January 1910, could be seen as a sensationalist tactic for selling newspapers.

484. As she left town that June, the anti-militarism campaign had already begun, but although she "could not stay long enough to take charge of it," she hoped Keller would join its ranks. In fact, Keller did share EG's ideas on suffrage, birth control, and anti-conscription, but not on anarchism itself. Later, in the early 1920s, she changed her focus to deaf and blind rights.

rotten [Los Angeles] County jail since March." They had been charged with writing articles on the insurrection in Mexico for the magazine *Regeneración* and distributing copies of the magazine through the U.S. mails; this was considered a periodical "tending to incite murder, arson, and treason." She worked hard to raise bail to prevent them from being "shipped to San Quentin to rot for a year or eighteen months, while the appeal was pending." Between her lectures in Los Angeles and the local *Mother Earth* subscribers of considerable means, her efforts on behalf of the Magóns were successful. After the funds for their release had been secured, a banquet imbued with a "marvelous spirit of comradeship and solidarity" was held in her honor. Revealing the prejudices of the times, Goldman characterized the Mexican revolutionaries as a "primitive people," with "a real appreciation of comradeship. No wonder the Mexicans have been able to hold out so long in their struggle for Land and Liberty" (see Letter to W. S. Van Valkenburgh, 17 July 1916).

She shared her thoughts with her friend Van Valkenburgh, including reflections on how strange it felt to be without Ben on her 1916 Los Angeles tour; it had been two and a half months, the longest separation since they had first met in 1908. Ben's letters conveyed his depression, which she assumed to be a side effect of a long prison stay. She never imagined that he might have fallen in love in the interim.[485]

### PREPAREDNESS DAY BOMBING

Goldman headed for San Francisco, a notoriously militant labor stronghold that had long been the center of bitter battles between workers and bosses, each side asserting its right to a closed or open shop. Just days after her arrival, the city was thrust into a panic. A Preparedness Day parade attracted throngs of marchers down Steuart Street off of Market Street. Without warning, a bomb exploded. Ten people were killed, and several others injured. High on the list of suspects were the city's prominent antiwar radicals and trade unionists, among them Alexander Berkman and Fitzi (M. Eleanor Fitzgerald), whose San Francisco magazine, *The Blast*, was a militant voice opposing war and its propelling force—industrial capitalism. The timing of Emma's visit triggered suspicion. Local residents, shaken to their very core, for the most part stayed away from political gatherings. She described her meetings as "poorly attended, and the audience terrorized to such an extent that I failed to lift them out of it except for rare occasions." She left California, desperate for a reprieve from the immediate hysteria and fallout from the bombing. The backlash aroused by the event seemed reminiscent of the aftermath of the Haymarket bombing, when suspects were tried and hanged; she resolved that those accused of setting off the Preparedness Day bomb would not share the same fate.

To address misconceptions about anarchism's relation to violence, Goldman and Berkman, along with the *The Blast* group, Group Freedom, Italian anarchist group

---

485. See *LA&EG*, p. 200 (pbk., p. 120).

Volonta, and the Union of Russian Workers, wrote a joint essay in *The Blast*. Countering those who chanted "down with the anarchists" when any act of violence took place, they argued that anarchists as well as labor unionists in fact defended the rights of workers and opposed "crime, poverty, and corruption in the world." To change such conditions anarchists "would do away with capitalism and introduce free and equal distribution. . . . It would be a society of real freedom, without coercion or violence, based on the voluntary communal arrangement, and in the spirit of Kropotkin: 'To each according to his needs; from each according to his ability.'" They asserted that "Anarchism means OPPOSITION to violence, by whomever committed, even if it be by the government." They pointed the finger of blame on the "millionaire . . . [who] builds a factory and robs his workers in a way that is much safer, more profitable and within the law." Insisting that only "the desperate man . . . to whom no other resort seems open [commits] violence." They defended those who commit violence for social reasons as "the last desperate struggle of outraged and exasperated human nature for breathing space and life."

Although historically such acts had been committed by anarchists, the group insisted that there were always individuals in "the Republican Party or the Presbyterian or Methodist Church" who have done the same without ever holding all of the members responsible for the acts of individuals within those institutions. Yet "many thousands of rebel workers, of Socialists, of Industrialists and Syndicalists, but above all of Anarchists, have lost work and even the chance of work, solely on the ground of their opinions." Thus, to counter the lust for revenge unleashed by the Preparedness Day bomb, especially against anarchists, the group of signers pointedly summed up their position: "We hate murder with a hatred that may seem absurdly exaggerated to apologists for war, industrial slaughter and Ludlow massacres, to callous acquiescers in governmental and plutocratic violence. . . . The guilt of these homicides lies upon every man and woman who, intentionally or by cold indifference, helps to keep up social conditions that drive human beings to despair. The man who flings his whole life . . . often at the cost of his own life, to protest the wrongs of his fellow-men is a saint compared to the active and passive upholder of cruelty and injustice" (see "Down with the Anarchists!" Essay in *The Blast*, 15 August 1916).

Goldman took to the road intending to solicit funds for the legal defense of "the San Francisco comrades." She went up the coast to Portland and Seattle. After heading north, she went on to Denver in anticipation of delivering lectures that would include a Russian drama course. Focus on the drama would be a relief from her harrowing time in San Francisco and would probably reach people with the means to support the San Francisco suspects' legal battle. Berkman went to New York, mobilized trade union support, and found a talented lawyer to plead the Preparedness Day case.[486] After she returned to New York, Goldman dictated a letter to Ellen Kennan. Fitzi not only acted as the scribe,

---

486. See Richard Frost, *The Mooney Case* (Stanford, Cal.: Stanford University Press, 1968).

but also added her own comments about "trying to convert the Chief of Police and head detectives of the Bomb Bureau and District Attorneys. But it is useless. . . . They belong to the cave men type, with no ideas at all of modern ideas, and people who really stand for something." Thus, three women, Emma, Fitzi, and Ellen Kennan, told of their troubles and shared their love and support, with the good humor and warmth that bolstered their resolve (see Letter to Ellen A. Kennan, 8 August 1916).

## ARRESTED AGAIN

Instead of finding calm upon her return to New York in October, Goldman found herself involved again with the New York City police over the issue of whether she had distributed birth control leaflets at the 20 May Union Square meeting before her tour out west.[487] Just as she was appearing as a subpoenaed witness in the defense of Bolton Hall, whose charges were then summarily dropped, Goldman was arrested on the street and charged with the same crime. Because she never hesitated to plead guilty and to accept the consequences of an act in which she had participated, Goldman was especially irate at the manner in which she was accosted by the police. She wrote to the editors of the *New York Herald* to alert them to "the unscrupulous methods of detectives who inconvenience, hound, persecute and arrest people without any redress whatever for those who have to suffer at the hands of the representatives of the law. . . . [W]hile the unfortunate victims are not able to expose the police methods, I am and I am of course, determined to do so" (see Letter to the *New York Evening Telegram*, 26 October 1916).

## "HELL BROKE LOOSE": LABOR VIOLENCE IN EVERETT

Shortly after her encounter with the police in New York, Goldman received an urgent letter from Minnie Parkhurst Rimer, the woman who had organized Goldman's meetings in Seattle just a few months before. Rimer wrote that "Hell broke loose in this part of the country yesterday." A shingle weavers' strike in Everett, Washington, attracted the support of a boatload of IWW members at the end of October. Those in the boat were met by vigilantes, who beat them. A meeting was called on 5 November to protest the violence of the vigilantes. When the next, larger boat arrived, gunshots erupted. Five young IWW men died, 48 were hospitalized, 20 of them critically injured, and 297 were jailed. A lumber manager and 2 officers were killed, further heightening the tension. Goldman shared her thoughts with her friend Agnes Inglis: "[With] all the mistakes the IWW are making, that movement has produced the finest and most heroic type of young American rebels,—in fact, I know of no one else who has made such an heroic fight for free speech as the boys belonging to the IWW."[488]

Goldman, with Reitman's help, began raising funds for those facing trial in the wake

487. Emma Goldman, "Emma Goldman's Defense."
488. EG to Agnes Inglis, 16 November 1916, *EGP*, reel 10.

of this bloody massacre. They decided to reprint Minnie Rimer's firsthand account in the December 1916 issue of *Mother Earth*, hoping that their readers would respond by spreading the word and contributing to the cause. Everett was harsh proof that the age of "progressive reform" had a violent side, painfully evident in each "battle field of the social war" (see "From the Battle Field of the Social War," Letter from Minnie Parkhurst Rimer, 6 November 1916).

In the same issue of *Mother Earth* that Goldman alerted her readers to the violence in Washington State against the IWW, she also reported on her own recent joust with the law. A New York judge denied her motion for a jury trial for her birth control arrest. She organized a mass letter-writing campaign to the district attorney against "the persecution and prosecution of one whose offense consists of standing for a worldwide movement" and included, as always, a solicitation for funds, especially for the trials and the necessary publicity accompanying them. She assured her readers that the birth control fight, like the protest in response to the violence against the IWW, was "worth making an effort, for the truth must prevail in the end."

## ON THE ROAD IN OMINOUS TIMES

Goldman was busy planning her upcoming 1917 tour incorporating topical issues from her previous lectures. Her lecture bill, which was published in *Mother Earth*, included "Anarchism and Human Nature: Do They Harmonize?" adding her voice to current debates about human nature, whether its determinants are innate or socially constructed, as in "The Education and Sexual Dwarfing of the Child."[489] She offered an alternative to the prevailing formality and restrictiveness of rote learning ("Obedience, A Social Vice") and repressive attitudes toward education about reproduction ("Celibacy or Sex Expression").[490] She shared her intentions with Agnes Ingles to speak about Russian drama as well as offer a series of lectures "tracing the ideal of Anarchism in the American classic period," among other topics.

On the surface it appeared that Goldman was continuing her political work as usual. But the mood in the country was ominously dark, and the intensity of repression against the IWW and other labor militants was fierce and spreading. The tactics had shifted from free speech rights to labor demands waged with militancy, thus drawing the ire of the authorities. Goldman confided in a letter to her friend Agnes that she fully expected to be arrested;[491] she knew that many of her European anarchist friends and correspondents, like Pierre Ramus and Guy Aldred, who had protested the war were now in prison.

489. EG gave several lectures on "Anarchism and Human Nature," a series in synchrony with concurrent discussions of social organization and human nature. See Chronology.

490. For specifics on lectures and debates on sex education, and other writings addressing this issue, see Chronology.

491. EG to Agnes Inglis, 16 November 1916, *EGP*, reel 10.

Even so, she had not fully comprehended how the war would permanently change life as she knew it in America.

## 4. A LONG VIEW: LIGHT DEFINING SHADOWS

Despite periodic jailing and police disruptions of her speeches, Emma Goldman enjoyed far greater freedom of expression from 1910–1916 than she would during the war years when Woodrow Wilson's crusade to make the world safe for democracy all but killed dissident expression in the United States. In these last peacetime years of the Progressive era, Goldman spread her ideas—as a lecturer, writer, theorist, public intellectual, and provocateur of universal freedom—in, and beyond, the United States. This volume is a representation of Emma Goldman from age forty-one to forty-seven, in her radical heyday and at the height of her powers as a famed (and infamous) revolutionary.

Though not swayed by her anarchism, many mainstream civil libertarians and radical intellectuals read and admired her passionate indictments of capitalism's injustices. Her writings fed a growing awareness and fear of the consequences of the widening class divide in industrial America.

Goldman's fiery speeches were intended to ignite fury about injustice and to incite the public either to take action or to empathize with those who did. Violence between labor and capital blazed across the country, with frequent fatalities on both sides. Unprecedented wealth accentuated dire poverty. Incremental reform continued to be a double-edged sword—both alleviating squalid conditions and suppressing the impetus for revolution.[492] Goldman's liberating vision of a world free from constraints and bound by mutual aid stood in stark contrast to the forced order of containment and control. Whether her vision was practical or realizable was less important than the optimism it instilled in her audiences, hope grounded in her abiding faith in the people.

Goldman stirred her listeners and readers, cut through external barriers, and appealed to core values born of justice, of shared humanity, and of the desire for freedom. While such expansiveness was integral to her understanding of anarchism, it went beyond categorical confines. When she expounded upon her "beautiful vision," few could deny its allure—whether or not they believed it to be attainable. The beauty she espoused stood in stark contrast to the ugliness of the way things were— the endemic hunger of the body and the spirit that Goldman so eloquently described. The more specific the critique to her audiences' experiences, the more engaged they became in her web of words and ideas. And yet always, it was the pathos, the longing for an elusive

---

492. Although the eight-hour day and wage reforms were enormous improvements, demands to alter the relations to power and cooperative control were rarely met.

harmony—internal and external—that touched the hearts and minds of her audiences, that allowed her to reach seekers regardless of class, gender, race, or country of origin.

In so doing, Goldman, too, was challenged to overcome her own judgmental divides. The same woman who mocked the pretenses of the middle class, the excesses of the rich, the passivity of the poor, the conformity of the many had to override her abstract disdain in addressing disparate audiences. To make a genuine connection, she appealed to the best in each individual—an attitude that often also rekindled what was best in them. No matter how scathing her critique, Goldman's lectures were uplifting, in part, due to the empowering trust she restored in those who otherwise felt powerless—even to dream.

This feeling of mutuality, of shared meaning—if only for a moment in time—was an intoxicating blend, not only for the audience, but for Goldman as well.

Many experienced her evening lecture as entertainment, a chance of a lifetime to hear the voice of a virtuoso of oppositional politics. For some, however, just the act of attending an Emma Goldman talk was a sign of their willingness to take risks, to enter into an experience that was living theater. An Emma Goldman event—whether she was poking holes in conventional ideas, hurling back insults, or taunting the police—was sure to be as exciting as it was unpredictable.

By 1910 Goldman was already a seasoned propagandist, a woman who knew her constituency, where she could make headway, and where she dare not tread. As an anarchist who was a Russian Jewish immigrant woman, she counted among her many quiet victories the welcome she received from American-born women and men to speak at their local drama clubs about the significance of European and Russian modern drama. She used it as an opportunity to build awareness of the relationship between internal and external freedom once again.

This third volume of *Emma Goldman: A Documentary History of the American Years* opens with Goldman's critique of the 1910 drive to halt white slave traffic, a public concern intended to protect poor women forced into the sex trade. Goldman's steadfast belief in a woman's right to control her own body was proven yet again by her willingness to go to jail in 1916 for the distribution of birth control information. Goldman's defense of prostitutes (though certainly not of the abduction of women for sexual hire) and of sexual expression outside of marriage and outside of gender norms were part of a wave of openness, as well as recurrent countervailing efforts to suppress sexual freedom.

Hers was a time when many women fought hard to win the right to vote,[493] and some even believed that vice would vanish under the influence of women's purity. Goldman challenged these claims arguing that women, as easily as men, could be co-opted by a

---

493. The National American Women's Suffrage Association had a hearing before Congress every year from 1869 to 1919. See Stanton-Anthony Selected Papers for background. See also Ellen C. Dubois, *Feminism and Suffrage: The Emergence of an Independent Women's Movement in America, 1848–1869* (Ithaca, N.Y.: Cornell University Press, 1978, 1999); *Women's Suffrage: A Survey, 1908–1912* (National Union of Women's Suffrage Societies, Manchester District).

government intertwined with the interests of a capitalist economy. While Goldman recognized the importance of equality, she believed that women's enslavement to the social and political conditions that kept them down could never be solved at a polling booth. In talk after talk, she addressed these aspects of women's freedom and independence— core values she strove to embody.

She spoke of anarchism not only as an abstract social and political philosophy, but also as a living force, linking her critique of society to key issues of the day.[494] For many, revolutionary transformation seemed within reach; though, for some, the fear of change felt equally palpable. Goldman wrestled with these contradictory hopes and fears by piecing together her Russian revolutionary past with the American tradition epitomized by Whitman's "Song of the Open Road." She adopted as her own what she believed to be the enduring egalitarian credo of the Declaration of Independence: freedom and justice for all.

Emma Goldman—the eloquent revolutionary, preacher, outlaw, gadfly, satirist, diviner of truths and consequences—voiced both hope and despair: hope for a total transformation of society, despair that nothing less could avert inevitable disaster in a system driven by greed and dependent on injustice. Both her warnings and her counsel rang true to those who risked looking at the world through her lens.

She relied on Ben Reitman, her tour manager (and lover), for careful planning, appropriate publicity, and well-placed lecture announcements as well as locating lecture halls and housing for "the guest speaker." Goldman's success during these years can be attributed in part to Reitman's talent as an organizer and all-around publicist. The two were a remarkably effective team. And yet, even as she braved inconsistent local laws in various cities on her tours, she chose not to expose herself to the uncertainty of communities that didn't already have a stronghold of anarchist enthusiasts. More strikingly, she never attempted to speak in the racist South to challenge lynching and the injustices of racism; paralyzed by fear, it was a decision she would later regret.

### RINGS OF FIRE

For many radicals living between 1910 and 1916 who were acutely aware of the intolerable conditions, the need for and possibility of revolution became paramount.[495] Puritanical crusaders against change found themselves surrounded by those who basked in a newfound freedom from constraint. Big cities were bustling. Massive numbers of women entered the industrial work force. New choices ignited new desires—extending beyond class, ethnic, racial, and gender barriers. The fight was on. Although anarchism did not have the influence of the growing socialist movement of the time,[496] nor did anarchism

---

494. See Chronology for array of EG lecture topics.
495. See, for example, the rhetoric of *The Blast*.
496. For example, Eugene V. Debs ran for president as a candidate of the Socialist Party ticket in 1900, 1904, 1908, 1912—and in 1920, behind bars, he received 3.4 percent of the votes. See also

have the organized strength of the union movements, it did have Emma Goldman—a woman who could shake her audiences out of complacency with resounding force. Although not at the center of all these concentric circles, she was among the very few who could bridge the spaces between them.

The war industry grew in size and influence between 1915 and 1916 as the United States became a source of arms for the European conflict. Moreover, the nation strengthened its own military—with training and supplies—to provide security should there be an attack. Labor unrest and strikes became increasingly more threatening to those in government and industrial sectors.[497] Acts of industrial sabotage, most often enacted by the Industrial Workers of the World, elicited coordinated bloody attacks on each side. Regardless of the impact upon low-wage workers, the government protected industrial production for war. Upon entry into the war, the government suppressed dissident antiwar ideas, regardless of its impact on civil liberties.

In Europe, the years of war were harsh on those who dared to express their dissent. Waves of anarchists, socialists, pacifists, and antiwar activists fled to the United States to escape their governments' acts of retribution. Many of those who could not leave were condemned to years in prison for their opposition to the war.[498]

Goldman made full use of her relative freedom of expression in those few years leading up to and just after the United States' entry into the First World War. Her speeches and writings on birth control, women's independence, anarchism, free speech, political violence, the hypocrisy of Puritanism, and drama, were among the most memorable of her American years.

Goldman, who had attempted to integrate elements of the European revolutionary political culture into the United States, would soon be swept away by transcontinental winds of repression. Her allies in middle-class America, including many civil libertarians, would retreat in fear. Worse yet, the force of unwavering unity across a broad

---

James Darsey, "Eugene Debs and American Class," in *A Rhetorical History of the United States*, vol. 6, *Rhetoric and Reform in the Progressive Era*, ed. J. Michael Hogan (Lansing: Michigan State University Press, 2003), p. 234, among many other fine works on Debs's impact and milieu. Howard Zinn, *A Power Governments Cannot Suppress* (San Francisco: City Lights Books, 2007), p. 234. Howard Zinn characterized the era of Debs as the first seventeen years of the twentieth century: "As economic stratification increased, the rhetoric of class struggle grew louder in American society [especially in the years before 1912]. Eugene V. Debs (1855–1926) lent a powerful voice to this fray [in a period] characterized by strikes, walkouts, and fiery rhetoric from members of the working class alienated and neglected by the booming capitalist society that belittled and crushed them. The socialist movement was extremely visible and popular throughout the country."

497. The American Federation of Labor stood strong against a Westinghouse military plant, even welcoming Goldman to the site of the strike.

498. Among Goldman's anarchist comrades imprisoned in these clampdowns on civil liberties accompanying the war were Rudolph Grossman (Austria); Tom Keel, Guy Aldred, Lillian Wolfe (England); Luigi Bertoni (Italy); and Alfred Rosmer (France). Goldman met some of these comrades at the International Anarchist Congress in Amsterdam in 1907, and others were among her many correspondents.

cross-section of people bonded by their demands for the right of free expression and for social justice, would soon dissipate. The war years would test Goldman's personal and political resilience.

*Light and Shadows, 1910–1916* reveals a portrait of a woman, not without her shadows, but essentially in the light of her life.

CANDACE FALK

EMMA GOLDMAN PAPERS

UNIVERSITY OF CALIFORNIA, BERKELEY

Volume 3, *Light and Shadows, 1910–1916*, like volumes 1 and 2, of the documentary edition of *Emma Goldman: A Documentary History of the American Years*, is a collection of critical selections from the comprehensive microfilm edition published by the Emma Goldman Papers in 1991. The book edition contains a number of documents discovered after, and in some cases as a result of, the publication of the microfilm edition. Facsimiles of original documents, transcribed for this volume, will be included in a forthcoming addendum reel to the comprehensive edition.

The documents are arranged chronologically. Date of authorship (for example, of a letter reproduced in a newspaper) takes precedence over date of publication. Documents dated by month and year with no indication of day of origination appear chronologically at the beginning of the month. Documents dated only by year appear at the beginning of the designated year. With correspondence, a place of authorship is also provided, in brackets if it does not appear on the original but has been inferred from information within the document or from another reliable historical source. Goldman correspondence takes precedence over other documents with the same date. Documents fall into three general categories: correspondence to and from Goldman, published writings (including newspaper transcriptions of interviews and lectures), and government reports.

Goldman's lectures began with the aim of attracting interest in anarchist ideas and culture, building a readership for *Mother Earth*, and providing a financial ballast for the magazine. The lectures were a platform for raising issues such as free speech, labor strikes, and birth control, and they provided an opportunity to publicize and raise money for an amazing array of trials and centers of political agitation. Her correspondence with friends and supporters across America and Europe reflects the personal dimension of her political work, as well as illustrating the ways in which her work informed her personal relationships. Her emotional and sexual involvement with her road manager, Ben Reitman, led to frequent, sometimes daily, correspondence between them—thus leaving an unusual number of Goldman-Reitman letters from which to select. The letters reveal a complex woman: as friend, lover, and organizer, making arrangements for talks throughout America while attempting to reconcile the contradiction between her vision of freedom in love and sense of being "an abject slave" to her passion for Reitman. The sheer volume of her correspondence is a tribute to the reach of her friends and supporters, ever expanding; as her own support of other causes intensified on tour, the letters also provided her with a format for reflection on contemporary events and insight into the evolution of new directions of anarchist involvement she championed.

A substantial number of documents are drawn from Goldman's *Mother Earth*, which was among many "little magazines" that influenced and shaped American radical culture before the First World War. The selection of Goldman's articles displays her development as a writer; during this period she published two books and eight pamphlets on cultural, political, and literary themes. Her reports from the road offer a firsthand perspective on localized radical history and struggles for free speech in the cities and towns of America, against the backdrop of contemporary national and international battles against repression. Other documents, drawn from both the radical and mainstream press, document Goldman's evolution in the public eye from an object of curiosity to a serious and challenging intellectual force.

The government documents represent the point of view of the main antagonist to Goldman's political career: the state. Surveillance reports and intergovernmental memos offer firsthand documentation of the official campaign against Goldman and the anarchist movement, a rare documentation of the interplay between those who strove for change and those who represented the power of the state to maintain law, order, and the status quo.

## TRANSCRIPTIONS

Goldman's correspondence of this period dramatically reflects her intellectual and linguistic development. The editors chose to transcribe Goldman's handwritten correspondence in a literal form: all misspellings and grammatical errors are preserved. Words and characters struck out in the original, indicating an abandoned thought or construction, are transcribed when legible with a strike-out bar through them. Certain idiosyncrasies have been standardized. For example, Goldman sometimes used a thin space between the end of a word and a possessive *s* in lieu of an apostrophe; the editors have chosen to standardize the punctuation in favor of readability. Obvious typographical errors (she began to use a typewriter in 1911) have usually been corrected.

Readability, the convenience of the researcher, and a desire to prevent unnecessary confusion have also informed the transcription policy. Certain elements in Goldman's correspondence that are less likely to be of interest to the student or historian have therefore been standardized:

1. A place and dateline is always provided, centered at the top of each document immediately following the document title, no matter where or if one appears in the original. The date and place are provided in square brackets when they do not appear in the original document. A double space in the dateline signifies a line break in the original.

2. The salutation and the complimentary close of letters are always set off from the body of the document.
3. Paragraphs are always indented.
4. Spacing between words is made regular. A single space is used between sentences, except when a punctuation mark is missing from the original. Empty lines between paragraphs have been closed.
5. In typewritten documents false starts at the end of a line have not been reproduced, and accidental keystrokes that have been typed over are not preserved in the transcription.
6. Interlineations and superscripts are brought down to the line.
7. Long dashes at the end of a line or paragraph have been rendered with an ordinary em dash.
8. Hyphens at the end of a line are not preserved unless they are normally part of the word.
9. The editors silently standardized the names of newspapers, books, articles, and abbreviations of organizations, and italicized titles of newspapers, books, and pamphlets, to facilitate accessibility to a general audience, while scholars can refer to the original version in the microfilm edition should they need more precise variants of the titles in context. Thus, for example, the vagaries of composition that would render Goldman's abbreviation of the newspaper *Arbeiter-Zeitung,* variously as "A.Z.," "Arb Z," "AZ.," A Z," have been standardized as *AZ,* with italics added to help clarify at a glance that this is a periodical, rather than a person or an organization. Similarly, various renderings of the acronym for the American Federation of Labor have been standardized as AFL.

In printed and third-party texts the editors have employed a less literal transcription policy. Obvious typos are silently corrected, as are misspellings. When of potential significance, a note with the misspelling of the original is attached at the first instance in a given document. Older or otherwise legitimate alternate spellings are preserved, however. Drop capitals are not preserved. Pagination marks are deleted.

## ANNOTATIONS

An unnumbered note immediately following each document provides information about the institutional location and the physical condition of the original. Information about excised portions of the original, alternate versions of the document, or accompanying matter such as photographs, illustrations, or printed stationery information is also noted here.

Footnotes elucidate particulars that appear or are alluded to in the body of a document, as well as offer the reader important historical background and context necessary to understanding the document.

Annotation is meant to provide the reader with the information necessary to adequately evaluate a document or a series of documents. This includes the clarification of names, dates, and events; cross-references to documents mentioned or cited in a given text; and alerts to vagaries in the original not reproducible in the transcription. When possible, notes may also provide missing voices in a particular discussion or debate, refer the reader to other sources in the microfilm and elsewhere that are directly related to a particular document, or add human color and texture of that time to the document. This editorial task has been done as thoroughly and consistently as possible, but the reader should be aware that both space considerations and the vast amount of relevant material within the microfilm edition have rendered complete citation in all documents impossible.

## APPENDIXES

The volume has a series of appendixes meant to guide the reader through Goldman's cultural, political, and social milieu. The biographical directory lists individuals who, in some way, influenced Goldman's life in a way that would justify a more extensive biographical entry than would be possible in a footnote. Biographical entries are meant to briefly summarize the individual's life, political activities, publications if any, and relationship to Goldman. The periodical directory offers the reader a selective bibliography of radical periodicals, chronicling the cultural and radical magazines and newspapers that either included or featured Goldman's work. An organizational directory contains information about the political and radical organizations that were formed throughout the period of this volume, connected and supporting, in various ways, Goldman's work and political vision.

Another appendix lists Goldman's own publications, as well as those by other authors published by Mother Earth Publishing Association, suggesting the importance of Goldman and *Mother Earth* as a source of English-language anarchist propaganda during this period. The Fund Appeals in *Mother Earth* in the appendix lists the funds and appeals published in *Mother Earth* between 1910 and 1916 and illustrates the central role of Goldman and *Mother Earth* in generating critical financial support. The funds and appeals offer a glimpse of both the methods and scope of political and social activity during this period.

## THE CHRONOLOGY

The Chronology presents both Goldman's activities and select cultural and political events, gathered from a variety of sources, including letters to and from Goldman, itineraries published in *Mother Earth,* contemporary newspaper accounts and leaflets, and memoirs of Goldman's friends and associates.

It remains a working document. Goldman's itineraries often were not realized; mistakes on dates, topics, and places were not uncommon, and some newspapers either grossly misrepresented or simply did not publicize her events, which made editorial corroboration of her public appearances exceptionally difficult. The chronology does reflect the incredible energy and vast territory of her travel and speaking engagements as well as the variety and scope of her lectures and political activities.

**DOCUMENT DESCRIPTIONS**

FORM

    A autograph

    P printed

    T typed

TYPE

    L letter

    D document (trial transcript, printed leaflet, etc.)

    Pc postal card

    W wire or telegram

SEAL

    S signed

    f fragment

    I initialed

    Sr signed with signature representation

    U unsigned

EXAMPLES OF DOCUMENT DESCRIPTIONS

| | |
|---|---|
| ALS | autograph letter signed |
| APcI | autograph postcard initialed |
| PLSr | printed letter with signature representation |
| TDS | typed document signed |
| TDSr | typed document with signature representation |
| TLf | typed letter fragment |
| TLI | typed letter initialed |
| TLS | typed letter signed |
| TLSr | typed letter with signature representation |
| TLU | typed letter unsigned |
| TWSr | typed wire with signature representation |

## REPOSITORIES, ARCHIVES, AND INSTITUTIONS

| | |
|---|---|
| AFB | American Federation for the Blind |
| CLU | University of California, Los Angeles, Department of Special Collections |
| CSmH | Huntington Library, San Marino, Calif. |
| CtY-B | Beinecke Rare Book and Manuscript Library, Yale University, New Haven, Conn. |
| CtY-S | Sterling Memorial Library, Yale University, New Haven, Conn. |
| CU-B | Bancroft Library, University of California, Berkeley |
| DLC | Library of Congress, Washington, D.C. |
| DNA | National Archives, Washington, D.C. |
| GA RF | Gosudarstvennyi arkhiv Rossiiskoi Federatsii (State Archive of the Russian Federation [formerly TsGAOR, Central State Archive of the October Revolution]), Moscow |
| ICarbS | Morris Library, Southern Illinois University, Carbondale |
| IISH | International Institute of Social History, Amsterdam |
| IU-U | University of Illinois, Chicago |
| MBU | Boston University, Boston |
| MCR | Schlesinger Library, Radcliffe College, Cambridge, Mass. |
| MH-H | Houghton Library, Harvard University, Cambridge, Mass. |
| MiU | Labadie Collection, Department of Rare Books and Special Collections, University of Michigan Library, Ann Arbor |
| NjP | Mudd Manuscript Library, Princeton University, Princeton, N.J. |
| NNC | Butler Library, Columbia University, New York |
| NNU | Tamiment Institute Library, New York University, New York |
| NYPL | Rare Books and Manuscripts Division, New York Public Library |
| WHi | Wisconsin Historical Society, Madison, Wisconsin |

## OTHER ABBREVIATIONS

| | |
|---|---|
| AB | Alexander Berkman |
| EG | Emma Goldman |
| IWW | Industrial Workers of the World |
| *ME* | *Mother Earth* |
| BR | Ben Reitman |
| *EGP*, reel # | Candace Falk et al., eds., *The Emma Goldman Papers: A Microfilm Edition* (Alexandria, Va.: Chadwyck-Healey Inc., 1991), reel #. |
| *LA&EG* | Candace Falk. *Love, Anarchy and Emma Goldman.* Rev. ed. New Brunswick, N.J.: Rutgers University Press, 1990, 1999. |
| *LML* | Emma Goldman. *Living My Life.* 1931. Reprint, New York: Da Capo Press, 1970. |

Essay in *MOTHER EARTH*

New York, January 1910

# The White Slave Traffic

Our reformers have suddenly made a great discovery: the white slave traffic. The papers are full of these "unheard of conditions" in our midst, and the lawmakers are already planning a new set of laws to check the horror.[1]

How is it that an institution, known almost to every child, should have been discovered so suddenly? How is it that this evil, known to all sociologists, should now be made such an important issue?

It is significant that whenever the public mind is to be diverted from a great social wrong, a crusade is inaugurated against indecency, gambling, saloons, etc. And what is the result of such crusades? Gambling is increasing, saloons are doing a lively business through back entrances, prostitution is at its height, and the system of pimps and cadets is but aggravated.[2]

To assume that the recent investigation of the white slave traffic by George Kibbe Turner[3] and others (and by the way, a very superficial investigation), has discovered anything new is, to say the least, very foolish. Prostitution was and is a widespread evil, yet mankind goes on its business, perfectly indifferent to the sufferings and distress of the victims of prostitution. As indifferent, indeed, as mankind has so far remained to our industrial system, or to economic prostitution.

Only when human sorrows are turned into a toy with glaring colors will baby people become interested,—for a while at least. The people are a very fickle baby that must have

---

1. The term "white slavery" was coined by writer and journalist George Kibbe Turner (1869–1952) in an article, "The City of Chicago: A Study of the Great Immoralities" (*McClure's Magazine*, April 1907). The article asserted that Chicago brothels were supplied with prostitutes by an organization composed largely of Russian Jews—a claim that fueled already staunch anti-immigrant and anti-Semitic sentiments in the United States. Turner also wrote the exposé on prostitution "Daughters of the Poor" (*McClure's Magazine*, November 1909).

2. The term "cadet," used by champions of the anti-prostitution cause during this period, denoted a pimp. As with the prostitutes involved with the "white slave traffic," the cadets were often depicted as Eastern-European Jews or, in some cases, African Americans ("dark cadets").

3. George Kibbe Turner's article "Daughters of the Poor" (*McClure's Magazine*, November 1909), an exposé of prostitution and the apparent high volume of "white slave" traffic, spurred nationwide vice investigations. Chicago congressman James R. Mann, chairman of the House Committee on Interstate and Foreign Commerce, proposed federal legislation, based on the Constitution's interstate commerce clause, to end white slavery. The White Slave Traffic Act (Mann Act), signed into law in 1910, allowed federal prosecution of those accused of using violence or intimidation to force women into prostitution.

new toys every day. The "righteous" cry against the white slave traffic is such a toy. It serves to amuse the people for a little while, and it will help to create a few more fat political jobs—parasites who stalk about the world as inspectors, investigators, detectives, etc.

What really is the cause of the trade in women? Not merely white women, but yellow and black women as well. Exploitation, of course: the merciless Moloch of capitalism that fattens on underpaid labor, thus driving thousands of women and girls into prostitution. With Mrs. Warren[4] these girls feel, "Why waste your life working for a few shillings a week in a scullery, eighteen hours a day?"

Naturally, our reformers say nothing about this cause. George Kibbe Turner and all other scribbles know the cause well enough, but it doesn't pay to say anything about it. It is so much more profitable to play the Pharisee, to pretend an outraged morality, than to go to the bottom of things. Yet no less an authority than Dr. Sanger, the author of "The History of Prostitution,"[5] although not a radical, has this to say:

"A prolific cause of female depravity can be found in the several tables, showing the description of the employment pursued and the wages received by the women previous to their fall, and it will be a question for the political economist to decide how far mere business consideration should be an apology on the part of employers for a reduction in their rates of remuneration, and whether the savings of a small percentage on wages is not more than counterbalanced by the enormous amount of taxation enforced on the public at large to defray the expenses incurred on account of a system of vice, *which is the direct result in many cases of insufficient compensation of honest labor.*"

The economic reason given for prostitution in the above quotation can be found in all works of any consequence dealing with the question. Nor is it necessary to seek information in books; one has but to observe everyday life to realize that there are thousands of girls working for two or three dollars a week, withering away in factories and shops, while life passes by in all its joy and glory, leaving them behind. What else are they to do? However, our present-day reformers would do well to look into Dr. Sanger's book. There they will find that out of 2,000 cases under his observation, but few came from the middle classes, from well-ordered conditions, or pleasant homes. By far the largest majority were working girls and working women. Some driven into prostitution through sheer want, others because of a cruel, wretched life at home, others again because of thwarted and crippled physical natures (which I will speak of again later on). Also it will do the maintainers of purity and morality good to learn that out of 2,000 cases 490 were

---

4. An allusion to George Bernard Shaw's play *Mrs. Warren's Profession* (written 1893, first produced 1902), which challenged contemporary prejudice against prostitution. In *Social Significance of the Modern Drama* EG refers to the play as "the red rag to the social bull" (p. 186).
5. William W. Sanger, *The History of Prostitution: Its Extent, Causes, and Effects Throughout the World* (New York: Harper & Brothers Publishers, 1859). Original note in EG's text read: "It is a significant fact that Dr. Sanger's book has been excluded from the U.S. mails. Evidently the authorities are not anxious that the public be informed as to the true cause of prostitution."

married women, women who lived with their husbands.[6] Evidently there was not much of a guarantee for their safety and purity in the sanctity of marriage.

The very last to cry out against prostitution is our "respectable" class, since it was that class that ushered in prostitution, from Moses to Trinity Church.[7] Dr. H. Ploss,[8] Dr. Alfred Blaschko,[9] Dr. W. W. Sanger, and other eminent writers on this subject convincingly prove that prostitution originated with the so-called upper classes. I quote Dr. Sanger:

"Our most ancient and historical records are believed to be the books of Moses; according to them it must be admitted that prostitutes were common among the Jews, many centuries before Christ. Moses appears to have connived at the intercourse of Jewish young men with foreign prostitutes. He took an Ethiopian woman himself. Assyrian women, Moabites, Midianites, and other neighbors of the Jews established themselves as prostitutes in the land of Israel. Jephtha, the son of a prostitute, became none the less Chief of Israel." Moses evidently believed that therein lay the greatest safeguard for the daughters of his own people. We shall see presently that the Christians were not so considerate of their own daughters, since they did not employ foreigners for that purpose.

The history of the Christian Church will also serve as a history of prostitution, since the two always went hand in hand and furnished thereby great revenues for the Church.

Dr. Sanger cites the case of Pope Clement II., who issued a bull that all prostitutes were to pay a certain amount of their earnings, or that those living on prostitution were compelled to give half their income to the Church. Pope Sixtus IV. received 20,000 ducats from a single brothel, which, incidently, he himself had built. Nor is it unknown that a great many cloisters and nunneries were in reality nothing else than brothels.

In modern times the Church is a little more careful in that direction. At least, it does not openly demand tribute from prostitutes. It finds it much more profitable to go in for real estate, like Trinity Church, for instance, to rent out death traps at an exorbitant price to those who live off and on prostitution.

---

6. In his book Dr. Sanger reports that of the 2,000 prostitutes he surveyed, 490 were married, although only 71 still lived with their partners.
7. New York City's Trinity Parish was heavily criticized by the New York press following allegations in 1895, and again in 1909, that Trinity's properties were unsanitary and a "threat to health and morals," an implied recognition that some properties were used for prostitution. A special committee appointed by the senate of the State of New York, and later Trinity's own special committee of the vestry, found that several of Trinity Corporation's tenements failed to meet health standards set by city ordinances.
8. Hermann Heinrich Ploss (1819–1885) was a German medical doctor and anthropologist whose most influential work was *Das Weib in der Natur- und Völkerkunde* (Leipzig: Th. Grieben, 1885), an ethnographic study of female anatomy, sexuality, and behavior.
9. Alfred Blaschko (1858–1922) was a German physician and author whose published works addressed health issues relating to prostitution. He helped establish the first German Society for the Fight Against Venereal Diseases, in Berlin (1902). His works include *Hygiene der Prostitution und der venerischen Krankheiten* (Jena: Fischer, 1893–1901), *Syphilis und Prostitution von Stendpunkte der Oeffentlichen, Gesundheitspflege* (Berlin: S. Karger, 1893), and *Die Prostitution im 19. Jahrhundert* (Berlin: Verlag der Socialistischen Monatshefter, [1900?]).

**United States Post Office**

NEW YORK, NEW YORK

JAN 15 1910

Enc.                                   January 14, 1910.


Mr. W.S. Mayer,

    Post Office Inspector-in-Charge,

      New York, N.Y.

Sir:

      I enclose herewith a copy of the
January, 1910, issue of "Mother Earth," which is
regarded as unmailable under Section 497, P.L.& R.,
on account of the matter contained in the article
on pages 344 to 351 under the caption "The White
Slave Traffic."

      Eighty pounds of this issue mailed
January 13, have been withheld from despatch and
will be retained awaiting advice from you as to
the disposition to be made of the same.   Twenty
pounds were mailed on the 12th instant.

           Very respectfully,


           Postmaster.

M-f

Letter from postmaster to the U.S. Post Office Inspector-in-Charge. (U.S. National Archives, Record Group 28)

NEW YORK........Jan...25,..10......19....

Assistant Attorney General

Post Office Dpt.

Washington, D. C.

OFFICE OF
Asst. Attorney General,
RECEIVED
JAN 27 1910
POST OFFICE DEPARTMENT.

Dear Sir:

We have just found out that the January issue of
"Mother Earth" has been held up in the N.Y.Post Office.

We understand that the matter is in the hands of
Mr. Comstock, but so far we have not been able to ascertain
the cause for this action. Nor had we been notified by the
Post Office (or by any other official of the Dpt.) that
the magazine had been held up. Do not the regulations of
the Dpt. provide that the publisher be notified whenever
an issue is held up? Why has it not been done in this case?

We urgently request you to look into this matter,
and to notify us at once as to the reasons for the above
action; also kindly instruct the N.Y.Postmaster and Mr.
Comstock to submit to us, at once, the reasons of their
objections to the January issue of our magazine, that we
may know what action to take in the matter.

Requesting an immediate reply,

We are, very truly,

per  A. Berkman

E/B

Letter from Alexander Berkman, an editor of *Mother Earth,* to the Post Office Assistant Attorney General, requesting a written justification from Anthony Comstock for restricting mail access to the January 1910 issue of the
magazine. Shortly after receipt of this letter, the Post Office released its hold. (U.S. National Archives, Record
Group 28)

Much as I should like to, my space will not admit speaking of prostitution in Egypt, Greece, Rome, and during the Middle Ages. The conditions in the latter period are particularly interesting, inasmuch as prostitution was organized into guilds, presided over by a Brothel Queen. These guilds employed strikes as a medium of improving their condition and keeping a standard price. Certainly that is more practical a method than the one used by the modern wage slave in society.

Never, however, did prostitution reach its present depraved and criminal position, because at no time in past ages was prostitution persecuted and hounded as it is to-day, especially in Anglo-Saxon countries, where Phariseeism is at its height, where each one is busy hiding the skeletons in his own home by pointing to the sore of the other fellow.

But I must not lose sight of the present issue, the white slave traffic. I have already spoken of the economic cause, but I think a cause much deeper and by far of greater importance is the complete ignorance on sex matters. It is a conceded fact that woman has been reared as a sex commodity, and yet she is kept in absolute ignorance of the meaning and importance of sex. Everything dealing with that subject is suppressed, and people who attempt to bring light into this terrible darkness are persecuted and thrown into prison. Yet it is nevertheless true that so long as a girl is not to know how to take care of herself, not to know the function of the most important part of her life, we need not be surprised if she becomes an easy prey to prostitution or any other form of a relationship which degrades her to the position of an object for mere sex gratification.

It is due to this ignorance that the entire life and nature of the girl is thwarted and crippled. We have long ago taken it as a self-evident fact that the boy may follow the call of the wild, that is to say that the boy may, as soon as his sex nature asserts itself, satisfy that nature, but our moralists are scandalized at the very thought that the nature of a girl should assert itself. To the moralist prostitution does not consist so much in the fact that the woman sells her body, but rather that she sells it to many.

Having been looked upon as a mere sex-commodity, the woman's honor, decency, morality, and usefulness have become a part of her sex life. Thus society considers the sex experiences of a man as attributes of his general development, while similar experiences in the life of a woman are looked upon as a terrible calamity, a loss of honor and of all that is good and noble in a human being. This double standard of morality has played no little part in the creation and perpetuation of prostitution. It involves the keeping of the young in absolute ignorance on sex matters, which alleged "innocence," together with an overwrought and stifled sex nature, helps to bring about a state of affairs that our Puritans are so anxious to avoid or prevent. This state of affairs finds a masterly portrayal in Zola's "Fecundity."[10]

Girls, mere children, work in crowded, overheated rooms ten to twelve hours daily

10. Emile Zola, *Fecondite* (Paris: Charpentier, 1899). One of three finished pieces of the socialist work *Les Quatres Evangiles* (The Four Gospels).

at a machine, which tends to keep them in a constant over-excited sex state. Many of these girls haven't any home or comforts of any kind; therefore the street or some place of cheap amusement is the only means of forgetting their daily routine. This naturally brings them into close proximity with the other sex. It is hard to say which of the two factors brings the girl's over-sexed condition to a climax, but it certainly is the most natural thing that a climax should follow. That is the first step toward prostitution. Nor is the girl to be held responsible for it. On the contrary, it is altogether the fault of society, the fault of our lack of understanding, of lack of appreciation of life in the making; especially is it the criminal fault of our moralists, who condemn a girl for all eternity because she has gone from "the path of virtue"; that is, because her first sex experience has taken place without the sanction of the Church or State.

The girl finds herself a complete outcast, with the doors of home and society closed in her face. Her entire training and tradition are such that the girl herself feels depraved and fallen, and therefore has no ground to stand upon, or any hold that will lift her up, instead of throwing her down. Thus society creates the victims that it afterwards vainly attempts to get rid of.

Much stress is laid on white slaves being imported into America. How would America ever retain her virtue if she didn't have Europe to help her out? I will not deny that this may be the case in some instances, any more than I will deny that there are emissaries of Germany and other countries luring economic slaves into America, but I absolutely deny that prostitution is recruited, to any appreciable extent, from Europe. It may be true that the majority of prostitutes of New York City are foreigners, but that is only because the majority of the population is foreign. The moment we go to any other American city, to Chicago or the middle West, we shall find that the number of foreign prostitutes is by far a minority.

Equally exaggerated is the belief that the majority of street girls in this city were engaged in this business before they came to America. Most of the girls speak excellent English, they are Americanized in habits and appearance,—a thing absolutely impossible unless they have lived in this country many years. That is, they were driven into prostitution by American conditions, by the thoroughly American custom for excessive display of finery and clothes, which, of course, necessitates money, money that can not be earned in shops or factories. The equanimity of the moralists is not disturbed by the respectable woman gratifying her clothesophobia by marrying for money; why are they so outraged if the poor girl sells herself for the same reason? The only difference lies in the amount received, and of course in the seal society either gives or withholds.

I am sure that no one will accuse me of nationalist tendencies. I am glad to say that I have developed out of that, as out of many other prejudices. If, therefore, I resent the statement that Jewish prostitutes are imported, it is not because of any Judaistic sympathies, but because of the fact inherent in the lives of these people. No one but the most superficial will claim that the Jewish girls migrate to strange lands unless they have some tie or relation that brings them there. The Jewish girl is not adventurous. Until recent years, she had never left home, not even so far as the next village or town, unless it were to visit some relative. Is it then credible that Jewish girls would leave their parents or families, travel thousands of miles to strange lands, through the influence and promises of strange forces? Go to any of the large incoming steamers and see for yourself if these girls do not come either with their parents, brothers, aunts, or other kinsfolk. There may be exceptions, of course, but to state that a large number of Jewish girls are imported for prostitution, or any other purpose, is simply not to know the Jewish psychology.

On the other hand, it speaks of very little business ability on the part of importers of the white slaves, if they assume that the girls from the peasant regions of Poland, Bohemia, or Hungary in their native peasant crude state and attire would make a profitable business investment. These poor ignorant girls, in their undeveloped state, with their shawls about their heads, look much too unattractive to even the most stupid man. It therefore follows that before they can be made fit for business, they, too, must be Americanized, which would require not merely a week or a month, but considerable time. They must at least learn the rudiments of English, but more than anything else they must learn American shrewdness, in order to protect themselves against the many uniformed cadets, who prey on them and fleece them at every step.

To ascribe the increase of prostitution to alleged importation, to the growth of the cadet system, or similar causes, is highly superficial. I have already referred to the former. As to the cadet system, abhorrent as it is, we must not ignore the fact that it is essentially a phase of modern prostitution,—a phase accentuated by suppression and graft, resulting from sporadic crusades against the social evil.

The origin of the cadets, as an institution, can be traced to the Lexow investigation in New York City, in 1894.[11] Thanks to the moral spasm, keepers of brothels, as well as unfortunate victims of the street, were turned over to the tender mercies of the police. The inevitable consequence of exorbitant bribes and the penitentiary followed.

While comparatively protected in the brothels, where they represented a certain value, the unfortunate girls now found themselves on the street, absolutely at the mercy of the graft-greedy police. Desperate, needing protection and longing for affection, these girls naturally proved an easy prey to cadets, themselves the result of the spirit of our commercial age. Thus the cadet system was the direct outgrowth of police persecution, graft,

11. In the early 1890s, muckraker Lincoln Steffens and photographer Jacob Riis investigated accusations made by Reverend Charles Parkhurst that city officials, including police, were corrupt and complicit in the proliferation of vice in New York City. In 1894, in response to the scandal, the New York State senate appointed Senator Clarence Lexow to head an investigation. The Lexow Committee found rampant corruption, including evidence that police officers took bribes in exchange for not enforcing prostitution laws, thus allowing prostitution to flourish without fear of arrest. The committee published its findings and proceedings in an 1895 report, *Report of the Special Committee Appointed to Investigate the Police Department of the City of New York, Lexow Committee Report* (Albany: James B. Lyon, State Printer, 1895).

and attempted suppression of prostitution. It were sheer folly to confute this modern phase of the social evil with the causes of the latter.

The serious student of this problem realizes that legislative enactments, stringent laws, and similar methods can not possibly eradicate, nor even ameliorate this evil. Those best familiar with the subject agree on this vital point. Dr. Alfred Blaschko, an eminent authority, convincingly proves in his "Prostitution im 19. Jahrhundert" that governmental suppression and moral crusades accomplish nothing save driving the evil into secret channels, multiplying its dangers to the community. In this claim he is supported by such thorough students as Havelock Ellis,[12] Dr. H. Ploss, and others.

Mere suppression and barbaric enactment can serve but to embitter and further degrade the unfortunate victims of ignorance and stupidity. The latter has reached its highest expression in the proposed law to make humane treatment of prostitutes a crime, punishing anyone sheltering a prostitute with five years imprisonment and $10,000 fine. Such an attitude merely exposes the terrible lack of understanding of the true causes of prostitution, as a social factor, as well as manifesting the Puritanic spirit of the Scarlet Letter days.[13]

An educated public opinion, freed from the legal and moral hounding of the prostitute, can alone help to ameliorate present conditions. Wilful shutting of eyes and ignoring of the evil, as an actual social factor of modern life, can but aggravate matters. We must rise above our foolish notions of "better than thou," and learn to recognize in the prostitute a product of social conditions. Such a realization will sweep away the attitude of hypocrisy and insure a greater understanding and more humane treatment. As to a thorough eradication of prostitution, nothing can accomplish that save a complete transvaluation of all accepted values—especially the moral ones—coupled with the abolition of industrial slavery.

*Mother Earth* 4 (January 1910): 344–51. This article first appeared as a *Mother Earth* pamphlet in late 1909 and then later, with significant revisions, as "The Traffic in Women," published in EG's *Anarchism and Other Essays* (1910).

12. Havelock Ellis (1859–1939) was an English psychologist, physician, socialist, sex reformer, and author engaged in the scientific study of the varieties of sexual behavior. EG often referred to, and drew from, his work in her lectures and essays.
13. A reference to Nathaniel Hawthorne's novel *The Scarlet Letter* (1850), set in seventeenth-century Puritan New England, in which a woman is stigmatized by her adulterous relationship and forced to brandish a scarlet *A* on her dress across her chest.

My Dear Miss Goldman:

Thank you for yours 5th. instant. I have been horribly busy these days.

I am not prepared to head a fund to be collected for enforcement of free speech.[1] This does not say, however, that I would not subscribe to such a fund,[2] but I can take no lead-ing part in it whatever, as my time is taken up here, and I return to England shortly.

You will remember what I said to you regarding Dr. Reitman.[3] I have never met the man, and I am in no way prejudiced against him, but particulars of his past record have reached me of such a character that I could not have anything to do with such a free speech fund at all, if his services are to be retained in connection therewith or in con-nection with your own work on the same line.[4]

My information comes from a source that I consider entirely reliable, and I am unwill-ing to discuss the matter, being perfectly satisfied on the points I bring before you.

I should think that you would make a serious mistake in bringing a lawyer from San Francisco to help you in your work, though that is your own lookout.[5]

Believe me, with all good wishes,

Yours very truly,

Joseph Fels

All this is Confidential of course—

1. The Free Speech Fund (May 1909–May 1910) was the successor to the Free Speech Defense. Joseph Fels, along with other prominent liberals such as Alice Stone Blackwell and Alden Freeman, was a major contributor. The money collected was used to cover legal fees, publicity meetings, and expenses, as well as to support free speech fights around the country, including those in Buffalo, Chicago, Detroit, Philadelphia, and Spokane.
2. Joseph Fels had been an enthusiastic and generous supporter of EG's free speech battle. In the fall of 1909 he wrote to the editor of the *Philadelphia Bulletin*, suggesting that "the city of Philadelphia should hide its head in shame" for not allowing EG to speak there. The letter was reprinted in the pamphlet *The Suppression of Free Speech* (New Haven, Conn.: Alden Freeman, 1909), edited by Alden Freeman.
3. BR had met EG in Chicago on 13 March 1908. By the time of this letter BR was Goldman's tour man-ager and lover.
4. Interestingly, in the same letter to the *Bulletin* (see note 2 above), Fels not only confirmed that he was "one of the heaviest contributors to a fund ensuring Miss Goldman a hearing wherever she chooses to speak from a public platform . . ." but also stated, "I am glad to know that one man, at any rate [Dr. Reitman] is willing to stand up and fight for her if necessary."
5. Possibly a reference to San Francisco attorneys Ernest E. Kirk and Cameron King, who successfully defended EG and BR in San Francisco in 1909 when they had been charged with conspiracy. See vol. 2, *Making Speech Free,* pp. 396–409.

Alexander Berkman, ca. 1910. Goldman's closest friend, comrade, and previous lover; editor of *Mother Earth* with primary responsibility for editing the magazine while Goldman and Reitman were away from the office on lecture tours. (Library of Congress)

TLS, Emma Goldman Archive, IISH. On stationery of the Office of Fels & Co. Addressed to Miss Emma Goldman, Box 47, Sta. D, New York, N.Y. Handwritten postscript.

Article in **MOTHER EARTH**

*New York, February 1910*

## Light and Shadows in the Life of an Avant-Guard

An avant-guard[1] of many years of public activity? How discouraging. Yet if we consider that Anarchism is the only social theory that has undertaken to transvalue[2] all values, we will see at once that the position of its exponents must needs remain that of the avant-guard, for some time to come.

Traditions and habits cling with great tenacity, both to man and institutions. Not merely because every effort of to-day is being bent on perpetuating the past, but because the past has a most marvelous capacity of not letting go.

Thus we see that the most radical, aye, the most advanced, rarely outgrow the old.

It is but a comparatively short period, considered in the light of historic events, that Anarchism, the reconstructor of social life, the transvaluator of all values, has made its advent on the intellectual horizon of the world.

Its task was stupendous, indeed. The Rock of Ages, huge and immovable, blocked its way. Yet unafraid, serene and proud, Anarchism began its onslaught. To-day it is a living, working force, most hated and most beloved of all theories that have come to rebuild the world.

The wonder is not that it has accomplished so little; the wonder is that it has done so much. Therefore the life of the avant-guard, with all its shadows, can never lose its light, its rich warm light.

Of the shadows, I have talked on more than one occasion. In fact, during the last two years *Mother Earth* has reported nothing but gloom.

1. By the mid-nineteenth century the term "avant garde," which originated in France, was commonly used to refer to the most innovative and radical elements of developing artistic and political communities. A self-proclaimed avant-garde movement arose there during the 1890s, consisting primarily of politically radical artists, writers, thinkers, and activists who linked the breaking of artistic tradition with the creation of a new society. Many, including Octave Mirbeau, Felix Feneon, and Camille Pisarro, were sympathetic to anarchism. Journals such as *Les Entretiens poltiques et littèreires* (Political and Literary Conversation, Paris 1890–1893), *L'Endehors* (On the Outside, Paris, 1891–1894) and *La Revue Blanche* (The White Review, Paris 1889–1903) reflected this fusion. Interestingly, a leading French anarchist paper, *L'Avant Garde*, was published 1877–1878.
2. EG used the concept of "transvaluation," borrowed from Nietzsche, to express her belief in the importance of the transformation of all values, especially moral. Such a transvaluation would be essential in creating a new anarchist society.

In 1908 my tour was affected by the crisis and its inevitable result: outraged humanity manifesting itself in the acts of Averbuch and Silverstein.[3]

The police, like the forest beasts, at the sight of blood became mad for more. Who but the avant-guard of Anarchism could be better prey? Anarchist meetings were closed, and Anarchist speakers suppressed. My tour, though strong enough to withstand every obstacle, has rendered *Mother Earth* very little financial assistance.

The avant-guard, like the wicked, finds no rest. In the early Fall of 1908 another tramp was undertaken. By that time the crisis had thoroughly whipped people into submission, completely breaking their will; poverty and despair have no interest in life and life's problems.[4] Then, too, it was the period of the presidential election, which in this "free land" has become a greater national calamity than the coronation of the Russian Tsar.[5] This tour, too, was a failure.

I had almost despaired of a change. Everything seemed to conspire to turn the shadows of life into black clouds, shutting out faith and hope.

It seemed useless to begin a tour again, and without visible means of maintaining *Mother Earth*, I had almost decided to give up the struggle.

But the power of perseverance overcomes all difficulties.

When the indefatigable Ben Reitman wired me from Chicago: "Police consent to let you speak in this city. Telegraph dates," all disappointments of the past two years were forgotten. The future once more held out new possibilities.

That one should have to depend on police permission in a country where liberty is an every-day slogan, is not a cheering aspect. Still, it is better to meet the enemy in the open than to be overtaken by him unawares. Time and again labor, energy, and money were spent on the arrangements of meetings, only to see it all wasted through police

---

3. EG refers to the 1908 bank crisis, and resulting unemployment. Lazarus Averbuch (1889–1908) was a Russian Jewish immigrant who was killed on 2 March 1908 by Chicago chief of police George Shippy, in "self defense," while allegedly attempting an assassination. He was assumed, without evidence, to be an anarchist. A roundup of Chicago anarchists followed, along with an attempt by the press to link EG to a nationwide anarchist conspiracy. Selig Silverstein (1889–1908) was a Russian Jewish New York anarchist and member of the Anarchist Federation of America, who was responsible for the 28 March 1908 bomb in New York's Union Square at a demonstration of the unemployed. Intended for the police, the bomb exploded in his hand, killing one bystander immediately and Silverstein within two weeks of the incident. AB was arrested and suspected of being involved in the explosion but was later quickly released. See vol. 2, *Making Speech Free*, pp. 281–83 and pp. 297–99 for further information on the two incidents.

4. The idea that those suffering from extreme poverty were unable to participate in struggles for social change because all their mental and physical energy was taken up with trying to survive is a consistent theme in Goldman's writing. See, for example, "Letter to Solidarity," 15 July 1898 (pp. 329–30); "A Short Account of My Late Tour" (pp. 337–39); and Interview in the *Philadelphia North American*, 11 April 1901 (pp. 440–45), in vol. 1, *Made for America*.

5. The candidates for president in 1908 were Republican William Howard Taft, who received 51.7 percent of the popular vote; Democrat William Jennings Bryan, 43 percent of the popular vote; and Socialist candidate Eugene Debs, 2.8 percent of the popular vote.

interference. Experience has taught us this lesson: Since freedom of speech is no longer everyone's right without fear or favor, it is best to ascertain beforehand where it will meet with the least interference.

We had barely begun our tour when Detroit placed itself on record against free speech.

Oh, spirit of Robert Reitzel, where are thou?—and you who gloried in the song of that lark of liberty, you who worshipped at the shrine, has the last note of his song died away that you submit to the Russianization of your city? Has your love of freedom been a mere reflection of Reitzel's genius, leaving you poor and empty now that he is no more. You will soon have the opportunity to prove whether the work of the *Der Arme Teufel*[6] has been a strong factor or a mere passing fancy. We are coming to Detroit to assert our right of free expression.

In Buffalo the police are evidently still peril-stricken by the shadow of that lone boy whom they had done to death before Christian justice placed him in the electric chair.[7] Else it is hard to account for their dread of the free voice. The energetic effort of a true friend of liberty, Mr. Fred Schulder,[8] has been in vain. And yet not altogether, as his own letter will prove.

Dear Emma:—

Yours of the 9th, with clipping, reached me yesterday.

After having seen the mayor twice, his secretary three times, and the Chief of Police three times, I have not succeeded in getting a promise that you will be allowed to speak in Buffalo.

Yesterday Chief Regan[9] told me that he would have to be compelled by the courts before he would consent to your speaking, but I pressed the matter so hard that he finally asked me to see him again to-day and get a definite reply. Told the clerk of my engagement, and he went to see the Lord at once. Coming back he informed me that the Chief could not see me this morning, as he had been subpoenaed to court and would have to leave at once; but that at any rate "She can't speak"; I should come in at 2 P.M. if I wanted to see him. I went to see a friend whom I know to be in thorough sympathy with Free Speech. I told him of the result of my various interviews, and that I would like to have someone with me as a witness if I saw the Chief again. I thought as a last resort I would ask him if he would permit you to recite the Lord's Prayer in Buffalo. His answer being either yes or no, he would have placed himself in a position to

---

6. German American anarchist editor, poet, and critic Robert Reitzel (1849–1898) lived in Detroit and edited *Der Arme Teufel* (The Poor Devil). For more on Reitzel and *Der Arme Teufel*, see vol. 1, *Made for America*, pp. 553 and 564.

7. A reference to Leon Czolgosz, who assassinated President William McKinley in September 1901 in Buffalo, New York.

8. Fred Schulder (1874–1961) German-born anarchist individualist and for some time a single-taxer. Schulder was the companion of anarchist Adeline Champney. An activist in the anarchist movement, Schulder acted as a sales representative for Benjamin Tucker's *Liberty* and helped organize meetings for EG in Cleveland, where he lived. EG regularly stayed with Champney and Schulder during her visits to Cleveland. Interestingly, Champney and Schulder had helped organize the 5 May 1901 meeting there, where Leon Czolgosz heard EG speak.

9. Leo Regan was the Buffalo chief of police.

be made the laughing stock of my friend. My friend felt sure that the Chief would only quibble; as there is no paper here that would dare to say anything derogatory of the police department, he thought it would be useless. Furthermore, he said that if he should come out in this matter, the police would find a way to injure his business. Partly owing to Mr. B's advice, and partly owing to the fact that for several days I have had a severe cold which seems to amount to a slight attack of grippe, and the weather alternating snow and rain, with slush ankle deep, I decided to stay indoors this afternoon and nurse my cold. I may write to the mayor, but it will probably be of no avail.

I never before appreciated the corrupting influence of the political machinery—what cowards it makes of persons! Why, one sleek eel-like politician told me that he was not sure but what he was a philosophical Anarchist himself. But of course in his position, etc. I never call myself a "philosophical," and when someone else describes me thus, I usually laugh at it; but after seeing cringing and scheming politicians, personas without a backbone, applying this term to themselves, I shall feel a shiver whenever I hear that combination of words.

My friend has learned the truth of what I have maintained for many years, namely, that the term "Philosophic Anarchist" is really an apology for cowardice that craves to appear interesting.

Columbus, O., can boast of an intelligent mayor; at least he is intelligent enough to know the difference between Socialism and Anarchism.

"If Emma Goldman were a Socialist I would let her speak. But she is an Anarchist." Like Gen. Funston, the mayor knows that Socialism perpetuates government, that it is therefore not so dangerous to the position of an army officer or a mayor as Anarchism, that contains no place for either.[10]

Those who live in New York and count among their friends Socialists like Leonard D. Abbott, Annie and Rose Strunsky, English Walling,[11] etc., have no idea of the material that goes to make up the party Socialists in the Middle West. Certainly a more conservative, retrogressive, bigoted set of people is hardly conceivable.

In Chicago the editor of the *Daily Socialist* would not endanger the opportunity of vote getting by announcing the fact that Free Speech was again to assert itself in that city; yet he is quite willing to charge double rates for E.G.'s ads.[12] Naturally, saloons, banks, and

---

10. George S. Marshall was mayor of Columbus 1910–1911. EG refers to General Frederick Funston's prosecution of U.S. army soldier William Buwalda, who was court-martialed and imprisoned for shaking EG's hand in San Francisco in 1908. See vol. 2, *Making Speech Free*, pp. 321–31.

11. During this time Leonard Abbott moved toward anarchism. William English Walling, Anna Strunsky Walling, and her sister Rose Strunsky were identified with the left wing of the Socialist Party.

12. Algie Martin Simons (1870–1950) was a socialist author, editor, and political leader on the right of the Socialist Party. Simons attended the founding conference of the Industrial Workers of the World in 1905 and edited the *International Socialist Review* until 1908 and the *Chicago Daily Socialist* until 1910. William English Walling worked to remove Simons—along with Victor Berger, Morris Hillquit, Robert Hunter, and John Spargo—from the Socialist Party's national executive board on grounds that they were trying to transform the party into a conservative labor party. Only Simons was removed in the 1910 party election. BR attacked Simons in the March 1910 edition of

other crooked business are more important to the Socialists of Chicago than the right of a human voice to be heard.

In Milwaukee the Socialist ward heeler Berger would not take our ads.[13] How could he soil his clean, pure, white political soul by such a thing? In his righteous indignation he urges "that some one ought to get after the Chicago *Daily Socialist* for accepting and printing a big advertisement of an Emma Goldman meeting."

When two thieves quarrel the honest man comes to his own. Possibly when autocrat Berger will get after autocrat Simons, the poor, deluded party subjects will learn to value their independence.

In Hannibal, Mo., a Socialist judge, Abner S. Smith,[14] whose Socialist activities consist in ordering people dispossessed if they fail to feed the landlord, hastens to assure the people of that city that Socialists are above all law abiding citizens. "We believe in laws and in obeying them, but of course we believe the people should have part in framing them." How is this for a follower of Karl Marx, who died in hopes that his theory would revolutionize the world.

And with all this compromise, with all this cowardice, with all this cringing servility to public opinion—defeat, nothing but defeat. Too bad. Too bad.

If human beings were not better than parties, one could have to despair of the future. But the consciousness that there are Socialists with character and personality often makes up for all the sins of the party politician. Several of such precious rarities we have met in Madison, Wis. I will speak of them later.

The first ray of light made itself felt in Cleveland. English meetings in that city have always been mediocre, but when January 9th came, three days after Ben Reitman had reached Cleveland, the meeting surpassed the highest expectations. Two large audiences came, not out of curiosity, but interested to learn the truth about the greatest crime of the 20th century committed by the Catholic Church. The subject was Francisco Ferrer and the Modern School.

That the heroic death of that tragic figure at Montjuich continues to arouse widespread indignation is proved by the multitudes that come to hear about the life and work of that man.

---

*Mother Earth* for not supporting the Chicago free speech fight. Simons would go on to denounce William Haywood at the 1912 national convention of the Socialist Party for advocating sabotage. Together with Marcus Hitch he translated Wilhelm Liebknecht's *No Compromise No Political Trading* (Chicago: C. H. Kerr, 1903) and Karl Kautsky's *The Social Revolution* (Chicago: C. H. Kerr, 1910), and was the author of *The American Farmer* (Chicago: C. H. Kerr, 1906) and *Social Forces in American History* (New York: Macmillan, 1911).

13. Right-wing socialist Victor Berger published the weekly Milwaukee Socialist weekly *Die Wahrheit*, as well as the socialist daily *Vorwaerts* (1892–1898). Beginning in 1911 he would publish the English-language daily *Milwaukee Leader* (1911–1929).

14. Abner Smith (b. 1851) was a Hannibal, Missouri, socialist. He was chief clerk of the Thirty-sixth General Assembly in the 1890s. He was a justice of the peace and a member of the first ward of the Marion County section of the Socialist Party's County Central Committee.

By dispelling the lies and calumnies which continue to appear in the Catholic press of America about Ferrer, I hope to make his name and work a living, working force in our midst, thus paying my tribute in a small measure to the memory of our dead comrade.[15]

A large Yiddish meeting closed our successful visit in Cleveland.

In Toledo the gloom of the city and the mirror-like polish of the icy sidewalks could not obscure the light that followed. A meeting arranged within twenty-four hours again attracted a large audience, and everything moved smoothly. Even I, on my way from the hall to the hotel; so smoothly, indeed, that I landed on one of the mirrors, leaving its icy glass intact, but nearly breaking my back. How little reform does reform the broken arms, legs, and backs of the people, Toledo bears witness.

Chicago has been thoroughly swept by that hurricane, Ben L. Reitman. During three weeks, single handed, with friends and foes against him, with a conspiracy of silence on the part of the Chicago press, Reitman proved to the satisfaction of all that one determined individual can move mountains.

The success of the meeting in Chicago meant a great deal to our doctor friend. This is the city in the streets of which he spent his childhood. It was here, too, that he became a part of our so-called underworld. It was in Chicago that he obtained a pass to respectable society, in the form of a doctor's certificate. In Chicago, too, he learned the glory of American citizenship by receiving his first baptism of police clubs during the unemployed parade. It was there he was made to appreciate the true meaning of Free Speech, dependent on the police department. Yes, the success of the meetings meant more to him than many people can realize. So he worked as only a man with a great purpose can work, with the result that never in years, not even on the occasion of Peter Kropotkin's visit, was there such marvelous success.

Six English and three Yiddish meetings, crowded every night regardless of the wretched Chicago weather. Over four thousand people paid admission, and a tremendous amount of literature sold, thanks to the energy and skill of Dr. Reitman. But the most valuable feature of the campaign is the reorganization of the old Social Science Club into a young, lusty fighter with new workers and systematic English weekly meetings. No wonder our comrades, the most timid even, became rejuvenated. Inspired by the zeal of one, all worked faithfully. Little Dr. Yampolsky, Wm. Nathanson, B. Weinninger, Anna and Jake Livshis, Edith Adams, F. Weber, and other comrades whose names I cannot remember.[16]

---

15. EG spoke on Francisco Ferrer 9–10 January 1910. She also wrote the essay "Francisco Ferrer" (*Mother Earth*, November 1909) and went on to help establish the New York–based Francisco Ferrer Association in June 1910.

16. Edith Adams was a Chicago anarchist who helped arrange EG's meetings in the city. She was a member of the Chicago Social Science Club, a distributor of *Mother Earth* in Chicago, and a contributor to *Winn's Firebrand* published by Ross Winn. Dr. Rebecca Miriam (Beckie) Yampolsky was a Chicago anarchist and early advocate of birth control. Yampolsky was the companion of Dr. William Nathanson. She was a friend of EG and in 1908 treated EG's sudden illness when EG was in

Milwaukee was the next stopping-place. The same fine results. Three excellent meetings, arranged in a few days. Added to that was the joy of decent accounts in several daily papers, conservative papers, mark you, not the Socialist one.

Madison, Wis., has had a great charm for me the last few years because of its historical library. But what I really found there is extraordinary indeed. Certainly a better equipped and better managed institution I have never seen in any other city in America. No other library has such a collection of books, papers, and magazines on the labor question, trade unionism, Socialism, and Anarchism. Yes, even Anarchism, that most hated, most tabooed and misunderstood theory.[17]

During the few hours that I could spend in the library, thanks to the generous assistance of Mr. Andrews, the chief research worker,[18] I saw collections of the earliest Anarchist papers, books, and pamphlets in America. Complete files of the *Alarm, Fackel, Vorbote, Chicago Arbeiter Zeitung, Free Society, Liberty, Freiheit, Mother Earth,* and scores of others.[19] Also numerous pamphlets dating almost half a century back. In fact, a perfect mint for the earnest student. If the liberal endeavor of this historical library will continue, it bids fair to become for America—in a small measure—what the British Museum is for England.

In all my travels through the length and breadth of this land I found its university cities the most bigoted, arrogant, and conservative. Madison, Wis., is undoubtedly a happy exception. The progressive spirit among professors and students is unusual indeed. Profs. Ross,[20] Commons,[21] Yastrow,[22] and others are making history in America. Thanks

---

Chicago. She also arranged, with Ben Reitman, the use of the Hobo College Hall for EG to speak. EG met BR for the first time in Yampolsky's house on 13 March 1908. Yampolsky contributed to the publication fund for the *Selected Works of Voltairine de Cleyre* (New York: Mother Earth Publishing Association, 1912). Dr. William Nathanson (1883–1963) was a Chicago anarchist, writer, philosopher, and translator. From 1910 to 1911, with Voltairine de Cleyre, Nathanson ran a short-lived Modern Sunday School in Chicago. Edith Adams, Yampolsky, Nathanson, and Annie and Jake Livshis were all anarchists and members of the Chicago Social Science Club. For more on the Social Science Clubs, see vol. 2, *Making Speech Free*, pp. 564–65.

17. The library of the State Historical Society of Wisconsin began collecting labor and radical material around the turn of the twentieth century.

18. A reference to John B. Andrews (1889–1943) the progressive economist. Andrews, though not employed by the library, was at this time engaged in a research project at the library.

19. *The Alarm, Die Brandfackel, Vorbote, Chicago Arbeiter Zeitung, Free Society, Liberty,* and *Freiheit* were early American anarchist papers. For more information on these papers, see Directory of Periodicals in vols. 1 and 2.

20. Edward Alsworth Ross (1866–1951), sociologist and writer, was professor at Stanford University from 1893 to 1900. In continuous conflict with the university's conservative benefactress, Jane Lathrop Stanford, he was dismissed in 1900 for his outspoken opinions, including advocacy of free silver, opposition to corporatism, and objection to the use of migrant Chinese labor in railroad construction, a position inimical to the Stanford family investment in the Union Pacific Railroad, which was then under construction. Following Ross's termination, nearly a half dozen more faculty resignations and dismissals followed at Stanford, some in protest; these ignited a debate over the importance of freedom of expression in a university subject to the control of its business backers. Ross was later hired as a professor at the University of Nebraska in 1901 and the University

to them the American student is becoming humanized, and socialized. He feels an interest in other things besides baseball, football, and scabbing. That university men should turn out in large numbers to hear Emma Goldman was more than some citizens of Madison could stand. Since we left that city the *Democrat*, a yellow sheet, has been attacking the university most venomously.[23] I am convinced, however, that its barking will not intimidate the progressive element. Nor will it hamper it in its commendable desire to learn the truth from right sources. Surely Prof. Ross, who has withstood the various attacks upon his right to think independently and to interpret modern sociology, both in Stanford[24] and the Nebraska University, is not likely to be disturbed in his march by anything the *Democrat* may say.[25] It was a great treat to meet Prof. Ross. His wonderful physique with its large, generous lines, his broadminded views of social events, and his great humanism, were refreshing after meeting so many pygmies who are infesting the American colleges.

---

of Wisconsin in 1906. His works include *Social Control* (1901), *Foundations of Sociology* (1905), *Sin and Society* (1907), and *Social Psychology* (1908), as well as the 1927 work *Standing Room Only?*, in which Ross warned of the dangers posed to American society by immigrants and other "socially undesirable" groups. His position, in contrast to many of his more progressive views, was that race was a major determinant in human development; he repudiated the racial prejudice inherent in those ideas shortly before his death. In 1910 Ross's announcement of EG's lectures, both in the city of Madison and in his university classes, as well as his intention to take EG on a tour of the campus, sparked a debate between the progressive Wisconsin faculty and the more reactionary regents, a disagreement resolved by a demand for Ross's public apology. In the aftermath, the graduating class of 1910 proposed a memorial tablet (suggested first by Lincoln Steffens) with an 1894 quote from the University of Wisconsin Board of Regents expressing the university's dedication to academic freedom. The proposal was rejected by the regents, and the plaque remained in storage until 1915, when it was placed on Bascom Hall on campus.

21. John R. Commons (1862–1945) was a prominent labor economist at the University of Wisconsin between 1904 and 1932. EG met Commons during her 1910 visit to the campus and recognized him as "an exception to the average American educator." With Wisconsin progressive governor Robert M. La Follette, Commons established labor and antitrust laws and public utility regulations between 1905 and 1931, which served as models for similar legislation across the nation. His four-volume *History of Labor in the United States* (1918–1935, written collaboratively with others) remains a landmark in American labor historiography.

22. Joseph Jastrow (1863–1944), author of several scholarly and popular books on psychology, earned the first doctoral degree in psychology in the United States in 1886. Two years later, Jastrow joined the faculty of the University of Wisconsin in the department of experimental and comparative psychology. Eschewing his interest in research, Jastrow committed himself to public mental health and shifted his focus to the popularization of psychological theory.

23. Several papers, including the *Madison Democrat*, denounced the university and members of its faculty for accommodating (and thus, it was held, sympathizing with) Goldman. References to EG's purported influence on Leon Czolgosz, McKinley's assassin, were particularly widespread among the condemnations. See, for example, *Beloit Daily Free Press*, 31 January 1910.

24. See note 20 above.

25. In addition to the condemnations by the *Madison Democrat* and other Wisconsin papers, at least one, the *Wausau Record-Herald*, explicitly demanded that the university fire Ross. Compelled to make a statement to the press, Ross explained that, while he did not believe in anarchism, he did believe in free speech (*Milwaukee Free Press*, 29 January 1910).

The inspiration of our short stay in Milwaukee[26] was the Socialist Students' Club, whose members tower mountain-high above their political leader. Both Dr. Reitman and myself were invited to their round table at the Y.M.C.A. (holy horrors!), where we were asked to address the Club. The doctor spoke of the relation between the educator and agitator, and I made a few remarks on the difference between the students of Russia and America. One member of the Club helped faithfully at our own meetings,[27] in a true fraternal spirit. Thus our visit to Madison was not only very interesting and profitable, but it was also a very delightful one. A sleigh ride in that very beautiful country, with all the glory of a white winter, bore me back to the never-to-be-forgotten joys of the Russian troika, dashing along through the cold, the music of its bells re-echoing through forest and field. For this childhood day in Madison I am indebted to a friend of former days, who is now professor at the University and a respectable citizen of the place.[28]

The light continues in its bright colors, even while I write this in the city of St. Louis, the success of which I will describe at another time.[29]

The life of the avant-guard,—how rich, how full, how all absorbing. The only life worth living.

EMMA GOLDMAN.

*Mother Earth* 4 (February 1910): 383–91.

---

## LIGHT AND SHADOWS IN THE LIFE OF AN AVANT-GUARD

### By EMMA GOLDMAN.

---

26. EG was in Milwaukee on 23–24 January 1910.
27. After the talk at the YMCA, EG was well received at her 26 and 27 January evening lectures at the local Knights of Pythias lodge. Before a large and orderly crowd that included students, professors, and state officials, EG concluded her first talk by saying she was "convinced" the university "contains many professors and students who are bona fide anarchists. Perhaps they do not realize this fact. Perhaps they may not even know that their ideas of the existing order of things are anarchistic until someone like me happens along to tell them the truth. . . . There are many others who recognize that they at heart are anarchists, but for social political or economic reasons they dare not come out in the open and say so" (*Madison Loyal Tribune*, 5 February 1910).
28. At the conclusion of the second night's lecture, the subject of which was "The Drama as a Disseminator of Revolutionary Ideas," EG told the university audience that she had been invited by a member of the Wisconsin faculty, who was also an old friend, to return next summer as his guest "to avail myself of the advantages of your library for a month." The *Chicago Record-Herald* (8 February 1910) reported that Eduard Prokosch (1876–1938), a young professor, had invited EG to stay with him and his family for the summer. Prokosch later denied that he had extended the invitation or that he was the prospective host mentioned by Emma Goldman in her lecture.
29. EG lectured in St. Louis 2–10 February.

Article in **MOTHER EARTH**

*New York, March 1910*

# The Free Speech Fight

FRIENDS:—

Two years have passed, and sometimes two years make a difference. Let us look back two years, and see a man by the name of George Shippy[1] at his height. "Shippy was an ideal Chief of Police." The newspapers praised him, and he had the confidence of the people of Chicago.

Two years have gone: Shippy is down and out. The newspapers have bitterly attacked him; they have unmercifully condemned him, he has no longer the confidence of the people of Chicago.

Two years ago Emma Goldman was hounded and persecuted. Two years ago she went to the Anthropological Society,[2] and a hundred policemen followed to prevent her from speaking. To-night, Emma Goldman addresses a Chicago audience without a uniformed policeman in the hall.

I don't know whether Emma Goldman has the confidence and respect of the people of Chicago, but I am sure that she has the confidence of a small number of people in Chicago who know that the persecution and hounding she was subjected to was unjustifiable.

Let us look back again, and see the changes which have taken place; let us see the steps that were responsible for the former Chief of Police Shippy being down and out, and Emma Goldman being able to speak.

Two years ago to-morrow the unemployed had a parade which it was my pleasure to lead. Shippy as Chief of Police issued orders to stop that parade.[3]

A month after that parade the notice appeared in the Chicago newspapers that Emma Goldman would come here. The next morning the papers came out with a statement from Chief of Police Shippy, refusing to allow Emma Goldman to talk.

Those two incidents changed the history of Chicago. Let us go back to the parade. The day of the parade Chicago looked like an armed city. Many unemployed were clubbed by the order of Chief of Police Shippy. At that time there lived in Chicago a young Russian

---

1. George Shippy (1855–1913), Chicago police chief (1907–1908), alleged that he was the victim of an anarchist assassination attempt by Lazarus Averbuch in March 1908, claiming he killed his attacker in self-defense. He resigned his position within two months of the affair and died five years later.
2. For a fuller account of EG's difficulty finding a venue for her 1908 Chicago lectures, see Interview in the *Chicago Inter Ocean*, 8 March 1908, vol. 2, *Making Speech Free*, pp. 284–87.
3. BR led a march of the unemployed workers in Chicago on 23 January 1908, during which he was beaten by the Chicago police.

Jew, who had been in the city but a few months, by the name of Harry Averbuch.[4] He, I am inclined to believe, stood on the street corner and saw the police club the unemployed. It is possible that he was not there. If he was not there, he at least read the accounts of how the police clubbed the people. Like all thinking Russians he must have been terribly outraged. A month later he read that the police—George Shippy—will not allow Emma Goldman to speak. He saw that free speech is being suppressed. He came from Russia, a land of tyranny and despotism; he believed that when he came to America things would be different, there would be free speech. He found that it is not so. In one month he learned that there was here just as much tyranny, just as much suppression of free speech as in Russia.

Harry Averbuch then took it upon himself to right what he thought was a great wrong.[5] He did go to Shippy's house, he was armed, he did have a revolver, and he did attempt to kill George Shippy. Those who have the impression from newspapers, especially the Socialist press, that Averbuch was not armed are mistaken. I have authentic proof that young Averbuch did go to Shippy's house and attempted to kill him, and I am inclined to think that he shot Shippy's son. The result of this boy going to Shippy's house was the Shippy killed him, and probably it was a case of self-defense.

Averbuch acted alone, Averbuch consulted no one. He did not need to consult any one: he saw the police club men and he saw the police suppress free speech; he was of a delicate temperament, he thought it rested upon him to remedy this great wrong and he took his life in his own hands. He was a very brave man. To Harry Averbuch I tender my very profound respect.

He was a foreigner: he did not know, as you and I know, that it is a mistake to attempt to kill a policeman, because a man may be Chief of Police to-day and three weeks later he may be tending bar. He did not know that a man may be the Mayor of Chicago and three months from now be in the penitentiary.[6] He did not know that; nevertheless he did this thing. He may have been very foolish; it was very foolish of him to lose his valuable young life, but nevertheless I, for one, refuse to condemn Averbuch. I think he was a brave man; I think he was a much braver man than George Shippy.

You all read the papers. When Emma Goldman was stopped most of you agreed it was all right. There was nothing done, or very little done, to secure for Emma Goldman her right of free speech. I want to bring out another point. In New York City a man similar to Shippy, by the name of Bingham, General Bingham, who was Chief of Police, clubbed the unemployed;[7] he suppressed meetings, and another boy who had only been here for a few years attempted to avenge the police outrage. He threw a bomb and lost

4. For more on Averbuch, see "A Letter to *The Public* of Chicago," Appeal, 6 March 1908, in vol. 2, *Making Speech Free*, pp. 281–83.
5. There is no extant evidence to suggest that Averbuch went to Shippy's house as a consequence of the suppression of free speech in Chicago.
6. In Chicago no mayor from 1893 to 1927 was imprisoned; however Police Chief George Shippy did resign within two months of the shooting incident (see, above, note 1).
7. General Theodore A. Bingham was police commissioner of New York City from 1 June 1906 to 1 July 1909.

Cartoon in the *Reno Evening Gazette*, April 1910, warning the public that Emma Goldman and Ben Reitman were on the loose. Goldman presented her controversial ideas about "Anarchy" and "Love and Marriage" in Reno on 17 April 1910. (*Reno Evening Gazette*)

his life. The point that I wanted to drive home to you is that the arbitrariness of the police in clubbing the unemployed and suppressing free speech caused Averbuch and Silverstein[8] to lose their lives.

Was Averbuch an Anarchist? What is an Anarchist? An Anarchist is one who knows something about Anarchist philosophy and who accepts that. I have been with the Anarchists nearly two years and I know most of them, the Italians, the Spaniards, the Jewish and the English, and I have never heard of an Anarchist preaching violence, nor have I read any such advice in the Anarchist writings. Averbuch may have been an Anarchist, but I think not. From what I can find out, he knew little about Anarchist principles. He had gone to a few Anarchist meetings, but those meetings were literary

8. For information on anarchist Selig Silverstein see "Emma Goldman Blames Police," Article in *Chicago Tribune*, 29 March 1908, in vol. 2, *Making Speech Free*, pp. 297–99.

meetings and he learned nothing about violence. So the point I bring home to you is this: Averbuch may have been an Anarchist and he may not have been one, but if he was an Anarchist it was not the principles of Anarchism that drove him to violence.

After the police had suppressed Emma Goldman, I attempted in a small way to secure the right of free speech for her. I did not know the meaning of free speech then, it was merely a fancy with me; now free speech means my life. I went to Milwaukee to hear Emma Goldman speak. She spoke in German; I did not understand her well. I went to Minneapolis to hear her speak and afterwards I said, "If that is Anarchism, I am an Anarchist," and since that time, nearly two years ago, I have been with Emma Goldman.

My relations and my friends are here: some of the boys I went to school with, some of the doctors who taught me medicine, some of the girls I played with, and some of the girls that know me very well. I want to use five minutes and take you to other cities where I have been with Emma Goldman. We went to St. Paul, then to Seattle, and then to California; no disturbance. We came back from the Coast and went to New York; no disturbance. I thought that Chicago was the only city in America where she had trouble. We started on another tour. We went to Indianapolis, the police of that city stopped her. We went to Washington. In Bellingham, Washington, Miss Goldman and I got off the train; the police were there with a warrant, charging us with creating a riot; they put us under $1,000 bail. We came to San Francisco; there was a new Chief of Police, and he arrested Emma Goldman, myself, and another friend on the charge of being Anarchists and denouncing the government as unnecessary.[9] We had a jury trial and the jury freed us. The Court held it was not a crime to denounce the government or being an Anarchist. I went back to New York and found there have been dozens of meetings stopped. I found in Worcester, Mass.,[10] in Burlington, Vt.,[11] in Buffalo,[12] Detroit,[13] in about twenty cities the police had suppressed Emma Goldman. Now I want to tell you why the police suppressed Emma Goldman. Emma Goldman says, and I think it is true, that compared with the newspapers the police are angels. The newspapers in America are largely responsible for the suppression of free speech. Now let me tell you how it was they stopped her in Detroit.

---

9. Jesse Brown Cook (1860–1938) was chief of police in 1909 after the death of William Biggy in late 1908 (see vol. 2, *Making Speech Free*). For an account of EG's encounter with San Francisco law enforcement and the San Francisco free speech fight see Circular letter, 26 January 1909, pp. 403–4; and To *Mother Earth*, 2 February 1909, pp. 405–9 in vol. 2, *Making Speech Free*.

10. In September 1909 EG was unable to find a hall to speak at in Worcester, Massachusetts. Mrs. Eliot White, the wife of an Episcopal minister, offered her house and lawn for EG's talk. When EG was locked out of Beaver Hall on 8 September, she took up Mrs. White on her offer. Despite attempts by the police to interfere with the meeting, EG was able to give her public lecture on private property.

11. EG was scheduled to speak at city hall on 3 September 1909 in Burlington, Vermont. The mayor banned her from speaking in city-owned buildings and continued to thwart her plans even when EG found alternative venues. The mayor's efforts were successful; EG never spoke in Burlington on this tour.

12. Early in January 1910, Fred Schulder attempted to obtain permission for EG to speak in Buffalo. He was unsuccessful.

13. On 3 January 1910, Police Commissioner Croul notified BR that EG would not be allowed to speak in Detroit. In mid-February, however, EG returned and delivered lectures in Detroit without police interference.

In Detroit a newspaper man went to the Commissioner and said, "Emma Goldman is coming to town, that awful Anarchist; the police have stopped her around the country, she will probably start a riot." The police Commissioner did not see the joke; he had a faint recollection of meetings being suppressed, and he goes to his Chief Assistant, a fine good natured Irishman, and he says, "Emma Goldman is coming to town, what do you think about her?" "Oh, she is an Anarchist, she told Czolgocz to kill McKinley." So the Chief of Police suppresses free speech, and the newspapers make a sensation.

Shippy played in the hands of the *Tribune* and *Journal*. The *Tribune* and *Journal* praised Shippy. He was a great man two years ago, but the same newspapers are the ones that are responsible for Shippy's downfall. Whenever a newspaper praises a policeman, look out! They will slip him one some time. I am not up here to condemn Shippy; it was a big hit when he stopped free speech. The newspapers knew Emma Goldman, many of the editors of the dailies and cosmopolitan magazines know her, and in towns where newspapers have an influence and a clever reporter, the newspaper or reporter can induce the police to stop free speech. The papers in Spokane, the Spokane *Chronicle* and *Review* are responsible for those 450 men being in jail to-day. I have learned to understand, I can understand the police, I can be lenient with them, but with the newspapers I cannot.

I want to impress on your minds this idea: Everybody reads the *Daily News* and *Tribune,* and they believe them. These newspapers deceive the people and urge the police to violence. The *Tribune*, the *Record-Herald*, the *Inter Ocean*, the *Journal*, and the *News* are the papers in Chicago that are responsible for the misrepresentation of Anarchism, as well as for the hanging of the Anarchists in '87, and are the greatest enemies the people of Chicago have.

Just a few minutes more, and I have finished. When the police suppress Emma Goldman, whether in Detroit, or Buffalo, or Indianapolis, New York, or Burlington, the Free Speech Committee takes up the fight. It circulates free speech literature and tries to create public sentiment. Let us take Boston, for instance. I went to see some Single Taxers, radicals, and Socialists there, and said, "The police are about to suppress Emma Goldman. Will you be with us in a free speech fight?" Now I am going to attack the Socialists. I saw in Boston the Executive Committee of the Socialist party, Jim Carey[14] and other members. I said to them, "Emma Goldman believes in liberty; we want justice, we want free speech; will you help us?" Carey said, "To hell with the Anarchists, to hell with freedom and free speech, we want Socialism." You may think this is an exception; not at all. I am convinced that if Simons[15] were Mayor and Barney Berlin[16] Chief of Police of Chicago, Emma Goldman would not speak here.

14. James F. Carey was president of the Common Council of the Socialist Labor Party in Haverhill, Massachusetts, and was elected to the Massachusetts State legislature in 1899. By 1912 he was on the right of the Socialist Party and chaired the 1912 Socialist Party convention.
15. Algie Simons edited the *Chicago Daily Socialist* until 1910.
16. Barney Berlin was an Illinois socialist and member of the 1905 Socialist Party's national executive committee with Victor Berger.

Some of the Socialists will take exception to this. In Haverhill, Mass., the officials of the town are Socialists, or rather they were. There was a Socialist Mayor and a number of the aldermen were Socialists. The Socialists in Haverhill refused to come out for freedom of speech. They said, "If the police want to stop Emma Goldman we don't care, unless they stop us." That has happened in every city in America, and I say to you that the Socialist party in America, as an organization, refuses to back us in our fight for free speech. I am speaking of the party as an organization; some of the members are all right. Debs[17] is a Socialist and he is a member of the Free Speech Committee, and the Chairman of the Committee is a Socialist. When we went to Simons, here in Chicago, he refused to aid the free speech fight. I said to the local Socialists: "If we can't get a hall, will you let us have your hall?" They would not have anything to do with us. "Will you appeal for her in your paper?" No. They talk about the suppression of Warren a great deal in the *Appeal*;[18] not a word has been said about Emma Goldman. We want the radical papers and the Socialists to defend free speech. If you will read the paper published here by Louis Post,[19] you will get the truth about the free speech fight; if you will read the *Mirror*[20] of St. Louis, you will there get the truth, too; also in the *New York Call* and many other valuable papers which have come out for Emma Goldman. I have not asked the Socialists to support Emma Goldman, because she does not need them. All we have asked them, as liberals and radicals, was to support our free speech fight.

Now, friends, my life's work I hope will always be with Emma Goldman and the great cause of human liberty.

*Mother Earth*, March 1910: 23–28. By Dr. Ben L. Reitman, with a footnote stating: "Police stenographic report of an address delivered by Dr. Reitman at Chicago, Jan. 19th, 1910."

17. Eugene V. Debs was five times the Socialist candidate for president, standing in 1900, 1904, 1908, 1912, and 1920. He often supported those who were politically left of the Socialist Party.
18. Fred Warren (1872–1959) was the editor of the socialist weekly *Appeal to Reason*. The paper, which ran 1894–1917, was first published in Kansas City (1894) and then in Girard, Kansas, by Julius A. Wayland. It was the most successful American socialist paper, with a paid circulation of 760,000 by 1913. After the kidnapping of Moyer, Haywood, and Pettibone in February 1906, Warren offered a reward in the paper for the capture of Kentucky's ex-governor William Taylor, who had been indicted for the murder of his successor. Warren was then arrested in 1907 and charged with violating the postal regulation prohibiting the mailing of any envelope which printed threatening or defamatory language. When his case came to trial in May 1909, he was convicted and sentenced to six months' hard labor and fined $1,500. He then took his case to the circuit court of appeals, which upheld his conviction, but soon after, on 1 February 1911, President William Howard Taft waived Warren's jail term and reduced the fine to $100. Warren refused to pay the fine except in the form of 400 subscriptions to the *Appeal to Reason*.
19. A reference to Louis Post's Chicago paper, the *Public*.
20. The *St. Louis Mirror* (1895–1920), a daily newspaper edited during this period by William Marion Reedy. An admirer and supporter of EG, Reedy published *Emma Goldman, The Daughter of a Dream* (St. Louis, 1908). From 1913 to 1920 the paper was called *Reedy's Mirror*.

Article in the *SIOUX CITY DAILY TRIBUNE*

*Sioux City, Iowa, 23 March 1910*

## Anarchy Believes in Mild Violence

**Miss Goldman Advocates It Against Capitalism
But Doesn't Believe in Bombs.**

Cause of All Suffering

Blames Centralized Wealth for All Grief and Pain of World—
Far Different Woman Than Might Be Supposed.

Violence against capitalism, which she says robs men of love, life and the pursuit of happiness, was advocated in no uncertain terms by Miss Emma Goldman, in her lecture on "Anarchism and What It Stands For," before a mixed audience in Labor temple last night. Personal violence, with dynamite, clock bombs and hand grenades, is not part of her creed. A large audience heard her and applauded riotously when she scored a telling point.

She was introduced by Ben Reitman, "King of the Hoboes," whose vagabondish appearance is interesting even if one knows nothing of his remarkable history.

**LIKE OTHER FOLKS.**

As the hour approached for the much talked of woman to arrive, heads were craned back toward the door. At last among a group who came in at the door walked a little woman, unless whose face could be seen, could not have been picked out from any other woman in the audience. Her general appearance did not differentiate her in any way from women seen on the street every day. There were no red flags pinned to her jacket, nor did red ribbon flaunt from her hat. In fact, that part of her apparel was not one that faddish women would rave about. A close fitting dark coat on her stoutish figure served to give the impression that she was shorter than she really is. She stepped behind a screen in the room and presently marched up the aisle with a firm, heavy stride. In the light the tremendous virility of the woman could be seen in every facial characteristic. This tenuous woman has no time for false braids and puffs and wore her hair in the simplest coiffure. Beauty hints are not in her line. She wore a severe white laundered shirt waist, with a flat Dutch collar and a black voile skirt. But if you were in the audience last night perhaps you did not notice her dress at all. Her face claims attention all the time.

First you will notice the severe lines of her face. She rarely smiles. A half suspicion of a smile may hover for an instant after a telling point driven home by satire, but it quickly disappears with continued imprecations against government that rules by violence, always on the side of the "vested" interests. A pair of glasses perched high on her puggish nose cannot hide the glint of battle that ever shines from her eyes. Even in repose her mouth is hard set, with lips pressed tight together. It is the mouth of a leader, with fighting lines at the corners. Her brow is high, her chin is firm and her complexion has the unrouged, unpowdered glow of health.

### CLAIMING THEIR OWN.

Capital and government were the two objects of the wrath of Miss Goldman in outlining a primer skeleton of anarchism. She declared that anarchism wants the men who make the wealth to claim it.

Capitalism, she said, places men in a rut that they never can climb out of. It makes then automatons, cogs in a machine, and it frowns on individual initiative. She pointed out present economic inequality and advocated the general strike. She cited examples of the individual and social instinct abnormally developed and said that anarchism looked to the harmonizing of these two instincts.

"The function of government is to foster crime," she said. She attacked the militarism of the nation which she said is always on the side of capital.

### FIGHTING TO EXIST.

"What are the 175,000 men in Philadelphia striking for today?[1] Are they striking for automobiles, mistresses and a life of dissolute ease? No, they are struggling for a right to live, educate their children and exist as they should have the right to exist. People tell us, with proud mien, of the schools that our government gives us, but what do they teach? Do they teach that hearts beat alike all over the world, that all blood is red and that tears hurt alike in every corner of the world? No, they teach that the world is made of thousands of little specks surrounded by an iron fence with a policeman with a club in his hand and a preacher with a prayer book, inside. That you must take one of these or perish."

1. On 27 February 1910 the Philadelphia Central Labor Union called a general strike in support of streetcar operators, who were protesting the dismissal of several members of the union. On 5 March, after union demands were not met, tens of thousands of workers walked out. The Pennsylvania State Federation of Labor voted to call for a statewide walkout of every industry, a proposal that was pocket-vetoed by the federation president. Two articles by Voltairine de Cleyre in the February and March 1910 issues of *Mother Earth* examine the Philadelphia strike in detail. The strike began to break down when, on 22 March, bricklayers and textile workers returned to work. The city's general strike was officially called off by the Central Labor Union on 27 March.

## BACK TO WEBSTER.

Finally Miss Goldman defined anarchism, anarchy and anarchist.

Anarchism is the philosophy of a new social order based on liberty unrestricted by man-made law, the theory that all forms of government are based on violence—hence wrong and harmful, as well as unnecessary.

Anarchy is the absence of government; disbelief in and disregard of invasion and authority based on coercion and force; a condition of society regulated by voluntary agreement instead of government.

Anarchist: 1. A believer in anarchism; one opposed to all forms of coercive government and invasive authority.

2. One who advocates anarchy, or absence of government, as the ideal of political liberty and social harmony.[2]

Miss Goldman will speak tonight on the subject of "Love and Marriage" at the court house.

The *Sioux City Daily Tribune,* 23 March 1910.

2. These exact definitions appeared regularly in *Mother Earth,* and the definition of anarchism was printed on all *Mother Earth* stationery.

If "what is has to be must be" Why make an effort for the new? Why struggle and face every obstacle? Why write books? Why publish M E? Why do the disagreeable thing?

No, I do not believe in this theory "what has to be must be." It's an excuse for cowards and weaklings. All my life, I have resisted it fought it, defied it. All my life I strove for the ideal, <u>all my life</u>, I have refused to accept the cruel hideous reality. It is too late for me to adjust myself to the anything, that kills my ideal inch by inch and day by day, <u>I will not, I can not.</u>

I have been so very miserable, that I postponed my return N to N Y. Am leaving to day for Albany, where I will meet Alex.[1] I have wired him to meet me there and return with me by boat.

I hope you have succeeded in arranging the trip, or that, you have written to N Y. I know you will hate to stay in Chicago. I hope you will not have to. As for myself—Ah well, it is no use—I know that you give as much as you can, I am not blaming or censuring you. Only, I can not reconcile myself to it. I'd rather do without reality if my ideal is forever to be abused insulted, spate upon, dragged through the mud.—

Please see about my laundry, let me know soon, whether I may hope for it.

EMMA

ALS, IU-U.

1. A reference to AB.

Hobo dearest.

What a baby boy you are, so naive so very much of a child. I really ought not to get angry with you. If only you had not awoken the woman in me, the savage primitive woman, who craves the man's love and care above every thing in the World.

I have a great deep mother instinct for you baby mine, that instinct has been the great redeeming feature in our relation. It has helped me on more than one occasion to overlook your boyish irresponcible pranks. But my maternal love for you is only one part of my being, the other 99 parts, consists of the woman the intense, passionate savage woman, whom you have given life as no one else ever has. I think therein lies the key to our misery and also to our great bliss, rare as it may be. I love you with a madness that knows no bounds, no excuses, no rivals no patience, no logic. I want your love your passion, your devotion your care. I want to be the centre of your thoughts your life your every breath. Anything that takes you away even for a moment drives me insane and makes my life an absolute hell. Because I love you so, I crave your care. I actually want you to take care of me. No one ever has, you know. I have always taken care and provided for others. I never wanted anyone to take care of me. But with you I long for it, oh so much. Not in the sense of earning money, but in the sense of little considerations and thoughtfulness, in the sense of relieving me of little burdens. My love for you has grown, has become stronger with time, because you have relieved me of so many things. But I want more, I know you can give it. And when you do not, when you become careless or indifferent, I suffer suffer untold agonies. That you can spend an hour at luncheon with a woman, who means nothing to you while you race me to death, as the ordinary husband does is such pain and sorrow to me, as you can never understand. It is not jealousy, because if it were, why should I feel miserable if you can spend a night with silly actors? No it is not jealousy, it's only a terrible savage craving to give you everything to receive everything from you, that's all. I have been thinking that there is something deeper in a woman's clinging to the man she loves. It is the soothing feeling of safety, of having some human being who delights in making you happy, in finding nothing too hard in his effort for you.

I never missed it never cared for it, never imagined I would need it until you came into my life, until you awakened that side of my nature, that side of my spychology

You see, my precious you have given life to a force that you do not know how to handle, how to meet, hence the conflicts, hence the lack of harmony and peace. And until you will know how to deal with this tremendous force, I fear, we never will have harmony. You say, "take me in charge when I get into a lot and love me." Has it even occurred to you darling mine, that that is precisely what I miss in you. I have felt it so terribly on that day in Milwaukee,[1] when my nerves were on edge and my whole being quivered. Where was your great love that would sooth and comfort. You acted like a slave driver. You laughed and jeered and forced me to the block. You made me realize that no matter how miserable I will be, I need not look for comfort and tenderness from you. Yet you say, I do not love you enough. Why Hobo you can not possibly believe that in earnest. I have proved my love for you in a million ways; in care, in tenderness in understanding. I have shown it in patience with your escapades, with your irresponcibilities with your ways. Oh, it has not been easy, it has been a life and death struggle. But I have always come out victoriously ready to forget and to receive you. But you, you dear never have. When I suffered most and needed you most, you were hard cruel and impatient, even brutally unfaire.

You do not know how I have suffered in my struggle with 210.[2] You have never known and understood. On the contrary you hurt my feelings a million times, and became angry when I resented it.

I do not reproach you, I only want you to know, that I too crave tenderness and understanding. Why do you never give it to me, why? I think you love, but why do you never share it? The only time you came near it is in our embrace. Oh, you are wonderful then you are sublime then, you led me right out of everything, into a new and beautiful World, you fill all my desires, all my wants. But that moment is so rare in our life now and the other is so cold so hard so cruel, I can not begin to tell you the misery, the dispair I go through. Yet with all that I love you, I have grown away from everything and everybody and have saturated myself with your image with the consciousness of you. It is really funny, when you say you feel yourself an outsider in N Y. It is absurd in the light of real facts.

You know, how I used to feel about 210 when we first met. Surely you must have noticed how I have gradually grown away. And now, on my return I had to face the inevitable, I feel a stranger an absolute stranger in 210. It is not the fault of my friends, certainly not H,[3] he is kinder and more tender than ever. I have linked my life with yours, have saturated my body and mind with you. That's why 210, means nothing to me anymore. If not for M E I would immediately discontinue the present arrangements. As it is, I have definitely decided to give up the flat before I go on a tour again, to get an office for M E with H to look after. And when I return to N Y, to get a studio for myself. As I

---

1. EG was lecturing in Milwaukee 23–24 January 1910.
2. Refers to 210 East Thirteenth Street, EG's apartment and the office of *Mother Earth*. The apartment was shared with AB and his companion Rebecca Edelsohn, Max Baginski, Hippolyte Havel, housekeeper Rhoda Smith, and a steady flow of others. Challenging work, deadline pressures, and personal relationships in crowded living quarters were a volatile combination.
3. EG's friend and comrade Hippolyte Havel, who lived at 210 East Thirteenth Street and worked on *Mother Earth*.

write you you have torn me out root and all of my native soil, and if your love will not become more tender, I shall continue to be a weary wanderer chasing for the impossible, a life with you, a real harmonous beautiful useful life—

Dearest mine, I have written a sort of a confession, I want you to know me, to understand me. Will you ever?

If you have sent a special, I will not get it until Tuesday or Wednesday. I left the house 1:30 P M there was no special then. I hope I will get a letter from you Monday in the village else, it will be hell to wait until Th Tuesday, 3 days. Of course, dear I knew you will not get your passage. You say, I have no faith in you. I have all the faith in the World in you but not in your judgement. I know you act by emotions and they are never realiable in every day affaires. Any way, I will send your passage Monday. I hope you can be in N Y Thursday evening. I want you Hobo, more than anything else in the World.

So far only 27 paid subscription have come for the book.[4] But we have about 50 orders, all as good as money. I am disappointed that I have not received one single substancial contribution. But it may come yet.

Mrs Yarmuth and Mrs Case, my Seattle friends have sent me a most magnificant scarf, the most beautiful I have ever had. I have quite a collection now. By the way, one old friend remembered my birthday, Mead,[5] you remember him, do you not? He came on the 27th about 9 P M with a beautiful bunch of roses and a volume of Gorki. Only Hobo, wrote a misely little note not a telegram even. Strange Hobo. Yet you always said you can get money in Chicago.

My baby boy, says lots of things he can not carry out. That's the beauty and charm about you dear, you are so delightfully optimistic and irresponsible.

Good by precious cruel lover mine.

Come to your Mommy wayward one, I long for you, I love you, yes I do.

MUMMY

ALS, IU-U.

4. A reference to EG's *Anarchism and Other Essays* (New York: Mother Earth Publishing Association, 1910). EG had announced her upcoming book to *Mother Earth* subscribers in order to gain advance sales. The circular, dated 24 June 1910, gave a list of chapters or "lectures" that were somewhat different from the published book. "What I Believe," "Anarchism Versus Socialism," "Direct Versus Political Action," "Crime and Criminals," and "The White Slave Traffic," all advertised in the circular, failed to appear in the final volume.
5. Possibly T. F. Meade, a New York anarchist and subscriber to *Mother Earth*; Meade contributed an article on Giordano Bruno to the May 1907 issue of the magazine.

Dᴇᴀʀ Cᴏᴍʀᴀᴅᴇ

This will introduce Dr Ben L Reitman, who's name you have probably seen in M E.

He is not long in our ranks, 2 years, but has proven very efficent as an organizer of meetings and a distributor of our literature. Also he has done great work with the unemployed here which resulted in a very severe and brutal attack on R by the police. He is one of the few Americans, who has completely abandoned himself to our propaganda. Needless to say, he is eager to meet you.[1]

Our friend will give you all the news about our work.

We hope you are well, and that Sophie and Sasha[2] are in good health. We would be so happy to hear from you, if only through a letter.

Fʀᴀᴛᴇʀɴᴀʟʟʏ

Eᴍᴍᴀ Gᴏʟᴅᴍᴀɴ

ALS, GA RF

1. In July 1910 BR traveled to London, where he met with Peter Kropotkin, Errico Malatesta, and Guy Aldred, among others.
2. Kropotkin's wife, Sophia Kropotkin (1856–1938). The daughter of a well-to-do Jewish family, who met Peter Kropotkin in Geneva in 1878 while studying biology at the University of Bern. They married the same year. She was a political activist in her youth. After her marriage she devoted herself almost entirely to Kropotkin and his political work. Sasha is the diminutive for Alexandra, Kropotkin's daughter (1887–1966). In the original letter EG wrote Sasha's name in Cyrillic script.

## To BEN L. REITMAN

*New York, 1 August 1910*

HOBO MY PRECIOUS.

I came to the City yesterday. The strain of waiting for news from you, seems more tense on the farm. Somehow, I think if I am in N Y, I am closer to you and will hasten your letter to me. That, of course is foolish. But is not my entire love for you foolish? Anyway, I am here to stay until Wednesday, maybe I will get something until then. I am so damned nervous, I can not be on the farm, until I hear from you. After, it may not be so trying.

I have done nothing since I wrote you last, except, that my three Mss, Psychology, Ferrer and Mariage, are now complete to be type-written.[1] I think they are good, the one on Marriage & Love, is the most brilliant I suppose because I have so little of it. Well, are not all great things merely in the ideal. Thus my ideal of love will die with me, never realized. Perhaps it is well it should be so.

This week, I will probably do nothing. I am here until Wednesday, then I shall have a visitor with me or rather two. Annie Livshis and her boy[2] are here. ~~They are~~ Annie has always been so beautiful to me, that I feel I must reciprocate in a small measure at least. She and Pete will stay with me over Sunday. Then too, I will not feel so lonely, I can talk to Annie about you. I can not and care not to do it with others. Next week, I will be able to continue my work. I might do 3 Mss again, if all goes well. That will give Stella,[3] six to begin with. While she is doing them, I hope to do the others, the two most important ones Anarchism and the drama, will necessitate most time.[4] I hope to do them all ~~nex~~ this month to send them to several Publ houses by Sept 10. I will not be able to wait with it until you return, dear. I must give the houses ample time to bring it out in Dec, if the book is accepted. If not they will have a chance to let me know, by the 1st of Oct, when we could begin our own publishing.

The 1st of Oct, it makes me feel chilly, that I should have to be without you for another

---

1. EG's essays "The Psychology of Political Violence," "Francisco Ferrer and the Modern School," and "Marriage and Love" were first published in EG's *Anarchism and Other Essays* (New York: Mother Earth Publishing Association, 1910).
2. Annie Livshis was a Chicago anarchist and friend of both EG and Voltairine de Cleyre. Her deaf and mute son, Peter Livshis, was also an anarchist. He was a friend of Voltairine de Cleyre. In 1915 his letters to *Land and Liberty* were published in the paper, which he helped distribute in Chicago. His article on the Chicago school strike was published in the *International Socialist Review* in March 1916.
3. A reference to Stella Comyn (Cominsky), EG's favorite niece, who often worked as a secretary and typist for EG.
4. A reference to her essays "Anarchism: What It Really Stands For" and "The Drama: A Powerful Disseminator of Radical Thought," both published in *Anarchism and Other Essays*.

2 months.[5] A nice mess, my love for you has made of me. A complete dependent for life's joy, on "a mere man. I feel like kicking myself all over. Oh, Hobo dear, I am an idiot. I love you so, I want you so, I could swim across just to have a peep at my ugly mean, selfish treacherous good for nothing lover, who's "techinique even is down and out. Come kiss me boy, I love you inspite of your faults, or because of them since you have no virtues worth loving. Dearest, nothing will become of our bookstore.[6] Harry[7] goes to St Louis tomorrow to join his brother in a moving picture show business. He will not return, I am sure. As to fixing up a store for Havel, that would be insanity, only another burden on my shoulders which would swallow up every cent we make just like M E. I do not propose to do it.

If we were not to tour and you could take charge of it, that's a different thing. But that is out of the question. Of course we shall tour and if my deepest desire comes through, I do not intend to return to N Y soon. [Illegible] want to go away with you, to Hell, rather than to be in N Y without you. No, we will not go into debts for bookstore, but if I can find a reasonable place to fix up an office for M E I will do that, to get rid of the flat.

God is certainly good to your Mommy. Beckie came out for two weeks. She followed your example went down the hill on the Bycicle and almost killed herself. Her face is in a terrible condition all swollen and bruised.

It will take at least two weeks to put it in condition, which means, she must be out on the farm. She is really not in the way, she is helpful and quiet, only the expence, the awful expence, it eats me up. $20 per week to live out on the farm. 5 people, you know. Then H expence in the City, the rent for the flat. Not a damned cent coming in for M E and only mesely 3–4 $ per week for the book.

I hate to write you all this, dear, you might think, I begrudge your trip. Indeed not, lover mine. I only wish we had the means for you to enjoy it in a more liberal way. I want my boy to know, how Mommy feels under all the weight and how little she can rest. Dear heart your argument that I ought not to do all these things, is about as valid, as if I say I ought not to love Hobo.

How can I refuse Alex or Havel a share in money if they are affilliated with M E? How am I to say to Alex, he ought not to have Beckie, or how am I to dispose of Mickie?[8]

---

5. BR left for Europe in July 1910 and planned to return in October of that year.
6. Plans were being made to incorporate a bookstore into the *Mother Earth* office to raise funds to supplement their income and disseminate anarchist literature and other material. Nothing, however, would come of this venture until the *Mother Earth* Bookstore was founded in early 1918 by Stella Comyn in Greenwich Village.
7. In his unpublished autobiography, "Roll Back the Years: Odyssey of a Libertarian" (edited by John Nicholas Bethel, New York University, Tamiment Library), Harry Kelly writes that he left New York in a "fit of depression."
8. AB, his companion Rebecca Edelsohn, Hippolyte Havel, and Herman Mikhailovitch all worked in the *Mother Earth* office and were supported, along with EG, BR, and Max Baginski, through sales of the magazine.

That's the rule dear. So long as I have M E, I must have an editor, I must have somebody to take care of things.

If only I could get myself to get rid of the magazine, I would be free from everything connected with it. You are the first to object to the discontinuation of the magazine, are you not?

Oh, I am tired, tired to death, of everything. I hope Alex can get on his feet with his book.[9] Oh, I would be so happy. Yesterday he finished the 1st part of it, 70 pages 30 000 words. He has done wonderful work, has surpassed all our expectation. If he continues in the same way, the book will be epoch making, at any rate it will be the first of that kind in revolutionary histor literature. I am so glad, that he is succeeding. It is one of the things that gives me strength to endure the burdens. I want with all my heart to complete my struggle for Alex by having induced and helped the book. He is entitled to some reward for the terrible 14 years—

Your Mommy is a queer Mommy, she can never exclude those, who have been in her life, not even you, precious.

Of course, dear you will see the various publishers book-store or no book-store.

A few days more and I will hear from Hobo. Do you know, that this is the first time in 2 1/2 years have that have been without news from you so long?

Dearest sweetheart lover, I think of you every month minute. I want you so much. As to the t b and m—I must suppress them all the day time. They do not believe in limited free speech. If I'd let them, they would talk me crazy—

Precious Hobo, inclosed your weekly "allowence. I wonder how you manage dear. Mommy is getting poorer every day. I sent Golm $100 the first since I returned by the time, I have paid the butcher, laundry grocer rent, several books I need for my lectures another $60 will be gone. 160 to 180 drawn since my return means $340. We have now, about $300 in the bank. That does not include the money for the book, about $100 also used up.

I fear, dear, that I will not be able to send you the cash for return, unless some good Fairies visit me. I will have to stick my sister for a ticket and pay her during the Winter, of course it will be second cabin. In that case, you will have to set a certain date for sailing and let me know a month in advance. Unless you really want to stay longer, I would like you to be bak by the 20th of Sept. I want to be on the farm with you, alone for one week at least. Do you? Sep is beautiful on the farm. By the 1st of Oct you will have to begin pushing the Ferrer meeting possibly also a few of our own. Let me know soon, if this arrangement suits you.

WITH LOVE DEEP AND SUBLIME. MOMMY. T-B M FOR HOBO

---

9. A reference to Berkman's ongoing work on his book *Prison Memoirs of an Anarchist*, which would be published by Mother Earth Publishing Association in 1912.

P S. Have just written Keell[10] to send me at once a copy of Blair Smith's[11] Direct Action and Heroines of Russia by Prelooker.[12] The latter I need for a lecture, get Keell to hurry them on.

ALS, IU-U. On *Mother Earth* stationery.

Ben Reitman, ca. 1910. Goldman's publicist, tour manager, and lover. (Library of Congress)

10. Thomas Keell was the editor of *Freedom*, an anarchist communist newspaper based in London.
11. J. Blair Smith, Scottish author of the pamphlet *Direct Action Versus Legislation* (Bridgeton, Scotland: Free Action Group, 1899; London: Freedom Press, 1909, Freedom Pamphlet No. 29).
12. *Heroes and Heroines of Russia; Builders of a New Commonwealth* (London: Simpkin, Marshal, Hamilton, and Kent, 1908) by Jaakoff Prelooker (1860–1935), an English author's sympathetic account of the revolutionary movement in Russia. His other works include *Russian Flashlight* (London: Chapman and Hall, 1911) and *The New Israelite* (London: Simpkin, Marshal, Hamillton and Kent, 1903). In a later letter to Tom Keell she said of the book, "It is old and stale and has not even the merit of good journalism." EG to Tom Keell, 31 August 1910, *EGP*, reel 68.

HOBO MY DARLING.

I got two letters from you to day, of the 18th, 19 & 20th. They made me very unhappy. You say in one of them, that a Socialist asked you "what are the Anarchists doing except talking". I wonder dear, if you know, how well this applieys to you? Here you go on shouting violence, yet are you ready to commit an act? If not, how can you consistantly go on urging others and endangering their lives?

You talk anarchy and claime to be one, yet you never for one moment act like an anarchist. You invade a private gethering, call the people all kinds of names and yet wonder, that they are indignant or disgusted with you. Dear Hobo, I do not mean to be unkind or to scold you really not, but only mean to show you, that you justify the opposition to anarchism. and Now, dear will you not remember once for all that anarchism, if it means anything at all means non invasion. You can no more force yourself and your ideas on a private gethering of people, than you can on a private flat at least not as an anarchist. Certainly the Socialists are rotten and I am the last one to spare them, but it would never occur to me to go into Berger's home, or to a tea he is giving to upraid and denounce him.[2] If you can do such a thing or justify it, why are you opposed to governments? That's precisely what government is doing, forcing you to accept its invasion. You shout for free speech but you are estounded if people insist upon there freedom to be Socialists, or any other ist. Dear, dear Hobo I fear you have not learned anything after all, I fear that all your reading has not taught you, that anarchism can not depend on your mood, but that it is a theory based on reason and judgement. You my dear do not reason, you merely follow your mood which invariably leads to disaster for yourself and others. You say Kennedy avoids you.[3] I do not wonder. You go about talking violence, why should he discredit himself in associating with you? He probably does not believe in violence. He must therefore find your talk very foolish and out of place.

As to our position on Violence, dear neither Kropotkin nor Berkman nor I, ever denied that conditions drive a man to Violence and that every real revolutionary change

---

1. EG had fallen and broken her kneecap at Ossining on 13 August. She was hospitalized in Manhattan 19–26 August 1910.
2. A reference to Wisconsin socialist Victor Berger, identified with the right wing of the Socialist Party.
3. Bart Kennedy (1861–1930) was an English author and early radical hobo-tramp. His *Slavery: Pictures from the Depths* (London: A. Treherne, 1905) was an important radical political novel, an extract from which, "The Logic of Revolutions," was published in the April 1908 *Mother Earth*. Other works include *A Man Adrift* (1899), *A Sailor Tramp* (1902), and *A Tramp's Philosophy* (1908). EG presumably had met Kennedy on a trip to Europe, in either 1895, 1900, or 1907.

necessitates the use of Violence. Never in all my life have I denied that in public. As to Alex, dear he has proven his position better than you and I. What we do insist upon and maintain in this, Violence is only the last medium of individual and social redress. If no other method is left, violence is not only justifiable, but imperative, not because anarchism teaches it, but because human nature does and must resist repression. Anarchism does teach you to get closer to human nature to understand why acts are committed but it does not teach you to kill and rape. The latter depend on res spell governement and not freedom. Dear, I have told you that a million times. You have heard me repeating it on the platform many times, yet you yourself go on confounding one thing with another and you are suprised if people resent it. Besides the question of violence has become an obsession with you. Like all your obsession, it is based on feeling merely and not on sense or logic. I tell you Ben you are playing with fire, you will get yourself into prison for absolutely nothing at all and the worst of it, you will not serve anarchism. Oh, Hobo dear boy, I wish you could see it, I wish you would realize how much harm you are really doing. I wish you would tell me dearest, is violent talk a proof of lack of respectability or does it show a revolutionary spirit? Kropotkin may not talk violence, but never once in his life has the old man expressed a word of condemnation against an act of violence. I know Kropotkin is conventional in every way, but I also know it is not of cowardice or gain, but because of his disposition and his invironment. Besides, how is he to blame if people write to or about him as the philosopher or thinker. He knows and the World knows K is a Revolutionist defending revolutionary action, why need he care? The same is true of Malatesta. If 50 people would discribe him as an Angel, he still remains a revolutionist because his every act proves him to be one.[4]

Now dear, you must allow people to act and think as they see fit and not as you. Therein lies the beauty of anarchism. Reedy[5] may discribe me as he pleases. That is the side he sees in me whether I am or am not a revolutionist you not depend on what Reedy writes, but on myself. So long as I resist every convention and law imposed upon me I am a Revolutionist. As to the method I employ, that depends too not on anarchism but on the time, place and condition. Intellegent Violence. Why the very idea of it, implys discretion judgement as to time and place, do you ever exercise it? You go about like a steer smashing blindly everything before you and when people resented you are surprised![6] Of course dear, I realize your right to talk in your own way. But I can not help being wretched because your way is so childish and irresponcible. I want you to be useful, I

4. In July 1910 BR had traveled to London. In the October 1910 *Mother Earth* BR contributed an article, "A Visit to London," in which he described his meeting with Kropotkin: "The conversation, though instructive, was brief and guarded, and centered entirely on the growth of Anarchism, which my host measured by the ever increased output of Anarchist literature."

5. William Marion Reedy, editor and publisher of the *St. Louis Mirror*, who wrote about EG in his essay *The Daughter of the Dream* (1908).

6. See EG's 25 September 1914 letter to BR, below, which also addresses the differences in their attitudes toward violence.

want you to do good work, I want you to become a power in the movement. But if you continue following your mood only, I know that you will undo in 5 minutes whatever good you may previously have done in 5 hours, and I suffer, I suffer like Hell.

You will forgive me dear, but I really do not believe you ought to speak in public until you have thoroughly digested and reasoned out your ideas.

You say you like Aldred, yet he too disapproves of your talk.[7] How then do you expect older and more thoughtful people to agree with you?

But enough, I know you will resent what I have already said as scolding. If you only knew how it hurts to criticise anything you do. Oh, if you only knew.

About my book dear. I have already informed you, that I will not make a special lecture on Direct Action. I will deal with methods in my Anarchism paper,[8] not of course in your sense. I certainly do not intend to say people ought to go and kill or throw bombs. No indeed not, I see no sense in that. Besides as have agreed with me some time ago. People do not commit an act because you tell them too, they are too damned cowardly for that.

I shall revise the W Slave Traffic.[9] But not Patriotism.[10] Why on Earth should I drag the Socialists in to it. If I were to write about them in relation to Patriotism there would be some sense in that, but my pamphlate is a study on Patriotism not on the Socialists. I hope with you dear that my book will prove a real contribution. I certainly will save no pain in making it one. So far, I think I have succeeded. I think I have done unusually good work in the 5 lectures. How the other five will turn out we'll see. Just at present, I am crippled, absolutely helpless.

Stewart[11] was just here, said I can be taken home, but the cast put on by one of the

7. English anarchist Guy Aldred (1886–1963) was twenty-four years old in 1910. Aldred was a member of the freethought movement, and in 1907 he contributed to the *Voice of Labour*, a London-based syndicalist paper, and helped create both the Industrial Union of Direct Actionists, an early syndicalist organization, and later the Communist Propaganda Group (1917), which attempted to blend anarchism and Marxism. Aldred would be imprisoned for ten months in 1910 for printing an edition of the *Indian Sociologist* (an Indian nationalist paper), which was banned in the wake of the assassination in London of Sir Curzon Wylie, aide de camp to the secretary of state for India, by Madan Lal Dhingra. In court he defended the publishing of the paper as an exercise of his right to free speech. Aldred edited the *Herald of Revolt* between 1910 and 1914 while contributing to many other freethought and political papers. He edited the *Spur* in 1914 and contributed two articles to *Mother Earth*, an essay on the economic conditions that force workers to join the army (1914), and an appeal for financial support (1915). In May 1916 Aldred was imprisoned for fifteen months for refusing conscription. He was in correspondence with both EG and AB between 1906 and 1916.

8. Probably the speech delivered many times by EG, which later evolved into "Anarchism: What It Really Stands For," published as part of *Anarchism and Other Essays* in 1910.

9. EG's essay "The White Slave Traffic," which was first published as a pamphlet in 1909, then as an article in the January 1910 *Mother Earth* (see above); it was revised significantly and published as "The Traffic in Women" in EG's first book, *Anarchism and Other Essays* (1910).

10. EG's essay "Patriotism: A Menace to Liberty" was published as a pamphlet by the Mother Earth Publishing Association in October 1908. It was later published in *Anarchism and Other Essays* (New York: Mother Earth Publishing Association, 1910). See vol. 2, *Making Speech Free*, pp 372–83 for a transcript of this essay.

11. EG received medical treatment for her broken kneecap from Dr. Stewart at St. Vincent's Hospital

interns is no good. I will have to go through the same misery. Stewart's assistant will come tomorrow to 210 to do it & Stewart will come Monday. Anyway I can go home, that is some gain.

I will finish this at the house to night.

210 9 PM

Hobo my own lover darling. Do not be angry with Mommy, I do not mean to be angry or scolding, but I love you. I want you to be great and big.

I was brought home an hour ago, all exhausted. Oh it was terrible, why were you not here to help. I can not write anymore, I am too worn. Roe is here Hapgood and Van der Weyde,[12] they just came, I can not write anymore.

Hobo my own, I love you. I want you with all my being. Come.

YOUR MOMMY ALWAYS

ALS, IU-U.

---

in New York City, where she was laid up. In *Living My Life*, she claims that the same doctor also treated William McKinley after he had been shot by Leon Czolgosz.

12. EG's friends Gilbert Roe, Hutchins Hapgood, and William Van der Weyde were free speech advocates and economic and social liberals. Gilbert Roe was a lawyer and treasurer of the Free Speech League as well as a longtime supporter of EG and AB. William Manley Van der Weyde (1870–1928), a professional photographer, also engaged in a number of radical causes, most notably the Ferrer Association and the Thomas Paine National Historical Association.

## From **ADELINE CHAMPNEY**

*Cleveland, Ohio, 4 September 1910*

MY DEAR EMMA:—

I hope you are out of the Hospital before this. I am very sorry to hear of your accident,[1] and so is Fred.[2] He asks me to give you his love, and to say if the niece whom you mention as being with you is Stella,[3] then he wishes to be remembered to her. Fred is spending the day with a very dear chum who is soon to leave Cleveland. I have been wishing to write you before, but seem to keep so busy all the time, and in the evenings I get so tired and sleepy. I have a little time now, before it is time to go to the Freethought Society,[4] and I am resolved to write to you.

First, we both thank you for mentioning Dr. Hailmann.[5] After some inquiry, Fred found him and is delighted with him. He expects to call on him today with his friend, who is training to be a teacher. Dr. Hailmann will speak at the Ferrer Memorial, which we have decided to hold a week late in order to have Voltairine for our principle speaker.[6] Voltairine will stay with me, while in Cleveland, and she has very kindly consented to speak at the Freethought Society.[7] Things are progressing very well, only Fred can not be here; but he will be in Buffalo at the time of her meetings there, so he will see and hear Voltairine. I have never met her, and I look forward to the visit with her. Streit and Schilling[8] and Rovner and one of the Italian boys were here last week, and they and doubtless others will contribute to having Voltairine come.

1. EG fell and broke her kneecap on 13 August 1910. See Letter to Ben Reitman, 26 August 1910, above.
2. A reference to Adeline Champney's companion, individualist anarchist Fred Schulder.
3. Stella Comyn (Cominsky) was EG's niece, who often assisted her with secretarial work.
4. Adeline Champney was a member of the Cleveland Freethought Society, a liberal discussion club.
5. Dr. W. N. Hailmann (1836–1920) was a member of the Normal Training School of Cleveland, Ohio, and an advocate of unstructured educational environments. His written works include *Application of the Principles of Psychology to the Work of Teaching* (Boston: W. Small, 1884); *Education of the Indian* (New York: J. B. Lyon Company, 1904); and a translation of Friedrich Fröebel's *The Education of Man* (New York: D. Appleton, 1887). Dr. Hailmann also contributed an article titled "The School and Life: Excerpts" from an article published by the *New York Post* to the September 1910 issue of *Mother Earth*.
6. Voltairine de Cleyre reported in *Mother Earth* ("Tour Impressions," January 1911) that the Cleveland Ferrer memorial meeting, held on 21 October, was successful despite a storm that limited attendance to 120 people. She mentioned that a man named Professor Bourland, of Cleveland University, addressed the meeting about the current political situation in Spain.
7. De Cleyre addressed a meeting of the Cleveland Freethought Society on 23 October, which was the Sunday following the Ferrer memorial meeting.
8. Cleveland-based anarchist Emil Schilling. It was Schilling who suspected President McKinley's assassin, Leon Czolgosz, of being an agent provocateur, having met him during 1901. This suspicion was printed in the 1 September 1901 edition of *Free Society*, five days before Czolgosz shot McKinley.

My own paper on Ferrer at the Freethought Society will be little more than an introduction to the larger meeting. It will come on the 9th., probably. I hope to have the pamphlet which the Ferrer Ass'n. are getting out before that.[9] I shall try to get them interested, and then Voltairine will do the rest. By the way, Dr. Hailmann says he has been following the work of Ferrer for the last three or four years. Dr. Hailmann promised Fred to come to hear me, and I look forward to meeting him. Fred says in addition to being apparently very liberal, he is very cordial and friendly. How fine it is to find such men among our educators! It makes us realize that the world does move on, in spite of institutions.

In the same mail with your letter I received one from Alex, in which he spoke of bringing out my article, What Is Worth While, soon, and asking for suggestions as to dividing it. Your letter seemed to question your being able to bring it out for some time yet. Apparently there was a difference of opinion between editor and publisher. I hardly know where to cut it, the structure seems to require that it should remain intact. I think your judgment, if it must be brought out in two parts, will be as good as mine.[10] I will look it over, and see what I think about it.

As for the pamphlet, I am anxious to have you get it out, as you can spread it all over the country, and if you use it in the magazine, of course that saves the cost of composition for the pamphlet.[11] You say it will cost you $35.00 for 2000 copies, and that if half of that could be raised, you could do it, after printing it in M.E. Now, some friends have raised a little fund, and Fred and I will make up the rest and send you $17.50, as soon as you are ready to publish it, if you will let me have 500 copies. I hope you can see your way clear to do this as I'd like to get into the good company you are scattering broadcast over the country.—Just here I was threatened with an interruption,—Streit, Baginski, Carl Nold[12] and some others from Detroit appeared, but finding Fred away did not come in. I am rather glad, for two of them were smoking, and I hate smoke, especially in my own house. And I hate to seem in-hospitable by asking visitors not to smoke. I am not used to it, and after they are gone, I have to air everything for a day before I am comfortable. I suppose those who take it as a matter of course have no idea how offensive it is to others. The only ones who have ever smoked in this apartment, are Streit and Joseph Fels.[13]

9. Presumably a reference to one of three pamphlets published by the Ferrer Association in 1910: *The Rational Education of Children*, the *Program of the International League for Rational Education of Children*, Voltairine de Cleyre's *The Modern School* (both of which were reprinted in *Mother Earth* the same year), or *Francisco Ferrer: His Life Work and Martyrdom*, edited by Leonard Abbott.

10. Champney's essay "What Is Worth While?" eventually appeared in *Mother Earth* in three parts in the November and December issues of 1910 (vol. 5, nos. 9 and 10) and in the January 1911 issue (vol. 5, no. 11).

11. Mother Earth Publishing Association printed Champney's essay "What Is Worth While" as a pamphlet in 1911.

12. Probably Max Baginski's brother, Richard Baginski, who like Carl Nold lived in Detroit.

13. A reference to prominent single-taxer and free speech supporter Joseph Fels.

Curiously enough, very few if any of my friends smoke. My little English friend,[14] Sec. of the Freethought Society, smokes, but not when he is here or even when he is coming here, often. He was in a short time ago, having lamed his back and being on a few days vacation, and he said to me—"I wanted a cigar this afternoon, but I also wanted to come and see you, and I decided that would be worth more." I have never made any aggressive objection to his smoking, but in a general way, he knows my dislike and disapproval. Once in a while he vows he will bring in some cigarettes and teach me to smoke. "You miss a whole lot, Adeline, and besides, it's more social!" I told him if I could find something as distasteful to set him doing, I'd try it!

Well, I'm taking up your time with a gossipy letter! I must get my boy and myself dressed and go out. I am on the Program committee of the Society, with an aggressive and tyrannically inclined Socialist,[15] and our little Sec. It is a peculiar arrangement, extremes meet and pivot upon the young Englishman. It amuses me whenever I think of it.

Our Society is a lot more liberal than many so-called Freethought Societies, but it is not worth very much time; but I have to have some place to go and see folks and get intellectual stimulation. And there are a lot of young men in it, some of them worth while. I am respected and feared, and looked on askance, by many; both because of my out and out Anarchism, and still more because of my unconventional life.[16] But I think I have an influence, and it is needed, as the president is the afore spoken-of despotic Socialist. He admires me and hates me at once. And the more he appreciates my ability, the more he distrusts my influences. But he's always most friendly and courteous. My little Englishman is a sort of weather-vane, vacillating between the two. Being a woman, I think I keep the wind blowing from the liberal quarter more than half the time. It is all very amusing. One must amuse one's self in this tragic world, or one would lose one's sanity!

I did not meet the Pohl's[17] when I was in Buffalo; they were out of town. But I have heard of many courageous and out and out things that Dr. Pohl has done and—paid for sometimes, too. I am glad you met them.

14. Possibly a reference to Cyril J. Bath (1889–1978), recording secretary of the Cleveland Freethought Society. In 1918 Bath would start the successful Cyril Bath Company, a popular stretch forming industrial enterprise.

15. A reference to socialist Isador Ladoff, president of the Cleveland Freethought Society. Ladoff's works include *The Passing of Capitalism, and the Mission of Socialism* (Terre Haute, Ind.: Debs Publishing, 1901); *American Pauperism and the Abolition of Poverty* (Chicago: C. H. Kerr, 1904); and *Socialism, the Antichrist* [1907?].

16. Champney had divorced her husband and had two children out of wedlock with her companion, Fred Schulder, who for much of the time did not live with Champney.

17. Dr. Pohl later arranged EG's 8–9 January 1911 meetings in Buffalo, N.Y.

Well, dear, I glad you are busy! I am sorry for the accident and the enforced rest. But don't take it too hard. Try to get a little real rest out of it, if such a thing is possible.

We all send love,

SINCERELY,
ADELINE

The only place I can find to separate the article is on page 9—"Out of the past have come down to us many maxims—etc." That is near the middle and does not make an intolerable break in continuity.

TLS, IISH, Emma Goldman Archive. On letterhead of the Cleveland Freethought Society, with officers' names and addresses, including Isador Ladoff, president; H. Berkowitz, treasurer; Helen M. Jefferies, corresponding secretary; and Cyril J. Bath, recording secretary. The postscript was handwritten.

Article in the *NEW YORK TIMES*

*New York, 2 November 1910*

## Comstock Heckled at Labor Temple

### Vice Crusader Is Made the Storm Centre for Anarchists' Questions.

Justifies His Work

Emma Goldman, Dr. Reitman, and Others Try in Vain
to Get Him to Admit Himself a Persecutor.

Anthony Comstock stood up yesterday before an audience at the Labor Temple, Fourteenth Street and Second Avenue, and replied to a volley of questions fired at him by Emma Goldman, Dr. Reitman, and their sympathizers. The debate got so hot and Reitman was so negligent of the rules of the meeting that Mr. Comstock threatened as a peace officer of the county to take him off to jail, and a young Scotchman demanded if there were not men enough in the church to punish the "millionaire hobo"[1] for his irreverence, but in the end the meeting closed with no worse effects than Mr. Comstock's loss of his train to Summit.

Mr. Comstock told the story of his fight for the adoption of the laws against the use of the mails for obscene literature and pictures and spoke especially of the convention of "so-called liberals, free thinkers, and free lovers" which had met to obtain their repeal.[2] As soon as he had finished the Rev. Charles Stetzle,[3] the Chairman, invited questions, the rule of the debate being that no man might ask a second question while there was any one else wishing the floor.

"Is it true that you have sent 1,000 people to jail," demanded Dr. Reitman at once, "for spreading necessary information about sex?"

"No," replied Mr. Comstock shortly.

"Yes," shouted Emma Goldman.

---

1. The reporter appears to have confused BR with socialist James Eads How, who founded the International Brotherhood Welfare Association and was known as the "millionaire hobo."
2. After its second convention in October 1877, the National Liberal League presented a petition in February 1878 signed by 70,000 people protesting the Comstock Act. Although the league was unanimously opposed to the Comstock Act, some of its members proposed reforming the law while others insisted on its repeal.
3. Reverend Charles Stetzle, a liberal labor activist, wrote the pro-labor article "The Idealism of the People" in the October 1910 *International Ladies Garment Worker*.

"And drove as many to suicide?" Reitman went on.[4]

"I have acted only according to the rules of the law," retorted Comstock.

"Who furnished you the perjured testimony?" demanded Emma Goldman.

"I have not used perjured testimony," said Mr. Comstock. "Your remarks are indecent and uncalled for."

A burst of applause followed this rebuke but Miss. Goldman was on her feet in a minute armed with a lengthy list of questions on a sheet of paper.

"Do you believe it honest for you to assume, in your investigations, the fictitious name of Max Jansen?"[5] she asked.

"As a Post Office Inspector I am entitled to any name I please," said Comstock. "I am not too stupid as to write a publisher and say I am a Post Office Inspector and will you please forward to me any obscene books you may be sending out?"

### SAYS SHE REPRESENTS THE TRUTH.

A roar of laughter greeted Mr. Comstock's retort, but through it Miss Goldman shouted: "Do you realize that purity is truth?"

"Who do you represent?" cried some one in the hall.

"I represent the truth," replied Miss Goldman, who wanted to know how it could be if Mr. Comstock had for forty years been inspecting obscene literature that his mind remained pure.

"A man can remain pure," said the vice hunter, "if he keeps his will under subjection, and obeys always the laws of God and morality."

The name of Robert Ingersoll then came up, and Mr. Comstock declared that he could prove that his was the first name on the petition asking the repeal of the laws against the use of the mails for obscene literature.[6]

"Do you say that Mr. Ingersoll was in favor of obscene literature?" demanded his interrogator.

---

4. In October 1902 freethought and free love advocate and writer Ida Craddock committed suicide the night before beginning her five-year sentence for obscenity, after suffering repeated instances of persecution by Comstock.

5. The fictitious name used by Comstock was actually Max Johnson. According to *Mother Earth* (November 1910), Comstock's ruse was discovered by German American anarchist George Bauer after Comstock, under the guise of Johnson, entrapped Bauer, the manager of the German-language anarchist paper *Freiheit*, by requesting that two Ferrer memorial pictures advertised in the paper (one of which displayed, among other things, a drawing of a nude woman as the representation of humanity breaking free of her bonds) be sent to him by mail. Bauer complied and was subsequently arrested, although he was released the next day when the grand jury refused to indict him.

6. Freethinker Robert Ingersoll, the first vice president of the National Liberal League, signed the above-mentioned petition (see note 2) calling for reform, but not repeal, of the Comstock Act. In 1880 the League again spoke out against the Comstock Act, this time calling for repeal of the law. Ingersoll resigned from his post in protest, refusing to sign the call for repeal. He argued that the league should be fighting for reform of the laws, not against Comstock himself, an effort he believed would only weaken the political power of the liberal movement.

"I say that his name was first on the petition. I am not running from loud-mouthed infidels and back-biters," said Mr. Comstock.

He declined to be led into a discussion as to how such knowledge should be disseminated without knowing what he was speaking about, and pointed out that matters fit for a medical work would cause the arrest of a man who displayed them in his shop window.

"Well, what harm would they do?" called some one. A shout from the audience went up, and the question was disregarded. Another man from the back of the hall demanded:

"Isn't prudery the chief cause of immorality?"

"Such a question is too absurd to be answered," said Mr. Comstock. He went on to speak of the decisions of the English courts in some cases and declared that unnecessary details that would tend to degrade the morals of those who read them might render a book illegal.

"Do you consider Boccaccio's 'Decameron'[7] obscene?" said some one.

"It has been so held by the courts for years," said Mr. Comstock.

"Well, you can buy it on the bookstalls on the Bowery. I saw three there to-day."

## WILLING TO BUY THEM AT $5 EACH.

"I beg your pardon. You can't find it in this city. I'll give you $5 for every copy you bring me," said Mr. Comstock.

"You can make $15 easy money there," put in Mr. Stetzle.

"What about Leo Tolstoy's[8] 'Resurrection'?" came from another earnest inquirer.

"I don't pass on what I haven't seen," responded Mr. Comstock.

Then a man declared that a director of physical culture had been fined in New Jersey as the result of having extracts from his magazine read to the jury,[9] and asked whether thousands of dollars in fines could not be obtained by reading to an equally unintelligent jury extracts from the Bible.

Mr. Comstock sidestepped by entering on a defense of New Jersey juries. They were, he declared, composed of farmers of a highly intelligent type, well read and well informed.

To the suggestion that after forty years of fighting vice it was strange that he found still so much to do, Comstock retorted that his task to-day is hard because of the license

7. Giovanni Boccaccio (1313–1375) Italian writer and humanist. His *Decameron* (1348–1353) was a collection of one hundred stories, some of which could be considered quite bawdy, told by young men and women escaping the plague in Florence in 1348.
8. Leo Nikolayevich Tolstoy's *Resurrection* (1899) included references to prostitution.
9. A reference to the case of Bernarr Macfadden, editor of *Physical Culture* magazine and director of the Physical Culture Colony in New Jersey. In 1907 he was arrested, tried, and sentenced to two years in prison and fined $2,000 for publication of *Wild Oats*, a John Coryell (writing under the pseudonym Dr. Robert H. Welford) novel warning of the effects of sexually transmitted disease. Macfadden was eventually pardoned by President Taft in 1909. The assertion that Macfadden was fined for reading excerpts of the magazine to the jury is unsubstantiated.

that prevailed before he began his agitation, and that there is less than half the obscene literature for sale in New York to-day than in many of the small cities of the country.

Reitman now began to be anxious to ask another question, and the Chair would not recognize him. He persisted, and Mr. Comstock burst out:

"I am a peace officer of this county. I will take you into custody and charge you with disorderly conduct."

"Go ahead," cried Reitman.

### IMPOSSIBLE TO DESCRIBE THEM.

"And you call this an open forum," shouted Emma Goldman. A shout went up from the audience, but Mr. Stetzle managed to restore order. Then a young girl said simply:

"I don't quite understand. Will you kindly tell us what these obscene books are?"

"It would be impossible," declared Mr. Comstock hurriedly. "It would be shameful for me or any one else to try to describe them publicly."

John D. Denton, the social secretary of the temple, rushed up the aisle. He shook a paper toward the platform and cried:

"Mr. Comstock, Mr. Comstock, please stop. A point of order. Never have I seen such rebellion, such disorder. I call on you as a peace officer to place these people under arrest."

It looked for a moment as if there might be real trouble, and many women rose and ran to the door. When the excitement subsided a serious young German near the front asked earnestly:

"Do you think that Bernard Shaw's works are all right for me to read?"[10]

Mr. Comstock had not read them and was not ready to pass on them offhand. He then explained that in his opinion no one should acquaint a child with the facts of life but his mother.

"How far ought school children go to the Metropolitan Art Gallery?"

"I do not know," replied Mr. Comstock. In the next minute he was roused to anger by a questioner, who wanted to know if it was right to place in the hands of a child the Bible.

"I will not consider, I will not listen to such remarks on the Word of God," said Mr. Comstock. "There is nothing in it that cannot be taken in the right spirit."

"He has avoided the question," came a voice amid shouts of indignation. Miss Goldman was signaling the Chairman wildly, but he passed her over for some one who asked:

10. Irish socialist playwright and literary critic George Bernard Shaw (1856–1950). Shaw was greatly admired by anarchist Benjamin Tucker, who claimed to have introduced Shaw to American readers through the publication of a lengthy article by Shaw in the 27 July 1895 issue of Tucker's paper, *Liberty*. Shaw was also admired by EG, who especially respected and admired his efforts to expose the hypocrisy of Christianity. EG included analysis of two of his plays, *Mrs. Warren's Profession* (1902) and *Major Barbara* (1905), in her lectures and in her book *The Social Significance of The Modern Drama* (1914). It was Shaw who coined the term "Comstockery" to describe the censorship that Comstock was attempting to enforce.

"Is the opera 'Salome'[11] a moral play for children?"

A general laugh drowned whatever Mr. Comstock may have said, and as Miss Goldman was still waving her paper at Mr. Stetzle he closed the meeting in spite of her protests.

"We may all have our views on art," said the Chairman, "but as we walk down Fourteenth Street and see Hell open before our eyes we want some one to hit somebody square between the eyes. I believe Mr. Comstock is the man who is doing that."

"Well, I've missed my train now," said Mr. Comstock as a vote of thanks to him was passed. "I might as well have stopped and fought it out."

*New York Times*, 2 November 1910, p. 8.

---

11. *Salome* (1903) was an opera by Richard Strauss based on Oscar Wilde's play of the same name. The first American production was at the New York Metropolitan Opera House on 22 January 1907. A public outcry at what was considered by some to be the opera's decadence (especially Salome's dance of the seven veils) limited the run of the opera to one, or according to some accounts two, performances.

# THE
# JAPANESE MARTYRS.

Original Editoral Staff of "Yorozu Cho-ho."

PRICE ONE PENNY.

FREEDOM PRESS, 127 OSSULSTON STREET, LONDON, N.W.

Cover of pamphlet memorializing the Japanese anarchists, executed for their alleged attempt to assassinate the Emperor of Japan after the international outcry on their behalf in December 1910 failed to save them. Kōtoku Shūsui is on the left in the photograph. Freedom Press, January 1911 (Kate Sharpley Archive)

Article in the *NEW YORK CALL*

New York, 12 November 1910

## Japanese Radicals Condemned to Die

### Americans Protest Against Barbarous Treatment of Modern Scholars and Thinkers.

Recent news from Japan states that a number of Socialists and anarchists have been condemned to death, and are to be executed for conspiracy against the imperial family of Japan.[1]ūū

The following telegram has been sent to the Japanese ambassador at Washington in the hope of intervention in their behalf before the day of execution.

Ambassador of Japan. Washington D.C.

In the name of humanity and international solidarity, we protest most energetically against the outrageous and unjust sentence upon our friend Denjiro Kotoku and his comrades. Are you trying to imitate Spain and Russia in their barbarous method against intellectuals?

EMMA GOLDMAN

HIPPOLYTE HAVEL

ALEXANDER BERKMAN

DR. BEN L. REITMAN

SADAKICHI HARTMANN[2]

1. On 26 May 1910 a plot to assassinate Emperor Mutsuhito of Japan was discovered by the Japanese government. Kōtoku Shūsui, Kanno Suga, and twenty-six other socialists and anarchists were arrested and charged with complicity in the plot. Although Kōtoku was aware of the plot, apparently he was not directly involved. The assassination attempt was conceived by Miyashita Takichi (1875–1911), a factory worker drawn to both socialism and to anarchism; Kanno Sugga, Kōtoku's estranged common-law wife and a militant anarchist; Niimura Tadao (1887–1911), a follower of Kōtoku; and Furukawa Rikisaku (1884–1911), who was recruited by Kanno. Miyashita built a bomb and turned it over for safekeeping to his friend Shimizu Taichio, who later betrayed the group by informing the police of the plot. The trial, which began on 10 December 1910, was closed to the public and resulted in twelve death sentences, including those of Kōtoku and Kanno, who were executed 24 and 25 January, respectively. Twelve others were sentenced to life in prison, and two were sentenced to terms of military service.

2. Hippolyte Havel, who took an active interest in the Japanese treason case, was instrumental in raising awareness and organizing public protest in the United States. He later published a collection of correspondence between Kōtoku and San Francisco radical Albert Johnson (reprinted in the August, September, and November 1911 issues of *Mother Earth*). He also wrote an article published in the 28 November 1910 *Call*, "Facts Regarding Japanese Radicals: Supplied by Oriental Information Agency and Consul General of Japan." EG commented on Havel's interest in the case: "Havel is developing

The subjoined letter, protesting against Japan's summary method of proceeding against her radical scholars and thinkers is being circulated among labor unions, political, literary and radical groups through the United States:

Dear Friend—In the name of humanity and international brotherhood we currently beg of you to protest energetically to the Japanese ambassador in Washington against the unjust and barbarous penalty of death pronounced upon Dr. Denjiro Kotoku, his wife,[3] and twenty-four other Socialists and anarchists.[4]

Dr. Kotoku, his wife, and their friends were brought before a court specially appointed for the purpose, judged guilty of plotting against the imperial family and sentenced to death. The fact that it was an unusual judicial procedure shows the proof of the alleged crimes was weak.

Denjiro Kotoku is a man who elevated himself to intellectual pursuits and has tried to popularize "Western" ideas in Japan. His "crime" consists in spreading radical ideas and for translating the works of Karl Marx, Leo Tolstoy, Peter Kropotkin and Michael Bakunin.[5] As a leader of the "Left" in the social revolutionary movement in Japan, he was called the "friend of the Kropotkinists." We are convinced the charge of conspiracy against the emperor is false.

Kotoku's condemnation marks the climax of the reaction against liberal ideas which has taken place in Japan during the last few years. Mr. Takayama, the leader of the Socialist party in Japan, has recently protested to western civilization against the persecutions of the Liberals in Japan.[6]

---

wonderful facilities. He wrote the inclosed letter to the Call and other papers and is just crazy on the Japanese case. I never saw him so interested in anything" (EG to BR, 29 November 1910, *EGP*, reel 4). Sadakichi Hartmann, an anarchist, artist, and writer active at the New York Ferrer Modern School, was born in Japan.

3. Kanno Suga was not the wife of Kōtoku, though she was, at one time, his companion. Kanno was forced into marriage at age seventeen and left her husband in 1902. By 1903 she had become politically active and by 1908 was moving in anarchist circles. She was arrested after a demonstration in June 1908. Upon her release from prison in August 1908, she ended her relationship with the still imprisoned anarchist Arahata Kanson (1887–1981). In 1909, she began to live with Kōtoku and helped him publish the journal *Jiyu Shiso* (Free Thought). The journal was outlawed from its first issue. Their relationship was severed in 1911 in part due to disagreement over her support of the assassination plot.

4. Ultimately, twelve were executed, the death sentences of the others commuted to prison terms. Besides those directly involved in the assassination attempt, those arrested and tried included Morichita Umpei (1881–1911), a member of the Heiminsha circle; Uchiyama Gudo (1874–1911), an anarchist and Zen monk; socialists Niimura, U. Nitta, and Sakai Toshihiko; and sixteen others.

5. Kōtoku translated Leo Tolstoy's antiwar essay "Kuiaratameyo" (Repent!) with Sakai Toshihiko in the socialist pacifist journal *Heimin Shimbun* in August 1904, during the Russo-Japanese war. He also translated, with Sakai, Karl Marx's *Communist Manifesto* in *Heimin Shimbun*, November 1904. He later translated Arnold Roller's *Social General Strike* (1907) and Kropotkin's *Conquest of Bread* (1909). There is no extant evidence that he translated any of Bakunin's work.

6. Actually Sen Katayama (1859–1933) a prominent Japanese socialist and author of *The Labor Movement in Japan* (Chicago: Charles H. Kerr & Company Co-Operative, 1918). Katayama published "Government Oppression in Japan" in the *International Socialist Review* 11, no. 2 (August 1910), a letter in the German-language socialist paper *Vorwärts* (28 August 1910), "How Japan Is Civilizing the Formosa Heathen" in the *International Socialist Review* 11 (October 1910), and "The Japanese Miner" in the *International Socialist Review* 11 (February 1911).

We, the international soldiers of freedom, are not willing to have our friends in Japan fall victims to the reactionary forces. Shall the Japanese government imitate the barbarous methods of Spain and Russia and do to death their scholars and thinkers?[7] We must act vigorously in the cause of humanity and civilization and we hope you will not fail to send an urgent protest to the Japanese ambassador.[8]

HUTCHINS HAPGOOD

LEONARD ABBOTT

EMMA GOLDMAN

HIPPOLYTE HAVEL

SADAKICHI HARTMANN

ALEXANDER BERKMAN

DR. BEN L. REITMAN

*New York Call*, 12 November 1910.

7. A reference to the 1909 execution of Spanish anarchist and Modern School educator Francisco Ferrer, as well as to the prevalent persecution of radical thinkers in Russia during this period.
8. In the circular version of this letter, sent out by the *Mother Earth* office, Rose Strunsky's name was included in the list of signatories (see circular in Jack London Collection, CSmH). Strunsky, a prominent socialist and writer, was also an original member of the Kōtoku defense, organized after the arrest of protesters at the Kōtoku Protest Conference on 29 January 1911, at Webster Hall in New York.

My darlingest Hobo

You know what it is to be at 210 one day.[1] Madness complete. It would take hours to tell you all I did to day and I am so tired I can hardly sit up. Still, I want my precious to know everything. To begin with, I wrote about 20 letters to day, part in behalf of the Japanese case which is steadily growing[2] part in behalf of someone. I will tell you later. First about the Japanese case. I have taken Lyric Hall instead of Terrace Lyceum.[3] I have the promis of several people to help financially, besides we will make a collection. We must give the meeting an American character and that can not be done on the East side. Foote, Dr Leverson[4] and others will give money. If we can raise enough after the meeting expences are covered we may send a cable to Japan.[5] I wonder dear, if you will care to do something in Chicago in the matter. You did not seem very interested and if you'd rather not never mind, dear.

Now as to the second part of the day's ordeal. The first greeting on my arrival yesterday, was a letter from Victor Dave.[6] He and his sick wife have been evicted from their

---

1. The *Mother Earth* office, at 210 East 13th Street, New York.
2. On 1 June 1910 the Japanese anarchist Kōtoku Shūsui and twenty-five other Japanese anarchists and socialists were arrested and charged with crimes against the throne (an alleged assassination plot) punishable by death. See "Japanese Radicals Condemned to Die," Article in *New York Call*, 12 November 1910, above.
3. This meeting took place on 12 December 1910 at Lyric Hall. Speakers included EG, Leonard Abbott, Bayard Boyesen, Arthur Bullard, Elizabeth Gurley Flynn, Hippolyte Havel, along with Saul Yanovsky (Yiddish), Max Baginski (German), Arturo Caroti (Italian), Michel Dumas (French), Jaime Vidal (Spanish), and Vaclar Rejsek (Bohemian).
4. Probably Dr. M. R. Levenson of 506 West 135th St., New York, a subscriber to *Mother Earth*. Dr. Edward Bond Foote Jr. was a financial supporter of EG, the Free Speech League, and a variety of other radical causes. For Foote Jr.'s earlier work see vol. 2, *Making Speech Free*, p. 522.
5. At the 12 December 1910 protest meeting at Lyric Hall EG took up a collection in order to send a protest telegram to the Japanese prime minister. The telegram stated "We the libertarians of New York in mass meeting assembled, protest emphatically against the sentence barbarously passed Kōtoku and his comrades." EG also collected money for the families of those executed; in May 1911 EG contacted Tokijiro Kato, and in April 150 yen was sent through Kato to the families of the executed anarchists and socialists in Japan.
6. Belgian-born anarchist writer and editor Victor Dave (1845–1922) was an associate of Peter Kropotkin, Johann Most, Michael Bakunin, and others. Dave spent much of his life in London and Paris and briefly edited *Freiheit* (1884) and contributed to *Humanité Nouvelle* in 1887. EG first met Dave in Paris in 1900, and together they participated in the Neo-Malthusian Congress. Dave was the author, with E. Belfort Bax and William Morris, of *A Short Account of the Commune of Paris* (London: Socialist League Office, 1886). In 1914 he would advise Margaret Sanger on the publication of her paper the *Woman Rebel*. Dave sided with Kropotkin during the First World War and signed the February 1916 Manifesto of the Sixteen in support of the Allies. For more on Dave, see vol. 1, *Made for America*, p. 526.

home and the belongings sold at auction, he begs for help. I wrote letters to people, who remember his part in the movement and put his case before them. I also sent to Ballard,[7] who met Dave in Paris he gave me $5. I sent Dave's letter to Hutch.[8] Perhaps in that way, I can get a little money together for this old warrier who was the teacher of Most[9] and a great figure in the movement for so many years. Of course, I will have to add something, short as we are. Dave's letter brought the possibility of old age and helplessness before me, and made me shudder. What if I could no longer do anything and were dependent? Oh, Hobo, my darling life is terrible, especially the old life of a revolutionist.

Letters and visitors were not all Mommy did. I went to the Dentist, who gave me a raking headache with drilling my tooth. I must go again tomorrow before I go to the farm. The real work on the tooth will begin Saturday, I will have to have a crown after it is treated, will also have to have other teeth attended to, which means an unexpected expence. I also saw a few places for the Ferrer Centre, too dear or unavailable. Boyesen came as I asked him but not Leonard.[10] The latter may not have gotten my letter. Bayesen is to call a meeting of the Exect for Dec 5th after noon, he is also to prepare a very short statement to go on a circular like your outcast get up,[11] of the things done and what we intend to do. We will also have the financial account a call for help and the announcement of the large meeting Jan 5th.[12] The matter will first be placed before the Committee and then ordered about 10 000 copies to flood the City radical element.

I have not forgotten our own meetings, dearest mine. Mickie[13] has distributed cards at M Franks and Brooklyn Philosophical yesterday. The Rand school W F M Hall and

7. Arthur Bullard, journalist and socialist, traveled widely in Africa, Europe, and Asia and wrote several books under the pseudonym Albert Edwards, notably *A Man's World* (New York: Macmillan, 1912) and *Comrade Yetta* (New York: Macmillan, 1913).

8. EG probably hoped Hutchins Hapgood, in his capacity as a columnist for the *New York Commercial Advertiser*, could publicize Dave's case.

9. Dave was probably Johann Most's introduction to anarchism. Dave helped Most edit *Freiheit* in London before the paper moved to New York in 1883, and he was a staunch proponent of propaganda by the deed.

10. The Ferrer Center Modern School of the Francisco Ferrer Association opened in January 1911 at 6 St. Marks Place. It was first organized as an adult center directed by Bayard Boyesen with Sunday and evening classes. Leonard Abbott was president of the Ferrer Association.

11. On 17 November 1910 BR hosted Outcast Night at Pacific Hall, New York City. Celebrating outcasts and outsiders, the event included speakers such as Sadakichi Hartmann and Hippolyte Havel. EG attended the event but did not speak.

12. The inauguration of the Francisco Ferrer Center was held on 5 January 1911 at Webster Hall, 119 East 11th Street. EG, Leonard Abbott, Bolton Hall, Bayard Boyesen, AB, Gilbert Roe, and Grace Potter spoke.

13. Herman Mikhailovitch, also referred to by EG as "Mickie," attached himself to EG's 1910 tour by offering to arrange her 29 March through 31 March lectures in Omaha, but in the process he was arrested for distributing the handbills advertising EG's meetings. He later worked around the *Mother Earth* office, served as secretary at the Ferrer Association, and once gave a speech at a Ben Reitman–organized hobo gathering. Over time he and EG clashed, which precipitated his expulsion from EG's circle.

a meeting to day.[14] Have also sent out many cards to our subscribers. I am expecting a very large Tolstoy[15] meeting both in Jewish and English and of course, the Engl card advertises my three lectures.

Tomorrow I go to the Farm to finish my Essay and if possible to write my reply to Volt for M E.[16] I will also have to write part of the Comments or all, so you can imagine what I have before me still, I will get through if only, I have my darling's love and cooperation.

I thought of you so much dear, all day. I wonder how you fared to day in Pittsburg,[17] if you got out to night I suppose, I will have a letter, I hope so.

Sweetheart, the inclosed letter came open, H tells me it was not even sealed I think.

Lover precious, my own great companion in work and struggle, I love you awfully much, so do the m—the t-b and every inch of me. Come close to me dearest, and let me rest, I is tired.

Good night. Hobo's Mommy

over

Hobo my dear. So far no letter from you. I hope it will come later, before I leave. I am in great misery with my jaw, did not sleep all night. Must go to the Dentist again. I dread going out on the farm with this ache, but I must, I have all the lecture material outside.

I may write again dear before, I leave, or from the farm.

With love for my own precious
Mommy

ALS, IU-U. On letterhead of *Mother Earth*.

14. EG lists a number of radical centers in New York. The Brooklyn Philosophical Society was a freethought organization for which Theodore Schroeder served as president and at which EG was invited to speak on several occasions. The Rand School of Social Science, founded in 1906 by George Davis Herron and Carrie Rand, was owned and operated by the American Socialist Society. The Rand School educated both socialists and the general public about socialism. The WFM Hall was the hall of the Women's Trade Union League.

15. EG lectured, in both English and Yiddish, on Leo Tolstoy as part of her lecture series on modern drama during her 1911 lecture tour.

16. EG wrote a response to Voltarine de Cleyre's lecture tour report, published in the December 1910 *Mother Earth*, in which de Cleyre criticized the move toward bringing anarchist propaganda to the middle and upper classes, rather than maintaining the focus on the working class. For EG's response see "A Rejoinder," Article in *Mother Earth*, December 1910, below.

17. Reitman was probably making arrangements for EG's meetings in Pittsburgh, held 11–14 January 1911.

My dear Miss Wald

My attention has been called to the case of Miss Welinsky, Monlifiero Home nurse who is held as insane in the Bellevue Hospital.

I learn that the girl is really not ill, but has been sent away for making some disclosures as to the cruel conditions prevelent at the Home. I understand Mr Schiff[1] has something to do with the case.

I wonder; if you could look into the case: The girl is poor and has no one. If there is any truth in the information I have been given, it would be a most terrible blunder. Perhaps you can do something.[2]

I am inclosing a letter printed in the <u>Call</u> to day also a circular which I sent out which will show you that Japan is about to follow the terrible methods of Western Europe.[3] I know both Dr Kotoku and Mme Kano through correspondence and am sure they are not guilty of the charge of conspiracy.

Mme Kano is the first woman in Japan held for a political offence. I am trying to get up some kind of a protest which might have some beneficial influence.[4]

1. Jacob Schiff (1847–1920) was a banker and philanthropist who financed much of Wald's early public health work, including the purchase of the building in New York City that housed the Henry Street Settlement. Anna Volinsky, who had worked at the Montefiore Home for Chronic Invalids in New York, apparently as a solicitor, was arrested on 17 October 1910 on charges of threatening Schiff (president of the home) with a pistol, and being of unsound mind. Declared insane, she was eventually committed, on 30 November, to the Manhattan State Hospital, where she killed herself on 2 January 1911.

2. In her reply, Wald suggested that EG's story was based on false information. The doctor who made the diagnosis, Wald wrote, "is above suspicion and could not possibly be influenced by anything but his judgement as to the condition of a patient." In a subsequent letter EG thanked Wald for correcting her mistake. Lillian Wald to EG, 5 December 1910; EG to Wald, 15 December 1910; *EGP*, reel 4.

3. The letter was the 28 November 1910 article by Havel, "Facts Regarding Japanese Radicals" in the *New York Call*; the circular EG refers to was reprinted in the 12 November 1910 *New York Call*. See "Japanese Radicals Condemned to Die," Article in the *New York Call*, 12 November 1910, above.

4. On 12 December 1910, EG participated in a New York meeting organized to protest the Japanese court's decision and solicited the support of prominent U.S. liberals in an effort to send several telegrams of protest to the Japanese government. She later helped raise money for the families of those who were executed in Japan. *Mother Earth* led the way in publicizing the events, dedicating the February 1911 issue to Kōtoku and his comrades. EG added a lecture on the subject to her spring speaking tour. On 6 December a protest meeting in San Francisco featured speeches by Jack London and the socialist Austin Lewis. Protests on the issue were held in cities across the United States, including Boston, St. Louis, Los Angeles, Seattle, and Portland, and in countries around the world, including France, England, Switzerland, and Austria. Lillian Wald, too, became involved in the Kōtoku case and corresponded directly with people she had met while touring Japan earlier in 1910.

You know it was just such a protest, which saved Babushka, and Tchaikovsky from death.[5] A number of friends have protested to the Ambassador in Washington. I wonder if you could not do the same. I ask this on purely humanitarian grounds as against Capital punishment.

Will be happy to hear from you.

Sincerely

Emma Goldman

ALS, Lillian Wald Papers, NN. On *Mother Earth* stationery.

---

5. In March 1910 the Russian government charged Catherine Breshkovskaya ("Babushka") and Nikolai Chaikovsky with treason for attempting to lead an armed rebellion against the Russian government. Their case spurred public protests in the United States and England and a petition drive for leniency. Although the accused expected the death penalty, Chaikovsky was acquitted, while Breshkovskaya was sentenced to perpetual exile in Siberia on the charge of engaging in "criminal activity in a revolutionary organization," namely the Russian Socialist Revolutionary Party (PSR).

MY DEAR JACK AND CHARMIAN

You have probably already seen some mention of the fate of ~~six~~ 26 comrades under death sentence in Japan.

I am inclosing material which will acquaint you with the case more fully. It seems to be a repitition of the Ferrer case, as Dr Kotoku and his wife Mme Kano are both educators and literary people. Kotoku was once in San Francisco. Did you run accross him.[1] Anyway, it is most unlikely that he has plotted against the Emperial family, though personally I should in no way consider that a crime. I don't believe you would either.

We are leaving nothing undone to arouse public interest, we have already succeeded in a measure. Dec 12th we are to have a big meeting which will probably cable its protest to Japan. Will you send us a line dear?[2] We are very eager to line up all revolutionists in this matter, as we have in that of Ferrer. Perhaps we can help to save the 26 lives.[3]

Please send anything you deem fit, at once in time for our meeting. I often think of you both and your dream place.[4] May I come again next Spring? I begin my pilgrimage in Jan. The road is full of thorns and one's soul bleeds, but there is no rest, onward ever onward is the watchword

WITH LOVE TO BOTH.

EMMA GOLDMAN

Remember me very kindly to Nakata.[5]

ALS, Jack London Collection, CSmH. On *Mother Earth* stationery. Date stamped in upper-right corner: December 5th 1910.

1. After spending five months in jail for his opposition to the Russo-Japanese War, socialist writer and activist Kōtoku Shūsui left Japan for San Francisco, where he stayed from December 1905 until June of the following year. Witnessing firsthand the mutual cooperation in the wake of the San Francisco earthquake influenced Kōtoku's conversion from socialism to anarchism, a political trajectory already in process while he was in prison. No record has been found to verify whether or not Kōtoku and socialist author Jack London or his wife Charmian ever met. Kōtoku's diary of his visit to San Francisco makes no mention of any meeting between them.
2. EG and eleven others spoke on behalf of Kōtoku and his co-defendants at a meeting in New York on 12 December 1910. The organizers read letters of protest from various American radicals and socialists, including a telegram from Jack London to the Japanese ambassador dated 24 November 1910.
3. A meeting supporting Kōtoku was held in San Franscico on 6 December 1910, sponsored by London and socialist Austin Lewis. A total of $800 was collected and sent to Japan.
4. EG had visited Jack and Charmian London at their ranch, Beauty Ranch, near Glen Ellen, California, earlier that year. The proposed 1911 visit never materialized. Their next meeting was in New York two years later.
5. Yoshiatsu Nakata was the Londons' housekeeper at the time of EG's visit.

Article in *MOTHER EARTH*

New York, December 1910

# A Rejoinder

It is not often that I take issue with my friend Voltairine de Cleyre. But there are a few points in her report[1] which I cannot permit to pass unchallenged.

Comrade Voltairine states that she speaks of the propaganda ("if there be any") "from short experience and impression." Yet she finds it necessary to emphasize the "seeking of respectable halls, respectable neighborhoods, etc." I have always known her to be cautious in passing opinions, and I am therefore surprised that a mere impression should warrant her in suggesting that we are seeking for "respectable halls, respectable people," etc.

The fact that the man who arranged a meeting for her in Rochester (by the way, *not* an Anarchist) has tried to sandwich her between bourgeois speakers, or that she was advertised in Buffalo as a Tolstoian Anarchist, is by no means proof that we are all following the same lines, or that "we have gone woefully wrong."

I have traveled the length and breadth of this country for many years; have been to the Coast four times within a short period, and I can assure Comrade Voltairine that no one connected with my work has sought for "respectable" patronage. Of course, if by "respectable halls" is meant clean halls, I plead guilty to the charge. I confess that I prefer such places, partly for sanitary reasons, but mainly because the workers themselves—the American workers—will not go to a dilapidated, dirty hall in an obscure quarter of the city. In that respect the people Voltairine wants to reach are probably the most bourgeois in America. I have again convinced myself of it the other day in Baltimore, where the American workers would not attend my meetings because the hall was in the "nigger" district. Strange as it may seem, the people who came were, what Voltairine would call, respectables.

I agree with our Comrade that our work should be among "the poor, the ignorant, the brutal, the disinherited men and women." I for one have worked with them and among them for twenty-one years. I therefore feel better qualified than Voltairine to say

---

1. Voltairine de Cleyre reported in the December 1910 issue of *Mother Earth* on her speaking tour, which began in New York on 7 October and concluded with her annual Haymarket speech in Chicago on 11 November. In her "Tour Impressions" de Cleyre argued that anarchists should direct their message to the workers, not to the middle and upper classes. De Cleyre wrote, "while I cannot now express a fixed opinion on so short experience, my impression is that our present propaganda (if there is any) is a woeful mistake. I am more than ever convinced that our work should be with the workers, not with the bourgeoisie. If these latter choose to come, very well, let them. But I should never approve of this seeking after 'respectable halls,' 'respectable neighborhoods,' 'respectable people,' etc., etc."

what may be accomplished in their ranks. After all, my friend knows the masses mainly from theory.[2] I know them from years of contact in and out of the factory. Just because of that knowledge I do not believe that our work should be only with them. And that for the following reasons:

The pioneers of every new thought rarely come from the ranks of the workers. Possibly because the economic whip gives the latter little opportunity to easily grasp a truth. Besides, it is an undisputed fact that those who have but their chains to lose cling tenaciously to them.

The men and women who first take up the banner of a new, liberating idea generally emanate from the so-called respectable classes. Russia, Germany, England, and even America bear me out in this. The first conspiracy against the Russian despot originated in his own palace, with the Decembrists[3] representing the nobility of Russia. The intellectual pioneers of revolutionary and Anarchist ideas in Germany came from the "respectables." The women who are to-day enduring the hunger strike for their ideas, in England, are also not from the ranks of the workers. The same holds good in regard to almost every country and every epoch.

Far be it from me to belittle the poor, the ignorant, the disinherited. Certainly they are the greatest force, if only they could be awakened from their lethargy. But I maintain that to limit one's activities to them is not only a mistake, but also contrary to the spirit of Anarchism. Unlike other social theories, Anarchism builds not on classes, but on men and women. I may be mistaken, but I have always been of the opinion that Anarchism calls to battle all libertarian elements as against authority.

That to limit oneself to propaganda exclusively among the oppressed does not always bring desired results, is borne out by more than one historical proof. Our Chicago comrades propagated only among the workers; in fact, cheerfully gave their lives for the oppressed. Where were the latter during the eighteen terrible months of the judicial farce? Were not the Chicago Anarchists shamefully betrayed by the very organization which Parsons and Spies[4] helped to build up—the Knights of Labor?[5] And has not the

---

2. EG's comment is not quite fair to de Cleyre, who, although she may never have been a garment factory worker as EG had been, nevertheless spent much of her life living and working as a tutor with the immigrant poor in Philadelphia and Chicago in a condition of abject poverty.

3. Led by military officer Pavel Ivanovich Pestel, the "Decembrists," so called after their failed 14 December 1825 attempt to prevent Tsar Nicholas from ascending the throne, issued one of the first serious threats to Russia's monarchy. After spending time in Europe, some Russian soldiers, on their return, joined secret societies calling for the abolition of serfdom and the establishment of a constitutional democracy. The revolt was brutally suppressed by Tsar Nicholas, who ordered the hanging of Pestel and others and the exile of many more to Siberia.

4. A reference to the Haymarket anarchists Albert Parsons (1848–1887), American anarchist and editor of the *Alarm*, and August Vincent Theodore Spies (1855–1887), German American editor of the *Chicago Arbeiter-Zeitung*. Parsons had been a member of the Knights of Labor from 1874. Spies, however, was a member for only a brief time, "principally because I never liked secrecy or ceremonies in an organization" (*Knights of Labor*, 6 and 13 November 1886).

5. Although Parsons and Spies were or had been members of the Knights of Labor in the wake of the Haymarket Square bombing, the organization, led by Terence V. Powderly, immediately repudiated

spirit of that time drifted into conservative channels, as represented by the American Federation of Labor? The majority of its members, I am sure, would hesitate not a moment to relegate Voltairine or myself to the fate of our martyred comrades.

John Most[6] worked for twenty-five years exclusively among the workers. He certainly never sought for "respectables." Indeed, the poorer and more wretched the atmosphere, the more eloquently Most spoke. Where are the results of his propaganda? Why was the man so utterly forsaken in the last years of his activities? Why cannot the *Freiheit*, in spite of all desperate efforts, be maintained?[7]

I think the answer to these questions can easily be found in the very thing Voltairine so fervently advocates—the propaganda exclusively among the workers. Yes, that is, in my opinion, the reason why we have in the past made so little headway. The economic factor is, I am sure, very vital. Possibly that accounts for the fact that a great many radicals lose their ideals the moment they succeed economically. Voltairine surely knows as well as I that hundreds of Anarchists, Socialists, and rabid revolutionists who were ardent workers twenty years ago are now very respectable, indeed much more respectable than the very people to whom Voltairine objects. That, however, should not discourage the true propagandist from working among the disinherited, but it should teach him the vital lesson that spiritual hunger and unrest are often the most lasting incentives.

Anarchism excludes no one and gives no one a mortgage on truth and beauty. Above all, Anarchism, as I understand it, leaves the propagandist free to choose his or her own manner of activity. The criterion must at all times be his or her individual judgement, experience, and mental leanings. In the Anarchist movement there is room for every one who earnestly desires to work for the overthrow of authority, physical as well as mental.

Emma Goldman.

*Mother Earth* 5 (December 1910): 325–28. This rejoinder was translated into German and reprinted, omitting all reference to Voltairine de Cleyre, in *Der Sozialist* (Berlin). See "Gegen einseitige Klassen-Propaganda" (Against a one-sided class-propaganda), 1 March 1911, *EGP*, reel 47. EG develops these ideas in her 1914 essay "The Intellectual Proletarian," which seeks to show that all workers, whether manual or intellectual, could be considered proletarian and therefore necessary for the social revolution.

---

any connections to anarchism. The Chicago Knights were in fact in the forefront of this distancing effort, declaring, "We are sure we voice the sentiment of the entire organization when we say we hope that Parsons, Spies, Most, Fielding [Fielden] and the whole gang of outlaws will be blotted from the surface of the earth" (*Knights of Labor*, 8 May 1886).

6. A reference to German anarchist Johann Most, considered among the most influential anarchists of his time, who from the turn of the century onward gradually lost much of his audience and readership. He died on 17 March 1906 while on a speaking tour.

7. *Freiheit*, the newspaper founded by Johann Most, ceased publication in 1910, just four years after his death.

MY DEAR MR BALDWIN.

What have you done to my friend Harry Kelly?[1] You must have hypnotised him, he is so taken with you. I can not really blame him, I would be myself, if I did not fear to shock you.

Mr Kelly writes me he had spoken to you about my coming visit to St Louis, and the chance of getting some decent Hall. I am very anxious to get a cleaner place than Druids Hall, but I fear $50 for the Memorial Hall, if we can get it is altogether too much for E G.[2]

It is very kind of you to say, I have left a good impression in St Louis.[3] But I know from experience, impressions rarly cover expences. You see, I want to have more than one meeting in St Louis, I must therefore have a more reasonable place. Can you suggest one? Perhaps there is some neat Hall about 500 capacity that could be got, for say, $25, that would really be the highest. I am writing Mr Reedy at the same time, would you confer with him.

Mr Kelly will be back in your City in time to attend to the proper advertising, if you would just help with the Hall I should deem it a great favor. I mean to place tickets for advance sale. I know a number of St. Louis friends who will help with that, I am sure Mr Reedy will also.

Am frightfully busy reading proofs on my book[4] and preparing my new lecture course.

I hope that you are well.

SINCERELY, EMMA GOLDMAN

ALS, ACLU Archives, NjP. On *Mother Earth* stationery. Addressed at top to Mr. Roger N. Baldwin, St. Louis, Mo.

1. Roger Baldwin and Harry Kelly both lived in St. Louis.
2. Baldwin answered EG's letter on 10 December 1910, stating that he would look into more appropriate halls.
3. EG lectured in St. Louis from 3 February through 10 February 1910. She returned to St. Louis in February 1911.
4. *Anarchism and Other Essays* (New York: Mother Earth Publishing Association, 1910).

Ben L Reitman

Baby[1] arrived three pm has beautiful body hope be soul is also worth while specimen mailed special wayward but precious father also twelve shipped mother still unnerved from strain but busy preparing for last ordeal in newyork roses greeted the new born and brought cheer to

Mommy Mickey
850pm

TWSr, IU-U. Western Union telegram addressed to Ben L. Reitman, M.D., 3429 Wood St.

1. A reference to the publication of *Anarchism and Other Essays* (New York: Mother Earth Publishing Association, 1910). On a circular dated 24 June 1910, EG had announced the upcoming book to *Mother Earth* subscribers in order to solicit advance sales of the book, listing twelve prospective essay titles (see *EGP*, reel 3). Although EG's letter stated that "no essential change will be made" in the contents of the book," she raised the final number of essays from twelve to thirteen and omitted the titles "What I Believe," "Anarchism Versus Socialism," and "Crime and Criminals." In their place, she included four new essays titled "The Hypocrisy of Puritanism," "Patriotism: A Menace to Liberty," "Minorities Versus Majorities," and "Prisons: A Social Crime and Failure." In addition, she revised two of the preliminary titles, changing "The Traffic in Women" to "The White Slave Traffic" and the subtitle of "The Drama" to from "The Strongest Dissemination of Radical Thought" to "A Powerful Disseminator of Radical Thought."

To Elizabeth Gurly Flynn.[1] The first American woman rebel. I send these Essays[2] in the hope that they may help her onward ever onward towards our great ideal.

EMMA GOLDMAN

ALS, Elizabeth Gurley Flynn Papers, NNU.

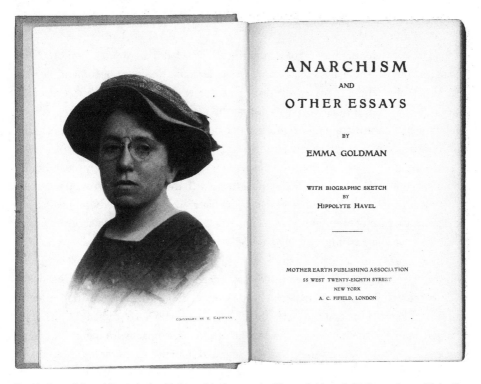

Frontispiece of *Anarchism and other Essays*, with photograph of Emma Goldman by Kajiwara, first published by the Mother Earth Publishing Association in 1910.

1. Prominent IWW organizer and speaker Elizabeth Gurley Flynn.
2. EG inscribed a copy of the newly published *Anarchism and Other Essays* to Flynn.

Essay published by **MOTHER EARTH PUBLISHING ASSOCIATION**

*New York, 1911*

# The Psychology of Political Violence

To analyze the psychology of political violence is not only extremely difficult, but also very dangerous. If such acts are treated with understanding, one is immediately accused of eulogizing them. If, on the other hand, human sympathy is expressed for the *Attentäter*,[1] one risks being considered a possible accomplice. Yet it is only intelligence and sympathy that can bring us closer to the source of human suffering, and teach us the ultimate way out of it.

The primitive man, ignorant of natural forces, dreaded their approach, hiding from the perils they threatened. As man learned to understand Nature's phenomena, he realized that though these may destroy life and cause great loss, they also bring relief. To the earnest student it must be apparent that the accumulated forces in our social and economic life, culminating in a political act of violence, are similar to the terrors of the atmosphere, manifested in storm and lightning.

To thoroughly appreciate the truth of this view, one must feel intensely the indignity of our social wrongs; one's very being must throb with the pain, the sorrow, the despair millions of people are daily made to endure. Indeed, unless we have become a part of humanity, we cannot even faintly understand the just indignation that accumulates in a human soul, the burning, surging passion that makes the storm inevitable.

The ignorant mass looks upon the man who makes a violent protest against our social and economic iniquities as upon a wild beast, a cruel, heartless monster, whose joy it is to destroy life and bathe in blood; or at best, as upon an irresponsible lunatic. Yet nothing is further from the truth. As a matter of fact, those who have studied the character and personality of these men, or who have come in close contact with them, are agreed that it is their super-sensitiveness to the wrong and injustice surrounding them which compels them to pay the toll of our social crimes. The most noted writers and poets, discussing the psychology of political offenders, have paid them the highest tribute. Could anyone assume that these men had advised violence, or even approved of the acts? Certainly not. Theirs was the attitude of the social student, of the man that knows that beyond every violent act there is a vital cause.

Björnstjerne Björnson, in the second part of *Beyond Human Power*, emphasizes the

---

1. Assassin or would-be assassin, in German. The term, especially in anarchist circles, refers to an anarchist who commits a conscious act of violence directed against a powerful individual—often royalty or a government leader—identified with acts of political repression.

fact that it is among the Anarchists that we must look for the modern martyrs who pay for their faith with their blood, and who welcome death with a smile, because they believe, as truly as Christ did, that their martyrdom will redeem humanity.[2]

François Coppée, the French novelist, thus expresses himself regarding the psychology of the *Attentäter*:

"The reading of the details of Vaillant's execution left me in a thoughtful mood. I imagined him expanding his chest under the ropes, marching with firm step, stiffening his will, concentrating all his energy, and, with eyes fixed upon the knife, hurling finally at society his cry of malediction. And, in spite of me, another spectacle rose suddenly before my mind. I saw a group of men and women pressing against each other in the middle of the oblong arena of the circus, under the gaze of thousands of eyes, while from all the steps of the immense amphitheater went up the terrible cry, *Ad leones!* and, below, the opening cages of wild beasts.

"I did not believe the execution would take place. In the first place, no victim had been struck with death, and it had long been the custom not to punish an abortive crime with the last degree of severity. Then, this crime, however terrible in intention, was disinterested, born of an abstract idea. The man's past, his abandoned childhood, his life of hardship, pleaded also in his favor. In the independent press generous voices were raised in his behalf, very loud and eloquent. 'A purely literary current of opinion' some have said, with no little scorn. *It is, on the contrary, an honor to the men of art and thought to have expressed once more their disgust at the scaffold.*"[3]

Again Zola, in *Germinal* and *Paris*, describes the tenderness and kindness, the deep sympathy with human suffering, of these men who close the chapter of their lives with a violent outbreak against our system.[4]

Last, but not least, the man who probably better than anyone else understands the psychology of the *Attentäter* is M. Hamon,[5] the author of the brilliant work, *Une Psychologie du Militaire Professionel*, who has arrived at these suggestive conclusions:

2. American journalist Alvan Sanborn (1866–1966) comments in *Paris and the Social Revolution* (1905), a work excerpted in *Mother Earth*, July–September 1906, that in *Over Ævne, I (Beyond Our Power, I*, 1883) Norwegian freethinker and author Bjørnstjerne Bjørnson (1832–1910) "emphasized . . . that it is among propagandists *par le fait* of anarchy that we must look for the modern martyrs, for the men who witness their faith with their blood, who sacrifice themselves unreservedly for their fellow-men, who welcome death with smiles and outstretched arms because they are confident that their martyrdom will usher the redemption of mankind." EG identified the second part of his play as a portrayal of an anarchist *Attentat*.

3. This is an excerpt from "French Opinion of Vaillant and His Act," *Liberty*, 24 March 1894, vol. 9, no. 49, whole issue no. 283 (New York). The François Coppée selection originally appeared in *Le Journal* (Paris), 8 February 1894.

4. French writer, novelist, naturalist, and social critic Émile Zola (1840–1902). In *Germinal* (1885) the character Souvarine epitomizes the nihilist and *Attentäter*. In his work *Paris* (1898) the anarchist character Salvat evokes Vaillant. Zola's major work was a twenty-novel history of the Rougon-Macquart family (1871–1893).

5. Augustin Hamon (1862–1945), French sociologist, critic, and editor. An anarchist militant during the 1890s, he was a delegate to the London congress of the Second International in 1896. Vestiges of

"The positive method confirmed by the rational method enables us to establish an ideal type of Anarchist, whose mentality is the aggregate of common psychic characteristics. Every Anarchist partakes sufficiently of this ideal type to make it possible to differentiate him from other men. The typical Anarchist, then, may be defined as follows: A man perceptible by the spirit of revolt under one or more of its forms,—opposition, investigation, criticism, innovation,—endowed with a strong love of liberty, egoistic or individualistic, and possessed of great curiosity, a keen desire to know. These traits are supplemented by an ardent love of others, a highly developed moral sensitiveness, a profound sentiment of justice, and imbued with missionary zeal."

To the above characteristics, says Alvin F. Sanborn, must be added these sterling qualities: a rare love of animals, surpassing sweetness in all the ordinary relations of life, exceptional sobriety of demeanour, frugality and regularity, austerity, even, of living, and courage beyond compare.[6]

"There is a truism that the man in the street seems always to forget, when he is abusing the Anarchists, or whatever party happens to be his *bête noir* for the moment, as the cause of some outrage is just perpetrated. This indisputable fact is that homicidal outrages have, from time immemorial, been the reply of goaded and desperate classes, and goaded and desperate individuals, to wrongs from their fellow-men, which they felt to be intolerable. Such acts are the violent recoil from violence, whether aggressive or repressive; they are the last desperate struggle of outrage and exasperated human nature for breathing space and life. And their cause lies not in any special conviction, but in the depths of human nature itself. The whole course of history, political and social, is strewn with evidence of this fact. To go no further, take the three most notorious examples of political parties goaded into violence during the last fifty years: the Mazzinians in Italy,[7] the Fenians in Ireland,[8] and the Terrorists in Russia.[9] Were these

---

his early attachment to anarchism played an important part in the manner in which he framed his four decades of activity in the Socialist Party in Brittany and his participation in the French Resistance during World War II. He edited *L'Humanité nouvelle* (1897–1907), was a translator and critic of Irish playwright George Bernard Shaw, and authored, among other books, *Psychologie du militaire professionnel* (1894), *Psychologie de l'anarchiste-socialiste* (1895), and *Le Socialisme et le congrès de Londres* (1897). EG first met Hamon in Paris in 1896, after which they maintained a correspondence. See vol. 1, *Made for America*, pp. 239, 257, and 280 for examples.

6. This sentence is a direct quotation from Alvan Sanborn's *Paris and the Social Revolution* (Boston: Small, Maynard, 1905), p. 156.

7. The Mazzinian were followers of Giuseppe Mazzini (1805–1872), an Italian nationalist and political thinker who founded the organization Giovine Italia (Young Italy) to promote Italian unification under a republican form of government. He later founded Young Switzerland and Young Europe, counterparts to Giovine Italia, to spread the principles of equality and brotherhood throughout Europe. Uprisings in Milan (1853) and Genoa (1857), though unsuccessful, were organized in part by Mazzini.

8. An Irish nationalist organization formed in 1858. After it attempted several attacks against the British in 1867, its leaders were arrested, and the group disbanded. The Fenians were reconstituted as the Irish Republican Brotherhood in 1873.

9. Between 1879 and 1881, Narodnaya Volya (the People's Will), a Russian terrorist organization, assas-

people Anarchists? No. Did they all three even hold the same political opinions? No. The Mazzinians were Republicans, the Fenians political separatists, the Russians Social Democrats or Constitutionalists. But all were driven by desperate circumstances into this terrible form of revolt. And when we turn from parties to individuals who have acted in like manner, we stand appalled by the number of human beings goaded and driven by sheer desperation into conduct obviously violently opposed to their social instincts.

"Now that Anarchism has become a living force in society, such deeds have been sometimes committed by Anarchists, as well as by others. For no new faith, even the most essentially peaceable and humane the mind of man has yet accepted, but at its first coming has brought upon earth not peace, but a sword; not because of anything violent or anti-social in the doctrine itself; simply because of the ferment any new and creative idea excites in men's minds, whether they accept or reject it. And a conception of Anarchism, which, on one hand, threatens every vested interest, and, on the other, holds out a vision of a free and noble life to be won by a struggle of existing wrongs, is certain to rouse the fiercest opposition, and bring the whole repressive force of ancient evil into violent contact with the tumultuous outburst of a new hope.

"Under miserable conditions of life, any vision of the possibility of better things makes the present misery more intolerable, and spurs those who suffer to the most energetic struggles to improve their lot, and if these struggles only immediately result in sharper misery, the outcome is sheer desperation. In our present society, for instance, an exploited wage worker, who catches a glimpse of what work and life might and ought to be, finds the toilsome routine and the squalor of his existence almost intolerable; and even when he has the resolution and courage to continue steadily working his best, and waiting until new ideas have so permeated society as to pave the way for better times, the mere fact that he has such ideas and tries to spread them, brings him into difficulties with his employers. How many thousands of Socialists, and above all Anarchists, have lost work and even the chance of work, solely on the ground of their opinions. It is only the specially gifted craftsman, who, if he be a zealous propagandist, can hope to retain permanent employment. And what happens to man with his brain working actively with a ferment of new ideas, with a vision before his eyes of a new hope dawning for toiling and agonizing men, with the knowledge that his suffering and that of his fellows in misery is not caused by the cruelty of fate, but by the injustice of other human beings,—what happens to such a man when he sees those dear to him starving, when he himself is starved? Some natures in such a plight, and those by no means the least social or the least sensitive, will become violent, and will even feel that their violence is social and not anti-social, that in striking when and how they can, they are striking, not for themselves, but for human nature, outraged and despoiled in their persons and in

---

sinated several government officials and repeatedly attempted to take the life of Tsar Alexander II, finally succeeding on 1 March 1881.

those of their fellow sufferers. And are we, who ourselves are not in this horrible predicament, to stand by and coldly condemn these piteous victims of the Furies and Fates? Are we to decry as miscreants these human beings who act with heroic self-devotion, sacrificing their lives in protest, where less social and less energetic natures would lie down and grovel in abject submission to injustice and wrong? Are we to join the ignorant and brutal outcry which stigmatizes such men as monsters of wickedness, gratuitously running amuck in harmonious and innocently peaceful society? No! We hate murder with a hatred that may seem absurdly exaggerated to apologists for Matabele massacres,[10] to callous acquiescers in hangings and bombardments, but we decline in such cases of homicide, or attempted homicide, as those of which we are treating, to be guilty of the cruel injustice of flinging the whole responsibility of the deed upon the immediate perpetrator. The guilt of these homicides lies upon every man and woman who, intentionally or by cold indifference, helps to keep up social conditions that drive human beings to despair. The man who flings his whole life into the attempt, at the cost of his own life, to protest against the wrongs of his fellow-men, is a saint compared to the active and passive upholders of cruelty and injustice, even if his protest destroy other lives besides his own. Let him who is without sin in society cast the first stone at such a one."[11]

That every act of political violence should nowadays be attributed to Anarchists is not at all surprising. Yet it is a fact known to almost everyone familiar with the Anarchist movement that a great number of acts, for which Anarchists had to suffer, either originated with the capitalist press or were instigated, if not directly perpetrated, by the police.

For a number of years acts of violence had been committed in Spain, for which the Anarchists were held responsible, hounded like wild beasts, and thrown into prison. Later it was disclosed that the perpetrators of these acts were not Anarchists, but members of the police department. The scandal became so widespread that the conservative Spanish papers demanded the apprehension and punishment of the gang-leader, Juan Rull,[12] who was subsequently condemned to death and executed. The sensational evidence, brought to light during the trial, forced Police Inspector Momento to exonerate completely the Anarchists from any connection with the acts committed during a long period. This resulted in the dismissal of a number of police officials, among them Inspector Tressols, who, in revenge, disclosed the fact that behind the gang of police

---

10. In March 1896 the natives of Rhodesia (now Zimbabwe) rose in rebellion against the imperial forces of the British South Africa Company in Matabeleland. The rebellion spread to neighboring Mashonaland in June. By 1897 the uprisings had been violently crushed by British imperial forces leaving thousands dead, the majority of whom were Africans.
11. An excerpt from Charlotte M. Wilson's *Anarchism and Outrage* (London: *Freedom* Pamphlet No. 8, 1893).
12. Juan Rull and his family were part of a network of police informants in Barcelona who threw bombs and then collected fees for implicating anarchists as perpetrators of violence. The scandal was revealed after Rull's arrest in 1907.

bomb-throwers were others of far higher position, who provided them with funds and protected them.[13]

This is one of the many striking examples of how Anarchist conspiracies are manufactured.

That the American police can perjure themselves with the same ease, that they are just as merciless, just as brutal and cunning as their European colleagues, has been proved on more than one occasion. We need only recall the tragedy of the eleventh of November, 1887, known as the Haymarket Riot.[14]

No one who is at all familiar with the case can possibly doubt that the Anarchists, judicially murdered in Chicago, died as victims of a lying, bloodthirsty press and of a cruel police conspiracy. Has not Judge Gary[15] himself said: "Not because you have caused the Haymarket bomb, but because you are Anarchists, you are on trial."

The impartial and thorough analysis by Governor Altgeld of that blotch on the American escutcheon verified the brutal frankness of Judge Gary. It was this that induced Altgeld to pardon the three Anarchists, thereby earning the lasting esteem of every liberty-loving man and woman in the world.[16]

When we approach the tragedy of September sixth, 1901, we are confronted by one of the most striking examples of how little social theories are responsible for an act of political violence. "Leon Czolgosz, an Anarchist, incited to commit the act by Emma Goldman."[17] To be sure, has she not incited violence even before her birth, and will she not continue to do so beyond death? Everything is possible with the Anarchists.

Today, even, nine years after the tragedy, after it was proved a hundred times that Emma Goldman had nothing to do with the event, that no evidence whatsoever exists to indicate that Czolgosz ever called himself an Anarchist, we are confronted with the same lie, fabricated by the police and perpetrated by the press. No living soul ever heard

---

13. Barcelona police, including Chief Tresols and "Memento," worked with the Duque de Bivina and Governor Francisco Manzano, among other officials, in orchestrating terrorist attacks by agents provocateurs, among them members of the Rull family.

14. On 11 November 1887, four of the five Haymarket anarchists were executed (Louis Lingg had killed himself the preceding night). The Haymarket incident occurred on 4 May 1886.

15. A reference to Joseph E. Gary (1821–1906), Cook County Superior Court justice who presided over the 1886 Haymarket trial. Elected to the bench in 1863, he served until his death.

16. In June 1893 Governor John P. Altgeld pardoned the surviving Haymarket anarchists, Samuel Fielden, Oscar Neebe, and Michael Schwab, effectively ending his own political career. His detailed statement issued with the pardons, *Reasons for Pardoning Fielden, Neebe, and Schwab* (Chicago, 1893), was published and circulated for many years by anarchists and socialists, including the Free Society Publishing Association (1899), Lucy Parsons (1915), C. H. Kerr (1896), and New York Labor News (1894).

17. On 6 September 1901 anarchist Leon Czolgosz was arrested immediately after the shooting of President William McKinley in Buffalo, New York. Czolgosz's trial began on 24 September 1901 and lasted two days. He was executed on 29 October 1901. See "Assassin's Trail . . . Emma Goldman's Words Drove Him to Murder," Article in the *San Francisco Chronicle*, 8 September 1901, in vol. 1, *Made for America*.

Czolgosz make that statement, nor is there a single written word to prove that the boy ever breathed the accusation. Nothing but ignorance and insane hysteria, which have never yet been able to solve the simplest problem of cause and effect.

The President of the free Republic killed! What else can be the cause, except that the *Attentäter* must have been insane, or that he was incited to the act.

A free Republic! How a myth will maintain itself, how it will continue to deceive, to dupe, and blind even the comparatively intelligent to its monstrous absurdities. A free Republic! And yet within a little over thirty years a small band of parasites have successfully robbed the American people, and trampled upon the fundamental principals, laid down by the fathers of this country, guaranteeing to every man, woman, and child "life, liberty, and the pursuit of happiness." For thirty years they have been increasing their wealth and power at the expense of the vast mass of workers, thereby enlarging the army of the unemployed, the hungry, homeless, and friendless portion of humanity, who are tramping the country from east to west, from north to south, in a vain search for work. For many years the home has been left in the care of the little ones, while the parents are exhausting their life and strength for a mere pittance. For thirty years the sturdy sons of America have been sacrificed on the battlefield of industrial war, and the daughters outraged in corrupt factory surroundings. For long and weary years this process of undermining the nation's health, vigor, and pride, without much protest from the disinherited and oppressed, has been going on. Maddened by success and victory, the money powers of this "free land of ours" became more and more audacious in their heartless, cruel efforts to compete with the rotten and decayed European tyrannies for supremacy of power.

In vain did a lying press repudiate Leon Czolgosz as a foreigner. The boy was a product of our own free American soil, that lulled him to sleep with,

> My country, 'tis of thee,
> Sweet land of liberty.

Who can tell how many times this American child had gloried in the celebration of the Fourth of July, or of Decoration Day, when he faithfully honored the Nation's dead? Who knows but that he, too, was willing to "fight for his country and die for her liberty," until it dawned upon him that those he belonged to have no country, because they have been robbed of all that they have produced; until he realized that the liberty and independence of his youthful dreams was but a farce. Poor Leon Czolgosz, your crime consisted of too sensitive a social consciousness. Unlike your idealless and brainless American brothers, your ideals soared above the belly and the bank account. No wonder you impressed the one human being among all the infuriated mob at your trial—a newspaper woman[18]—as a visionary, totally oblivious to your surroundings. Your large, dreamy eyes must have beheld a new and glorious dawn.

---

18. Quite possibly Katherine Leckie (b. Kingston, Canada; d. 1930), a Chicago journalist and editor. EG recalls, in *Living My Life*, Leckie having visited her during her brief incarceration in Chicago just

Now, to a recent instance of police-manufactured Anarchist plots. In that bloodstained city, Chicago, the life of Chief of Police Shippy was attempted by a young man named Averbuch.[19] Immediately the cry was sent to the four corners of the world that Averbuch was an Anarchist, and that the Anarchists were responsible for the act. Everyone who was at all known to entertain Anarchist ideas was closely watched, a number of people arrested, the library of the Anarchist group confiscated, and all meetings made impossible. It goes without saying that, as on various previous occasions, I must needs be held responsible for the act. Evidently the American police credit me with occult powers. I did not know Averbuch; in fact, had never before heard his name, and the only way I could have possibly "conspired" with him was in my astral body. But, then, the police are not concerned with logic or justice. What they seek is a target, to mask their absolute ignorance of the cause, of the psychology of the political act. Was Averbuch an Anarchist? There is no positive proof of it. He had been but three months in the country, did not know the language, and, as far as I could ascertain, was quite unknown to the Anarchists of Chicago.

What led to his act? Averbuch, like most young Russian immigrants, undoubtedly believed in the mythical liberty of America. He received his first baptism by the policeman's club during the brutal dispersement of the unemployed parade. He further experienced American equality and opportunity in the vain efforts to find an economic master. In short, a three months' sojourn in the glorious land brought him face to face with the fact that the disinherited are in the same position the world over. In his native land he probably learned that necessity knows no law—there was no difference between a Russian and an American policeman.

The question to the intelligent social student is not whether the acts of Czolgosz or Averbuch were practical, any more than whether the thunderstorm is practical. The thing that will inevitably impress itself on the thinking and feeling man and woman is that the sight of brutal clubbing of innocent victims in a so-called free Republic, and the degrading, soul-destroying economic struggle, furnish the spark that kindles the dynamic force in the overwrought, outraged souls of men like Czolgosz or Averbuch. No amount of persecution, of hounding, of repression, can stay this social phenomenon.

But, it is often asked, have not acknowledged Anarchists committed acts of violence? Certainly they have, always however ready to shoulder the responsibility. My contention is that they were impelled, not by the teachings of Anarchism, but by the tremendous pressure of conditions, making life unbearable to their sensitive natures. Obviously, Anarchism, or any other social theory, making man a conscious social unit, will act as a leaven for rebel-

---

after the McKinley assassination. Leckie wrote for the *Chicago Chronicle* in 1901 and later for the *Chicago American* and the *New York Evening Journal*. Leckie was associate editor (with Theodore Dreiser) of the *Delineator* and editor of both *New Idea Woman's Magazine* and the *Housekeeper*. She was also a member of a number of radical organizations, including the International Workers' Defense League in 1916, Greenwich Village's Heterodoxy Club, and the Women's Trade Union League.

19. See "The Free Speech Fight," Article in *Mother Earth*, March 1910, below.

lion. This is not a mere assertion, but a fact verified by all experience. A close examination of the circumstances bearing upon this question will further clarify my position.

Let us consider some of the most important Anarchist acts within the last two decades. Strange as it may seem, one of the most significant deeds of political violence occurred here in America, in connection with the Homestead strike of 1892.[20]

During that memorable time the Carnegie Steel Company organized a conspiracy to crush the Amalgamated Association of Iron and Steel Workers. Henry Clay Frick, then Chairman of the Company, was intrusted with that democratic task. He lost no time in carrying out the policy of breaking the Union, the policy which he had so successfully practiced during his reign of terror in the coke regions. Secretly, and while peace negotiations were being purposely prolonged, Frick supervised the military preparations, the fortification of the Homestead Steel Works, the erection of a high board fence, capped with barbed wire and provided with loopholes for sharpshooters. And then, in the dead of night, he attempted to smuggle his army of Pinkerton thugs into Homestead, which act precipitated the terrible carnage of the steel workers. Not content with the death of eleven victims, killed in the Pinkerton skirmish, Henry Clay Frick, good Christian and free American, straightway began the hounding down of the helpless wives and orphans, by ordering them out of the wretched Company houses.

The whole country was aroused over these inhuman outrages. Hundreds of voices were raised in protest, calling on Frick to desist, not to go too far. Yes, hundreds of people protested,—as one objects to annoying flies. Only one there was who actively responded to the outrage at Homestead,—Alexander Berkman. Yes, he was an Anarchist. He gloried in that fact, because it was the only force that made the discord between his spiritual longing and the world without at all bearable. Yet not Anarchism, as such, but the brutal slaughter of the eleven steel workers was the urge for Alexander Berkman's act, his attempt on the life of Henry Clay Frick.

The record of European acts of political violence affords numerous and striking instances of the influence of environment upon sensitive human beings.

The court speech of Vaillant, who, in 1894, exploded a bomb in the Paris Chamber of Deputies,[21] strikes the true keynote of the psychology of such acts:

"Gentlemen, in a few minutes you are to deal your blow, but in receiving your verdict I shall have at least the satisfaction of having wounded the existing society, that cursed

---

20. The "strike" (in reality, a lockout) at the Homestead Steel Works, owned by industrialist Andrew Carnegie, began in the summer of 1892 after the company refused to negotiate with the workers' union, the Amalgamated Association of Iron and Steel Workers.

21. Auguste Vaillant (1861–1894) was a French anarchist, who on 9 December 1892 threw a bomb in the Paris Chamber of Deputies. Although no one was killed and only a few people suffered minor injuries, Vaillant was executed on 6 February 1894. At his trial he declared, "the deputies are responsible for all society's afflictions." Vaillant's bomb throwing led to the passage of the anti-anarchist *lois scélérates* and inspired the Italian Santo Caserio's assassination of French President Sadi Carnot in June 1894. The text of the argument Vaillant presented to the court was widely circulated in pamphlet form and reprinted by Benjamin Tucker in *Liberty*, 24 February 1894.

society in which one may see a single man spending, uselessly, enough to feed thousands of families; an infamous society which permits a few individuals to monopolize all the social wealth, while there are hundreds of thousands of unfortunates who have not even the bread that is not refused to dogs, and while entire families are committing suicide for want of the necessities of life.

"Ah, gentlemen, if the governing classes could go down among the unfortunates! But no, they prefer to remain deaf to their appeals. It seems that a fatality impels them, like the royalty of the eighteenth century, toward the precipice which will engulf them; for woe be to those who remain deaf to the cries of the starving, woe to those who, believing themselves of superior essence, assume the right to exploit those beneath them! There comes a time when the people no longer reason; they rise like a hurricane, and pass away like a torrent. Then we see bleeding heads impaled on pikes.

"Among the exploited, gentlemen, there are two classes of individuals: Those of one class, not realizing what they are and what they might be, take life as it comes, believe that they are born to be slaves, and content themselves with the little that is given them in exchange for their labor. But there are others, on the contrary, who think, who study, and who, looking about them, discover social iniquities. Is it their fault if they see clearly and suffer at seeing others suffer? Then they throw themselves into the struggle, and make themselves the bearers of the popular claims.

"Gentlemen, I am one of these last. Wherever I have gone, I have seen unfortunates bent beneath the yoke of capital. Everywhere I have seen the same wounds causing tears of blood to flow, even in the remoter parts of the inhabited districts of South America, where I had the right to believe that he who was weary of the pains of civilization might rest in the shade of the palm trees and there study nature. Well, there even, more than elsewhere, I have seen capital come, like a vampire, to suck the last drop of blood of the unfortunate pariahs.

"Then I came back to France, where it was reserved for me to see my family suffer atrociously. This was the last drop in the cup of my sorrow. Tired of leading this life of suffering and cowardice, I carried this bomb to those who are primarily responsible for social sufferings.

"I am reproached with the wounds of those who were hit by my projectiles. Permit me to point out in passing that, if the bourgeois had not massacred or caused massacres during the Revolution, it is probable that they would still be under the yoke of the nobility. On the other hand, figure up the dead and wounded of Tonquin, Madagascar, Dahomey, adding thereto the thousands, yes, millions of unfortunates who die in the factories, the mines, and wherever the grinding power of capital is felt.[22] Add also those

22. The Franco-Prussian War (1870–1871) fomented nationalist rivalries among the industrial states of Europe, especially France and Germany, thus stimulating the scramble to occupy Africa and Asia. Under the Third Republic (1870–1940), France expanded its empire into North and West Africa, Madagascar, the Middle East, and Indochina. Following the bombardment of the port of Tamatave

who die of hunger, and all this with the assent of our Deputies. Besides all this, of how little weight are the reproaches now brought against me!

"It is true that one does not efface the other; but, after all, are we not acting on the defensive when we respond to the blows which we receive from above? I know very well that I shall be told that I ought to have confined myself to speech for the vindication of the people's claims. But what can you expect! It takes a loud voice to make the deaf hear. Too long have they answered our voices by imprisonment, the rope, rifle volleys. Make no mistake; the explosion of my bomb is not only the cry of the rebel Vaillant, but the cry of an entire class which vindicates its rights, and which will soon add acts to words. For, be sure of it, in vain will they pass laws. The ideas of the thinkers will not halt; just as, in the last century, all the governmental forces could not prevent the Diderots and the Voltaires from spreading emancipating ideas among the people, so all the existing governmental forces will not prevent the Reclus,[23] the Darwins, the Spencers,[24] the Ibsens,[25] the Mirabeaus,[26] from spreading the ideas of justice and liberty which will annihilate the prejudices that hold the mass in ignorance. And these ideas, welcomed by the unfortunate, will flower in acts of revolt as they have done in me, until the day when the disappearance of authority shall permit all men to organize freely according to their choice, when we shall each be able to enjoy the product of his labor, and when those moral maladies called prejudices shall vanish, permitting human beings to live in harmony, having no other desire than to study the sciences and love their fellows.

"I conclude, gentlemen, by saying that a society in which one sees such social inequalities as we see all about us, in which we see every day suicides caused by poverty, prostitution flaring at every street corner,—a society whose principal monuments are barracks and prisons,—such a society must be transformed as soon as possible, on pain of being eliminated, and that speedily, from the human race. Hail to him who labors, by no matter what means, for this transformation! It is this idea that has guided me in my duel with authority, but as in this duel I have only wounded my adversary, it is now its turn to strike me.

in 1883, Madagascar ceded control of external affairs and certain land, rent, and occupation rights in a treaty with France in 1885. In 1870 France sent 30,000 troops to Tonkin (northern Vietnam); the Vietnamese signed the treaty of Hué in June 1884 recognizing their nation's status as a French protectorate. France spent the next decade trying to suppress Vietnamese resistance in the north. Dahomey was captured in 1894.

23. Jean Jacques Élisée Reclus (1830–1905), French anarchist communist and geographer and leading theorist of an anarchist communism distinguished by unusual tolerance and generosity to other anarchist ideas.

24. Herbert Spencer (1820–1903), English philosopher and sociologist. He advocated the importance of the individual over society and of science over religion, and he argued for an extreme form of economic and social laissez-faire.

25. A reference to Norwegian-born dramatist and poet Henrik Ibsen.

26. Octave Mirbeau (1848–1917) was a French journalist, novelist, and playwright. See also "Priestess of Anarchism Becomes Dramatic Seer," Interview in the *San Francisco Bulletin*, 16 January 1909, in vol. 2, *Making Speech Free*, pp. 396–402.

"Now, gentlemen, to me it matters little what penalty you may inflict, for, looking at this assembly with the eyes of reason, I can not help smiling to see you, atoms lost in matter, and reasoning only because you possess a prolongation of the spinal marrow, assume the right to judge one of your fellows.

"Ah! gentlemen, how little a thing is your assembly and your verdict in the history of humanity; and human history, in its turn, is likewise a very little thing in the whirl-wind which bears it through immensity, and which is destined to disappear, or at least to be transformed, in order to begin again the same history and the same facts, a veri-tably perpetual play of cosmic forces renewing and transferring themselves forever."[27]

Will anyone say that Vaillant was an ignorant, vicious man, or a lunatic? Was not his mind singularly clear, analytic? No wonder that the best intellectual forces of France spoke in his behalf, and signed the petition to President Carnot, asking him to com-mute Vaillant's death sentence.

Carnot would listen to no entreaty; he insisted on more than a pound of flesh, he wanted Vaillant's life, and then—the inevitable happened: President Carnot was killed. On the handle of the stiletto used by the *Attentäter* was engraved, significantly,

### VAILLANT!

Santa Caserio[28] was an Anarchist. He could have gotten away, saved himself; but he remained, he stood the consequences.

His reasons for the act are set forth in so simple, dignified, and childlike a manner that one is reminded of the touching tribute paid Caserio by his teacher of the little vil-lage school, Ada Negri, the Italian poet, who spoke of him as a sweet, tender plant, of too fine and sensitive texture to stand the cruel strain of the world.[29]

"Gentlemen of the Jury! I do not propose to make a defense, but only an explanation of my deed.

"Since my early youth I began to learn that the present society is badly organized, so badly that every day many wretched men commit suicide, leaving women and children in the most terrible distress. Workers, by the thousands, seek for work and cannot find it. Poor families beg for food and shiver with cold; they suffer the greatest misery; the little ones ask their miserable mothers for food, and the mothers cannot give them, because

27. The text quoted here by EG is the statement Vaillant read at his trial on 10 January 1894. It was printed in *Liberty*, 24 February 1894, vol. 9, no. 47, whole issue no. 281.

28. Italian anarchist Santo Caserio (1873–1894) assassinated French President Sadi Carnot in Lyon on 24 June 1894 to avenge the execution of Auguste Vaillant on 6 February 1894. He was immediately arrested and executed on 16 August. His act led to the passage of the third of three Exceptional Laws (or what anarchists referred to as the *lois scélérates*) on 26 and 27 July 1894.

29. Ada Negri (1870–1945), Italian poet and novelist and teacher at the elementary school of Motta Visconti in Pavia from 1888 to 1892. She was rumored to have been Caserio's teacher. She won the Milli Prize for poetry in 1894 and the Mussolini Prize for artistic achievement in 1931. Her major literary works on social issues include *Fatalita* (Fatality, 1892), *Tempeste* (Storms, 1895), *Maternita* (Motherhood, 1904), *Dal profondo* (From the Depths, 1910), and *Esilio* (Exile, 1914).

they have nothing. The few things which the home contained have already been sold or pawned. All they can do is beg alms; often they are arrested as vagabonds.

"I went away from my native place because I was frequently moved to tears at seeing girls of eight or ten years obliged to work fifteen hours a day for the paltry pay of twenty centimes. Young women of eighteen or twenty also work fifteen hours daily, for a mockery of remuneration. And that happens not only to my fellow countrymen, but to all workers, who sweat the whole day long for a crust of bread, while their labor produces wealth in abundance. The workers are obliged to live under the most wretched conditions, and their food consists of a little bread, a few spoonfuls of rice, and water; so by the time they are thirty or forty years old, they are exhausted, and go to die in the hospitals. Besides, in consequence of bad food and overwork, these unhappy creatures are, by hundreds, devoured by pellagra—a disease that, in my country, attacks, as the physicians say, those who are badly fed and lead a life of toil and privation.

"I have observed that there are a great many people who are hungry, and many children who suffer, whilst bread and clothes abound in the towns. I saw many and large shops full of clothing and woolen stuffs, and I also saw warehouses full of wheat and Indian corn, suitable for those who are in want. And, on the other hand, I saw thousands of people who do not work, who produce nothing and live on the labor of others; who spend every day thousands of francs for their amusement; who debauch the daughters of the workers; who own dwellings of forty or fifty rooms; twenty or thirty horses, many servants; in a word, all the pleasures of life.

"I believed in God; but when I saw so great an inequality between men, I acknowledged that it was not God who created man, but man who created God. And I discovered that those who want their property to be respected, have an interest in preaching the existence of paradise and hell, and in keeping the people in ignorance.

"Not long ago, Vaillant threw a bomb in the Chamber of Deputies, to protest against the present system of society. He killed no one, only wounded some persons; yet bourgeois justice sentenced him to death. And not satisfied with the condemnation of the guilty man, they began to pursue the Anarchists, and arrest not only those who had known Vaillant, but even those who had merely been present at any Anarchist lecture.[30]

"The government did not think of their wives and children. It did not consider that the men kept in prison were not the only ones who suffered, and that their little ones cried for bread. Bourgeois justice did not trouble itself about these innocent ones, who do not yet know what society is. It is no fault of theirs that their fathers are in prison; they only want to eat.

"The government went on searching private houses, opening private letters, forbid-

---

30. In the aftermath of Vaillant's action in December 1893, the French government mounted a campaign to suppress anarchist activities, passing the first two of three *lois scélérates* (exceptional laws). The first imposed imprisonment and fines for journalists convicted of provoking violence. The second criminalized any formal or informal connections to anarchism or associations with anarchists.

ding lectures and meetings, and practicing the most infamous oppressions against us. Even now, hundreds of Anarchists are arrested for having written an article in a newspaper, or for having expressed an opinion in public.

"Gentlemen of the Jury, you are representatives of bourgeois society. If you want my head, take it; but do not believe that in so doing you will stop the Anarchist propaganda. Take care, for men reap what they have sown."[31]

During a religious procession in 1896, at Barcelona, a bomb was thrown. Immediately three hundred men and women were arrested. Some were Anarchists, but the majority were trade unionists and Socialists. They were thrown into that terrible bastille, Montjuich, and subjected to most horrible tortures. After a number had been killed, or had gone insane, their cases were taken up by the liberal press of Europe, resulting in the release of a few survivors.

The man primarily responsible for this revival of the Inquisition was Cánovas del Castillo, Prime Minister of Spain. It was he who ordered the torturing of the victims, their flesh burned, their bones crushed, their tongues cut out. Practised in the art of brutality during his régime in Cuba, Cánovas remained absolutely deaf to the appeals and protests of the awakened civilised conscience.

In 1897 Cánovas del Castillo was shot to death by a young Italian, Angiolillo.[32] The latter was an editor in his native land, and his bold utterances soon attracted the attention of the authorities. Persecution began, and Angiolillo fled from Italy to Spain, thence to France and Belgium, finally settling in England. While there he found employment as a compositor, and immediately became the friend of all his colleagues. One of the latter thus described Angiolillo: "His appearance suggested the journalist, rather than the disciple of Guttenberg. His delicate hands, moreover, betrayed the fact that he had not grown up at the 'case.' With his handsome frank face, his soft dark hair, his alert expression, he looked the very type of the vivacious Southerner. Angiolillo spoke Italian, Spanish, and French, but no English; the little French I knew was not sufficient to carry on a prolonged conversation. However, Angiolillo soon began to acquire the English idiom; he learned rapidly, playfully, and it was not long until he became very popular with his fellow compositors. His distinguished and yet modest manner, and his consideration towards his colleagues, won him the hearts of all the boys."[33]

Angiolillo soon became familiar with the detailed accounts in the press. He read of the great wave of human sympathy with the helpless victims at Montjuich. On Trafalgar Square he saw with his own eyes the results of these atrocities, when the few Spaniards,

31. An excerpt from the speech made by Santo Caserio at his trial. The text appeared in *Anarchy on Trial* (London: *Freedom* Pamphlet No. 9, 1896).

32. Michele Angiolillo (1871–1897) was an Italian anarchist who shot and killed Antonio Cánovas del Castillo, prime minister of Spain, on 8 August 1897, at the Santa Agueda baths.

33. A description of Michele Angiolillo taken almost verbatim from an article by A. Derlitzki entitled "Angiolino," which appeared in *Mother Earth* 1 (October 1906). This was the only article by one A. Derlitzki printed in *Mother Earth*.

who escaped Castillo's clutches, came to seek asylum in England. There, at the great meeting, these men opened their shirts and showed the horrible scars of the burned flesh. Angiolillo saw, and the effect surpassed a thousand theories; the impetus was beyond words, beyond arguments, beyond himself even.[34]

Señor Antonio Cánovas del Castillo, Prime Minister of Spain, sojourned at Santa Agueda. As usual in such cases, all strangers were kept away from his exalted presence. One exception was made, however, in the case of a distinguished looking, elegantly dressed Italian—the representative, it was understood, of an important journal. The distinguished gentleman was—Angiolillo.

Señor Cánovas, about to leave his house, stepped on the veranda. Suddenly Angiolillo confronted him. A shot rang out, and Cánovas was a corpse.

The wife of the Prime Minister rushed upon the scene. "Murderer! Murderer!" she cried, pointing at Angiolillo. The latter bowed. "Pardon, Madame," he said, "I respect you as a lady, but I regret that you were the wife of that man."

Calmly Angiolillo faced death. Death in its most terrible form—for the man whose soul was as a child's.

He was garrotted. His body lay, sun-kissed, till the day hid in twilight. And the people came, and pointing the finger of terror and fear, they said: "There—the criminal— the cruel murderer."

How stupid, how cruel is ignorance! It misunderstands always, condemns always.

A remarkable parallel to the case of Angiolillo is to be found in the act of Gaetano Bresci, whose *Attentat* upon King Umberto made an American city famous.[35]

Bresci came to this country, this land of opportunity, where one has but to try to meet with golden success. Yes, he too would try to succeed. He would work hard and faithfully. Work had no terrors for him, if it would only help him to independence, manhood, self-respect.

Thus full of hope and enthusiasm he settled in Paterson, New Jersey, and there found a lucrative job at six dollars per week in one of the weaving mills of the town. Six dollars per week was, no doubt, a fortune for Italy, but not enough to breathe on in the new country. He loved his little home. He was a good husband and devoted father to his *bam-*

34. In May 1897 in London a "Spanish Atrocities Committee" formed in response to recent accounts by Spanish anarchists of the harrowing conditions and torture in Montjuich prison. On 22 August the committee arranged a mass meeting in Trafalgar Square providing a platform for Francisco Gana and other Montjuich prisoners to expose the horrors of their experiences. The Trafalgar Square meeting, which EG credits in her essay as the catalyst for Angiolillo's *Attentat* against Spanish prime minister Antonio Cánovas del Castillo, actually took place two weeks after the assassination, by which time he had already been tried and executed.

35. Gaetano Bresci assassinated King Umberto (1844–1900) in 1900. After ascending the throne in 1878, Umberto was the target of three assassination attempts. The first two attacks, presumed to be the result of anarchist conspiracies, prompted inconclusive investigations. After Umberto's assassination, the town of Paterson, New Jersey, where Bresci lived, became synonymous with militant anarchism in the eyes of the public.

*bina*, Bianca, whom he adored. He worked and worked for a number of years. He actually managed to save one hundred dollars out of his six dollars per week.

Bresci had an ideal. Foolish, I know, for a workingman to have an ideal—the Anarchist paper published in Paterson, *La Questione Sociale*.[36]

Every week, though tired from work, he would help set up the paper. Until late hours he would assist, and when the little pioneer had exhausted all resources and his comrades were in despair, Bresci brought cheer and hope, one hundred dollars, the entire savings of years. That would keep the paper afloat.

In his native land people were starving. The crops had been poor, and the peasants saw themselves face to face with famine. They appealed to their good King Umberto; he would help. And he did. The wives of the peasants who had gone to the palace of the King, held up in mute silence their emaciated infants. Surely that would move him. And then the soldiers fired and killed those poor fools.

Bresci, at work in the weaving mill at Paterson, read of the horrible massacre. His mental eye beheld the defenceless women and innocent infants of his native land, slaughtered right before the good King. His soul recoiled in horror. At night he heard the groans of the wounded. Some may have been his comrades, his own flesh. Why, why these foul murders?

The little meeting of the Italian Anarchist group in Paterson ended in a fight. Bresci had demanded his hundred dollars. His comrades begged, implored him to give them respite. The paper would go down if they were to return him his loan. But Bresci insisted on its return.

How cruel and stupid is ignorance. Bresci got the money, but lost the good will, the confidence of his comrades. They would have nothing more to do with one whose greed was greater than his ideals.

On the twenty-ninth of July, 1900, King Umberto was shot at Munzo. The young Italian weaver of Paterson, Gaetano Bresci, had taken the life of the good King.

Paterson was placed under police surveillance, everyone known as an Anarchist hounded and persecuted, and the act of Bresci ascribed to the teachings of Anarchism. As if the teachings of Anarchism in its extremest form could equal the force of those slain women and infants, who had pilgrimed to the King for aid. As if any spoken word, ever so eloquent, could burn into a human soul with such white heat as the life blood trickling drop by drop from those dying forms. The ordinary man is rarely moved either by word or deed; and those whose social kinship is the greatest living force need no appeal to respond—even as does steel to the magnet—to the wrongs and horrors of society.

If a social theory is a strong factor inducing acts of political violence, how are we to

36. *La Questione Sociale* was a weekly Italian-language anarchist newspaper in print from 15 July 1895 to 21 March 1908. Bresci briefly served as the editor of the paper and was a key financial supporter. Banned from the mails in 1908 on the grounds of obscenity, it reappeared the same year with the new title *L'Era Nuova*.

account for the recent violent outbreaks in India, where Anarchism has hardly been born. More than any other old philosophy, Hindu teachings have exalted passive resistance, the drifting of life, the Nirvana, as the highest spiritual ideal. Yet the social unrest in India is daily growing, and has only recently resulted in an act of political violence, the killing of Sir Curzon Wyllie by the Hindu, Madar Sol Dhingra.[37]

If such a phenomenon can occur in a country socially and individually permeated for centuries with the spirit of passivity, can one question the tremendous, revolutionizing effect on human character exerted by great social iniquities? Can one doubt the logic, the justice of these words:

"Repression, tyranny, and indiscriminate punishment of innocent men have been the watchwords of the government of the alien domination in India ever since we began the commercial boycott of English goods. The tiger qualities of the British are much in evidence now in India. They think that by the strength of the sword they will keep down India! It is this arrogance that has brought about the bomb, and the more they tyrannize over a helpless and unarmed people, the more terrorism will grow. We may deprecate terrorism as outlandish and foreign to our culture, but it is inevitable as long as this tyranny continues, for it is not the terrorists that are to be blamed, but the tyrants who are responsible for it. It is the only resource for a helpless and unarmed people when brought to the verge of despair. It is never criminal on their part. The crime lies with the tyrant."[38]

Even conservative scientists are beginning to realize that heredity is not the sole factor moulding human character. Climate, food, occupation; nay, color, light, and sound must be considered in the study of human psychology.

If that be true, how much more correct is the contention that social abuses will and must influence different minds and temperaments in a different way. And how utterly fallacious the stereotyped notion that the teachings of Anarchism, or certain exponents of these teachings, are responsible for the acts of political violence.

Anarchism, more than any other social theory, values human life above things. All

37. The first partition of Bengal by the English in 1905 spurred five years of extreme revolutionary nationalist activity in India. Young nationalists formed terrorist organizations using bombing as their strategic means for creating the fear that would ultimately liberate India from British imperialism. On 1 July 1909 Madan Lal Dhingra (ca. 1887–1909) shot and killed Lieutenant Colonel Sir William Curzon-Wyllie, political aide-de-camp to India's secretary of state, Lord John Morley, in London. Dhingra associated with Indian revolutionary leaders, including Vinayak Damodar Savarkar, founder of the Free India Society, and Shyamji Krishna Varma, president of the India Home Rule Society and founder of the *Indian Sociologist* (the society's publication) and of India House (the hub of the Indian nationalist movement in London).
38. In the original note EG cited "The Free Hindusthan" as the source of the quotation. The *Free Hindustan*, an English-language Indian nationalist bimonthly journal (whose motto was "Resistance to tyranny is service to humanity and a necessity of civilization"), was founded by Taraknath Das and Surrendra Mohan in March 1908. The paper was first published in Vancouver, then moved to Seattle the same year, and finally to New York in 1909. Lack of funds forced the closure of the publication in November 1910.

Anarchists agree with Tolstoy in this fundamental truth: if the production of any commodity necessitates the sacrifice of human life, society should do without that commodity, but it cannot do without that life.[39] That, however, nowise indicates that Anarchism teaches submission. How can it, when it knows that all suffering, all misery, all ills, result from the evil of submission?

Has not some American ancestor said, many years ago, that resistance is obedience to God?[40] And he was not an Anarchist even. I would say that resistance to tyranny is man's highest ideal. So long as tyranny exists, in whatever form, man's deepest aspiration must resist it as inevitably as man must breathe.

Compared to wholesale violence of capital and government, political acts of violence are but a drop in the ocean. That so few resist is the strongest proof how terrible must be the conflict between their souls and unbearable social iniquities.

High strung, like a violin string, they weep and moan for life, so relentless, so cruel, so terribly inhuman. In a desperate moment the string breaks. Untuned ears hear nothing but discord. But those who feel the agonized cry understand its harmony; they hear in it the fulfillment of the most compelling moment of human nature.

Such is the psychology of political violence.

PD. New York: Mother Earth Publishing Association (210 East 13th Street), 1911. Pamphlet.

39. Leo Tolstoy, in *The Slavery of Our Times* (1900), writes: "If, in order that London or Petersburg may be lighted by electricity, or in order to construct exhibition buildings, or in order that there may be beautiful paints, or in order to weave beautiful stuffs quickly and abundantly, it is necessary that even a very few lives should be destroyed, or ruined, or shortened—and statistics show us how many are destroyed—let London or Petersburg rather be lit by gas or oil; let there rather be no exhibition, no paints, or materials, only let there be no slavery, and no destruction of human lives resulting from it." (p. 63)
40. "Rebellion to tyrants is obedience to God" was the motto on Thomas Jefferson's seal.

Essay published by **MOTHER EARTH PUBLISHING ASSOCIATION**

*New York, 1911*

# Marriage and Love

The popular notion about marriage and love is that they are synonymous, that they spring from the same motives, and cover the same human needs. Like most popular notions this also rests not on actual facts, but on superstition.[1]

Marriage and love have nothing in common; they are as far apart as the poles; are, in fact, antagonistic to each other. No doubt some marriages have been the result of love. Not, however, because love could assert itself only in marriage; much rather is it because few people can completely outgrow a convention. There are today large numbers of men and women to whom marriage is naught but a farce, but who submit to it for the sake of public opinion. At any rate, while it is true that some marriages are based on love, and while it is equally true that in some cases love continues in married life, I maintain that it does so regardless of marriage, and not because of it.

On the other hand, it is utterly false that love results from marriage. On rare occasions one does hear of a miraculous case of a married couple falling in love after marriage, but on close examination it will be found that it is a mere adjustment to the inevitable. Certainly the growing-used to each other is far away from the spontaneity, the intensity, and beauty of love, without which the intimacy of marriage must prove degrading to both the woman and man.

Marriage is primarily an economic arrangement, an insurance pact. It differs from the ordinary life insurance agreement only in that it is more binding, more exacting. Its returns are insignificantly small compared with the investments. In taking out an insurance policy one pays for it in dollars and cents, always at liberty to discontinue payments. If, however, woman's premium is a husband, she pays for it with her name, her privacy, her self-respect, her very life, "until death doth part." Moreover, the marriage insurance condemns her to life-long dependency, to parasitism, to complete uselessness, individual as well as social. Man, too, pays his toll, but as his sphere is wider, marriage does not limit him as much as woman. He feels his chains more in an economic sense.

Thus Dante's motto over Inferno applies with equal force to marriage. "Ye who enter here leave all hope behind."[2]

That marriage is a failure not but the very stupid will deny. One has but to glance over

---

1. See "Marriage," Essay in the *Firebrand*, 18 July 1897, in vol. 1, *Made for America*, for EG's early thoughts on marriage. Many of EG's earlier ideas are developed in more detail there.
2. The quotation comes from Dante's *Inferno*, canto 3, line 9. In Italian, "Lasciate ogne speranza, voi

the statistics of divorce to realize how bitter a failure marriage really is. Nor will the stereotyped Philistine argument that the laxity of divorce laws and the growing looseness of woman account for the fact that: first, every twelfth marriage ends in divorce; second, that since 1870 divorces have increased from 28 to 73 for every hundred thousand population; third, that adultery, since 1867, as ground for divorce, has increased 270.8 per cent; fourth, that desertion increased 369.8 per cent.[3]

Added to these startling figures is a vast amount of material, dramatic and literary, further elucidating this subject. Robert Herrick, in *Together*;[4] Pinero, in *Mid-Channel*;[5] Eugene Walter, in *Paid in Full*,[6] and scores of other writers are discussing the barrenness, the monotony, the sordidness, the inadequacy of marriage as a factor for harmony and understanding.

The thoughtful social student will not content himself with the popular superficial excuse for this phenomenon. He will have to dig down deeper into the very life of the sexes to know why marriage proves so disastrous.

Edward Carpenter[7] says that behind every marriage stands the life-long environment of the two sexes; an environment so different from each other that man and woman must remain strangers. Separated by an insurmountable wall of superstition, custom, and habit, marriage has not the potentiality of developing knowledge of, and respect for, each other, without which every union is doomed to failure.

Henrik Ibsen,[8] the hater of all social shams, was probably the first to realize this great truth. Nora leaves her husband, not—as the stupid critic would have it—because she is tired of her responsibilities or feels the need of woman's rights, but because she has come to know that for eight years she had lived with a stranger and borne him children.

---

ch'intrate." Many translations exist; one common version by Henry Wadsworth Longfellow is "All hope abandon, ye who enter here!"

3. The statistics EG quotes here match data published in *Special Reports of the Census Office: Marriage and Divorce 1867–1906*.

4. Robert Herrick (1868–1938) was a novelist and English professor at the University of Chicago. His novel *Together* (1908) offered a critique of the institution of marriage.

5. Sir Arthur Wing Pinero (1855–1934) was an English dramatist. He is best known for *The Profligate* (1889) and *The Second Mrs. Tanqueray* (1893). In *Mid-Channel* (1909), one in a series of plays from 1889 to 1909 in which Pinero depicts the plight of women in Victorian society, a wife is prepared to forgive her husband's infidelity, but he will not forgive hers.

6. Eugene Walter was an American dramatist. Paid in Full (1908) was his first success. The play concerns a man who steals from his employer, then deceives his wife about the illegitimate source of his income. When he is found out, he asks for and receives her help, but it costs them their marriage and the husband's life. EG would go on to write about Walter in *The Social Significance of the Modern Drama* (1914).

7. Edward Carpenter (1844–1929) was an English author, poet, and social activist. Frequently referenced by EG, Carpenter was an early advocate of women's equality and homosexual emancipation. EG's talk on homosexuality, "The Intermediate Sex," was taken from the title of one of Carpenter's works, *The Intermediate Sex: A Study of Some Transitional Types of Men and Women* (London: Swan Sonnenschein, 1908).

8. Henrik Ibsen (1828–1906) was a Norwegian playwright. Nora is a character in his most famous work, *A Doll's House* (1879). During this time EG frequently lectured on Ibsen's plays.

Can there be anything more humiliating, more degrading than a life-long proximity between two strangers? No need for the woman to know anything of the man, save his income. As to the knowledge of the woman—what is there to know except that she has a pleasing appearance? We have not yet outgrown the theologic myth that woman has no soul, that she is a mere appendix to man, made out of his rib just for the convenience of the gentleman who was so strong that he was afraid of his own shadow.

Perchance the poor quality of the material whence woman comes is responsible for her inferiority. At any rate, woman has no soul—what is there to know of her? Besides, the less soul a woman has the greater her asset as a wife, the more readily will she absorb herself in her husband. It is this slavish acquiescence to man's superiority that has kept the marriage institution seemingly intact for so long a period. Now that woman is coming into her own, now that she is actually growing aware of herself as a being outside of the master's grace, the sacred institution of marriage is gradually being undermined, and no amount of sentimental lamentation can stay it.

From infancy, almost, the average girl is told that marriage is her ultimate goal; therefore her training and education must be directed towards that end. Like the mute beast fattened for slaughter, she is prepared for that. Yet, strange to say, she is allowed to know much less about her function as wife and mother than the ordinary artisan of his trade. It is indecent and filthy for a respectable girl to know anything of the marital relation. Oh, for the inconsistency of respectability, that needs the marriage vow to turn something which is filthy into the purest and most sacred arrangement that none dare question or criticize. Yet that is exactly the attitude of the average upholder of marriage. The prospective wife and mother is kept in complete ignorance of her only asset in the competitive field—sex. Thus she enters into life-long relations with a man only to find herself shocked, repelled, outraged beyond measure by the most natural and healthy instinct, sex. It is safe to say that a large percentage of the unhappiness, misery, distress, and physical suffering of matrimony is due to the criminal ignorance in sex matters that is being extolled as a great virtue. Nor is it at all an exaggeration when I say that more than one home has been broken up because of this deplorable fact.

If, however, woman is free and big enough to learn the mystery of sex without the sanction of State or Church, she will stand condemned as utterly unfit to become the wife of a "good" man, his goodness consisting of an empty brain and plenty of money. Can there be anything more outrageous than the idea that a healthy, grown woman, full of life and passion, must deny nature's demand, must subdue her most intense craving, undermine her health and break her spirit, must stunt her vision, abstain from the depth and glory of sex experience until a "good" man comes along to take her unto himself as a wife? That is precisely what marriage means. How can such an arrangement end except in failure? This is one, though not the least important, factor of marriage, which differentiates it from love.

Ours is a practical age. The time when Romeo and Juliet risked the wrath of their fathers for love, is no more. If, on rare occasions, young people allow themselves the luxury of romance, they are taken in care by the elders, drilled and pounded until they become "sensible."

The moral lesson instilled in the girl is not whether the man has aroused her love, but rather is it, "How much?" The important and only God of practical American life: Can the man make a living? Can he support a wife? That is the only thing that justifies marriage. Gradually this saturates every thought of the girl; her dreams are not of moonlight and kisses, of laughter and tears; she dreams of shopping tours and bargain counters. This soul poverty and sordidness are the elements inherent in the marriage institution. The State and the Church approve of no other ideal, simply because it is the one that necessitates the State and Church control of men and women.

Doubtless there are people who continue to consider love above dollars and cents. Particularly is this true of the class whom economic necessity has forced to become self-supporting. The tremendous change in woman's position, wrought by that mighty factor, is indeed phenomenal when we reflect that it is but a short time since she has entered the industrial arena. Six million women wage workers;[9] six million women, who have the equal right with men to be exploited, to be robbed, to go on strike; aye, to starve even. Anything more, my lord? Yes, six million wage workers in every walk of life, from the highest brain work to the mines and railroad tracks; yes, even detectives and policemen. Surely the emancipation is complete.

Yet with all that, but a very small number of the vast army of women wage workers look upon work as a permanent issue, in the same light as does man. No matter how decrepit the latter, he has been taught to be independent, self-supporting. Oh, I know that no one is really independent in our economic treadmill; still, the poorest specimen of a man hates to be a parasite; to be known as such, at any rate.

The woman considers her position as worker transitory, to be thrown aside for the first bidder. That is why it is infinitely harder to organize women than men. "Why should I join a union? I am going to get married, to have a home." Has she not been taught from infancy to look upon that as her ultimate calling? She learns soon enough that the home, though not so large a prison as the factory, has more solid doors and bars. It has a keeper so faithful that naught can escape him. The most tragic part, however, is that the home no longer frees her from wage slavery; it only increases her task.

According to the latest statistics submitted before a Committee "on labor and wages, and congestion of population," ten per cent of the wage workers in New York City alone are married,[10] yet they must continue to work at the most poorly paid labor in the world. Add to this horrible aspect the drudgery of housework, and what remains of the protection and glory of the home? As a matter of fact, even the middle-class girl in marriage can not speak of her home, since it is the man who creates her sphere. It is not impor-

9. The 1900 census lists 5.3 million female workers. The 1910 census, at the time not yet available to EG, lists 8.1 million.
10. An article in the *New York Times* on 13 September 1910 (p. 4) summarizes the details of the report.

tant whether the husband is a brute or a darling. What I wish to prove is that marriage guarantees woman a home only by the grace of her husband. There she moves about in his home, year after year, until her aspect of life and human affairs becomes as flat, narrow, and drab as her surroundings. Small wonder if she becomes a nag, petty, quarrelsome, gossipy, unbearable, thus driving the man from the house. She could not go, if she wanted to; there is no place to go. Besides, a short period of married life, of complete surrender of all faculties, absolutely incapacitates the average woman for the outside world. She becomes reckless in appearance, clumsy in her movements, dependent in her decisions, cowardly in her judgment, a weight and a bore, which most men grow to hate and despise. Wonderfully inspiring atmosphere for the bearing of life, is it not?

But the child, how is it to be protected, if not for marriage? After all, is not that the most important consideration? The sham, the hypocrisy of it! Marriage protecting the child, yet thousands of children destitute and homeless. Marriage protecting the child, yet orphan asylums and reformatories overcrowded, the Society for the Prevention of Cruelty to Children[11] keeping busy in rescuing the little victims from "loving" parents, to place them under more loving care, the Gerry Society. Oh, the mockery of it!

Marriage may have the power to bring the horse to water, but has it ever made him drink? The law will place the father under arrest, and put him in convict's clothes; but has that ever stilled the hunger of the child? If the parent has no work, or if he hides his identity, what does marriage do then? It invokes the law to bring the man to "justice," to put him safely behind closed doors; his labor, however, goes not to the child, but to the State. The child receives but a blighted memory of its father's stripes.

As to the protection of the woman,—therein lies the curse of marriage. Not that it really protects her, but the very idea is so revolting, such an outrage and insult on life, so degrading to human dignity, as to forever condemn this parasitic institution.

It is like that other paternal arrangement—capitalism. It robs man of his birthright, stunts his growth, poisons his body, keeps him in ignorance, in poverty, and dependence, and then institutes charities that thrive on the last vestige of man's self-respect.

The institution of marriage makes a parasite of woman, an absolute dependent. It incapacitates her for life's struggles, annihilates her social consciousness, paralyzes her imagination, and then imposes its gracious protection, which is in reality a snare, a travesty on human character.

If motherhood is the highest fulfillment of woman's nature, what other protection does it need, save love and freedom? Marriage but defiles, outrages, and corrupts her fulfillment. Does it not say to woman, Only when you follow me shall you bring forth life? Does it not condemn her to the block, does it not degrade and shame her if she refuses to

---

11. The New York Society for the Prevention of Cruelty to Children, also known as the Gerry Society after founder Elbridge Thomas Gerry (1834–1927), was active in establishing and enforcing New York's child labor laws. The society inspired hundreds of similar organizations around the world, many of which, including the NYSPCC, are still active today.

buy her right to motherhood by selling herself? Does not marriage only sanction motherhood, even though conceived in hatred, in compulsion? Yet, if motherhood be free of choice, of love, of ecstasy, of defiant passion, does it not place a crown of thorns upon an innocent head and carve in letters of blood the hideous epithet, Bastard? Were marriage to contain all the virtues claimed for it, its crimes against motherhood would exclude it forever from the realm of love.

Love, the strongest and deepest element in all life, the harbinger of hope, of joy, of ecstasy; love, the defier of all laws, of all conventions; love, the freest, the most powerful moulder of human destiny; how can such an all-compelling force be synonymous with that poor little State and Church-begotten weed, marriage?

Free love? As if love is anything but free! Man has bought brains, but all the millions in the world have failed to buy love. Man has subdued bodies, but all the power on the earth has been unable to subdue love. Man has conquered whole nations, but all his armies could not conquer love. Man has chained and fettered the spirit, but he has been utterly helpless before love. High on a throne, with all the splendor and pomp his gold can command, man is yet poor and desolate, if love passes him by. And if it stays, the poorest hovel is radiant with warmth, with life and color. Thus love has the magic power to make of a beggar a king. Yes, love is free; it can dwell in no other atmosphere. In freedom it gives itself unreservedly, abundantly, completely. All the laws on the states, all the courts in the universe, cannot tear it from the soil, once love has taken root. If, however, the soil is sterile, how can marriage make it bear fruit? It is like the last desperate struggle of fleeting life against death.

Love needs no protection; it is its own protection. So long as love begets life no child is deserted, or hungry, or famished for want of affection. I know this to be true. I know women who became mothers in freedom by the men they loved. Few children in wedlock enjoy the care, the protection, the devotion free motherhood is capable of bestowing.

The defenders of authority dread the advent of a free motherhood, lest it will rob them of their prey. Who would fight wars? Who would create wealth? Who would make the policeman, the jailer, if woman were to refuse the indiscriminate breeding of children? The race, the race! shouts the king, the president, the capitalist, the priest. The race must be preserved, though woman is degraded to a mere machine,—and the marriage institution is our only safety valve against the pernicious sex awakening of woman. But in vain these frantic efforts to maintain a state of bondage. In vain, too, the edicts of the Church, the mad attacks of rulers, in vain even the arm of the law. Woman no longer wants to be a party to the production of a race of sickly, feeble, decrepit, wretched human beings, who have neither the strength nor moral courage to throw off the yoke of poverty and slavery. Instead she desires fewer and better children, begotten and reared in love and through free choice; not by any compulsion, as marriage imposes. Our pseudo-moralists have yet to learn the deep sense of responsibility toward the child, that love in freedom has awakened in the breast of woman. Rather would she forego forever the glory of motherhood than bring forth life in an atmosphere that breathes only destruction and death. And if she does become a mother, it is to give to the child the deepest and best her being can yield. To grow with the child is her motto; she knows that in that manner alone can she help build true manhood and womanhood.

Ibsen must have had a vision of a free mother, when, with a master stroke, he portrayed Mrs. Alving.[12] She was the ideal mother because she had outgrown marriage and all its horrors, because she had broken her chains, set her spirit free to soar until it returned a personality, regenerated and strong. Alas, it was too late to rescue her life's joy, her Oswald; but not too late to realize that love in freedom is the only condition of a beautiful life. Those who, like Mrs. Alving, have paid with blood and tears for their spiritual awakening, repudiate marriage as an imposition, a shallow, empty mockery. They know, whether love last but one brief span of time or for eternity, it is the only creative, inspiring, elevating basis for a new race, a new world.

In our present pygmy state love is indeed a stranger to most people. Misunderstood and shunned, it rarely takes root; or if it does, it soon withers and dies. Its delicate fiber can not endure the stress and strain of the daily grind. Its soul is too complex to adjust itself to the slimy woof of our social fabric. It weeps and moans and suffers with those who have need of it, yet lack the capacity to rise to love's summit.

PDU, Mother Earth Publishing Association (210 East 13th Street), 1911. Pamphlet.

---

12. Mrs. Alving is a character in Henrik Ibsen's play *Ghosts* (1881). Oswald is Mrs. Alving's son. The play addresses issues of marriage, incest, and euthanasia. EG here refers to the finale of the play (act 3).

Essay published by **MOTHER EARTH PUBLISHING ASSOCIATION**

*New York, 1911*

# Anarchism

## What It Really Stands For

### Anarchy.

Ever reviled, accursed, ne'er understood,
Thou art the grisly terror of our age.
"Wreck of all order," cry the multitude,
"Art thou, and war and murder's endless rage."
O, let them cry. To them that ne'er have striven
The truth that lies behind a word to find,
To them the word's right meaning was not given.
They shall continue blind among the blind.
But thou, O word, so clear, so strong, so pure,
Thou sayest all which I for goal have taken.
I give thee to the future!
Thine secure
When each at least unto himself shall waken.
Comes it in sunshine? In the tempest's thrill?
I cannot tell—but the earth shall see!
I am an Anarchist! Wherefore I will
Not rule, and also ruled I will not be!

JOHN HENRY MACKAY.[1]

The history of human growth and development is at the same time the history of the terrible struggle of every new idea heralding the approach of a brighter dawn. In its tenacious hold on tradition, the Old has never hesitated to make use of the foulest and cruelest means to stay the advent of the New, in whatever form or period the latter may have asserted itself. Nor need we retrace our steps into the distant past to realize the

---

1. John Henry Mackay (1864–1933), Scottish-born German anarchist individualist. His novel *The Anarchists*, set in London's anarchist milieu in 1897, was published by Benjamin Tucker in 1891. Under the pseudonym Sagita, Mackay was one of the earliest proponents of man-boy love. The poem "The Anarchists" is taken from his collection of poetry *Sturm* (1888). It was first published in English in Tucker's paper *Liberty* (no. 216, 30 January 1892), translated by Harry Lyman Koopman.

enormity of opposition, difficulties, and hardships placed in the path of every progressive idea. The rack, the thumbscrew, and the knout are still with us; so are the convict's garb and the social wrath, all conspiring against the spirit that is serenely marching on.

Anarchism could not hope to escape the fate of all other ideas of innovation. Indeed, as the most revolutionary and uncompromising innovator, Anarchism must needs meet with the combined ignorance and venom of the world it aims to reconstruct.

To deal even remotely with all that is being said and done against Anarchism would necessitate the writing of a whole volume. I shall therefore meet only two of the principal objections. In so doing, I shall attempt to elucidate what Anarchism really stands for.

The strange phenomenon of the opposition to Anarchism is that it brings to light the relation between so-called intelligence and ignorance. And yet this is not so very strange when we consider the relativity of all things. The ignorant mass has in its favor that it makes no pretense of knowledge or tolerance. Acting, as it always does, by mere impulse, its reasons are like those of a child. "Why?" "Because." Yet the opposition of the uneducated to Anarchism deserves the same consideration as that of the intelligent man.

What, then, are the objections? First, Anarchism is impractical, though a beautiful ideal. Second, Anarchism stands for violence and destruction, hence it must be repudiated as vile and dangerous. Both the intelligent man and the ignorant mass judge not from a thorough knowledge of the subject, but either from hearsay or false interpretation.

A practical scheme, says Oscar Wilde, is either one already in existence, or a scheme that could be carried out under the existing conditions;[2] but it is exactly the existing conditions that one objects to, and any scheme that could accept these conditions is wrong and foolish.[3] The true criterion of the practical, therefore, is not whether the latter can keep intact the wrong or foolish; rather it is whether the scheme has vitality enough to leave the stagnant waters of the old, and build, as well as sustain, new life. In the light of this conception, Anarchism is indeed practical. More than any other idea, it is helping to do away with the wrong and foolish; more than any other idea, it is building and sustaining new life.

The emotions of the ignorant man are continuously kept at a pitch by the most bloodcurdling stories about Anarchism. Not a thing too outrageous to be employed against this philosophy and its exponents. Therefore Anarchism represents to the unthinking what the proverbial bad man does to the child,—a black monster bent on swallowing everything; in short, destruction and violence.

Destruction and violence! How is the ordinary man to know that the most violent element in society is ignorance; that its power of destruction is the very thing Anarchism is combating? Nor is he aware that Anarchism, whose roots, as it were are part of nature's

---

2. Oscar Wilde (1854–1900), Irish playwright and libertarian socialist, published his influential work *The Soul of Man Under Socialism* in 1891. Both this work and *The Ballad of Reading Gaol* (1898) were influential in radical circles. *Mother Earth* reprinted an extract from *De Profundis* in 1906. The preceding is a direct quotation from *The Soul of Man Under Socialism*.
3. The quoted passage appears with no textual variations in Wilde's *The Soul of Man Under Socialism*.

forces, destroys, not healthful tissue, but parasitic growths that feed on the life's essence of society. It is merely clearing the soil from weeds and sagebrush, that it may eventually bear healthy fruit.

Someone has said that it requires less mental effort to condemn than to think. The widespread mental indolence, so prevalent in society, proves this to be only too true. Rather than to go to the bottom of any given idea, to examine into its origin and meaning, most people will either condemn it altogether, or rely on some superficial or prejudicial definition of non-essentials.

Anarchism urges man to think, to investigate, to analyze every proposition; but that the brain capacity of the average reader be taxed too much, I also shall begin with a definition, and then elaborate on the latter.

Anarchism:—The philosophy of a new social order based on liberty unrestricted by man-made law; the theory that all forms of government rest on violence, and are therefore wrong and harmful, as well as unnecessary.

The new social order rests, of course, on the materialistic basis of life; but while all Anarchists agree that the main evil today is an economic one, they maintain that the solution of that evil can be brought about only through the consideration of *every phase* of life,—individual, as well as the collective; the internal, as well as the external phases.

A thorough perusal of the history of human development will disclose two elements in bitter conflict with each other; elements that are only now beginning to be understood, not as foreign to each other, but as closely related and truly harmonious, if only placed in proper environment: the individual and social instincts. The individual and society have waged a relentless and bloody battle for ages, each striving for supremacy, because each was blind to the value and importance of the other. The individual and social instincts,— the one a most potent factor for individual endeavor, for growth, aspiration, self-realization; the other an equally potent factor for mutual helpfulness and social well-being.

The explanation of the storm raging within the individual, and between him and his surroundings, is not far to seek. The primitive man, unable to understand his being, much less the unity of all life, felt himself absolutely dependent on blind, hidden forces ever ready to mock and taunt him. Out of that attitude grew the religious concepts of man as a mere speck of dust dependent on superior powers on high, who can only be appeased by complete surrender. All the early sagas rest on that idea, which continues to be the *leit-motif* of the biblical tales dealing with the relation of man to God, to the State, to society. Again and again, the same motif, *man is nothing, the powers are everything.* Thus Jehovah would only endure man on condition of complete surrender. Man can have all the glories of the earth, but he must not become conscious of himself. The State, society, and moral laws all sing the same refrain: Man can have all the glories of the earth, but he must not become conscious of himself.[4]

---

4. This idea is taken directly from Michael Bakunin's *God and the State.* Bakunin recounts the biblical story of Adam and Eve to demonstrate Jehovah's wish "that man, destitute of all understanding of himself, should remain an eternal beast, ever on all-fours before the eternal God, his creator and

Anarchism is the only philosophy which brings to man the consciousness of himself; which maintains that God, the State, and society are non-existent, that their promises are null and void, since they can be fulfilled only through man's subordination. Anarchism is therefore the teacher of the unity of life; not merely in nature, but in man. There is no conflict between the individual and the social instincts, any more than there is between the heart and the lungs: the one the receptacle of a precious life essence, the other the repository of the element that keeps the essence pure and strong. The individual is the heart of society, conserving the essence of social life; society is the lungs which are distributing the element to keep the life essence—that is, the individual—pure and strong.

"The one thing of value in the world," says Emerson, "is the active soul; this every man contains within him. The soul active sees absolute truth and utters truth and creates."[5] In other words, the individual instinct is the thing of value in the world. It is the true soul that sees and creates the truth alive, out of which is to come a still greater truth, the reborn social soul.

Anarchism is the great liberator of man from the phantoms that have held him captive; it is the arbiter and pacifier of the two forces for individual and social harmony. To accomplish that unity, Anarchism has declared war on the pernicious influences which have so far prevented the harmonious blending of individual and social instincts, the individual and society.

Religion, the dominion of the human mind; Property, the dominion of human needs; and Government, the dominion of human conduct, represent the stronghold of man's enslavement and all the horrors it entails. Religion! How it dominates man's mind, how it humiliates and degrades his soul. God is everything, man is nothing, says religion. But out of that nothing God has created a kingdom so despotic, so tyrannical, so cruel, so terribly exacting that naught but gloom and tears and blood have ruled the world since gods began. Anarchism rouses man to rebellion against this black monster. Break your mental fetters, says Anarchism to man, for not until you think and judge for yourself will you get rid of the dominion of darkness, the greatest obstacle to all progress.

Property, the dominion of man's needs, the denial of the right to satisfy his needs. Time was when property claimed a divine right, when it came to man with the same refrain, even as religion, "Sacrifice! Abnegate! Submit!" The spirit of Anarchism has lifted man from his prostrate position. He now stands erect, with his face toward the

---

his master." For more on EG's reference to this argument, see also "Anarchist Laws," Essay in *Die Brandfackel,* October 1894, in vol. 1, *Made for America.*

5. Ralph Waldo Emerson, American essayist, poet, and philosopher, spoke these words in "The American Scholar," an oration delivered before the Phi Beta Kappa Society at Cambridge, Massachusetts, on 31 August 1837 and later published in essay form. The original quotation reads "The one thing in the world, of value, is the active soul. This every man is entitled to; this every man contains within him, although in almost all men obstructed and as yet unborn. The soul active sees absolute truth and utters truth, or creates."

light. He has learned to see the insatiable, devouring, devastating nature of property, and he is preparing to strike the monster dead.

"Property is robbery," said the great French Anarchist, Proudhon.[6] Yes, but without the risk and danger to the robber. Monopolizing the accumulated efforts of man, property has robbed him of his birthright, and has turned him loose a pauper and an outcast. Property has not even the time-worn excuse that man does not create enough to satisfy all needs. The A B C student of economics knows the productivity of labor within the last few decades far exceeds normal demand a hundredfold. But what are normal demands to an abnormal institution? The only demand that property recognizes is its own gluttonous appetite for greater wealth, because wealth means power: the power to subdue, to crush, to exploit, the power to enslave, to outrage, to degrade. America is particularly boastful of her great power, her enormous national wealth. Poor America, of what avail is all her wealth, if the individuals comprising the nation are wretchedly poor? If they live in squalor, in filth, in crime, with hope and joy gone, a homeless, soilless army of human prey.

It is generally conceded that unless the returns of any business venture exceed the cost, bankruptcy is inevitable. But those engaged in the business of producing wealth have not yet learned even this simple lesson. Every year the cost of production in human life is growing larger (50,000 killed, 100,000 wounded in America last year); the returns to the masses, who help to create wealth, are ever getting smaller. Yet America continues to be blind to the inevitable bankruptcy of our business of production. Nor is this the only crime of the latter. Still more fatal is the crime of turning the producer into a mere particle of a machine, with less will and decision than his masters of steel and iron. Man is being robbed not merely of the products of his labor, but of the power of free initiative, of originality, and the interest in, or desire for, the things he is making.

Real wealth consists in things of utility and beauty, in things that help to create strong, beautiful bodies and surroundings inspiring to live in. But if man is doomed to wind cotton around a spool, or dig coal, or build roads for thirty years of his life, there can be no talk of wealth. What he gives to the world is only gray and hideous things, reflecting a dull and hideous existence,—too weak to live, too cowardly to die. Strange to say, there are people who extol this deadening method of centralized production as the proudest achievement of our age. They fail utterly to realize that if we are to continue in machine subserviency, our slavery is more complete than was our bondage to the King. They do not want to know that centralization is not only the death knell of liberty, but also of health and beauty, of art and science, all these being impossible in a clock-like, mechanical atmosphere.[7]

6. Pierre-Joseph Proudhon (1809–1865) was a French social theorist and an early and influential proponent of anarchist mutualism. His *Qu'est-ce que la Propriete?* (What Is Property? An Inquiry into the Principle of Right and of Government, Benjamin Tucker, 1840) defined anarchism as a distinct political theory.
7. Compare EG's statements on wealth and production in *A Beautiful Ideal* (Chicago: J. C. Hart, 1908): "Man has been degraded into a mere part of a machine and all that makes for spontaneity, for

Anarchism cannot repudiate such a method of production: its goal is the freest possible expression of all the latent powers of the individual. Oscar Wilde defines a perfect personality as "one who develops under perfect conditions, who is not wounded, maimed, or in danger."[8] A perfect personality, then, is only possible in a state of society where man is free to choose the mode of work, the conditions of work, and the freedom to work. One to whom the making of a table, the building of a house, or the tilling of soil, is what the painting is to the artist and the discovery to the scientist,—the result of inspiration, of intense longing, and deep interest in work as a creative force. That being the ideal of Anarchism, its economic arrangements must consist of voluntary productive and distributive associations, gradually developing into free communism, as the best means of producing with the least waste of human energy. Anarchism, however, also recognizes the right of the individual, or numbers of individuals, to arrange at all times for other forms of work, in harmony with their tastes and desires.

Such free display of human energy being possible only under complete individual and social freedom, Anarchism directs its forces against the third and greatest foe of all social equality; namely, the State, organized authority, or statutory law,—the dominion of human conduct.

Just as religion has fettered the human mind, and as property, or the monopoly of things, has subdued and stifled man's needs, so has the State enslaved his spirit, dictating every phase of conduct. "All government in essence," says Emerson, "is tyranny."[9] It matters not whether it is government by divine right or majority rule. In every instance its aim is the absolute subordination of the individual.

---

originality, for the power of initiative, has been either dulled or completely killed in him until he is but a living corpse, dragging out an aimless, spiritless and idealess existence.

"Man is here to be sacrificed upon the altar of things, heaps and heaps of things, that are as dark and dull as the human machines that have produced them.

"Yet how can we talk of social wealth when the production of that wealth can be attained only at the expense of human lives, thousands and thousands of human lives? And what are these lives worth without the power of initiative, of spontaneity?"

8. In *The Soul of Man Under Socialism,* Oscar Wilde writes, "What I mean by a perfect man is one who develops under perfect conditions; one who is not wounded, or worried, or maimed, or in danger."

9. EG is possibly referring to a quotation from Emerson's 1841 essay "Politics," where he addresses the nature of the state and government: "But our institutions, though in coincidence with the spirit of the age, have not any exemption from the practical defects which have discredited other forms. Every actual state is corrupt. Good men must not obey the laws too well. What satire on government can equal the severity of censure conveyed in the word *politic,* which now for ages has signified *cunning,* intimating that the State is a trick?" Excerpts from this essay, including a portion of this quotation, were published in *Mother Earth* in June 1913. The essay was also referred to by Lillian Browne in her essay "Emerson the Anarchist," published in the December 1909 edition of *Mother Earth.* Voltairine de Cleyre addressed what she saw as the ultimate failure of American democracy, in contrast to the ideals conceived by the framers of the Constitution, in her essay *Anarchism and Other Traditions* (New York: Mother Earth Publishing Association, 1909). She believed that a true democratic state was impossible because the "essence of government" is that it is easily corruptible by interest and force.

Referring to the American government, the greatest American Anarchist, David Thoreau, said: "Government, what is it but a tradition, though a recent one, endeavoring to transmit itself unimpaired to posterity, but each instance losing its integrity; it has not the vitality and force of a single living man. Law never made man a whit more just; and by means of their respect for it, even the well disposed are daily made agents of injustice."[10]

Indeed, the keynote of government is injustice. With the arrogance and self-sufficiency of the King who could do no wrong, governments ordain, judge, condemn, and punish the most insignificant offenses, while maintaining themselves by the greatest of all offenses, the annihilation of individual liberty. Thus Ouida[11] is right when she maintains that "the State only aims at instilling those qualities in its public by which its demands are obeyed, and its exchequer is filled. Its highest attainment is the reduction of mankind to clockwork. In its atmosphere all those finer and more delicate liberties, which require treatment and spacious expansion, inevitably dry up and perish. The State requires a taxpaying machine in which there is no hitch, an exchequer in which there is never a deficit, and a public, monotonous, obedient, colorless, spiritless, moving humbly like a flock of sheep along a straight high road between two walls."[12]

Yet even a flock of sheep would resist the chicanery of the State, if it were not for the corruptive, tyrannical, and oppressive methods it employs to serve its purposes. Therefore Bakunin repudiates the State as synonymous with the surrender of the liberty of the individual or small minorities,—the destruction of social relationship, the curtailment, or complete denial even, of life itself, for its own aggrandizement. The State is the altar of political freedom and, like the religious altar, it is maintained for the purpose of human sacrifice.[13]

In fact, there is hardly a modern thinker who does not agree that government, organized authority, or the State, is necessary *only* to maintain or protect property and monopoly. It has proven efficient in that function only.

Even George Bernard Shaw, who hopes for the miraculous from the State under

10. Henry David Thoreau (1817–1862), American writer, poet, abolitionist, and philosopher, wrote in his 1849 essay "Civil Disobedience," "Law never made men a whit more just; and, by means of their respect for it, even the well-disposed are daily made the agents of injustice."

11. Ouida was the pen name of English novelist Marie Louise de la Ramee (1839–1908). The following quoted passage appears in the essay "The State as an Immoral Factor," published in Ouida's volume of collected essays *Views and Opinions* (London: Methuen, 1895). Most of the essays in this collection were originally published in the *Fortnightly Review* or the *North American Review*, though the details of original publication date and place of this particular essay are unclear.

12. The preceding quoted sentences do not appear contiguously in Ouida's essay. The first three sentences appear on page 361 of *Views and Opinions* (London: Methuen, 1895); EG has inserted commas and omitted the word "liberal" between "require" and "treatment" in the third sentence. The final sentence, which begins "The State requires," appears on page 348; the original text includes the additional words "unanimously and" before "humbly like a flock of sheep."

13. This argument is propounded in Bakunin's *God and the State* (1882).

Fabianism, nevertheless admits that "it is at present a huge machine for robbing and slave-driving of the poor by brute force."[14] This being the case, it is hard to see why the clever prefacer wishes to uphold the State after poverty shall have ceased to exist.

Unfortunately there are still a number of people who continue in the fatal belief that government rests on natural laws, that it maintains social order and harmony, that it diminishes crime, and that it prevents the lazy man from fleecing his fellows. I shall therefore examine these contentions.

A natural law is that factor in man which asserts itself freely and spontaneously without any external force, in harmony with the requirements of nature. For instance, the demand for nutrition, for sex gratification, for light, air, and exercise, is a natural law. But its expression needs not the machinery of government, needs not the club, the gun, the handcuff, or the prison. To obey such laws, if we may call it obedience, requires only spontaneity and free opportunity. That governments do not maintain themselves through such harmonious factors is proven by the terrible array of violence, force, and coercion all governments use in order to live. Thus Blackstone is right when he says, "Human laws are invalid, because they are contrary to the laws of nature."[15]

Unless it be the order of Warsaw after the slaughter of thousands of people, it is difficult to ascribe to governments any capacity for order or social harmony. Order derived through submission and maintained by terror is not much of a safe guaranty; yet that is the only "order" that governments have ever maintained. True social harmony grows naturally out of solidarity of interests. In a society where those who always work never have anything, while those who never work enjoy everything, solidarity of interests is nonexistent; hence social harmony is but a myth. The only way organized authority meets this grave situation is by extending still greater privileges to those who have already monopolized the earth, and by still further enslaving the disinherited masses. Thus the entire arsenal of government—laws, police soldiers, the courts, legislatures, prisons,—is strenuously engaged in "harmonizing" the most antagonistic elements in society.

The most absurd apology for authority and law is that they serve to diminish crime. Aside from the fact that the State is itself the greatest criminal, breaking every written and natural law, stealing in the form of taxes, killing in the form of war and capital pun-

14. EG quotes socialist playwright George Bernard Shaw's "The Impossibilities of Anarchism," published in *Socialism and Individualism*, a volume of Fabian essays published as part of the Fabian Socialist Series (no. 3) in 1911 (New York: John Lane Company). Shaw's essay was originally delivered as a lecture at a meeting of the Fabian Society on 16 October 1891. The full quotation reads "I fully admit and vehemently urge that the State at present is a huge machine for robbing and slave-driving the poor by brute force."

15. Sir William Blackstone (1723–1780), professor of law at Oxford University in England, in his *Commentaries on the Laws of England,* discusses human laws and the laws of nature in a section entitled "On the Nature of Laws in General": "This law of nature, being coeval with mankind and dictated by God Himself, is of course superior in obligation to any other. It is binding over all the globe in all countries, and at all times: no human laws are of any validity, if contrary to this; and such of them as are valid derive all their force, and all their authority, from this original."

ishment, it has come to an absolute standstill in coping with crime. It has failed utterly to destroy or even minimize the horrible scourge of its own creation.

Crime is naught but misdirected energy. So long as every institution of today, economic, political, social, and moral, conspires to misdirect human energy into wrong channels; so long as most people are out of place doing the things they hate to do, living a life they loathe to live, crime will be inevitable, and all the laws on the statutes can only increase, but never do away with, crime. What does society, as it exists today, know of the process of despair, the poverty, the horrors, the fearful struggle the human soul must pass on its way to crime and degradation. Who that knows this terrible process can fail to see the truth in these words of Peter Kropotkin:

"Those who will hold the balance between the benefits thus attributed to law and punishment and the degrading effect of the latter on humanity; those who will estimate the torrent of depravity poured abroad in human society by the informer, favored by the Judge even, and paid for in clinking cash by governments, under the pretext of aiding to unmask crime; those who will go within prison walls and there see what human beings become when deprived of liberty, when subjected to the care of brutal keepers, to coarse, cruel words, to a thousand stinging, piercing humiliations, will agree with us that the entire apparatus of prison and punishment is an abomination which ought to be brought to an end."[16]

The deterrent influence of law on the lazy man is too absurd to merit consideration. If society were only relieved of the waste and expense of keeping a lazy class, and the equally great expense of the paraphernalia of protection this lazy class requires, the social tables would contain an abundance for all, including even the occasional lazy individual. Besides, it is well to consider that laziness results wither from special privileges, or physical and mental abnormalities. Our present insane system of production fosters both, and the most astounding phenomenon is that people should want to work at all now. Anarchism aims to strip labor of its deadening, dulling aspect, of its gloom and compulsion. It aims to make work an instrument of joy, of strength, of color, of real harmony, so that the poorest sort of man should find in work both recreation and hope.

To achieve such an arrangement of life, government, with its unjust, arbitrary, repressive measures, must be done away with. At best it has but imposed one single mode of life upon all, without regard to individual and social variations and needs. In destroying government and statutory laws, Anarchism proposes to rescue the self-respect and independence of the individual from all restraint and invasion by authority. Only in freedom can man grow to his full stature. Only in freedom will he learn to think and move, and give the very best in him. Only in freedom will he realize the true force of the social bonds which knit men together, and which are the true foundation of a normal social life.

---

16. This quotation is paraphrased from Peter Kropotkin's *Law and Authority* (London: International Publishers, trans. H. Seymour, 1886).

But what about human nature? Can it be changed? And if not, will it endure under Anarchism?

Poor human nature, what horrible crimes have been committed in thy name! Every fool, from king to policeman, from the flatheaded parson to the visionless dabbler in science, presumes to speak authoritatively of human nature. The greater the mental charlatan, the more definite his insistence on the wickedness and weaknesses of human nature. Yet, how can any one speak of it today, with every soul in a prison, with every heart fettered, wounded, and maimed?

John Burroughs has stated that experimental study of animals in captivity is absolutely useless.[17] Their character, their habits, their appetites undergo a complete transformation when torn from their soil in field and forest. With human nature caged in a narrow space, whipped daily into submission, how can we speak of its potentialities?

Freedom, expansion, opportunity, and, above all, peace and repose, alone can teach us the real dominant factors of human nature and all its wonderful possibilities.

Anarchism, then, really stands for liberation of the human mind from the dominion of religion; the liberation of the human body from the dominion of property; liberation from the shackles and restraint of government. Anarchism stands for a social order based on the free grouping of individuals for the purpose of producing real social wealth; an order that will guarantee to every human being free access to the earth and full enjoyment of the necessities of life, according to individual desires, tastes, and inclinations.

This is not a wild fancy or an aberration of the mind. It is the conclusion arrived at by hosts of intellectual men and women the world over; a conclusion resulting from the close and studious observation of the tendencies of modern society: individual liberty and economic equality, the twin forces for the birth of what is fine and true in man.

As to methods. Anarchism is not, as some may suppose, a theory of the future to be realized through divine inspiration. It is a living force in the affairs of our life, constantly creating new conditions. The methods of Anarchism therefore do not comprise an iron-clad program to be carried out under all circumstances. Methods must grow out of the economic needs of each place and clime, and of the intellectual and temperamental requirements of the individual. The serene, calm character of a Tolstoy will wish different methods for social reconstruction than the intense, overflowing personality of a

17. John Burroughs (1837–1921), American essayist and nature writer, wrote for several periodicals, including the New York *Leader*. In his essay "In the Noon of Science," published in *The Summit of the Years* (Houghton Mifflin, 1913), Burroughs discusses the subjection of animals to laboratory testing: "We may know an animal in the light of all the many tests that laboratory experimentation throws upon it, and yet not really know it at all. We are not content to know what the animal knows naturally, we want to know what it knows unnaturally. We put it through a sort of inquisitorial torment in the laboratory, we starve it, we electrocute it, we freeze it, we burn it, we incarcerate it, we vivisect it, we press it on all sides and in all ways, to find out something about its habits or its mental processes that is usually not worth it. Well, we can gain a lot of facts, such as they are, but we may lose our own souls" (51–52).

Michael Bakunin or a Peter Kropotkin. Equally so it must be apparent that the economic and political need of Russia will dictate more drastic measures than would England or America. Anarchism does not stand for military drill and uniformity; it does, however, stand for the spirit of revolt, in whatever form, against everything that hinders human growth. All Anarchists agree in that, as they also agree in their opposition to the political machinery as a means of bringing about the great social change.

"All voting," says Thoreau, "is a sort of gaming, like checkers, or backgammon, a playing with right and wrong; its obligation never exceeds that of expediency. Even voting for the right thing is doing nothing for it. A wise man will not leave the right to the mercy of chance, nor wish it to prevail through the power of the majority."[18] A close examination of the machinery of politics and its achievements will bear out the logic of Thoreau.

What does the history of parliamentarism show? Nothing but failure and defeat, not even a single reform to ameliorate the economic and social stress of the people. Laws have been passed and enactments made for the improvement and protection of labor. Thus it was proven only last year that Illinois, with the most rigid laws for mine protection, had the greatest mine disasters. In States where child labor laws prevail, child exploitation is at its highest, and though with us the workers enjoy full political opportunities, capitalism has reached the most brazen zenith.

Even were the workers able to have their own representatives, for which our good Socialist politicians are clamoring, what chances are there for their honesty and good faith? One has but to bear in mind the process of politics to realize that its path of good intentions is full of pitfalls: wire-pulling, intriguing, flattering, lying, cheating; in fact, chicanery of every description, whereby the political aspirant can achieve success. Added to that is a complete demoralization of character and conviction, until nothing is left that would make one hope for anything from such a human derelict. Time and time again the people were foolish enough to trust, believe, and support with their last farthing aspiring politicians, only to find themselves betrayed and cheated.

It may be claimed that men of integrity would not become corrupt in the political grinding mill. Perhaps not; but such men would be absolutely helpless to exert the slightest influence in behalf of labor, as indeed has been shown in numerous instances. The State is the economic master of its servants. Good men, if such there be, would either

---

18. The quoted material is from Henry David Thoreau's 1849 essay "Civil Disobedience." EG has collapsed the following lengthy paragraph of Thoreau's essay into the abbreviated paragraph appearing above:

"All voting is a sort of gaming, like checkers or back-gammon, with a slight moral tinge to it, a playing with right and wrong, with moral questions; and betting naturally accompanies it. The character of the voters is not staked. I cast my vote, perchance, as I think right; but I am not vitally concerned that that right should prevail. I am willing to leave it to the majority. Its obligation, therefore, never exceeds that of expediency. Even voting for the right is doing nothing for it. It is only expressing to men feebly your desire that it should prevail. A wise man will not leave the right to the mercy of chance, nor wish it to prevail through the power of the majority."

remain true to their political faith and lose their economic support, or they would cling to their economic master and be utterly unable to do the slightest good. The political arena leaves one no alternative, one must either be a dunce or a rogue.

The political superstition is still holding sway over the hearts and minds of the masses, but the true lovers of liberty will have no more to do with it. Instead, they believe with Stirner that man has as much liberty as he is willing to take. Anarchism therefore stands for direct action, the open defiance of, and resistance to, all laws and restrictions, economic, social, and moral. But defiance and resistance are illegal. Therein lies the salvation of man. Everything illegal necessitates integrity, self-reliance, and courage. In short, it calls for free, independent spirits, for "men who are men, and who have a bone in their backs which you cannot pass your hand through."[19]

Universal suffrage itself owes its existence to direct action. If not for the spirit of rebellion, of the defiance on the part of the American revolutionary fathers, their posterity would still wear the King's coat. If not for the direct action of a John Brown[20] and his comrades, America would still trade in the flesh of the black man. True, the trade in white flesh is still going on; but that, too, will have to be abolished by direct action. Trade unionism, the economic arena of the modern gladiator, owes its existence to direct action. It is but recently that law and government have attempted to crush the trade union movement, and condemned the exponents of man's right to organize to prison as conspirators. Had they sought to assert their cause through begging, pleading, and compromise, trade unionism would today be a negligible quantity. In France, in Spain, in Italy, in Russia, nay even in England (witness the growing rebellion of English labor unions)[21] direct, revolutionary, economic action has become so strong a force in the battle for industrial liberty as to make the world realize the tremendous importance of labor's power. The General Strike, the supreme expression of the economic consciousness of the workers, was ridiculed in America but a short time ago. Today every great strike, in order to win, must realize the importance of the solidaric general protest.[22]

Direct action, having proved effective along economic lines, is equally potent in the environment of the individual. There a hundred forces encroach upon his being, and only persistent resistance to them will finally set him free. Direct action against the

19. The original quotation from Henry David Thoreau's 1849 essay "Civil Disobedience" reads "Oh for a man who is a *man,* and, as my neighbor says, has a bone in his back which you cannot pass your hand through!"

20. John Brown (1800–1859), radical American abolitionist, led the raid on Harper's Ferry in 1859 in an attempt to secure weapons to distribute to slaves for armed rebellion. Brown was tried for murder, slave insurrection, and treason in the state of Virginia, for which he was hanged on 2 December 1859. EG associated John Brown with a current of anti-statist tradition in the United States.

21. From 1910 to 1914 a wave of strikes and violent industrial conflict shook England. In 1910 coal miners struck in South Wales, in 1911 transport workers struck in Liverpool, and in 1912 both the first national miners' strike and a huge transport workers' strike took place in London.

22. EG develops her ideas on direct, revolutionary, and economic action in her essay "Syndicalism: Its Theory and Practice," published in *Mother Earth,* January–February 1913.

authority of the law, direct action against the invasive meddlesome authority of our moral code, is the logical, consistent method of Anarchism.

Will it not lead to a revolution? Indeed, it will. No real social change has ever come about without a revolution. People are either not familiar with their history, or they have not yet learned that revolution is but thought carried into action.

Anarchism, the great leaven of thought, is today permeating every phase of human endeavor. Science, art, literature, the drama, the effort for economic betterment, in fact every individual and social opposition to the existing disorder of things, is illumined by the spiritual light of Anarchism. It is the philosophy of the sovereignty of the individual. It is the theory of social harmony. It is the great, surging, living truth that is reconstructing the world, and that will usher in the Dawn.

PDU, Mother Earth Publishing Association, 1911.

DEAR COMRADE:

I have read your book[1] with great attention. I am afraid the <u>Nuova Era</u>[2] is right in think-ing it will be little read except by those who would attend your lectures, but, as this peri-odical also says, it will, with careful study by the most intelligent of our comrades and some bourgeois of inquiring mind. I received your circulars, and will mail them as often as I write letters. I enclose a list of persons in Eau Claire to whom sending them, in one cent envelopes, might possibly pay. Mrs. Anastad you know already. Among your points which particularly attracted my attention are the evolutionary methods of free indus-try (p. 61); the identity of Anarchist violence with all other of a revolutionary kind (p. 90); the expose of bogus conspiracies (pp. 92, 3) the analysis of patriotism (pp. 134–5). (During the campaign of 1896, I heard a Bryan orator tell that the house of Belmont is Schoeneberg in Germany,[3] and [ . . . ] as you say of the rich Americans, belongs equally to all countries—I suppose it is Kaloros in Greece, and Bonnydune in Scotland.)

The secret motive of governments for increasing their armaments—a sufficiently dangerous experiment in these anti-patriotic days; the aims of anti-militarism (pp. 147–8); what you say on Ibsen's and Carpenter's remarks about marriage as affected by the psychology of sex,[4] (p. 235); the pernicious affect of marriage on labor, (p. 239); the real secret of Kings' and priests' aversion to sexual freedom, (p. 243); the importance of Art in our movement (pp. 247–49); the nullity of the mob, and all-ness of the indi-vidual in reform, (pp. 269–70). What you say about prostitution (pp. 185-7-193) points in the right direction: but there is something deeper. Prostitution is a positive insti-

---

1. A reference to EG's *Anarchism and Other Essays*. C. L. James's page references correspond to the first edition, published in 1910 by Mother Earth Publishing Association.
2. A reference to the Italian-language anarchist paper *L'Era Nuova* (1910–1917), published in Paterson, New Jersey.
3. A reference to a supporter of William Jennings Bryan (1860–1925), a leader and gifted orator of the Democratic Party and nominee for President in 1896. Bryan cinched the nomination with his famous "Cross of Gold" speech at the Democratic Party convention. Bryan proposed free and unlim-ited coinage of silver in order to remedy the economic ills of farmers and industrial workers. He was defeated by the Republican nominee, William McKinley.
4. In her essay "Marriage and Love" EG, echoing the ideas of Edward Carpenter and Henrik Ibsen, states that marriage brings together radically opposite individuals destined to remain forever strang-ers. According to her interpretation of Carpenter, men and women are so different, they are practi-cally unknowable to each other. Drawing from Ibsen, EG argues that married women are further degraded because they are expected to repress their natural sex instinct. See "Marriage and Love," Essay published by Mother Earth Publishing Association, January 1911, above.

tution. It is the oldest institution. It is the primitive form of sex-slavery (Moterman, Primitive Marriage;[5] Bachofen, Mutterrecht;[6] Lubbock—(now Lord Avebury—Origin of Civilization.[7] Marriage in all forms, polyandrous, polygamous, and monogamious, is only a graft upon this stem, inoculated for the benefit of Chiefs, nobles, and rich men, whom the bourgeois, of course, have imitated, and caricatured, but the proletariat much less; so that it is now the pet "duty", of the middle class, shirked, as a bore, by the rich whom it has ceased to suit, and never thoroughly naturalized among the homeless-gang-laborers. Marriage is the branch on which grow redundant population, patriotism, militarism, and class. But prostitution is the stem on which marriage itself grows, and without which, as is well known, it cannot exist. No reform, whether called Anarchism or something else, will succeed, (in effecting its ostensible purpose) if it does not go down to the root of sex-slavery. The earliest development of sex-slavery, prostitution, you know of course, is rather invigorated than weakened by tearing and hacking. It must be poisoned for peoples' taste, by showing that it is the stem on which marriage grows, I mean especially for womens' by showing them that it is not a sporadic evil which they can ignore or treat with philanthropic sprinklings, but the state of their sex as such since the evolution of human society—marriage being only a modification, which requires perpetuation of the unmodified kind. Your biography was very interesting to me. I have a thousand times heard the statement about sex-slavery of working-girls, on p. 14; but it always seemed to me incredible that even working girls, who adopted prostitution, should be such fools as to work hard also. I can understand a grisette,[8] milliners' apprentice, waitress, and etc—whose work is light, ekeing out the wages with paid and secret amours, but not a sewing-girl's accommodating bosses for permission to work "from early morning till late at night" because she could sell herself so much better. I have myself observed that the Anarchists are mainly instrumental in securing the success, moral as well as financial, of most of the radical undertakings. (p. 37) They are the

5. James probably intended to refer to John F. McLennan (1827–1881), the Scottish lawyer who formulated a theory of the evolution of the marriage instinct, suggesting a natural progression from a period of promiscuity to a stable matriarchal state. McLennan's *Primitive Marriage* was published in 1865.

6. Johann Jakob Bachofen (1815–1887), Swiss philologist, anthropologist, and author of *Das Mutterrecht: Eine Untersuchung uber die Gynaikokratie der alten Welt nach ihrer religiosen und der rechtlichen Natur* (1861; later published as *Mutterrecht and Urreligion*, 1954). Through his analysis of Roman, Greek, and Egyptian mythology, Bachofen concluded that the patriarchal structure of society dominant throughout Western history was a relatively recent invention, predated by a more primitive matriarchal culture.

7. Sir John Lubbock (1834–1913), English banker, statesman, and naturalist, member of Parliament from 1870, and made Baron Avebury in 1900. An evolutionist, his works include *The Origin of Civilisation and the Primitive Condition of Man: Mental and Social Condition of Savages* (1882); *Ants, Bees, and Wasps* (1882); *Pre-historic Times as Illustrated by Ancient Remains: and the Manners and Customs of Modern Savages* (1886); *The Pleasures of Life* (2 vols., 1887–1889); *On Municipal and National Trading* (1907); and *Marriage, Totemism and Religion: An Answer to Critics* (1911).

8. A young working girl.

reserve of the labor army—the best, most experienced troops, brought up at the crisis; but whose real importance is, and should be, little known to the enemy. It tickled me to think of your five o'clock "aesthetic tea" among the nobs, under the name of Miss Smith.[9] I hope that you will write your own biography yet.

Two phenomena most encouraging to judicious advocates of our cause were forcibly brought before me while reading your life and writings. One is the generally tolerant spirit of Anarchism. It gives no encouragement to Teufelsdroeck's[10] mania for "building"—it merely pulls down obstacles to <u>growth</u>. Every tub must stand on its own bottom. Now, for example, my daughters, because they are my daughters, care no more for institutions than myself. But they think one zealot in the family is quite enough. Why should I blame them? They have kept the pot boiling since my health failed; and that is a pretty fair division of labor.

The other encouraging phenomenon is the sporadic distribution of our ideas among outsiders (p. 38). Never mind if they do steal our thunder. That Colorado judge[11] who popularized the suspended sentence, has given law and order a deadly wound; for their strength is the idiotic fear of criminals among the masses,—"them-asses",—who think their exploiters necessary to their safety. When they learn, as they are learning, that common crime is not dangerous, they will cease to excuse the organized crime of society.

It is human nature to desire appreciation, however, though I do my utmost to consider only usefulness, I suppose Kropotkin's French <u>Revolution</u> has quite superceded mine.[12] Well. I soothe my conceit by reflecting that mine did much to put the idea in his head.

TLU, Emma Goldman Archive, IISH. The following written in EG's hand along left margin of first page: "one of the most scholarly anarchists in the US," referring to American scholar and anarchist Charles Leigh James.

9. James is referring to anecdotes about EG in Hippolyte Havel's introduction to *Anarchism and Other Essays*. The incident referred to occurred in 1905 when EG was tour manager for the theater company of Russian actor and director Pavel Orlenev, for whom she acted as interpreter at New York society functions, under the name "Miss E G Smith."
10. A character in Thomas Carlyle's *Sartor Resartus* (1833–1834).
11. Progressive Colorado reformer and first judge of Denver's Juvenile Court (1900–1927) Benjamin Barr Lindsey. Lindsey was influential in the establishment of a separate juvenile court system, believing that rehabilitation treatment was more effective than the isolation of prison time. He advocated the use of the suspended sentence—a sentence that the judge provides will not be enforced if the defendant performs certain services, makes restitution to persons harmed, or serves probation time. See also note 10 in Letter from William T. Holmes, 8 November 1912, below.
12. James's *History of the French Revolution* (Chicago: Abe Isaak, 1902) was published after being serialized in *Free Society* from 14 April 1901 through 29 December 1901. Peter Kropotkin's *The Great French Revolution* was published by G. P. Putnam and Sons in 1909.

I am glad to get a bit of the literature. We will give Anarchy & Malthus as a premium with the book.[1] Trade a few hundred Modern Schools with the Ferrer Ass. for Life of Ferrer.[2] If we have any kind of a trip we ought to sell most of your small pamphlets. We must push Modern Science & Anarchism[3] this trip. Be sure and bring Ballad of Reading Gaol & Soul of Man with you.[4] They ough to go in Catalogue[5]—we ough to carry Frank Harris' Bomb.[6] Beside, Eltzbacher,[7] Conquest of Bread[8] and if we would see Putman[9] he would give us 30–60 days to pay for books. And we could buy in great French Revolutions.[10]

Take James' French Revolution[11] and Kelso's Government analyzed[12] out of the office & put them in your private library.

I will write Lucy Parsons[13] about having the speeches delivered to me in Chicago that is if you care to have them.

We ough to carry Brieux Plays[14] with us there is 60¢ on each book and we will get time to pay for them. We might put Archer life of Ferrer. but it is too heavy.

Sorry we are all out of right to disbelieve.[15]

I think for the next Anarchy vs. Socialism pamphlet.[16] We will print a verbatim report

1. BR proposed that they offer C. L. James's pamphlet *Anarchy and Malthus* (New York: Mother Earth Publishing Association, 1910) with the purchase of EG's *Anarchism and Other Essays*.
2. BR is referring to Francisco Ferrer's *The Modern School* (New York: Mother Earth Publishing Association, 1909) and William Archer's *The Life, Trial, and Death of Francisco Ferrer* (London: Chapman and Hall, 1911).
3. Peter Kropotkin, *Modern Science and Anarchism* (New York: Mother Earth Publishing Association, 1908).
4. Oscar Wilde, *Ballad of Reading Gaol* (1898) and *Soul of Man Under Socialism* (1899).
5. From 1911 a catalogue of Mother Earth Publishing Association books and pamphlets, "together with a list of works distributed by *Mother Earth*," was intermittently published.
6. Frank Harris, *The Bomb* (New York: Mitchell Kennerley, 1909).
7. Paul Eltzbacher, *Anarchism* (New York: Benjamin Tucker, 1908).
8. Peter Kropotkin, *Conquest of Bread* (New York: G. P. Putnam and Sons, 1906).
9. This is a reference to G. P. Putnam, a New York publisher.
10. Peter Kropotkin, *The Great French Revolution* (New York: G. P. Putnam and Sons, 1909).
11. C. L. James, *History of the French Revolution* (Chicago: A. Isaak Jr., 1902).
12. John R. Kelso, *Government Analyzed* (Longhorn, Colorado: E. D. Kelso, 1892).
13. Lucy Parsons, ed., *The Famous Speeches of the Haymarket Martyrs* (Chicago: Lucy Parsons, 1909).
14. Eugène Brieux, *Three Plays by Brieux*, with preface by Bernard Shaw, English versions by Mrs. Bernard Shaw, St. John Hankin, and John Pollock (New York: Brentano's, 1911), was distributed by mail order through *Mother Earth* magazine.
15. Edwin J. Kuh, *The Right to Disbelieve* (New York: Mother Earth Publishing Association, 1910).
16. W. C. Owen, *Anarchy Versus Socialism* (New York: Mother Earth Publishing Association, 1910).

of one of your debates that you have with some good man. Lewis is anxious to debate with you.[17] I missed him yesterday.

I want to see a volume of debates of yours published some day. Have its Mother Earth give it to Buckley[18] yet.

Be sure and put away one of all the pamphlet the M.E. publishes.

ALS, IU-U.

17. Arthur Morrow Lewis (1873–1959), Chicago member of the Socialist Party and a popular lecturer on Marxism. Lewis had a regular Sunday lecture on socialism at the Garrick Theater in Chicago for many years. In fact, EG did not debate Lewis on the subject of direct action versus political action until 7 March 1912.
18. A reference to Buckley & Wood, binders and distributors of *Mother Earth*.

My dearest Mommy—

All packed up ready to go. I will be so glad to see you—Oh it seems as if I will never be unkind or neglectful of you again. Your pathetic letter reminded me that we were strangers, Yes we are strangers my great foolish love for you has never made me unfold my self to you. Oh if I could love you and have you as I really want to—It often seems to me that I will never be able to make you understand me and love me as I want to be loved. To have a home, to have peace and quiet—to have you in beauty and great delight. Oh will that ever be, I hope so.

How can I be pregnant when I am not married the little girl asked.

How can we be unhappy and worried when we love each other.

Oh to understand. You don't know me. I want to pet and humor you. I want to be a loving sweetheart. But when we are together business propaganda so many things interfere.

You are such a powerful creature it is difficult to be a simple lover to you. Your passion is so strong so glorious that fate provides that I never can have enough. Oh lover I come to you full of hope and life. full of burning desire for the big lovely mountains full of [madly?] for the sweet tasting treasure box. I come to you full of love for you. I come as your admirer your lover your manager—

Baby I want you I love you.

Oh just love me. Understand me. Take the Mountains and treasure box Willie is starved and waiting.

Mommy I love you
Hobo

Book account.

Received from Mother Earth 112 copies

Sold—51 copies

Left with A.G. Mc.Glurg[1] on consignment 20 copies

| " | " | Marie's book Shop " | " | 6 | " |
| " | " | Edith Adams.— | | 5 | " |
| " | " | Sam Savis | | 2 | " |

---

1. This is a reference to the Chicago publishing company and bookstore A. C. McClurg and Company.

| | | |
|---|---|---|
| Sold to Public Library | 1 | " |
| "   " [illegible] Library | 1 | " |
| Left at home | 8 | " |
| taking with me. | 7 | " |
| Gave free- | 11 | " |
| Ind Free Speech Com | | |
| Dr Montgomery | | |
| Brother 1 | | |
| Stenographer 1 | | |
| Edith Adams-1 | | |
| Jew girl Miss [illegible] | | |
| Mail man 1 | | |
| Elevator man 1 | | |
| Ian [illegible] | | |
| Woman 1 | | |

—1

I left the books with A.G. Mc McGlurg and [illegible] book shop which are the two lead-ing book stores in Chicago on consignment that is the <u>way</u> all publishers do <u>now</u>. When I get the card out I will announce that books can be had at these stores. Edith <u>Adams</u> will act as our agent and take in the meeting. Sam Savis will also <u>help</u>. If I had felt <u>bet-ter</u> and had a little more life and the holidays were not on I am sure I would have sold the <u>lot</u> but I have advertised the <u>book</u>[2] greatly and at least 50 people said they would buy the <u>book</u> latter.

I am surprised that the book go slow in NW—How did Reedy's [ad?] <u>work</u>.[3] We make a hit yet.

The new pamphlet is fine. I think the <u>Psychology of Violence</u> will sell well. The new <u>pamphlets</u>[4] have <u>one</u> bitter <u>dissipointment</u> you did not put in Definition of Anarchy <del>Anarchy</del> <u>Anarchism</u>[5]—I think it is a damn shame not to do it. I wrote Berkman that it would help

2. EG, *Anarchism and Other Essays* (New York: Mother Earth Publishing Association, 1910).
3. William Marion Reedy's paper, the *St. Louis Mirror*, favorably reported on her work, advertising her appearances in St. Louis and describing in detail her visit in the 9 March 1911 issue. The *Mirror* pub-lished an ad for EG's book in the 17 November 1910 issue.
4. EG, *Psychology of Political Violence* (New York: Mother Earth Publishing Association, 1911).
5. The definitions of "anarchy" referred to by BR regularly appeared in *Mother Earth*: "anarchy" was defined as "the absence of government; disbelief in, and disregard of, invasion and authority based on coercion and force; a condition of society regulated by voluntary agreement instead of govern-ment." "Anarchist" was defined as a "believer in Anarchism; one opposed to all forms of coercive government and invasive authority; an advocate of Anarchy, or absence of government, as the ideal of political liberty and social harmony." "Anarchism" was defined as "the philosophy of a new social order based on liberty unrestricted by man-made law; the theory that all forms of government rest

much to put these deffinitions in all pamphlets that come out. But he is so much of an artist and has no little idea of the <u>importance</u> of pouplarizing these terms that he did not do it. These <u>definition</u> are to be on the Catalogue of books that we are getting out. I was glad to get the review in the <u>Globe</u>[6] send me a <u>copy</u> of all reviews that come out as I go to book <u>sellers</u> and to Libraries they will be extremely <u>useful</u>.

<u>Also</u> <u>please</u> be sure to make up a new scrap book of all the <u>reviews</u> get every line good or bad make the paper and keep it in a <u>book</u>. So when we publish your autobiograph or any new book we will have these reviews to show the <u>publishers</u>—and I feel sure you will have no trouble to find a publisher for your new <u>books.</u>

Why was the list of literature left off of our new pamphlet.

ALS, IU-U. On *Mother Earth* stationery. Location at top, "At home on the eve of departure."

---

on violence, and are therefore wrong and harmful, as well as unnecessary." This definition of "anarchism" also appeared on *Mother Earth* stationery.

6. A review of *Anarchism and Other Essays* (New York: Mother Earth Publishing Association, 1910) appeared in the *New York Globe* in January 1911.

DEAR FRIEND:

Enclosed please find announcements of my Lectures in Chicago.[1]

Dr. J. Greer,[2] of 52 Dearborn St., has kindly lent his office as the distribution depot of our cards. If you care to help make the meetings known, you can do so by calling or writing to Dr. Greer for cards, and distribute them in your section of the city, or among your friends. Also we have reserved seats for advance sale. Dr. Greer will supply you with as many as you would like to sell.

Every assistance you can give, I will greatly appreciate. Please address me until February 5th, Randolph Hotel, Detroit, Mich.

SINCERELY,

EMMA GOLDMAN

The meetings will take place Feb 12, 13, 14, 15 & 16th Hod Carriers Hall, Harrison and Halsted.

TLS, Floyd Dell Papers, ICarbS. Handwritten postscript.

1. Floyd Dell (1887–1969) American socialist poet, journalist, and playwright lived in Chicago until 1913, when he moved to New York City. Dell was a member of the 1909 Free Speech Committee. Dell wrote for the *Tri-City Workers Magazine* and edited the *Friday Literary Review* in 1911. In 1913 he moved to New York, where he was associated with the Greenwich Village bohemian movement. Dell was a member of the New York Liberal Club, which produced three of his plays. He was editor of the *Masses*, for which he wrote extensively, and an editor and regular contributor to *New Review*. He contributed once to *Mother Earth*, in 1909. In 1912 he wrote a chapter, "Socialism and Anarchism in Chicago," for *Chicago Its History and Its Builders a Century of Marvelous Growth*, vol. 2 (Chicago: J. S. Clarke, 1912). His various writings on feminism often referred to EG and her work, including his book *Women as World Builders: Studies in Modern Feminism* (Chicago: Forbest, 1913), which included a chapter on Beatrice Webb and EG, and he was criticized for his portrait of EG by Margaret Sanger in the *Woman Rebel*. He was also associated with the Provincetown Players, which performed a number of his plays.
2. Dr. J. H. Greer (1851–1921) was a Chicago physician, anarchist, and author. He was a financial supporter of *Mother Earth* and other anarchist publications, including the *Selected Works of Voltarine de Cleyre* (New York: Mother Earth Publishing Association, 1914). Greer often hosted EG on her visits to Chicago. He contributed once to *Mother Earth* (November 1912) on the subject of the Haymarket anarchists. His writings on birth control, which were widely circulated, include *Talks on Nature. Important Information for Both Sexes. A Treatise on the Structure, Functions and Passional Attractions of Men and Women. Anatomy, Physiology, Hygiene. A True Marriage Guide* (Chicago: J. H. Greer, 1910); and, most importantly, *A Physician in the House* (Chicago: M. A. Donahue, 1897), reprinted many times.

My dear Mr Baldwin

I just heard from Mr Kelly[1] to the effect that he was compelled to go out of town again for a few days. That is too bad since I do not like to impose on you anything you feel, you ought not to do.

I am very anxious to book Hibernian Hall,[2] now as you have not mentioned my name to the care taker of the place, he may refuse when the poor culprit is announced. What do you suggest? Will you consult with Mr Reedy, have written him a few days ago and I am writing him again, now. His Catholic spirit may smooth matters over. Please see him, I put my fate in the keeping of you two good Angels.

Write me soon ther here, or General Delivery Toledo, will be there the 28th.[3]

Sincerely

Emma Goldman

ALS, ACLU Archives, NjP. On stationery of the Claypool Hotel, Indianapolis, Indiana.

1. A reference to Harry Kelly, American anarchist, editor, printer, and lecturer, who was living in St. Louis at this time.
2. A reference to the social hall for the St. Louis chapter of the Hibernians, an Irish-Catholic fraternal organization.
3. Baldwin had written EG the same day, informing her that he had asked a Miss Martin, director of the St. Louis Beethoven Dance Conservatory and a friend of William Marion Reedy, to organize EG's lectures in the city in 1911.

MY DEAR HUTCH

Let me congratulate you on your splendid review in <u>The Bookman</u>.[1] It is the first thing you have written about me which is free from the ordinary journalistic tricks. I am indeed very grateful that it is so, not so much for my sake as for your own. You are altogether too fine dear, to write cheap things. I know one can not escape it in a cheap World. And yet it seems a pity, especially in your case. You have such a store of human sympathy, something so warm and glowing that it is often a marvel to me, how little it asserts itself in your criticisms or reviews of people.

In your <u>Bookman</u> article, you cease to be Hapgood the newspaper man. You are Hutch the very human tender Hutch who thrilled me so the night at the Boulevard[2] and many times before at 210.[3] I can not begin to tell you how happy that tone in your write up has made me. Not because of what ever praise it contained really not. Rather is it, because I felt that you have at last looked to the soul of E G the public character. It took you many years to do it, old man, but I am glad you got there at last. Possibly, a few years longer, will bring you still closer to E G. I hope so anyway.

Don't you think we are rather slow in knowing each other Hutchie boy? We two, with such a World wide reputation for getting sweethearts—It seems to me it's harder to live down one's reputation, than to live up to it.

1. Hutchins Hapgood reviewed EG's *Anarchism and Other Essays* (New York: Mother Earth Publishing Association, 1910) in the *Bookman: An Illustrated Magazine of Literature and Life* (New York 32 [February 1911]: 639–40). Hapgood and EG had a friendly, and rather flirtatious, relationship during the period of this volume.
2. Café Boulevard was the meeting place of the Sunrise Club, a New York liberal lecture and dining club founded in 1890 by the individualist anarchist E. C. Walker, where Hapgood spoke on occasion. EG was often invited to speak at the Sunrise Club, though AB, considered an activist and not a lecturer, was not invited to speak. Walker (1849–1931) was also an active member of the National Liberal League and a free speech advocate. He was a New York agent for *Mother Earth* and had previously edited *Lucifer the Lightbearer* (1882–1888, with Moses Harman) and *Fair Play* (1888–1909, with Lillian Harman). Walker also served as an editorial contributor to Benjamin Tucker's journal *Liberty* (1906–1908), after submitting letters and articles to the paper from 1885 onward. Walker signed the widely circulated letter sent to *Justice* in 1911 protesting the allegation that EG was a police spy. His works during this period include *The One-Issue Secularism: A Life Member's Letter to the American Secular Union Congress in Chicago* (Los Angeles: S. W. Davis, 1910), *Marriage and Prostitution* (New York: Edwin C. Walker, 1913), and *The Ethics of Freedom* (New York: E. C. Walker, 1913). For more details on Walker, see vol. 2, *Making Speech Free*.
3. Refers to 210 East 13th Street, which was both the office of *Mother Earth* and EG's shared apartment. In January 1911 EG moved the offices of *Mother Earth* and her residence from 210 East 13th Street to a larger building at 55 West 28th Street.

I liked your brother[4] even more when I met him at my second meeting. His face was a study. He sat right in front of me, when I spoke on the drama. He had such a kindly expression, it made me feel quite at home in the little Church. But of course I could not mistake him for you, dear.[5]

Yes, it was T Snyder who helped in our triumph.[6] He certainly left not a stone unturned. But the Churches had nothing to do with him. The two ministers volunteered themselves.

Tom is a wonderful chap. What a pitty the men I might love, have wives I like. You may ask, what difference does it make? Well, if I thought the wives free it might not matter. But somehow I hate to get my joy at the expence of others. Or possibly it is altogether a very selfish reason. I hate to be an incident in a man's life—

Well if I could explain motives, I should be a very wise woman. As it is I am a woman alright, too much for my own good, and not wise.

Affectionately

Emma

PS. The "Wild Man"[7] is learning for the first time, he knows me, the pain, that he has caused others so long. The possibility of my caring and associating with anyone else. Human nature is a strange mixture Hutch. And the Wild Man is very human. That's why you and I feel so close to him, is it not?

ALS, CtY-B. On stationery of the Randolph Hotel, Detroit, Michigan.

4. William Powers Hapgood (1872–1960) was the president of Columbia Conserve Company of Indianapolis. The company was a grower and canner of tomatoes and a model of cooperative management and ownership until it failed in 1910; it was later reorganized in 1916.
5. EG was lecturing in Indianapolis, where William Hapgood lived, on 24 January. See note 6 below.
6. Thomas F. Snyder and his wife, Katherine, were friends of EG's who lived in Indianapolis. After initially being denied a venue by all the halls in Indianapolis EG was finally able to speak when an orthodox preacher, Reverend Nelson, offered the Pentecost Tabernacle Church. Following this engagement, EG also spoke at the Universalist Church in Indianapolis. See also Letter to Hutchins Hapgood, 23 February 1911, below.
7. A reference to BR, who was a friend and drinking companion of Hapgood at this time.

## To HUTCHINS HAPGOOD

*Peoria, Illinois, 23 February 1911*

DEAREST HUTCH.

My silence is not due to the fact that you failed to do justice to my letter. I simply did not wish to inflict My wretched moods on you, else I should have written often.

I wish, I could get hold of you some times just to talk to you and have you drive away the clouds.

I must be getting old Hutchie, dear, I see nothing but clouds most times, or is it my own fancy? I can not tell, I only know I have grown so damnably sensitive to all kinds of impressions, as if my soul were covered with tissue paper. Fate, or the devil must have entered into some sort of a conspiracy, when I was thrust into the public arena, I realize more and more how deficiant I am for that. And yet I am not much fit for a private life. Truth is, I am pretty much of an abartion Hutchie boy. I find life hard to endure under all circumstances. You see, I am not as lucky as you, I too do not like myself, still less do I like life, or that which we call life. I wish I were ein Königkind[1] somewheres in the woods, basking in love and flowers and mad forgetfulness. I don't say I should be contented long it would depend on the love and flowers I suppose.

Just fancy wishing for such things, yet standing in ugly dirty Hall facing dull people, with your soul inside out for everyone to stick a dirty thumb into it.

I don't exactly know what ails you, dear boy, but I think the element of reckless defiance to circumstances is sadly lacking among all the younger middle class generation in America. I meet so many, who are very thoughtful, they are utterly out of keeping with the old, lean strongly towards the new, but in most cases they balance in the air. I think they are very much fettered by a puritanic past, which makes them slow and methodical, unable to throw off the weight of traditions. Perhaps, I am mistaken, but that is my impression. I am not so sure that pain would civilize our wild man,[2] in the way he needs to be civilized, it may make him harder. At any rate, I do not like to try him. Not so much for his sake, as My own. Contrary to my reputation, I never could enter into a momentary relationship. Every experience meant more to me than the birth of a child. I have always paid much more than I got out, which is no one's fault, but My own, possibly I am too insatiable I don't know. Ou[t]side of yourself no one has attracted me so strongly as Tom,[3] since I know Ben and yet could not give way simply because of the dread of

---

1. Königkind, meaning literally "a child of the king," is a phrase that often appears in German fairy tales to characterize those who are coddled and carefree.
2. EG is referring to BR. See also Letter to Hutchins Hapgood, 31 January 1911, above.
3. Thomas Snyder, married to Katherine Snyder, EG's friend in Indianapolis. See Letter to Hutchins Hapgood, 31 January 1911, above.

pain which is sure to be mine. I feel about T, as I have often of you, too much involved in it, and I am not one to step lightly over people's soul, nor am I easily content to be a medium of a moment's pleasure. I could do it much easier, when I was younger, youth is so self centered. Some times though I feel like scattering everything to the winds and just drink from the cup of life until all is a blank. I am a queer specimen Hutchie, darling. It's only fortunate my friends do not know me, or I would be lonelier than I am now.

We go from here to St Louis. Billy Reedy[4] is experimenting for me with The "Fashionable" arranged two meetings at an exclusive Hall with $1 admission, that I may address the ladies who think they are thinking.[5] It's cruel to make them see that they are not, but thought is cruel, is it not?

I always have three lectures for the "common" folk, so you need not fear I am turning into a snob.

Always glad to hear from you, dear.

AFFECTIONATELY,

EMMA

Remember me kindly to Neith[6] and Bertha if she is still with you. How is the boy?[7]
All of next week you can reach me The Maryland Hotel St Louis Mo.

Hapgood Family papers, American Literature Manuscript Collections, Beinecke Rare Book and Manuscript Library, Yale University.

4. EG is referring to William Marion Reedy.
5. EG spoke at the Wednesday Club Auditorium, which belonged to the Wednesday Club, an organization of St. Louis society women, on 28 February and 2 March, on the topics "Tolstoi—Artist and Rebel" and "Galsworthy's *Justice*," events orchestrated by Reedy and by Alice Martin, a member of the club; see also Letter to Roger Baldwin, 24 January 1911, above. The club was subsequently denounced by the Reverend James W. Lee of the St. John's Methodist Church, South, who claimed that allowing EG to rent the club's building was "as bad as letting it out to the worst burglar that ever broke into a house, or to the veriest thief that ever ran away to Canada with the money of widows and orphans in his pocket, or to the worst assassin that ever killed a king or shot a president of the United States." While some club members supported EG's right to speak, many either agreed with Lee or denied any responsibility for the renting of the hall.
6. A reference to Neith Boyce Hapgood (1872–1951), Hutchins's wife and a feminist author, journalist, and playwright. In 1898 she was an assistant to Lincoln Steffens at the New York *Commercial Advertiser*, where she met and in June 1899 married Hutchins Hapgood. She was a founding member of the Provincetown Players and wrote four plays for the theater group. The Hapgoods' home in Provincetown was the first venue of the theater group, and Boyce's play *Constancy*, about the love affair of John Reed and Mabel Dodge Luhan, was one of the first two plays performed. Her works include *The Forerunner* (1903), *The Folly of Others* (1904), *Eternal Spring* (1906), and *The Bond* (1908). She also contributed to *Revolt* (1916).
7. The Hapgoods had two sons, Boyce (1901–1918) and Charles Hutchins (1904–1982). Charles had contracted polio in 1910.

DEAREST NUNA

I suppose it will be of little consolation to you, when I tell you, I carry your letter with me always meaning to write, not out of duty, but because I love you and always think of you. And yet it is true, only one leading as mad a life as I has but little opportunity to partake of love and friendship. These precious elements need repose and quiet, I have neither.

However, perhaps it must be so, I am really getting to be a fatalist.

We have been racing from place to place always busy, always in anxiety. I can not say, we have had good results, somehow we do not get ahead. The reasons? There are many, absolute silence on the part of the press in most Cities, (except as in Pitts, attacks, when I have gone), poor Halls bad weather and considerable opposition on the part of my dear comrades. Every thing together helps to complicate matters so that I sometimes feel as if I could endure it no longer. And yet you see, I go on, I can not help otherwise. everything in me rebels against the idea of submitting to things. Indeed the greater the obstacles the more I am driven on, driven by some uncontrolable force within me which will not let me rest.

With all that, I grow more miserable every day. It is no one's fault, just my unfortunate sensitiveness which seems to increase with every hour. I guess, I must be getting old. I certainly never knew the agony of soul in former years. But now, ah my dear, I can not discribe it, it's beyond words.

Every little thing burns my flesh and tears my nerves to pieces. I dare say the good "Lord" will make place for me in Heaven, for verily I suffer Hell every hour of my existence.

This is not a cheerful letter, is it dearest? But what's the use of having a friend if you can not unload your misery on him. I do not permit myself such a luxury too often do I? That is only because, I have few friends.

Since I wrote the report in M E nothing of much interest has happened.[1] Detroit was awful in every way.[2] Ann Arbor was fair, the students though still boisterous were less vindictive.[3] Also, I have the pleasure of knowing, that my last year's visit has induced a

---

1. See "On the Trail" in *Mother Earth*, February 1911.
2. This is in reference to EG's lecture series in Detroit at Stabbler Hall and Freemen Hall from 31 January through 5 February 1911. She also spoke in Ann Arbor on 4 February.
3. In *Living My Life* (p. 445) EG recalled that at her lectures at the University of Michigan in Ann Arbor in 1910 she "was confronted with five hundred university rowdies in our hall, whistling, howling, and acting like lunatics." Students broke chairs and raided the literature table.

Professor to announce a course on Anarchism for this year. I am corresponding with the gentleman and have sent him a lot of material.[4]

I had a good meeting in Grand Rapids, my first visit there and spent a day with my ex soldier boy Wm Buwaldo.[5]

Who dare say, that character is not stranger than circumstances? Buwaldo was 15 years in the army, fought in the Philopeans, went through the usual cruel soul distroying drill of barrak life. But he remained as fine and sweet as a delicate flower. With a thoughtfulness and consideration, that are simply wonderful.

He is on a farm with an old step mother his father having died last year.

Though he longs to go out into the World, a free man, he remains on the farm, because as he says, "Why should I burden others with my cares." The woman is very old and no one to look after her. But he does not waste his time, he studyies, has developed marvelously and is altogether a great chap. I am prouder of having made Buwaldo think, than of anything I have accomplished through my public work.

Chicago. Well, I'd better not write about it. Purgatory is a pleasant place compared, with the horrors I endured there. Do you remember Mrs Alving telling the pastor the escapades of her husband the scene in the dining room, when she heard the same scene repeated by her son.[6] Призракий[7] Chicago is saturated of Призракий, the most horrible spooks imaginable—

We are on our way to St Louis, where I am to address "fashionable" women in a fashionable Hall. It is to be $1 admission. Reedy and a certain Miss Martin are managing that affaire.[8] But I also have three other meetings for the "Common" folk.[9] It's all so amusing dear, if only I could laugh—

I am so glad you have started something for the Japanese victims. I don't remember any other event that so effected me, as the murder of the 12 souls, especially the little woman, whom I knew through correspondence. She has translated my Tragedy of Woman's Emancipation."[10] Somehow our Russian heroines seem of sturdier stuff,

4. EG is referring to Robert Mark Wenley (1861–1929), professor of philosophy at the University of Michigan.

5. William Buwalda (1869–1946) was a U.S. Army soldier in the engineers corps, who attended EG's lecture on "Patriotism" in San Francisco in 1908. He was court-martialed and imprisoned for shaking EG's hand while he was in uniform. See vol. 2, *Making Speech Free*, p. 513.

6. A reference to the second act of Henrik Ibsen's play *Ghosts* (1881).

7. Prizraki (English transliteration) is "ghosts" in Russian.

8. William Marion Reedy and Alice Martin organized lectures for EG at the exclusive Women's Wednesday Club in St. Louis. EG spoke on "Tolstoy—Artist and Rebel" on 28 February and "Galsworthy's *Justice*" on 2 March. In the March 1911 edition of *Mother Earth* she described the society club as "a parasitic class of women who do not know what to do with their time."

9. EG delivered three lectures at the Odeon Recital Hall in St. Louis on 26 February and 1 March.

10. A reference to Kanno Suga, the Japanese anarchist who was executed on 25 January 1911 for plotting to assassinate the emperor. No evidence of this translation has been found, and, in fact, in her prison diaries (1910–1911) Kanno mentions that she was only just beginning to study English. EG is most likely confusing her with Noe Ito (1895–1923), who would publish a translation of "The

therefore their death never effected me so terribly. But this delicate flower tender and yielding as Japanese women are, what glorious courage, what simple faith to die, as she has died—

I wish you success dear Nun, I hope you will carry the undertaking to a successful end.

Yes, Rasnick[11] is a bore, he really is a very petty piece of humanity, but I admire his devotion to the Agitator, or rather to Fox.[12] It merely proves that even small souls, may sometimes be capable of a big emotion. I hardly think I shall cross Rasnick's path, he does not like me, he is not alone in that.

Sadikichi[13] is a strange Critter, a bit too frozen for me, but he is certainly talented.

Well dear I must close, have a lot to do yet and I am not at all well. I must have caught cold, I am sore all over, inside and outside.

Ben[14] just came in with flowers, it's criminal to get them now, but it's the only bit of color I have, so I don't mind Ben extravaggence.

Write me when you feel like, your letters are always welcome.

WITH LOTS OF LOVE
EMMA

Remember me kindly to George[15] and Liza.[16] Ben sends love to you.

ALS, MCR. On stationery of the New National Hotel, Peoria, Illinois.

---

Tragedy of Women's Emancipation" as a supplement to her paper *Seito* (Bluestocking) in 1913 (and later name her children Emma 1 and Emma 2).

11. Dr. Martin Rasnick was a dentist who lived and practiced in Home Colony from around 1911 to 1913. His companion, Esther Abramovitz, went on to live with Jay Fox and, later, William Z. Foster. He offered both political and financial support to the paper.

12. The *Agitator* (1910–1912) was edited by Jay Fox.

13. This is a reference to the German-Japanese anarchist author and artist Sadakichi Hartmann, who had frequently contributed stories to *Mother Earth*.

14. EG is referring to BR.

15. Russian-born anarchist and single-taxer George Seldes (1860–1931) was Nunia's husband at this time.

16. Liza could possibly be Nunia's sister.

Editorial in *MOTHER EARTH*

*March 1911*

# Our Sixth Birthday

With this issue *Mother Earth* begins her sixth journey through life.

Five years! What an infinitesimal drop in the ocean of eternity; yet how terribly long a time when travelled on a hard, thorny road. With a world of ignorance and prejudice to battle against, a thousand obstacles to overcome, hosts of enemies to face, and with but few friends, *Mother Earth* has withstood, for five years, the storm and stress of the firing line, and has wavered not.

More than once was she stabbed by the enemy, and hurt by the thrusts of the well-meaning; more than once was her body bruised, her flesh torn by conflicting forces; yet never has she fallen by the wayside, nor her ardor been subdued.

Now that *Mother Earth* begins her sixth journey, it behooves us to halt a moment and to ponder the question: Was the struggle and pain worth while? has the magazine justified the expectations that gave it life?

Not long ago a friend wrote to us: Why don't you give up? Why waste your time and energy in a lost cause? *Mother Earth* has not reached the people you had hoped to reach, nor does the magazine satisfy even some of our own comrades, because—as they say—more reading matter than is contained in *Mother Earth* can be had in the ordinary magazines, for ten cents.

Viewed from the dominant standpoint of success, our friend is right. In that sense *Mother Earth* has failed. Our circulation is still far from the fifty-thousand mark; our subscribers, too, do not represent the multitudes. Nor is our financial rating such that we need feel any anxiety lest a Wall Street panic break our bank. Again, *Mother Earth* has lost in avoirdupois; it began as a heavyweight of sixty-four pages, but is now reduced to the lightweight class.

But since when do Anarchists measure success by quantity? Are numbers, weight, or following the true criterion of success? Should not the latter consist, first of all, in adherence to the chosen purpose, no matter at what cost? Indeed, the only success of any value has been the failure of men and women who struggled, suffered, and bled for an ideal, rather than give up, or be silenced.

*Mother Earth is* such a success. Without a party to back her, with little or no support from her own ranks, and consistently refusing to be gagged by a profitable advertising department, she has bravely weathered the strain of five years, stormy enough to have broken many a strong spirit. She has created an atmosphere for herself which few Anarchist publications in America have been able to equal. She has gathered around her a coterie of men and women who are among the best in the country, and, finally, she has acted as a leaven of thought in quarters least expected by those who are ready with advice, yet unable to help.

Many an editor of our better-class dailies has found in *Mother Earth* a source of information and inspiration, and though they would be loathe to admit it, it is nevertheless true that they have used our magazine for copy on numerous occasions. That, among other things, may help to account for the decided change in the tone of the press towards Anarchism and Anarchists.

But for want of space many instances could be cited, showing how well and widely *Mother Earth* is read by journalists and writers, and what is thought of her merits by those who value quality above quantity.

As to the original *raison d'être* of *Mother Earth*, it was, first of all, to create a medium for the free expression of our ideas, a medium bold, defiant, and unafraid. That she has proved to the fullest, for neither friend nor foe has been able to gag her.

Secondly, *Mother Earth* was to serve as a gathering point, as it were, for those, who, struggling to free themselves from the absurdities of the Old, had not yet reached firm footing. Suspended between heaven and hell, they have found in *Mother Earth* the anchor of life.

Thirdly, to infuse new blood into Anarchism, which—in America—had then been running at low ebb for quite some time.

All these purposes, it may be said impartially, the magazine has served faithfully and well.

We cannot claim for *Mother Earth* hosts of followers, but she has made some friends whose steadfast devotion and generosity has accomplished greater results than would have been possible with a large income. Besides, our magazine would have long ere this been self-supporting, were it not for the many other issues drawing upon its resources.

We have created an American Anarchist propaganda literature,[1] which has consumed the largest part of the magazine's income; indeed, it is this, more than anything else, which has been such a drain on our funds.

On the whole, we feel that our fighter has more than justified its existence. True, *Mother Earth* is far from perfect; but, after all, it is the striving for, rather than the attainment of, perfection which is the essence of all effort, of life itself.

The struggle is ever before us. With increased determination and greater enthusiasm *Mother Earth* enters upon the sixth year, confident that her friends need no other

---

1. By 1911 Mother Earth Publishing Association had published EG's book *Anarchism and Other Essays* (New York: Mother Earth Publishing Association, 1910; 2nd ed. 1911) and seven of her pamphlets, as well as seventeen pamphlets by other authors.

assurance than that the magazine will continue on the great Open Road, with face ever turned toward the Dawn.[2]

Emma Goldman,
Alexander Berkman.

*Mother Earth* 6 (March 1911): 2–4.

2. A reference to the Walt Whitman poem after which the magazine was originally to be named. See Letter to Max Metzkow, 20 January 1906, vol. 2, *Making Speech Free*, p. 168.

## Are Kotoku Protests Justified?

3 February 1911

MY DEAR MISS GOLDMAN.

I have just received notice of the "Kotoku Protest Conference Defense Committee."[1] It begins: "The judicial murder by the Japanese government of twelve Anarchists and Socialists"—I have seen no evidence that they are anything but what some people here would call Philosophical Anarchists and very little that they are Socialists; it is certainly unfair to them and confusing to others to lump them all as "Anarchists and Socialists." Anarchy and Socialism seem to me (as to Tucker)[2] to be opposite poles of thought, and I think it should be remembered that twelve of them are still in jail awaiting the arbitrary disposal of the Japanese authorities. It appears to me that for Anarchists to meet as such, and protest as such,* and to dub them Anarchists with the meaning *Terrorist* that is ordinarily, though erroneously, understood by the word "Anarchist," is practically to stab them in the back. The threat in this resolution is particularly ill advised.

I have no doubt whatever that the Anarchistic expressions of sympathy, with the threat of violence that is sent out under that name, would only prejudice the Japanese officials against the prisoners, and there is no question that those are reported.

I joined in these protests because I saw clearly that they would be made anyhow by the Anarchists and, if they were to refrain, probably by hardly anybody else; and as my name is known in connection with some conservative matters, I hoped that it might have a palliative effect. If it had been a question, however, of whether the withholding of my name would have tended to stifle the protest under the much misunderstood name of "Anarchist," I should certainly have withheld it[3]—not from any lack of sympathy, but

---

1. The Kōtoku Defense Committee, of which AB was secretary treasurer, included both anarchist and socialist activists, including BR, EG, Hippolyte Havel, Rose Strunsky, Jaime Vidal, and Louis Fraina.
2. Benjamin R. Tucker contrasted anarchist socialism and anarchist individualism in his pamphlet *State Socialism and Anarchism* (1888), suggesting that anarchism and socialism were incompatible and contradictory.
3. Bolton Hall, a lawyer and prominent single-taxer. This was not the first time Hall had been reticent to lend his name to the efforts to protest the high treason affair. According to Japanese government reports (Confidential Report No. 36, 23 November 1910, from Kokichi Mizuno, consul general in New York to Baron Yasuya Uchida, Japanese ambassador to the United States), at a 22 November meet-

because it seems to me a means ill-adapted to the end that we wish to attain, or at least proposed, namely—to save those persons who under pretext of conspiracy are being punished for the expression of their opinions.

For the same reason I think that the appeal of the Protest Conference will injure those who remain alive, more than any money we can raise will help them.

Yours very truly,
Bolton Hall

*Mr. Hall is in error. The protest meeting was not held by "Anarchists, as such." The call to organize the Kotoku Protest Conference was issued by Local New York, S. L. P.[4] The participants and speakers at the protest meeting represented all shades of radicalism.—Ed. [of Mother Earth]

11 February 1911

My Dear Mr. Hall.

As your letter could not go in the March issue of Mother Earth, and also because I was very busy, I delayed answering yours of the 3rd instant.

To say that I was surprised at the contents of your letter is to express it mildly. I had hoped from you, of all people, that, after knowing me for something like ten years and a great many others who hold the same ideas as I, you would have developed out of the notion that the Anarchists are divided into philosophics and terrorists. But I see that you are still in the thralldom of the superstition so common among a great many people.

Now, as a matter of fact, there is not an Anarchist in the whole world who propagates violence, except that all agree—even such ultra respectables as Mr. Tucker[5]—that we have the right to resist oppression.

The term "Philosophic Anarchists," as Fred Schulder justly said, is merely a cloak for a great many who hate to be considered fools, and yet haven't the courage to admit that they are opposed to present society.[6] It is not used in any other country except America,

---

ing EG and others adopted the proposal to protest to the Japanese ambassador, hold another protest meeting, and visit the Japanese consul general in New York demanding clarification of the facts of the Kōtoku Incident. After the proposals were adopted, of the three representatives nominated to visit the Japanese consul general in New York, only Hall declined. The other two nominees, Leonard Abbott and Bayard Boyesen, visited the consul general on 23 November.

4. The Socialist Labor Party (SLP) was a Marxist party founded in 1876.

5. See "Are Kotoku Protests Justified?," 3 February 1911, above.

6. Individualist anarchist Fred Schulder wrote a letter to EG, which was printed in the Mother Earth article "Light and Shadows in the Life of an Avant-Guard," February 1910, above. In the letter, Schul-

and was adopted largely for the very reason that Schulder refers to. It is quite true that there are Anarchists, Individualists and Communists, but these terms only differentiate the particular economic arrangements of society under Anarchism. But to class them into philosophic and terrorist Anarchists is, to my mind, very absurd. Surely you cannot accept that classification merely because of the popular notion of it. Would you, because the popular notion were that Single Tax meant taking away the land from the people, accept this meaning? As a free man, you must be interested in what you stand for. Of course you would try to dissuade the public from its misconception. But you would not give yourself another name merely to satisfy public opinion. Would you? I think that the term "Anarchist" is quite broad enough to cover whatever concept we may have of a society based on individual freedom and collective opportunity. If the public does not understand it, it is my business to educate it, but it cannot be my business to give myself another name merely because the public is ignorant.

Now, as to why the Anarchists have combined in an active protest against the terrible murder in Japan.[7] The Japanese who were recently killed proclaimed themselves as Anarchists without any extra qualification to it. As a matter of fact they were known as "Kropotkinists," because they have translated Kropotkin's works.[8] They were and still are bitterly attacked by the Marxian Socialists,[9] just as we are attacked by them in this country. It certainly would have been downright betrayal to the Japanese victims if their only comrades, the Anarchists, had not taken an active part in their behalf. The very fact that they stood quite isolated in Japan is more reason why we here and in Europe should have expressed as loudly as possible our sympathy with them; at least it must have been something inspiring to know that their comrades all over the world were with them.

I should, of course, be very sorry to hurt those who are still alive and in the hands of the Japanese authorities; but I am quite confident that they would not want me to keep silent

---

der criticized those who call themselves "philosophical Anarchists" and wrote: "After seeing, cringing and scheming politicians, persons without a backbone, applying this term to themselves, I shall feel a shiver whenever I hear that combination of words."

7. Kōtoku Shūsui and ten other Japanese anarchists and socialists were executed on 24 January 1911. Kanno Suga was executed on 25 January. After their executions, protest and memorial meetings were held by socialists and anarchists, including a ceremony on 25 January 1911 in Oakland, California, at Japanese socialist Sakutaro Iwasa's home (also the location of the local Japanese paper); at a meeting on 29 January 1911 in New York at which five people were arrested, leading to the formation of the Kōtoku Defense Committee; and at a public meeting held on 12 February 1911 in San Francisco, at which M. Myrata, Alex Horr, James H. Barry, Leo B. Mihan, Joseph Brown, Sakutaro Iwasa, and Terry Carlin spoke.

8. Kōtoku Shūsui translated both Arnold Roller's *Social General Strike* (1907) and Peter Kropotkin's *Conquest of Bread* (1909).

9. Most Japanese anarchists had been social democrats before Kōtoku's conversion to anarchism by 1906, and they were often subject to criticism by socialists, many of whom were their earlier political comrades. For example, Katayama Sen (1859–1933), a leading Japanese socialist, claimed that "the socialist movement of Japan is somewhat crippled and hindered on account of anarchistic views held by some who profess to be . . . socialists." See *Shakai Shimbun*, 15 September 1907, p. 1.

simply because I could buy their release by denying them. I am quite sure that were I in their place I should utterly repudiate the sympathy and assistance of any set of so-called "liberals," if they gave it to me on the condition that they would deny my Anarchism.

You may lend your name to the protest if you wish, or not—that, of course, is for you to decide. But I cannot believe that you will be like many others who claim to be liberals or radicals; namely, that you would withdraw your name because the people there are Anarchists, or because the Anarchists here have joined their brothers in a protest. If liberalism means anything at all, it means faith in the ideal of liberty, especially in the right of the individual to entertain an ideal of liberty, no matter how little understood by the public at large. At any rate it seems to me that whatever we have accomplished in the past in the way of liberty has been thanks to the staunch and faithful adherence of the pioneers of an idea to their principles.

You know that as well as I, Mr. Hall, and I hope that you will not expect us to betray our principles, or our comrades, because of some petty gain we might accomplish from the conservative element.

This may seem a little harsh to you. I am sure I do not mean to be, especially with you; but, to tell the truth, I am tired of the compromise that seems to be the fundamental effort of every man and woman in this country.[10] I repudiate any such means of gaining recognition for myself, or of buying redress for those whom I call my comrades. I assure you if the people in Japan would have denied their ideas I should have been very grieved, but I would not have claimed them, because then it would have meant going directly against their desires; but so long as they are brave enough to stand up for the truth, why should I, or my comrades here, be expected to join in the popular howl against them?

Yours very truly,
Emma Goldman.

New York, 13 February 1911

My Dear Miss Goldman.

I thought that I had made my letter clear, but yours makes it clearer—that I had not. I have added a few words in the further, though probably futile, effort to make it plain to the careless reader.

You can do whatever you like as to publishing my letter, as revised, and your answer, modified as it will be to accord with the changes in mine.

---

10. Criticism of any form of "strategic" political compromise was common in the pages of *Mother Earth* during these years. In his three-part series on "The Failure of Compromise," in the November 1909, June 1910, and July 1910 issues, AB systematically argued that political compromise could never lead to social and economic emancipation.

I have also made some notes on yours. My objection was and is to *methods*; your letter seems to assume that it is to *principles* (on which there is no disagreement between us).

Language seems to me to be merely one method of communication and the best language that which best conveys our thought and feeling.

If I could find another name that would avoid the misunderstanding of the words "Single Tax" I *would* certainly substitute that. In England our movement is called "Taxation of Land Values," or "Ground Rent Taxation."[11]

But as we already have taxation of land values here, though only a little of it, the change would create a new difficulty while removing a part of the old one.

Still we often debate changing.

Yours cordially,
Bolton Hall.

*Mother Earth* 6 (April 1911): 57–61.

11. In England the single-tax movement was represented by the United Committee for the Taxation of Land Values, which was founded in 1907 and published the magazine *Land Values* as a vehicle for clarifying and spreading its ideas.

# Emma Goldman in Hearty Sympathy

We wage a campaign of education, not only through *Regeneración* but by unremitting correspondence, especially with recognized leaders of radical thought. Recently we published the letters that have passed between Samuel Gompers and Ricardo Flores Magón,[1] and that sent to Eugene V. Debs.[2] This week we reproduce one written last month to Emma Goldman,[3] and the whole-souled reply it immediately evoked. Copies of the correspondence, published in leaflet form, are being distributed at all meetings held by Emma Goldman on her present western tour. The letter sent her runs as follows:

DEAR FRIEND AND FELLOW-FIGHTER IN THE CAUSE OF HUMAN LIBERTY:—

I write urging you to exercise on behalf of my countrymen in Mexico the influence you wield over a large section of the American public. Need I spend my breath in telling you that we are fighting the world-wide battle of human emancipation; that our cause is your cause; that we are struggling for what every intelligent man and woman knows as being absolutely indispensable for human happiness and development? I think I need not.

It is well known—has been proved beyond all peradventure of doubt—that, at the behest of the money power, hundreds of thousands of my countrymen have been driven from the lands on and by which they and their forefathers had lived since our history began.[4] Thus they have

---

1. Ricardo Flores Magón wrote to Samuel Gompers on 11 March 1911, arguing that the cause of the Partido Liberal Mexicano (PLM) was also the cause of the AFL and urging Gompers to speak out on behalf of the PLM against U.S. intervention in Mexico. Magón's appeal was published in *Mother Earth* 6 (April 1911): 48–49. Gompers's response, published on 1 April 1911 in *Regeneración*, professed "intense interest" in the PLM's cause but minimized the seriousness of the American military maneuvers then taking place on the Mexican border, thus tacitly declining Magón's request for specific aid.
2. Ricardo Flores Magón wrote to Eugene V. Debs on 13 January 1910 from territorial prison in Florence, Arizona. Debs had initiated this correspondence on 30 December 1909, at which time Flores Magón asked Debs to help raise funds for the defense of jailed PLM members, and reiterated his request in a letter to Debs on 6 April 1911. This letter was published on 15 April 1911 in *Regeneración*.
3. This letter, dated 13 March 1911, was reprinted in *Mother Earth* 6 (April 1911): 48–49, and in the *Agitator* on 15 April 1911, p. 4, with minor variations. *EGP*, reels 5, 47.
4. Land laws passed under Mexican president Porfirio Díaz in 1883 encouraged the transfer of ownership of rural lands to both foreign investors and to the Mexican elite. The 1883 law encouraged companies to survey public lands by offering one-third of the land surveyed as an outright grant, and making the other two-thirds available at discounted prices. By 1894 foreign companies held title to

been forced into such Hells as the tobacco plantations of the Valle Nacional[5] and the hemp plantations of Yucatan, or driven into exile across the American border, where they struggle desperately for a starvation wage. Somehow or other men and women must live; or, at least, try to live.

What will become of these millions of men and children[6] if the money power has its way? What will be the result if it succeeds in trampling them beneath the heel of militarism? And what will be the effect on the character and standing of the American nation if it suffers itself to be the obedient tool of the money power, and stands before the world the avowed defender of chattel slavery of the most atrocious type? Surely, to ask these questions is to answer them.

The American public does not understand; it cannot see the picture in its awful reality, for it is misled by the wilful misrepresentations of those who, having gigantic money interests at stake, are sparing no effort to delude it.

So long as the money power thought the struggle in Mexico was merely to displace one Dictator with another it looked on indifferently; for such struggles have been frequent in the history of Latin peoples, and they alter nothing. But today it understands quite clearly that its own selfish interests are in the balance; that we are fighting for the restoration of millions and millions of acres of land, given away to foreign syndicates by the fraudulent connivance of Díaz' unspeakable government, and entirely without the consent of the rightful owners, the people; that we are determined that the poor shall come once more into what is justly their own. Therefore today the money powers in America, backed by the money powers of the world, are calling the American nation to arms.[7]

In such a crisis will you be silent? I think not; indeed I know you cannot be.

Yours for human emancipation,
R. Flores Magón.

In reply we received the following, being a copy of a manifolded letter Emma Goldman is mailing to all her correspondents.[8] Jack London and other noted writers on the social question are pursuing a similar course. The letter follows:

Dear Friend—

Enclosed is copy of letter received from Ricardo Flores Magón, president of the "Junta" of the Mexican Liberal Party. It speaks for itself and makes, to me at least, irresistible appeal.

---

20 percent of the Mexican land mass. By 1910 a few wealthy families owned much of Mexico's productive land.

5. Valle Nacional is located in Oaxaca.

6. The *Mother Earth* version reads "men, women and children."

7. In March 1911 President William Howard Taft ordered 20,000 soldiers to the border to curtail the illegal export of munitions to Mexican rebels. In a letter to the army chief of staff, General Leonard Wood, Taft explained that he sent troops to protect American investments in Mexico (which he estimated were valued over $1 billion) and the lives of 40,000 Americans who lived in Mexico or near the border.

8. EG's response was dated 19 March 1911.

The leading facts connected with the Mexican revolution are well known, thanks largely to the measures taken recently by the government of the United States, at the behest of Wall Street. Through countless articles and such well-authenticated books as Turner's "Barbarous Mexico,"[9] it has been proved beyond all doubt that slavery of an inconceivably brutal type is rampant in Mexico, and is supported mainly by American dollars. Thus this country has become once more a partner in that very chattel slavery which, less than two generations ago, it shed blood and treasure freely to overthrow, once and forever.

The American public would not tolerate for one moment that partnership if it understood the situation clearly; but it is being duped and misled daily by a press owned body and soul by the money power. Our struggle is against this terribly powerful combination, and, Herculean though the task may be, the education of the public is the one imperative duty of the hour. Accordingly I urge you, above all things, to devote all the time and money you can spare to the education of the public on this Mexican question; doing so without delay, for time is precious.

Write to your friends; send letters and articles to the papers; use your own brains and think out for yourself the various ways in which you can be of service. And DO IT NOW.

MONEY MUST BE CONTRIBUTED, and for this we must look to an awakened public conscience. You will awaken that conscience best by yourself making sacrifices for this, which is our common cause.

Send all money and communications to *Regeneración* (organ of the Mexican Liberal Party), 519 E. 4th St., Los Angeles, Cal. You may rest assured that every cent will be expended honestly and judiciously, for these people thoroughly understand the situation and have proved their sincerity by years of exile, imprisonment and heroic labor.

This is not the special cause of Socialists, Anarchists, Single Taxers, Trades Unionists, or other individual wings of the great army of discontent. It is a straight case of millions of our fellow creatures having been driven from the lands on which they and their forefathers had lived for generations, in order that absentee syndicates may reap colossal fortunes by indescribable revolting slavery. I believe it to be the most brutal instance on record of absolutely heartless expropriation by that money power which worships the dollar alone, and is deaf, dumb and blind to the claims of human life.

No question of "isms" is involved. There is a plain call to universal duty.

The fight for human liberty in Mexico cannot but affect most profoundly the labor movement in this country and throughout the world. Thought will be engendered and apathy dispelled; the road will be cleared for fundamental changes. The more successful the struggle

---

9. John Kenneth Turner's *Barbarous Mexico* was a muckraking account of Porfirio Díaz's regime based on Turner's extensive fact-finding journeys through Mexico in 1908 and 1909. The book for the first time exposed the American public to brutal labor conditions in Mexico and played a significant role in undermining Díaz's popularity in the United States. Turner attacked Mexico's slave plantation system in the Yucatan, the displacement of the Yaqui Indians, the regime's intolerance of dissent, and U.S. and European assistance to Díaz. Although *Barbarous Mexico* was published in book form in March 1911 (Chicago: Charles H. Kerr), Turner had previously published articles that would eventually make up parts of the book in *American Magazine* (October and November 1909), *Appeal to Reason* (1910), *International Socialist Review* (December 1910; January and April 1911), and *Pacific Monthly* (September 1910 and February 1911).

there, the easier it will be for every one of us here. We should reciprocate, going to the very edge of our opportunities.

Either this revolution will succeed or it will fail. In the former case, human liberty will gain, inestimably. In the latter case another gallant effort will be drowned in blood, and the struggle for emancipation will have an incalculably serious setback. Whichever way the struggle goes every one of us will be affected.

In your own self-interest, therefore, as well as for the sake of our common humanity, I send you this appeal. I feel confident I shall not send in vain.

YOURS FOR HUMAN LIBERTY AND A LIFE WORTH LIVING,
EMMA GOLDMAN.

*Regeneración* (Los Angeles), 22 April 1911, p. 4.

Article in the *FRESNO MORNING REPUBLICAN*

*Fresno, California, 14 May 1911*

## Emma Goldman Comes to Preach "Anarchism" to I.W.W.'s

### Female Agitator Full of Sympathy for Mexican Insurrectos.

Takes Contradictory Stand on Dynamiting Cases;
Supports McNamara.

Emma Goldman arrived in Fresno yesterday afternoon to give a couple of lectures under the auspices of the I.W.W.'s. Miss Goldman was accompanied by her manager, Ben Reitman, who carries the big stick in business matters. Miss Goldman received several visitors at the Fulton hotel during the afternoon, but reserved the evening for her private labors. These consisted largely of keeping up with her correspondence, about which she seemed greatly concerned.

"I am glad to be in Fresno just now," she said. "The I.W.W. boys have made a good fight here and have demonstrated the effectiveness of jail-stuffing as a method of winning such fights."[1] Miss Goldman appeared somewhat worn by travel, although she hurried about and walked to the post office for her mail.

Her short almost slight figure was clothed in a plain traveling dress, and had her hair plainly combed back, showing her strong Balto-Slavic features with heavy brows, and large mouth and jaws. It was a face masculine rather than coarse, of the stern type of the battler against heavy odds.

She spoke part of the time in the technical language of semi-scientific books on sociology, and then in a lecture room manner spoke of the "Mexican insurrectos and their American brothers," as she had met them at Tia Juana.[2] "All the people of Mexico are against the dictator, they will win, and a free republic will be established. They are not well enough educated for anything more yet," she said.

1. A reference to the IWW strategy of deliberately courting arrest for their outdoor organizing efforts, thus crowding the local jails. Each member would demand a separate trial by jury when arrested. The aim of the strategy was to slow down, to the point of stopping, the entire local legal and administrative system and in the process increase the cost on local taxpayers, until it was impractical for the local government to prosecute demonstrators. This tactic worked particularly well during the Fresno free speech fight, where after a six-month struggle the ban on street meetings was rescinded.
2. Although there is no extant evidence corroborating EG's assertion that she met PLM rebels in Tijuana, she mentions meeting PLM members in border towns in a number of letters.

Miss Goldman denied any design on her part to arrive in Los Angeles at the same time as the McNamara brothers.[3] "We arrived there on the same afternoon, but it was just a coincidence," she said. "I did not try to communicate with them. I never saw such concentrated solidarity on the part of the union men of the country to stand behind an accused member. I have heard many say they were for the accused men, right or wrong."

Miss Goldman talked with apparent pleasure of her girlhood, saying she was born in Russia, though of German parentage. At 3 she went with her parents to Germany,[4] where she received a high school education. "I've knocked about this country a good bit," she said, "and I've learned what many a working man has learned—that the boasted freedom is a myth." There was a certain affability in her manner, when she warmed up to the subjects of human rights and wrongs. On the other hand, she said she could excuse a man for blowing up his fellow workers, while destroying a bitter opponent's property.

Miss Goldman will talk on "Anarchism" at I.W.W. hall at 3 o'clock this afternoon. At 8 o'clock she will give her views on "Marriage and Love."[5]

*Fresno Morning Republican,* 14 May 1911, p. 11.

3. James B. and John J. McNamara were indicted in 1911 for the 1 October 1910 bombing of the printing plant of the anti-union *Los Angeles Times*; the bombing killed twenty-one people. To ensure that the brothers stood trial in Los Angeles, the Burns detective organization illegally transported James B. McNamara from Detroit and John J. McNamara from Indianapolis on 24 April 1911. EG arrived in Los Angeles on 30 April. The case became a cause célèbre in the labor movement and the political left, attracting nationwide attention to the labor conflict in Los Angeles and fueling the Los Angeles mayoral campaign of socialist candidate Job Harriman.
4. Accounts of EG's early years vary, but it is more likely that she moved to Germany between 1875 and 1877, at which time she would have been between the ages of six and eight.
5. The *Fresno Morning Republican* published a short report on EG's meeting the following day, announcing, "Anarchist Leader Opposes Religion, Capitalism and Government" (*Fresno Morning Republican,* 15 May 1911, *EGP,* reel 47).

DEAR COMRADE—

I have your very kind letter of May 2nd. Needless to say, I was very happy to hear from you. I appreciate only too well how swamped you must be and not always enjoying the very best of health. I should not want to add to your labors, only sometimes it becomes necessary to communicate with one who has for many years been our teacher.

I absolutely agree with you, dear Comrade, that there is no reliance in the intellectual interest of most people, especially those who depend upon their livelihood through their intellectual pursuits, yet at the same time I feel it is important to urge these people on if only to make a stand. After all, each one can only give as much as he is capable. So long as we are not blinded to that fact, it would be folly not to accept what they can give.

Needless to say, I feel with you that our "starting-point", the people, is correct, but unfortunately it is the most difficult thing on earth to get to them. If they are unorganized they seem to be steeped in superstition to the extent of excluding the slightest interest in ideas. If they are organized, they become like automatons, moving at the dictates of their leaders. In either case, the opposition to anarchism, in this country at any rate, is much stronger among the working-people than it is in the ranks of the intellectuals, and yet Heaven only knows for more than thirty years anarchism has been carried to the masses. In fact, at least twenty of the twenty-three years that I have been active I have spent in the working-men's ranks. My first experience with the police was due to my connection with the cloakmakers union and its strike in 1893 which resulted in my year's imprisonment.[1] The same has been the case all along. Last spring, before the cloakmakers declared a general strike,[2] I made a regular campaign through their various branches speaking in behalf of that great weapon and so it has been constantly. Yet with all that, I must face the inevitable; we have failed to strike root in the ranks of the workers, except in an indirect way.

---

1. EG was arrested in August 1893, charged with incitement to riot for speaking at a demonstration of the unemployed. She was found guilty and sentenced to one year at Blackwell's Island penitentiary. This arrest and imprisonment was not related to involvement with the cloakmakers' union. See vol. 1, *Made for America*, pp. 144–89.
2. Abraham Rosenberg, president of the International Ladies' Garment Workers' Union, led a general strike of the cloakmakers to demand a minimum-wage scale and union recognition. In preparation for six months, the strike involving 70,000 workers began on 7 July and ended on 2 September 1910, with both sides claiming victory. From EG's letters and papers from late summer 1910, it appears she was in Ossining, New York, working on *Anarchism and Other Essays* from July 1910 and then in the hospital recuperating from her broken kneecap, which she injured on 13 August. No extant evidence suggests she spoke to striking cloakmakers at that time.

My visit to California, which I am now concluding and which has been crowned with marvelous success both in the attendance and the tremendous sale of literature, I have for the first time in my public career seen a spark of interest in our ideas. In connection with the kidnapping and the arrest of the two McNamaras[3] I found that the workers have finally awakened to the importance of direct action in opposition to the political corruption. It is very encouraging indeed and yet I cannot deny that even that interest lacks the fundamental knowledge of anarchism as a world thought. But at any rate the beginning is made and will, no doubt, bear fruit. However, it means a constant grind on the firing-line.

Thank you very much for your kind appreciation of my book[4] and Mother Earth. The purpose of the former was to have something which would be simple and apply to the American economic struggle. Never for one moment did I make myself believe that it is going to fill the place in the theoretical discourses of our ideas. One who stands in the fight has little time for theorizing. I am glad to say that the book has been very favorably reviewed, though not extensively so.[5] The pettiest and most wilful reviews appeared in the socialistic papers, of course.[6] They are a bad lot in America, much more so than even in Europe, although I do not think that there is a socialistic writer in this country who would have the audacity to make the statements that have appeared in "Justice" of May 13th,[7] which you have probably seen. It would really be very funny if it were not so tragic to accuse one who has been hounded by the police for nearly a quarter of a century of being in the service of the latter, but then I should not complain. If a great spirit

3. See note 3, "Emma Goldman Comes to Preach 'Anarchism' to I.W.W.'s," Article in the *Fresno Morning Republican*, 14 May 1911, above.

4. EG is referring to her recently published *Anarchism and Other Essays* (New York: Mother Earth Publishing Association, 1910).

5. For reviews see, for example, *Conservator* 50 (January 1911): 172–73; *Public* (10 February 1911), pp. 138–39; *Current Literature* 50 (February 1911): 176–78; *Freedom* (February 1911), p. 14; *Bookman* 32 (February 1911): 639–40; *San Francisco Call* (26 March 1911).

6. See, for example, *International Socialist Review* 11 (February 1911): 501. The reviewer described her essay "Anarchism: What It Really Stands For" as a "'horrible example' of the metaphysical method of reasoning from unproved assumptions to fantastic conclusions." In fairness, however, the reviewer goes on to claim that "the other essays" are much better than the first, and contain much that is worth reading.

7. An article in *Justice*, the official publication of the Social Democratic Party of England, accused EG of being an agent provocateur: "Emma Goldman has had a remarkable free run in the United States for a good many years and some people have wondered how it is that this female firebrand should carry on her propaganda of violence so long and with such impunity. But it is not generally known that Emma Goldman is in the pay of the police, though the fact has leaked out recently. At one time she was employed by Mr. A. E. Olarovsky of the Russian Secret Police in San Francisco as an agent and a spy. It is the same, we may be sure, with nine cases out of ten with those 'prominent' Anarchists who only kill with their mouths, who are never on hand when an outrage occurs and who manage to escape so mysteriously when their associates are arrested." *Justice* 13 (May 1911): 7.

like Bakunin could be accused by Marx and Engels of being a police spy,[8] I should be content in getting the same dose, but it is tragic just the same.

I hope that you have quite recovered by this time and are able to continue your valuable task you have undertaken. It surely must be an interesting work which I should like to read very much indeed. I dare not burden you with any request to write for Mother Earth, but if we could get an occasional letter I am sure it would be of great interest to our readers.

With kindest regards to Sophia and Sasha,[9]

FRATERNALLY,

EMMA GOLDMAN

P.S. What is your attitude towards the Mexican revolution? I am sure you must have been following it up through the European papers. I have been able to study the situation at close range having been at the border-line for some time. Whatever the outcome will be, I think it is a most marvelous event. The most genuine uprising of the people since the Paris commune. I am sending you a copy of an appeal which has just been issued by the Liberal Junta,[10] by the way composed entirely of anarchists. I hope you can find time to say something about it in Freedom[11] or Temps Nouveau.[12] Surely if Bakunin, Cafiero[13]

---

8. In July 1846 Karl Marx had published in his paper, *Neue Rheinische Zeitung*, the accusation that the novelist George Sand had proof that Russian anarchist Michael Bakunin was a Russian spy. The paper later published Sand's denial and Bakunin's protest.

9. A reference to Peter Kropotkin's wife, Sophia Kropotkin.

10. This is possibly the "Manifesto to the Workers of the World," issued by the Organized Junta of the Partido Liberal Mexicano (PLM) on 3 April 1911 from Los Angeles, California (*Regeneración*, 8 April 1911). The manifesto included an appeal for financial support. Excerpts were later reprinted in the July 1911 edition of *Freedom*.

11. Freedom (1886–1927), a London-based anarchist communist newspaper, frequently reported on the Mexican Revolution, printing articles and letters by PLM members, including Ricardo Flores Magón and William C. Owen. Honoré Joseph Jaxon (1861–1952), secretary of the Chicago Mexican Liberal Defense League, went to England from August 1911 to March 1912 on behalf of the PLM and also contributed articles to *Freedom* on the Mexican situation.

12. *Les Temps Nouveaux* (Paris, 1895–1914), an anarchist communist weekly edited by Jean Grave and one of the leading French anarchist newspapers. Jean Grave's editorial critical of the PLM appeared in the 29 March 1912 *Les Temps Nouveaux* and prompted Kropotkin's response in defense of the PLM in early April.

13. Bakunin and Carlo Cafiero both participated in revolutionary struggles of their period. Bakunin was instrumental in some of the European revolutions of 1848 and the Dresden insurrection in 1849. Cafiero (1864–1892), an Italian anarchist, helped organize and participated in Italian insurrection attempts in 1874 and 1877. He was the principal agent in Italy for the General Council of the First International and was later a key organizer behind the creation, in August 1872, of the anarchist Italian Federation of the International Workingmen's Association. Cafiero and French anarchist Élisée Reclus edited and published a section of Bakunin's "The Knouto-Germanic Empire and the Social Revolution" manuscript, which they found among his papers after his death. Published as *Dieu et l'état* (God and the State) (Geneva: Imprimerie Jurassienne, 1882), this pamphlet

and other of our brave comrades could participate in the revolutionary attempts of the past, we too ought to take our place with the Mexicans who are fighting a truly heroic battle, the more so because they are being attacked not only by the politicians of Mexico, like Madero,[14] but even by the socialist politicians of this country and of course by the United States government. I fear that unless they are given aid the revolution will be drowned in the blood of the poor Mexican peons. The poorer the people, the greater the price, always.

Am sending you the Pacific Monthly containing an able article by Kenneth Turner,[15] the author of Barberous Mexico and the man who has rendered the Mexican people great service.

I still have a hard months work before me, will be in N Y June 30 th.

TLS, GA RF, fond 1129, opis' 2, delo 978, listy 5–6. Partially autographed postscript.

---

became Bakunin's most popular work. It was first translated into English by Benjamin Tucker in 1883 and was reprinted by Mother Earth Publishing Association in 1916.

14. Francisco Madero (1873–1913) was the president of Mexico (1911–1913) and a key figure in the Mexican Revolution. A Mexican aristocrat unsuccessful in his early attempt to enter politics, he wrote *La Sucesión Presidencial en 1910* calling for political change in Mexico. Madero ran in 1910 against the ruling Porfirio Díaz, who had him jailed before the election. After his release Madero, working with a broad coalition including the PLM, called on the Mexican people to overthrow the Díaz regime, and in November 1910 fighting broke out across the country. Madero was elected president in 1911, winning the support of the American socialists. However, fighting continued as the PLM and other organizations demanded even more extensive social and economic changes. Madero was eventually overthrown by a military revolt and then assassinated on 22 February 1913.

15. John Kenneth Turner's "The Mexican Revolution" appeared in *Pacific Monthly* 25 (June 1911): 609–26.

MY DEAR CHARMIAN:—

I should have answered your note of the 25th of May sooner but for the fact that I knew of your absence from home. I think you are probably now returning from your trip which I hope has been as pleasant as you and Jack expected.[1]

As to the sentence in my letter, I cannot understand how you could possibly have interpreted its meaning that my fight is the only fight.[2] I am sure that if you knew me better you would know that I am altogether too little self-conscious to assume that my method of fighting is the only one.

What I really meant is this: ~~that~~ there is a fighting under fire, another one in safety. The writer's method of fighting especially when he has arrived, as Jack certainly has, is not combined with a great deal of stress and danger. Whereas the agitator's method must inevitably remain so, since he is always on the battlefield and therefore confronted by all kinds of dangers.

To tell the truth I am inclined to think that the writer does more effective work than the speaker. I have infinite faith in the written word, but that does not do away with the fact that whereas, one in Jack's position can get some recreation, can enjoy the country's beauty or arrange his life in harmony with himself, one in my position cannot.

Yes, my meetings on the coast have been very successful. In fact, if not for that month, I should have had to borrow money to get back to New York. As it is I have enough to take me home and keep Mother Earth Alive over Summer. I have also succeeded in paying off part of the cost of my book[3] but I still owe a considerable amount of money. However, I understand that he who cannot make debts is not considered successful from a business point of view.

Dear, I am enclosing an exact copy of an article which appeared in the London

---

1. Charmian London (née Kittredge) (1871–1955), socialist and editor, was the wife of the novelist Jack London. She met him in 1902 and became his editorial assistant and secretary in 1904, before their marriage in 1905. She wrote for the socialist paper *Wilshire's* and was a founding member of the Women's Socialist Society in Oakland, California. She also published *Log of the Snark* (1915) about the Londons' adventures in the South Pacific. After Jack London's death in 1916, she published several works about their life together, most notably *The Book of Jack London* (1921).
2. In a letter to Jack London the previous month EG wrote that she was sorry she could not visit the Londons, but "pleasures and peace are only meant for writers not for fighters" (EG to Jack London, 23 May 1911, *EGP*, reel 5).
3. EG, *Anarchism and Other Essays* (New York: Mother Earth Publishing Association, 1910).

"Justice," the Social Democratic paper.[4] The thing speaks for itself for ordinarily I have never paid the slightest attention to any attack, no matter whence it came. Thus it isn't at all unusual for Socialist papers to accuse me of being in the employ of the Capitalistic class, mainly for the purpose of hurting the Socialistic movement. All that seemed very trivial to me, but this article is so scurrilous and of such wide-spread consequence that it cannot be passed in silence.[5] I have therefore sent copies to a number of Socialists who have known me for years and who are able to say how true the miserable accusation is. I understand that Walling, Annie Strunsky, the Stokes, and several others, have sent their protest to "Justice."[6]

Possibly Jack and you do not know me so well as the above mentioned, but nevertheless I hope that you can conscientiously join the protest. It will interest you both to know that in response to the first protest which was sent from the London Anarchists, "Justice" still reiterated the story, claiming that they had reliable proof yet failing to give the proof. Also that their informant, who by the way, fails to sign his name, has this to say "The information concerning Emma Goldman was conveyed by definite statement to that effect made in my hearing by Mr. A. E. Olarovsky himself."[7]

Oralarovsky is supposed to be the representative of the Russian government in whose employ I am supposed to have been. Just think of a Socialist taking the word of a Russian official as against one who, whatever the difference is, has been in the revolutionary movement for twenty-two years.

If not for the inconsistency it would take but a very short time to force the "Justice" people to retract. The libel laws in England are very severe, but it goes without saying that I would not invoke the law in my behalf. I do, however, mean to force to these black-

---

4. Justice was the official organ of the Social Democratic Federation.
5. The 13 May article claimed that EG was a Russian spy employed by A. E. Olarovsky of San Francisco. In June Leonard Abbott sent *Justice* editor Harry Quelch a protest letter signed by twenty-four prominent intellectuals and radicals. The letter, which maintained that "there is not an iota of truth in the charge," was printed in the 8 July issue of *Justice*, but the newspaper continued to defend the original article while refusing to release the name of the informant. Jack London also penned a protest that was published in the London anarchist paper *Freedom* two months later. He wrote: "As a socialist who knows Emma Goldman well, and who is proud to call her a 'friend,' I am writing to protest against the attack on her, published in the columns of *Justice*. . . . Either you are ignorant of Emma Goldman or are dreadfully misinformed, or are both." EG wrote to London: "I won't thank you for your prompt protest sent to *Justice*, but I do want you to know that I appreciate your friendship very much." See Letter to Peter Kropotkin, 29 May 1911, above, and Letter to Jack London, 26 September 1911, below.
6. William English Walling, Anna Strunsky Walling, Rose Pastor Stokes, and J. G. Phelps Stokes signed the protest letter to *Justice* editor Harry Quelch. EG had sought out prominent American socialists to defend her against the socialist paper's accusation.
7. Alexandre Epitketovich Olarovsky (d. 1910) was a Russian diplomat who served in the United States between 1881 and 1887. He was appointed the Russian consul general to San Francisco on 26 January 1881, and later served as the consul general in New York until 1887, when he became consul general to Siam. By 1907 he had retired from active duty due to ill health, and he died in 1910. V. Kushpel, director of the Archive of Foreign Affairs of Russian Empire, letter, 9 June 2000, to EGP.

mailers morally, either to give proofs, or to retract. I will be very glad to hear from you and Jack relative to this matter. I will treat of the whole thing in the next issue of Mother Earth[8] and hope by that time to have a note from you.

Affectionately,
Emma Goldman

TLS, Jack London Collection, CSmH.

8. EG wrote about these events in "Socialist Calumny," *Mother Earth* 6 (July 1911): 135–39.

## To the International Mexican Meeting in Cooper Union Assembled:—

Dear Friends:—

I regret deeply that I cannot be with you on this great occasion,[1] not so much for my own sake but that I could tell you of the wonderful heroism and the hardihood of the men who are at this moment fighting for life and liberty. It is not an exaggeration when I say that the Mexican Revolution is, in many respects, even more sublime than the great uprising in Russia of a few years ago.[2] In that country men and women coming from the higher station in society had for more than fifty years consecrated their lives in behalf o[f] the emancipation of the Russian masses; besides the latter had the sympathy and approval of the whole civilized world. Not so, the Mexicans. There have never been the Kropotkins, the Peravskajas, the Breskovskys, the Sosanoffs,[3] and scores of others to lend the great cause their wonderful intellectual and spiritual power. The agitation for liberty in Mexico is but of very recent date and yet without any aid. Without much preparation, outraged humanity in Mexico has risen like a mighty giant. The revolutionary fire has spread all over the country, nor will it be extinguished until the people have gotten back their precious heritage, the land.[4]

Probably never in the history of the economic struggle has a movement stood so iso-

---

1. This rally was organized by the New York Mexican Revolution Conference, a group that was founded in 1911 and met weekly at the Ferrer Center. The organization supported and sent funds to the Partido Liberal Mexicano (PLM). This 26 June 1911 rally was called to voice sympathy for the Mexican revolutionists and ask that the United States government not interfere with the revolution or assist Mexican presidential candidate Francisco Madero. The rally was chaired by Leonard Abbott. Speakers included AB, Harry Kelly, Joseph Ettor, Max Baginski, and Jaime Vidal. A similar Mexican Liberal Defense Conference had also been founded that year by Voltairine de Cleyre in Chicago. Throughout the spring and summer of 1911 EG worked to raise funds for the PLM. At this time EG was on a lecture tour in the west. In May she spoke on the Mexican Revolution while in Los Angeles and collected funds to send to the PLM.
2. EG is referring to the Russian Revolution of 1905.
3. Sophia Perovskaya, Catherine Breshkovskya, and Egor Sazanov were three Russian revolutionaries whom EG admired.
4. In the "Programa del Partido Liberal y Manifesto a la Nación," issued on 1 July 1906, the PLM demanded that all unproductive lands be taken from landowners and redistributed to the peasants. By 1911, however, the PLM fully turned away from this reformist approach to land distribution in favor of the demand to abolish all private property.

lated and jammed in by forces bent on its destruction. As formerly the tyrant Diaz[5] with his clique, so has the new aspirant for power, Madero,[6] declared war on the Mexican people. Added to that is the U. S. government, ever ready to perform the hangman's job at the behest of Wall Street.[7] And now comes the blow from quarters least expected. The very people who have for years proclaimed themselves as the heralds of the revolutionary cause, expecially of the economic emancipation of the masses—the political Socialists— have turned traitors to their p[os]itions and traitors to the eternal spirit of revolution. They too, have joined the enemy in declaring that the Mexican rebels are bandits.[8] The shame of it! The criminal outrage of it!

In the name of all that is sacred in the revolutionary struggle of the past—in the name of the great martyrs who have died on the altar of liberty and emancipation—I appeal to

5. José Porfirio Díaz (1830–1915) was military general and president of Mexico (1877–1880, 1884–1911) and Oaxacan governor (1880–1884). Díaz's regime, though he was elected, functioned like a dictatorship, with the congress reduced to subservience and the constitution amended in 1890 to allow him an indefinite number of reelections. His government regularly imprisoned opponents and censored the press. As the nation advanced industrially, with massive foreign investments mostly from the United States, the building of railroads and exports rose, along with the gap between the rich and poor. These inequalities and Díaz's seemingly endless rule ignited opposition from labor, liberals, and radicals alike and grew into the Mexican Revolution of 1911, which ended his regime. Díaz submitted his resignation to the Mexican Congress on 25 May 1911 and fled to Paris. Francisco León de la Barra became the interim president.

6. During the 1910 Mexican presidential election Díaz imprisoned the opposition candidate, Francisco Madero. Madero issued the Plan of San Luis Potosi, calling for a revolution to overthrow Díaz to begin on 20 November 1910. Initially the PLM supported Madero. By the time of this meeting, however, the PLM and the Zapatistas had denounced Madero. After Díaz resigned armed peasant groups, some associated with the PLM, continued to seize land and fight with local authorities. Madero dispatched troops to Baja California via the U.S. railways to crush the PLM revolt in Baja; his order included a public endorsement of the shooting of the peasant rebels. He was elected president of Mexico in October 1911.

7. In March 1911 President William Howard Taft ordered 20,000 soldiers to the border to curtail the illegal export of munitions to Mexican rebels. In a letter to the army chief of staff, General Leonard Wood, Taft explained that he sent troops to protect American investments in Mexico (which he estimated were valued over $1 billion) and the lives of 40,000 Americans who lived in Mexico or near the border. On 14 June 1911 PLM members, including Ricardo Flores Magón and his brother Enrique, were arrested by U.S. federal agents in Los Angeles under U.S. neutrality laws.

8. American socialists were early supporters of the Mexican Revolution and the PLM. Throughout 1910 and into 1911 *Appeal to Reason* and Eugene Debs personally backed the cause of the Mexican peasants and worked for the release of Ricardo Flores Magón and other PLM organizers held in U.S. prisons. In April 1911 the Socialist Party executive committee passed a resolution, which appeared in the April 1911 *International Socialist Review*, strongly protesting the U.S. government's support of the Díaz dictatorship. However, by May 1911, as the anarchist tendency of the PLM grew and in the wake of various events surrounding the Baja invasion, *Appeal to Reason* declared the revolution over and supported Madero. In editorials *Appeal to Reason* noted that although Madero could only be expected to establish capitalism, they considered this a step in the right direction away from dictatorship and were unwilling to support the PLM's anarchism. In April and May of 1911 the socialist *New York Call* labeled Madero a tool of American capital, but refused to support the Baja activities. The paper attacked the PLM leadership as "a group of bandits," and ridiculed Ricardo Flores Magón for staying safely in the United States instead of leading the Baja uprising.

you, men and women, to assist the Mexican revolution, to come to the moral and financial support of the brave men and women in Mexico who are fighting such a heroic struggle, who are facing no end of difficulties and hardships, and yet who have never wavered for one moment since the revolution began. Surely you cannot allow the reactionary forces to drown the efforts for liberty in the blood of its martyrs. The thing most needed at the present moment is money—but also the assurance of your solidaric sympathy, which I hope you will not deny to our Mexican brothers. The revolution must go on until the people have taken posession of the land—until they can go back to Mother Earth and draw from her generous bosom new life and new hope. "Long live the Eternal Spirit of Revolution! Long live Anarchy!

TLU, Box 2, folder 3, Emma Goldman Papers, MBU.

Cover of *Regeneración* magazine honoring Enrique and Ricardo Flores Magón, among other members of the Junta of El Partido Liberal Mexicano (PLM)—The Mexican Liberal Party, 1911. (Pitzer College, Anarchy Archives)

How strange is love, how complecated is human nature. Years ago I read The Life of Mary Wallstoncraft.[1] Her weak and humiliating love life with Imlay, was the most terrible thing to me.

Mary Wollstoncraft the most daring woman of her time, the freest and boldest exponant of liberty, of free love the slave of her passion for Imlay.[2] How could anyone forgive such weakness?

Thus I reasoned many years ago. Today? E G the Wallstoncraft of the 20th Century even like her great sister, is weak and dependent, clinging to the man, no matter how worthless and faithless he is.[3] What an irony of fate.

I see but one way of pulling myself together from the agony of doubt, that always assails me, when I leave you in Chicago. Activity, propaganda. That is my salvation. That is the only force which reconciles me to my mad passion for you.

Perhaps, if Mary could have found a work companion in Imlay she would not have attempted to drown herself, nor would her life been wrecked through that one great passion.

And you are such a wonderful worker Hobo, so true and devoted, so completely wrapped up in the work. If not for that side in you, I should have long dispaired. Well, let's then work, if our love is such a miserable failure.

I have taken up the Mexican work. The Conference[4] consistant of a few willing but stupid boys has done nothing so far, except spending whatever little it has raised. I had a special meeting yesterday and woke the boys up from their lazy sleep.[5]

---

1. Probably a reference to Elizabeth Robbins Pennell, *The Life of Mary Wollstonecraft* (Boston: Robert Brothers, 1884).

2. Mary Wollstonecraft met Gilbert Imlay, an American businessman, in France in 1793. Although not legally married, they lived together throughout 1793 and had a daughter together, Fanny, in 1794. Imlay's repeated infidelity, however, led him to end the relationship, apparently causing Wollstonecraft to attempt suicide. Wollstonecraft later met William Godwin in 1796 and married him in 1797.

3. EG's November 1911 lecture "Mary Wollstonecraft, Her Tragic Life and Her Struggle for Freedom" focused on Wollstonecraft's personal life. EG saw herself and Wollstonecraft as pioneers of modern, independent womanhood but also as women who could not transcend their common demon of jealousy.

4. The New York Mexican Revolution Conference, founded in 1911, met weekly at the Ferrer Center to build public support and collect money for the Partido Liberal Mexicano (PLM). See also Letter to the International Mexican Meeting, 23 June 1911, above.

5. EG had recently received a letter from W. C. Owen in Los Angeles, calling for EG's help and support of PLM members who had recently been arrested. On 23 July 1911 she wrote to BR "the second letter is from Owen. A desperate appeal for help. *Regeneración* must be kept up in order to represent the

This is the program

1) A big demonstration on Union Square for the latter part of August[6]

2) Committees to canvas Union for money. Four, have been organized and will begin next week.

3) Lectures on the Mexican situation with stereopticon [scenes?] to be started at once. Have already written to Owen[7] for slides or pictures.

4) Myself to lecture at Chautauqua places if that can be arranged.[8]

I have sent to Chautauqua N Y for a list of places. I think these propositions can be carried out and will help raise money and arouse interest in the Mexican Revolution. But to make them a great success, <u>you must</u> do the work. I know no one else, who is as capable. You see dear boy, my faith in your manageral genius can not be shaken.

Will you take charge of the work? If so you will have to come to N Y of course. I go to the farm Friday for next week, probably the last week too. Then I will return to throw all my energies into the Mexican cause during all of August and part of Sept.

I shall therefore want you to come to N Y by Aug 10th. By that time the arrangements for the Union Square meeting will be under way for you to do the rest. Also we may have our slides ready and the Hall rented.

Will my manager write me by Special delivery, what he thinks of these arrangements and if he will come on to take charge of them. As to my lover, he is still in the embrio. Will he ever be born into radiant maturity? To strive for it is worth the struggle, because struggle is life.

HOBO, MY HOBO
MOMMY.

ALS, IU-U.

---

real revolution. . . . I have called a special Mexican conference, will try to organize committees to go to the unions" (EG to BR 23 July 1911, *EGP*, reel 5).

6. The Union Square meeting, intended to arouse support for the Mexican Revolution, took place on 26 August 1911. EG spoke (in German), and BR chaired the meeting. Other speakers included Bernard Sernaker (in Yiddish), William Thurston Brown (in English), Jaime Vidal (in Spanish), Max Baginski (in German), and Samuel Boris (in Russian).

7. Anarchist W. C. Owen became editor of the English-language page of *Regeneración*, in March 1911.

8. There is no record of EG speaking at the Chautauqua Institute, a nondenominational adult education center in western New York. In a letter to BR on 28 July 1911 EG wrote that she had received a catalog from the institute and felt that it seemed too conservative to be a place to raise money for the PLM.

My precious Hobo.

Why are you not here with me so I can lean and look accross the sea. I am going out only to return by train. Beckie is ill and can not be left alone.[1] It is terrible how fate always conspires against the possibilities of rest and peace. But after all one does not neglect an animal when it is ill. I hope to be able to go out again Monday and stay all week.

I am indeed strange lover dear. So very strange, I do not even recognize myself. 30 years I walked through life serenely sure of myself in all conditions and circumstences. I dared Lucifer himself, never knew weakness, never failed to live up to what seemed right to me.

Then, a great element of nature came along, a Cyclone that swept accross the plane of my existence tearing me root and all from my usual sure position. It twisted my soul and turned my brain until all that was gone. Only one thing remained the elemental force, it is in my very blood now, the master power of my thought and actions. It is my love for you my Hobo and nothing else counts.

If ever our correspondence should be published, the World would stand aghast. That I, EG, the "strong revolutionist, the dare devil, the one who has defied laws and convention, should have been as helpless as a shipwrecked crew on the foaming ocean. It is indeed the irony of fate.

You are the foaming ocean out of which rise mountain high the mad waves of my love they carry me swiftly along the life and hope, then dash me down, for such is the purpose of the waves. Yes, indeed, I am strange dear.

And so you want to remain in Chicago until Sept. Well dear, you must know best what you want. The work here needs you it needs you absolutely and will not succeed with out you. And I? Oh Hobo! Hobo! If only you would know.—

I would like to take the day trip on the boat to Albany and go back with you at night, it is such a wonderful trip and would be still more wonderful with you. When shall it be? You could get your tickets to Albany and I would have our boat tickets, and state room ready. Let me know, dear boy.

I leans and looks accross the sea until it seems that no one's left behind, but you and

---

1. A reference to Rebecca Edelsohn, AB's companion. In 1911 Edelsohn became pregnant, and BR performed an abortion for her in September. In letters to BR during September 1911 EG discussed Edelsohn's operation and the trouble BR could get into if any problems occurred (see *EGP*, reel 5). Later in 1911 AB transcribed a letter in his diary that EG sent to Edelsohn after the operation, comforting her for her loss.

me. Hobo I hold you I cling to you until we are glewed into one. Until my love and passion covers your body and burns your soul. Until the life essence streeming from you that precious essence absorbs in my blood. Until, until, but oh how poor are words. Hobo, my beloved Hobo. Can you not hear me?

Mommy

July 29th 9 PM
Back in NY tired and weary and oh so lonely.

ALS, IU-U. On *Mother Earth* stationery.

Dear Emma,—

Am grieved very much over Winn's condition and will do what I can for him. Have sent him a mite to-day without saying anything about Madam's letter to you or that I know of his needs or condition.[1] I myself have been hors du combat for several weeks. Nerves have collapsed.

Now as to your assumption that I have any enmity against you. I feel hurt that you, the least of all, should be boorish, discourteous, and unjust, especially to comrades who have always done all they could to make your work and personal ambitions successful, and it is more than I expected and somewhat surprising. After I had taken the initiative among the local comrades in making it possible for you to speak in Detroit in the face of the tyranny of the police, it was, to say the least, untactful to attack me with others in the press and say the ungracious things you did.[2] If you like this sort of thing, why all right,

---

1. A reference to Ross Winn, Tennessee-based anarchist. His wife, Gussie, had written to EG requesting financial help while her husband, who had devoted himself to the anarchist movement, was in ill health. In response EG organized a support fund, sending copies of Gussie Winn's letter to several anarchists, including Labadie. In a cover letter she told Labadie, "I hope that your personal feeling against me will not hinder you from helping me in the task of raising some money for our faithful comrade Ross Winn." Another, later letter asked for financial help to support an anonymous comrade (Ross Winn), who was ill and needed help to support his family. The letter was signed by Dr. J. H. Greer, D. Finkler, Voltairine de Cleyre, Theodore Appel, Vincent St. John, and W. E. Trautmann. See Gussie Winn to EG, 12 July 1911, *EGP*, reel 5; EG to Joseph Labadie, 27 July 1911, Ibid.; Circular to EG, 30 November 1911, Ibid.

2. In a letter written to Labadie on 10 August 1911 EG stated that she was not referring to him while criticizing Detroit anarchists—a reference to the following attack by EG of Detroit anarchists, included in a lecture tour account in the March 1910 *Mother Earth*:

   "Detroit, Mich., was conquered after all. Alas, it was not the spirit of Robert Reitzel that helped. Of that there is not more. An erstwhile lickspittle of Reitzel, who in a foolish moment was induced to join the committee for free speech, took to his heels when he learned that we actually came to test the situation. Another whose claim to radicalism consists of silly stunts, was still more 'liberal': he kept in the background. Only one remained true to the spirit of *Der arme Teufel*—Conrad Pfeifer; but even he was worried lest the 'mighty be offended.'

   "The saviors of free speech in Detroit were, as usual, the single taxers, urged on by Mr. Ingram, the most spirited of them all.

   "Ridicule is a tremendous weapon against authority; thus Tsar Croul of Detroit may have come down from his throne for fear of appearing ridiculous. At any rate, our meetings did take place. Yet not without great loss of time and considerable expense. However, it was worth it all, not merely because of the material and moral success, but for the sake of our comrades there.

   "Carolus Nold, the erstwhile stormer, wastes his life in the mental atrophy of German *Vereinsmeierei* (club life). Too bad for the boy who could still do much in a healthier atmosphere. My visit to Detroit bears me out. Carl became rejuvenated. He threw himself with the old fire in the work, as in

but I don't like it. It does not seem to me necessary to spit fire at every one one meets, especially at those who have grown gray in the movement and who on every occasion have stood faithfully by their guns, even long before you knew there was a social movement. I repeat, I don't like it, and don't have to approve of it in those who do. If you think you are doing any good for either yourself or the movement by such conduct, why just go ahead and take the consequences. In my own modest way I have not found it necessary to use either invective or abuse of anybody to propagate Anarchism. I leave this for the Archists,[3] those who themselves are always correct in their conduct and leave nothing unsaid or undone to impress this on their auditors or readers, who would censor the behavior of others. It goes without argument that none of us have the wonderful gifts of oratory, keenness of perception, wide and varied and abtruse knowledge, unbounded courage and limitless moral rectitude of never flinching in the face of fire as has our own peerless Emma. Nature does not make a marvelous man or woman every day, and we are willing to grant these splendid virtues to you, but why you should find it necessary to emphasize the difference between us poor mortals and yourself we cannot for the life of us understand.

I have been trying to avoid saying these things to you, but you seem to invite it. You have referred to it several times, and so far I have said nothing, as I tho' the least said the better.

As to Nold, Carl Schmidt[4] et al, whom you have vilified, they are amply able to care of themselves. I desire to say this, however, that they are my friends and I reciprocate in the most loyal, unyielding friendship and resent unreservedly any detraction from their high worth and character.

Yours for love and truth and freedom,

Jo Labadie

TLSr, Joseph A. Labadie Papers, MiU. Various handwritten corrections.

----

the days when his spirit was as young as his years." EG, "Light and Shadows in the Life of an Avant-Guard," *Mother Earth*, February 1910, p. 19, above.

Nold, in a 1911 letter, stated that he and his associates had intervened with the police on EG's behalf, thus making possible the six successful meetings during EG's 1910 visit to Detroit. Nold concluded bitterly, "I'll be frank with you. Emma's not about propaganda anymore, it's all dollars and cents. The Jew in her, which she'd suppressed for years, is now suddenly, with Reitman's help, coming to the fore again." Carl Nold to Max Metzkow, 14 February 1911, Joseph Ishill Papers, MH-H.

3. "Archism" was a term used by some anarchist individualists (notably Benjamin Tucker), who identified it as the polar opposite of anarchist communism. Dora Marsden (1882–1960), English editor of the *Freewoman* and the *Egoist*, in 1914 defined an *archist* as "one who seeks to establish, maintain and protect by the strongest weapons at his disposal the law of his own interests" (*Egoist*, 1, no. 18).

4. Carl Schmidt (1856–1934), German-educated, Detroit-born "millionaire" tanner. Schmidt was a leading Republican, and a friend of Clarence Darrow and Eugene Debs. He was also a benefactor and friend of Joseph Labadie, giving him land and money to support his work. He was persuaded by Labadie to ignore the police opposition and support EG's right to speak in Detroit in February 1910. Schmidt was also a financial contributor to the *Mother Earth* Free Speech Fund (1906–1909).

## To JOSEPH A. LABADIE

*New York, 10 August 1911*

My dear Jo. Labadie:—

I am so glad I gave you an opportunity to get rid of your gall. It isn't a very good element to have. It destroys one's health and good spirits, and I should hate to know that I had been instrumental in doing that. But, joking aside, Old Man, I can tell you that I was never more innocent as in the storm my criticism of the Detroit radicals is concerned.[1] First of all, let me tell you right here, and I can do so with an easy conscience, since it is so long you will not accuse me of trying to get on the good side of your nature. As a matter of fact, it was Siegel[2] and not you, and I said as much to Dr. Clausen[3] when I was in Detroit last time. I couldn't possibly have meant you, because you had attended the first meeting, and however little your Anarchism or method of propaganda may have appealed to me, I never could have considered you a backslider. As to the others, I have nothing to retract. The very manner N.[4] reacted upon my criticism proves himself to be precisely the man I described him to be. No matter what N. would have said about me, it would never affect my interest in the propaganda, nor would I refuse to participate in any education, just because N. happens to be connected with it. Yet so very petty did he show himself, that when the Ferrer Association wrote to him about a memorial last year,[5] he refused to have anything to do with it because I suggested him as the right person to approach. I shall not waste a word on Carl Sch.[6] To me he is nothing else than an ordinary exploiter, with this distinction, that while the ordinary man who lives off the sweat of his fellow men makes no pretense to humanitarianism and radicalism, he does, and that is the thing which I cannot stand. But with all that, dear boy, I don't see why you should be angry. I take it you believe in free speech and in the right of one's

1. See Letter from Joseph A. Labadie, 3 August 1911, above.
2. Dr. Tobias Sigel was a Detroit anarchist who taught Esperanto and physical education at the Detroit Modern School. An associate of both Robert Reitzel and Johann Most, Sigel translated Most's *The God Pestilence* into Esperanto (ca. 1900–1909) and published a three-volume collection of essays from *Der Arme Teufel*, *Der Armen Teufels Gesammelte Schriften* (with an introduction by Max Baginski; Detroit: Reitzel Klub, 1913).
3. Dr. Emma Clausen, a published poet and a contributor to *Mother Earth*, was EG's friend and often her host in Detroit. See also vol. 2, *Making Speech Free*.
4. EG is referring to Detroit anarchist Carl Nold. See Letter from Joseph Labadie, 3 August 1911, above.
5. At EG's suggestion, the Francisco Ferrer Association sponsored memorial dinners in cities throughout the country on 13 October 1910 to mark the first anniversary of Ferrer's execution and to raise money for the establishment of Modern Schools.
6. EG is referring to Detroit Republican Carl Schmidt. See note in Letter from Joseph Labadie, 3 August 1911, above.

opinions. Why, then, may I not express my opinions? If I am proven wrong, I shall be glad to retract what I have said. But until then I shall have to stick to my original idea about the two men. However in the face of all the great things that happen in the world this is a very unimportant matter. Much more important to me is the way in which you have responded to my appeal for Ross Winn.[7] You are a dear, Jo., and I am sorry if I have hurt you. Now as to the real purpose of this letter. I am trying to arrange a few dates for William Thurston Brown[8] along the route from New York to Portland, Oregon. You probably have read or heard of him, but at any rate I want you to know that he was the first to start a Modern School in America and that he is now preparing to take charge of a Modern School in Portland, Oregon. Also he has developed out from the political clap trap into revolutionary libertarian lines and is otherwise a very able and charming man. He is to speak in Phila., Buffalo, Chicago and other cities. And I wondered if you could not arrange a lecture for him in Detroit. If you will not tell Carl that I am back of this proposition, he is sure to help, and so would all of our subscribers, once you start the ball a-rolling.[9] Brown can be in Detroit September 11th. You can choose from the following lectures: "Ibsen's Message to Woman", "Does America Need the Modern School?", "Reform or Revolution, Which?", "How Capitalism Has Hypnotized Society." Brown has decided on these dates partly because he wants to do some propaganda in the east and also as a means of raising his fare to Oregon. Therefore, you will do well to plan the meeting in a way that might leave a surplus for Brown. Please write him directly at Rand School, 112 E. 19th St., New York City. Needless to say I am always glad to hear from you.

Fraternally,

Emma Goldman

TLS, Joseph A. Labadie Papers, MiU. On *Mother Earth* stationery with Labadie autographed notation adding, "Answered Sept. 30, 1911" at top of page.

7. EG is referring to Ross Winn, an American anarchist who was ill. See Letter from Joseph A. Labadie, 3 August 1911, above.
8. Modern School educator William Thurston Brown founded a Modern School in Salt Lake City, Utah, in 1910.
9. Carl Nold taught at the Detroit Modern Sunday School.

MY DEAR JACK LONDON.

Have you heard from the Justice people?[1] I have not, except the repition of the hidious charge. I think Quelch[2] probably realises, he has made an awful blunder, but has neither decency nor courage to retract. Else it is hard to explain, how he would ignore the protests even of his own comrade, and they have sent bulks of them. I know your letter has not appeard, nor has George Herron's,[3] nor in fact a great many others'. on the other hand, Quelch goes on repeating "I am morally sure" as if that were enough.

Rose Strunsky, has been to see Hyndman, to get something from him?[4] I am inclosing an axact quotation from her letter dealing with that part. If that is not the hight of biggotry and mad fanaticism, I do not know what is. And these are the redeemers of the human race the moulders of a new society. The Tcar himself could not be more despotic. Evedently, there is but one thing left to do, to give Mr Quelch and Hyndman a dose of direct action, which t they certainly will get, if ever I go to London.

Dear boy, I am inclosing an announcement of Alex Berkman's forthcoming book,[5] not so much because I wish to relieve you of yuor money, though, everything thankfully accepted. But, it is for another reason, that I am sending you the circular.

You as the only revolutionary American writer, can not help but appreciate the first revolutionary literary American book, dealing with American economic struggle, as viewd through one, who spent 14 years, as, a "political in an American prison. And, I am certain that Berkman's work, aside of its literary value, is the first American human document of its kind, which can not but appeal, to one of your temperement.

---

1. London wrote to *Justice* protesting their accusation that EG was a police spy. The letter was published in the September 1911 London *Freedom*. See Letter to Peter Kropotkin, 29 May 1911, and Letter to Charmian London, 23 June 1911, above.
2. Harry Quelch (1858–1913) was an English socialist and member of the Social Democratic Federation, as well as editor of the party's journal, *Justice*, from 1886 to 1913 and translator of Marx's *The Poverty of Philosophy* (Chicago: Charles H. Kerr, 1910).
3. EG is referring to Professor George D. Herron, a Christian socialist.
4. EG asked Rose Strunsky, Anna Strunsky Walling's sister then in London, to visit Henry Mayers Hyndman (1842–1921) on her behalf. EG hoped that Hyndman, the leader of the Social Democratic Federation, for which *Justice* was the official organ, could be persuaded to pressure *Justice* editor Harry Quelch to either substantiate his charge that EG was a Russian spy or to print a retraction. In *Living My Life* (p. 482) EG states that Hyndman apparently agreed, but he never fulfilled his promise.
5. In September EG sent out a circular to announce the near completion of AB's book, titled "Autobiography of an Anarchist," and to ask for financial assistance to send the book to their printer. The book was later published as *Prison Memoirs of an Anarchist* (New York: Mother Earth Publishing Association, 1912).

I know you are a busy man, imposed upon a grea deal, yet, I make bold to ask you a favor, a very great favor. Would you read Berkman's Mss.? Both B, and myself have faith in your literary sincerity, and would be so happy to get your verdict. Then, too, if the book appeals to you strongly, perhps, you would feel moved to write the preface.[6] This is realy Berkman's idea, but as he is busy finishing his last part, I am writing for him.

There is a bare possibility, that Mitchell Kennerly may publish the book,[7] if not, we want to try a few more Publ. just for our own satisfaction. Who do you think should be seen at Mc Millans,[8] if at all? In any event, we will publish it ourselves, if I have to beg borow or steal, no effort can be too much for something, which represents a life time of sorroww and pain.

Now dear Jack, do not hasited, to be perfectly fra free with you answer we will understand frank with your answer, we will understand.

Don't mind my typewriting, have just only begun recently, but I will do better, when next I write.

Love to Charmian[9] and yourself.

Emma

TLS, CSmH, Jack London Collection. On *Mother Earth* stationery. After "moved to write the preface" a note appears in London's hand: "if he'll stand for my preface? Sure. But first I must read ms." At "Mitchell Kennerly" London comments, "if I have a preface they may. They've got guts."

6. London did write the requested preface, but it was highly critical of anarchism in general and of AB's assassination attempt in particular, characterizing the latter as "silly." In his rejection of the preface, Berkman wrote, "I'm awfully sorry, but I can't take it as it stands. It more than damns me with faint praise. And your attack on Anarchists, of course, is—to my mind—entirely out of place in an *introduction* of—<u>not</u> an Anarchist, but a psychic, a human document." Instead Hutchins Hapgood wrote the introduction, in which he, too, described AB's book as "a human document."
7. Mitchell Kennerley (1878–1950), English-born New York publisher and book-auction house president. Kennerley launched his own imprint in 1906, publishing new literature and radical authors, including Edward Carpenter, Frank Harris, Edna St. Vincent Millay, George Meredith, and H. G. Wells. From 1910 to 1916 he also published the *Forum*, whose contributors included Reginald Wright Kauffman, John Reed, and Rose Strunsky.
8. The Macmillan Company was London's publisher.
9. EG is referring to London's wife, Charmian London.

**Essay in *MOTHER EARTH***

*New York, October 1911*

# October Twenty-Ninth, 1901

It was in St. Louis, the 6th of September, 1901. I was just entering a street car, after a day's hard work soliciting orders for a firm.[1] Suddenly my ears caught the sound, "Extra, extra, the President shot!" I was too fatigued and miserable to heed the cry; besides, one is so used to newspaper "extras," one rarely stops to investigate.

At dinner in a friend's house I learned that President McKinley had been shot by a man by the name of Nieman.[2] One of our company remarked jokingly, "I should not be surprised if they will connect you with the act." The man spoke more prophetically than he realized.

The following morning I started on my day's task, which promised to be particularly hard, as I had to employ my skill to induce a business house to close a large order. It took all morning to settle the matter and left me even more dejected than the previous day. I dragged myself to the nearest restaurant and, while waiting to be served, I looked at the papers. There it was, in large black headlines, "President McKinley shot by an Anarchist, Leon Czolgosz—the man confessed to having been incited by Emma Goldman—the house of the publisher of the Anarchist paper *Free Society* raided—8 Anarchists arrested to be held until Emma Goldman is found—detectives sent to all parts of the country to arrest the dangerous woman."[3]

The whole thing seemed so absolutely preposterous that it took me some time to realize its significance; but after an hour's reflection, while I sat in the restaurant with people discussing E. G. around me, I decided to make for Chicago that very evening. It was not easy to get away, without arousing suspicion. My St. Louis friends had arranged a small dinner party for me on that same date, the 7th. To leave abruptly would have caused an inquiry as to my whereabouts, which under the circumstances had to be avoided. I therefore went through with the affair, and then made the night train for Chicago.

Ten years have passed since that terrible time,—terrible, because it disclosed, as in a flash, the savagery, the blind fury, the yellow human soul. Not only the knavish soul of the newspaper clique, nor yet the brutal soul of the police; nor even the mob soul, so appalling in its massiveness. But more than all else, it was the soul of the so-

---

1. To supplement her income, EG worked for her former lover Edward Brady as a representative of his woodworking company while she traveled on her lecture tour. On 6 September EG visited stationery and novelty shops in St. Louis to solicit orders for Brady.
2. Leon F. Czolgosz's alias was Fred C. Nieman.
3. There is no extant evidence to show that any St. Louis newspaper used this exact headline.

called radicals, manifesting itself in such contemptible cowardice and moral weakness, that impressed me with never-to-be-forgotten vividness. They, more than the yellow Hearsts,[4] more than the prostitute press, more than the mad public, proved the loudest defamers of the boy who had dared to strike the blow.

But for them Leon Czolgosz would not have been dragged to the block, like a sheep to slaughter. But for them, his last moment would not have been agonized by the consciousness of being deserted, betrayed, forsaken by his own brothers, even like Christ.

"All men are equal before the law," is one of our slogans. What a farce, what hypocrisy! The case of Leon Czolgosz has stamped this American boast as a lie. Indeed, there is no parallel in the annals of this country, where a human being has received less equality, less justice, less fair play, less humanity, than did this truest American child, Leon Czolgosz. From the very moment when he was nearly beaten to death on the Exposition grounds by a fury-drunk mob and the police, until he was dragged to the "trial," this modern Christ was forced to go through a thousand Golgothas. Not a kind word, not a human touch, during all those awful days between September 6th and October 29th,[5] when in the name of a "merciful God" and a "just law" he was done to death.

True, the law was observed,—Leon Czolgosz was assigned two lawyers to "defend" his case.[6] This farce must have made the angels weep. As if even a child did not know that the victim would be denied the simplest human rights. And the lawyers! What a disgrace to the human species, how despicably, how cringingly they acted! A defence, indeed! Ferocious beasts might have shown more humanity. What pigmies these worthy disciples of Justice represent compared with the man who defended Francisco Ferrer![7]

Spain is an autocracy ruled by the military and clerical rod. In 1909 anti-military uprising ran high, creating the same excitement, the same fury, the same savage craving for victims as with us in September, 1901. More,—there was the blood-thirsty monster of 1,800 years, the Catholic Church, ready to devour its prey. Ferrer's lawyer had everything to lose and nothing to gain. Yet, how daring, how sympathetic was that man!

William Archer in his "Life of Ferrer," tells how the man disliked taking the case, because of his antagonism to his client.[8] But Ferrer had chosen him,—one more example of the superior sense of justice even of an autocracy to our free country. The former grants the privilege to choose your defender, the latter imposes legal aid, which by its

---

4. Newspapers owned by the Hearst family included the *New York Journal*, the *San Francisco Examiner*, and the *Chicago American*.
5. These are the dates of Czolgosz's arrest and execution.
6. Czolgosz was defended by Robert C. Titus and Loran L. Lewis, two court-appointed state defenders.
7. Ferrer was defended by Captain Francisco Galcerán Ferrer.
8. According to Archer in *The Life, Trial, and Death of Francisco Ferrer* (London: Chapman and Hall, 1911), Ferrer chose Captain Francisco Galcerán Ferrer from a long list of possible defenders because of the similarity in their names. Galcerán Ferrer, a stranger to his client, admitted his initial repugnance toward Ferrer's anti-militarism, but was quickly won over upon meeting him.

Flyer advertising a protest meeting in New York "against the growing Religious Superstition"—a theme Emma Goldman addressed often during the period of this volume. (Kate Sharpley Archive)

very dependency upon the court must be partial and unfair. He came, unprejudiced, big and fine, with the sublime mission of pleading for a human life as the sole consideration. With earnestness and devotion this man pleaded for his client as if for his own life, carrying everyone with him in the soul-stirring appeal.

True, Francisco Ferrer was innocent of the charge for which he was tried; Czolgosz was not. But, as far as the court and his accusers were concerned, Ferrer was as guilty as his American comrade. Then, too, he was before a military court, subject to absolute methods of procedure. Not so the court that tried Leon Czolgosz. It pretends fair play, impartiality, justice, democracy. Yet it remained for this court to sit in judgment over a man morally and physically bound, blindfolded and gagged, a pitifully helpless human prey, turned over to the block. Were America glorious with a thousand noble deeds, her brutal inhumanity to the boy in Buffalo would forever condemn her as the most savage and cruel nation of the world.

Ten years have passed since the hideous hour of October 29th, but the spirit of Leon Czolgosz is not dead. How could it be, with its roots in the depths of the ever-growing conflict between the disinherited millions and the possessors of the earth?

"I did it for the good of the people," were the last words of the solitary youth in the death-chair of Auburn prison.[9] But the people knew him not, the people passed him by in blind hatred. Yet with all that, he was flesh of their flesh and blood of their blood. He suffered for them, endured humiliation for them, gave his life for them. His tragedy consisted in his great and intense love for the people, but unlike many of his brother slaves he could neither submit nor bow his neck. Thus he had to die.

It is said that I inspired the act. I repudiate the charge. Not because I would not take my stand with this victim of our time, but because I know that he whose hatred of injustice and tyranny burns at white heat is beyond external influences. And Leon Czolgosz must have hated tyranny, else he could never have died such an heroic death. No, he could not have remained so serene, so wonderfully oblivious to all the trivialities of his surroundings.

It is this death, solitary and sublime, that will always stand out as the great symbol in my recollection of that sombre figure of October 29th, 1901.

Emma Goldman.

*Mother Earth* 6 (October 1911): 232–35.

9. According to the 30 October 1901 edition of the *New York Times*, Czolgosz's last words were "I killed the President because he was an enemy of the good people—the working people. I am not sorry for my crime. I'm awfully sorry I could not see my father."

Interview in the
## *NEW YORK GLOBE AND COMMERCIAL ADVERTISER*

*New York, 9 October 1911*

## Labor's Seeress Predicts a Commune
## If M'Namaras Die

### Deaths Quickly Avenged Should Forces of Capitalism Succeed in Executing the Two Brothers, Says Emma Goldman.

#### Anarchist, But Has No Peer As Authority

Working World Has Grown Vastly More Radical, She Finds, and
Conviction Spells Another Haymarket, or Worse

Another "Haymarket," born of a workingmen's enmity, will convulse America if the McNamara brothers are found guilty of being dynamitards and their lives forfeited to the law, according to the keenest student of labor evolution in the world.[1]

"Should the forces of capitalism which seem determined to execute these two brothers succeed," says this authority, "their deaths will be quickly avenged."

It detracts not a whit from the value of this opinion to disclose that its author is Emma Goldman, frankly and aggressively an anarchist. Herein, however, lies the reason why the utmost weight attaches to her deliberately formed dictum. She is not welcome in labor circles. Her name is anathema. She is the pariah whenever chance association links the two causes. Despite that, this keen-minded woman knows more about the American labor movement than any disciple in it.

In her own thorough way, preaching her ideal of "Anarchism, the Moving Spirit of the Labor Movement," which is the title to one of her lectures, she has in the twenty years of

---

1. Many anarchists, including EG, AB, and Voltairine de Cleyre, marked the execution of the Haymarket anarchists in 1887 as a significant factor in their turn toward radicalism. Here EG warns that the trial of labor organizers James and John McNamara has the potential to ignite the flames of violence. The McNamara brothers were on trial for their alleged involvement in the *Los Angeles Times* building explosion on 1 October 1910. The trial began 11 October 1911 with Clarence Darrow as the defense attorney. Though the McNamaras initially pleaded not guilty, they would later change their plea to one of guilty, surprising many of their radical and trade union supporters. EG repeated a variant of this comparison between the Haymarket trial and the McNamara *Los Angeles Times* bombing trial in "On the Trail" in the June 1911 edition of *Mother Earth*. For a fuller account of the McNamaras' trial see "Emma Goldman Comes to Preach Anarchism to the IWW's," Article in *Fresno Morning Republican*, 14 May 1911, and Letter to Peter Kropotkin, 29 May 1911, above.

her stormy petrel experience gained a knowledge of the movement and the value of the personal equations as they are found in its leaders which make her paramount.

### NOTHING OF VIRAGO.

Anybody expecting to find a fire-eating virago breathing death and vengeance to rulers and the destruction to all established social orders will never recognize this type in Emma Goldman. Now passing her forty-second year, of moderate blonde type, with the clear healthy complexion of a girl of fifteen, strong features and wearing glasses, rather short and just a little stout, she looks very much like a school teacher.

Soft-spoken and carefully weighing each question, she gives a deliberate answer and once she tells you her [lines missing] several weeks in and around Los Angeles, where the McNamaras will be placed on trial next Wednesday, Emma Goldman was found to-day in her apartment of three or four rooms five flights up (rear) in the big tenement house at 210 East Thirteenth street, where she has resided for years.

Her tiny suite is both a home and the headquarters of the international propaganda she conducts. There she edits and arranges for the publication of her monthly magazine, *Mother Earth*, one of the most radical monthlies in the world and which has subscribers in practically every country.

She talks about the labor movement just as she does the drama, art, or problems of maternity, and makes in each instance a thorough analysis. She has made a special study of the McNamara case and has a lecture on it which she calls "The McNamara Case and Burns[2]—Government by Spies."

### DOUBTS CONVICTION.

"I do not believe," she said to-day, "that it will be possible to get a jury in California to convict John J. McNamara, the secretary of the Bridge and Structural Ironworker's Union, and his brother, who were kidnapped from Indiana and are charged with conspiracy and the dynamiting of the Los Angeles Times Building, in which several lives were lost.

"I very much doubt if even the radicals here in the east have more than a faint conception of how thoroughly aroused labor is in the middle and far west on this McNamara case. It is wonderful. You know I am not over popular with the majority of the labor union people, and am opposed to the socialists perhaps more than any others, but I found all grades of unionists united in this fight.

"Gompers has gone further in this fight than any of us supposed he was capable of going. He has gone from one end of California to the other denouncing the kidnapping of the McNamaras.[3]

"If Burns has a strong case against them, as he has led many to believe, he made a

2. William J. Burns was the private detective whose agency was responsible for arresting the McNamara brothers. EG would deliver this lecture in late October and early November in New York City.
3. American Federation of Labor president Samuel Gompers lectured throughout the West Coast dur-

great mistake when he kidnapped these men in violation of all law and rushed them incommunicado across the country. He had a far better chance to convict them in Indiana, as no man in California is so cordially disliked as Gen. Harrison Grey Otis, the owner of the building they are accused of dynamiting.[4] A very small number of merchants and manufacturers are supporting him for class reasons. He was for years the tool of the Southern Pacific and has opposed the people on every issue.

### ADMIRES GAMENESS.

"Personally, I must say that I admire him while hating what he stands for. He is such a superb fighter. In this day of spineless men and general submission to all kinds of abuses it does me good to see a man with a backbone and full of fight even if he is on the other side.

"The country has made wonderful progress on radical lines in twenty years. I am as much of an anarchist as ever, yet I recently spoke in Ann Arbor, Mich., and received a magnificent reception from the students and professors, although but two years ago the same students did all they could to break up my meetings.[5]

"I have just ended a tour including fourteen university towns and cities with a like result. It is not that Emma Goldman is one particle less radical, but that the country has made intellectual progress.

"If they should execute the McNamaras the capitalists will have a rude awakening. They will find the temper of the people very different from that of the days of the Chicago anarchists. Then the trades unions were absolutely indifferent and their own leaders smothered what resentment was displayed.

"It has been said that anybody who prophesies shows that he can also be a fool, but I feel safe in saying that we will have a mighty social upheaval if the McNamaras are

---

ing the fall of 1911, publicizing the case of the McNamaras. He withdrew his support, however, after they pleaded guilty.

4. Harrison Gray Otis (1837–1917) was a newspaper publisher and owner and publisher of the *Los Angeles Times*. Otis was described by Eugene Debs as early as April 1895 in a speech as a "monumental liar and cowardly sneak." Otis acquired part interest (1882) and then full control (1886) of the *Los Angeles Times*, and directed the paper through the end of World War I. He championed the declaration of war against Spain in 1898 and served briefly as a major general. He fiercely opposed labor unions and made his newspaper a voice of ultraconservative Republicanism, "industrial freedom," and the open shop. To work against organized labor, Otis also organized the Merchants and Manufacturers Association, a powerful organization that controlled business and industry in Los Angeles. On 1 October 1910 the offices of the *Los Angeles Times* were bombed by James B. McNamara with the aid of David Caplan and Matthew A. Schmidt. Otis headlined the case relentlessly and kept the search for the bombers on the front page throughout the fall and winter of 1910 and 1911. Later, Otis was in close contact with the San Diego vigilantes, speaking at a banquet of businessmen in late November 1911, just before the 8 January 1912 passage of an anti-street-speaking ordinance, urging businessmen's suppression of street speaking there.

5. Students heckled EG at a lecture on the University of Michigan's Ann Arbor campus on 19 February 1910. For EG's account of the meeting see *Mother Earth* 5 (March 1910): 20–21.

executed. The country had a fair specimen of the aroused working class in the trials of Moyer and Haywood, which trials I believe were conducted in a far fairer spirit than is conceivable in the McNamara case."[6]

### EVERY IRISHMAN'S CAUSE.

"There is another important factor," she continued. "The McNamaras are Irish, and the Irish of the United States keenly resent the way they have been treated. Now everybody knows that the Irish by nature are fighters, and few realize how solidly they are backing the McNamaras in this fight. I believe that this fact cannot be too strongly emphasized. If anything happens to the McNamaras there will be individual Irishmen who will see that they are avenged.

"The majority of the people of Los Angeles are satisfied that the Times building was destroyed by a gas explosion, as gas had been escaping in asphyxiating quantities for days. Dynamite experts brought in by the police have declared that nothing like the results of the explosion could have been caused by dynamite. They said everything went to prove that it was something like gas, which detonates much more slowly."[7]

*New York Globe and Commercial Advertiser,* 9 October 1911.

6. EG is referring to the trial of labor organizers William D. Haywood and Charles Moyer for the murder of ex-Idaho governor Frank Steunenberg. Together with George Pettibone they were acquitted in 1907.
7. A reference to the contemporary assertion by various labor and radical organizations, including the California State Federation of Labor, that the explosion was caused by leaking gas, not dynamite. See, for instance, *International Socialist Review,* November 1910; and the *Proceedings of the California State Federation of Labor 1910.*

Ben just arrived

DEAR.

I suppose you'll have to stay in, well, let's hope it will soon be over. I shall miss you more than I can tell dear.

I would suggest the dedication to be "To all who struggle against boundage I dedicate this book."[8]

It gose without saying that the prisoners are included. I would write more but I am disturbed now.

I am with you in spirit dear.

AFFECT.

E.

ALI, Emma Goldman Archive, IISH.

---

8. The actual dedication to *Prison Memoirs of an Anarchist* reads: "To all those who in and out of prison fight against their bondage." First published in September 1912, Berkman's memoirs were promoted in a circular distributed by EG in September 1911 soliciting subscriptions to the book and providing a preliminary list of chapter headings. In the published edition of *Prison Memoirs*, however, these chapter headings were dramatically altered and expanded, suggesting that in the intervening months Berkman substantially revised the form and content of his memoirs.

"Pesterer no. 19," caricature of Emma Goldman addressing a crowd of "working men and working women," shouting her abhorrence of constant surveillance of those who voice dissent. She points to the police scattered throughout her audience as men whose "souls are completely colonized" and yells "A curse on this order, a curse, a curse !!!" Yiddish humor periodical, *Der Groysser Kundes* (the *Big Stick*) August 1911. (Labadie Collection, University of Michigan)

From **BEN L. REITMAN**

*Chicago, 14 January 1912*

## At Home

MOMMY MINE.

"Three weeks" in Chicago and how long it seems. It is a beautiful Sunday morning. The cold snap is over. It has been from 2 to 16 below 0 for 10 day. There is a soft white covering on Chigago's dirty Streets and If I could I would love to take mommy sleigh riding and talk to you about life and art and technique. I remember many rides we have had. but not enough. Remember the ride in Fargo N. D., Fresno Calif., Boise Idaho, do you recall the auto ride in Frisco one wild night. Remember the auto ride with Walsh, in Kansas City[1] & with that [Prison] man in Los Angeles.[2] Dearest our life on the road has'nt been all bad. has it. I want more and more of it. I wanted to write something intelligently to you about Orleneff.[3] I think I understand your feeling in the matter. (but personally I cant see how you can attach your self to a worthless Hobo when there are such men as Orleneff and Hutch[4] and other to love) and I am glad you are interested in him. Really I am happy that the plays of his give you pleasure. I wish I might sit by you to enjoy with you.

I don't see why Orleneff could'nt travel around the county as a free lance. It isn't necessary for him to work for land Lords and manager. I wish it were possible for us all to travel together. We could have a [Suhail] hall or theatre in the Jewish district for him and English hall for Momy and you could be of so much help to him if you were in town with him. Why could'nt he travel around giving reading and sketchs of his plays. He would be under small expense and get his art before the people and if you could act as

---

1. Possibly Francis (Frank) Patrick Walsh (1864–1939), a prominent Kansas City trial lawyer, well-known labor attorney, and advocate of social reform. In 1913 he led the Commission on Industrial Relations' investigation of labor unrest. After Billings's conviction, Walsh worked with the International Workers' Defense League's defense of Tom Mooney and spoke at the December 1916 Carnegie Hall fund-raising meeting for Mooney and Billings. Walsh refused the request to act as Mooney's attorney in the preparedness trial, although years later he would become his chief counsel.
2. Possibly a reference to Griffith J. Griffith, secretary and treasurer of the Los Angeles–based Prison Reform League.
3. A reference to Russian actor Pavel Nikolaevich Orlenev, then touring the United States. EG had in 1905 been the publicity agent for Orlenev's theater company.
4. Hutchins Hapgood, with whom EG maintained a flirtatious relationship.

translater. I can't see why it isn't possible to make some sort of a deal that way. I think he would enjoy such a free lance trip across the county.

I want to help him if I can. I see by the Papers that J. Fox has been found guilty and will have to pay $1000.00 fine.[1] A woman was foreman of the jury. An other argument in favor of suffrage. That is damm shame. The Goverment will gather in all the Anarchist in one way or an other. I would'nt be surprised if some of Mother Earth family get it soon. I am so glad Mother Earth has been kept in N. Y. we ought never move our business away from N. Y. I am concerned about the new inditement of J. & J. in Los Angeles.[2] I wonder what Steffens has to say now.[3]

"We must work while it is day, for the time cometh that we will not be permitted to work any more."[4]

Be careful dear heart and have the other careful especially the woman. We can never tell when the hounds will spring at our throats. As you know, before this thing is over, I feel sure that Anarchism will be made the "goat" and while "The Anarchist propoganda has passed the stage of ridicule and willful misunderstanding" We must be on the look out. No matter what happens to us we must see that Mother Earth Publishing ass. ~~will~~ continues. I hope you will carefully arrange thing in N. Y. and talk to Kelly & Roe[5] and others that you have confindence in to continue the work if all of us are taken away. To

1. As a result of his article in the *Agitator* ("The Nudes and the Prudes," reprinted in *Mother Earth*, March 1912) in defense of nude swimming at Home Colony, Washington, Jay Fox became the center of a major obscenity trial that stretched from 1911 to 1915. First arrested for the article in 1909, he was found guilty of violating the Comstock Act and sentenced to two months in prison. Fox's bail, pending appeal, was set at $1,000. The case was appealed to the Washington Supreme Court and the U.S. Supreme Court, where the original sentence was upheld.

2. Clarence Darrow, James and John McNamara's attorney, was indicted on two counts of jury tampering and bribery in connection with the McNamara trial in January 1912. Darrow's first trial, which began 5 May 1912, resulted in a verdict of not guilty. His second trial, which eventually began in January 1913, ended in a hung jury on 8 March 1913, after which the prosecution dropped all charges with the proviso that Darrow should no longer practice law in California.

3. Lincoln Steffens, hoping to write about the motives that fueled the *Los Angeles Times* building explosion as a vehicle for explaining the causes of industrial violence, acted as a mediator between the prosecution and the McNamaras as they negotiated a settlement. The McNamaras agreed to plead guilty; in return, they were to be given short prison sentences and the prosecution (and the Los Angeles Merchants and Manufacturers Association) promised there would be no further prosecutions in the case. However, this agreement was broken: James was convicted of murder and sentenced to life imprisonment, and John was convicted of conspiracy to murder and given fifteen years. In 1913 thirty-eight members of the International Association of Bridge and Structural Iron Workers union were convicted in Indianapolis for transporting dynamite or conspiring to transport dynamite. In 1915 Matthew A. Schmidt was convicted of first-degree murder and sentenced to life imprisonment, and in 1916 David Caplan was convicted of voluntary manslaughter and received a ten-year sentence. Steffens was criticized bitterly by EG, BR, AB, and others for his gullibility and naïveté in his role as a go-between.

4. The actual quotation reads: "Work while it is called today; for the night cometh, wherein no man can work." Thomas Carlyle, *Sartor Resartus*, book 2, chapter 9.

5. A reference to anarchist Harry Kelly, who contributed to and helped edit *Mother Earth*, and Gilbert Roe, a lawyer and free speech advocate who also often worked with EG.

quote you again "people are beginning to realize the significance and wide import of Anarchism."[6]

Baby I want your work to live to have an influence on the new Society. I am so glad I am an Anarchist. the more I see of life the more I read the more I am confident the Anarchism is the greatest factor in the building of a good world.

And the thing that will make Anarchism a force in our lives and our literature.

I am glad I am your manager.

Mother Earth comes it is a good number I am glad to see Miss Raney poem.[7]

The "Right to live"[8] is good it would made a good lecture. I hope you will change the book Ad. next month it ought to be change ever month it wont cost any thing.[9] That Wanted notice of Mother Earth should be cut out and a large notice of May 1910 inserted.[10] I tried to tell you that in a previous letter. I miss Havel article and I miss your. I don't think it good policy for you to be too busy to have an article every month.[11] If you are willing to struggle to raise money I don't see why you are not willing to write an article every month. I am glad James article is about finished.[12] I liked what you wrote about Orleneff.[13] I hope you will make arrangement for Mother Earth to be a "great number" every issue. Dear I don't mean to be harshly critical. I am so much interested and when I realize what you can do. I hate to see any thing less than your best.

I have an other obsession in my brain. I want to go rabbit hunting for a few day. I want to run around in the snow this is give me a chance to get a little target practice that I need. My Brother has a hunting license and several guns. I am going to try and raise the price of a trip. Maybe I will go to Iowa or to Bill Buwalda place.[14] Wish me and Mommy could go to gether and be free for a [illegible] week and shoot bugs and grass hoppers and do it.

Just had my Brother's kid out giving them a sleigh ride.

---

6. This is a quotation from EG's short article "The New Year," which was published in the January 1912 edition of *Mother Earth*.
7. Rebekah E. Raney's poem "Blaming the Fester" appeared in the January 1912 *Mother Earth* (vol. 6, no. 11).
8. Max Baginski's article "The Right to Live," which appeared in the January 1912 *Mother Earth* (vol. 6, no. 11), claimed that the right to live was a basic tenet of anarchism: "When everything, every essential of life is the monopoly of a certain class . . . [t]he demand of the right to live is the most revolutionary demand of our day."
9. A reference to the advertisement of books available for purchase through the office of *Mother Earth*.
10. At the end of the January 1912 issue, BR addressed a query to readers asking for back issues of *Mother Earth*, explaining that the staff was in the process of collecting and binding volumes of *Mother Earth*.
11. No article by Hippolyte Havel or EG appeared in the January 1912 *Mother Earth*; however, an introductory editorial letter, "The New Year" by EG, did appear.
12. A reference to *Economy as Viewed by an Anarchist*, by C. L. James, which was intermittently serialized in *Mother Earth* from September 1910 to January 1912, although the final chapter was never published.
13. An unsigned article, "Paul Orleneff," appeared in the January 1912 *Mother Earth*.
14. By this time, William Buwalda was living on the family farm in Hudsonville, Michigan.

I been writing to Momy and play with the kids all morning and it is soon time to get my lunch and go to the Lewis lecture he has a debate with Barnad today. On "has Religion helped or hindered progress." Barnard will defend <u>Religion</u>.[15] I had a terrible time at his meeting last <u>Sunday</u> they threatened to have me arrested for selling <u>pamphlets</u>. I am going to try again today to sell Anarchy VS <u>Socialism</u>.[16]

Herman Kuehn[17] talk a[smeared] the Open Forum[18] tonight on the Delusion of Natural Right. I go there.

Now my sweetheart I love you and want to hold you close and want to count the Mountains, and hold them close, thre long weeks since I saw Lady treasur box. I have never forgotten her beauty or fragence, she is always close to me.

I hope you will always want me and you will remember that you are my great glorious <u>lover</u>.

Have a good time in N. Y. and rest and live.

Momy take me me for I love you
Hobo

"It may be that fate will give the life and ~~love~~ leave to row once more

Set some strong man free for fighting as I awhile take his oar[19]—

God be thanked—what'er comes after, I have lived and toiled with men!"

Kipling. Galley Slave

ALS, IU-U.

15. A lecture and debate between socialist Arthur M. Lewis and Christian anarchist and poet William Francis Barnard. Barnard was a contributor to *Free Society* and *Mother Earth* and author of *The Moods of Life: Poems of Varied Feeling* (Chicago: The Tooks Press, 1905), *The Tongues of Toil and Other Poems* (Chicago: Fraternal Press, 1911), and *Mind over Mind* (Cleveland: The Artcraft Printing Co., 1919). The debate took place at the Garrick Theater in Chicago.
16. Reitman refers to William C. Owen's *Anarchy Versus Socialism* (New York: Mother Earth Publishing Association, 1910).
17. Herman Kuehn was a Minneapolis-based anarchist individualist and single-taxer.
18. The Open Forum in Chicago was led by anarchist Hulda Potter Loomis.
19. The actual Kipling line reads: "Set some strong man free for fighting as I take awhile his oar," from "The Galley-Slave," published in *Departmental Ditties and Other Verses*, 1886.

# MOTHER EARTH

### Monthly Magazine Devoted to Social Science and Literature
#### Published Every 15th of the Month

EMMA GOLDMAN, Proprietor, 55 West 28th Street, New York. N. Y.
Entered as second-class matter April 9, 1906, at the post office at New York, N. Y.,
under the Act of Congress of March 3, 1879.

| Vol. VI | OCTOBER, 1911 | No. 8 |
|---|---|---|

# Lectures by Emma Goldman

## Sunday Evenings, 43 E. 22nd Street

October    15.—Anarchism, the Moving Spirit in the Labor Movement.

October    22.—Maternity, A Drama by Brieux. (Why the poor should not have children.)

October    29.—Government by Spies. (The MacNamara Case and Burns.)

November  5.—The Failure of Christianity.

November 12.—Art and Revolution.

November 19.—Communism, the most Practical Basis for Society.

### Meetings will begin at 8 P. M.

Questions and Discussion.

Single Tickets, 25c. Course of six lectures $1.00. For sale at

## Mother Earth, 55 West 28th Street

These lectures will also be delivered in Jewish, at Terrace Lyceum, 206 East Broadway, every Sunday at 3 P. M., beginning Sunday, October 15th.

The week days during October and November are to be devoted to neighboring cities. Comrades desiring to arrange for dates will please communicate with me at once.

BEN L. REITMAN.

Notice in *Mother Earth* for an Emma Goldman lecture series representative of the broad range of topics she addressed. Note that she often delivered her talks in Yiddish in the afternoon and in English in the evening. (Kate Sharpley Archive)

Article in the *DENVER DAILY NEWS*

*Denver, 17 April 1912*

## Sex Problem Talks Fill Hall to Doors, Says Emma Goldman

### Noted "Anarchist" Discusses Modern Day Questions in "Safe and Sane" Interview; Says She Has Preached Ideas Now Being Exploited in Magazines.

By Alice Rohe.

"It is really quite interesting to note," said Emma Goldman yesterday afternoon, "that when I come to Denver my lectures upon the great, sweeping, broad subjects of economics are very poorly attended, but when I lecture upon sex subjects the hall is packed. At my last visit I counted fifteen automobiles in front of the dingy, cheap little hall in which I talked."

"And do you regard this as a sign of awakening thought or of minds looking for something they think will be not—nice?" I asked. Miss Goldman smiled rather strangely and replied:

"Whatever the motive was that brought those people to that lecture, they appeared extremely interested and expressed a deep interest in the remarks.

"Indeed, I attribute it to the slow but sure awakening. You cannot imagine the changes that have come in the last ten years. Positively, when I talked upon sex subjects ten years ago I was ill for days afterwards. The experience of looking into those leering faces, of talking to people who grasped only what they thought to be a discussion of the lewd, of the immoral, was too much for me. I was only preaching the very things that are being discussed today in literature and in universities.

"Yes, indeed, in colleges," continued Miss Goldman. "My very dear friend, Dr. Ulrich, a woman of great learning and advanced views, is now instructor of eugenics in the University of Minnesota.[1] Do you regard that as a step in advance?"

**ALL IN LITERATURE.**

The most insistent thought that keeps coming into one's mind when talking to Emma Goldman, called in terror, by the unthinking, a red-handed anarchist, recognized by the dispassionate as one of the greatest intellectual forces of the day, is that these views

---

1. The only Ulrich in the medical school at the University of Minnesota during this period was a man, Dr. Henry Ulrich. There is no indication in his biography that he lectured on or studied eugenics.

which she has been preaching for the past twenty years are being served to us with great flourish of mental pyrotechnics in our recent "advanced" literature.

This thought, that when Emma Goldman makes a statement it is regarded as shockingly anarchistic, but when Ellen Keyes[2] or Karin Michaelis[3] express the same view it is regarded as the message of the "emancipated," was so overpowering yesterday afternoon that I asked Miss Goldman what she thought about it.

"The pioneer in any movement is bound to be branded by conventionality," said Miss Goldman, "and the acceptance of ideas which were regarded as anarchistic, as food for discussion in clubs today shows the slow but sure awakening of the feminine mind, at least."

## REFERS TO *CHANTECLER*.

"Do you, in view of all the things you have endured for the sake of your ideas and beliefs, regard your struggle as worth while? Do you consider the struggle against the dark wall of dense ignorance for the illuminating of the few worth while?"

Miss Goldman smiled. "Do you remember the lines in *Chantecler*,[4] where the Cock discovers that he does not cause the sun to rise?" she inquired. He was content to announce the coming of the dawn.

"Mary Wollstonecraft," continued Miss Goldman, "preached what I am preaching years ago. She was the real pioneer, and whenever I have encountered difficulties I look back at this brave woman who lived in convention-bound England at a time when it was far more difficult to gain self-expression than it is even now."[5]

Miss Goldman indeed does not regard suffrage in Colorado as advancing the general

2. Ellen Karolina Sofia Key (1849–1926), a Swedish feminist author and free love advocate, profiled in Floyd Dell's *Women as World Builders; Studies in Modern Feminism* (Chicago: Forbes, 1913) and quoted in the *Woman Rebel* (1914). Her works, especially *Love and Marriage* and *The Century of the Child*, were translated into many languages and were especially popular in their Yiddish editions. Her books include *The Century of the Child* (New York: G. P. Putnam's Sons, 1909); *Love and Marriage*, which includes a critical and biographical introduction by Havelock Ellis (New York: G. P. Putnam's Sons, 1911); *The Woman Movement*, also with an introduction by Havelock Ellis (New York: G. P. Putnam's Sons, 1912); and *The Renaissance of Motherhood* (New York: G. P. Putnam's Sons, 1914). Key's social analysis suggested that women could attain their greatest individual development through contributing to society as mothers, though Key called for a social restructuring of motherhood, wherein, for example, the state fully economically supports women during their childbearing years. In her educational theory outlined in *The Century of the Child*, Key emphasizes the need for the natural development of children's intellects in a climate of education that encourages curiosity, obedience, and rationality.
3. Katharina Marie Michaelis Satrangeland (Karin Michaelis) (1872–1950), prolific and popular Danish author and feminist. Michaelis was best known for her novel *The Dangerous Age: Letters and Fragments from a Woman's Diary*, which was first serialized in the *Revue de Paris* (1911) and reviewed in the August 1911 edition of *Current Literature*. She was a friend of the author Agnes Smedley and EG during EG's exile years.
4. *Chantecler* (1910), a play by Edmond Rostand, reviewed by EG in the *Denver Post*, 23 April 1912. EG's review later appeared in her book *The Social Significance of the Modern Drama* (1914).
5. In late 1911 EG wrote a lecture manuscript, titled "Mary Wollstonecraft, Her Tragic Life and Her Struggle for Freedom," which she delivered on numerous occasions.

cause of women particularly, for she holds that here and in other suffrage[6] states the women are afraid to advance on account of their political positions. The ballot, she says, has not developed them mentally.

"Women in states where suffrage does not exist are more fearless in self-expression than in these states where they have the franchise. Those women fighting in England,[7] while they may cease to develop after the battle is won, are making great strides, for they are sacrificing everything for their ideas and their ideals."

### STRIKE OF THE SEX.

"What do you consider the greatest question, the greatest upheaval of the present day? Is it not the woman movement?" I inquired.

"It is indeed," replied Emma Goldman. "We may call present conditions the strike of the sex.

"The important thing for women to consider, however, is that the economic emancipation of the race is absolutely interwoven with sex enslavement. Economic conditions must be solved along with the woman question. Woman has too long been a commodity instead of a creative force; today, however, she is solving her questions herself and the individual emancipation is the forerunner, of course, of a more universal emancipation."

The recent newspaper articles all over the country in regard to Karin Michaelis' startling assertion that a woman has the right to motherhood when she desires brought to mind the fact that Emma Goldman, "anarchist," accused of immoral teaching, has long asserted this now newspaper admitted contention.

"Why, I think the same as I have always thought," said Emma Goldman. "Karin Michaelis is bringing out no new idea. I assert that until women may bear children when they please the future race will be just that much retarded."

### QUESTION OF MOTHERHOOD.

"Motherhood should be a desired event in a woman's life. She should have the right to bring into the world offspring by a man she loves. She should not be forced to bear children against her will because she wears a gold band on her left hand. All of which

6. At this time the states that had granted suffrage to women were Wyoming (1869), Colorado (1893), Utah (1895), Idaho (1896), Washington (1910), and California (1911); Oregon, Arizona, and Kansas granted suffrage in 1912.
7. A reference to the direct-action tactics of the suffragettes then taking place in England. Those around *ME* were most impressed by the tactics of the suffragettes, if not their stated aims. In his article "The Suffragettes" in the February 1910 *ME* Hippolyte Havel writes, "No other political group has ever used such tactics except the Anarchists. And with what ingenuity and effect the suffragettes have employed this method." One of the suffragettes' most prominent members, Emmeline Pankhurst (1858–1928), would tour the United States in 1913. English women finally secured the right to vote in 1928.

merely reverts to the subject of eugenics, a science which may be taught in other universities than Minnesota and which will tend to the betterment of the coming generation."

The teaching of sex hygiene in the schools and the open discussion by the Mothers' congress of Denver Miss Goldman regards as encouraging signs.[8]

"If only those in authority knew how to direct the awakening of sex in adolescence into the right channels we would have art and music and literature, the beautiful expressions of this forte, instead of the ugly motifs which ignorance breeds in our convention-bound system," she said.

Tonight, at East Turner hall, Emma Goldman gives her lecture, "Sex, the Great Element of Creative Work." Concerning this she maintains, with scientists, it is so tremendous a power that its development into vice through ignorance is a crime of society.

A quiet, bomb-throwingless, bloodless conversation was this interview with Emma Goldman, a woman who has read beyond the belief of the busy workers' ideas, a thinker who has, through her insistence upon telling the truth, expressed her ideas regardless of conventions.

So far as the Nemesis policeman who has pursued the plain-spoken Emma Goldman, he may be found in other guises where women fearlessly express their ideas, only, of course, he does not always wear a uniform and carry a club.

*Denver Daily News*, 17 April 1912, p. 12. The author of this article, Alice Rohe (1876–1957), born in Lawrence, Kansas, was a drama and book critic for various newspapers in the United States and abroad and a member of the Heterodoxy Club of Greenwich Village in New York City.

---

8. The National Congress of Mothers, founded in 1897, had changed its name and become the National Congress of Mothers and Parent-Teacher Associations in 1908 and published the *Child Welfare Magazine* (1909–1928). The organization worked for child welfare and later became the more focused Parent Teacher Association (PTA).

## Article in the *DENVER POST*

*Denver, 21 April 1912*

## Suffrage Dealt Blow by Women of Titanic

### Emma Goldman Inquires to Know If Equality Is Demanded Only at Ballot Box—Human Nature Came Into Own in Men.

By Emma Goldman.

Barring all sensational and conflicting reports of the Titanic horrors[1] there are two features which seem to have been overlooked altogether. One is, the part woman has played in the terrible disaster, which to say the least, is in keeping with centuries of her training as a mere female.

With all the claims the present-day woman makes for her equality with man, her great intellectual and emancipatory achievements, she continues to be as weak and dependent, as ready to accept man's tribute in time of safety and his sacrifice in time of danger, as if she were still in her baby age.

"The men stood aside to let the ladies go first." What about the ladies? What about their love superior to that of the men? What about their greater goodness? Their demand to equal rights and privileges? Is this to be found only at the polls, or on the statutes? I fear very much that the ladies who have so readily accepted the dictations of the men, who stood by when the men were beaten back from the life-boats, have demonstrated their utter unfitness and inferiority, not merely to the title of man's equal, but to her traditionary fame of goodness, love and self-sacrifice.

It is to be hoped that some there were among the steerage victims at least, who preferred death with those they loved to life at the expense of the loved ones.

The second feature is this: To die for those we love is no small matter in a world where each is for himself and the devil take the hindmost. But to die for those far removed from us by a cold and cruel social and material gulf—for those who by their very position must needs be our enemies—for those who, a few moments before the disaster prob-

---

1. The White Star luxury liner *Titanic* struck an iceberg and sank on 14–15 April 1912, resulting in the loss of over 1,500 passengers. Although the survival statistics indicate that women were allowed into the lifeboats first, there is debate over whether it was the male passengers who allowed the women to go first or the crew who refused to allow men to enter the lifeboats. The discrepancy between first- and third-class passengers was evident in the survival statistics, suggesting that the wealthier passengers had been given preference in the limited assignment of lifeboats, although eyewitness accounts are rather unclear and contradictory on how this happened.

ably never gave a thought to the toilers and pariahs of the ship—is so wonderful a feat of human nature as to silence forever the ridiculous argument against the possibilities of human nature. The average philistine forever prates of how human nature must be coerced and beaten; how it must be kept in check and disciplined. How little he knows of the grandeur of human nature has never before been so magnificently demonstrated as by the crew of the Titanic, the sailors, stokers, workers, and drones belonging to the disinherited of the earth!

With neither club or statute to compel them, I wonder what induced these men to go to their death with greater fortitude than do soldiers on the battlefield? Why, it is human nature, stripped of all social artifice, of the deadening and dulling chase for material gains. Human nature, come into its own! Into its deep social kinship which so far has only expressed itself in great stress but which points to still greater possibilities for the future, when man shall no longer his brother maim!

*Denver Post,* 21 April 1912, p. 8.

THE OCCASION OF THE SEASON
A GREAT DEBATE ON
Direct Action VERSUS Political Action
AT CARNEGIE HALL 57th Street and Seventh Avenue
Friday Evening, February 2, 8 o'Clock

# ANARCHISM

⌐ VS ⌐

SOCIALISM

BETWEEN

EMMA GOLDMAN,
the world's most famous and
greatest Anarchist.
FOR DIRECT ACTION.

SOL FIELDMAN,
Socialist orator and
debater.
FOR POLITICAL ACTION.

Flyer for a debate on anarchism versus socialism held between Emma Goldman and Sol Fieldman of the Socialist Party of America at Carnegie Hall. Goldman often debated prominent socialists, drawing large crowds hungry for clarification and excited to witness a spirited fight. (EGP, Third Party Newsclippings File)

MY DEAR MR. BONFILS:—

Since I received your very kind letter, I have gone through the horrors of hell, as you probably know by this time from the telegraphic dispatches. I am unable, at this particular moment to give all the details that happened in San Diego during my one day's stay there.[1] I have attempted in as cool and impartial manner as I am capable of giving some idea as to what was really done to Dr. Reitman and myself and I hope that you can see your way clear in printing the article in the next Sunday edition of The Post.[2] As to payment, you can do as you please about it. Aside of all the physical torture that we have endured, the experiences in that California City has cost something like $75.00, the Doctor being robbed of every stitch of clothes and made to walk thirty miles in a naked condition, not to speak of the fact that we have lost considerable because of our meeting being suppressed. But in sending you the article, I am not so much concerned in the money side, as I am in the desire that your readers in Denver and wherever your paper reaches, should know the absolute truth and nothing but the truth of the conditions prevalent in San Diego.[3]

Please remember that the things which have been meted out to Dr. Reitman and myself have been going on now for over two months, only that the unfortunate victims of the mob in San Diego have so far been half-starved, obscure victims beings of our present social injustice and that as a result, few papers would credit what they had to say. You have met me Mr. Bonfils, so have a great many people in Denver. You will therefore believe me when I tell you that what I have said in the article is not only uncolored,

1. For the details of EG and BR's experience in San Diego, see the "The Outrage of San Diego," Article in *Mother Earth*, June 1912, below.
2. EG wrote to *Denver Post* co-owner and editor Frederick Gilmer Bonfils (1861–1933) asking that he publish an article she wrote about her experiences at San Diego; the article was not printed, but a copy of the article EG sent to Dr. E. B. Foote identifies it as "The Outrage of San Diego." Bonfils, rumored to have previously been a lottery con man, edited a newspaper known for its sensationalist journalism and dramatic style of reportage.
3. Although no article by EG was published in the *Denver Post*, newspapers across the country carried the story of EG and BR's experience in San Diego. See, for example, "San Diego Bars Reitman Angry Citizens Drive Anarchist from City," *St. Louis Post Dispatch*, 15 May 1912; "Tar for Dr. Reitman, Emma Goldman Fled," *New York Times*, 16 May 1912; "Vigilantes Oust Two Anarchists," *Chicago Tribune*, 16 May 1912; "Federal Inquiry on Reitman Government Takes Up Attacks on IWW Men at San Diego," *New York Times*, 18 May 1912; "Begins IWW Inquiry Federal Grand Jury Takes Up San Diego Riots," *New York Tribune*, 19 May 1912.

The San Diego

**16 PAGES 16** Home Edition

FULL LEASED WIRE SERVICE O' THE UNITED PRE

THIRTY-FIRST YEAR   WHOLE NO. 9628                     WEDNESDAY, MAY 15, 1912.

# TARRY COAT FOR DR. REITMAN
# AS EMMA GOLDMAN LEAVES CITY

## ANARCHISTS LEAVE IN THE EARLY MORNING AFTER A DEMONSTRATION

Crowds at Grant Hotel Threaten Both; Miss Goldman Spirited Out to Train; "Star Spangled Banner" Sung by Crowd; Socialists in Convention Want Matter Looked Into; Miss Goldman in Los Angeles.

### Winner in California Primary

KNIGHTS ON

Front-page article in the *San Diego Sun* reporting the tarring of Ben Reitman by "vigilantes," on 14 May 1912, one of many ongoing features in the newspaper on the Free Speech fight raging in the city at that time. (Doe Library, University of California, Berkeley)

but as a matter of fact, does not give half the side of the occurrence. The other half is not printable.

The Governer of the State of California has sent a personal representative who has taken sworn testimony of the most incriminating character,[4] but so terrible has been the pressure so far brought to bear by a priveliged class of money mongers, that even

4. California governor Hiram Warren Johnson (1866–1945) was an attorney and founding member of the Progressive Party in 1912; he was the vice presidential running mate on Theodore Roosevelt's unsuccessful 1912 Progressive ticket. Johnson built his reputation on his successful prosecution of San Francisco political boss Abe Ruef, on breaking the Southern Pacific Railroad's domination of California politics, and on securing progressive legislative reform. Johnson appointed Harris Weinstock to act as his special commissioner to investigate the events in San Diego. Weinstock's investigations concluded on 21 April 1912, after he had taken extensive oral evidence from both sides. Published in mid-May 1912, Weinstock's report, *Report of Harris Weinstock Commissioner to Investigate the Recent Disturbances in the City of San Diego, California to his Excellency Hiram W. Johnson, Governor of California, Sacramento, 1912* (printed nearly in full in the *San Francisco Bulletin* of 18 May), took an equivocal position. The report both condemned the IWW tactics and denounced the vigilantes, suggesting, also, that the police in San Diego exercised "needless brutality."

that testimony has not been given to the public. I am hoping to get ahold of it soon and if I do will submit it to you, provided you will be brave enough to publish it, of which I am sure I have no doubt. But meanwhile, I ask you in behalf of the hundreds of victims who have endured torture and indignities at the hands of that blood-thirsty mob of San Diego and also in behalf of the principles of fair play and freedom of expression, to publish my article on our San Diego experience.

I thank you very much indeed for your kind appreciation of my ability and also for the good will you express in wishing to help me to come before the Public. I agree with you that it is largely a matter of lack of understanding, but unless some papers are as brave as you have been to give the truth a hearing, I do not see how the people are ever to know what the ideal I stand for really represents.

If nothing interferes, I hope to avail myself of the opportunity you wish to give me during the month of July. I would like you, if possible, to let me know in advance just what line of articles you want me to write. It would save considerable time, as I could prepare material in advance.

About the McNamara proposition, I will see what I can do. Of course, it depends entirely on the two men. If they do not want me to make public my interview with them,[5] I certainly could not do it, but if they consent, I mean to submit it to you and then let you do whatever you please with it. The Posts of April 30th, Tuesday,[6] have not arrived. The Fargo express Company seem to know nothing about it. I am very anxious to get them and would ask you to please make another shipment to my name, of Jefferson Square Hall, Golden Gate Avenue, The Terminal Hotel San Francisco, Cal. Also, if possible, I would like another fifty each of every issue containing my articles. I have large demands for them from almost every part of Europe and this country.

Thanking you for your great kindness and hoping that you will print the article. If you do, I should want five 100 hundred copies sent to the San Francisco address.

VERY SINCERELY,
EMMA GOLDMAN

TLS, IU-U. Addressed to Fred G. Bonfils, the *Denver Post*, Denver, Colo.

---

5. There is no extant public record of this interview by EG with John and James McNamara.
6. The *Denver Post* of 30 April had published the last of three articles by EG on "the social unrest," titled, "Greed of Capital Basis of Social Unrest Today," 30 April 1912.

MY DEAR MR. WOOD:

I suppose you have read of the patriotic insanity now prevalent in San Diego which has resulted in the tarring, beating and also some other tortures of Ben Reitman, and the mobbing of myself. We are not sorry for our experience because it has forced a situation that has been going on for three months[1] to a national issue.

I have gone through much in my life and have seen police and mob brutality on more than one occasion, but the conditions in San Diego are beyond anything I have ever experienced. If only the workers would learn the use of direct action from their enemies matters might come to a break soon. As it is, the Industrial Workers and other victims have practiced passive resistance while the good Christians and patriotic citizens are exercising direct action.

It seems to me that something must be done, and that soon, to bring pressure upon the City of San Diego; and unless it be wide-spread publicity, I do not know what else could be done. With that in view, I am sending you some clippings giving you the account of our experience, and also a copy of an article which I have sent to "The Denver Post",[2] hoping that you may make use of some of it for the Portland papers, or possibly "The Pacific Monthly".[3]

I am also enclosing tickets to my forthcoming lectures which will begin June 2d at Christensen's Hall.[4] You may be able to interest some of your friends. Apropos of my coming: I intend to start a drama class while in Portland which I have done with great success in a number of cities.[5] I mean by that a series of afternoon talks on the drama

---

1. The San Diego City Council first banned street speaking in a forty-eight-block area at the center of town on 8 January 1912. This ordinance was followed by one passed on 13 February, which gave the police the right to disperse crowds of people anywhere within the city limits. The police began vigorously enforcing this law on 28 March, arresting large numbers of IWW members.

2. No account of the San Diego incident appeared in the *Denver Post*.

3. The *Pacific Monthly*, published in Portland, Oregon, from October 1898 until December 1911, when it was acquired by the more conservative *Sunset Magazine*. Wood, who had been a regular contributor to the *Pacific Monthly*, did not write for *Sunset Magazine*.

4. EG was scheduled to speak 2 June at Christiansen's Hall in Portland, Oregon, on the topics "Anarchism the Moving Spirit in the Labor Struggle" and "The Failure of Christianity."

5. In 1911 and early 1912 EG gave lectures on the drama in several U.S. cities, including Dayton, Indianapolis, Chicago, and New York. These drama lectures focused primarily on two plays, Eugene Brieux's *Maternity* and Henrik Ibsen's *An Enemy of the People*. In April EG initiated a modern drama course in Denver, with the help of Ellen A. Kennan, a teacher at the Denver East Side High School, and Ida Kruse McFarlane, a Denver professor of English literature and drama and head of the Department of English Literature at the University of Denver. The class continued to meet in

---

as a great social educator. This isn't intended to be for the public at large, but mainly for professional people who, as you know, need education much more than working people do. May I count on your assistance? I mean, would it be possible for you to interest a number of people in my drama classes? Perhaps some of the people who attended Brown's course could be interested.[6]

We leave here on the 29th of May. If you have any suggestions to make I would be glad to hear from you until then.

Sincerely,
Emma Goldman

TLS, Charles Erskine Scott Wood Papers, CU-B.

---

her absence under the direction of McFarlane. EG returned to Denver in late June and continued the course four nights a week for two weeks beginning 2 July.

6. William Thurston Brown was the founder and organizer of a short-lived but active Modern Day School, associated with the Ferrer Association in Portland, Oregon. The school opened in October 1911, on the second anniversary of Ferrer's execution, and closed within two years of its founding.

My dear Mr. Schroeder:

As usual you are the most prompt and generous of my friends,[1] of which I thank you very much. I haven't yet heard from Dr. Foote and if his condition is as bad as you say, it is most likely that I will not hear from him.[2] However, whether I do or not I feel that unless your contribution comes from the Free Speech fund,[3] I have no right to it, because I know that you are not engaged in the cupon-cutting business. I have written you day before yesterday, enclosing $200, on account of my debt to you, and when you write me in reply, I hope you will be perfectly frank with me about the check which I returned herewith. If the money comes from the Free Speech fund and you want me to have it, I will take the amount off the hundred dollars I owe you; but I do not feel justified to accept anything coming from your own pocket as long as I do not absolutely need it.

It is a great pity that people are never interested in things further than their noses; else the San Diego situation should have aroused the whole country. Think of it! Day before yesterday a fellow by the name of Parsons got up in the unrestricted quarter and quoted a passage of the Bible.[4] For that he was most brutally kicked about and finally arrested. Isn't that going some? Well, I don't care about how the eastern people feel in the matter.[5] I am devoting most of my time to arouse public interest and I am glad to

---

1. Theodore Schroeder was by 1912 the principal administrator of the Free Speech League and a regular financial supporter of EG and *Mother Earth*.
2. At the time of this letter Edward Bond Foote Jr. was already very ill with neuritis, a condition that gradually paralyzed him. He died on 12 October 1912.
3. Edward Bliss Foote (1829–1906) had left a large portion of his inheritance to his son, Edward Bond Foote, specifying that it be used to protect and secure freedom of speech and press. In his will he wrote, "give generously from the proceeds of my estate to all good movements for the maintenance of free press, free speech and free mails, the cause of heredity (i.e., stirpiculture, eugenics), liberalism, etc." (Foote and his contemporaries used terms such as "stirpiculture," the production of pure races or stocks by careful breeding, and "eugenics" to justify the need for what was later known as birth control.) The Free Speech League, established in 1902, had by 1906 been reinvigorated by Theodore Schroeder, the secretary of the league. In 1908 Foote Jr. established a fund for Schroeder and the league, allowing Schroeder to dedicate himself completely to the league and making its work more effective. *Mother Earth* and EG encouraged the creation of the fund, collecting funds for the Free Speech League at meetings, publishing collection details, and encouraging donations.
4. On 28 May 1912 IWW member A. B. Carson, in a test of the ordinance against public speaking in certain parts of San Diego, stood on a soapbox one hundred feet outside the prohibited area and read from the Bible. Carson was then accosted by police officer A. L. Hathaway, and when he attempted to run away, he was followed by a group of vigilantes, arrested, and taken into custody "for his own safety."
5. A reference to the apparent lack of interest on the part of people in the eastern United States to the brutality of the San Diego free speech fight.

say I have succeeded some, and mean to keep it up as long as I am on the coast. ~~I am~~
We are going to Portland and Seattle, having dates for the next two weeks,[6] and if at all
possible, we mean to go back to San Diego.[7] It is really for that reason that I was anxious
to have you speak to Dr. Foote, but I understand, of course, that it is quite impossible
in his present condition. I hope he writes. You can reach me until June 16th, General
Delivery, Seattle.

EMMA GOLDMAN

TLS, Morris Library, ICarbS.

6. In Portland EG gave a series of lectures sponsored by the Portland Modern School from 1 June to 6
   June, then lectured in Seattle from 9 June to 16 June, before traveling back east.
7. EG and BR did not return to San Diego until the following year. On 20 May 1913 they traveled to
   San Diego, where they were immediately arrested, put in jail, and then placed on a train back to Los
   Angeles for their own safety.

Ben Reitman on the day after he had been abducted by vigilantes from his hotel in San Diego, taken to Escondido, stripped, covered in tar and sage-brush, and left naked in the desert. Rare photograph, likely taken by a government agent with notation on the back identifying the store from which his new clothing was purchased. (Attorney General US Webb Records, California State Archives).

Article in ***MOTHER EARTH***

New York, June 1912

# The Outrage of San Diego

Fifty years ago a young lawyer looked out from his office window and saw a well-dressed, infuriated, mad, screaming mob, dragging a man by a rope along the streets of Boston. That man was Lloyd Garrison, and the young lawyer America's greatest orator, Wendell Phillips.[1] So tremendous was the impression made upon Phillips by the terrible, savage sight in an American city, that he became the fiery exponent of the great human cause for which Lloyd Garrison had been assaulted by the mob on that day.

Since then we have no doubt advanced along the lines of intellectual and social endeavor. Certainly we have learned that justice and truth, for which both Wendell Phillips and Lloyd Garrison made such a brave and gallant fight, represent great ideals, now being accepted by millions of people.

But if Lloyd Garrison and Wendell Phillips had been in San Diego a little before 1 o'clock on the 14th of May, 1912, they would have realized that very little, if anything, has changed since their time. There was the same well-dressed, howling, hooting, and blood-thirsty mob, the only difference being that the victims were two Anarchists instead of Abolitionists.[2] Equally so they would have realized that it is to-day as great a crime to work for the emancipation of the white slave as it was to work for the cause of the black slave fifty years ago.[3]

---

1. This incident, in which a mob of respectable Boston citizens violently dragged William Lloyd Garrison through the streets for being a spokesman for abolition and editor of the *Liberator*, took place on 21 October 1835. William Lloyd Garrison (1805–1879) was an American abolitionist and reformer. He helped organize the New England Anti-Slavery Society (1832) and American Anti-Slavery Society (1833). Believing that every man had the God-given right to be free from bondage, Garrison renounced the Church and State, calling the U.S. Constitution a "pro-slavery document." Garrison helped edit *The Genius of Universal Emancipation* (1821–1839) and later published the anti-slavery paper the *Liberator* (1831–1865). Initially, Garrison was a believer in nonviolent resistance, and EG considered him a courageous and principled American whose position on religion and government resonated with the essence of the anarchist tradition. As a result of this incident Wendell Phillips (1811–1884) entered the abolitionist movement. He contributed to the *Liberator* and in 1840 was a delegate to the World Anti-Slavery Convention in London. A member of the American Anti-Slavery Society, Phillips also campaigned for women's suffrage, the rights of labor, and the abolition of capital punishment. He would later be an enthusiastic supporter of the Russian revolutionaries of the 1870s and 1880s.
2. EG removed a clause from the end of this sentence that had appeared in a previous draft: "and the mob did not have the rope."
3. EG entirely excluded a paragraph from the final essay that appeared in a draft: "However, I do not so much condemn the mob, as it neither reasons nor is it very eminable to reason, but I do

On my previous trips to California I never failed to speak in San Diego, and I have never been disturbed. This time I had a double reason for visiting that city. First, to lecture;[4] and, secondly, to learn for myself of the outrages which had been committed against the I. W. W. men during the last three months.[5] Dr. Reitman and I could have slipped in quietly, but we had nothing to hide. Besides, we wanted to give the authorities a chance to make good their claim that they were not in league with the savagery and cruelties committed by the so-called patriotic citizens of San Diego.

We wrote the Mayor,[6] notifying him of the time and the place of the lectures, and asking him to keep his subordinates from suppressing the right of free speech. In reply we heard from Chief of Police Wilson,[7] ordering us to stay away from San Diego. As we

---

condemn those who, for months past have filled the people of San Diego with prejudice and with blood-curdling stories and with the spirit of vengeance. Those who have done so do not represent ~~rebels~~ rabble, but boast of belonging to the so-called better class of citizens, lawyers, doctors, real estate men, the police and one of the leading papers and I say this ~~not without any absolute truth,~~ but because I have been there and have been able to get sufficient data that would send every one of them up to the penitentiary for years, if there were a Judge and jury in San Diego brave enough to accept the ~~case~~ evidence."

4. According to a draft of this article, EG had intended to discuss Henrik Ibsen's *An Enemy of the People* and Eugène Brieux's *Maternity*, both of which were often the subject of her modern drama lectures and were later analyzed in detail in *The Social Significance of the Modern Drama* (1914). She was not planning to directly address the situation of the IWW in San Diego.

5. In early February San Diego police began arresting IWW members and other activists for violating a new ordinance, which rescinded their right to give public talks on street corners in a designated area of the city's downtown district. Political and religious groups affected by the ban formed the California Free Speech League. The San Diego free speech fight was among the most violent of the IWW campaigns against local anti-street-speaking laws waged since 1909 throughout the western United States. The laws were often initiated and supported by merchant and manufacturing associations and designed to prevent the IWW from organizing unskilled and migrant laborers. "Wobblies" came to San Diego from all over the United States, intent on speaking in public places, then peacefully surrendering to mass arrests, packing the local jails, and overwhelming the courts. This strategy had succeeded in Spokane and Fresno, where the laws against street speaking were repealed in response to the onslaught of Wobbly demonstrators. City authorities in San Diego, however, responded with more restrictive ordinances and harsher tactics, in conjunction with tacit approval of vigilante squads that included leading San Diego businessmen and professionals. California newspaper magnate John D. Spreckels (who owned the pro-vigilante *San Diego Union*) and his Los Angeles counterpart, Harrison Gray Otis, leaders in the open-shop movement (a movement to keep businesses union free), supported sensationalist fears, fueling the brutality and violence. Wobblies were taken out of San Diego prisons at night by vigilantes and beaten, trains rolling into the city carrying its members were stopped, and suspected members were expelled and attacked. The San Diego atrocities continued for months, resulting in several deaths, provoking appeals to the state government by organized labor, and in April 1912 resulting in an investigation under Governor Hiram Johnson by Harris Weinstock. Despite Weinstock's report (which likened the breach of civil liberties in San Diego to those in tsarist Russia) and extensive coverage in the national press, neither state nor federal government decisively intervened in the conflict. Although threats by California attorney general U. S. Webb against vigilante leaders put an end to much of the overt violence, the suppression of free speech in San Diego continued. Upon EG and BR's return to San Diego in May 1913 they were jailed immediately, pursued by a mob, and again forced to leave the city without holding their scheduled meeting.

6. James E. Wadham was mayor of San Diego from 1911 to 1913.

7. Jefferson "Keno" Wilson (1862–1934), San Diego police chief from 3 May 1909 until 10 January 1917.

could not possibly recognize the high-handed authority of this uniformed cossack, we determined to carry out our schedule as originally planned.

On arriving in the city we saw a large crowd, but paid no further attention to it, quietly passing to the auto-bus of the U. S. Grant Hotel. Then the mob outbreak began, the moment our presence became known. I shall not attempt to describe the language, the madness, the atrocities that raged around us. It seemed as if the entire city had turned into an insane asylum.

But for the pluck of the chauffeur, we would have been mobbed there and then. He raced at wild speed, with several cars full of vigilantes in mad pursuit, screaming, yelling, and cursing the chauffeur. Finally we reached the U. S. Grant Hotel, in our company being Mr. and Mrs. E. E. Kirk. Mr. Kirk, though under indictment himself, showed wonderful bravery in meeting us at the depot[8]—an act which was certainly as heroic as that of Wendell Phillips, who rushed out to the rescue of Lloyd Garrison.

No objection was made at the hotel. We were assigned to our rooms and, after some rest, we went down to the grill-room for our luncheon. Everything seemed quiet, when about 4 P.M. the head clerk announced that he would have to transfer us to other rooms, as the vigilantes had gotten hold of the registry and were determined to get us out of the hotel. Later the manager himself, Mr. Holmes, arrived, assuring us that we were perfectly safe under his roof, but that he could not permit us to go down to the lobby or restaurant, or anywhere in the hotel, which meant nothing less than incarceration. Again we waited for some time to map out a plan of action, but at 7.30 P.M. the horror of our reception was repeated, only in a more hideous manner.

Five thousand people, preceded by a hundred autos, with fashionably-dressed women

---

Beginning in 1884, Wilson worked in a range of law enforcement positions in Southern California, including constable and city marshal of Oceanside, U.S. Customs deputy collector and inspector, and in 1899 patrolman for the San Diego Police Department. As chief of police, Wilson presided over the police action against the IWW demonstrations in San Diego in 1912, which included mass arrests, deportations from the city, and the use of fire hoses to break up crowds. He was also aware of, if not complicit in, the outbreaks of vigilante violence in San Diego that included the kidnapping of and violence against Ben Reitman. Public reaction to police tactics led to Wilson's expulsion from the office of police chief in 1917, after which he served as a desk sergeant and then as deputy U.S. marshal of the San Diego office.

8. Socialist attorney Ernest E. Kirk (1872–1950) had successfully defended EG and BR in San Francisco in 1909 against charges of conspiracy (see vol. 2, *Making Speech Free*, pp. 405–9), after which he remained in close contact with them. He acted as their personal attorney, chaired EG's 1911 meetings in San Diego, and at EG's request rented the hall for her May 1912 lecture series. As the attorney of the California Free Speech League, he represented the IWW during the San Diego free speech fight (1912–1913). While staying at the U. S. Grant Hotel, Kirk received death threats from the mob assembled outside. For his participation in the San Diego free speech campaign, Kirk was charged with criminal conspiracy to violate San Diego city ordinance 4623—the ban on public speaking downtown—ultimately spending six months in jail and paying a $300 fine. See *People of the State of California v. Ernest E. Kirk*: Affidavit, 18 May 1912 (*EGP*, reel 56). Kirk's brief at his trial was later published as *Is Free Speech Right or Wrong: Brief of E. E. Kirk Before the Common Council of San Diego* (San Diego: San Diego Local of the Socialist Party, 1912). The Kirks were not mentioned in EG's initial draft of this article.

and men as their occupants, with American flags, their riot-whistles creating a deafening noise, surrounded the hotel. Five hundred of these maniacs, led by a good Christian and American patriot, Francis Bierman, reporter on the *San Diego Union*, entered the hotel lobby, unfurled the American flag, compelled everybody to sing the "Star Spangled Banner" as an inspiration for their heroic work, then walked up to Manager Holmes and demanded: "Turn over the two damned Anarchists to us, or we will take you." Mr. Holmes replied that he couldn't do that. That it was the custom of the hotel to protect its guests; but that if they would quiet down, he would see Miss Goldman and induce her to leave the city. Thereupon the committee said they would wait, but would return, reinforced, raid the hotel, drag every guest out of the rooms until they would locate us. If they should fail in that, Mr. Holmes would have to pay for it with his life.

About 10 o'clock Mr. Holmes came to us and told us that he could no longer guarantee our safety, but that if we would leave he would give us protection. That we refused to do. Equally so, to act upon his suggestion to ask the Chief of Police for protection. We said that when we decided to go, we would leave as we had arrived—openly and without the support of the authorities. While we were discussing the matter, we were interrupted by violent knocks on the door, and a man (whom we took for a detective, but who afterwards proved to be a vigilante) stepped in and informed Mr. Holmes that the Chief of Police, with other men from the department, were at Mr. Holmes' office and demanded to see us.

Strange to say, Reitman showed greater intuition than myself, immediately suspecting foul play. He said that the Chief should come to us, but to avoid argument I suggested that we go down to the office of Mr. Holmes. There we found six men; one, a certain J. M. Porter,[9] I recognized as the leading vigilante of the afternoon mob, and also the one who threatened E. E. Kirk's life in my presence in the hotel lobby. We were then informed that the Chief was in the next room and would see me first. Even then I did not suspect the conspiracy to which the police and even Mr. Holmes himself had lent a willing hand. How could I? We were not in Russia. We were in San Diego, in an American city, in the leading hotel of the town, at 10 o'clock in the evening. How could I for a moment suspect that human beings would be so bestial and degenerate as to commit a thing which would put to shame even Russia?

My conversation with the Chief of Police, his assistant, the head of detectives, and some other officers lasted but a few minutes. They offered their protection, which I refused, telling the Chief that all he had to do was to invoke the ordinance which has made it a felony to gather in the business districts of the city and for which three hun-

---

9. John M. Porter was a wealthy real estate developer and building contractor who, with the reporter Francis Bierman, headed the vigilante mob known as the Citizens' Committee. He was charged with contempt of court in May 1912, after IWW attorney Fred H. Moore petitioned for a citation against Porter and fifteen other vigilantes for interfering with an officer of law in discharge of his duties and also for protection of the court from violence after Porter verbally threatened Moore. Porter was later released by the Superior Court. Porter was identified by Ernest E. Kirk as one of the vigilantes who threatened him outside the U. S. Grant Hotel on 14 May.

dred I. W. W. men had been beaten, clubbed, arrested, and subjected to every cruelty and indignation imaginable. But the Chief replied that he couldn't do that, because the mob had outgrown his power. I then suggested that he resign, as he declared himself unfit to be a protector of so-called law and order. I asked him to let me speak to the mob from the window, as the office was on the first floor. I have faced mobs before in my life and have invariably succeeded in soothing them. But even that he wouldn't do, and so the conversation came to an end, the Chief giving me the cheerful assurance that he would turn me over to the mob the following morning. I replied that if I had to die, I was just as willing to die at the hands of the mob as at the hands of the police.

I immediately went to the room where I had left the Doctor. I found it locked, and then I suddenly realized the whole contemptible conspiracy. I demanded that the door be opened, and of course there was no Ben Reitman. I turned to the Chief of Police and told him that if any serious injury should come to Reitman, or if he should lose his life, I would hold the Chief responsible for it; and, furthermore, that I would come to San Diego and take his miserable life; nor would I run away, as I am always ready to stand the consequences for anything I say or do. The brave Chief grew pale and said, "Why, we had nothing to do with it. You know yourself, we were in the next room." Which only added to his cowardice, as the whole wretched business was carried out with the consent and connivance of the police department.

For four hours I paced the floor of my room in agony, not knowing what had become of Ben Reitman, and knowing still less what to do, because I could not communicate with our friends in San Diego, as that would have meant turning them over to the police. At 2 A.M., May 15th, the house detective and another man came to the room. Nature does create some freaks. The man with the house detective had a most wonderful face, kind, tender, and human, but he introduced himself as a detective. He reminded me of a beautiful woman with a rotten soul. He said that he would not lie in telling me that he came from Ben Reitman, but that he was given absolute assurance on the part of some authoritative people that no harm had come to him, although he had been taken out of town and was now on his way to Los Angeles. I then called up Mrs. Estelle Kirk, giving the name of the detective, whom she evidently knew, as she told me that he was the only decent man in the entire department; that therefore it might be possible that he was telling the truth. But I did not feel inclined to believe, as I never yet have found a detective who can tell the truth. But the manager of the hotel begged and pleaded with me to leave. He said that he had sheltered us as long as he could; that he didn't ask us to come in the first place; that we were taking undue advantage of him; and that we were ruining the hotel and jeopardizing his life—all of which was true. I felt I had no right to drive the man into a still more desperate position, and therefore I decided to leave on the 2:45 train for Los Angeles. I ordered a taxi. On the way to the depot I could see nothing of a suspicious character. The streets were deserted, and San Diego had returned to its normal sleepy state.

I was just about to enter the car when six automobiles with the same maniacs—patriotic citizens—whisked up to the station, and then I felt myself bodily lifted up by the trainmen, pushed into the car, and the door locked. The train did not pull out for another eight minutes, the most terrible, the most hideous eight minutes of my life. There were the good Christian, law-abiding, respectable citizens, and the howl they raised, the language they used, the efforts they made to break into the train, are beyond description, beyond anything that the most depraved human beings could be capable of. After a seemingly endless trip, in the desperate hope that Reitman would join me at some of the stations, I finally landed in Los Angeles, only to find that he had not arrived. Later I learned of the horrible things that happened to him, the details of which our readers will find in his own article.[10]

I have, of course, been interfered with on previous occasions in a number of American cities. Free speech in this country depends entirely on the whims and arbitrary will of ignorant police officials. But it was left to San Diego, a town which Nature herself has intended man to be happy and peaceful in, to suppress the right of free speech and assemblage and to outrage every vestige of personal liberty in a manner which would have put to shame the Spanish Inquisition. It was left to citizens who swear by law and order to break not only their own written laws, but every principle of decency and humanity.

Ostensibly the organization now known as the I. W. W. is responsible for the excitement and the bloodthirsty attitude of the people of San Diego. But after all, that is the indictment made against every organization and idea which the popular mind has not yet accepted. But whether the I. W. W. be right or wrong, they cannot possibly be so wrong as the people of San Diego who are brutally suppressing the right of free expression and who are committing acts of violence and outrage which would put every one of them, including the entire police department, into the penitentiary for life, if the judiciary of that city were not as cowardly and craven as its citizens.

Men and women who are not ready to listen to contrary opinion on any given subject, thereby condemn themselves to the grossest ignorance and the most outrageous tyranny. If what the I. W. W., or any other undesirable, have to say is wrong, it will die of itself a much quicker death than if these people are beaten, clubbed, tarred, and driven out like wild beasts. Nor can anything I stand for be killed by mob-butchery or by police violence. The issue of Free Speech is one of the most vital and fundamental in America, and the very moment any given section of the country undertakes to suppress freedom of expression, it at the same time undermines every principle of liberty and condemns itself to death.

Fortunately for Reitman, he had money and his return ticket to Los Angeles. He could at least help himself somewhat after the terrible experience. But what about the hundreds of men, without friends or money, who were subjected to the same terrible outrage, except that their bodies were not burned or tarred? I understand that the Savior of

10. On the night of 14 May vigilantes, including businessmen, doctors, and lawyers, took Reitman twenty miles outside of town, stripped and tortured him, burning "IWW" into his buttocks with a lighted cigar. Covered with tar and sagebrush, he was made to kiss the American flag, forced to sing the national anthem, and then beaten before being left to make his way to Los Angeles in his underwear and vest. See Ben L. Reitman, "The Respectable Mob," *Mother Earth* 7 (June 1912): 109–14.

the Christian people said, "Whatsoever ye do unto the least of these my children, ye do unto me." And yet the people who call themselves Christians and worship the memory of Christ, continue in a brutal, savage manner to outrage life, to beat and club men, to drive them out of town, to leave them penniless and without food on the deserts of California.

Verily, man's power of endurance is a very elastic thing, or the vigilantes would have long ere this been given a dose of their own medicine.

However, it has been said that if there is one innocent man in a city, that city will be saved. And there is such a man in San Diego—Mr. George Edwards,[11] who is at the head of the Music Institute. At the critical moment, when even the bravest people lost their courage, this man, who had never before seen or heard me, offered me his hall for a lecture. I felt, however, that to accept Mr. Edwards' kindness and hospitality would have meant to endanger his life, which I certainly could not do. But it was his spirit of kindliness and the great friendship shown by the Kirks that gave the only spark of life and warmth in that benighted, maddened town, San Diego.

Life under our present system is not so great a thing that he who has an ideal and loves liberty should not be willing to part with it. But life in San Diego is worse than death. I cannot believe that the number of intelligent people in the United States is so small that they could not bring moral pressure upon that city to stop its atrocities. It was the intelligent minority which forced the Southern planter to stop his murderous treatment of the black man. Surely the same can be done to-day. It is with that in view that this article is written, and not in complaint of anything we have endured. It is also because I feel that the crimes, the savagery, and the unspeakable cruelties perpetrated by the San Diego thugs, with the connivance of the police and the support of the *San Diego Union* and *Tribune*, must be brought to an end. Crime begets crime, and violence inevitably gives birth to violence.[12] If San Diego is justified in violence, why not its victims? To avoid both, I appeal to all fair-minded and liberty-loving people throughout the country to join in a determined campaign against San Diego and its horrors.

Emma Goldman.

*Mother Earth* 7 (June 1912): 115–22. Widely circulated among English-speaking anarchists, this article was also translated into Italian, appearing under the title "Contro la Vandea!" in *Cronaca Sovversiva* on 1 June 1912.

11. George Edwards, with a small group of San Diego residents, in 1912 established the Open Forum, a free speech organization to counter the activities of the city's vigilantes. By EG's third visit to the city in 1915, the Open Forum's membership had grown to several hundred, according to Edwards's article in *Mother Earth* (July 1915). Also a musician and composer, he set to music Voltairine de Cleyre's poem "The Hurricane" (1913), Olive Schreiner's short piece "A Dream of Wild Bees," and Dostoyevsky's "The Grand Inquisitor" from *The Brothers Karamozov*.
12. In a letter sent to the *New York World* (16 May 1912) and published in the June 1912 *Mother Earth*, AB, Harry Kelly and Hippolyte Havel echoed EG's words and warned that the violence of the San Diego vigilantes may be answered in kind, stating, "Violence begets violence. Terror from above breeds terror below. . . . We feel that the Anarchists and other social rebels will be forced, as a matter of self-defense, to answer violence with violence."

DEAR COMRAD:

No doubt the papers of Austria[1] have reported the events of San Diego, California,[2] as they have really been of national importance. I shall not attempt to describe the horror of the twenty-four hours that we were made to go through while in that City. I am, however, sending you clippings, which give a fairly accurate account of the things that happened there. Besides that we have sent a lot of material to "Mother Earth" which will appear in our current issue.

Things have certainly changed since you have been here dear Comrad, and if they go on in the same way pretty much longer we will have a skirmish that the privileged class least expects. There is a most wonderful awakening all through the country in behalf of our ideas, especially in behalf of the radical methods which we have propagated for so many years, direct action and the general strike. Their efficacy was demonstrated in the Lawrence, Mass. strike, in fact to such an extent that the capitalist press is up in arms against us and the I. W. W. because of the very force of our tactics.[3] The pity is that the ranks of the I. W. W. are sadly lacking in able and intellectual men and women, and also

1. Rudolf Grossman (1882–1942; aliases Kl. Morleit, Fr. Stürmer, and Pierre Ramus) was an Austrian anarchist and editor of *Der Zeitgeist*. Grossman was arrested on 18 June 1902, with Luigi Galleani and William MacQueen, for "inciting to riot" at a violent demonstration during a strike in Paterson, New Jersey. See vol. 2, *Making Speech Free*, pp. 91–94. Jumping bail a short time after, Grossmann fled first to England and then to Vienna. There he continued his political work under the pseudonym Pierre Ramus. After settling in Austria, Grossmann edited *Wohlstand für Alle* (Wealth for All) (1907–1914). He was active in the birth control movement in Vienna. Following the outbreak of World War I, Grossmann would be imprisoned for anti-militarist activities. Grossmann corresponded with EG during the period of this volume and contributed to *Mother Earth* in December 1913, writing the report "Anarchism in German-Speaking Countries."

2. A reference to EG and BR's experiences in San Diego during the IWW free speech fight there.

3. On 11 January 1912 3,500 textile mill operatives, the majority of whom were women, marched out of the Everett Mill in Lawrence, Massachusetts, to protest a wage cut. Workers in other mills followed, and by 13 January more than 23,000 mill workers, coordinated in large part by IWW organizers, were met with brutal attacks by the police and the militia—effectively imposing martial law. The troops, under the command of Colonel Sweester, would occupy the city until 23 February, when the police department resumed the task. On 29 January an onlooker was killed during a clash between strikers and the police. The next day, strike leaders Joseph Ettor and Arturo Giovannitti were blamed for the death and arrested on the charges of incitement to riot and as accessories to murder. Mill owners were forced to settle with the strikers in late February, securing a substantial victory for the workers by the time the strike was officially over on 14 March. Although EG did not actively participate in the Lawrence strike, she collected more than $950 for the strikers.

that the political spook is still rampant, although they have repudiated it from their party program,[4] but after all it is a young movement, and certainly is full of great promise.

When in New York I always follow up your work through your papers, but I can never do so while en route as I am busy every minute with our own immediate work.

How are you, and how is the movement growing in your part of the country? Write me a long letter and tell me all about it. I am intensely interested of course.

I do not know at this moment when I will be back in New York as I may remain in Denver, Colorado for a month to comply with the unusual request of a daily paper, the Denver Post, to contribute a series of articles on the Social Unrest and our ideas.[5] Certainly we do move, if a capitalist paper will offer an Anarchist, and especially such a one as myself, its columns for anarchist propaganda.

Hoping that you will give the San Diego struggle the widest publicity, and make your readers conversant with the work we are doing,

FRATERNALLY YOURS,
EMMA GOLDMAN

TLS, Pierre Ramus Archive, IISH. Handwritten at top: "Genosse Grossman" (Comrade Grossman).

4. At the IWW convention in 1908 delegates had voted by a small margin (35 to 32) to remove all reference to political action from the preamble of their constitution. The October 1908 *Mother Earth* praised the spirit of the revolutionary element among the delegates. See vol. 2, *Making Speech Free*, pp. 558–59.
5. EG contributed three articles on social unrest to the *Denver Post*. The articles, which appeared on 26, 28, and 30 April 1912, were "Nation Seethes in Social Unrest," "Woman Center of Social Storm Which Is Sweeping Us Along," and "Greed of Capital Basis of Social Unrest Today."

Interview in the *INDUSTRIAL WORKER*

*Spokane, Wash., 6 June 1912*

# Emma Goldman and Ben Reitman Tell of San Diego Experience.

**[By Caroline Nelson].**

The most fearless woman in America today undoubtedly is Emma Goldman. She told me that her first "crime" was committed in Russia when she was only eight years old. It happened in her own home. Her folks were farmers and had a servant girl, who got herself into trouble and was promptly kicked out into the cold world without any means.[1] Emma forthwith robbed her mother's strong-box and handed the proceeds to the outcast. I am not an anarchist because I can't subscribe to their philosophy, but I can admire a little woman who fought for years all alone for what is to her most sacred, and who went calmly on to fight in the teeth of all opposition.[2] A dozen women of the Emma Goldman type in the labor movement could give the movement a boost that would make it leap ahead with lightning speed. Unfortunately for our working men today the working women are not revolutionary and mostly have the absurd idea that by construing the workers' philosophy to mean nothing but a little reform they can do a whole lot of good. The socialist women in general are nothing short of a lot of geese, that confine themselves to cackling about uplifting the workers, and sprawl before upperclass or professional women who will condescend to grace their meeting to hand them out a little respectability. Not so Emma Goldman, she stands by her guns through thick and thin, and goes with the police to jail with the same defiance that she mounts the platform to speak to a hostile audience, if need be.

She says that she went to San Diego in the midst of the free speech fight to compel the capitalistic press of the country to take notice of it which she knew it would be com-

---

1. *LML* makes no mention of EG's family being farmers. Rather EG's father is identified as an innkeeper and a shopkeeper. The inn was in the rural Baltic town of Popelan.
2. The author of this article, Caroline Nelson (1868–1951), was a West Coast radical IWW organizer and birth control advocate. As an IWW reporter for *Industrial Worker*, she wrote articles on subjects that included antiracist tracts, reports on labor disputes, and birth control advocacy. Nelson spoke with EG at an antiwar meeting and presided over a birth strike meeting in 1914. She contributed articles to the *International Socialist Review* (between 1912 and 1914), the *Woman Rebel*, and *The Blast* (1916). And she wrote the pamphlets *Nature Talks on Economics: A Manual for Children and Teachers in Socialist Schools* (Chicago: C. H. Kerr, 1912), *Aggressive Unionism* (Tacoma, Wash.: S. T. Hammersmark, 1914), and *Living or Dead Labor Unions* . . . (Kansas City, Mo.: Labor Union Educational League, 1916).

pelled to do, not because she is respectable, but because she is the most disreputable woman in America. Her object was certainly accomplished. In her own way of telling it, the listener is brought face to face with the fact that our civilization has hoisted into power the most savage and brutal members in society, who drop their veneer of culture at the least provocation. Miss Goldman said in part of her experiences in San Diego:

"I have seen mobs many times, but I have never seen such a yelling mob of thousands of well-dressed people as the one which greeted us at the depot in San Diego. We had engaged rooms at the U. S. Grant Hotel and we managed to get on the automobile hotel bus. Six private automobiles followed. They were filled with upper class women who hooted and yelled: 'Give up that anarchist, we will strip her naked; we will tear out her guts.' Many other things were said by those 'cultured' women which could not be repeated in public. The working men having charge of the hotel automobile raced for their life to save us from the vigilantes, which closed in on us at every turn. At last we got to the hotel to our rooms. The mob was held at bay by the hotel manager outside. But after a while they stormed the hotel and demanded that we be delivered over to them. The manager told them that it was his custom to protect his guests. They then told him that they would ruin him and tear down the building to get us.

"Finally a hotel clerk came to us and said that the chief of police wanted to see us. We told him to send the police to our rooms, but he said that we must come down and see him in a private room. We went with the clerk, and I was taken by myself to a room where the chief of police, Wilson,[3] and a man that looked like a detective were awaiting me. 'We want you to sign a document demanding the protection of the police,' said Wilson. 'I shall do no such thing,' I said. 'The mob is beyond our control,' said Wilson. 'If the mob is beyond your control,' said I 'you are not fitted for your office and had better resign. Let me speak to the mob. I have soothed more than one mob.' But the chief of police refused to allow me to speak to the mob and the interview ended.

"When I returned to our rooms I found that Ben Reitman had been kidnaped by the vigilantes. I then returned to the chief of police and declared that I should hold him personally responsible for Reitman's life, that if any harm came to him he would have to pay for it, that I would come back to San Diego to take his life myself. Whereupon the official began to shake in his knees and declared that he had nothing to do with the kidnaping of Reitman.

"The manager again came to my room and said that he could not protect me from the mob, and asked me to leave the hotel, that I had no right to stay there and ruin him, as he had not asked me to come. I decided to leave on the next train for Los Angeles. The mob outside the hotel again followed me up in their automobiles. I reached the train and just as I stepped on the ground the vigilantes closed in on me and were on the point of grab-

3. San Diego police chief Jefferson "Keno" Wilson. For more information on Wilson, see "The Outrage of San Diego," Article in *Mother Earth*, June 1912, above.

bing me when the trainmen rescued me and lifted me on board the train and slammed the car door in the face of the howling mob."

Ben Reitman's story is almost unbelievable. He says: "The moment Miss Goldman was out of the way a half dozen men clutched hold of me. One put his hand over my mouth. They threw me in a waiting automobile in the bottom and began to torture me and hysterically calling me by the vilest names. One of the men urinated on me, while others held me down. They took me twenty miles out in the desert where they stopped and threw me out. Immediately they tore off my clothes and threw me on the ground and with tar taken from a can traced I.W.W. on my back and a doctor burned the letters in with a lighted cigar. I was then allowed to put on my underclothes because the Christian gentlemen thought I might meet some ladies and shock them. I was also allowed to put on my vest. Then I was made to run the gauntlet of fourteen of these ruffians, who told me that they were not working men, but doctors, lawyers, real estate and business men. They tortured me and humiliated me in the most unspeakable manner. One of them was to put my cane in my rectum. Three hundred I.W.W.'s had gone through a similar torture before me by these Christian gentlemen."

Emma Goldman declared that she had seen many mobs, but in no instance had the mobs been made up of working people, but always of the respectable citizens.

Anyhow the whole state of California is stirred up over this San Diego free speech fight. Spreckles' *Call* in San Francisco and his papers in San Diego[4] have done all they could to stir this mess into a patriotic stew, but the whole working class of every brand of organization is on to the game, and knows it is a class struggle. This fight is the greatest thing that ever happened in California to promote class consciousness. Everybody is asking what is the I.W.W. Let the good fight go on. All we need is to capture the workers' mind, when we have that we have all. And one of the best ways to capture it, is to make the capitalist press advertise what we stand for. All activities lead to revolution. Peace and submission is our greatest enemy at this stage of the game.

*Industrial Worker* (Spokane, Washington), 6 June 1912, p. 4.

4. John Spreckels was a prominent San Diego businessman who published the *San Francisco Call* and the *San Diego Union*. See also "The Outrage of San Diego," Article in *Mother Earth*, June 1912, above.

## To BEN L. REITMAN

*Denver, 13 July 1912*

HOBO MINE.

What do you think of Mommy getting up at seven all by herself? And I went to bed at one, too, ain't I smart? And what do you think is the my morning prayer? Hobo, I love you and I am glad I will see you soon.

I have lots to do to day, packing, straightning my things, make my notes of "King Hunger" for this afternoon,[1] see a lot of people and do a lot of odds and ends. Now, that I am going to leave, I am sorry because of the class, everybody has become so intensely interested that I was asked to stay longer and if I did, not one of my pupils would stop I am sure. I met some rather striking women and also a few men, the "Tausigs"[2] for instance, friends of Miss Kennan. He is a Physician and attended every evening class, his wife is a very interesting woman of some mind of her own. Altogether I could certainly build up a big drama school. But, I should never be content with that kind of work alone.

The newspapers have completely boycotted me, the "Post" too has drawn in its horns. The last time I saw Bonfils,[3] I could feel the frost in the air and while he did put in a notice, it was stuck away, so that one could hardly see it. Your friend Gurly[4] has acted like a S——. He did not even have the courage to say he would not bring anything, but promised every time, I even went to him myself once and though he faithfully said he would, he had not a word. One thing is certain, Hobo, if my public work would depend on going after the news papers, I would give up the job, I loath it and feel as if I were prostituting myself, in fact I have never all these years given them the satisfaction and I never will again. Hobo, is born for it just as he is born to be a manager, he is not born to love Mommy, that's why he does it so badly, almost as badly, as I do when I have to ask the papers for favors.

I heard Dr Stanley Hall[5] last night, Mrs James, one of my pupils, a friend of Ida's,

---

1. Leonid Andreyev's play *King Hunger* (1907) was the subject of EG's evening lecture.
2. Dr. Arnold S. Taussig (1867–1930) and Gertrude H. Taussig (1872–1948) attended EG's drama class in Denver. He was a noted heart surgeon and an authority on tuberculosis. She was a socialite from a prominent Denver family. They were married in 1908. She studied music for several years in New York and Berlin and was a director of the Children's Hospital of Denver and the organizer of the first hospital school there. They were part of Ellen Kennan's circle of friends.
3. The *Denver Post* was known for its questionable and sensationalist journalism and outrageous publicity stunts. The paper published three articles by EG 26–30 April 1912 on "The Social Unrest." For information on Frederick Gilmer Bonfils (1861–1933), see Letter to Fred G. Bonfils, 16 May, above.
4. Boyd Gurley was editor of the *Denver Express*, founded in 1906 by Edward W. Scripps.
5. Dr. Granville Stanley Hall (1844–1924) was a psychologist, educator, and first president of Clark University. He established the *American Journal of Psychology* (1887). A founding president of the

took me in her car, Ida, Fred Mc Farland, Mrs Stahl, the sister of Mrs Kassler, Dr, and Mrs Black[6] were with us. They realy went because I announced the lecture and urged them to go and then they gave me a roasting. It realy was awful. Gad, when I think the kind of men that teach in this country, I actually believe myself to be a "Genius". In the first place, he has aged terribly since we saw him, his delivery is abominal and they tell me it never was better, and the stuff.

He spoke on "The Present Statues, Methods and Results of Moral Prophylaxix, Sex Teachings." He was introduced by a minister and of course, was evidently afraid to move "The Church will teach Sex, "We need Sex instruction, to preserve Chastity, Morality and Religion." And a lot such other rot, it was awful. Our own people were there and if questions had been permitted they would have wiped the floor with the "Professor. It realy makes me sick to think the kind of "Authorities America has. But with all that, I said to Ida, "every little thing helps, said the Irish woman when she pissed in Ocean." He did emphacyzed the importence of sex, in fact gave almost as much credence to it as I, and for that audience of his it was worth a good deal, as it would not get it otherwise. But, Oh! if only I could have gotten up, if only I could have such an audience, but that will never be I fear.

Hobo mine, I wonder if I will hear from you to day, I had no letter yesterday, I will not mail this until later, so I can add a few words. This will reach you Monday morning and at 2. P. M. if the train is on time Hobo will meet me, is you glad I am coming?

---

American Psychological Association in 1892, he emphasized sexuality in his child development theories and was instrumental in bringing Sigmund Freud and psychoanalysis to the United States, featuring Freud and Jung at a conference at Clark University in 1909 and later publishing Freud's lectures in the *American Journal of Psychology* (April 1910). He was best known for his "recapitulation theory," which posited that the developmental stages of individual children mirror the development of the human race over history. EG first heard Hall speak in Worcester in 1909. His works include *Adolescence* (New York: D. Appleton, 1904) and *Educational Problems* (New York: D. Appleton, 1911). Cora Bennett Stevenson, a teacher at the New York Ferrer School from May 1913 to July 1914, was a follower of Hall and applied his theories to her method of teaching there.

6. Fred McFarlane (1884–1962) and Ida Kruse McFarlane (1871–1940) were wealthy friends and benefactors of EG's. Fred McFarlane attended EG's drama class and was the secretary treasurer of McFarlane-Eggers Machinery Company. He was also a supporter of the Central City Opera House in the Denver area. Ida Kruse McFarlane was a professor of English literature and drama and head of the Department of English Literature at the University of Denver. Mrs. McFarlane had an early career as an actress and performed under the stage name Ida Eskus. She had studied the new social drama and trends in literature while visiting Scandinavia. In April 1912 McFarlane continued teaching EG's Denver class on modern drama after EG left. Mrs. Stahl was a wealthy Denver resident and subscriber to *Mother Earth*. She was married to George Stahl (1870–1932), who was assistant secretary of Vindicator Consolidated Gold Mining Company in Cripple Creek. Mrs. Charles M. (Grace Maria) Kassler (1872–1952) was a Denver socialite who attended EG's lectures. She was an influential promoter of adult education in Denver, helping to found the Denver Labor College and the Parent Teacher Association. Dr. Melville Black (1866–?) was professor of ophthalmology at the Medical Department of the University of Colorado. All attended EG's drama lectures in Denver at the suggestion of EG's friend Ellen Kennan, who was a Denver schoolteacher.

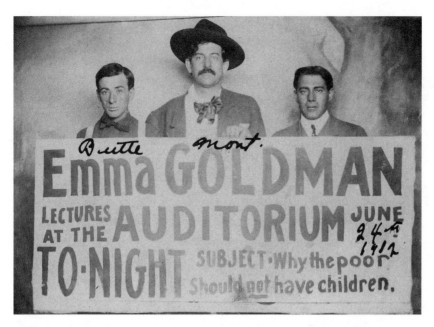

Ben Reitman and two locals holding a large placard for Goldman's (provocatively titled) lecture about the challenge of poverty for those without access to birth control, Butte, Montana, 24 June 1912. (University of Illinois at Chicago)

The inclosed letter will show you that things are pretty rotten in San. Diego.[7] I had intended to send the balance of the money to Bauer,[8] but in the first place, he has not acknowledged the receipt of the money sent from Butte, and in the second place I decided to wait, until they begin public speaking again, I certainly do not want the money to go for no other purpose than for lawyers and political campaining, do you?

Until Monday then my Hobo, The T. B. and M. are starved so you had better prepare plenty of W. wine and other things that go with it. I want a real feast, as in the old long ago, when Hobo first met me.

Dear, dear Hobo, I loves you very much,
Mommy

P S. Dear just got your letter, will talk about everything Monday. I hope and pray you

7. No extant enclosure has been found.
8. Kasper Bauer was a Southern California socialist and editor of the Los Angeles–based socialist paper *Common Sense* (1904–1909). Bauer was treasurer of the California Free Speech League in 1912 during the IWW San Diego free speech fight.

will be <u>cautious</u> with your Monday morning visiter. I never heard of such recklessness in my life and really think it impardonable. But certain people will not learn until it is too late.

The Rock Iland dear, I am coming on.

WITH LOVE
M

TLI, Emma Goldman Archive, IISH. Autographed postscript.

Dear Comrade Grossman.

I am now in the country with comrade Berkman who is currently writing the last chapter of his book.[1] The book was almost as great a torture as the 14 years of prison both for Berkman as well as for me. But with perseverance everything can be withstood. I have a little time just now and want to use it to respond to your letter.

The fact that you have endured and have remained active speaks a great deal for your courage and enthusiasm, I wish we had more of your kind. Unfortunately we have nothing of the sort here. And now we have lost both Voltairine and comrade Russ Winn, who died a week ago.[2] Practically the only truly active American anarchists.

Nonetheless, our ideas are certainly perceptible here, in journals as well as in the workers' movement. That brings me to your comments in Wohlstand Fuer Alle.[3] In the article about San Diego you write among other things "our comrade E. G. is not to be begrudged for devoting herself entirely to agitation on behalf of anarchism." What exactly do you mean by this? Do you think, dear comrade, that I am not propagating anarchism because I, let's say, speak about the modern drama? I can not accept that you are so petty. Anyway I would like you to know that I am always speaking about anarchism and from an anarchistic standpoint, regardless of what topic I am dealing with. If that were not the case such things as San. Diego would not happen to us and I would not have been so bitterly persecuted all these years. Indeed, I do not believe that it is an exaggeration to say that everything that is known in America about anarchism is due to my agitation. Even Volt was well-known only in the most narrow circles.

Apropos with regard to Voltairine, you don't seem very well informed about her either. You write that Volt. loves children. Indeed it is a known fact that Volt. can not stand children, and has for years now repudiated her own child. That of course says nothing against her. She was not at all a hypocrite, and she didn't feign maternal love any more than she did any other, and it was in this where her merit lay. I have touched on these points because you, dear friend, are not well informed with regard to our activities and the comrades in this country. Don't take offense.

We have all kinds of large events planned for this winter, the 25 year memorial for

---

1. AB's *Prison Memoirs of an Anarchist* (New York: Mother Earth Publishing Association, 1912).
2. Voltairine de Cleyre died 20 June 1912, and Ross Winn, 8 August 1912.
3. *Wohlstand für Alle* (Wealth for All) was a bimonthly anarchist newspaper edited by Pierre Ramus (the pen name of Rudolf Grossman) from 1907 to 1914 in Klosterneuberg, near Vienna.

our Chicago comrades[4] with a special edition of M.E. 70th birthday celebration of com-rade Kropotkin with an extra edition of M.E[5] and in addition a series of new lectures and obviously Berkman's book, which will be shipped out by the end of next month, you will receive a copy as soon as possible. I will also send you an article about the work of comrade Ross Winn;[6] I'm at work on it right now.

Heartfelt greetings also to your girlfriend.

In solidarity.
Emma Goldman

Lieber Genosse Grossman.

Ich bin jetzt auf dem Lande mit Genosse Berkman der momentan das lezte Kapital seines Buches schreibt. Das Buch war beinahe eine ebenso grosse Qual wie die 14 Jahre Gefaengniss fuer Berkman sowohl wie feur mich. Aber mit Ausdauer erlebt man Alles. Habe gerade etwas Zeit und will dieselbe dazu benuetzen um Ihren Brief zu beantworten.

Dass Sie sich durchgerungen haben und immer thaetig sind spricht viel fuer Ihren Muth und Begeisterung, ich wuenschte wir haetten mehr von dieser Sorte. Hier haben wir leider Niemanden. Und jezt haben wir sowohl Voltairine als auch Genosse Riss Winn der vor einer Woche gestorben ist verlohren. Fast die einzigen wirklich thaetigen Amerianischen Anarchisten.

Immerhin, unsere Ideen machen sich hier stark bemerkbar, sowohl in Zeitschriften als auch in der Arbeiter Bewegung. Das bringt mich zu einer Ihrer Bemaerkungen Im "Wohlstand Fuer Alle. In dem Bericht ueber San Diego, schreiben Sie unter Andern "Es ist unserer Genossen E. G. nicht vergoonnt sich ganz der Agitation das Anarchismus zu widmen" Was meinten Sie eigentlich damit? Glauben Sie Liber Genosse dass ich nicht den Anarchismus propagiere weil ich sagen wir, ueber das moderne Drama spreche? Ich

4. A memorial meeting for the Haymarket anarchists was held 11 November 1912 at the Manhattan Lyceum in New York City. The free event was chaired by AB, and the speakers included EG, Frank Jordan, and Harry Kelly in English, as well as Ludovico Caminita in Italian, August Lott in German, William Shatoff in Russian, and Voline (V. M. Eikhenbaum) in Yiddish. The meeting was sponsored by many anarchist groups, including the *Mother Earth* group, the *Freie Arbeiter Stimme* association, *Golos Truda* group, the Federated Anarchists of America, the Bread and Freedom group, Francisco Ferrer Association, group *L'Era Nuova*, and several IWW branches, among others.
5. The December 1912 *Mother Earth* was issued in celebration of Kropotkin's seventieth birthday. *Mother Earth* and *Freie Arbeiter Stimme* also arranged a birthday celebration, held 7 December 1912 at Carnegie Hall. Speakers (in six languages) included William English Walling, Anna Strunsky, EG, James F. Morton, AB, Harry Kelly, Saul Yanovsky, Abe Cahan, Dr. Solotaroff, L. Deutsch, Jaime Vidal, Michel Dumas, and M. Resjek. The meeting was chaired by Leonard Abbott.
6. EG wrote an obituary of Ross Winn for the September 1912 edition of *Mother Earth*, and she helped establish a fund to support Winn's widow, Gussie, and their children.

kann nicht annehemen dass Sie gar so engherzig sind. Jedenfals moechte ich dass Sie wissen, dass ich, ganz gleich welches Thema behandle, immer ueber den Anarchismus und vom anarchistischen StandPunkt spreche. Wen dem nicht so war wuerden solche Dinge wie San. Diego uns nicht passieren und wuerde ich nicht nach all diesen Jahren so bitter verfolgt werden. ueberhaupt, ich glaube nicht dass es Uebertreibung ist wenn ich sage, dass was man in America ueber den Anarchismus weiss meiner Agitation zu verdanken ist. Den sogar Volt war nur im engsten Kreis bekannt.

Apropos wegen Voltairine, auch ueber sie scheinen Sie nicht sehr orientiert zu sein. Sie schreiben dass Volt. Kinder sehr gerne hatte. Nun ist das eine bekannte Thatsache dass Volt. Kinder nicht ausstehen konnte und ihr eigenes Kind jahrelang nicht anner-kannte. Was ja nicht gegen sie spricht. Sie war eben keine Heuchlerin und hat die Mutter Liebe ebenso wenig geheuchelt wie Aller Andere, darin gerade lag ihr Verdinst. Ich habe diese Punkte nur beruehrt weil Sie lieber Freund nicht gut orientieet sind im Bezug auf unsere Thatigkeit und Genossen in diesem Lande. Nichts fuer Ungut.

Wir haben fuer diesen Winter allerhand grosse Unternehmungen vor, 25jaehrige GedenkFeier unserer Chicagoer Genossen mit Spezial Nummer M.E. 70 jaehrige Geburtstags Feier Genosse Kropotkins mit extra M.E Ausgabe und ausserdem wine Reihe neuer Vortraege, und selbstverstaendlich Berkmans Buch das schon Ende nachs-ten Monats versand werden wird, Sie bekommen sofort eine copy. Werde Ihnen auch eine article ueber die Thaetigkeit Genosse Ross Winn senden, bin gerade and der Arbeit. Herzliche Gruess auch an Ihre Freundin.

SOLIDARISCH.
EMMA GOLDMAN

TLS, Pierre Ramus Archive, IISH. Translated from the German.

DEAREST:—

It is so very, very sweet of you to address me with endearing terms. I assure you that no one in the world appreciates such expressions of endearment more than myself, especially when they emanate from such a tower of strength as yourself. I suppose that the reason that you are such a tower of strength is that you are thoroly purged from all superstition. I note where you say that love should not mean worship as that smacks too much of slavishness for you. I discuss that matter because I naturally wanted to find just what your definition of the term meant.

In speaking of having known intimately more men than I can count on my fingers I meant that it appalled me to think that a woman would do such a thing for mercernary reasons. You will agree with me that that is a most horrible thing and appalling. I believe that it is nobody's business if a woman has loved a hundred men. I myself have so little vitality that it is positively injurious to my health to love many people with intensity but that may be due to my defective nerve adjustment caused from one of my immediate progenitor's alcoholism and also to my own alcoholism which my environment helps along.

Certainly I do not mind a criticism from you. You would not criticize if I were not worth it. Now, is that subtle flattery? Once there was a man named Mr. Smith and Mr. Smith said to Mr. Jones, "Mr. Jones, I have heard a very nice thing about you and it is that you are the only man in the world who cannot be flattered." Mr. Jones wore a pleased grin for about a week; he would have worn it longer only he could not find his collar button one day.

I will never mind criticism from you because I love you and believe you to be a thoroly sincere person and also I learn things from your criticism.

You must have magnificent physical strength, dearest. How can you always be so calm and how can you always view all sides of a question so dispassionately?

I have been very sick this week. Fred[1] and I had a terrific quarrel and also a "terrific" reconciliation and also I got drunk. When I say drunk I mean drunk since I cannot touch one drop of liquor with out drinking a couple of quarts. I am quite contrite and am suffering my punishment out. Fred and I beat each other and I am all over bruises. We are both sorry and are going to try over again. We are both hulks of humanity who

---

1. Fred was Almeda's partner.

were started out wrong in life. Fred has been away from work again so that we will be quite poor for some time.

The socialists have launched their new paper this week.[2] It is an improvement from the last because it is filled with extracts from the writings of Debs.[3] I wonder what they would do if they had to draw upon their own imagination? The editorial column states that the sixth page shall be devoted to religeous questions, articles by noted Theologians etc., on burning issues. Devoted to religeous questions and they claim that they do not have anything to do with religeon one way or another. I shall certainly not concede anything to their limitations but shall give them hell.

If it is agreeable to you I would like to come to you the night of September 1st 2nd, arriving at the ~~Jersey station~~ New York Terminal Sept. ~~2nd~~ 3rd at 8.08 A. M. Let me know at what time to meet you and where.

Lovingly, lovingly,
Almeda

Sept. 3rd will be the day after Labor Day, won't it? If that is not convenient to you just let me know. Please do not inconvenience yourself by going to New York so early in the morning to meet me but let me know what time of the day you wish to meet me and where.

I do not regard men like Berkman and Reitman as strangers; they are brothers. I hope Mr. Reitman's hurts that he received in Cal. are better and also that he managed to get a couple of licks back while the performance was going on. But I s'pose that in a case of that kind it is best to be passive. To be passive sometimes means that we will reach our goal more quickly.

Enclosed find scedule.[4]

TLS, Anna Baron Papers, MBU.

2. Possibly the *Eye Opener*, a socialist newspaper published in Chicago by Frank O. Anderson from 1912 to 1920.
3. A reference to socialist leader Eugene Debs.
4. No extant enclosure has yet been found.

My DEAR, DEAR NUNYA.

Your agonized cry has gripped my soul more than I am capable of discribing. I am sure you are mistaken when you say I have ever brushed a similar outpouring from you, aside, if I did I do not rememeber it, nor could it have been as serious, or it would have effected me as your last letter has, it would have stirred me as much.

Indeed, I have known all along that you were sexually starved, I knew that years ago when Ben pressed you so hard. I am sure if he had shown tact and had been more gentle you would have responded at the time. And how can it be otherwise for a woman of your intense temperement? You have lived a life of contenence so long, it is a wonder to me that some great passion has not swept you off your feet long ago.

You ask me for advice, dearest girl, how can I give it in such a situation? There was a time in my life when I should have considered it preposterious for a free woman to love a conservative man. But I have learned through great stress of my own, that love has nothing what soever to do with ideas, habits or traits. I know that through my life with Ben, which until this moment has continued to be a vulcano in spite of all his short comings. Of course, Ben has undergone a marvelous change and is more in harmony with my work than any man I have ever known, but we are still, and probably will be miles apart in our tastes always will be seperated in our tastes, in everything.

The same may be with you, what has the man's ideas to do with your love for him? If you realy think he responds to your passion you ought to follow what seems to be a tremendious force in your life. He may become more advanced and radical through your relations with him, as Ben has become advanced and developed. But, there is one thing you must bear in mind, there is no peace in the struggle. I mean the difference between you both, will of necessity cause eternal friction and bring much heart ache into your life.[1] That too, I know dear. But, Schöpenhauer was right when he said, "for every grain of happyness we pay with a life time of agony."[2]

There is one thing which seems to present itself as a sort of solution, why do you not sitisfy your craving for the man's love? I mean why do you not enter into a relationship

---

1. The person in question was probably Fred Merrick, Pittsburgh publisher of the socialist and IWW paper *Justice*. (See also Letter from Ben Reitman, 17 January 1912, *EGP*, reel 5.)
2. German philosopher Arthur Schopenhauer (1788–1860). Schopenhauer was identified with a "philosophy of pessimism," the belief that suffering far outweighed fleeting states of pleasure and happiness.

with him? Must you break all comradely ties with George because of it?[3] Must you live in one house with the other man? Why not continue to work and share as you have for so many years with George, and simply meet the other? In that way, you would be able to test yourself and his love, you would be able to find out whether your obsession for him is but temporary or lasting, whether it is not as often happens, a mere physical attraction.

Of course, George may not want that, but if he is big, he will act as I have with Beckie when she became Alex sweatheart,[4] or as the men who have been in my life before Ben have acted. It may not have been easy for them, but they realized that I must follow an impelling force.

Or if that is impossible, why do you not go away with him for a time, surely he will not expect that you should marry him, though some socialists are conservative enough for that. At any rate, if he realy cares for you he will not bother much about such trifles. The main thing is, that you should be able to see the man in freedom and follow your longing for him without let or hindrence, if for no other reason, to see if your love for him is realy vital, which we can never know under presure. Can you not arrange that dear? And must you if that is done break with the past? That would be a great pitty because of the fine comradeship that existed betwene you and George.

Dearest, all this may seem so inediquate, but how can one advise in such a matter? It is impossible. The only thing one can do is to suggest but in the last analysis you must follow your own bent. If it is a matter of a place I should be so glad to give you the use of our little farm, I must go into town the 9th until the 21st, you could be here with him absolutely undisturbed for two weeks, something you both need to find yourselvs. Would you like that? Surely there is no need of acting like all conventional people, begin house keeping and such nonsense, why not show him what freedom can do for two lovers? I am at your servise if you wish to come. I do not know what else I can say, I hope I have not said too much already. To me love has always been such a sensitive matter, I disliked preying in the love life of any one. But you will understand, will you not dear?

My dear dear Freind, I have reread your letter and I can only say what I have said in the begining, love has nothing to do with a man's opinions or views. It may help to develope him as in Ben's case but you will have to pay a very costly prise for it, namely much pain and heartache, but with all that I believe you ought to follow the call of your heart, whether the man is a political socialist or no socialist at all. The fact that he was able to arouse you so, proves that it was the man and not his ideas, why then not take the man and let his ideas alone?

Or is he so conventional that he would insist on marriage? If so I fear his love is not much and perhaps you had better go away, In either case I would be very happy to be of assistence to you in any way I can.

---

3. George Seldes, Nunia Seldes's husband, was a Russian-born single-taxer and anarchist.
4. A reference to the relationship between Rebecca Edelsohn and AB, which began in 1907.

We have returned to our little wild place, it is glorious here. I had hoped it would be for the whole month of Sept. but my sister is coming to N.Y the tenth with her girl who sails for Europe the 18th.[5] Of course I will have to be there that week. I shall be out here until the 9th however, write me dear.

WITH MUCH, MUCH LOVE.
EMMA

TLS, IU-U. Last ten words handwritten. Addressed to Mrs. N. Seldes, 1801 Centre Ave., Pittsburg, Pa.

5. A reference to EG's sister, Lena Cominsky, and her niece, Stella Cominsky.

MY GREAT AND WONDERFUL LOVER.

I raced off a letter to you a while ago and then reread yours of yesterday. It is like the strain of some wonderful music, something of Bethooven's both strong and sweet. What a bad lover you are not to write me such letters often. Why, you would put new vigour into my soul. Dearest Hobo mine, why can you not disclose the beauty of your soul to me more often? You do not know what it means to me to look into that tender soul of yours even if you do not believe in "souls."

I thank you darling for the prevelege of giving me at least an occasi[onal] glimps, it is as exquisite as the color of the woods now, so rich and soothing and passionate. As I wrote you this morning, I slept badly to night, for no special reason. I read my two manuscripts, "Anarchism and Vice[1] to our friends out here and they were inthusiastic, but of course that proves little. They love me and are not in a position to give an unbiased opinion. I read them more for my own practice to get the thought thoroughly ground into my mind. I do not think I would read them to you, for fear that you would not like them which would add to my dread of lectu[ring]. I let you judge by the delivery and only hope you may not be too severe on me. See, baby mine, I want your approval so, I hate to do poor work. Better not expect too much.

Darling boy, I want with all my heart that we may succeed with free meetings, for your sake more than anything else but also because I want to put to shame some of my friends who have misjudged you. But I am not sanguine enough to believe we will succeed. I am simply too conscious of our material conditions. We owe Goldman[2] over $500, we already owe Schroeder[3] $300, Boyesen[4] $75. We need $300 for Goldman before we can get a single copy of the book and we have not as much in the bank. Now why deceive ourselves? You know as well as I my darling that nothing comes to us from the sky, we must grind out everything from our tongues and brain, you as well as I.

In former times, the agitation was carried on a small scale, with the <u>Free Society</u> or the <u>Freiheit</u>[5] set up gratis and all the work done freely, therefore free meetings were pos-

---

1. Probably "Vice, Its Cause and Cure" and "The Psychology of Anarchism." EG added both topics to her repertoire around this time, lecturing on both in New York City on 6 October 1912.
2. Goldman was the printer of *Mother Earth, Anarchism and Other Essays*, and *Prison Memoirs of an Anarchist*.
3. Theodore Schroeder was the lawyer and organizer of the Free Speech League.
4. Bayard Boyesen was a lecturer at Columbia University. His independent wealth enabled him to teach full-time at New York's Ferrer school after EG recruited him around 1911.
5. *Free Society*, edited by Abe Isaak, was the principle English-language anarchist communist weekly at

sible, also the Germans when they were interested were very liberal with contributions. But all that is no more. To day every step costs like Hell. Here is our actual expence, M.E. printing, mailing, office and telephone, outside of office postage, $150 per month. Your mother and Max[6] receive from $60 to 70 per month. Our own expences, for rent and mere living, outside of anything extra $25. per week, $100 per month. That does not include clothing or any other outside expence. Le[t] us say $300 per month.

Now as to reciepts, you know about them best, we have never at any time gotten in the office more than $200 per month and that at the hight of the Winter, out of that not one hundred can be counted as profits. The other two hundred comes from meetings, or borrowed money paid back from meetings. These are hard disagreable facts darling. I hate to place them before you at this particular moment when you are so enthused with the free meetings idea. But nevertheless I must, so that you go about it with open eyes. Forgive me if it hurts.

I have thought hard and deeply how we might simplify our lives and reduce expences so we can realy free our work from commercialism. For until we succeed in doing that we must have some income. Can you suggest a way? As long as Alex[7] works on M.E he is entitled to get his living and to keep the woman he loves. I may not like the idea but in justice to Alex I must submit to it. Of course, we can not dismiss your mother, I'd rather not eat myself. Remains therefore only Max. Believe me it is not because he mean so much to me that he gets the paltry few Dollars, but because he is doing work for the magazine, which so long as I can not entirely devote myself to it, he will have to do because Alex is not enough interested, nor yet has the necessary confidence in himself to do. Besides, even if Max would never write a line, I should still want to assist him, because he is so utterly helpless in this system.

As to our own expence, we might reduce it if we could live out here and I mean to do it some day, but so long as we have neither a horse or other method of rapid conveyence, you could not commute, nor could I. Here are the circumstances which must be met, dear heart, so you know that admission or a substantial sustaining fund is imperative to keep the machinery oiled.[8] Let's hope we will get the latter. But do not be disappointed if we don't, and if we must have admission. Meanwhile, dearest I suggest that

---

the turn of the century. The paper was published in San Francisco November 1897–1901, in Chicago February 1901–1904, and in New York 27 March 1904–20 November 1904. *Freiheit*, an important German-language American anarchist paper, was founded by Johann Most, edited for a time by Max Baginski, and ceased publication in 1910. For more on *Free Society* and *Freiheit* see vol. 1, *Made for America*, pp. 565 and 566.

6. Max Baginski was one of the editors of *Mother Earth*.

7. Alexander Berkman worked as editor of *Mother Earth* from his release from prison in 1906 until 1914. At the time of this letter he lived at the *Mother Earth* office with his partner, Rebecca Edelsohn.

8. A serial letter from EG was sent to *ME* supporters in September 1912 asking for a sustaining fund to allow her meetings to be free of charge. In the letter she argued that charging admission "kept away the very people who need enlightenment most." See Letter to Dear Friend, September 1912, *EGP*, reel 6.

you do not mention on the cards the admission part, we can then remain free until the last moment.

Have you sent the ad to the <u>Freie Arb Stimme</u>?[9] I hope so and also that you have stated admission for the Jewish lectures. I know you never forget anything sweetheart, but you have so much to do, it may have slipped your mind. In that case we will have to send in a large ad in the <u>F. A. S</u> for next week.

Lover, I do hope you can come out Saturday afternoon, I am writing Max that you want to be relieved in the afternoon, you might let him begin Saturday, say from two, you could then get here about four and spend until Sunday morning with me. I want you more than all else now, I really need your love and tenderness to help me in my work, because I need a stimulant and you are the strongest I know of. Do let me know if I may expect you and what time, perhaps I can have Rousseau[10] meet you. If you do come bring out the black Jewish bread and some meet, a roast of Lamb or Veal, we have everything else.

Dearie, dearie, how inconsistent to expect everybody else not to smoke because you are better finer and happyer without it? Why the great difference between us and Carry Nations[11] or other Governmentalist is that we do not want any one to do as we do, that we grant him the liberty to live his own life in his own way. Smoking may be as bad for Alex as it is for you, though I doubt it, still, you would not want him to follow you would you? You do not believe in uniformity do you? Of course not. I don't either, else every woman would love my Hobo, which I should not like at all.

Apropos of seducing woman's soul, yes you could dearest, more than any one else I know, if you would not make straight for the extreme end of her soul, which you do in the form of your language. If you would only take it for granted that she has a soul, or if not that you can help develope it, then you would begin from that end and succeed, I am sure. Because you certainly have as much sweetness and tenderness as Hutch, but you rarely show it to most women. I know you will some day, because you are growing, bigger and finer every day. Yes you are and I am proud of you Hobo mine.

And now to work, I am starting on my anti political lecture[12] after lunch and will keep at it until it's typewritten which may take all night, but I like to work that way. Tomorrow

9. *Freie Arbeiter Stimme* was a Yiddish-language anarchist paper in New York with a large and loyal readership.

10. Probably David Rousseau, who was a New York social reformer, populist, and state socialist. Apparently based in Ossining, New York, he was interviewed on 29 March 1894 in the *Ossining Morning Advertiser*. The interview was later reprinted as a pamphlet, *A Nation of Fools, David Rousseau Gives His Views on the Social Problem* (Ossining, N.Y.: 1894), in which he advocated the socialist ideas of Edward Bellamy.

11. Carry Amelia Moore Nation (1846–1911), American temperance crusader and women's rights advocate. EG also refers to her in "A Character Study of Emma Goldman," in the 11 April 1901 *Philadelphia North American*; see vol. 1, *Made for America*.

12. Possibly her lecture "The Dupes of Politics," which was first given in October 1912. See *EGP*, reel 55.

I will write more Hobo. Come take the M. and T-B.[13] they want you. press close to me and let me feel the passionate burning T[14] on the T.B it is ecstatic and maddening. Oh, I love you boy, I love you.

TL, IU-U. Last seven words handwritten.

13. EG and Reitman often used code for the sexually explicit parts of their correspondence. "M" and "TB" were code for "mountains" and "treasure box."
14. Code for "tongue."

EMMA AND ALEX, MY DEAR COMRADES:

With absorbing interest I have read the book,[1] but now that I have undertaken to tell of it language utterly fails me. If I could meet Comrade Alex face to face, my arm about his neck, my hand clasping his, and so standing he could look into my eyes perhaps he could there read the feeling and thought that I cannot express in words. Before Emma's letter and the book came, I had been worrying over my own petty troubles. How infinitesimal they now appear in comparison with our dear Comrade's experiences. I am somehow reminded of that memorable day in November when Comrade Parsons[2] tried my soul, when he said to me: "Comrade, I couldn't live a year in State prison under a life sentence. I should either commit suicide or go insane". And so I have also felt. I am but a weakling, and the horror of such an existence would be more than I could bear.

Did you not receive a letter from me, Comrade Berkman? I have a distinct recollection of <u>intending</u> to write to you shortly after you were taken to the pen, and I believe I did write; but much sickness & trouble have impaired my memory, so that I cannot be certain. Perhaps in my then state of feeling I expressed myself too freely and my letter was not delivered to you.

I instantly recognized the "Yankee" in the account of the tunnel.[3] In the light of that experience the name "Mole" which he assumed while in Denver had a peculiar significance. I understand that Vella K—[4] has entirely severed all radical connections of late years, but is again living in Chicago.

I am glad, Emma, that you don't think I have become entirely an apostate. It was

---

1. William T. Holmes (1851–1928) was an American anarchist active in Chicago during the Haymarket affair and after. By 1912 he had ceased to be active in the anarchist movement and was living in Farmington, New Mexico, where, together with Lizzie Holmes, he owned a peach orchard. An occasional contributor to *Mother Earth*, the *Agitator*, and *Instead of a Magazine*, he joined the Socialist Party in 1915. Holmes refers here to Berkman's *Prison Memoirs of an Anarchist* (New York: Mother Earth Publishing Association, 1912), which dealt with events that occurred while Holmes was still active in the anarchist movement.
2. Haymarket anarchist Albert Parsons, who was a close friend of Holmes. Parsons was executed on 11 November 1887.
3. In a 10 May 1900 letter published in AB's *Prison Memoirs*, referring to the plan to tunnel him out of prison, Berkman wrote: "Tell 'Yankee' [Harry Gordon] and 'Ibsen' [Eric B. Morton] and our Italian comrades what I feel—I know I need not explain it further to you. No one realizes better than myself the terrible risks they are taking, the fearful toil in silence and darkness, almost within hearing of the guards." Harry Gordon was secretary and treasurer of the Alexander Berkman Defense Association; Eric B. Morton, a San Francisco–based anarchist, helped EG smuggle guns to Russia in 1905.
4. Vella Kinsella was a Chicago anarchist and singer who performed at anarchist meetings in Chicago,

Frontispiece to the first edition of Alexander Berkman's *Prison Memoirs of an Anarchist,* published by the Mother Earth Publishing Association, 1912. (Kate Sharpley Archive)

reported to me that you told I had withdrawn from the movement because I was getting rich and found it didn't <u>pay</u> to have such affiliations. Surely my past record ought to preclude such an assumption. If you knew how "rich" I am getting you would smile at the ridiculous charge. The actual fact is we are nearer the verge of want today than at any time in many years. We have utterly failed to make good on our peach Orchard, are deeply in debt, I am a partial invalid, and am unable to get work enough to make a decent living.

Sam Fielden[5] is still at La Veta, Colorado, where I also made my home for several

including various Haymarket memorials. In the plot to tunnel AB out of prison she pretended to be Eric B. Morton's wife, singing and playing piano to cover the noise of the digging.

5. Samuel Fielden (1847–1922) English-born anarchist and one of the Haymarket defendants. Pardoned in June 1893 by Governor John Altgeld, Fielden went back to work in Chicago before inheriting money that allowed him to buy an isolated ranch in Colorado. He was still in contact with William Holmes when he died on 7 February 1922. See also vol. 1, *Made for America.*

years. I am afraid Sam has become indifferent and penurious in his old age. He and Harry (his son) have 800 acres of land, between them, many head of cattle and other tangible evidences of wealth, yet he lives in a miserable hut, in squalor and unclean. His wife died a few months ago, and his daughter, Alice, now keeps house for him. Poor Alice; a good girl, a beautiful character; but she cannot persuade the old man to live like a decent being or to provide her with even a comfortable home. Of course this is strictly confidential between us and should go no further. I am sorry that he did not respond to your request for an article.

Referring once more to the book. I wish it could be placed in the hands of every humane prison official in the country. Thos. Tynan,[6] warden of the Colo. State prison at Canon City, Colo. Governor George W. P. Hunt[7] of Arizona and R. B. Sims,[8] Hunt's Supt. of the Arizona penitentiary at Florence, Ariz., Gov. West of Oregon,[9] Supt. Ray Baker of the Nevada pen. and other officials who have tried with marked success the "honor" system of treating criminals. I suppose the new plan originated with Judge Lindsey of Denver,[10] whose novel treatment of the "bad" boys brought before him has won for him international renown, but it has been adopted in many of our Western prisons and has certainly marked a new departure in prison reform.

Next Monday is the memorable Eleventh of November; our martyrs' great anniver-

6. Thomas J. Tynan, appointed deputy warden of Colorado State Prison in March 1909 and warden in 1911, a position he held until 1915. Prisoners worked under unarmed guards and without chains under Tynan, who asserted "by removing the continual threat of arms, by eliminating oppression and brutalities, by establishing a system of graded rewards for cheerfulness and industry, the penitentiary has been given a wholesome, helpful atmosphere." Tynan was also an advocate of vocational training and recreational activities for the prisoners.

7. George W. P. Hunt (1859–1934), American politician who served as president of the Arizona legislative council (1905–1909), as president of the Arizona Constitutional Convention (1910), and as the first governor of the state of Arizona (1912–1917).

8. Robert B. Sims (1876–1951), a framer of the Arizona constitution in 1910 and superintendent of the Arizona State Prison in Florence from 1912 to 1922.

9. Oswald West (1873–1960), progressive reformer and Democrat. West was governor of Oregon from 1911 to 1915 and a prolific contributor to various Oregon newspapers and journals.

10. Benjamin Barr Lindsey (1869–1943), Colorado reformer, was a leading figure of the Progressive Party and first judge of Denver's Juvenile Court (1900–1927), where he instituted many reforms. He later supported the Ludlow coal mine strikers in 1913–1914, traveled to Europe as part of Henry Ford's Peace Party in 1915, and, as a proponent of suffrage and birth control, presided over Margaret Sanger's and EG's birth control meetings in Denver in 1916. A 1914 poll ranked Lindsey among the ten greatest living Americans. He was forced from his position in 1927 when the Ku Klux Klan briefly gained control of Denver politics, after which he left Denver and settled in Los Angeles. His works include *The Problem of the Children and How the State of Colorado Cares for Them, A Report of the Juvenile Court of Denver* (Denver: The Merchants Publishing Company, 1904); *The Beast*, with Harvey J. O'Higgins (New York: Doubleday, Page, 1910), which detailed his fight against corruption in Denver; *The Uplift Book of Child Culture* (Philadelphia: Uplift Publishing Company, 1913); and *Children in Bondage; a Complete and Careful Presentation of the Anxious Problem of Child Labor—Its Causes, Its Crimes and Its Cure*, with Edwin Markham and George Creel (New York: Hearst's International Library, 1914).

sary. You will be commemorating that event, I presume, on Sunday the 10th.[11] About twelve years have passed since I have been able to take part in such a meeting. How I wish I could be with you in the flesh, as I shall be in the spirit on Sunday next. I shall expect to read an account of the meeting in Mother Earth.

Dear Girl, I have read of your troubles and triumphs over the country. I have grieved over your misfortunes and rejoiced over your successes. After long arduous service such as you have given to the Cause should come peace and rest. That these blessings may fall to your lot is the earnest wish of

YOUR FAR AWAY COMRADE
WILL HOLMES

ALS, Alexander Berkman Archive, IISH. Addressed at top to Emma and Alex.

---

11. The memorial meeting in New York was held on Monday, 11 November 1912, at the Manhattan Lyceum. See also Letter to Rudolf Grossman, 23 August 1912, above.

Tribute in *MOTHER EARTH*

*December 1912*

# Peter Kropotkin

Those who constantly prate of conditions as the omnipotent factor in determining character and shaping ideas, will find it very difficult to explain the personality and spirit of our Comrade Peter Kropotkin.

Born of a serf-owning family and reared in the atmosphere of serfdom all about him, the life of Peter Kropotkin and his revolutionary activity for almost fifty years stand a living proof against the shallow contention of the superior potency of conditions over the latent force in man to map out his own course in life. And that force in our comrade is his revolutionary spirit, so elemental, so impelling that it permeated his whole being and gave new meaning and color to his entire life.

It was this all-absorbing revolutionary fire that burned away the barriers that separated Kropotkin, the aristocrat, from the common people, and flamed a clear vision all through his life. It filled him, the child of luxury, of refinement, the heir of a brilliant career, with but one ideal, one purpose in life—the liberation of the human race from serfdom, from all physical as well as spiritual serfdom.[1]

How faithfully he has pursued that course, only those can appreciate who know the life and work of Peter Kropotkin.

Another very striking feature characteristic of this man is that he, of all revolutionists, should have the deepest faith in the people, in their innate possibilities to reconstruct society in harmony with their needs.

Indeed, the workers and the peasants are, to Kropotkin, the ones to hand down the spirit of resistance, of insurrection, to posterity. They, unsophisticated and untampered by artificiality, have always instinctively resented oppression and tyranny.

With Nietzsche, our comrade has continually emphasized that wherever the people have retained their integrity and simplicity, they have always hated organized authority as the most ruthless and barbaric institution among men.

Possibly Kropotkin's faith in the people springs from his own simplicity of soul—

---

1. Kropotkin, along with a number of young people interested in radical reform in Russia, was a member of the Chaikovsky Circle. Founded in 1869 in St. Petersburg, the Chaikovsky Circle was a study and self-education circle named after N. V. Chaikovsky, one of its leading members. Its program stressed the necessity of unifying intellectuals, peasants, and workers in the political struggle against the tsarist autocracy. Kropotkin's membership in the Chaikovsky Circle was his first revolutionary activity; later, in 1874, he was arrested for illegal activities against the tsarist government.

**25th ANNIVERSARY**
of the
**CHICAGO MARTYRDOM**
will be commemorated
MONDAY, NOVEMBER 11th, 8 P. M.
AT MANHATTAN LYCEUM
EAST 4th STREET, NEAR 3rd AVENUE.

*Speakers in English, German, Jewish*
*Italian, Spanish, Russian and Bohemian.*

**Preliminary Announcement**
*The*
Anniversary of the seventieth birthday
*of*
Comrade Peter Kropotkin
will be celebrated at
CARNEGIE HALL
NEW YORK
Saturday, December 7th, 1912, 8 P M.

GRAND ANARCHIST
**BALL AND REUNION**
Arranged by
MOTHER EARTH
Will take place
Christmas Eve. December 24th, 1912, 8 P. M.
In the large and beautiful
ROYAL LYCEUM
10-12-14 West 114th Street, New York
(2 blocks South of Lenox Subway)
*Tickets 35 Cents.   -   -   -   -   Hat-Check 15 Cents.*

Poster announcing three upcoming events: the 25th anniversary of the execution of the Chicago Anarchists (note the array of international speakers); Peter Kropotkin's seventieth birthday; and an annual anarchist celebration. (Kate Sharpley Archive)

a simplicity which is the dominant factor of his whole make-up. It is because of this, even more than because of his powerful mentality, that Revolution, to Peter Kropotkin, signifies the inevitable sociologic impetus to all life, all change, all growth. Even as Anarchism, to him, means not a mere theory, a school, or a tendency, but the eternal yearning, the reaching out of man for liberty, fellowship, and expansion.

Possibly this may also explain the truly human attitude of Peter Kropotkin toward the *Attentäter*.[2] Never once in all his revolutionary career has our comrade passed judgment on those whom most so-called revolutionists had only too willingly shaken off—partly because of ignorance, and partly because of cowardice—those who had committed political acts of violence.

Peter Kropotkin knew that it is generally the most sensitive and sympathetic personality that smarts most under our social injustice and tyranny, personalities who find in the act the only liberating outlet for their harassed soul, who must cry out, even at the expense of their own lives, against the apathy and indifference in the face of our social crimes and wrongs. More than most revolutionists, Peter Kropotkin feels deeply with the spiritual hunger of the *Attentäter*, which culminates in the individual act and which is but the forerunner of collective insurrection—the spark that heralds a new Dawn.

But Peter Kropotkin does more. He also feels with the social pariah, with him who through hunger, drudgery, and lack of joy strikes down one of the class responsible for the horror and despair of the pariah's life. This was particularly demonstrated in the case of Luccheni,[3] who was denounced and denied by nearly all other radicals. Yet no one can possibly have such an abhorrence of violence and destruction of life, as our Comrade Peter Kropotkin; nor yet be so tender and sympathetic to all pain and suffering. Only that he is too universal, too big a nature to indulge in shallow moral censorship of violence at the bottom, knowing—as he does—that it is but a reflex of organized, systematic, legal violence on top.

Thus stands Peter Kropotkin before the world at the age of seventy: the most uncompromising enemy of all social injustice; the deepest and tenderest friend of oppressed and outraged mankind; old in years, yet aglow with the eternal spirit of youth and the undying faith in the final triumph of liberty and equality.

*Mother Earth* 7 (December 1912): 325–27.

---

2. "Assassin or would-be assassin," in German. The term, especially in anarchist circles, describes an anarchist who commits a conscious act of violence directed against a powerful individual—often royalty or a government leader.

3. Luigi Luccheni (1873–1910) was an Italian anarchist who assassinated Empress Elizabeth of Austria in Geneva on 10 September 1898, stabbing her to death with a sharpened file. Luccheni supposedly planned to assassinate the Duke of Orleans, who was planning to visit Geneva, but when the duke did not come, Luccheni assassinated the empress, who happened by coincidence to be in Geneva, instead. Kropotkin refused to condemn Luccheni or individuals like him, "driven mad by horrible conditions" (Kropotkin in *Freedom*, October 1898). In a letter to the *New York World* EG repudiated Luccheni's act, pointing out that because the empress was not a political enemy of anarchism, the violence was senseless and reflected badly on anarchists in general. Luccheni, who was sentenced to life in prison, hung himself in 1910. For the reaction of EG and other anarchists in America to the assassination, see "New York Anarchist Leaders Denounce the Murder of Austria's Empress," To the *New York World*, 18 September 1898, in vol. 1, *Made for America*, pp. 346–48.

Essay in *MOTHER EARTH*

New York, January–February 1913

# Syndicalism: Its Theory and Practice

In view of the fact that the ideas embodied in Syndicalism have been practised by the workers for the last half century, even if without the background of social consciousness; that in this country five men had to pay with their lives because they advocated Syndicalist methods as the most effective in the struggle of labor against capital;[1] and that, furthermore, Syndicalism has been consciously practised by the workers of France, Italy and Spain since 1895,[2] it is rather amusing to witness some people in America and England now swooping down upon Syndicalism as a perfectly new and never before heard-of proposition.

It is astonishing how very naïve Americans are, how crude and immature in matters of international importance. For all his boasted practical aptitude, the average American is the very last to learn of the modern means and tactics employed in the great struggles of his day. Always he lags behind in ideas and methods that the European workers have for years past been applying with great success.

It may be contended, of course, that this is merely a sign of youth on the part of the American. And it is indeed beautiful to possess a young mind, fresh to receive and perceive. But unfortunately the American mind seems never to grow, to mature and crystallize its views.

Perhaps that is why an American revolutionist can at the same time be a politician. That is also the reason why leaders of the Industrial Workers of the World continue in the Socialist party, which is antagonistic to the principles as well as to the activities of the I.W.W.[3] Also why a rigid Marxian may propose that the Anarchists work together

---

1. A reference to the Haymarket anarchists.
2. The date EG uses here, 1895, marks the birth of the French Confédération Générale du Travail (CGT). Louis Levine called the CGT "the first important manifestation of the revolutionary tendency in the syndicalist movement in France" in his book *The Labor Movement in France* (New York: Columbia University, 1912), although in fact syndicalists and workers' organizations existed prior to its formation. In 1911 the Spanish syndicalist union, the Confederación Nacional de Trabajo (CNT), was founded, followed in 1912 by its Italian counterpart, the Unione Sindacale Italiana (USI).
3. From its formation in 1905 the IWW defined itself as a labor union based on class struggle without affiliation to any particular political party. In September 1908 at the IWW's fourth annual convention the organization voted by a small margin to remove all reference to political action from its constitution. The Socialist Party, in contrast, sought support as a traditional electoral party. Despite the potential antagonisms over strategy, many members of the IWW were also members of the Socialist Party.

with the faction that began its career by a most bitter and malicious persecution of one of the pioneers of Anarchism, Michael Bakunin.[4] In short, to the indefinite, uncertain mind of the American radical the most contradictory ideas and methods are possible. The result is a sad chaos in the radical movement, a sort of intellectual hash, which has neither taste nor character.

Just at present Syndicalism is the pastime of a great many Americans, so-called intellectuals. Not that they know anything about it, except that some great authorities— Sorel,[5] Bergson[6] and others[7]—stand for it: because the American needs the seal of authority, or he would not accept an idea, no matter how true and valuable it might be.

Our bourgeois magazines are full of dissertations on Syndicalism. One of our most conservative colleges has even gone to the extent of publishing a work of one of its students on the subject, which has the approval of a professor.[8] And all this, not because Syndicalism is a force and is being successfully practised by the workers of Europe, but because—as I said before—it has official authoritative sanction.

As if Syndicalism had been discovered by the philosophy of Bergson or the theoretical discourses of Sorel and Berth,[9] and had not existed and lived among the workers long before these men wrote about it. The feature which distinguishes Syndicalism from most philosophies is that it represents the revolutionary philosophy of labor conceived and born in the actual struggle and experience of the workers themselves—not in uni-

4. Michael Bakunin joined the International Workingmen's Association (IWA) in 1868. Engaged with Marx in a bitter dispute over the structure and organization of the International, Bakunin and his supporters were expelled at the 1872 congress at the IWA in the Hague.

5. Georges Sorel (1847–1922), a trained engineer, wrote on social and economic issues from a socialist and revolutionary syndicalist perspective. Best known for *Réflexions sur la violence* (Reflections on Violence) (Paris: Librairie de "Pages libres," 1908), a work advocating the use of violence, culminating in a general strike, to create an opening for the establishment of a moral, equitable society run by the proletariat. Sorel was later associated with the nationalist syndicalist movement in France and collaborated with members of the monarchist movement Action Française, until around 1914.

6. Henri Bergson (1859–1941) was a French philosopher. His works on political economy influenced Georges Sorel, who borrowed Bergson's terminology and regularly quoted him in his own work. Bergson rejected the primacy of intellectual and scientific rationalism at the expense of the metaphysical and attempted to incorporate intuition and consciousness into Darwin's biological theories in order to understand social systems and behaviors more clearly.

7. In the pamphlet edition of this essay the text reads: "Sorel, Lagardelle, Berth and others." Hubert Lagardelle (1875–1958) was a socialist in 1899 when he launched *La Jeunesse socialiste*; he later was drawn to the ideas of revolutionary syndicalism.

8. A reference to anarchist scholar Lewis Lorwin (Levine), who contributed his article "Syndicalism" to the liberal magazine *North American Review* in 1912. Columbia University published Lorwin's PhD thesis, "The Labor Movement in France: A Study in Revolutionary Syndicalism" (Columbia University, 1912) as part of a larger work, *Studies in History, Economics and Public Law* (New York: Columbia University Press, 1917). Columbia professor Franklin H. Giddings wrote a favorable introduction to Lorwin's work.

9. Edouard Berth (1874–1939) was a French intellectual whose writings during this period, *Les nouveau aspects du socialisme* (Paris: M. Riviere, 1908) and others, focused on the working class and on revolutionary syndicalism.

versities, colleges, libraries, or in the brain of some scientists. *The revolutionary philosophy of labor,* that is the true and vital meaning of Syndicalism.

Already as far back as 1848 a large section of the workers realized the utter futility of political activity as a means of helping them in their economic struggle.[10] At that time already the demand went forth for direct economic measures, as against the useless waste of energy along political lines. This was the case not only in France, but even prior to that in England, where Robert Owen, the true revolutionary Socialist, propagated similar ideas.[11]

After years of agitation and experiment the idea was incorporated by the first convention of the *Internationale*, in 1867, in the resolution that the economic emancipation of the workers must be the principal aim of all revolutionists, to which everything else is to be subordinated.[12]

In fact, it was this determined radical stand which eventually brought about the split in the revolutionary movement of that day, and its division into two factions: the one, under Marx and Engels, aiming at political conquest; the other, under Bakunin and the Latin workers, forging ahead along industrial and Syndicalist lines.[13] The further development of those two wings is familiar to every thinking man and woman: the one has gradually centralized into a huge machine, with the sole purpose of conquering political power within the existing capitalist State; the other is becoming an ever more vital revolutionary factor, dreaded by the enemy as the greatest menace to its rule.

It was in the year 1900, while a delegate to the Anarchist Congress in Paris, that I first came in contact with Syndicalism in operation.[14] The Anarchist press had been discussing the subject for years prior to that; therefore we Anarchists knew something about Syndicalism. But those of us who lived in America had to content themselves with the theoretic side of it.

10. The 1848 February Revolution in France, which overthrew the monarchy of Louis Philippe and established the Second Republic, catalyzed popular uprisings in several western and central European states, including the Hapsburg Empire, the German states, and Italy. Each of these revolutions, however, was eventually defeated.

11. Robert Owen (1771–1858) was a British utopian socialist who immigrated to America, where he founded several cooperative communities, including the New Harmony Colony in Indiana (founded in 1825). Some historians would disagree with EG's assessment of Owen's eschewing of political activity as futile, because he was known to have on occasion submitted his social reform proposals to government officials and worked with them.

12. The first convention of the International Workingmen's Association actually took place in 1865 in London. The first congress was held in 1866 in Geneva.

13. Bakunin was a significant influence on IWA members in western European (referred to by EG as Latin) countries. In 1868 he founded the International Alliance of Social Democracy, which had branches in Spain, Italy, and Switzerland. The term "syndicalist," as EG used it, was not in use in 1872, becoming part of common usage only in the early twentieth century.

14. Though EG came as a delegate, the 1900 anarchist congress in Paris was halted by the police before it began. For more on the 1900 anarchist congress (International Congress of Revolutionary Working People) see vol. 1, *Made for America*, pp. 416–21.

In 1900, however, I saw its effect upon labor in France: the strength, the enthusiasm and hope with which Syndicalism inspired the workers. It was also my good fortune to learn of the man who more than anyone else had directed Syndicalism into definite working channels, Fernand Pelloutier. Unfortunately, I could not meet this remarkable young man, as he was at that time already very ill with cancer.[15] But wherever I went, with whomever I spoke, the love and devotion for Pelloutier was wonderful, all agreeing that it was he who had gathered the discontented forces in the French labor movement and imbued them with new life and a new purpose, that of Syndicalism.

On my return to America I immediately began to propagate Syndicalist ideas, especially Direct Action and the General Strike.[16] But it was like talking to the Rocky Mountains—no understanding, even among the more radical elements, and complete indifference in labor ranks.

In 1907 I went as a delegate to the Anarchist Congress at Amsterdam and, while in Paris, met the most active Syndicalists in the *Confédération Général du Travail:* Pouget,[17] Delesalle,[18] Monatte,[19] and many others. More than that, I had the opportunity to see Syndicalism in daily operation, in its most constructive and inspiring forms.

15. Fernand Pelloutier (1867–1901) was a journalist and socialist who, disillusioned by leftist party politics, moved toward anarchism and syndicalism. He was general secretary of the Fédération Nationale des Bourses du Travail from 1895 until his death in 1901 from leukemia.

16. Before traveling to Europe in November 1899, EG regularly lectured on trade unionism. After her return her lectures included topics such as "Anarchism and Trade Unionism" and "Cooperation a Factor in the Industrial Struggle." EG did not, however, begin lecturing specifically on syndicalism until after her trip to Europe in 1907. While in Europe she attended the International Anarchist Congress in Amsterdam, where syndicalism was strongly endorsed by a number of anarchists present. She returned to the United States in October 1907 and began delivering a lecture entitled "Syndicalism: A New Phase in the Labor Movement" in January 1908. The topic however was dropped from her lectures until November 1912. Her lecture on syndicalism had a range of titles, including "Syndicalism, the Hope of the Worker"; "Syndicalism in Theory and Practice"; "Syndicalism, the Strongest Weapon of Labor"; and "Syndicalism, the Modern Menace to Capitalism." See "The International Anarchist Congress," Article in *Mother Earth*, October 1907, in vol. 2, *Making Speech Free*, p. 234, for EG's report of the congress, including a fuller explanation of syndicalism.

17. Émile Pouget (1860–1931) was a leading member of the CGT. In 1900 he founded the CGT publishing organ, *La Voix du peuple*, with Fernand Pelloutier. He had also been editor of the anarchist paper *Père Peinard* (Cool Daddy) See vol. 1, *Made for America*, pp. 552 and 567.

18. Paul Delesalle (1870–1948) was an anarchist, revolutionary syndicalist militant, and precision toolmaker. He was the assistant secretary of the Fédération Nationale des Bourses du Travail and of the CGT bourses section from 1897 to 1908, and a drafter of the Charter of Amiens. Delesalle was arrested in 1907 for his protest against the French government's deployment of troops in the Midi. He left the CGT in 1908 and opened a bookstore. He was also a regular contributor to *Les Temps nouveaux* (New Times) and *La Voix du peuple* (The Voice of the People). His many pamphlets include *La Confédération générale du Travail* (1907) and *Syndicat et Syndicalisme* (1909).

19. Pierre Monatte (1881–1960), a French anarcho-syndicalist influenced by Émile Pouget, played a central role in the 1907 International Anarchist Congress in Amsterdam, where he argued that syndicalism was the best strategy for revolutionary change. He fled to Switzerland in 1908 to escape arrest for his involvement in the strike at Villeneuve-Saint-Georges. He returned to Paris and worked as a librarian for the Confédération Générale du Travail. He founded the magazine *La*

I allude to this, to indicate that my knowledge of Syndicalism does not come from Sorel, Bergson or Berth, but from actual contact with and observation of the tremendous work carried on by the workers of Paris within the ranks of the *Confédération*. It would require a volume to explain in detail what Syndicalism is doing for the French workers. In the American press you read only of its resistive methods, of strikes and sabotage, of the conflicts of labor with capital. These are no doubt very important matters, and yet the chief value of Syndicalism lies much deeper. It lies in the constructive and educational effect upon the life and thought of the masses.

The fundamental difference between Syndicalism and the old trade union methods is this: while the old trade unions, without exception, move within the wage system and capitalism, recognizing the latter as inevitable, Syndicalism repudiates and condemns present industrial arrangements as unjust and criminal, and holds out no hope to the worker for lasting results from this system.

Of course Syndicalism, like the old trade unions, fights for immediate gains, but it is not stupid enough to pretend that labor can expect humane conditions from inhuman economic arrangements in society. Thus it merely wrests from the enemy what it can force him to yield; on the whole, however, Syndicalism aims at, and concentrates its energies upon, the complete overthrow of the wage system. Indeed, Syndicalism goes further: it aims to liberate labor from every institution that has not for its object the free development of production for the benefit of all humanity. In short, the ultimate purpose of Syndicalism is to reconstruct society from its present centralized, authoritative and brutal state to one based upon the free, federated grouping of the workers along lines of economic and social liberty.

With this object in view, Syndicalism works in two directions: first, by undermining the existing institutions; secondly, by developing and educating the workers and cultivating their spirit of solidarity, to prepare them for a full, free life, when capitalism shall have been abolished.

Syndicalism is, in essence, the economic expression of Anarchism. That circumstance accounts for the presence of so many Anarchists in the Syndicalist movement. Like Anarchism, Syndicalism prepares the workers along direct economic lines, as conscious factors in the great struggles of to-day, as well as conscious factors in the task of reconstructing society along autonomous industrial lines, as against the paralyzing spirit of centralization with its bureaucratic machinery of corruption, inherent in all political parties.

Realizing that the diametrically opposed interests of capital and labor can never be reconciled, Syndicalism must needs repudiate the old rusticated, worn-out methods of trade unionism, and declare for an open war against the capitalist régime, as well as against every institution which to-day supports and protects capitalism.

---

*Vie Ouvière* (Worker's Life, Paris, 1909–1914). Although opposed to the First World War, Monatte was drafted and chose to serve in the military.

As a logical sequence Syndicalism, in its daily warfare against capitalism, rejects the contract system, because it does not consider labor and capital equals, hence cannot consent to an agreement which the one has the power to break, while the other must submit to without redress.

For similar reasons Syndicalism rejects negotiations in labor disputes, because such a procedure serves only to give the enemy time to prepare his end of the fight, thus defeating the very object the workers set out to accomplish. Also, Syndicalism stands for spontaneity, both as a preserver of the fighting strength of labor and also because it takes the enemy unawares, hence compels him to a speedy settlement or causes him great loss.

Syndicalism objects to a large union treasury, because money is as corrupting an element in the ranks of labor as it is in those of capitalism. We in America know this to be only too true. If the labor movement in this country were not backed by such large funds, it would not be as conservative as it is, nor would the leaders be so readily corrupted. However, the main reason for the opposition of Syndicalism to large treasuries consists in the fact that they create class distinctions and jealousies within the ranks of labor, so detrimental to the spirit of solidarity. The worker whose organization has a large purse considers himself superior to his poorer brother, just as he regards himself better than the man who earns fifty cents less per day.

The chief ethical value of Syndicalism consists in the stress it lays upon the necessity of labor getting rid of the element of dissension, parasitism and corruption in its ranks. It seeks to cultivate devotion, solidarity and enthusiasm, which are far more essential and vital in the economic struggle than money.

As I have already stated, Syndicalism has grown out of the disappointment of the workers with politics and parliamentary methods. In the course of its development Syndicalism has learned to see in the State—with its mouthpiece, the representative system—one of the strongest supporters of capitalism; just as it has learned that the army and the church are the chief pillars of the State. It is therefore that Syndicalism has turned its back upon parliamentarism and political machines, and has set its face toward the economic arena wherein alone gladiator Labor can meet his foe successfully.

Historic experience sustains the Syndicalists in their uncompromising opposition to parliamentarism. Many had entered political life and, unwilling to be corrupted by the atmosphere, withdrew from office, to devote themselves to the economic struggle— Proudhon,[20] the Dutch revolutionist Nieuwenhius,[21] John Most[22] and numerous others.

---

20. French social theorist and anarchist Pierre-Joseph Proudhon was elected to the Constituent Assembly of the Second Republic in June 1848, before being imprisoned for criticizing Louis-Napoleon.
21. Ferdinand Domela Nieuwenhuis was an anarchist and syndicalist who had been a preacher prior to 1879. He was the first socialist member of the Dutch parliament in 1888, where he became disenchanted with parliamentarianism and gravitated toward anarchism.
22. Johann Most was elected into the Reichstag (German parliament) in 1874 and 1878 before he became an anarchist.

While those who remained in the parliamentary quagmire ended by betraying their trust, without having gained anything for labor. But it is unnecessary to discuss here political history.[23] Suffice to say that Syndicalists are anti-parliamentarians as a result of bitter experience.

Equally so has experience determined their anti-military attitude. Time and again has the army been used to shoot down strikers and to inculcate the sickening idea of patriotism, for the purpose of dividing the workers against themselves and helping the masters to the spoils. The inroads that Syndicalist agitation has made into the superstition of patriotism are evident from the dread of the ruling class for the loyalty of the army, and the rigid persecution of the anti-militarists. Naturally, for the ruling class realizes much better than the workers that when the soldiers will refuse to obey their superiors, the whole system of capitalism will be doomed.

Indeed, why should the workers sacrifice their children that the latter may be used to shoot their own parents? Therefore Syndicalism is not merely logical in its anti-military agitation; it is most practical and far-reaching, inasmuch as it robs the enemy of his strongest weapon against labor.

Now, as to the methods employed by Syndicalism—Direct Action, Sabotage, and the General Strike.

DIRECT ACTION.—Conscious individual or collective effort to protest against, or remedy, social conditions through the systematic assertion of the economic power of the workers.[24]

Sabotage has been decried as criminal, even by so-called revolutionary Socialists.[25] Of course, if you believe that property, which excludes the producer from its use, is justifiable, then sabotage is indeed a crime. But unless a Socialist continues to be under the influence of our bourgeois morality—a morality which enables the few to monopolize the earth at the expense of the many—he cannot consistently maintain that capitalist property is inviolate. Sabotage undermines this form of private possession. Can it therefore be considered criminal? On the contrary, it is ethical in the best sense, since it helps society to get rid of its worst foe, the most detrimental factor of social life.

Sabotage is mainly concerned with obstructing, by every possible method, the regular process of production, thereby demonstrating the determination of the workers to give according to what they receive, and no more. For instance, at the time of the French railroad strike of 1910, perishable goods were sent on slow trains, or in an opposite direction of the one intended.[26] Who but the most ordinary philistine would call that a crime?

---

23. This sentence was omitted in the pamphlet edition.
24. This definition first appeared in the April 1912 edition of *Mother Earth*.
25. At the 1912 Socialist Party convention an amendment was passed that expelled members who opposed political action or advocated sabotage. This was an effort to weed out radical members of the party, including prominent IWW leader William Haywood. Haywood was officially recalled from the Executive Committee in early 1913, which prompted his own resignation from the party.
26. In October 1910 French railway workers called for a general strike, the culmination of their growing

If the railway men themselves go hungry, and the "innocent" public has not enough feeling of solidarity to insist that these men should get enough to live on, the public has forfeited the sympathy of the strikers and must take the consequences.

Another form of sabotage consisted, during this strike, in placing heavy boxes on goods marked "Handle with care," cut glass and china and precious wines. From the standpoint of the law this may have been a crime, but from the standpoint of common humanity it was a very sensible thing. The same is true of disarranging a loom in a weaving mill, or living up to the letter of the law with all its red tape, as the Italian railway men did, thereby causing confusion in the railway service. In other words, sabotage is merely a weapon of defense in the industrial warfare, which is the more effective, because it touches capitalism in its most vital spot, the pocket.

By the General Strike, syndicalism means a stoppage of work, the cessation of labor. Nor need such a strike be postponed until all the workers of a particular place or country are ready for it. As has been pointed out by Pelloutier, Pouget, as well as others, and particularly recent events in England,[27] the General Strike may be started by one industry and exert a tremendous force. It is as if one man suddenly raised the cry "Stop the thief!" Immediately others will take up the cry, till the air rings with it. The General Strike, initiated by one determined organization, by one industry or by a small, conscious minority among the workers, is the industrial cry of "Stop the thief," which is soon taken up by many other industries, spreading like wildfire in a very short time.

One of the objections of politicians to the General Strike is that the workers also would suffer for the necessaries of life. In the first place, the workers are past masters in going hungry; secondly, it is certain that a General Strike is surer of prompt settlement than an ordinary strike. Witness the transport and miner strikes in England: how quickly the lords of State and capital were forced to make peace. Besides, Syndicalism recognizes the right of producers to the things which they have created; namely, the right of the workers to help themselves if the strike does not meet with speedy settlement.

When Sorel maintains that the General Strike is an inspiration necessary for the people to give their life meaning, he is expressing a thought which the Americans have never tired of emphasizing. Yet I do not hold with Sorel that the General Strike is a

---

dissatisfaction with working conditions. To demonstrate the importance of their work to everyday life, they adopted tactics that included misdirecting goods. After dynamite was found on the Marseilles railway lines, ex-socialist minister of the interior Aristide Briand declared a military state of emergency, thereby mobilizing all the railway workers. Workers were forced to resume work (under threat of court-martial), and the strike committee was arrested. The strike was broken within one week. Mocking the phenomenon of a socialist strike breaker, Guy Aldred compiled a number of Briand quotes under the title "The Anarchist Sayings of Aristide Briand" in the February 1911 *Mother Earth.*

27. From 1910 to 1914 a wave of strikes and violent industrial conflict shook England. In 1910 coal miners struck in South Wales, in 1911 transport workers struck in Liverpool, and in 1912 both the first national miners' strike and a huge transport workers' strike in London rocked the country.

"social myth," that may never be realized.[28] I think that the General Strike will become a fact the moment labor understands its full value—its destructive as well as constructive value, as indeed many workers all over the world are beginning to realize.

These ideas and methods of Syndicalism some may consider entirely negative, though they are far from it in their effect upon society to-day. But Syndicalism has also a directly positive aspect. In fact, much more time and effort is being devoted to that phase than to the others. Various forms of Syndicalist activity are designed to prepare the workers, even within present social and industrial conditions, for the life of a new and better society. To that end the masses are trained in the spirit of mutual aid and brotherhood, their initiative and self-reliance developed, and an *esprit de corps* maintained whose very soul is solidarity of purpose and the community of interests of the international proletariat.

Chief among these activities are the *mutualitées*, or mutual aid societies, established by the French Syndicalists.[29] Their object is, foremost, to secure work for unemployed members, and to further that spirit of mutual assistance which rests upon the consciousness of labor's identity of interests throughout the world.

In his "The Labor Movement in France," Mr. L. Levine states that during the year 1902 over 74,000 workers, out of a total of 99,000 applicants, were provided with work by these societies, without being compelled to submit to the extortion of the employment bureau sharks.[30]

These latter are a source of the deepest degradation, as well as of most shameless exploitation, of the worker. Especially does it hold true of America, where the employment agencies are in many cases also masked detective agencies, supplying workers in need of employment to strike regions, under false promises of steady, remunerative employment.

The French Confédération had long realized the vicious rôle of employment agencies as leeches upon the jobless worker and nurseries of scabbery. By the threat of a General Strike the French Syndicalists forced the government to abolish the employment bureau sharks, and the workers' own *mutualitées* have almost entirely superseded them, to the great economic and moral advantage of labor.[31]

Besides the *mutualitées*, the French Syndicalists have established other activities

---

28. Sorel expounded this theory in *Réflexions sur la violence* (Reflections on Violence), which was first published in a series of articles in the French paper *Le Mouvement Socialiste* in 1906. An English-language edition of the book was published in New York by the publisher B. W. Huebsch in 1912.

29. Formed in the nineteenth century, "mutual aid" or "friendly" societies were precursors to trade unions—securing work for the unemployed and offering financial and social aid to workers and their families.

30. Louis Levine, *The Labor Movement in France: A Study in Revolutionary Syndicalism* (New York: Columbia University, 1912), p. 73.

31. In 1904 the French senate abolished employment bureaus in response to the CGT-supported campaigns in defense of protesting workers. Pressures building from numerous confrontations between police and workers, and a food-industry strike, influenced the senate's passing of the legislation.

tending to weld labor in closer bonds of solidarity and mutual aid. Among these are the efforts to assist workingmen journeying from place to place. The practical as well as ethical value of such assistance is inestimable. It serves to instill the spirit of fellowship and gives a sense of security in the feeling of oneness with the large family of labor. This is one of the vital effects of the Syndicalist spirit in France and other Latin countries. What a tremendous need there is for just such efforts in this country! Can anyone doubt the significance of the consciousness of workingmen coming from Chicago, for instance, to New York, sure to find there among their comrades welcome lodging and food until they have secured employment? This form of activity is entirely foreign to the labor bodies of this country, and as a result the traveling workman in search of a job— the "blanket stiff"—is constantly at the mercy of the constable and policeman, a victim of the vagrancy laws, and the unfortunate material whence is recruited, through stress of necessity, the army of scabdom.

I have repeatedly witnessed, while at the headquarters of the Confédération, the cases of workingmen who came with their union cards from various parts of France, and even from other countries of Europe, and were supplied with meals and lodging, and encouraged by every evidence of brotherly spirit, and made to feel at home by their fellow workers of the Confédération. It is due, to a great extent, to these activities of the Syndicalists that the French government is forced to employ the army for strikebreaking, because few workers are willing to lend themselves for such service, thanks to the efforts and tactics of Syndicalism.

No less in importance than the mutual aid activities of the Syndicalists is the cooperation established by them between the city and the country, the factory worker and the peasant or farmer, the latter providing the workers with food supplies during strikes, or taking care of the strikers' children. This form of practical solidarity has for the first time been tried in this country during the Lawrence strike,[32] with inspiring results.

And all these Syndicalist activities are permeated with the spirit of educational work, carried on systematically by evening classes on all vital subjects treated from an unbiased, libertarian standpoint—not the adulterated "knowledge" with which the minds are stuffed in our public schools. The scope of the education is truly phenomenal, including sex hygiene, the care of women during pregnancy and confinement, the care of home and children, sanitation and general hygiene; in fact, every branch of human knowledge— science, history, art—receives thorough attention, together with the practical application in the established workingmen's libraries, dispensaries, concerts and festivals, in which the greatest artists and literateurs of Paris consider it an honor to participate.

One of the most vital efforts of Syndicalism is to prepare the workers, *now*, for their rôle in a free society. Thus the Syndicalist organizations supply its members with text-

---

32. A reference to the 1912 textile workers' strike in Lawrence, Massachusetts, where strikers' children were cared for by supporters in other towns while the strike in Lawrence continued. See EG to BR, 24 January 1912, *EGP*, reel 6.

books on every trade and industry, of a character that is calculated to make the worker an adept in his chosen line, a master of his craft, for the purpose of familiarizing him with all the branches of his industry, so that when labor finally takes over production and distribution, the people will be fully prepared to manage successfully their own affairs.

A demonstration of the effectiveness of this educational campaign of Syndicalism is given by the railroad men of Italy, whose mastery of all the details of transportation is so great that they could offer to the Italian government to take over the railroads of the country and guarantee their operation with greater economy and fewer accidents than is at present done by the government.

Their ability to carry on production has been strikingly proved by the Syndicalists, in connection with the glass blowers' strike in Italy.[33] There the strikers, instead of remaining idle during the progress of the strike, decided themselves to carry on the production of glass. The wonderful spirit of solidarity resulting from the Syndicalist propaganda enabled them to build a glass factory within an incredibly short time. An old building, rented for the purpose and which would have ordinarily required months to be put into proper condition, was turned into a glass factory within a few weeks, by the solidaric efforts of the strikers aided by their comrades who toiled with them after working hours. Then the strikers began operating the glass-blowing factory, and their cooperative plan of work and distribution during the strike has proved so satisfactory in every way that the experimental factory has been made permanent and a part of the glass-blowing industry in Italy is now in the hands of the cooperative organization of the workers.

This method of applied education not only trains the worker in his daily struggle, but serves also to equip him for the battle royal and the future, when he is to assume his place in society as an intelligent, conscious being and useful producer, once capitalism is abolished.

Nearly all leading Syndicalists agree with the Anarchists that a free society can exist only through voluntary association, and that its ultimate success will depend upon the intellectual and moral development of the workers who will supplant the wage system with a new social arrangement, based on solidarity and economic well-being for all. That is Syndicalism, in theory and practice.

*Mother Earth* 7 (January–February 1913): 373–78, 417–22. This essay also appeared as a pamphlet under the title *Syndicalism: The Modern Menace to Capitalism* (Mother Earth Publishing Association, 1913); a truncated version entitled "Syndicalism" was published in Charles T. Sprading's anthology, *Liberty and the Great Libertarians* (Los Angeles: Golden Press, 1913), 506–13. See *EGP*, reel 48.

33. The Italian glassblowers were organized in a mutual aid society before 1900, when they formed the Federation of Italian Bottle-Blowers, an organization that negotiated agreements with the Glass Trust, an alliance of four companies and three independent factories. The federation called a strike when a factory, known as "the Glass," refused to negotiate with the new organization. The federation launched a cooperative bottle factory to offer work to the strikers. "The Glass" eventually merged its plant into the Glass Trust, and in its first year the cooperative plant turned a profit, spurring several new cooperative factories, which eventually dominated the production of the nation's glass.

Pamphlet published by
## MOTHER EARTH PUBLISHING ASSOCIATION
*New York, March 1913*

## Victims of Morality

Not so very long ago I attended a meeting addressed by Anthony Comstock, who has for forty years been the guardian of American morals. A more incoherent, ignorant ramble I have never heard from any platform.[1]

The question that presented itself to me, listening to the commonplace, bigoted talk of the man, was, how could anyone so limited and unintelligent wield the power of censor and dictator over a supposedly democratic nation? True, Comstock has the law to back him. Forty years ago, when Puritanism was even more rampant than to-day, completely shutting out the light of reason and progress, Comstock succeeded, through shady machination and political wire pulling, to introduce a bill which gave him complete control over the Post Office Department[2]—a control which has proved disastrous to the freedom of the press, as well as the right of privacy of the American citizen.

Since then, Comstock has broken into the private chambers of people, has confiscated personal correspondence, as well as works of art, and has established a system of espionage and graft which would put Russia to shame.[3] Yet the law does not explain the

---

1. On 1 November 1910 EG, BR, and others attended a meeting at the Labor Temple, Second Ave in New York City where Anthony Comstock spoke. EG and BR intervened in the meeting and criticized Comstock for his promotion of laws intended to deny the use of the mails for what he arbitrarily classified as "obscene" literature and pictures. For a report of this meeting see "Comstock Heckled at Labor Temple," Article in the *New York Times*, 2 November 1910, above.

2. In 1873 Anthony Comstock lobbied Congress to pass a law that banned from the mail any "obscene, lewd, or lascivious" items, including contraceptive information. The law became known as the Comstock Law, and Anthony Comstock was made the special post office official charged with enforcing the law. In addition to making the mailing of "obscene, lewd, or lascivious" items illegal, the law also gave the post office authority to suppress and destroy materials at its discretion. Comstock also used this authority to prosecute a wide range of progressive and radical publications.

3. Anthony Comstock would actively solicit materials, under false names, that he deemed indecent in order to prosecute the publishers for the mailing of obscene materials.

   As early as 1877 Comstock wrote to anarchist Ezra Heywood under a false name requesting a copy of *Cupid's Yokes*, Heywood's free love pamphlet. Heywood was arrested by Comstock and convicted, although he was pardoned within the year. In 1910 Comstock arrested New York anarchist George Bauer, the manager of *Freiheit*, after requesting under a false name two copies of a Francisco Ferrer memorial painting through the mail; the charges against Bauer were dropped. (See note 5 in "Comstock Heckled at Labor Temple," Article in the *New York Times*, 2 November 1910, for more on this incident.) In December 1914 a Comstock agent would visit William Sanger's apartment pretending to be a friend of Margaret Sanger's and request a copy of a birth control pamphlet. Sanger was then arrested by Comstock in early 1915 and convicted, eventually serving a thirty-day sentence. In

power of Anthony Comstock. There is something else, more terrible than the law. It is the narrow puritanic spirit, as represented in the sterile minds of the Young-Men-and-Old-Maid's Christian Union, Temperance Union, Sabbath Union, Purity League,[4] etc. A spirit which is absolutely blind to the simplest manifestations of life; hence stands for stagnation and decay. As in antebellum days, these old fossils lament the terrible immorality of our time. Science, art, literature, the drama, are at the mercy of bigoted censorship and legal procedure, with the result that America, with all her boastful claims to progress and liberty is still steeped in the densest provincialism.

The smallest dominion in Europe can boast of an art free from the fetters of morality, an art that has the courage to portray the great social problems of our time. With the sharp edge of critical analysis, it cuts into every social ulcer, every wrong, demanding fundamental changes and the transvaluation of accepted values.[5] Satire, wit, humor, as well as the most intensely serious modes of expression, are being employed to lay bare our conventional social and moral lies. In America we would seek in vain for such a medium, since even the attempt at it is made impossible by the rigid régime, by the moral dictator and his clique.

The nearest approach, however, are our muckrakers, who have no doubt rendered great service along economic and social lines.[6] Whether the muckrakers have or have not helped to change conditions, at least they have torn the mask from the lying face of our smug and self-satisfied society.

Unfortunately, the Lie of Morality still stalks about in fine feathers, since no one dares

---

addition, Comstock boasted of his harassment and persecution of people under the authority of the Comstock Act. As early as 1881 he already counted fifteen suicides as a result of his efforts. Many held him responsible for the suicide of freethought and free love advocate Ida Craddock, who after her third arrest and facing a second imprisonment by Comstock committed suicide in October 1902. In her suicide note she blamed Comstock's persistent persecution for her action.

4. EG refers to the Young Men's Christian Association (YMCA), the National Women's Christian Temperance Union (WCTU), the American Sabbath Union, and the American Purity Alliance, all Christian reform organizations. The YMCA was established in the United States in 1851 and was intended to protect young men from the vice present in cities; it was as a member of the YMCA Committee for the Suppression of Vice that Anthony Comstock began his paid career in vice suppression. The WCTU was founded in 1874 and was devoted to the suppression of alcohol consumption. The American Sabbath Union, organized in 1888, was dedicated to the preservation of the Sabbath for worship. The American Purity Alliance, founded in Baltimore in 1895, was dedicated to a Christian purification of social life, especially through the elimination of prostitution.

5. "Transvaluation" in Nietzsche's philosophy is the process by which one set of values is challenged and replaced by another. It is quite simply a total reassessment of morality. The first article on Nietzsche in *Mother Earth* appeared in March 1907 and was written by Helene Stoecker, a German feminist and sexual reformer. In November 1912 the works of Friedrich Nietzsche began to be advertised for sale by the magazine, and in January 1913 an article by B. M. (possibly Max Baginski) on Nietzsche's work appeared; the article discussed Nietzsche's attack upon Christian morality.

6. "Muckrakers" was the name given to investigative journalists who wrote exposés on municipal and corporate corruption. They were typically considered to be allied with the Progressive movement. Some of the most famous journalists associated with muckraking were Upton Sinclair, Lincoln Steffens, and Ida Tarbell.

to come within hailing distance of the holy of holies. Yet it is safe to say that no other superstition is so detrimental to growth, so enervating and paralyzing to the minds and hearts of the people, as the superstition of morality.

The most pathetic, and in a way discouraging, aspect of the situation is a certain element of liberals, and even of radicals, men and women apparently free from religious and social spooks. But before the monster of Morality they are as prostrate as the most pious of their kind—which is an additional proof to the extent to which the morality worm has eaten into the system of its victims and how far-going and thorough the measures must be which are to drive it out again.

Needless to say, society is obsessed by more than one morality. Indeed, every institution of to-day has its own moral standard. Nor could they ever have maintained themselves, were it not for religion, which acts as a shield, and for morality, which acts as the mask. This explains the interest of the exploiting rich in religion and morality. The rich preach, foster, and finance both, as an investment that pays good returns. Through the medium of religion they have paralyzed the mind of the people, just as morality has enslaved the spirit. In other words, religion and morality are a much better whip to keep people in submission, than even the club and the gun.[7]

To illustrate: The Property Morality declares that that institution is sacred. Woe to anyone that dares to question the sanctity of property, or sins against it! Yet everyone knows that Property is robbery;[8] that it represents the accumulated efforts of millions, who themselves are propertyless. And what is more terrible, the more poverty stricken the victim of Property Morality is, the greater his respect and awe for that master. Thus we hear advanced people, even so-called class-conscious workingmen, decry as immoral such methods as sabotage and direct action, because they aim at Property.

Verily, if the victims themselves are so blinded by the Property Morality, what need we expect from the masters? It therefore seems high time to bring home the fact that until the workers will lose respect for the instrument of their material enslavement, they need hope for no relief.

7. EG's attack on morality seems to draw a significant influence from the work of Max Stirner. In *Der Einzige und Sein Eigenthum* Stirner rejects the idea of an objective good and evil in favor of a life centered on oneself. Stirner's book was popular in individualist anarchist circles, and in particular was promoted in Benjamin Tucker's *Liberty*. Tucker published the first English-language translation, by Steven T. Byington, in 1907. The edition was generally less popular, although well known, among anarchist communists. Max Baginski wrote a review of Tucker's edition, in the May 1907 *Mother Earth*, in which he praised the book, criticized individualist anarchists, and discusses Stirner's attack on morality that "forges the chains of man's subjugation," much along the lines that EG does here. Contrast that, however, with the emphasis on the importance and need for morals and ethics as promoted in Peter Kropotkin's pamphlet *Anarchist Morality* (1891), which *Mother Earth* reprinted from November 1916 to March 1917, and as a pamphlet in 1917.

8. EG is referring here to Pierre-Joseph Proudhon's famous maxim "property is robbery," which he puts forth in his work *Qu'est-ce que la propriété?* (Paris: Brocard, 1840); an English-language translation was published by Benjamin Tucker: *What Is Property?* (Princeton, Mass.: B. R. Tucker, 1876).

* * *

However, it is with the effect of Morality upon women that I am here mostly concerned. So disastrous, so paralyzing has this effect been, that some even of the most advanced among my sisters never thoroughly outgrow it.

It is Morality which condemns woman to the position of a celibate, a prostitute, or a reckless, incessant breeder of hapless children.

First, as to the celibate, the famished and withered human plant. When still a young, beautiful flower, she falls in love with a respectable young man. But Morality decrees that unless he can marry the girl, she must never know the raptures of love, the ecstasy of passion, which reaches its culmination expression in the sex embrace. The respectable young man is willing to marry, but the Property Morality, the Family and Social Morality decree that he must first make his pile, must save up enough to establish a home and be able to provide for a family. The young people must wait, often many long, weary years.

Meanwhile the respectable young man, excited through the daily association and contact with his sweetheart, seeks an outlet for his nature in return for money. In ninety-nine cases out of a hundred, he will be infected, and when he is materially able to marry, he will infect his wife and possible offspring. And the young flower, with every fiber aglow with the fire of life, with all her being crying out for love and passion? She has no outlet. She develops headaches, insomnia, hysteria; grows embittered, quarrelsome, and soon becomes a faded, withered, joyless being, a nuisance to herself and everyone else. No wonder Stirner preferred the grisette to the maiden grown gray with virtue.[9]

There is nothing more pathetic, nothing more terrible, than this gray-grown victim of a gray-grown Morality. This applies even with greater force to the masses of professional middle-class girls, than to those of the people. Through economic necessity the latter are thrust into life's jungle at an early age; they grow up with their male companions in the factory and shop, or at play and dance. The result is a more normal expression of their physical instincts. Then too, the young men and women of the people are not so hide-bound by externalities, and often follow the call of love and passion regardless of ceremony and tradition.

But the overwrought and oversexed middle class girl, hedged in her narrow confines with family and social traditions, guarded by a thousand eyes, afraid of her own shadow—the yearning of her inmost being for the man or the child, must turn to cats,

---

9. "Now the habit of renunciation cools the heat of your desire, and the roses of your youth are growing pale in the chlorosis of your heavenliness. The soul is saved, the body may perish! O Lais, O Ninon, how well you did to scorn this gray virtue! One free *grisette* against a thousand virgins grown gray in virtue!" Max Stirner, *The Ego and His Own*, p. 63. This passage was quoted at greater length by Max Baginski in his review of Benjamin Tucker's edition of *The Ego and His Own* in the May 1907 *Mother Earth*.

dogs, canary birds, or the Bible Class. Such is the cruel dictum of Morality, which is daily shutting out love, light, and joy from the lives of innumerable victims.

Now, as to the prostitute. In spite of laws, ordinances, persecution, and prisons; in spite of segregation, registration, vice crusades, and other similar devices, the prostitute is the real specter of our age. She sweeps across the plains like a fire burning into every nook of life, devastating, destroying.

After all, she is paying back, in a very small measure, the curse and horrors society has strewn in her path. She, weary with the tramp of ages, harassed and driven from pillar to post, at the mercy of all, is yet the Nemesis of modern times, the avenging angel, ruthlessly wielding the sword of fire. For has she not the man in her power? And, through him, the home, the child, the race. Thus she slays, and is herself the most brutally slain.

What has made her? Whence did she come? Morality, the morality which is merciless in its attitude to women. Once she dared to be herself, to be true to her nature, to life, there is no return: the woman is thrust out from the pale and protection of society. The prostitute becomes the victim of Morality, even as the withered old maid is its victim. But the prostitute is victimized by still other forces, foremost among them the Property Morality, which compels woman to sell herself as a sex commodity for a dollar per, out of wedlock, or for fifteen dollars a weeks, in the sacred fold of matrimony.[10] The latter is no doubt safer, more respected, more recognized, but of the two forms of prostitution the girl of the street is the least hypocritical, the least debased, since her trade lacks the pious mask of hypocrisy; and yet she is hounded, fleeced, outraged, and shunned, by the very powers that have made her: the financier, the priest, the moralist, the judge, the jailor, and the detective, not to forget her sheltered, respectably virtuous sister, who is the most relentless and brutal in her persecution of the prostitute.

Morality and its victim, the mother—what a terrible picture! Is there indeed anything more terrible, more criminal, than our glorified sacred function of motherhood? The woman, physically and mentally unfit to be a mother, yet condemned to breed; the woman, economically taxed to the very last spark of energy, yet forced to breed; the woman, tied to a man she loathes, whose very sight fills her with horror, yet made to breed; the woman, worn and used-up from the process of procreation, yet coerced to breed, more, ever more. What a hideous thing, this much lauded motherhood! No wonder thousands of women risk mutilation and even prefer even death to this curse of the cruel imposition of the spook of Morality. Five thousand are yearly sacrificed upon the

10. The comparison of marriage to prostitution was a common one in free love circles, for example in Ezra Heywood's journal the *Word*, in Benjamin Tucker's *Liberty*, and in *Lucifer the Lightbearer*. See also, "Marriage, Essay in the *Firebrand*," 18 July 1897, vol. 1, in which EG states that "[t]he sole difference between her [the prostitute] and the married woman is, that the one has sold herself into chattel slavery during life, for a home or a title, and the other one sells herself for the length of time she desires."

altar of this monster, that will not stand for prevention but would cure abortions. Five thousand soldiers in the battle for their physical and spiritual freedom, and as many thousands more who are crippled and mutilated rather than bring forth life in a society based on decay and destruction.

Is it because the modern woman wants to shirk responsibility, or that she lacks love for her offspring, that drives her to the most drastic and dangerous means to avoid bearing children? Only shallow, bigoted minds can bring such an accusation. Else they would know that the modern woman has become race conscious, sensitive to the needs and rights of the child, as the unit of the race, and that therefore the modern woman has a sense of responsibility and humanity, which was quite foreign to her grandmother.

With the economic war raging all around her, with strife, misery, crime, disease, and insanity staring her in the face, with numberless little children ground into gold dust, how can the self and race-conscious woman become a mother? Morality can not answer this question. It can only dictate, coerce, or condemn—and how many women are strong enough to face this condemnation, to defy the moral dicta? Few, indeed. Hence they fill the factories, the reformatories, the homes for feeble minded, the prisons, the insane asylums, or they die in the attempt to prevent child-birth. Oh, Motherhood, what crimes are committed in thy name! What hoses are laid at your feet, Morality, destroyer of life!

Fortunately, the Dawn is emerging from the chaos and darkness. Woman is awakening, she is throwing off the nightmare of Morality; she will no longer be bound. In her love for the man she is not concerned in the contents of his pocketbook, but in the wealth of his nature, which alone is the fountain of life and of joy. Nor does she need the sanction of the State. Her love is sanction enough for her. Thus she can abandon herself to the man of her choice, as the flowers abandon themselves to dew and light, in freedom, beauty, and ecstasy.

Through her re-born consciousness as a unit, a personality, a race builder, she will become a mother only if she desires a child, and if she can give to the child, even before its birth, all that her nature and intellect can yield: harmony, health, comfort, beauty, and, above all, understanding, reverence, and love, which is the only fertile soil for new life, a new being.[11]

---

11. EG's use of eugenics concepts like "race" and "race building" were not at all unusual among free love advocates at this time. These ideas of a free, or anarchist, eugenics, were advocated by Moses Harman, Ezra Heywood, Lois Waisbrooker, and others. An early anarchist student of eugenics ideas was the individualist Stephen Pearl Andrews. The free lovers were also interested in the supposed advances in humanity that would be wrought by the free selection of partners by women. This idea was advocated by, among others, Stephen Pearl Andrews (see *Love, Marriage, and Divorce* [Boston: B. R. Tucker, 1889]), Ezra Heywood, and, in non-anarchist circles, Alfred Russell Wallace (see *Social Environment and Moral Progress* [New York: Cassel, 1913], pp. 147–49). EG seems particularly concerned here with the assumed prenatal, rather than hereditary, influence of a mother upon her child, an idea that, while largely rejected by biologists even today, was examined by, among others, Havelock Ellis in volume 5 of his *Studies in the Psychology of Sex* (Philadelphia: F .A. Davis, 1906) as well as in *The Problem of Race-Regeneration* (New York: Moffat, Yard, 1911).

Morality has no terrors for her who has risen beyond good and evil. And though Morality may continue to devour its victims, it is utterly powerless in the face of the modern spirit, that shines in all its glory upon the brow of man and woman, liberated and unafraid.

PD. Published as a pamphlet titled *The Victims of Morality and the Failure of Christianity* by Mother Earth Publishing Association in 1913, and originally published as "Victims of Morality" in *Mother Earth*, March 1913, pp. 19–24.

**Essay in *MOTHER EARTH***

*New York, April 1913*

# The Failure of Christianity

The counterfeiters and poisoners of ideas in their attempt to obscure the line between truth and falsehood, find a valuable ally in the conservatism of language.

Conceptions and words that have long ago lost their original meaning, continue through centuries to dominate mankind. Especially is this true if these conceptions have become a common-place, if they have been instilled in our beings from our infancy as great and irrefutable verities. The average mind is easily content with inherited and acquired things, or with the dicta of parents and teachers, because it is much easier to imitate than to create.

Our age has given birth to two intellectual giants, who have undertaken to transvalue the dead social and moral values of the past, especially those contained in Christianity. Friedrich Nietzsche and Max Stirner[1] have hurled blow upon blow against the portals of Christianity, because they saw in it a pernicious slave morality, the denial of life, the destroyer of all the elements that make for strength and character. True, Nietzsche has opposed the slave-morality idea inherent in Christianity in behalf of a master morality for the privileged few.[2] But I venture to suggest that his master idea had nothing to do with the vulgarity of station, caste, or wealth. Rather did it mean the masterful in human possibilities, the masterful in man that would help him to overcome old traditions and worn-out values, so that he may learn to become the creator of new and beautiful things.

Both Nietzsche and Stirner saw in Christianity the leveler of the human race, the breaker of man's will to dare and to do. They saw in every movement built on Christian morality and ethics attempts not at the emancipation from slavery, but for the perpetuation thereof. Hence they opposed these movements with might and main.

Whether I do or do not entirely agree with these iconoclasts, I believe, with them, that Christianity is most admirably adapted to the training of slaves, to the perpetuation of a slave society; in short, to the very conditions confronting us to-day. Indeed, never

---

1. German philosophers Friedrich Nietzsche and Max Stirner influenced the formulation of Goldman's arguments against religion. Stirner's *The Ego and His Own* (1844) was serialized in the anarchist newspaper *Liberty* and published in book form in 1907 by Benjamin Tucker, in an English translation by Steven T. Byington. EG often reprinted works by Nietzsche in *Mother Earth* and spread his ideas in her lectures. This essay was also heavily influenced by Bakunin's *God and the State*, originally published in English by Benjamin Tucker in 1883 and later published by Mother Earth Publishing Association in 1916.
2. See Nietzsche's *The Genealogy of Morals* (1887).

could society have degenerated to its present appalling stage, if not for the assistance of Christianity. The rulers of the earth have realized long ago what potent poison inheres in the Christian religion. That is the reason they foster it; that is why they leave nothing undone to instill it into the blood of the people. They know only too well that the subtleness of the Christian teachings is a more powerful protection against rebellion and discontent than the club or the gun.

No doubt I will be told that, though religion is a poison and institutionalized Christianity the greatest enemy of progress and freedom, there is some good in Christianity "itself." What about the teachings of Christ and early Christianity, I may be asked; do they not stand for the spirit of humanity, for right and justice?

It is precisely this oft-repeated contention that induced me to choose this subject, to enable me to demonstrate that the abuses of Christianity, like the abuses of government, are conditioned in the thing itself, and are not to be charged to the representatives of the creed. Christ and his teachings are the embodiment of submission, of inertia, of the denial of life; hence responsible for the things done in their name.

I am not interested in the theological Christ. Brilliant minds like Bauer,[3] Strauss,[4] Renan,[5] Thomas Paine,[6] and others refuted that myth long ago. I am even ready to admit that the theological Christ is not half so dangerous as the ethical and social Christ. In proportion as science takes the place of blind faith, theology loses its hold. But the ethical and poetical Christ-myth has so thoroughly saturated our lives, that even some of the most advanced minds find it difficult to emancipate themselves from its yoke. They have rid themselves of the letter, but have retained the spirit; yet it is the spirit which is back of all the crimes and horrors committed by orthodox Christianity. The Fathers of the Church can well afford to preach the gospel of Christ. It contains nothing dangerous to the régime of authority and wealth; it stands for self-denial and self-abnegation, for penance and regret, and is absolutely inert in the face of every indignity, every outrage imposed upon mankind.

3. Bruno Bauer (1809–1902) was a Hegelian German theologian who claimed there was no historical Jesus, asserting that Christianity was a religious construct of the early Christians. In the 1840s, as a member of the Young Hegelians of Berlin, Max Stirner belonged to an informal debating society over which Bauer presided.

4. David Friedrich Strauss (1808–1874) was a German theologian. His controversial work *Das Leben Jesu* (The Life of Jesus) (1835–1836) explored the Gospels as a historical text, rejecting any trace of the supernatural in his interpretation. (His book was translated into English in 1848 by Mary Anne Evans, better known by the pen name George Eliot.)

5. Ernest Renan (1823–1892) was a French liberal philosopher, skeptic, Bible critic, and orientalist. His seven-volume series, *History of the Origins of Christianity* (1863–1882), which included *The Life of Jesus* (1863), *The Apostles* (1866), *Saint Paul* (1867), *The Antichrist* (1873), *The Gospels* (1877), *The Christian Church* (1879), and *Marcus Aurelius* (1882), was virulently denounced by the French Catholic Church. An icon of the freethought movement, he was honored at his death by members of the International Freethought Federation, who sent a telegram of condolence to his widow.

6. In *Age of Reason* (1794, 1796) Thomas Paine (1737–1809) argued that although Jesus Christ actually may have existed, the histories about him were likely myths written by others for their own personal and political interests.

Here I must revert to the counterfeiters of ideas and words. So many otherwise earnest haters of slavery and injustice confuse, in a most distressing manner, the teachings of Christ with the great struggles for social and economic emancipation. The two are irrevocably and forever opposed to each other. The one necessitates courage, daring, defiance, and strength. The other preaches the gospel of non-resistance, of slavish acquiescence in the will of others; it is the complete disregard of character and self-reliance, and therefore destructive of liberty and well-being.

Whoever sincerely aims at a radical change in society, whoever strives to free humanity from the scourge of dependence and misery, must turn his back on Christianity, on the old as well as the present form of the same.

Everywhere and always, since its very inception, Christianity has turned the earth into a vale of tears; always it has made of life a weak, diseased thing, always it has instilled fear in man, turning him into a dual being, whose life energies are spent in the struggle between body and soul. In decrying the body as something evil, the flesh as the tempter to everything that is sinful, man has mutilated his being in the vain attempt to keep his soul pure, while his body rotted away from the injuries and tortures inflicted upon it.

The Christian religion and morality extols the glory of the Hereafter, and therefore remains indifferent to the horrors of the earth. Indeed, the idea of self-denial and of all that makes for pain and sorrow, is its test of human worth, its passport to the entry into heaven.

The poor are to own heaven, and the rich will go to hell. That may account for the desperate efforts of the rich to make hay while the sun shines, to get as much out of the earth as they can: to wallow in wealth and superfluity, to tighten their iron hold on the blessed slaves, to rob them of their birthright, to degrade and outrage them every minute of the day. Who can blame the rich if they revenge themselves on the poor, for now is their time, and the merciful Christian God alone knows how ably and completely the rich are doing it.

And the poor? They cling to the promise of the Christian heaven, as the home for old age, the sanitarium for crippled bodies and weak minds. They endure and submit, they suffer and wait, until every bit of self-respect has been knocked out of them, until their bodies become emaciated and withered, and their spirit broken from the wait, the weary endless wait for the Christian heaven.

Christ made his appearance as the leader of the people, the redeemer of the Jews from Roman dominion; but the moment he began his work, he proved that he had no interest in the earth, in the pressing immediate needs of the poor and the disinherited of his time. What he preached was a sentimental mysticism, obscure and confused ideas lacking originality and vigor.

When the Jews, according to the gospels, withdrew from Jesus, when they turned him over to the cross, they may have been bitterly disappointed in him who promised them so much and gave them so little. He promised joy and bliss in another world, while the people were starving, suffering, and enduring before his very eyes.

It may also be that the sympathy of the Romans, especially of Pilate,[7] was given Christ because they regarded him as perfectly harmless to their power and sway. The philosopher Pilate may have considered Christ's "eternal truths" as pretty anaemic and lifeless, compared with the array of strength and force they attempted to combat. The Romans, strong and unflinching as they were, must have laughed in their sleeves over the man who talked repentance and patience, instead of calling to arms against the despoilers and oppressors of his people.

The public career of Christ begins with the edict, "Repent, for the Kingdom of Heaven is at hand."

Why repent, why regret, in the face of something that was supposed to bring deliverance? Had not the people suffered and endured enough; had they not earned their right to deliverance by their suffering? Take the Sermon on the Mount, for instance. What is it but a eulogy on submission to fate, to the inevitability of things?

"Blessed are the poor in spirit, for theirs is the Kingdom of Heaven."

Heaven must be an awfully dull place if the poor in spirit live there. How can anything creative, anything vital, useful and beautiful come from the poor in spirit? The idea conveyed in the Sermon on the Mount[8] is the greatest indictment against the teachings of Christ, because it sees in the poverty of mind and body a virtue, and because it seeks to maintain this virtue by reward and punishment. Every intelligent being realizes that our worst curse is the poverty of the spirit; that it is productive of all evil and misery, of all the injustice and crimes in the world. Every one knows that nothing good ever came or can come of the poor in spirit; surely never liberty, justice, or equality.

"Blessed are the meek, for they shall inherit the earth."

What a preposterous notion! What incentive to slavery, inactivity, and parasitism! Besides, it is not true that the meek can inherit anything. Just because humanity has been meek, the earth has been stolen from it.

Meekness has been the whip, which capitalism and governments have used to force man into dependency, into his slave position. The most faithful servants of the State, of wealth, of special privilege, could not preach a more convenient gospel than did Christ, the "redeemer" of the people.

---

7. Pontius Pilate was the Roman prefect of Judea who handed over Jesus Christ for crucifixion.
8. The Sermon on the Mount was a sermon said to have been delivered by Jesus Christ on a Galilee mountainside. Considered the occasion of the largest gathering of followers of Jesus, the sermon imparted the essence of Christ's teachings, including "Blessed are those who mourn, for they shall be comforted" (Matthew 5:4); "Blessed are the meek, for they shall inherit the earth" (Matthew 5:5); "Blessed are those who hunger and thirst for righteousness, for they shall be filled" (Matthew 5:6); "Blessed are the merciful for they shall obtain mercy" (Matthew 5:7); "Blessed are the pure in heart, for they shall see God" (Matthew 5:8); "Blessed are the peacemakers, for they shall be called sons of God" (Matthew 5:9); and "Blessed are those who are persecuted for righteousness' sake, for theirs is the kingdom of heaven" (Matthew 5:10).

"Blessed are they that hunger and thirst for righteousness, for they shall be filled."

But did not Christ exclude the possibility of righteousness when he said, "The poor ye have always with you?" But, then, Christ was great on dicta, no matter if they were utterly opposed to each other. This is nowhere demonstrated so strikingly as in his command, "Render to Cesar the things that are Cesar's, and to God the things that are God's."

The interpreters claim that Christ had to make these concessions to the powers of his time. If that be true, this single compromise was sufficient to prove, down to this very day, a most ruthless weapon in the hands of the oppressor, a fearful lash and relentless tax-gatherer, to the impoverishment, the enslavement, and degradation of the very people for whom Christ is supposed to have died. And when we are assured that "Blessed are they that hunger and thirst for righteousness, for they shall be filled," are we told the how? How? Christ never takes the trouble to explain that. Righteousness does not come from the stars, nor because Christ willed it so. Righteousness grows out of liberty, of social and economic opportunity and equality. But how can the meek, the poor in spirit, ever establish such a state of affairs?

"Blessed are ye when men shall revile you and persecute you, and say all manner of evil against you falsely, for my sake. Rejoice, and be exceedingly glad: for great is your reward in heaven."

The reward in heaven is the perpetual bait, a bait that has caught man in an iron net, a strait-jacket which does not let him expand or grow. All pioneers of truth have been, and still are, reviled; they have been, and still are, persecuted. But did they ask humanity to pay the price? Did they seek to bribe mankind to accept their ideas? They knew too well that he who accepts a truth because of the bribe, will soon barter it away to a higher bidder.

Good and bad, punishment and reward, sin and penance, heaven and hell, as the moving spirit of the Christ-gospel have been the stumbling-block in the world's work. It contains everything in the way of orders and commands, but entirely lacks the very things we need most.

The worker who knows the cause of his misery, who understands the make-up of our iniquitous social and industrial system can do more for himself and his kind than Christ and the followers of Christ have ever done for humanity; certainly more than meek patience, ignorance, and submission have done.

How much more ennobling, how much more beneficial is the extreme individualism of Stirner and Nietzsche than the sick-room atmosphere of the Christian faith. If they repudiate altruism as an evil, it is because of the example contained in Christianity, which set a premium on parasitism and inertia, gave birth to all manner of social disorders that are to be cured with the preachment of love and sympathy.

Proud and self-reliant characters prefer hatred to such sickening artificial love. Not because of any reward does a free spirit take his stand for a great truth, nor has such a one ever been deterred because of fear of punishment.

"Think not that I come to destroy the law or the prophets. I am not come to destroy, but to fulfill."

Precisely. Christ was a reformer, ever ready to patch up, to fulfill, to carry on the old order of things; never to destroy and rebuild. That may account for the fellow-feeling all reformers have for him.

Indeed, the whole history of the State, Capitalism, and the Church proves that they have perpetuated themselves because of the idea "I come not to destroy the law." This is the key to authority and oppression. Naturally so, for did not Christ praise poverty as a virtue; did he not propagate non-resistance to evil? Why should not poverty and evil continue to rule the world?

Much as I am opposed to every religion, much as I think them an imposition upon, and crime against, reason and progress, I yet feel that no other religion had done so much harm or has helped so much in the enslavement of man as the religion of Christ.

Witness Christ before his accusers. What lack of dignity, what lack of faith in himself and in his own ideas! So weak and helpless was this "Saviour of Men" that he must needs the whole human family to pay for him, unto all eternity, because he "hath died for them." Redemption through the Cross is worse than damnation, because of the terrible burden it imposes upon humanity, because of the effect it has on the human soul, fettering and paralyzing it with the weight of the burden exacted through the death of Christ.

Thousands of martyrs have perished, yet few, if any, of them have proved so helpless as the great Christian God. Thousands have gone to their death with greater fortitude, with more courage, with deeper faith in their ideas than the Nazarene.[9] Nor did they expect eternal gratitude from their fellow-men because of what they endured for them.

Compared with Socrates[10] and Bruno,[11] with the great martyrs of Russia, with the Chicago Anarchists,[12] Francisco Ferrer,[13] and unnumbered others, Christ cuts a poor figure indeed. Compared with the delicate, frail Spiridonova[14] who underwent the most ter-

9. Literally "from Nazareth," a term used to describe both Jesus and his followers.
10. Socrates (469–399 BC) was sentenced to death after being tried for allegedly corrupting young people and for religious heresies.
11. Giordano Bruno (1548–1600), Italian philosopher and early freethinker whose works *Spaccio de la Bestia Trionfante* (Expulsion of the Triumphant Beast) and *La Cena de le Ceneri* (The Ash Wednesday Supper), both published in 1584, attacked both Aristotelian and Christian tendencies in contemporary thought. Tried by the Church for heresy and burned at the stake, Bruno was memorialized as an icon of the freethought movement. The anarchist newspaper *Lucifer the Lightbearer* was dated EM (Era of Man), from the death date of Bruno, rather than the birth of Christ.
12. A reference to the Chicago Haymarket anarchists executed in 1887.
13. Francisco Ferrer was executed by the Spanish government on 13 October 1909, on the official charge of being "author and chief of the rebellion" of the July 1909 general strike in Barcelona called by *Solidaridad Obrera*, in which churches were burned, thousands were injured, and more than 200 workers were killed.
14. Maria Aleksandrovna Spiridonova (1885–1941) was a Russian revolutionary who in 1906 assassinated the tsarist general Luzhenovsky, known for his brutal repression of the peasantry. Spiridonova was beaten and raped by the general's guards before being exiled to Siberia. Spiridonova had joined the Socialist Revolutionary Party (PSR) as a youth from Russia's gentry elite, and upon her release and return to Petrograd in 1917 she represented the party in the Constituent Assembly.

rible tortures, the most horrible indignities, without losing faith in herself or her cause, Jesus is a veritable nonentity. They stood their ground and faced their executioners with unflinching determination, and though they, too, died for the people, they asked nothing in return for their great sacrifice.

Verily, we need redemption from the slavery, the deadening weakness, and humiliating dependency of Christian morality.

The teachings of Christ and of his followers have failed because they lacked the vitality to lift the burdens from the shoulders of the race; they have failed because the very essence of that doctrine is contrary to the spirit of life, exposed to the manifestations of nature, to the strength and beauty of passion.

Never can Christianity, under whatever mask it may appear—be it New Liberalism, Spiritualism, Christian Science, New Thought, or a thousand and one other forms of hysteria and neurasthenia—bring us relief from the terrible pressure of conditions, the weight of poverty, the horrors of our iniquitous system. Christianity is the conspiracy of ignorance against reason, of darkness against light, of submission and slavery against independence and freedom; of the denial of strength and beauty, against the affirmation of the joy and glory of life.

*Mother Earth* 8 (April 1913): 41–48. For a verbatim draft of this essay, see *EGP*, reel 48. Also issued in pamphlet form along with "Victims of Morality" (1913) and with "The Philosophy of Atheism" (ca. 1913). See *EGP*, reel 48. EG delivered numerous lectures on "The Failure of Christianity" beginning in 1911 in New York City (5 November). In 1912 she spoke on the subject in St. Louis (25 February), Los Angeles (6 May), Portland (2 June), and New York City (22 December). She lectured on the subject on two occasions in 1913 (8 June and 21 December) under the revised heading "The Antichrist Friederich Nietzsche: Powerful Attack upon Christianity."

---

She would later serve more than twenty years' imprisonment in Siberia and would be shot by the Bolsheviks in 1941.

My dear Miss Kennan.

I have your good letter of March 29th, also the one sent Gen. Del. to this City, inclosed. The reason I failed to get the latter sooner, is that I had my mail addressed to the Hotel and not the P O.

Indeed, I do not mind your frank statement regarding the prejudice against Dr Reitman. I was aware all along that such prejudice existed, but, to me it spoke against the people who judged by externals, rather than against Dr Reitman, although I know that he does make a great many unecessary breaks.

However, you are mistaken regarding the letter to be sent out. There was no intention to have Dr Reitman's name, either prominant, or in any other form appear on the letter. That is pricisely the reason why I asked you and Mrs Mc.Farlane, to sign the letter, since it is impossible to send it unsigned and would be tactless for me to sign it.

I shall be very glad for you to manage the Nietzsche course,[1] but just what do you mean by that, if our friends do not even want to sign a simple announcement? No doubt they have their reasons, (have not yet heard from either), how are we to reach people about the course? I will be glad to hear what you suggest. Let me hear from you soon. I leave here for Minneapolis Friday.[2] Gen. Del will reach me there.

I hope you understand dear Miss Kennan, that I do not want you or my other friends to do anything, which you would rather not do for whatever resson. Not even for the sake of success do I want my friends to be compelled to do anything against their desire.

There is one other thing, I have all my life struggled against prejudice and have never made concessions to it. I feel that I could not do it at this late day even for the sake of success, which would mean the most terrible failure to me. But that does not mean dear friend, that I want to impose Dr Reitman on any one.

If you feel you can sign the letter, not the kind I sent you but one setting forth the Nietzsche course, I will mail the letter to you as soon as it is done, if not we will have to let things run their course and depend on the sale of tickets, of which I inclose a dozen, am sending to Mrs Mc Farlane, Kassler and Taussig[3] each the same number, also to some of our other subscribers.

Let me hear from you soon and please do not feel that I am in the least hurt because

---

1. EG delivered several lectures on Nietzsche from 29 April through 1 May 1913 at the Denver Women's Club.
2. EG was scheduled to lecture in Minneapolis from 6 to 9 April 1913.
3. Grace Kessler was a Denver resident who subscribed to *Mother Earth* (as Mrs. C. Kessler). Her hus-

of the reference to Dr Reitman, he can take care of himself, I am sure. It merely occurs to me that people who start with prejudice may not get much out of Nietzsche who faught prejudice as no other man has.

With kindest regards to Miss Nafe.[4]

CORDIALLY

EMMA GOLDMAN

TLS with handwritten corrections, Emma Goldman Archive, IISH. On stationery of the Lexington Hotel, Chicago, Ill.

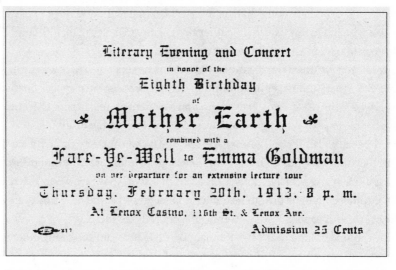

Card announcing a farewell gala for Emma Goldman, a combined literary evening and concert, at the Lenox Casino, New York, before she embarked on her annual cross-country lecture tour. (Kate Sharpley Archive)

---

band, Charles M. Kessler, owned Kessler Investment Company in Denver, Colorado. Gertrude H. Taussig was a Denver resident and Kennan's friend.
4. Gertrude Nafe lived with Kennan and, like Kennan, was a high school teacher. She was a teacher of English and contributed a number of stories and reports to *Mother Earth*.

Dear Comrade:

I am writing this letter away from our office, therefore, cannot speak for the rest of our comrades, Berkman, Baginski, Havel and Harry,[1] but I do know that we were all very happy indeed, to get your two letters, one dated December 21st and the other of February 4th. We were ~~pretty~~ glad of the assurance in your two letters that you are feeling much better and have now recovered from your attack.[2] You can imagine, dear comrade, what the news of your illness meant to us, especially as we felt that possibly we had been instrumental in overtaxing your energies. But now, that you are with us again, we rejoice in the great tribute paid you from all parts of the world.

Indeed, I was very glad to hear of the testimonials sent you from Russia. While my whole life is rapt up in the American struggle, almost as if I had been born here, still my soul is in Russia, and probably will never be anywhere else. Did I ever tell you, dear comrade, that years ago when Gershuni and Thaikovsky were in New York,[3] I came near going to Russia? At that time it seemed as if I could not endure life in America, when the struggle was so intense in Russia, and Gershuni wanted me to go very much. Indeed, had made all arrangements for me to go and the one thing which prevented the plan was a question asked me by Thaikovsky, as to what defense I would make should I come before court in Russia. That is, whether I would say "I am an Anarchist." Needless to say, I told him that that would be exactly what I would state, and of course the S. R. could not back me.[4] Thus, I remained here, whether for good or evil.

I am giving you this little bit of experience, that you may know how deeply my sympathies are with the Russian struggle and always will be, although my life is so intense that I rarely get time to listen to my own voice, as to where I most crave to be.

I have been on the road again since the 21st of February, and I am sorry to say that the

1. AB, Max Baginski, Hippolyte Havel, and Harry Kelly worked at the *Mother Earth* office in New York City.
2. In November 1901 Kropotkin had suffered a severe heart attack, marking the beginning of a progressive physical decline punctuated by periods of physical frailty.
3. In 1905 Russian member of the Socialist Revolutionary Party (PSR) Gregori Gershuni was sentenced to exile in Siberia after he was arrested for conspiring to assassinate Interior Minister D. S. Sipiagin. He escaped through China to the United States and visited New York in early 1907. Nikolai Chaikovsky was also in New York at the time, lecturing as a representative of the PSR.
4. The adopted program of the PSR advocated socialism achieved through a democratic republic based on general franchise and the conversion of Russia into a federative state. The PSR's brand of socialism-populism, unlike anarchism, embraced democratic socialism and often focused on the concerns and needs of Russia's peasantry.

tour this time has not proven satisfactory, either in point of attendance or in the quality of the audiences. I cannot ascribe it to any other cause except the usual reaction from the political tension which follows every Presidential election in the United States. During the campaign the people are excited almost to the breaking point. They concentrate all their hopes and expectations on their political candidate, and when the election is over, a mental apathy and spiritual indifference sets in, which nothing will overcome. Time after time the people go through the same fuss, and yet they will not learn how utterly stupid the whole performance is. The thing that makes our position in this country so very desperate is that everybody outside of the Anarchists perpetuate the political spook, even the I. W. W., who are doing splendid work in a way, and are really developing a wonderful type of American proletarians; even they have never yet definitely declared themselves against politics, and Bill Haywood who is the most earnest of the members continues to play with fire by sticking in the Socialist Party.[5] You can see for yourself, dear comrade, how very much alone we stand and how difficult and trying is our position.

Of course, a change has taken place towards our ideas. There is no longer the blind hatred and unreasonable opposition of ten or fifteen years ago, although, it requires just the least little bit of an inducement, as that in San Diego,[6] for the old brutalities to break loose, but on the whole we do get a hearing and we are treated with great respect, which is something gained, but not enough to satisfy one who stands on the firing line. It is therefore not at all strange that I should feel completely worn out on this trip. I have come to the point where I will have to, by sheer necessity, discontinue the annual tours and concentrate myself on New York and "Mother Earth."

Comrade Berkman's book has been widely and favorably reviewed, and yet with it all, it does not sell well.[7] Hard to tell why. We still have the whole burden of the cost on our backs, which will probably take at least another year to dispose of, but with it all, we do not regret for one minute having published it; even if it only reaches the few, it will continue to live among them, and that is all one may hope for a great work.

It is hardly necessary for you to write to the comrade who sent you the paper knife.

5. At the 1908 convention of the Industrial Workers of the World (IWW) the preamble to the union's constitution was changed to remove reference to political action. Many members, however, remained in the Socialist Party of America (SPA). In 1912 the SPA passed an amendment requiring its membership to pledge their opposition to sabotage, violence, and all illegal action. The imposition of the oath forced William Haywood to choose between the SPA and the IWW, and he withdrew from SPA activities.

6. During the 1912 IWW free speech fights in San Diego, vigilantes attacked and threatened radicals. In May 1912 while organizing EG's lectures in San Diego, BR was kidnapped by vigilantes, who were under police protection, and taken to La Penasquitos ranch, about twenty miles north of San Diego. He was tarred and "sagebrushed" with the letters "IWW" burned into his rear with a cigar and forced to kiss the American flag while singing "The Star Spangled Banner." See "The Outrage of San Diego," *Mother Earth*, June 1912 (above).

7. AB's *Prison Memoirs of an Anarchist* was published in 1912 by Mother Earth Publishing Association. For an example of a review see *Current Literature* 53 (December 1912).

However, his name is John Spies, and his address is Box 1307, Care of Frank Monroe, Denver, Colorado.[8] I see him every evening, as he attends all my lectures. He is very happy, indeed, to have given you some pleasure with his work. He is a great artist and would be a tremendous addition to a free society, but under our present regime he must eek out a bear existence in the most deadening factory atmosphere. Such is the lot of a great many who would render so much service to the world if they had a chance.

Well, dear comrade, I do not wish to write too much, because I do not want to tax your strength in reading what I have to say. I hope, profoundly, that you may continue to do your great work for many, many years longer. We need you badly because there is no one to take your place, and you must know that you have been a tremendous factor in Anarchist thought and ideas.

Give my love to Sophie and Sasha,[9] also to Shapiro[10] and any of the other comrades who are interested in knowing about our life and work.

I expect to be back in New York by the end of July, as I am now on the way to the Coast which will take about two months to cover.

YOURS FRATERNALLY,
EMMA GOLDMAN

TLS, with autograph corrections, Peter Kropotkin Collection, GA RF. Addressed from the Roslyn Hotel, Denver.

8. John Spies, Frank A. Monroe, and Lena Monroe were Denver anarchists and subscribers to *Mother Earth*.
9. His wife, Sophia Kropotkin, and their daughter, Sasha (the diminutive for Alexandra).
10. Alexander Schapiro (1882–1946) was a Russian-born anarchist who lived in London. Schapiro represented the Jewish Anarchist Federation at the 1907 Anarchist Congress in Amsterdam, where he was made a member of the International Correspondence Bureau.

My dear Friend:—

Got your wire signed by the other faithful ones this morning. Not for one moment did I doubt your devotion and interest, and yet when the message came it made me very happy. We never realize how much our friends mean to us until we are surrounded by enemies, and the time spent in San Diego,—Tuesday, May the 20th,—was even more hideous than last year.[1] I suppose when you wired you had only read of our arrest which took place the moment we left the train but the more horrible thing came later. The mob as bloodthirsty and infuriated, surrounded the jail because it knew that it was backed by the police. For four endless hours, I heard the fire alarm ringing in my ears with the shouts for Ben Reitman. There is no doubt in my mind that had the mob gotten to Ben, it would not have meant only tarring but death; besides, the police were determined to force us out of the city, so, under the circumstances, there was nothing else to do but to go. However, the experience has made me more resolute than ever to go back to San Diego if it takes me the rest of my life until I have established free speech but if I go again I will go alone as it is almost beyond human power to move freely when you have those dear to you depending for their lives upon every one of their movements.

My meetings here have been tremendously successful. In fact, the most successful I have ever had in Los Angeles. I close tomorrow night but most likely I will return for another two weeks as I have a guaranteed offer of fifty subscribers to a drama course.[2] It is not definite; I will know more about it before I leave. However, I have two weeks' work in San Francisco and if I do come back to this city it will be when I am through with San Francisco.

There are many things I should like to talk to you about but I have a great deal to do

1. EG and BR arrived in San Diego at 4:40 a.m., were arrested immediately, and were taken to the police station. The police station was mobbed, and to ensure their safety they were escorted to the train station, as the angry crowd followed them, for a Santa Fe Railroad train back to Los Angeles at 1:10 p.m. This experience, coupled with the brutal treatment he had encountered in San Diego a year before, traumatized BR.

2. From 12 to 23 May EG delivered lectures in Los Angeles on topics including "Revolutionary Labor Methods," "The Failure of Democracy," "The Russian Drama," and "The Modern Drama." After lecturing in San Francisco EG returned to Los Angeles, and on 16 June began a drama lecture series at Choral Hall.

and so will close, grateful for all your beautiful friendship. Remember me with love to Edith Chase[3] and the others. I am writing Gertrude myself.[4]

WITH MUCH LOVE,
EMMA GOLDMAN

For the next two weeks, you can address me, General Delivery, San Francisco.

TLS, Emma Goldman Archive, IISH. Addressed to Miss Ellen Kennan, 701 East 14th Avenue, Denver, Colorado.

3. Edith Chase was a Denver high school teacher at East Side High School, a colleague of both Ellen Kennan and Gertrude Nafe, and a subscriber to *Mother Earth*.
4. Gertrude Nafe was Kennan's friend and roommate.

DEAR FRIEND

I had hoped by this time to be able to write you difinitely when we might reopen in L A. But I am at a loss just now.[1]

I find a terrible reaction in this City, as a result of the muddled outcome of the McNamara, Darow & Indianapolis[2] cases. More than ever I am convinsed of the logic of the anarchist position against compromise. It's simply heartbreaking to see what Darow has made of the one supreme opportunity of his life and how his weakness and compromise have influenced labor all along the line.

Under the circumstances I am not at all sure if I can get into the unions. Those who might help me are bitterly pessemistic and the others are too cowardly to stand for the things they know, I would say.

However, I have not yet given up hope completely. In any event, we are coming back to L A if the drama venture can be assured. I am writing to Mr Elsworth about the Egan Auditorium for that purpose, he has probably phoned you or will do so, when he has seen the man.[3]

As to the single admission I think I will give 9 lectures instead of eight in the course for $5 with M E and charge 50 c admission. This will give me more time to do justice to the work I mean to take up and will also be greater inducement for those who want to take the course.

The main thing now is to get as many subscribers as you can. I know you & Mrs Gerson will do that. Perhaps you can induce Mr & Mrs Johnson to interest their friends and also the Clarks who know a lot of people.

---

1. Gerson (1872–1960) was a Los Angeles–based doctor and social reformer.
2. On 1 December 1911 John McNamara, secretary-treasurer of the International Association of Bridge and Structural Iron Workers (IABSIW), and his brother James pleaded guilty to charges for the October 1910 *Los Angeles Times* building explosion, under the condition that the state would halt the prosecution of other labor organizers associated with the case. On 28 December 1912, however, at a federal trial in Indianapolis, thirty-eight men, nearly all officials in the IABSIW, were found guilty of either entering into a conspiracy to carry dynamite and nitroglycerine on passenger trains or aiding and abetting the transportation of the explosives. In addition, the McNamaras' attorney, Clarence Darrow, was indicted in January 1912 and tried twice for tampering with and bribing the jury. Although he was found not guilty, in the first trial, which began 5 May 1912, his second trial, which began in November 1912, ended in a hung jury on 8 March 1913, after which the prosecution dropped the charges. See Letter from BR, 14 January 1912, above.
3. Elmer Ellsworth was a Los Angeles friend and supporter, who helped arrange EG's meetings in that city.

You may state that I mean to take up new material and go into it thoroughly. For instance Strindberg who is a great master can hardly be approached in less than 2 evenings. In fact, I devoted 4 lectures to him in Denver. Then there is Bjornson and Ibsen a number of Germans I did not mention, Pinero, 2 new plays of Galsworthy, several of Shaw. The Russians of course and if we have time, I should want to speak of Synge. Anyhow the material is really inexhaustible and could easy comprise several months, not only 9 talks.[4]

Please write me how you feel about the outlook of the number of subscribers and how much they may be depended upon. Also if we may hope for a large free meeting in the Auditorium.

Remember me kindly to Mrs. Gerson & other friends.

FRATERNALLY

EMMA GOLDMAN

ALS, T. Perceval Gerson Papers, CLU. Street address, 1153 Eddy St., written after signature.

---

4. EG held a nine-lecture drama course from 16 June to 3 July 1913 at Choral Hall, Temple Auditorium Building, in Los Angeles under the auspices of the drama club. She spoke on the following dramatists and writers: Henrik Ibsen, August Strindberg, Hermann Sudermann, Gerhart Hauptmann, Otto Hartleben, Maurice Maeterlinck, Eugene Brieux, Pierre Wolff, A. W. Pinero, George Bernard Shaw, John Galsworthy, Charles Rann Kennedy, J. M. Synge, W. B. Yeats, Lady Gregory, Lennox Robinson, T. C. Murray, Leo Tolstoy, Anton Chekov, Maksim Gorky, Evgenii Chirikov, and Leonid Andreyev.

בעקאנטמאכונג

די בעריהמטע אנארכיסטין

עמא גאלדמאן

וועט האלטען א לעקטשור אין אידיש

דאנערסטאג דעם 17-טען יולי, 1913

טהעמא

מוטערשאפט

זאלען קבצנים האבען פיעלע קינדער
יעס בריינג

די לעקטשור וועט שטאטפינדען אין

## JEFFERSON SQUARE BUILDING
### 925 GOLDEN GATE AVE.

דיזע טהעמא איז איינע פון די שטארקסטען פון עמא גאלדמאנ'ס לעקטשורס
אן אין. בי פערלאנג געהאלטען געווארען 20 מאל אין דער שטאדט ניו
יארק צו אונגעהייערע גרויסע פערזאמלונגען (מעננער און פרויען).

איינטריט 15 אן 25 סענט     אנפאנג 8 אוהר אבענד

עמא גאלדמאן האלט אפ לעקטשורס אין ענגליש. אין דיזען
בילדינג. יעדען ווענד... אבאנמ... מיטוואך אן פרייטאג.

Majestic Press ⬤ 315 Hayes St.

Announcement: Well-known anarchist woman, Emma Goldman, will lecture on "Motherhood," a variant of her provocative talk on "Why (and Whether) the Poor Should Not Have Children," delivered by popular demand over 20 times to distinguished audiences of men and women in New York. It can be heard in Yiddish in San Francisco at 8 PM at Jefferson Hall, 925 Golden Gate Avenue, admission 15 or 25 cents. Four other Goldman lectures will be delivered in English that week, same time, same building, July 1913. (Emma Goldman Papers Project)

## Article in the *SEATTLE POST-INTELLIGENCER*

*Seattle, 12 August 1913*

# Emma Goldman Lauds the Hobo

### Says He's to be Envied for His Resistance to "Machine"; 200 Hear Her Talk.

Two hundred persons paid admission to hear Miss Emma Goldman speak at Finnish Socialist hall last night. There was no sign of disturbance in or about the hall. One lonely patrolman stood in the rear and had nothing to do.

"We do not have to preach violence," declared Miss Goldman. "What we are preaching is education against violence which is epitomized in our modern society in war, capital punishment, prisons, capitalism and plutocracy. The hobo is a man to be envied as he has the courage to resist the machine that would rob him of his birthright. He rides in a box car, but is as honorable a globe trotter as he who rides in a private car.

### FINE IDEALS DESTROYED.

"The grinding mill of the present system which makes a man hate labor because he has no relation to the work he is doing drives out all that is fine and good, and makes him cunning, shrewd and contemptible. These are the only weapons of character he has to win his bread. Our children are educated to make the best of their environment; all that is idealistic and good is ground out, and leaves the brute who will do anything to get ahead.

"Society rushes in a mad chase after vulgar wealth, and the poor hang to the coat-tails of the rich and think they may get what they desire if they vote, pray and work long enough.

### TRUTH FEARED, NOT DYNAMITE.

"The press, the good citizen and the patriot fear the truth much more than they do dynamite. They repudiate the ideal that man must become independent, yet if they should study the history of any country or race they would find that the terrific longing of mankind is liberty. Despots cannot see that this dominant factor must assert itself. The working man has never felt the ecstasy of giving and receiving under freedom without government, law and the policeman's club!"

Miss Goldman took occasion to say that Socialism would not solve present problems, as the unit in Socialism must give up individuality so the mass might accomplish its aim. She declared she was not an I.W.W.,[1] but that anarchy advocated direct action.

## REITMAN SELLS HER BOOKS.

Miss Goldman was late in appearing, and Dr. Ben L. Reitman, her manager, offered her books and lectures, and copies of Ibsen and Brieux for sale before the lecture.

Miss Goldman speaks tonight in Finnish Socialist hall on the modern drama.

*Seattle Post-Intelligencer*, 12 August 1913, p. 13.

---

1. Although by 1908 the Industrial Workers of the World (IWW) had eliminated any reference to political action from the preamble to its constitution and focused the union's attention on organizing workers on the job and advocating sabotage in the workplace, tactics which EG applauded as direct action, she was one of the few American anarchist communists who never formally joined the organization. See Directory of Organizations.

Article in the *BUTTE MINER*

Butte, Montana, 29 August 1913

## "Anarchist Queen" with Ambitious Dream

### Miss Emma Goldman Has Scheme to Build Theaters for Development of Local Talent.

Establishment of theaters and stage societies in Butte, Spokane and every other large city of the country for the development of local talent, the production of modern plays with accentuated social and human significance, and for the overthrow of the present "one star" system is the next mission on which Miss Emma Goldman, characterized as the "queen of the anarchists," is to venture.

Her plan of action in this respect has been outlined in every city where she has lectured on her speaking tour, which closed in Butte last night, and yesterday she again repeated the hope of her efforts in her next venture. She lauded the work of the English stage societies, which, she declared, have been instrumental in developing much dramatic talent that would otherwise have been lost to the world, and the music teachers' association of Los Angeles in developing local musical talent.

"With my present tour ended tonight," said Miss Goldman, "I shall arrange for the publication of my new book, 'The Social and Revolutionary Significance of the Modern Drama.'[1]

"My next tour, which probably will be made within a few months, will be devoted to an effort to fulfill my ambition for the establishment of theaters in every large city for the presentation of the modern radical dramas bearing upon the great social problems of the day.

"The stage today is the most important place for putting before the people the great pressing social and economical questions, and I shall try to induce every city to provide a place in which modern drama, dealing with the social problems of the world, may be presented.

"I do not intend to give up the lecture platform in the work that I have done so long. I will take that up later."

Miss Goldman spoke twice at the local Auditorium yesterday. In the afternoon

---

1. Published in 1914 by R. G. Badger, Boston, EG's *The Social Significance of the Modern Drama* synthesized many themes discussed in her modern drama lectures and classes and included chapters on the Scandinavian drama, the German drama, the French drama, the English drama, the Irish drama, and the Russian drama.

her topic was, "The Physiology of Anarchy,"[2] and in the evening, "The Danger of the Growing Power of the Church."

It was her seventh visit to Butte, and she declared herself well pleased with her stay. She had several friends in the city, and outside of time occupied by her lecture engagements, she spent her time with them. She was accompanied by Dr. Ben Reitman.

*Butte Miner,* 29 August 1913.

2. The lecture title, "The Physiology of Anarchy," as published in the *Miner,* appears to be a typographical error. This is the only appearance of a lecture with this exact title or with the term "physiology" in the title. However on numerous occasions EG delivered lectures with titles containing the term "psychology," such as "The Psychology of Anarchism," "The Psychology of War," and "The Psychology of Political Violence."

MY OWN MY, PRECIOUS, MY ONLY LOVER IN ALL THE WORLD.

I just came to the office and found your letter, the first real expression of your love since I have left you, or rather since we were on the train from Butte. Darling mine, it is idle talk to prove to you that you never have or will be "one of my lovers", but the only lover, who has absorbed every nerve and atom of my being in six and half years. The one and only lover, who filled my whole being at the exclusion of all else.

It is good of you to say, "have other lovers, I long for tenderness, for affection, for the thousand and one things, that make love worth having. I know you have it in you, but somehow it shows itself rarely to me, which of course, may be my fault, I don't know. I only know that I long for it, not from other men, but you, you alone. From my big, wild, black haired savage lover. Hobo, darling, precious one, I love you madly and want you still more madly.

I have just come back from uptown, was at our new house, it is a dream, I am sure you will like it.[1] I have read carefully what you say in your letter darling, I want you and mother, truly dearest. But with it all, I too have a sad feeling, a fear, your mother may not like it and just do it for your sake. I know it would be terrible to me if she thought, she is being shoved away. However we will try it. And please lover mine, if at any time, she feels she'd rather be a away with you in her own little Apt, be perfectly at liberty to tell me so.

Now as to the arrangement of the house, the office will be in the frontroomm basement, just like at the Ferrer,[2] it's right from the street and will keep the rest of the house clean, it is a beautiful room, much longer than our present office, but not so wide. Back of that is a large kitchen, light and leading out into a beautiful yard.

Next is what we call the parlor floor, a long parlor, almost the size of the Ferrer, only more beautiful and with a parkquet floor. I will take that, and Hobo can always come to Mommy and love her, with no one back of us to disturb our great and wonderful love, as it is at times. Back of this room, is a magnificent dinning room, it will be a joy to eat there, a dumb waiter leading from the kitchen to send up the food.

On the first floor are two rooms and the bath, which I have rented to Stella and Saxe,

---

1. On 1 October 1913 EG moved from 210 East 13th Street, where she had lived for ten years, to 74 West 119th Street. She established a household incorporating the offices of *Mother Earth* and living space for herself, AB, BR, her housekeeper Rhoda Smith (Smithy), her nephew Saxe Commins, her niece Stella Comyn (Cominsky), and Ida Reitman (BR's mother, to whom he was deeply devoted). Rebecca Edelsohn and M. Eleanor Fitzgerald at times also lived in the house.
2. The Francisco Ferrer Association's offices, at 63 East 107th Street in Manhattan, incorporated a day school, space for evening lectures, a small café, and living quarters.

for which she pays fourty Dollars per month, including light and laundry? The bath is on the same floor which we will all use, but there is a seperate "Tante Meyer"[3] from the kitchen and we expect to put one in on the second floor. The second floor has four rooms, three are not large and the reason I have in mind the larger room for Alex is that you will want to be with your mother and there are two rooms together close by. Alex will have the front room and Smithy the one between. That will give your mother absolute privacy, yet leave the dining room and kitchen open to her, always. When you come and you do not like the arrangements, we can manage differently. But if you and mother are in the house, we will have no one else, except the floor for Stella, which is quite private.

If we were not touring and were in N Y all years, I should not think of having Stella, but with six months absense, we can not afford $70 rent, besides Stella is dreadfully lonely and has begged me to take her in.

This night I wrote you it would be foolish to ship your furniture, but since I got your letter and have seen how much it means to you and mother, I decided it is best you send what you want, what difference does it make if it costs a little more, your joy and comfort and especially the feeling of your mother realy mean more to me. If we have too much we will send it to the farm.

Ship everything you have on the list direct to the house, 74 W 119th St, near Lenox Ave. It will be alright lover, if you leave the 27th, it would get you here the 28th, Sunday and Monday we would move. Mother could stay the one night at 210, or a Hotel if she prefers. As to your expenses, you will not have enough, if you must spend $85 for shipping goods. Is Lew[4] likely to contribute anything for your mother? He could pay her fare, but if you hate to ask him Let it go, write me how much you absolutely need.

Hobo mine, I do hope all will be well and harmounious at our new house, Oh I want peace and harmony so much and I want my lover, my darling comrade co-worker, friend and sweetheart, I want you more than everything else in the World and I want our work. Indeed, indeed dearest you can run Mother Earth in your own way, or to be still more explicit let's run it together. You know yourself that I have always consented to your plans, even if at first, I did not agree. Your remarks about my friends are very unkind and anything but big. Havel may be a druncard, but he can write and knows the movement. Alex maybe a temperanmental weakling which by the way, you should not take objections to but he still can be depended upon in time of police trouble, and Max may not have office ability, but he could not be bullied by the authorities And these are very vital things for an anarchist office.

However I agree with you, they are no good for the practical side, we need Lioness[5]

3. Tante Meyer (Aunt Meyer) is a playful Yiddish euphemism for "toilet."
4. Lew Reitman was BR's brother.
5. M. Eleanor Fitzgerald was known as "the Lioness" for her red mane of hair. Also known as "Fitzi," she was a former lover of BR who lived in South Dakota before moving to New York to work at the *Mother Earth* office.

for that, but we will need someone else for the other. I am inclosing copy of letter which I wrote to her day before yesterday, I did not send it until to-day because I wanted to hear from you first. If she does not come in response to this letter I am sorry, but I can not help it, I must be frank with her and myself. I think however she will come. I suppose she will have to get a room, because we have none in the house, at least not while we are in N Y. When we two are gone she could live in the house and be with mother. Anyway you can write her to come if you wish it.

Hobo dearest, precious lover, come to me, the m. want you, the t-b crys for you,[6] and I am calling you, come to me I love you, I adore you, you are my all my own.

PASSIONATELY

MOMMY.

After rereading my letter of last night, I tore it up. I was depressed & lonely and try as I may, my letter came out gloomy and I do not want to burden Hobo.

Come to Mommy quick, I got something, red & juicy hot & passionate for you. Lover, lover, I hold you. Mommy

TLS, IU-U. Handwritten postscript. On Mother Earth Publishing Association stationery.

6. EG and BR often refer to EG's "m" (mountains) and "t-b" (treasure box).

Dear Mabel Dodge.

I write first to remind you of our social for Tom Mann for next Monday at 9 P M.[1] You are coming are you not? By the way, please ask Reed[2] for me in case he has forgotten.

Now to another matter. I am sending under seperate cover a package of cards announcing my Sunday lectures, will you call the special attention of your friends on Thursday to the lecture of Sunday Dec 14th, on "The Intellectual Proletarians,"[3] as it deals largely with the people who go to such affairs as yours and others and are making a desperate struggle to exist. I hope you can come too

Sincerely

Emma Goldman

TLS, CtY-B. On Mother Earth Publishing Association stationery.

1. Tom Mann (1856–1941) an industrial syndicalist, trade unionist, and a leader of the English labor movement, who, beginning in the late 1880s, was a strong advocate of the eight-hour day. Mann moved to Australia in 1901, where he shifted from supporting state socialism to syndicalism before his return to Britain in 1910. His pamphlet *The Way to Win* (Broken Hill, Australia: Barrier Daily Truth Press, 1909) advocated for trade union activity over parliamentary politics and expressed disapproval of dual unionism (i.e., creating another trade organization in opposition to the AFL). In Manchester he was instrumental in the founding of the Industrial Syndicalist Education League and edited the organization's newspaper, *The Industrial Syndicalist* (July 1910–May 1911). In 1911 Mann led the transport workers' strike in Liverpool; after urging soldiers to restrain from shooting the striking workers, he was charged with sedition. Mann joined the British Socialist Party in 1916. He occasionally contributed to *Mother Earth*, including the tenth-anniversary souvenir edition, and once, to *The Blast*. Although he maintained a cordial relationship with the Industrial Workers of the World (IWW) and lectured at many local halls, he opposed its policy of dual unionism. EG's social gathering in honor of Mann's U.S. lecture tour took place on 15 December 1913.
2. John Reed (1887–1920) was an American socialist, journalist, and author. At this time, he was Dodge's companion.
3. Goldman's lecture, a version of which was published in the February 1914 edition of *Mother Earth*, was delivered at the Harlem Masonic Temple in New York City.

## To EDNA KENTON

*[New York], 18 December 1913*

My dear Edna:—

I did not want to bother you Monday night with practical matters, as I wanted you to enjoy and to get to know Tom Mann.[1] But I write now to ask you to get me a good list of names as we are getting out an announcement of my Drama Lectures, at Berkley Theatre, and I would like to reach as many people as possible.[2]

I think that I told you that we have engaged Berkley Theatre as sort of a venture and as we have no means to advertise extensively, we must depend upon the assistance of our friends. Will you let me hear from you very soon? Do not forget New Year's Eve. We will have an affair at the house and a dance of course. I am supposed to provide good male dancers, but I know so few good males on general principles, that I will have to turn to my women friends, hoping that they are more fortunate than I. If you know of such miracles, bring them along, but not too many at a time.

Affectionately,
Emma Goldman

TLS, NNC. Addressed to Miss Edna Kenton, 240 West 15th Street, New York City. On Mother Earth Publishing Association stationery.

---

1. Edna Kenton (1876–1954) was an author, suffragist, lecturer, and friend of EG. She was a member of the Greenwich Village Heterodoxy Club, a critic for the *Bookman*, and a *Mother Earth* subscriber. Her works include *What Manner of Man* (Indianapolis: Bowen-Merrill, 1903) and *Clem* (New York: Century, 1907). Kenton's later political scholarship focused on the relationship between Jesuit missionaries and Native Americans. On 15 December 1913 she attended a social held in honor of the British syndicalist Tom Mann, organized in part by EG. For more on Mann see Letter to Mabel Dodge, 8–10 December 1913, above.
2. EG delivered a drama lecture series from 11 January to 15 March 1914 at the Berkeley Theatre in New York City.

**MOTHER EARTH PUBLISHING ASSOCIATION**
55 WEST TWENTY-EIGHTH STREET
NEW YORK
74 WEST 119TH STREET

December 27, 1913.

Theodore Dreiser,
3609 Broadway,
New York City.

My dear Dreiser:-

I have arranged for a house party and a
New Year's dance for Wednesday evening, December 31st,
and would like you to be among us to kick out the old
year and meet the new. Any time after ten o'clock
P.M. will do. Let me know if I may expect you.

Sincerely,

Do bring Miss Hayman along.

Emma Goldman

Emma Goldman's typewritten note to Theodore Dreiser inviting him to a house party and New Year's Eve dance on 31 December 1913. Emma Goldman knew Dreiser through mutual friends in Greenwich Village. (Van Pelt Library, University of Pennsylvania, Dreiser Collection)

My dear Dreiser:—

I have arranged for a house party and a New Year's dance for Wednesday evening, December 31st, and would like you to be among us to kick out the old year and meet the new. Any time after ten o'clock P.M. will do. Let me know if I may expect you.[1]

Sincerely,

Emma Goldman

Do bring Miss Hayman along.

TLS, Theodore Dreiser Collection, University of Pennsylvania. On Mother Earth Publishing Association stationery. Addressed to Theodore Dreiser, 3609 Broadway, New York City.

1. Theodore Dreiser (1871–1945) was a prominent socialist journalist, novelist, poet, and dramatist. An advocate for freedom of expression, he was a drama critic, correspondent, investigative reporter, and special feature writer for the *St. Louis Globe-Democrat*, the *St. Louis Republic*, the *Pittsburgh Dispatch*, and the *New York World* (1871–1895). He edited the magazine *Ev'ry Month* (1895–1897) and was also a freelance journalist for magazines such as *Munsey's*, *Cosmopolitan*, *Success*, *McClure's*, *Harper's*, and *Scribner's*. Dreiser was subeditor of the *New York Daily News* (1904), editor of *Smith's Magazine* and *Broadway Magazine* (1905), and editor-in-chief of the Butterick publications—*Delineator, Designer, New Idea*, and *English Delineator* (1907–1910). At the time of this letter Dreiser was an associate of Greenwich Village political radicals Max Eastman and Floyd Dell. By this time he had already published the novels *Sister Carrie* (1900) and *The Financier* (1912) and his account of his travels in Europe, *A Traveler at Forty* (1913).

## *The Social Significance of the Modern Drama*

In order to understand the social and dynamic significance of modern dramatic art it is necessary, I believe, to ascertain the difference between the functions of art for art's sake and art as the mirror of life.

Art for art's sake presupposes an attitude of aloofness on the part of the artist toward the complex struggle of life: he must rise above the ebb and tide of life. He is to be merely an artistic conjurer of beautiful forms, a creator of pure fancy.

That is not the attitude of modern art, which is preëminently the reflex, the mirror of life. The artist being a part of life cannot detach himself from the events and occurrences that pass panorama-like before his eyes, impressing themselves upon his emotional and intellectual vision.

The modern artist is, in the words of August Strindberg,[1] "a lay preacher popularizing the pressing questions of his time." Not necessarily because his aim is to proselyte, but because he can best express himself by being true to life.

Millet,[2] Meunier,[3] Turgenev,[4] Dostoyevsky,[5] Emerson,[6] Walt Whitman, Tolstoy, Ibsen, Strindberg, Hauptmann and a host of others mirror in their work as much of the spiritual

---

1. August Strindberg (1849–1912), Swedish playwright, actor, and novelist. EG discusses several of his plays, including *The Father* (1887) and *Miss Julie* (1888; described as *Countess Julie* by EG), in *The Social Significance of the Modern Drama*. EG viewed him as "relentlessly honest" and defended him against charges of misogyny. The quotation appears in the preface to Strindberg's play *Miss Julie*.
2. Jean-Francois Millet (1814–1875), French artist whose *The Man with a Hoe* (1863) was one of several of his paintings depicting peasants at work.
3. Constantin Meunier (1831–1905), Belgian sculptor and painter whose artworks, which often focused on labor, include *The Mine*, a three-part painting, and *Monument to Labor*, a series of bronze and stone statues and reliefs.
4. Ivan Turgenev (1818–1883) Russian novelist, poet, and playwright who in his novel *Fathers and Sons* (1862) drew a literary portrait of Bazarov, the nihilist.
5. Fyodor Dostoyevsky (1821–1881), Russian novelist, journalist, and short-story writer. His works include *Crime and Punishment* (1866) and *The Brothers Karamazov* (1879–1880). He used the anarchist Nechayev as a model for the character Pyotr Verkhovensky in his novel *The Possessed* (1869–1872).
6. Ralph Waldo Emerson (1803–1882) was an American essayist, poet, and philosopher. Emerson founded the Concord-based New England Transcendentalism Circle, of which Thoreau was also a member. Emerson emphasized individualism and the rejection of traditional authority. For EG he was part of the American intellectual tradition of individual freedom from the authority of the state. Excerpts from his works were printed in *Mother Earth* and, in tandem with Thoreau, he was a topic of one of her lectures. His works include *Essays* (Boston: James Munroe, 1841), *Representative Men* (Boston: Phillips, Sampson, 1850), *May Day and Other Pieces* (Boston: Ticknor and Fields, 1867), and *Society and Solitude* (Boston: Osgood, 1874).

and social revolt as is expressed by the most fiery speech of the propagandist. And more important still, they compel far greater attention. Their creative genius, imbued with the spirit of sincerity and truth, strikes root where the ordinary word often falls on barren soil.

The reason that many radicals as well as conservatives fail to grasp the powerful message of art is perhaps not far to seek. The average radical is as hidebound by mere terms as the man devoid of all ideas. "Bloated plutocrats," "economic determinism," "class consciousness," and similar expressions sum up for him the symbols of revolt. But since art speaks a language of its own, a language embracing the entire gamut of human emotions, it often sounds meaningless to those whose hearing has been dulled by the din of stereotyped phrases.

On the other hand, the conservative sees danger only in the advocacy of the Red Flag. He has too long been fed on the historic legend that it is only the "rabble" which makes revolutions, and not those who wield the brush or pen. It is therefore legitimate to applaud the artist and hound the rabble. Both radical and conservative have to learn that any mode of creative work, which with true perception portrays social wrongs earnestly and boldly, may be a greater menace to our social fabric and a more powerful inspiration than the wildest harangue of the soapbox orator.

Unfortunately, we in America have so far looked upon the theater as a place of amusement only, exclusive of ideas and inspiration. Because the modern drama of Europe has till recently been inaccessible in printed form to the average theater-goer in this country, he had to content himself with the interpretation, or rather misinterpretation, of our dramatic critics. As a result the social significance of the Modern Drama has well nigh been lost to the general public.

As to the native drama, America has so far produced very little worthy to be considered in a social light. Lacking the cultural and evolutionary tradition of the Old World, America has necessarily first to prepare the soil out of which sprouts creative genius.

The hundred and one springs of local and sectional life must have time to furrow their common channel into the seething sea of life at large, and social questions and problems make themselves felt, if not crystallized, before the throbbing pulse of the big national heart can find its reflex in a great literature—and specifically in the drama—of a social character. This evolution has been going on in this country for a considerable time, shaping the wide-spread unrest that is now beginning to assume more or less definite social form and expression.

Therefore, America could not so far produce its own social drama. But in proportion as the crystallization progresses, and sectional and national questions become clarified as fundamentally social problems, the drama develops. Indeed, very commendable beginnings in this direction have been made within recent years, among them "The Easiest Way," by Eugene Walter,[7] "Keeping Up Appearances," and other plays

7. Eugene Walter (1874–1941), American playwright. EG wrote a favorable review of his work *The Easiest Way* in the May 1909 *Mother Earth*, considering it "the first American work of dramatic art."

by Butler Davenport,[8] "Nowadays" and two other volumes of one-act plays, by George Middleton[9]—attempts that hold out an encouraging promise for the future.

The Modern Drama, as all modern literature, mirrors the complex struggle of life,—the struggle which, whatever its individual or topical expression, ever has its roots in the depth of human nature and social environment, and hence is, to that extent, universal. Such literature, such drama, is at once the reflex and the inspiration of mankind in its eternal seeking for things higher and better. Perhaps those who learn the great truths of the social travail in the school of life, do not need the message of the drama. But there is another class whose number is legion, for whom that message is indispensable. In countries where political oppression affects all classes, the best intellectual element have made common cause with the people, have become their teachers, comrades, and spokesmen. But in America political pressure has so far affected only the "common" people. It is they who are thrown into prison; they who are persecuted and mobbed, tarred and deported. Therefore another medium is needed to arouse the intellectuals of this country, to make them realize their relation to the people, to the social unrest permeating the atmosphere.

The medium which has the power to do that is the Modern Drama, because it mirrors every phase of life and embraces every strata of society,—the Modern Drama, showing each and all caught in the throes of the tremendous changes going on, and forced either to become part of the process or be left behind.

Ibsen, Strindberg, Hauptmann, Tolstoy, Shaw, Galsworthy and the other dramatists contained in this volume represent the social iconoclasts of our time. They know that society has gone beyond the stage of patching up, and that man must throw off the dead weight of the past, with all its ghosts and spooks, if he is to go foot free to meet the future.

This is the social significance which differentiates modern dramatic art from art for art's sake. It is the dynamite which undermines superstition, shakes the social pillars, and prepares men and women for the reconstruction.[10]

Emma Goldman

TDS, from *The Social Significance of the Modern Drama*, pp. 3–8.

8. Benjamin Butler Davenport (1871–1958), American playwright, actor, and theater manager. In 1911–1912 he built the Bramhall Playhouse, self-described as "the First Free Theatre in the World." His play *Keeping up Appearances* appeared in 1910.
9. George Middleton (1880–1967), American playwright and author. His works include *The Sinner* (1907), *Nowadays* (New York: Henry Holt, 1914), and *Polly with a Past* (New York: Henry Holt, 1914).
10. EG first began lecturing on the modern drama in 1907 in a talk on "The Revolutionary Spirit of the Modern Drama." She continued to speak frequently on the subject throughout 1908, 1909, and 1910, under such headings as "The Drama: The Strongest Disseminator of Radicalism"; "The Drama as a Disseminator of Revolutionary Ideas"; and "Drama and Its Effect on Radicalism." In 1912 EG taught a series of drama classes through the Women's Club in Denver, and in 1913 she delivered lectures on Russian, German, French, and English drama. The title of her October 1913 lecture in New Jersey, "The Social and Revolutionary Significance of Modern Drama," was later transformed into the title of her 1914 book, *The Social Significance of the Modern Drama*.

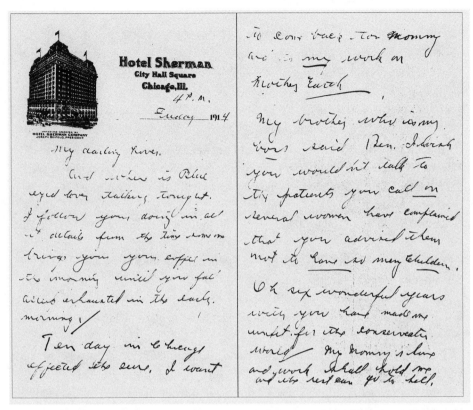

First pages of letter from Ben Reitman to Emma Goldman, expressing his frustration with a situation that feels intolerable, his strong impulse to end their relationship, and admission that he might come crawling back, Fri. 4 PM n.d. 1914. (UI-C)

MOMMY.

You always write me long letters.—and I answer "What do you want me to say"?—Now I have something to say. First I have decided to leave New York—<u>absolutely and for good.</u> Mother will go to Chicago[1] Thursday and I will ship the <u>furniture</u> to <u>Chicago</u>. I don't need to pay its <u>freight.</u>

Today I wrote my Brother[2] that he must relieve me of taking care of Mother for a <u>while.</u>

I am determined not to have the care of Mother or any one else for a while. Not even if Mother has to go to <u>the poor house.</u>

I am going to leave N.Y. Thursday. I may go to Mich. and try and find Lee <u>in the woods.</u> I want to get a rest away from the world. I have no plans no hope no ambition <u>no</u> sweet heart calling or needing <u>me.</u>

I want to get away from Mother & work and evey thing. If I can't stand it I crawl back and <u>ask</u> to be forgiven.

I may tramp again[3] I don't know & I don't care. I feel that if once I get rid of all the burdens and responsibilities I shall be free.

I am 35 <u>years old</u>, and I haven't any thing and I am only the janitor[4] or clown. I don't amount to a damm in the movement, and I <u>know</u> it no one takes me <u>serious</u>, The <u>kindest</u> thing they can say about me is that I can sell literature you are a power Berkman is a force and Reitman is a <u>joke.</u>

I will be forgotten in 3 months or <u>less.</u> There is nothing to me. So I had to act and <u>serve</u>, and I did serve you and the movement as well as I knew how. Every activity of my brain's every thought I had during the last 6 years was <u>yours.</u>[5] It was a voulentay service and it came natural and I have no <u>regrets.</u>

But now it is <u>over.</u> You poor woman made a silly crack diagnosis, thinking the trouble was due to mother. No—No—you will have to guesse <u>again.</u>

I have'nt any pride for I know my self. I am ignorant and superfical—I don't think

---

1. BR's mother, Ida Reitman, who had moved to New York to live with BR and EG, was originally from Chicago.
2. Lew Reitman, BR's brother, was a Chicago businessman.
3. BR spent an early part of his life tramping through the United States and Europe.
4. In 1898 BR worked as a lab assistant for Dr. Maximilian Herzog, who was working on the etiology of syphilis at Chicago's Polyclinic Laboratory.
5. BR first met EG in 1908.

in my head. I am a <u>coward</u> or afraid of death or <u>jail</u>. Maybe I am. But you must let me express my <u>confusion</u>. You called me a <u>coward</u> again and again when I was thinking of your safty and your meeting. You stabed me with the taunt that I spoiled Phila.[6] & San Diego[7] when I thought I was puting one over on the <u>police</u>. You robbed me of my joy in getting the <u>best of the police</u>. On that trip back from <u>Paterson</u>[8] when I needed a kind word, you and Berkman made me feel like a whipped cur and you discussed my recurring <u>cowardice.</u>

On Jan 1st during the few fun moments I slept. When I woke up <u>irritable</u> something happened, a big abscess was forming in my <u>intestines</u>. Latter it broke. When I refer to how my Intestine or Stomach or cigeretts, affected me, you scoff me and are not <u>helpful</u>, and called me brutal and a coward.

You keep reminding me how much you give up for me and how I draw your very heart's blood out and ect.

And so forth and so on.—

It had to come to an end some <u>time</u>. And now is as good as any.

I feel sure that your meeting will be successful and little effort will be needed to keep them up. Lioness[9] can take care of all my work (if not what difference) the little literature I sell is not worth half the bother, and ect.

It does'nt matter what <u>happens</u>. I am going away. If I don't have money to send Mother away she will shift for her self.

There is little else to say. I don't understand & you don't understand what difference does it make.

If I can't live my life without you I beg you to take me back a la Beck & Sasha[10]—and if you won't take me—

Well let the future take care <u>of that.</u>

It is'nt necessary to write me—I know you are always right—At least I have never heard you admidt you were wrong or unjust or unkind since I have been with you.

Hobo

ALS, IU-U. Addressed from 146 Lenox Ave, New York.

6. A reference to the events of Philadelphia in 1909 when EG reluctantly went to court to try to win the legal right to free speech in that city and BR staged a number of publicity events that both EG and Voltairine de Cleyre did not approve of. For further details see vol. 2, *Made for America*, pp. 454–56.

7. A reference to the San Diego vigilantes' brutal treatment of BR during the 1912 San Diego free speech fight. See "Outrage of San Diego," Article in *Mother Earth*, June 1912, above. On 16 May 1912 BR spoke at a Los Angeles meeting to protest the actions of San Diego vigilantes during which he made crude allusions to his body, causing the crowd to laugh at his descriptions. Both Charles Sprading and EG felt he had destroyed the outrage of the crowd against the vigilantes for the sake of humor.

8. A free speech protest held in Paterson, New Jersey, on 5 January 1914. EG, AB, and BR had spoken alongside Leonard Abbott, Gilbert Roe, and Bolton Hall.

9. A reference to M. Eleanor Fitzgerald, who became office manager of *Mother Earth* in 1914.

10. A reference to Rebecca Edelsohn and Alexander Berkman's relationship.

Article in **MOTHER EARTH**

*New York, January 1914*

## Self-Defense for Labor

If the workers of America were sufficiently developed mentally and conscious of the spirit of solidarity, the events of the last few months would compel them to go on a general strike or use more effective means of self-defense against their masters.

From North to South, from East to West the country re-echoes with the numberless brutalities and cold-blooded outrages perpetrated against labor, which must well nigh tax the patience of the most timid, let alone those who still have warm blood in their veins.

Yet, all that is being done in reply to the daily crimes committed by the parasitic class and its State and municipal hirelings, the authorities, is—investigations,[1] everlasting investigations. The latter only tend to distract the attention of the people from the real issue, which is that the workers in this country are absolutely at the mercy of their masters.

We have barely caught our breath after the horrors enacted in West Virginia,[2] when the news comes of the brutalities in the hop fields of Wheatland, Calif.,[3] in the mines

---

1. Demands for congressional hearings were frequently made in the aftermath of labor violence or disturbance. The Women's Trade Union League led a campaign to investigate working conditions in factories following the Triangle Shirtwaist fire in 1911. The governor of New York created a Factory Investigating Commission following the fire to conduct statewide hearings. In March 1912 a congressional hearing investigating the Lawrence textile mill strike was demanded by Wisconsin socialist congressman Victor Berger. In November 1913 Congressman Edward Keating introduced a resolution calling for a congressional investigation into the Colorado miners' strike. The resolution was passed on 27 January 1914.

2. On 18 April 1912 West Virginia coal miners at Paint Creek walked out in order to gain recognition for the United Mine Workers of America. Miners at nearby Cabin Creek joined the strike soon after. Governor William E. Glasscock declared martial law and called in troops on three separate occasions. Mine operators brought in mine guards from the Baldwin-Felts Detective Agency to evict miners and their families from company homes. On 7 February 1913 mine operators and the county sheriff, traveling in an armored train, open fired on a miners' tent colony at Holly Grove on Paint Creek, killing striker Cesco Estep. The miners won what was to be a short-lived victory in the summer of 1913.

3. In the summer of 1913 workers at the Durst hop ranch in Wheatland, California, met to protest substandard wages and dangerous working conditions, drafting ten demands for improvement. After ranch owner Ralph Durst rejected the petition, former IWW organizer Richard "Blackie" Ford, with other IWW members, argued for a general strike. On 3 August, Durst, backed by the local district attorney and sheriff's deputies, confronted a second protest meeting. Shots were fired, many were injured, and five men were killed in the riot that followed, including District Attorney Ed Manwell, who was also Durst's personal attorney; two sheriff's deputies; and two workers. Ford and Herman

in Trinidad, Colorado,[4] and Calumet, Michigan.[5] In all these places the police, the militia, and armed gangs of citizen thugs are carrying on a reign of terror that would put to shame the Black Hundreds of Russia.[6] In Wheatland, numbers of hop-pickers have been massacred and many more wounded; in Colorado Moyer is foully attacked, shot in the back and driven out of town,[7] and Mother Jones is forcibly deported from Trinidad;[8] not to mention the other outrages perpetrated against the strikers in Michigan and Colorado.

Yet, not a voice is raised in protest. The law winks its eye, and not a single thug is apprehended or punished. On the contrary, it is the strikers who are dragged before the bar of justice. On the 12th of this month four workers will have to stand trial in Marysville, California, for the riot caused by the police.[9] During the strike at the Durst hop ranch, at Wheatland, 23,000 hop-pickers who came in response to a "want ad," found themselves confronted with conditions suited only for cattle. They were placed in quarters unfit for habitation and compelled by the hired slave-drivers to keep at work without rest and without proper food to sustain their exhausted energies. Not even water was provided, and as the heat was terrific, these peons were forced to buy lemonade (five cents per glass) from a member of the Durst family. Unable to bear things any longer, the men sent to Durst a delegate, who was brutally assaulted and beaten up. Then

Suhr were arrested, tried, and found guilty in January 1914 for the deaths and sentenced to life imprisonment. Although no one ever determined who was responsible for the violence, the "Wheatland Hop Riot" sparked a major anti-IWW campaign throughout California.

4. The United Mine Workers intensified its organizational efforts in southern Colorado in 1912, resulting in a strike against the Colorado Iron and Fuel Company from 1913 to 1914. The strike centered around the company town of Trinidad, where evicted miners set up tent colonies. One such colony was the site of the infamous Ludlow Massacre. For more on the Ludlow Massacre and its effects see "En Route," Article in *Mother Earth*, June 1914; and note 18 to "Preparedness, the Road to Universal Slaughter," Article in *Mother Earth*, December 1915, below.

5. Beginning in July 1913, Michigan copper workers struck against twenty-one mine operators, including the Calumet and Hecla Mining Company, resulting in several violent clashes between workers, sheriff's deputies, and anti-union vigilantes. During the strike, more than seventy people, most of whom were children, died in the chaos following a false fire alarm at the union's 1913 Christmas Eve party. Although the circumstances of the false alarm are disputed, a local Finnish-language socialist paper blamed the tragedy on an intruder from the company-sponsored Citizens' Alliance. The funeral procession received nationwide attention in the press. On 12 April 1914 the strikers voted to return to work.

6. The Black Hundred was a militant right-wing organization active in Russia from the beginning of the 1900s. It supported tsarist rule of Russia, was strongly anti-anarchist and anti-socialist, and took part in anti-Semitic activities including the pogrom of October 1905. See also vol. 2, *Making Speech Free*, pp. 252–53.

7. Charles H. Moyer, president of the Western Federation of Miners, actually was attacked not in Colorado but while visiting Michigan during the 1913 copper strike.

8. Mary Harris "Mother" Jones was deported three times and detained twice by local authorities during the Colorado Fuel and Iron strike of 1913–1914.

9. Richard "Blackie" Ford and Herman Suhr stood trial in Marysville, California, on 24 January 1914. They were indicted on charges of murder for the deaths of District Attorney E. T. Manwell and Deputy Sheriff Reardon during the Wheatland riot. Both were sentenced to life imprisonment.

the men struck. Immediately the local authorities made common cause with the slave-owners. They were also aided by the Burns' detectives[10] and the Citizens' Alliance[11] and finally by the National Guard, under the command of Adjutant General Forbes.[12] This legal outfit broke into a meeting of strikers and opened fire without the least provocation, killing two workers and wounding a great many others, among them District Attorney Manwell and Deputy Sheriff Reardon, who later died. Since then a number of hop pickers have been kept in jail and subjected to every torture known to the "third degree." One of the men was kept fourteen days without sleep in order to force from him a confession. As the result of this treatment one of the victims attempted suicide, while another, who had lost his arm in the police riot, found the tortures so unbearable that he hanged himself. All this happened, not on the rubber plantations of the far Congo, but in our own free America.

This treatment of labor is no longer an exception. It has become the rule all over the country. Similar horrors have been going on in Michigan and Colorado till they have now reached the climax where brutal assaults and forcible deportation are the order of the day. One of the latest victims is Mother Jones, regarding whose deportation General Chase[13] gave out the following statement:

> Mrs. Jones was met at the train this morning by the military escort acting under instructions not to permit her to remain in this district. The detail took charge of Mrs. Jones and her baggage, and she was accompanied out of the district under guard after she had been given breakfast. The step was taken in accordance with my instructions to preserve peace in the district. The presence of Mother Jones here at this time cannot be tolerated. She had planned to go to the Ludlow tent colony of strikers to stop the desertion of union members. If she returns she will placed in jail and held incommunicado.

The presence of Mother Jones must have indeed been dangerous to the masters of General Chase, since he so obligingly disposed of her. Just as the presence of Moyer seems to have been very unpleasant to the mine-owners of Calumet. Having resorted to the club and all-around terrorism to break the spirit of the Calumet strikers, and having failed of their purpose, the mine barons planned the deportation of Moyer and carried it out with that brutality which only law-abiding citizens are capable of. It is to be hoped that Moyer, who is one of the most peaceful and conservative leaders in the Western

10. Deputy sheriffs and Burns detectives traveled throughout California with "John Doe" warrants for mass arrests of migrant workers and IWW members.
11. The Citizens' Alliance movement, composed of employers and business and professional men, financially backed employers during strikes, lobbied for antilabor legislation, and worked to weaken the movement for unionization.
12. Brigadier General Edwin Alexander Forbes (ca. 1860–1915) served as adjutant general of the California National Guard from 4 January 1911 until his death on 18 June 1915. He became known as the "Father of the California Cadet Corps."
13. General John Chase of the Colorado National Guard was sent to Trinidad by Governor Elias M. Ammons on 28 October 1913 to quell the labor unrest.

Federation of Miners, will now realize that the mailed fist of the law is raised, not only against Anarchists and I. W. W. men, but also against the respectable element in the labor movement if they dare assert their rights.

But whether the criminal assault upon the President of the Western Federation of Miners will prove a lesson to him or not, surely the workers of Calumet and of the rest of country cannot much longer remain in ignorance as to the real condition of affairs. They can no longer hope for protection from the government—no, not even from the federal authorities since they, too, serve only King Mammon. Neither have they anything to expect from the good will of the public. If nothing else, then reasons of sheer self-defense would justify the workers to arm themselves for their own protection and that of their families against the outrages practiced upon them.

At a negro meeting in Washington, D. C., Rev. I. N. Ross[14] called upon his hearers to fight for their political, social and industrial rights. "To prepare for war in times of peace is the policy of this nation," he argued. "It should be your policy, if you wish to free yourself from the oppression and break the fetters of this era of new slavery."

It is not often that an Anarchist can agree with a Christian gentleman; but I heartily concur in this case, except that I feel that it is not only the negro who must learn to fight against the oppression, the fetters of the era of the new slavery, but also the white man, the workers at large. They owe it to themselves, to the cause of labor, and above all to their own self-respect and dignity that they should no longer submit meekly to the indignity, injustice and crimes heaped upon them.

*Mother Earth* 8 (January 1914): 328–31. EG discussed the same subject in a talk called "The Awakening of Labor," delivered in 1914 on her yearly lecture tour.

14. The Reverend Isaac Newton Ross (1856–1927) was a minister in the African Methodist Episcopal Church and pastor of Ebenezer Baptist Church in Baltimore, Maryland.

"PATRIOTISM IS THE LAST REFUGE OF A SCOUNDREL!"—*Samuel Johnson*

# MONSTER ANTI - MILITARY
# MASS MEETING

## SUNDAY NIGHT, MAY 3
### At East Turner Hall, 2132 Arapahoe St.
### ADMISSION FREE

To Protest Against the Outrages committed upon the Working Class of Colorado by the Thugs and State Hirelings; Against the Importation of Federal Troops, and Against this country's War with Mexico.

# WORKINGMEN REMEMBER

Whenever a country has gone to War the Workingmen and Women have always been the losers, and whenever Federal Soldiers have Invaded a Strike Region, Workers Have been KILLED and the Strike has been LOST.

## DON'T BE FOOLED

### Come All Who Are Against Exploitation and Murder

## SPEAKERS
### EMMA GOLDMAN      S. MEYERS and Others

#### DR. BEN R. REITMAN, Chairman
Anti-Militarist League of Denver.

NOTE—Emma Goldman will deliver a Series of Lectures on the Revolutionary Significance of the Modern Drama, from May 4 to 9, at 8:00 p.m., in Building Trades Club Hall, 1749 Arapahoe Street.

Poster announcing meeting in Denver, organized by the Anti-Militarist League to protest the Ludlow Massacre of 20 April 1914 as well as the impending threat of war with Mexico. (Emma Goldman Papers Project)

My dear dear Miss Kennan:—

I am not going to make any apologies for my long silence, because I know that in the goodness of your heart you have not condemned me. I assure you that it was not lack of interest or love for you which made it impossible for me to write until now. But a thousand and one things which seem hard to bear and which one does not want to load upon other people's shoulders. However, I determined to write you today, though if my letter does not read very cheerful you will know that it is because Monday is my "Katzen Jammer day",[1] and I haven't even the excuse of enjoying the charms of Bacchus. The thing which causes my Monday depression is my Sunday's lectures.[2] They wear me out completely,—a sort of a spiritual and mental drunk, which takes twenty-four hours to overcome. But then you will take my affection for you rather than the gloom which may prevail over this letter.

Since I wrote you last we have sent out a second circular letter to our subscribers asking for subscription for the Drama book.[3] We did that because we came to the conclusion that we need hope for nothing from the people who attended the Drama Lectures. Not that I have ever believed that the interest of these people goes further then their skin. But I am convinced now that it does not strike root to any extent, except of course with those who feel deeply on the pressing questions of the day, and to whom the Drama is only a powerful vehicle of expression, and these are the people we have heard from in response to our second circular letter. Altogether we must have received $400.00 for the book, which wouldn't be very much but for the fact that we have finally changed our printer and have thereby reduced the cost of printing almost in half.

Under the circumstances, I think that we will be able to get the book out by the first part of April as far as the money consideration goes. But the preparation of the material is, of course, another matter. I am doing that now and am moving along very slowly. You see I have my Sunday lectures entirely different material to treat of, than the one I am preparing for the book. That means that I am compelled to throw myself from one thing into another which is the same sensation as the effect of hot and cold water, but then I must plod along the best I can, and hope to the fairies for the rest.

1. "Hangover day" or "morning after the night before" in German.
2. EG was scheduled to give a series of Sunday lectures on modern drama at the Berkeley Theatre in New York City (23 West 44th Street). At the time of this letter EG had already given two lectures on the Scandinavian drama (11 and 18 January) and one on the German drama (25 January).
3. EG's *The Social Significance of the Modern Drama* (Boston: Richard G. Badger, 1914).

I am sorry to say that my Sunday lectures are not very gratifying, owing to the difficulty in getting a Hall, we foolishly went into a Theatre, and while we payed only $35.00, which is very little for New York conditions, we will have to discontinue the lectures in that place for the attendance does not cover expenses.[4] We will probably go to the Woman's Trade Union League for the balance of the course.

My tour this year will not begin until April as I cannot leave New York until my book is completed and ready for sale. By the way, it will sell at $1.00, outside of postage of course. And while I am on the point of money, I wish to say that I will not have to call on the friends who have pledged money until the end of next month, when the material will be turned over to the printer. Also about another matter: I wonder if you are not pressed for funds, because I am not able to return my loan at the present. I hope that you can conveniently wait until I get to Denver, when I might be able to turn over the proceeds of my meetings to you in order to cover the loan. But of course if you are pressed, please do not hesitate to let me know. I might be able to make different arrangements and to relieve you of the burden.

I don't know whether Miss Rankin is attending my lectures.[5] She has never again shown up after that first visit. I hope that I have not disappointed her too much. But if she heard the lectures she, no doubt has written you, Let me know about her.

The situation in the Colo. mine strike is certainly terrible. Still more terrible that all the radicalism of Colorado is of no avail to counteract the despotic measures of the authorities. What on earth do the women do with their vote,[6] if they cannot even muster up energy to make such Russian actions as kidnapping Mother Jones impossible.[7] One almost dispairs of any change in this country. Mainly, however, of the workers themselves. After all, the mine owners could not act as they do, if the workers were not such cringing slaves, and their leaders such lickspittals. I must say that I am disgusted.

Bill Haywood has returned from Europe, but is not well at all.[8] I am afraid that the

---

4. EG gave a series of lectures on drama every Sunday between 11 January and 15 March 1914 at the Berkeley Theatre, 23 West 44th Street, in New York City.
5. Mary Alice Rankin, a teacher in Denver at the Lowell School and a friend of Ellen Kennan's.
6. Colorado was the first state to grant women suffrage through a general election with a law passed on 7 November 1893, and it was the second state, after Wyoming, to grant women suffrage. Wyoming was admitted to the union in 1890 with a women's suffrage provision.
7. A reference to the 1913–1914 Colorado coal miners' strike and to the arrest of eighty-three-year-old Mary "Mother" Jones (1830–1930), who as a labor organizer for the United Mine Workers, visited Ludlow, Colorado, in 1914. Mother Jones spent nine weeks in prison and was then expelled from the state, after which she returned to the site of the strike and was subsequently imprisoned again. For more see "En Route," Article in *Mother Earth*, June 1914, below.
8. After the Paterson strike ended, William Haywood, ill and exhausted after playing a leading role in the events in and around the strike, was taken to Europe to recuperate by Jessie Ashley.

experience of the Patterson Strike has left a terrible dent upon the man.[9] Perhaps, also, the disappointment with his own comrades. I hardly need tell you of the psychology of the mob. Had the Patterson strike succeeded Bill Haywood would have been acclaimed as a god, but since it failed, Bill Hayward was made to feel the responsibility. Yet no one worked harder and more devotedly than he. It takes an iron constitution to survive the struggle with your enemies and even more than that to survive the misunderstanding of your friends. It is a great pity that Bill Haywood has not more determination to break lose from all party lines and start out on his own hook. That is the only way to serve the cause of freedom.

I have heard from Gertrude,[10] and will use the sketch she sent me as soon as we have space in MOTHER EARTH. Give her my love please, and remember me kindly to Edith Chase, also Mr. Ferrari,[11] and take my love for yourself. I am always very glad to hear from you even if I cannot write often. I know that you will understand and forgive.

AFFECTIONATELY,
EMMA GOLDMAN

TLS, Emma Goldman Archive, IISH.

9. On 25 February 1913 workers at silk mills in Paterson, New Jersey, walked out of the factory after the manufacturers refused to sign a contract for wage increases, with Detroit IWW Local 25. By 27 February 5,000 weavers (one-third of those employed in Paterson's silk mills) had stopped working. By late March the strike was subdued briefly when manufacturers agreed to wage increases (but refused to recognize the Detroit IWW). Fueled by the recent victory at Lawrence and the manufacturers' retraction of their contract, the strike resumed on 4 April. Although the strike was nonviolent, many picketers were arrested, jailed, and fined. Despite substantial public support, including the Paterson Strike Pageant at Madison Square Garden on 7 June (an event that lost money) and the evacuation of strikers' children to sympathizers' homes in New York, the strike was eventually broken and was over by 22 August 1913.

10. Gertrude Nafe was a friend of Ellen Kennan's.

11. Edith Chase was a Denver high school teacher at East Side High School with Ellen Kennan and Gertrude Nafe, and a subscriber to *Mother Earth*. Robert Ferrari was a Denver lawyer who was also an Italian vice consul, a birth control advocate, a friend of Ellen Kennan's, and a subscriber to *Mother Earth*.

Essay in *MOTHER EARTH*

New York, February 1914

## Intellectual Proletarians

The proletarization of our time reaches far beyond the field of manual labor; indeed, in the larger sense all those who work for their living, whether with hand or brain, all those who must sell their skill, knowledge, experience and ability, are proletarians. From this point of view, our entire system, excepting a very limited class, has been proletarianized.

Our whole social fabric is maintained by the efforts of mental and physical labor. In return for that, the intellectual proletarians, even as the workers in shop and mine, eke out an insecure and pitiful existence, and are more dependent upon the masters than those who work with their hands.

No doubt there is a difference between the yearly income of a Brisbane[1] and a Pennsylvania mine worker. The former, with his colleagues in the newspaper office, in the theater, college and university, may enjoy material comfort and social position, but with it all they are proletarians, inasmuch as they are slavishly dependent upon the Hearsts, the Pulitzers, the Theater Trusts, the publishers and, above all, upon a stupid and vulgar public opinion. This terrible dependence upon those who can make the price and dictate the terms of intellectual activities, is more degrading than the position of the worker in any trade. The pathos of it is that those who are engaged in intellectual occupations, no matter how sensitive they might have been in the beginning, grow callous, cynical and indifferent to their degradation. That has certainly happened to Brisbane, whose parents were idealists working with Fourier in the early co-operative ventures.[2]

1. A reference to Arthur Brisbane (1864–1936), American writer and newspaper editor known for his sensationalist style. He was the son of utopian socialist and reformer Albert Brisbane (1809–1890). In 1883 he worked on the *New York Sun* and then on Joseph Pulitzer's *New York World*. In 1897 William Randolph Hearst appointed him managing editor of the *New York Journal*, where he dramatically increased circulation and became one of the most widely read columnists and the highest paid editor of his day. He played a major editorial role in the *Journal*'s promotion of the Spanish-American War.

2. Arthur Brisbane's father, Albert Brisbane, was an early utopian socialist and follower of Charles Fourier (1772–1837), the French social theorist whose vision of the ideal society centered on small associationist communities with communal production and communal sharing of housekeeping functions. American communities based on his ideas were founded in Red Bank, New Jersey, and Brook Farm, Massachusetts (1841–1846). Albert Brisbane studied under Fourier in France for two years, and in the late 1830s began working to popularize Fourierism in the United States, in part through his columns on Fourierism (which Brisbane called Associationism) in the *New York Tribune*. In her draft of "Historic Development of Anarchism" (1933), EG cited Fourier to explain the

Brisbane, who himself began as a man of ideals, but who has become so enmeshed by material success that he has forsworn and betrayed every principle of his youth.

Naturally so. Success achieved by the most contemptible means cannot but destroy the soul. Yet that is the goal of our day. It helps to cover up the inner corruption and gradually dulls one's scruples, so that those who begin with some high ambition cannot, even if they would, create anything out of themselves.

In other words, those who are placed in positions which demand the surrender of personality, which insist on strict conformity to definite political policies and opinions, must deteriorate, must become mechanical, must lose all capacity to give anything really vital. The world is full of such unfortunate cripples. Their dream is to "arrive," no matter at what cost. If only we would stop to consider what it means to "arrive," we would pity the unfortunate victim. Instead of that, we look to the artist, the poet, the writer, the dramatist and thinker who have "arrived," as the final authority on all matters, whereas in reality their "arrival" is synonymous with mediocrity, with the denial and betrayal of what might in the beginning have meant something real and ideal.

The "arrived" artists are dead souls upon the intellectual horizon. The uncompromising and daring spirits never "arrive." Their life represents an endless battle with the stupidity and the dullness of their time. They must remain what Nietzsche calls "untimely," because everything that strives for new form, new expression or new values, is always doomed to be untimely.[3]

The real pioneers in ideas, in art and in literature have remained aliens to their time, misunderstood and repudiated. And if, as in the case of Zola, Ibsen and Tolstoy,[4] they compelled their time to accept them, it was due to their extraordinary genius and even more so to the awakening and seeking of a small minority for new truths, to whom these men were the inspiration and intellectual support. Yet even to this day Ibsen is unpopular, while Poe,[5] Whitman and Strindberg have never "arrived."

The logical conclusion is this: those who will not worship at the shrine of money, need not hope for recognition. On the other hand, they will also not have to think other people's thoughts or wear other people's political clothes. They will not have to proclaim as true that which is false, nor praise that as humanitarian which is brutal. I realize that

---

stifling of spontaneity by the capitalist economic system, arguing that only by emancipating labor from the coercion of daily work will the imagination to create a system that supports social harmony be possible. Fourier's major work, *Theorie des quatre mouvements et des destinees generales: Prospectus et annonce de la decouverte*, was published in 1808. Albert Brisbane and Fourier co-authored *General Introduction to Social Science* (New York: C. P. Somerby, 1876).

3. Between 1873 and 1876 German philosopher Friedrich Nietzsche published four short essays, including "David Strauss, the Confessor and the Writer," "The Uses and Disadvantages of History for Life," "Schopenhauer as Educator," and "Richard Wagner in Bayreuth," known collectively as *Untimely Meditations*.

4. EG often referred to the works of Émile Zola, Henrik Ibsen, and Leo Tolstoy in her written work and lectures.

5. Edgar Allan Poe (1809–1849), American poet, short-story writer, and literary critic.

those who have the courage to defy the economic and social whip are among the few, and we have to deal with the many.

Now, it is a fact that the majority of the intellectual proletarians are in the economic treadmill and have less freedom than those who work in the shops or mines. Unlike the latter, they cannot put on overalls, and ride the bumpers to the next town in search of a job. In the first place, they have spent a lifetime on a profession, at the expense of all their other faculties. They are therefore unfitted for any other work except the one thing which, parrot-like, they have learned to repeat. We all know how cruelly difficult it is to find a job in any given trade. But to come to a new town without connections and find a position as teacher, writer, musician, bookkeeper, actress or nurse, is almost impossible.

If, however, the intellectual proletarian has connections, he must come to them in a presentable shape; he must keep up appearances. And that requires means, of which most professional people have as little as the workers, because even in their "good times" they rarely earn enough to make ends meet.

Then there are the traditions, the habits of the intellectual proletarians, the fact that they must live in a certain district, that they must have certain comforts, that they must buy clothes of a certain quality. All that has emasculated them, has made them unfit for the stress and strain of the life of the bohemian. If he or she drink coffee at night, they cannot sleep. If they stay up a little later than usual, they are unfitted for the next day's work. In short, they have no vitality and cannot, like the manual worker, meet the hardships of the road. Therefore they are tied in a thousand ways to the most galling, humiliating conditions. But so blind are they to their own lot that they consider themselves superior, better, and more fortunate than their fellow-comrades in the ranks of labor.

Then, too, there are the women who boast of their wonderful economic achievements, and that they can now be self-supporting. Every year our schools and colleges turn out thousands of competitors in the intellectual market, and everywhere the supply is greater than the demand. In order to exist, they must cringe and crawl and beg for a position. Professional women crowd the offices, sit around for hours, grow weary and faint with the search for employment, and yet deceive themselves with the delusion that they are superior to the working girl, or that they are economically independent.

The years of their youth are swallowed up in the acquisition of a profession, in the end to be dependent upon the board of education, the city editor, the publisher or the theatrical manager. The emancipated woman runs away from a stifling home atmosphere, only to rush from employment bureau to the literary broker, and back again. She points with moral disgust to the girl of the redlight district, and is not aware that she too must sing, dance, write or play, and otherwise sell herself a thousand times in return for her living. Indeed, the only difference between the working girl and the intellectual female or male proletarian is a matter of four hours. At 5 a.m. the former stands in line waiting to be called to the job and often face to face with a sign, "No hands wanted." At 9 a.m. the professional woman must face the sign, "No brains wanted."

Under such a state of affairs, what becomes of the high mission of the intellectuals, the poets, the writers, the composers and what not? What are they doing to cut loose from their chains, and how dare they boast that they are helping the masses? Yet you know that they are engaged in uplift work. What a farce! They, so pitiful and low in their slavery themselves, so dependent and helpless! The truth is, the people have nothing to learn from this class of intellectuals, while they have everything to give to them. If only the intellectuals would come down from their lofty pedestal and realize how closely related they are to the people! But they will not do that, not even the radical and liberal intellectuals.

Within the last ten years the intellectual proletarians of advanced tendencies have entered every radical movement. They could, if they would, be of tremendous importance to the workers. But so far they have remained without clarity of vision, without depth of conviction, and without real daring to face the world. It is not because they do not feel deeply the mind- and soul-destroying effects of compromise, or that they do not know the corruption, the degradation in our social, political, business, and family life. Talk to them in private gatherings, or when you get them alone, and they will admit that there isn't a single institution worth preserving. But only privately. Publicly they continue in the same rut as their conservative colleagues. They write the stuff that will sell, and do not go an inch farther than public taste will permit. They speak their thoughts, careful not to offend any one, and live according to the most stupid conventions of the day. Thus we find men in the legal profession, intellectually emancipated from the belief in government, yet looking to the fleshpots of a judgeship; men who know the corruption of politics, yet belonging to political parties and championing Mr. Roosevelt.[6] Men who realize the prostitution of mind in the newspaper profession, yet holding responsible positions therein. Women who deeply feel the fetters of the marital institution and the indignity of our moral precepts, who yet submit to both; who either stifle their nature or have clandestine relations—but God forbid they should face the world and say, "Mind your own damned business!"

Even in their sympathies for labor—and some of them have genuine sympathies— the intellectual proletarians do not cease to be middle-class, respectable and aloof. This may seem sweeping and unfair, but those who know the various groups will understand that I am not exaggerating. Women of every profession have flocked to Lawrence,[7] to Little Falls,[8] to Paterson,[9] and to the strike districts in this city. Partly out of curiosity,

6. Probably a reference to Theodore Roosevelt's Progressive Party, aka Bull Moose Party, formed following Roosevelt's break with the Republican Party in 1912.
7. A reference to the 1912 strike of textile workers in Lawrence, Massachusetts, that took place between 11 January and 14 March 1912. For more on the strike see Letter to Rudolf Grossman, 4 June 1912, above.
8. On 10 October 1912, 1,500 textile mill workers—70 percent of whom were women—walked out of the Phoenix and Gilbert Knitting Mills in Little Falls, New York, in response to wage cuts. With the help of the IWW, workers staged parades, pickets, and meetings, which were increasingly met with police brutality, mass arrests, and, eventually, total suppression. George Lunn, the socialist Mayor of Schenectady, was arrested on 15 October while addressing the strikers. On 30 October all IWW organizers, speakers, and committee members were arrested and jailed. The strike ended on 2 January 1913 on terms—including wage increases—devised by state mediators.
9. The 1913 Paterson silk workers strike. See note 9 in Letter to Ellen A. Kennan, 26 January 1914, above.

often out of interest. But always they have remained rooted to their middle-class traditions. Always they have deceived themselves and the workers with the notion that they must give the strike respectable prestige, to help the cause.

In the shirtwaistmakers' strike professional women were told to rig themselves out in their best furs and most expensive jewelry, if they wanted to help the girls.[10] Is it necessary to say that while scores of girls were manhandled and brutally hustled into the patrol wagons, the well-dressed pickets were treated with deference and allowed to go home? Thus they had their excitement, and only hurt the cause of labor.

The police are indeed stupid, but not so stupid as not to know the difference in the danger to themselves and their masters from those who are driven to strike by necessity, and those who go into the strike for pastime or "copy." This difference doesn't come from the degree of feeling, nor even the cut of clothes, but from the degree of incentive and courage; and those who still compromise with appearances have no courage.

The police, the courts, the prison authorities and the newspaper owners know perfectly well that the liberal intellectuals, even as the conservatives, are slaves to appearances. That is why their muckraking, their investigations, their sympathies with the workers are never taken seriously. Indeed, they are welcomed by the press, because the reading public loves sensation, hence the muckraker represents a good investment for the concern and for himself. But as far as danger to the ruling class is concerned, it is like the babbling of an infant.

Mr. Sinclair would have died in obscurity but for "The Jungle,"[11] which didn't move a hair upon the heads of the Armours,[12] but netted the author a large sum and a reputa-

10. The New York shirtwaist makers' strike of 1909, "The Uprising of the Twenty Thousand," began as a spontaneous walkout by several shops in lower Manhattan but became industry-wide by late November 1909. The workers were mostly teenage girls, eastern European Jewish and Italian immigrants who worked under harsh conditions, including an oppressive subcontracting system. Faced with a mass walkout, the shirtwaist makers' Local 25 of the International Ladies' Garment Workers' Union (ILGWU) relied on organizational support from the New York Women's Trade Union League (WTUL), the Fareynigte Idishe Geverkshaftn (United Hebrew Trades), and the Socialist Party (SP). In early November Mary Dreier, a wealthy New York socialite and president of the WTUL, was arrested on a picket line that was plagued by company-hired strikebreakers and police and backed up by courts intent on intimidating women strikers. Press coverage of Dreier's arrest (an apologetic judge later dismissed the charges against her) helped to generate public interest in the strike and reinforced the strategy of placing WTUL "allies" on the picket line as witnesses. Eventually, wealthy reformers and socialist radicals differed too much to work together in the strike coalition, which in the end may have contributed to the failure of the strike to achieve its central aim—the closed shop—although their initial participation did dramatically increase the number and influence of socialists in Local 25 and the ILGWU.
11. Upton Sinclair's novel *The Jungle* (1906; first published in *Appeal to Reason*, 1905) was a muckraking account of the meatpacking industry.
12. The Armour & Company empire was founded by Philip Danforth Armour (1832–1901) in 1863 when he co-founded a meatpacking business in Milwaukee. In the 1870s the business was centered in Chicago, expanded to East Coast cities, and began exporting meat products to Europe. Armour was noted as an innovator in the meatpacking industry for his use of animal waste products, the sale of canned meat, and innovation in several slaughtering techniques. The reputation of Armour &

tion. He may now write the most stupid stuff, sure of finding a market. Yet there is not a workingman anywhere so cringing before respectability as Mr. Sinclair.

Mr. Kibbe Turner would have remained a penny-a-liner but for our political mud-slingers, who used him to make capital against Tammany Hall.[13] Yet the poorest-paid laborer is more independent than Mr. Turner, and certainly more honest than he.

Mr. Hillquit would have remained the struggling revolutionist I knew him twenty-four years ago, but for the workers who helped him to his legal success.[14] Yet there is not a single Russian worker on the East Side so thoroughly bound to respectability and public opinion as Mr. Hillquit.

I could go on indefinitely proving that, though the intellectuals are really proletarians, they are so steeped in middle-class traditions and conventions, so tied and gagged by them, that they dare not move a step.

The cause of it is, I believe, to be sought in the fact that the intellectuals of America have not yet discovered their relation to the workers, to the revolutionary elements which at all times and in every country have been the inspiration of men and women who worked with their brains. They seem to think that they and not the workers represent the creators of culture. But that is a disastrous mistake, as proved in all countries. Only when the intellectual forces of Europe had made common cause with the struggling masses, when they came close to the depths of society, did they give to the world a real culture.

With us, this depth in the minds of our intellectuals is only a place for slumming, for newspaper copy, or on a very rare occasion for a little theoretic sympathy. Never was the latter strong or deep enough to pull them out of themselves, or make them break with their traditions and surroundings. Strikes, conflicts, the use of dynamite, or the efforts

---

Company was somewhat marred by scandals of 1898–1899 when a company packing house was charged with selling tainted beef. By the early 1890s Philip Danforth Armour's wealth was estimated at $50 million (about $20 billion in current value), and he remains today among the forty wealthiest people in American history.

13. George Kibbe Turner (1869–1952) was a writer and editor for *McClure's Magazine* during the era of progressive reform journalism. Turner exposed the corrupt practices of the Democratic Party machine in New York City municipal politics in his article "Tammany's Control of New York by Professional Criminals" (June 1909). Turner began his career as a reporter for the *Springfield (Mass.) Republican*, were he worked from 1891 to 1906. Turner then became a writer and editor for *McClure's Magazine*. His major articles for *McClure's* include "Galveston: A Business Corporation" (October 1906), "The Confession and Autobiography of Harry Orchard" (July–November 1907, published as a book in 1907), "The City of Chicago: A Study of the Great Immoralities" (April 1907), "Tammany's Control of New York by Professional Criminals" (June 1909), and "Daughters of the Poor" (November 1909). Turner co-wrote a series with John Moody titled "The Masters of Capital in America" (1910–1911). After 1912 Turner devoted himself to fiction, publishing three novels and contributing short stories and serial novels to *McClure's* until 1917.

14. Morris Hillquit (1869–1933), a Jewish immigrant born Moishe Hillkowicz, was a socialist, trade unionist, politician, and labor lawyer. He served as the International Ladies' Garment Workers' Union's general counsel after 1913 and defended its leaders against murder charges in connection with a 1910 strike. He represented the right wing in factional battles (1911–1912) within the Socialist Party of America.

of the I. W. W. are exciting to our intellectual proletarians, but after all very foolish when considered in the light of the logical, cool-headed observer. Of course they feel with the I. W. W. when he is beaten and brutally treated, or with the MacNamaras,[15] who cleared the horizon from the foggy belief that in America no one needed use violence. The intellectuals gall too much under their own dependence not to sympathize in such a case. But the sympathy is never strong enough to establish a bond, a solidarity between him and the disinherited. It is the sympathy of aloofness, of experiment.

In other words, it is a theoretic sympathy which all those have who still enjoy a certain amount of comfort and therefore do not see why anyone should break into a fashionable restaurant. It is the kind of sympathy Mrs. Belmont has when she goes to night courts.[16] Or the sympathy of the Osbornes, Dottys and Watsons[17] when they had themselves locked up in prison for a few days. The sympathy of the millionaire Socialist who speaks of "economic determinism."

The intellectual proletarians who are radical and liberal are still so much of the bourgeois regime that their sympathy with the workers is dilettante and does not go farther

15. James and John McNamara, who pleaded guilty to the bombing of the *Los Angeles Times* building in 1910. The trial and case brought to light the ongoing violence between the International Association of Bridge and Structural Iron Workers (IABSIW) union, of which the McNamaras were active members, and the National Erectors Association (NEA). Between 1905 and 1910, the IABSIW dynamited about 150 NEA-affiliated buildings and bridges, without injury or loss of life, as part of an ongoing conflict over open and closed shops.

16. Alva Erskine Smith Vanderbilt Belmont (1853–1933) was a wealthy New York socialite and, after 1908, a leader in the women's suffrage movement. She gave generously of her time and money to various suffrage organizations. Among the many causes Belmont supported was the Women's Trade Union League during the 1909 and 1916 garment industry strikes. The incident EG alludes to occurred on 20 December 1909, when Belmont bailed out four striking women from jail and remained with them in the New York Night Court until 2:45 a.m. Still, the next day EG issued a caveat against blanket support of such efforts, warning that Belmont's "contributions will not harmonize capital and labor. They will harm the labor movement, which, to be successful, must be entirely independent." Belmont also helped rescue the financially strapped *Masses* in 1912.

17. EG refers to prison reformers Thomas Mott Osborne, Madeleine Zabriskie Doty, and Elizabeth C. Watson. Thomas Mott Osborne (1859–1926) was an industrialist, grandnephew of William Lloyd Garrison, and mayor of Auburn, New York. In 1913 he entered Auburn prison for a week, disguised as prisoner Tom Brown, and in reaction to his firsthand experience he organized the Mutual Welfare League, an inmate-run organization to help manage the prison. He was vice president of the Anti-Imperialist League (1908–1921) and warden of Sing Sing prison in New York State from 1914 to 1916. He wrote *Society and Prisons* (New Haven: Yale University Press, 1916) and *Within Prison Walls: Being a Narrative of Personal Experience During a Week of Voluntary Confinement in the State Prison at Auburn, New York* (New York: Appleton, 1916). Madeleine Zabriskie Doty (1879–1963) was a lawyer, journalist, author, and social reformer with a special interest in child welfare. She was active in Greenwich Village's Liberal Club. As a member of New York's 1913 Prison Reform Commission, she spent one week in Auburn Women's Prison with co-investigator Elizabeth C. Watson gathering information for a report on prison conditions. Her works include *Society's Misfits* (New York: The Century Company, 1916). Later, in 1919, she would marry Roger Baldwin. Elizabeth C. Watson (1886–1951) was a field investigator for the New York State Department of Labor. With Madeline Doty, she spent one week in 1913 inside Auburn Women's Prison to gather information for a report on prison conditions for New York's Prison Reform Commission.

than the parlor, the so-called salon, or Greenwich village.[18] It may in a measure be compared to the early period of the awakening of the Russian intellectuals described by Turgenev in "Fathers and Sons."[19]

The intellectuals of that time, while never so superficial as those I am talking about, indulged in revolutionary ideas, split hairs through the early morning hours, philosophized about all sorts of questions and carried their superior wisdom to the people with their feet deeply rooted in the old. Of course they failed. They were indignant with Turgenev and considered him a traitor to Russia. But he was right. Only when the Russian intellectuals completely broke with their traditions; only when they fully realized that society rests upon a lie, and that they must give themselves to the new completely and unreservedly, did they become a forceful factor in the life of the people. The Kropotkins, the Perovskayas, the Breshkovskayas, and hosts of others repudiated wealth and station and refused to serve King Mammon.[20] They went among the people, not to lift them up but themselves to be lifted up, to be instructed, and in return to give themselves wholly to the people. That accounts for the heroism, the art, the literature of Russia, the unity between the people, the mujik and the intellectual. That to some extent explains the literature of all European countries, the fact that the Strindbergs, the Hauptmanns, the Wedekinds, the Brieux, the Mirbeaus,[21] the Steinlins[22] and Rodins[23] have never dissociated themselves from the people.

Will that ever come to pass in America? Will the American intellectual proletarians ever love the ideal more than their comforts, ever be willing to give up external success for the sake of the vital issues of life? I think so, and that for two reasons. First, the proletarization of the intellectuals will compel them to come closer to labor. Secondly, because of the rigid regime of puritanism, which is causing a tremendous reaction against conventions and narrow moral ties. Struggling artists, writers and dramatists who strive to create something worth while, aid in breaking down dominant conventions; scores of women who wish to live their lives are helping to undermine our morality

18. A reference to Mabel Dodge's salon and Greenwich Village bohemians. See Letter to Mabel Dodge, 8–10 December 1913, above.
19. Ivan Turgenev's novel *Fathers and Sons* (1861).
20. Peter Kropotkin, Sophia Perovskaya, and Catherine Breshkovskaya all had common roots in Russia's gentry elite and, in EG's eyes had all renounced their privilege and dedicated their lives to the working people of Russia.
21. August Strindberg, Gerhart Hauptmann, Frank Wedekind, Eugene Brieux, and Octave Mirbeau were all European authors whom EG often commented on in her lectures and written work, especially that dealing with the modern drama.
22. Théophile Alexandre Steinlen (1859–1923) was a Swiss-born French painter and illustrator for the journals *Mirliton*, *Assiette au Beurre*, *Chat Noir*, and *Gil Blass*. His later works were often satirical social critiques, depicting the poverty of the Paris working class and the violence of the First World War.
23. Auguste Rodin (1840–1917) was a French sculptor whose works include *The Age of Bronze* (1876); *St. John the Baptist* (1878); *The Gates of Hell* (unfinished), out of which evolved *Adam and Eve* (1881); *The Kiss* (1886); *The Thinker* (1879–1900); and *The Burghers of Calais* (1894).

of to-day in their proud defiance of the rules of Mrs. Grundy. Alone they cannot accomplish much. They need the bold indifference and courage of the revolutionary workers, who have broken with all the old rubbish. It is therefore through the co-operation of the intellectual proletarians, who try to find expression, and the revolutionary proletarians who seek to remould life, that we in America will establish a real unity and by means of it wage a successful war against present society.[24]

*Mother Earth* 8 (February 1914): 363–70.

24. The term "intellectual proletarian" was used by Gustave Hervé in *Patriotism and the Worker: Being a Speech Delivered on 30 December 1905 at the Trial of the Paris Anti-Militarists* (first published in the United States by the IWW in 1912). EG also discusses the intellectual proletarian in the afterword to her *My Further Disillusionment in Russia* (New York: Doubleday, 1924), pp. 166–67: "It is true that most intellectuals consider themselves a class apart from and superior to the workers, but social conditions everywhere are fast demolishing the high pedestal of the intelligentsia. They are made to see that they, too, are proletarians, even more dependent upon the economic master than the manual worker. Unlike the physical proletarian, who can pick up his tools and tramp the world in search of a change from a galling situation, the intellectual proletarians have their roots more firmly in their particular social environment and cannot so easily change their occupation or mode of living. It is therefore of utmost importance to bring home to the workers the rapid proletarization of the intellectuals and the common tie thus created between them. If the Western world is to profit by the lessons of Russia, the demagogic flattery of the masses and blind antagonism toward the intelligentsia must cease."

DEAREST,

I returned from Brownsville a while ago[1] and though it is late I want to write to you. I did not do so to day, had to read Irish plays and go to Bronsv.

I had a good meeting thanks to Judin[2] the only faithful soul left the others have gone back. Such is life, a process of elimination.

My own boy, just because I know the "strange bond between you and your mother and the influence she has over you" I do not wish you to come back. I do not wish you ever again to be placed in the position where you must be torn between your feelings for her & me. Neither do I ever again want to be in a position where I must struggle for my happyness with your mother. It is altogether too sordid and I have had enough of it.

I am not at all deceived as to what I did for you. I know I meant to give you much and if I failed it is not because I have not tried. You say I might have been more patient. Well, dear heart perhaps if you will stop to consider the things that happened in your life since March 1908, you will not think me quite lacking in patience.

If we could live alone in a flat! Isn't that rather contra[dictory] whe[n] you say yourself that the[re i]s a "strange bond between you a[nd] your mother." So long a[s] that exists you must live with her, dearest. I would not even if I could have it otherwise. It would not be fair to her nor you. Besides [I] know you too well old man I know that several months away from your mother unless it be on the road (and now I have no faith even in that) would necessitate your going to your mother, so why deceive oursel[ve]s?

"Security" Hobo, [how] can you expect that with me[?] My life must of necessity remain insecure always and what is more, I do not wish it otherwise. Security means stagnation I hope I shall never get to that.

On the other hand, you must have security, because you must make your mother comfortable which our work has evidently prevented you from doing. Is it therefore not most logical that you should seek security. You see dearest heart, I am not blind and I must face facts. Walt Whitman says in one of his poems, I believe it is in the Open Road

---

1. EG participated in a debate in Brownsville, a working-class district on the outskirts of Brooklyn, on the 16th or 17th of February 1914, and returned again for a lecture on the Irish playwright Synge on the 21st.
2. Probably William Judin, a Russian-born Jewish anarchist, based at times in both New York and Chicago, who later became secretary of the International Propaganda Group. Judin was part of the group that published the monthly *Social War* (1917) and *Social War Bulletin* (1918) in Chicago.

"Who gose with me, may not halt or seek comforts. He will find a hard road condamnation and few friends."[3]

I fear dearest, EG & security do not hitch together, why then hitch with EG? You have given me much my Hobo. I know you did it gladly. I have no claim on you when others have—

Dearie what makes you think ~~EVT~~ Sasha[4] ever doubted your capacity to find jobs? He may not have believed that business and propaganda go together. But he always knew you'd make a success of any business. Neither Sasha nor anyone else ever believed that you were in the work because you could get no job, so be at ease on this score.

And so you think I have not pushed you as much as I did Sasha? Perhaps not. But dearest that's only because you can do the pushing so much more than I, or any one I have ever known. Indeed, I seemed very passive compared with your wonderful activity.

I am afraid dear that your opposition to Sasha makes you say unkind things. I wonder how dependent you would have been with 14 years of your life curtailed. Besides Sasha is dependent because he has done one line of work all his life. Perhaps if you had been in the movement 25 years cut off, from the outside World and the commercial grind, you'd find it just a little more difficult to drop everything and find jobs. I am not defending Sasha, I am only calling your attention to certain things you have overlooked. Being in the movement all one's life, is like being married all one's life, it incapacitates one for others things, that's one of the reason why you would be wise to get away from it, before it's too much in your blood.

My Hobo EG does not need a manager nor does ME. EG needs a lover, a man whose love is big enough to defy the World. The manager must be incidental. I have come to think that our main tragedy dearies is due, to the fact that you were my manager first & always and incidentally my lover. That is the source of all our friction, all misunderstanding, EG work was your aim and EG was the means to that aim. Oh not for yourself, God forbid, but because you were infatuated with the work.

Well, I fear that can never be again, at least I hope not. Work must come out of love and comradeship, since the other way did not work.

The only real come back is from the living not the dead, dearest—Good night! May you find happyness and joy and forgetfulness from every pain I have ever caused you Hobo mine.

Your Mommy.

"It is still where the Dead are My soul too is still" and something in my heart upset it all—

ALS, IU-U.

---

3. The lines nearest to these are in Whitman's "Song of the Open Road" in *Leaves of Grass* (Philadelphia: David McKay, 1900): "He going with me must go well arm'd / He going with me goes often with spare diet, / Poverty, angry enemies, desertions."
4. Alexander Berkman and Ben Reitman had an often contentious relationship, rooted in stylistic difference as well as their disagreement over tactics and methods of propaganda.

Article in the *NEW YORK TIMES SUNDAY MAGAZINE*

*New York, 29 March 1914*

# So-Called I. W. W. Raids
# Really Hatched by Schoolboys

**Real History, Told for First Time, of the Latest Movement Against
Society—A Product, Not of the I. W. W. Nor of the Anarchists,
but of the Ferrer School Where Three Pupils Originated It.**

By Charles Willis Thompson.

It will be very much to the advantage of the conservative people of this town to learn
more than they have yet taken the trouble to learn about the continuing and growing
demonstrations which have been loosely lumped under the head of "I. W. W. raids." It
is always to the advantage of a person who is attacked to know why he is attacked, who
is attacking him, and where he may expect the next blow.

And this is an attack—an attack on the social system. Its aim is nothing less than
revolution.

It has been taken lightly by this careless town, but it should not be taken lightly. It is
the most serious demonstration that the revolutionary element has made in this country
since the demonstrations in Chicago in 1886, which ended in the conflict between the
police and the revolutionists in Haymarket Square, the throwing of the famous bomb,
and the hanging of the Anarchist leaders.

The conflict was brought about when the police attempted to break up one of the
revolutionary meetings. The leaders of the present movement openly say that a similar attempt to-day will bring about the same result. The blame, they say, will be on the
shoulders of the police; as long as the police do not interfere with them there will be no
bloodshed; if the police do, there will be.

"I don't know whether it was consciously done or not," said Emma Goldman to me
the other day, and she smiled significantly as she said it, "but it was a very diplomatic
move on the part of the authorities not to interfere last Saturday with the Union Square
meeting and the parade on Fifth Avenue. I really congratulate the Mayor on that, congratulate him sincerely—if it was consciously done.

"Because you know that when hungry people are driven to desperation they can't reason. They ought not to be expected to, either."

Detective James J. Gegan is one of the policemen assigned to the following of the so-
called raiders. He has been on the "case" ever since Tannenbaum began his movement

on the churches,[1] and has watched it day by day. After the Fifth Avenue demonstration[2] of which Miss Goldman thus spoke, he said:

"It is evident that the men downtown (meaning his official superiors) do not recognize the seriousness of this movement. We who follow them from day to day see that they are gaining strength, and unless they are checked serious consequences may result."

### REAL HISTORY OF MOVEMENT.

The public appearance a week ago of Emma Goldman, Alexander Berkman, and the other anarchist leaders in this movement started by Frank Tannenbaum and heretofore called an I. W. W. movement, startled our careless town. The consternation it excited led to a lot of bewildered attempts to account for it, all of them entirely wrong. The favorite notion appeared to be that Big Bill Haywood and the I. W. W. had started the movement, using Tannenbaum as a tool, and that the anarchists had suddenly stepped in and wrested it away from them.[3]

Believing that his movement is a matter of much importance to everybody, and particularly to the class that is menaced by it, I shall here set down the real history of the movement, which is printed now for the first time, and its aims. It will disturb some preconceptions, but it will be the truth.

This movement was not originated either in the councils of the I. W. W. nor those of the anarchists. It originated in a centre of social disaffection which hitherto has not been mentioned in connection with it—the Ferrer School, at 63 West 107th Street.[4]

Emma Goldman and Alexander Berkman did not suddenly swoop upon it after they

1. Frank Tannenbaum was an anarchist, IWW member, and frequenter of the New York Ferrer Center. On 27 February 1914 Tannenbaum led the first of a series of marches of unemployed men to churches demanding food and shelter. On one such visit to a Catholic church, the Church of St. Alphonsus on 4 March 1914, a minor riot ensued and 190 people were arrested. Tannenbaum was charged with incitement to riot and sentenced to one year in prison. Following this conviction a number of organizations sprang into existence to continue the movement of the unemployed.
2. The Fifth Avenue demonstration, an event organized by the Ferrer Center's Conference of the Unemployed, was a parade of the unemployed that followed a mass meeting in Union Square on 21 March 1914; at the meeting EG, AB, and Carlo Tresca spoke. The parade marched from the Union Square meeting to the Ferrer Center, where food was distributed to the unemployed.
3. Beginning in the winter of 1913 a severe economic depression, marked by increasing numbers of unemployed, swept the United States. In New York demonstrations of the unemployed were common. Organizers of the many demonstrations and rallies included frequenters of the Ferrer Center and anarchists such as Frank Strawn Hamilton, Charles Robert Plunkett, Arthur Caron, AB, and Frank Tannenbaum. Following Tannenbaum's arrest, a number of unemployed workers' groups were organized, including A Labor Defense Committee founded by Elizabeth Gurley Flynn, Carlo Tresca, and William Haywood at Mary Heaton Vorse's apartment; an IWW Unemployed Union of New York; and the Conference of the Unemployed, formed at the Ferrer Center, with Joseph J. Cohen as secretary. Although AB coordinated all these groups and played a key role in organizing their demonstrations, in an article in the April 1914 *Mother Earth* he openly criticized prominent socialists and IWW leaders for failing to support Tannenbaum's defense and failing to support the unemployed movement.
4. The New York Ferrer Modern School was the school and center of the Francisco Ferrer Association, located at 63 East 107th Street, New York City, not 63 West 107th Street as the article states.

saw its progress and the opportunities it afforded. They were privy to it from the beginning. The real originators of it told her their intentions before they made a move.

There were no leaders, either of the I. W. W. nor of the anarchists, sitting in darkness in the background and pulling the strings. The conception and the execution were those of young men, mostly hardly more than boys, never before prominent in any revolutionary camp. The I. W. W. and anarchist leaders alike—the Haywoods and the Goldmans—deliberately and purposely stayed out of it, out of both the direction and the execution of it, and left everything to these youngsters. They knew all that was going on, of course.

For nearly thirty years—ever since the outbreak of the Chicago Anarchists—the revolutionary leaders have been hoping and cudgeling their brains for some move that would dramatize discontent as effectively as the strike that preceded the Haymarket collision had done. It finally came, not from them, but from the audacious brains of these boys, and was hatched in the Ferrer School, an institution less than four years old.

The soil, they exultantly say, is better prepared for the revolutionary seed than at any time in all these thirty years. The social discontent has grown and made itself felt to such an extent that now the authorities are more cautious in meeting it. In illustration of this growth they point to these two pictures:

First, of a little, blond-haired, blue-eyed girl addressing a meeting of the unemployed in Union Square and quoting Cardinal Manning's Maxim: "Necessity knows no law, and the starving man has a natural right to a share of his neighbor's bread." She added, "Ask for work. If they do not give you work, ask for bread. If they do not give you work or bread, then take bread." The community was thrown into a panic; the girl was arrested, tried, convicted, and sentenced to serve a year on Blackwell's Island. This was in 1893.[5]

Second, of a little, blond-haired, blue-eyed woman addressing a meeting of the unemployed in Union Square and saying: "March down to the Mayor. March down to the police. March down to the other city officials. Make them tell you what they are going to do to give you food and shelter. Go to the churches, go to the hotels and restaurants, go to the bakeshops, and tell them they must give you something to keep you from starving." Her hearers formed in line and marched down Fifth Avenue, jeering the churches and the homes of the rich. No arrests were made. This was in 1914.[6]

The girl in Union Square in 1893 was Emma Goldman. The woman at Union Square in 1914 was Emma Goldman. What has made the difference in 21 years?

"Times have changed," replied Emma Goldman when I asked her this question. "Even the courts would not send a person to jail for a year for such an utterance, if made to-day, as I served a year for making then.

---

5. The reporter refers to the events surrounding an 1893 protest against unemployment in which EG, then just twenty-four years old, was arrested and imprisoned. For a narrative of EG's 1893 arrest, trial, and imprisonment, including the attribution of her words to English theologian Cardinal Henry Edward Manning (1808–1892), see vol. 1, *Made for America*, pp. 144–82.
6. A reference to the 21 March 1914 demonstration and parade of the unemployed in New York City at which the forty-five-year-old EG addressed the crowd.

"There is a great difference between the quality of the unemployed themselves then and now. Then it was just simply a blind groping, and now it is a consciousness that they are entitled to a share of the good things of life."

### "INTELLECTUAL PROLETARIAT."

"Then it is remarkable, the change of the intellectual class toward the condition of labor. That is due to the fact that in the last ten years an intellectual proletariat has been developed in this country. There is a tremendous contingent of professional men and women everywhere who are proletarians."

"In sympathy with the proletariat, you mean?" I inquired.

"No, indeed—proletarians themselves. They have to walk around looking for jobs. The only difference between them and the men who work with their hands is the number of hours. The danger to present-day society is greater from these intellectual proletarians than from the unemployed, because they have tasted the good things of life and know what they are missing."[7]

This movement, begun in the Ferrer School, is defined by Leonard D. Abbott, the President of that institution, as "a dramatic gesture of the unemployed." He explained the aim of it thus:

"The whole value of this church-raiding system lies in its advertising the issue of the unemployed in a way that is compelling and that makes everybody think. These tactics are an effort of the more adventurous spirits to dramatize the whole issue."

It originated with three or four "Ferrer School boys," one of whom was Tannenbaum. All of them attended the evening classes there, and the Ferrer School claims them as its product and is proud of them. Tannenbaum was not a representative in any authorized sense of either the I. W. W. or the Anarchists, though he was well known to the leaders of both. The whole idea was his own and that of his chums at the school, whose names are withheld by the school authorities for perfectly understandable reasons.

None of them at first contemplated the church-raiding scheme or any of the subsequent developments. Their plan at first was simply to organize a few meetings to agitate the unemployment issue, and the shape the movement afterward took was simply a rather rapid evolution.

They informed Emma Goldman of their plans and asked her to raise money in aid of them. She has been delivering, all Winter, a series of successful lectures at the Berkeley Lyceum on the subject of the modern drama.[8] She made her appeal for funds at one of these lectures and collected about $40.

Tannenbaum and his associates at first undertook to hold their meetings in a hall,

7. For more on EG's views on the "intellectual proletariat" see her essay in *Mother Earth*, "The Intellectual Proletarians," February 1914, above.
8. EG gave a series of lectures on the modern drama every Sunday between 18 January and 15 March 1914 at the Berkeley Theatre, 23 West 44th Street, in New York City.

but did not have money enough to keep them up. They then resorted to open-air meetings, and the idea of moving on to the churches grew out of that. It was an inspiration of the Ferrer School boys.

The Hebrew Trades[9] and the Socialists called a conference of the unemployed, but when it was held the radical element of the I. W. W. and the Anarchists appeared and took possession of the meeting, and the Socialists and the Hebrew Trades withdrew.[10] This was the night Tannenbaum was arrested, and since then the extremists have been in full control of the movement. When the young leaders were arrested the work was carried on by men like them. The capture of one of these youthful disturbers simply made a breach into which another was ready to step. And the movement grew.

These young men are not of the ignorant type that one would expect. The most prominent of them, with the exception of Tannenbaum, are men of education and culture. Some of them are writers, poets, artists.

### MOVEMENT HAS A POET.

Aside from Tannenbaum, the most prominent are Joe O'Carroll and Douglas Dixon. Adolph Wolff is called by Mr. Abbott "the poet of the movement." Dixon studied at Cambridge University. O'Carroll comes of excellent people in Dublin. He is unemployed and has tuberculosis; his parents induced priests in this country to interest themselves in him, but O'Carroll, because of his beliefs, resisted their aid and joined the Ferrer School boys.[11] All three are poets—of the class of "intellectual proletarians" of which Emma Goldman spoke to me. Wolff is a sculptor as well as a poet.

"He," said Mr. Abbott, "is the first creative spirit that has come out of the Ferrer School. His poems"—Wolff has published a volume of them which made some talk— "were written at my literary class."[12]

9. The United Hebrew Trades was an organization founded by Morris Hillquit and Bernard Weinstein. According to Hillquit in his book *Loose Leaves from a Busy Life* (New York: Macmillan, 1934), the organization promoted "(1) mutual aid and cooperation among the Jewish trade unions of New York; (2) organization of new unions; (3) the propaganda of Socialism among the Jewish workers."

10. The Conference of the Unemployed was actually based at the Ferrer Center, and the treasurer of the organization was anarchist Joseph J. Cohen.

11. Joseph O'Carroll was a New York Irish American IWW organizer and a frequenter of the New York Ferrer Center. He was active in the 1913–1914 unemployment demonstrations, when, on 4 April, at the second rally organized by the Conference of the Unemployed in Union Square, he was severely beaten and arrested by the police (probably saved from death only by Rebecca Edelsohn who placed herself between O'Carroll and the police batons). O'Carroll spent months in the hospital recovering from the beating, which was loudly protested by EG and others. He would later physically attack the informant, Donald Vose, at Matthew Schmidt's trial in late 1915.

12. Adolf Wolff (1883–1944) was a Belgian-born sculptor, poet, and anarchist. He attended literature courses at the Ferrer Center, and his poetry appeared in the first issue of the *Glebe* (New Jersey; September 1913) under the title "Songs, Sighs and Curses." His collected poems, *Songs of Rebellion, Songs of Life, Songs of Love* (New York: A. and C. Boni, 1914), contained many of the poems which appeared in the *Glebe* along with thirty other previously unpublished pieces.

### EMMA GOLDMAN'S DREAM.

The leaders of the Anarchists and the I. W. W. kept ostentatiously out of the movement at first, but were delighted with it; not merely because it was in line with their ideas, but because it was a fulfillment of the hope they had always entertained—that by the constant sowing of discontent the younger element would at last rise itself, without waiting for leaders. It had always been their dream to bring about social changes, as one of them expressed it, "through the working-men themselves, as opposed to the Socialist conception, which does everything through the State."

Through all the twenty-one years since Emma Goldman was sentenced to jail for her vain effort to disturb the apathy of the unemployed, this has been her dream. She was delighted when she saw, as she believed, a beginning of an approximation toward reality, and she, like Haywood of the I. W. W., stayed out and let them have full swing.

But she kept on aiding the movement by raising money, though she confined herself to that. "It has been a great joy to me," she told me, "to see boys, some of them not much more then children, show so much organizing capacity and so much self-control, and I didn't want to step in. I knew that if Mr. Berkman or I did step in, the whole attention of the public would be fixed on us. Besides, I was terribly busy. I had just finished the manuscript of a book on the social significance of the modern drama, which a Boston house is going to bring out,[13] and I had pledged myself to have every line in by March 20. I was busy with my lectures, too, and it was a physical impossibility to do anything for them."

Haywood, too, kept his hands off. He came to town and was the guest of honor at a meeting of social rebels at the Fifth Avenue home of Mrs. Mabel Dodge,[14] but with the other I. W. W. leaders he stayed in the background as ostentatiously as did the anarchist chiefs.

On Saturday, a week ago, Miss Goldman and Berkman of the Anarchists, and Carlo Tresca of the I. W. W.,[15] came to the front and the Union Square meeting, which so excited the crowd that it marched down Fifth Avenue. Berkman says 500 were in line. Of those who were at the Union Square meeting Miss Goldman estimates that fully half were "rebels," as she calls them, the others being the unidentified unemployed.

This parade may have been made up in the same proportions of rebels and unemployed, but it was the rebels who led, inspired and guided it. Fifty of them were women, Anarchist women—"our girls," as Miss Goldman always calls them.

"I was not in the Fifth Avenue demonstration," she said. "I left two hours before it

---

13. EG's book *The Social Significance of the Modern Drama* (Boston: Richard G. Badger, 1914).
14. An article published later, in the 12 May 1914 *New York Times*, suggested that IWW organizers Bill Haywood and Frank Hamilton had been entertained at Mabel Dodge's home as part of a conference on the unemployed.
15. Italian anarchist and IWW organizer Carlo Tresca played an active part in the unemployed movement and, unlike other IWW members such as Bill Haywood who distanced themselves and the organization from the anarchists killed in the 4 July 1914 Lexington Avenue explosion, defended the dead anarchists, claiming one of them, Arthur Caron, was an IWW member.

began, and I didn't know it was to take place. When they got to the Ferrer Association headquarters they called me up and told me how they had marched and how spirited the boys were, and they were taken over to the Ferrer Association and given food and money and tobacco—I had collected money for them at Union Square.

"Mr. Berkman told me that all this talk of our girls spitting in the faces of women was nonsense. Our girls wouldn't do such a thing. The demonstration was inspired, but orderly. They did make demonstrations before the churches and the synagogues, but the quality of these boys is demonstrated in this wonderful fact—when they reached Mount Sinai Hospital they marched in absolute silence for two blocks so as not to disturb the sick people. Not a single paper mentioned that, because it would give these boys a little semblance of being human."

### CONSTRUCTIVE ANARCHISM.

The Ferrer School, which thus produced this "dramatic gesture of the unemployed," was described to me by its President, Mr. Abbot, as "a laboratory in which new social theories are tested." It is the first institution, he says, "devoted to the constructive side of anarchism."[16] It is less than four years old, and it is turning out, and is intended to turn out, graduates filled with a settled discontent with the present social system and a determination to end it.

In the day classes there are between thirty and forty children, under the tutelage of Mrs. Cora Bennett Stephenson.[17] Back of it are men and women of that class of "intellectuals" to which Miss Goldman looks so hopefully. At the evening classes, which are of course designed for young people older than those in the day classes, lectures are given, of which an idea may be gained from a list of some of those given in the last five weeks.

Among them, then, were lectures by Elizabeth Gurley Flynn, the I. W. W. leader, on the Paterson strike, in which she was arrested; by Louis Levine and Andre Tridon[18] on

16. In 1919 Ferrer organizers Harry Kelly and Leonard Abbott would publish a short-lived anarchist newspaper titled *Freedom: A Journal of Constructive Anarchism*. At this time all prewar anarchist publications had been banned, and many anarchist publishers and editors, including AB and EG, were in jail facing deportation. Years later, a book by Russian exile and anarchist Gregory Maximoff, *Constructive Anarchism* (Chicago: Maximoff Memorial Publication Committee, 1952), published after his death, would revisit and reiterate the philosophy behind Abbott and Kelly's newspaper.

17. Cora Bennett Stephenson (b. 1872) was an American socialist and teacher dismissed from her Illinois public school position for protesting Ferrer's execution in 1909. She joined the New York Ferrer Modern School as a teacher in 1913 but left in the aftermath of the 4 July 1914 Lexington Avenue bombing. She was a member of the editorial board of the literary journal *Smart Set* after 1914. Her works include the novel *The Hand of God* (Boston: Ball Publishing, 1909) and an opera, *A Lovers' Knot* (London: New York: G. Schirmer, 1916).

18. Lewis Levitzki Lorwin (Louis Levine) would become an authority on the French labor movement. He was a speaker at the second-anniversary dinner of the Ferrer Association on 14 June 1912 and taught syndicalism to adult classes at the Ferrer Center. Andre Tridon (1877–1922) was a French socialist and secretary of the socialist and literary magazine *Masses*. He spoke at the Ferrer school

syndicalism; by Edwin Markham[19] on poetry; by Gutierrez, the Mexican revolutionist,[20] on Mexico; by Clarence S. Darrow, the McNamaras' lawyer, on Voltaire; by Emma Goldman, Berkman, and others. Robert Henri and George Bellows[21] conduct the art class. Among those back of the enterprise are Lincoln Steffens, Hutchins Hapgood, Gilbert E. Roe, Theodore Schroeder, Bolton Hall, Alden Freeman,[22] and others of the "intellectual" class.

---

and contributed to the *International*, the *Industrial Worker*, and the *Smart Set*. His *The New Unionism* (New York: B. W. Huebsch, 1913) was an early study of revolutionary syndicalism; in it he expressed his critique of anarchism as an ideology.

19. Edwin Markham (1852–1940) was an American poet, best known for his poem "The Man with the Hoe," originally published in the *San Francisco Examiner*, 15 January 1899, and later published in *The Man with the Hoe and Other Poems* (New York: Doubleday & McClure, 1899).

20. Lazano Gutierrez de Lara was a Mexican revolutionary and educator who acted as John Kenneth Turner's guide through Mexico, helping him gather facts for his articles and his book *Barbarous Mexico* (1910). Gutierrez edited *Regeneración* in Los Angeles after Ricardo Flores Magón was arrested in 1907, until he too was arrested, forcing the magazine to temporarily cease publication in January 1908. In 1909 he was again arrested in Los Angeles and charged with disturbing the peace; released, he was immediately rearrested on orders from the federal government's Department of Commerce and Labor, and threatened with deportation under the anti-anarchist laws. He escaped deportation, claiming he was a socialist, not an anarchist. He was a lecturer at the New York Ferrer Modern School in 1914. He wrote, with Edgcumb Pinchon, *The Mexican People: Their Struggle for Freedom* (New York: Doubleday, Page, 1914), and he contributed the article "Story of a Refugee" to *Pacific Monthly* 25, no. 1 (January 1911).

21. A reference to artist, author, and philosophical anarchist Robert Henri (1865–1929). Henri was part of the group known as "the Eight," which in March 1908 staged an independent art show after their work was rejected by the National Academy of Design. The group was known for their opposition to the authority of the academy and commitment to freedom of expression. In November 1911 Henri began lecturing at the Ferrer Center once a week at the invitation of EG, an affiliation that would last until the center closed its doors in 1918. Many pupils from the classes he taught with George Bellows at the Ferrer Center, including Adolf Wolff, Man Ray, and George Weber, would go on to be famous in the world of American art. In 1912 Henri donated paintings in support of the Lawrence strike. In March and April 1915 Henri painted three portraits of EG, which were subsequently destroyed in 1934 by the heir to Henri's estate, his sister-in-law. A member of the Birth Control Committee, Henri worked with Leonard Abbott to plan a mass meeting at Carnegie Hall in 1916. As a member of the New York Publicity Committee for the International Workers' Defense League, he also helped organize a fund-raising meeting at Carnegie Hall for Mooney and Billings in 1916. Henri contributed to the tenth-anniversary souvenir edition of *Mother Earth* as well as the article "Isadora Duncan and the Libertarian Spirit" to the April 1915 issue of the *Modern School*, in which he favorably compared Duncan to Walt Whitman, seeing them both as figures holding "the deep philosophy of freedom and of dignity, of simplicity and of order." He also contributed to Horace Trabel's *Conservator*.

George Bellows (1882–1925) was an artist and member of the Ashcan School. Bellows was a student of Robert Henri's who joined him as an instructor at the Ferrer Center in 1912 and also helped organize the Armory Show in 1913. Like Henri, Bellows donated paintings in support of the Lawrence strike. Bellows also joined the art staff of the *Masses* in 1912, contributing illustrations until the magazine ceased publication in 1917. And like Henri, he was a member of the 1916 New York Publicity Committee for the International Workers' Defense League and helped organize a fundraising event at Carnegie Hall for Mooney and Billings.

22. Lincoln Steffens, Hutchins Hapgood, Gilbert E. Roe, Theodore Schroeder, Bolton Hall, and Alden Freeman were all liberals associated with EG. Hall, Roe, and Freeman were founding members of

These were the classes which Tannenbaum and his colleagues attended, it was where they got their ideas, and it was in this building and after one of the lectures that they conceived and laid out their plans. From there they went to Emma Goldman's, twelve blocks away, and asked her aid in getting money.

As the movement gathered strength the I. W. W. and the Anarchists joyously fell in with it, and not they alone, but all the apostles of discontent of whatever creed. Miss Goldman told me a surprising thing, which was that among those who aided in the raid on the churches were many who were neither Anarchists nor I. W. W. men, but simply Freethinkers in religion.

"That," she said, "was the particular phase that appealed to them, not the industrial feature of the subject. They certainly succeeded in doing rather better anti-religious work than some of the Secularists; they placed the church where Ingersoll[23] couldn't have placed it."

The flames were assiduously fanned from two headquarters, those of the I. W. W. on West Street and those of the Anarchists at 313 Grand Street.[24] They work independently and are not in all respects harmonious.

### FOOD, NOT POLITICS, WANTED.

"The break that is coming between the two elements," said one of them, "is largely over the question of organization. The conference of the unemployed on Grand Street realizes the impossibility of organizing the unemployed, and simply stands for demonstrations that will picture the issue vividly. The I. W. W. are trying to organize the movement. On that point clashes have come.

"It has had the effect, too, of making sharper the division between the Socialists and the I. W. W., for the I. W. W. very sensibly used the argument, 'What are your political methods going to do for the unemployed who are actually suffering? They want food, not politics.'"

On this matter of "dramatizing the issue" the leaders of the revolt believe that wherever they show their ragged regiments the picture is painted on the mind of every one who sees them. They are, these leaders say, a forlorn and miserable looking crowd, who will touch quickly the understanding of any spectator to whom unemployment has been merely a name.

"If you had seen the way they ate the sandwiches at the Ferrer School you would have no doubt about their being hungry," said Leonard Abbott.

---

the Francisco Ferrer Association. All except Bolton Hall were members of the Free Speech League. Lincoln Steffens was a frequenter of the Ferrer Center and was present at the 21 March 1914 unemployed mass meeting and the 4 April 1914 meeting at which many anarchists were violently beaten by the police.

23. Robert Ingersoll was probably the most influential American freethinker of the nineteenth century.

24. The *Mother Earth* offices were at West 119th Street, the IWW Unemployed Union of New York was at East 4th Street, and the Ferrer Center was located at 63 East 107th Street.

"That crowd at Union Square," said Emma Goldman, "was the most forlorn gathering of human beings I ever laid my eyes on. They were cold and hungry; they shivered incessantly. One of these men is in the last stages of tuberculosis; he has six children; the other day he was thrown out of his miserable garret, where rags and junk were his furniture.

"We aim to call attention to the unemployed. Something must be done for men like that one. If I owned a restaurant, or even a platform, and the unemployed came there, I would let them make use of it as much as possible—because," she added significantly, "the other way is a stupid way, it doesn't pay.

"Will this lead to disorder? That will depend on the police. I don't believe the unemployed will submit silently to being clubbed.

"They do not want to cause a rumpus. But if the police beat them up, I think the time is past when people will submit to it. I think the editorial in *The Times* last Monday was more of an incitement to riot than anything I have said. It told the police to use violence.[25] The editor must know that the police need no such incitement.

"There are enough people of kindly instincts, of all classes, to assist the unemployed, if they can be made to see what unemployment means. Then the people would not be driven to desperation. But if there are to be arrests by the police on the one side, and resistance by the people on the other, who can foresee the result?"

So little has been heard of the anarchists of late years that it struck the town with astonishment to see their sudden reappearance in menacing numbers. It has been so often said that they are dying out that their strength was amazing.

But if they are dying out, it does not manifest itself in their outward appearance. Five years ago Berkman and Emma Goldman got out their little magazine, *Mother Earth*, in a poor little tenement on East Twelfth Street. Later they were able to take an office on West Twenty-eight Street and present a much smarter appearance. Now they have a whole house, a brownstone one, at 74 West 119th Street, where they have several assistants.

Yearly Miss Goldman tours the country, delivering her lectures in the principal cities. When she began them she was frequently arrested; now she meets with no interference, and her audiences grow. There are forty or fifty publishing houses in the country which get out revolutionary literature exclusively. A new one was recently started in this city, the Rabelais Press, run by a man named Rampapas.[26] Anarchism may be dying out,

25. The editorial in the *New York Times* said, among other things, "We urge the Mayor to take action in the matter without delay and Commissioner McKay to order the police to break up such meetings as that of Saturday and enforce the law against all unlicensed parades and street demonstrations. All the trouble can be stopped now by a few determined policemen with heavy clubs who know that the will of the people is behind them. If it is allowed to develop, infantry, cavalry, and artillery many be needed."

26. John Rompapas was a Greek anarchist and publisher, as well as an importer of cigars. He founded the Rabelais Press in 1914, which published Hippolyte Havel's *Revolutionary Almanac* (1914), his own philosophical autobiography, *Book of My Life* (1914), and Margaret Sanger's *What Every Girl*

but if one searches for signs of its moribund condition he is likely to find things that will disagreeably astonish him.

## SHE NEVER RUNS AWAY.

She is going on her usual tour on March 30, and Dr. Ben Reitman, her manager, is in Chicago now arranging it. This accounts for the otherwise inexplicable fact that this picturesque and fiery rebel's name has not appeared in the reports of the Tannenbaum movement. "If he had been here you would have heard of him," said Miss Goldman, with a flash in her eyes unusual with her. In conversation, whatever she may be on the platform, she is the quietest and most impassive of talkers.

In newspaper discussions of these things there are often references to the "Goldman-Berkman group of Anarchists." The term is a misnomer; there is no such group, or rather the term implies divisions that do not exist. Emma Goldman and Alexander Berkman are the leaders of all the Anarchists, not only in this city but in the whole country.

Another favorite delusion is that these rebels, in times of stress, are in hiding somewhere, from which they emerge to create trouble and then disappear again. After the Union Square meeting and the Fifth Avenue march it was reported that Emma Goldman had "fled from the city for the week-end." She was, in fact, delivering a lecture in Newark.

"As if any one ever heard of Emma Goldman running away!" she said disdainfully. "Every one knows where I live, and any one who doesn't can ask the police—they know."

Emma Goldman, like many of her followers, was converted to Anarchism by the hanging of the four Chicago Anarchists after the Haymarket outbreak. That outbreak was the culmination of just such demonstrations as are being carried on now. These demonstrations continued until the Chicago police undertook to break up a meeting held in Haymarket Square to discuss the unemployed situation of the day; one of the crowd threw a bomb, and seven policemen were killed. Seven of the Anarchist leaders were convicted of incendiary utterances and four were hanged; one blew his brains out on the day appointed for his execution, and two were sentenced to life imprisonment, but were pardoned after the excitement of the time had died down.

That execution is always in the minds of the revolutionary leaders, but it does not daunt them. It made an Anarchist of Emma Goldman; after it Berkman assaulted Henry C. Frick and served sixteen years in prison for it.[27] Haywood has since been on

---

*Should Know* (1914) and *What Every Mother Should Know* (1914). He also donated seed money for Havel's *The Social War* (1913) and Sanger's journal the *Woman Rebel* (1914). Rompapas frequented both the Ferrer Center and Mabel Dodge's salon, and contributed to the funeral expenses for the Lexington Avenue bombers in 1914. He was also the author of *Greek Language Self Taught* (New York: Atlas Book Store, 1916).

27. AB served fourteen years of his sentence.

trial for his life.[28] Elizabeth Gurley Flynn[29] has served a prison term. Whatever is before them, it cannot frighten them or turn them aside. They are unafraid and indomitable. As Emma Goldman says, the police know where she lives, and no one ever heard of her running away.

This is the situation. This is the history and the meaning of what we are now seeing. This is what confronts the social order. Is it, or is it not, worth serious thought?

*New York Times Sunday Magazine*, 29 March 1914, p. 2. The author of this article, Charles Willis Thompson (1871–1946) was a New York journalist, chief of the Washington bureau of the *New York Times* during the Theodore Roosevelt presidency, and a prominent reporter during the First World War. Thompson also interviewed EG for the *New York Times* on 30 May 1909; see vol. 2, *Making Speech Free*.

28. On 30 December 1905 former Idaho governor Frank Steunenberg was killed by a bomb that exploded as he opened the front gate of his house. On 17 February 1906 Western Federation of Miners (WFM) leaders Charles Moyer, William "Big Bill" Haywood, and George Pettibone were arrested in Colorado without warrants on suspicion of conspiracy in the murder. They were jailed on 6 March, where they remained for almost a year. See note in "As to 'Crammer of Furnaces,'" Article in *Mother Earth*, December 1906, vol. 2, *Making Speech Free*.

29. IWW organizer Elizabeth Gurley Flynn's involvement in the Spokane, Washington, IWW free speech fight led to her arrest on 30 November 1909 for criminal conspiracy (for editing the IWW paper *Industrial Worker* while its regular editors were in jail). After spending one night in jail she was was released after money for her bail was raised. The ninety-day sentence she received at her first trial was overturned on appeal.

DEAR MARGARET:—

I am enclosing money order for $3.70, the first bundle of W.R. you sent me.[1] I am grateful to you I am sure for the contribution you have made to Mother Earth of the second bundle. You evidently did not understand my letter. I asked you to send me more copies to this city, as I am all out of those I had; but it is too late now, and, if possible, I want you to send by express 50 copies or more to Ruth Allson, 1034 18th Ave. N.E., Minneapolis, Minn.[2] I will be in Minneapolis all of next week and I should like to circulate the paper in that city.

It was quite impossible for me to get subscribers because when people heard that the paper was held up they would not subscribe for it for fear that it will not be continued.[3] Besides, I think it will be very difficult even if you should get a distributing depot in every city. In a small town it might be workable, but in a city like Chicago it would be quite impossible for any one to carry the copies to each subscriber, as they are all removed from each other by long distances. I therefore am much afraid that you will buck up against a difficulty which will make the continuance of the little fighter impossible, unless it is released from the postal authorities. Of course as long as I am touring I can reach a great many people. I should want at least 500 copies of your paper sent to Los Angeles by express, and I am sure that I can use more than 50 of the first and second issues for Denver. You can send me a hundred of each, but I do not see how you are going to work it, unless the copies can be sent to each subscriber.

I don't think you ought to give 5 cents on a copy to agents. It is entirely out of the ordinary run of discounts. 4 cents ought to be the highest. We only give 3 on copies of Mother Earth and 4 cents on bundles. If you give too much discount you will not be able to maintain your work.

I was interested in your account of your neighbors. It is hardly credible that such a thing should occur in a city like New York; but I find that I am not surprised at anything that will happen in this country. As a matter of fact, the people themselves are so dense that they are capable of greater outrage than even the police. The best proof of

1. Margaret Sanger began publishing the revolutionary feminist and birth control paper the *Woman Rebel* in March 1914.
2. Ruth S. Olson was a correspondent of EG'S and distributor of *Mother Earth* who helped arrange EG's Minneapolis lectures from 1911 to 1915.
3. The *Woman Rebel* was held up in the mails for its inclusion of content in violation of the Comstock anti-obscenity law, as birth control information was considered obscene.

that is the lynching in the south[4] and the horrors committed by the vigilantes in San Diego[5] and other cities. Of course the people help, but mob brutality, which is the result of ignorance, is by far more terrible than police brutality which might be reasoned with occasionally.

I do hope that you will survive the antagonism of your neighbors, and if not do move to a different part of the city. I certainly hope that you can keep up the paper. It is a very brave attempt and the first commenced by a woman in this country. I want to help all I can, but, as I said before, it will be very difficult to reach individuals unless the magazine can go by mail. I am trying to find somebody who will take the sale of your publication for Chicago. Have not been able to discover anyone yet, but I may before I leave the city.

There are so many meetings here, and if any one would undertake the work he would find it worth while; in fact even from a material point of view I am going to see who I can get.

I leave here for Madison, Wis., Saturday. Then go to Minneapolis for a week. General Delivery will reach me.

I am glad to hear that the meeting last Saturday on Union Square proved such a great success and that our boys got away with their heads unbroken.[6]

With much love.

Fraternally,

Emma Goldman

TLS, Margaret Sanger Papers, DLC. On Lexington Hotel stationery. "Replied 19 April 1914" handwritten on first page of letter. Addressed to Miss Margaret Sanger, 34 Post Ave., New York City.

4. As well as a general comment this could possibly be a reference to the 31 March 1914 lynching that had just taken place in Wagoner County, Oklahoma. The victim was 17-year-old Marie Scott, whose brother had killed one of the two white men who had assaulted her.
5. See "Outrage of San Diego," Article in *Mother Earth*, June 1912, above, for an account of the 1912 San Diego free speech fight.
6. On Saturday, 11 April, a peaceful rally was held in Union Square, organized by the Conference of the Unemployed. The previous week, on 4 April, another rally organized by the Conference of the Unemployed had ended in violence, with many protesters, including Joe O'Carroll, Adolf Wolff, and Arthur Caron, brutally beaten by the police. See "Self-Defense for Labor," Article in the *New York Times Sunday Magazine*, 29 March 1914, above.

Cover of April 1914 issue of *Mother Earth* magazine emblazoned with the black flag of anarchy and hunger, a symbol of the erupting mass demonstrations by the unemployed—particularly in New York throughout the spring of 1914. (Kate Sharpley Archive)

## Emma Goldman in Defense
## of Modern Women's Fashions

### Anarchist Gives Ideas of Why Sisters Should Do As They Please.

Declares That Originality in Dress Is Certain Sign
of Brains in Wearer.

"No, I don't think women's fashions are too eccentric. Some are rather pretty, I think, some are sensible and some are—"

A typical French shrug of shoulders and uplift of palms, which might have been interpreted, "I don't care what they wear," completed Emma Goldman's defense of women's fashions.

Emma Goldman, whom one associates in one's mind with bombs, mobs and revolution, yesterday afternoon valiantly defended women's love of dress and her temptation to be an imitator of her French sister no matter to what extreme lengths this desire of imitation may lead her.

Emma Goldman is a Bohemian.[1] You see that by her dress and by her indifference to conventions. She was modishly dressed as she sat in her room in the Chamberlain hotel, but comfort had been her main thought. Her suit of blue was tailor made, her low shoes were of latest design, her white embroidered waist was cut low in neck, her stockings were silk. But her independence of conventionality of dress was expressed in the absence of any restriction of body by stays or girdles. She moves naturally and easily; crosses one knee upon another with a grace that few of her middle weight build could copy.

### NO ANARCHISTIC LOOK.

Looks like an anarchist and militant womanhood? Not much. Emma Goldman reminds one of the old type of womanhood. She has strong nerve energy. She has eyes that are like the sea—gray, gray blue, cold, piercing, with an occasional sunny half light. She is positive, direct, assertive, but womanly.

---

1. Bohemia (in 1914 a location within the Czech Republic) was characterized as the romantic home of the Gypsies. The term "Bohemian," first used in Paris in the 1830s, evolved to identify those who rejected bourgeois social mores. By the time it was incorporated into colloquial English, in the mid-nineteenth century, its meaning also took a more literary and artistic cast.

In an hour's intimate interview yesterday Emma Goldman said not one word about anarchy. She talked of woman—her place in the world, her right to say whether or not she should be the mother of sons to be killed in war—her place in social service and, finally, her right to dare to choose what she wore irrespective of the opinion of any man.

Miss Goldman, who is simply a free lance in thought, with no faith in political institutions, is original in her attitude toward the woman problem and her dress.

"Why should anything so unimportant as woman's dress be discussed?" Miss Goldman asked with some asperity.

"Yes, why?" meekly echoed the reporter. One doesn't contradict Miss Goldman. The directness of the look and the seagreenness of the eyes forbid it.

"Yes, why?" she continued. "Women should have the right to dress as they please. Just because one person dares to do anything a little different from his neighbor he is considered eccentric. It makes no difference if he makes a garden or builds a fence differently. We seem to think that we should be modeled alike from the same clod of clay. But we are not.

## ONE IDEA OF DRESS.

"The trouble is," Miss Goldman paused in meditation of the subject in which she had become surprisingly interested. She crossed her knees, pushed back the soft brown hair from her forehead, and completed the sentence. "The trouble is people have become used to the idea of a uniformity of dress. They expect women to all dress exactly alike. When one woman becomes independent of this thought she puts on something which does not conform exactly to what the uniform of women's dress is supposed to be—therefore, mark you, she is unusual, she is different from her sisters, she is a strange, new being whom the people cannot understand. Now why should not women dress as they please? Doesn't it seem preposterous that she cannot dress as she desires to dress and leave the world out of it? Clothing is physical covering, not a part of a person. I am more concerned about the brain of woman than about her dress. Every time I see a woman who has dared to be independent in dress—even if she is extremely dressed—I am glad of it. I know she has brains and has dared to prove it."

*Des Moines (Iowa) Register and Leader,* 26 April 1914, p. 5.

Printed by permission of S. T. Kajiwara

EMMA GOLDMAN

# THE
# SOCIAL SIGNIFICANCE
# OF THE MODERN
# DRAMA

EMMA GOLDMAN

BOSTON: RICHARD G. BADGER
TORONTO: THE COPP CLARK CO., LIMITED

Frontispiece of Emma Goldman's *The Social Significance of the Modern Drama*—a collection of essays primarily related to contemporary issues addressed by modern playwrights in Europe and Russia, an R.G. Badger publication, 1914.

MY DEAR MR. BROWNE:

I have your two letters, but have been terribly busy, therefore, could not write. I am sure I am very glad to have been able to do a little for your venture.[1] I only wish it were more. I feel confident that you would have far greater success, if you would give the people Modern plays which have a bearing on their own lives. After all, we cannot expect the people who are occupied by economic difficulties to interest themselves in Greek tragedies. I think, however, that you could combine both though, if you would only devote half the time to the Modern Drama.

I am rather anxious to know how the Gabler performances came off.[2] Did you have good attendance? How was the Norwegian Interpreter. I will be glad to hear from you at your convenience.

I am here until the 10th of May and then go to Los Angeles for an indefinite time. My address in that city will be Hotel Astoria, Third and Olive Streets.

Remember me to Mrs. Browne and all the members of the Little Theater.[3]

SINCERELY,

EMMA GOLDMAN

TLS, Van Valkenburgh–Browne Papers, MiU. Addressed to Mr. Maurice Browne, The Chicago Little Theatre, Fine Arts Building, Chicago, Illinois.

1. Maurice Browne (1881–1955) was an English actor, director, and producer. In 1912, inspired by Laura Pelman, director of the Hull House Players, he and his wife, Ellen van Valkenburgh, founded the Chicago Little Theatre. Early productions included Wilfrid Wilson Gibson's *Womenkind* and William Butler Yeats's *On Brails Strand*. EG met Browne through Margaret Anderson in 1914.
2. Henrik Ibsen's *Hedda Gabler* was the final production of the Little Theatre's second season. Borgny Hammer, a Norwegian actor, played the title role (in English). The performance's unprecedented financial success allowed the theater to start its third season debt free and with enough reserves to extend its reach.
3. Opening night was 12 November 1912 for the Chicago Little Theatre, located on Michigan Avenue in a small rear room on the fourth floor of the Fine Arts Building (also the building of Margaret Anderson's *Little Review*). Intended to enhance the cultural life of Chicago, the Little Theatre staged plays spanning a wide range of genres and topics, and became especially known for its innovative and experimental pieces. Wracked with financial problems, it closed its doors in 1917.

My dear Margaret:

I have your two letters of the 11th and 19th, also 200 copies May W.R. I wrote Alex[1] to call you up and ask whether you had sent April copies to Los Angeles, as they did not arrive and I'd like to make sure.

The May issue is good and if you can only keep up, I am sure the paper will become a force. It sells splendidly, as the subject you are treating is really the main thing people are interested in. Not one of my lectures brings out such a crowd as the one on the birth strike and it is the same with the W.R. It sells better than anything we have.

Inclosed is a money order for $10.50, credit me as follows. $7.50 for 150 Rebels, of which you sent 50 to Minneapolis, and 200 to Denver, for the balance of the Denver shipment and the May issue to this city, I will remit in a little while. $3 are for the Denver subs. I expect to get some subs here too. By the way, if you have a few numbers of the first issue you can spare, send them to me, several people who will subscribe want it.

About the Neo Malthusian leagues, it is a splendid idea but why must it be done secretly?[2] I think it ought to be started openly and that people ought to be taught to go to prison if need be. I do not believe the American psychology is fit for conspiratory work, too many agents of J. J. Burns[3] about who would only cause mischief. If I can speak about the subject openly why can people not organize openly? I think it would help to break the Comstock control,[4] besides I don't think there is a law dealing with that question.

If you could arrange, my suggestion would be that you make a tour, talk about prevention, organize leagues and take the paper with you. I am inclined to think you'd have a tremendous success. Perhaps you might start the preliminary work during the summer and start out in the fall, or begin with N.Y. you have no idea what the personal element

1. EG distributed Margaret Sanger's paper, the *Woman Rebel*, during her cross-country lecture tours. While on these tours, she left the management of the *Mother Earth* office to AB and others.
2. The Neo-Malthusian League was a European birth control organization visited by Sanger while in Europe the previous year. The April 1914 *Woman Rebel* announced, "Neo-Malthusian Leagues are being formed throughout the United States," as well as an invitation to readers to "write for information if you are interested in forming one in your vicinity." The July 1914 issue of the *Woman Rebel* announced the formation of a recently organized Birth Control League, which appears to have existed only on paper.
3. The detective William J. Burns, whose agency was responsible for arresting the McNamaras, as well as Matthew Schmidt and David Caplan.
4. EG refers to the control the Comstock anti-obscenity laws (1873, 1876) had over lectures and publications promoting birth control.

means in reaching people, in that way, you could kill two flies with one stroke, circulate the paper, sell pamphlets and also organize the leagues.

My meetings here have been good but nothing what they were last year. Unemployment has left the country in pretty bad condition. I have opened a drama course last night,[5] don't know how it will pan out. It did not look very encouraging to begin with. But we are used to ups and downs. If only I did not feel so wretched, but I caught a terrible cold in Denver which affected my throat and I can not shake it off. But I will survive I suppose.

We are here until the 11th of June, then in S.F. General Del. I will need at least hundred of the May W.R. for S.F. if you can get the June out in time, of the latter I shall want two hundred.[6]

WITH LOVE.

EMMA.

TLSr, Margaret Sanger Letters, DLC. "COPY" typed at top of first page.

---

5. EG's drama course was scheduled for 1 to 5 June 1914 in Los Angeles.
6. The June issue of the *Woman Rebel* included an excerpt from EG's essay "Woman Suffrage," first published in *Anarchism and Other Essays* (New York: Mother Earth Publishing Association, 1910).

Drawing on the cover of May 1914 issue of *Mother Earth*, reflecting the journal's concern about the growing patriotic fervor threatening to overpower individual liberty. (Kate Sharpley Archive)

Article in *MOTHER EARTH*

*New York, June 1914*

# En Route

The wave of unemployment, which has swept the country from coast to coast, is only now making itself felt in all its paralyzing effect.[1]

Of course the workers were the first to feel the death-like grip of unemployment. Never earning more than enough to satisfy their immediate needs, the masses were not able to stand the "vacation" so generously thrust upon them by our insane capitalist régime. Hence the terrible distress in the ranks of the workers.

As usual, the kept press denied the scope of the poverty and want which loomed like a black spectre all winter upon the horizon of the economic struggle. But now it is being conceded everywhere—even by the most stupid upholders of present conditions—that the siege of hard times has been the worst in many years.

Especially is this true of Denver which, on the decline for the past several years, now looks like a veritable graveyard. Even the horrors of Ludlow[2] did not wake it up for long,

---

1. From winter 1913 through 1915 the United States was in a severe economic depression with massive unemployment; over one-quarter of a million people were out of work in New York alone.

2. In early 1913 the United Mine Workers began an organizing drive in southern Colorado mines owned by the Colorado Fuel and Iron Company (of which John D. Rockefeller Jr. was the principal stockholder). The company refused to negotiate a contract with the union. After the shooting of a UMW organizer in August 1913 the intensity of the organizing escalated, and at the miners' convention in Trinidad, at which Mother Jones spoke, the miners voted to strike. On 23 September 1913 roughly 90 to 95 percent of the miners (11,000 men) went on strike; they left the mine camps with their families, relocating to tent colonies set up by the union. The largest of the colonies, consisting of 400 tents housing about 1,000 people was at Ludlow, about eighteen miles outside Trinidad.

   The strike was marked by violence from the beginning. The Baldwin-Felts detective agency, which had been hired by Colorado Fuel and Iron Company before the strike had begun, immediately began harassing the strikers. On 17 October 1913 one man was killed and a ten-year-old boy was left with nine bullets in his leg. Later that month 190 armed guards with machine guns and rifles heading for the Ludlow colony were intercepted by armed strikers, and one guard was killed. By 28 October 1913, when Colorado governor Elias M. Ammons declared martial law and called in the National Guard, at least nine men had been killed. After a winter of violent skirmishes between the strikers and the National Guard, with escalating violence and mounting tension on both sides, the Colorado governor recalled most of the National Guard. Those who remained were employed by either the mining company or the detective agency. On the morning of 20 April 1914 (following Ludlow camp leader and strike organizer Louis Tinkas's discussion with the Colorado National Guard leader, Major Hamrock) National Guardsmen and detectives began firing into the tents at the Ludlow colony with machine guns. This firing continued throughout the day; some strikers fired back, and by the end of the day the tents were set on fire by the militia. Figures vary as to the actual death toll, but ten men and one child were killed in the tents from machine gun fire, including Louis Tinkas and

though there was a slight ripple. Most people are so wrapped up in their own little lives, especially when material distress is added to poor health (and Denver at its best is but a large sanitarium)[3] that their interest in the murder of women and children was only of passing moment. Besides, why worry when the Federal troops can be had for the asking?[4] And so, as on previous occasions, the average Denverite threw the responsibility on the government and went about his own little worries.

Under the circumstances our meetings were better than might be expected, though they were not large. In all we had seven propaganda lectures and eleven drama talks.[5] Nothing of particular interest occurred except for the huge anti-military meeting attended by a most enthusiastic audience of two thousand.[6] The event was especially significant because of the speech of a High School youth, young Elsberg—intense, earnest and strong—a gratifying and encouraging contrast to the High School boys who joined the militia and became a party to the crimes in Ludlow.

The second important event was the Free Speech fight we started in behalf of the Industrial Workers of the World.[7]

---

other strike leaders; Tinkas appears to have been deliberately murdered. At least two women and eleven children were found burned to death the next day. The event became known as the Ludlow Massacre, and it led to a "call to arms" from the United Mine Workers. Open armed revolt of miners in southern Colorado broke out and lasted eight days, until President Woodrow Wilson sent in federal troops. The Colorado Federation of Labor called on workers to "organize the men in your community in companies to protect the workers in Colorado against the murder and cremation of men, women and children by armed assassins in the employ of coal corporations. . . . Gather together for defensive purposes all arms and ammunition legally available." In New York both Carlo Tresca for the IWW and AB for the Anti-Militarist League made calls for volunteers and financial donations to send "men, arms and ammunition" to Colorado.

3. Many tuberculosis patients traveled to places with a high altitude and clean mountain air to treat their lung disease. In 1910 Denver anarchist Julia May Courtney wrote that the "reason for intellectual sloth is the fact that Denver is the Mecca for consumptives. The sanitariums are filled for the most part with those who in all probability will not recover" (*Mother Earth*, June 1910).

4. On 28 April 1914 President Woodrow Wilson sent federal troops to Colorado at the request of Governor Ammons and ordered "all persons engaged in or connected with said domestic violence and obstruction of the laws to disperse and retire peaceably to their respective abodes on or before the 30th day of April, instant." Once federal troops arrived, the strike lost momentum but was not officially called off until December 1914.

5. EG spoke in Denver from 28 April through 9 May 1914, delivering a series of lectures on the "Revolutionary Significance of the Modern Drama" as well as other topics.

6. On 3 May EG spoke at a meeting called by the Anti-Militarist League of Denver, to protest the use of federal troops in the Colorado mining strike and the invasion of Mexico by U.S. forces. The meeting took place at East Turner Hall, 2132 Arapahoe Street, Denver, and was chaired by BR.

7. The IWW free speech fight was fought over the right of IWW organizers and members to engage in street speaking in Denver. Under the name of the Free Speech League, IWW members and their lawyers questioned the constitutionality of the law requiring groups to obtain permits before speaking on the streets. In Julia May Courtney's article "Denver" in the June 1914 *Mother Earth*, she writes of the free speech victory in which "the police and commissioners of Denver completely backed down, giving the IWW the right to speak when, where and what they pleased." Interestingly, the previous year there had also been an IWW free speech fight in Denver. From 26 December 1912 to 1 May 1913 IWW members from all over the West had converged on Denver in the wake of the revocation and

On our arrival we found that twenty-seven had already been arrested and railroaded to the county jail. During our stay about thirty more were picked up, yet not a line of publicity anywhere, and absolute indifference among the organized workers and the Socialists.

Only when we threatened to start street speaking and secured Whitehead and Vogl,[8] both radicals and splendid men, to take up the I. W. W. cases, did we succeed in bringing the gross brutality of the police to the notice of the public. Two days before we closed our course, thirty of the boys were discharged and the original twenty-seven released from jail.[9]

As on another memorable occasion in Los Angeles after the funeral procession of Mikolaschek,[10] we arranged a feast for the released I.W.W. The tables were heavily laden with all sorts of good stuff to eat and drink, contributed by our faithful friends and two hundred boys had the time of their lives with song, dance and general fellowship.

The main result of the Free Speech agitation is the right won by the I.W.W. to speak on the street. It is but fair to say that the credit is due entirely to Ben Reitman, as I was incapacitated to do much owing to a severe cold. Ben, with his usual zeal once he is interested in an issue, worked day and night until every I.W.W. was released. On the day they were let go it was again Ben who met them at the jail, marched them, singing, through the street, into the nearest restaurant for a general feed. It is hardly necessary to state that it was his great joy to have accomplished so much. But unfortunately the Denver I.W.W. local has proven itself as petty as many other locals who cheerfully accept the assistance and solidarity of the Anarchists and then cast them aside. Thus we had no sooner left Denver than the local decided that *Mother Earth* and other Anarchist literature must not be handled by its members. What a pity that the I.W.W. must imitate the politicians.

The last two visits to Denver have been anything but worth while. However, we could not pass it by because of the group of friends in that city. There is no other group

---

denial of all applications for street-speaking permits. The Wobblies had been arrested in overwhelming numbers and filled the jails until they won the right to obtain permits to speak on public streets.

8. In a letter to Theodore Schroeder reporting on the situation in Denver, BR wrote, "Whitehead and Vogl were the lawyers and they did splendid work. They want to make a test case of the right of the police to issue permits" (Ben Reitman to Theodore Schroeder, 10 May 1914, Theodore Schroeder Papers, University of Illinois, Carbondale). Julia May Courtney also wrote of Whitehead and Vogl, "Too high praise cannot be given the law firm of Vogl and Whitehead, who forced the city to admit that they had no ordinance permitting arrest for street-speaking; and that the arrest of individuals for vagrancy is Unconstitutional" ("Denver," *Mother Earth*, June 1914). Whitehead and Vogl had shown their support of free speech in the past—in May 1910 *Mother Earth* reported that the firm, through A. Vogl, donated $10 to the Free Speech Fund.

9. Of their work, BR wrote to Schroeder, "It is needless to tell you EG . . . raised the money for the lawyers got people interested and I did the press work" (BR to Theodore Schroeder, 10 May 1914, Theodore Schroeder Papers, Southern Illinois University, Carbondale).

10. In the first week of May, during the San Diego free speech fight of 1912, IWW member Joseph Mikolasek had been killed. On 13 May 1912 IWW members and others held a funeral and demonstration in Los Angeles at which EG spoke.

of its size that has proven so faithful and generous to our work. Ellen E. Kennan, staunch and big-hearted, had charge of the arrangements. With her worked Gertrude Nafe, Edith Chase, Frank and Lina Monroe, John Spies, loyal unto death, Julia May Courtney,[11] Bert Brown, A. Horowitch, Wm. Kley, and a number of other friends. Their efforts, their splendid comradeship, and deep devotion have always compensated us for whatever disappointments we have met in Denver, and will continue to be the lure to bring us back.

From Denver we went to Salt Lake City for two meetings, arranged by a faithful few: Nelson Johnson, Lenquist and others. There is a proposition on foot to have us back for a drama course, on our return East. We hope our friends will make it possible.

We are now closing a three weeks' stay in Los Angeles, and will write about it in next issue.

We open at San Francisco, at Mission Turn Hall, 18th St., near Valencia, on Sunday, June 14th, 3 P.M.

*Mother Earth*, June 1914.

11. Ellen Kennan became president of the local Free Speech League during the Denver free speech fight. Gertrude Nafe, Edith Chase, Frank and Lena Monroe, John Spies, and Julia May Courtney were all Denver anarchists or friends and supporters of EG.

DEAR MARGARET:

I received your telegram, and also yours of the 6th inst. Both found me in a very depressed state of mind, and not wishing to communicate those spirits to you, I did not write. I feel better at this moment, largely, I think, because our meetings have picked up somewhat. Therefore I want to answer a few points raised in your letter.

First of all, however, please credit me with the enclosed express money order for $15 for the three hundred copies of "The Woman Rebel" of which you sent one hundred to Denver and two hundred to Los Angeles.[1] For those sent to this city, I will remit later. If only the authorities were not so stupid, they would realize that they are doing you more good by holding up the paper than any amount of money could do. "The Woman Rebel" is the best seller of anything we've got, just because it is known that the paper has been held up. But then, the authorities will die stupid.

Send ten copies of the paper every month to

Perry E. McCullough,

4023 Winter St.,

Los Angeles.[2]

He has undertaken the agency and will increase the number as the demand grows. I also succeeded in getting several subscribers in that city for you, but there is a little misunderstanding regarding the payment. I have to first ascertain from the girl who took down the names as to who paid and who did not. Will send you the names in a few days. Meanwhile, you can send "The Woman Rebel" to Mrs. Harriet Gerson,[3] #1011 W.P. Story Bldg., Los Angeles. They would like the first number if possible. They will remit, I am sure.

Of course I will try to get an agent for the paper in this city. Have already secured several subscriptions.

The idea of first organizing the newer Malthusian leagues before spreading information is very good.[4] The backbone of the stupid postal law will be broken only when there

---

1. EG promoted and distributed Margaret Sanger's paper, the *Woman Rebel*, while on her cross-country lecture tour.
2. Perry McCullough was also a subscriber to *Mother Earth* and friend of EG. Interestingly, he was married to the daughter of Chris Evans (1847–1917), a famous California train robber and author of the utopian novel *Eurasia* (San Francisco: James H. Barry, n.d.).
3. Harriet Gerson was the wife of EG's friend and supporter T. Perceval Gerson.
4. The April 1914 issue of the *Woman Rebel* (vol. 1, no. 2) printed the announcement "Neo-Malthusian

is enough intelligent determined opinion against it. That is why I advised your coming out with all the information in the paper before you have built it up, because if you will have readers interested enough in making a fight in case you go to prison, it is worth while going there; but not otherwise.

I am glad to hear that Caroline Nelson has become interested in your line of work.[5] I think she will be able to do a great deal for you, especially in the industrial centers where she is known. Besides she will have the assistance of the I.W.W. which I have not. I wonder if you know how terribly narrow they are towards anyone who doesn't subscribe to their god "The One Big Union". But Caroline Nelson will be supported by them, I am sure and therefore will be able to do much for the paper, and also for your tour in the future.

About myself, there isn't much to say. Our meetings have been most discouraging all along, altho the last few we have had in this city have improved somewhat. I am to continue here for the next three weeks in the course of Drama lectures[6] and as we have succeeded in securing a centrally located hall, we are most hopeful of results. Certain it is that the country is stricken by the results of the unemployment of last winter and the radical movement by a sort of a mental apathy. That applies to every shade of opinion. Most of the I.W.W. and others, including the Anarchists, haven't enough spirit to kill a fly, let alone to offer resistance to the increased reactionary tendencies infesting the country. Perhaps it is the quiet before the storm. I hope so anyway; but it is hell to be confronted with such a state of affairs. However, we must go on to the very end.

WITH MUCH LOVE.

EMMA.

P.S. Do not fail to send me the June issue of the "Woman Rebel."

TLSr, Margaret Sanger Papers, DLC. Marked "Copy." Second and third pages both marked "Page 3." Addressed to Margaret H. Sanger, 34 Post Ave., New York City.

---

Leagues are being formed throughout the United States" as well as an invitation to readers to "write for information if you are interested in forming one in your vicinity."
5. Caroline Nelson was an IWW reporter and organizer who became active in the birth control movement in 1914. For more on Nelson see note 2 in "Emma Goldman and Ben Reitman Tell of San Diego Experience," Interview in the *Industrial Worker*, 6 June 1912.
6. EG delivered a series of drama lectures in San Francisco at the Odd Fellows Hall between 22 June and early July 1914.

Alexander Berkman (and friend Helen Goldblatt) arriving at Tarrytown, New York, in June 1914 to take part in a protest outside the home of John D. Rockefeller Jr. in response to his refusal to publicly acknowledge or express regret for the role his company played in the massacre of children, women, and strikers in Ludlow. (Library of Congress)

Emma Goldman

General delivery Seattle

Everything all right Been so rushed have not written B on eighth day hunger strike[1] Tarrytown trial tomorrow[2] Received your remittance for note The other hundred paid Grayzel[3] Much love and good wishes

Sasha

TWS, Emma Goldman Papers MBU. On stationery of Western Union Night Letter, delivered at 12:25 a.m., 28 July.

1. Rebecca Edelsohn declared a hunger strike on 20 July 1914 after her ninety-day jail sentence for an antiwar speech earlier that year was upheld.
2. The trial of those arrested on 30 May 1914 while attempting to hold an open-air demonstration at Fountain Square in Tarrytown, New York, near Rockefeller's home, to express public outrage for his role in the Ludlow Massacre. During the Tarrytown free speech fight eleven men and one woman were arrested and charged with blocking traffic and holding a street meeting without a permit. The protesters were surrounded by the entire Tarrytown police force, and one by one the speakers were arrested as they began to address the crowd until all were detained. Among those arrested were Maurice Rudome, Rebecca Edelsohn, Arthur Caron, Charles Plunkett, Jack Isaacson, Frank Mandese (who was also detained by the police on the night of the Lexington Avenue explosion when he was found on the grounds of the Rockefeller estate), Louis Pastorella, Charles Berg, Adolph Aufricht, Joseph Secunda, Vincenzo Fabriciano, and Jack Butler. The next day AB, Helen Goldblatt, David Sullivan, Harry Wilkes, Joe De Rosa, and others traveled to Tarrytown and again tried, to no avail, to speak. This time De Rosa, Sullivan, and Wilkes were arrested and AB was "badly bruised by police violence" but not arrested. Later that night when almost twenty more Italian and Spanish anarchists arrived to reinforce AB on the speaker's platform, they were beaten and forcibly put on a train back to New York City. The trial for all except Edelsohn, who was already in prison for her April arrest, was held on 28 July. Mandese, Plunkett, Secunda, Fabriciano, Isaacson, Pastorella, and Rudome were sentenced to sixty days in prison, while David Sullivan, who was later discovered to be a police spy, was sentenced to thirty days. De Rosa was released immediately. Wilkes was discharged, and Aufricht was released with a suspended sentence. Edelsohn, whose trial for her Tarrytown arrest was finally held on 29 October, was acquitted of all charges. The arrests and police brutality with which the protesters were met helped precipitate events that led to the Lexington Avenue bomb explosion on 4 July 1914, which killed Caron, Carl Hanson, Berg, and Marie Chavez.
3. This could possibly be a misspelling of Max Maisel, the New York bookseller who published and sold radical literature.

Alexander Berkman addressing a mass meeting in Union Square on 11 July 1914 to honor the three anarchists killed the week before in the accidental explosion of a bomb intended for Rockefeller's estate. (Library of Congress)

DEAR DOCTOR:

It was stupid of me not to tell you who Rebecca Edelsohn is and what she has done, but I thought you knew all about her through Mother Earth.[1] She is the girl who was most active in the Rockefeller Mourners' Campaign,[2] but she was arrested for anti-military talks, placed on a bond of $300, if she promised to behave, but she refused; she was then sent up for 90 days.[3] The Free Speech League appealed her case, but as might have been expected the decision of the lower court was sustained.[4] She then declared a hunger-

1. EG had written to Gerson on 24 July 1914, after receiving a telegram from AB regarding Rebecca Edelsohn's hunger strike. Edelsohn had begun a hunger strike on 20 July 1914. Her case was covered extensively in both the mainstream New York press and *Mother Earth* from her initial arrest in April through the end of her month-long hunger strike on 20 August 1914. Dr. Theodor Perceval Gerson was a Los Angeles–based physician and social reformer. Gerson was a friend and correspondent of EG's who helped organize some of her Los Angeles meetings. Gerson was also a birth control advocate; he corresponded with Margaret Sanger in 1916, obtained her birth control pamphlets, and became president, after Georgia Kotsch, of the Los Angeles Birth Control League in early 1917. He was a member of a group of important liberals in the city, the Los Angeles Severance Club, founded in 1906 by abolitionist and suffragist Caroline Severance; he served as president from 1917 until his death. In 1916 he invited the Flores Magón brothers to speak before the club at one of its bimonthly meetings, and he had in fact taken an earlier interest in the brothers' activities, examining the ill Ricardo when he was in prison. A member of the California State Medical Society and the Los Angeles County Medical Association, Gerson would later serve as the director of the Southern California American Civil Liberties Union.
2. The Rockefeller Mourners' Campaign, also known as the Free Silence Movement and then the Tarrytown free speech fight, was initiated by Upton Sinclair following the Ludlow Massacre. After John D. Rockefeller Jr. refused to speak with Upton Sinclair about Ludlow on 28 April 1914, Sinclair, his wife, and four other women staged a demonstration of complete silence and nonresistant mourning in front of the Standard Oil Company in New York. Sinclair and others were arrested. Leonard Abbott, AB, and other anarchists and Ferrer School associates assumed the leadership and coordination of the movement upon Sinclair's imprisonment. On 10 May the Free Silence League disbanded, but anarchist and IWW agitators moved the protests from New York City to the Rockefeller estate in Tarrytown, New York, where protests and a free speech fight continued through June.
3. Edelsohn was first arrested, with Samuel Hartman, on 22 April 1914 for her antiwar speech, part of the ongoing agitation of the Anti-Militarist League, at Franklin Statue (Printers' Row) in New York City. An angry mob disturbance erupted, but she refused to stop speaking when ordered to by the police. She was then arrested for disturbing the peace and disrespecting the American flag. On 24 April she was sentenced to a $300 bond on the condition that she keep the peace for ninety days. She refused the injunction on her right to speech and therefore faced a jail sentence of ninety days. In court she announced she would begin a hunger strike in protest of the injustice of the court. Edelsohn became the first person in the United States to use a hunger strike (then a popular tactic with suffragettes in England) as a strategy for political protest.
4. Edelsohn was released after forty-eight hours when Leonard Abbott and the Free Speech League, the

strike which she has kept up ever since, at least until August 8th when I last heard from Berkman. The papers, thanks to Commissioner Davis,[5] have given out all sorts of false statements, that she is eating on the sly and similar things which are done to discredit the girl. When that didn't help, they placed her under a rigid regeme, no mail no visitors, in fact no communication with the outside world; but she is sending out letters nevertheless; that's how Mr. Berkman keeps in touch with her.[6] Now, if you can arouse some interest, especially among women, to send protests to the commissioner, I will be very grateful I am sure. Send them direct to New York and also inform Mr. Berkman of whatever communications may be sent to Katherine Davis.[7]

I have closed the most interesting visit here and am off for Butte tomorrow morning.[8] Will be there only a few days; then for a week to Chicago, where you can reach me at the Lexington Hotel, 22nd and Michigan Boulevard. After that, New York.

Thank you very much for the kind letter you wrote to the "lady." There is one thing, however, that I want to correct you about. I was not born into a hostile environment and I have not inherited bitterness, because it just so happens that my people were never persecuted. I got most of my hostility in "the land of freedom and promise." I wish you would emphasize that next time you write, because I got my anarchism not in Russia but in the United States.

I am glad you are seeing our friends and keeping in touch with them. Sorry to hear

---

International Defense Conference (an organization for the legal defense of those "arrested in connection with the class struggle"), and her lawyer appealed for a retrial, and on 24 April she was released on bail. Edelsohn's case was retried on 20 July. The sentencing of the original judge was upheld, and she again declared a hunger strike, which she sustained for thirty-one days, until her release on 30 August upon payment of bond by M. Eleanor Fitzgerald and AB; both feared that Edelsohn's life would be in danger if she continued the hunger strike.

5. New York City commissioner of corrections Katherine B. Davis (1860–1935) was a social reformer known for her innovation and rigor in the field of prison administration. She began her career as a settlement house social worker, serving as head of St. Mary's Street College Settlement in Philadelphia 1893–1897. Davis served as the prison matron of Bedford Hills Reformatory for Women in New York from 1901 to 1914, when she became the first woman appointed the New York City commissioner of corrections (1914–1915); she was also the first woman to be appointed to any cabinet-level position in New York City government. Though known as a reformer, she faced heavy criticism from many for the tactics during her administration. *Mother Earth* in June 1914 reported that Davis's great deeds included holding Marie Ganz incommunicado during her two months' imprisonment for attempting to attack John D. Rockefeller Jr. Rebecca Edelsohn charged Davis with turning the workhouse at Blackwell's Island into a veritable hell. She was also criticized by Margaret Sanger in her journal the *Woman Rebel* on a number of occasions. Davis later served as director of the Bureau of Social Hygiene of the Rockefeller Foundation.

6. Edelsohn also contributed correspondence sub rosa to the *Woman Rebel* ("One Woman's Fight," August 1914) while in prison.

7. In EG's previous letter she had asked Gerson to contact the president of the Civic Club in Los Angeles to gather the support of prominent women for Edelsohn and protest against her forced feeding.

8. EG lectured in Portland from 5 to 18 August before traveling to Butte, Montana, where she lectured from 16 to 19 August. Her topics included "Anti-War" and "Birth Control."

that Jack White[9] is ill, but he was drinking rather heavily when I was in Los Angeles. It is strange what effect experience has on some people. I had the impression that the boy has gone to pieces since his few months in jail.[10]

Give my love to Mrs. Gerson and to all our friends.

CORDIALLY,
EMMA GOLDMAN

TLS, T. Perceval Gerson Papers, CLU.

9. Jack White, also spelled "Whyte," was an IWW organizer arrested, charged, and found guilty of criminal conspiracy during the San Diego free speech fight in 1912. His appeal for support of the San Diego IWW free speech fight was published in the March 1912 *Mother Earth*, as was his speech before the court at his trial for criminal conspiracy ("To Hell with Your Courts," September 1912). He also helped organize meetings for EG in Los Angeles after her return from San Diego in 1912 and collected money for the California Free Speech League, organized during the San Diego free speech fight.

10. A reference to White's imprisonment for six months on charges of criminal conspiracy to violate the anti-street-speaking ordinance during the San Diego free speech fight in 1912.

Cover of September 1914 issue of *Mother Earth* by Man Ray, portraying the impending sacrifices of engagement in the war as tantamount to crucifying Christ on a cross-like pole of the American flag, its stars and stripes merging into the prison garb of future anti-war activists and perhaps prisoners of war.

DEAR EM—

Yes, it is a pity that the present atmosphere prevails in the house. Nor has it anything to do with Fitz or B.[1] I had hoped for something different, but I saw in your letters that you were not pleased, for some reason, with the N.Y. activities.

Well, you remember when I was helping you to finish your book,[2] just at the end, I joined the Unemplo. movement.[3] You said the other day that but for B., I would not have participated. But you know that Moisu was here at the time & B. was entirely out of the field. Well, when I gave some of my time to the Unempl., you kicked and we almost had a fuss about it.

Well, you may not have liked the activities in N.Y.—that is one's pleasure to form his own opinion in the matter. What mine is, you know. It simply happened to be a psycho-logic moment & I think it did a lot of propaganda.[4] That I was an actor in it, is only inci-dental. The papers will naturally make a fuss over the most prominent name involved.

Of course, you are welcome to your own opinion in this matter, but I must say you did not show a big spirit in your attitude. I'm sorry to say it.

So, from your letters I saw that when you come the situation here will be just what it is now.

Nor have you shown a big spirit in your attitude to Fitz or B. I thought you might be

---

1. M. Eleanor Fitzgerald was the current companion of AB and office manager of *Mother Earth*. Rebecca Edelsohn was AB's former companion; she also worked at *Mother Earth* and was involved in various anarchist activities in New York. Both women also lived in the house attached to the offices of *Mother Earth*.

2. EG's *The Social Significance of the Modern Drama* was published in 1914.

3. The unemployment movement, of which AB was a driving force, began in the winter of 1913. The movement staged marches, parades, rallies, and demonstrations, eventually integrating its efforts with those of the Anti-Militarist League and the Tarrytown free speech fight, in response to the events in Ludlow, Colorado, in 1914. See also Letter from AB, 27 July 1914; and Letter to T. Perceval Gerson, 13 August 1914, above.

4. AB refers to his unemployment, anti-militarist, and Tarrytown activities, which culminated in the 4 July 1914 Lexington Avenue explosion. The idea of a "psychological moment" necessary for the indi-vidual act of violence to turn into open revolt and revolution was something that was often explored by EG and AB. Acts of violence were judged by their ability to use such psychological moments to further the revolutionary potential for anarchism. In 1892 Johann Most argued that AB's *Attentat* on Henry Clay Frick was not valid because it was not backed by a similar psychological moment of the masses of American workingmen, and in 1901 AB followed a similar argument in criticizing Leon Czolgosz's assassination of President William McKinley; for more on these events, see vol. 1, *Made for America*, pp. 484–88.

interested enough to befriend B., to have a talk with her about her activities, her plans, her hunger stri[ke,] etc.[5] It's tragic to think that <u>you</u> have acted this way. You've given B.—as well as Fitz—the cold shoulder.

Of course, you cannot overcome your dislikes. But you should have been the Anarchist <u>first</u>—the Anarchist interested & encouraging the activities of the younger generation.

Well, I have no quarrel with you on this, dear, but it has pained me—not for B's or F's sake, but for your own. You did not act big.

Now, as to B. You still imagine, it seems, that she is my sweetheart. But that's not important. But I thought you wanted her to stay here & recuperate. At least you wrote so. She has many places to stay, I assure you. But she did not want to leave at your coming, because you planned to take her to the farm with you and because she thought it would hurt you if she leaves right after or before your arrival.

I assure you, you never understood B. She has far more nobility of character than you would admit, and if it were not [B] but some one else [wh]o did what she did, [y]ou'd be in ecstacy over the young com[r]ade.

Now, you are perfectly right in wanting B. to leave. I know you don't enjoy her presence & there is no reason why she should stay [un]der such circumstances. [N]or does B. herself [li]ke the atmosphere. [Yo]u are making it pretty chilly, my dear E.

Your good friend Smithy[6] is so unpleasant for Fitz that she had to take rooms away fr[om] here. I have also arranged to have a roo[m] in F.'s place. We will move in in a day or two & then B. goes with us. So, dear, you don't have to worry about that.

And the anti-milit. work could be done in the Center[7] as soon as we make arrangements about it, which will be done before we move out of here.

Now, as to M. E.[8]—yes, dear, we both feel a change must be made. I have been intending to speak with you about it. I have been thinking about a tour also, but first I have some other things to attend to. And one of the purposes of my tour would be to organize

---

5. After being arrested twice for street speaking and refusing to pay her fine both times Edelsohn went to jail. She then declared a hunger strike in protest of the infringement on her freedom of speech. The August 1914 *Woman Rebel* printed some of her letters from prison and an article by Alexander Berkman about her experience, "Becky Edelsohn: The First Political Hunger Striker in America," in the August 1914 *Mother Earth*. See also Letter to T. Perceval Gerson, 13 August 1914, above, for more about Edelsohn's activities.

6. Rhoda Smith was EG's housekeeper.

7. The Anti-Militarist League was founded at the Ferrer Center but was based at the offices of *Mother Earth*, 74 West 119th Street, New York City. AB proposes that upon his moving, the league's activities could take place at the Ferrer Center instead of 74 West 119th Street. The last activity of the league appears to have been a benefit ball and bazaar, held on 24 October 1914, for the Rangel-Cline defense and for Italian anti-militarists.

8. The March 1915 *Mother Earth* was the last to list AB as editor; thereafter, EG was both publisher and editor. After traveling across the country AB moved to California in order to help in the work of defending anarchists David Caplan and Matthew Schmidt, who were being tried for their connection with the 1910 bombing of the *Los Angeles Times* building. In 1916 AB and M. Eleanor Fitzgerald began publishing *The Blast* from San Francisco.

groups in the cities I visit. But of that we can speak later. The first thing needed is to get some one else as editor for M. E. For I'd need a couple of months for myself. Well I've been interrupted [ . . . ] but I want you to know that whatever misunderstandings there are between us, I am always, yours the same

Sasha

ALS, MBU-EGP.

MY DEAREST.

Life is an eternal merry go around only it is rarely merry. 25 years ago when I came to N Y I lived in a furnished room. To day I have gotten back to the starting point.

I have settled with my landlord, he got $100 to the $70 security and has released me. It may interest you to know that never at any time was he ready to give me a bonus, so we have lost nothing in refusing his offer last year.

Well if I had remained I would have been compelled to spend $175 on the furnace roof, pluming & coals and would have had the terrific expense for another year. I simply could not endure that thought, so I have settled and $100 blood money were turned over to the landlord. I shall move Wednesday as my new place will not be ready until then.[1]

As I have written you the new place consists of one huge room with three windows on the street, seperate entrance from the Hall way, that will be the office. Another room not quite so large with 2 windows in the yard, also seperate entrance from Hall, that will be my room for the present at any rate. There is also a toilet on the floor with a little room for a kitchenette. There is but one other floor over ours which is empty at present.

I am taking from the house only what I have in my room and our office outfit, the rest I will give away or sell, as I shall never again set up a household unless I can do it in harmony and that will never be in my life.

I am sorry that you do not "relish" N Y for the Winter but I am afraid if you want me you will have to come to N Y as I could and would not remain in Chicago, now at any rate. It is my definite determination to take full charge of M E the coming Winter and see what I can do with it, therefore I mean to come back here. Needless to say, I shall want you to come with me, but only when you can do so gladly and above everything else in the World.

Hobo dearest, you evidently did not understand my letter about the Lexing. affaire.[2] I will therefore repeat it as we two must understand each other dear, before we go ahead.

---

1. In late September 1914 the *Mother Earth* office (which doubled as EG's apartment) moved from 74 West 119th Street to 20 East 125th Street, in New York City after the dissolution of the large *Mother Earth* household that had included AB, EG, BR, M. Eleanor Fitzgerald, Rebecca Edelsohn, EG's niece Stella Comyn, and others.
2. On 4 July 1914 a bomb intended for John D. Rockefeller Jr. accidentally exploded at Lexington Avenue in New York City and killed four people, including Charles Berg, Arthur Caron, and Carl Hanson—anarchists known well by AB from protests in Tarrytown, their shared involvement in the unemployed protests of 1914, and participation in Ferrer Center activities. One woman who was not involved with the plot, Marie Chavez, was also killed. At the mass memorial demonstration, held 11

I do not know what is changing your attitude towards violence. I know you are still in the formative stage and will have more than one change in life. I would not for the World want you to go contrary to your conviction. On the other hand I must absolutely insist that my position is not against violence and never will be unless I become weak minded. When I said the Lex affaire was to be regretted I only meant that the place was ill and stupidly chosen.[3] But not for one moment did I mean to imply that I am opposed to the thing itself. Further more, even if I did not approve of the motive purpose, I should still be on the side of the actionists because I hold that if society makes no provision for the individual, society must take the consequences. This position ought not to be new to you my Hobo, you have heard me make that stand always nor do I intend to go back on it.[4]

Please don't think I am pleading in behalf of Sasha. Really not. I know he has and will make blunders, I know he is obsessed by the importence of his particular work. I know he has done things without even as much as consulting us. But that has nothing to do with my position on violence, dear.

I assure you my lover I want to build up ideas that will count, but if I am to do it by denying or going back on what I know to be logically, historically and inevitably true, I shall prefer to tear down rather than build up.

Believe me darling, in disagreeing with you, I do not mean to imply that you are afraid or that you have been influenced. But I do mean to say that you are emotional and meta physical, hence you must have all sorts of changes. Now, my ideas have been derived through years of thought, study, struggle suffering and percecution they are bred in my blood and until I am proven otherwise, no one shall change my attitude.

I have no intention of giving up the Magazine, on the contrary I am going to so simplify my life, that I can devote myself to M E more than ever before without trailing about the country. I hope I may some day be free from debts, I shall make a desperate attempt towards that end. With $20 rent per month & Alex shifting for himself, also with no new literature printed, we can get rid of debts, if we have any kind of a success in Chicago & the coming Winter. By next spring we will see, if we have gotten ahead, I at least shall not go on a tour for a year. I need rest, I need mental repose, I need a whole year away from the platform.

I know best why my work has been poor last year, I am worn out and 7 incessant years of talking are to blame for it. I mean to make a stop soon, if possible next Spring, but my debts must be paid first, I am sick of them.

-------

July in New York, a telegram signed by EG and BR sent from San Francisco was read: "Our deepest sympathy with all oppressed of the world, of whom our dead comrades were the conscious and brave spokesmen. We honor the memory of our dead comrades, the victims of the capitalist system and the martyrs of labor."

3. The bomb exploded in the apartment of anarchist Louise Berger, half-sister of Charles Berg, at 1626 Lexington Avenue between 103rd and 104th Streets, an area of tenements populated mainly by recently arrived immigrants.

4. Compare this letter to EG's 26 August 1910 letter to Ben Reitman above, which also deals with their attitudes toward violence.

Dearest, you will not mind my speaking frankly will you dear, we must understand each other, life will be more bearable.

I had planned to write an article about Margaret Anderson,[5] but I have no time and am not in the right spirit. But I will have a notice and also an ad not because of what she is doing for me, but because she is making a brave stand and I want to encourage her.

Dearest, why bother about her "poets"? I think the girl is well able to take care of herself, besides each one must learn to mould his own life no one can do it for us.

I do not intend to have an appeal for the N Y meetings. I have written you several times dear, our subs have been taxed to the limit I can not now worry them again. Besides we have attempted free meetings here you know with what results.

I am well satisfied with Lenox Casino, especially as we have the Ballroom which is beautiful, and no musik on top, we can have it for about $6 per afternoon Sunday $4 for cards and advertising that would make it $10 per meeting. Why then beg and appeal, I am tired of it.

Had a letter from Johnson he is willing to back Grand Rapids meetings, but he must keep in the back ground. Have written Buwalda to day asking if he will undertake the arrangements.

Now when can we be in Grand Rapids? Are we to go there from Chicago or on our way back? What other City can we strike between Chicago & Detroit, we will need about 10 days for Grand Rapids Detroit & Ann Arbor. We could then spend a few days in Indianapolis, I will see what I can do about some backing there for free meetings. Then about the 1st week of Dec in St Louis, Fishman & Falkenberg will be home. Ben[6] writes he can not get in before the 12th and we can not wait so long. Tell me definitely when we can leave Chicago, also if we are to go to Peoria for Oct 25th, or shall it be when we are through with Chicago.[7]

Hobo my Hobo, I love you but I am weary with the World, with people, with myself. I shall be cheerful soon have patience dear.

Your Mommy

ALS, IU-U. On Mother Earth Publishing Association stationery.

5. Margaret Caroline Anderson (1886–1973) was a journalist, author, critic, bohemian, and founder and editor of the *Little Review*. EG and Anderson first met in April 1914 when Anderson attended an EG lecture in Chicago. Anderson launched the literary periodical *Little Review* in Chicago in March 1914. The magazine reflected her interest in psychoanalysis, feminism, and anarchism, and was instrumental in bringing new and avant-garde modern literature to the United States. EG supported the *Little Review*, publishing advertisements for it in *Mother Earth*. A friend and correspondent of EG's, Anderson published EG's writing in the *Little Review*, and contributed to the tenth-anniversary souvenir edition of *Mother Earth*. Anderson praised EG in the May 1914 issue of the *Little Review*, which according to Anderson created a scandal and the loss of the magazine's financial backer. No article by EG on Anderson appeared in *Mother Earth*.

6. Probably Ben Capes (1883–1964), a traveling salesman and anarchist from St. Louis who often helped organize meetings for EG.

7. EG was scheduled to lecture in Chicago between 23 October and 15 November, in Detroit on 20 and 22–24 November, in Ann Arbor on 21 November, in Grand Rapids on 26 November, in St. Louis on 29 November to 6 December, and in Indianapolis on 8–9 December.

MY DEAR MR. STIEGLITZ;—

I don't know how much you are interested in music but as an artist, I am sure you do not exclude its joys.[1] At any event, I am calling your attention to a concert to be given by David Hochstein,[2] a violinist at Aeolian Hall, Friday evening, Jan. 15. The young man, who is my nephew, by the way, has just returned from Europe, but as he came back unheralded, it will mean uphill work to get a footing in this country. No one will appreciate what that means more than you, who have had such a tremendous struggle yourself. I am anxious that you should hear him play, not because I am related to him, but because he is a great artist. I speak from knowledge, as I heard him two weeks ago in his native town, Rochester. I have tickets on sale. I hope you will attend the concert, also interest your circle of friends. Any suggestion you can make to help to call attention to David Hochstein will be gratefully received.

SINCERELY,

EMMA GOLDMAN

I wonder if you will permit us to put a window card in the Photo Secession Galleries,[3] announcing the concert?[4]

TLS, CtY-B. On Mother Earth Publishing Association stationery.

---

1. Alfred Stieglitz (1864–1946) was an American photographer and the art director of three galleries in New York. Gallery "291" exhibited Matisse in 1908, Cezanne in 1910, and Georgia O'Keefe, his future wife, in 1915. He was a promoter of the 1913 Armory Show, an event often credited with introducing modern European art to the United States, and an editor of the avant-garde journal *Camera Work* (1903–1917).
2. David Hochstein (1892–1918) was the son of EG's half-sister Helena and a child-prodigy violinist. He enlisted in the army in 1917 and was killed in France shortly before the armistice.
3. Stieglitz's Little Galleries of the Photo-Secession, also known as "291," was located at 291 Fifth Avenue.
4. Stieglitz wrote back on 8 January, saying that he would attend the concert and that he was "only too glad to display a window card if you will send it up. Or at least if I cannot display it, as we never display any announcements of any kind, I shall at least see to it that the visitors see it" (Steiglitz to EG, 8 January 1915, *EGP*, reel 8).

# International Anarchist Manifesto on the War

Europe in a blaze, twelve million men engaged in the most frightful butchery that history has ever recorded; millions of women and children in tears; the economic, intellectual, and moral life of seven great peoples brutally suspended, and the menace becoming every day more pregnant with new military complications—such is, for seven months, the painful, agonizing, and hateful spectacle presented by the civilized world.

But a spectacle not unexpected—at least, by the Anarchists, since for them there never has been nor is there any doubt—the terrible events of to-day strengthen this conviction—that war is permanently fostered by the present social system.[1] Armed conflict, restricted or wide-spread, colonial or European, is the natural consequence and the inevitable and fatal outcome of a society that is founded on the exploitation of the workers, rests on the savage struggle of the classes, and compels Labor to submit to the domination of a minority of parasites who hold both political and economic power.

The war was inevitable. Wherever it originated, it had to come. It is not in vain that for half a century there has been a feverish preparation of the most formidable armaments, and a ceaseless increase in the budgets of death. It is not by constantly improving the weapons of war, and by concentrating the mind and the will of all upon the better organization of the military machine that people work for peace.

Therefore, it is foolish and childish, after having multiplied the causes and occasions of conflict, to seek to fix the responsibility on this or that government. No possible distinction can be drawn between offensive and defensive wars. In the present conflict, the governments of Berlin and Vienna have sought to justify themselves by documents not less authentic than those of the governments of Paris and Petrograd. Each does its

---

1. The First World War sparked a split in the international anarchist movement between those who supported France and England against what was perceived as German aggression, and those who opposed war on principle (Max Nettlau was one of the few anarchists who supported Austria-Hungary). In October 1914 Peter Kropotkin expressed his support for France and England in the journal *Freedom*. The next month's issue included Errico Malatesta's opposition to Kropotkin. Respected and long-standing militant anarchists lined up on both sides. The antiwar group's manifesto was first published in the March 1915 issue of *Freedom* and the March 1915 issue of *Cultura Obrera*, and then two months later in *Mother Earth*. The next year, those in support of England, France, and their allies published their "Manifesto of the Sixteen" (named for the number of signatories, though the actual number was fifteen, as a place name had been mistaken for a person) in *La Bataille* (14 March 1916), a French syndicalist daily; signatories included Kropotkin, Jean Grave, Paul Reclus, Victor Dave, and Christiaan Cornelissen.

very best to produce the most indisputable and the most decisive documents in order to establish its good faith and to present itself as the immaculate defender of right and liberty, and the champion of civilization.

Civilization? Who, then, represents it just now? Is it the German State, with its formidable militarism, and so powerful that it has stifled every disposition to revolt? Is it the Russian State, to whom the knout, the gibbet, and Siberia are the sole means of persuasion? Is it the French State, with its *Biribi*,[2] its bloody conquests in Tonkin, Madagascar, Morocco, and its compulsory enlistment of black troops?[3] France, that detains in its prisons, for years, comrades guilty only of having written and spoken against war? Is it the English State, which exploits, divides, and oppresses the populations of its immense colonial Empire?

No; none of the belligerents is entitled to invoke the name of civilization, or to declare itself in a state of legitimate defense.

The truth is, that the cause of wars, of that which at present stains with blood the plains of Europe, as of all wars that have preceded it, rests solely in the existence of the State, which is the political form of privilege.

The State has arisen out of military force, it has developed through the use of military force, and it is still on military force that it must logically rest in order to maintain its omnipotence. Whatever the form it may assume, the State is nothing but organized oppression for the advantage of a privileged minority. The present conflict illustrates this in the most striking manner. All forms of the State are engaged in the present war; absolutism with Russia, absolutism softened by Parliamentary institutions with Germany, the State ruling over peoples of quite different races with Austria, a democratic constitutional régime with England, and a democratic Republican régime with France.

The misfortune of the peoples, who were deeply attached to peace, is that, in order to avoid war, they placed their confidence in the State with its intriguing diplomatists, in democracy, and in political parties (not excluding those in opposition, like Parliamentary Socialism). This confidence has been deliberately betrayed, and continues to be so, when governments, with the aid of the whole of their press, persuade their respective peoples that this war is a war of liberation.

We are resolutely against all wars between peoples, and in neutral countries, like Italy, where the governments seek to throw fresh peoples into the fiery furnace of war, our comrades have been, are, and ever will be most energetically opposed to war.

The role of the Anarchists in the present tragedy, whatever may be the place or the

---

2. "Biribi" is a term that refers to the French practice of forcing men with prison records to serve in special punitive battalions, known for their brutal disciplinary practices.
3. Compulsory enlistment of black African troops in the French army began with a 1912 decree regulating the first draft plan for West Africa. By the end of the war well over 100,000 Afro-French subjects had served in the army. See also note on the French conquest of Africa and Southeast Asia in "Psychology of Political Violence," Essay published by Mother Earth Publishing Association, January 1911 above.

situation in which they find themselves, is to continue to proclaim that there is but one war of liberation: that which in all countries is waged by the oppressed against the oppressors, by the exploited against the exploiters. Our part is to summon the slaves to revolt against their masters.

Anarchist action and propaganda should assiduously and perseveringly aim at weakening and dissolving the various States, at cultivating the spirit of revolt, and arousing discontent in peoples and armies.

To all the soldiers of all countries, who believe they are fighting for justice and liberty, we have to declare that their heroism and their valor will but serve to perpetuate hatred, tyranny, and misery.

To the workers in factory and mine it is necessary to recall that the rifles they now have in their hands have been used against them in the days of strike and of revolt, and that later on they will be again used against them in order to compel them to undergo and endure capitalist exploitation.

To the workers on farm and field it is necessary to show that after the war they will be obliged once more to bend beneath the yoke and to continue to cultivate the lands of their lords and to feed the rich.

To all the outcasts, that they should not part with their arms until they have settled accounts with their oppressors, until they have taken land and factory and workshop for themselves.

To mothers, wives, and daughters, the victims of increased misery and privation, let us show who are the ones really responsible for their sorrows and for the massacre of their fathers, sons, and husbands.

We must take advantage of all the movements of revolt, of all the discontent, in order to foment insurrection, and to organize the revolution to which we look to put an end to all social wrongs.

No despondency, even before a calamity like the present war. It is in periods thus troubled, in which many thousands of men heroically give their lives for an idea, that we must show these men the generosity, greatness, and beauty of the Anarchist ideal: Social justice realized through the free organization of producers; war and militarism done away with forever; and complete freedom won, by the abolition of the State and its organs of destruction.

Signed by—Leonard D. Abbott, Alexander Berkman, L. Bertoni,[4] L. Bersani, G. Bernard, G. Barrett,[5] A. Bernardo, E. Boudot,[6] A. Calzitta, Joseph J. Cohen,[7] Henry

---

4. Luigi Bertoni (1872–1947) was an Italian writer, translator, and editor who at a young age began writing for the Geneva anti-clerical paper *La Vespa*. He had moved to Geneva in 1891 and became involved with the labor movement and later the anarchist movement. Bertoni founded the Geneva bilingual journal *Il Riveglio/Le Réveil* in 1900 and was editor until 1947, during which time he was arrested many times by Swiss authorities. Bertoni translated Kropotkin into Italian and Malatesta into French and was the author of many pamphlets.

5. George Barrett (born Ballard; 1888–1917) was a Scottish anarchist and political street speaker. He

Combes,[8] Nestor Ciele van Diepen, F. W. Dunn,[9] Ch. Frigerio,[10] Emma Goldman, V. Garcia,[11] Hippolyte Havel,[12] T. H. Keell,[13] Harry Kelly, J. Lemaire,[14] E. Malatesta,[15] H. Marques, F. Domela Nieuwenhuis,[16] Noel Panavich, E. Recchioni,[17] G. Rijnders,[18]

---

was a founder of the Glasgow Anarchist Group and publisher of the Glasgow-based *Anarchist* from 1912 to 1913. His pamphlets *The Anarchist Revolution* (London: Freedom Press, 1920) and *Objections to Anarchism* (London: Freedom Press, 1921) were published posthumously.

6. Edouard Eugène Boudot (b. 1886) was a French cartoonist who in 1912 became acting secretary of the Anarchist Communist Federation (FCA) along with Henry Combes. In 1912 he was among the founders of the journal *Le mouvement anarchiste*. Boudot was arrested several times and imprisoned for avoiding conscription.

7. Joseph J. Cohen (1878–1953) was an anarchist educator and editor of *Freie Arbeiter Stimme* (1923–1932). After immigrating in 1903 from Russia to Philadelphia he was taught English by Voltairine de Cleyre. In 1905 he helped found the Radical Library and acted as the driving force behind the establishment of the Modern School of Philadelphia. Cohen became an organizer of the Ferrer School in New York in December 1913 and was instrumental in its relocation to Stelton, New Jersey.

8. Henry Emmanuel Jules Combes (1887–1925) was a French stenographer and anarchist who collaborated on *Le Libertaire* in 1912 and served as managing editor of *Le Mouvement Anarchiste*. He was acting Anarchist Communist Federation (FCA) secretary following the arrest of Louis Lecoin in 1912. Charged with organizing anti-militarist campaigns, he fled to England where he remained throughout the war.

9. Fred Dunn (1884–1925) was an English anarchist and editor of the *Voice of Labour* from 1914 to 1916. As a war resister, he took refuge in the United States, where he taught at the Modern School at Stelton.

10. Carlo Frigerio (1878–1966) was an Italian anarchist and typesetter who assumed the editorship of *Il Risveglio/Le Réveil* following Luigi Bertoni's death in 1947.

11. Vicente Garcia (alias Pamiro; 1866–1930) was a Spanish anarchist who accompanied Malatesta on a tour on the northern Spanish regions in 1897. He spent the latter half of his life in England, where he was associated with *Freedom* and served as a correspondent for many Spanish-language anarchist papers.

12. Hippolyte Havel was a Czech-born anarchist-communist. He was actively involved with both *Mother Earth* and the Ferrer Center.

13. Thomas Keell (1886–1938) was an English anarchist and editor of *Freedom*. In June 1916 he and his companion, Lilian Wolfe, were imprisoned briefly for publishing an article defying the British wartime Military Service Act of 1916.

14. Jules André Lemaire (1874–1957) was a French anarchist militant, member of the leather-workers' union, and manager (until 1906) of the Amiens anarchist newspaper *Germinal*. In 1906 Lemaire was sentenced to eighteen months in prison for publishing an anti-militarist article. In 1914 he deserted from the army, fleeing to Spain and then England, where he would live in exile for fourteen years.

15. Errico Malatesta (1853–1932) was an influential Italian anarchist. Opposed to war, he wrote articles against Kropotkin's stance. The articles included "Anarchists Have Forgotten Their Principles" (printed in *Mother Earth*, January 1915) and "Pro Government Anarchists" (reprinted in *The Blast*, 15 May 1916); both articles were widely reprinted and circulated in the anarchist press.

16. Ferdinand Domela Nieuwenhuis (1846–1919) was a Dutch anarchist and pacifist. A prominent anti-militarist, he contributed a number of articles to *Mother Earth*, including "To the Anti-Militarists, Anarchists, and Free Thinkers" (February 1915), in which he outlined his belief in the power of a general strike of an international brotherhood of workers to end the war.

17. Emidio Recchioni (1864–1924) was an Italian anarchist arrested in June 1894 in connection with the shooting of Italian prime minister Crispi and sentenced to three years' imprisonment. He worked with Malatesta to found *L'Agitazione*. Later he was again arrested but this time escaped. Recchioni was also a contributor to *L'Adunata dei Refrattari* and *La Protesta* (under the pen name "Nemo").

18. G. Rijnders (1876–1950) was a Dutch anarchist who published Arnold Roller's *Social General Strike* and *Direct Action*, and later served as editor of *De Vrije Socialist*.

I. Rochtchine,[19] A. Savioli, A. Schapiro,[20] William Shatoff,[21] V. J. C. Schermerhorn,[22] C. Trombetti, P. Vallina,[23] G. Vignati, Lillian G. Woolf,[24] S. Yanowsky.[25]

This manifesto is published by the International Anarchist movement, and will be printed in several languages and issued in leaflet form.

London, 1915.

*Mother Earth* 10 (May 1915): 119–22. Published in *Freedom* (March 1915) and *Cultura Obrera* in Spanish (March 1915).

19. Iuda Solomnovich Roshchin (born Grossman; 1883–1934) was a Russian anarchist and anti-syndicalist and brother of Abram Solomnovich. He lectured in southern Russia on behalf of the anarchist All-Russian Congress, and later collaborated with the Bolsheviks.

20. Alexander Schapiro (1882–1946) was a prominent Russian-born anarchist. He was active in the London anarchist movement with Kropotkin, Malatesta, and Rudolf Rocker and was interned in England during World War I.

21. William Shatoff (b. 1887) was a Russian anarchist and organizer for the Union of Russian Workers in New York City. He was also active in the Ferrer Center and the Anarchist Red Cross before returning to Russia in 1917, where he died in the Stalinist purge of the late 1930s.

22. Nicolaas J. C. Schermerhorn (1866–1956) was author of *Vrijheid en persoonlijkheid*.

23. Vallina Martínez (alias Pedro; 1879–1970) was a Spanish anarchist and physician. Sentenced to eight years' imprisonment for anarchist propaganda, he fled to France and settled in Paris in 1902. He attended the Amsterdam Anarchist Congress in 1907. After being expelled from France he lived in London from 1908 to 1914, later seeking refuge in Mexico, where he devoted himself to medicine and anarchist propaganda.

24. Lilian Gertrude Wolfe (b. Woolf; 1875–1974) was an English anarchist and companion of Thomas H. Keell, who helped found the English Anti-Conscription League in 1915. She was imprisoned while pregnant for printing Fred Dunn's "Defying the Act," an article exposing the injustice of The Defense of the Realm Act, which was passed in August 1914 and granted the English government executive power to suppress published criticism of the state, to imprison without trial, and to commandeer all economic resources for the war effort.

25. Saul Yanovsky was a Jewish anarchist and editor, from 1899 to 1919, of *Freie Arbeiter Stimme*. He later changed his position to one of support for England and France.

## To ELLEN A. KENNAN

*Cleveland, Ohio, 6 May 1915*

MY DEAREST ELLEN:—

I got your letter the day I left New York. Couldn't take the time to write you then but will not delay any longer. I can't begin to tell you how glad I am that you have saved me from the Normal Hall.[1] It was the most oppresive dump and always made me feel as if some-body were clutching at my throat. If the Marble Hall[2] is anything like what it used to be, it will be pleasant to speak there. I hope, though, that they are sporting a little plat-form now, because in the past I had to stand in the body of the house and as the gods have not made me very tall and people come not only to hear but also to see, it made it very embarrassing all around.

As Reitman always attends to the cards,[3] I have written to ask him to let you know how many to print; also to send you the cut which goes on the back of the card. You will probably hear from him before this reaches you. In any event, you can order 7,000 cards and keep the composition standing in case we want more. Please order them at once and see that I receive a package of about 200 to Chicago any time before I leave there, which will be the 18th of this month. I want the Denver subscribers to get the announcement and the tickets at least two weeks in advance. As soon as I reach Chicago, I will send you tickets which you, Gertrude and Edith Chase might be able to sell.[4]

I am so glad May Courtney still feels the same interest in my work. I had begun to dispair because she wrote not a line for a whole year and said nothing during Berkman's stay.[5] I was very anxious to learn what impression his work has made on her. I confess I was amused to hear that she is busy fighting a medical bill. I thought she had outgrown the faith in politics. I sometimes think that the political bug is a more dangerous germ than the religious bug. I notice that the most advanced people still cling to the ragged edges of the ballot.

I am so glad you are interested in the subjects I have sent. I am sure the one on the

1. EG lectured at the Normal Hall in Denver on 23 and 24 April and 7 July 1912 and 26 and 27 April 1913.
2. EG delivered a series of lectures at the Marble Hall in Denver between 30 May and 2 June 1915.
3. Cards announcing upcoming EG events, and other materials publicizing EG's lectures, were often handled by BR.
4. Gertrude Nafe and Edith Chase were friends of Ellen Kennan and supporters of EG.
5. AB went on a lecture tour in 1915. He reached Denver in February, where he delivered twelve lec-tures, including "Crime and Punishment." He would return to Denver again in 1915, to raise money and support for David Caplan and Matthew Schmidt, setting up a local chapter of the International Workers' Defense League. Gertrude Nafe became the first secretary of the local Denver league.

intermediate sex[6] will interest you also, because I am speaking about it from entirely a different angle than Ellis Forel, Carpenter[7] and the others, and that mainly because of the material I have gathered during the last half dozen years through my personal contact with the intermediate, which has lead me to gather the most interesting material.

The beginning of my tour has been wonderful. Tremendous meetings in Philadelphia and Washington, D.C. I am to return for 2 weeks to our govermental grinding mill— Washington, D.C. Also had a big meeting in Pittsburgh. Last night in this city was not very encouraging, which is not due to the people of Cleveland[8] but to the mismanagement of those who have arranged the meetings. Tomorrow night I leave for Chicago for a week's lectures.[9] After that I will go for a few days to Margaret Anderson's shack on Lake Bluff.[10] I want to tell you much about Margaret Anderson. She is certainly a rare specimen and has a great literary future before her.

I am looking forward with great joy to being with you in your apartment. I only hope that my stay will not inconvenience you. You know what a irregular creature I am and that I keep such terribly late hours. Please don't let me impose upon you in any way, but I do want to be with you as that will be the only chance I have to get thoroughly acquainted with one who has endeared herself to me as you have. Do write again soon, c/o Lexington Hotel, and I will do the same, making various suggestions as to the best way for distributing cards. Remember me affectionately to Gertrude, Edith and also to Mr. Farrare.[11]

With lots of love,

Emma

TLS, Emma Goldman Archive, IISH. Addressed to Miss Ellen A. Kennan, 1301 Logan Ave., Denver, Colo.

6. EG began delivering her lecture on homosexuality, "The Intermediate Sex," in 1915.
7. Havelock Ellis, Auguste Forel, and Edward Carpenter all wrote on the subject of homosexuality. Havelock Ellis engaged in the scientific study of the varieties of sexual behavior, which he considered the outstanding social matter of his time. Ellis's *Sexual Inversion* (1897) offered a sympathetic study of homosexuality. Auguste Forel (1848–1931) was a Swiss sexologist, neuroanatomist, psychiatrist, and entomologist. He was known for his investigations of brain structure and his social reform work in the prevention of syphilis and alcoholism, work that combined medical and sociopolitical viewpoints. His book *The Sexual Question* (New York: Rebman, 1908) called for the abolition of sex laws and promoted the legal equality of the sexes; free availability of contraceptives; and the legalization of incest, bestiality, and homosexual marriage. Edward Carpenter's book *The Intermediate Sex* was first published in America by Mitchell Kennerley in New York in 1912.
8. EG spoke at the Pythian Temple in Cleveland.
9. EG delivered a series of lectures at the Fine Arts Building in Chicago between 9 and 16 May 1915.
10. In 1915 Margaret Anderson rented a small house on the shore of Lake Michigan in Lake Bluff, Illinois, and lived there with her sister and with her lover-companion, Harriet Dean.
11. Robert Ferrari, Denver lawyer, Italian vice consul, birth control advocate, friend of Ellen Kennan's, and *Mother Earth* subscriber.

## To CHARLES ERSKINE SCOTT WOOD

*Los Angeles, 18 June 1915*

My dear Mr. Wood:—

I have written Kitty[1] a long letter asking her to speak to you about the Schimdt and Caplan case.[2] At the time I did not know that you were still in San Francisco. I felt that if there was one man who could save the situation it was you, and being deeply interested in the fate of the two men, I am naturally very eager to have you go on the case.[3]

Since I have come to Los Angeles, I find the same crooked methods have been employed as in the McNamara case. It is a miracle to me how little people will learn from experience, and that a man like Lincoln Steffens,[4] who ought to know better, will repeat the same foolish thing. I wonder how much people will have to pay before they will realize that there is nothing to be hoped for from the money power.

I suppose that you know all about the Schmidt and Caplan defense,—prosecution would be a better term for it, because those who claim to be the friends of the boys would have their way, I haven't any doubt that they would both be delivered to the gallows.[5] Fortunately, the boys themselves do not want to go through the mess of several years ago[6] and are therefore very eager to have you defend them. I hope that you will not

1. Katherine Beck ("Kitty" or "Kitten") was Wood's secretary and a friend of EG.
2. Matthew Schmidt and David Caplan were arrested in February 1915 for their part in the 1910 *Los Angeles Times* building explosion. The two had been in hiding since October 1910 and were apprehended through Detective William Burns and Donald Vose, the son of a longtime anarchist who went to work for Burns; he used his connections in the anarchist community to uncover the hiding places of Caplan and Schmidt. Schmidt and Caplan were extradited to California, where they were charged with murder and set to be tried in Los Angeles.
3. Caplan and Schmidt had been working to convince Wood to take their case. In early June, following Wood's visit with them in Los Angeles, they would write to him a number of times in an effort to induce him to take the case. See Schmidt and Caplan to CES Wood, 9 June 1915, 21 June 1915, and 22 July 1915, CES Wood Papers, CU-B.
4. Lincoln Steffens had traveled to Los Angeles in 1911 to help mediate between the McNamara brothers and the *Los Angeles Times* in an effort to foster industrial peace. However the severe sentences given to the McNamara bothers caused many to distrust his efforts. For more on Steffens's role in the McNamara brothers' trial see Letter from Ben Reitman, 14 January 1912, above.
5. Wood himself was suspicious of the motives of those in charge of Caplan and Schmidt's defense. He wrote in a personal letter that he had told the two, "I would make every effort to come into the case; but I am satisfied that the local counsel and the managers have no desire to have me in, possibly for the same reason that they finally concluded I was not the man for the McNamaras." See letter to Helen Todd, 27 May 1915, CES Wood Papers, CU-B.
6. A reference to the McNamara brothers' trial and eventual plea of guilty. For details on the case and

refuse. I appreciate the responsibility and the strain it would mean for you, but it is a wonderful chance, Mr. Wood, to fight for a great cause with open weapons.

I am here until the first of July, and then go to San Francisco for three weeks or a month.[7] I shall be located at the Scottish Rite Hall, but till then I can be reached at The Streicher Apartment, 454 Figueroa St. Los Angeles. Will you not write me a letter and tell me what you think of the Schmidt and Caplan proposition, and also whether you will take the case.[8]

Those of us who want to work in behalf of the boys would have greater confidence and deeper enthusiasm to go about the country arousing interest for them if we knew that a man who is not merely a lawyer, but above everything else is a man, is in charge of the defense.[9] I confess that I would not be able to do any thing otherwise, because I

---

EG's opinion see "Emma Goldman Comes to Preach 'Anarchism' to the I.W.W.'s," Article in the *Fresno Morning Republican*, 14 May 1911, and Letter to Peter Kropotkin, 29 May 1911, above.

7. EG had been in Los Angeles giving a series of lectures since 6 June, also traveling to San Diego in what was her first lecture tour there since the free speech fight in 1912. While in Los Angeles she spoke at a meeting for Caplan and Schmidt at the Los Angeles Labor Temple and held a fund-raising social for their defense. Her last lecture date in Los Angeles was 30 June 1915. EG gave her first lecture in San Francisco on 4 July. She remained in San Francisco through her last lecture date in that city, 29 July 1915.

8. On 17 July 1915 Wood wrote to Caplan and Schmidt, informing them that he would not be able to take the case because their defense fund and committee did not have enough money to allow him to become engaged in the case. He wrote, "I, also, am a wage-slave of only a little greater freedom." See C. E. S. Wood to Matthew Schmidt and David Caplan, 17 July 1915, C. E. S. Wood Papers, CU-B.

9. Wood at first refused to travel to Los Angeles to take part in the defense due to both time and financial constraints, although later he did go to Los Angeles to meet with Caplan, Schmidt, Lincoln Steffens, and Olaf Tveitmoe. See letter to Fremont Older, 6 March 1915, and to Fred H. Moore, 24 May 1915, CES Wood Papers, CU-B. Tveitmoe (1865–1923) was a Norwegian American editor and a powerful labor organizer in California. Tveitmoe was the editor of the San Francisco Building Trades Council newspaper, *Organized Labor* (1900–1980), and he helped to organize the state Building Trades Council in 1901, becoming general secretary of the council from 1901 to 1922. Tveitmoe first encountered Detective William Burns in 1907 when Tveitmoe, then serving on the board of supervisors, was nominally involved in the Ruef graft case, a major bribery case in San Francisco. In 1910 when the state Building Trades Council was working on a campaign to make all of California a closed shop, Tveitmoe left San Francisco for Los Angeles to become president of the General Campaign Strike Committee for the unionizing of Los Angeles. Sometime in 1910 Tveitmoe introduced the McNamara brothers to David Caplan and Matthew Schmidt, who helped the brothers purchase the dynamite used to bomb the *Los Angeles Times* building. He was indicted on federal charges in 1911 with thirty-eight other union men suspected of conspiracy in the bombing. Found guilty in December 1911 and sentenced to six years in prison, Tveitmoe appealed the case, and in January 1914 his sentence was reversed. A new trial was ordered and then abandoned when no new evidence was found. Tveitmoe later worked closely with the Caplan-Schmidt Defense League helping to raise money and organize the defense, although some, such as Wood and Berkman, found him too much the politician and suspected him of being most interested in keeping himself free from further charges at the expense of Caplan and Schmidt.

am sick to the very heart of lawyers who like sharks take possession of every labor case and drain it dry and in the end accomplishing nothing. I do hope that you will write me.

Remember me affectionately to Mary and Sara.[10]

Faithfully,

Emma Goldman

TLS, Charles Erskine Scott Wood Papers, CU-B. The letter was written in care of Wood's companion, suffragist Sara Bard Field.

10. Sara Bard Field was Wood's companion, and her sister, Mary Field Parton (1878–1969), was a radical labor reporter who had covered the McNamara trial.

# MOTHER EARTH

VOL. X.            MAY, 1915           No. 3

BILLY
SUNDAY
TANGO

Cover of May 1915 issue of *Mother Earth* by Robert Minor, mocking Billy Sunday, the popular evangelist who considered sexuality and sensuality a sin, dancing with Jesus. The "Billy Sunday Tango" was a popular performance piece at *Mother Earth* socials. (Kate Sharpley Archive)

Article in the *OREGONIAN*

Portland, Oregon, 7 August 1915

## Emma Goldman Is Put Under Arrest

### Distributing Unlawful Literature Charged Against Anarchist Speaker.

Manager Accused Also

Speaker Taken From Hall Just After She Had Been Introduced by
Colonel C. E. S. Wood and Had Begun to Speak.

Emma Goldman, the anarchist speaker, was arrested at 9 o'clock last night while speaking in the Turn Halle at Fourth and Yamhill streets. The arrest was made on a warrant charging Miss Goldman and Dr. Ben Reitman, her business manager, with distributing literature on birth control.

Miss Goldman had just begun her address on the subject of "Birth Control: How and Why Small Families Are Best." She was introduced by Colonel C. E. S. Wood,[1] her attorney.

Scarcely had she concluded her opening remarks when Patrolman Martin, in plain clothes, walked up the aisle to the stage, followed by Mr. Reitman. Miss Goldman had already warned the audience that her arrest had been threatened.

"Here comes an officer to arrest me now," cried Miss Goldman.

The audience, which crowded the lower floor of the hall, waited in hushed expectancy. The officer produced a warrant, which Colonel Wood insisted that the policeman read himself.

"Yes, read it! Read it!" shouted the crowd.

The policeman, much embarrassed by the publicity, began in a low voice, and was greeted with cries of "louder!"

Colonel Wood rose on the stage and held up his hand for silence.

"This officer is only obeying his order," Colonel Wood said. "Let us be courteous to him!"

The crowd broke into cheers, which continued while Miss Goldman descended from the stage.

The arrest was threatened yesterday afternoon, and was the result of a letter and cir-

---

1. Philosophical anarchist C. E. S. Wood was a friend and supporter of EG and often chaired her meetings in Portland. Wood served as EG's lawyer in 1915, defending her against the birth control charges.

cular mailed to Mayor Albee yesterday.[2] The circular is said to have been devoted to birth control. The Mayor submitted the question to City Attorney LaRoche,[3] who held that the information in the circular was such that its distribution violated the city ordinances.

Police Chief Clark summoned Mr. Reitman, and warned him that Miss Goldman would be arrested if she attempted to speak. A conference between the attorneys followed, and the city authorities decided to base their charge on the alleged distribution of improper literature.[4]

The complaint to the authorities was made by Mrs. Josephine de Vare Johnson,[5] 318 Oregonian building.

Miss Goldman was released on $500 cash bail, negotiated by Colonel Wood. Mr. Reitman was unable to raise that sum, and was still in prison at a late hour. After her release Miss Goldman announced that she would attempt to speak again on the same subject tonight.

*Oregonian*, 7 August 1915, p. 12.

2. Harry Russell Albee was mayor of Portland from 1913 to 1917.
3. Walter P. LaRoche was the Portland city attorney from June 1913 to September 1920.
4. The leaflet in question, *Why and How the Poor Should Not Have Many Children* (1916), was probably written by BR, although William Robinson claimed authorship, and included practical birth control information.
5. Josephine DeVore Johnson (variously spelled as DeVare) was the daughter of Reverend John DeVore, a Methodist preacher, and the widow of William Carey Johnson, a prominent Oregon judge and staunch Republican, and she was a self-proclaimed purity crusader. In a letter to the mayor's secretary, she protested EG's planned lectures, especially on birth control and homosexuality, and took it upon herself to recommend sanctions against EG, many of which were later imposed by Portland officials. She also procured the pamphlet on birth control for which EG and BR were convicted and fined, and testified for the prosecution at EG's trial.

## Article in *OREGON JOURNAL*

*Portland, Oregon, 8 August 1915*

# Emma Goldman Is Fined $100 in City Court

### Dr. Ben Reitman, Woman's Manager, Given Equal Punishment for Circulating Birth Control Circular.

#### Appeals to be taken by Both Defendants

#### Prosecutor Declines to Read Pamphlet Aloud in Court Room.

Emma Goldman, the anarchistic lecturer, and Dr. Ben Reitman, her manager, were each fined $100 by Acting Municipal Judge F. W. Stadter this morning, after they had been convicted of a charge of distributing a pamphlet on birth control in the course of Emma Goldman's series of meetings here.

Reitman and Emma Goldman were arrested while the latter was speaking at Turnhall, Fourth and Yamhill streets, last night, in the presence of a crowd of 250 people. Colonel C.E.S. Wood furnished $500 cash bail for Miss Goldman, but Reitman was forced to spend the night in jail.

### AUDIENCE IS DISAPPOINTED.

An immense crowd gathered at the municipal building this morning for the trial, and the atmosphere was tense with suppressed curiosity that existed among the spectators in the packed courtroom. When Deputy City Attorney L. E. Latourette declined to read aloud the pamphlet[1] that caused all the trouble, audible signs of disappointment were heard from all parts of the room.

"Portland is setting itself up as an Anthony Comstock, and old Madame Grundy,"[2] asserted Colonel Wood, in his argument. The city had disgraced itself by the action, and the trial of the woman, he declared, was a prostitution of justice.

---

1. The pamphlet in question was *Why and How the Poor Should Not Have Many Children*, written by BR, although William J. Robinson also claimed authorship.
2. Mrs. Grundy is a fictional character first portrayed in Thomas Morton's *Speed the Plough* (1798) as an arbiter of social etiquette. Later, her name came to signify prudishness and is associated with censorship and social convention.

## COLONEL WOOD RAISES BAIL.

Colonel Wood said he had personally raised the $500 cash demanded last night, on his own check, but cashiers of his checks were unable to furnish the $500 cash necessary for the release of Reitman.

The defense admitted most of the allegations of the prosecution, that the meeting was a public one, that Emma Goldman had spoken, and that Ben Reitman was her manager.

Reitman, characteristically garbed in a large Stetson hat, black flowing tie, blue suit and soft shirt, was brought out from the prisoner's cage after the trial started, and in his testimony personally took the responsibility for passing the pamphlet around among the few persons in the audience who received it. Emma Goldman, Reitman and three of the witnesses for the defense refused to be sworn, but affirmed the necessary oath that preluded their testimony.[3]

## KNEW NOTHING OF PAMPHLET.

The offense on which they were convicted took place Tuesday night, and Emma Goldman said she was speaking at that time on "Friedrich Nietzsche, the Intellectual Storm Center of Europe."[4] She knew nothing of the distribution of the birth control pamphlet, she said, and would have objected had she known, because she said she wanted to personally take the responsibility for any information disseminated at one of her meetings.

In this statement she was corroborated by Reitman, who said he knew that she objected to the statement, but that it was one of his lines of publicity, aside from his work as her manager and business associate.

In substantiation of this statement, Reitman said: "We are anarchist propagandists, and the proceeds of our sales go to further the cause of anarchism. We are together in this, but I personally advance other ideas and theories, which have nothing whatever to do with her work."

## CIRCULAR NOT POSTED.

Other witnesses for the defense, all of whom testified that the circular was not publicly posted and that it was not generally distributed among the spectators, were Mrs. S. K. Black, Mrs. M. T. Oatman, 547 Fifth street; Mrs. Pauline B. C. Summers, 1103

---

3. By law, those testifying in court must take an oath that reads, "I swear that I will speak the truth, the whole truth and nothing but the truth." However, as EG did here, they may substitute "I affirm" for "I swear" for political or religious reasons.
4. This lecture was delivered at Turn Hall. Ironically EG was arrested three days later, just before delivering her lecture "Birth Control: How and Why Small Families Are Best."

East Twenty-third street north; H. C. Uthoff,[5] 501 Schuyler street, and Mrs. Flora L. Foreman,[6] 726 Belmont street.

## BONDS FIXED AT $200.

Acting Municipal Judge Stadter[7] held that the circular was fully covered by the ordinance, and that it was a violation. After he had found them guilty, he fixed a bond, allowing the appeal of the case to the circuit court, at $200 for each defendant.[8] This was at once furnished out of the $500 cash bail for Emma Goldman.

During the trial, Deputy City Attorney Latourette said that the city did not know the nature of the circular until late yesterday. The warrant for the two was at once issued.

## WILL DEFY CHIEF'S ORDER.

Chief of Police Clark said this morning that Miss Goldman would not be allowed to talk again in Portland. The orders came from the mayor's office, he said. As he was leaving the court dock, Reitman turned to the reporters' table and told them that Miss Goldman would speak again tonight.[9]

Mrs. Josephine DeVore Johnson was the complainant named in the warrant. Patrolman Lee Martin and Detective Howell made the arrests last night, and there was much commotion in the hall when Colonel Wood insisted that Patrolman Martin read aloud the warrant. Just previously Chief Clark[10] had informed Reitman that he would be arrested if a meeting was held last night.

Several officers about the police station were called on the carpet before Chief Clark this morning, when an explanation was demanded why no one was on hand about 6 o'clock last night to issue the complaint and warrant.

*Oregon Journal,* 8 August 1915, pp. 1, 8.

5. H. C. Uthoff was the organizer of the Portland Birth Control League, which was formed in May 1915.
6. Flora Forman was an Oregon public school teacher and member, since 1911, of the Socialist Party. Foreman would be arrested and convicted in 1918 under the Espionage Act for refusing to contribute to the Red Cross and speaking to school children about anti-militarism.
7. F. W. Stadter, who was acting as municipal judge of Portland in place of Judge John Stevenson, made and signed the judgments against EG and BR for "distributing bills relating to the prevention of conception."
8. The case against EG and BR was dismissed 13 August 1915 by Judge William Gatens, who said, "There is too much tendency to prudery nowadays. We are shocked to hear things uttered that we are familiar with in our every-day life."
9. EG gave a lecture that night at Turn Hall, "Variety or Monogamy, Which?"
10. John Clark, chief of the Portland Police Department 1913–1917.

**CITY OF PORTLAND,**
*Plaintiff,*

*vs.*

~~Emma Goldman~~
~~and Ben Reitman~~
*Defendant.*

**Undertaking on Appeal**

A judgment having been given on the ....9th.... day of ....August.... 191 5 whereby ....Emma Goldman.... was condemned to pay a fine of $....100.00.... and in default thereof, to serve a period of ....fifty.... days in the jail of the City of Portland, Multnomah County, Oregon; and ~~he~~—she having appealed from said judgment, and has been duly admitted to bail in the sum of ....200.00.... We, ....Herman Conrad Uthoff.... residing at ....501 Schuyler.... County of ....Mult.... State of Oregon, occupation ....Farmer.... and ....Harry Labowich.... residing at ....291 Broadway.... County of ....Mult.... State of Oregon, occupation ....Cashier.... hereby undertake that the above named ....Emma Goldman.... shall in all respects abide and perform the orders and judgments of the appellate court upon the appeal, and shall pay all costs awarded against ~~him~~—her on the appeal and render ~~himself~~—herself in execution of any judgment rendered against ~~him~~—her on the appeal or if ~~he~~—she fail to do so in any particular, then we will pay to the State of Oregon, the sum of $....200.00....

IN WITNESS WHEREOF, we,—I have hereunto set our hands and seals—my hand and seal this....9.... day of ....Aug.... 191 5

*Herman Conrad Uthoff*

*Harry Labowich*

taken and acknowledged before me this ....9th.... day of ....August.... 191 5

*J. W. Stadter*
acting **Municipal Judge for the City of Portland.**

Goldman and Reitman challenged their arrest and fine for the distribution of birth control literature in Portland, Oregon. This legal document, signed by two men who personally paid twice the amount of Goldman's fine, served as a collateral guarantee, should she lose the appeal and fail to comply with the pending ruling of the appellate court. (Archives of Multnomah County Circuit Court, Oregon)

Modern ideas on War, Labor and the Sex Question are revolutionizing thought. If you believe in learning things yourself, it will pay you to hear

# Emma Goldman

Who will deliver a Series of Lectures in Portland on Vital Subjects at

## Portland, Subject and Dates:

Sunday, August 1st, 3 P. M.

### THE PHILOSOPHY OF ANARCHISM

Sunday, August 1st, 8 P. M.

### THE "POWER" OF BILLY SUNDAY

Monday, August 2nd, 8 P. M.

### MISCONCEPTIONS OF FREE LOVE

Tuesday, August 3rd, 8 P. M.

### FRIEDRICH NIETZSCHE—The Intellectual Storm Center of Europe

Wednesday, August 4th, 8 P. M.

### JEALOUSY—Its Cause and Possible Cure

Thursday, August 5th, 8 P. M,

### ANARCHISM AND LITERATURE

Friday, August 6th, 8 P. M.

### THE BIRTH CONTROL (Why and How Small Families Are Desirable)

Saturday, August 7th, 8 P. M.

### THE INTERMEDIATE SEX (A Discussion of Homosexuality)

Sunday, August 8th, 3 P. M.

### WAR AND THE SACRED RIGHT OF PROPERTY

Sunday, August 8th, 8 P. M.

### VARIETY OR MONOGAMY—WHICH?

ADMISSION 25 CENTS

8 Lectures With MOTHER EARTH, Subscription $2.50

OVER

## Scandinavian Socialist Hall, 4th and Yamhill

Flyer advertising the impressive range of issues Emma Goldman planned to address in her 1915 lecture series in Portland. (Emma Goldman Papers Project)

To the *SPUR*

New York, 16 October 1915

# New York Letter

Over here the war-spirit is growing, and manifesting itself in an evil-smelling measure called "preparedness." Not only will the sweat of the masses be used to bolster up capitalistic and militaristic methods, but even our youth in the schools are to be poisoned through the organisation of military drills and training. The "Socialists" are doing their anti-war agitation in the same half-hearted way they oppose every clamorous idea. They are opposed to war, if it is for plunder, but are in favour of war, of course, if it is for defence.

The Birth Control movement is gaining ground and requires constant attention.

Comrade Berkman has been doing wonderful work in behalf of Caplan and Schmidt.[1] He was successful particularly in arousing the Jewish workers, the Hebrew Trades coming out strong for the boys.[2] The trial is now on and every effort is being made to dispose of our comrades, as in the case of the McNamaras.[3]

The I.W.W. are disrupted pretty much, and are losing what little ground they gained in the past. But for a few, the Anarchists are quarreling as to whether Kropotkin is right or wrong in his position.[4] All the more reason to increase our efforts, which accounts for my going out on a lecture tour again so soon. I am going away for two months' speaking between New York and Chicago,[5] and will take in a number of cities on the way. I hope to have large meetings when I speak against "Preparedness."

---

1. AB was touring the country to raise funds and support for the defense of David Caplan and Matthew Schmidt under the auspices of the Caplan-Schmidt Defense League and the International Workers' Defense League.

2. The United Hebrew Trades, founded in 1888 by eastern European Jewish immigrant workers on New York's Lower East Side, was the first significant Jewish union in the United States. Morris Hillquit was among its founding members. According to AB's 1915 reports to *Mother Earth*, the Arbeiter Ring was also supportive of the Caplan-Schmidt Defense League.

3. James and John McNamara had been tried and convicted for the bombing of the *Los Angles Times* building. Caplan and Schmidt were arrested in February 1915, charged with aiding and abetting the plot to bomb the *Los Angeles Times* building. On 12 January 1916 Schmidt was sentenced to life in prison, and on 5 December 1916 Caplan was given a ten-year sentence after being found guilty of voluntary manslaughter.

4. A reference to Peter Kropotkin's position in support of England and France in the war. See "International Anarchist Manifesto on the War," Manifesto in *Mother Earth*, May 1915, above.

5. From late October to December EG lectured in Baltimore, Washington, D.C., Pittsburgh, Detroit, Ann Arbor, Chicago, and other cities on a variety of topics, including "Preparedness, the Road to Universal Slaughter."

So you see, dear comrade Aldred, we are not lagging behind, but doing full measure. Keep up your good work against war and conscription,[6] and do send us your paper regularly. With best wishes and kindest regards to all comrades of *The Spur*, yours fraternally,

EMMA GOLDMAN.

The *Spur* (London), December 1915, p. 56. The *Spur*, an English anarchist journal, ran intermittently between June 1914 and April 1921. The paper was edited by Guy Aldred and later Rose Witcop while Aldred was interned for conscientious objection to World War I. The *Spur* described itself as a journal of anarchist socialism. It finally ceased publication when its offices in Glasgow and London were raided by the police in March 1921 and Aldred was sentenced to a year in prison for distributing seditious material. In 1915 Rudolf Rocker wrote a series of antiwar articles for the paper.

6. In May 1916 Guy Aldred, editor of the *Spur*, was imprisoned for fifteen months for refusing conscription.

## To LEON MALMED

*Pittsburgh, 11 November 1915*

DEAR LEON.

Am writing this on a very memorable and important day in my life. We have a com-memoration meeting,[1] wish you were with us.

My meetings here have been most gratifying, especially the appreciation of our lit-erature, Ben sold $119 in 3 meetings.

To day at noon, I spoke in front of one of the largest canon factories, the Westing house, we got several thousand workers to listen on Preparedness,[2] it would have done your heart good.

We have a lovely group here most of them young Americans. I stopped at the home of the Loans Grace & Tom,[3] most beautiful people. For the first time in a long time, I really enjoyed staying with comrades. You see dear, I am not quite spoiled by Hotels.

The comrades hope to get 200 subs for a drama course, they already have 40. I am to come for one night a week. The same in Washington and two nights in Phil.

That will keep me runing as follows. N Y Engl meeting Sunday night, train for Pittsburg. Lecture Monday night, train for Washingt. Lecture, train for Philadelphia. Lectures Wed & Thursday. Friday train for NY. Jewish lecture. Only rest Saturday & all day Sunday. That will last 7 weeks. Don't you think I ought to be rich at the end?[4]

Really dear, I only think of a home when I am in NY, when I am on the road and see young people in the movement, I feel young again and forget everything.

I shall be very glad to see you at the end of Dec & have a few days with you. I hope you'll be very successful with your new store and gain enough to travel again. But what-ever you will do Leon dear I shall always be your true friend and comrade.[5]

The L A papers now openly call Donald a Burns detective, star witness.[6] It's too awful.

1. That evening EG spoke at an "International Meeting to Commemorate the Death of Our Chicago Comrades" (a memorial meeting for the Haymarket anarchists) at Montefero Hall in Pittsburgh. Other speakers included Jacob Margolis and William Wycis (in Polish).
2. EG spoke at a public street meeting on "Preparedness" to the workers of the East Pittsburgh West-inghouse armaments factory, maker of gun shells.
3. Grace and Tom Loan, mentioned in Ben Reitman's "Three Hundred and Twenty-One Lectures" in the January 1916 issue of *Mother Earth*, helped organize EG's lectures in Pittsburgh.
4. During January, February, and March 1916 EG traveled between New York, Washington, Pittsburgh, and Philadelphia delivering lectures in a series on modern drama.
5. Anarchist Leon Malmed owned a delicatessen in Albany, New York. Malmed left his family in 1915 to accompany EG, AB, and BR on a West Coast tour.
6. Donald Vose (also Meserve; 1892–1945), the son of Gertie Vose, an anarchist at Home Colony and an informant for the William Burns Detective Agency. In 1915 he informed on David Caplan and

He sold our boys for $2500. Oh I'd give years of my life, if he'd never put his dirty foot in our house.

Write me to Detroit.

Affectionately

Emma

While you are in N Y do not fail to go to the Arts Student Bldg an exhibition of Portraits mine is there.[7] Anna[8] will probably know where it is.

ALS, MCR.

---

Matthew Schmidt, who were in hiding after being indicted for complicity in the *Los Angeles Times* bombing of 1910. Eugene O'Neill based the character Don Parrit in *The Iceman Cometh* (1946) on Vose. EG wrote a passionate account of his betrayal of her trust in *Mother Earth* (January 1916) titled "Donald Vose: the Accursed."

7. EG sat for a portrait for Robert Henri (1865–1929), important member of the realist Ashcan School of painting. She met Henri in 1911 and convinced him to teach what became a popular art class at the Ferrer Center.

8. Anna Baron (1895–1939) was a Russian-born American immigrant and former secretary to film producer Cecil B. DeMille in New York. Baron worked as EG's secretary and later, from 1915 to 1916, as business manager of the *Mother Earth* office. Baron collected funds through the Anarchist Red Cross for the unemployed movement and the Anti-Militarist League (1914) and acted as secretary of the Anarchist Forum (1914–1915).

**OPPORTUNITY !**

"Opportunity," cover of the September 1915 issue of *Mother Earth* by artist Robert Minor. Former President Teddy Roosevelt seizes the opportunity to promote readiness for combat. (Kate Sharpley Archive)

Essay in *MOTHER EARTH*

*New York, December 1915*

# Preparedness, the Road to Universal Slaughter

Ever since the beginning of the European conflagration, the whole human race almost has fallen into the deathly grip of the war anesthesis, overcome by the mad teaming fumes of a blood soaked chloroform, which has obscured its vision and paralyzed its heart. Indeed, with the exception of some savage tribes, who know nothing of Christian religion or of brotherly love, and who also know nothing of dreadnaughts, submarines, munition manufacture and war loans, the rest of the race is under this terrible narcosis. The human mind seems to be conscious of but one thing, murderous speculation. Our whole civilization, our entire culture is concentrated in the mad demand for the most perfected weapons of slaughter.

Ammunition! Ammunition! O, Lord, thou who rulest heaven and earth, thou God of love, of mercy and of justice, provide us with enough ammunition to destroy our enemy. Such is the prayer which is ascending daily to the Christian heaven. Just like cattle, panic-stricken in the face of fire, throw themselves into the very flames, so all of the European people have fallen over each other into the devouring flames of the furies of war, and America, pushed to the very brink by unscrupulous politicians, by ranting demagogues, and by military sharks, is preparing for the same terrible feat.

In the face of this approaching disaster, it behooves men and women not yet overcome by the war madness to raise their voice of protest, to call the attention of the people to the crime and outrage which are about to be perpetrated upon them.

America is essentially the melting pot. No national unit composing it, is in a position to boast of superior race purity, particular historic mission, or higher culture. Yet the jingoes and war speculators are filling the air with the sentimental slogan of hypocritical nationalism, "America for Americans," "America first, last, and all the time." This cry has caught the popular fancy from one end of the country to another. In order to maintain America, military preparedness must be engaged in at once. A billion dollars of the people's sweat and blood is to be expended for dreadnaughts and submarines for the army and the navy, all to protect this precious America.[1]

The pathos of it all is that the America which is to be protected by a huge military force is not the America of the people, but that of the privileged class; the class which

---

1. On 9 October 1915 William Gibbs McAdoo, secretary of the treasury in the cabinet of President Woodrow Wilson, submitted an estimate of $1.25 billion in government expenditures for the next fiscal year, a figure that included a $1.5 million increase for national defense.

robs and exploits the masses, and controls their lives from the cradle to the grave. No less pathetic is it that so few people realize that preparedness never leads to peace, but that it is indeed the road to universal slaughter.

With the cunning methods used by the scheming diplomats and military cliques of Germany to saddle the masses with Prussian militarism, the American military ring with its Roosevelts,[2] its Garrisons,[3] its Daniels,[4] and lastly its Wilsons,[5] are moving the very heavens to place the militaristic heel upon the necks of the American people, and, if successful, will hurl America into the storm of blood and tears now devastating the countries of Europe.

Forty years ago Germany proclaimed the slogan: "Germany above everything. Germany for the Germans, first, last and always. We want peace; therefore we must prepare for war. Only a well armed and thoroughly prepared nation can maintain peace, can command respect, can be sure of its national integrity."[6] And Germany continued to prepare, thereby forcing the other nations to do the same. The terrible European war is only the culminating fruition of the hydra-headed gospel, military preparedness.

Since the war began, miles of paper and oceans of ink have been used to prove the barbarity, the cruelty, the oppression of Prussian militarism. Conservatives and radicals alike are giving their support to the Allies for no other reason than to help crush that militarism, in the presence of which, they say, there can be no peace or progress in Europe.[7] But though America grows fat on the manufacture of munitions and war loans to the Allies to help crush Prussians the same cry is now being raised in America which, if carried into national action, would build up an American militarism far more terrible than German or Prussian militarism could ever be, and that because nowhere

---

2. After 1912 Theodore Roosevelt devoted much of his time to the military preparedness movement.

3. Lindley Miller Garrison (1864–1932) was secretary of war under Woodrow Wilson from 1913 to 1916.

4. Josephus Daniels (1862–1948) was owner and publisher of the North Carolina *News and Observer*, and secretary of the navy from 1913 to 1921.

5. Politician and president of the United States Woodrow Wilson (1856–1924). Wilson was elected governor of New Jersey in 1910 and president of the United States in 1912. As president he opposed intervention in the Mexican Revolution for a policy of "watchful waiting," against the wishes of American and European business interests, but in April 1914 he took a more aggressive role against the Mexican war. Wilson also tried to stay out of the European war that began in 1914 and used American "neutrality" as a campaign slogan in the 1916 election; his record of progressivism and peace helped him win reelection in 1916. However, after the sinking of the *Lusitania* in May 1915 Wilson ordered Secretary Garrison to prepare for a larger military. Garrison's proposal, "A Proper Military Policy for the United States," called for the expansion of the regular army and the creation of a national reserve "continental army" of 400,000 volunteers, a plan that encountered opposition and was rejected by Wilson, prompting Garrison's resignation on 10 February 1916.

6. EG makes reference to German nationalism and patriotism that was influenced by Bismarckian ideologies. Otto von Bismarck reached the peak of his political power and influence in 1871, when he became chancellor of the German Empire.

7. Among those who supported the Allies against the "German militarism" that EG refers to were anarchists Peter Kropotkin, Jean Grave, Paul Reclus, Victor Dave, and Christiaan Cornelissen.

in the world has capitalism become so brazen in its greed and nowhere is the state so ready to kneel at the feet of capital.

Like a plague, the mad spirit is sweeping the country, infesting the clearest heads and staunchest hearts with the deathly germ of militarism. National security leagues, with cannon as their emblem of protection, naval leagues with women in their lead have sprung up all over the country, women who boast of representing the gentler sex, women who in pain and danger bring forth life and yet are ready to dedicate it to the Moloch War.[8] Americanization societies with well known liberals as members,[9] they who but yesterday decried the patriotic clap-trap of to-day, are now lending themselves to befog the minds of the people and to help build up the same destructive institutions in America which they are directly and indirectly helping to pull down in Germany— militarism, the destroyer of youth, the raper of women, the annihilator of the best in the race, the very mower of life.

Even Woodrow Wilson, who not so long ago indulged in the phrase "A nation too proud to fight,"[10] who in the beginning of the war ordered prayers for peace, who in his proclamations spoke of the necessity of watchful waiting, even he has been whipped into line. He has now joined his worthy colleagues in the jingo movement, echoing their clamor for preparedness and their howl of "America for Americans." The difference between Wilson and Roosevelt is this: Roosevelt, a born bully, uses the club; Wilson, the historian, the college professor, wears the smooth polished university mask, but underneath it he, like Roosevelt, has but one aim, to serve the big interests, to add to those who are growing phenomenally rich by the manufacture of military supplies.

8. The National Security League was formed on 1 December 1914 in New York to advance the cause of military preparedness. The Navy League, formed in 1902 in the wake of the country's territorial expansion after the Spanish-American War, worked closely with the Army League and the National Security League at the forefront of the preparedness movement. A civilian organization with ties to the military and war-related industries, the Navy League educated the public on the importance of a strong U.S. fleet and exerted pressure on Congress for increased military appropriations. The Women's Section of the Navy League, formed in July 1915, was part of a year-long propaganda campaign to influence public opinion before Congress convened in December. Among the tasks the women were responsible for was that of distributing 1 million copies of the preparedness pledge.

9. Americanization organizations, whose presence intensified with the increase of eastern and southern European immigrants and the escalation of war in Europe, included social scientists, settlement workers, and Progressive reformers. These organizations worked to quicken the assimilation of immigrant families, often targeting immigrant mothers and training them to adopt American middle-class standards of family organization, child care, nutrition, and hygiene, as well as promoting rallies, patriotic naturalization ceremonies, and Fourth of July celebrations. Prominent women reformers were involved with the Americanization cause; these included notably Sophonisba Breckinridge and Frances Kellor, both suffragists and immigration assimilation workers in Chicago, and Katharine Bement Davis, New York City corrections commissioner and prison reformer.

10. On 10 May 1915 (just three days after the sinking of the *Lusitania*), speaking in Philadelphia before an audience of naturalized Americans, Wilson stated: "There is such a thing as a man being too proud to fight. There is such a thing as a nation being so right that it does not need to convince others by force that it is right." The full text of the speech was printed in the *New York Times* on 11 May 1915.

Woodrow Wilson, in his address before the Daughters of the American Revolution, gave his case away when he said, "I would rather be beaten than ostracized."[11] To stand out against the Bethlehem, du Pont, Baldwin, Remington, Winchester metallic cartridges and the rest of the armament ring means political ostracism and death.[12] Wilson knows that; therefore he betrays his original position, goes back on the bombast of "too proud to fight" and howls as loudly as any other cheap politician for preparedness and national glory, the silly pledge the navy league women intend to impose upon every school child: "I pledge myself to do all in my power to further the interests of my country, to uphold its institutions and to maintain the honor of its name and its flag. As I owe everything in life to my country, I consecrate my heart, mind and body to its service and promise to work for its advancement and security in times of peace and to shrink from no sacrifices or privation in its cause should I be called upon to act in its defence for the freedom, peace and happiness of our people."

To uphold the institutions of our country—that's it—the institutions which protect and sustain a handful of people in the robbery and plunder of the masses, the institutions which drain the blood of the native as well as of the foreigner, and turn it into wealth and power; the institutions which rob the alien of whatever originality he brings with him and in return gives him cheap Americanism, whose glory consists in mediocrity and arrogance.

The very proclaimers of "America first" have long before this betrayed the fundamental principles of real Americanism, of the kind of Americanism that Jefferson had in mind when he said that the best government is that which governs least; the kind of America that David Thoreau worked for when he proclaimed that the best government is the one that doesn't govern at all;[13] or the other truly great Americans who aimed to make of this country a haven of refuge, who hoped that all the disinherited and oppressed people in coming to these shores would give character, quality and meaning to the country. That is not the America of the politician and munition speculators. Their America is powerfully portrayed in the idea of a young New York Sculptor;[14] a hard cruel hand

---

11. On 11 October 1915, speaking in Washington at the "silver jubilee celebration" of the Daughters of the American Revolution, Wilson criticized pro-war "hyphenated Americans," stating: "I would a great deal rather be obliged to draw pepper up my nose than to observe the hostile glances of my neighbors. I would a great deal rather be beaten than ostracized. I would a great deal rather endure any sort of physical hardship if I might have the affection of our fellow-men." The full text was printed in the *New York Times* on 12 October 1915.

12. The Bethlehem Steel Corporation was the second-largest steel producer in the United States and the world's largest shipbuilding organization. The DuPont company, one of the largest companies in the world and a leading manufacturer of explosives, was ordered in 1910 to break up its monopoly on the munitions industry.

13. Although probably not the words of Thomas Jefferson, this quotation is often attributed to him. The "motto" also appears in Henry David Thoreau's *Civil Disobedience* (Boston: Ticknor and Fields, 1866). In his essay Thoreau asserts that "government is best which governs not at all."

14. Quite possibly a reference to anarchist sculptor and poet Adolf Wolff, who was known to have created anti-militarist artwork, including poetry, drama, and sculpture.

with long, lean, merciless fingers, crushing in over the heart of the immigrant, squeezing out its blood in order to coin dollars out of it and give the foreigner instead blighted hopes and stulted aspirations.

No doubt Woodrow Wilson has reason to defend these institutions. But what an ideal to hold out to the young generation! How is a military drilled and trained people to defend freedom, peace and happiness? This is what Major General O'Ryan has to say of an efficiently trained generation: "The soldier must be so trained that he becomes a mere automation; he must be so trained that it will destroy his initiative; he must be so trained that he is turned into a machine. The soldier must be forced into the military noose; he must be jacked up; he must be ruled by his superiors with pistol in hand."[15]

This was not said by a Prussian Junker; not by a German barbarian; not by Treitschke or Bernhardi,[16] but by an American Major General. And he is right. You cannot conduct war with equals; you cannot have militarism with free born men; you must have slaves, automatons, machines, obedient disciplined creatures, who will move, act, shoot and kill at the command of their superiors. That is preparedness, and nothing else.

It has been reported that among the speakers before the Navy League was Samuel Gompers.[17] If that is true, it signalizes the greatest outrage upon labor at the hands of its own leaders. Preparedness is not directed only against the external enemy; it aims much more at the internal enemy. It concerns that element of labor which has learned not to hope for anything from our institutions, that awakened part of the working people which has realized that the war of classes underlies all wars among nations, and that if war is justified at all it is the war against economic dependence and political slavery, the two dominant issues involved in the struggle of the classes.

Already militarism has been acting its bloody part in every economic conflict, with

---

15. General John F. O'Ryan (1874–1961) commanded the New York National Guard in 1915. On 20 October 1915, in an address to the New York Technology Club at their "war luncheon," General O'Ryan stated: "The greatest value of a trained soldiery came from the process which made them mere automation, trained to do the bidding of their officers. The first thing that must be done is to destroy all initiative, and that, with the training, fits men to be soldiers. . . . The recruit does not know how to carry out orders. His mental state differs from that of the trained soldier, who obeys mechanically. We must get our men so that they are machines, and this can be done only as the result of a process of training. . . . We have to have our men trained so that the influence of fear is overpowered by the peril of an uncompromising military system, often backed up by a pistol in the hands of an officer. . . . The recruits have got to put their heads into the military noose. They have got to be 'jacked up'—they have got to be 'bawled out.'"

16. Heinrich von Treitschke (1834–1896) was a popular writer and professor of history at the University of Berlin. He was an ardent German nationalist and anti-Semite who supported the Bismarckian policy of a united Germany under Prussia and was best known for his *Deutsche Geschichte im XIX. Jahrhundert* (German History in the Nineteenth Century, 1874–1894, 5 vols.). Friedrich von Bernhardi (1849–1930) was a German general who advocated increased military spending in his influential book *Deutschland und der nächste Krieg* (1911) (*Germany and the Next War*, 1912).

17. No record has been found of Samuel Gompers addressing the Navy League prior to 1916. He was, however, moving toward an endorsement of militarism in 1915. He made his first speech in favor of military preparedness at a National Civic Federation meeting in New York City in January 1916.

the approval and support of the state. Where was the protest of Washington when "our men, women and children" were killed in Ludlow?[18] Where was that high sounding outraged protest contained in the note to Germany? Or is there any difference in killing "our men, women and children" in Ludlow or on the high seas? Yes, indeed. The men, women and children at Ludlow were working people, belonging to the disinherited of the earth, foreigners who had to be given a taste of the glories of Americanism, while the passengers of the *Lusitania* represented wealth and station[19]—therein lies the difference.

Preparedness, therefore, will only add to the power of the privileged few and help them to subdue, to enslave and crush labor. Surely Gompers must know that, and if he joins the howl of the military clique, he must stand condemned as a traitor to the cause of labor.

Just as it is with all the other institutions in our confused life, which were supposedly created for the good of the people and have accomplished the very reverse, so it will be with preparedness. Supposedly, America is to prepare for peace; but in reality it will be the cause of war. It always has been thus—all through blood-stained history, and it will continue until nation will refuse to fight against nation, and until the people of the world will stop preparing for slaughter. Preparedness is like the seed of a poisonous plant; placed in the soil, it will bear poisonous fruit. The European mass destruction is the fruit of that poisonous seed. It is imperative that the American workers realize this before they are driven by the jingoes into the madness that is forever haunted by the spectre of danger and invasion; they must know that to prepare for peace means to invite war, means to unloose the furies of death over land and seas.

That which has driven the masses of Europe into the trenches and to the battlefields is not their inner longing for war; it must be traced to the cut-throat competition for military equipment, for more efficient armies, for larger warships, for more powerful cannon. You cannot build up a standing army and then throw it back into a box like tin soldiers. Armies equipped to the teeth with weapons, with highly developed instruments

18. During the Colorado coal strike of 1913–1914, the Colorado National Guard, along with guards from the Baldwin-Felts Detective Agency, the group hired by the mine operators of John D. Rockefeller Jr.'s Colorado Fuel and Iron Company to break the strike, clashed with the 11,000 miners and their families who were living in tent colonies set up by the United Mine Workers in September 1913. Colorado governor Ammons declared martial law on 28 October, and on 20 April violence escalated when the National Guard sprayed the Ludlow tent colony with machine gun fire. Most accounts number the dead at thirteen strikers, two women and eleven children. Sixty-six men, women, and children were killed by the time the strike was officially called off in December 1914. The union never won recognition, and no guard was ever indicted for the Ludlow deaths. For further details on the Ludlow strike see also "En Route," Article in *Mother Earth*, June 1914, above.

19. On 7 May 1915 a torpedo from a German submarine sank the British luxury liner *Lusitania* killing 1,198 people, including approximately 130 Americans. The *Lusitania* was also carrying thousands of cases of three-inch shells and millions of rounds of rifle and other small-arms ammunition. This incident sparked an increase in support from the American public for military preparedness.

of murder and backed by their military interests, have their own dynamic functions. We have but to examine into the nature of militarism to realize the truism of this contention.

Militarism consumes the strongest and most productive elements of each nation. Militarism swallows the largest part of the national revenue. Almost nothing is spent on education, art, literature and science compared with the amount devoted to militarism in times of peace, while in times of war everything else is set at naught; all life stagnates, all effort is curtailed; the very sweat and blood of the masses are used to feed this insatiable monster—militarism. Under such circumstances, it must become more arrogant, more aggressive, more bloated with its own importance. If for no other reason, it is out of surplus energy that militarism must act to remain alive; therefore it will seek an enemy or create one artificially. In this civilized purpose and method, militarism is sustained by the state, protected by the laws of the land, is fostered by the home and the school, and glorified by public opinion. In other words, the function of militarism is to kill. It cannot live except through murder.

But the most dominant factor of military preparedness and the one which inevitably leads to war, is the creation of group interests, which consciously and deliberately work for the increase of armament whose purposes are furthered by creating the war hysteria. This group interest embraces all those engaged in the manufacture and sale of munition and in military equipment for personal gain and profit. For instance, the family Krupp, which owns the largest cannon munition plant in the world; its sinister influence in Germany, and in fact in many other countries, extends to the press, the school, the church and to statesmen of highest rank. Shortly before the war, Carl Liebknecht, the one brave public man in Germany now, brought to the attention of the Reichstag that the family Krupp had in its employ officials of the highest military position, not only in Germany, but in France and in other countries.[20] Everywhere its emissaries have been at work, systematically inciting national hatreds and antagonisms. The same investigation brought to light an international war supply trust who cares not a hang for patriotism, or for love of the people, but who uses both to incite war and to pocket millions of profits out of the terrible bargain.

It is not at all unlikely that the history of the present war will trace its origin to this international murder trust. But is it always necessary for one generation to wade through oceans of blood and heap up mountains of human sacrifice that the next generation may learn a grain of truth from it all? Can we of to-day not profit by the cause which led to the European war, can we not learn that it was preparedness, thorough and efficient preparedness on the part of Germany and the other countries for military aggrandizement and material gain; above all can we not realize that preparedness in America must and will lead to the same result, the same barbarity, the same senseless sacrifice

20. In 1913 German social democrat Karl Liebknecht revealed that the Krupp armaments firm was bribing the staff of the German war department.

of life? Is America to follow suit, is it to be turned over to the American Krupps, the American military cliques? It almost seems so when one hears the jingo howls of the press, the blood and thunder tirades of bully Roosevelt, the sentimental twaddle of our college-bred President.

The more reason for those who still have a spark of libertarianism and humanity left to cry out against this great crime, against the outrage now being prepared and imposed upon the American people. It is not enough to claim being neutral; a neutrality which sheds crocodile tears with one eye and keeps the other riveted upon the profits from war supplies and war loans, is not neutrality. It is a hypocritical cloak to cover the countries' crimes. Nor is it enough to join the bourgeois pacifists, who proclaim peace among the nations, while helping to perpetuate the war among the classes, a war which in reality, is at the bottom of all other wars.

It is this war of the classes that we must concentrate upon, and in that connection the war against false values, against evil institutions, against all social atrocities. Those who appreciate the urgent need of co-operating in great struggles must oppose military preparedness imposed by the state and capitalism for the destruction of the masses. They must organize the preparedness of the masses for the overthrow of both capitalism and the state. Industrial and economic preparedness is what the workers need. That alone leads to revolution at the bottom as against mass destruction from on top. That alone leads to true internationalism of labor against Kaiserdom, Kingdom, diplomacies, military cliques and bureaucracy. That alone will give the people the means to take their children out of the slums, out of the sweat shops and the cotton mills. That alone will enable them to inculcate in the coming generation a new ideal of brotherhood, to rear them in play and song and beauty; to bring up men and women, not automatons. That alone will enable woman to become the real mother of the race, who will give to the world creative men, and not soldiers who destroy. That alone leads to economic and social freedom, and does away with all wars, all crimes, and all injustice.

*Mother Earth* 10 (December 1915): 331–38. EG entered this essay as evidence in her 1917 trial to exhibit the consistency of her views on conscription. *Goldman & Berkman v. United States*, Transcript of Trial, U.S. Supreme Court (25 September 1917), pp. 408, 513–18, *EGP*, reel 59.

Margaret Sanger, ca. 1915, remarkably effective birth control organizer who, early on, was mentored by Emma Goldman. (Library of Congress)

MY DEAR.

I wrote you a long letter from Chicago yesterday.[1] To day I heard that our good friends Schroeder & others[2] are urging you to plead guilty.[3]

That would be too awful. Just kill the movement you have helped to advance in 50 years. I hope you will do no such a thing. That you will be as brave as you have so far.

Dear dear Girl, I appreciate your state of mind, I feel deeply all you have gone through since you began your work.[4] But at the same time I feel that it would be a great impardonable error were you now to allow yourself to be beaten. To compromise when there is no need of it.

You have friends all over the country. You can have what ever means will be needed to fight. You have aroused the interest, as no one ever has. Think of losing it all by declaring yourself guilty.[5] Don't do it.

I have a suggestion to make to you. Hold out until I come back the 23rd of this month. Then go away with me for 2 weeks to Lakewood or some place. I am terribly tired and need a rest. We'd both gain much and I would help you find yourself.

What do you think to this? Let me know.

1. In the letter EG included a money order for $40, collected at one of her lectures on birth control, and promised to send all proceeds from her lectures on birth control to raise money for Sanger. See EG to Sanger, 7 December 1915, *EGP*, reel 9.
2. Theodore Schroeder was the lawyer of the Free Speech League. The "others" included anarchists and single-taxers James F. Morton and Bolton Hall, socialist editor Max Eastman, Dr. James Warbasse, and lawyers Simon H. Pollock and Samuel Untermeyer.
3. In August 1914 Margaret Sanger was indicted for publishing a philosophical defense of assassination and eleven articles on birth control that were deemed obscene under the Comstock Law. In October 1914 she fled to Europe to escape arrest. The indictment was still outstanding when Sanger returned to New York a year later. Many lawyers and supporters advised Sanger to plead guilty, accept a plea bargain, and promise never to break the law again. Sanger hesitated, not wishing to concede to the association of birth control with obscenity. She believed that "the issue involved [was] to raise the entire question of birth control out of the gutter of obscenity and into the light of human understanding." Sanger to my Friends and Comrades, 5 January 1916, Joint Legislative Committee Records (Lusk Committee), New York State Records Division.
4. Sanger's daughter, Margaret (Peggy), became ill with pneumonia while at the Stelton Modern School and died at Mt. Sinai Hospital in New York on 6 November 1915.
5. The federal prosecutor, wary of making a martyr of Sanger and thereby furthering her cause, dropped his charges against her on 18 February 1916.

Page from Emma Goldman's letter to Margaret Sanger, 8 December 1915, urging her not to plead guilty at her forthcoming trial for violating federal postal laws governing the distribution of birth control information, and instead to take the likely prison sentence as an opportunity to bring more attention to the larger impact of this unjust law. (Margaret Sanger Papers, DLC)

But in any event don't decide right now what ~~you want~~ to do about your case, don't. Write me Gen Del Indianapolis Ind.

WITH LOVE. E G

ALI, Margaret Sanger Papers, DLC. On stationery of the Marquette Hotel, St. Louis. In an endorsement at the top of the letter, Sanger later wrote: "Emma Goldman 1915"; and at the end of the letter, "Emma Goldman who had heard that the lawyers Etc were putting pressure on me to plead guilty."

My dear Mr. Wood:—

I congratulate you on the splendid article in THE BLAST on "What's the matter with labor."[1] It is positively the best thing that has been written on the subject in a long while. It is significant to me that a non workingman; I mean of course as used in the narrow sense, should have such a wonderful insight in the defects of the labor movement and labor. I would reprint the article in MOTHER EARTH but for the fact that THE BLAST goes to the same people so that it would only mean taking up space for a repetition.[2] But you need not think that you are going to escape me in that way.

This month we close the first decade of the existence of MOTHER EARTH. The March number begins the journey on the second decade.[3] I wonder if it will ever reach the number of years it has in the past. I am preparing to get out a special issue and want an article from you. Something dealing with the contribution from your point of view, MOTHER EARTH has made to the general radical movement. Such as the free speech, education, the labor struggle or whatever subject you would care to write about. I want it to be more impersonal, leaving poor me out of the question as the last March number was entirely too eulogistic.[4] Rather do I want something which will express the place of

1. Charles Erskine Scott Wood's article "What Is the Matter with Labor" appeared in the 22 January edition of *The Blast*. The article was originally a letter written to California labor leader Olaf Tveitmoe following Matthew Schmidt's sentencing to life imprisonment. Writing on 5 January 1916, he argued against Tveitmoe and other labor leaders' strategy of denying any illegal actions in the defense of Caplan and Schmidt: "I believe the only value of force or violence is as it promotes an idea, and if you deny to the act of force and violence all the idea and responsibility back of it, what good has been done? The doer becomes a mere criminal and the idea is repudiated and smothered out of sight." AB had wanted to print the letter in *The Blast*, as had James H. Griffes in his magazine, *Everyman*. Wood refused to have the letter printed by AB, but he did rework it as the article "What Is the Matter with Labor." The article began "Labor lacks solidarity. . . . Here, in my opinion, is the missionary work for true labor leaders,—to bring the masses of Labor to a conception of their strength in unity; the absolute necessity for a completely united labor." See C. E. S. Wood to Olaf Tveitmoe, 5 January 1916, C. E. S. Wood Papers, CSmH; C. E. S. Wood to J. H. Griffes, 15 January 1916, C. E. S. Wood Papers, CU-B; *The Blast*, 22 January 1916.

2. EG did, however, call special attention to Wood's article in the February 1916 issue of *Mother Earth*, reporting, "The first and second issue of *The Blast* have arrived. Hail to *The Blast*! The second number was especially fine, the most telling article being by our Friend C. E. Wood."

3. EG began publishing *Mother Earth* in March 1906, and 1916 marked the eleventh year of the magazine's continued publication.

4. No special issue of *Mother Earth* was published in March 1916. However, an article by Wood, "The Great American Scapegoat," was published in July 1916 with a special note that it had been delayed. In the article Wood wrote, "*Mother Earth* has written, spoken, begged, threatened and gone to jail

MOTHER EARTH in the economic and esthetic struggle of America. I am sure you will be able to contribute something very fine. I must however, have all material together not later than the 20th of Feb. I am therefore writing long in advance so that you should not have to rush at the last minute.

Berkman sent me a copy of the letter which you wrote to him about Caplan.[5] It was splendid but I could have told you in advance that C. will not be able to act upon it even if he wanted to, and from a letter he wrote you I am inclined to think he doesn't even want to.[6] You see, the case has been so terribly botched that it is impossible for Caplan now to make any kind of a stand without making Mat. appear ridiculous.[7] The tragedy of it that these two men should have to be sacrificed to save the hide of unscrupulous labor leaders.[8] It is too revolting. Still more revolting that everyone of us should be gagged by it instead of crying out against the betrayal which is being enacted in California.

---

for Freedom. Freedom everywhere and at all times." The previous year, 1915, EG had published a special souvenir issue in March celebrating the tenth year of *Mother Earth*. In that issue Wood had contributed the tribute article "The Rebel Press."

5. On 15 January 1916 Wood wrote a letter to AB outlining his idea for David Caplan's defense. He suggested that Caplan dispense with all lawyers and allow himself to be represented by a court-appointed lawyer. He argued that "Caplan standing alone ought to arouse sympathy for him with the public and the jury" as well as emphasizing the fact that the prosecutors were not court appointed but paid for by the National Erectors Association. He warned that it was a dangerous step to take, "but legal and technical defences don't seem to have done any good so far." See C. E. S. Wood to AB, 5 January 1916, C. E. S. Wood Papers, CU-B.

6. On 2 January 1916, just days after Schmidt was found guilty, Caplan wrote to Wood asking him to take charge of his case. He wrote of Schmidt's trial, "To my mind his trial was not conducted in the manner it should have been conducted, I had hoped that more of economic struggle would be brought out in the trial. I want my trial to be as radical as it can be made, want as much as possible the class struggle brought out and exposed to the light." EG then wrote to Wood on 1 February asking him to take the case and trying to explain Caplan's change of mind: "I cannot quite reconcile this with his request now that you look after his interests, except that in his position all of us would have a great many changes of ideas. I don't know how you feel about the case but I think Dave is right when he says that it would be suicidal for him to go into court alone now." Wood then wrote to EG on 8 February, explaining that it was too late for him to enter the case and reiterating his belief that the best defense would be publicity and propaganda about the conditions that were bringing about labor violence. Finally EG wrote to Wood on 21 February, "I wasn't very hopeful when I wrote you asking that you should take it. I know that with the whole matter having been messed up it was not likely that you will go into it. But I wrote for Caplan's sake and also to ease my own mind. I don't know what is going to become of the boy since he is in the hands of the same people who delivered Schmidt into the hands of the hangman." See David Caplan to C. E. S. Wood, 2 January 1916; EG to C. E. S. Wood, 1 February 1916; C. E. S. Wood to EG, 8 February 1916; EG to C. E. S. Wood, 21 February 1916, C. E. S. Wood Papers, CU-B.

7. Matthew Schmidt, who had been convicted of murder on 30 December 1915 for his part in the *Los Angeles Times* bombing, was sentenced on 12 January 1916 to life in prison; his case was argued purely on the evidence, and there were no discussions of labor relations and the class war.

8. Many, including EG, AB, and Wood, believed that Schmidt and Caplan were sacrificed to protect others, including labor leaders such as Tveitmoe and Anton Johannsen. Johannsen (b. 1872), like Tveitmoe, was a San Francisco labor organizer, and he was also sympathetic to anarchism. He was a member of the United Brotherhood of Carpenters and Joiners and an organizer for the California Buildings Trades Council (1909–1914). Hutchins Hapgood cast him as the anonymous subject

I hope that you are well and that you will let me hear from you soon.

Always faithfully,

Emma Goldman

Dearest Kitten:—

I know unless you are going to be after Mr. W. I will never get the article and I do want to have it. Besides, what's the good of having a friend like you unless you can use that friendship for "political pull." You owe me a letter anyway kid. When are you going to write? With loads of love, E

TLS, Charles Erskine Scott Wood Papers, CU-B. On Mother Earth Publishing Association stationery, New York.

---

of the book *The Spirit of Labor* (1907). Johannsen presided over EG's 26 May 1912 meeting in San Francisco at the Labor Council Hall. He had been active since 1910, immediately preceding the *Los Angeles Times* building explosion, in the campaign to organize Los Angeles trades. Suspected of conspiracy in the plot to bomb the building, Johannsen was indicted for interstate transport of dynamite (although the charges were later dropped). He helped organize the efforts to support and defend the McNamara brothers. Later an associate of AB's in San Francisco, he contributed articles to *The Blast* and worked to organize support for Mooney and Billings as well as Caplan and Schmidt. Like Tveitmoe, he faced criticism from anarchists for his handling of the Caplan and Schmidt defense. Regarding Tveitmoe, Wood wrote, "Labor-leaders, like other leaders, must be held to the responsibility of the job they assume and they should be attacked for either their ignorance or their betrayals, or any other unfitness." EG explained her views of labor leaders in the Caplan-Schmidt case: "The labor leaders, the pseudo radicals and even the socialists perpetuate the ignorance of labor, cater to its weakness and compromise with its cowardice. So it will probably take another fifty years of hard knocks of actual contact such as the McNamaras and Schmidt have had before labor will venture to make a determined step." See Wood to J. H. Griffes, 15 January 1916; EG to C. E. S. Wood; C. E. S. Wood Papers, CU-B.

Essay in *MOTHER EARTH*

*New York, February 1916*

# The Philosophy of Atheism

To give an adequate exposition of the Philosophy of Atheism, it would be necessary to go into the historical changes of the belief in a Deity, from its earliest beginning to the present day. But that is not within the scope of the present paper. However, it is not out of place to mention, in passing, that the concept God, Supernatural Power, Spirit, Deity, or in whatever other term the essence of Theism may have found expression, has become more indefinite and obscure in the course of time and progress. In other words, the God idea is growing more impersonal and nebulous in proportion as the human mind is learning to understand natural phenomena and in the degree that science progressively correlates human and social events.[1]

God, today, no longer represents the same forces as in the beginning of His existence; neither does He direct human destiny with the same iron hand as of yore. Rather does the God idea express a sort of spiritualistic stimulus to satisfy the fads and fancies of every shade of human weakness. In the course of human development the God idea has been forced to adapt itself to every phase of human affairs, which is perfectly consistent with the origin of the idea itself.

The conception of gods originated in fear and curiosity. Primitive man, unable to understand the phenomena of nature and harassed by them, saw in every terrifying manifestation some sinister force expressly directed against him; and as ignorance and fear are the parents of all superstition, the troubled fancy of primitive man wove the God idea.

Very aptly the world renowned atheist and anarchist, Michael Bakunin, says in his great work *God and the State*: "All religions, with their gods, their demi-gods, and their prophets, their messiahs and their saints, were created by the prejudiced[2] fancy of men who had not attained the full development and full possession of their faculties. Consequently, the religious heaven is nothing but the mirage in which man, exalted by ignorance and faith, discovered his own image, but enlarged and reversed—that is

1. Compare this with Michael Bakunin, *God and the State*: "Their God is not the vigorous and powerful being, the brutally positive God of theology. It is a nebulous, diaphanous, illusory being that vanishes into nothing at the first attempt to grasp it." *God and the State* (Boston: Benjamin Tucker, 1882; British ed., Tunbridge Wells: Science Library, 1883) was a highly influential work among anarchists. EG follows its ideas closely in this essay. Mother Earth Publishing Association also published *God and the State* in 1916.
2. The Mother Earth Publishing Association edition of *God and the State* reads "credulous" here.

divinised.[3] The history of religions, of the birth, grandeur, and the decline of the gods who had succeeded one another in human belief, is nothing, therefore, but the development of the collective intelligence and conscience of mankind. As fast as they discovered, in the course of their historically-progressive advance, either in themselves or in external nature, a quality,[4] or even any great defect whatever, they attributed them to their gods, after having exaggerated and enlarged them beyond measure, after the manner of children, by an act of their religious fancy. * * * With all due respect, then, to the metaphysicians and religious idealists, philosophers, politicians or poets: the idea of God implies the abdication of human reason and justice; it is the most decisive negation of human liberty, and necessarily ends in the enslavement of mankind, both in theory and practice."[5]

Thus the God idea revived, readjusted, and enlarged or narrowed, according to the necessity of the time, has dominated humanity and will continue to do so until man will raise his head to the sunlit day, unafraid and with an awakened will to himself. In proportion as man learns to realize himself and mold his own destiny theism becomes superfluous. How far man will be able to find his relation to his fellows will depend entirely upon how much he can outgrow his dependence upon God.

Already there are indications that theism, which is the theory of speculation, is being replaced by Atheism, the science of demonstration; the one hangs in the metaphysical clouds of the Beyond, while the other has its roots firmly in the soil. It is the earth, not heaven, which man must rescue if he is truly to be saved.

The decline in theism is a most interesting spectacle, especially as manifested in the anxiety of the theists, whatever their particular brand. They realize, much to their distress, that the masses are growing daily more atheistic, more anti-religious; that they are quite willing to leave the Great Beyond and its heavenly domain to the angels and sparrows;[6] because more and more the masses are becoming engrossed in the problems of their immediate existence.

How to bring the masses back to the God idea, the spirit, the First Cause, etc.—that is the most pressing question to all theists. Metaphysical as all these questions seem to be, they yet have a very marked physical background. Inasmuch as religion, "Divine Truth," rewards and punishments are the trade-marks of the largest, the most corrupt

---

3. The Mother Earth Publishing Association edition has the spelling "divinized."
4. The Mother Earth Publishing Association edition reads "a power, a quality" here.
5. Not quoted in an earlier draft of this essay. Asterisks are also not present.
6. EG is paraphrasing a line from Heinrich Heine's *Deutschland: Ein Wintermärchen* here: "Den Himmel überlassen wir / den Engeln und den Spatzen" (Caput I). Note also Johann Most's use of the same quotation in *Die Gottespest* (The God Pestilence), where he writes, speaking of the rich: "It is not surprising then, that those who are rich and mighty enough to enjoy paradise on earth should laughingly proclaim with Heine:
   'The angels and the birds may own
   The heavens for themselves alone.'"

Ben Reitman and Anna Baron (the general secretary) in the *Mother Earth* office, ca. 1915. The poster on the wall above Ben Reitman is an appeal on behalf of the Caplan-Schmidt case, and larger portraits, from left to right, are of Proudhon and Robert Reitzel. Between the portraits is a print by Boardman Robinson. (Cleveland Public Library)

and pernicious, the most powerful and lucrative industry in the world, not excepting the industry of manufacturing guns and munitions. It is the industry of befogging the human mind and stifling the human heart.[7] Necessity knows no law; hence the majority of theists are compelled to take up every subject, even if it has no bearing upon a deity or revelation or the Great Beyond. Perhaps they sense the fact that humanity is growing weary of the hundred and one brands of God.

How to raise this dead level of theistic beliefs is really a matter of life and death for all denominations. Therefore their tolerance; but it is a tolerance not of understanding but of weakness. Perhaps that explains the efforts fostered in all religious publications to combine variegated religious philosophies and conflicting theistic theories into one denominational trust. More and more, the various concepts "of the only true God, the only pure spirit, the only true religion" are tolerantly glossed over in the frantic effort

7. An earlier draft reads "It is the human heart" in place of this sentence.

to establish a common ground to rescue the modern mass from the "pernicious" influence of atheistic ideas.

It is characteristic of theistic "tolerance" that no one really cares what the people believe in, just so they believe or pretend to believe. To accomplish this end, the crudest and vulgarest methods are being used. Religious endeavor meetings and revivals with Billy Sunday[8] as their champion—methods which must outrage every refined sense, and which in their effect upon the ignorant and curious often tend to create a mild state of insanity not infrequently coupled with eroto-mania. All these frantic efforts find approval and support from the earthly powers; from the Russian despot to the American President; from Rockefeller and Wanamaker[9] down to the pettiest business man. They know that the capital invested in Billy Sunday, the Y.M.C.A., Christian Science, and various other institutions will return enormous profits from the subdued, tamed, and dull masses.[10]

Consciously or unconsciously, most theists see in gods and devils, heaven and hell, reward and punishment, a whip to lash the people into obedience, meekness and contentment. The truth is that theism would have lost its footing long before this but for the combined support of Mammon and power. How thoroughly bankrupt it really is, is being demonstrated in the trenches and the battlefields of Europe today.

Have not all theists painted their Deity as the god of love and goodness? Yet after thousands of years of such preachments the gods remain deaf to the agony of the human race. Confucius cares not for the poverty, squalor and misery of the people of China. Buddha remains undisturbed in his political indifference to the famine and starvation of the outraged Hindoos; Jahve[11] continues deaf to the bitter cry of Israel; while Jesus refuses to rise from the dead against his Christians who are butchering each other.

---

8. Billy Sunday, born William Ashley (1862–1935), was a Christian revivalist preacher. He was ordained a minister by the Chicago Presbytery in 1903. His performances at rallies were unconventional. He would jump around all over the stage crashing fists on chairs and other accessories while a choir and musicians would serve as an entourage. Sunday preached hard work, godly living, the holiness of motherhood, and divine love; he railed against theater, dancing, card playing, and most famously alcohol (he called himself the sworn enemy of booze and said that its only place was in hell).

9. John Wanamaker (1838–1922) wealthy and influential department store pioneer and postmaster general 1889–1893.

10. Note the similarity to EG's "Victims of Morality" (*Mother Earth*, March 1913): "This explains the interest of the exploiting rich in religion and morality. The rich preach, foster, and finance both, as an investment that pays good returns. Through the medium of religion they have paralyzed the mind of the people, just as morality has enslaved the spirit. In other words, religion and morality are a much better whip to keep people in submission, than even the club and the gun." See also Johann Most's *Die Gottespest* (The God Pestilence): "And yet the rich and mighty foster and nourish divine idiocy and religious stupidity. It is, in fact, part of their business; it is really a question of life or death to the domineering and exploiting classes whether the people at large are dumfounded religiously or not. With religious lunacy stands and falls their power. The more man clings to religion, the more he believes—the more he believes, the less he knows. The less he knows, the more stupid he is—the more stupid, the easier he may be governed."

11. Alternate spelling of "Yahweh."

The burden of all song and praise, "unto the Highest" has been that God stands for justice and mercy. Yet injustice among men is ever on the increase; the outrages committed against the masses in this country alone would seem enough to overflow the very heavens. But where are the gods to make an end to all these horrors, these wrongs, this inhumanity to man? No, not the gods, but MAN[12] must rise in his mighty wrath. He deceived by all the deities, betrayed by their emissaries, he, himself, must undertake to usher in justice upon the earth.

The philosophy of Atheism expresses the expansion and growth of the human mind. The philosophy of theism, if we can call it a philosophy, is static and fixed. Even the mere attempt to pierce these mysteries represents, from the theistic point of view, non-belief in the all embracing omnipotence, and even a denial of the wisdom of the divine powers outside of man. Fortunately, however, the human mind never was, and never can be, bound by fixities. Hence it is forging ahead in its restless march towards knowledge and life. The human mind is realizing "that the universe is not the result of a creative fiat by some divine intelligence, out of nothing, producing a masterpiece chaotic in perfect operation," but that it is the product of chaotic forces operating through aeons of time, of clashes and cataclysms, of repulsion and attraction crystalizing through the principle of selection into what the theists call, "the universe guided into order and beauty." As Joseph McCabe well points out in his *Existence of God*: "a law of nature is not a formula drawn up by a legislator, but a mere summary of the observed facts—a bundle of facts. Things do not act in a particular way because there is a law, but we state the law because they act in that way."[13]

The philosophy of Atheism represents a concept of life without any metaphysical Beyond or Divine Regulator. It is the concept of an actual, real world with its liberating, expanding and beautifying possibilities, as against an unreal world, which, with its spirits, oracles, and mean contentment has kept humanity in helpless degradation.

It may seem a wild paradox, and yet it is pathetically true, that this real, visible world and our life should have been so long under the influence of metaphysical speculation, rather than of physical demonstrable forces. Under the lash of the theistic idea, this earth has served no other purpose than as a temporary station to test man's capacity for immolation to the will of God.[14] But the moment man attempted to ascertain the nature of that will, he was told that it was utterly futile for "finite human intelligence" to get beyond the all-powerful infinite will. Under the terrific weight of this omnipotence, man has

12. Spelled "Man" in an earlier draft.
13. *The Existence of God*, Inquirers Library no. 1 (London: Watts, 1913), chapter 5, p. 77. EG omits "Martineau disdainfully calls it" after "bundle of facts" from her quotation of McCabe's text. Joseph McCabe (1867–1955) was an English atheist, freethinker, and rationalist writer and lecturer. Other works by McCabe during this period include *The Martyrdom of Ferrer* (1910), *The Story of Evolution* (1912), and *The Tyranny of Shams* (1916).
14. Compare with Bakunin in *God and the State*: "the perpetual immolation of humanity to the insatiable vengeance of the divinity."

been bowed into the dust,—a will-less creature, broken and sweating in the dark. The triumph of the philosophy of Atheism is to free man from the nightmare of gods; it means the dissolution of the phantoms of the beyond. Again and again the light of reason has dispelled the theistic nightmare, but poverty, misery and fear have recreated the phantoms—though whether old or new, whatever their external form, they differed little in their essence. Atheism, on the other hand, in its philosophic aspect refuses allegiance not merely to a definite concept of God, but it refuses all servitude to the God idea, and opposes the theistic principle as such. Gods in their individual function are not half as pernicious as the principle of theism which represents the belief in a supernatural, or even omnipotent, power to rule the earth and man upon it. It is the absolutism of theism, its pernicious influence upon humanity, its paralyzing effect upon thought and action, which Atheism is fighting with all its power.

The philosophy of Atheism has its root in the earth, in this life; its aim is the emancipation of the human race from all God-heads, be they Judaic, Christian, Mohammedean, Budhistic, Brahministic, or what not. Mankind has been punished long and heavily for having created its gods; nothing but pain and persecution have been man's lot since gods began. There is but one way out of this blunder: Man must break his fetters which have chained him to the gates of heaven and hell, so that he can begin to fashion out of his reawakened and illumined consciousness a new world upon earth.

Only after the triumph of the Atheistic philosophy in the minds and hearts of man will freedom and beauty be realized. Beauty as a gift from heaven has proved useless. It will, however, become the essence and impetus of life when man learns to see in the earth the only heaven fit for man. Atheism is already helping to free man from his dependence upon punishment and reward as the heavenly bargain-counter for the poor in spirit.[15]

Do not all theists insist that there can be no morality, no justice, honesty or fidelity without the belief in a Divine Power? Based upon fear and hope, such morality has always been a vile product, imbued partly with self-righteousness, partly with hypocrisy. As to truth, justice, and fidelity, who have been their brave exponents and daring proclaimers? Nearly always the godless ones: the Atheists; they lived, fought, and died for them. They knew that justice, truth, and fidelity are not conditioned in heaven, but that they are related to and interwoven with the tremendous changes going on in the social and material life of the human race; not fixed and eternal, but fluctuating, even as life itself. To what heights the philosophy of Atheism may yet attain, no one can prophesy. But this much can already be predicted: only by its regenerating fire will human relations be purged from the horrors of the past.

Thoughtful people are beginning to realize that moral precepts, imposed upon humanity through religious terror, have become stereotyped and have therefore lost

---

15. An earlier draft of this essay ends at this point.

all vitality. A glance at life today, at its disintegrating character, its conflicting interests with their hatreds, crimes, and greed, suffices to prove the sterility of theistic morality.

Man must get back to himself before he can learn his relation to his fellows. Prometheus chained to the Rock of Ages is doomed to remain the prey of the vultures of darkness.[16] Unbind Prometheus, and you dispel the night and its horrors.

Atheism in its negation of gods is at the same time the strongest affirmation of man, and through man, the eternal yea to life, purpose, and beauty.

*Mother Earth* 10 (February 1916): 410–16. Also published as a pamphlet with the essay "Failure of Christianity" by Mother Earth Publishing Association in 1916. The first published advertisement for this pamphlet occurs in the April 1916 *Mother Earth*.

16. Prometheus, a Titan of Greek myth, offended Zeus by giving the gift of fire to mankind and was chained to Mt. Caucasus, where every day an eagle would eat his liver. Each night his liver would grow so he could endure the same punishment every day. In the eyes of some radicals and freethinkers Prometheus was seen as the rebel god.

MY DEAR HELEN KELLER:—

I should really address you as comrade, but for the fact that so much abuse has resulted from that very endearing term. But I feel towards you that way nevertheless.[1] I have heard you speak at Carnegie Hall last month[2] and I want you to know that it was one of the most stirring events in my life. How very stirring you will realize if you bear in mind that my life has not run very smoothly. I am not going to indulge in the shallow praises which must be a common place to you, that you are a remarkable woman. But I do want you to know that I appreciate more than I can tell your wonderful spirit, especially the spirit which has enabled you to keep in touch with the great pulse of life—the revolutionary movement. Few people I know who have no handicaps whatever, have demonstrated such a clear vision and such a deep grasp of the tremendous conflict going on in society today as you have in that wonderful Carnegie Hall address of yours.

I am sending you some literature on Anarchism, for ought I know you are conversant with it already, because it seems impossible for a woman of your deep feelings and tremendous mind to have remained unaware of the most persecuted, hounded, misunderstood and yet far reaching philosophy for the social reconstruction. Nevertheless, I am sending you a few things including the magazine which we are publishing, if only to come close to you in that way.

Some day I hope I will meet you, but for the present we are both very busy people. I lecture about six times a week in and out of New York and no doubt you too are tremendously occupied. Meanwhile, however, I want you to know that I am very proud of you, the more so because for twenty-five years I have been searching, searching deligently to find one truely big, brave American woman. Unfortunately I have not discovered very many. You are among the very few.

FRATERNALLY,

EMMA GOLDMAN

TLS, Helen Keller Papers, AFB. On Mother Earth Publishing Association stationery. Addressed to Helen Keller Wrentham, Mass.

1. Helen Keller had joined the Socialist Party in 1909, and following the Lawrence textile strike, she joined the IWW in 1912.
2. On 5 January 1916 Keller delivered a speech titled "Strike Against War" at a meeting sponsored by the Woman's Peace Party and the Labor Forum. She called for an uprising of the workers against the preparedness movement and for a strike against all war industries.

My Dear Sir:—

In view of the fact that the Birth Control question is now dominant before the American public, I hope that you will not permit your prejudice against anarchism and myself as its exponent to refuse me fair play. I have lived and worked in New York City for twenty-five years. On more than one occasion I have been misrepresented in the press and anarchism has been made to appear hideous and ridiculous. I am not complaining; I am merely stating a fact which you, I am sure, know as well as I.

But now the question involved in my arrest which took place Friday, February 11th[1] and which is to be heard Monday, February 28th is birth control, a world wide movement sponsored and supported by the greatest men and women through Europe and America, such as Prof. August Forel, Havelock Ellis, George Bernard Shaw, H. G. Wells,[2] Dr. Drysdale[3] in Europe and in America by Prof. Jacobi,[4] Dr. Robinson and many others. A movement which has originated in minds of people who were both scientific and humanitarian, and which at the present time is backed by science, sociology and economic necessity. Certainly you will not refuse me a hearing in behalf of such an issue.

I have lectured on birth control for years; many times in New York and other cities, before representative audiences. At almost every meeting plain clothes men were present taking copious notes. It was therefore no secret that I am sponsoring birth control and the necessity of imparting knowledge on this most vital question.

1. EG was arrested on 11 February as she was about to enter Vorwart (Forward) Hall, in New York City, where she was scheduled to lecture on the "Philosophy of Atheism." She was charged with lecturing the previous Tuesday, 8 February, on a medical question (birth control) in defiance of the law; she was released on $500 bail.
2. Herbert George Wells (1866–1946) was an English socialist who was a novelist, journalist, and popular historian. An extract from Wells's *In the Days of the Comet* (1906), titled "The Modern Newspaper," was reprinted in the April 1906 *Mother Earth*. His book *The Future in America* (London: Chapman and Hall, 1906) contained an interview with imprisoned English anarchist William MacQueen and an account of Gorky's aborted tour of America in 1906. See "To the Strikers of Paterson," Letter to *La Question* Sociale, in vol 2., *Making Speech Free*, pp. 91-94.
3. Which Drysdale EG is referring to is unclear. Dr. Alice Vickery Drysdale (1844–1929), president of the Malthusian League, and her son Dr. Charles Vickery Drysdale (1874–1961), secretary of the league, were freethinking, liberal utilitarians dedicated to the advocacy of birth control and the small family.
4. Abraham Jacobi (1830–1919) was a physician-reformer who observed that medical problems were frequently rooted in social and economic conditions. He was president of the American Medical Association and known as the "father of pediatrics." Dr. William J. Robinson persuaded him to endorse contraception in his 1912 presidential address before the American Medical Association.

Friday, February 4th, I again delivered this lecture in Forward Hall, New York, when three thousand people attempted to crowd the place. As a result of this popular clamor for knowledge on birth control, another meeting was arranged for Tuesday, February 8th at the New Star Casino. Again an eager throng attended. The meeting was orderly and everything went off as peacefully and intelligently as on all other occasions when I lecture if not interfered with by the police. Then on Friday, February 11th, just as I was about to enter the Forward Hall to deliver a lecture on Atheism, a subject which has no bearing at all upon birth control, I was arrested, taken to a filthy station house, then hustled into a patrol wagon, rushed to the Clinton Street jail, there searched in the most vulgar manner by a course looking matron in the presence of two detectives, a thing which would outrage the most hardened criminal. Then I was locked up in a cell until my bondsman released me on five hundred dollars bail.

Now all this was unnecessary in as much as I am too well known in the country to run away. Besides, one who has stood the brunt for an ideal for twenty-five years is not likely to run away. A summons would have been enough. But because I happen to be Emma Goldman and the exponent of Anarchism, the whole brutality of the New York police had to be employed in dealing with me, which only goes to prove that everything else in society advances except the Police Department. I confess I was credulous enough to believe that some change had taken place since my last arrest in New York City, which was in 1906, but I discovered my mistake.[5]

However, this is not vital, but what is of importance and that which I hope you will place before your leaders is the fact that the methods of persecution on the part of the reactionary element in New York City in relation to any modern idea pertaining to birth control have evidently not ended with the death of Anthony Comstock. His successor, wanting to ingratiate himself, is leaving nothing undone to make any intelligent discussion of that vital subject possible. Unfortunately, he and the police are evidently not aware that birth control has reached such dimensions that no amount of persecution and petty chicanery can halt its sweep.

It is hardly necessary to point out that whatever may be the law on birth control, those like myself who are disseminating knowledge along that line are not doing so because of personal gain or because we consider it lewd or obscene. We do it because we know the desperate condition among the masses of workers and even professional people, when they cannot meet the demands of numerous children. It is upon that ground that I mean to make my fight when I go into court. Unless I am very much mistaken, I am sustained in my contention by the fundamental principles in America, namely, that when a law

5. EG was arrested on 30 October 1906 with a number of other anarchists while attending a New York anarchist meeting called to protest police suppression of a 27 October meeting that had been called to discussion the actions of Leon Czolgosz. EG was held on two charges of criminal anarchy for articles published in *Mother Earth*, and for inciting to riot. She was arraigned and then released the following day.

has outgrown time and necessity, it must go and the only way to get rid of the law is to awaken the public to the fact that it has outlived its purposes and that is precisely what I have been doing and mean to do in the future.

I am planning a campaign of publicity through a large meeting in Carnegie Hall[6] and through every other channel that will reach the intelligent American public to the fact that while I am not particularly anxious to go to jail, I should yet be glad to do so, if thereby I can add my might to the importance of birth control and the wiping off our antiquated law upon the statute.

Hoping that you will not refuse to acquaint your readers with the facts set forth here.

SINCERELY YOURS,

TLU, Emma Goldman Archive, IISH. On Mother Earth Publishing Association stationery. Reprinted in *Mother Earth* 11 (March 1916): 426–30.

6. This birth control mass meeting took place on 1 March 1916. Speakers included Margaret Sanger, Leonard Abbott, Gilbert E. Roe, Theodore Schroeder, Bolton Hall, John Reed, Anna Strunsky Walling, Dr. William J. Robinson, and Dr. A. L. Goldwater.

VOL. 1          SAN FRANCISCO, SATURDAY, FEBRUARY 12, 1916          No. 5

The Boss's wife can buy information to
limit her family.

The Boss can buy your children to supply his factories with cheap labor.

Cover of *The Blast* by Lydia Gibson mocking the role of the medical profession in maintaining the class nature of the distribution of birth control information. (the *Blast*)

DEAR COMRADE:—

If I will wait until I have time, I'll never get to writing you at length. So I have decided to get the bull by the horn especially as I want to acquaint you with two or three things which will prove of interest to you. If you ever thought for a moment that the people who backed Margaret Sanger[1] in her struggle will do anything in my case, please get that out of your head. They have demonstrated that last night at the so called "Jubile"[2] meeting for Margaret Sanger that they are not really interested in birth control or if they are it is only when it can be kept within respectable channels.

This is what happened. Bob Minor,[3] who probably felt that the meeting should take up my case made a motion on the floor that I be asked to speak and be sent for from the hall where I was delivering my weekly Sunday lecture.[4] The audience applauded but not one single person had the courage to get up and sustain him in his proposition while the chairman a Mrs. Cothren,[5] one of the hard and impossible feminists literally rode over Bob Minor and went right on with the proceedings as if no suggestions were made at all. The tragic part of it is that Margaret Sanger was on the platform and hadn't courage enough to speak up, that after all the work the anarchists have done for her and Sanger.[6] Please dear comrade do not think that I expect her or anyone else to be grateful. I am only citing the case because it proves again that the anarchists are merely used to fetch

---

1. In 1915 a tactically moderate organization, the National Birth Control League, was established. The organization consisted of mainly middle-class feminists and reformers and framed the fight for birth control information as an issue of free speech. This organization and Sanger were eventually able to attract liberal and progressive supporters who shied away from association with EG.
2. The meeting was a celebration of the dismissal on 14 February 1916 of the federal indictment against Sanger. It was held at the Bandbox Theatre, 257 East 57th St., New York City, on 21 February 1916. Speakers included Dr. A. L. Goldwater, who also spoke at EG's birth control meetings; Helen Todd, a suffragette who was later on the board of directors of the New York Women's Publishing Company, which published the *Birth Control Review*; and Sada Cowan, the playwright.
3. Robert Minor was an anarchist cartoonist and contributor to various radical periodicals.
4. EG lectured on "Birth Control" at the Harlem Masonic Temple on 20 February 1916.
5. Marion B. Cothren (b. 1880) was a lawyer, lecturer on feminism (often listed on lecture bills as Mrs. Frank Cothren), and member of the Heterodoxy Club in Greenwich Village. From 1918 she was president of the New York Women's Publishing Company, the publisher of Margaret Sanger's *Birth Control Review*.
6. William Sanger, Margaret Sanger's husband, was arrested on 19 January 1915 for giving an under-cover Comstock agent a copy of the pamphlet *Family Limitation*. After his request for a trial by jury was denied twice, on 10 September 1915 William Sanger was found guilty of distributing indecent literature and offered a choice of a $150 fine or thirty days in prison; he chose prison.

the chestnuts out of the fire and that when they are in trouble they need not hope for any support from those who pose as liberals and radicals.

Personally, I am pleased that the lines are drawn; I want no fashionable women to trail after me. To use all their pull and position including their sex to hypnotize men in office in order to have a case dismissed. That's really what happened in Margaret Sanger's case and while I do not mean for a moment to imply that Margaret approved of it, I mean to say that she did not disapprove of it. As you know, silence is a sign of consent. Besides, the dismisal of a case is no victory to me since the law continues on the statute and if some poor bogger should get into trouble he will be sent up very quickly without anybody raising a voice. That's what has happened in the past; that's what has happened in Bill Sanger's case.

As for me, I am going to have it fought out come what may. I am not foolish enough to think that I will succeed in helping to wipe off the law. But at least I will succeed in attracting attention to birth control rather than to myself. I am going into court next Monday without a lawyer though I do have Gilbert Roe who has been a friend of mine for twenty years prepare the technical side of the case as I haven't the time or inclination to look after that part. I cannot now discuss the mode of procedure but you will hear of it.

I see that you have written to Herman Keene.[7] Good. Write to everyone else you know as that will save me time. I am terribly rushed with a thousand and one things especially as this is MOTHER EARTH week and my trial comes up next week. We have secured Carnegie Hall for a big protest meeting March 1st. We will have to work terribly hard to fill it as I expect little publicity from the papers. I sent the enclosed letter to all the papers in the city. So far only the <u>Globe</u> brought the matter verbatum. The <u>Tribune</u> had one paragraph and none of the other papers have said anything so you can see that it will mean hard struggle and fight for every inch. I wish you could be here on the 1st of March. I have put a photo aside for you but want to wait until I have time and peace of mind to write something on it. Will send it to you then.

With kindest regards to the big and little girls,

AFFECTIONATELY,
EMMA

TLS, Emma Goldman Archive, IISH. On Mother Earth Publishing Association stationery.

7. Herman Kuehn was editor of *Instead of a Magazine*, a paper to which Van Valkenburgh contributed.

My dearest Faithful Ellen:—

Your letter of Feb. 20th with check for $20 enclosed received. Thank you dear for your splendid effort in my behalf. I would have answered immediately but I wanted to be able to tell you the outcome of my preliminary hearing. I went into court without a lawyer. I mean to continue without one to the end. Of course I was held, but nevertheless the preliminary hearing already gave me opportunity to do a tremendous amount of propaganda in behalf of Birth Control. Enclosed clippings are from the <u>Call</u> and the <u>New York Herald</u>. The latter is very remarkable considering the fact that the <u>Herald</u> represents the most reactionary element in this city.

Tonight is the great event, the meeting at Carnegie Hall.[1] The first time in the history of New York and in fact in America, the issue of Birth Control will be frankly thrashed out in such a place as Carnegie Hall by radical men and women. That in itself is worth having been arrested for. The weather is wonderful and to judge by the advance sale of tickets, I think we will have a crowded house. I wish you were with us dear and that I were as inspired as I have been in San Francisco before the Religious Congress.[2] But I am terribly tired out and my brain feels so weary. Yesterday, while I was writing my article for MOTHER EARTH, I felt that if I stretch my brain a little further, it would burst, so I took the bus and rode down town looking at every silly shop window in order to distract my mind from the thousand and one things I am doing. However, I will try my best tonight, as it really means a supreme moment.

I am going to try to pull out the trial until we are through with our winter's work as I want to leave MOTHER EARTH secure in case I have to go to prison. I am not going to allow a little thing like a year's imprisonment to undermine the work I have been doing for years. Don't think I am in anyway worried or disturbed regarding the outcome. As I wrote Berkman today, for years I have been engaged in a wild chase with no opportunity to collect my thoughts or to hold an inventory of myself.[3] And if I shall have to go to prison, I will take it as a god's sent opportunity for a general overhauling of myself.

---

1. A mass meeting in support of EG and birth control agitation took place on 1 March 1916 at Carnegie Hall. Other speakers included Free Speech League members Gilbert Roe, Theodore Schroeder, and Bolton Hall.
2. EG spoke on "The Philosophy of Atheism" before the Congress of Religious Philosophy on 29 July 1915. The congress, at the Civic Auditorium in San Francisco, was held during the San Francisco Exposition and brought together religious philosophers from all over the country. See *LML*, p. 560.
3. To this date the letter is no longer extant.

But on the other hand, I shall not go without a fight and it is going to be revolutionary and determined. Much more so than others could possibly make it who haven't yet outgrown the necessity of respectability.

If there is anything at all that will save the situation, it is country wide publicity, so I want you to get together our faithful ones and organize a campaign for Denver which shall consist of meetings, of a circular or manifesto issued from Denver, of letters and articles to the press and letters and resolutions, the more the marrier sent to Edward Swann,[4] District Attorney. By the way, he is District and not City Attorney. Also, if money can be raised, it will help a great deal. I want very much to go to my trial without a lawyer just as I have at my hearing. But I will have to have somebody to prepare the technical side and besides that I will have to have a great deal of publicity all of which will cost money. But I do not want to exploit you and the people who have already contributed. There must be any number of women who could be approached for contributions and letters. That's the main thing. To organize a Committee that would visit women with lists, get their names and contributions, both of which will help us tremendously.

So far we have heard from Mrs. Kessler.[5] We sent $5.00. By the way, call them up and ask them to hold up the check. Ben lost his valet with some checks and some cash, fortunately not a very large amount. The Cohen check was among them. Mary Levine[6] wrote that she would send money later on. Please give her my love and let her read this letter as she can do a tremendous amount. Also give my love to Gertrude and tell her I have received her letter and her check was not among the lost ones. Dear, I shall have to avail myself of you as the depot for the news we will send to Denver as it is physically impossible for us to write all the details to everyone separate. But will keep you posted regularly.

With a great deal of love and much gratitude for your devotion.

AFFECTIONATELY,

EMMA

P.S. Ben wishes to be rememberd and wished you were here to read him some stories. Please, also call up Mrs Kessler say I have her letter and will write soon.

TLS, Emma Goldman Archive, IISH. On Mother Earth Publishing Association stationery. Last line of postscript handwritten.

---

4. Edward Swann (1862–1945) was a Florida-born New York politician and lawyer. Swann served as a representative in Congress from 1902 to 1903. In 1908 he was elected judge of the Court of General Sessions in New York City, a position he held until 1916. From 1916 to 1922 he was the district attorney for New York County.
5. Mrs. Grace (Charles M.) Kassler was a Denver friend and supporter of EG's.
6. Mary Levin was a birth control advocate as well as a probation officer at the Juvenile Court in Denver. She contributed to the Caplan-Schmidt Defense Fund while AB was in Denver in 1915. A friend of EG's, she was also a subscriber to *Mother Earth*.

DEAR MR. SCHROEDER

I had hoped to see you yesterday, therefore did not write. I am sorry you can not go to Washington, the meeting would have meant a great support to my case.[1]

Yes the article will do.[2] I will send it to our printer earlier and ask him to make proofs to you, please do not delay returning it. The price I will get when it has appeared in M E.

I am so utterly at varyance with you and other American Radicals as to getting results that I can see in Robinson's attitude nothing but weakness.[3] The same applys to your position as to the Free Speech League.[4]

This clamoring for results has made every radical movement bloodless and what is most significant the compromise and trimming of all these movements have led to no results whatever.

Nothing but determination and logical adherence to the fundemental principle of the issue can ever lead to results. The Birth Control issue is the best example. It has been propagated for 50 odd years yet it came to the fore only when the law was defied not before.

---

1. Following EG's series of lectures in Washington, D.C., in early 1916, Schroeder had been invited to speak before the recently formed Washington, D.C., Birth Control League by anarchist Lillian Kisliuk, secretary of the league and friend of EG. At that time he was unable to travel to Washington.
2. The abstract of Schroeder's 1 March Carnegie Hall speech appeared in the April 1916 *Mother Earth*. EG had solicited the speeches of Schroeder, William Robinson, and Dr. A. L. Goldwater from their Carnegie Hall meeting to appear in the April 1916 issue of *Mother Earth*, which was devoted to the birth control issue.
3. In a previous letter to Schroeder EG complained of William Robinson's desire not to have the birth control agitation associated with herself and anarchism because it would antagonize other doctors, stating, "Here I am introducing a plan in behalf of freedom of speech and press and every form of human expression; here I am about to be tried for the very thing that men like Robinson stand for and yet the moment my name is mentioned, they throw their hands up in holy horror. These men are simply hopeless. But then, it is just as well that we should know what their pretence is" (EG to Theodore Schroeder, 10 March 1916, Ralph Ginzburg Collection, WHi). Robinson was director of the Genito-Urinary Diseases Department at the Bronx Hospital in New York and among the first American physicians to advocate birth control. He often shared a platform with EG, though his arguments were rooted in the eugenics movement and he considered homosexuality "a sign of degeneracy." He was, however, a member of the 1916 Birth Control Committee and was probable author of the leaflet *Why and How the Poor Should Not Have Many Children*, which was regularly distributed at EG's meetings.
4. Schroeder was the attorney and author of pamphlets and books for the Free Speech League. As a representative of the Free Speech League, Schroeder resisted tying the league to any political position, and he cautioned Leonard D. Abbott against political affinities.

However I am anarchist enough to let others be saved in their own way but I refuse to have their way save me, hence I shall not bother with Dr. Robinson.[5]

Sincerely,
Emma Goldman

ALS, Ralph Ginzburg Collection, WHi. On Mother Earth Publishing Association stationery.

5. In a later letter EG clarified her position regarding Robinson and other reformers, assuring Schroeder that she did not wish to have others agree with her methods, nor would she condemn others because their methods were different from hers. She wrote, "My objection to these people is only to their hypocricy. I mean by that that they claim to stand for the principle of liberty which includes unlimited free speech and expression and immediately when any one proceeds to express himself, he is coersed or silenced by these apostiles of liberty. I have no patients with that kind of liberty" (EG to Theodore Schroeder, 6 April 1916, Theodore Schroeder Papers, ICarbS).

"Emma Goldman Gets Her Deserved Punishment," cartoon illustration of a sweatshop boss pointing and saying: "Listen to this scandal! I must have kids working for me and she just preaches against having children. To jail with her!" The newspaper at Emma Goldman's feet reads "Lecture: How to Protect Yourself from Having Too Many Children." Yiddish humor periodical, *Der Groysser Kundes* (the *Big Stick*) February 1916. (Labadie Collection, University of Michigan)

Appeal in *MOTHER EARTH*

*New York, April 1916*

## An Urgent Appeal to My Friends

In her contribution on the subject of Birth Control my friend Rebekha Raney takes issue with me on the efficacy of *Mother Earth* appearing as a special Birth Control number.[1] Since Rebekha and I believe in free speech I take the liberty to tell her that her objections are based on considerable naïveté regarding radicals and their beliefs.

Not only is there a number of *M. E.* readers who do not believe in Birth Control, but a great many radicals everywhere have excommunicated me from their lives because I discuss the subject and devote space in *Mother Earth* to it.

In justice to my critics I wish to say that their objections are due largely to the fact that they look upon Birth Control only as a very small phase in a much larger social setting; namely the freedom of expression in life, labor and art which is constantly being interfered with and curtailed by the reactionary forces.

Yet I hold Birth Control to be a tremendously important phase, first because it is tabooed and the people who advocate it are persecuted. Secondly it represents the immediate question of life and death to masses of people. That is the principal reason for the present issue of *Mother Earth*. There is another one, my own arrest.[2] I have no other medium of communication with the public at large except through our magazine. If our readers doubt this, the conspiracy of silence which has so far been observed by the conservative and even the so-called radical press should convince them of this fact.

Since my preliminary hearing, February 28th, hardly an allusion to my case has appeared in any of the papers. A few protest meetings have taken place, one in Seattle, Washington, on February 27th, one in San Francisco, on March 10th,[3] and our own in Carnegie Hall on March 1st.[4] For the rest there has been a dead silence.

That is exactly what the authorities want. But if they build upon that as a safe basis

---

1. Rebekah Raney was a San Francisco–based anarchist and birth control advocate. Her article "The Crowbar vs. Words," was printed, following EG's essay "The Social Aspect of Birth Control," in the April 1916 issue of *Mother Earth*. In her essay Raney suggests that people who read *Mother Earth* already believe in birth control.
2. EG was arrested on 11 February 1916 and charged with lecturing on February 8 on birth control.
3. The San Francisco meeting was announced by AB in *The Blast*. According to *The Blast*, birth control information was eagerly sought at the "enthusiastic" meeting, and $53.65 was raised to print and distribute a leaflet on the "Prevention of Conception."
4. See Letter to Ellen Kennan, 1 March 1916, above, for a description of the Carnegie Hall meeting. Speeches delivered there by Dr. William Robinson, Dr. A. L. Goldwater, and Theodore Schroeder were printed in the April 1916 *Mother Earth*.

to railroad me they will find themselves woefully mistaken, as I am quite determined to give them considerable trouble. The first step is this issue of *Mother Earth* which treats the Birth Control question from every angle; historic, scientific, social, economic and above all from the point of view of Woman, which of them all is the most decisive.

Friends, do you want to help through the medium of publicity? If so, send for bundles of *Mother Earth*, spread the magazine in meetings, among your friends, everywhere that will arouse interest in my case.

Now for the larger work. Before I go before Special Sessions I want to make an adequate and strong defense which is subsequently to be published and circulated in an edition of 100,000 copies.[5] Between now and the trial we must carry on a propaganda campaign through letters and circulars. Lastly and in a measure the most important, if the outcome of my trial is against me *Mother Earth* will remain without the main source of subsistence. I must repeat once more that our magazine though much better placed than heretofore is not self supporting and would discontinue if I should stop lecturing. But I cannot permit that, not after ten terrible years of struggle. *MOTHER EARTH MUST BE SECURED.*

Friends, I ask not for myself but for the one thing dearest in all the world to me, my work, our work the larger and more important aspect of which Birth Control is indeed a small phase—Anarchism, the complete economic and social emancipation of man. For this I ask your support.

Send your contributions at once to The Emma Goldman Defense Committee, 20 East 125th St., N. Y. City. Write letters, arrange protest meetings, pass strong resolutions, have them signed and sent to the District Attorney, Edward Swann.[6]

*Mother Earth* 11 (April 1916): 450–51.

---

5. There is no extant evidence that this mass printing of her official statement ever happened.
6. New York County district attorney Edward Swann was the prosecuting attorney in her case.

Essay in *MOTHER EARTH*

*New York, April 1916*

# The Social Aspects of Birth Control

It has been suggested that to create one genius nature uses all of her resources and takes a hundred years for her difficult task. If that be true, it takes nature even longer to create a great idea. After all, in creating a genius nature concentrates on one personality whereas an idea must eventually become the heritage of the race and must needs be more difficult to mould.

It is just one hundred and fifty years ago when a great man conceived a great idea, Robert Thomas Malthus,[1] the father of Birth Control. That it should have taken so long a time for the human race to realize the greatness of that idea, is only one more proof of the sluggishness of the human mind. It is not possible to go into a detailed discussion of the merits of Malthus' contention, to wit, that the earth is not fertile or rich enough to supply the needs of an excessive race. Certainly if we will look across to the trenches and battlefields of Europe we will find that in a measure his premise was correct. But I feel confident that if Malthus would live to-day he would agree with all social students and revolutionists that if the masses of people continue to be poor and the rich grow ever richer, it is not because the earth is lacking in fertility and richness to supply the need even of an excessive race, but because the earth is monopolized in the hands of the few to the exclusion of the many.

Capitalism, which was in its baby's shoes during Malthus' time has since grown into a huge insatiable monster. It roars through its whistle and machine, "Send your children on to me, I will twist their bones; I will sap their blood, I will rob them of their bloom," for capitalism has an insatiable appetite.

And through its destructive machinery, militarism, capitalism proclaims, "Send your sons on to me, I will drill and discipline them until all humanity has been ground out of them; until they become automatons ready to shoot and kill at the behest of their masters." Capitalism cannot do without militarism and since the masses of people furnish the material to be destroyed in the trenches and on the battlefield, capitalism must have a large race.

In so called good times, capitalism swallows masses of people to throw them out

---

1. Thomas Robert Malthus (1766–1834) was an eighteenth-century English clergyman and economist whose influential *Essay on the Principle of Population* (London: J. Johnson, 1798) calculated that the human population was increasing to a number greater than the earth could support, and he argued for the limitation of population growth through sexual abstinence.

again in times of "industrial depression." This superfluous human mass, which is swelling the ranks of the unemployed and which represents the greatest menace in modern times, is called by our bourgeois political economists the labor margin.[2] They will have it that under no circumstances must the labor margin diminish, else the sacred institution known as capitalistic civilization will be undermined. And so the political economists, together with all sponsors of the capitalistic regime, are in favor of a large and excessive race and are therefore opposed to Birth Control.

Nevertheless Malthus' theory contains much more truth than fiction. In its modern aspect it rests no longer upon speculation, but on other factors which are related to and interwoven with the tremendous social changes going on everywhere.

First, there is the scientific aspect, the contention on the part of the most eminent men of science who tell us that an overworked and underfed vitality cannot reproduce healthy progeny. Beside the contention of scientists, we are confronted with the terrible fact which is now even recognized by benighted people, namely, that an indiscriminate and incessant breeding on the part of the overworked and underfed masses has resulted in an increase of defective, crippled and unfortunate children. So alarming is this fact, that it has awakened social reformers to the necessity of a mental clearing house where the cause and effect of the increase of crippled, deaf, dumb and blind children may be ascertained. Knowing as we do that reformers accept the truth when it has become apparent to the dullest in society, there need be no discussion any longer in regard to the results of indiscriminate breeding.

Secondly, there is the mental awakening of woman, that plays no small part in behalf of Birth Control. For ages she has carried her burdens. Has done her duty a thousand fold more than the soldier on the battlefield. After all, the soldier's business is to take life. For that he is paid by the State, eulogized by political charlatans and upheld by public hysteria. But woman's function is to give life, yet neither the state nor politicians nor public opinion have ever made the slightest provision in return for the life woman has given.

For ages she has been on her knees before the altar of duty as imposed by God, by Capitalism, by the State, and by Morality.[3] To-day she has awakened from her age-long sleep. She has shaken herself free from the nightmare of the past; she has turned her face towards the light and is proclaiming in a clarion voice that she will no longer be a party to the crime of bringing hapless children into the world only to be ground into dust by the wheel of capitalism and to be torn into shreds in trenches and battlefields.

2. A reference to labor market surpluses, which lower wages by keeping the supply of labor artificially high. Karl Marx and other economists argued that these surpluses make workers desperate for jobs and willing to accept low wages, and the workers' consequent powerlessness enables capitalism to thrive.
3. For more on EG's criticism of morality see *Victims of Morality*, Pamphlet Published by Mother Earth Publishing Association, March 1913, above.

And who is to say her nay? After all it is woman who is risking her health and sacrificing her youth in the reproduction of the race. Surely she ought to be in a position to decide how many children she should bring into the world, whether they should be brought into the world by the man she loves and because she wants the child, or should be born in hatred and loathing.

Furthermore, it is conceded by earnest physicians that constant reproduction on the part of women has resulted in what the laity terms, "female troubles": a lucrative condition for unscrupulous medical men. But what possible reason has woman to exhaust her system in everlasting child bearing?

It is precisely for this reason that women should have the knowledge that would enable her to recuperate during a period of from three to five years between each pregnancy, which alone would give her physical and mental well-being and the opportunity to take better care of the children already in existence.

But it is not woman alone who is beginning to realize the importance of Birth Control. Men, too, especially working men, have learned to see in large families a millstone around their necks, deliberately imposed upon them by the reactionary forces in society because a large family paralyzes the brain and benumbs the muscles of the masses of working men. Nothing so binds the workers to the block as a brood of children and that is exactly what the opponents of Birth Control want. Wretched as the earnings of a man with a large family are, he cannot risk even that little, so he continues in the rut, compromises and cringes before his master, just to earn barely enough to feed the many little mouths. He dare not join a revolutionary organization; he dare not go on strike; he dare not express an opinion. Masses of workers have awakened to the necessity of Birth Control as a means of freeing themselves from the terrible yoke and still more as a means of being able to do something for those already in existence by preventing more children from coming into the world.

Last, but not least, a change in the relation of the sexes, though not embracing very large numbers of people, is still making itself felt among a very considerable minority. In the past and to a large extent with the average man to-day, woman continues to be a mere object, a means to an end; largely a physical means and end. But there are men who want more than that from woman; who have come to realize that if every male were emancipated from the superstitions of the past nothing would yet be changed in the social structure so long as woman had not taken her place with him in the great social struggle. Slowly but surely these men have learned that if a woman wastes her substance in eternal pregnancies, confinements and diaper washing, she has little time left for anything else. Least of all has she time for the questions which absorb and stir the father of her children. Out of physical exhaustion and nervous stress she becomes the obstacle in the man's way and often his bitterest enemy. It is then for his own protection and also for his need of the companion and friend in the woman he loves that a great many men want her to be relieved from the terrible imposition of constant reproduction of life, that therefore they are in favor of Birth Control.

From whatever angle, then, the question of Birth Control may be considered, it is the most dominant issue of modern times and as such it cannot be driven back by persecution, imprisonment or a conspiracy of silence.

Those who oppose the Birth Control Movement claim to do so in behalf of motherhood. All the political charlatans prate about this wonderful motherhood, yet on closer examination we find that this motherhood his gone on for centuries past blindly and stupidly dedicating its offspring to Moloch.[4] Besides, so long as mothers are compelled to work many hard hours in order to help support the creatures which they unwillingly brought into the world, the talk of motherhood is nothing else but cant. Ten per cent. of married women in the city of New York have to help make a living. Most of them earn the very lucrative salary of $280 a year. How dare anyone speak of the beauties of Motherhood in the face of such a crime?

But even the better paid mothers, what of them? Not so long ago our old and hoary Board of Education declared that mother teachers may not continue to teach.[5] Though these antiquated gentlemen were compelled by public opinion to reconsider their decision, it is absolutely certain that if the average teacher were to become a mother every year, she would soon lose her position. This is the lot of the married mother; what about the unmarried mother? Or is anyone in doubt that there are thousands of unmarried mothers? They crowd our shops and factories and industries everywhere, not by choice but by economic necessity. In their drab and monotonous existence the only color left is probably a sexual attraction which without methods of prevention invariably leads to abortions. Thousands of women are sacrificed as a result of abortions because they are undertaken by quack doctors, ignorant midwives in secrecy and in haste. Yet the poets and the politicians sing of motherhood. A greater crime was never perpetrated upon woman.

Our moralists know about it, yet they persist in behalf of an indiscriminate breeding of children. They tell us that to limit offspring is entirely a modern tendency because the modern woman is loose in her morals and wishes to shirk responsibility. In reply to this, it is necessary to point out that the tendency to limit offspring is as old as the race. We have as the authority for this contention an eminent German physician Dr. Theilhaber[6] who has compiled historic data to prove that the tendency was prevalent

4. In the Bible Moloch was a Canaanite and Phoenician god to whom children were sacrificed.
5. The official policy of the New York City Board of Education allowed married women to work as teachers only if they had been widowed or separated from their husbands for more than three years. Teachers who failed to report their marriages and eventually became pregnant were dismissed. The idea that only single women should teach was widespread, and in 1914 only three large school systems in the country allowed teachers to return after a maternity leave. Between 1914 and 1915 opposition to this general policy was led by Henrietta Rodman's Feminist Alliance, with the legal counsel of Gilbert Roe, and by 1915 the Board of Education officially allowed the return to the classroom of teachers who had become pregnant, after a mandated two-year maternity leave.
6. Felix Theilhaber (1884–1956) was a Berlin doctor and sexologist. He was among the first doctors to call for a liberalization of birth control and of the laws pertaining to sex. His writings include *Der*

among the Hebrews, the Egyptians, the Persians and many tribes of American Indians. The fear of the child was so great that the women used the most hideous methods rather than to bring an unwanted child into the world. Dr. Theilhaber enumerates fifty-seven methods. This data is of great importance in as much as it dispels the superstition that woman wants to become a mother of a large family.

No, it is not because woman is lacking in responsibility, but because she has too much of the latter that she demands to know how to prevent conception. Never in the history of the world has woman been so race conscious as she is to-day. Never before has she been able to see in the child, not only in her child, but every child, the unit of society, the channel through which man and woman must pass; the strongest factor in the building of a new world. It is for this reason that Birth Control rests upon such solid ground.

We are told that so long as the law on the statute books makes the discussion of preventives a crime, these preventives must not be discussed.[7] In reply I wish to say that it is not the Birth Control Movement, but the law, which will have to go. After all, that is what laws are for, to be made and unmade. How dare they demand that life shall submit to them? Just because some ignorant bigot in his own limitation of mind and heart succeeded in passing a law at the time when men and women were in the thralls of religious and moral superstition, must we be bound by it for the rest of our lives? I readily understand why judges and jailers shall be bound by it. It means their livelihood; their function in society. But even judges sometimes progress. I call your attention to the decision given in behalf of the issue of Birth Control by Judge Gatens of Portland, Oregon. "It seems to me that the trouble with our people to-day is, that there is too much prudery. Ignorance and prudery have always been the millstones around the neck of progress. We all know that things are wrong in society; that we are suffering from many evils but we have not the nerve to get up and admit it, and when some person brings to our attention something we already know, we feign modesty and feel outraged."[8] That certainly is the trouble with most of our law makers and with all those who are opposed to Birth Control.

I am to be tried at Special Sessions April 5th. I do not know what the outcome will be, and furthermore, I do not care. This dread of going to prison for one's ideas so prevalent

---

*Untergang der deutschen Juden* (Munich: E Reinhardt, 1911), *Das Sterile Berlin eine Volkswirtschtliche Studie* (Berlin: E. Marquardt, 1913), and *Die Schadigung der Rasse Durch Sozials und Wirtschaftliches Aufsteigen Bewiesen an den Soziale Aufsteigen den Familien Gefahren* (Berlin: L. Lamm, 1914).

7. The Comstock Act, officially called the Act for the Suppression of Trade in, and Circulation of, Obscene Literature and Articles of Immoral Use, was passed in 1873 and amended in 1876. The act prohibited the production, sale, loan, and exhibition of any "obscene" or "immoral" material and specifically referred to items concerning contraception and abortion.

8. William Gatens (1867–1927), a progressive district judge of Multnomah County, Oregon, from 1909 to 1922. In 1915 he upheld EG and BR's appeal following their 7 August arrest and 8 August conviction in Portland for distributing "literature of an illegal character," and on 13 August, overturned their conviction and sentence (both had been fined $100). See "Emma Goldman Is Fined $100 in City Court," Article in the *Oregon Journal*, 8 August 1915, above. EG quotes the decision of the circuit court, over which Gatens presided.

among American radicals, is what makes the movement so pale and weak. I have no such dread. My revolutionary tradition is that those who are not willing to go to prison for their ideas have never been considered of much value to their ideas. Besides, there are worse places than prison. But whether I have to pay for my Birth Control activities or come out free, one thing is certain, the Birth Control movement cannot be stopped nor will I be stopped from carrying on Birth Control agitation. If I refrain from discussing methods, it is not because I am afraid of a second arrest, but because for the first time in the history of America, the issue of Birth Control through oral information is clear-cut and as I want it fought out on its merits, I do not wish to give the authorities an opportunity to obscure it by something else. However, I do want to point out the utter stupidity of the law. I have at hand the testimony given by the detectives, which, according to their statement, is an exact transcription of what I spelled for them from the platform. Yet so ignorant are these men that they have not a single contracept spelled correctly now. It is perfectly within the law for the detectives to give testimony, but it is not within the law for me to read the testimony which resulted in my indictment. Can you blame me if I am an anarchist and have no use for laws? Also, I wish to point out the utter stupidity of the American court. Supposedly justice is to be meted out there. Supposedly there are to be no star chamber proceedings under democracy, yet the other day when the detectives gave their testimony, it had to be done in a whisper, close to the judge as at the confessional in a Catholic Church and under no circumstances were the ladies present permitted to hear anything that was going on. The farce of it all! And yet we are expected to respect it, to obey it, to submit to it.

I do not know how many of you are willing to do it, but I am not. I stand as one of the sponsors of a world-wide movement, a movement which aims to set woman free from the terrible yoke and bondage of enforced pregnancy; a movement which demands the right for every child to be well born; a movement which shall help free labor from its eternal dependence; a movement which shall usher into the world a new kind of motherhood. I consider this movement important and vital enough to defy all the laws upon the statute-books. I believe it will clear the way not merely for the free discussion of contracepts but for the freedom of expression in Life, Art and Labor, for the right of medical science to experiment with contracepts as it has in the treatment of tuberculosis or any other disease.

I may be arrested, I may be tried and thrown into jail, but I never will be silent; I never will acquiesce or submit to authority, nor will I make peace with a system which degrades woman to a mere incubator and which fattens on her innocent victims. I now and here declare war upon this system and shall not rest until the path has been cleared for a free motherhood and a healthy, joyous and happy childhood.

*Mother Earth* 11 (April 1916): 468–75.

To the *LITTLE REVIEW*

Queen's County Jail, April 1916

# Letters from Prison

## Emma Goldman

What am I doing? I am watching human misery. There is no misery so appalling as imprisoned misery. It is so helpless, so humiliated.

Yes, I think the prisoners do love me, at least those who have been thrown in with me. It is so easy to get their love. The least bit of kindness moves them—they are so appreciative. But what can one do for them?

Do you remember that passage from Galsworthy's *Justice* in which some one says to Falder: "No one wishes you harm"?[1] Therein lies the pathos. No one wishes these social victims harm. The Warden and Matron here are exceptionally kind. And yet the harm, the irreparable harm, is done by the very fact that human beings are locked up, robbed of their identity, their self-respect, their self-hood.

Oh, I am not sorry I was sentenced. In fact I am glad. I needed to get to these pariahs who are the butt of all the horrors. It would be well if every rebel were sent to prison for a time; it would fan his smouldering flame of hate of the things that make prisons possible. I am really glad.

. . . We are awakened at six and unlocked at seven in the morning. Then comes breakfast, of which I have so far eaten only oatmeal with what pretends to be milk. The coffee or tea I have not managed to get down. At seven-thirty we are taken out into the yard. I walk up and down like one possessed, to get the exercise. At eight-thirty we are back, and the women keep themselves busy scribbling; but my girls will not let me do that; I must talk to them. (The Warden, by the way, is reading my *Anarchism*, and the Matron my *Social Significance of the Modern Drama*.) In fact, I seem to have more devotion here than on the outside. At eleven we have dinner, and at four in the afternoon supper—which I will describe to you when I come out. Then we are locked up until seven A.M.—fifteen hours, the hardest of all to bear. Do you remember the line in *The Ballad of Reading Gaol*: "Each day a year whose days grow old"?[2] To me it is "each night a year whose nights grow long." I have always loved the night, but jailed nights are ghastly things.

---

1. John Galsworthy (1867–1933), an English novelist and playwright whose play *Justice* (1910) addressed the horrors of prison life and aroused public interest in prison reform. The line EG quotes is from act 4.
2. The actual quotation is "And that each day is like a year, / A year whose days are long." from Oscar Wilde's *The Ballad of Reading Gaol* (London, 1898).

The lights are on until nine P.M., and we can read and write all day—which is a godsend. Also this prison is one of the cleanest in the country.

. . . What on earth have I done that people should go into such ecstasies? No one raves because you breathe; why rave if you take a determined stand when that means the very breath of life to you? Really I feel embarrassed with all the love and devotion and adulation for so little a thing, so infinitesimal compared with the truly heroic deeds of the great souls. My only consolation is that the fight is not at an end and that I may yet be called upon to do something really great. But for the present it is hardly worth the fuss.

Today is Sunday and we were taken out to the yard for a walk. It was a glorious day, marred only by the monotony of the stripes and the spiritless slouching figures. Yet the sky excluded no one; its glorious blue spread over them all, as if there were no sorrows in all the world and man was never cruel to his kind.

The days pass quickly between the study of my fellow prisoners, my letters, and other writing. The evenings are taken up with reading. But jailed nights are so oppressive. They lie like stone upon your heart. The thoughts, the sobs, the moans that emerge like pale shadows from every human soul. It is stifling. Yet people talk of hell. There is no more threatening thing in all the world than the hell of jailed nights.

Good morning. Another crazing night has gone. . . .

*Little Review* 3 (April 1916): 17–18.

My dear Jake:—

I hope you received our night letter this morning and that the telegram sent to Dave[1] together with $100 addressed to the County Jail reached him. We had a very large and enthusiastic meeting,[2] Only one of the East side high mucky mucks kept his word, Penkin.[3] But he spoke very well indeed. On the whole the meeting was very spirited and pledged its willingness to assist provided Dave will stand his grounds and you will make a revolutionary fight. Needless to say I have all the confidence in the world in you and I am sure Dave too would be energetic if only those rotten leaders were not there to break his spirit. They are sure to succeed if they keep on telling him stories about the support the delegates of the labor convention have promised. Dave must be made to understand that there is no reliance on anything they say. It seems to me he ought to know it by this time.

I am glad that you infused some life into the San Francisco boys. Of course I cannot really blame them if they were unwilling to do anything. Why should they exhert themselves to feed such lawyers as those who have butchered Mat?[4] Now they will have some encouragement; at least they will know as far as you are concerned, the fight will be worth while. It was your telegram that really inspired the audience much more than anything that was said, the assurance that Dave is determined to make a revolutionary stand. Though the workers have not much courage themselves, they nevertheless hate to see one of their own weekkneed, so let us hope we will not be disappointed in Dave as we have been in the others.

1. David Caplan was a Russian-born anarchist who was arrested with Matthew A. Schmidt in connection with the 1910 *Los Angeles Times* bombing. Margolis was acting as Caplan's defense attorney.
2. On 2 April 1916 EG chaired a meeting at the Star Casino in New York City to protest the sentence of life imprisonment on Matthew A. Schmidt and encourage David Caplan, both charged with conspiracy to blow up the *Los Angeles Times* building.
3. Jacob Panken (1879–1968) was a socialist accountant, lawyer, labor leader, and the first socialist municipal court judge (elected in 1917). He lived on New York's Lower East Side. Born in Kiev, Russia, he emigrated to Connecticut with his peasant family. Panken was a close associate of Eugene Debs, Morris Hillquit, and Fiorello H. La Guardia, and he took credit for introducing La Guardia to the labor movement in New York City. He was president of the socialist *Jewish Daily Forward* and founder of the first American women's labor union, the Waistmakers' Union, which became the International Ladies' Garment Workers' Union. After the 1913 Paterson silk strike was defeated he criticized the tactics of the IWW, arguing that its goal of "social revolution" was hurting the strikers and making it impossible to win any concessions from the factory owners. His most notable work was *Socialism for America* (New York: Rand School Press, 1916).
4. Matthew Schmidt was found guilty on 12 January 1916 of first-degree murder and sentenced to life in prison for his part in the *Los Angeles Times* bombing.

For the first time in a long while, I have a new proof of the mob psychology. As I wrote you, the meeting was very spirited and everything went on alright, each speaker reiterating the right of the worker to strike and to use every method for his defense and a great many other phrases and then some little boys who are on strike at the Forward[5] asked to be given the floor to state their case and immediately pendimonium broke lose. Of course, most of the trade unions are connected with the Forward so they dread to do or say anything that will displease that political institution. Besides that there were a lot of Forward adherents, so of course they could not stand for two little boys, both ragged and half starved to say anything in their behalf. The tragic part is that even anarchists howled with the mob, ready to tear me to pieces because I gave the boys the floor. It was sickening. And these are the people who are to usher in a new society! Well, at this critical moment when you need all your energy and spirit, I do not want to discourage you. Besides, you know the mob yourself. But I feel as if I had gone through a steam roller.

Please Jake, keep us posted regularly what is going on. We must supply the papers here. It would be still better if you could send at least a weekly report to the Jewish papers, the New York Folks Zeitung[6] and the Call,[7] though the latter is the most despicable. Let me hear from you soon. Good luck.

EMMA

TLS, Emma Goldman Archive, IISH. On Mother Earth Publishing Association stationery.

5. The two boys were part of the contingent of newspaper carriers striking against the socialist *Jewish Daily Forward*, a sponsor of the meeting called to raise money for David Caplan's defense. For a newspaper report of this event see "Socialists Rebel at Emma Goldman," *New York Times*, 3 April 1916, p. 22.
6. The *New York Volkszeitung* was a German-language socialist daily published from 1878 to 1932.
7. The *New York Call* was a socialist daily published from 1909 to 1923.

ME VERY DEAR COMRADE:—

I got your night message and also your generous contribution to my defense, $100. I wish I could find words to express my deep emotions which you awoke in my soul. Believe me dear comrade it is not the $100 which stirred me so, although, strange as it may seem to you, you are the second person who in all my life of twenty-six year's activity ever contributed such a sum to my work, yet it isn't the money at all, it is the spirit which prompted you to send the contribution. The lovely feeling of comradeship which made you realize without being told that in the struggle with the powers that be, money is needed.

I wonder why people lack so much intuition and sensitiveness to the means of others? Why they compel one to use a sledge hammer to wake them up from their complacency and their dull indifference? Why they cannot see that the struggle for an ideal is hard enough without having to go through the constant material worry? Perhaps it is because, they have all their physical senses dulled through the monotony and sordidness of life.

You dear comrade have all reasons to feel very rich indeed because you are endoued with such an amount of feeling which so few of us have who boast of being able to see and hear and use the human voice. Your inner world must be very colorful, else you could not respond so quickly to those who struggle for their ideal. I consider the opportunity I had in hearing and seeing you one of the greatest events in my life because it has been instrumental in opening up our correspondence and I hope in bringing us personally together some of these days. Meanwhile I am proud of your friendship and comradeship and deeply greatful for your generosity.

You will see by the enclosed that my case has been set for April 20th, when the trial is definitely to take place. I know too much of the courts to expect anything in the way of justice. When I looked into the faces of the Judges I realized that there is nothing to hope for from these dull hard humans who as Bernard Shaw says are paid so much a year for judging others. Why would they not grow hard and dull? My hope is centered on the agitation and the direct action we are going to carry on and which we have already done in a measure. Today I have received the glad news that owing to direct action a comrade of ours in San Francisco[1] was set free for distributing information on birth con-

---

1. Joseph Macario, a San Francisco Italian anarchist active in the Volonta (Will) group, was sentenced to six months in jail on 30 March 1916 for distributing birth control information. His sentence was reversed the next day by Judge John J. Sullivan, after protests by Rebekah Raney and a group of prominent San Francisco women. The judge explained his reversal as a misunderstanding. The

trol among the unfortunate, poverty stricken Italian women. And would you believe it, the Judge said: "If the Anarchists have done this work, they have done good work". We are progressing some, don't you think? I have sent for the verdict of the Judge as it will certainly have considerable bearing on my case. After all judges go by precedent. I will keep you posted as to the development of the case.

I am sending you with this letter our Special issue of MOTHER EARTH.[2] I hope it will be sent to you so you can read it before you get back. If this reaches you in time and you haven't yet done so, please write a letter of protest to the District Attorney, Edward Swann[3] and to the presiding Judge before whom I am to be tried, O'Keefe. I am sure that will have some effect. Also, if it is not burdening you too much, please send me a copy of the protest you will mail, as I shall want to use it for MOTHER EARTH.

If you get back late in May I am afraid I shall not see you, unless I am in prison and then I hope you will come to pay me a visit. Otherwise, I shall have to start on my annual lecture tour by the 15th of the month. But I shall want to hear from you at your earliest convenience.

FRATERNALLY AND DEVOTEDLY,
EMMA GOLDMAN

TLS, Helen Keller Archives, AFB. On Mother Earth Publishing Association stationery.

---

letter Raney wrote to the judge was later published in the 15 April 1916 edition of *The Blast* with an accompanying article by David Leigh. The incident does not appear to have been reported in San Francisco mainstream newspapers.

2. The April 1916 *Mother Earth* was a special issue dedicated to birth control.

3. Keller wrote to Edward Swann on 7 April 1916 asking him to take a personal interest in the case and hoping that "the law and public opinion of your state will support you in finding that it is not a crime to teach mothers how to prevent the conception of children."

## To JACOB MARGOLIS

*New York, 6 April 1916*

My dear Jake:—

I got your letter of March 31st. On your arrival in Los Angeles you must have found several letters from me. I also wrote you on Monday which you will get before this reaches you. Through all my letters you will know what has been accomplished so far and what we intend to do further. I certainly hope that Luke North gave you money.[1] If not wire me as soon as this reaches you and I will see that the Caplan Schmidt Defense Conference[2] sends you money. As a matter of fact they were going to send more than $100 to Caplan, but I insisted that whatever money is still on hand should be kept for you as we are responsible for your reembursement. Now let me know immediately if you need money and it will be sent.

I was not at all disappointed at the reception you received from the crucked politician Harriman.[3] I know him for years and know that he is rotten. It isn't so much crucked-

1. EG sent money to Luke North, president of the Los Angeles International Workers' Defense League, to forward to Margolis. Margolis was serving as defense attorney for David Caplan. Luke North, the pen name of James Hartness Griffes, was a Los Angeles–based single-taxer and libertarian. Besides being president of the Los Angeles branch of the International Workers' Defense League, North was secretary of the Anti–Capital Punishment League; an attorney on the Flores Magón brothers' defense; and a leader in the Great Adventure, which was organized to add a single-tax amendment to the California Constitution. Griffes published and edited the magazine *Everyman* (1906–1909, 1913–1919) in association with the Single Tax Club of Los Angeles (EG contributed the article "The Child and Its Enemies" to the December 1914 issue). He was featured in Charles Sprading's anthology, *Liberty and the Great Libertarians* (Los Angeles: Golden Press for Charles Sprading, 1913), and was a contributing author, as Luke North, to *The Blast* and, as James Griffes, to *Instead of a Magazine*. North's works include *Rubaiyat of Cheerfulness* (Los Angeles: The Golden Press, 1907), *Every Man Has His Price; A Play in Four Acts* (Los Angeles: The Golden Press, 1910), and *The White Flame; A Play* (Los Angeles: The Golden Press, 1910). He wrote the foreword to, and published, *The Plea of Clarence Darrow in His Own Defense to the Jury [That Exonerated Him of the Charge of Bribery]* at Los Angeles, August 1912 (Los Angeles: Golden Press, 1912).

2. The Caplan-Schmidt Defense League was a Los Angeles–based organization founded to aid and provide defense for David Caplan and Matthew A. Schmidt, who were arrested in February 1915 for helping the McNamara brothers purchase dynamite to bomb the *Los Angeles Times* building on 1 October 1910.

3. Socialist Job Harriman (1861–1925) was a California socialist politician, lawyer, and utopian colonist. Harriman took part in the McNamara brothers' case and was a lawyer for Matthew Schmidt. Harriman was the Socialist Labor Party candidate for California governor in 1898, before moving to the Social Democratic Party and serving as Eugene Debs's running mate in the 1900 campaign for president. Harriman was a powerful and influential member of the State Executive Committee of the Socialist Party, and he worked in Los Angeles to create a party that united the socialist and labor bodies for greater political power. Harriman defended Ricardo Flores Magón and his associates after their arrest in Los Angeles in 1907. In 1910 Harriman, along with Clarence Darrow, defended the McNamara brothers against charges of bombing the *Los Angeles Times* building. At the time, in 1911,

ness as cowardice. It is simply apphalling how cringing they all are. I knew what is awaiting you when I asked you to go. I shouldn't have suggested going into the mess to any
other person but you, but I know you are a fighter and that you will come out victorious
if only Dave[4] will stand his ground. If he doesn't there will be nothing lost as far as you
are concerned as you will have gathered enough material to show up the utter rotteness
of the labor movement in this country. The one to pay will be Dave because he will get
absolutely no assistance if the people in the East find out that he has gone back on his
word. So I can only hope for his sake that he will stand firm.

The papers in this city have had not a word about the opening of the trial. I will try to
get some Los Angeles papers by Saturday. But in any event I expect to get a letter from
you early next week to tell me just what happened. I hope it hasn't been postponed again.

You will see by the enclosed that my trial is definitely set for April 20th. As I have
told you repeatedly, I will not have a lawyer. I have no faith whatever in the legal side of
the case and there is no one here, not even Roe,[5] who will fight it on any other ground.
If you hadn't gone to California I should most likely have had you here. As it is, I will
fight it out myself. I have sent today for the decision of the Judge in the case of our Italian
Comrade in San Francisco.[6] It is certainly a most remarkable decision and may have
some bearing with the Judges here, though I confess since I saw their faces yesterday, I
haven't much hope. At any rate I shall make a fight.

Let me hear from you again soon.

Faithfully,

Emma

TLS, Emma Goldman Archive, IISH. On Mother Earth Publishing Association stationery.

---

Harriman was also the socialist candidate for mayor of Los Angeles. After winning the primary election on 31 October 1911 Harriman was overwhelmingly defeated in the general election on 5 December
1911, which occurred just five days after the McNamara brothers' surprise guilty plea. In 1913 he again
ran for mayor and was again defeated. In 1914 Harriman helped found the utopian colony of Llano del
Rio in Southern California, and in 1915 he was one of the attorneys who defended Matthew Schmidt
in his trial for the *Los Angeles Times* bombing. Harriman's published writings include *The Class War
in Idaho; the Horrors of the Bull Pen. An Indictment of Combined Capital in Conspiracy with President
McKinley, General Merriam and Governor Steunenberg, for Their Crimes Against the Miners of the Coeur
de'Alenes* (New York: Volks Zeitung Library, 1899); *The Socialist Trade and Labor Alliance Versus "Pure
and Simple" Trade Union; A Debate held at Grand Opera House, New Haven, Conn., November 25, 1900,
between Daniel De Leon representing Socialist Trade and Labor Alliance and the Socialist Labor Party, and
Job Harriman Representing the "Pure and Simple" Trade Union and Social Democratic Party* (New York:
New York Labor New Company, 1900); and *Lewis-Harriman Debate: Socialist Party vs. Union Labor
Party: Simpson Auditorium, Los Angeles, California* (Los Angeles: Common Sense Pub. Co., 1906).
4. EG is referring to David Caplan.
5. Attorney Gilbert Roe represented William and Margaret Sanger in a case of charges for distributing
birth control information, and he helped AB avert a five-year sentence stemming from a frame-up
by the police for AB's involvement in the unemployed demonstrations in 1914.
6. Joseph Macario was a San Francisco–based Italian anarchist who was tried for distributing birth
control literature. See Letter to Helen Keller, 6 April 1916, above, for more information on Macario's
case.

DEAR COMRADE

It behooves an heathan like myself to be in prison on this holy day when Christ hath risen: What a farce it is to see the poor outcast creatures with their faith and their believes. It appears nowhere so hideous to me as in a place like this.

Are you terribly suprised at the verdict? I am not. I knew it would mean a conviction. I was however surprised with the sentence. No doubt the protest had some effect.[1] I understand that the Judge & District Attourney were swamped with letters, telegrams and resolutions.

But the most solitary effect was created by the dinner on the Eve of the trial[2] and the demonstration at the Court. Both were indeed inspiring.

The dinner brought together whatever is best and genuine in the radical movement in N Y. Artists, Doctors Rebels of every discription. The tone was wonderful and the speaches great. Rose Pastor Stokes spoke and gave out the pamphlate.[3] The latter created a storm of inthusiasm which I have seldom seen at such a gathering.

At the trial fully a thousand people gathered in the Court room, Court corridors and around the building. It was a great demonstration. No wonder the Judges and Court Attendents were so courteous, you would not have believed you were in Court at all.

As to my defense you will read that in M E, so I will not go into it.[4] I want you to know however that I was able to bring out the social and economic side of the movement as was never done in a N Y Court. I am sure I never would have been able to do so with a lawyer. One thing is certain the 15 days I received were given me to save the face of the Procecution.

1. Before the trial, EG, fearing severe punishment, asked her friends and supporters to write letters of protest to New York City district attorney Edward Swann and to organize an Emma Goldman Defense Committee Fund. See also EG to Theodore Schroeder, 6 April 1916, *EGP*, reel 9; EG to Helen Keller, 6 April 1916; EG to Bolton Hall, 6 April 1916, *EGP*, reel 9; and W. S. Van Valkenburgh to EG, 9 April 1916, *EGP*, reel 9.
2. The dinner took place 19 April 1916 at the Brevoort Hotel in New York City. Those present included Robert Henri, George Bellows, Robert Minor, John Sloan, Dr. A. L. Goldwater, and Dr. B. Liber. Speakers included EG, Harry Kelly, and Rose Pastor Stokes. Reports of the meeting were included in the May 1916 birth control issue of *Mother Earth*.
3. Stokes passed out the pamphlet *Why and How the Poor Should Not Have Many Children*, which contained practical birth control information; the pamphlet was written by BR, but William Robinson also claimed authorship.
4. Much of the May 1916 *Mother Earth* was devoted to the issue of birth control and to EG's 20 April 1916 trial, including a complete transcript, "Emma Goldman Before the Bar: The People of the State of New York Against Emma Goldman April 20, 1916."

So here I am and would you believe it I am glad to be here. There is no place on Earth which arouses one's intense abhorence of authority as prison. It were well if many of our radical could get to prison occasionally it would do them good I am sure.

I don't think that the Judges even were foolish enough to believe they will stop me from discussing Contercepts. Not until the law ceases to operate will I be appeased. I am sure much propaganda was done, but I am not as foolish as M S[5] to believe the law is dead, it is nothing of the kind.

Another Carnegie Hall[6] meeting is being arranged for May 6th. I come out the 5th. It will be a sort of reception and renewed challenge to the law. How I wish you could be with us. Is there no chance at all your runing over by boat for Saturday and Sunday? It would be wonderful if you could.

Rose P Stokes and others are going to give out information as to myself wait and see. Meanwhile one large protest meeting has already taken place Friday and another one is taking place to night. These are my regular lecture evenings turned into protest meeting.

You see dear Comrad we are forging the fire while it's hot, we're determined not to let go until a real victory is achieved.

You're not worrying about me, are you? I am quite alright. I have turned into a good Jewish, am getting Matzas sent in, as I am not going to be here long enough to get used to the <u>bread</u>. Tell the truth I have felt very little need for food so far which is fortunate. It will protect my stomach and reduce my fat—Call up Leon[7] and remember me to him. He's so busy with Delicattessen, he seems to have little time for other matters. Kindest regards to the family.

Faithfully

EG

P S. You can write me every day, but <u>of course all ingoing and outcoming mail is read.</u>

ALI, Emma Goldman Archive, IISH.

---

5. EG is referring to birth control advocate Margaret Sanger.
6. The meeting took place on 5 May. EG and others spoke, including Harry Weinberger and Rose Pastor Stokes, who had also distributed the pamphlet *Why and How the Poor Should Not Have Many Children*.
7. Leon Malmed was a mutual friend of EG and Van Valkenburgh.

## To SARA BARD FIELD

*Queens County Jail, 28 April 1916*

My dear Sara

I got your letter it was sent to me from our office after it was opened, since all in coming and out going mail are read here.[1]

I appreciate beyond words the interest and assistance you and my other friends gave me. But really dear, it is so little I have done. When I think of the heroic deeds of some Russian women I feel ashamed to receive so much devotion. My only consolation is that in the great human struggle every little thing has its place.

I am glad of my arrest and the outcome of the trial. First because of the response from so many friends and the fact that even conservative women came to the fore. Secondly because of the opportunity to again come close to our social victims. Really it is worth the inconvenience to know for instance that so many women in S F were ready to sign the pamphlate.[2] As to my stay here I would not have missed it for the World.

Of course the fight is not yet over. Reitman was arrested yesterday on the same charge violation of section 1142.[3] It will probably go harder with him. Besides there will be many more before long, as we do not intend to stop so soon.

---

1. Sara Bard Field (1882–1974) was a Portland- and San Francisco–based suffragist and poet. After returning in 1902 from a mission in Burma (Myanmar) with her minister husband she lived in Cleveland during single-taxer Tom Johnson's administration and became increasingly involved in reform activities. After moving to Portland in 1910 Field became involved in suffrage politics in the West. She worked as the paid state organizer for the Oregon campaign that won women's suffrage in 1912, building a reputation as a skilled orator. Field traveled to Los Angeles in 1911 to report on the *Los Angeles Times* bombing trial of the McNamara brothers for the (Portland) *Oregon Journal*; in Los Angeles she lived with her sister, Mary Field, who was a companion of Clarence Darrow and was also covering the trial for *American Magazine*. In 1913 and 1914 she worked for suffrage in Nevada. In 1914 she moved to San Francisco and became the companion of C. E. S. Wood, although the two would not live together until 1918. Active in the Congressional Union, she helped found its successor, the National Woman's Party, and traveled across the country collecting signatures for a petition to President Wilson in support of women's suffrage (September–December 1915). She supported EG and her birth control agitation (1916), though their relationship was more one of political affinity than friendship. On 20 July 1916, two days before the Preparedness Day parade bombing in San Francisco, she spoke, along with William McDevitt and others, at an anti-preparedness demonstration sponsored by pacifists and labor unions. In fall 1916, under the auspices of the International Workers' Defense League, she spoke at a meeting with Robert Minor and William A. Spooner, secretary-treasurer of the Alameda County Central Labor Council, for Mooney and Billings, after EG, who was scheduled to speak, could not make it to the West Coast in time. Field also contributed articles on birth control to the tenth-anniversary souvenir edition of *Mother Earth* and to *The Blast*.
2. Forty women of San Francisco signed a letter addressed to Judge George O'Keefe stating that they supported EG and would continue to distribute contraception information in defiance of the law. The letter was reprinted in the May 1916 edition of *Mother Earth*.
3. On 27 April at the office of *Mother Earth* BR was arrested for discussing and distributing literature

It will be curious to see what the authorities will do with women like Rose Pastor Stokes[4] and others of position. They will have to arrest them if only to make a showing. And yet I am not so sure. Anyhow it's going to be tried here.

Certain it is that no issue has grown to such size in so short a time as the birth control issue. Of course, I do not consider it the most important in the World, but it is important enough to fight it to a finish.

I am glad to have your cooperation and hope you will continue to help us so long as the fight is on.

It was one week yesterday since I came here. The days passed very quickly. Certainly we are advancing, the difference in conditions between 1893 when I did 10 months in the Pennetantiary is unbeleavable. There is some humanity now, there was none then. We are allowed to write and receive many letters and read all we want. The matrons are not quite so rigid and there are many more improvements. But humiliation continues, of course. What else are prisons for?

The nights however are very appalling. I don't believe anyone has ever adaquately pictured jailed nights with the silent tears and moans emerging like pale shadows from every cell. They are so oppressive, so stifling.

But that too will be passed soon. I will be released May 4th at 8 A M though it may be only for a short time. If not, I hope to see you in Calif in the Summer.

I had a very beautiful wire from Mr W[5] will write him tomorrow. In fact, I have had scores of letters and telegrams from all over the country, never knew I am such a popular "society Bell."

I wish you were with us Friday at Carnegie Hall, I think it will be a great event, a celebration a protest and a challenge. How is May and the baby?[6] Are they both quite well. My niece Stella has a lovely boy[7] and looks radiant. Motherhood agrees with some women. But how terrible the effect upon others? How are your little ones? Love to them and to you.

FAITHFULLY

E G

Your contribution was received.

ALI, C. E. S. Wood Collection, CSmH.

---

about birth control the previous Sunday (22 April) during a meeting at Harlem Masonic Temple. Section 1142 of the New York State law prohibited anyone from providing information about contraceptives. BR was found guilty of "unlawfully possessing printed matter of indecent character" and sentenced to sixty days in the workhouse. Reitman refused to appeal the case. See EG to Jacob Margolis, 5 May 1916, *EGP*, reel 9.

4. Rose Pastor Stokes was never arrested for distributing birth control information
5. Portland lawyer C. E. S. Wood was Field's companion.
6. Margaret Parton, who was the daughter of Mary Field Parton, Sara Bard Field's sister, was born in 1915.
7. Stella Comyn (Cominsky) Ballantine moved to Provincetown with her actor husband, Teddy Ballantine, and gave birth to her first son, Ian Ballantine, in the spring of 1916.

## To My Friends, Old and New

I have received so many letters while in jail and since then, that it is quite impossible for me to answer each one separately.[1] So I take the only medium of communication I have, *MOTHER EARTH*, to write to all of you, dear faithful friends.

I know that you are very anxious to learn how I fared in the Queen's County retreat and whether my imprisonment has "reformed" me. I shall try to give you my impressions as best I can in limited space. I said at the Carnegie Hall meeting May 5th:[2] "I am grateful to the authorities of New York for having sent me to jail." This may have seemed a mere phrase for effect, but I meant it absolutely and earnestly. I repeat the same now. I am deeply grateful to the authorities of New York City.

First, my imprisonment has advanced our cause as nothing I could have done had I gone up and down the country for a whole year lecturing before large audiences. It has brought to the fore scores of people; people I have never known or heard of before. So instead of reaching only the few, we are now able to reach thousands of men and women to whom Birth Control information has become a necessity and who are with us in our fight to break down the conspiracy of silence.

Secondly, my imprisonment has brought me in touch with the social victims, whom society first drives into crime and then hides behind closed bars in order to appease its conscience. What are the crimes of my fellow-prisoners and those like them who fill the prisons and jails all over the United States? Ignorance and poverty. "Poverty is the greatest of all crimes," says George Bernard Shaw in "Major Barbara."[3] Who can deny it? Only those who will not see, who prefer to remain blind among the blind.

I wish to cite a few cases to prove that it is poverty and ignorance and nothing else which make the social offender.

A woman, a mother of a twenty-months-old baby, works as chamber-maid in a hotel. She is young, she is beautiful. She is full of the joy of life. She sees other women arrayed in gorgeous clothes while she does not even make enough to buy the cheapest things.

---

1. EG was released from Queens County Jail on 4 May 1916 after serving fifteen days for lecturing on birth control at the Star Casino on 8 February.
2. This meeting, organized by BR to celebrate EG's release from jail as well as to address the birth control question, was chaired by Max Eastman. Speakers included BR, Harry Weinberger, Arturo Giovannitti, and Rose Pastor Stokes, who distributed leaflets on contraception from the platform.
3. A quote from George Bernard Shaw's preface "First Aid to Critics" from *John Bull's Other Island and Major Barbara* (New York: Brentano's, 1907).

She takes a skirt from a salesman's room. For that she is given an indeterminate sentence of one month to a year.

Oh, the cruelty of the indeterminate sentence! Only a mind parched with the stale virginity of a Katherine B. Davis could have conceived of such a law, which turns the prisoner over, body and soul, to the mercy of the prison and the parole authorities, and undermines her health and spirits with constant uncertainty and fear.

There is the criminal, who, poor in health and out of work, while at church picks up a pocket-book and is hauled by the owner of the purse before court. She is too ill and wretched to plead her own case, nor has she money to engage counsel. Sick and trembling, she stands before the dispenser of justice, who pronounces in routine fashion: "Six months workhouse." In this case the victim happens to be refined, sensitive and self-conscious. She is a woman who has always been self-supporting, who has always retained her pride and her self-respect. What does jail do to her? It crushes her absolutely and unfits her for a place in the world. What a mockery justice is!

There is a young girl of nineteen. At the age of sixteen, the most glorious and mysterious age, her "kind" mother placed her in the Bedford Reformatory[4] because she was "unruly and wayward." How is that ignorant mother to know that the adolescent stage is the awakening of spring; the time when nature in all her recklessness and wildness seeks expression, volcano-like, rushing forward. She has not been told by her mother, and who in turn does not understand her child. The young girl is placed in a reformatory. In this case the preparatory school of vice and crime. After a long stay in that hideous institution the girl is allowed to go out on parole. She is prepared for nothing else but the street, and as she is both young and beautiful, she finds willing arms to receive her from the street. Shortly after that she is again picked up and given one year in the penitentiary. When that time is up, she will probably be returned to the Bedford Reformatory, the place which originally marred her.

Then there is the case of Katherine. Only a Dickens or a Victor Hugo or a Dostoyevsky could adequately describe the pathos of this case. Katherine has been a drudge all her life. She does not have to tell you so. She looks it, every bit of her. The silent drudge who has given service all her life. For twenty-nine years Katherine dreams of New York. Ah, if she only could get to this magic city, New York! But she is a drudge and has two children to support. How will she ever realize her dream? Still, she goes on dreaming and for aught I know, it is this dream which puts color into her dreary life.

Suddenly the miracle of miracles happens. Katherine comes into a great fortune—$100 accident insurance. Fifty dollars goes to her children and with the other fifty Katherine goes to New York, equipped only with an address to someone in Yonkers. On arrival she goes to a café on the water front and is there directed to a cheap room

4. The Bedford Hills Reformatory for Women in New York was established in 1901. Katherine Bement Davis was a prison matron at the reformatory from 1914 to 1915.

# Birth Control Meeting

## Friday, May 5th, 1916
### 8 P. M.

## At CARNEGIE HALL
### 57th Street and 6th Avenue
#### TO WELCOME

# EMMA GOLDMAN
#### FROM PRISON

And demonstrate that locking up a propagandist does not prevent the dissemination of Ideas.

We still live in a Country, where it is a crime to teach people that which no one can deny, will make the world a better place in which to live.

### SPEAKERS:

| | |
|---|---|
| ROSE PASTOR STOKES | HARRY WEINBERG |
| PROMINENT DOCTORS | EMMA GOLDMAN |
| LEONARD D. ABBOTT | And Others |
| *MUSIC* | *THEODORE SCHROEDER, Chairman* |

## Admission 15, 25 and 50 Cents          Boxes $5.00

Tickets on sale at Mother Earth, 20 East 125th St.     Tel. Harlem, 6194

If you believe that all serious minded women and men should have the right to learn about Birth Control Methods and any thing else that will better their conditions, then you can not afford to miss this meeting.

Flyer for a birth control meeting on 5 May 1916 at Carnegie Hall, celebrating Emma Goldman's release from Queens County Jail after serving a fifteen-day sentence for the distribution of explicit birth control information. (Emma Goldman Papers Project)

---

over a saloon. On Sunday, with joy in her heart and the ecstasy of being in a magic city, Katherine goes back to the café has her food and one or two drinks, oblivious to the men sitting about in the same place. She returns to her rooms and begins to count her great capital of $41. Suddenly the door of her room is broken open and some one steals her capital. Katherine screams and rushes after the man, when she feels herself picked up and thrown down the flight of stairs. After a long time (it must have seemed very long to

Katherine) she comes to from her deadly faint and finds herself in a pool of blood with a gash in her forehead. She has forgotten her dream of twenty-nine years and even the loss of her $41 in her effort to scramble up the stairs and get into her room. There she lies for a week, with only the "kind landlady" to relieve her misery by a few cold compresses on her head and some wretched food to sustain her weakened condition.

After a week Katherine is back on her feet. A drudge is not accustomed to indulge in rest, even if deathly sick. She goes back to the streets of the magic city in a seedy state, to make her way to Yonkers. After miles of walking she gets to a vacant lot, faint with fatigue and hunger and takes a drink out of her flask to pull up sufficient strength to go further. But instead she falls asleep.

Suddenly she feels a burning pain in the sole of her foot and stares into the blurred eyes of a policeman. Katherine is arrested for vagrancy and drunkenness and given sixty days in the workhouse. That is the end of Katherine's dream of 29 years about New York. What grim and tragic material for a master brush or pen! But what does society do with Katherine? It casts her out on the dung heap called prisons. It neither has imagination nor humanity enough to grasp that Katherine's crime was only poverty, and how dare the poor have dreams?

Last, but not least, there are hundreds of drug victims who, thanks to the new law, are picked up every day, suddenly cut off from their habit, and thrust into jail for many months. There they are undernourished and indifferently left to fight out the mad craving which they have neither the strength nor vitality to overcome. When their time is up, their health is undermined; their will, never too strong, is completely broken. They cannot sustain their existence unless they have some stimulant, so they go back to their habit.

All these human pariahs find closed doors on their return to society. If they are not picked up by the police immediately, they are so within a very short time, and, again, the prison doors open and close upon them. After all, what would the authorities of New York and other cities do without these criminals? The Police Department, the Court, the District Attorney? They all thrive upon those whom poverty and ignorance drive into crime. The authorities cannot afford that crime should cease out of our midst, so they go on perpetuating our system which makes the criminal, and then hypocritically pretend that they are saving the system from the criminal.

Indeed, I am glad to have come close to this unfortunate human material. I found among them more humanity, a greater spirit of co-operation and helpfulness, than I would be likely to find among those who sit in judgment over them and send them to jail. Material which, if placed in a sane society, would do away with the terrible human waste and with all the tragedy and pain that is hidden away and barred "lest Christ should see how men their brothers maim."[5]

---

5. From Oscar Wilde's *Ballad of Reading Gaol*, part 5, stanza 3.

"READY TO GO
TO JAIL FOR
BIRTH-CONTROL"

Ben Reitman at the
Carnegie Hall Meeting

Sketched by
Boardman Robinson

Boardman Robinson's sketch of Ben Reitman speaking at the Carnegie Hall birth control meeting, 5 May 1916. (Bancroft Library, University of California, Berkeley)

Lastly, I have an additional proof, if proof were needed, that prison does not deter, that as far as the so-called common criminal is concerned, it does not cure him from the necessity of recommitting crimes. What else is he to do when he comes out with all the doors of society closed against him, without means of livelihood and without sympathy or understanding to greet him? Thus the prison is an endless circle wherein the prisoners move round and round, and all their prison experience does to them is to make them hate society more. True, they have no social background. Yet their hatred is sufficiently dangerous to undermine the ease of their tormenters.

As to the effect of prisons on criminals like myself, I do not have to tell you, dear friends, that it has only not lessened, but intensified, my devotion to our cause. The Birth Control agitation continues, now more than ever, even though a much heavier sentence was imposed upon our friend Ben Reitman than upon myself.[6] If the authorities were

6. On 8 May 1916 BR was sentenced to sixty days at Queens County Jail for distributing birth control pamphlets at his 23 April lecture.

foolish enough to think that they could stop it by giving me fifteen days or Reitman two months, they'll find themselves mistaken, as we have demonstrated in the marvelous meeting on Union Square, Saturday, May 20th, where a mass of humanity consisting of thousands clamored for Birth Control information.[7] So you see, dear comrades, that I am right in my appreciation of the service rendered by the authorities of New York to the Birth Control movement.

For the devotion and assistance you have given me, I could not, even if I tried, express what I feel. I hope to be able to prove to you through my actions what it has meant to me. I am starting out on my tour for the West on the first of June with a two-days stop in Cleveland and one day in Denver. Then for Los Angeles, where I hope to be until the early part of July. Letters will reach me there, care of Burbank Hall, 542 S. Main Street.

The work will continue until a free motherhood and a glorious childhood will be established. In this way we will set humanity free and create human arrangements which shall establish healthy and beautiful conditions for a healthy, beautiful and free race.

*Mother Earth* 11 (June 1916): 516–21.

7. EG, Anna Sloan, Leonard Abbott, Jessie Ashley, and Ida Rauh Eastman spoke about the birth control movement from a car in the midst of a huge crowd in Union Square, introduced by Bolton Hall. Jessie Ashley and Ida Rauh Eastman both read birth control information to the crowd, and numerous volunteers, both in the car and on the periphery of the crowd, distributed the birth control pamphlet *Why and How the Poor Should Not Have Many Children* and sold Margaret Sanger's *What Every Girl Should Know* and *What Every Mother Should Know*, as well as the June issue of the *Masses* (which included EG's speech at her 20 April trial).

My dearest Comrade:

I am terribly ashamed of myself to have kept you waiting so long for a reply to your wonderful letter and the enclosed contribution, which you so generously sent. It is only due to the fact that I was left with a lot of urgent work owing to the imprisonment of my comrade, Ben. L. Reitmann.[1] He has carried the brunt of the office and all of its details for 8 years on his back. I was almost beside myself with a thousand and one details connected with our office and the general propaganda, and as I had to prepare a number of lectures for my tour besides, you can readily imagine how much time there was left for anything else.

As I wrote you on a previous occasion, I could not, if I tried, express what your coming into my life has already meant or what it is going to mean.[2] I have had all sorts of people in my life; some have remained during my entire life and others have dropped out but somehow I was never so deeply moved as by your friendship and generosity. I think, perhaps, it is because I know what a terrible struggle you must have had. Yes indeed, it is a breach of *loyalty* on the part of those who call themselves radicals, not to join hands in a fight, especially if that fight is for Free Speech and Free Press, but then I have come across such things so often in my 26 years of experience, that I am no longer surprised. Most people that *who* call themselves radicals and socialists are so, only by name and not in their innermost beings. After all, no one can give more than he is capable and no one ought to expect more. Yes you are quite right, *when you say* only those are dangerous to the present society who propogate "direct action against *frightfulness* of the industrial conflict" and if anyone doubted that they had ample opportunity to convince themselves from the action of the authorities of New York. Because Rose Pastor Stokes[3] through her husband, is connected with the upper strata, the authorities did not proceed against her. Neither did they proceed against Ida Rauh Eastman and Jessie Ashley, although the two latter and with myself and others, stood up in an automobile in Union Square, Saturday May 20th and distributed 20,000 Birth Control circulars.[4]

---

1. On 8 May 1916 BR was sentenced to sixty days at Queens County Jail for distributing birth control pamphlets at his 23 April lecture.
2. In January 1916 EG attended one of Keller's lectures at Carnegie Hall in New York City. This could possibly have been her "Strike Against War" lecture delivered on 5 January under the auspices of the Women's Peace Party and the Labor Forum. See Letter to Helen Keller, 8 February 1916, above.
3. Rose Pastor Stokes (1879–1933) was a prominent socialist and wife of the wealthy reformer J. G. Phelps Stokes. At EG's birth control meeting on 5 May 1916 Stokes passed out birth control information but was never arrested.
4. Ida Rauh Eastman, Jessie Ashley, and Bolton Hall were all charged under Section 1142 of the New

Emma Goldman speaking in Union Square on 20 May 1916 to protest Ben Reitman's sentence of sixty days in Queens County Jail for distributing birth control literature. Although the audience appears to be composed of men, women were at the edges of the crowd distributing and receiving birth control information. (Library of Congress)

So in the last analysis the scapegoats continue to be anarchists. As I wrote to a friend only to-day if the time should come *when* I am no longer considered by the authorities "dangerous" I hope my friends will disown me. I hope I shall never live to see Anarchism become thoroughly respectable, for then I shall have to look for a new ideal.

Thank you again for your wonderful spirit and solidarity. One can afford to face the whole world with one like you for a friend. I am going to Los Angeles for a month where you can reach me c/o Burbank Hall, 542 So. Main Street, Los Angeles, Cal. After that for a month in San Francisco. In August I expect to go to Portland, Seattle, and cities on the way, and probably land in Denver early in September. I should love to see you

York State Law for handing out birth control information at the 20 May Union Square meeting. Ashley was tried on 30 October and was fined $50. Ida Rauh Eastman's and Bolton Hall's cases were eventually dismissed. See Letter in *Mother Earth*, June 1916, above; Letter to Anna Strunsky-Walling, 8 July 1916, below; and Letter to the *New York Evening Telegram*, 26 October 1916, below.

on the way and hope you will keep in touch with me, so I can keep you posted about my movements.

On your return to New York you will find a lot of anti-military spirit. Several of us got together to begin an anti-militarist campaign[5] but I could not stay long enough to take charge of it. I suppose our friends will see you about it.

Wishing you a joyous and restful summer, I remain

Deeply Devoted
Your friend and Comrade,
Emma Goldman

P S. En route to Denver. I had to finish this on the train, as the friend who took dictation did not finish the letter until late yesterday. That also explains the corrections.[6]

Faithfully
EG

TLS, Helen Keller Archives, AFB. Addressed to Miss Helen Keller, Wrantham, Mass. Autograph postscript.

5. *Mother Earth* began advertising anti-militarist literature in the May 1916 issue, including EG's pamphlets *Preparedness: The Road to Universal Slaughter* and *Patriotism: A Menace to Liberty*, Kropotkin's *War and Capitalism*, and George Barrett's *The Last War*. The advertisement ran in *Mother Earth* for the rest of 1916. The only article on the anti-militarist campaign, "Good Prospects for Anti-Militarism," appeared in the August 1916 issue.
6. In the transcription of this document, italicized words indicate EG's handwritten insertions to the typewritten letter.

My dearest Anna:

I was very glad to get your letter. No, I did not know your condition or I certainly should have refrained from asking you to participate in the activities of last spring in N. Y. What a strange girl you are to have so many kiddies, especially when you go through such a terrible ordeal during pregnancy. I can only hope that you really enjoy the whole procedure, and that your kiddies are strong and look upon life with a great deal of cheer. However, I understood that if you did not write or come it is because you had reasons for it. I have too much faith in you to ever doubt you.

I am closing a month's interesting work in this city. Have had a good attendance to all meetings, but the largest last Sunday on Birth Control.[1] It's almost phenomenal how this issue has attracted the attention of the people. I cannot begin to tell you the hundreds I receive and their pathetic nature. I wish I could have three meetings in the largest hall of every city, and besides that that I could go from village to village. I believe that there is nothing the people need so much as the knowledge of how to prevent bringing undesirable and undesired children to the world. I am to repeat the lecture tomorrow night, so great is the demand. I then go to San Francisco for a month, where I will be at the Gordon Alexander Apartments, 601 Sacramento Street.

We are going to make a big campaign for Ida Rauh and Bolton Hall.[2] I am sure she will get a postponement. Hall's trial comes up on the 7th of October, and I expect Ida's will take place about the same time. We certainly must do our utmost to have a victorious fight, and that can only be accomplished by a campaign of publicity and agitation.

---

1. On 2 July EG lectured on "Free or Enforced Motherhood: The Necessity for Birth Control." She repeated the lecture the following week, on 9 July, due to popular demand.
2. Ida Rauh Eastman's case, stemming from her participation in the 20 May Union Square demonstration in which she handed out birth control information, was set for 20 July but was postponed and eventually dismissed when it came to trial eighteen months later. Bolton Hall was also arrested and tried on similar charges stemming from the same event. Apparently there was widespread support of Hall and Eastman, as indicated by a petition submitted to District Attorney Edward Swann of New York City from "the men and women of Los Angeles," written on 2 July 1916, the same night that EG lectured in Los Angeles on "Free or Enforced Motherhood: The Necessity for Birth Control." The petition praised Hall and Eastman as "two people who have for years devoted themselves to the cause of human betterment" and demanded their release, adding "Be it further resolved that we pledge our support to the Birth Control Movement and to those who bravely stand the brunt in behalf of a healthier and better race." Bolton Hall's case also was discharged. See Letter to the *New York Evening Telegram*, 26 October 1916, below.

I hope, dear, that you will be feeling better from now on, and that you will have a comparatively restful and enjoyable summer.

WITH LOTS OF LOVE,
EMMA GOLDMAN

TLS, Anna Strunsky-Walling Papers, CtY-B. Addressed to Mrs. Anna Strunsky Walling, Nantucket, Massachusetts.

My dear Comrade:

. I was glad to get your letter of June 25th. I tried to write you several times but somehow "the spirit would not work." I had a very hard month in Los Angeles, partly because of the details of the meetings, which I had to attend to myself, being without Ben, and mainly because of a maddening attack of toothache trouble. Both are over now, so I will not worry you with an account. However, I want you to know that I had a successful stay; and also that for the first time in twenty years I had a few days to see the marvels of Southern California. I was always so rushed for time in the past that I never could allow myself a few days vacation. I did the trick this time and I was drunk with the beauty and the gorgeousness of Mlle. Nature. How little we in the East know of America and its vast possibilities!

The most important phase of my stay in Los Angeles was getting out the Magon Brothers on bail.[1] Both of the men are sick and have been languishing in that rotten County jail since March. Our people tried hard enough to get them out on bail but failed. They were convicted and sentenced while I was in the city. Their case was appealed and they were about to be shipped to San Quentin to rot for a year or eighteen months, while the appeal was pending; so there was nothing else to do but launch right into what seemed an insurmountable task, but we succeeded. Much to my amazement I discovered among my Los Angeles subscribers several people of considerable means, and I must say they came up handsomely. Evidently, Mother Earth has done something for them, so it is not living in vain.

I wish you would have been with me the evening when the Magons, their families and twenty other Mexicans gave me a banquet on a large field under the blue sky, and with their marvelous spirit of comradeship and solidarity to give the affair color and beauty.[2] It would have made you forget all the hopelessness of the mob you describe

---

1. Ricardo and Enrique Flores Magón were arrested and jailed on 18 February 1916 for using the mails to distribute material "tending to incite murder, arson, and treason" for articles they had written for *Regeneración*. (W. C. Owen was also indicted but evaded arrest because he happened to be in Washington State at the time, later fleeing to New York, then to London.) The trial began 31 May; both were found guilty and sentenced on 22 June 1916. Enrique received three years while, owing to his ill health, Ricardo's sentence was limited to one year and one day. *Mother Earth* printed appeals for assistance for the Magón brothers, as well as a reprint of a letter to EG from Enrique (written during their trial), and their statement upon sentencing. On 26 June EG and AB posted bail, giving the Magóns momentary freedom while they awaited their appeal.
2. The banquet was held 6 July at Ivanhoe Reservoir, near Silver Lake Reservoir, outside of Los Angeles. EG also mentioned this event in "Stray Thoughts" in the August 1916 *Mother Earth*.

marching in the preparedness parade in your city. Really, dear Comrade, only the primitive people have a real appreciation of comradeship. No wonder the Mexicans have been able to hold out so long in their struggle for Land and Liberty.

Your letter seemed very downcast. I do not blame you for being disgusted with the cowardice of the mass; but nevertheless you are mistaken when you say that the people joined the preparedness circus voluntarily. I know that pressure was brought to bear upon the workers nearly everywhere, in some places more direct than in others. They were threatened with their jobs and positions if they will not march. And while both give them not enough to live on, still they submitted to the pressure.

Your surprise over the American government and its change of policy with regard to Mexico[3] proves to me what a poison Democracy really is if it can have deceived even you. To have had faith in Wilson[4] shows to me how misleading the whole structure of government in America is. You are not the only one, dear Comrade, who was mislead. I must say that I was not deceived for a single moment. One has but to look at the smug face of Wilson to know that he is a hypocrite and cannot be trusted.

I suppose you have read the latest issue of <u>Everyman</u>. Poor Luke North,[5] he acts like a huckster, whose measley shop is endangered by competition. There you have the great friendships, which last only so long until you dare be yourself, and these radical friends come down with a sledge hammer. The joke of it is that I know no more about Berkman's article[6] than the man in the moon. In fact, I didn't even know of "The Great Adventure" until I came to Los Angeles. Not that I do not agree with Aleck's criticism; but fancy a man calling himself a radical, holding me responsible for what someone else does! Of course I do not mind his petty attack in <u>Everyman</u>. But I confess I was disgusted with Luke North when he refused to preside at the Magon meeting, although he was President of the Defense League. But then, why waste time on such small people?

Ben has gone on to Chicago and will leave from there for the Coast on Wednesday.

---

3. In March 1916 the United States changed the policy of nonintervention it had applied to the Mexican Revolution following Pancho Villa's raids in northern Mexico and Columbus, New Mexico. On 15 March 1916 President Woodrow Wilson ordered General John J. Pershing and 6,000 men into Mexico, a strategic interventionist stance that received congressional approval.

4. Disregarding the pressure from American and European business interests, President Woodrow Wilson opposed intervention in the Mexican Revolution in favor of a policy of "watchful waiting." In April 1914, however, he reversed his stance, taking a more aggressive role in the Mexican war.

5. In the July 1916 issue of Luke North's Los Angeles–based magazine *Everyman* he published an article titled "The Wide Open Conspiracy." The article was largely favorable to EG and *Mother Earth*, in spite of his criticism of her positive assessment of Nietzsche and of the militant political tactics of AB, especially his attempt on the life of Henry Clay Frick.

6. AB's article titled "The Great Adventure" in the 1 June 1916 issue of *The Blast* was a two-pronged criticism of the Great Adventure, a single-tax movement led by Luke North and Herman Kuehn in Los Angeles to add an amendment incorporating the single tax to the California constitution. AB asserted that real social change could not be achieved through the machinery of the state or courts and that the central problem was not the monopolization of land but rather the "monopoly of the mechanical means of production and distribution," which must be addressed as well.

Needless to say I am very glad, as it is the first time in eight years that I have been separated from the boy for ten weeks. He was the spirit of the work during all that time, so I am glad that he will take charge of it again. He has had rather a bad reaction since he came out. Has been terribly depressed, I think because he made a brave effort to be cheerful and adjust himself to the horrors of jail.

You have the July number so you know that your article about the Irish rebellion[7] finally got in. The idea of you suggesting that I wouldn't bring the article because I will not agree with your conclusion about violence. I wonder if you can write something for the August issue. If so, please send it to the office as soon as possible. It ought to be there about the 26th or 7th; and send me a copy. How about writing something on the change of heart on the part of the Administration, or any subject you feel deeply about? You know I believe that it is the only thing we can write well about, anyway. Will be glad to hear from you again soon. Kindest regards to Luther. Love to the children.

Fraternally,

Emma

TLS, Emma Goldman Archive, IISH.

7. Van Valkenburgh's "The Echo from Erin" was published in the July 1916 *Mother Earth*. In it he suggested that education rather than violence would bring about a united Ireland. The article ends with this assessment of the Easter uprising: "Their fruitless sacrifices should give courage and stimulation to the pursuit of more efficient means of casting off tyrannical authority at the cheapest possible price to the people."

My dear Ellen:—

I got your good letter yesterday, and while I have the chance, I hasten to reply. I know you will be glad to learn that for the moment, at least, Sasha and Fitzie are safe.[1] But one never knows what the wretched police will do next. I shall be more at ease after the new number of THE BLAST is out as I am worried that the authorities may proceed against. Not so much as for the material, but for the very powerful cartoon which Bob Minor has made.[2] But then, if one is to stop to consider what the authorities will do, it will be utterly impossible to go ahead with the work. We have always found it best to let the authorities go to hell and do our work in our own way.

The few weeks since July 22d have been a veritable hell. My meetings were poorly attended, and the audiences terrorized to such an extent that I failed to lift them out of it except for rare occasions.[3] I confess that I never was happier to get through with the meetings than I have been in the experience here. I am leaving for Portland on Sunday, and while I shall be glad to be out of California, I will be more anxious away than if I were here. There is not any doubt that the authorities are bound to hang our men. It will require a tremendous amount of effort to counteract the conspiracy of the Chamber of Commerce,[4] the Hearst outfit[5] and the police. Naturally, I should want to be on the spot to

---

1. On 22 July 1916 a bomb exploded during the Preparedness Day parade on Market Street in downtown San Francisco, killing ten people and injuring several others. Local police immediately rounded up and detained some of the city's most prominent radicals, searched the offices of *The Blast*, and threatened to arrest AB and M. Eleanor Fitzgerald. District Attorney Charles Fickert publicly alleged that AB was part of a radical conspiracy along with Thomas Mooney and Warren Billings, who, with others, were arrested a few days after the bombing and charged with first-degree murder.

2. Robert Minor's illustration for the cover of the 15 August 1916 *Blast* portrays "Preparedness" as a hulking figure in a military cap clutching rifle and bombs amidst cannons and supplicants. The caption reads "Worshiping the God of Dynamite."

3. EG lectured in San Francisco from 16 July and left the city on 13 August.

4. The San Francisco Chamber of Commerce was a conservative business group working in tandem with the police and detectives to find and prosecute those responsible for the bomb.

5. William Randolph Hearst (1863–1951), a newspaper publisher and politician, who owned and operated a number of newspapers and periodicals, including the *San Francisco Examiner*, the *New York Evening Journal*, and the *Chicago Examiner*. He was reputed to have sensationalized journalism by featuring lavish photographs and instituting the practice of banner headlines in his papers. Twice elected to the U.S. House of Representatives from New York City, he lost the election for governor of New York in 1906.

help, but I cannot do that unless, of course, Sasha should get into trouble. Then I should come back, no matter what happens.

We have accomplished a few things. One being that we got the Labor Unions to come out in favor of the men. The other that a defense committee was organized with Bob Minor as Secretary.[6] The third, that we induced a well-known lawyer[7] of the city to see Mooney, who was the only one so far without any assistance at all. You see Mooney had been considered a sort of a black sheep by the Labor forces here, except for a small minority of rebel workers in the Unions, because he is a tremendous fighter and radical.[8] But I am convinced that gradually the more thoughtful element of the Labor Unions will back him as well as the others. And by heavens it will be necessary in order to save them all.

Very soon a statement will be gotten out for the press. Some of it will be sent to you with the hope that you may be able through the newspaper women of Denver to get some publicity. I tell you, Dear, that it will be absolutely necessary to combine forces all over the country to save the men. It is a clear repitition of the 11th of November[9] since that time. The authorities know perfectly well that they do not have the right men, just because of it, they will use every crooked means to send those they have to the gallows. But we are not going to let them. And if we all combine, we are bound to succeed.

I may be able to come to Denver the latter part of August. I have decided once more to give up Yellowstone Park, partly because it is really too late to enjoy a stay there late in August, and also it would seem criminal to me to spend $100 or $150 at a time when THE BLAST is pushed to the wall and money is needed for the boys. I really couldn't enjoy it. So it is most likely I will be with you the last part of August rather than the time I had planned. Also I have great doubts about Seattle as our friends there find it so difficult to get a hall. If I fail to get suitable quarters in that city, I shall not go to Seattle at all, but will go directly from Portland to Denver.[10] Please go up to Marble Hall and see if the dates the last part of August to the 3d of September, inclusive are open, and what the lowest rental will be for a series of eleven lectures. That will give me a chance to deliver the Russian Course, and four on general topics.

6. By 10 September 1916 twenty-nine unions were represented by the International Workers' Defense League in San Francisco, including the Cigar Makers' Union No. 88, the Millmen's Union Nos. 42 and 550, the Piledrivers' Union No. 77, and the Waiters' Union No. 30.

7. Maxwell McNutt, who served as the lead attorney for the defense in the cases of both Mooney and Billings, visited Mooney in jail one week after the grand jury handed down indictments on 1 August 1916.

8. Thomas Mooney took part in several militant strikes in San Francisco, including a failed strike, on 14 July 1916, against the United Railroads of San Francisco, which created substantial animosity toward Mooney by business interests in the city.

9. The 11 November 1887 date was the execution date of the Chicago anarchists convicted of murder after the 1886 bombing in Haymarket Square.

10. EG did, in fact, speak in Seattle after 23 August, between her appearances in Portland and Denver.

Ben and I leave here Sunday. Write me General Delivery Portland, as you will not be able to reach me here in time. There are lots of things I would like to write you, but THE BLAST will be out tomorrow, and as it contains all that happened since the 22d, you will get an idea of everything. Remember me to all our friends.

AFFECTIONATELY,
EMMA


Dear Ellen Kennan:—

I am writing this letter for Emma. I want you to know that your little note of cheer and sympathy was gladly received. We have had a hard wearing week, but are still on top, and out of jail. I am very tired, though, from the experience. It would have done you good to see me trying to convert the Chief of Police and head detectives of the Bomb Bureau[11] and District Attorneys. But it is useless. Such an ignorant outfit I never came in contact with before. They belong to the cave men type, with no ideas at all of modern ideas, and people who really stand for something. I often think of you and love you much. Greet all the friends for me. Much love. Fitzie[12]

TLS, Emma Goldman Archive, IISH.


11. The San Francisco Bomb Bureau, founded on 23 July 1916, was headed by Captain Matheson and had more than a dozen detectives and officers assigned to it. The bureau speculated about the identities of the suspected bombers, eventually settling on Warren Billings, Thomas Mooney, Rena Mooney, Edward D. Nolan, and Israel Weinberg.
12. This note was written by M. Eleanor Fitzgerald.

"You and I Cannot Live in the Same Land," Robert Minor cover of the 1 July 1916 issue of *The Blast* portraying the government (in the wake of preparedness for war) cutting the throat of the free press (*The Blast*).

**Essay in *THE BLAST***

*San Francisco, 15 August 1916*

## Down with the Anarchists!

We must get rid of the Anarchists! They are a menace to society. Does not Hearst say so? Do not the M. & M.[1] and the gentlemen of the Chamber of Commerce, who have also declared war on Labor, assure us that the Anarchists are dangerous and that they are responsible for all our troubles? Does not every skinner of Labor and every grafting politician shout against the Anarchists? Isn't that enough to prove that the Anarchists are dangerous?

But why are all the money bags and their hirelings so unanimous in condemning the Anarchists? Generally they disagree on many questions and they bitterly fight each other in their business and social life. But on TWO questions they are always in accord.

What are those two questions that all the capitalists and profit mongers are always in perfect agreement on? They are these:

Smash the Labor Unions!

Hang the Anarchists!

WHY? Because the Labor Unions are cutting the bosses' profits by constantly demanding higher wages. And the Anarchists want to abolish the boss altogether.

Now, what is the matter with the Anarchists? What do you really know about them, except the lies and misrepresentations of their enemies—who are also the enemies of the workers and opposed to every advancement of Labor? If you stop to think of it, you really know nothing of the Anarchists and their teachings. Your masters and their press have taken good care that you shouldn't learn the truth about them. Why? Because as long as they can keep you busy shouting against the Anarchists, they are safe in their saddle on the backs of the people.

That's the whole secret.

What do the Anarchists really want? When you know that, you will be able to decide for yourself whether the Anarchists are your enemies or your friends.

The Anarchists say that it is not necessary to have murder and crime, poverty and

---

1. A reference to the Merchants and Manufacturers Associations of Los Angeles and San Francisco and the *San Francisco Examiner*, owned by William Randolph Hearst. Harrison Gray Otis, owner of the *Los Angeles Times*, was an important member of the Los Angeles Merchants and Manufacturers Association, which campaigned for the open shop and "industrial freedom." AB and EG believed that the San Francisco Merchant and Manufacturers Association was behind the frame-up of Mooney, Billings, and the others arrested.

corruption in the world. They say that we are cursed with these evils because a handful of people have monopolized the earth and all the wealth of the country. But who produces that wealth? Who builds the railroads, who digs the coal, who works in the fields and factories? You can answer that question for yourself. It is the toilers who do all the work and who produce all that we have in the world.

The Anarchists say: The products of Labor should belong to the producers. The Industries should be carried on to minister to the needs of the people instead of for profit, as at present. Abolishing monopoly in land and in the sources of production, and making the opportunity for production accessible to all, would do away with capitalism and introduce free and equal distribution. That, in turn, would do away with laws and government, as there would be no need for them, government serving only to conserve the institutions of today and to protect the masters in their exploitation of the people. It would abolish war and crime, because the incentive to either would be lacking. It would be a society of real freedom, without coercion or violence, based on the voluntary communal arrangement of "To each according to his needs; from each according to his ability."

That is what the Anarchists teach. Suppose they are all wrong. Are you going to prove it by hanging them? If they are wrong, the people will not accept their ideas, and therefore there can be no danger from them. But, if they are right, it would be good for us to find it out. In any case it is a question of learning what these Anarchists really want. Let the people hear them.

But how about violence? you say. Don't the Anarchists preach and practice violence and murder?

They don't. On the contrary, the Anarchists hold life as the most sacred thing. That's why they want to change the present order of things where everyone's hand is against his brother, and where war, wholesale slaughter in the pursuit of the dollar, bloodshed in the field, factory and workshop is the order of the day. The poverty, misery and bitter industrial warfare, the crimes, suicides and murder committed every day of the year in this country will convince any man of intelligence that in present society we have plenty of Law, but mighty little order or peace.

Anarchism means OPPOSITION to violence, by whomever committed, even if it be by the government. The government has no more right to murder than the individual. Anarchism is therefore opposition to violence as well as to government forcibly imposed on man.

The Anarchists value human life. In fact, no one values it more. Why, then, are the Anarchists always blamed for every act of violence? Because your rulers and exploiters want to keep you prejudiced against the Anarchists, so you will never find out what the Anarchists really want, and the masters will remain safe in their monopoly of life.

Now, what are the facts about violence? Crimes of every kind happen every day. Are the Anarchists responsible for them? Or is it not rather misery and desperation that drive people to commit such acts? Does a millionaire go out on the street and knock you down with a gaspipe to rob you of a few dollars? O, no. He builds a factory and robs his workers in a way that is much safer, more profitable and within the law.

Who, then, commits acts of violence? The desperate man, of course. He to whom no other resort seems open. Violence is committed by all kinds of people. Such violence is mostly for the purpose of theft or robbery. But there are also cases where it is done for social reasons. Such impersonal acts of violence have, from time immemorial, been the reply of goaded and desperate classes, and goaded the desperate individualists, to wrong from their fellow-men, which they felt to be intolerable. Such acts are the violent RECOIL from violence, whether aggressive or repressive; they are the last desperate struggle of outraged and exasperated human nature for breathing space and life. And their CAUSE LIES NOT IN ANY SPECIAL CONVICTION, BUT IN HUMAN NATURE ITSELF. The whole course of history, political and social, is strewn with evidence of this fact. To go no further, take the Revolutionists of Russia,[2] the Fenians and Sinn Feiners of Ireland,[3] the Republicans of Italy.[4] Were those people Anarchists? No. Did they all hold the same political opinions? No. But all were driven by desperate circumstances into this terrible form of revolt.[5]

Anarchists, as well as others, have sometimes committed acts of violence. Do you hold the Republican Party, or the Presbyterian or Methodist Church responsible for acts of individual members? It would be stupid to do so.

Under miserable conditions of life, any vision of the possibility of better things makes the present misery more intolerable, and spurs those who suffer to the most energetic struggles to improve their lot, and if these struggles only immediately result in sharper misery, the outcome is sheer desperation. In our present society, for instance, an exploited wage worker, who catches a glimpse of what work and life might and ought to be, finds the toilsome routine and the squalor of his existence almost intolerable; and even when he has the resolution and courage to continue steadily working his best, and waiting until new ideas have so permeated society as to pave the way for better times, the mere fact that he has such ideas and tries to spread them brings him into difficulties with his employers. How many thousands of rebel workers, of Socialists, of Industrialists and Syndicalists, but above all of Anarchists, have lost work and even the chance of work, solely on the ground of their opinions? It is only the specially gifted craftsman who, if he be a zealous propagandist, can hope to retain permanent employment. And what hap-

2. EG refers to the revolutionists in Russia as "Social Democrats" or "Constitutionalists" in her *The Psychology of Political Violence*, Essay published by Mother Earth Publishing Association, 1911, above.

3. EG refers to the Fenians, a mid-nineteenth-century Irish nationalist organization that attempted insurrections against the British in 1867, as "political separatists" in her essay *The Psychology of Political Violence*. Sinn Féin, Gaelic for "we ourselves," is the name of an Irish nationalist political party founded in 1905 for the purpose of freeing Ireland from the political control of Britain. On 24 April 1916 the Irish Republican Brotherhood began an armed insurrection in Dublin, demanding home rule for Ireland. The British government wrongly mislabeled this action, also known as the Easter Rising, as led by Sinn Féin.

4. EG refers to the Mazzinians in Italy as republicans in *The Psychology of Political Violence*.

5. This paragraph with minor changes, starting with the sentence "Such impersonal acts of violence have . . ." was taken directly from EG's 1911 essay *The Psychology of Political Violence*, published by Mother Earth Publishing Association (1911); see above for a transcription.

pens to a man with his brain working actively with a ferment of new ideas, with a vision before his eyes of a new hope dawning for fellows in misery is not caused by the cruelty of fate, but by the injustice of other human beings—what happens to such a man when he sees those dear to him starving, when he himself is starved? Some natures in such a plight, and those by no means the least social or the least sensitive, will become violent, and will even feel that their violence is social and not anti-social, that in striking when and how they can, they are striking, not for themselves, but for human nature, outraged and despoiled in their persons and in those of their fellow sufferers. And are we, who ourselves are not in this horrible predicament, to stand by and coldly condemn these piteous victims of the Furies and Fates? Are we to decry as miscreants these human beings who act with heroic self-devotion, often sacrificing their lives in protest, where less social and less energetic natures would lie down and grovel in abject submission to injustice and wrong? Are we to join the ignorant and brutal outcry which stigmatizes such men as monsters of wickedness, gratuitously running amuck in a harmonious and innocently peaceful society? NO! We hate murder with a hatred that may seem absurdly exaggerated to apologists for war, industrial slaughter and Ludlow massacres,[6] to callous acquiescers in governmental and plutocratic violence, but we decline in such cases of homicide as those of which we are treating, to be guilty of the cruel injustice of flinging the whole responsibility of the deed upon the immediate perpetrator. The guilt of these homicides lies upon every man and woman who, intentionally or by cold indifference, helps to keep up social conditions that drive human beings to despair. The man who flings his whole life into the attempt, often at the cost of his own life, to protest against the wrongs of his fellow-men, is a saint compared to the active and passive upholders of cruelty and injustice, even if his protest destroys other lives besides his own. Let him who is without sin in society cast the first stone at such a one.

*THE BLAST* GROUP
GROUP FREEDOM
ITALIAN ANARCHIST GROUP VOLONTA
UNION OF RUSSIAN WORKERS
Per ALEXANDER BERKMAN
EMMA GOLDMAN

*The Blast* (San Francisco), 15 August 1916, pp. 5–7. "Down with the Anarchists" was a popular title used by anarchists in the United States, beginning with the publication of a pamphlet by Johann Most around the turn of the twentieth century. It had also been the title of leaflet number 3 produced by the Anarchist Federation of New York in May 1908 (printed as "To Our Enemies" in the March 1908 edition of *Mother Earth*). This article from *The Blast* was reprinted in leaflet form.

6. On 20 April 1913 Colorado National Guardsmen volleyed machine-gun fire into the union tent village in Ludlow, Colorado. At least five miners, twelve children, and two women were killed. See "Preparedness, the Road to Universal Slaughter," Article in *Mother Earth*, December 1915, above.

## To the *NEW YORK EVENING TELEGRAM*

*New York, 26 October 1916*

DEAR SIR:

If you have any doubt of the tremendous growth of the birth control movement—the desperate methods employed by the New York Police Department in dealing with the birth control advocates should dispel that doubt. Not only do the police arrest everyone who openly discuss or distribute birth control information, but they frameup charges against innocent victims. Of course, perjury is nothing new with the police department, so it may not surprise you to learn that the old staid method is again being used in the most flagrant manner.

Friday, October 20, I was subpoenaed to appear as a witness for Mr. Bolton Hall, in his trial before Special Sessions, Department Six, for having distributed birth control circulars at the Union Square meeting on May 20.[1] Mr Hall was acquitted. Together with a number of friends, I left the court-house about 5:P.M., and had barely gotten to the sidewalk when I was arrested by Detective Price. When he was asked to show a warrant he said "it was unnecessary, that I was in his charge and would have to come along." Knowing from the past that a detective, even like the "Russian Black Hundred," is absolute, I went along to the Elizabeth Street station-house, and was there placed under $1,000.00 bail for having distributed birth control leaflets at the Union Square meeting May 20. Evidently the detective took no heed to the overwhelming testimony brought to bear in behalf of Mr. Bolton Hall, a testimony which, of course, will also be brought to bear in my behalf; ie, that neither Mr. Hall nor myself distributed birth control leaflets. The detectives were in a frameup and they straightway proceeded to carry out their decision.

You will recollect that last April, I was arrested for having given out birth control information; that I was tried and found guilty and that I preferred going to the Queen's County Jail rather than pay a fine of $100.00. With that in view it is hardly necessary for me to emphasize that I believe in the birth control issue, and that I believe in the necessity of giving people information. In other words, I am willing to take the consequences if I have been guilty of what the law pleases to call an offence. But as it is, I have not given out the circulars and, of course, do not intend to be arrested and thrown into jail simply because the New York detectives want to foolishly crown themselves with laurels of stemming the tide of the birth control agitation.

I am coming up for a hearing at the Fourth District Court, 57th Street, between

---

1. See Letter to Anna Strunsky Walling, 8 July 1916, note 2, above.

Lexington and Third Avenues, before Judge Barlow, October 27, at 10 O'clock A.M. I shall have with me numerous representatives men and women of New York City who have attended the meeting and are therefore in a position to testify whether, or not, I have given out the circulars. It therefore remains to be seen whether a judge on the New York Bench will prefer to take the testimony of a detective or men and women, well-known in professional and public affairs of our city. Should I be held for trial, I will, of course, bring the case before Special Sessions, or even higher, if need be. Somebody simply must put a stop to the unscrupulous methods of detectives who inconvenience, hound, persecute and arrest people without any redress whatever for those who have to suffer at the hands of the representatives of the law.

Will you call the attention of your readers to this new outrage which, of course, is only one of the many which happen every day in New York City, with this exception, that while the unfortunate victims are not able to expose the police methods, I am and I am of course, determined to do so.[2]

Yours truly,
Emma Goldman

TLU, Agnes Inglis Papers, MiU. Addressed to City Editor, *Evening Telegram*.

2. EG sent a similar letter to the editor of the *New York Evening Post*. She changed the last sentence to "that while the unfortunate victims are not in a position to expose the police methods but I am, and I intend to do so."

Cover of the 15 July 1916 issue of *The Blast,* working men portrayed as casualties of war preparedness.

From **MINNIE PARKHURST RIMER** in *MOTHER EARTH*

*Seattle, 6 November 1916*

# From the Battle Field of the Social War

My Dear Emma:

Hell Broke Loose in this part of the country yesterday as you have seen by the papers.[1]

I saw a telegram to-day from Ben, pledging support.[2] I am glad indeed to know he and you are so prompt and thoughtful. This is the time encouragement is needed.

My heart is very heavy to-day when I look at five of the I.W.W. boys, lying in the city morgue, young and beautiful specimens of manhood, just come in from the harvest fields many of them, and 48 more in the hospital, 20 of whom may die. But they are a splendid lot to-day at the Hall. I see no tears there to-day but a smile instead and a determined look.

Three[3] of the law and order squad in Everett are dead and 19 in the hospital.

We here have been denied the privilege of seeing either the wounded or those in jail of which there are 297. Habeas corpus proceedings were started to-day, so by Wednesday we will be able to see our prisoners.

---

1. On 30 October 1916 IWW members traveled by boat from Seattle to Everett to support striking shingle weavers in their conflict with company strike breakers and to assert the right of free speech. They were met at the dock by the local sheriff and his deputies and subsequently beaten by vigilantes. The IWW scheduled a meeting in Everett on 5 November to protest the police-sanctioned brutality of the vigilantes. More than 250 IWW members who returned to Everett on 5 November by boat were met with gunfire at the dock from deputies forewarned of the boat's arrival. Five IWW members were killed: Abraham Rabinowitz, Hugo Gerlot, Gustav Johnson, John Looney, and Felix Baran. Twenty-seven other IWW members were wounded, two deputies were killed, and twenty other local authorities were wounded. Who fired the first shot is still unknown. Upon the return of the boat to Seattle, seventy-four IWW members were arrested—one of whom was tried and later acquitted—for the first-degree murder of Deputy Jefferson Beard. Fred H. Moore was the chief counsel for the IWW defense. A massive publicity campaign mobilized national support for the defense of the arrested IWW members and resulted in their cases being dismissed in May 1917.
2. Minnie Parkhurst Rimer was a member of the IWW and founder of the Workers' Defense League of Seattle. She helped organize EG's meetings in Seattle in August 1915 and August to September 1916. From 1917 to 1919 she served as secretary to the Seattle Birth Control League. EG reprinted a second letter from Rimer (who after 1918 appears to have used her surname Parkhurst exclusively) in the June 1917 issue of Mother Earth. The letter reported on the link between the May Day events in Seattle and both the trial of the Everett strikers and the Mooney-Billings case in San Francisco.
3. Actually, two were killed. Lieutenant Charles O. Curtiss, a lumber company office manager, died instantly, and Deputy Sheriff Jefferson Beard died the next day.

Telegrams are coming from all over the country pledging support.

Affectionately,
Minnie Rimer

*Mother Earth* 11 (December 1916): 697.

Emma Goldman, ca. 1916.

**1910**

EARLY JANUARY

Fred Schulder unsuccessfully attempted to gain permission for EG to speak in Buffalo, New York.

JANUARY 3

Police Commissioner Croul informed BR that EG would not be allowed to speak in Detroit, Michigan.

JANUARY 9–10

EG lectured on Francisco Ferrer in **Cleveland**, Ohio.

JANUARY 12–15

EG was scheduled to lecture in **Toledo**, Ohio.

JANUARY 14

The January 1910 issue of *Mother Earth* was held by the postmaster because of Anthony Comstock's complaint about EG's essay "The White Slave Traffic," under Section 497 of the Postal Laws and Regulations Act of 1902. EG and AB were not informed of the hold and were alerted only by the complaints of subscribers who failed to receive the magazine.

JANUARY 17

EG spoke in the afternoon and evening on "Woman Suffrage" at German Hod Carriers' Hall in **Chicago**, Illinois.

JANUARY 23

EG lectured on "Francisco Ferrer and the Modern School" and "The Drama, the Most Powerful Disseminator of Radicalism" at

Freie Gemeinde Hall, 264 Fourth Street, in **Milwaukee**, Wisconsin. BR also spoke on "The Struggle for Free Speech."

JANUARY 24

EG was scheduled to speak in German on "White Slave Traffic in This and European Countries" in **Milwaukee**.

JANUARY 26

EG spoke on the difference between students in the United States and Russia in the afternoon to the socialist club of the University of Wisconsin in **Madison**. BR discussed "The Educator and the Advocate." In the evening she spoke at the Knights of Pythias Hall in **Madison**.

AB accompanied Anthony Comstock to the office of the district attorney to inquire about the hold of the January 1910 issue of *Mother Earth* by the post office. Inspector-in-Charge W. S. Mayer decided that the magazine included nothing legally objectionable. The following morning the *New York Times* reported that Comstock claimed the incident was a publicity scheme for *Mother Earth*.

JANUARY 27

EG spoke on "The Drama as a Disseminator of Revolutionary Ideas" and "Love and Marriage from an Anarchist Perspective" at the Knights of Pythias Hall in **Madison**.

JANUARY 29

The January 1910 issue of *Mother Earth* was released by the post office after Comstock was forced to withdraw his objections to "The White Slave Traffic."

**JANUARY 30**

Moses Harman died.

**JANUARY 31**

EG lectured in **Hannibal**, Missouri. The meeting was organized by the sole anarchist in Hannibal, A. H. Garner. The police insisted on taking the names of all who attended.

**FEBRUARY 2**

EG spoke on "Ferrer and the Modern School" at Druid's Hall, 9th and Market Streets, in **St. Louis**, Missouri.

**FEBRUARY 3**

EG was scheduled for an afternoon lecture either on "Woman Suffrage" or "The Modern Drama as a Revolutionary Agency" at Druid's Hall in **St. Louis**. At 8:15 p.m. she spoke on "Leo Tolstoy the Last Great Christian" at the Music and Arts Building, 347 Broadway, in **St. Louis**.

**FEBRUARY 4**

EG was scheduled to lecture in German on "The White Slave Traffic in America" at Druid's Hall in **St. Louis**.

**FEBRUARY 5**

EG spoke on "Art in Relation to Life" at Artists' Guild on Union Boulevard in **St. Louis**.

**FEBRUARY 6**

EG was scheduled to lecture on "Preachers and Purity" at 3 p.m. and in the evening on "The Drama," with special reference to local St. Louis events, at Druid's Hall in **St. Louis**. The evening lecture topics included Tolstoy's *Power of Darkness*, Ibsen's *Brand*, Galsworthy's *Strife*, Hauptmann's *Before Sunrise* and *Lonely Souls*, Gorky's *Pit*, Wedekind's *Spring's Awakening*, and Shaw's *Major Barbara*.

**FEBRUARY 10**

EG lectured at, and was entertained with BR by, the St. Louis Artists' Guild in **St. Louis**.

**FEBRUARY 14–18**

EG was scheduled for four lectures in **Detroit**, Michigan.

**FEBRUARY 19**

EG was scheduled to lecture on "The Influence of Drama on Anarchism" in the afternoon and on "Anarchism" in the evening at Johnson Tent Hall, 109 North Main Street, in **Ann Arbor**, Michigan.

**FEBRUARY 20**

EG spoke at a meeting in **Detroit**, Michigan.

**FEBRUARY 21**

EG was scheduled to lecture in **Buffalo**, New York.

**LATE FEBRUARY**

EG held three meetings in **Rochester**, New York.

**FEBRUARY 26**

EG met the liberal mayor of Toledo, Brand Whitlock, for the first time, at a lecture he delivered to the City Club in **Rochester**. In 1911 Whitlock became vice president of the Free Speech League.

**MARCH 5**

A general strike began in Philadelphia, precipitated by the perfunctory discharge of 600 trolley workers on 15 February.

**MARCH 9**

The Spokane City Council repealed the 1908 ordinance prohibiting street meetings.

**MARCH 11**

EG lectured on "The General Strike" in **Pittsburgh**, Pennsylvania.

**MARCH 18**

EG arrived in **Minneapolis**, Minnesota.

**MARCH 20**

EG was scheduled to lecture on "Tolstoy, Artist and Rebel" at 3 p.m. and on Galsworthy's *Justice* at 8 p.m. at McElroy's Hall, 723 Nicollet Avenue, in **Minneapolis**.

**MARCH 21**

EG was scheduled to lecture at McElroy's Hall in **Minneapolis**, 8 p.m.

**MARCH 22**

EG was scheduled to lecture on "Danger in the Growing Power of the Church" at Dania Hall, Cedar Avenue and Fifth Street, in **Minneapolis**, 8 p.m.

**MARCH 23**

EG was scheduled to lecture on "Victims of Morality" at Dania Hall in **Minneapolis**.

**MARCH 24**

EG was scheduled to speak at the Labor Temple in **Sioux City**, Iowa.

**MARCH 25**

EG was scheduled to speak at City Hall in **Sioux City**.

Later, EG arrived in **Omaha**, Nebraska.

**MARCH 26**

An amendment to the Immigration Act of 1907 passed Congress. The 1910 act, while not changing the language excluding anarchists, streamlined the methods of prosecution and deportation of excludable aliens and still forbade the entry of any anarchists into the United States.

**MARCH 27**

EG spoke on "Francisco Ferrer and the Modern School" at 3 p.m. and "The General Strike" at 8 p.m. at Fraternity Hall in **Omaha**. BR chaired the meeting.

**MARCH 28**

EG spoke on "Woman Suffrage" at 3 p.m. and "The White Slave Traffic" at 8 p.m. at the Lyric Theater in **Omaha**.

**EARLY APRIL**

EG spoke on "The Drama," "Ferrer," and "Marriage and Love" in **Denver**, Colorado.

**APRIL 1**

EG spoke on "Anarchy—What It Really Is" at Granada Hall in **Denver**.

**APRIL 7**

EG and BR arrived in **Cheyenne**, Wyoming.

**APRIL 8**

EG was scheduled to lecture on "Anarchism and What It Really Stands For" in the evening at Keefe Hall Annex in **Cheyenne**. EG and

BR were arrested, but they were released that night with aid from prominent Cheyenne residents and two attorneys. EG held an informal meeting in her room at the Metropolitan Hotel after her release.

**APRIL 9**

EG delivered the lecture scheduled for the previous night, without any intervention from the police.

**APRIL 10**

EG was scheduled to speak on "Marriage and Love" in the afternoon and "The Drama" in the evening at Fraternal Hall in **Cheyenne**.

**APRIL 12**

EG lectured in the evening on "Francisco Ferrer and the Modern School" at Eastman's Hall on State Street, in **Salt Lake City**, Utah. Reverend William Thurston Brown introduced her.

**APRIL 13**

EG was scheduled to speak in the evening on "The White Slave Traffic" at Eastman's Hall in **Salt Lake City**.

**APRIL 17**

EG spoke on "Anarchy" and "Love and Marriage" at Eagle Hall in **Reno**, Nevada.

**APRIL 18**

EG arrived in **Sacramento**, California. She visited the old anarchist George Pyburn. BR continued on to San Francisco, California.

**APRIL 24**

EG lectured on Francisco Ferrer at Jefferson Square Hall in **San Francisco**.

**APRIL 26**

EG lectured on John Galsworthy's *Strife* at Jefferson Square Hall in **San Francisco**.

**APRIL 28**

EG debated Edward Adams Cantrell, national lecturer for the Socialist Party, on "Resolved that collective regulation, and not free love, is a guarantee for a healthy race" at Jefferson Square Hall in **San Francisco**. EG argued for the negative and Cantrell for the positive.

EG visited Jack and Charmian London at their ranch in **Glen Ellen**, California.

**MAY 5**

EG was scheduled to lecture on "Francisco Ferrer, the Modern Martyr" at Burbank Hall in **Los Angeles**, California.

**MAY 6**

EG lectured on "The Spanish Inquisition in American Prisons" at Burbank Hall in **Los Angeles**.

**MAY 7**

EG spoke on "*Strife*, a Great Labor Drama" at Burbank Hall in **Los Angeles**.

**MAY 8**

EG was scheduled for an afternoon lecture on "The White Slave Traffic" and an evening lecture on "Art in Revolution and Life" at Burbank Hall in **Los Angeles**.

**MAY 9**

EG spoke on "Can Legislation Do Away with the White Slave Traffic?" at Germania Hall in **San Diego**, California.

**MAY 10**

EG was scheduled to debate Edward Adams Cantrell on "Resolved that socialism and not anarchy will solve the social problem" at Germania Hall in **San Diego**. Cantrell failed to appear for the debate.

**MAY 12**

EG debated Edward Adams Cantrell on "Woman Suffrage" at Burbank Hall in **Los Angeles**. In response to the success of the meetings, EG added a lecture, the ninth, to the schedule. While in Los Angeles, EG met with former prisoner and member of the Prison Reform League, Colonel Griffith J. Griffith, who, with W. C. Owen, published *Crime and Criminals* (Los Angeles: Los Angeles Prison Reform League, 1910).

**MAY 20**

EG was scheduled to lecture in **Portland**, Oregon.

**MAY 21**

EG was scheduled to lecture on "The General Strike" at Alisky Hall, 265 Morrison, in **Portland**.

**MAY 22**

EG lectured on "The Drama" at 3 p.m. and "Crime and Criminals" at 8 p.m. at Alisky Hall in **Portland**.

**MAY 24**

EG lectured on "The Crime and Sufferings of Francisco Ferrer" at Columbia Lodge Hall in **Seattle**, Washington.

**MAY 25**

EG lectured on "The White Slave Traffic" at Columbia Lodge Hall in **Seattle**.

**MAY 29**

EG lectured on "Francisco Ferrer and the Modern School" in the afternoon and "The General Strike" in the evening, at Academy Hall in **Spokane**, Washington.

**MAY 30**

EG lectured on "Crime and Criminals" in the evening at Academy Hall in **Spokane**.

**MAY 31**

EG and BR were struck by a freight train while driving in **Spokane**. EG was thrown from the car and badly bruised. BR was unharmed.

**SUMMER**

AB began writing *Prison Memoirs of an Anarchist* at EG's farm in Ossining, New York.

**JUNE 1**

EG lectured on "Marriage and Love" in the evening at Academy Hall in **Spokane**. Kōtoku Shūsui was arrested and charged with crimes against the throne, punishable by death in Japan. Following his arrest, hundreds of others were interrogated and arrested.

**JUNE 2**

EG arrived in **Butte**, Montana.

**JUNE 3**

The Francisco Ferrer Association was founded at the Harlem Liberal Alliance.

Speakers included Harry Kelly (chair), Jaime Vidal, Leonard Abbott, and AB.

**JUNE 5**

EG gave an afternoon lecture on "Francisco Ferrer and the Modern School" and an evening lecture on "The White Slave Traffic" at Carpenter's Union Hall in **Butte**. BR was scheduled to give a short talk and biography of EG prior to her talks.

**EARLY–MID JUNE**

EG was scheduled to lecture in **Bismarck** and **Fargo**, North Dakota.

**JUNE 18**

EG's lecture tour ended.

**JUNE 20**

EG was scheduled to speak in **Rochester**, New York.

**JUNE 22**

EG visited **Albany**, New York.

**JUNE 25**

Congress passed the White Slave Traffic Act, known as the Mann Act, prohibiting inter-state or international transport of women for "immoral purposes."

**JULY 2**

EG was working on *Anarchism and Other Essays* in **Ossining**, New York.

**JULY 20**

BR left for London, where he would meet with Errico Malatesta, Peter Kropotkin, and Guy Aldred.

**AUGUST 3**

Ricardo Flores Magón, Librado Rivera, and Antonio Villareal were released from Flor-ence prison, Arizona.

**AUGUST 13**

EG fell and broke her kneecap.

**AUGUST 19–26**

EG was being treated for a broken kneecap under an assumed name in St. Vincent's Hospital in **New York**.

**SEPTEMBER 3**

*Regeneración* was revived by Ricardo Flores Magón in Los Angeles, with a new English-language page.

**OCTOBER**

Subscribers to *Mother Earth* publications in Canada were denied receipt of materials by the Canadian authorities, on the grounds that the content was of a treasonable nature. BR returned from Europe.

**OCTOBER 1**

A bomb exploded in the alley behind the *Los Angeles Times* building, killing twenty-one people. Two other bombs failed to explode: one in the home of the *Los Angeles Times* pro-prietor, Harrison Gray Otis, and another in the home of the secretary of the Merchants and Manufacturers Association.

**OCTOBER 6**

Francisco Madero issued a call for a wide-spread uprising to occur on 20 November in Mexico. In a newspaper article he announced himself the acting president of the republic and named Ricardo Flores Magón vice presi-dent, a position that Flores Magón rejected.

**OCTOBER 13**

EG spoke at the one-year commemoration of the execution of Francisco Ferrer. The Ferrer Association was scheduled to hold a com-memoration meeting and dinner in Cooper Union in **New York**.

**OCTOBER 16**

The IWW announced an open-air meeting in Fresno, California, in defiance of local city ordinances. Nine were arrested; five more were arrested the following day.

**NOVEMBER**

EG was denied use of halls in **Washington, D.C.** The chief of police declared his intent to prevent EG from speaking.

San Diego police blocked meetings com-memorating the Haymarket anarchists.

**NOVEMBER 1**

EG, BR, and others attended a meeting at the Labor Temple, Second Avenue in **New York**, where Anthony Comstock spoke; they criticized Comstock for his promotion of laws intended to deny the use of the mails for what he arbitrarily classified as obscene literature and pictures.

**NOVEMBER 7**

Tolstoy died.

**NOVEMBER 8**

Victor Berger of Milwaukee became the first Socialist Party candidate elected to Congress.

**NOVEMBER 11**

EG was scheduled to speak in commemoration of the Haymarket anarchists at Terrace Lyceum, 206 East Broadway, in **New York**. Other speakers included Leonard Abbott and BR.

**NOVEMBER 12**

EG spoke at a meeting held at Lloyd Hall in **New York,** to protest the Japanese treason trial. The chairman, Leonard Abbott, read telegrams from Jack London, Eugene Debs, and Hulda Potter Loomis. Other speakers included Bayard Boyesen, Grace Potter, Arthur Bullard, Hippolyte Havel, Saul Yanovsky, Arturo Caroti, Jaime Vidal, Max Baginski, Michel Dumas, and Vacar Rejsek. The Kōtoku protests began after an article, signed by EG, Hippolyte Havel, AB, BR, and Sadakichi Hartmann, was published in the 12 November 1910 issue of the *New York Call*.

**NOVEMBER 13**

EG was scheduled to lecture in English on "Victims of Morality," 8 p.m., at the Women's Trade Union League, 43 East 22nd Street, in **New York**.

**NOVEMBER 17**

BR hosted "Outcast Night," a discussion of various types of social outcasts at Pacific Hall in **New York**. Speakers included Sadakichi Hartmann and Hippolyte Havel. EG was in attendance.

**NOVEMBER 20**

EG was scheduled to lecture in English on "The Danger of the Growing Power of the Church," 8 p.m., at the Women's Trade Union League in **New York**.

The Maderista uprising began in Mexico.

**NOVEMBER 22**

EG and others held a small meeting (about a hundred people) to address the case of Kōtoku in **New York**. EG compared Kōtoku to Ferrer, and she proposed to send a protest to the Japanese ambassador and visit the Japanese consul general in New York to clarify the events of the incident. The proposals were adopted, and Bolton Hall, Leonard Abbott, and Bayard Boyesen were nominated; Hall refused the nomination.

**NOVEMBER 23**

Leonard Abbott and Bayard Boyesen visited the consul general in New York. They were denied information on the Kōtoku incident.

**NOVEMBER 25**

EG delivered a lecture in Yiddish on "Victims of Morality" at Union Hall in **Baltimore**, Maryland.

**NOVEMBER 26**

EG was scheduled to give an afternoon lecture on "The Modern Drama" and an evening lecture on "Francisco Ferrer and the Modern School" at the Labor Lyceum, 1011 East Baltimore Street, in **Baltimore**.

**DECEMBER 4**

EG was scheduled to speak on "The Message of Anarchy," at 8 p.m. at East 22nd Street, in **New York**.

**DECEMBER 9**

A mob of more than 1,000 vigilantes attacked and beat IWW members and burned IWW tent headquarters and camp during an ongoing free speech battle in Fresno, California. EG lectured at the Terrace Lyceum in **New York**.

**DECEMBER 10**

The trial of Kōtoku and other defendants opened in the supreme court of Japan. Under Article 73 of the Criminal Code, Crimes

Against the Throne, the charges were punishable by death.

DECEMBER 11

EG was scheduled to speak on "Tolstoy the Rebel" at 2 p.m. at Lyric Hall in **New York**. Bayard Boyesen spoke on "Tolstoy the Teacher," and Grace Potter read from Tolstoy's work. The meeting was chaired by Leonard Abbott. In the evening EG was scheduled to speak on *The Awakening of Spring: a Tragedy of Childhood,* by Frank Wedekind at 43 East 22nd Street, in **New York**.

DECEMBER 12

EG spoke at a meeting to protest the trial of Kōtoku, at 8 p.m. at Lyric Hall in **New York**. Leonard Abbott, Bayard Boyesen, Arthur Bullard, Elizabeth Gurley Flynn, Hippolyte Havel, Saul Yanovsky (in Yiddish), Max Baginski (German), Arturo Caroti (Italian), Michel Dumas (French), Jaime Vidal (Spanish), and Vaclar Rejsek (Bohemian) also spoke.

DECEMBER 17

EG's first book, *Anarchism and Other Essays,* was published.

DECEMBER 18

EG was scheduled to speak on "The Parody of Philanthropy" at 43 East 22nd Street, in **New York**, 8 p.m. EG also attended a meeting on the Japanese treason trial in **New York**.

DECEMBER 24

EG attended the anarchist Grand Festival and Ball sponsored by *Mother Earth* and held at Grand Manhattan Hall, 311 Grand Street, in **New York**.

DECEMBER 29

The trial of Kōtoku and other Japanese anarchists ended.

DECEMBER 31

Ethel Duffy Turner became editor of the English-language section of *Regeneración.*

**1911**

JANUARY

The Partido Liberal Mexicano (PLM), with IWW support invaded Baja California; short-lived revolutionary communes were established in Mexicali and Tijuana. The IWW free speech fight in Fresno, California, continued. By this time, several hundred IWW members were imprisoned for attempting to hold public meetings. *Mother Earth*'s offices moved from 210 East 13th Street to 55 West 28th Street, in **New York**.

JANUARY 5

EG, Leonard Abbott, Bolton Hall, Bayard Boyesen, AB, Gilbert Roe, Rose Pastor Stokes, J. G. Phelps Stokes, Jack London, Hutchins Hapgood, Jaime Vidal, Upton Sinclair, Charles Edward Russell, and Grace Potter spoke at Webster Hall, 119 East 11th Street, to inaugurate the new Ferrer School located at St. Mark's Place in **New York**. Ferrer Center began its Sunday and evening classes.

JANUARY 6

EG was scheduled to lecture on Tolstoy in **Rochester**, New York.

JANUARY 8–9

EG was scheduled to speak in **Buffalo**, New York.

JANUARY 11–14

EG was scheduled to speak in **Pittsburgh**, Pennsylvania.

JANUARY 14

EG was scheduled to debate with Frederick Ruppel of the Allegheny Socialist Party local on "Socialism Against the Philosophy of Anarchism" at the Labor Temple, **Pittsburgh**. Hall managers cancelled the debate when it was discovered that another speaker was booked for the same night. However, EG debated with Ruppel that night to a packed hall in another venue, possibly at the Canton Auditorium.

EG was scheduled to present afternoon and evening lectures at the Pythian Temple in **Cleveland**, Ohio.

**JANUARY 16**

EG lectured in Yiddish on "The Eternal Spirit of Revolution" at Royle Hall in **Cleveland**.

**JANUARY 17–20**

EG was scheduled to speak in **Columbus**, Ohio.

**JANUARY 18**

EG was prevented from speaking at the United Mine Workers (UMW) convention in **Columbus**. Even though many members of the United Mine Workers supported EG's right to free speech, union leaders voted against allowing EG to address the convention.

Kōtoku and twenty-three co-defendants were sentenced to death by the supreme court of Japan for plotting against the throne. Two other defendants were sentenced, one to eight years and the other to eleven years in prison. Although the trial was held in camera, the reading of the verdict was a public session.

**JANUARY 19**

In the Kōtoku trial, twelve of the death sentences were commuted to life imprisonment. EG was scheduled to speak in **Columbus**.

**JANUARY 20**

EG was scheduled to speak in **Columbus**. EG was locked out of Memorial Hall, the location of the UMW convention.

**JANUARY 21–23**

EG was scheduled to speak in **Cincinnati**, Ohio.

**JANUARY 22**

A protest meeting was called by EG in response to the Japanese anarchists' death sentences.

**JANUARY 24**

EG spoke at the Pentecost Tabernacle, **Indianapolis**, Indiana. All halls initially refused,

but Reverend Nelson eventually offered his church to EG. Following her engagement at the Pentecost Tabernacle, EG spoke at the Universalist Church in **Indianapolis**.

Kōtoku and ten other Japanese anarchists were executed.

**JANUARY 25**

EG spoke on "Francisco Ferrer" at G.A.R. Hall in **Elyria**, Ohio.

Japanese anarchist Kanno Suga was executed.

**JANUARY 27**

EG was scheduled to lecture in **Dayton**, Ohio.

**JANUARY 28**

EG was scheduled to lecture in **Toledo**, Ohio.

**JANUARY 29**

EG lectured in **Toledo**. Robert Henri was in attendance.

Several thousand anarchists protested the executions of Kōtoku and the other Japanese anarchists at a meeting in Webster Hall, followed by a March down Broadway in New York. Speakers included Bayard Boyesen and AB. EG and BR sent a telegram of support.

PLM forces captured Mexicali, Baja California.

**JANUARY 31**

EG lectured on "Victims of Morality" at Staebler Hall, 257 Beaubien Street, in **Detroit**, Michigan.

**FEBRUARY 1**

EG spoke on "The Eternal Spirit of the Revolution" at Staebler Hall in **Detroit**, Michigan

**FEBRUARY 2**

EG spoke on "The Danger in the Growing Power of the Church" at Friedman's Hall, 392 Hastings Street, in **Detroit**, Michigan

**FEBRUARY 4**

EG lectured in **Ann Arbor**, Michigan.

**FEBRUARY 5**

EG lectured on " Justice" and "Tolstoy, the Artist and Rebel" at Friedman's Hall in **Detroit**.

**FEBRUARY 6–7**

EG was scheduled to speak in **Jackson**, Michigan.

**FEBRUARY 8–9**

EG was in **Grand Rapids**, Michigan, hosted by William Buwalda.

**FEBRUARY 12–16**

EG was scheduled to lecture in the afternoon and evening at Hod Carriers' Hall, Harrison and Green Streets, in **Chicago**.

**FEBRUARY 14**

Francisco Madero returned to Mexico to assume command of all revolutionary fighting forces.

**FEBRUARY 17**

EG was scheduled to speak in Yiddish in **Chicago**.

**FEBRUARY 19**

EG was scheduled for two meetings in English in **Chicago**.

**FEBRUARY 21**

EG spoke on "Anarchism—What it Really Stands For" in **Urbana**, Illinois.

**FEBRUARY 23**

EG was scheduled to speak in **Peoria**, Illinois.

**FEBRUARY 25**

In an editorial in *Regeneración*, Ricardo Flores Magón broke with Madero, accusing him of being a traitor. Flores Magón denied rumors that he would accept the vice presidency in a Madero government. Intercepted communications indicated that PLM forces throughout Mexico had joined or were coerced into Maderista armies.

**FEBRUARY 26**

EG was scheduled to deliver "The Eternal Spirit of Revolution" in the afternoon and "The Social Importance of Ferrer's Modern School" in the evening at Odeon Recital Hall in **St. Louis**, Missouri.

**FEBRUARY 28**

EG was scheduled to speak on "Tolstoy—Artist and Rebel" at Wednesday Club Auditorium

in **St. Louis**. On this visit to St. Louis EG met with Roger Baldwin and Robert Minor.

**MARCH 1**

EG spoke on "Victims of Morality" at Odeon Recital Hall in **St. Louis**.

**MARCH 2**

EG was scheduled to speak on "Galsworthy's *Justice*" at Wednesday Club Auditorium in **St. Louis**. Rental of the hall was controversial. Fresno, California, city officials repealed a ban on street speaking.

**MARCH 3**

EG was scheduled to lecture in Yiddish on Tolstoy in **St. Louis**.

**MARCH 4**

EG was scheduled to speak on "Victims of Morality" at Lyric Theatre in **Belleville**, Illinois. BR was scheduled to chair. Later, in **Staunton**, Illinois, town constables stopped EG in the train station but released her in time for her to address a small audience in a laundry building.

**MARCH 6–13**

EG spoke in **Milwaukee** and **Madison**, Wisconsin.

**MARCH 11**

The PLM appealed to Samuel Gompers of the American Federation of Labor for help and support.

**MARCH 13**

Ricardo Flores Magón appealed to EG for support of the revolutionary movement in Mexico.

**MARCH 14**

EG spoke in **St. Paul**, Minnesota.

**MARCH 16**

EG was scheduled to lecture on "Anarchy" at Owls Hall, 166 West Superior Street, in **Duluth**, Minnesota.

**MARCH 17**

EG spoke on "Marriage and Love" at Knights of Pythian Hall, 118 West Superior Street, in **Duluth**.

A meeting, along with a concert and ball, in

honor of the sixth birthday of *Mother Earth* was scheduled to take place at the Terrace Lyceum in New York.

**MARCH 19–22**

EG was scheduled to speak in **Minneapolis**, Minnesota.

**MARCH 21**

EG was scheduled to speak in **Milwaukee**, Wisconsin.

**MARCH 23**

The Free Speech League's formal incorporation was approved by Justice Giegerich of the Supreme Court.

**MARCH 24**

William C. Owen replaced Ethel Duffy Turner as editor of the English-language section of *Regeneración*.

EG was scheduled to speak in **Sioux City**, Iowa.

**MARCH 26**

EG lectured at 3:00 p.m. on "The Spirit of Revolution" at 8:00 p.m. at the Lyric Theater in **Omaha**, Nebraska.

**MARCH 27**

EG delivered a lecture in **Omaha**.

**MARCH 28–30**

EG was scheduled to speak in **Lincoln**, Nebraska.

**APRIL 3**

The PLM issued "Manifesto to the World's Toilers" in English and Spanish, setting out its revolutionary stance.

**APRIL 4**

EG spoke at Williamson's Hall in **Kansas City**, Missouri.

**APRIL 5**

EG spoke on "Marriage and Love" at Pythian Hall in **Kansas City**.

**APRIL 7**

EG was scheduled to speak in Yiddish at 1715 Oak Street, in **Kansas City**.

The Free Speech League was incorporated at Albany, New York, by Leonard Abbott (president), Brand Whitlock (vice president),

Lincoln Steffens, Bolton Hall, Gilbert E. Roe, Dr. E. B. Foote Jr. (treasurer), and Theodore Schroeder (secretary).

**APRIL 8**

A Prisoners' Ball, sponsored by the Anarchist Red Cross to benefit the "exiled and imprisoned comrades," was scheduled to take place at the Manhattan Lyceum in New York.

**APRIL 9**

EG spoke at 3 p.m. on "Anarchism and What It Really Stands For," and at 8 p.m. on "Marriage and Love," at Fraternal Aid Hall in **Lawrence**, Kansas. EG also spoke on "Why Laws Fail" to the Good Government Club, a group of law students, in **Lawrence**.

**APRIL 10**

EG spoke on "The Message of Anarchy" at Luken's Opera House in **Topeka**, Kansas.

**APRIL 11**

EG spoke on "Marriage & Love" at Luken's Opera House in **Topeka**.

**APRIL 14**

James B. McNamara and Ortie McManigal were arrested in Detroit on suspicion of causing the *Los Angeles Times* explosion of 1 October 1910.

**APRIL 16**

EG lectured on "Tolstoy" in the afternoon and "Revolutions" in the evening at Champs Hall in **Denver**, Colorado.

**APRIL 17**

EG lectured on "Church" at Champs Hall in **Denver**.

**APRIL 18**

EG lectured on "The Victims of Morality (Modern Monks and Nuns)" at Champs Hall in **Denver**.

**APRIL 22**

John J. McNamara, secretary-treasurer of the International Association of Bridge and Structural Iron Workers, was arrested in Indianapolis on suspicion of causing the explosion at the *Los Angeles Times* building of 1 October 1910.

EG was scheduled to debate socialist Murray King at the Federation of Labor Hall in **Salt Lake City**, Utah, but King was replaced by Philip Engle.

APRIL 23

EG was scheduled to give an afternoon and an evening lecture at the Federation of Labor Hall in **Salt Lake City**.

APRIL 30

EG was scheduled to speak in the afternoon and evening at Mammoth Hall in **Los Angeles**, California.

MAY 1–2

EG was scheduled to speak both evenings at Mammoth Hall in **Los Angeles**.

MAY 6

EG spoke at a social at Burbank Hall, 542 South Main Street, in **Los Angeles**; she sent the proceeds to support the Mexican Revolution.

MAY 7

EG was scheduled to speak on "Charity" at 3 p.m. and on "Revolution" at 8 p.m., in Mammoth Hall in **Los Angeles**.

MAY 8

Baja California was mostly under PLM control.

MAY 8–9

EG spoke twice at Germaine Hall in **San Diego**, California. Ernest E. Kirk chaired both meetings.

MAY 13

EG arrived in **Fresno**, California.

*Justice,* a Social Democratic Party newspaper in London, accused EG of being an agent provocateur in the employ of the police; claimed she had spied for A. E. Olarovsky of the Russian secret police in San Francisco; and argued that she was now trying to incite the Milwaukee socialists to engage in bomb throwing to provoke the police to crush them.

MAY 14

EG spoke on "Anarchism and What It Stands

For" at 3 p.m. and on "Marriage and Love" at 8 p.m. in **Fresno**.

MAY 16

EG was scheduled to speak in **San Francisco**, California.

MAY 20

EG spoke in the afternoon on "The Drama— A Powerful Disseminator of Radical Thought" and in the evening on "Anarchism and What It Really Stands For" in **Palo Alto**, California.

MAY 21

EG spoke on "The Eternal Spirit of the Revolution" at 3 p.m. and on "Victims of Morality" at 8 p.m. at Jefferson Square Hall in **San Francisco**, California.

Madero signed a peace treaty with Díaz, but the PLM refused to lay down its weapons.

MAY 24

EG debated Socialist William McDevitt in the Building Trades Auditorium in **San Francisco**.

MAY 25

Díaz stepped down as Mexican president and left for Paris.

MAY 26

EG and BR arrived in **Portland**, Oregon. EG was scheduled to begin a series of five lectures on 28 May.

MAY 29

EG spoke on "The Danger of the Growing Power of the Church" at Alisky Hall in **Portland**.

MAY 30

EG lectured in the afternoon on "The General Strike and the McNamara Case" and in the evening on "The Eternal Spirit of Revolution" at Alisky Hall in **Portland**. BR spoke on "Burns' Method of Securing Evidence."

MAY 31

EG spoke on "Victims of Morality" at Alisky Hall in **Portland**.

JUNE 1

EG delivered a lecture on "The General Strike" at the Labor Temple in **Portland**.

JUNE 3

C. L. James died.

JUNE 6

Madero dispatched troops to Baja California via the U.S. railways to crush the liberal revolt in Baja California.

JUNE 6

EG and BR were in **Spokane**, Washington.

JUNE 8

The third meeting of the New York Mexican Revolution Conference was held at the Ferrer Center in New York.

JUNE 14

Ricardo and Enrique Flores Magón and others were arrested at the *Regeneración* offices and charged with breaching the neutrality laws; all papers and equipment were seized.

MID-JUNE

EG spoke in **Colville**, Washington, and **Boise**, Idaho. She visited the Idaho penitentiary.

JUNE 23

Ricardo and Enrique Flores Magón were released on bail.

EG lectured on "The General Strike" at the Women's Club in **Denver**, Colorado.

JUNE 24

EG was scheduled to lecture on Wedekind's *The Awakening of Spring* at the Women's Club in **Denver**.

JUNE 25

EG was scheduled to debate Dr. Duren J. H. Ward, editor of *Up the Divide,* on "Anarchism Versus Socialism" in **Denver**.

JUNE 26

A mass meeting in support of the Mexican Revolution was scheduled at Cooper Union, New York. Speakers included Max Baginski, Joseph Ettor, Jaime Vidal, Harry Kelly and AB. The meeting was chaired by Leonard Abbott.

JUNE 30

Statement protesting charges made in *Justice* (London) that EG was a police spy, signed by Leonard Abbott, William English Walling,

Hutchins Hapgood, J. G. Phelps Stokes, William Marion Reedy, Alden Freeman, Bolton Hall, Rose Pastor Stokes, Theodore Schroeder, James F. Morton Jr., Edwin C. Walker, Daniel Kiefer, Rose Strunsky, and Hulda L. Potter Loomis.

EG spoke at a dinner held to celebrate the first anniversary of the Ferrer Association at the Café Boulevard in **New York**. Other speakers included Leonard D. Abbott, Hippolyte Havel, AB, and Harry Kelly.

SUMMER/FALL

EG spent time with AB at retreat in **Ossining**, New York. AB resumed work on *Prison Memoirs of an Anarchist.*

JULY

U.S. socialists broke with the Magónistas and supported Madero. Eugene Debs, in the *International Socialist Review,* called for education and organization, and distanced himself from the PLM.

JULY 5

The *New York Call,* a socialist paper, denounced the PLM in Baja California, labeling them bandits.

AUGUST 12

EG attended an excursion held by the Ferrer Association.

MID-AUGUST

EG and BR vacationed in **Old Orchard Beach**, Maine. She used the alias Miss Ida Crossman. They were scheduled to return to **New York** on 23 August.

AUGUST 26

EG spoke to gain support for the Mexican Revolution at a mass meeting at Union Square in **New York**. BR chaired the meeting; speakers included Bernard Sernaker (in Yiddish), William Thurston Brown (English), Jaime Vidal (Spanish), EG and Max Baginski (German), and Samuel Boris (Russian).

FALL

EG worked unsuccessfully to find a publisher for AB's book and decided to publish it through the Mother Earth Publishing Association. Gilbert Roe held a private benefit to raise money for the publication.

SEPTEMBER 23

PLM published a manifesto to replace the PLM program of 1906. The manifesto critiqued the principle of private property, which it targeted as the sole "reason for government and the church to exist" and declared "war against Authority, war against Capital, and war against the Church."

SEPTEMBER 26

EG solicited Jack London to write a preface for AB's *Prison Memoirs of an Anarchist.*

OCTOBER 1

EG was scheduled to speak at a mass meeting "to protest against the growing Religious Superstition" at Lyric Hall, 725 Sixth Avenue, in **New York**. Other speakers included Harry Kelly, Dr. M. Cohn, Max Baginski, Parker Sercombe, and Dr. B. Liber. The meeting was chaired by BR.

Francisco Madero was elected president of Mexico.

OCTOBER 11

The McNamara brothers' trial began in Los Angeles. Defense attorney Clarence Darrow entered a plea of "not guilty."

OCTOBER 13

EG was scheduled to speak at a mass meeting to commemorate the second anniversary of the death of Francisco Ferrer, at Murray Hill Lyceum, 34th Street and Third Avenue, in **New York**, 8 p.m.

OCTOBER 15

EG was scheduled to begin the first of a series of Sunday lectures to residents of Manhattan's Lower East Side. She spoke on "Anarchism, the Moving Spirit in the Labor Movement" at Terrace Lyceum, 206 East Broadway, at 3 p.m. in Yiddish and at 8 p.m. in English, in **New York**.

OCTOBER 22

EG was scheduled for the second in her Sun-

day lecture series, speaking on "*Maternity,* a Drama by Brieux (Why the Poor Should Not Have Children)," at Terrace Lyceum in **New York**.

OCTOBER 29

EG was scheduled for the third in her Sunday lecture series, speaking on "Government by Spies, the McNamara Case and Burns," at Terrace Lyceum in **New York**.

NOVEMBER 5

EG was scheduled for the fourth in her Sunday lecture series, speaking on "The Failure of Christianity," at Terrace Lyceum in **New York**.

NOVEMBER 12

EG was scheduled for the fifth in her Sunday lecture series, speaking on "Art and Revolution," at Terrace Lyceum in **New York**.

NOVEMBER 18

The *Mother Earth* annual fall gathering celebration was scheduled at Terrace Lyceum in **New York**.

NOVEMBER 19

EG was scheduled for the sixth in her Sunday lecture series, speaking on "Communism, the Most Practical Basis for Society," at Terrace Lyceum in **New York**.

NOVEMBER 20–25

EG was scheduled to speak in **Connecticut**.

NOVEMBER 24

EG spoke on Tolstoy at a meeting of the Russian Workers Group in **New York**.

NOVEMBER 26

By popular demand, EG's Sunday lectures continued, with EG speaking on "Mary Wollstonecraft, the Pioneer of Modern Womanhood" at 43 East 22nd Street, in **New York**, 8 p.m.

NOVEMBER 27–DECEMBER 3

EG was scheduled to speak in **Massachusetts**.

DECEMBER 1

The McNamara defense withdrew its pleas of not guilty and entered a guilty plea after Lincoln Steffens and Clarence Darrow brokered a deal.

DECEMBER 3

EG visited with Samuel Atkins Elliot Jr., grandson of the former Harvard University president, while in **Cambridge**, Massachusetts. EG was scheduled to speak on "Socialism Caught in Its Political Trap" for her Sunday lecture series at 43 East 22nd Street, in **New York**, and answered questions about the McNamara case.

DECEMBER 5

In Los Angeles John J. McNamara was sentenced to fifteen years and James B. McNamara to life imprisonment in San Quentin. The search continued for David Caplan and Matthew Schmidt, anarchists also suspected in the bombing.

A San Diego grand jury recommended that "Soapbox Row," a local area historically used for street speaking by single-taxers, Salvation Army, and Wobblies, be cleared and that street speaking be prohibited in the downtown area.

DECEMBER 10

EG spoke on "Sex, the Element for Creative Work," for her Sunday lecture series at 43 East 22nd Street in **New York**.

DECEMBER 17

EG gave a farewell lecture for her Sunday lecture series at 43 East 22nd Street, in **New York**.

DECEMBER 19–20

EG was scheduled to speak in **Schenectady**, New York.

DECEMBER 21

EG gave a lecture in Yiddish in **Albany**, New York.

DECEMBER 22

EG spoke in **Albany**.

**1912**

JANUARY 5

EG spoke in **Brooklyn**, New York.

JANUARY 8

EG spoke on "Woman's Inhumanity to Man" to the Sunrise Club at the Café Boulevard in **New York**.

The San Diego City Council passed an ordinance creating a restricted district (a forty-nine-block area in the center of town) where street meetings were prohibited, implying that street speaking could take place beyond its boundaries.

JANUARY 12

A widespread strike began in textile factories in Lawrence, Massachusetts, as wage slips revealed pay cuts.

JANUARY 14

EG spoke on "Love and Marriage" at the "Arbeiter Ring Lunch" in **New York**.

JANUARY 21

EG spoke in the afternoon in Yiddish at the New York Ferrer Association and in the evening at a Jewish meeting in uptown Manhattan in **New York**.

JANUARY 29

A bystander was killed at the Lawrence, Massachusetts, strike in a confrontation between police and strikers.

JANUARY 31

Joseph Ettor and Arturo Giovannitti, IWW organizers sent to Lawrence, Massachusetts, were charged with incitement to riot and accessories to murder, implicating them in the death of the Lawrence bystander.

FEBRUARY

The *Modern School* magazine launched.

FEBRUARY 2

EG debated socialist Sol Fieldman on "Direct vs. Political Action" at Carnegie Hall, **New York**. At the debate William Haywood made a plea for money for support of the textile strikers in Lawrence, Massachusetts, raising $532.

FEBRUARY 3

EG was scheduled to attend a meeting called by the Italian Socialist Federation to express support for the Lawrence strikers, at Union Square in **New York**, 4 p.m.; Haywood was also scheduled to speak.

**FEBRUARY 4**

EG debated Sol Fieldman again on "Direct vs. Political Action" at Republic Theater in **New York**, raising $143 for the Lawrence strikers in response to Elizabeth Gurley Flynn's appeal for funds.

**FEBRUARY 8**

A San Diego city ordinance restricting street meetings in the central business district went into effect, and forty-one IWW members were arrested for violating the ordinance.

**FEBRUARY 9**

Ettor and Giovannitti were arraigned for incitement to riot and as accessories to murder. The hearing lasted for eight days.

**FEBRUARY 10**

EG debated C. E. Ruthenberg on "Anarchy, or Direct Action—Socialism, or Political Action" at Pythian Temple, **Cleveland**, Ohio.

**FEBRUARY 11**

Lawrence strikers' children were taken to New York, and later to Jersey City, New Jersey; Philadelphia, Pennsylvania; and Barre, Vermont.

**FEBRUARY 11–12**

EG was scheduled to speak in **Cleveland**.

**FEBRUARY 13**

EG was scheduled to speak on "Anarchism the Moving Spirit in the Labor Struggle" at Owls Hall in **Lorain**, Ohio, 8 p.m.

The San Diego City Council passed an ordinance giving police the right to control movement and disperse assemblies in any part of the city, to take effect 28 March.

**FEBRUARY 14**

EG was scheduled to speak on "Maternity" at Grand Army of the Republic Hall in **Elyria**, Ohio, 8 p.m.

**FEBRUARY 16**

EG was scheduled to speak on "Maternity" at Labor Hall, **Columbus**, Ohio, 8 p.m.

**FEBRUARY 17**

EG was scheduled to speak on "Art and Revolution" at 3 p.m. and on "Anarchism, the Moving Spirit in the Labor Struggle" at 8 p.m., presumably at Labor Hall in **Columbus**.

**FEBRUARY 18**

EG debated socialist Frank Midney in the afternoon at Jewel Theater in **Dayton**, Ohio. The meeting was attended by 200 and resulted in Midney's two-year expulsion from the Dayton Socialist Party. EG spoke in the evening on "Motherhood."

**FEBRUARY 19**

AB and Jack London met to discuss London's preface to *Prison Memoirs of an Anarchist.*

**FEBRUARY 21**

EG was scheduled to speak on "Maternity" at Walhalla Hall in **Indianapolis**, Indiana, 8 p.m.

The judge found probable cause of guilt against Ettor and Giovannitti. As they awaited the grand jury, they were held without bail.

**FEBRUARY 22**

EG was scheduled to speak on "Art and Revolution" at 3 p.m. and on "Anarchism, the Moving Spirit in the Labor Struggle" at 8 p.m., presumably at Walhalla Hall in **Indianapolis**.

**FEBRUARY 23**

AB wrote to Jack London, thanking him but rejecting his preface for its unsympathetic remarks about anarchism, which he deemed inappropriate because *Prison Memoirs of an Anarchist* was "not an anarchist tract."

**FEBRUARY 25**

EG spoke in the afternoon on "Anarchy and Its Relation to the Workingman" and in the evening on "The Failure of Christianity" at Odeon Hall in **St. Louis**.

**FEBRUARY 26**

The recently formed California Free Speech League in San Diego staged a protest march to demand better treatment for the IWW members in jail.

**FEBRUARY 26–27**

EG was scheduled to deliver evening lectures at Druid's Hall in **St. Louis**.

**FEBRUARY 28**

EG was scheduled to lecture at Odeon Hall in **St. Louis**.

**MARCH 3**

EG was scheduled to speak on "Anarchism, the Moving Spirit in the Labor Struggle" at 3 p.m. and on "Art and Revolution" at 8 p.m. at Hod Carriers' Hall in **Chicago**.

**MARCH 4**

EG was scheduled to debate Arthur Lewis on "Direct Action Versus Political Action" in **Chicago**. She was also scheduled to speak on "*Maternity*, a Drama by Brieux (Why the Poor Should Not Have Children)" at Hod Carriers' Hall in **Chicago**, 8 p.m.

**MARCH 5**

EG was scheduled to speak on "Socialism Caught in the Political Trap" at Hod Carriers' Hall in **Chicago**, 8 p.m.

**MARCH 7**

EG was scheduled to debate Dr. Denslow Lewis about the usefulness of marriage at Hod Carriers' Hall in **Chicago**, 8 p.m. EG argued that "the institution of marriage is detrimental to society."

**MARCH 8**

EG debated Arthur M. Lewis about the usefulness of marriage at Hod Carriers' Hall in **Chicago**, 8 p.m. While in Chicago, EG held at least two Jewish meetings, and lectured on "Art and Revolution" and Rostand's *Chantecler.*

**MARCH 9**

EG was scheduled to speak on "Sex, the Great Element of Creative Work" at 3 p.m.

and on "Anarchy" at 8 p.m. at the Oakland Music Hall in **Chicago**.

**MARCH 10–11**

EG was scheduled to speak in **Milwaukee**, Wisconsin.

The IWW held a protest meeting in front of San Diego city jail. Police called in the fire department to disperse the crowd, spraying them with water from fire hoses.

**MARCH 14**

The victorious Lawrence strikers voted to return to work.

**LATE MARCH–EARLY APRIL**

According to *Mother Earth*, EG spoke in the following cities after Milwaukee: **Grand Rapids**, Michigan; **Detroit**, Michigan; **Ann Arbor**, Michigan; and **Madison**, Wisconsin.

**MARCH 26**

EG was scheduled to speak in **Minneapolis**, Minnesota.

**MARCH 29**

EG was scheduled to speak in **Omaha**, Nebraska.

**MARCH 28**

The San Diego police began enforcement of the recently enacted "move-on" ordinance.

**MARCH 29**

Ricardo and Enrique Flores Magón and W. C. Owen published an open letter to Jean Grave in *Les Temps Nouveaux* responding to the attack on the PLM that claimed it was not an anarchist organization. In early April Kropotkin joined the debate in the paper in an article supporting the PLM.

**APRIL 3**

IWW attorneys Fred Moore and Marcus Robbins wired California governor Hiram Johnson in an attempt to enlist his intervention on behalf of the IWW in San Diego.

**APRIL 5**

San Diego newspaperman Abram Sauer, editor of the *San Diego Herald*, was kidnapped from his home by local vigilantes for publishing affidavits of IWW men who had been beaten by local vigilantes.

APRIL 7

EG gave afternoon and evening lectures at Kaw Valley Socialist Club Hall, 807 Walnut Street, in **Kansas City**, Missouri.

APRIL 8

EG lectured on "Socialism Caught in the Political Trap," at Kaw Valley Socialist Club Hall in **Kansas City**.

APRIL 9

EG spoke on "Sex the Great Element of Creative Work" at Kaw Valley Socialist Club Hall in **Kansas City**.

APRIL 10

EG spoke on "The Failure of Christianity" at 934 Massachusetts Street in **Lawrence**, Kansas.

APRIL 11

EG lectured on "The Six Great Elements of Creative Work" at 934 Massachusetts Street in **Lawrence**.

APRIL 12

EG lectured on sex at 934 Massachusetts Street, in **Lawrence**. She suggested that a chair in eugenics be established at Kansas University in memory of Moses Harman.

APRIL 15

EG lectured on the Brieux play *Maternity* in **Denver**, Colorado.

Harris Weinstock was appointed by California governor Hiram W. Johnson to investigate "charges of cruelty and all matters pertaining to the recent disturbances in the city of San Diego."

APRIL 16

EG lectured in the evening on "Socialism Caught in the Political Trap" at East Turner Hall in **Denver**.

APRIL 17

EG was scheduled to lecture on "Sex, the Great Element of Creative Work" at East Turner Hall in **Denver**.

Harris Weinstock arrived in San Diego,

California, and met with local officials in the evening.

APRIL 18

EG lectured on Rostand's *Chantecler* in the ballroom of the Brown Palace Hotel in **Denver**. The lecture was chaired by Albert Vogle.

APRIL 18–20

Harris Weinstock conducted public hearings on the official investigation into the brutalities in San Diego.

APRIL 21

EG lectured in the afternoon on the "Possibilities of Human Nature" and in the evening on "Art and Revolution" at the Women's Club in **Denver**. IWW organizers, on their way to San Diego to fight for free speech, attended EG's talk; a collection was made to support them.

APRIL 22

EG attended a **Denver** production of Rostand's *Chantecler*, starring Maude Adams as Chantecler, in the evening at the Broadway Theater. EG reviewed the production as a *Denver Post* theater critic.

APRIL 23

EG began her 5 p.m. drama classes at the Women's Club and was scheduled to continue them daily for a week. Later in the evening, EG was scheduled to lecture on "Woman's Inhumanity to Man" at Normal Hall in **Denver**.

APRIL 24

EG taught a 5 p.m. drama class at the Women's Club, in **Denver**. Later in the evening, EG lectured on "The Drama" at Normal Hall in **Denver**.

APRIL 25

EG taught a class on French and German Drama at the Women's Club in **Denver**.

APRIL 26

EG taught a class on Russian drama at the Women's Club, completing her Denver lecture series, and the drama class was scheduled to give her a farewell reception at 35 East 18th Avenue in **Denver**.

EG's article "Nation Seethes in Social Unrest," the first of a three-part series by EG on social unrest, appeared in the *Denver Post*.

**APRIL 28**

EG gave two lectures at Socialist Hall in **Salt Lake City**, Utah. In her afternoon lecture she condemned labor leaders who renounced the McNamara brothers, calling them "yellow curs." In the evening she spoke on "Sex the Great Element of Creative Work."

EG's article "Woman Center of Social Storm Which Is Sweeping Us Along" appeared in the *Denver Post*.

**APRIL 29**

EG spoke on Rostand's *Chantecler* in the afternoon and "Shall the Poor Have Many Children" in the evening at Socialist Hall in **Salt Lake City**.

**APRIL 30**

EG's article "Greed of Capital Basis of Social Unrest Today," the third of three articles on social unrest, appeared in the *Denver Post*.

**MAY 1**

EG arrived in **Los Angeles**, California.

**MAY 3**

In the morning EG addressed several hundred members of the IWW at IWW headquarters in **Los Angeles**; she said she might visit San Diego, California, to aid the free speech fight.

**MAY 4**

EG was scheduled to address a street gathering in commemoration of the Haymarket anarchists in **Los Angeles**.

**MAY 5**

EG was scheduled to lecture on "Anarchism, the Moving Spirit in the Labor Struggle" at Mammoth Hall in **Los Angeles**.

**MAY 6**

EG was scheduled to lecture on "The Failure of Christianity," at Mammoth Hall in **Los Angeles**.

**MAY 7**

EG was scheduled to lecture on "Art and Revolution" at Mammoth Hall in **Los Angeles**.

IWW member Joseph Mikolasek was shot and mortally wounded by police in front of San Diego IWW headquarters.

**MAY 8**

EG was scheduled to lecture on "Woman's Inhumanity to Man" at Mammoth Hall in **Los Angeles**.

**MAY 9**

EG was scheduled to lecture on "Sex, the Great Element of Creative Work" at Mammoth Hall in **Los Angeles**.

**MAY 10**

EG was scheduled to lecture on "Communism, the Most Practical Basis for Society" at Mammoth Hall in **Los Angeles**.

**MAY 11**

EG was scheduled to lecture on "Socialism Caught in the Political Trap" at Mammoth Hall in **Los Angeles**.

A social and dance was scheduled at Burbank Hall in **Los Angeles**, in support of the San Diego free speech fight.

**MAY 12**

EG was scheduled to deliver two closing lectures on "Sex, the Great Element of Creative Life" and "Socialism Caught in the Political Trap" at Mammoth Hall in **Los Angeles**.

**MAY 12–18**

Delegates to the national Socialist Party convention in Indianapolis, Indiana, by a vote of 191 to 90, amended the Socialist Party constitution (Article 2, Section 6) to read that "any member of the Party who opposes political action or advocates crime, sabotage or violence as a weapon of the working class will be expelled." Adoption of the anti-sabotage amendment was perceived by some as a direct attack on William Haywood and other IWW members and supporters.

**MAY 13**

EG spoke in the morning at the funeral of Joseph Mikolasek at the IWW Headquarters in **Los Angeles**.

EG arrived by train in **San Diego**, California, in the afternoon, and was driven by bus, accompanied by Attorney Ernest E. Kirk and his wife, to the U.S. Grant Hotel, followed by an aggressive mob. An angry crowd of 2,000 surrounded EG's hotel; although she later admitted to fearing for her safety, she still refused police protection and declined to leave the city. BR, separated from EG by a ruse, was taken from the hotel by vigilantes, under police protection, to La Penasquitos Ranch, about twenty miles north of San Diego, where he was tarred and sage-brushed and had the letters IWW burned into his backside with a cigar. BR was also forced to kiss the American flag and sing "The Star Spangled Banner." EG, finding BR gone and having been told that he had been sent ahead to Los Angeles, boarded a train for Los Angeles in the middle of the night.

MAY 14–15

EG's lectures on "Ibsen's *Enemy of the People*" and "Brieux's *Maternity*" at the Socialist Hall in San Diego were canceled following the capture and abuse of BR and EG's departure to Los Angeles, on the 14th.

MAY 15

EG arrived at the Santa Fe depot in **Los Angeles**, California. BR arrived at the Santa Fe depot a few hours later and was greeted by members of the IWW.

MAY 16

The Citizens' Committee of San Diego informed proprietors of local printing establishments that they were not to accept matter submitted for publication by the editors of the *San Diego Herald* and the *Labor Leader,* which were sympathetic to the IWW and the socialists; San Diego vigilantes then destroyed the presses of the two newspapers. EG called a protest meeting on the San Diego outrages that evening at Walker Theater in **Los Angeles**. Speakers included Anton

Johannsen, McKilvey (secretary of the IWW local), Dr. Pandit, BR, and Charles Sprading.

MAY 17

EG and BR left **Los Angeles** for San Francisco. They had been given a summons by Assistant U.S. District Attorney Dudley W. Robinson before the federal grand jury that had been called to investigate the IWW.

MAY 18

EG and BR arrived in **San Francisco**. EG was greeted upon her arrival by the Mayor, reporters, and cameras, including two moving picture operators.

AB, Hippolyte Havel, and Harry Kelly signed a letter, published in the *New York World*, stating, "If the public sentiment of the country and the passive attitude of the press continue to encourage these outrages, we feel that the anarchists and other social rebels will be forced, as a matter of self-defense, to answer violence with violence."

MAY 19

EG gave the first of a series of lectures in the afternoon on "Anarchism, the Moving Spirit in the Labor Struggle," at Jefferson Square Hall in **San Francisco**; money was collected for the IWW members of San Diego and Los Angeles.

MAY 20

EG lectured at Jefferson Square Hall in **San Francisco**; money was collected for the IWW members of San Diego and Los Angeles.

MAY 25

EG was denied use of the socialist headquarters auditorium, Hamilton Hall, in **Oakland**, California.

After recommendation of Harris Weinstock to Governor Johnson and U.S. Attorney General Webb, the California attorney general arrived in San Diego to investigate the situation.

MAY 26

EG lectured on "Ibsen's *An Enemy of the People*" and on "Woman's Inhumanity to Man" at Trades Council Hall in **San Francisco**; BR reviewed the history of the fight waged in San Diego against the IWW and declared his intention to return to San Diego. The meeting was presided over by Anton Johannsen and attended by 1,000.

**MAY 30**

EG and BR spoke at Pythian Castle, **Sacramento**, California, about their recent experiences in San Diego. The *Sacramento Bee* published an editorial calling for the suppression of EG's speech and demanding her deportation from the United States.

**JUNE 1**

EG and BR arrived in **Portland**, Oregon, for a series of lectures sponsored by the Portland Modern School.

**JUNE 2**

EG spoke on "Anarchism the Moving Spirit in the Labor Struggle" at 3 p.m. and on "The Failure of Christianity" at 8 p.m. at Christensen's Hall in **Portland**. She was originally scheduled to speak at Alinsky Hall, but members of the Grand Army of the Republic protested giving their meeting place to EG.

**JUNE 3**

EG was scheduled to lecture on "*Maternity,* a Drama by Brieux (Why the Poor Should Not Have Children)" at Christensen's Hall in **Portland**.

**JUNE 4**

EG was scheduled to lecture on "Communism, the Most Practical Basis for Society" at Christensen's Hall in **Portland**.

Ricardo Flores Magón, among other members of the PLM junta, stood trial in Los Angeles for violating neutrality laws. The trial became notorious for paid perjured witnesses, a prejudiced judge, and a suspiciously feeble defense.

**JUNE 5**

EG lectured on "Sex, the Great Element of Creative Work" at Christensen's Hall in **Portland**.

**JUNE 6**

EG was scheduled to lecture on "Socialism Caught in the Political Trap" at Christensen's Hall in **Portland**.

**JUNE 9**

EG began a week-long series of lectures on anarchy and socialism in **Seattle**, Washington. The *Seattle Times* created a furor over anarchism: "Will not some patriots save Seattle from the treasonable utterances of EG?" Five hundred veterans of the Spanish-American War threatened to meet EG at the train station and drive her away. The Mayor refused requests to prevent EG from speaking but assigned police to her meetings to prevent an outbreak of trouble.

**JUNE 11**

EG was scheduled to lecture on "Art and Revolution" at Eiler's Recital Hall in **Seattle**.

**JUNE 12**

EG was scheduled to lecture on *Chantecler* at Eiler's Recital Hall in **Seattle**.

**JUNE 13**

EG was scheduled to lecture on "Communism, the Most Practical Basis for Society" at Eiler's Recital Hall in **Seattle**.

**JUNE 14**

EG was scheduled to lecture on "Sex, the Great Element of Creative Work" at Eiler's Recital Hall in **Seattle**.

**JUNE 15**

EG and BR were scheduled to lecture on "*An Enemy of the People*" and about the San Diego free speech fight at Eiler's Recital Hall in **Seattle**.

**JUNE 16**

EG was scheduled to lecture on "Socialism Caught in the Political Trap" at 3 p.m. and on "Woman's Inhumanity to Man" at Eiler's Recital Hall in **Seattle**.

**JUNE 19**

EG delivered a lecture at the IWW hall in **Spokane**, Washington, where she raised funds for free speech in San Diego and for

Ettor and Giovannitti. This was the first of three lectures she was to deliver in the city. A labor law was passed by Congress extending the eight-hour workday to all employees working under federal contract.

JUNE 20

Voltairine de Cleyre died.

JUNE 22

PLM members Ricardo and Enrique Flores Magón, Librado Rivera, and Anselmo Figueroa were all convicted on multiple counts of conspiracy to violate neutrality laws.

LATE JUNE

EG spoke at three indoor meetings and one outdoor meeting in **Butte**, Montana. While there, she learned of Voltairine de Cleyre's death.

JUNE 25

The convicted PLM members were sentenced to twenty-three months' imprisonment in the federal penitentiary at McNeil Island, Washington. Following their sentencing, riots erupted outside the courthouse in Los Angeles.

JUNE 27

EG was scheduled to arrive in **Denver**, Colorado.

JUNE 30

EG was scheduled to lecture about the San Diego free speech fight at Marble Hall in **Denver**.

JULY 2

EG spoke on the life of August Strindberg to twenty people on the opening night of her drama course. She was scheduled to teach classes on the modern drama from 4 to 5:30 p.m. for two weeks, four nights a week, at the Café Martin in **Denver**. Her intention to teach another course on eugenics was abandoned because of lack of public interest.

JULY 4

Enrique Flores Magón and others were transported from Los Angeles jail to McNeil Island,

Washington, to serve their twenty-three month term.

JULY 7

EG delivered a lecture on "Patriotism, a Menace to Liberty" at Normal Hall in **Denver**.

JULY 11

EG was scheduled to lecture on "Vice, Its Cause and Cure" in **Denver**.

JULY 13

EG lectured on "Andreyev's *King Hunger*" to her drama class in **Denver**.

MID-JULY

EG visited Voltairine de Cleyre's grave site at the Waldheim Cemetery in **Chicago** on her way back to New York.

JULY 22

EG was back at the *Mother Earth* office in **New York**.

JULY–OCTOBER

EG was recuperating from her tour at her farm in **Ossining**, New York. AB was working on the final chapter and revisions to *Prison Memoirs of an Anarchist*, which was to be published by September. BR was left in charge of the *Mother Earth* office.

AUGUST

The Syndicalist League of North America was founded by William Z. Foster.

AUGUST 8

Ross Winn died.

SEPTEMBER 30

The trial for Lawrence strike leaders Joseph Ettor and Arturo Giovannitti began in Salem, Massachusetts.

OCTOBER 6

EG was scheduled to lecture in **New York** in Yiddish on "The Psychology of Anarchism" at 2:30 p.m. at the Terrace Lyceum, and in English on "Vice" at 8 p.m. at the Lenox Casino.

OCTOBER 13

EG was scheduled to lecture on "The Psychology of Anarchism" at the Lenox Casino in **New York**.

**OCTOBER 20**

EG was scheduled to lecture on *Prison Memoirs of an Anarchist* at the Lenox Casino in **New York**.

**OCTOBER 26**

EG was scheduled to lecture on "Sex as an Element of Creative Work" at Madison Hall in **New York.**

**OCTOBER 27**

EG was scheduled to lecture on "The Dupes of Politics" at Lenox Casino in **New York**.

**OCTOBER 28**

EG spoke at a banquet held to celebrate the publication of AB's book at Café Boulevard, **New York**. Other speakers included Lincoln Steffens, William English Walling, Gilbert D. Roe, Hutchins Hapgood, Anna Strunsky Walling, Theodore Schroeder, Saul Yanovsky, William Thurston Brown, Hippolyte Havel, Leonard D. Abbott, Harry Kelly, Dr. H. Solotaroff, and Dr. Michael A. Cohn.

**NOVEMBER 3**

EG was scheduled to lecture on "Sex Sterilization of Criminals" in the afternoon at Terrace Lyceum and in the evening at Lenox Casino in **New York**.

**NOVEMBER 5**

Woodrow Wilson was elected president. Socialist Eugene Debs earned a popular vote of 900,672.

**NOVEMBER 10**

EG was scheduled to lecture on the question "What is the best and most successful weapon in the struggle of labor against capital?" at 3 p.m. at Terrace Lyceum, and on "Syndicalism" that evening at Lenox Casino in **New York**.

**NOVEMBER 11**

EG was among many speakers at the twenty-fifth anniversary of the executions of the Haymarket martyrs at 8 p.m. at Manhattan Lyceum East in **New York**. Other speakers included Franklin Jordan, Harry Kelly, Ludovico Caminita, August Lott, William

Shatov, with AB as the chairman. Participating organizations included *Mother Earth, Freie Arbeiter Stimme,* and *Golos Truda* and various trade union branches.

**NOVEMBER 17**

EG was scheduled to lecture on *King Hunger* by Leonid Andreyev at 2:30 p.m. at Terrace Lyceum, and in the evening at Lenox Casino in **New York**.

**NOVEMBER 22**

EG lectured in **New York**.

**NOVEMBER 24**

EG was scheduled to lecture in the afternoon on "The Failure of Democracy" at the Terrace Lyceum, and in the evening on the same subject at Lenox Casino in **New York**.

**NOVEMBER 26**

Ettor and Giovannitti were acquitted on all charges.

**NOVEMBER 28**

EG was scheduled to lecture on "The Resurrection of Alexander Berkman: *Prison Memoirs of an Anarchist*" at 3 p.m. and on "Syndicalism, the Hope of the Worker" at 8 p.m. at Caton's Hall in **Pittsburgh**, Pennsylvania.

**NOVEMBER 30**

EG was scheduled to speak on "Love and Marriage" in the afternoon and to debate Frank Midney on "Anarchism and Socialism" in the evening at Diamond Theatre in **New Castle**, Pennsylvania.

**LATE NOVEMBER**

EG planned to speak in the towns of **McKees Rocks** and **New Kensington**, Pennsylvania.

**DECEMBER**

A special commemorative edition of *Mother Earth* was published to celebrate Kropotkin's seventieth birthday.

**DECEMBER 1**

During a victory rally at New York's Harlem Casino celebrating the acquittal of Ettor and Giovannitti, William Haywood gave a speech that allegedly advocated direct action and sabotage. Controversy arose with the Socialist Party because there was no transcript of his speech to corroborate the allegations.

EG was scheduled to lecture on "Woman's Inhumanity to Man" at 3 p.m. at the Terrace Lyceum, and in the evening at Lenox Casino in **New York**.

DECEMBER 6

EG was scheduled to lecture on "What is the best weapon for the worker?" at 8 p.m. at the Metropolitan Singer Hall in **New York.**

DECEMBER 7

EG was one of the speakers scheduled for the international celebration of Peter Kropotkin's seventieth birthday arranged by *Freie Arbeiter Stimme* with *Mother Earth* to take place at Carnegie Hall in **New York**. Other speakers included W. English Walling, Anna Strunsky, James F. Morton, AB, Harry Kelly, Sal Yanovsky, and Dr. H. Solotaroff, with Leonard D. Abbott as chairman.

DECEMBER 8

EG was scheduled to lecture on "Economic Efficiency, the Modern Menace" at Lenox Casino in **New York**.

DECEMBER 11

EG and AB were scheduled to speak at the celebration of Peter Kropotkin's seventieth birthday at West Side Auditorium in **Chicago**, Illinois, 8 p.m.

DECEMBER 12

EG was scheduled to speak on "Syndicalism in Theory and Practice" at West Side Auditorium Annex in **Chicago**, 8 p.m.

DECEMBER 15

EG was scheduled to lecture on "*Damaged Goods* by Brieux," at Lenox Casino in **New York,** 8 p.m.

DECEMBER 22

EG was scheduled to lecture on "The Birth of Labor and the Failure of Christianity" at Lenox Casino in **New York**, 8 p.m.

DECEMBER 24

A grand ball and reunion, sponsored by

*Mother Earth*, was scheduled to take place at Royal Lyceum in **New York**.

DECEMBER 28

A charge against William Haywood for advocating sabotage and direct action in violation of Article 2, Section 6 of the Socialist Party constitution was issued by the national Socialist Party after being initiated by the New York State committee and seconded by New Jersey and District of Columbia socialists.

## 1913

JANUARY

Referendum D went out to Socialist Party members in the January edition of the *Socialist Party Monthly Bulletin* with the following comment: "Whereas W. D. Haywood, a member of the National Executive Committee, has stated in public meetings in New York City that he never advocated the use of the ballot by the workers, and instead advised them to use direct action and sabotage, violation of Article 2, Section 6, of the National Constitution; therefore be it 'Resolved, By the State Committee, representing the Socialist party of the State of New York, that W. D. Haywood is unworthy to remain any longer a member of the National Executive Committee, and the committee therefore initiates a motion for his recall from the National Executive Committee as provided by the National Constitution.'"

JANUARY 12

EG was scheduled to deliver the first lecture of the drama series, on "The Scandinavian Drama: August Strindberg, the Conflict of the Sexes," at Lenox Casino, 116th Street and Lenox Avenue, in **New York**, 8 p.m.

JANUARY 19

EG was scheduled to speak on "The German Drama: Gerhardt Hauptmann, the Social and Economic Struggle" at Lenox Casino in **New York**, 8 p.m.

Approximately 800 broad-silk weavers at the Doherty Company mill in Paterson, New Jersey, left work to protest the introduction of the multiple-loom system, leading to a drop in wages.

**JANUARY 26**

EG was scheduled to speak on "The German Drama (Continued): Arthur Schnitzler, Frank Wedekind, and Others, the Necessity of Sex Education" at Lenox Casino in **New York**, 8 p.m.

**FEBRUARY 1**

The strike at the Doherty Company mill in Paterson, New Jersey, became plant-wide.

**FEBRUARY 2**

EG was scheduled to speak on "The French Drama: Maeterlinck, Rostand, Mirbeau, and Brieux" at Lenox Casino in **New York**, 8 p.m.

**FEBRUARY 9**

EG was scheduled to speak on "The English Drama: George Bernard Shaw, Arthur Pinero, John Galsworthy, Charles Rann Kennedy, and Others" at Lenox Casino in **New York**, 8 p.m.

**FEBRUARY 12**

EG lectured in **Hartford**, Connecticut.

**FEBRUARY 14**

EG spoke in **Newark**, New Jersey.

**FEBRUARY 16**

EG was scheduled to speak at 8 p.m. on "The Russian Drama: Tolstoy, Chekov, Gorky, and Andreyev" at one of her two meetings in **Newark**.

**FEBRUARY 17–MARCH 5**

The Armory Show (an International Exhibition of Modern Art) opened at the 69th Regiment Armory at Lexington Avenue and 26th Street in New York. The show was instrumental in bridging the gap between contemporary American and European art.

**FEBRUARY 18**

IWW Local 152 voted approval for a general strike of all silk workers in Paterson, New Jersey.

President Francisco Madero was overthrown in Mexico.

**FEBRUARY 20**

*Mother Earth* held a gala: "Literary Evening and Concert in honor of the eighth birthday of *Mother Earth* Combined with a Fare-Ye-Well to Emma Goldman on her departure for an extensive lecture tour."

EG among many others was also scheduled to speak at Lenox Casino, 116th Street and Lenox Avenue, in **New York**, 8 p.m.

**FEBRUARY 22**

Francisco Madero was executed in Mexico City.

EG was scheduled to speak on "Sex Sterilization of Criminals" at Memorial Hall, 521 Superior Avenue N.W., in **Cleveland**, Ohio.

**FEBRUARY 23**

EG was scheduled to speak on "The Psychology of Anarchism" at 3 p.m. and on "Woman's Inhumanity to Man" at 8 p.m. at Memorial Hall in **Cleveland**.

**FEBRUARY 25**

EG was scheduled to speak on "Syndicalism, the Modern Menace to Capitalism" at Meredith Hall, corner of Jefferson and Michigan, in **Toledo**, Ohio.

Between 4,000 and 5,000 silk workers left work according to a prearranged plan, and the Paterson silk workers general strike began. Carlo Tresca, Elizabeth Gurley Flynn, and Patrick Quinlan were all arrested on charges of incitement to riot after speaking at a gathering of workers.

**FEBRUARY 26**

EG was scheduled to speak on "Woman's Inhumanity to Man" at Meredith Hall in **Toledo**.

**FEBRUARY 27**

EG was scheduled to speak on *Prison Memoirs of an Anarchist* at Prismatic Hall, 140 First Street, in **Detroit**, Michigan, 8 p.m.

**FEBRUARY 28**

EG was scheduled to speak on "Woman's

Inhumanity to Man" at Prismatic Hall in **Detroit**, 8 p.m.

MARCH 1

EG was scheduled to speak on "*Damaged Goods* by Brieux" at 3 p.m. and on "Syndicalism, the Modern Menace to Capitalism" at 8 p.m. at Woodmen's Hall, Main and Washington Streets, in **Ann Arbor**, Michigan.

MARCH 2

EG was scheduled to speak on "Syndicalism, the Modern Menace to Capitalism" at Duffy Hall, 64 Grand River Avenue, in **Detroit**, 8 p.m.

MARCH 4

EG was scheduled to speak on "The Failure of Democracy" at Germania Hall, 37 South Delaware Street, in **Indianapolis**, Indiana, 8 p.m.

MARCH 5

EG was scheduled to speak on "Syndicalism, the Modern Menace to Capitalism" at Germania Hall in **Indianapolis**, 8 p.m.

MARCH 6

EG was scheduled to speak on "Woman's Inhumanity to Man" at Germania Hall in **Indianapolis**, 8 p.m.

MARCH 8

By this date more than 23,000 textile workers were on strike in Paterson, New Jersey.

MARCH 9

EG was scheduled to lecture on "The Failure of Democracy" at Majestic Hall, Beaumont and Morgan Streets, in **St. Louis**, Missouri, 3 p.m.

MARCH 10

EG was scheduled to lecture on "Sex Sterilization of Criminals," at Majestic Hall in **St. Louis**, 8 p.m.

MARCH 11

EG was scheduled to lecture on "Syndicalism, the Modern Menace to Capitalism" at Majestic Hall in **St. Louis**, 8 p.m.

MARCH 12

EG was scheduled to lecture on AB's *Prison Memoirs of an Anarchist* at Majestic Hall in **St. Louis**, 8 p.m.

MARCH 13

EG was scheduled to lecture on "Woman's Inhumanity to Man" at Majestic Hall in **St. Louis**, 8 p.m.

MARCH 16

EG was scheduled to lecture on "The Failure of Democracy" at 3 p.m. and on *Prison Memoirs of an Anarchist* at 8 p.m. at Oakland Music Hall, 40th Street and Cottage Grove Avenue, in **Chicago**, Illinois.

MARCH 17

EG was scheduled to present a lecture on the modern drama at the Lexington Hotel, 22nd Street and Michigan Boulevard, at 5 p.m. and on "Sex Sterilization of Criminals" at Oakland Music Hall in **Chicago**, 8 p.m.

MARCH 18

EG was scheduled to present a lecture on the modern drama at the Lexington Hotel at 5 p.m. and to lecture on "Syndicalism, the Modern Menace to Capitalism" at Oakland Music Hall in **Chicago**, 8 p.m.

MARCH 19

EG was scheduled to lecture on the modern drama at the Lexington Hotel in **Chicago**, 5 p.m.

MARCH 20

EG was scheduled to continue her lecture series on the modern drama at the Lexington Hotel at 5 p.m. and on "The Psychology of Anarchism" at Oakland Music Hall in **Chicago**, 8 p.m.

MARCH 21

EG was scheduled to continue her lecture series on the modern drama at the Lexington Hotel at 5 p.m. and on "Woman's Inhumanity to Man" at Oakland Music Hall in **Chicago**, 8 p.m.

The forty-second anniversary of the Paris Commune was celebrated with a concert and speeches at the Terrace Lyceum, 206 East Broadway, in New York.

**MARCH 22**

EG was scheduled to continue her lecture series on the modern drama at the Lexington Hotel in **Chicago**, 5 p.m.

**MARCH 23**

EG was scheduled to speak on "Sex Sterilization of Criminals" at 3 p.m. and on "Syndicalism, the Modern Menace to Capitalism" at 8 p.m. at Freie Gemeinde Hall, 262–264 Fourth Street, in **Milwaukee**, Wisconsin.

**MARCH 24**

EG was scheduled to deliver a lecture in German on "Woman's Inhumanity to Man" at Freie Gemeinde Hall in **Milwaukee**, 8 p.m.

**MARCH 28–MARCH 30**

EG was scheduled to speak in **Des Moines**, Iowa.

**MARCH 30**

William Haywood and Adolph Lessig, a strike leader, were arrested on charges of unlawful assemblage and disorderly conduct while leading a group of strikers in Paterson, New Jersey, to a meeting in Haledon.

**MARCH–APRIL**

*Socialist Party Monthly Bulletin* (March–April) reported the results of the balloting and William Haywood's recall from the national executive committee by a vote of 22,495 to 10,944, a referendum that removed Haywood from the Socialist Party's highest administrative body for advocating direct action. Haywood left the party.

**APRIL 6**

EG was scheduled to lecture on "The Failure of Democracy" at 3 p.m. and on *Prison Memoirs of an Anarchist* at 8 p.m. at Federation Hall, 102 Washington Avenue, in **Minneapolis**, Minnesota.

**APRIL 7**

EG was scheduled to lecture on "Sex Sterilization of Criminals" at Federation Hall in **Minneapolis**, 8 p.m.

**APRIL 8**

EG was scheduled to lecture on "Syndical-

ism, the Modern Menace to Capitalism" at Federation Hall in **Minneapolis**, 8 p.m.

**APRIL 9**

EG was scheduled to lecture on "Woman's Inhumanity to Man" at Federation Hall in **Minneapolis**, 8 p.m.

**APRIL 13**

EG was scheduled to lecture on "Sex Sterilization of Criminals" at 3 p.m. and on "The Failure of Democracy" at 8 p.m. at Commercial Travelers' Hall, 12th and Central, in **Kansas City**, Missouri.

**APRIL 14**

In the afternoon EG gave the first in a series of four afternoon lectures on the drama at Commercial Travelers' Hall in **Kansas City**. EG lectured on "*Damaged Goods.* A Powerful Drama by Brieux Dealing with the Scourge of Venereal Disease."

**APRIL 15**

EG gave the second afternoon lecture on the drama and was scheduled to lecture on "Syndicalism, the Modern Menace to Capitalism" at Commercial Travelers' Hall in **Kansas City**.

**APRIL 16**

EG gave the third afternoon lecture on the drama and was scheduled to lecture on "Woman's Inhumanity to Man" at Commercial Travelers' Hall in **Kansas City**.

**APRIL 17**

EG gave the fourth and last afternoon lecture on the drama in **Kansas City**.

**APRIL 18–19**

EG was scheduled to lecture in **Coffeyville**, Kansas.

**APRIL 20**

EG was scheduled to deliver two lectures in **Lawrence**, Kansas.

**APRIL 21**

EG was scheduled to lecture on "Woman's Inhumanity to Man" at Knights of Pythias Hall, Sixth and Quincy, in **Topeka**, Kansas, 8 p.m.

APRIL 22

EG was scheduled to lecture on "Syndicalism, the Strongest Weapon of Labor." A discussion of "direct action, sabotage and the general strike" followed at Knights of Pythias Hall in **Topeka**, 8 p.m.

APRIL 25

EG was scheduled to deliver the opening lecture of a series, which would run until 1 May excluding Sunday, on Friedrich Nietzsche at the Women's Club in **Denver**, Colorado, 5 p.m. EG was scheduled for an opening evening lecture at Howe Hall in **Denver**, 8 p.m.

APRIL 26

EG was scheduled to lecture on Friedrich Nietzsche at the Women's Club, 5 p.m., and to lecture at Normal Hall in **Denver**, 8 p.m.

APRIL 27

EG was scheduled to lecture at Normal Hall at 3 p.m. and at Howe Hall in **Denver**, 8 p.m.

APRIL 28

EG was scheduled to lecture on Friedrich Nietzsche at the Women's Club, 5 p.m., and at Howe Hall in **Denver**, 8 p.m.

APRIL 29

EG was scheduled to lecture on Friedrich Nietzsche at the Women's Club, 5 p.m., and to lecture at Howe Hall in **Denver**, 8 p.m.

APRIL 30

EG was scheduled to lecture on Friedrich Nietzsche at the Women's Club, 5 p.m., and to lecture at Howe Hall in **Denver**, 8 p.m.

MAY 1

EG was scheduled to lecture on Friedrich Nietzsche at the Women's Club, **Denver**, 5 p.m., and to give the opening lecture in a drama series, similar to the previous year's series, in **Denver**, 8 p.m.

MAY 2–4

EG was scheduled to lecture on the drama in **Denver**, 8 p.m.

MAY 7

EG spoke at a memorial meeting for Joseph Mikolasek, an IWW member killed during the 1912 San Diego free speech fight, at the IWW Hall in **Denver**. Charles Cline also spoke.

MAY 8

EG was scheduled to lecture on the drama in **Denver**, 8 p.m.

MAY 12

EG lectured on "Revolutionary Labor Methods" at Burbank Hall in **Los Angeles**, California.

MAY 13

EG was scheduled to speak on Brieux's play *Woman as a Sex Commodity* at Burbank Hall in **Los Angeles**.

MAY 14

EG spoke on "The Failure of Democracy" at Mammoth Hall, 517 South Broadway, in **Los Angeles**.

MAY 15

EG lectured on *Prison Memoirs of an Anarchist* at Mammoth Hall in **Los Angeles**.

MAY 16

EG was scheduled to speak on "The Russian Drama: Tolstoy, Chekov, Gorky and Andreyev" at Burbank Hall in **Los Angeles**.

MAY 17

EG spoke on Brieux's play *Damaged Goods* at Mammoth Hall, **Los Angeles**.

MAY 18

EG was scheduled for an afternoon lecture on "Nietzsche's Anti-Christ" and an evening lecture on "The Modern Drama" at Mammoth Hall in **Los Angeles**.

MAY 19

EG lectured on "The Modern Drama" at Mammoth Hall in **Los Angeles**. Later, EG and BR left Los Angeles for San Diego, California.

MAY 20

EG was scheduled to lecture in the evening on "Ibsen's Play, *An Enemy of the People*" in **San Diego**, California. She and BR were arrested upon arrival in San Diego at 4:40 a.m. and, surrounded by a mob, taken to the police station under police protection and later escorted and placed aboard the afternoon train to Los Angeles "for their own safety."

**MAY 21**

EG spoke on "The French Drama and San Diego" at Mammoth Hall in **Los Angeles**.

**MAY 22**

EG spoke on the turn of events in San Diego at a rally against the "San Diego outrage" in **Los Angeles**. Speakers included C. T. Sprading and BR. EG was scheduled to speak on "The English Drama" at Mammoth Hall in **Los Angeles**.

**MAY 23**

EG lectured on "The English Drama" at Mammoth Hall **Los Angeles**.

**MAY 25**

EG was scheduled to speak on "Psychology of Anarchism" at 3 p.m. and on the "Social Significance of the Modern Drama" at 8 p.m. at Jefferson Square Hall in **San Francisco**, California.

**MAY 26**

EG was scheduled to speak on "Sex Sterilization" at Jefferson Square Hall in **San Francisco**, 8 p.m.

**MAY 27**

EG was scheduled to speak on "The Failure of Democracy" at Jefferson Square Hall in **San Francisco**, 8 p.m.

**MAY 28**

EG was scheduled to speak on *Prison Memoirs of an Anarchist* at Jefferson Square Hall in **San Francisco**, 8 p.m.

**MAY 29**

EG was scheduled to speak on "Syndicalism, the Strongest Weapon of Labor" at Jefferson Square Hall in **San Francisco**, 8 p.m.

**MAY 31**

An anarchist social and dance was scheduled to take place at Jefferson Square Hall in **San Francisco**, 8 p.m.

**JUNE 1**

EG spoke in the afternoon on "Syndicalism, the Strongest Weapon of Labor" at Building Trades Temple in **San Francisco**.

**JUNE 2**

The third annual dinner of the Francisco Ferrer Association was scheduled at Café Boulevard in New York. Speakers included Harry Kelly, AB, Hutchins Hapgood, Cora Bennett Stephenson, Hippolyte Havel, M. Weber, and James F. Morton Jr.

EG was scheduled to speak on "The Modern Drama, Ibsen and Strindberg" at Jefferson Square Hall in **San Francisco**.

**JUNE 3**

EG was scheduled to speak on "The German Drama" at Jefferson Square Hall in **San Francisco**.

**JUNE 4**

EG was scheduled to speak on "The French Drama" at Jefferson Square Hall in **San Francisco**.

**JUNE 5**

EG was scheduled to speak on "The English Drama" at Jefferson Square Hall in **San Francisco**.

**JUNE 6**

EG was scheduled to speak on "The English Drama, Cont'd: Stanley Houghton's *Hindle Wakes;* John Galsworthy, *The Wheels of Justice Crush All;* and Charles Rann Kennedy, *The Dignity of Labor*" at Jefferson Square Hall in **San Francisco**.

**JUNE 7**

EG was scheduled to speak on "The Russian Drama: Tolstoy, Chekov, Gorky and Andreyev" at Jefferson Square Hall in **San Francisco**.

*The Paterson Strike Pageant,* written by John Reed, was performed at Madison Square Garden in New York. It was a financial failure, losing rather than gaining money for the strikers.

**JUNE 8**

EG was scheduled to deliver her "farewell lectures" on "The Antichrist Friedrich Nietzsche: Powerful Attack upon Christianity" at 3 p.m. and on "The Child and Its Enemies: The Revolutionary Developments in Modern Education" at 8 p.m. at Jefferson Square Hall in **San Francisco**.

JUNE 15

EG was scheduled to speak on "Friedrich Nietzsche, the Anti-Governmentalist" at 3 p.m. and on "The Social Evil" at 8 p.m. at Mammoth Hall, 517 South Broadway, in **Los Angeles**, California.

JUNE 16

EG was scheduled to speak on "The Scandinavian Drama: Henrik Ibsen's *Brand, A Doll's House, Hedda Gabler,* and *The Master Builder*" at Choral Hall, Temple Auditorium Building, Fifth and Olive Streets, in **Los Angeles**, 8 p.m., under the auspices of the Drama Club.

JUNE 18

EG was scheduled to speak on "The Scandinavian Drama: August Strindberg's *Facing Death, The Dance of Death, Creditors,* and *Comrades*" at Choral Hall in **Los Angeles**, 8 p.m.

JUNE 19

EG was scheduled to speak on "German Drama: Herman Sudermann's *Magda, St. John's Fire;* Gerhart Hauptmann's *The Beaver Coat, Lonely Lives;* Gabriel Schilling's *Escape;* and Otto Hartleben's *The Moral Demand*" at Choral Hall in **Los Angeles**, 8 p.m.

JUNE 20

A memorial meeting was held to honor the first anniversary of the death of Voltairine de Cleyre at Forward Hall, 175 East Broadway, in New York, at 8 p.m. Speakers included Harry Kelly, AB, Hippolyte Havel, Sal Yanovsky, and C. B. Stephenson.

EG lectured in Yiddish on Brieux's *Maternity* at Rosen's Hall in **Los Angeles**.

JUNE 22

EG was scheduled to speak on "Economic Efficiency" at 3 p.m. and on "Art and Revolu-

tion" at 8 p.m. at Mammoth Hall in **Los Angeles**.

JUNE 23

EG was scheduled to speak on "French Drama: Maurice Maeterlinck's *Mary Magdalene* and *Monna Vanna,* Brieux's *Maternity,* and Wolfe's *The Lily*" at Choral Hall in **Los Angeles**, 8 p.m.

JUNE 25

EG was scheduled to speak on "English Drama: A. W. Pinero's *Mid Channel* and *The Thunderbolt*; George Bernard Shaw's *The Doctor's Dilemma* and *The Shewing-Up of Blanco Posnet*; John Galsworthy's *The Eldest Son*; and Charles Rann Kennedy's *The Servant in the House*" at Choral Hall in **Los Angeles**, 8 p.m.

JUNE 26

EG was scheduled to speak on "Irish Drama: J. W. Synge's *The Playboy of the Western World*; W. B. Yeats' *Where There Is Nothing*; Lady Gregory's *Spreading the News*; Lennox Robinson's *Harvest*; and T. G. Murray's *Birthright* and *Maurice Harte*" at Choral Hall in **Los Angeles**, 8 p.m.

JUNE 28

An evening anarchist social and dance to raise funds "for the purpose of publishing the works of Voltairine De Cleyre" was scheduled for Mammoth Hall in **Los Angeles**, in commemoration of the first anniversary of Voltairine de Cleyre's death.

JUNE 29

EG was scheduled to speak on "The Child and Its Enemies: The Revolutionary Developments in Modern Education" at 3 p.m. and on "Art and Revolution" at 8 p.m. at Mammoth Hall in **Los Angeles**.

JUNE 30

EG was scheduled to speak on "Russian Drama: Tolstoy's *The Power of Darkness* and *The Fruits of Enlightenment,* and Anton Chekov's *The Swan Song* and *The Cherry Orchard*" at Choral Hall in **Los Angeles**, 8 p.m.

EG was scheduled to speak in Yiddish on "The Russian Drama: Andreyev's *Anathema*, Anton Chekov's *The Swan Song*, and Chirikov's *The Chosen People*" at Rosen's Hall in **Los Angeles**.

**JULY 2**

EG was scheduled to lecture on "The Russian Drama, Continued: Maksim Gorky's *At the Bottom*, Chirikov's *The Chosen People*, and Leonid Andreyev's *Anathema* and *King Hunger*" at Choral Hall in **Los Angeles**, 8 p.m.

**JULY 3**

EG was scheduled to deliver a concluding lecture on Russian drama and to lead a general discussion and review on "The Social Significance of the Modern Drama" at Choral Hall in **Los Angeles**, 8 p.m.

**JULY 13**

EG was scheduled for lectures on "The Relation of the Individual to Society" at 3 p.m. and on "The Danger of the Growing Power of the Church" at 8 p.m. at Jefferson Square Hall, 925 Golden Gate Avenue, in **San Francisco**, California.

**JULY 14**

EG was scheduled to deliver the opening lecture on Dynamics of the Modern Drama on "The Scandinavian Drama: Henrik Ibsen's *Hedda Gabler, Doll's House*, and *The Master Builder*" at Jefferson Square Hall in **San Francisco**, 8 p.m.

**JULY 16**

EG was scheduled to deliver a lecture on "The Scandinavian Drama: Bjørnstjerne Bjørnson's *Beyond Human Power*, and August Strindberg's *Facing Death, Creditors*, and *Comrades*" at Jefferson Square Hall in **San Francisco**, 8 p.m.

**JULY 17**

EG was scheduled to lecture in Yiddish on "Motherhood, Should the Poor Have Many Children?" at Jefferson Square Hall in **San Francisco**.

**JULY 18**

EG was scheduled to lecture on "German Drama: Herman Sudermann's *Magda* and *St. John's Fire*, Gerhart Hauptmann's *Beaver Coat* and *Lonely Live*, *Gabriel Schilling's Escape*, and Otto Hartleben's *The Moral Demand*" at Jefferson Square Hall in **San Francisco**, 8 p.m. Paterson ribbon weavers voted to abandon the general strike and seek a shop-by-shop settlement. The strike dwindled as silk workers gradually returned to work.

**JULY 20**

EG was scheduled to deliver lectures on "Friedrich Nietzsche, the Anti-Governmentalist" at 3 p.m. and on "The Social Evil" at 8 p.m. at Jefferson Square Hall in **San Francisco**.

**JULY 21**

EG was scheduled to lecture on "French Drama: Maurice Maeterlinck's *Mary Magdalene* and *Monna Vanna*, Brieux's *Maternity*, and Wolfe's *The Lily*" at Jefferson Square Hall in **San Francisco**, 8 p.m.

**JULY 22**

EG debated Professor Maynard Shipley on "Anarchism vs. Socialism" at Jefferson Square Hall in **San Francisco**.

**JULY 23**

EG was scheduled to lecture on "English Drama: A. W. Pinero's *Mid Channel* and *The Thunderbolt*, George Bernard Shaw's *The Shewing-Up of Blanco Posnet*, John Galsworthy's *The Eldest Son*, and Charles Rann Kennedy's *The Servant in the House*" at Jefferson Square Hall in **San Francisco**, 8 p.m.

**JULY 25**

EG was scheduled to lecture on "Irish Drama: J. M. Synge's *The Playboy of the Western World*, W. B. Yeats' *Where There Is Nothing*, Lady Gregory's *Spreading the News*, Lennox Robinson's *Harvest*, and T. G. Murray's *Birthright* and *Maurice Harte*" at Jefferson Square Hall in **San Francisco**, 8 p.m.

**JULY 27**

EG was scheduled to lecture on "Beyond Good and Evil" at 3 p.m. and on "Art and Revolution" at 8 p.m. at Jefferson Square Hall in **San Francisco**.

**JULY 28**

EG was scheduled to lecture on "Russian Drama: Tolstoy's *The Fruits of Enlightenment* and Anton Chekov's *The Swan Song* and *The Cherry Orchard*" at Jefferson Square Hall in **San Francisco**, 8 p.m.

**JULY 29**

EG was scheduled to lecture on "The Russian Drama, Continued: Maksim Gorky's *At the Bottom*, Chirikov's *The Chosen People*, and Leonid Andreyev's *Anathema* and *King Hunger*" at Jefferson Square Hall in **San Francisco**, 8 p.m.

The *New York Call* announced the end of the Paterson conflict and the defeat of the strikers.

**JULY 30**

EG was scheduled to deliver the concluding lecture on "General Discussion of the Importance of the Modern Drama as a Social and Educational Medium" at Jefferson Square Hall in **San Francisco**, 8 p.m.

**AUGUST**

A biographical essay on EG written by Arahata Kanson was published in *Kindai Shiso* (Modern Thought) in Japan.

**AUGUST 2**

Adolph Lessig officially called off the Paterson strike.

**AUGUST 3**

EG lectured on "Syndicalism, the Strongest Weapon of Labor, Direct Action, and Sabotage" in the afternoon and on the sterilization laws adopted by the state of Oregon in the evening at Alisky Hall, 3rd and Morrison Streets, in **Portland**, Oregon.

**AUGUST 4**

EG was scheduled to speak on "Henrik Ibsen, the Struggle of the New Against the Old" and "August Strindberg, the Conflict of the Sexes" at Alisky Hall in **Portland**.

**AUGUST 5**

EG was scheduled to speak on "The German Drama: Gerhart Hauptmann, The Social and Economic Struggle; Frank Wedekind, The Need of Sex Instruction; and Ludwig Thoma, The Hypocrisy of Morals" at Mulkey Hall, Second and Morrison, in **Portland**.

**AUGUST 6**

EG was scheduled to speak on "The French Drama: Rostand's *Chantecler*, Maeterlinck's *The Bluebird*, and Brieux's *Damaged Goods*, on the Peril of Venereal Diseases" at Alisky Hall in **Portland**.

**AUGUST 7**

EG debated Professor W. F. Ries on "Socialism vs. Anarchism" at Arion Hall, 2311/2 Oak Street, in **Portland**.

The board of regents of the University of Washington decided to refuse EG permission to deliver a series of lectures on the campus in Seattle.

**AUGUST 8**

EG was scheduled to speak on "The English Drama: Shaw's *Mrs. Warren's Profession*, on Religion, Charity and Prostitution; Stanley Houghton's *Hindle Wakes*; Githa Sowerby, on the Tyranny of Institutions; and John Galsworthy, the Wheels of Justice Crush All" at Alisky Hall in **Portland**.

**AUGUST 9**

EG was scheduled to speak on "The Russian Drama: Tolstoy, Gorky, Chekov, and Andreyev" in **Portland**.

BR and Herman Michaelovitch were arrested for distributing flyers announcing EG's lectures the following Monday and Tuesday at the Socialist Hall, 31st Avenue and Madison Street, in Seattle, Washington.

**AUGUST 10**

EG spoke on "Violence and the Modern Drama" at the Finnish Socialist Hall in **Seattle**, Washington.

The Seattle Free Speech League was organized at the Labor Temple, 6th Avenue and University Street; it called on the governor of Washington to overturn the decision by the University of Washington's board of regents removing the "Open Forum" from the campus. BR spoke at the meeting.

AUGUST 11–12

EG spoke at Finnish Socialist Hall in **Seattle.**

AUGUST 17

Despite the Mayor's intention to prevent EG from speaking in Everett, she spoke in the afternoon on "Marriage and Love" and in the evening participated in a debate with socialist Minot "Maynard" Shipley on "Anarchy vs. Socialism" at Liberty Hall in **Everett**, Washington. It was EG's first visit to Everett since two years before, when city authorities had prevented her from speaking.

AUGUST 18 OR 19

EG was prevented from speaking at the University of Washington by the board of regents.

AUGUST 22

EG was scheduled to speak on "The Social and Revolutionary Significance of the Modern Drama" at McVay's Hall, 609 Trent Avenue, in **Spokane**, Washington.

AUGUST 24

EG spoke on "The Growing Danger of the Power of the Church" in **Butte**, Montana.

AUGUST 28

EG spoke on "The Psychology of Anarchy," and the "Growing Power of the Church" in **Butte**, marking the end of her lecture tour.

SEPTEMBER 11

Texas deputies attacked a group of PLM supporters led by J. M. Rangel as they were on their way to Mexico, and Silvestre Lomas was killed. The PLM group took two deputies hostage during the assault.

SEPTEMBER 13

An armed band captured and arrested all fourteen members of the PLM group on

charges of the murder of one of the deputies. All fourteen were convicted; Rangel was sentenced to ninety-nine years, and Charles Cline, an American IWW member, was sentenced to life imprisonment.

SEPTEMBER 23

A strike began in Colorado by miners working for the Colorado Fuel and Iron Company, owned by John D. Rockefeller Jr. Organized by the United Mine Workers, the miners moved their families to union tent colonies in the countryside away from mining camps.

OCTOBER

EG moved to 74 West 119th Street, a larger, ten-room house, with a parlor large enough to accommodate the seating of a hundred people. BR's mother, in poor health, moved in briefly and left as conflicts between her and EG grew. M. Eleanor Fitzgerald moved in and acted as secretary, and Rhoda Smith acted as housekeeper.

OCTOBER 12

EG spoke at a Francisco Ferrer memorial meeting, 8 p.m., at New Forward Hall, 165 East Broadway, in **New York.**

OCTOBER 18

A reunion concert and ball, sponsored by *Mother Earth*, took place at Lenox Casino in **New York**.

OCTOBER 26

EG spoke on "Anarchism" in the afternoon and on "The Social and Revolutionary Significance of the Modern Drama" in the evening at the Broad Street Theatre in **Trenton**, New Jersey.

OCTOBER 28

Martial law was declared in Colorado.

NOVEMBER 2

EG was scheduled to speak on "Our Moral Censors" at Harlem Masonic Temple in the Park and Tilford Building, 310 Lenox Avenue in **New York**, 8 p.m.

NOVEMBER 9

EG was scheduled to speak on "The Place of

Anarchism in Modern Thought" at Harlem Masonic Temple in **New York**, 8 p.m.

NOVEMBER 16

EG was scheduled to speak on "The Strike of Mothers" at Harlem Masonic Temple in **New York**, 8 p.m.

NOVEMBER 23

EG was scheduled to speak on "Friedrich Nietzsche, The Anti-Governmentalist" at Harlem Masonic Temple in **New York**, 8 p.m.

NOVEMBER 25

EG, AB, and BR attended an afternoon lecture addressed by Emmeline Pankhurst at Eltinge Theatre in **New York**.

NOVEMBER 30

EG was scheduled to speak on "Beyond Good and Evil" at Harlem Masonic Temple in **New York**, 8 p.m.

DECEMBER 7

EG was scheduled to speak on "The Individual and Society" at Harlem Masonic Temple in **New York**, 8 p.m.

DECEMBER 14

EG was scheduled to speak on "The Intellectual Proletarians" in **New York**.

DECEMBER 15

EG hosted a social for Tom Mann, who was touring America, in **New York**, 9 p.m.

DECEMBER 16

EG spoke on "The Spirit of Anarchism in the Labor Struggle" at IWW Institute Hall in **Paterson**, New Jersey, before a mass meeting of the IWW. Police interrupted and forced her off the platform, after she had been warned not to speak and advised to take the "earliest train out of town." The talk was attended by 2,000 IWW supporters, many of whom attempted to prevent the police from disbanding the lecture.

DECEMBER 21

EG was scheduled to lecture on "The Anti-Christ: Friedrich Nietzsche's Powerful Attack on Christianity" at Harlem Masonic Temple at 8 p.m. in **New York**.

DECEMBER 24

On Christmas Eve, the annual "Christmas Gathering of the *Mother Earth* Family" was celebrated with a dance at Mt. Morris Hall in **New York**.

DECEMBER 28

EG was scheduled to talk on "Why Strikes Are Lost" at Harlem Masonic Temple in **New York**.

## 1914

JANUARY

In the winter the United States was experiencing massive unemployment with more than a quarter of a million people out of work in New York City alone.

JANUARY 3

The Anarchist Red Cross held its annual Prisoners' Ball at the Harlem River Casino in New York.

JANUARY 4

EG was scheduled to speak on "The Awakening of Labor" at the Labor Temple in **Philadelphia**, Pennsylvania, an event organized by the Radical Library. At 7:30 p.m., before the lecture was scheduled to begin, the police drove everyone out of the lecture hall and locked the doors. The event was moved to the headquarters of the Radical Library, where EG spoke.

JANUARY 5

EG was among the speakers, along with Bolton Hall, Leonard D. Abbott, Gilbert Roe, AB, BR, Lincoln Steffens, Hutchins Hapgood, and Grace Potter, at a free speech protest held by the Free Speech League in the Institute Hall, 90 Main Street, in **Paterson**, New Jersey.

JANUARY 10

Grocer John G. Morrison and his son Arling were shot and killed at their store by two men in Salt Lake City, Utah.

JANUARY 11

EG delivered a lecture in the evening on "The

Scandinavian Drama: Henrik Ibsen's *Brand, Hedda Gabler,* and *The Master Builder*" at Berkeley Theatre, 23 West 44th Street, in **New York;** collections were taken for the unemployed.

JANUARY 13

Joe Hill (Joel Hägglund) was taken into custody in Salt Lake City for the murder of John G. Morrison.

JANUARY 18

EG was scheduled to speak in the evening on "The Scandinavian Drama: August Strindberg's *Facing Death, Mother Love,* and *Comrades*" at Berkeley Theatre in **New York.**

JANUARY 19

The Flores Magón brothers and other PLM members were released from prison on McNeil Island.

JANUARY 22

IWW member Joe Hill pleaded not guilty to the charge of first-degree murder of grocery store owner John G. Morrison.

JANUARY 25

EG was scheduled to speak in the evening on "The German Drama: Herman Sudermann's *Magda* and *The Fires of St. John*; Gerhart Hauptmann's *Beaver Coast, Lonely Lives*; and Gabriel Schilling's *Escape*" at Berkeley Theatre in **New York.**

FEBRUARY 1

EG was scheduled to speak in the evening on "The French Drama: Maurice Maeterlinck's *Monna Vanna* and *The Blue Bird,* Its Parallel to Edmond Rostand's *Chantecler;* Eugene Brieux's *The Three Daughters of M. Dupont,* and M. Wolfe's *The Lily*" at the Berkeley Theatre, **New York.**

FEBRUARY 8

EG was scheduled to speak in the evening on "The English Drama: A. W. Pinero's *Mid-Channel* and *The Thunderbolt* and George Bernard Shaw's *Widower's Houses* and *The Shewing-Up of Blanco Posnet*" at Berkeley Theatre in **New York.**

FEBRUARY 13

EG debated William Edlin, secretary of the Arbeiter Ring, under the auspices of the Radical Educational Club at the City Casino, 195 Chrystie Street, in **New York.**

FEBRUARY 15

EG was scheduled to speak in the evening on "The English Drama: John Galsworthy's *The Silver Box* and *The Eldest Son,* Stanley Houghton's *Hindle Wakes* and *The Younger Generation,* and John Masefield's *The Tragedy of Nan*" at Berkeley Theatre in **New York.**

FEBRUARY 16 OR 17

EG took part in a debate with Harry Walton in **Brownsville,** a district of Brooklyn, New York. The proceeds from the event, $25, were sent to the Rangel-Cline Defense Fund. The debate was reported in *Regeneración* on 28 February 1914.

FEBRUARY 21

EG lectured in **Brownsville.**

FEBRUARY 22

EG was scheduled to speak in the evening on "The Irish Drama: J. W. Synge's *The Playboy of the Western World;* W. B. Yeats's *Where There Is Nothing;* Lady Gregory's *Spreading the News;* Lennox Robinson's *Harvest;* and T. C. Murray's *Birthright* and *Maurice Harte*" at Berkeley Theatre in **New York.**

FEBRUARY 27

In New York 1,000 unemployed men, led by the young anarchist Frank Tannenbaum, marched to the Baptist Tabernacle at 164 Second Avenue to demand food and shelter.

FEBRUARY 28

In New York Tannenbaum led 600 unemployed men to the Labor Temple on East 14th Street, where they were given shelter.

MARCH

Margaret Sanger released the first issue of *Woman Rebel.*

MARCH 1

EG was scheduled to speak on "The American Drama: Mark E. Swan's *Her Own Money;* William Hurlbut's *The Strange Woman;* J. Rosett's *The Quandary* and *Middle Class;* and Edwin Davis Schoonmaker's *The American* at Berkeley Theatre in **New York**, 8 p.m.

MARCH 4

In New York Tannenbaum led a group of 200 unemployed men, including Arthur Caron, to the Church of St. Alphonsus on West Broadway. A riot ensued, leading to Tannnenbaum's arrest and one-year imprisonment on Blackwell's Island for "inciting to riot."

MARCH 6

EG was scheduled to speak in **Newark,** New Jersey.

MARCH 8

EG was scheduled to speak on "The Russian Drama: Leo Tolstoy's *The Distiller* and *The Fruits of Enlightenment;* Anton Chekov's *The Swan Song* and *The Cherry Orchard;* Maksim Gorky's *The Smug Citizens* and *Summer Folk;* and Leonid Andreyev's *Anathema*" at Berkeley Theatre in **New York**, 8 p.m.

MARCH 9

EG delivered a lecture in **Philadelphia**, Pennsylvania, organized by the Free Speech League.

MARCH 15

In the afternoon EG attended a meeting in honor of the ninth birthday of *Mother Earth,* with a celebration of the Paris Commune at Terrace Lyceum, 206 East Broadway, in **New York.** EG spoke at a "Farewell Evening" with a concluding lecture and general discussion and review of the modern drama at Berkeley Theatre in **New York**, presided over by Leonard Abbott.

MARCH 20

EG was scheduled to speak in **Brooklyn,** New York.

MARCH 21

EG, AB, Carlo Tresca, and others delivered speeches at a mass meeting in Union Square in **New York,** where the Conference of the Unemployed rallied; the demonstration continued up Fifth Avenue to the Ferrer Center, where the unemployed were fed.

MARCH 22

EG was scheduled for an afternoon lecture in **Newark,** New Jersey.

MARCH 27

EG was scheduled to debate in **New York**.

APRIL

EG's book *The Social Significance of the Modern Drama* was published.

APRIL 2

Margaret Sanger was informed that the March issue of the *Woman Rebel* violated Section 211 of the U.S. Criminal Code and was unmailable.

APRIL 3

BR reported that EG opened *Mother Earth*'s seventh-annual lecture tour on this date in **Chicago**, Illinois, with "three splendid Jewish meetings."

APRIL 4

The Conference of the Unemployed held a second rally in Union Square, but it was aggressively dispersed by the police. Arthur Caron and Joe O'Carroll, IWW unemployed organizers, were among those badly beaten.

APRIL 5

EG spoke on "The Conflict of the Sexes" at Workman's Hall in **Chicago.**

APRIL 6

EG was scheduled to deliver the first afternoon lecture in a series on the modern drama, beginning with "The Scandinavian Drama: Henrik Ibsen's *Hedda Gabler* and *The Master Builder,* and August Strindberg's *Comrades* and *The Link*" at Lexington Hotel, 22nd Street and Michigan Avenue, in **Chicago**. EG was scheduled to lecture in the evening on "Anarchism vs. Socialism" at International Labor Hall, 538 Wells Street, in **Chicago**.

APRIL 7

EG was scheduled to lecture in the afternoon on "The German Drama: Herman Sudermann's *The Fires of St. John;* Gerhart

Hauptmann's *Lonely Lives* and *Rose Bernd,* and Ludwig Thoma's *Morals*" at Lexington Hotel in **Chicago**. EG was scheduled to lecture in the evening on "Our Moral Censors" at International Labor Hall in **Chicago**.

**APRIL 8**

EG was scheduled to lecture in the afternoon on "The English Drama: John Galsworthy's *The Eldest Son* and *The Fugitive;* St. John Hankin's *The Last of the De Mullins;* John Masefield's *The Tragedy of Nan;* and J. C. Francis's *Change*" at Lexington Hotel in **Chicago**. EG was scheduled to lecture in the evening on "The Individual and Society" at International Labor Hall in **Chicago**.

**APRIL 9**

EG was scheduled to lecture in the afternoon on "The Irish Drama: J. W. Synge's *The Playboy;* W. B. Yeats' *Where There Is Nothing;* Lady Gregory's *Spreading the News;* Lenox Robinson's *Harvest* and *Birthright;* and T. C. Murray's *Maurice Harte*" at Lexington Hotel in **Chicago**. EG was scheduled to lecture in the evening on "The Hypocrisy of Charity" at International Labor Hall in **Chicago**.

**APRIL 10**

EG was scheduled to lecture in the afternoon on "The American Drama: Eugene Walter's *The Easiest Way;* Mark E. Swan's *Her Own Money;* William Hurlbut's *The Strange Woman;* and George Middleton's *Nowadays*" at Lexington Hotel in **Chicago**. In the evening she was scheduled to lecture on "Beyond Good and Evil" at International Labor Hall in **Chicago**.

**APRIL 11**

EG was scheduled to lecture on "The Russian Drama: Leo Tolstoy's *The Fruits of Enlightenment;* Anton Chekov's *The Swan Song* and *The Cherry Orchard;* Maksim Gorky's *The Smug Citizens;* and Leonid Andreyev's *Anathema*" at Lexington Hotel in **Chicago**, 4:30 p.m. At 8 p.m. she was scheduled to lecture

in German on "Anarchism and Labor" at International Labor Hall in **Chicago**. A third mass meeting of the Conference of the Unemployed was held in Union Square in New York, without a police permit.

**APRIL 12**

EG was scheduled to lecture in the afternoon on "The Mother Strike" at International Labor Hall in **Chicago**. In the evening she lectured on "The Anti-Christ" in **Chicago**.

**APRIL 19**

EG was scheduled to give two lectures in **Madison**, Wisconsin.

**APRIL 20**

Colorado National Guardsmen volleyed machine-gun fire into the union tent village in Ludlow, Colorado. Tents were set on fire. At least five miners, twelve children, and two women were killed. The event led to a series of demonstrations against the Rockefeller family at their home in Tarrytown, New York; in Colorado hundreds of miners took up arms and attacked mines.

**APRIL 21–24**

EG was scheduled to lecture in **Minneapolis**, Minnesota.

**APRIL 22**

Anarchist Rebecca Edelsohn was arrested for disorderly conduct at an antiwar meeting at Franklin's statue in New York. She was sentenced to a bond of $300 to keep the peace for ninety days. She refused and was sentenced to ninety days in the workhouse. Edelsohn then declared a hunger strike, becoming the first American political prisoner to declare a hunger strike in order to protest the injustice of her sentence. The Free Speech League took up her case after forty-eight hours, and she was released upon the application for a new trial.

**APRIL 23**

AB announced the formation of the Anti-Militarist League in New York and encouraged the formation of similar leagues throughout the country. He also continued to organize the unemployed.

**APRIL 26**

EG lectured in the afternoon on "The Mother Strike" at Trades Assembly Hall in **Des Moines**, Iowa. She left that night for Denver, Colorado.

**APRIL 28–MAY 2**

EG was scheduled to lecture on the drama in **Denver**, Colorado.

**APRIL 29**

Upton Sinclair and his wife organized a "Silent Parade" in front of Rockefeller's New York Standard Oil offices to protest the Ludlow Massacre, with Arthur Caron and Leonard D. Abbott among the marchers. Sinclair was arrested, along with four women. President Wilson sent federal troops to Colorado to restore order.

**APRIL 30**

Upton Sinclair and the four women arrested with him on 29 April refused to pay the fines for picketing and served three days in jail.

**MAY**

Donald Vose arrived at EG's apartment in New York with a letter of introduction from his mother and a letter purportedly addressed to Matthew Schmidt "from someone in Washington" (David Caplan).

**MAY 1**

EG was scheduled to speak on the drama in **Denver**, at a local Jewish meeting.

Upton Sinclair paid his fine and was released from the Tombs jail.

AB, Rebecca Edelsohn, and others took part in an International May Day celebration at Mulberry Bend Park under the auspices of the Anti-Militarist League. AB made a speech criticizing Rockefeller for his part in the Ludlow Massacre and urged a general strike; many in the crowd carried banners linking Ludlow to Mexico. The demonstration ended in a procession to Union Square,

where marchers joined socialists in a mass revolutionary demonstration.

**MAY 3**

EG was scheduled to speak at a meeting called to protest the use of federal troops in the Colorado mining strike and the growing threat of war with Mexico at a meeting at East Turner Hall, 2132 Arapahoe Street, in **Denver**, organized by the Anti-Militarist League of Denver.

Demonstrations occurred at Rockefeller's church in New York and at his country estate in Pocantico Hills.

**MAY 4–9**

EG was scheduled to deliver a series of evening lectures on "The Revolutionary Significance of the Modern Drama" in the Building Trades Club Hall, 1749 Arapahoe Street, in **Denver**.

**MAY 9**

EG delivered a concluding drama lecture in **Denver**, and attended a party for the IWW members released from jail. While in **Denver**, BR led a free speech victory march down 16th Street for the twenty-seven IWW members released from jail. A local Free Speech League was established in conjunction with the National Free Speech League.

**MAY 11**

EG left **Denver** for **Salt Lake City**, Utah, to lecture at two scheduled meetings.

**MAY 17**

EG was scheduled to speak in the afternoon on "Anarchism vs. Socialism" and in the evening on "Our Moral Censors" at Lincoln Hall, Walker Auditorium, 730 S. Grand Avenue, 3rd Floor, in **Los Angeles**, California.

**MAY 18**

EG was scheduled to speak on "The Individual and Society" at Lincoln Hall, Walker Auditorium in **Los Angeles**, 8 p.m.

AB, Rebecca Edelsohn, Harry Kelly, and others spoke for the Anti-Militarist League at Paterson, New Jersey, on "Thou Shalt Not Kill Either in Mexico or Colorado."

MAY 19

EG was scheduled to speak in the evening on "Beyond Good and Evil" at Burbank Hall, 542 S. Main Street, in **Los Angeles.**

MAY 20

EG was scheduled to speak in the evening on "Revolution and Reform—Which?" at Burbank Hall in **Los Angeles.**

MAY 21

EG was scheduled to speak in the evening on "The Intellectual Proletarians" at Lincoln Hall, Walker Auditorium in **Los Angeles.**

MAY 22

EG was scheduled to speak in the evening on "The Hypocrisy of Charity" at Burbank Hall in **Los Angeles.**

MAY 23

EG was scheduled to speak in the evening on "The Conflict of the Sexes" at Burbank Hall in **Los Angeles.**

MAY 24

EG was scheduled to speak in the afternoon on "The Place of the Church in the Labor Struggle" and in the evening on "The Mothers' Strike" at Lincoln Hall, Walker Auditorium in **Los Angeles.**

JUNE 1

EG was scheduled to speak in the evening on "The English Drama: George Bernard Shaw's *Widower's Houses* and *The Devil's Disciple,* and John Galsworthy's *The Pigeon*" at YPSL Hall, 116½ East Third Street, in **Los Angeles.**

JUNE 2

EG was scheduled to speak in the evening on "The English Drama: St. John Hankins' *The Last of the De Mullins;* John Masefield's *The Tragedy of Nan;* and John Oswald Francis' *Change*" at YPSL Hall in **Los Angeles.**

JUNE 3

EG was scheduled to speak in the evening on "The Irish Drama: J. M. Synge's *The Tinker's Wedding;* Lady Gregory's *McDonough's Wife;*

Lenox Robinson's *Patriots;* and Seamus O'Kelly's *The Bribe*" at YPSL Hall in **Los Angeles.**

JUNE 4

EG was scheduled to speak in the evening on "The American Drama: Eugene Walter's *The Easiest Way;* W. E. Swan's [Mark E. Swan's] *Her Own Money;* W. Hurlbut's *The Strange Woman;* and George Middleton's *Nowadays*" at YPSL Hall in **Los Angeles.**

JUNE 5

EG was scheduled to speak in the evening on "The Russian Drama: Leo Tolstoy's *The Fruits of Enlightenment,* Anton Chekov's *The Cherry Orchard,* and Leonid Andreyev's *Anathema* and *King Hunger*" at YPSL Hall in **Los Angeles.**

JUNE 14

EG spoke in the afternoon on "Revolution or Reform—Which?" and in the evening on "Our Moral Censors" at Mission Turn Hall, 18th Street near Valencia, in **San Francisco,** California.

JUNE 15

EG was scheduled to speak on "The Superman and the Revolution" at Mission Turn Hall in **San Francisco.**

JUNE 16

EG was scheduled to speak on "The Hypocrisy of Charity" at Mission Turn Hall in **San Francisco.**

JUNE 17

EG was scheduled to speak on "The Intellectual Revolutions" at Mission Turn Hall in **San Francisco.**

Joe Hill's trial began in Salt Lake City, Utah.

JUNE 18

EG was scheduled to speak on "The Conflict of the Sexes" at Mission Turn Hall in **San Francisco.**

JUNE 19

EG was scheduled to speak on "Anarchism vs. Socialism" at Mission Turn Hall in **San Francisco.**

**JUNE 20**

EG was scheduled to speak on "The Mothers' Strike" at Mission Turn Hall in **San Francisco**.

**JUNE 21**

EG was scheduled to speak in the afternoon on "Anti-Militarism: The Reply to War" and in the evening on "The Place of the Church in the Economic Struggle" at Mission Turn Hall in **San Francisco**.

**JUNE 22–JULY 8**

EG began a new series of lectures on the modern drama, reviewing the work of French, German, Russian, Scandinavian, English, and American playwrights at Odd Fellows Hall, 7th and Market Street, in **San Francisco**.

**JUNE 22**

EG was scheduled to speak on Ibsen's plays at Odd Fellows Hall in **San Francisco**.

**JUNE 28**

Joe Hill was convicted of murder.

Archduke Francis Ferdinand of Austria was murdered in Sarajevo, sparking a chain of events that led to World War I.

**JULY 1**

EG was the principal speaker at an afternoon meeting of the Sex Hygiene Congress at Merchant Exchange Building in **San Francisco**, sponsored by the University of California at Berkeley. She was scheduled to lecture on "Morality" at Odd Fellows Hall in **San Francisco**. She also attended a Radical Club dinner, where she challenged a government-employed professor, who was addressing the club on "Unemployment," to a debate sometime while she was in **San Francisco**.

**JULY 3**

EG lectured on "Free Love" at Odd Fellows Hall in **San Francisco**.

**JULY 4**

An explosion on Lexington Avenue in New York killed Arthur Caron, Carl Hanson, Charles Berg, and Marie Chavez. The three men were apparently planning to bomb John D. Rockefeller Jr.'s house in Tarrytown. Shortly after, the "To the Public" leaflet issued by the Francisco Ferrer Association disassociated the organization from the bomb.

**JULY 6**

EG was scheduled to lecture on "American Drama" at Odd Fellows Hall in **San Francisco**.

**JULY 8**

Joe Hill was sentenced to death.

EG delivered her final lecture in **San Francisco**.

**JULY 11**

EG arrived in **Eureka**, California, with BR. She lectured in the evening at Woodman Hall in **Arcata**, California.

Anarchists and others met in Union Square, New York, to mourn the deaths of Arthur Caron, Charles Berg, and Carl Hanson. Speakers included AB, Leonard Abbott, Rebecca Edelsohn, and Elizabeth Gurley Flynn. A telegram of solidarity was sent by EG and BR. It was a politically charged event with 1,000 policemen on hand.

**JULY 12**

EG lectured on "Anarchism and Why It Is Misunderstood" at 3 p.m. and on "The Place of the Church in the Economic Struggle" at 8 p.m. at Brett Hall in **Eureka**, California.

**JULY 13**

EG was scheduled to lecture in **Fortuna**, California.

**JULY 14**

EG lectured on "The Birth Strike" at Brett Hall in **Eureka**.

**JULY 18**

BR was arrested for distributing handbills announcing EG's lectures. He was released immediately after agreeing to stop handing them out in **Portland**, Oregon.

**JULY 19**

EG was scheduled to lecture in the afternoon on "Strikes, New and Old Methods" at Scandinavian Socialist Hall (aka Turn Hall) at 4th and Yamhill in **Portland**. EG also was scheduled to speak that evening at 8 p.m. in the same location, on a subject to be announced.

**JULY 20**

EG was scheduled to lecture on "The Scandinavian Drama: Henrik Ibsen, Liberty, the Great Constructive Force; August Strindberg, The Conflict of the Sexes, and Bjørnstjerne Bjørnson, Beyond Our Might" at Scandinavian Socialist Hall in **Portland**.

Rebecca Edelsohn was sent to jail after refusing to pay a $300 bond to keep the peace, stemming from her 22 April arrest. She began a thirty-one-day hunger strike in prison.

**JULY 21**

EG was scheduled to lecture on "Russian Drama: Leo Tolstoy, The Sham of Culture; Anton Chekov, The Hope for a New Society, and Leonid Andreyev, Man's Lack of Faith in His Own Power" at Library Hall, Tenth and Taylor Streets in **Portland**.

**JULY 22**

EG was scheduled to lecture on "The American Drama: Eugene Walter, Woman as a Sex Commodity; M. E. Swan, The Economic Equality of Woman; W. Hulburt, The Inconsistency of Pseudo-Radicals; and George Middleton, The Slavery of Traditions" at Scandinavian Socialist Hall, **Portland**.

**JULY 23**

EG was a guest at the single-tax luncheon at 148 Fifth Street at noon in **Portland**. EG was scheduled to lecture on "English Drama: Bernard Shaw, The Source of Charity; John Galsworthy, The Futility of Reform and the Double Standard of Morality; John Masefield, The Cruelty of the Law; and Francis, The Struggle Between the Old and Young" at Scandinavian Socialist Hall, **Portland**.

**LATE JULY**

EG spoke on "Intellectual Proletarians" at a meeting at the Portland Public Library in **Portland**, arranged and presided over by C. E. S. Wood. She also was scheduled to speak on

"The Immorality of Prohibition and Continence" in **Portland**.

**JULY 26–AUGUST 3**

EG was scheduled to hold meetings in **Seattle**, Washington.

**AUGUST 4**

EG spoke on "The Birth Strike—Why and How the Poor Should Not Have Children" at Eagles' Hall, 13th and E Streets, in **Tacoma**, Washington.

At midnight Britain declared war on Germany, marking the official beginning of World War I.

**AUGUST 5–13**

EG was scheduled to lecture in **Portland**, Oregon. While in Portland EG participated in a benefit social for Rangel and Cline and Ford and Suhr; $34 was raised, and other speakers included Covington Hall. EG also took part in an anti-militarist meeting.

**AUGUST 6**

EG was scheduled to speak at an anti-military mass meeting at Scandinavian Socialist Hall, Fourth and Yamhill Streets, in **Portland**.

**AUGUST 13**

EG closed her lecture series in **Portland**.

**AUGUST 14**

EG left **Portland** for **Butte**, Montana.

**AUGUST 16–19**

EG held five meetings in **Butte**. Topics included war and birth control.

**AUGUST 25**

Margaret Sanger was indicted on three counts of obscenity for publishing the March, May, and July issues of the *Woman Rebel* and one count of inciting to murder and assassination for publishing "In Defense of Assassination" by Herbert Thorpe in the July issue.

**SEPTEMBER 1**

Joe Hill's petition for a new trial was denied.

**SEPTEMBER 15**

EG was back in **New York.**

While visiting EG, Matthew Schmidt met Donald Vose. Also present were Lincoln Steffens and Hutchins Hapgood.

The October issue of the London *Freedom* printed "A Letter on the Present War" by Peter Kropotkin in which he indicated his support for England and France against German aggression. Kropotkin's stance split the international anarchist movement, which traditionally had been anti-militarist and opposed to nationalism.

The *Mother Earth* office moved to 20 East 125th Street in New York.

The fifth-anniversary commemoration of Francisco Ferrer's death by the Ferrer Association was held at Forward Hall in New York.

A bomb was found at Church of St. Alphonsus, and a bomb exploded at St. Patrick's Cathedral in New York. Police tried to link the bombs to Tannenbaum's IWW church raids of the previous year.

EG left **New York** for Chicago, Illinois.

EG was scheduled to speak in Yiddish on "The Psychology of War" at Hod Carriers' Hall, Harrison and Green Streets, in **Chicago**.

EG was scheduled to lecture in the afternoon on the Scandinavian drama; topics included Ibsen's *Specter* and Strindberg's *The Father* and *The Friend* (Comrade), the first of a series of Yiddish lectures on the modern drama at Workman's Hall, 12th Street, in **Chicago**.

In the evening, EG's first propaganda lecture on "War, and the Sacred Right of Property" was scheduled at East End Hall, Erie and Clark Streets, in **Chicago**.

EG spoke on "The Immorality of Prohibition and Continence" at East End Hall in **Chicago**.

EG was scheduled to open a lecture series in the evening with "Introduction: The Modern Drama as a Mirror of Individual, Class and Social Rebellion Against the Tyranny of the Past," at Fine Arts Building, 410 South Michigan Avenue, in **Chicago**.

EG was scheduled to deliver a propaganda lecture on "The Betrayal of the International" at East End Hall in **Chicago**.

EG was scheduled to speak on "The Scandinavian Drama: Henrik Ibsen's *The Comedy of Love;* August Strindberg's *Lucky Pehr;* and Hjalmar Bergstrom's *Karen Borneman* and *Lyndgard and Co.*" at Fine Arts Building in **Chicago**.

Margaret Sanger fled the country by train to Montreal, Canada, to escape charges against her.

EG was scheduled to hold a meeting in Yiddish on "The False Pretenses of Culture" at Hod Carriers' Hall in **Chicago**.

EG was scheduled to speak on "The German Drama: Gerhardt Hauptmann's *Hannele;* Hermann Sudermann's *The End of Sodom;* and Max Halbe's *Youth*" at Fine Arts Building in **Chicago**.

EG was scheduled to deliver in the afternoon a drama lecture in Yiddish on Hauptmann's *The Singing Bells;* Ekman Tudarman's [Hermann Sudermann's] *Magda;* Frank Wedekind's *Fruhlings Erwachen* (Spring's Awakenings); and Marx Heldge's [Max Halbe's] *The Youth* at Workman's Hall in **Chicago**.

EG spoke in the evening on "The Psychology of War" at Fine Arts Building in **Chicago**.

**NOVEMBER 2**

EG was scheduled to lecture on "The Sham of Culture" at East End Hall in **Chicago**.

**NOVEMBER 3**

EG was scheduled to speak on "The French Drama: Eugene Brieux's *The Red Robe*, Paul Hervieu's *In Chains*, Henry Beque's *The Vultures*, and Henry Bataille's *Plays*" at Fine Arts Building, **Chicago**.

Margaret Sanger sailed for England from Canada, fleeing charges.

**NOVEMBER 4**

EG was scheduled to lecture on "The Tsar and 'My Jews'" at East End Hall in **Chicago**.

**NOVEMBER 5**

EG was scheduled to lecture on "The Italian and Spanish Drama: Gabrielle D'Annunzio's *The Daughter of Jorio*; Guiseppe Giacosa's *The Sacred Ground*; and Jose Echegaray's *The Great Galcotto*" at Fine Arts Building in **Chicago**.

**NOVEMBER 6**

EG was scheduled for an evening Yiddish lecture on "The Tsar and 'My Jews'" at Hod Carriers' Hall in **Chicago**.

**NOVEMBER 7**

EG was scheduled to lecture on "The English Drama: George Bernard Shaw's *Misalliance* and *Fanny's First Play*; Charles Rann Kennedy's *The Idol Breaker*; and John Galsworthy's *The Mob*" at Fine Arts Building in **Chicago**. The PLM published an open letter to the workers of the United States encouraging them to back the struggle of the working class in Mexico. The letter was reprinted in the April 1915 issue of *Mother Earth*.

**NOVEMBER 8**

EG was scheduled for a drama lecture in the afternoon in Yiddish on Jacob Gordin's *The Shita*, Sholem Asch's *The God of Revenge*, and David Pinski's *The Family Tria* at Workman's Hall in **Chicago**. EG spoke in the evening on "War and 'Our Lord'" (also titled "Religion and the War") at Fine Arts Building in **Chicago**.

**NOVEMBER 9**

EG was scheduled to deliver a propaganda lecture on "The Misconceptions of Free Love" at East End Hall in **Chicago**.

In the early morning, AB was arrested in New York for felonious assault of a police officer after an altercation took place between the police and anarchists on their way home from a farewell dinner for AB, who was about to leave on a nationwide lecture tour. Four other people, including *Golos Truda* editor William Shatov, were also arrested and charged with disorderly conduct. Three were sentenced to ten days in the workhouse, and one chose to pay a $10 fine.

**NOVEMBER 10**

EG was scheduled to speak on "The American Drama: Plays by Butler Davenport, George Middleton, and Others, to Be Announced Later" at Fine Arts Building in **Chicago**.

AB was released on $1,000 bail provided by the father of Andrea Ciofalo, a member of the New York Bresci group. AB left New York for Pittsburgh, the first engagement on his lecture tour.

**NOVEMBER 11**

EG and other speakers were scheduled for the twenty-seventh anniversary of the Haymarket anarchists commemoration at East End Hall in **Chicago**.

**NOVEMBER 12**

EG was scheduled to speak on "The Jewish Drama: Jacob Gordin's *The Slaughter*; Sholem Asch's *The God of Vengeance*; David Pinski's *The Zwee Family*; and Max Nordau's *A Question of Honor*" at Fine Arts Building in **Chicago**.

**NOVEMBER 13**

EG was scheduled to speak at an evening Yiddish propaganda meeting on "The False Fundamentals of the Free Love" at Hod Carriers' Hall, **Chicago**.

NOVEMBER 14

EG was scheduled to speak on "The Russian Drama: Maksim Gorky's *Summer Folk;* Anton Chekov's *The Three Sisters;* and Leonid Andreyev's *The Life of Man* and *Savva*" at Fine Arts Building in **Chicago**.

NOVEMBER 15

EG was scheduled to deliver a drama lecture in the afternoon in Yiddish on Tolstoy's *The Living Dead;* Gorky's *The Night Asylum* (*The Lower Depths*); Chekhov's *The Cherry Orchard;* and Andreyev's *King Hunger* at Workman's Hall in **Chicago**. EG was scheduled to speak in the evening on "The Tsar and 'My Jews'" at Fine Arts Building in **Chicago**.

EG spoke on "The Relationship of Anarchism to Literature" at the Chicago Press Club luncheon.

NOVEMBER 20

EG spoke on "War" in **Detroit**, Michigan.

NOVEMBER 21

EG spoke in the afternoon and evening in **Ann Arbor**, Michigan.

NOVEMBER 22

EG spoke on "War and Its Relation to Property" at Turner Hall in **Detroit**.

NOVEMBER 23

EG spoke on "Misconceptions of Free Love" at Arbeiter Hall in **Detroit**.

NOVEMBER 24

EG spoke on "The War and Our Lord" at Prismatic Hall in **Detroit**.

NOVEMBER 26

EG spoke in **Grand Rapids**, Michigan, at two meetings arranged by the Analyser Club with William Buwalda among the organizers.

NOVEMBER 29–DECEMBER 6

EG was scheduled to speak on topics including "War and the Sacred Right of Property," "The Sham of Culture," "The Misconceptions of Free Love," and "The Psychology of Anarchism" at Trade Union Central Federation Hall in **St. Louis**, Missouri. Propaganda meetings took place in the afternoons and

evenings of Sunday 19 November and Sunday 6 December. Altogether, EG spoke at eight English and two Yiddish meetings.

DECEMBER

*Regeneración* suspended publication because of lack of funds.

DECEMBER 1

The National Security League was formed in New York to advance the cause of military preparedness.

DECEMBER 8

EG spoke on "War and the Sacred Rights of Property" at Germania Hall in **Indianapolis**, Indiana.

DECEMBER 9

EG spoke on "Misconceptions of Free Love" at Germania Hall in **Indianapolis**.

The strike of miners in Colorado had dwindled and was effectively called off by the United Mine Workers of America. Sixty-six men, women, and children had been killed.

DECEMBER 9–10

EG was scheduled to lecture in **Cincinnati**, Ohio.

DECEMBER 13

EG was scheduled to deliver English lectures in the afternoon and evening at Pythian Temple in **Cleveland**, Ohio.

DECEMBER 14

EG was scheduled to deliver a Yiddish lecture at Royal Hall in **Cleveland**.

DECEMBER 15–18

EG spoke in **Pittsburgh**, Pennsylvania, at a meeting organized by Jacob Margolis.

DECEMBER 19

A Comstock agent visited William Sanger's studio, pretending to be a friend of Margaret Sanger; upon his request William Sanger gave him a copy of her pamphlet *Family Limitation.*

DECEMBER 20

EG spoke on "The War" at the Victoria Theatre in **Rochester**, New York, an afternoon event organized by Miriam Cominsky, EG's niece.

**DECEMBER 22**

EG spoke on the birth strike to a packed meeting at Rochester Labor Lyceum in **Rochester**.

**DECEMBER 24**

EG was back in **New York**.

**DECEMBER 31**

EG hosted a New Year's Eve party at the *Mother Earth* office in **New York**.

**1915**

**JANUARY 8**

EG was scheduled to speak in **Newark**, New Jersey.

**JANUARY 10**

EG was scheduled to speak in the evening on "War, and the 'Sacred' Right of Property," at Harlem Masonic Temple, 310 Lenox Avenue, between 125th and 126th Streets, in **New York**.

**JANUARY 15**

EG attended violin concert by her nephew David Hochstein at Aeolian Hall in **New York**.

**JANUARY 17**

EG was scheduled to speak in the evening on "The Betrayal of the International" at Harlem Masonic Temple in **New York**.

**JANUARY 18**

EG was scheduled to speak on "War, and the 'Sacred' Rights of Property" at Van Loon Hall, 120 Madison Avenue near South Pearl Street, in **Albany**, New York.

**JANUARY 19–20**

EG was scheduled to speak in **Albany** and **Schenectady**, New York.

**JANUARY 19**

Anthony Comstock agent returned to William Sanger's studio with Comstock. Sanger was arrested, charged with distributing a copy of Margaret Sanger's pamphlet on *Family Limitation*, and taken to court and arraigned, with bail set at $500.

**JANUARY 20**

William Sanger was bailed out of jail with funds raised by Leonard Abbott and Gilbert Roe.

**JANUARY 22**

EG was scheduled to speak in **Newark**, New Jersey.

**JANUARY 24**

EG spoke in the evening on "The Misconceptions of Free Love" at Harlem Masonic Temple in **New York**.

**JANUARY 29**

EG was scheduled to lecture in Yiddish in **Boston**, Massachusetts.

**JANUARY 30**

EG delivered "two independent lectures," one in the afternoon and one in the evening in **Boston**; one was arranged by the Freedom Group and "comrade Block," and the other, in Yiddish, by the Working People's Institute of Boston.

**JANUARY 31**

EG was scheduled to speak in the evening on "The Sham of Culture" at Harlem Masonic Temple, 310 Lenox Avenue, between 125th and 126th Streets, in **New York**.

**FEBRUARY 7**

EG was scheduled to speak on "The War and Our Lord," at Harlem Masonic Temple in **New York**, 8 p.m.

**FEBRUARY 13**

Matthew Schmidt was arrested on the streets of New York after Donald Vose informed the authorities of his whereabouts.

**FEBRUARY 14**

EG was scheduled to speak on "The Tsar and 'My Beloved Jews,'" at the Harlem Masonic Temple in **New York**, 8 p.m.

**FEBRUARY 16**

EG was scheduled to deliver "Introduction: The Modern Drama as a Mirror of Individual, Class and Social Rebellion Against the Tyranny of the Past" at Van Loon Hall in **Albany**, New York.

EG was scheduled to speak at the Socialist Press Club in **New York.**

David Caplan was arrested on Bainbridge Island, a few miles from Seattle, where he had been hiding. Donald Vose had informed the authorities of his whereabouts.

**FEBRUARY 20**

The *Mother Earth* ball, "Red Revel," took place in the evening at Lenox Casino in **New York.**

**FEBRUARY 21**

EG was scheduled to speak in the evening on "The Immorality of Prohibition and Continence" at Harlem Masonic Temple in **New York;** she was probably at an afternoon meeting as well.

**FEBRUARY 23**

EG was scheduled to speak on "The Scandinavian Drama: Henrik Ibsen, The Struggle of the New Against the Old, and August Strindberg, The Conflict of the Sexes" at Van Loon Hall in **Albany,** New York.

**FEBRUARY 24**

EG planned to lecture on "Anarchism," "The War," and "The Birth Strike" in **Schenectady,** New York.

**FEBRUARY 28**

EG was scheduled to speak in the evening on "Woman and War," at Harlem Masonic Temple in **New York.**

**MARCH**

The International Anarchist Manifesto on the War, signed by EG, AB, Errico Malatesta, and more than thirty other anarchists from the United States, England, the Netherlands, Italy, Russia, France, and Spain, was issued from London. This antiwar position repudiated Peter Kropotkin's support, announced in 1914, of England and France against Germany.

**MARCH 2**

EG was scheduled to speak on "The German Drama: Gerhart Hauptmann: The Social and Economic Struggle" and "Frank Wedekind:

The Need of Sexual Instruction" at Van Loon Hall in **Albany,** New York.

Frank Abarno, a member of the Bresci anarchist group, and Amedero Polignani, an undercover policeman, placed a bomb in St. Patrick's Cathedral. Abarno was immediately arrested, as was his friend and associate Carmine Carone, who was at home. Both men were charged with conspiracy to bomb the cathedral.

**MARCH 4**

William Sanger and attorney Gilbert Roe requested a jury trial for his birth control case; the request was denied.

**MARCH 7**

EG was scheduled to speak on "Anarchism and Literature" at Harlem Masonic Temple, 310 Lenox Avenue, between 125th and 126th Streets, in **New York.**

**MARCH 8**

EG held a meeting for the "Italian Boys' Defense," a defense committee for Frank Abarno and Carmine Carone.

**MARCH 9**

EG was scheduled to speak on "The French Drama: Rostand and Maeterlinck: *Chantecler* and *The Bluebird;* Mirbeau, The Tragedy of Material Success, and Brieux's *Damaged Goods*" at Van Loon Hall in **Albany,** New York, sponsored by the Social Science League.

**MARCH 11**

The tenth anniversary of *Mother Earth* was celebrated at Berkeley Theatre, 22 West 44th Street, in **New York,** with music and drama. Speakers included EG, Leonard Abbott, and Bolton Hall.

**MARCH 12**

EG spoke at a meeting for William Sanger's defense in **Albany,** New York.

**MARCH 14**

EG was scheduled to speak on "Feminism, a Criticism of Woman's Struggle for the Vote and 'Freedom'" at Harlem Masonic Temple in **New York.**

**MARCH 15**

The trial of William Sanger was scheduled to begin, but it was postponed until 12 April; Gilbert Roe was Sanger's attorney.

**MARCH 16**

EG was scheduled to speak on "The English Drama: G. Bernard Shaw's *The Doctor's Dilemma;* John Galsworthy's *Strife;* Charles Rann Kennedy's *Servant in the House;* and Sir Arthur Pinero's *The Thunderbolt*" at Van Loon Hall in **Albany**, New York.

**MARCH 18**

EG and H. M. Kelly were English speakers at a celebration of the forty-fourth anniversary of the Paris Commune in the evening at Lenox Casino, Lenox Avenue and 116th Street, in **New York**. Carlo Tresca spoke in Italian, Pedro Esteve in Spanish, William Shatov in Russian, and Michael Cohn in Yiddish.

**MARCH 21**

EG was scheduled to speak on "Nietzsche, the Intellectual Storm Center of the Great War" at Harlem Masonic Temple in **New York**.

**MARCH 23**

EG was scheduled to speak on "The Russian Drama: Tolstoy's *The Power of Darkness;* Chekov's *The Swan Song;* Gorky's *Summer Folk;* and Andreyev's *Anathema*" at Van Loon Hall in **Albany**, New York.

**MARCH 27**

The International Masquerade Ball, under the auspices of *Golos Truda*, was scheduled to take place at the Manhattan Lyceum in New York.

**MARCH 28**

EG lectured on "Limitation of Offspring" at Harlem Masonic Temple in **New York**. She also spoke to 600 people on family limitation at the Sunrise Club in **New York**.

**MARCH 29**

EG held a Jewish meeting in **New York**.

**MARCH 30**

EG was scheduled to speak on "The Italian and Spanish Drama: Gabrielle D'Annunzio's *The Daughter of Jorio;* Guiseppe Giacosa's *The Sacred Ground;* and Jose Echegaray's *The Great Galeotto*" at Van Loon Hall in **Albany**, New York.

Invited by students of Columbia College, EG was scheduled to lecture on "The Message of Anarchism" at Union Theological Seminary, Broadway and 120th Street, in **New York**, later cancelled by union officials because EG was ill.

**APRIL**

The organizing junta of the PLM, including the Flores Magón brothers, appealed to the readers of *Mother Earth* for solidarity with the workers of Mexico and the Mexican revolutionary movement.

EG posed for a portrait by Robert Henri in **New York**.

**APRIL 1**

EG was scheduled to speak on "The Birth Strike" in **Schenectady**, New York.

**APRIL 2**

EG was scheduled for Jewish meeting in **Albany**, New York.

**APRIL 6**

EG spoke before the students of the Theological Seminary at Columbia College in **New York**, a meeting rescheduled from 30 March.

**APRIL 7**

EG debated Isaac Hourwich as a fund-raiser for the Ferrer School on "Social Revolution Versus Social Reform" in **New York**.

**APRIL 9**

A celebration of the anniversary of *Mother Earth* was scheduled to take place at the Labor Temple in **Brownsville**, New York. Frank Abarno and Carmine Carbone were found guilty and sentenced to six to twelve years in prison.

**APRIL 11**

EG was scheduled to speak on "The Intermediate Sex" at Harlem Masonic Temple in **New York**.

**APRIL 12**

The trial of William Sanger, originally scheduled to begin 15 March, was again postponed.

**APRIL 13**

EG was scheduled to speak on "The American Drama: Butler Davenport, George Middleton, and Eugene Walter's *The Easiest Way*" at Van Loon Hall in **Albany**, New York.

**APRIL 15**

EG was scheduled to speak on "War and Private Property" at a public conference at Laster Hall, 34 Andrew Street, in **Lynn**, Massachusetts; BR was also scheduled to speak.

**APRIL 16**

EG addressed a meeting of 1,000 people in **Lynn**.

**APRIL 18**

EG was scheduled to speak on "Man—Monogamist or Varietist?" at Harlem Masonic Temple in **New York**.

**APRIL 19**

EG was scheduled to speak against the Billy Sunday movement at Turn Hall, on Van Houten Street, in **Paterson**, New Jersey.

**APRIL 20**

EG was scheduled to speak on "The Jewish Drama: Jacob Gordin's *The Slaughter;* Sholem Asch's *The God of Vengeance;* David Pinski's *The Zwee Family;* and Max Nordau's *A Question of Honor*" at Van Loon Hall in **Albany**, New York, the last of the series.

**APRIL 28**

A farewell dinner for EG was hosted by Carlo Tresca and others in **New York**.

**APRIL 29–30**

EG spoke on "Billy Sunday" in English and on "The Limitation of Offspring" before a Jewish audience in **Philadelphia**, Pennsylvania.

**MAY 2**

EG spoke on "The Limitation of Offspring" in **Washington, D.C.**, under the auspices of the Liberal Discussion Club. Catholic socialist Mahoney tried and failed to prevent her from speaking; he harassed the owners

of public halls where EG might speak and urged the police to intervene.

**MAY 3**

EG spoke at a Jewish meeting arranged by Leon Malmed in **Baltimore**, Maryland.

**MAY 4**

EG was scheduled to speak on "Limitation of Offspring" in **Pittsburgh**, Pennsylvania. She May have spoken instead on "The Message of Anarchy," a lecture EG formerly delivered under the name of "Psychology of Anarchism."

**MAY 5–7**

EG was scheduled to speak at Pythian Temple in **Cleveland**, Ohio.

**MAY 7**

RMS *Lusitania* was sunk by German submarine off the coast of Ireland.

**MAY 9**

EG was scheduled to speak on "Nietzsche, the Intellectual Storm Center of the European War" at the Fine Arts Assembly Room, Fine Arts Building in **Chicago**, Illinois.

**MAY 10**

EG was scheduled to speak on "Is Man a Varietist or Monogamist?" at the Fine Arts Assembly Room, Fine Arts Building in **Chicago**.

**MAY 11**

EG was scheduled to speak on "Jealousy" at the Fine Arts Assembly Room, Fine Arts Building in **Chicago**.

**MAY 12**

EG was scheduled to speak on "Social Revolution vs. Social Reform" at the Fine Arts Assembly Room, Fine Arts Building in **Chicago**.

**MAY 13**

EG was scheduled to speak on "Feminism (A criticism of the Modern Woman's Movements)" at the Fine Arts Assembly Room, Fine Arts Building in **Chicago**.

**MAY 15**

EG spoke on "The Intermediate Sex (A study of Homosexuality)" at the Fine Arts Assembly Room, Fine Arts Building in **Chicago**.

**MAY 16**

EG spoke on "The Limitation of Offspring" at the Fine Arts Assembly Room, Fine Arts Building in **Chicago**.

The Ferrer Modern School moved from New York to Stelton, New Jersey.

**MAY 21**

EG delivered a lecture in **Milwaukee**, Wisconsin, arranged by Yiddish comrades.

**MAY 22**

EG lectured to two large student audiences in **Madison**, Wisconsin.

**MAY 23**

EG was scheduled to speak on "The Philosophy of Anarchism" in the afternoon and on "Misconception of Free Love" in the evening in **Minneapolis**, Minnesota.

**MAY 24**

EG was scheduled to speak on "Birth Control, Why and How Workers Should Have Small Families" in the evening in **Minneapolis**.

**MAY 25**

EG spoke on "The Modern School and the Child" in **St. Paul**, Minnesota, under the auspices of the Liberal Alliance League.

**MAY 26**

EG was scheduled to speak in **St. Paul**.

**MAY 28**

Joe Hill's case was appealed in Salt Lake City, Utah.

**MAY 30**

EG was scheduled to speak in the afternoon on "Friedrich Nietzsche, the Intellectual Storm Center of the European War," and in the evening on "Misconceptions of Free Love" at Marble Hall, 1514 Cleveland Place, in **Denver**, Colorado.

**MAY 31**

EG was scheduled to speak in the evening on "Jealousy, Its Cause and Possible Cure" at Marble Hall in **Denver**.

**JUNE 1**

EG was scheduled to speak in the evening on "The Intermediate Sex (A Discussion of Homosexuality)" at Marble Hall in **Denver**.

**JUNE 2**

EG was scheduled to speak in the evening on "Limitation of Offspring. Why and How Small Families are Preferable" at Marble Hall in **Denver**.

**JUNE 3**

Joe Hill's appeal failed. Three judges decided there was no cause to grant a new trial or reverse the jury's verdict.

**JUNE 6**

EG was scheduled to present an afternoon lecture on "Psychology of War" and an evening lecture on "The Follies of Feminism" at Burbank Hall in **Los Angeles**, California.

**JUNE 8**

EG was scheduled to speak at Burbank Hall in **Los Angeles**.

**JUNE 9**

EG was scheduled to speak on "War" at Burbank Hall in **Los Angeles**.

**JUNE 12**

EG was scheduled to speak on "Jealousy" at Burbank Hall in **Los Angeles**.

**JUNE 17**

EG was scheduled to deliver a lecture on birth control at Rosen's Hall in **Los Angeles**.

**JUNE 18**

EG was scheduled to lecture at Burbank Hall in **Los Angeles**.

**JUNE 19**

EG was scheduled to lecture on "Prohibition" at Burbank Hall in **Los Angeles**.

**JUNE 20**

EG spoke in the morning on "Ibsen's *An Enemy of the People*" (a lecture she had twice been prevented from delivering in San Diego), in the afternoon on "Nietzsche and the War," and in the evening on the Sanger case at Fraternal Brotherhood Hall in **San Diego**, California. She was accompanied by AB; BR did not return this time.

Walter Moore, one of the 1912 vigilantes and

a member of the city council, proposed that the city appropriate $3,000 to "entertain" her again, but members of the Open Forum convinced the newly elected Mayor to state publicly that anyone who harassed EG would invite the attention of the police.

JUNE 22–27

EG was scheduled to lecture at Burbank Hall in **Los Angeles**, California. During her stay in Los Angeles she spoke at a Caplan-Schmidt meeting at Labor Temple and held a Caplan-Schmidt social. She was invited by Dr. T. Perceval Gerson to speak at the Severance Club (named after Caroline M. Severance, co-worker of Susan B. Anthony and Julia Howe).

JUNE 22

EG was scheduled to lecture on "Birth Control" at Burbank Hall in **Los Angeles**.

JUNE 23

EG was scheduled to speak at Burbank Hall in **Los Angeles**.

JUNE 26

An anarchist ball was held at Burbank Hall in Los Angeles.

JUNE 27

EG was scheduled to lecture on "War and Church" at 3:00 p.m. and on "Anarchism and Literature" at 8:00 p.m. at Burbank Hall in **Los Angeles**.

JUNE 30

EG lectured on "Feminism" before the Woman's City Club in **Los Angeles**.

JULY 4

EG lectured in the afternoon on "The Psychology of War" at Scottish Rite Hall, Van Ness Avenue and Sutter Street, **San Francisco**, California.

JULY 5

EG lectured in the afternoon on "The Misconceptions of Free Love" at Scottish Rite Hall in **San Francisco**.

JULY 6

EG was scheduled to lecture in the evening on "War and the 'Sacred' Right of Property" at Scottish Rite Hall in **San Francisco**.

JULY 7

EG lectured in the evening on "Jealousy, Its Cause and Possible Cure" at Scottish Rite Hall in **San Francisco**.

JULY 8

EG was scheduled to lecture in the evening on "The Betrayal of the Spirit of the International" at Scottish Rite Hall in **San Francisco**.

JULY 9

EG lectured in the evening on "The Follies of Feminism (A criticism of the Modern Woman's Movement)" at Scottish Rite Hall in **San Francisco**.

JULY 10

EG lectured in the evening on "The Immorality of Prohibition and Continence" at Scottish Rite Hall in **San Francisco**.

JULY 11

EG was scheduled to lecture in the evening on "The Philosophy of Anarchism" at 3 p.m. and on "Billy Sunday and His 'Power'" at Scottish Rite Hall in **San Francisco**.

JULY 12

EG lectured in the evening on "Monogamy or Variety, Which?" at Scottish Rite Hall in **San Francisco**.

JULY 13

EG was scheduled to lecture in the evening on "The Sham of Culture" at Scottish Rite Hall in **San Francisco**.

JULY 14

EG was scheduled to lecture in the evening on "Women and War" at Scottish Rite Hall in **San Francisco**.

William Sanger again requested a jury trial for his birth control case, and the request was again denied.

JULY 16

EG was scheduled to lecture in the evening on "The Modern School and the Child" at Scottish Rite Hall in **San Francisco**.

## JULY 17

EG was scheduled to lecture in the evening on "The Intermediate Sex, a discussion of Homosexuality" at Scottish Rite Hall in **San Francisco**.

## JULY 18

EG was scheduled to lecture in the afternoon on "Religion and the War" at Averill Hall, 1254 Market Street near Larkin, in **San Francisco**.

## JULY 18

EG was scheduled to lecture in the evening on "Revolution or Reform" at Averill Hall in **San Francisco**.

## JULY 19

EG was scheduled to lecture in the evening on "Birth Control (Why and How Small Families Are Preferable)" at Averill Hall in **San Francisco**.

## JULY 20

EG was scheduled to lecture in the evening on "Anarchism and Literature" at Averill Hall in **San Francisco**.

## JULY 21

EG lectured in the evening on "Our Moral Censors" at Averill Hall in **San Francisco**.

## JULY 23

EG was scheduled to lecture in the evening on "The Tsar and 'My Beloved Jews'" at Averill Hall in **San Francisco**.

## JULY 24

An anarchist social and ball was held in the evening at Averill Hall in **San Francisco**. EG was in attendance.

## JULY 25

EG was scheduled to lecture on "The Right of the Child Not to Be Born" at 3 p.m. and on "Nietzsche, the Intellectual Storm Center of the War" at 8 p.m. at Averill Hall in **San Francisco**.

## JULY 29

EG spoke on "The Philosophy of Atheism" to the Congress of Religious Philosophy at the Civic Auditorium in **San Francisco**.

## AUGUST 1–8

EG was scheduled for a lecture series to be chaired by C. E. S. Wood at Scandinavian Socialist Hall, Fourth and Yamhill, in **Portland**, Oregon.

## AUGUST 1

EG lectured in the afternoon on "The Philosophy of Anarchism" at 3 p.m. and on "The 'Power' of Billy Sunday" at Scandinavian Socialist Hall in **Portland**.

## AUGUST 2

EG was scheduled to speak in the evening on "Misconceptions of Free Love" at Scandinavian Socialist Hall in **Portland**.

Joe Hill again sentenced to be executed; the date set was 1 October.

## AUGUST 3

EG presented a lecture in the evening on "Nietzsche and War" at Scandinavian Socialist Hall in **Portland**, a meeting chaired by C. E. S. Wood.

## AUGUST 4

EG spoke in the evening on "Jealousy—Its Cause and Possible Cure" at Scandinavian Socialist Hall in **Portland**.

## AUGUST 5

EG was scheduled to speak on "Anarchism and Literature," at Scandinavian Socialist Hall in **Portland**.

## AUGUST 6

EG and BR were arrested at 9 p.m. in **Portland** for distributing literature on birth control. EG was arrested just after she had been introduced by C. E. S. Wood to a large crowd on the lower floor of Scandinavian Socialist Hall and had started her talk on Nietzsche. EG had been warned that afternoon by the police chief that she would be arrested because of a birth control circular that had been distributed. Her arrest was prompted by a citizen's complaint. EG was released on $500 cash bail, provided by Wood, and she announced that she would try to speak on the subject of birth control on 7 August, while BR was still in jail.

**AUGUST 7**

EG and BR were fined $100 for distributing birth control information in **Portland**. The prosecution claimed that the birth control circulars were distributed on the prior Tuesday evening at EG's talk on Nietzsche. BR admitted to distributing them, but said it was without EG's knowledge. EG and BR decided to appeal their case. Chief of Police Clark proclaimed that EG would not be allowed to speak again in Portland. She spoke in the evening on "The Intermediate Sex (A Discussion of Homosexuality)" at Scandinavian Socialist Hall, in a meeting attended by, among others, plainclothes policemen, a deputy district attorney, and a deputy city attorney.

**AUGUST 8**

EG was scheduled to speak in the afternoon on "War and the 'Sacred' Right of Property," and in the evening on "Variety or Monogamy, Which?" at Scandinavian Socialist Hall in **Portland**.

**AUGUST 10**

EG spoke on "The Sham of Culture" at Portland Public Library in **Portland**.

**AUGUST 13**

The case against EG was dismissed in a Portland court by Judge William Gatens, who was quoted as saying, "There is too much tendency to prudery nowadays. We are shocked to hear things uttered that we are familiar with in our every-day life." EG was represented by C. E. S. Wood.

**AUGUST 14–24**

EG was scheduled to speak in **Seattle**, Washington.

**AUGUST 15**

EG spoke on "War and the Sacred Right of Property" in the afternoon and "The Power of Billy Sunday" in the evening at IWW Hall in **Seattle**.

**AUGUST 23**

EG spoke at a meeting for Caplan and Schmidt in **Seattle**.

**SEPTEMBER 10**

William Sanger was tried and convicted for distributing indecent literature and served a thirty-day jail sentence in lieu of paying a $150 fine.

**SEPTEMBER 16**

EG was scheduled to speak on a "Message to Labor from Our Two Comrades in Jail in Los Angeles: Caplan and Schmidt" at an international mass meeting at Harlem Casino, 116th Street and Lenox Ave, in **New York**.

**SEPTEMBER 18**

In Salt Lake City, Utah, Joe Hill's attorneys applied for the commutation of his sentence to life imprisonment, a petition that was denied.

**SEPTEMBER 21**

Anthony Comstock died.

**SEPTEMBER 30**

President Wilson intervened in the Joe Hill case, asking and receiving a postponement of the execution until the Swedish minister had time to speak to the governor of Utah. Elizabeth Gurley Flynn and Mrs. J. Sargent Cram, the wife of a prominent Democrat, had asked President Wilson through his secretary to intervene and grant Joe Hill a reprieve.

**OCTOBER 3**

EG spoke on Caplan and Schmidt at Forward Hall in **New York**.

**OCTOBER 4**

The trial of Matthew A. Schmidt, accused of murder in the *Los Angeles Times* bombing, began in the superior court of Los Angeles. EG lectured about Caplan and Schmidt in **Brownsville**, New York.

**OCTOBER 6**

Margaret Sanger arrived in New York, after fleeing to England to escape charges.

**OCTOBER 10**

William Sanger was released from prison.

EG was scheduled to report on her cross-country tour at a *Mother Earth* autumn festival at Harlem Casino in **New York**.
The Utah Board of Pardons terminated the reprieve of Joe Hill.

**OCTOBER 18**

Joe Hill's date of execution was set, for the third time, for 19 November.

**OCTOBER 26**

EG lectured on "Preparedness, the Road to Universal Slaughter" in **Philadelphia**, Pennsylvania, hosted by the Free Speech League with Theodore Schroeder.

**OCTOBER 27**

EG lectured on "Birth Control" in **Philadelphia**.

**LATE OCTOBER**

EG lectured on "Friedrich Nietzsche, the Intellectual Storm Center of Europe" and in Yiddish on "Misconception of Free Love" sometime during her **Philadelphia** tour.

**OCTOBER 29**

*Regeneración* resumed publication from the outskirts of Los Angeles, after having been suspended in December for lack of funds.

**OCTOBER 30–31**

EG lectured in **Baltimore**, Maryland.

**NOVEMBER 1**

EG spoke on "Friedrich Nietzsche, the Intellectual Storm Center of the European War" at Pythian Temple in **Washington, D.C.**

**NOVEMBER 2**

EG spoke on "Victims of Morality" at Pythian Temple in **Washington, D.C.**

**NOVEMBER 3**

EG lectured on "Anarchism Versus Socialism" at Pythian Temple in **Washington, D.C.**

**NOVEMBER 4**

EG lectured on "Sex, the Great Element of Creative Work" at Pythian Temple in **Washington, D.C.**

**NOVEMBER 5–7**

EG was scheduled to speak at Pythian Temple in **Washington, D.C.**, but was prohibited from delivering her talk by the hall's managers.

**NOVEMBER 8**

EG lectured in the evening on "Birth Control or the Prevention of Conception" at Montefero Hall, 2616 Fifth Avenue, in **Pittsburgh**, Pennsylvania.

**NOVEMBER 9**

EG lectured in the evening on "Preparedness, the Road to Universal Slaughter" at Montefero Hall in **Pittsburgh**.

**NOVEMBER 10**

EG lectured in the evening on "Feminism, a Discussion of the Follies of the Woman's Rights Movement" at Montefero Hall in **Pittsburgh**.

**NOVEMBER 11**

EG lectured on "Preparedness" at noon at a street meeting in **Pittsburgh** to shell makers outside the Westinghouse armaments factory. In the evening EG spoke at the International Meeting to Commemorate the Death of Our Chicago Comrades, at Montefero Hall in **Pittsburgh**. Additional short speeches were given by Jacob Margolis and William Wycis (in Polish).

**NOVEMBER 12**

EG lectured in the evening on "The Immorality of Prohibition and Continence," at Montefero Hall in **Pittsburgh**.

**NOVEMBER 13**

EG was scheduled to lecture on birth control and on Nietzsche at Woodman's Hall, Main and Washington Streets, in **Ann Arbor**, Michigan. Ann Arbor police were unsuccessful in their attempt to stop the lecture on birth control.

**NOVEMBER 14**

EG was scheduled to lecture in the evening on "The Philosophy of Atheism" at Turner Hall, 136 Sherman Street, in **Detroit**, Michigan.

**NOVEMBER 15**

EG was scheduled to lecture in the evening

on "The Right of the Child Not to Be Born" at Turner Hall in **Detroit**.

NOVEMBER 16

EG was scheduled to lecture in the evening on "Friedrich Nietzsche, the Intellectual Storm Center of the European War" at Turner Hall, **Detroit**.

NOVEMBER 17

EG was scheduled to lecture in **Akron**, Ohio.

NOVEMBER 18

EG was scheduled to lecture in **Youngstown**, Ohio.

NOVEMBER 19

Joe Hill was executed by a Utah firing squad. EG was scheduled to lecture in the evening in Yiddish at the Workingmen's Hall, West 12th and Miller Streets, in **Chicago**, Illinois.

NOVEMBER 21

EG was scheduled to lecture in the afternoon in Yiddish at Workingmen's Hall and in the evening on "Preparedness, the Road to War and Disaster" at Fine Arts Theatre, 410 South Michigan Avenue, in **Chicago**.

NOVEMBER 23

EG was scheduled to lecture in the evening on "The Right of the Child Not to Be Born" at Fine Arts Theatre in **Chicago**.

NOVEMBER 25

EG was scheduled to lecture in the evening on "The Message of Anarchism" at Fine Arts Theatre in **Chicago**.

A large funeral procession for Joe Hill took place in Chicago. An estimated 30,000 were in attendance, including William Haywood. EG sent a wreath in support.

NOVEMBER 26

EG was scheduled to deliver a lecture in Yiddish at Workman's Hall in **Chicago**.

NOVEMBER 27

EG lectured in the evening on "Sex, the Great Element of Creative Art" at Fine Arts Theatre in **Chicago**.

NOVEMBER 28

EG was scheduled to lecture in the afternoon

to a Yiddish audience at Workman's Hall in **Chicago**. EG was scheduled to lecture in the evening on "The Philosophy of Atheism" at Fine Arts Theatre in **Chicago**.

NOVEMBER 30

EG lectured in the evening on "Victims of Morality" at Fine Arts Theatre in **Chicago**.

DECEMBER 1

EG lectured, perhaps in Yiddish, on "Birth Control" in **Chicago**.

DECEMBER 2

EG was scheduled to lecture in the evening on "Nietzsche and the German Kaiser" at Fine Arts Theatre in **Chicago**.

DECEMBER 3

EG lectured in Yiddish in **Chicago**.

DECEMBER 4

EG lectured in the evening on "Birth Control" at Fine Arts Theatre in **Chicago**.

DECEMBER 5

EG was scheduled to lecture in the evening on "Beyond Good and Evil" at Fine Arts Theatre in **Chicago**.

DECEMBER 8–12

EG delivered five lectures, including one on birth control at Open Forum in **St. Louis**, Missouri.

DECEMBER 14–15

EG held two meetings at Odeon Hall, Metropolitan Music Building, corner of Pennsylvania and North Streets in **Indianapolis**, Indiana.

DECEMBER 15

The Margaret Sanger trial was scheduled to begin but was postponed until 18 January 1916. The defense attorney counseled Margaret Sanger to plead guilty and accept a plea bargain offered by the U.S. attorney.

DECEMBER 16–17

EG was scheduled to lecture at Masonic Cathedral in **Columbus**, Ohio. Mayor Karb and Chief of Police Carter banned EG from speaking because "she was not considered a fit person to lecture on either one of the subjects announced."

DECEMBER 18

EG lectured at Kayser Hall in **Akron**, Ohio.

DECEMBER 19

EG lectured afternoon and evening at Pythian Temple, Huron Road in **Cleveland**, Ohio.

DECEMBER 20

EG lectured to a Yiddish audience at Royal Hall in **Cleveland** and became ill with the grippe (influenza).

DECEMBER 21

EG lectured in **Youngstown**, Ohio.

DECEMBER 22

EG arrived in **New York**, ill with the grippe, and spent two weeks in bed.

DECEMBER 30

Matthew Schmidt was found guilty of murder in the first degree.

LATE DECEMBER–EARLY JANUARY

EG was ill and was advised to find better accommodations, as she did not have a bath. She was not allowed to stay at the Theresa Hotel, which sparked a number of protests in the press, including one from Harry Weinberger. EG eventually obtained a furnished apartment at West 133rd Street, in New York.

## 1916

JANUARY 7

EG gave the opening lectures in Yiddish at Forward Hall in **New York**.

JANUARY 9

EG spoke on "Preparedness: A Conspiracy Between the Munitions Manufacturers and Washington" at Harlem Masonic Temple in **New York**.

JANUARY 10

EG delivered a lecture in Yiddish on "The Right of the Child Not to Be Born" at Royal Hall in **Philadelphia**, Pennsylvania.

JANUARY 11

EG was scheduled to speak on "Victims of

Morality" at North Broad Street Drawing Rooms in **Philadelphia.**

JANUARY 12

EG lectured on her "Personal Interpretation of Anarchy" at the Civitas Club, a women's club in **Brooklyn**, New York.

Matthew A. Schmidt was sentenced to life imprisonment.

JANUARY 15

AB's periodical, *The Blast*, commenced publication in San Francisco. AB and Fitzi had moved to San Francisco in late 1915.

JANUARY 16

EG spoke on "The Child's Right Not to Be Born" at Masonic Temple in **New York.**

JANUARY 18

EG was scheduled to speak on "The Message of Anarchism" at North Broad Street Drawing Rooms in **Philadelphia**, Pennsylvania. Margaret Sanger's trial was scheduled to begin but was postponed, first to 24 January and then to 14 February.

JANUARY 19

EG was scheduled to speak on "The Scandinavian Drama" at Perpetual Building Association Hall in **Washington, D.C.**

JANUARY 20

EG was scheduled to speak on "The Scandinavian Drama" at Conservatory of Music in **Pittsburgh**, Pennsylvania.

JANUARY 23

EG was scheduled to speak on "The Message of Anarchism" at Harlem Masonic Temple in **New York**.

JANUARY 25

EG was scheduled to speak on "Misconceptions of Free Love" at North Broad Street Drawing Rooms in **Philadelphia**, Pennsylvania.

JANUARY 26

EG was scheduled to speak on "The German Drama" at Arcade Hall in **Washington, D.C.**

JANUARY 27

EG was scheduled to speak on "The German

Drama" at Conservatory of Music in **Pittsburgh**, Pennsylvania.

President Wilson launched a national campaign to generate support for preparedness with three rousing speeches in New York.

**JANUARY 30**

EG was scheduled to speak on "The Philosophy of Atheism" at Harlem Masonic Temple in **New York**.

**FEBRUARY 1**

EG was scheduled to speak on "The Philosophy of Atheism" at North Broad Street Drawing Rooms in **Philadelphia**, Pennsylvania.

**FEBRUARY 2**

EG was scheduled to speak on "The French Drama" at Arcade Hall in **Washington**, **D.C.**

**FEBRUARY 3**

EG was scheduled to speak on "The French Drama" at Conservatory of Music in **Pittsburgh**, Pennsylvania.

President Wilson delivered the final speech of the preparedness campaign in St. Louis, Missouri.

**FEBRUARY 4**

EG lectured on birth control at Forward Hall in **New York**.

**FEBRUARY 6**

EG was scheduled to speak on "Sex: The Great Element of Creative Art" at Harlem Masonic Temple in **New York**.

**FEBRUARY 8**

EG lectured on birth control at Star Casino in **New York**.

**FEBRUARY 9**

EG was scheduled to speak on "The English Drama" at Arcade Hall in **Washington**, **D.C.**

**FEBRUARY 10**

EG was scheduled to speak on "The English Drama" at Conservatory of Music in **Pittsburgh**, Pennsylvania.

**FEBRUARY 11**

EG was scheduled to lecture on the "Philosophy of Atheism" at Vorwart Hall in **New York**. She was arrested as she was about to enter the building and charged with violating

Section 1142 of the New York State Penal Code for lecturing the previous Tuesday, 8 February, on a medical question (birth control) in defiance of the law; she was released on $500 bail.

**FEBRUARY 13**

EG was scheduled to speak on "Nietzsche and the German Kaiser" at Harlem Masonic Temple in **New York.**

**FEBRUARY 16**

EG was scheduled to speak on "The American Drama" at Arcade Hall in **Washington**, **D.C.**

**FEBRUARY 17**

EG was scheduled to speak on "The American Drama" at Conservatory of Music in **Pittsburgh**, Pennsylvania.

**FEBRUARY 18**

The federal prosecutor dropped charges brought against Margaret Sanger in August 1914 for subject matter published in the *Woman Rebel*.

Ricardo and Enrique Flores Magón were indicted by a grand jury for using the mails to distribute material "tending to incite murder, arson, and treason." Ricardo and Enrique were arrested; Enrique resisted and was beaten to the point of requiring stitches for his wounds. William C. Owen, in Washington State at the time, escaped arrest and fled to England.

**FEBRUARY 20**

EG spoke on "Birth Control" at Harlem Masonic Temple in **New York.**

A meeting was held for Margaret Sanger in New York to celebrate the dropping of charges against her. In attendance was Robert Minor, who made a motion for EG to talk, suggesting that she be called away from the Harlem Masonic Temple where she was speaking. The motion was not sustained, and the request was ignored.

**FEBRUARY 23**

EG was scheduled to speak on "The Russian Drama" at Arcade Hall in **Washington**, **D.C.**

EG was scheduled to speak on "The Russian Drama" at Conservatory of Music in **Pittsburgh**, Pennsylvania.

**FEBRUARY 27**

EG was scheduled to speak on "*The Ego and Its Own* (a Review of Max Stirner's Book)" at Harlem Masonic Temple in **New York**.

**FEBRUARY 28**

EG's preliminary hearing in connection with the charges made at her arrest on February 11 occurred before Judge Simms. EG moved for dismissal but was refused and instead was "held over for Special Sessions."

**MARCH 1**

EG spoke at a birth control mass meeting held at Carnegie Hall in **New York**; she announced that she was also lecturing every Sunday night at Harlem Masonic Temple in **New York**. Other speakers included Margaret Sanger, Leonard Abbott, Gilbert E. Roe, Theodore Schroeder, Bolton Hall, John Reed, Anna Strunsky Walling, Dr. William J. Robinson, and Dr. A. L. Goldwater.

**MARCH 5**

EG spoke on "*The Ego and Its Own* (a Review of Max Stirner's Book)" at Harlem Masonic Temple in **New York**.

**MARCH 6**

The Birth Control and Anti-Censorship Association was organized by EG and Leonard Abbott at an evening meeting in **New York**. The organization became known as the Birth Control Committee of New York; its members included Anna Sloan, Marie Jennie Howe, Robert Henri, and Dr. William J. Robinson, with Abbott as its secretary.

**MARCH 7**

EG was scheduled to speak on "The Irish Drama: John Millington Synge, William Butler Yeats, Thomas Cornelius Murray" at Conservatory of Music in **Pittsburgh**, Pennsylvania. This was the beginning of a second drama course in Pittsburgh.

**MARCH 8**

EG was scheduled to speak on "The Irish Drama," including T. C. Murray's *Maurice Harte;* Seamus O'Kelly's *The Bribe;* Rutherford Mayne's *The Red Turf,* and Lennox Robinson's *The Patriots* at Arcade Hall in **Washington, D.C.**

AB organized a mass meeting in San Francisco, California, protesting the Flores Magón brothers' arrest.

**MARCH 9**

EG was scheduled to speak on "The Message of Anarchism" at Arcade Hall in **Washington, D.C.**

**MARCH 10**

A mass meeting was held in San Francisco to protest EG's arrest on charges of disseminating information on birth control.

**MARCH 11**

*Mother Earth* Ball was to be held to celebrate the eleventh anniversary of the magazine, at Harlem Casino in **New York**.

**MARCH 12**

EG was scheduled to speak on "The Family" at the Harlem Masonic Temple in **New York.** A meeting was scheduled to raise funds for David Caplan at 3 p.m. in New York.

**MARCH 14**

EG was scheduled to speak on "Irish Drama Continued: O'Kelly, Mayne, Robinson" at the Conservatory of Music in **Pittsburgh**, Pennsylvania.

David Caplan's trial, originally scheduled to begin on this day, was postponed until 5 April.

**MARCH 15**

EG was scheduled to speak on "Italian and Spanish Drama" including Gabriele D'Annunzio's *The Daughter of Jorio;* Guiseppe Giacosa's *The Stronger* and *Sacred Ground;* and Jose Echegaray's *The Great Galetto* at Arcade Hall in **Washington, D.C.**

MARCH 16

EG was scheduled to speak on "The Intermediate Sex" at Arcade Hall in **Washington, D.C.**

MARCH 19

EG was scheduled to speak on "The Scandinavian Drama" at Harlem Masonic Temple in **New York.**

MARCH 21

EG was scheduled to speak on "Italian and Spanish Drama" at Conservatory of Music in **Pittsburgh**, Pennsylvania.

MARCH 22

EG was scheduled to speak on "The Jewish Drama," including Jacob Gordon's *The Slaughter;* Sholem Asch's *The God of Vengeance;* and David Pinski's *The Family Tsvi* at Arcade Hall in **Washington, D.C.**

MARCH 23

EG was scheduled to speak on "Nietzsche and the German Kaiser" at Arcade Hall in **Washington, D.C.**

MARCH 24–27

EG spoke sometime during this period at the Hungry Club in **Pittsburgh**, Pennsylvania.

MARCH 26

EG was scheduled to speak on "The German Drama" at Harlem Masonic Temple in **New York.**

MARCH 28

EG was scheduled to speak on "Friedrich Nietzsche, the Intellectual Storm Center of the Great War" at the Conservatory of Music in **Pittsburgh**, Pennsylvania.

MARCH 29

EG was to attend a social dance and performance at Arcade Hall in **Washington**, D.C.

MARCH 30

EG was scheduled to speak on "The Right of the Child Not to Be Born" at Arcade Hall in **Washington, D.C.**

APRIL 2

EG was scheduled to speak on "The French Drama" including Henry Becque's *The Vul-*

*tures* and Paul Hervieu's *Modesty,* at Harlem Masonic Temple in **New York.**

EG chaired a meeting at the Star Casino in **New York** to protest the life imprisonment of Matthew A. Schmidt and encourage David Caplan on the eve of his trial. Both men were being tried on charges that they had conspired to blow up the *Los Angeles Times* building. The socialists at the meeting became unruly when the striking newsboys of the *Jewish Daily Forward* expressed their desire to present a petition to the meeting. The anarchists accused the socialists of wanting to suppress the newsboys because the socialists favored the paper in the dispute. EG abandoned the platform.

APRIL 5

David Caplan's trial began.

EG's hearing for her 11 February arrest began.

APRIL 9

EG was scheduled to speak on "The English Drama," including George Bernard Shaw's *Fanny's First Play* and *Androcles and the Lion;* St. John Hankin's *The Last of the DeMullins;* Granville Barker's *Waste;* and John Galsworthy's *The Mob* at Harlem Masonic Temple in **New York**.

APRIL 16

EG was scheduled to speak on "The Irish Drama," including Seamus O'Kelly's *The Bribe;* Rutherford Mayne's *The Red Turf;* Lenox Robinson's *The Patriots;* and J. M. Synge's *The Tinker's Wedding* at Harlem Masonic Temple in **New York.**

APRIL 19

A banquet was given for EG at the Hotel Brevoort in **New York** on the eve of her trial. Those in attendance included Harry Kelly, Rose Pastor Stokes, Whidden Graham, John Cowper Powys, Alexander Harvey, Robert Henri, George Bellows, Randal Davey, John Sloan, Robert Minor, Boardman Robinson, and John Francis Tucker.

**APRIL 20**

EG was tried before Judges O'Keeffe, Moss, and Herbert (special sessions) for lecturing on birth control; she was sentenced to serve fifteen days in Queens County Jail, after refusing to pay a $100 fine.

**APRIL 21**

EG was serving her sentence in the Queens County Jail in Queens, **New York**.

**APRIL 22**

Oscar Neebe, the Haymarket anarchist, died in Chicago.

**APRIL 23**

BR delivered EG's lecture on birth control at Harlem Masonic Temple in New York, where he also distributed birth control pamphlets.

**APRIL 24**

The Easter Rebellion broke out in Dublin.

**APRIL 27**

BR was arrested at the *Mother Earth* office in New York for distributing pamphlets on birth control on 23 April.

**MAY 4**

EG was released from jail.

**MAY 5**

EG spoke at a birth control meeting at Carnegie Hall in **New York**; Rose Pastor Stokes distributed pamphlets on birth control. In attendance were Max Eastman (editor of the *Masses*), Alois Trnka, Harry Weinberger, Arturo Giovannitti, Dr. Cecile L. Greil, and Horace Traubel.

**MAY 8**

BR was tried on charges stemming from his 27 April New York arrest for distributing birth control pamphlets. He was sentenced to sixty days in the workhouse and sent to Queens County Jail, with a scheduled release date of 6 July.

**MAY 20**

EG attended a meeting to protest BR's imprisonment at Union Square in **New York**. In a statement in the *New York Times* she anticipated the meeting as a test of how extremely

the district attorney's office discriminated against poor people, as exhibited by the restraint and hesitance to arrest wealthy demonstrators like Rose Pastor Stokes.

**MAY 21**

The trial of Ricardo and Enrique Magón began in Los Angeles, California. Ricardo was unable to attend due to poor health; the judge denied the reading of a defense statement.

**MAY 27–28**

A conference was held to celebrate the first anniversary of the Modern School's move to **Stelton**, New Jersey. Speakers included EG, William Thurston Brown, and Harry Kelly.

**MAY 31**

EG spoke at a celebration of the anniversary of Walt Whitman's birthday at the twenty-third annual meeting of the Walt Whitman Fellowship at the Hotel Brevoort in **New York**. Other speakers included Hamlin Garland, Alexander Harvey, Everett Martin, Horace Traubel, Rose Pastor Stokes, Clement Wood, William Davenport, Percival Wicksell, John Butler Yeats, Alfred Kreymborg, Helen Hoyt, William Sanger, and John Weichsel.

**JUNE 2**

Iron ore miners went on strike in the Mesabi Range in northern Minnesota calling for an eight-hour day and other demands; soon 30,000 miners were on strike. The IWW was called on for support. Carlo Tresca and others were sent to help organize the strikers, who were of many different nationalities.

**JUNE 3**

EG lectured on "Free or Forced Motherhood" at Moose Hall in **Cleveland**, Ohio.

**JUNE 4**

EG spoke on birth control to an audience in Yiddish at Royal Hall in **Cleveland**.

**JUNE 7**

EG spoke on "The Right of the Child Not to Be Born" at Upper Howe Hall in **Denver**, Colorado.

EG began a series of lectures with a speech on "Anarchism and Human Nature, Do They Harmonize?" at Burbank Hall in **Los Angeles**, California. The lectures were organized by AB.

JUNE 12

EG was scheduled to speak on "The Family, Its Enslaving Effect upon Parents and Children" at Burbank Hall in **Los Angeles**.

JUNE 13

EG spoke on "Art and Revolution: The Irish Uprising" at Burbank Hall in **Los Angeles**.

JUNE 14

EG spoke on "Preparedness, the Road to Universal Slaughter" at Burbank Hall in **Los Angeles**. The meeting coincided with a preparedness parade that took place the same day in Los Angeles.

JUNE 15

EG was scheduled to speak on "Friedrich Nietzsche and the German Kaiser" at Burbank Hall in **Los Angeles**.

The Modern School Association of North America was established at a conference at Stelton, New Jersey; Harry Kelly was named chairman, and Leonard Abbott, secretary.

JUNE 17

EG was scheduled to speak on "The Right of the Child Not to Be Born" at Burbank Hall in **Los Angeles**.

JUNE 18

EG was scheduled to speak on "The Philosophy of Atheism" at Burbank Hall in **Los Angeles**.

JUNE 22

Enrique Flores Magón was given a $1,000 fine and three years in prison for each count, to run concurrently; Ricardo Flores Magón was given the same fine and one year and one day on each count. The shorter prison time was because of his poor health.

JUNE 26

Ricardo Flores Magón was freed on bail pending an appeal. Bail was posted by EG and AB.

JUNE 30

Margaret Sanger was arrested in Portland, Oregon, for selling birth control pamphlets.

JULY 1

Enrique Flores Magón was freed on bail pending an appeal.

A social dance was held to benefit the defense of David Caplan and the Flores Magón brothers in **Los Angeles**. It was attended by EG and the Flores Magón brothers.

JULY 2

EG lectured on "Free or Enforced Motherhood: The Necessity for Birth Control" in **Los Angeles**.

JULY 3

Armed deputies and guards raided a private home in the Mesabi Range in Minnesota without warrants; a battle broke out, and two guards were killed.

JULY 4

At 3 a.m. IWW organizers, including Carlo Tresca, Joseph Schmidt, and Frank Little, were arrested in the Mesabi Range. They were charged with first-degree murder of armed deputies in a nearby town. Although they were not present at the scene of the crime, authorities claimed that their speeches incited the violence that caused the killing.

JULY 6

EG attended a banquet held in her honor by the families of the Flores Magón brothers in **Silver Lake**, California.

JULY 7

A birth control meeting to welcome BR's release from prison was scheduled at the Harlem Casino in New York.

JULY 9

EG repeated her popular lecture on "Free or Enforced Motherhood: The Necessity for Birth Control" in **Los Angeles**, California. During her stay in **Los Angeles** EG delivered four lectures on anarchism and American literature, especially the works of Emerson, Thoreau, and Whitman.

**JULY 16**

EG delivered a speech on "Anarchism and Human Nature, Do They Harmonize?" at Averill Hall in **San Francisco**, California.

**JULY 18**

EG was scheduled to deliver a speech on "The Family, Its Enslaving Effect upon Parents and Children" at Averill Hall in **San Francisco**.

**JULY 19**

EG was scheduled to deliver a speech on "Art for Life" at Averill Hall in **San Francisco**.

**JULY 20**

An anti-preparedness mass meeting was held at the Dreamland Rink in **San Francisco**. Sponsors included Paul Scharrenberg, Olaf Tveitmoe, and members of the International Workers' Defense League. EG postponed her lecture on "Preparedness the Road to Universal Slaughter."

**JULY 21**

EG was scheduled to deliver a speech on "Friedrich Nietzsche and the German Kaiser" at Averill Hall in **San Francisco**.

**JULY 22**

A bomb exploded during the Preparedness Day parade in San Francisco, killing ten people and injuring forty. The press immediately blamed labor organizers and anarchists. EG was scheduled to speak on "The Philosophy of Atheism" at Averill Hall in **San Francisco**, California. In fact, she spoke on "Preparedness," the lecture she had postponed from 20 July, in response to the bomb that had exploded earlier that day.

**JULY 23**

EG was scheduled to speak on "The Philosophy of Atheism" in **San Francisco**.

**JULY 25**

EG spoke on "Free Love" in **San Francisco**.

**JULY 26**

EG spoke on the bomb explosion of 22 July in **San Francisco**.

Warren K. Billings, Israel Weinberg, and Edward Nolan were arrested in association with the San Francisco preparedness parade bombing.

**JULY 27**

Thomas J. Mooney and Rena Mooney were arrested in Guerneville, California, while returning to San Francisco from holiday, after notifying police of their whereabouts once they read in the *San Francisco Examiner* that Thomas Mooney was a wanted man.

**JULY 29**

The offices of *The Blast* were raided without a warrant by police officials; the California subscription list of *Mother Earth* was seized, along with other material relating to EG. AB and M. Eleanor Fitzgerald were taken to police headquarters, questioned, and threatened with arrest.

**JULY 31**

EG spoke on "Free or Forced Motherhood: The Need of Birth Control" in **Oakland**, California.

**AUGUST 7**

EG met with AB and others in the office of *The Blast* in **San Francisco** to help the International Workers' Defense League defend the five Preparedness Day parade bombing suspects.

**AUGUST 13**

EG left **San Francisco** for Portland, Oregon.

**AUGUST 17**

EG began a series of four lectures on "Anarchism and Human Nature" at Scandinavian Socialist Hall, Fourth and Yamhill Streets, in **Portland**. EG was also scheduled to speak on "The Gary System in the Public Schools," "Preparedness," and "Birth Control" while in **Portland**.

**AUGUST 18**

EG lectured on "Education" at Scandinavian Socialist Hall in **Portland**.

**AUGUST 27**

EG lectured on "Anarchism and Human Nature, Are They Opposed to Each Other?" at

3 p.m. and on "The Educational and Sexual Dwarfing of the Child" at 8 p.m. at Tivoli Theatre, **Seattle**, Washington.

**AUGUST 28**

EG lectured on "Walt Whitman, the Beauty of Sex Expression" at Tivoli Theatre, **Seattle**.

**AUGUST 29**

EG was scheduled to lecture on "Preparedness, the Road to Universal Slaughter" at Tivoli Theatre, **Seattle**.

**AUGUST 30**

EG lectured on "Free or Forced Motherhood? The Need of Birth Control" at Tivoli Theatre in **Seattle**. That evening she and BR left Seattle for a vacation in **Yellowstone National Park**.

**SEPTEMBER 10**

EG was scheduled to speak on "Anarchism and Human Nature" at Marble Hall in **Denver**, Colorado.

**SEPTEMBER 11**

EG was scheduled to begin a series of afternoon lectures; her first was "Russian Literature: The Voice of Revolt (Introduction)" at Adams Hotel in **Denver**.

The trial of Warren K. Billings began in San Francisco.

**SEPTEMBER 12**

EG was scheduled to speak on "Russian Literature: The Voice of Revolt (Turgenev)" at Adams Hotel in **Denver**.

**SEPTEMBER 13**

EG was scheduled to speak on "Russian Literature: The Voice of Revolt (Tolstoy)" at Adams Hotel in **Denver**.

**SEPTEMBER 14**

EG was scheduled to speak in the afternoon on "Russian Literature: The Voice of Revolt (Dostoyevsky)" at the Adams Hotel and in the evening on "The Educational and Sexual Dwarfing of the Child" at Marble Hall in **Denver**.

**SEPTEMBER 15**

EG was scheduled to speak on "Russian

Literature: The Voice of Revolt (Chekhov)" at Adams Hotel in **Denver**.

**SEPTEMBER 16**

EG was scheduled to speak on "Russian Literature: The Voice of Revolt (Gorky)" at Adams Hotel in **Denver**.

**SEPTEMBER 17**

EG was scheduled to speak in the afternoon on "Russian Literature: The Voice of Revolt (Andreyev)" at Adams Hotel in **Denver**. She was also scheduled to speak in the evening on "Free or Forced Motherhood: The Why and How of Birth Control" in Marble Hall in **Denver**.

The Mesabi Range strike in Minnesota was called off by the central strike committee.

**SEPTEMBER 18**

EG was scheduled to speak on "Russian Literature: The Voice of Revolt (Artzibashev)" at the Adams Hotel in **Denver**. She was also scheduled to speak on "Free or Forced Motherhood: The Why and How of Birth Control" to the Denver Birth Control League in **Denver**, where BR discussed methods of birth control.

**OCTOBER 7**

Warren Billings was sentenced to life in prison.

**OCTOBER 16**

In the Brownsville district of Brooklyn Margaret Sanger opened the first birth control clinic in America.

**OCTOBER 20**

Bolton Hall was acquitted on the charge of distributing birth control pamphlets at a 20 May meeting held at Union Square in New York to protest BR's imprisonment for advocating birth control in the same place. EG was arrested on the same charge when she appeared to testify on Hall's behalf, and was released on $1,000 bail.

**OCTOBER 23**

The second trial of David Caplan began after the first trial ended in a hung jury.

Warren Billings was convicted of first-degree murder.

**OCTOBER 26**

Margaret Sanger was entrapped by a female detective posing as a mother of four children desperate for birth control information; she was arrested for distributing birth control information from her clinic.

**OCTOBER 27**

EG's hearing for her 20 October arrest before Judge Barlow was at 10 a.m.; she waived examination and tried to be awarded a jury trial but was refused. She would eventually go to trial on 8 January 1917, and be acquitted. Margaret Sanger was freed on bail.

**OCTOBER 30**

A boat full of forty IWW members arrived in Everett, Washington, from Seattle to support the AFL shingle weavers strike; they were arrested and later beaten by vigilantes.

**EARLY NOVEMBER**

AB returned to New York to organize support for the Mooney and Billings case; he hired an attorney for the defense, W. Bourke Cockran.

**NOVEMBER 5**

The IWW scheduled a meeting in Seattle in response to repression of striking workers' free speech and the violence on 30 October. A boat with 250 IWW members attempted to dock in Everett and was met by a group of vigilantes and deputies. Shots were fired, prompting the IWW boat to turn back. Five IWW members and two deputies were killed, thirty-one IWW members and twenty deputies were wounded, and an unknown number drowned in an event that became known as Everett's "Bloody Sunday."

**NOVEMBER 7–8**

In the presidential election Allen Benson, the Socialist Party candidate won 585,113 votes, 3.2 percent of the total vote.

**NOVEMBER 11**

EG spoke at a memorial meeting for the Chicago anarchists at East End Hall in **Chicago,**

Illinois. William D. Haywood, Theodore Appel, and Lucy E. Parsons also spoke; BR was chairman.

**NOVEMBER 12**

EG was scheduled to lecture on Russian Literature: "The Life Struggle and Martyrdom of Russian Literature" in Recital Hall at the Fine Arts Building in **Chicago.**

**NOVEMBER 13**

EG lectured on "Free or Forced Motherhood? (The Why and How of Birth Control)" at East End Hall in **Chicago.**

**NOVEMBER 14**

EG was scheduled to lecture on Russian Literature: "Ivan Turgenev, the Eternal conflict Between the Old and Young Generations" in Recital Hall at the Fine Arts Building in **Chicago.**

**NOVEMBER 15**

EG was scheduled to lecture on Russian Literature: "Leo Tolstoy, Artist and Prophet" in Recital Hall at the Fine Arts Building in **Chicago.**

Margaret Sanger was arrested at the reopened Brownsville clinic for maintaining a public nuisance.

**NOVEMBER 16**

EG was scheduled to lecture on "Anarchism and Human Nature: Are They Opposed to Each Other?" at East End Hall in **Chicago.**

**NOVEMBER 17**

EG was scheduled to lecture on Russian Literature: "Fyodor Dostoyevsky, the Psychologist of Misery and Poverty" in Recital Hall at the Fine Arts Building in **Chicago.**

**NOVEMBER 18**

EG was scheduled to lecture on Russian Literature: "Anton Chekov, the Idealist" in Recital Hall at the Fine Arts Building in **Chicago.**

**NOVEMBER 19**

EG held a meeting on birth control in the afternoon in **Chicago.** In the evening EG lectured on Russian Literature: "Maksim

Gorky, the Voice of Revolt" in Recital Hall of the Fine Arts Building in **Chicago**.

**NOVEMBER 20**

EG was scheduled to lecture on "The Intermediate Sex (A Discussion of Homosexuality)" at East End Hall in **Chicago**.

The tenth IWW national convention began at Bush Temple in Chicago. A resolution was adopted openly declaring the IWW's opposition to the First World War, patriotism, nationalistic sectionalism, and militarism.

**NOVEMBER 21**

EG was scheduled to lecture on Russian Literature, "Leonid Andreyev, the Iconoclast" at Recital Hall, Fine Arts Building, **Chicago**.

**NOVEMBER 22**

EG was scheduled to lecture on "The Educational and Sexual Dwarfing of the Child" at East End Hall, **Chicago**.

**NOVEMBER 23**

EG was scheduled to lecture on Russian Literature: "Michael Artzibashev, the Liberator of Sex" at Recital Hall of the Fine Arts Building in **Chicago**.

**NOVEMBER 27**

Margaret Sanger's trial for distributing birth control information and for maintaining a public nuisance began, but was then postponed pending the judge's decision about whether or not to go to the grand jury.

**NOVEMBER 28**

EG was scheduled to speak on "Family Life, a Prison for Parents and Child" at North-side Auditorium in **Milwaukee**, Wisconsin. The meeting was organized by the Milwaukee Anarchist Group.

**DECEMBER 2**

EG spoke at a meeting at Carnegie Hall in **New York** to protest the conviction of Warren K. Billings and arrest of Edward D. Nolan, Thomas J. Mooney, Israel Weinberg, and Rena Mooney, charged with bombing the San Francisco Preparedness Day parade on 22 July. The meeting was called by the

United Hebrew Trades with addresses by Frank Walsh, Max Eastman, Max Pine (secretary of the Hebrew Trades), Arturo Giovannitti, Patrick Quinlan, and AB. That afternoon, a demonstration took place at Union Square on behalf of Thomas Mooney and of Carlo Tresca, among others, who were arrested on the Mesabi Range.

**DECEMBER 4**

EG was scheduled to speak on "Leo Tolstoy, Artist and Prophet, and Fyodor Dostoyevsky, the Psychologist of Misery and Poverty" at Woodman's Hall in **Ann Arbor**, Michigan.

**DECEMBER 5**

EG was scheduled to speak on "Anton Chekov, the Idealist, and Maksim Gorky, the Voice of Revolt" at Woodman's Hall in **Ann Arbor**.

**DECEMBER 6**

EG was scheduled to speak on "Leonid Andreyev, the Iconoclast" at Woodman's Hall in **Ann Arbor**.

**DECEMBER 7**

EG was scheduled to speak on "Michael Artzibashev, the Liberator of Sex" at Woodman's Hall in **Ann Arbor**.

**DECEMBER 8**

EG was scheduled to speak in **Detroit**, Michigan.

**DECEMBER 10**

EG was scheduled to speak on "Anarchism and Human Nature: Do They Harmonize?" at 3 p.m. and on "The Life and Struggle of Russian Literature: Leo Tolstoy, Artist and Prophet" at 8 p.m. at Pythian Temple in **Cleveland**, Ohio.

**DECEMBER 11**

EG was scheduled to speak on "The Educational and Sexual Dwarfing of the Child" at Moose Hall in **Cleveland**.

**DECEMBER 12**

EG spoke on "Is Birth Control Harmful: a Discussion of the Limitation of Offspring" at Moose Hall, **Cleveland**. BR was arrested for "calling for volunteers to distribute birth control literature." He was placed under $1,000 bail, and the money was quickly raised by friends.

DECEMBER 13

EG was scheduled to speak on "Tolstoy" at Century Club in **Rochester**, New York.

DECEMBER 14

EG was scheduled to speak on "Ibsen's *Ghosts* and *An Enemy of the People*" at Recital Hall in **Rochester**.

DECEMBER 15

EG spoke on "August Strindberg's *The Father* and *Countess Julia*" at Recital Hall in **Rochester**, where BR was arrested for distributing birth control literature; an illegal pamphlet on contraceptives was supposedly discovered inside William J. Robinson's book *Limitation of Offspring*.

David Caplan was found guilty of voluntary manslaughter for his role in the *Los Angeles Times* bombing.

DECEMBER 17

EG was scheduled to speak on "Anarchism and Human Nature: Do They Harmonize?" at Labor Lyceum in **Rochester**.

DECEMBER 18

EG was scheduled to speak on "The Educational and Sexual Dwarfing of the Child" at Labor Lyceum in **Rochester**.

DECEMBER 19

EG was scheduled to speak on "Free or Forced Motherhood?: The Need of Birth Control" at Labor Lyceum in **Rochester**.

BR was in court.

DECEMBER 28

David Caplan was given the maximum sentence of ten years in prison.

DECEMBER 31

The offices of *The Blast* were again raided in San Francisco, California. Police confiscated letters, manuscripts, and files in an effort to find evidence to connect AB with the Preparedness Day bombing.

**Abbott, Leonard Dalton** (1878–1953) American radical, freethinker, and anarchist. An early member of the Socialist Party of America, he later became involved in the anarchist movement. Abbott was the founding president of the Francisco Ferrer Association (1910), an active lecturer at the New York Ferrer Modern School, president of the Thomas Paine National Historical Association (1910), an active member of the Freethinkers of America, and a leader in the movement to have the Free Speech League incorporated in 1911. In 1910 he signed a letter to the Japanese ambassador in protest of the death sentence passed upon Kōtoku and other Japanese anarchists. In 1911 Abbott initiated a protest letter to *Justice* countering the allegation that EG was a tsarist spy. He also took an active role in the New York Mexican Revolution Conference, which took place at the Ferrer Center. He assisted with Margaret Sanger's defense through the Free Speech League after her magazine, the *Woman Rebel*, was suppressed and she was charged with obscenity (1914–1915). Through the Free Speech League he was active during the Tarrytown free speech fight in 1914. Abbott was also a major financial contributor to the Anti-Militarist League and to the funeral expenses for Berg, Caron, and Hanson, who died in the Lexington Avenue explosion in 1914. He met Rosa Yuster at the Ferrer Modern School, and they were married after the birth of their second child in 1915. He was secretary of the Birth Control Committee (1916) and of the Emma Goldman Defense Fund (1916). A regular contributor to *Mother Earth*, including the tenth-anniversary souvenir edition, he also contributed to the *Truth Seeker*, the *International*, and *Revolt*. Abbott was associate editor of *Current Literature* (1905–1925), editor with J. William Lloyd and C. L. Swartz of *Free Comrade* (1912), and editor with Harry Kelly of *Modern School* in 1912. Written works include *Francisco Ferrer: His Life, Work, and Martyrdom* (ed. Abbott; Francisco Ferrer Association, 1910), *What Ferrer Taught in His Schools* (Current Literature Publishing, 1910), and *The Detroit Francisco Ferrer Modern School* (with William Thurston Brown; New York: Herold Press, 1912).

**Anderson, Margaret Caroline** (1886–1973) American author, literary critic, magazine publisher, and bohemian. Born in Indianapolis, Indiana, to a wealthy family, Anderson grew up in Youngstown, Ohio, and Columbus, Indiana, and visited Lake Wawasee, Indiana, during summers. From 1903 to 1906 she studied piano at Western College for Women in Oxford, Ohio, but she did not graduate. Bored by life in the Midwest, she moved to Chicago with her sister in 1908, where she worked as a literary critic for the *Interior* (later the *Continent*) and the *Chicago Evening Post*'s *Friday Literary Review*, edited by Floyd Dell. She also worked in a bookstore and for the *Dial*, where she learned about the process of assembling and publishing a journal. In March 1914 she founded the literary journal the *Little Review*. The magazine reflected her interests in psychoanalysis, feminism, and anarchism, and was instrumental in bringing new and avant-garde modern literature to the United States. EG first met Anderson in Chicago in April 1914, and they became friends and correspondents. EG supported the *Little Review* by publishing advertisements for it in *Mother Earth*. Anderson published EG's writings in the *Little Review*, helped sponsor her lectures, and contributed to the tenth-anniversary souvenir edition of *Mother Earth* in March 1915.

**Andreyev, Leonid Nikolayevitch** (1871–1919) Russian author, lawyer, crime reporter, and editor. Friend and protégé of Maksim Gorky, he had his first volume of stories published by Gorky's publishing house. Works include *Savva* (1906), *King Hunger* (1907), *The Seven Who Were Hanged* (1907), and *The Pretty Sabine Women* (1912). The play *King Hunger*, featured in EG's lectures and her book *The Social Significance of the Modern Drama* (1914), was first published in English in the quarterly magazine *Poet Lore* (1911). However, his play *Anathema* (1909) was the one that EG would later consider his most thought-provoking work. See also vol. 2, *Making Speech Free*.

**Angiolillo, Michele** (referred to in some newspaper accounts as "Golli") (1871–1897) Italian anarchist, shot and killed Antonio Cánovas del Castillo, prime minister of Spain, on 8 August 1897, at the Santa Agueda baths. The son of a tailor, he worked as a compositor before leaving Foggia in October 1883, spending time in Marseilles and Barcelona under the name José Santos. He became interested in anarchism while in Coromina and traveled again to Marseilles before being expelled. He later frequented anarchist circles in Belgium and London. He testified that he had acted independently in the assassination of Cánovas, an act he intended as revenge for the 4 May 1897 executions at Montjuich prison of five anarchists linked by the Spanish government to the Corpus Christi day bombing of 7 June 1896. Denied the right to speak of anarchism or the wars in Cuba and the Philippines at his trial, he was sentenced to death by garrote and executed on 20 August 1897. He was the subject of a Voltairine de Cleyre short story, "The Heart of Angiolillo" (1898), which was reprinted in *Selected Works of Voltairine de Cleyre* (1914). See also vols. 1 and 2.

**Ashley, Jessie** (1861–1919) Wealthy suffragette, socialist lawyer, and, for a time, companion of William Haywood. A regular contributor to the *Woman's Journal*, she wrote on feminism, labor, and the McNamara trial. Ashley was treasurer of the National American Woman Suffrage Association until 1912, when she lost her bid for reelection, reportedly because she was a socialist. She served as legal counsel for the Little Falls strikers (1912–1913) and was head of the Paterson Defense League (1913), raising money for the legal defense of the strike leaders. In 1913 EG provided Ashley with an introduction to Victor Dave during her trip to Europe with Bill Haywood. In 1914, along with Mabel Dodge, Ashley loaned Margaret Sanger money to publish the *Woman Rebel*, and in 1915 she was on the editorial board of the socialist *New Review*. She also contributed financially to the *Mother Earth* Sustaining Fund. She spoke at the Union Square birth control meeting on 20 May 1916 and was arrested, with Bolton Hall and Ida Rauh, for handing out birth control leaflets.

**Baginski, Max** (1864–1943) German anarchist and editor. Baginski was co-founder of *Mother Earth*, and co-editor of *Freiheit* (1906–1910) with Henry Bauer after the death of Johann Most in 1906. He worked as a publicist in New York for left journals, including German-language workers' papers, *Mother Earth*, and his own short-lived journal, *Internationale Arbeiter Chronik* (seven issues, 30 March–23 September 1914). Baginski was a frequent contributor to *Mother Earth* on topics ranging from syndicalism to European literature. In 1913 he wrote the introduction to the three-volume collection of Robert Reitzel's work *Des Armen teufel gesammelte Schriften* (Detroit: Reitzel Klub, 1913). His works also include *Syndikalismus; Lebendige, keine todten Gewerkschaften* (New York: Bauer, [1909?]).

**Bakunin, Michael** (1814–1876) Russian revolutionary and foremost theorist of Russian anarchism. He was a hugely influential and iconic figure of international anarchism. A leading force in the opposition to Marx in the International Workingmen's Association (First International), Bakunin first described himself as an anarchist in the mid-1860s (although not in writing until 1867). His principal works are *Statism and Anarchy* (1873) and *God and the State* (1882). *God and the State* was originally translated into English and published by Benjamin Tucker in Boston (in England, Tunbridge Wells: Science Library, 1883). It was published again in 1896 (Columbus Junction, Iowa: E. H. Fulton, 1896) and again in 1900 (San Francisco: Isaak, 1900). Mother Earth Publishing Association republished the work in 1916, incorrectly identifying it as the first American edition. Tucker also serialized Bakunin's *The Political Theology of Mazzini and the International*, translated by Sarah E. Holmes, in *Liberty* from 18 September 1886 to 18 June 1887. In April 1880 Ezra Heywood's paper the *Word* published Bakunin's *The Gospel of Nihilism*. Albert Parsons published abstracts from Bakunin's *Catechism of a Revolutionary* in the *Alarm* on 23 January 1886, and *Woodhill and Claflin's Weekly* in New York City also published some of Bakunin's writings. Bakunin died in Bern, Switzerland, on 1 July 1876. See also vols. 1 and 2.

**Baldwin, Roger Nash** (1884–1981) St. Louis-based reformer. Baldwin resided in St. Louis from 1906 to 1917, where he was an active proponent of progressive social reform and was involved in the formation of St. Louis' first interracial group, the Committee for Social Service Among Colored People. From 1906 to 1910 he served on the faculty of Washington University, where he established the university's sociology department. In 1910 he served as president of the State Conference for Social Welfare and secretary of the St. Louis Civic League. From 1907 to 1910 he was chief probation officer for the St. Louis juvenile court. Baldwin helped organize EG's 1911 lectures in St. Louis; however, reluctant to become too involved, he had Alice Martin do most of the planning (in *Living My Life* EG gives all the credit to Martin and William Marion Reedy). In 1916 Baldwin was involved in his first free speech fight when he supported the right of Margaret Sanger to speak on birth control after protests against her erupted throughout the city.

**Bellows, George** (1882–1925) American artist and member of the Ashcan School. Bellows was a student of Robert Henri, who in 1912 joined him as an instructor at the Ferrer Center, where one of their pupils was Man Ray. Bellows donated paintings in support of the Lawrence strike. He joined the art staff of the *Masses*, directed by John Sloan, in 1912, contributing illustrations until the magazine ceased publication in 1917. Bellows also helped organize the 1913 Armory Show. As a member of the 1916 New York Publicity Committee for the International Workers' Defense League, he helped organize a fund-raising event at Carnegie Hall for Mooney and Billings. Among his most famous works are his boxing scenes, such as *Both Members of the Same Club* (1909; National Gallery of Art, Washington, D.C.) and *Stag at Sharkey's* (1909; Cleveland Museum of Art), and the portraits of his wife and children, including *Emma and Her Children* (1922; Museum of Fine Arts, Boston).

**Berg, Charles** (alias Peter Fischer) (1891–1914) Latvian anarchist. He fought with the "Fighting Squad" and the "Forest Brethren" anarchist guerrilla groups in the Baltic region during the 1905 Russian Revolution, and after the revolution he helped smuggle guns and ammunition across the border. A merchant seaman, he met Carl Hanson in Hamburg, where the two traveled together and eventually arrived in New York in 1911. In New York Berg joined the Lettish Anarchist Group and in 1913 became one of the founding members of the Lettish Anarchist Red Cross. He was assistant treasurer of the Conference of the Unemployed at the Ferrer Center during 1913 and 1914. He helped organize the Tarrytown protests following the Ludlow Massacre in 1914. Along with Rebecca Edelsohn, Arthur Caron, and others he was arrested for attempting to make public speeches at Fountain Square in Tarrytown, and he was killed in the Lexington Avenue explosion on 4 July 1914.

**Berger, Victor L.** (1860–1929) Socialist, state congressman, and U.S. congressman beginning in 1910. Born in Austria-Hungary, Berger settled in Milwaukee in 1878. He co-founded the Socialist Party of America. By 1910 he was playing a critical role in the socialist control of Milwaukee. He established the weekly *Socialist Democrat Herald* in 1901 (an earlier version of his daily the *Milwaukee Leader*, which began in 1913). The first socialist elected to the U.S. Congress (1911–1913), during his term he supported a measure to maintain the constitutional rights of the McNamara brothers and sponsored hearings on the 1912 Lawrence strike. He condemned the use of violence as a political tactic and denounced the IWW as anarchical and threatening to the socialist labor movement. EG met him once and found him intolerant of her ideas, although he had came to her defense in Chicago during 1907 when her meetings were suppressed. His publications include *Madam, How Will You Feed Your Family?* (Chicago: Socialist Party, 1910), *What Should We Do to Be Saved* (Milwaukee: Social Democratic Pub., 1910), *Broadsides of Victor Berger* (Milwaukee: Social-Democratic Pub., 1912).

**Berkman, Alexander** (1870–1936; born Ovsej Berkman) A Lithuanian-born anarchist, a leading organizer for various causes, an editor, and an author. He was EG's closest comrade politically and a lifelong friend. AB served as editor of *Mother Earth* from 1907 to 1915. In 1910 he was a founding member of the Francisco Ferrer Association and the following year was one of the first teachers at the New York Ferrer Modern School. During 1911 AB worked to finish his book, *Prison Memoirs of an Anarchist*, which was published by Mother Earth Publishing Association in 1912. AB continued anarchist agitation through organizations and individuals associated with the Ferrer Center. In 1912 he worked with Harry Kelly and Jaime Vidal to organize the Alexander Aldamas Defense Fund. (Aldamas was a Marine Firemen's Union member who was charged with murdering three police officers during a strike.) AB also supported the IWW, speaking at Paterson strike meetings in 1913. In 1913 and 1914 he was instrumental in the unemployed movement in New York, organizing the Conference of the Unemployed. In 1914 AB organized the Anti-Militarist League and subsequently served as secretary-treasurer. Through the league he helped collect money for the Rangel-Cline Defense Fund and Italian revolutionaries, as well as for the victims of the Ludlow Massacre and the striking Colorado Miners. During the summer of 1914 AB organized small groups in Tarrytown, New York, the home of Rockefeller's country estate, to protest his anti-union practices. Fifteen people, including Rebecca Edelsohn and Arthur Caron, were arrested when they spoke against the wealthy philanthropist. Evidence suggests that AB was the main organizer of the planned bomb attack on Rockefeller's home in Tarrytown. On 4 July 1914 the bomb exploded prematurely at a tenement building on Lexington Avenue in New York City, killing anarchists Carl Hanson, Charles Berg, and Arthur Caron. AB arranged a mass memorial demonstration at Union Square for the three men. During the following months personal and political tension appeared to arise between Berkman and EG. AB was arrested on 9 November 1914 for felonious assault of a police officer after an altercation took place between the police and anarchists on their way home from a farewell dinner for AB, who was about to leave on a nationwide lecture tour. Four other people, including *Golos Truda* editor William Shatov, were also arrested and charged with disorderly conduct. AB's $1,000 bail was provided by the father of Bresci Group member Andrea Ciofalo. AB left New York on 10 November 1914 to begin his lecture tour. Charges against him were later dropped with the help of his lawyer, Gilbert Roe.

AB planned to use the lecture tour as an opportunity to help establish anti-militarist leagues in various cities and scout a location for a possible move. With his companion at the time, M. E. Fitzgerald, AB remained on tour for most of 1915. While in Los Angeles he became heavily involved in the Caplan-Schmidt Defense League. He was chosen by the league to organize local groups, appeal to labor unions for support, and collect aid on his return trip to New York City. AB and Fitzgerald returned to New York for a few weeks in September before moving to San Francisco. On 15 January 1916 they published the first issue of *The Blast*. AB immediately began helping to organize mass demonstrations in San Francisco to support groups and causes such as the Partido Liberal Mexicano (PLM) and anti-militarism. AB was a signatory of the International Anarchist Manifesto on the War, an antiwar document issued from London in March 1915. After the 22 July 1916 Preparedness Day bomb in San Francisco he took an active role in organizing through the International Workers' Defense League for the defense of the five arrested in connection to the explosion. A week after the explosion and later on New Year's Eve 1916, *The Blast* offices were raided by police trying to collect evidence to implicate AB as an organizer of the bombing. He was later indicted in connection with the case. Additional publications during the 1910–1916 period include *Selected Works of Voltairine de Cleyre* (New York: Mother Earth Publishing Association, 1914), which he compiled and edited after her death.

**Billings, Warren Knox** (1893–1972) Militant industrial unionist and self-described anarchist. In March 1913 Billings arrived in San Francisco from New York. In San Francisco he was active in a shoe workers' strike, working as an undercover scab for the radical Boot and Shoe Workers' Union, during which he met Thomas Mooney. He was also active in the Pacific Gas & Electric strike during the summer of 1913 and was employed as an investigator for the San Francisco local union of electrical workers, locating guards of electrical towers and stealing dynamite. He was arrested by Pinkerton detectives in September 1913 for transporting dynamite on a streetcar in Sacramento during the PG&E strike. He was sentenced to a two-year imprisonment in Folsom Penitentiary and released on bail in December 1914. Billings was acquainted with AB, Edward Nolan, and other San Francisco anarchists, and he boarded at the San Francisco home of Belle Lavin, who had six years earlier boarded Matthew Schmidt before the bombing of the *Los Angeles Times* building in 1910. He was arrested in San Francisco on 24 July 1916, two days after the Preparedness Day bombing, which killed nine people. Billings was indicted on first-degree murder charges, along with Tom Mooney and his wife, Rena Mooney, Israel Weinberg, and Edward Nolan. Despite a lack of reliable physical evidence and the contradictory accounts of witnesses, he was found guilty of murder. On 5 October 1916 he was sentenced to life imprisonment in Folsom Prison. Billings remained in the background while Mooney fought continually for his own release and became a cause célèbre among the American left, particularly the Communist Party. Billings was released soon after Mooney, when his sentence was commuted to time served on 16 October 1939. He worked as a watchmaker in San Francisco until his death in 1972.

**Bjørnson, Bjørnstjerne** (1832–1910) Norwegian freethinker, poet, playwright, novelist, and theater director. His earlier work examined and celebrated Norwegian identity, while his later work (after 1870) addressed issues of political liberty and social inequality. He was a stage director in Bergen (1857–1859) and director of the Oslo (1865–1867) and Christiania (1866–1871) theaters. He was editor for the newspaper *Aftenbladet* (1859–1860; he was forced to resign for his reformist articles) and for the *Norkst Folkeblad* (1866–1871). Bjørnson was awarded the Nobel Prize for literature in 1903. His work was featured regularly in EG's drama lectures. Major works include *Mellem Slagene* (Between the Battles, 1857), *Maria Stuart i Skotland* (Mary Stuart in Scotland, 1864), *En Fallit* (A Bankruptcy, 1875), *Redaktören* (The Editor, 1875), *En handske* (A Gauntlet, 1883), *Over aevne, I* (Beyond Our Power, I, 1883), and *Geografi og Kjaerlighed* (Love and Geography, 1885). Bjørnson's play *Over aevne, II* (Beyond Our Power, II, 1895) addressed labor strife and the anarchist movement.

**Boyesen, Bayard** (dates unknown) American scholar and educator and the son of Hjalmar Hjorth Boyesen, a leading American Ibsen scholar. Instructor of English and comparative literature at Columbia University, he was forced to resign in 1911 after the school's president censured him for associating with EG and other anarchists, and for his poem "Song of Solidarity," which was published in *Francisco Ferrer: His Life, Work, and Martyrdom* (New York: Francisco Ferrer Association, 1910). In 1911, upon EG's request, he became the first director of the day school at the New York Ferrer Modern School and secretary of the Francisco Ferrer Association of New York. EG wrote of him, "He really is a great fellow and the only man in this country who as a teacher can adequately perpetuate the Spirit of Ferrer" (EG to BR, 27 July 1911, *EGP*, reel 3]. By the end of 1912 Boyesen had distanced himself from politics and moved to a family farm in Massachusetts, although he later sheltered Matthew Schmidt at EG's request. He wrote a review of AB's *Prison Memoirs of an Anarchist* (New York: Mother Earth Publishing Association, 1912) in the February 1913 *Mother Earth*. He contributed articles to *Monthly News Letter* (1910), the *Modern School* (1912), *Others* (1916), and occasionally to *Mother Earth* (1911–1912). His works include *The Marsh: A Poem* (Boston: R. G. Badger, 1905), *Prospectus of the Francisco Ferrer Association of New York* (New York: Francisco Ferrer Association, 1911), *The Modern School in New York* (New York: Francisco Ferrer Association, 1911).

**Bresci, Gaetano** (1869–1901) Italian-born American anarchist. He apprenticed as a silk weaver in Milan, where he first joined the anarchist movement. In early 1898, he settled in Paterson, New Jersey, where he worked as a silk weaver. Bresci gravitated toward the anti-*organizzatori* affinity group in West Hoboken, New Jersey. He was a subscriber and benefactor of *L'Aurora*, the West Hoboken anti-*organizzatori* paper edited by Giuseppe Ciancabilla. In May 1900 he left his home in West Hoboken to assassinate King Umberto of Italy to avenge the victims of government repression in Milan and Sicily. Bresci fulfilled his mission at Monza on 29 July 1900, and he died in prison the following year, reportedly by suicide.

**Breshkovskaya, Catherine** (1844–1934) Russian revolutionary and a founder of the Socialist Revolutionary Party. After a short trial in March 1910 she was sentenced to perpetual exile for "criminal activity in a revolutionary organization," and the sentence caused an outcry from some sectors of the American press. EG regarded Breshkovskaya as a hero and model of the Russian female revolutionist; however, their relationship would sour following the Russian Revolution in 1917 and Breshkovskaya's vocal criticism of the Bolsheviks. Her reminiscences, *The Little*

*Grandmother of the Russian Revolution* (Boston: Little, Brown), were published in 1918, edited by Alice Stone Blackwell. See also vol. 2, *Making Speech Free.*

**Brieux, Eugene** (1858–1932) French playwright best known for his plays *Red Robe* (1900); *Damaged Goods* (1902), a controversial discussion of venereal disease first produced in the United States in 1913; and *Maternity* (1903). *Damaged Goods* and *Maternity* were featured in EG's *The Social Significance of the Modern Drama* (1914) and in her modern drama lectures between 1911 and 1915.

**Brown, William Thurston** (1861–1938) Christian socialist, for a time member of the Socialist Party, and Modern School educator. He served as director of Modern Schools in Salt Lake City (1910), Portland (1911), and Chicago (1916), and as principal and director of the Modern School in Stelton, New Jersey (1916–1919). While at Stelton, Brown was editor of the *Modern School.* He lectured at the New York Freethought Society (January–April 1913). He was the author of *Socialism and Primitive Christianity* (Chicago: C. H. Kerr, 1910). His pamphlets published by the Portland, Oregon, Modern School include *The Need of Religion as a Means of Knowing the Real Value of Things* (1910), *Love's Freedom and Fulfillment* (1911), *The Moral Basis of the Demand for Free Divorce* (1911), *The Evolution of Sexual Morality* (1911), *What Socialism Means as a Philosophy and as a Movement* (1911), *The Tragedy of Shakespeare and the Tragedy of Ibsen: A Study in Ethical Values* (1911), *Socialism and the Individual: An Interpretation of Oscar Wilde's "The Soul of Man Under Socialism"* (1911), *Walt Whitman: Poet of the Human Whole* (1911), and *The Church and Human Progress: The Convincing Witness of History* (1911).

**Burns, William J.** (1861–1932) American private detective and president of the William J. Burns Detective Agency, which he founded in 1909. In 1910 Burns was hired by the McClintock-Marshall Company and the National Erectors Association to hunt dynamiters who had blown up several bridges; Burns blamed union workers for inciting the explosions through their protests against the open shop. Arriving in Los Angeles on the day of the *Los Angeles Times* building explosion, he was hired and offered a $100,000 reward, by George B. Alexander, mayor of Los Angeles, to investigate the bombing. Burns built the case against the McNamara brothers, David Caplan, and Matthew A. Schmidt. In order to track Caplan Burns infiltrated the anarchist Home Colony in Washington State by posing as a surveyor; later, he convinced Donald Vose to travel to New York, infiltrate the anarchist community, and find Schmidt. Burns was indicted by a grand jury on the charge of kidnapping John J. McNamara. He regularly used spies and undercover agents as part of his operations, many of which were directed against the labor movement. One such operation was an attempt to infiltrate the Francisco Ferrer Association after the 4 July 1914 Lexington Avenue explosion. He was known for targeting members of the IWW, and he eventually accused Samuel Gompers of the AFL of being involved in the Los Angeles bombing "conspiracy." He wrote *The Masked War* (New York: George H. Doran, 1913), an account of the *Los Angeles Times* bombing investigation.

**Caplan, David** (ca. 1870–1930s) Russian-born anarchist and student radical before being expelled from Russia. He arrived in New York around 1890 and lived in Philadelphia and Chicago, where he met Matthew A. Schmidt. Later, he moved to Portland, Oregon, during which time he probably visited Home Colony, and then to San Francisco. In San Francisco he ran a grocery, distributed anarchist literature, and was apparently a close associate of Eric B. Morton. In 1910 he and Schmidt were introduced by San Francisco labor leader Olaf A. Tveitmoe to James B. McNamara, who was planning for the bombing of the *Los Angeles Times* building. With McNamara and Schmidt, Caplan helped purchase the dynamite, which they brought to a house rented by Caplan in San Francisco before transporting it to Los Angeles. Following the bombing, he went into hiding on Bainbridge Island, Washington, near Home Colony. His hiding place appears to have been known to some Home Colony residents, for Donald Vose, son of Home Colony resident Gertie Vose, visited him and told William J. Burns where he was hiding. Caplan was arrested on 18 February 1915, five days after Schmidt was arrested in New York. The Caplan and Schmidt cases were often covered in the pages of *Mother Earth*, and EG and AB worked to raise funds for their defense. Caplan's first trial, which began 5 April 1916 in Los Angeles, ended in a hung jury, and his second trial, which began 23 October 1916, resulted in a verdict of voluntary manslaughter and a sentence of ten years in prison. Caplan began serving his sentence on 10 January 1917; he served six years and six months and was released on 10 July 1923.

**Caron, Arthur** (d. 1914) Of part Native American descent, a machinist, engineer, and anarchist. Caron was a frequent visitor to the Ferrer Center. He was a member of the IWW New York unemployed workers' local and active in the movement of the unemployed in the winter of 1913. He was arrested with Frank Tannenbaum at a demonstration of the unemployed at the church of St. Alphonsus. Caron was badly beaten by the police in the Union Square demonstration of the unemployed on 4 April 1914. He was an active organizer in the Rockefeller protest campaign, which grew out of Upton Sinclair's Free Silence movement after the Ludlow Massacre; he was instrumental in moving the protest to the village of Tarrytown, near Rockefeller's country home. During the free speech fight that developed in Tarrytown he was arrested, along with Becky Edelsohn and Charles Berg, on 30 May 1914 for trying to hold a public meeting there. Released on bail pending trial on 8 June 1914, Caron was stoned by local citizens during a police-condoned riot at an aqueduct, which was adjacent to Tarrytown but owned by the city of New York, on 22 June 1914 when he tried to speak. He was killed, along with Berg and Carl Hanson, in the Lexington Avenue explosion of 4 July 1914, when a bomb intended for Rockefeller's estate exploded in their tenement apartment.

**Carpenter, Edward** (1844–1929) English author, poet, social reformer, libertarian socialist, proponent of women's equality, and homosexual. Along with John Addington Symonds, Carpenter was an early advocate of homosexual emancipation. In 1877 he met Walt Whitman, whose poetry he believed alleviated the shame associated with homosexuality. His unrhymed poem and major work, *Towards Democracy* (1883), reflects Whitman's influence. The title of his book *The Intermediate Sex* (London: S. Sonnenschein, 1908; New York: Mitchell Kennerley, 1912) was adopted as the title of a frequently delivered lecture by EG on homosexuality. An active supporter of birth control, he met Margaret Sanger when she visited England in 1914. Hippolyte Havel reviewed Carpenter's *The Drama of Love and Death* (New York and London: Mitchell Kennerley, 1912) in the September 1912 edition of *Mother Earth*. Carpenter wrote a tribute to Kropotkin that was published in the December 1912 *Mother Earth* on Kropotkin's seventieth birthday, and the preface to the English edition of AB's *Prison Memoirs of an Anarchist* (1925). Also a pacifist, Carpenter wrote antiwar tracts, including *Healing of Nations and the Hidden Sources of Their Strife* (London: G. Allen & Unwin, 1915; New York: C. Scribner's Sons, 1915) and *Never Again!* (Manchester: National Labour Press, 1916). His autobiography, *My Days and Dreams* (New York: Scribner's), was published in 1916.

**Comstock, Anthony** (1844–1915) American reformer and founder of the Society for the Suppression of Vice in 1872. He was the post office official charged with enforcing the Comstock Act, the obscenity law bearing his name. As a special unpaid postal inspector with the power to enter any post office and confiscate any material he deemed obscene, he sometimes used fictitious names when investigating progressive and radical publications, including works of literature like Whitman's popular *Leaves of Grass*, Tolstoy's *Kreutzer Sonata*, and anything in print about birth control, in order to suppress them. Comstock's crusade was marked by conflict with anarchists and freethinkers. *Discontent, Lucifer the Lightbearer,* and *Mother Earth* were among the many papers he barred from the mails. EG sharply criticized his role as a censor in many of her lectures and essays, including the essays "The Hypocrisy of Puritanism" (in *Anarchism and Other Essays* [New York: Mother Earth Publishing, 1910]) and *Victims of Morality* (New York: Mother Earth Publishing Association, 1913). His only published work after 1900 was *Race Track Infamy: or, Do Gamblers Own New York State; a Scathing Exposure of How the Constitution of New York State Is Flagrantly Violated by Common Gamblers* (New York: printed by author, 1904). See also vols. 1 and 2.

**Comyn, Stella** (born Stella Cominsky; married name Stella Comyn Ballantine) (1886–1961) EG's niece and one of her closest relatives. Comyn worked as a records clerk at the U.S. embassy in Paris in 1907; EG visited her during her trip to Europe that year. A minor stir was caused when government agents investigating EG discovered Comyn was the niece of EG. There are conflicting stories about her departure from the embassy: she was asked to leave or she resigned because she wanted to return to America. She eventually returned to New York with the Hapgoods in 1908. During this period Comyn worked as EG's secretary and lived at the *Mother Earth* household, 74 West 119th Street, New York. In September 1910 she began working as a secretary for Eugene Walter, author of the play *The Easiest Way*. Comyn wrote a review of Edgar Lee Masters's *Spoon River Anthology* in the November 1915 *Mother Earth*. Comyn spent the summer of 1916 in Provincetown with her husband, English actor Edward "Teddy" Ballantine, and was one of the founders of the Provincetown Players. Also in 1916 she gave birth to the couple's son, Ian Ballantine.

**Coryell, John Russell** (1851–1924) American author, educator, and anarchist. EG describes him and his wife, Abby Coryell, as generous contributors to the movement and two of her closest American friends; both were members of the Sunrise Club. He was the originator of the popular Nick Carter detective series and the Bertha M. Clay romance series. He was arrested on 6 January 1907 at a *Mother Earth* meeting with EG and AB for "propagating anarchist ideas." A lecturer at the New York Ferrer Center, he and his wife were the first teachers at the New York Ferrer Modern School day school for children in 1911. He was a frequent contributor to *Mother Earth* under his own name and one of his many pseudonyms, Margaret Grant, and a contributor to *Lucifer the Light Bearer* and *Physical Culture*; he published and edited his own short-lived journal, *The Wide Way*, in 1907–1908. He also authored the pamphlets *Love and Passion* (New York: Corwill, 1907), *Making of Revolution* (New York: Corwill, 1908), *Sex Union and Parenthood and What Is Seduction?* (New York: Mother Earth Publishing Association, ca. 1900–1909), and *The Rent Strike* (New York: Corwill, n.d.).

**Courtney, Julia May** (1873–1951) Denver cashier and anarchist sympathizer. She helped form the Denver branch of the Ferrer Association (1911). Courtney gathered subscription lists for *Regeneración* (1911), distributed Margaret Sanger's the *Woman Rebel* (1914) in Denver, and contributed to the Caplan-Schmidt Defense Fund (1915). She also subscribed to *Mother Earth* and contributed the articles "Remember Ludlow" and "Denver" in 1914. She later became a chiropractor.

**de Cleyre, Voltairine** (1866–1912) American anarchist, freethinker, poet, lecturer, and teacher. Together with EG and Lucy Parsons, she was a leading anarchist spokeswoman of the period. After corresponding with AB while he was in prison she helped him adjust to life after his release and was instrumental in the completion of his *Prison Memoirs of an Anarchist* (1912). Berkman returned the favor and edited a posthumous volume of her writings, *Selected Works of Voltairine de Cleyre* (1914). Her relationship with EG was complex, and they clashed over the issue of who constituted the proper audience for anarchist propaganda during a de Cleyre lecture tour in the fall of 1910. She corresponded regularly with EG during this period. De Cleyre's private letters, however, reflect suspicions about EG's financial honesty and rigor. Nonetheless, in 1911 she joined the signatories of the widely circulated letter to *Justice* protesting the journal's accusation that EG was a tsarist spy. By 1911 de Cleyre's activism was focused almost exclusively on the Mexican Revolution. As treasurer of the Chicago-based Mexican Liberal Defense Conference, she raised funds for the Partido Liberal Mexicano (PLM) by lecturing and distributing copies of *Regeneración*, and in July 1911 she became the Chicago correspondent to *Regeneración*. Shortly before her death she began learning Spanish in hopes of moving to Los Angeles to immerse herself in the Mexican struggle. In the last nineteen months of her life she lived in Chicago with Annie and Jake Livshis, and for two months she taught at the Modern School there. She wrote for foreign-language anarchist papers such as *Di Fraye Gezelshaft*, *Volne Listy* (a Bohemian anarchist paper), and *Freie Arbeiter Stimme*. In 1911, concerned that anarchists did not have enough practical experience in educating children to properly manage a school, she turned down an offer from Leonard Abbott to become business manager of the Ferrer Association. In 1912 she wrote in the *Agitator* her support for the McNamara brothers after their confession, "The McNamara Storm" of 15 January 1912, and protested against the treatment of the IWW members during the free speech fight in San Diego. Also in 1912 she worked on a translation of Louise Michel's memoirs. In the months following her 20 June 1912 death a flood of memorials were published within the anarchist press celebrating her life, including articles by Hutchins Hapgood in the *Globe and Commercial Advertiser* (21 June 1912), by unknown writers in *Regeneración* (one in English and one in Spanish, 22 June 1912), by Saul Yanovsky and de Cleyre's former student Joseph J. Cohen in *Freie Arbeiter Stimme* (22 June 1912 and 28 June 1912, respectively), by Jay Fox in the *Agitator* (15 July 1912), by Luigi Galleani in *Cronaca Sovversiva* (27 July 1912), by an unknown writer in *Freedom* (August 1912), and by Joseph Kucera in *Why* (August 1913). The July 1912 *Mother Earth* was a memorial issue dedicated to de Cleyre, as was the September 1913 issue of *Herald of Revolt*. A committee of anarchists, including Leonard Abbott, Harry Kelly, Joseph Kucera, Saul Yanovsky, and Margaret Perle McLeod, formed the Voltairine de Cleyre Publication Fund to raise money to publish her selected works, and shortly after her death Annie Livshis published a pamphlet, *In Memoriam: Voltairine de Cleyre* (Chicago, 1912). During this period her work was published by Mother Earth Publishing Association (New York), including *The Dominant Idea* (1910), *The Mexican Revolt* (1911), *Direct Action* (1912), and *Selected Works of Voltairine de Cleyre* (edited by Alexander Berkman with a biographical sketch by Hippolyte Havel, 1914). She also translated Franscico Ferrer's "The Modern School" for the November 1909 *Mother Earth*; the essay was later published as a pamphlet by Mother Earth Publishing Association (1909). A collection of her writings, *Selected Stories* (Seattle: The Libertarian Magazine, 1916), was published by Cassius Cook. She was buried at Waldheim Cemetery in Forest Park, Illinois, close to the Haymarket memorial.

**Debs, Eugene** (1855–1926) American labor and political leader who was Socialist Party candidate for president of the United States in 1900, 1904, 1908, 1912, and 1920. Debs remained sympathetic to the IWW until 1913, when he criticized the union for being an "anarchist organization." Although he supported the general strike and advocated industrial unionism, he did not advocate sabotage and thus did not protest when Haywood was ousted from the party in 1913. Debs and the socialist paper *Appeal to Reason* (of which he was editor) would support Madero after the split between the PLM and the Maderoists in Mexico in 1911. Although Debs admired the work of the Partido Liberal Mexicano (PLM), he was uncomfortable with its refusal to identify itself as anarchist, and he supported Madero after the revolution of 1910. He took a militant antiwar stand, opposing preparedness and warning working men against being used as tools of the capitalist war machine. He refused the 1916 Socialist Party presidential nomination and instead became editor of *Rip-Saw* in order to write against the war. Debs wrote several pamphlets, including *Liberty* (Chicago: Charles H. Kerr, 1911), *Unionism and Socialism* (Chicago: Charles H. Kerr, 1912), *Tom Mooney Sentenced to Hang: An Appeal to the Organized Workers of America* (San Francisco: Tom Mooney Molders Defense Committee, 1916), and *Labor and Freedom: The Voice and Pen of Eugene V. Debs* (St. Louis: P. Wagner, 1916). See also vols. 1 and 2.

**Eastman, Ida Rauh** (1877–1970) Greenwich Village socialist, member of the Heterodoxy Club, sculptor, poet, and actress. She visited Russia in 1907–1908 and later met Kropotkin in Switzerland. She shared an apartment with Madeline Doty before marrying Max Eastman in 1911. Rauh was assigned by the Women's Trade Union League to study the causes of the Triangle Shirtwaist fire of 1911 and suggest remedies. She was a founder of and actress in the Provincetown Players. Rauh spoke at a Union Square birth control mass meeting with EG on 20 May 1916 and was arrested with Jessie Ashley and Bolton Hall for distributing birth control information later that year. She was also a member of the publicity committee for the International Workers' Defense League's mass meeting in New York City to aid the Mooney-Billings case (1916).

**Edelsohn, Rebecca "Becky"** (ca. 1891–1973) New York anarchist, anti-militarist, and companion of AB for a time. Edelsohn was involved in the 1914 unemployment movement demonstrations and protests. She worked closely with AB on behalf of the Anti-Militarist League, serving as secretary of the league's fund-raising ball in late 1914. On 22 April 1914 she was arrested for giving an antiwar speech at Franklin's statue in New York City. At her trial she refused the stipulation of a gag on her public speaking, and when sent to the workhouse for ninety days, she became the first prisoner in the United States to announce in court that she would undertake a hunger strike, to protest her sentence of a $300 fine or jail term. Leonard Abbott and the Free Speech League took over her defense, petitioning for and winning a retrial, after which she was released on bail. She took part in the Tarrytown free speech fight against Rockefeller. She was again arrested, this time with fourteen other protesters, including Arthur Caron, at Tarrytown, New York, for protesting outside the Rockefeller estate on 30 May 1914. Edelsohn was one of the speakers at the memorial for the anarchists who were killed in the Lexington Avenue explosion on 4 July 1914. On 20 July 1914 at her second trial for her 22 April arrest, her original conviction was upheld, and she again declared a hunger strike when sent to prison. This time maintaining her hunger strike for thirty days, she was held at Blackwell's Island; Commissioner of Corrections Katherine Davis withheld all information concerning her case in an effort to break her strike. She was released on 30 August 1914 when, fearing she would not survive if she remained on a hunger strike, M. Eleanor Fitzgerald paid her $300 bond. On 29 October 1914 she conducted her own defense and was acquitted for her part in the 30 May Tarrytown protest. Edelsohn's 1914 report of her time in the workhouse, "Hunger Striking in America," was one of her occasional contributions to *Mother Earth*. She also contributed prison letters to the *Woman Rebel* (August 1914). The 29 January 1916 issue of *Revolt* and the February 1916 issue of *The Blast* announced her imminent lecture tour across the country; her topics included "Society and the Individual," "Science and Social Questions," "Morality," "Militarism," and "Feminism."

**Ellis, Henry Havelock** (1859–1939) English psychologist, physician, socialist, sex reformer, and author. He engaged in the scientific study of the varieties of sexual behavior. Ellis considered "the sexual problem" the outstanding social problem of his time. His *Sexual Inversion* (1897) offered a sympathetic study of homosexuality. The book, labeled obscene by British authorities, became the first in his seven-volume *Studies in the Psychology of Sex* (1897–1928). His book *The Task of Social Hygiene* (1912) rejected revolutionary change and linked women's sexual liberation and pleasure to social harmony and stability. EG referred to his work in her lectures and quoted him in essays—including "Prisons: A Social Crime and Failure," "Traffic in Women," and "Patriotism: A Menace to Liberty"—published in her book *Anarchism and Other Essays* (1912). Ellis's other works include *The Problem of Race Regeneration* (1911), *The World of Dreams* (1911), and *The Forces Warring Against War* (1914).

**Ferrer y Guardia, Francisco** (1859–1909) Spanish anarchist and educator. Founder of the Escuela Moderna (Modern School) in Barcelona (1901–1906). He was a significant benefactor in the development of anarchism in Spain, founding *La Huelga General* in 1902 with Ignacio Clavia, with support from Anselmo Lorenzo and Ricardo Mella. In 1907, with Anselmo Lorenzo, Jose Prats, and Enrique Puget, he launched *Solidaridad Obrera*, which became the organ of the Confederacion National Trabajero (CNT). He founded the International League for the Rational Education of Children in Paris in 1908. He was suspected, though never convicted, of involvement in anarchist attempts to assassinate the king in 1905. Ferrer was executed by the Spanish government on 13 October 1909 on the official charge of being "author and chief of the rebellion" in the July 1909 general strike in Barcelona called by *Solidaridad Obrera*, in which churches were burned, thousands were injured, and more than 200 workers were killed. Ferrer was not actually in Barcelona during "the Tragic Week," and his arrest and execution caused an international outcry from anarchist, radical, and liberal circles. The protest of Ferrer's execution led in the United States to the creation of the Francisco Ferrer Associations and numerous Modern Schools. By the first anniversary of his death there were twenty-five Ferrer Associations in the United States, attracting a variety of political figures, including EG, AB, Harry Kelly, Leonard Abbott, William Thurston Brown, James F. Morton, and E. B. Foote Jr. Ferrer edited *L'École Rénovée* (France 1908–1909) and was the author of *The Modern School*, which was reprinted by Mother Earth Publishing Association (1909), and *The Origin and Ideals of the Modern School* (London: Watts, 1913).

**Fitzgerald, Margaret Eleanor** (1877–1955) known affectionately as "Fitzie" or "the Lioness" for her red hair, was a close friend of EG and AB and manager of *Mother Earth* and later *The Blast*. A teacher, she planned in 1898 to become a missionary for the Seventh Day Adventists. She became interested in anarchism and the labor movement in 1901 and 1902 after spending time as an advance sales agent for traveling chautauquas. Fitzgerald was a lover and then a friend of BR. She worked at *Mother Earth*, first as secretary and then as assistant editor. She lived at the *Mother Earth* household at 74 West 119th Street, New York. Fitzgerald became AB's companion and political comrade and moved with him in 1915 to San Francisco, where she worked as manager and assistant editor of *The Blast* (1916). She was an active organizer in the defense of both Caplan-Schmidt and Mooney-Billings.

**Flores Magón, Enrique** (1887–1954) anarchist and younger brother of Ricardo Flores Magón. He was a co-founder of the Partido Liberal Mexicano (PLM) and its first treasurer. Although less well known than his elder brother, he was nonetheless a constant presence on the junta of the PLM and the editorial board of *Regeneración*. He and Ricardo were arrested in Los Angeles in June 1911 for violating the Neutrality Act, which prohibits the organization of military actions against countries toward which the United States is neutral. Their trial began on 4 June 1912 and lasted until the 22nd, when they were found guilty. Three days later they were sentenced to twenty-three months in prison; they were released on 19 January 1914. Enrique was arrested again in February 1916 with his brother for mailing "indecent" material (that is, material that tended "to incite arson, murder, or assassination"), and he was sentenced on 22 June 1916 to three years' imprisonment. Although Ricardo and Enrique had remained in jail throughout the trial, they were released pending appeal to the U.S. Circuit Court after EG helped to raise bail. In 1916 and 1917 Enrique frequently wrote articles and dispatches for *Mother Earth*, reporting on his and Ricardo's 1916 trial.

**Flores Magón, Ricardo** (1873–1922) Journalist, co-founder of the Partido Liberal Mexicano (PLM), and prominent Mexican anarchist. He abandoned his legal studies to fight the rule of Mexico's president Porfirio Díaz. The Mexican government's suppression of the liberal movement forced Ricardo, with a number of his comrades, into exile in the United States, where they formed the PLM in 1905. In the United States they faced frequent detention and denial of postal privileges. Ricardo was arrested in 1907 in Los Angeles with Modesto Díaz, Librado Rivera, and Antonio Villarreal, and they were all sent to prison in Arizona. *Regeneración* was reestablished in Los Angeles after their release in 1910. Following the start of the Mexican revolution, the PLM found it necessary to clarify its differences with other factions, particularly that of Francisco Madero. The PLM, which had been pushed by Ricardo toward an anarchist position, issued a new manifesto on 23 September 1911 in which its anarchist communism became evident, although it continued to avoid the use of the word "anarchism." On 14 June 1911 Ricardo, Enrique, Librado Rivera, and Anselmo Figueroa were arrested in Los Angeles for violations of the Neutrality Act, for which indictments were not issued until 8 July. The trial began on 4 June 1912, and much attention was given to PLM connections to U.S. radicals. On 22 June all four were found guilty, and on the 25th they were sentenced to twenty-three months in prison, which they served at McNeil Island in Washington. During their imprisonment the publication of *Regeneración* was contin-ued by Teodoro Gaytán, Blas Lara, and William C. Owen. The imprisoned men were released four months early, on 19 January 1914, and Ricardo and Enrique resumed work on the paper. Under pressure from the Mexican government of Venustiano Carranza the United States began investigations of *Regeneración*. On 18 February 1916 an indictment was issued against the editors, Ricardo, Enrique, and Owen, for transporting indecent materials in the mails. Although Owen avoided arrest in Washington, Ricardo and Enrique were arrested in Los Angeles. Ricardo was hospitalized at the time and sentenced to spend one year and one day in prison in consideration of his health, while Enrique was sentenced to three years. AB organized a mass meeting in San Francisco on 8 March 1916 to protest their case. AB and EG were instrumental in the defense of the Flores Magóns during their 1916 trial, through articles in *The Blast* and *Mother Earth*, the arrangement of mass meetings, and EG's lecture engagements in Los Angeles, which helped to raise money for bail. In June 1916 Ricardo and Enrique were released on bail while their cases were appealed.

**Flynn, Elizabeth Gurley** (1890–1964) American IWW organizer and radical. Flynn met EG in 1905 through her friend Fred Robinson, son of Dr. William J. Robinson. In 1906, at the age of fifteen, she spoke at the Socialist Club in New York on "Women Under Socialism." Flynn joined the IWW and attended her first IWW convention in 1907. She was active in the IWW free speech fights in Spokane, Washington, and Missoula, Montana, in 1909. Flynn helped organize and support, among many others, the 1912 Lawrence textile strike and the 1913 Paterson, New Jersey, silk strike. During the Lawrence strike she met Carlo Tresca, who would be her companion until 1925. Flynn spoke at the memorial rally for the victims of the Lexington Avenue bomb explosion in July 1914. She was an organizer of the New York unemployed movement in the winter of 1913–1914, and spoke regularly at unemployed movement demonstrations in New York. The song "Rebel Girl" was written for her by Joe Hill, whom she visited in prison during her lecture tour in April 1915. Flynn met with President Woodrow Wilson to request—unsuccessfully—his intervention in Utah on behalf of Hill. She was a member of the Heterodoxy Club in Greenwich Village and a supporter of birth control for working women. During the summer of 1916 Flynn was sent by the IWW to the Mesabi Range ironworkers' strike in Minnesota after the police arrested Tresca and other IWW organizers for the murder of a deputy sheriff and an innocent bystander. William D. Haywood's refusal to allocate adequate funds for the men's defense and a disagreement over the plea bargain accepted by the defendants created tension between the two organizers. In late 1916 Flynn went to Seattle to raise funds for the IWW men arrested in connection with the Everett massacre. Flynn was a contributor to *Solidarity* and the *International Socialist Review*, and she was the author of *Sabotage, the Conscious Withdrawal of the Workers' Industrial Efficiency* (Cleveland: IWW Publishing Bureau, 1915).

**Foote, Dr. Edward Bond Jr.** (1855–1912) Prominent physician and free speech and birth control advocate. He founded and edited *Dr. Foote's Health Monthly* (New York, 1876–1896) with his father, Edward Bliss Foote. Foote was an advocate of a single tax, free thought, prison reform, sexual freedom, eugenics, and especially free speech. He was one of the original founders of the Free Speech League, secretary and organizer of the New York Liberal Club, also known as the Manhattan Liberal Club, and treasurer of the Ferrer Association. Foote contributed to the general Free Speech Fund and was instrumental in the 19 April 1911 incorporation of the Free Speech League. He was a guiding spirit of the Free Speech League, had been active in the league since its inception in 1902, and was president in 1909 and treasurer in 1913. He was treasurer of numerous other organizations, including the Thomas Paine National Historical Association and the American Secular Union. He was active in many of the same causes as EG, and *Mother Earth* published a warm obituary praising his belief in freedom of speech. The Free Speech League published a memorial booklet upon his death edited by Theodore Schroeder, *Edward Bond Foote Biographical Notes and Appreciatives* (Riverside, Conn.: Hillacre Press for the Free Speech League, 1913).

**Fox, Jay** (1870–1961) Irish-born American anarchist, organizer, and syndicalist. Present during the 1886 Haymarket affair, Fox was one of several prominent Chicago anarchists and was a delegate at the founding convention of the IWW in 1905. He later voiced criticism of the organization in the *Agitator* and the *Syndicalist* for its nonsyndicalist philosophies and refusal to work with already existing unions. Fox withdrew from the IWW in late 1912. He was a resident of the anarchist colony at Home, Washington, beginning in 1910. As a result of his article in the *Agitator* ("The Nudes and the Prudes," reprinted in *Mother Earth* in March 1912) in defense of nude swimming, he became the center of a major obscenity trial (1911–1915). Fox was editor of the *Agitator* (Home, Washington, 1910–1912), renamed the *Syndicalist* (Chicago, 1913), a conduit for European syndicalist thought, including that of Herve and Pouget. He also contributed to the *Demonstrator*, the first issue of *Freedom* (San Francisco, 1910), *Revolt* (1916), the *Alarm* (1916), and *Mother Earth*. Fox died at Home, Washington, on 8 March 1961.

**Freeman, Alden** (1862–1937) Political reformer and homosexual son of the treasurer of the Standard Oil Company. He was an organizer and secretary of the reform group Citizens Union of East Orange, New Jersey (1902–1908). Freeman attended a 1909 EG lecture on Ibsen, which was broken up by the police. Outraged by the suppression of free speech, he invited EG to his estate to give the lecture, which led to a friendship between the two. Freeman was a member of the Free Speech League (1911–1914), a founding member of the Francisco Ferrer Association (1910), and a substantial contributor to the Ferrer Center and Modern School, underwriting rent on the center and paying Principal Will Durant's salary in 1911. Also in 1911 he signed the widely circulated letter sent to *Justice* protesting its accusations that EG was a Russian police spy. He withdrew his support of the Ferrer Center and cut his ties with anarchists after the 4 July 1914 Lexington Avenue explosion, not wanting to be associated with violence. Freeman was also a substantial contributor to the *Mother Earth* Sustaining Fund (1909–1913) and an occasional contributor to the magazine. His works include *A Year in Politics* (1906), *The Fight for Free Speech, a Supplement to Law-Breaking by the Police* (editor; East Orange, N.J.: East Orange Record Press, 1909), and *The Forerunners of Woodrow Wilson* (with Hester E. Hosford, 1914).

**Galsworthy, John** (1867–1933) English novelist and playwright. He won the Nobel Prize for literature in 1932 for plays on controversial ethical and social issues. His works include *The Silver Box* (1906), *Strife* (1909), *Justice* (1910), and *The Pigeon* (1914). The latter three were discussed in EG's *The Social Significance of the Modern Drama* (1914) and in her modern drama lectures.

**Gompers, Samuel** (1850–1924) English-born American labor organizer who was president of the American Federation of Labor (AFL) (1886–1894 and 1896–1924), a body of craft unions open to skilled workers. He perceived the IWW as a socialist threat that would undermine the skilled workers and their unions. He warned all AFL affiliates of possible IWW infiltration and instructed members to refuse IWW cooperation and not to support IWW strikes. He was criticized strongly by socialists and revolutionaries, including contributors to *Mother Earth*, who faulted the AFL's celebration of Labor Day instead of May Day. Gompers supported the McNamara brothers until their guilty plea, raising thousands of dollars for their defense, inducing Clarence Darrow to be their lawyer, and traveling to the West Coast in the fall of 1911 to rally support for them. He was a member of the Factory Investigation Committee after the Triangle Shirtwaist fire (1911). Gompers was attacked by anarchists and socialists for supporting military preparedness in 1916, although he did support the case for a new trial after Mooney's death sentence (1916). In November 1916, after the shootings in Everett, Washington, Gompers called on the government to support working-class people there. His publications of this period include *Labor in Europe and America* (New York: Harper and Brothers, 1910), *The McNamara Case Also, an Appeal for Funds to Secure a Fair and Impartial Trial* (Washington, D.C.: McNamara Ways and Means Committee, 1911) and *Socialist Methods Versus Trade Union Methods* (Washington, D.C.: American Federation of Labor, 1912).

**Gorky, Maksim (pseudonym of Alexey Maximovich Peshkov)** (1868–1936) Russian novelist and a conceptual founder of Russian socialist realism who was widely acclaimed Russia's first proletarian writer. Gorky joined the Russian Social Democratic Labor Party (RSDLP) while living in St. Petersburg between 1899 and 1906. He contributed most of the revenue from his writings to the party; for a period his donations were one of the party's main sources of income. He settled in Capri as a political exile in 1906 after failing in his mission to collect funds abroad for the RSDLP. While in Capri he began extensive correspondence with Lenin, wrote for the party's publications, and attended the Fifth Party Congress in London. In 1913, after a general declaration of amnesty, he returned to Russia where he became the founding editor of *Letopis* (Chronicles; 1915–1917). His publications during the period of this volume include *Submerged* (Boston: R. G. Badger, 1915) and the autobiographical work *My Childhood* (New York: The Century Co., 1915). EG discussed his play *A Night's Lodging* (Boston: Poet Lore, 1905) in *The Social Significance of the Modern Drama* (1914). See also vol. 2, *Making Speech Free*.

**Hall, Bolton** (1854–1938) Irish-born American single-taxer, social reformer, lawyer, land reformer, and philosophical anarchist. Although not always in agreement with EG's politics, he remained her loyal admirer and supporter. Hall protested against the death sentence of Kōtoku (1910) in a letter to the Japanese ambassador. He also signed the widely circulated 1911 letter sent to *Justice* protesting its accusations that EG was a Russian police spy. A supporter of the Ferrer Center and New York Ferrer Modern School, he was treasurer of the Ferrer Association in 1911. He was a public advocate for birth control and was arrested in 1916 with Ida Rauh and Jessie Ashley for distributing birth control literature at a Union Square mass meeting. Hall's writing appeared frequently in *Mother Earth*, including the tenth anniversary souvenir edition. Hall's writing also appeared in the *Agitator*, the *American Journal of Eugenics*, the *Arena*, *Discontent*, *Joseph Fels Fund Bulletin*, *Land and Liberty*, *Life* magazine, the *Public*, the *Single Tax Review*, the *Syndicalist*, and the *Toiler*. His works of this period include *What Tolstoy Taught* (New York: B. W. Huebsch, 1911), *The Mastery of Grief* (New York: H. Holt, 1913), *Thrift* (New York: B. W. Huebsch, 1916), and *The Psychology of Sleep* (New York: Moffatt Yard, 1916).

**Hanson, Carl** (d. 1914) Latvian-born revolutionary. Hanson was a close friend of Charles Berg, whom he met in Hamburg working as a merchant seaman. He came to New York in 1911 and worked as a carpenter. He was a founding member of the Lettish Anarchist Red Cross in New York in December 1913. He was involved in the Anti-Militarist League and the Tarrytown free speech fight against Rockefeller in 1914. Hanson was killed with Arthur Caron, Charles Berg, and Marie Chavez in the Lexington Avenue explosion on 4 July 1914.

**Hapgood, Hutchins** (1869–1944) American liberal journalist, author, and bohemian. Hapgood was a speaker at the New York Ferrer Center and a supporter of the Free Speech League. In 1911 he signed the letter to the Japanese ambassador protesting the execution of Kōtoku and the other Japanese anarchists. He and his wife, Neith Boyce Hapgood, were founding members of the Provincetown Players in 1915. Hapgood was a close friend of EG and contributed articles to *Mother Earth*. He wrote a favorable review of EG's *Anarchism and Other Essays* in the *Bookman* (February 1911) and the introduction to AB's *Prison Memoirs of an Anarchist*. Hapgood was a regular contributor to the *Globe and Commercial Advertiser* (New York) and also contributed to *Revolt*, the *International*, and *Collier's*. His publications from this period include *Types from City Streets* (New York: Funk and Wagnalls, 1910), *Fire and Revolution* (New York: Free Speech League, 1912), *A Cold Enthusiast* (Hillacre, Riverside, Conn.: privately printed, 1913). See also vol. 2, *Making Speech Free*.

**Hartmann, Sadakichi** (1867–1944) German-Japanese anarchist poet, author, painter, critic, and drinking companion of Hippolyte Havel. Hartmann signed the letter sent to the Japanese ambassador protesting the death penalty for Japanese anarchists in 1911. He was an occasional teacher at the Modern School, a contributor to Alfred Stieglitz's influential modernist journal, *Camera Work*, and a regular contributor of articles to the *Altrurian, Forum,* and *The Blast*. He also published his own art magazine, *Stylus*. His books include *Landscape and Figure Composition* (New York: Baker and Taylor, 1910), *The Whistler Book* (Boston: C. Page, 1910), *Permanent Peace, Is It a Dream?* (New York: Guido Bruno, 1915), and *Tanka and Haikai: 14 Japanese Rhythms* (New York: Guido Bruno, 1915). *Mother Earth* often published his short stories. See also vol. 2, *Making Speech Free*.

**Havel, Hippolyte** (1869–1950) Czech-born anarchist-communist propagandist. He lived in New York and was actively involved with the Ferrer Center, speaking there regularly. Also a major character in Greenwich Village, he was the companion of Polly Holladay and worked as a cook in her restaurant. In 1910 he signed the letter urging people to protest the death penalty passed on Kōtoku and other Japanese anarchists, and he was instrumental in organizing their defense and publicizing their case, writing articles in the *New York Call* and in *Mother Earth*, including "Justice in Japan" and "The Kōtoku Case," as well as editing the correspondence of Kōtoku and Albert Johnson. In February 1911 Havel left his editorial position at *Mother Earth*, and during the summer and fall of 1911 visited Paris. In 1912 he helped found the Ferrer Center's Syndicalist Educational League, of which he was secretary and Harry Kelly treasurer. Havel wrote the biographical sketches for EG's *Anarchism and Other Essays* (New York: Mother Earth Publishing Association, 1910) and Voltairine de Cleyre's *Selected Works* (New York: Mother Earth Publishing Association, 1914). He edited *The Revolutionary Almanac* (New York: Rabelais Press, 1914) and the journal *Revolt* (1916), which was published in the basement of the New York Ferrer Center, and wrote *Bakunin* (New York: The Centenary Commemoration Committee, 1914). He also contributed to the magazine *Camera Work*. See also vols. 1 and 2.

**Haywood, William "Big Bill"** (1869–1928) Organizer of American labor, the Socialist Party, and the IWW. In 1907 Haywood drifted away from the IWW, believing it ineffective, and instead began working with the Socialist Party. He was a delegate to the 1910 International Socialist Conference in Copenhagen. Haywood became active with the IWW again in 1911 after he abandoned his support for political reform and as the IWW was moving to the forefront of industrial conflict, successfully organizing workers across the country. Conflict within the Socialist Party of America

(SPA)—in which an amendment was passed forcing all members to vow a loyalty oath opposing sabotage, violence, and all illegal action, ostensibly a choice between the SPA and the IWW—led to Haywood's break with the SPA in 1913. He was recalled from the National Executive Committee for a speech he made in 1912 in which he advocated direct action and sabotage, and he left the party after his recall. He occasionally stayed at the *Mother Earth* office while in New York. He also attended Mabel Dodge's salon, where he once debated with EG, AB, and William English Walling; Haywood spoke for syndicalism, EG and AB for anarchism, and Walling for socialism. He was a powerful organizer and orator for the IWW and the principal agitator for the textile workers striking in Lawrence (1912) and silk workers striking in Paterson (1913). After Vincent St. John's retirement from the IWW in 1914 Haywood was elected as the general secretary-treasurer of the union. He was the companion of Jessie Ashley after 1912. Haywood was a temporary editor of the *Miner's Magazine*, a contributing editor to *International Socialist Review* (1906–1913), and a regular contributor to *Solidarity* and the *Industrial Worker*. He was the author, with Frank Bohn, of *Industrial Socialism* (Chicago: Charles H. Kerr, 1911).

**Henri, Robert** (1865–1929) American painter, art teacher, philosophical anarchist, and author. He was part of the group known as The Eight, which in March 1908 staged an independent art show after their work was rejected by the National Academy of Design. The group was known for their opposition to the authority of the academy and commitment to freedom of expression. In November 1911 Henri began lecturing at the Ferrer Center once a week at the invitation of EG, an affiliation that would last until the center closed its doors in 1918. Many pupils from the classes he taught with George Bellows at the Ferrer Center would go on to be famous in the world of American art, including Adolf Wolff, Man Ray, and George Weber. He donated paintings in support of the Lawrence strike (1912). In March and April 1915 Henri painted three portraits of EG, which were destroyed in 1934 by his sister-in-law, the heir to his estate. A member of the Birth Control Committee, Henri worked with Leonard Abbott to plan a mass meeting at Carnegie Hall in 1916. As a member of the New York Publicity Committee for the International Workers' Defense League, he also helped organize a fund-raising meeting at Carnegie Hall for Mooney and Billings in 1916. Henri contributed to the tenth-anniversary souvenir edition of *Mother Earth*. He wrote an article, "Isadora Duncan and the Libertarian Spirit," for the April 1915 issue of the *Modern School*, in which he favorably compared Duncan to Walt Whitman, seeing both as figures holding "the deep philosophy of freedom and of dignity, of simplicity and of order." He also contributed to the *Conservator*.

**Hillquit, Morris (born Moishe Hillkowicz)** (1869–1933) Jewish immigrant, socialist, trade unionist, politician, and labor lawyer. He represented the right wing in factional battles in 1911–1912 within the Socialist Party of America. A lawyer in a series of legal battles, he served as the International Ladies' Garment Workers' Union's general counsel after 1913 and defended its leaders against murder charges in connection with a 1910 strike. He was also instrumental in shaping the socialist antiwar position, having authored the party's official antiwar manifesto in 1915, and in 1917 he would lead the largely socialist People's Council, a radical group that held mass meetings in Madison Square Garden to call for peace. He was active politically as Socialist Party nominee for Congress in New York's Twentieth District in 1916. His works include *Socialism Summed Up* (New York: H. K. Fly, 1912), *Socialism in Theory and Practice* (New York; Macmillan, 1914), *The Double*

*Edge of Labor's Sword* (with Samuel Gompers and Max J. Hayes; Chicago: Socialist Party, National Office, 1914), and *Socialism: Promise or Menace?* (with John A. Ryan; New York: Macmillan, 1914).

**Ibsen, Henrik** (1828–1906) Norwegian-born dramatist and poet. Ibsen's drama often centered around middle-class characters and presented an intense psychological analysis of their reaction to social pressures. Ibsen worked as stage director in the Norwegian Theater in Bergen (1851–1857) and as artistic director of the Kristiania Theater (1857–1862). He went on to found the Norwegian Company with his friend and colleague Bjørnstjerne Bjørnson in 1859. Major works include *Brand* (1866), *A Doll's House* (1879), *An Enemy of the People* (1882), *Hedda Gabler* (1890), *The Master Builder* (1891), and *Ghosts* (1881). The August 1915 issue of *Mother Earth* reprinted his poem "To My Friend, the Revolutionary Orator." Ibsen's work was also featured prominently in EG's drama lectures and in her book *The Social Significance of the Modern Drama* (1914). Ibsen's character Doctor Stockman in *An Enemy of the People* was seen by some anarchists, including EG, as epitomizing individual resistance against the mass. To others, such as Errico Malatesta, he was the symbol of bourgeois egoism.

**Ingersoll, Robert** (1833–1899) Prominent American freethinker, orator, and writer. Ingersoll served as the attorney general of Illinois, 1867–1869, but gave up politics in order to devote himself to practicing law and lecturing throughout the country on rationalism, humanism, and intellectual freedom. Ingersoll achieved national fame as a brilliant orator and powerful writer, but he was attacked regularly by supporters of church and religion for his identification as an agnostic. He was influenced by Voltaire and Paine. His writings evidence support for blacks, women, and workers, but Ingersoll was critical of EG and anarchism in general. He was an influential member of the National Liberal League until 1880, when he resigned as vice president because he favored modification of the Comstock laws, rather than a full repeal as others in the league supported. His works include *The Gods* (1872), *Some Mistakes of Moses* (1879), and *Why I Am an Agnostic* (1896). See also vol. 1, *Made for America*.

**Inglis, Agnes Ann** (1870–1952) Anarchist curator of the Labadie Collection at the University of Michigan at Ann Arbor (1924–1952). Initially a socialist and suffragist, she worked at settlement houses, including the Franklin Street Settlement House in Detroit and Graham Taylor's Commons in Chicago. On returning to Michigan she worked at the YMCA in Ann Arbor. Inglis became an anarchist after reading EG's writings. She met EG perhaps as early as 1912 and organized EG's meetings in Ann Arbor in November 1915 and at the University of Michigan in 1916. She organized a birth control league complete with a clinic in Ann Arbor (1916). Inglis contributed financially to the war fund of *The Blast* and to the International Workers' Defense League's fund for Mooney and Billings.

**James, Charles L.** (1846–1911) American scholar and anarchist. He lived a relatively secluded life in Eau Claire, Wisconsin, but was seen by EG, Voltairine de Cleyre, and others as the most learned American anarchist. He developed for Voltairine de Cleyre the reading outline for the Philadelphia Social Science Club. This outline later became the foundation for James's "Vindication of Anarchism," which was serialized in *Free Society* in 1903; Abe Isaaks Jr. and Natasha Notkin planned to publish the piece in book form after his death but never did. He contributed articles to many other anarchist publications, including *Alarm*, *Lucifer the Lightbearer*, and *Mother Earth*, which serialized his essays "Anarchism and Malthus" from April 1909 to

August 1909 and "Economy as Viewed by an Anarchist" from September 1912 to January 1913. His works include *The Law of Marriage, An Exposition of Its Uselessness and Injustice* (Chicago: C. L. James, 1870), *Manual of Transcendental Philosophy* (Boston: W. White, 1871), *The Future Relation of the Sexes* (St. Louis: C. L. James, 1872), *Anarchy: A Tract for the Times* (Eau Claire, Wisc.: Eau Claire Book and Stationery, 1886), *Degeneracy* (Eau Claire, Wisc.: C. L. James, n.d., ca. 1880–1889), *An Appeal to the Women of America in Behalf of Liberty and Justice. To and For the Prosecuted and Persecuted Defenders of the Wives and Mothers of Our Land* (Topeka, Kansas: Moses Harman, 1891), *Origin of Anarchism* (Chicago: A. Isaak Jr., 1902), *History of the French Revolution* (Chicago: A. Isaak Jr., 1902), and *Anarchy and Malthus* (New York: Mother Earth Publishing Association, 1910).

**Kanno Suga** (1881–1911) Japanese militant anarchist, editor, and journalist who wrote under the pen name "Sugako." She joined Christian and socialist opponents of the Russo-Japanese War in 1904, becoming part of the Heiminsha group led by Sakai Toshihiko and Kōtoku Shūsui. She worked for the newspapers *Muro Shimpo* (Muro News) in 1906 and *Tokyo Dempo* (Tokyo Telegraph) in 1907. Kanno was diagnosed with tuberculosis in 1907. After the brutal police beating of political demonstrators in June 1908, known as the Red Flag Incident, she was convinced that peaceful reform was impossible in Japan, and she converted to anarchism. In 1909 she co-founded, with her then companion Kōtoku, the journal *Jiyu Shiso* (Free Thought) and subsequently spent three months in jail for violating censorship laws. While Kanno was in jail, officials discovered the plot to assassinate the emperor (May 1910). Unlike Kōtoku, whose knowledge of the assassination plot was secondhand, Kanno indicated in her diaries that she was directly involved in the Great Treason Incident and perhaps even a central organizer, although publicity by the government and press was focused on Kōtoku. The trial of twenty-six anarchists, many of whom were implicated only by association, began in December 1910, and eleven of the accused, including Kōtoku, were executed on 24 January. Kanno was executed the following day.

**Keell, Thomas H.** (1866–1938) Prominent English anarchist and editor. He corresponded regularly with EG and AB, acting as a British conduit for news of their activities. Keell edited the *Voice of Labour* and served as a delegate to the International Anarchist Congress in Amsterdam in 1907, where he met EG. He met BR in London in 1910. In 1913 he became acting (and later, permanent) editor of the London journal *Freedom*. Keell opposed Kropotkin's pro–World War I position and signed the International Anarchist Manifesto on the War. In June 1916 he and his partner, Lilian Wolfe, were imprisoned briefly for publishing an article defying the British wartime Military Service Act of 1916. He also contributed an article about the 1912 arrest of Errico Malatesta to the July 1912 *Mother Earth*.

**Keller, Helen** (1880–1968) American socialist and spokeswoman for the blind and deaf. Keller joined the Socialist Party in 1909 in Massachusetts and the IWW in 1912. She corresponded with, was interviewed by, and wrote for various socialist and mainstream newspapers, including the *New York Call*, the *Ladies Home Journal*, and the *New York Times*. In 1913 she published a controversial collection of essays, *Out of the Dark*, which examined and defended her belief in socialism. Keller was involved with the Heterodoxy Club of Greenwich Village, a group of prominent progressive women founded in 1912. In the fall of 1915 Keller began her campaign against World War I. On 5 January 1916 EG attended one of Keller's lectures against preparedness at Carnegie Hall in New York City. They began corresponding a month later, after EG wrote to Keller praising her lecture. In April 1916 Keller wrote several letters to District Attorney Edward Swann of New York and to the *New York Call* supporting EG's birth control agitation and protesting her arrest. Keller and EG often corresponded in support and admiration of each other's work but would meet only briefly, in 1917. Keller maintained her support for radical movements throughout her life.

**Kelly, Henry May "Harry"** (1871–1953) American anarchist, printer, lecturer, and a founder of the Ferrer Association in New York and the Modern School at Stelton, New Jersey. He served as chairman of the 3 January 1910 meeting establishing the Francisco Ferrer Association, and with Stewart Kerr, the association's secretary, he served as founding editor of the organization's bulletin, *News Letter* (1910). Kelly was a founding member of the Ferrer Modern School in 1911 and remained influential in shaping school policy, especially its 1915 move to Stelton, New Jersey. In March 1911 he joined Abe Isaak's Aurora Colony in Lincoln, California, near Sacramento. After three months he was called back to New York by Leonard Abbott to serve as an organizer of the Ferrer Association. In response to the harsh treatment of EG and BR in the 1912 San Diego free speech fight he issued, with AB and Hippolyte Havel, a statement to the press that anarchists and social rebels would "answer violence with violence." In 1912 he organized a testimonial dinner for AB in honor of the recently released *Prison Memoirs of an Anarchist*. At a Ferrer Association dinner in October 1914 Kelly and AB quarreled over the question of what the anarchist position on war ought to be. Kelly defended Kropotkin's position in support of the Allies, although he would eventually sign the International Anarchist Manifesto on the War. He contributed regularly, under both "Harry Kelly" and "Henry May," to *Freedom* and *Mother Earth*, including the latter's tenth-anniversary souvenir edition. He was also an editor, with Leonard Abbott, of the *Modern School* (1912). Kelly contributed to *Everyman* (1914), *The Blast* (1916), and *Revolt* (1916).

**Kennan, Ellen A.** (ca. 1873–ca. 1950) Teacher at Denver East Side High School and correspondent of EG. She was a friend and roommate of Gertrude E. Nafe. Kennan was EG's main Denver contact, helping her organize her lectures and drama classes there. She contributed to the Caplan-Schmidt Defense Fund and *The Blast* war fund, and wrote articles for *Mother Earth* in 1916.

**Kōtoku, Denjiro (Shūsui)** (1871–1911) Japanese anarchist-communist and journalist. He was a major conduit for European socialist and anarchist thought in Japan. Kōtoku was one of the founders of the Japanese Social Democratic Party (1901) and the Japanese Socialist Party (1906), both of which were banned by the government. During the Russo-Japanese War (1904–1905) he translated articles by Tolstoy, *Sixteen Years in Siberia* by Menshevik Lev Deich, and *The Communist Manifesto*. By 1905 he was writing about Catherine Breshkovskaya and supporting the Russian Socialist Revolutionary Party's policy of violence. Kōtoku served a five-month sentence in the same year for "disturbing public peace and order." In late 1905 and early 1906 he visited Seattle and San Francisco, where he met Russian exiles, and after the 1906 San Francisco earthquake he witnessed cooperation and mutual aid in action—an experience that reinforced his understanding of Kropotkin's ideas. He was also influenced during this time by Jean Grave's *Moribund Society and Anarchism*. Just before his return to Japan, a group of Japanese militants in Berkeley, California, using a program framed by Kōtoku, founded the Shakai Kakumeito (Social-Revolutionary Party), which supported the tactics of terrorism. Kōtoku appears to have corresponded with EG, AB, and Kropotkin, and he translated the latter's *Conquest of Bread* (1909). Influenced by anarcho-syndicalism, he translated Arnold Roller's *Social General Strike* (1907). He was allegedly involved in a plot to assassinate the Japanese emperor in 1910, which resulted in his execution, in January 1911, along with eleven other anarchists, including his former companion, Kanno Suga. EG and other anarchists, including Hippolyte Havel, played a major role in American protest that followed, including organization of the Kōtoku Protest Conference Defense Committee Fund (of which AB was secretary) and help with publicity on the case. A selection of his letters was published in *Mother Earth* (July–September 1911), edited by Hippolyte Havel.

**Kropotkin, Peter** (1842–1921) Russian revolutionary, geographer, geologist, and principal theorist of anarchist communism. He wrote the entry "Anarchism" in the *Encyclopaedia Britannica* in 1910. Although he was revered by many anarchists, EG and AB, writing in *Mother Earth* and *The Blast*, objected to his support of the Allies in World War I, against what he saw as German militarism. Kropotkin was a signatory of the Manifesto of the Sixteen in 1916 supporting the war, a position published earlier in the October 1914 issue of the London *Freedom*. The December 1912 issue of *Mother Earth* paid tribute to his life and work on his seventieth birthday. In November 1916 *Mother Earth* began serializing his "Anarchist Morality," which ran each month through March 1917. The only book of his published in English during the period of this volume was a reprint of his 1905 *Russian Literature*, reissued as *Ideals and Realities in Russian Literature* (New York: A. A. Knopf, 1915).

**Kuehn, Herman** (1853–1918) Minneapolis anarchist-individualist, single-taxer, and land reformer. He was an associate of Luke North and Joseph Labadie. Kuehn sometimes wrote under the pen names Evelyn Gladys and Willard Grosvenor. He was a member of the Minneapolis Fellowship of Freedom (1912), a philosophical anarchist and land reform organization of which Labadie was secretary. Kuehn contributed financially to the *American Journal of Eugenics* and wrote articles for the *Demonstrator*, *Land and Liberty* (1914), and *The Blast* (1916). He was editor of the anarchist journal *Fellowship Clearing House* (1 February–16 April 1915), which became *Instead of a Magazine* (1915–1916). Kuehn went on to edit the anarchist journal *Free Lance* (1916), which displayed the banner subhead "Resistance to Tyranny Is the First Law of Patriotism." He moved to Los Angeles in 1916, becoming treasurer of Luke North's Great Adventure campaign for a single-tax amendment to the California constitution, centered around the paper *Everyman*. As Evelyn Gladys, he wrote three collections of essays on social and economic issues, including *The Problem of Worry: Principles of Scientific Mutualism Applied to Modern Commerce* (Chicago: N. B. Irving, 1901), *Shoes, Pigs and Problems* (Chicago: C. H. Kerr, 1905), and *Thoughts of a Fool* (Chicago and London: E. P. Rosenthal and Company, 1905).

**Labadie, Joseph Antoine** (1850–1933) American individualist-anarchist, printer, labor organizer, editor, journalist, and civil servant on the Detroit water board. He participated in a wide range of radical campaigns and organizations. Labadie helped organize EG's Michigan lectures, though especially between 1909 and 1911 he expressed discomfort with EG's activism on issues of sexuality and her outspoken defense of Leon Czolgosz. He was secretary of the Fellowship of Freedom (1912–1916), the group that backed Herman Kuehn's *Instead of a Magazine*. Labadie contributed an article on Haymarket to *Mother Earth* in 1912. His donation of personal and political papers to the University of Michigan at Ann Arbor in 1912 became the foundation of a world-class radical and labor archive. See also vol. 2, *Making Speech Free*.

**Livshis, Annie Mindlin** (1864–1953) Russian-born, Jewish Chicago anarchist and companion of Jake Livshis. In 1886 she immigrated to the United States, where her brothers were already members of the anarchist movement in New York and followers of Johann Most. Annie Mindlin was a member of the Pioneers of Liberty and then a homesteader in Kansas for a short time before meeting and marrying Jacob "Jake" Livshis. For a time the couple worked in the garment industry in Chicago, where in 1890 they helped organize the first formal Jewish trade union in the city. The Livshises were founding members of the Edelstadt group and later the Chicago Social Science Club (1911). She was a friend of EG and a close friend of Voltairine de Cleyre, who lived with the Livshises during the last nineteen months of her life. In 1914 Livshis collected money for the Rangel-Cline Defense Fund. She also contributed money to the publication fund for *Selected Works of Voltairine de Cleyre* in 1912 and wrote and published *In Memoriam: Voltairine de Cleyre* (Chicago: Annie Livshis, 1912).

**Livshis, Jake** (dates unknown) Russian-born, Jewish Chicago anarchist, cigar maker, and husband of Annie Livshis. Together with Annie, he provided Voltairine de Cleyre with a home during the last nineteen months of her life. Livshis was a member of the Social Science Club of Chicago (1911). He contributed to the publication fund for *Selected Works of Voltairine de Cleyre* in July 1912, as well as to a host of other causes and support groups.

**London, Jack** (1876–1916) prominent American novelist and socialist. He met and befriended EG during her 1908 San Francisco tour. Prompted by EG, he wrote to the Japanese ambassador to protest the death sentence imposed on Kōtoku and the Japanese anarchists. In 1911, also at EG's request, he wrote a letter to the English socialist magazine *Justice* to protest its accusation that EG was a spy for the Russian police. EG solicited London to write the preface to AB's *Prison Memoirs*, but AB and EG rejected his piece because of its critical attitude toward anarchism. London was a member of the Francisco Ferrer Association, a lecturer at the New York Ferrer Modern School, and a supporter of the Flores Magón brothers. Among his many works *The Iron Heel* (New York: Macmillan, 1908) was especially important in radical circles. Max Baginski reviewed his novel *Adventure* in the September 1911 *Mother Earth*. See also vol. 2, *Making Speech Free*.

**Luhan, Mabel Dodge** (1879–1962) Wealthy New York patron, known for her Greenwich Village salon, located at 23 Fifth Avenue. From 1913 to 1915 her salon served as a forum for ideas on feminism, literature, birth control, eugenics, politics, and Freudian psychoanalysis. Dodge wrote articles on psychoanalysis and politics for *Camera Work*, the *International*, and the *Masses*. She contributed a poem to *Mother Earth* (April 1913). She claimed she was the source of the idea for the 1913 Paterson Strike Pageant, a reenactment of the silk workers' strike, which John Reed, her lover at the time, helped foster. Dodge met EG through Hutchins Hapgood and invited her to the salon, where EG's presentation on anarchism failed to hold the interest of the guests.

**Maisel, Max N.** (1872–1959) Owner of a bookshop at 424 Grand Street in New York City, where he published and sold anarchist works, European literature, and Yiddish translations. He was a New York agent for anarchist periodicals (including *Mother Earth*), he sold tickets for EG's lectures in New York, and he was a founding member of the Kropotkin Literary Society (1912), which published Yiddish translations of anarchist works. He also published Margaret Sanger's pamphlets *What Every Mother Should Know* and *What Every Girl Should Know* in 1916. See also vol. 2, *Making Speech Free*.

**Malatesta, Errico** (1853–1932) Influential Italian anarchist. In May 1912, while living in England, Malatesta was charged with criminal libel for circulating a leaflet that suggested that an ex-anarchist named Ballelli was a spy for the Italian police. During his trial emphasis was placed on the fact that Malatesta had supplied a bottle of gas to the infamous Sidney Street gang, a group of Latvian anarchists in London. He was sentenced to three months' imprisonment and recommended for deportation. A substantial campaign, supported by such figures as Thomas Mann and Guy Aldred, prevented his deportation. After his release he began editing from London the Italian anarchist newspaper *Volonta*, published in Ancona. Malatesta returned to Italy during the summer of 1913. In June 1914 he addressed an anti-militarist protest meeting in Ancona, which ended in a clash with police and the death of three unarmed demonstrators. In response a general strike was called by the General Confederation of Labor, Unione Sindacale Italiana, and the Railwaymen's Union. Malatesta helped organize unsuccessful anarchist revolts during the strike, also known as the "Red Week," centered around the Emilia-Romagna and Le Marche region. After the failure of the uprisings, he fled to London. In response to Kropotkin's pro-war stance Malatesta wrote articles for *Freedom*, including "Anarchists Have Forgotten Their Principles" (November 1914, reprinted in the January 1915 *Mother Earth*) and "Pro Government Anarchists" (April 1916, reprinted in the 15 May 1916 *Blast*). Both articles were widely reprinted and circulated in the anarchist press. With EG and AB, Malatesta was a signatory of the International Anarchist Manifesto on the War (1915). He also contributed to *Mother Earth*, usually on the situation in Italy. Publications during this period include *Anarchistes de gouvernement* (a French translation of "Pro Government Anarchists," 1916). See also vol. 2, *Making Speech Free*.

**Malmed, Leon** (born Leon Bass and mistakenly named Malmed by a U.S. immigration officer; 1881–1956) Russian-born anarchist and owner of a delicatessen in Albany, New York. He was a member of the Albany anarchist group Germinal. Malmed left his family in 1915 to accompany EG, AB, and BR on a West Coast tour, during which he was arrested in Portland, Oregon, for distributing birth control material. Malmed was a financial supporter of *Mother Earth* and a lifelong friend, companion, and correspondent of EG. He appears in *LML* as Leon Bass. See also vol. 2, *Making Speech Free*.

**Margolis, Jacob** (1885–1959) Pittsburgh labor and IWW lawyer who identified himself as a syndicalist and anarchist. He represented, for a short time, David Caplan. However, they could not agree on the line of defense, and Margolis returned to Pittsburgh. In 1913 he spoke at an IWW meeting with Joseph Ettor. In 1915 he spoke with EG at a preparedness lecture in Pittsburgh, and in 1916 he organized her Pittsburgh drama course. He also contributed to *The Blast* in 1916. Margolis was disbarred in 1920 after testifying before a U.S. Senate committee on radicalism in the labor movement.

**McNamara, James Barnabas** (1882–1941) Printer and paid dynamiter for the International Association of Bridge and Structural Iron Workers (IABSIW). James McNamara, together with Ortie McManigal, dynamited nonunion construction sites in an operation directed by his brother, John J. McNamara. He was responsible for the 1910 dynamiting of the *Los Angeles Times* building, which killed twenty people. He was arrested for the bombing in Detroit on 14 April 1911 by the William J. Burns Detective Agency, which had been employed by the National Erector's Association, an industry group. He had obtained the dynamite for the bombing with the aid of two anarchists, David Caplan and Matthew A. Schmidt, who went underground and remained free until 1915. The McNamara brothers were widely seen as victims of a frame-up, and their case was compared to the earlier one of Moyer, Haywood, and Pettibone. Their defense effort, which was supported by Samuel Gompers, was directed by Clarence Darrow. The evidence against them, though, was apparently damning, and on 1 December 1911 they pleaded guilty, James pleaded guilty to the bombing of the *Times* building and John to the dynamiting of the Llewellyn Iron Works in Los Angeles. Their confessions seem to have been a result of negotiations between Lincoln Steffens, Clarence Darrow, E. W. Scripps, and the prosecution. Many radicals and liberals complained that the prosecution reneged on the deal by giving the McNamaras harsher sentences than promised and by continuing to pursue David Caplan and Matthew Schmidt. On 5 December 1911 J. B. was sentenced to life in prison at San Quentin, where he died on 8 March 1941.

**McNamara, John Joseph** (1876–1941) Labor organizer, lawyer, and secretary-treasurer of the International Association of Bridge and Structural Iron Workers (IABSIW). He directed dynamiting operations against nonunion construction sites in an effort to unionize the structural iron industry. A practicing Catholic and supporter of the American Federation of Labor, he seems to have had few ties to radicalism. John McNamara was arrested in Indianapolis in 1911 by detective William J. Burns in connection with the 1910 *Los Angeles Times* building explosion and was illegally extradited to California. Sentenced to fifteen years in prison on 5 December 1911, John McNamara was released 10 May 1921. After release from prison he went back to work for the IABSIW as the business agent of the Indianapolis local. He died on 7 May 1941 in Butte, Montana, just two months after his brother, who had died in prison. See also the entry for James Barnabas McNamara, above.

**Michel, Louise** (1830–1905) French anarchist, teacher, and writer. Heroine of the Paris Commune who transferred her activism to anarchism. Michel joined the *La Revolution Sociale* circle in Paris. She contributed to *Les Temps Nouveaux* and *Le Libertaire* and wrote essays, novels, poetry, history, and an opera, as well as her memoirs. EG met Michel in London in 1895, where they spoke on the same platform. See also vols. 1 and 2.

**Minor, Robert** (1884–1952) Anarchist illustrator and artist, and later a key figure in the Communist Party. He joined the Socialist Party in 1907 but moved philosophically toward anarcho-syndicalism after a year spent in Paris studying art (1912–1913). He was chief cartoonist for the *St. Louis Post-Dispatch* (1910) and in 1913 became a cartoonist for the *New York Evening World*, while concurrently contributing to *Mother Earth*. An aggressive opponent of American entrance into World War I, he was fired from the *New York Evening World* in 1915 for his refusal to tone down the antiwar position of his art. During 1915 the *Masses* began publishing his cartoons, many of which protested the war in Europe and America's imminent involvement. Minor was the treasurer and primary organizer of the International Workers' Defense League, which provided aid and publicity to the defense of Thomas Mooney and Warren Billings (1916–1918). He coordinated the first mass meeting to protest the arrests of Mooney and Billings, at Dreamland Rink in San Francisco in September 1916. He regularly contributed illustrations, and occasionally articles, to *Mother Earth*, as well as to *The Blast* and *Revolt*.

**Mirbeau, Octave Henri Marie** (1848–1917) French playwright, novelist, and anarchist who wrote regularly for anarchist periodicals. He originally advocated and published right-wing views, and he volunteered to serve in the French army during the Franco-Prussian War. However, by the mid-1880s, after exposure to the works of Tolstoy and Kropotkin, he had abandoned militarism and his former stance in favor of anarchism. Mirbeau's *The Torture Garden* (1899) was a savage attack on government. He wrote more than 1,200 short stories and articles, including three semi-autobiographical novels: *Le Calvaire* (1886), *L'Abbé Jules* (1888), and *Sébastien Roche* (1890). All three reflected his anarchism, but *L'Abbé Jules* was the most explicit. In 1900 Benjamin Tucker translated his *Le Journal d'une femme de chamber* as *A Chambermaid's Diary* (New York: Benjamin Tucker), upon which it was confiscated by the U.S. postmaster under the Comstock Act for its sexually explicit satirical content.

**Mooney, Thomas J.** (1882–1942) Molder by trade, militant socialist, and trade unionist. In 1907 Mooney traveled to Europe, where he was drawn to socialism. Upon his return in the winter of 1907 he began formal study of socialism, and in 1908 he joined the Socialist Party of Stockton, California. Mooney was a passenger on the "Red Special" promotional train for Eugene V. Debs's 1908 presidential campaign. He was a circulation manager and later publisher of the socialist militant worker paper *Revolt* (San Francisco, 1911–1912). He briefly joined the IWW in March 1910 but let his membership lapse, though he maintained ties with IWW leaders, including William D. Haywood, Elizabeth Gurley Flynn, Vincent St. John, and West Coast organizer George Speed. In 1912 Mooney was a delegate to the International Molders' Union convention. Mooney was involved in the 1913 Frank & Hyman Shoe Company strike, where he met Warren K. Billings, a young labor militant. Mooney was also active in the Pacific Gas and Electric (PG&E) strike of 1913, which caused extensive damage to PG&E property, including eighteen attacks with dynamite. He had ties to San Francisco anarchists, including Eric B. Morton and Edward Nolan, and he served as secretary of the International Workers' Defense League in 1916, actively working for the defense of Matthew Schmidt and David Caplan. Acquainted with AB, he helped with production of *The Blast*; he attended *Blast* picnics and wrote one article for the paper. In 1916 he tried to organized the motormen and conductors of the United Railroads of San Francisco, and an unsuccessful strike was attempted on 14 July 1916. For this and other activity he was under the surveillance of Martin Swanson, a private detective who worked for a detective agency employed by PG&E. Swanson suspected Mooney of being involved in the dynamiting of PG&E electric towers. Swanson suggested Mooney, Mooney's wife Rena, Billings, Israel Weinberg, and Edward Nolan to San Francisco district attorney Charles Fickert as suspects for the Preparedness Day bombing of 22 July 1916, which killed ten people and wounded forty. All were arrested in the days following. Although he was never arrested, attempts were made to label AB as the coordinator behind the bombing, including an unsuccessful attempt to extradite him from New York in July 1917. Despite contradictory witnesses and a lack of solid physical evidence, Mooney was convicted of murder and sentenced to death. AB and EG were among the first to come to the defense of Mooney and Billings in the pages of *The Blast* and *Mother Earth*, insisting on their innocence and the conspiracy of antilabor interests to frame them. The death sentence was commuted to life imprisonment following national protests as well as protests in Russia arranged by AB through anarchists, including Louise Berger, who had returned to take part in the revolution. His case was for years to be a cause célèbre of the American and international left, and especially of the Communist Party, with which Mooney's defense was allied by convenience, if not by ideology. Mooney was granted a full and unconditional pardon by Governor Culbert Olson of California on 7 January 1939, after twenty-two years in prison.

**Morton, Eric B.** (d. ca. 1930) Norwegian-born American anarchist. Morton was nicknamed both "Eric the Red," after the hero of an Icelandic saga, and "Ibsen," after the Norwegian playwright, in AB's *Prison Memoirs of an Anarchist* (1912). Morton was often involved in clandestine anarchist activities, including attempting to tunnel AB out of prison in 1901 and helping EG and Catherine Breshkovskaya smuggle guns into Russia during the 1905 Russian revolution. Morton moved to San Francisco, where he edited the short-lived *Freedom* (1910–1911). He signed the widely circulated letter sent to *Justice*, protesting the accusation that EG was a Russian police spy in 1911. He was a member of the millmen's union, sat on the San Francisco Building Trades Council, and served as a delegate to the San Francisco Labor Council. David Caplan listed Morton as his cousin on his application to be a special police officer, and Morton sometimes lived with Caplan's family. He was for a time suspected of complicity in the *Los Angeles Times* building bombing but was never arrested. Morton was involved in the Caplan-Schmidt Defense League, acting as publicity manager and collecting funds from Los Angeles. He later served as associate editor of *The Blast* (San Francisco, 1916–1917), and his poem "The Golden Rule," a reference to the ongoing labor-capital war being waged in California, introduced the premier issue in January 1916. His poem "Caplan and Schmidt," signed Eric the Red, was published in the September 1915 *Mother Earth*.

**Most, Johann** (1846–1906) German-born anarchist propagandist who was imprisoned several times for his speeches and publications. At the invitation of anarchist Justus Schwab, Most immigrated to the United States in December of 1882 and settled in New York City. He resumed the publication of *Freiheit*, which was notorious for advocating propaganda by deed, until his death in 1906. Most died during a propaganda tour in Cincinnati on 17 March 1906 and was memorialized by Max Baginski in the March 1906 and March 1911 issues of *Mother Earth*. See also vol. 1, *Made for America*, for more on his relationship with EG and the American anarchist movement.

**Moyer, Charles H.** (1866–1937) American labor leader who was president of the Western Federation of Miners (WFM; 1902–1916). Although the WFM was known for its militant radicalism, Moyer often advocated moderation and negotiation. He was arrested, along with William Haywood and George Pettibone, for the murder of the former governor of Idaho, Frank Stuenenberg, but he was released in 1908 after both Haywood and Pettibone were acquitted. Moyer emerged from prison much more conservative. Although present at the 1905 founding convention of the IWW, Moyer withdrew the WFM from the IWW because the IWW was too radical. After at one time being close to Haywood, Moyer removed him from the WFM in 1908 and became more sympathetic toward AFL strategy, reaffiliating the WFM with the AFL in 1911, which it had left in 1897. The WFM changed its name in 1916 to the International Union of Mine, Mill, and Smelter Workers but experienced a steady decline in membership, causing Moyer to resign in 1926.

**Nafe, Gertrude E.** (dates unknown) School teacher at East Side High School in Denver, Colorado, and a friend and roommate of Ellen Kennan. She was secretary of the Denver branch of the International Workers' Defense League for Caplan and Schmidt in 1915, and she contributed funds to the Caplan-Schmidt Defense Fund. An occasional contributor to *Mother Earth*, Nafe wrote a short story for the tenth-anniversary souvenir edition and an article on the Ludlow Massacre and the striking miners, "Colorado," for the June 1914 issue.

**Nettlau, Max** (1865–1944) Prominent anarchist historian and author. His inherited wealth enabled him to devote himself to collecting and studying anarchist history. He was acquainted with EG,

Kropotkin, Errico Malatesta, Rudolf Rocker, Victor Dave, and Élisée Reclus, among others. Nettlau wrote for the London *Freedom*, including most of the international notes and the annual "Reviews of the Year." He edited the revised edition of Bakunin's *God and the State* (London: Freedom Press, 1910). Nettlau contributed the essay "Anarchism: Communist or Individualist?—Both" to the July 1914 *Mother Earth*; this was a republication from the March and May 1914 editions of *Freedom* and displayed his move away from strict anarchist communism. Although his attitude toward World War I was complex, he essentially supported Germany and Austria-Hungary. His correspondence with EG continued but was sporadic during this period. See also vol. 1.

**Nietzsche, Frederick** (1844–1900) German philosopher admired by anarchists not only for his critique of both Judeo-Christian morality and the State but also as a supporter of the supremacy of the individual against social and political constraints. His work was often republished in *Mother Earth* and also was the basis of a regular element in EG's lectures on culture and politics. EG identified with Nietzsche's desire to reevaluate, or transvalue, all accepted values. Editions of his work were advertised in and sold through *Mother Earth*. His major works include *Thus Spoke Zarathustra* (1883–1885), *Beyond Good and Evil* (1886), *On the Genealogy of Morals* (1887), and *Ecce Homo* (written in 1888 but first published in 1908).

**Nieuwenhuis, F. Domela** (1846–1919) Dutch anarchist pacifist. He worked with Christiaan Cornelissen and others to form the syndicalist organization National Arbeids Sekretariat in 1893. He attended the International Anarchist Congress in 1907 and signed the International Anarchist Manifesto on the War in 1915. A committed anti-militarist, he contributed a number of articles to *Mother Earth* including "To the Anti-Militarists, Anarchists, and Free Thinkers," February 1915, in which he outlined his belief in the power of a general strike of an international brotherhood of workers to end the war. See also vols. 1 and 2.

**Nold, Carl** (1869–1934) German-born anarchist who was imprisoned with AB in 1893. Nold settled in Detroit in the 1890s, where he became an active force in the anarchist community. He worked with Joseph Labadie, taught at the Detroit Modern Sunday School, contributed financial support to various publishing endeavors, including the *Selected Works of Voltairine de Cleyre* and *Land and Liberty*. He wrote for various anarchist publications, including the *Demonstrator, Discontent,* and *Mother Earth*. See also vol. 1.

**Orlenev, Pavel** (1869–1932) Russian actor and head of the St. Petersburg Players. EG, under the pseudonym E. G. Smith, became the troupe's manager for a time in the fall of 1905. In appreciation of her help Orlenev, before returning to Russia in 1906, gave a benefit performance of Ibsen's *Ghosts* to help launch *Mother Earth*. Orlenev and his theater troupe returned to New York in January 1912, where they performed Ibsen, Dostoyevsky (*Crime and Punishment*), and Shakespeare (*Hamlet*). EG wrote an unsigned short piece in appreciation of Orlenev; it appeared in the January 1912 *Mother Earth*. See also vol. 2, *Making Speech Free*.

**Owen, William Charles** (1854–1929) English socialist and later anarchist and land reformer. He contributed to the Free Speech Defense Fund and to the general Free Speech Fund (1906–1910) and was a member of the 1909 Free Speech Committee. While working as a police-court reporter in Los Angeles, he conducted an investigation for the Prison Reform League, which was the basis of the book *Crime and Criminals* (1910), an indictment of the California prison system. In 1910 Owen began working with and supporting the Partido Liberal Mexicano (PLM) and the Flores Magón brothers, and in 1911 he began editing the English-language page of *Regeneración*. First from Los Angeles and later San Francisco, he issued regular news on their situation through his Free Press Service and his journal, *Land and Liberty*. Owen supported Kropotkin's pro-Allies stance in 1915 and criticized EG, AB, and other antiwar anarchists in *Land and Liberty*. In 1915 he opened a bookshop in San Francisco with Irish anarchist John Creaghe. In 1916 he was accused, with the Flores Magón brothers, of using the mails to transmit materials inciting "murder, deliberate arson and treason." In Washington State at the time, Owen was able to escape arrest; he later traveled to New York and then London, where he remained. He contributed to the *Agitator* (1911–1912), *Freedom* (London; 1911–1914), the Los Angeles socialist paper *Western Comrade* (1914), and *Mother Earth*, writing mainly on the Mexican Revolution and anarchist theory, as well as reporting on the *Los Angeles Times* explosion and its aftermath. He edited his own paper, *Land and Liberty* (May 1914–June 1915) in Hayward, California. His works include *Crime and Criminals* (Los Angeles: Prison Reform League, 1910), *Anarchism Versus Socialism* (New York: Mother Earth Publishing Association, 1910), *The McNamara Case and Socialism, Have the Socialists Made Good?* (Los Angeles: *Regeneración*, 1911 or 1912), and *The Mexican Revolution: Its Progress, Causes, Purpose and Probable Results* (Los Angeles: *Regeneración*, 1912). See also vol. 1, *Made for America*.

**Paine, Thomas**  (1737–1809) English writer, freethinker, and humanitarian. Paine was influential in shaping public opinion during the American Revolution and an active participant in the French Revolution. His major writings include *Common Sense* (1776), *The Rights of Man* (1791–1792), and *Age of Reason* (1794, 1796). Many anarchists and freethinkers, including Leonard Abbott, James F. Morton, and individualist anarchist E. C. Walker joined the Thomas Paine National Historical Association. EG and other anarchists identified with his hostility to established religion and his attempt to keep government as small as possible.

**Parsons, Lucy**  (1853–1942) Chicago anarchist and widow of Haymarket martyr Albert Parsons. Parsons was a close friend and associate of Carl Nold, and in 1912 she helped form the Syndicalist League of North America with William Z. Foster and Jay Fox. During the winter of 1913–1914 she also worked to organize the unemployed and remained dedicated to reversing the record of the Haymarket case. Parsons engaged in a series of lecture tours during the period of this volume, during which she was arrested in Los Angeles in 1913 for selling literature without a license, in San Francisco in 1914 for speaking before a gathering of the unemployed, and in Chicago in 1915 for leading a hunger demonstration (her bail payment was arranged by Jane Addams). Parsons traveled to Minnesota to help organize the Mesabi Range strike in the summer of 1916, and she spoke with EG, Theodore Appel, William Haywood, and BR at the annual 11 November Haymarket memorial meeting that same year. Parsons contributed to the *Agitator, Syndicalist*, and the *Industrial Worker*; wrote for the first issue of *Land and Liberty* in 1914; and helped edit the *Alarm* in 1915–1916. She also edited a 1915 edition of *Altgeld's Reasons for Pardoning Fielden, Schwab and Neebe*.

**Pelloutier, Fernand**  (1867–1901) French anarchist and syndicalist. He was general secretary, after 1895, of the Fédération Nationale Des Bourse du Travail. He authored *L'organisation corporative et l'anarchie* (1896) and *Histoire Des Bourses du travail, orgine, institutions, avenir* (1902).

**Perovskaya, Sophia** (1853–1881) Russian revolutionary, populist. A member of the Chaikovsky Circle, and later a leader of Narodnaya Volya (People's Will), a clandestine socialist group that emerged out of a split in the populist Zemlya i Volya (Land and Liberty party) and embraced assassination as a political strategy. On 13 March 1881 Perovskaya stationed her co-conspirators in Narodnaya Volya along the route of Alexander II's travel and signaled them when he was in range of their bombs. Arrested on 22 March 1881, she was hung on 15 April 1881, the first woman political prisoner in Russia to be executed. She became a symbol of courage and self-sacrifice for many young revolutionaries both in Russia and in the United States and was especially admired by EG.

**Post, Louis Freeland** (1849–1928) Liberal Chicago lawyer, influential single-tax editor, and civil servant. Post founded and edited the *Public* (Chicago, 1898–1913), a liberal single-tax journal in which he reported sympathetically on EG, defending her and her free speech fights. He served as assistant secretary of labor through Woodrow Wilson's two administrations. His works during this period include *The Open Shop and the Closed Shop* (Cincinnati: Joseph Fels Fund of America, 1912); *Origin and Progress of the Single Tax Movement* (Brooklyn: Single Tax Information Bureau, 1913); *Trusts, Good and Bad* (Chicago: The Public, 1914); and *A Study of Land Value Taxation* (Cincinnati: Joseph Fels Fund Commission, 1915). See also vols. 2 and 4.

**Pouget, Jean Joseph (known as Émile)** (1860–1931) French syndicalist, author, and editor. Pouget moved to syndicalism after being a strong proponent of propaganda by the deed. Pouget's works include *Grève générale réformiste et Grève générale révolutionnaire* (The Reformist General Strike and the Revolutionary General Strike, 1902), and with Emile Pataud *How We Shall Bring About the Revolution* (trans. Fred and Charlotte Charles, Oxford: New International Publishing, 1913). Other works translated into English include *The Basis of Trade Unionism* (London: Freedom Press, 1908) and *Sabotage* (trans. Arturo M. Giovannitti, Chicago: Charles H. Kerr, 1913). See also vols. 1 and 2.

**Proudhon, Pierre-Joseph** (1809–1865) French social theorist and an early and influential proponent of anarchist mutualism. Author of *What Is Property? An Inquiry into the Principle of Right and of Government* (1840) and *System of Economic Contradictions: or the Philosophy of Misery* (1846), aong others.

**Raney, Rebekah Elizabeth** (dates unknown) San Francisco–based anarchist who helped arrange meetings for EG in that city. She was a trained nurse and an active advocate and distributor of birth control material. In 1915 she started working as a stenographer for the *San Francisco Chronicle*. In 1916 she wrote a letter, later published in *The Blast*, to Judge Sullivan protesting Joseph Macario's sentence of six months in jail for distributing birth control information. The successful campaign prompted Macario's release the next day. A contributor of articles to *Mother Earth*, she would criticize EG for focusing exclusively on birth control in the April 1916 issue, arguing that the issue of birth control needed to be taken beyond the limits of the radical press for real change to occur.

**Reclus, Jean Jacques Élisée** (1830–1905) Geographer and French anarchist-communist theorist. Born into the family of a dissident Protestant pastor, his anarchist communism distinguished itself by unusual tolerance and generosity to other anarchist beliefs. He was originally a follower of Proudhon, but he became closely involved with Bakunin in the 1860s, and also Jean Grave. Imprisoned after the Paris Commune (1871) and sentenced to ten years' banishment, he moved to Switzerland, where he wrote his monumental *Nouvelle géographie universelle* (published in English as *The Earth and Its Inhabitants*, 19 vols.; London: J. S. Virtue, 1876–1894). He placed particular emphasis on the free associative action of individuals, and in *Lé Revolté* he advocated propaganda by the deed, but he was dismayed by the "verbal violence" rife in the anarchist circles of Paris and Lyon. Reclus wrote numerous works on anarchism, including the widely translated and reprinted pamphlets *An Anarchist on Anarchy* (Boston: B. R. Tucker, 1884) and *Evolution and Revolution* (London: W. Reeves, 1884). From 1894 on he lived in Belgium and taught at a university founded in his honor. See also vols. 1 and 2.

**Reed, John** (1887–1920) American socialist, journalist, author, and poet. A Harvard graduate (1910), he worked as a journalist in New York, writing for *American Magazine* (1911) and *Metropolitan Magazine* (1913). His book of poetry, *A Day in Bohemia or Life Among the Artists* (Riverside, Conn.: printed author, Hillacre Bookhouse, 1913), was instrumental in defining Greenwich Village life. He published short stories and served as temporary editor of the *Masses*. He worked closely with Mabel Dodge, writing the script and helping produce the Paterson Strike Pageant for the striking silk workers (1913). Reed traveled with Dodge to Europe in the summer of 1913. He also traveled to Mexico during the revolution (December 1913–1914), meeting and spending time with Francisco "Pancho" Villa; he later documented his experiences in articles for the *Masses, Metropolitan Magazine,* and in his book *Insurgent Mexico* (New York, London: D. Appleton, 1914). Reed probably met EG at Mabel Dodge's salon. He was a founding member of the Provincetown Players. His other works include *The War in Eastern Europe* (New York: Charles Scribner's Sons, 1916) and the play *Freedom* (New York: Provincetown Players Second Series, 1916).

**Reedy, William Marion** (1862–1920) Editor and publisher. He edited the *Mirror* (St. Louis; 1893–1920), which from 1910 on was known as *Reedy's Mirror*. Reaching its height in 1913–1915, the paper played an important role in American letters, introducing writers such as Edgar Lee Masters and publishing the *Spoon River Anthology* (1914). The paper also included a section titled "Reflections," which Reedy himself wrote, presenting his thoughts on the political and news issues of the day to his readers. Reedy was active in the political arena as a close confidant to Presidents Theodore Roosevelt (1901–1909) and William Howard Taft (1909–1913) and their cabinet members. Although registered as a Democrat, he always wrote and voted without loyalty to party, focusing on the issues instead and thus inspiring St. Louis to an independent movement in politics. Although he never advocated socialism and was not an anarchist, Reedy championed the individual, believing that it was not men en masse but individual labor and thought that ran the country. He advocated the single tax, claiming it as the only way to equalize tax law and solve the social and political ills of society. Reedy contributed to the tenth-anniversary souvenir edition of *Mother Earth*.

**Reitman, Ben** (1879–1942) Chicago gynecologist, hobo, and companion of EG. He met EG in March 1908 and moved to New York in fall 1908. He credited EG with turning him into an anarchist during this period and acted as her tour manager and advance agent for her lectures. He traveled to London in 1910 and met anarchists Peter Kropotkin, Errico Malatesta, Rudolph Rocker, Thomas Keell, Guy Aldred, and others; his "Revolutionary Notes from America" appeared in the June 1911 *Freedom*. In 1912 he was brutally mistreated by vigilantes during the San Diego free speech fight, an experience that profoundly affected him. BR left his duties at the *Mother Earth* office in early 1914 but reunited with EG later that year in Chicago, again assuming his place as her tour manager. He was arrested four times for distributing birth control information during this period: in Portland, Oregon, on 6 October 1915, a charge later dismissed by the judge; in New

York City, on 23 April 1916, a charge for which he was sentenced to sixty days in the workhouse (May–June 1916); in Cleveland, on 12 December 1916; and in Rochester, New York, on 15 December 1916. He contributed tour reports and articles regularly to *Mother Earth* and had a piece in the tenth-anniversary souvenir edition. In late 1916 BR moved to Chicago to live with his companion, Anna Martindale. See also vol. 2, *Making Speech Free*.

**Reitzel, Robert** (1849–1898) German-born American anarchist poet, critic, and translator. Reitzel was founder and editor of the radical literary journal *Der arme Teufel* (The Poor Devil, 1884–1900). He was a staunch supporter of the imprisoned Haymarket anarchists and later of AB during his confinement. In the 1890s Reitzel became friends with EG, who visited him shortly before his death. His posthumous publications include *Das Reitzel-Buch einem Vielgeliebten zum Gedachtniss* (ed. Martin Drescher; The Reitzel-Book: In Memory of a Loved-One; Detroit, 1900), *Abenteuer eines Grunen* (Adventures of a Greenhorn: An Autobiographical Novel; Chicago: Mees, Deuss, 1902), and *Des Armen Teufel* (ed. Max Baginski; That Poor Devil; Detroit: Reitzel Klub, 1913). See also vols. 1 and 2.

**Robinson, Dr. William Josephus** (1867–1936) American physician, medical journalist, and editor. He was director of the Genito-Urinary Diseases Department at the Bronx Hospital in New York. Robinson was one of the first American advocates of birth control. He often shared a platform with EG, though his arguments were rooted in the eugenics movement, and he considered homosexuality "a sign of degeneracy." He was a member of the 1916 Birth Control Committee. His publications include *Never-Told Tales* (New York: Critic and Guide, 1908); *Sexual Problems of To-day* (New York: Critic and Guide, 1912); *Sex Morality: Past, Present and Future* (New York: Critic and Guide, 1912); *A Practical Treatise on the Causes, Symptoms, and Treatment of Sexual Impotence and Other Sexual Disorders in Men and Women* (New York: Critic and Guide, 1913); *Fewer and Better Babies or the Limitation of Offspring* (New York: Eugenics Publishing, 1915); *The Treatment of Gonorrhea and Its Complications in Men and Women* (New York: Critic and Guide, 1915); *Sex Knowledge for Women and Girls; What Every Woman and Girl Should Know* (New York: Race Betterment League, 1916); and *Sex Knowledge for Men, Including a Program for Sex Education of the Boy* (New York: Critic and Guide, 1916). Robinson also edited *Altruria*, a philosophical freethought paper (1907–1908), *The Medico-Pharmaceutical Critic and Guide* (title varies, 1903–1936; a medical journal in which he advocated birth control and adopted an antiwar position), and he was on the advisory council of the socialist magazine *New Review*. He contributed to Moses Harman's *American Journal of Eugenics* and occasionally to *Mother Earth* on the subject of birth control.

**Rockefeller Jr., John D.** (1874–1960) Son of industrialist John D. Rockefeller Sr. After graduating from Brown University in 1897 Rockefeller Jr. joined his father's business, going on to represent the elder Rockefeller's interests after his official retirement that same year. Rockefeller Jr. would later serve in leadership positions for many companies, including his father's (Standard Oil) and J. P. Morgan's United States Steel Corporation. Rockefeller Jr. strongly opposed unions and pushed for the open shop. At the time of the Ludlow Massacre in April 1914 he was serving on the board of directors of Colorado Fuel and Iron Company and had a controlling interest in the company, one of the mine operators involved in the incident. The preceding strike had been caused in part by the anti-union policies of Colorado Fuel and Iron Company and other mine operators. Rockefeller Jr. defended his company's actions in resisting the organization of miners and denied culpability in the deaths that took place in the unrest. Following the Ludlow Massacre, anarchist Marie

Ganz stormed Rockefeller Jr.'s New York office, intent on killing him. That same year a group of anarchists and IWW members, including Arthur Caron, AB, and Rebecca Edelsohn, traveled to his home in Tarrytown, New York, to protest the actions of the militia at Ludlow. The protesters were immediately arrested and jailed when they attempted to speak, treatment that may have in part accounted for the bomb, intended for Rockefeller's estate, that went off in an apartment on Lexington Avenue. The Anti-Militarist League first began protest against Rockefeller's Standard Oil after calls for American intervention in the Mexican Revolution (Standard Oil, under the name Waters-Pierce, controlled 90 percent of the of the wholesale and retail trade in oil in Mexico). See also vol. 2, *Making Speech Free*.

**Rocker, Rudolf** (1873–1958) German anarchist historian, writer, and activist. From 1895 on he lived in London with his lifelong companion, Milly Witcop. In London's East End he learned Yiddish and joined the Jewish anarchist and trade union movement. Rocker met EG at her East End lecture during her first trip to London, and they became correspondents and comrades. In 1896 he began writing for *Arbeiter Fraynd* (Worker's Friend), the weekly central organ of Yiddish activism, and he founded *Germinal*, a theoretical and literary monthly, that same year. Rocker became editor of *Arbeiter Freund* in 1898. In 1912 he assisted the successful sweatshop strike in London's East End, turning *Arbeiter Freund* into a daily to serve the striking workers. Rocker opposed World War I and in 1914, at the start of the war, he was arrested, charged as an enemy alien, interned until 1918, and then deported to the Netherlands. An article written from jail and opposing Kropotkin's pro-war stance, was published in the *Spur* and reprinted in *Mother Earth* in 1916. See also vols. 1 and 2.

**Roe, Gilbert Ernstine** (1865–1929) New York lawyer and author. His legal work consisted of bankruptcies, commercial and construction contracts, and personal injury cases, although he also represented defendants in numerous free speech cases for little or no pay for the Free Speech League. He was a charter member of the New York Liberal Club and a member of the 1909 Free Speech Committee. Roe was vice president of the Free Speech League at the time of its incorporation (1911). An original member of the Francisco Ferrer Association (1910), he lectured there on law and American government. He signed the widely circulated 1911 letter to *Justice* protesting its accusation that EG was a Russian police spy. He was legal counsel to Margaret Sanger in 1914 when the Comstock Act banned the mailing of the *Woman Rebel*, and he defended William Sanger in 1915 at his trial for distributing Margaret Sanger's pamphlet *Family Limitation*. In 1915 Roe helped AB avert a five-year sentence stemming from a frame-up by the police for AB's involvement in the unemployed demonstrations the year before. He was a substantial financial contributor to the Mother Earth Sustaining Fund, and he wrote for the tenth-anniversary souvenir edition of *Mother Earth*. His publications include *Our Judicial Oligarchy* (New York: B. W. Huebsch, 1912) and *Reasonable Restrictions upon Freedom of Assemblage* (New York: Free Speech League, 1915).

**Roosevelt, Theodore** (1858–1919) President of the United States from 1901 to 1909. He was vice president under William McKinley and became president after McKinley's assassination, then served a full term after he was elected to the office in 1904. Influenced by American naval theorist Alfred Thayer Mahan, Roosevelt asserted that the United States needed a strong navy in order to cultivate and protect its interests. In 1912 Roosevelt was presidential candidate for the newly formed Progressive Party (aka Bull Moose Party). After losing the election to Woodrow Wilson, Roosevelt devoted much of his time to writing his autobiography and after 1914, to the military preparedness movement.

**Sanger, Margaret Higgins** (1879–1966) New York nurse, socialist, and birth control reformer. Sanger started her career as a nurse and socialist and in 1912 began writing a column on sex education for the *New York Call*, "What Every Girl Should Know." EG influenced her ideas about birth control, and Sanger moved toward anarchism. She sent her children to the New York Ferrer Modern School and later to the Modern School at Stelton, New Jersey. She took a leading part in supporting the Lawrence strike of 1912 and the Paterson strike of 1913, which she wrote about in Hippolyte Havel's *Revolutionary Almanac* (1914). In March 1914 Sanger began publishing the *Woman Rebel*, which in August of that year led to her indictment on nine charges of violating the Comstock Act. She jumped bail in October 1914 and fled to England. After Sanger returned to the United States in October 1915 charges against her were dropped following the death of her five-year-old daughter from pneumonia. She then toured America extensively, speaking on birth control as well as opening America's first birth control clinic in Brownsville, Brooklyn, in October 1916. After nine days the clinic was raided, and the staff, including Sanger, were arrested. She and her sister spent thirty days in jail, where her sister, Ethel Byrne, following Rebecca Edelsohn's lead, engaged in a hunger strike in protest. Sanger subsequently moved away from anarchism and never acknowledged EG or anarchism's influence on her ideas about birth control. She wrote the pamphlets *What Every Mother Should Know* (New York: Rabelais Press, 1914), *Family Limitation* (New York: privately printed, 1914), *What Every Girl Should Know* (New York: Max Maisel, 1915), and *Methods of Birth Control* (New York, 1915). She wrote a letter to *Land and Liberty* (September 1914) and wrote articles on the progress of her birth control agitation to *Mother Earth* (1914–1916). She also wrote articles for *Freedom*, the *Modern School* magazine, *International Socialist Review*, *The Blast*, and *Revolt* and was on the advisory board of *Revolt*.

**Sanger, William** (1873–1961) American architect, painter, and socialist. He was married to Margaret (Higgins) Sanger from 1902 to 1921, and the couple had three children. In 1911 the Sangers moved to New York City, where they met EG and became part of the radical bohemian circle there. In 1912 Sanger was an active member of the Syndicalist Education League, a short-lived organization headed by Hippolyte Havel and Harry Kelly. He was a member of the Socialist Party and supported the IWW, and both he and his wife participated in the 1913 Paterson Strike Pageant. While his wife was in Europe in 1914, Sanger was tricked into selling a Comstock agent a Margaret Sanger pamphlet on birth control, *Family Limitation*. He was arrested in early 1915 and was twice denied requests for jury trials. Sanger was tried and convicted in September and given the choice of a $50 fine or jail. Sanger chose jail and spent thirty days in the Tombs, a jail in New York City. A pamphlet about his trial would be published: *Jailed for Birth Control: The Trial of William Sanger, September 10, 1915* (New York: Birth Control Review, 1917), edited with an introduction by James Waldo Fawcett.

**Schapiro, Alexander** (1882–1946) Prominent Russian-born anarchist. With Kropotkin, Malatesta, and Rocker, he was active in the London anarchist movement. He spoke eight languages: Bulgarian, Turkish, Spanish, English, French, Russian, German, and Yiddish. Schapiro represented the Jewish Anarchist Federation of London at the 1907 International Anarchist Congress in Amsterdam, where he was made a member of the Anarchist Federation Correspondence Bureau. He signed the International Manifesto Against the War in 1915 and was interned during the war. He contributed one article to *Mother Earth*, in 1916.

**Schmidt, Matthew A.** (1881–1963) American anarchist, woodworker, and mechanic. Schmidt was a subscription agent for *Mother Earth* in 1906 in Chicago, where met David Caplan. He and Caplan were introduced to James B. McNamara in San Francisco by Olaf A. Tveitmoe, a local labor leader. Schmidt, McNamara, and Caplan purchased dynamite to bomb the *Los Angeles Times* building. The dynamite was brought to a house rented by Caplan in San Francisco before being transported to Los Angeles. Following the bombing, Schmidt was named in criminal indictments and went into hiding in New York City. EG introduced him to Donald Vose, the son of EG's friend and fellow anarchist Gertie Vose. Donald Vose was working for William J. Burns as a spy, and he told Burns where Schmidt was hiding. On 13 February 1915 Schmidt was arrested on the streets of New York City. Schmidt was found guilty of murder on 30 December 1915 and sentenced to life at San Quentin Prison on 12 January 1916. He was paroled in 1939 and later pardoned by California governor Culbert Olson, on 22 December 1942. Following his release from prison, he married Elizabeth Livermore, a social worker and member of a prominent San Francisco family. After her death in 1954 he may have managed a labor radio station in Chicago. He died in 1963 in Wisconsin. He contributed the articles "'orrors, 'orrors!" (October 1915) and "The 'Liberty Bell' and Liberty" (August 1915) to *Mother Earth*.

**Schroeder, Theodore Albert** (1864–1953) Attorney, legal scholar, and free speech advocate. He was a principal theoretician for the Free Speech League and secretary at the Free Speech League's legal incorporation in 1911. Schroeder was a member of the 1909 Free Speech Committee, president of the Brooklyn Philosophical Society, and a member of the New York Liberal Club and the Sunrise Club. He signed the 1911 letter sent to *Justice* protesting its accusations that EG was a Russian police spy. Schroeder helped develop the defense for Jay Fox in Washington (1911) following his prosecution for publication of the article "The Nudes and the Prudes" in the *Agitator*. He also worked on the 1912 San Diego free speech fight, the 1914 Denver free speech fight for EG and BR, and the 1916 *Blast* case. He frequently contributed articles on free speech to *Mother Earth*, including the tenth-anniversary souvenir edition, and to *Physical Culture*. His books and pamphlets include *Freedom of the Press and "Obscene" Literature: Three Essays* (New York: Free Speech League, 1906); *Liberty of Speech and Press Essential to Purity Propaganda. An Address Prepared for the National Purity Conference and to be Delivered October 10th, 1906* (New York: Free Speech League, 1906); *Much Needed Defense for Liberty of Conscience, Speech and Press, with Special Application to Sex Discussion* (New York: Free Speech League, 1906); *The Criminal Anarchy Law* (New York: Mother Earth Publishing Association, 1907); *Our Vanishing Liberty of the Press* (New York: Free Speech League, 1907); *Unconstitutionality of All Laws Against "Obscene" Literature Asserted in a Brief* (New York: Free Speech League, 1908); *"Due Process of Law" in Relation to Statutory Uncertainty and Constructive Offences, Giving Much Needed Enlightenment to Legislators, Bar and Bench* (New York: Free Speech League, 1908); *Free Press Anthology* (New York: Free Speech League, 1909); *A Lobby for Liberty* (New York: Free Speech League, 1910); *Erskine on the Limits of Toleration* (New York: Mother Earth Publishing Association, 1911); *Obscene Literature and Constitutional Law, a Forensic Defense of Freedom of the Press* (New York: Free Speech League, 1911); *Protest of the Free Speech League Against the Passage of Senate Bill No. 1790, Assembly Bill No. 650, New York Legislature, 1911, Which Proposes to Penalize Certain Medical Advertising and Intelligence* (New York: Free Speech League, 1911); *Table of Cases Involving Obscenity and Kindred Statues* (New York: Free Speech League, 1911); *Conflict Between Religious Morals and Ethical Science, Being a Study in the Uncertainty of the Moral*

*Test of the Crime* (New York Free Speech League, 1911); *Free Speech for Radicals* (New York: Free Speech League, 1912; reprinted in 1916 with an overview of the free speech fights he and the league had been involved in since 1900); *The Free Speech Case of Jay Fox* (New York: Free Speech League, 1912); *Concerning the Free Speech Anthology* (New York: Free Speech League, 1912); *Edward Bond Foote, Biographical Notes and Appreciatives* (New York: Free Speech League, 1913); *Methods of Constitutional Construction. The Synthetic Method Illustrated on the Free Speech Cause of the Federal Constitution. With Three Supplements Bearing on the Rights of Revolutionists by James Mill, J. L. De Lolme and John Cartwright* (New York: Free Speech League, 1914); *Our Prudish Censorship Unveiled* (New York: Free Speech League, 1915); *McNamaras: Martyrs or Criminals* (New York: Free Speech League, 1915); *Presumption and Burden of Proof as to Malice in Criminal Libel* (New York: Free Speech League, 1915); and *Theodore Schroeder in Defense of a Chinese* (New York, 1916).

**Seldes, George S.** (1860–1931) Russian-born freethinker, revolutionary utopian, single-taxer, and anarchist. Seldes attempted to establish a utopian collective farm in Alliance, New Jersey, but it failed due to local lack of interest. After moving to Philadelphia he became a druggist and studied law. Seldes was well read and was fluent in eleven languages. A prominent member of the Friends of Russian Freedom, he supported the 1905 uprising against the tsar and corresponded with such notable revolutionaries as Tolstoy and Kropotkin. He was also an ardent advocate of education; he tried to build a library for farmers of New Jersey and later took part in building the Stelton Modern School and the Mohegan Colony and school. Nunia Seldes was his second wife. See also vol. 2, *Making Speech Free*.

**Seldes, Nunia Berman** (dates unknown) Pittsburgh friend and correspondent of EG. Nunia was a close friend of EG; as EG explained to Seldes, "there have been so few women in my life, that I could care much about. You have sort of woven yourself around my heart, I feel it more and more every time I meet you. Unfortunately my public life leaves little room for privacies with any one worth while" (EG to Nunia Seldes, 15 January 1911, *EGP*, reel 4.) She was a financial supporter of anarchist causes, including the *Mother Earth* Sustaining Fund, the Kōtoku Defense Committee Fund, and the *Blast* War Fund. She was married to George Seldes.

**Sloan, John** (1871–1951) American socialist and artist. He was a member of the Eight (1908), a group of leading progressive artists of the avant-garde. Sloan was later associated with the Ashcan School of realist art, influenced by Robert Henri. He joined the Socialist Party in 1910. From 1911 to 1916 he served as art editor of the *Masses*. Sloan was a member of the Publicity Committee of the International Workers' Defense Committee for the Mooney-Billings case in 1916. He spoke at the 1916 Walt Whitman celebration. Contrary to EG's recollections in *Living My Life* (1931), Sloan maintained that he never taught at the Ferrer Modern School. He heard EG lecture numerous times and described her in his diary as "a really great woman."

**Stokes, Rose Pastor** (1879–1933) American socialist and later communist. Stokes was born in Poland and raised in poverty in London. In 1890 she and her family immigrated to the United States, and at age eleven she began working as a cigar maker. In 1903 she started work as a journalist at the *Yiddishes Tageblatt* in New York City. She interviewed J. G. Phelps Stokes, a wealthy reformer who was working in a settlement house on the Lower East Side, and they married in 1905 in a highly publicized wedding. Stokes was a prominent speaker of the Intercollegiate Socialist Society, which was led by her husband (1907–1917). She was a member of the 1909 Free Speech

Committee, and *Mother Earth* reprinted her October 1909 letter in support of free speech, which was read at a mass meeting in Philadelphia. She signed the widely circulated 1911 letter to *Justice* protesting its allegation that EG was a police spy. She was an active supporter of the New York restaurant and hotel workers' strikes of 1912 and the Paterson strike of 1913. A birth control advocate, she delivered a speech in support of EG upon her release from prison in 1916. She attracted considerable attention when her wealth and social status thwarted attempts to have her arrested for distributing practical contraceptive information. Her works include a drama, *The Woman Who Wouldn't* (New York: The Knickerbocker Press, 1916), about an unmarried mother and labor militancy. She also co-translated into English, with Helena Frank, a volume of Yiddish poetry by Morris Rosenfeld, *Songs of Labor and Other Poems* (Boston: R. G. Badger, 1914).

**Tannenbaum, Frank** (1893–1969) Anarchist, IWW member, and frequenter of the Ferrer Center. He organized a series of marches of the unemployed movement upon churches in New York demanding food and shelter. Tannenbaum was imprisoned for a year for inciting to riot after leading the unemployed to St. Alphonsus Catholic Church on 4 March 1914. His actions were admired by EG and AB. Upon his release he distanced himself from anarchism and went on to become a prominent Latin American scholar at Columbia University. He wrote an article on his imprisonment for the June 1915 issue of the socialist magazine *New Review*.

**Thoreau, Henry David** (1817–1862) American writer, poet, abolitionist, and philosopher. A naturalist, he lived the doctrine of New England transcendentalism as expressed by Ralph Waldo Emerson. Thoreau began work as a teacher, but he resigned when asked to use corporal punishment on his students. In 1838 he opened a private school in Concord, Massachusetts, based on the principles of transcendentalism. After his brother became ill and died of lockjaw Thoreau went into seclusion at Walden Pond for more than two years and in 1854 published *Walden* about this experience. He came to town once during this time and was arrested for intentionally refusing to pay the poll tax, an experience that prompted him to write "Resistance to Civil Government" (1849), later known as "On the Duty of Civil Disobedience." He supported John Brown and the abolition movement. EG considered Thoreau a vital part of the latent anarchist impulse in the American political tradition. Along with Emerson, he was the topic of one of EG's lectures and was often referred to in her writings.

**Tolstoy, Leo (Count Lev Nikolayevich)** (1828–1910) Russian writer. Tolstoy is best known for his literary works, including *War and Peace* (1869), *Anna Karenina* (1877), and *The Death of Ivan Illyich* (1884). His later writings include the influential philosophical essays *Confession* (1884), *What Then Must We Do?* (1886), *The Kingdom of God Is Within You* (1894), and *The Slavery of Our Times* (1900). Some of the profits from his last novel, *Resurrection* (1899–1900), were donated to Jane Addams's Hull House. Anarchists admired Tolstoy's compassion for the poor and his anti-government ideology, although he condemned all catalysts of violence, including revolutionary activity. Anarchists also celebrated his rejection of institutionalized religion, despite his advocacy of Christian love as the primary means of improving society (although they admired the anti-militarism that it fueled in his work). Tolstoy's ideas were popularized in the United States by Ernest Crosby and Benjamin Tucker. Four of Tolstoy's essays were published in *Mother Earth*, as well as an obituary, which called him "the prophet of a new era." EG also quoted him regularly in her articles and essays. See also vol. 2, *Making Speech Free*.

**Traubel, Horace** (1858–1919) American poet and journalist. He was the companion of Walt Whitman and one of the three literary executors to his estate. Traubel was founding editor and publisher of the *Conservator* (1890–1919), a journal dedicated to keeping the memory of Walt Whitman alive. A dedicated socialist and advocate of free speech, he wrote favorably about EG and her book *Anarchism and Other Essays* (1910) in the *Conservator*, and he invited EG to speak at a number of the annual Walt Whitman celebrations. Traubel was a member of the 1909 Free Speech Committee and contributed an antiwar article to *The Blast*. His publications include *With Walt Whitman in Camden* (3 vols.; Boston: Small, Maynard, 1906–1914), *Optimos* (New York: B. W. Huebsch, 1910), and *Collects* (New York: A. & C. Boni, 1914). *Mother Earth* published his letter in defense of free speech, written during the free speech fight in Philadelphia, in the October 1909 issue.

**Tresca, Carlo** (1879–1943) Italian-born socialist and IWW organizer. After being convicted of libel in Italy in 1904 Tresca fled to the United States. By 1910 he had settled in New Kensington, Pennsylvania, and was editing *L'Avvenire,* an Italian-language socialist newspaper. He was imprisoned for nine months in 1911–1912 for libel against a priest. After his release he went to Lawrence, Massachusetts, and became a lead organizer for the Ettor-Giovannitti Defense Committee. In Lawrence he met Elizabeth Gurley Flynn, and they began a companionship that would last for more than ten years. Tresca was active as an IWW organizer in strikes in Little Falls, New York (1912), New York City (1913), and Paterson, New Jersey (1913). He worked with EG and AB during the unemployed movement in New York City (1914) and the Tarrytown demonstrations (1914). Tresca defended Arthur Caron, as an IWW member, after the Lexington Avenue explosion when other IWW members denounced him. He worked with AB to organize the 11 July 1914 memorial meeting, at which he spoke. In 1916 Tresca was arrested during the Mesabi Range strike in Minnesota for his alleged involvement in the murder of a sheriff's deputy. The charges were later dropped.

**Tucker, Benjamin R.** (1854–1939) American individualist anarchist and publisher and editor of the individualist anarchist paper *Liberty.* Tucker's influence on American anarchism, once substantial, had by 1906 diminished dramatically. The last issue of *Liberty* appeared in April 1908. Shortly after his paper ceased publication, he moved to France and then in 1914, to Monaco. Living in Europe, he sided with the Allies during World War I. See also vols. 1 and 2.

**Turgenev, Ivan** (1818–1883) Russian writer, dramatist. Turgenev wrote novels instead of plays to answer the tsarist policy of censoring controversial performances. He was influenced by Nikolai Vasilievich Gogol. The main character in his novel *Rudin* (1855) was based on Russian anarchist Michael Bakunin. Other works include *A Sportsman's Sketches* (1852), *A Nest of Gentlefolk* (1859), *On the Eve* (1860), and *Fathers and Sons* (1862), whose character Bazarov is both a revolutionary agnostic and nihilist. *Mother Earth* reprinted "The Reporter" and "The Beggar" in 1906.

**Turner, John** (1864–1934) British anarchist, lecturer, journalist, and founder and president (1912–1924) of the Shop Assistants' Union. His sister, Lizzie, also an anarchist, was the companion of Thomas H. Bell, a Scottish-born associate of EG. Turner was the printer and publisher of *Freedom* (London: 1895–1907) and contributed to the *Shop Assistant* (London). In the July, August, and September 1911 editions of *Freedom* Turner defended EG against accusations published in the

London *Justice* by social democrats that she was a Russian police spy (see "'Justice' and Emma Goldman," *EGP*, reel 2). See also vols. 1 and 2.

**Turner, John Kenneth** (1879–1948) American socialist journalist involved in Mexican revolutionary affairs and supportive of the Partido Liberal Mexicano (PLM). While a reporter for the *Los Angeles Express* in 1908, Turner first met Ricardo Flores Magón and other members of the PLM through Job Harriman in Los Angeles, where they were being held for violation of neutrality laws. With John Murray, he became active in the Mexican Revolutionists Defense League. Posing as a wealthy businessman, he visited Mexico in 1909 with Mexican revolutionary Lázaro Gutiérrez de Lara and wrote a series of articles in *American Magazine* and *Appeal to Reason* on the Díaz regime; the articles were later collected in a book, *Barbarous Mexico* (Chicago: Charles H. Kerr, 1911). *Mother Earth*, in the August 1910 issue, said that Turner's articles in *Appeal to Reason* were "of the first importance to all revolutionists and should be studied carefully." Turner's wife, Ethel Duffy Turner, became the editor of the English-language page of *Regeneración* in 1910. Turner helped to acquire munitions for the PLM and IWW members who briefly held Baja California. By 1916, in a decided turn away from the PLM, Turner was celebrating the rise of Venustiano Carranza as a victory for socialism.

**Van Valkenburgh, Warren Starr** (1884–1938) American Anarchist, bookkeeper, and accountant who wrote under the pseudonym Walter Starrett and was a close friend of Leon Malmed. Van Valkenburgh met EG at Schenectady, New York, where he arranged a meeting for her although he was still a member of the Socialist Party of Schenectady at the time. He contributed to *Mother Earth*, *The Blast*, *Instead of a Magazine*, and *Revolt* and enjoyed a regular correspondence with EG. He was also a member of the Sociology Club of Schenectady between 1914 and 1918.

**Vidal, Jaime** (dates unknown) Spanish-born anarchist and personal friend of Francisco Ferrer. He was influential in the organization of the Ferrer Association in New York and spoke at the 3 June 1910 inaugural meeting. He was active in the anarchist movement in New York and taught at the Ferrer Center. He was the Spanish organizer for the Marine Transport Workers Union in New York City, an IWW-affiliated union with anarchist influence. Vidal was also a member of the Rangel-Cline Defense Committee, treasurer of the Alexander Aldamas Defense Committee (of which Harry Kelly was secretary), and strongly supported the PLM. He contributed to *Cultura Obrera* and edited the paper *Fuerza Consciente: Revista ilustrada dedicada a la Propaganda Anarquica y Revolucionaria* from New York and San Francisco in 1913–1914, before it was suppressed by the authorities.

**Wald, Lillian** (1867–1940) Nurse, social worker, and founder of the Henry Street Settlement on New York's Lower East Side. Wald worked on behalf of various causes benefitting women and children, including the Women's Trade Union League and the federal Children's Bureau, which she helped create in 1912. With the outbreak of World War I Wald felt compelled to commit publicly to the pacifist cause. Co-founder of the American Union Against Militarism (1914), she later served as a liaison between President Woodrow Wilson and the Women's International League for Peace and Freedom (formerly the Women's Peace Party). In *LML* EG cites Wald as being one of the first American women she had met who was interested in the economic condition of the masses. See also vol. 2, *Made for America*.

**Walling, Anna Strunsky** (1879–1964) Russian-born San Francisco socialist, author, and friend of EG. She published, with Jack London, a novel in the form of letters, *The Kempton-Wace Letters*, a debate on the nature of love (1903). She helped establish the 1905 Friends of Russian Freedom group in San Francisco and just before the outbreak of the Russian Revolution of 1905 traveled to Russia, where she met and married William English Walling (1906). She sent the necessary funds to retain Ernest E. Kirk to defend EG, BR, and Alex Horr during their free speech fight in San Francisco (January 1909). Walling was a member of the 1909 Free Speech Committee and an occasional contributor to *Mother Earth*. She signed the widely circulated letter sent to *Justice* protesting its allegation that EG was a Russian police spy, as well as the 1911 letter to the Japanese ambassador in Washington protesting the death sentences passed on Kōtoku and the other Japanese anarchists. She was a friend and correspondent of EG and AB. Her works include the novel *Violette of Pere Lachaise* (New York: Frederick A. Stokes, 1915).

**Walling, William English** (1877–1936) American socialist and author. In 1904 he was introduced to Catherine Breshkovskaya by EG. He spent two years in Russia (1905–1907), where he interviewed the leaders of the revolution, including Lenin and Gorky, and met and married Anna Strunsky. In 1909 he joined the Free Speech Committee and cofounded the NAACP. Before joining the Socialist Party in 1910 he accused Victor Berger, Morris Hillquit, Robert Hunter, and Algie Simons of secretly planning to turn the Socialist Party into a reformist labor party; a struggle for power ended with the expulsion of the most radical group of the party, including William Haywood, at the 1912 convention. He signed the 1911 widely circulated letter sent to *Justice* protesting the allegations that EG was a Russian police spy. He wrote for the December 1912 Kropotkin seventieth-birthday issue of *Mother Earth* and contributed funds to the funeral expenses of the Lexington Avenue bombers in 1914. He was also a contributor to the *International Socialist Review*. His books include *Russia's Message* (New York: Doubleday, Page, 1908), which was reviewed favorably by Hippolyte Havel in *Mother Earth*; *The Larger Aspects of Socialism* (New York: Macmillan Company, 1913); and *Progressivism—and After* (New York: Macmillan Company, 1914).

**Weinberg, Israel** (dates unknown) Executive board member of the Jitney Bus Operators' Union in San Francisco. He was indicted on first-degree murder charges along with Thomas Mooney, Warren Billings, Rena Mooney, and Edward Nolan for the bombing of the Preparedness Day parade in San Francisco on 22 July 1916 and was accused by the prosecution of driving the jitney bus that Mooney allegedly took to the site of the bombing. He subscribed to *The Blast*, and attended a picnic for *The Blast* on 4 July 1916 with Tom Mooney, but he did not claim to be an anarchist or to be involved in radical activity in San Francisco. He said that his only relationship to Tom and Rena Mooney was that his son took music lessons from Rena Mooney, and he often gave them free rides on his jitney. Weinberg was held in jail until his release on bail in March 1918.

**Weinberger, Harry** (1886–1944) American attorney, single-taxer, and anarchist sympathizer. He was a member of the Brooklyn Philosophical Society and of the Republican Party until 1916. Weinberger met EG after he wrote to newspapers protesting the refusal of a Cleveland hotel to allow her accommodation. He was special assistant attorney general of New York from 1909 to 1914 and was the attorney for EG, AB, Tom Mooney, Ricardo Flores Magón, and BR. He defended EG in 1916 after her arrest for lecturing on birth control in defiance of Section 1142 of the New York Penal Code. As a member of the 1916 New York Publicity Committee for the International

Workers' Defense League, he helped to organize a fund-raising meeting at Carnegie Hall for Mooney and Billings. He was also counsel for the Provincetown Players. He was an occasional contributor to *Mother Earth* and a lifelong friend of EG.

**Whitman, Walt** (1819–1892) American poet, journalist, and essayist, best known for his collection of poems *Leaves of Grass* (1855), revised and reissued in three different editions in his lifetime. The collection was often banned on grounds of obscenity under the Comstock Act, especially the poem, "A Woman Waits for Me." Whitman held numerous jobs while writing and editing for periodicals, including the *Brooklyn Eagle* (1846–1848) and the *Brooklyn Times* (1857–1858). During the Civil War Whitman worked first as a clerk in Washington and then as a nurse, caring for both Union and Confederate wounded. He later worked as a clerk in the Department of the Interior and in the attorney general's office. A paralytic stroke in 1873 forced Whitman to give up his work. At the time of his death his poetry was more popular in Europe than in the United States.

His work had enormous influence throughout the American freethought and radical movements of the late-nineteenth and early-twentieth centuries. His friend Robert Ingersoll delivered a passionate oration at Whitman's funeral. Benjamin R. Tucker was an early champion of *Leaves of Grass*, and EG had originally planned to name *Mother Earth* (itself a Whitmanesque title) *The Open Road* after Whitman's influential poem of the same name. Whitman's works include *Sequel to Drum Taps* (1865), *Democratic Vistas* (1871), and *Specimen Days and Collect* (1882–1883). A ten-volume edition of his complete writings was published in 1902.

**Winn, Ross** (1872–1912) American anarchist. He attended the National Convention of Reform Clubs and Trade Unions, 27–29 September 1897, which was also attended by Eugene Debs, Jay Fox, and EG. He represented the Texas branch of the Industrial Army. Winn published the newspaper *Winn's Firebrand* (1902–1910; Mount Juliet, Tennessee and then Sweden, Texas), later renamed *Advance a Monthly Freelance* (1910–1912, Mount Juliet, Tennessee). He was also an occasional contributor to *Mother Earth*. He died in 1912, and in her obituary in the September 1912 edition of *Mother Earth* EG described him as "one of the most earnest, sincere, and able American Anarchists."

**Wolff, Adolf** (1883–1944) Belgian sculptor, poet, and anarchist. He taught at the New York Ferrer Center, wrote for the *Modern School* magazine, and contributed articles to the *International* and to *Mother Earth*. He took part in the 1914 unemployment activities, as well as the Rockefeller and Tarrytown protests. He was sentenced to thirty days in prison on 17 September for taking part in the Tarrytown protests, in violation of the parole from his unemployment demonstration arrest. He created a bronze urn called *The Fighting Eagle* that commemorated and held the ashes of Charles Berg, Carl Hanson, and Arthur Caron, who were killed in the 4 July 1914 Lexington Avenue explosion. On 24 October 1914 the Anti-Militarist League staged his one-act anti-militarist play. Wolff briefly served as an art reviewer for the *International* (1913–1914). His poetry appeared in *Others* (1915–1916) and the *Glebe* (New Jersey), including one, "Songs, Sighs and Curses," in the first issue (September 1913). His collected poems, *Songs of Rebellion, Songs of Life, Songs of Love* (New York: A. & C. Boni, 1914), comprised many of the poems that appeared in the *Glebe*, along with thirty other previously unpublished pieces.

**Wood, Charles Erskine Scott** (1852–1944) Portland lawyer, writer, poet, social reformer, and philosophical anarchist. Wood met EG in 1908 and often chaired EG's meetings when she was in Portland. Wood met his future partner, Sara Bard Field, in early 1911 in Portland through Clarence Darrow. He refused Darrow's request to work on the McNamara brothers' defense in 1911, although he remained close to the case and offered advice and recommendations, as well as speaking at a public protest meeting in Portland on 8 October 1911. He was also asked to defend Caplan and Schmidt, but in the end refused, although again he offered advice and recommendations. In 1915 he sponsored and successfully defended EG after her arrest in Portland for speaking on birth control. On 4 April 1916 he spoke at a defense meeting for Caplan and Schmidt in San Francisco with Tom Mooney, AB, Edward Nolan, William McDevitt, Carlo Tresca, and Ed Morgan. In June 1916 he chaired Margaret Sanger's first lecture in Portland, and when she and others were arrested for distributing her pamphlet *Family Limitation* (1914), Wood acted as their defense lawyer. In November 1916 Wood advised and supported, although he refused to take the case, IWW members in Everett, Washington, charged with murder. He was a prolific contributor to journals, including *Everyman*, *The Blast*, and *Mother Earth*, including the tenth-anniversary souvenir edition. His books include *The Poet in the Desert* (1915), which EG distributed on her lecture tours.

**Yanovsky, Saul** (1864–1939) Jewish anarchist, lecturer, and editor of the Yiddish papers *Di Abend Tsaytung* (The Evening Newspaper; 1906), *Freie Arbeiter Stimme* (1899–1919), and *Di Fraye Gezelshaft* (1910–1911). Yanovsky was a founder of the Jewish anarchist group Pioneers of Liberty. He was perceived by EG as "despotic" and by AB as rigid and "dictatorial." However, *Freie Arbeiter Stimme* did sponsor some of EG's lectures. Yanovsky later moderated his politics, especially in regard to Kropotkin, whom he came to support. A capable administrator and organizer, he put *Freie Arbeiter Stimme* on a sound financial footing. Under his editorship the paper published many prominent European writers as well as spotlighting new Yiddish writers. It also moved to a more conciliatory and less anti-religious anarchism. By 1914 the paper had reached a circulation of about 20,000. Originally a signatory of the anarchist "Manifesto Against the War" in 1915, he later supported England, France, and their allies against Germany.

***The Agitator: A Semi-monthly Advocate of the Modern School, Industrial Unionism and Individual
Freedom*** Home [Colony], Wash.: November 1910–November 1912, semi-monthly. Anarchist paper
edited by Jay Fox. It argued for the end of dual unionism and for militants to work in the AFL
rather than the IWW. It reported on the violations of EG's constitutional right to free speech in
Washington, D.C. in 1910. W. C. Owen favorably reviewed *Anarchism and Other Essays* in January
1911. The paper was printed on the same printing press earlier used by Ezra Heywood on his
paper the *Word* (1872–1890, 1892–1893). Contributors included Ricardo Flores Magón, William
Z. Foster, EG, Harry Kelly, Joseph Labadie, James F. Morton, William C. Owen, and Vincent St.
John. It was succeeded by the *Syndicalist* (Chicago) beginning in January 1913.

***The Alarm*** Chicago: vol. 1, no. 1 (October 1915)–vol. 1, no. 11 (August 1916), monthly. Anarchist paper
published by the "International Propaganda Group of Chicago," edited by Aaron Barron, then
V. Dolen and Lucy E. Parsons, and managed by Theo Appel. In the spring of 1916 it was suppressed
and barred from mail delivery under Section 211 of the Criminal Code. It merged in 1917 with
*Revolt*, which had also been suppressed under the same law, to form the *Social War* (Chicago),
edited by Hippolyte Havel. Contributors included Jay Fox, Nina Van Zandt-Spies, and Henri Zisly;
it printed the work of William Thurston Brown, Ralph Chaplin, John H. Edelman, Ricardo Flores
Magón, William C. Owen, Jules Scarceriaux, and Ross Winn.

***American Journal of Eugenics*** Chicago: July 1907–January/February 1910, monthly. The successor to *Lucifer the Lightbearer* (see vols. 1 and 2). It was edited and published by Moses Harman.
Anarchist journal promoting eugenics as an element of its advocacy of sexual and emotional
freedom. Contributors included J. William Lloyd, James F. Morton, Lizzie Holmes, and John
R. Coryell. After Harman's death in 1910 the April 1911 edition of *Mother Earth* printed Lillian
Harman's announcement that *Mother Earth* could serve as a substitute periodical for the unex-
pired subscriptions to the *American Journal of Eugenics* and a source for obtaining other works
by Moses Harman.

***Appeal to Reason*** Kansas City, Mo.: August 1895–1896; Kansas City, Kans.: 1896; Girard, Kans.:
1897–1922, mostly weekly. Independent socialist paper founded and edited during this period
by Julius Augustus Wayland, who was strongly supportive of Eugene V. Debs and the Socialist
Party. A popular paper, promoted aggressively, its circulation rose to 275,000 by 1907. It promoted
Flores Magón as a revolutionary, calling attention to his publication, *Regeneración*, although by

1911 it criticized him and withdrew active support of the PLM. In May 1912 Debs wrote an article in condemnation of the San Diego authorities' treatment of EG and BR, while simultaneously clarifying his opposition to most representatives of anarchism. Contributors included Eugene V. Debs, Kate Richards O'Hare, Charlotte Perkins Gilman, Upton Sinclair, and Ernest Untermann.

***The Blast: A Revolutionary Labor Weekly*** San Francisco, Calif.: 15 January–15 March 1916, weekly; 15 March 1916–15 September 1916, semi-monthly; then irregularly until March 1917; New York: May 1917–June 1917, monthly. West Coast anarchist newspaper, conceived as a nonsectarian revolutionary labor periodical and often critical of San Francisco and Los Angeles labor leaders. It was edited by AB and Eric B. Morton, with M. Eleanor Fitzgerald and Carl Newlander. It was influential in raising awareness and funds for the defense of David Caplan and Matthew Schmidt, and later of Tom Mooney and Warren Billings. Its mission was described in the first issue: "To blast the bulwarks of slavery and oppression is of primal necessity. It is the beginning of really lasting construction. Thus will *The Blast* be destructive. And *The Blast* will be constructive." *The Blast* published many antiwar articles and an ongoing column by AB to introduce children and young adults to anarchist ideas. Contributors included Leonard D. Abbott, Charles Ashleigh, Sara Bard Field, Enrique Flores Magón, EG, Sadakichi Hartmann, Harry Kelly, Herman Kuehn, Jacob Margolis, Robert Minor, Caroline Nelson, Tom Mooney, Luke North, Edgcumb Pinchon, Margaret Sanger, Horace Traubel, Warren Van Valkenburgh, and Charles Erskine Scott Wood.

***Bruno's Weekly*** New York: 1915–1916, weekly. Greenwich Village art and literature periodical subtitled *Edited by Guido Bruno in His Garret on Washington Square* and containing work by Adolf Bohm, Frank Harris, Sadakichi Hartmann, and Hippolyte Havel. *Bruno's Weekly* was the successor to *Bruno's Greenwich Village* and was itself superseded by *Bruno's Chap Books* and *Bruno's* (1917), *Bruno's Bohemia* (1918), *Bruno's Review of Two Worlds* (1920), and *Bruno's Review of Life Love and Letters*. The *Weekly* contained book reviews, stories, poetry, and articles on politics and people. The June 1916 article "Anarchists in Greenwich Village" expressed support for anarchism and for EG. Later that month the paper alerted its readers to *Mother Earth*'s coverage of EG's and BR's imprisonment for their advocacy of birth control.

***Cronaca sovversiva: Ebdomadario anarchico di propaganda rivoluzionaria*** (The Subversive Chronicle: An Anarchist Weekly of Revolutionary Propaganda) Barre, Vt.: 6 June 1903–1912, weekly; Lynn, Mass.: 1912–1918; Providence, R.I.: May 1919. Militant Italian-language anarchist communist newspaper, edited by Luigi Galleani under the pseudonyms Grigi Galleani, Luigi Pimpino, Mentana, and Tramp. Associates included Andrea Salsedo, Carlo Valdinoci, and Constantino Zonchello; contributors included Umberto Colarossi, Raffaele Schiavina, and later Bartolomeo Vanzetti. While in Barre, the paper was printed by an IWW-organized printer. It moved to Lynn, Massachusetts, in 1912, where Galleani had a devoted Italian-immigrant following. Although the newspaper was the mouthpiece of Galleanists, it also served as a communication center for other Italian anarchist groups and individuals. The paper reprinted selected anarchist works by Peter Kropotkin, Élisée Reclus, and Michael Bakunin. Max Stirner's *Ego and Its Own* was intermittently excerpted in the newspaper. It published articles by EG, news of her lecture tours, and advertisements for *Mother Earth* events.

***Cultura obrera*** (Workers' Culture) New York: 1911–1927, weekly. Spanish-language anarchist periodical (briefly affiliated with the IWW from 1913 to 1914), edited by Pedro Esteve, then Roberto

Muller. Subtitled *ortavoz de los Obreros Industriales del Mundo* (Voice of the IWW) and then *Periodico obrero, de doctrina y de combate* (The teaching and fighting newspaper). It reported on labor news, especially activities of maritime and cigar workers. It maintained a firm editorial stance against World War I. It reported regularly on EG's activities. Contributors included AB, Maria Echevarria, George Gallart, Peter Kropotkin, Anselmo Lorenzo, Ricardo Flores Magón, Terrida del Marmol, and Jaime Vidal.

**Current Literature** New York: July 1888–December 1912, monthly; name changed to *Current Opinion*, January 1913. Journal edited by Edward J. Wheeler (1905–1922), with associate editor Leonard Abbott from 1905 to 1925. It included frequent features on modern European literature and sympathetically reviewed EG's work. Along with *Poet Lore,* it introduced EG to much of the modern European literature addressed in her lectures. In February 1911 it published an in-depth review of EG's *Anarchism and Other Essays,* as well as praise for AB's *Prison Memoirs of an Anarchist* in 1912 and the need for revision of the prison methods that it exposed.

**L'Era Nuova** (New Era) Paterson, N.J.: 1908–1917, weekly. Italian-language anarchist periodical, the successor to *La Questione Sociale,* edited by Camillo Rosazza, Ludovico Caminita, Franz Widmer, and others. Subtitled *Periodico settimanale,* and *A Newspaper Devoted to the Interests and Welfare of the Working Class.* Contributors included AB, Jay Fox, and F. Saverio Merlino.

**Everyman** Los Angeles, Calif.: 1906–1909, 1913–1919, monthly; name changed from *Apostle of Cheerfulness* in May 1908. Journal published and edited by James H. Griffes (pen name Luke North) in association with the Single Tax Club of Los Angeles. *Everyman* published Clarence Darrow's statement before the jury in his second trial in the May 1913 issue; the statement was later produced as a pamphlet, with an introduction by Luke North, *The Plea of Clarence Darrow in His Own Defense to the Jury (That Exonerated Him of the Charge of Bribery) at Los Angeles, August 1912* (Los Angeles: Golden Press, 1912). The paper favorably reviewed *The Social Significance of the Modern Drama* in its April and May 1914 issues. In December 1914 it published a special edition on the Modern School, edited by Leonard Abbott with contributions by EG. It initiated the single-tax "Great Adventure," a movement to add a single-tax amendment to the California constitution, and condemned capital punishment, taking an active interest in the work of the Anti-Capital Punishment League.

**Free Comrade** Wellesley, Mass.: 1910–1912, monthly. Anarchist and socialist newspaper edited by Leonard D. Abbott and J. William Lloyd, who were often the sole contributors. *Free Comrade* reviewed *Mother Earth* favorably and featured EG regularly. Lloyd's review of *Anarchism and Other Essays* included strong criticism of some of EG's ideas while maintaining his overwhelming support for her actions.

**Freedom** San Francisco, Calif.: vol. 1, no. 1 (November 1910)–1911, monthly. Anarchist paper edited by Eric B. Morton. *Freedom* described itself as "a monthly journal devoted to the destruction of superstition and the uplift of the under-dog." The first and only issue included a memorial tribute to Francisco Ferrer. Contributors included Jay Fox, Alexander Horr, and William McDevitt.

**Freedom** London: 1886–1928, 1929–present under various titles. Widely read English-language anarchist communist paper. *Freedom* was published weekly, fortnightly, or monthly depending on funding. It was edited by Alfred Marsh 1895–1914. Contributors included Peter Kropotkin,

W. C. Owen, Ricardo Flores Magón, Harry Kelly, and Lucy Parsons. The journal included an "International Notes" section for the dissemination of anarchist-related news. It favorably reviewed EG's *Anarchism and other Essays,* and in the summer of 1911 reprinted letters from Jack London, Leonard Abbott, and others protesting the socialist journal *Justice*'s accusation that EG was a Russian police spy. In 1912 it reprinted EG's articles on the IWW free speech fight in San Diego, including reports on the vigilante attack on Ben Reitman and EG's expulsion. BR also contributed in 1912 while he was visiting England. During World War I *Freedom* adopted an antiwar position after its featured debate between Kropotkin, who feared Germany's aggressive militarism and supported the Allies, and Malatesta, who argued that anarchists should be dedicated anti-militarists engaged in battle only for social revolution. In 1915 the journal published the International Anarchist Manifesto on the War, which protested the war and called for social revolt; signatories included EG, Abbott, AB, Cohen, Havel, and Malatesta. The paper was distributed in the United States through *Mother Earth.*

**Freie Arbeiter Stimme** (Free Voice of Labor) New York: July 1890–1894, weekly; 1899–1977. Yiddish-language anarchist newspaper (the German transliteration also appeared on the masthead), edited by Saul Yanovsky from 1899 until 1919. *Freie Arbeiter Stimme* published labor news, literary criticism, and cultural criticism, as well poetry and translations of novels. Among the paper's contributors were Peter Kropotkin, Johann Most, Max Nettlau, Rudolf Rocker, and poet Morris Winchevsky; it also published translations of Leonid Andreyev, Henrik Ibsen, Octave Mirbeau, George Bernard Shaw, Ivan Turgenev, and Oscar Wilde. The paper advertised EG's talks, but EG had little interaction with the paper, as her relationship with Yanovsky was always strained. Yanovsky and the paper were initially antiwar, signing the International Anarchist Manifesto Against the War, although Yanovsky later moved toward Kropotkin's position of support for England and France.

**Herald of Revolt: An Organ of the Coming Social Revolution** London: vol. 1, no. 1 (December 1910)– vol. 4, no. 5 (May 1914), monthly. Anarchist paper edited by Guy Aldred and from 1912 co-edited by Henry Sara. The masthead featured quotations from Herbert Spencer, Karl Marx, and Jesus Christ, illustrating Aldred's attempt to synthesize anarchism and Marxism. The paper featured original translations of Michael Bakunin by Karl Lahr, letters by Walker C. Smith and Cassius V. Cook, and contributions from Lahr, Henry Sara, and Rose Witcop; EG was a regular correspondent. The paper was succeeded by the *Spur.*

**Industrial Worker** Spokane, Wash.: 18 March 1909–4 September 1913, weekly; Seattle, Wash.: 5 February 1910–21 May 1910, 1 April 1916–4 May 1918, 16 July 1919–21 November 1931; Everett, Wash.: 7 May 1919–9 July 1919, weekly. Published by the Spokane locals of the Industrial Workers of the World until 15 December 1910, when it became a publication of the General Executive Board. *Industrial Worker* was edited by A. E. Cousins, Fred W. Heslewood, Otto Justh, John F. Leheney, Joseph O'Neil, P. R. Schleis, Hartwell S. Shippey, Walker C. Smith, and James Wilson. In addition to reporting on the activities of the IWW the *Industrial Worker* discussed the ideas of revolutionary syndicalism, the IWW's relationship to the AFL, and the rights of all workers regardless of race. Although the IWW was not an anarchist organization, the paper was sympathetic to various anarchist campaigns, including those of Francisco Ferrer and the Modern School, the Kōtoku Shusui Defense Fund, and the Partido Liberal Mexicano (Mexican Liberal Party). EG subscribed to *Industrial Worker* and sent *Mother Earth* to the newspaper's offices. In July 1909 BR collected subscriptions for the paper. *Industrial Worker* advertised EG's lectures in Spokane whenever she spoke there and occasionally reported on her subsequent activities. The 6 June 1912 edition featured a long interview by Caroline Nelson with EG after the San Diego incident. In July 1913 the General Executive Board suspended Walker C. Smith as editor of the paper, without specifying reasons for their decision. Smith was heavily critical of the board and an advocate of decentralizing the administration of the organization. The paper soon folded, leaving *Solidarity*, owned and operated by the General Executive Board, as the principal IWW English-language newspaper. *Industrial Worker* resumed publication in April 1916 with Thomas Whitehead as temporary editor. The first edition stated that it was a new paper, "not a revival of the old." J. A. MacDonald took over as editor in May 1916. Contributors included Charles Ashleigh, Eugene V. Debs, Justus Ebert, Joseph Ettor, Elizabeth Gurley Flynn, Joe Hill, William D. Haywood, Tom Mann, Caroline Nelson, and Vincent St. John.

***Instead of a Magazine*** Minneapolis, Minn.: No. 1 (1 February 1915)–no. 35 (29 May 1916). An anarchist, individualist, and single-tax journal, edited and published by Herman Kuehn, that ran for thirty-five issues. The magazine described itself as "devoted to no Cause or Cult. It is an open forum for the discussion of topics of sociologic import. Its editor frankly admits skepticism of the efficacy of every mooted substitute for voluntary cooperation." Contributors included Cassius V. Cook, William Holmes, Luke North, and Warren Van Valkenburgh. In late June 1918, after *Mother Earth Bulletin* was suppressed by the postal authorities, Stella Ballantine attempted to publish a mimeographed sheet called *Instead of a Magazine* describing her visit with EG in prison; the postal authorities refused to accept it.

***International Socialist Review*** Chicago: July 1900–February 1918. A popular socialist monthly, the *Review's* subtitle was changed from *A Monthly Journal of Socialist Thought* to *The Fighting Magazine of the Working Class* in August 1910. The change reflected the magazine's shift from a theoretical socialist journal to a popular socialist monthly representing the views of left-wing socialism and industrial unionism. The *Review* was critical of anarchism and craft unionism as well as of the right wing of the Socialist Party. The editor during this period was Charles H. Kerr; associate editors included William E. Bohn, William D. Haywood, Max Hayes, Robert Rives La Monte, Leslie E. Marcy, Mary E. Marcy, and Phillips Russell. Contributors included Charles Ashleigh, Joseph E. Cohen, Clarence S. Darrow, Eugene V. Debs, Elizabeth Gurley Flynn, Jim Larkin, Tom Mann, James F. Morton Jr., John Murray, Caroline Nelson, John Reed, Margaret Sanger, Vincent St. John, William Trautmann, John Kenneth Turner, Jaime Vidal, and William English Walling. It also published the work of Ralph Chaplin, Joe Hill, and Jack London. Although the *Review* was generally unambiguous in its hostility toward anarchism, the February 1911 issue included a sympathetic but critical review of EG's *Anarchism and Other Essays*, attacking her theoretical reasoning but asserting that the essays were "worth reading" and ultimately supporting her "heroic fight for free speech."

***Land and Liberty: An Anti-Slavery Journal*** Hayward, Calif.: vol. 1, no. 1 (1 May 1914)–vol. 1, no. 15 (July 1915), monthly. Anarchist newspaper with the motto "Slavery must go," edited by William C. Owen. *Land and Liberty* covered and supported the Flores Magón brothers, the PLM, and the Mexican Revolution. Critical of EG and AB's stance against World War I, it agreed with Peter

Kropotkin in his support of the Allied forces. It was also critical of EG's speeches and writings in *Mother Earth* about the war.

***Little Review*** Chicago: March 1914–May 1916, November 1916; San Francisco: June–July 1916 (one issue); New York: 1917–1926; Paris: 1929 (final issue), monthly. Avant-garde literary periodical with a playful and often elitist tone, edited by Margaret Anderson, Jane Heap, and Ezra Pound, and later by Jules Romain, John Rodker, and Francis Picabia. *Little Review* was published as a quarterly in 1921 and then sporadically until 1926. It took a favorable tone toward EG's work and character, and published her lecture schedule in Chicago in 1914. It published a mixed but favorable review of *The Social Significance of the Modern Drama* in October 1914. It published EG's essay "Preparedness: The Road to Universal Slaughter" in December 1915, the same month it appeared in *Mother Earth*. In May 1916 it published excerpts of EG's letters from prison after her incarceration for distributing birth control information. It also published AB's article on the Caplan and Schmidt cases and Robert Minor's article on the Mooney and Billings cases. Margaret Anderson especially supported Mooney and Billings, and was critical of San Francisco labor leaders. Contributors included AB, Floyd Dell, Theodore Dreiser, EG, Clarence Darrow, Ben Hecht, Ernest Hemingway, Robert Minor, Louise Bryant, and Carl Sandburg.

***The Masses*** New York: vol. 1 (January 1911)–December 1917, suspended due to staffing problems September–November 1912, monthly. Continued as the *Liberator* in 1918. Radical political and cultural magazine that linked art and literature to revolutionary politics and the labor movement, calling itself "A monthly magazine devoted to the interests of the working people." The *Masses* was edited by Thomas Seltzer, Horatio Winslow, Piet Vlag, and, from 1912 to 1917, Max Eastman. Contributing editors included John Reed, Mary Heaton Vorse, Floyd Dell, and William English Walling. Contributors included Sara Bard Field, Elizabeth Gurley Flynn, C. E. S. Wood, and Bolton Hall. It featured the art of George Bellows, Henry J. Glintenkamp, Boardman Robinson, and Art Young. It was organized as a cooperative, and artists and writers who contributed to the magazine also shared in its management. The paper followed the Ludlow strikers' story, the McNamara case, and the Tom Mooney proceedings. In 1912 it featured a small editorial on BR's "unspeakable" treatment in San Diego, but it equated the mob action to anarchist direct action; it did not mention EG's presence. The *Masses* absorbed the *New Review* in 1916 and began publishing a section entitled "Masses Review." Throughout 1916 it followed the arrests and trials of those involved in birth control advocacy and claimed that the law in force only gave "a convenient pretext for the arrest of anybody whom the authorities desire, for any other reason, to have in their power." It printed the full text of EG's speech at her 20 April trial in defense of her right to lecture on birth control, followed by generally sympathetic accounts of EG's other political activities. The periodical took a firm antiwar stance, publishing many articles and political cartoons condemning militarism and capitalist interests.

***The Modern School*** New York; Ridgefield, N.J.; Stelton, N.J.: 1912–1922, irregular monthly/ quarterly. Anarchist publication of the Modern School, successor to *Monthly News Letter* of the Francisco Ferrer Association. It described itself as "A monthly magazine devoted to advanced ideas in education." It was edited by Lola Ridge, Leonard Abbott, Harry Kelly, William Thurston Brown, Carl Zigrosser, and Frank V. Anderson, assisted by Manuel Komroff and Adolf Wolff. Contributors included John R. Coryell, Will Durant, Elizabeth Ferm, Charlotte Perkins Gilman, Michael Gold (Irwin Granich), Hutchins Hapgood, David Lawson, Man Ray, Margaret Sanger, Lincoln Steffens, Horace Traubel, and Max Weber.

**Monthly News Letter** New York: 1910–1911, monthly. Newsletter of the Francisco Ferrer Association, edited by Harry Kelly and Stewart Kerr. Contributors included Leonard Abbott, Bayard Boyesen, and Hutchins Hapgood. This short-lived newsletter reported on the goals, ideals, and progress of the Francisco Ferrer Association. It was succeeded by the *Modern School*.

**Mother Earth: Monthly Magazine Devoted to Social Science and Literature** New York: March 1906–August 1917, monthly. Anarchist journal published by EG and edited variously by EG, Max Baginski, AB, and Hippolyte Havel. Baginski was the usual author of the "News and Comments" section, and AB edited the magazine from 1907 to 1915. According to Harry Kelly, "A half dozen of the faithful gathered at the offices of Dr. Solotaroff, on East Broadway, to discuss ways and means of launching a new publication based upon libertarian principles. . . . The original intention was to make a magazine similar to *L'Humanite Nouvelle,* that brilliant and scholarly publication issued in Brussels" ("Mother Earth 1905–1915," *Mother Earth*, March 1915). The first issue of the magazine had a print run of 3,000, which sold out within a week, followed by a second printing of 1,000. Contributors included Leonard Abbott, Adeline Champney, John R. Coryell, Voltairine de Cleyre, Floyd Dell, Jay Fox, Bolton Hall, Sadakichi Hartmann, C. L. James, Harry Kelly, Peter Kropotkin, William C. Owen, BR, Lola Ridge, Theodore Schroeder, John Kenneth Turner, and Charles Erskine Scott Wood; it also published letters of Francisco Ferrer, and Kōtoku Shūsui. The July 1912 issue was dedicated to the recently deceased Voltairine de Cleyre; the December 1912 issue, to a celebration of Peter Kropotkin's seventieth birthday; the July 1914 issue, to the anarchists Caron, Berg, and Hanson, killed in the Lexington Avenue explosion; the March 1915 issue, a special souvenir edition, to a celebration of the tenth year of *Mother Earth;* and the April 1916 issue, to coverage of birth control agitation. In 1916 the IWW paper *Solidarity* offered its readers a joint subscription, for $1.50, to *Solidarity* and *Mother Earth*.

**New Review** New York: January 1913–June 1916, weekly (monthly from May 1913). Socialist journal edited by Herman Simpson and, from May 1914, by a board whose members included Frank Bohn, William Bohn, W. E. B. Du Bois, Floyd Dell, Max Eastman, Louis C. Fraina, Arturo Giovannitti, Arthur Livingston, Walter Lippmann, Herman Simpson, Robert H. Lowie, William English Walling, Helen Marot, Albert Sonnichsen, and Robert Rives La Monte. Contributors included Karl Kautsky, Louis Levine, Anton Pannekoek, Rose Strunsky, Horace Traubel, and John Kenneth Turner. Unfavorable references to anarchism in the journal included Pannekoek's two-part January and February 1913 article, "Socialism and Anarchism." *New Review* merged with the *Masses* in July 1916.

**Poet Lore** Boston: vol. 1, no. 1 (1889)–present, semi-monthly. A periodical featuring literature, poetry, and criticism. It was published by Richard G. Badger and the Gorham Press, which was also the publisher of EG's *The Social Significance of the Modern Drama*. Along with *Current Literature, Poet Lore* introduced EG to many authors whom she incorporated into her modern drama lecture series, including Strindberg, Andreyev, and Bjørnson.

**The Public** Chicago: no. 1 (April 1898)–no. 1125 (December 1919), weekly. This single-tax weekly described itself as a "national journal of fundamental democracy and a weekly narrative of history in the making." Contributors included Adeline Champney, Harry Weinberger, Charles Erskine Scott Wood, Charlotte Perkins Gilman, and BR. Throughout this period the weekly chronicled nationwide attempts by the police and government to prevent EG's meetings and strongly advocated the right to free speech, especially in the editorials "The Persecution of Emma Goldman" (1909) and "Emma Goldman and the Law" (1916). It published Bolton Hall's favorable review of *Anarchism and Other Essays* in February 1911. Llewellyn Jones's review of AB's *Prison Memoirs of an Anarchist* in January 1913 was a scathing attack on AB's choice of topic and his egotistical and unscientific style.

**Regeneración** (Regeneration) Mexico: 1900–?; San Antonio, Texas: 1904; St. Louis: 1905–1906; Los Angeles: 1910–1918. Spanish-language liberal opposition, then anarchist, paper, edited by the Mexican revolutionary Ricardo Flores Magón, at times with Juan Sarabia, Librado Rivera, and Antonio Villarreal. The English segment was edited first by Alfred Sanftleben, then by Ethel Duffy Turner, and finally by William C. Owen. The paper featured EG, regularly reported on her lectures, and acknowledged in print the donations it received from her meetings. Owen and the Flores Magón brothers were indicted and the Flores Magón brothers arrested and imprisoned, charged with using the mails to transmit materials inciting "murder, deliberate arson and treason."

**Revolt: The Voice of the Militant Worker** San Francisco: vol. 1, no. 1 (1 May 1911)– no. 53 (11 May 1912), weekly. A left-Socialist paper, edited by Cloudesley Johns, Austin Lewis, William McDevitt, and Nathan L. Griest. Tom Mooney, whose promotional efforts were largely responsible for its circulation of 1,500, was listed as publisher from July 1911, and eventually as the paper's only named staff member. Contributors included Frank Bohn, William Thurston Brown, William D. Haywood, Charles H. Kerr, Jack London, Tom Mann, Caroline Nelson, Vincent St. John, Rose Pastor Stokes, Walker C. Smith, Rose Strunsky, and William English Walling.

**Revolt** New York: 1 January 1916–11 March 1916, weekly. An anarchist paper, subtitled *The Stormy Petrel of the Labor Movement*, edited by Hippolyte Havel with the help of Jack Isaacson and published in the basement of the Ferrer Center. Volume 1, numbers 1–8 were all suppressed and barred from mail delivery under Section 211 of the Criminal Code, after being designated as "vile, indecent, filthy, obscene literature with an amendment which applies to the advocacy of murder, arson, and assassination." The editorial advisory board and contributors included Benjamin De Casseres, Moritz Jagendorf, David Rosenthal, Adolf Wolff, Michael Gold, Leonard Abbott, Harry Kelly, Max Weber, Robert Minor, and Margaret Sanger. The paper, from the first issue, claimed to be aimed at all "rebels," "workers," "outcasts," "dreamers," and "searchers of truth and light." Its goal was to "interpret the new tendencies in art, science, literature, and in the revolutionary labor movement." The 19 February 1916 issue reported on Emma Goldman's arrest for birth control agitation.

**Solidarity** New Castle, Pa.: 1909–1913; Cleveland: 1913–1917; Chicago: 1917; weekly. Owned and published weekly by C. H. McCarty and B. H. Williams as the eastern organ of the IWW until April 1913, when the paper moved to Cleveland. *Solidarity* was then published by the IWW Publishing Bureau, and the paper's ownership was transferred to the General Executive Board. It was edited by B. H. Williams, with associate editors that included C. H. McCarty and Justus Ebert. *Solidarity* reported primarily on the organizing activities of the IWW and the trials of indicted members. Contributors included members from the General Executive Board, Joseph Ettor, Helen Keller, Elizabeth Gurley Flynn, and Carlo Tresca. The paper reprinted an appeal by the Kōtoku Protest Conference on 11 February 1911. At the eighth-annual IWW convention in 1913 Williams proposed that the *Industrial Worker* and *Solidarity* consolidate and publish out of Cleveland. After Walker C. Smith was removed by the General Executive Board as editor of *Industrial Worker*, the paper folded, leaving *Solidarity* as the principal IWW English-language newspaper. By 1915 the paper was the official organ of the IWW. Because *Solidarity* was published under the supervision of the General Executive Board, the paper adamantly advocated the centralization of the organization. B. H. Williams reviewed EG's book *Anarchism and Other Essays* in the 4 March 1911 edition. In 1916 the paper offered its readers a joint subscription, for $1.50, to *Solidarity* and *Mother Earth*. The paper occasionally reprinted material from *Mother Earth*.

***The Syndicalist*** Chicago: vol. 3, no. 1 (1 January 1913)–vol. 3, no. 14 (1–15 September 1913), semi-monthly. A syndicalist paper, the successor to the *Agitator*. It was edited by Jay Fox and managed by William Z. Foster and was closely associated with Foster's Syndicalist League of North America, although it was nominally published by the Syndicalist Publishing Association. Contributors included J. W. Fleming, J. W. Johnstone, William C. Owen, and Jules Scarceriaux. It advertised EG's upcoming lectures and favorably reviewed AB's *Prison Memoirs*.

***Toiler: A Monthly Review of International Syndicalism*** Kansas City, Mo.: vol. 1, no. 1 (October 1913)–vol. 3, no. 1 (January 1915), mostly monthly. A paper of the Syndicalist Educational League of Kansas City, associated with the Syndicalist League of North America. It advocated "boring from within" the AFL in an effort to turn its member organizations into revolutionary syndicalist unions. It was edited by Max Dezettel with Otto E. Cook, and at times with Earl R. Browder. It published the work of Pedro Esteve, Bolton Hall, Anton Johannsen, Louis Levine, Jack London, Tom Mann, Caroline Nelson, W. C. Owen, Émile Pouget, and Arnold Roller. Contributors included William Z. Foster, Jay Fox, J. W. Johnstone, and Jean E. Spielman.

***Why*** Tacoma, Wash.: January 1913–February 1914, monthly; March 1914–July 1914, semi-monthly. It sported numerous mastheads, including "No consecrated absurdity would have stood its ground if man had not silenced child's objections" for much of 1913. An anarchist newspaper with close ties to the IWW. It was edited by Mrs. Frances Moore, Samuel T. Hammersmark, and finally Eugene Travaglio. Contributors included Jay Fox, Joseph Labadie, William C. Owen, Jules Scarceriaux, Joseph Kucera, and Horace Traubel.

***The Woman Rebel*** New York: March 1914–October 1914, monthly. A revolutionary socialist and anarchist paper, edited by Margaret Sanger. Subtitled *No Gods—No Masters* and *A monthly paper of militant thought*. It raised the subject of birth control and female emancipation in an anti-capitalist context. After the first issue Sanger was notified that the government deemed it unmailable. She continued to publish and in August was indicted for violating obscenity statutes for the March, May, and July issues, specifically for several articles on sexuality and "A Defense of Assassination" by Herbert Thorpe. Contributors included Rebecca Edelsohn, Helen Keller, Lily Gair Wilkinson, and Rose Witcop. The journal reprinted excerpts from EG's "Love and Marriage" and Voltairine de Cleyre's "Direct Action" in its first issue and an excerpt from EG's "Woman Suffrage" in the June 1914 issue.

**Anarchist Federation**  At the 1907 International Anarchist Congress in Amsterdam an Anarchist International Federation was created. It was composed of anarchist groups, federations, and individuals in order to foster communication among anarchists around the world. A bureau of correspondence, consisting of five members with Alexander Schapiro acting as secretary, was organized to assume the task of maintaining communication. The bureau published the *Bulletin de L'Internationale Anarchist*; the first issue, February–March 1908, was published in London and contained extracts from delegates' reports from the congress and information on the state of the anarchist movement in various countries.

The American Anarchist Federation was founded in 1908 by AB and J. C. Behr, who became secretary and treasurer, respectively. Based in New York, it was identified variously as the Anarchist Federation of America, the Anarchist Federation of New York, or simply the Anarchist Federation. In the January 1908 *Mother Earth* the Anarchist Federation announced that its purpose was to bring together anarchist individuals and groups, act as an educational bureau, propagate anarchism through bulletins, seek "participation in the every-day social life of the people," involve itself in labor unions, promote direct action and the general strike, and work as a collection fund for the defense of radical political prisoners. The Anarchist Federation affiliated itself with the International Anarchist Federation.

In 1910 the Anarchist Federation donated money to the Partido Liberal Mexicano (PLM; Mexican Liberal Party); corresponded with the bureau of correspondence of the International Anarchist Federation in Paris; and circulated a manifesto—published in the November 1910 *Mother Earth* and signed by EG, Bolton Hall, Leonard Abbott, Hippolyte Havel, Dr. Juliet H. Severance, Dr. Charles Andrews, AB, and BR—in solidarity with the McNamara brothers.

On 25 January 1914 the Anarchist Federation of Brooklyn held an international mass meeting at the Manhattan Casino to protest the harsh sentences of Rangel, Cline, and the other PLM members arrested and charged with the 1913 shooting of a Texas sheriff. H. M. Woolman, president of the Anarchist Federation of Brooklyn, presided over the meeting, reviewed the case, read from a pamphlet by Jake Oppenheimer, and warned against the dangers of racial prejudice. Pedro Esteve spoke on the history of the Mexican Revolution, and Bernard Sernaker spoke in Russian on conditions that necessitated the use of force.

In February 1914, at its meeting at Club Avanti, the newly titled International Anarchist Communist Federation, formerly the International Anarchist Federation, chose new secretarial officers: Max Charnick to represent English and Yiddish anarchists, and Joseph Libita to represent Italian and Spanish anarchists. The meeting brought together members of Friends of Art and Education, Club Avanti, the Russian Progressive Circle, and members of the group centered around the Spanish-language paper *Cultura Obrera,* edited by Pedro Esteve. Members of the federation rearticulated their objective as promoters of anarchist communist propaganda, and as a vehicle for organized protest against government persecution of anarchists across the country. In the spring of 1914 they invited anarchist groups in the United States and Canada to join their attempts to streamline propaganda efforts. The organization focused on the specific legal cases of Rangel and Cline and the defense of the other Texas PLM prisoners, and on the case of the Italian anti-militarist Augusto Massetti, who was being held in a psychiatric hospital for shooting his colonel to avoid fighting in the war.

Anarchist Federations representing Yiddish groups published a number of journals, including *Dos Fraye Vort* (The Free Word) (New York, 1911), published monthly by the Federated Anarchists Groups in America and edited by J. A. Maryson; *Di Frayhayt* (Freedom) (New York, 1913–1914) published monthly by the Federated Anarchists Groups and edited by L. Barone; and *Di Fraye Tsukunft* (The Free Future) (New York, 1915–1916), published irregularly by the Anarchist Federation of America. See also vol. 2, *Making Speech Free.*

**Anarchist Red Cross**   The Anarchist Red Cross (ARC) was organized by European and American anarchists to aid imprisoned anarchists and other radicals in Russia who received no assistance from established revolutionary groups in that country. The first and strongest group in the United States was formed in New York in 1907 by former Russian prisoners H. Weinstein and J. Katzenelenbogen. The organization published *Di Shtime fun di Russishe Gefangene* (The Voice of the Russian Prisoners) (monthly, New York, 1913–ca. 1916, edited by Alexander Zager). Other branches were organized in Chicago (1909), Philadelphia (1911), Detroit (1914), and Baltimore. The New York Latvian branch of the Anarchist Red Cross, organized in December 1913 was founded by Carl Hanson, Charles Berg, and Hanson's half-sister, Louise Berger.

The organization collected large sums of money for distribution in Russia. Fund-raising activities centered around various annual Arestanten Balls (Prisoners' Balls), which were popular and lucrative events in New York, Chicago, and Philadelphia. The Chicago group also organized the Bauren Ball (Peasants' Ball) and published a humorous yearly bulletin by the same name. *Mother Earth* advertised the first-annual Arrestanten Ball to be held in New York on 17 March 1911. Later, EG, Louise Berger, and Anna Baron collected funds under the auspices of the Anarchist Red Cross and passed them to the Unemployed and Anti-Militarist League Fund, to help the strikers at Ludlow and the protesters at Tarrytown. The ARC disbanded in 1917, following the announcement from the Russian revolutionary front that all political prisoners had been freed. At the urging of EG, AB, and Alexander Shapiro, the ARC regrouped in Berlin at the end of 1921 and resumed its mission.

**Anti-Militarist League**   The Anti-Militarist League was founded at the New York Ferrer Center in 1914 by anarchist members of the Conference of the Unemployed, including Rebecca Edelsohn, Leonard Abbott, AB, and M. Eleanor Fitzgerald, "for the purpose of calling public attention to Colorado, as well as to stem the fever of jingoism fanned by the capitalist press" (*Mother Earth,* May 1914). The league's office was located at 74 West 119th Street, and the official letterhead declared that "War is a quarrel between two thieves" and urged "Insurrection rather than war." The Anti-Militarist League was dedicated not only to the fight against war and militarism, especially the threat of impending war with Mexico, but also to foment domestic insurrection, armed if necessary. AB served as the league's secretary-treasurer and announced the formation of the league to the press on 23 April, three days after the Ludlow Massacre.

That same day, Edelsohn and Samuel Hartman were sentenced to $300 bonds to keep the peace after their arrest the previous day at an informal protest against war with Mexico at Franklin's statue in New York City. While speaking, Edelsohn had asserted that the flag of the United States was not worth fighting for. At her hearing the next day Edelsohn refused to accept the offer of release in exchange for a moratorium on political speaking, instead declaring a hunger strike in protest; in the process she became the first woman in America to undertake a public display of a hunger strike as a strategy for political protest.

AB announced to the press on 28 April that the league was holding nightly meetings and weekly mass meetings to raise funds for the striking miners in Colorado to purchase guns and ammunition, as well as to recruit a volunteer regiment to assist the strikers. He announced the establishment of a "war fund" in *Mother Earth* to supply the Colorado strikers with money and, when necessary, "with men, arms and ammunition" (*Mother Earth,* May 1914). AB, under different pseudonyms, also wrote several articles about the league in *Mother Earth,* including "Anti-Militarist Activities in New York," and "Anti-Militarist Propaganda." The league also organized fund-raising activities, including balls, bazaars, and the sale of general strike buttons, and it held a 1 May 1914 rally in New York's Mulberry Bend Park, attended by AB, Marie Ganz, Rebecca Edelsohn, and Regina Wolff. The league also raised money for the Rangel-Cline Defense Fund and for activities of anarchists in Europe protesting against World War I; on 24 October 1914 it held a ball and bazaar to benefit both Rangel-Cline and Italians supporting the anti-militarist Augusto Massetti. On 24 May 1914 the league took an active part in the International Protest Rally for Massetti, at which AB, Rebecca Edelsohn, and Harry Kelly spoke, along with N. Cuneo and Pietro Allgra in Italian, Jose Rubio in Spanish, and Leopold Bergman in Yiddish.

Many members of the Anti-Militarist League joined the Tarrytown protests against Rockefeller in May and June 1914, and—along with anarchist groups from Philadelphia, Trenton, Paterson, Newark, Hoboken, and Albany, as well as New York City—participated in the mass memorial at Union Square on 11 July 1914 for the victims of the Lexington Avenue bomb.

Other Anti-Militarist League branches were founded throughout the county, including one in Denver, where a mass meeting on 3 May 1914, sponsored by the Anti-Militarist League of Denver, was chaired by BR with speakers EG and S. Meyers, among others. The meeting handbill read "To Protest Against the Outrages committed upon the Working Class of Colorado by Thugs and State Hirelings; Against the Importation of Federal Troops, and Against this country's War with Mexico. Workingmen Remember Whenever a country has gone to War the Workingmen and Women have always been the losers, and whenever Federal Soldiers have Invaded a Strike Region, Workers Have been KILLED and the Strike has been Lost."

The Anti-Militarist League of Paterson, New Jersey, sponsored a mass meeting on 18 May 1914, at which AB, Rebecca Edelsohn, Harry Kelly, and others spoke. Like the Denver meeting, this meeting combined protest of the state's use of force against the striking miners in Ludlow with protest against calls for war with Mexico. The handbill for the meeting read "Thou Shalt Not Kill, Either in Mexico or Colorado" and urged workers to "Refuse to be a murderer for the benefit of the rich blood-suckers. But, if you want to fight join the cause of Labor against Capital and help us defend the Colorado Mine Workers who are being ruthlessly slaughtered by the very masters who urge you to protect their interests in Mexico."

**Arbeiter Ring** The Arbeiter Ring was a Jewish fraternal organization and a critical force within the Jewish labor movement. It was founded by cloakmakers Sam Greenberg and Harry Lasker and former communard M. Goldreich in 1892 in New York, to protect Jewish immigrants from harsh working conditions in sweatshops. The organization became a nationwide federation in 1900. Nonpartisan and primarily socialist, the organization included many active anarchists. Some branches, including the Radical Library Group in Philadelphia, were exclusively anarchist. Unlike other fraternal orders it was founded on principles of social reform and mutual aid, and it emphasized labor organization rather than secret rituals. Members pledged to deny support to any political party that preserved wage slavery and to create their own programs of technical and cultural education. The educational committee published a monthly magazine, *Der Freund*, and Yiddish books, and it established Yiddish schools for children; both AB and Harry Kelly taught Sunday school classes at the Arbeiter Ring in the years before the Ferrer Center was established in New York. The organization's numbers grew when it expanded out of New York's East Side and created local branches in other parts of New York, the United States, and Canada. By 1916 it had grown to more than 600 branches and more than 52,000 members. In 1915 branches supported AB's tour for the Caplan-Schmidt Defense League. In *Mother Earth* AB described the Arbeiter Ring as an organization that was "progressive and revolutionary, [and] can always be relied upon to aid in every labor struggle." The group donated large sums to radical organizations in need of financial assistance. The officers in 1916 included Abe Epstein, president, and Meyer London, legal adviser.

**Birth Control Leagues** Birth control information had been disseminated with infrequent arrests and little government legal restriction during much of the nineteenth century. The Comstock Act of 1873, revised in 1876, defined, among other things, contraceptive information as obscene and illegal.

In 1876 Edward Bliss Foote, the author of a popular medical treatise, *Medical Common Sense* (1858), which included information on birth control (and instructions for obtaining it from him), was among the first to be prosecuted under the new law. In his defense Foote argued that contraceptive information was medical in nature and therefore not obscene, an argument that would remain the foundation of many subsequent free speech fights for access to birth control information. In 1906 another early birth control advocate, William J. Robinson, advertised in his journal, the *Critic and Guide*, the availability of birth control information, which he would provide only to other doctors.

In 1914 the fight for access to birth control information and contraceptives escalated with the publication of Margaret Sanger's journal the *Woman Rebel*, with its advocacy of legal and accessible birth control for working-class and poor women as part of its larger vision of a general social revolution. EG supported Sanger, helping to distribute her journal and lecturing on the subject of birth control. She continued distributing practical contraceptive information, including both Sanger's pamphlet, *Family Limitation* (1914), and another, *Why and How the Poor Should Not Have Many Children*, which was written by William Robinson, although authorship was claimed by BR. The May 1916 issue of *Mother Earth* was devoted to birth control. As birth control agitation became more concentrated, Comstock and other government agents escalated their efforts to thwart the distribution and circulation of "obscene" material. In response to this suppression various birth control organizations were formed.

**Birth Control League of America** In the July 1914 issue of the *Woman Rebel,* after Sanger had been warned that the first issue of the *Woman Rebel* violated Section 211 of the U.S. Criminal Code and was banned from the mails, she announced the formation of the Birth Control League of America. The purpose of the organization was to "carry on an extensive, nation wide campaign of education, of literature, to prove to the workers that it is to their interests to have a thorough knowledge and understanding of the means for regulating the size of their families" and to agitate for repeal of state and federal laws against the dissemination of birth control information and render aid to those prosecuted under the laws. Sanger issued a call to her sympathizers to join or form like-minded leagues. This organization appears to have existed on paper only and was never active.

**National Birth Control League** When Sanger fled the country in 1914 to avoid facing trial for her obscenity indictment, other groups quickly formed to continue the work for birth control. The National Birth Control League (1915–1919) was organized on 31 March 1915 by Mary Ware Dennett and a group of mostly middle-class socialists and liberals. Dennett served as secretary, Clara Gruening Stillman as treasurer, and Gertrude Minturn Pinchot as the first president; other members included Jessie Ashley, Bolton Hall, and Lincoln Steffens, all united in their dedication to changing the law to allow free dissemination of birth control information. This relatively conservative group was interested in changing birth control laws and did not endorse direct action and never participated in illegal dissemination of practical information. Unlike Sanger, Dennett and her group did not limit contraceptive dispensation to doctors or nurses and instead framed the argument as an issue of free speech, asserting that birth control information should be accessible to everyone. The National Birth Control League published *The National Birth Control League; a Brief Statement of What It Stands For* (New York: Co-Operative Press, 1915). When Sanger declined a position on the league's executive board, it refused to raise financial support for her defense, thus straining relations between Sanger and the National Birth Control League.

**Portland Birth Control League** The Portland Birth Control League (1915–1918) was founded in response to Sanger's general call in the *Woman Rebel* and EG and BR's birth control work in Portland. The group, organized by H. C. Uthoff, sought to stimulate discussion of birth control and repeal the laws criminalizing the dissemination of information. It supported EG and BR when they were arrested in October 1916. According to IWW journalist and birth control activist Caroline Nelson, they met at the public library. H. C. Uthoff wrote an article on birth control in William Robinson's the *Critic and Guide.* The group published a pamphlet in 1915 titled *The Birth Control League: A Brief Statement of What It Stands For.* The National Birth Control League based its statement of intent on the Portland league's statement of principles.

**San Francisco Birth Control League** The San Francisco Birth Control League (1915), while not as active as the Portland Birth Control League, was organized at roughly the same time. Caroline Nelson, a member of the league, reported that although it was founded with the intention to distribute information to poor and working-class women, its members were mostly professional and middle-class women, who themselves already had access to the information.

A Los Angeles Birth Control League was also organized in California by socialist Georgia Kotsch, who also worked to organize the Rangel-Cline defense and was an active worker for suffrage in California.

**Birth Control League of Massachusetts** The Birth Control League of Massachusetts (1916) developed from the Allison Defense League, formed after the arrest of Van K. Allison. Allison, a Fabian socialist, was sentenced to three years in prison (later reduced to three months) after being arrested in July 1916 for giving an undercover police agent a copy of *Why and How the Poor Should Not Have Many Children*. The Birth Control League of Massachusetts was co-founded by the sisters Blanche Ames Ames and Jessie Ames Marshall with the intention of "promoting rational parenthood." The group started as a defense association for Allison and evolved into the Birth Control League of Massachusetts, publishing "a short statement on birth control" in 1916. The group was aided by the legal advice of Theodore Schroeder, with whom the League corresponded.

**Birth Control Committee** The Birth Control Committee (1916) of New York City was organized to support EG in her trial on charges of disseminating birth control information; many anarchist sympathizers joined, among them Anna Sloan, Marie Jennie Howe, Robert Henri, Dr. William J. Robinson, and Leonard Abbott, the group's secretary. The group hosted a birth control mass meeting, which was a public welcome upon EG's release from prison on 20 May 1916. Scheduled to speak at this meeting were such notables as Max Eastman (who later canceled on the grounds that he refused to share a stage with BR), Rose Pastor Stokes, Arturo Giovannitti, Harry Weinberger, Leonard Abbott, Theodore Schroeder, and EG. It initiated an Emma Goldman Defense Committee in April 1916 and a Birth Control Defense Fund in May of the same year.

**New York Birth Control League** In late 1916 the New York Birth Control League (1916–1918) was founded. Dr. Frederick Blossom, a member of the Socialist Party, was both its primary organizer and the managing editor of Sanger's *Birth Control Review* (first published February 1917 in the league's office). Formed in December 1916, after Margaret Sanger's October arrest for opening a birth control clinic in Brooklyn, the New York Birth Control League offered financial support for Sanger's trial, worked to amend state and federal laws to allow physicians and registered nurses to disseminate birth control information, and advocated birth control as a critical means for safeguarding women's health and promoting social welfare.

**Committee on Birth Control of New York** Theodore Schroeder set forth the group's mission statement in his speech at the Carnegie Hall mass meeting for birth control: "I am in favor of amending Section 1142 of the Penal Code of the State of New York to permit duly licensed physicians to prescribe for their patients methods of preventing conception."

**Caplan-Schmidt Defense League** The Caplan-Schmidt Defense League was a Los Angeles–based organization founded to aid the defense for David Caplan and Matthew A. Schmidt, who were arrested in February 1915 for allegedly helping the McNamara brothers purchase dynamite to bomb the *Los Angeles Times* building on 1 October 1910.

The Caplan-Schmidt Defense League argued that an agreement between labor and capital in Los Angeles, made in the McNamara brothers' trial, had been broken by the arrest of Caplan and Schmidt. Thus, their defense campaign was framed in terms of the ongoing war between labor and capital. The executive committee was made up of labor leaders from San Francisco and Los Angeles and included I. W. Cowles; Edward D. Nolan, who was later arrested following the Preparedness Day bombing in 1916; C. F. Grow, representing the Los Angeles Central Labor Council; and Tom Barker, representing the Los Angeles Building Trades Council. Eric B. Morton served as secretary of publicity after AB's services were refused. Also involved peripherally were John Kassel, Pete Isaak (son of Abe and Mary Isaak), and George Speed.

In June 1915 AB forged a strong connection between the Caplan-Schmidt Defense League and the San Francisco International Workers' Defense League, and he wrote a number of letters under the auspices of the Caplan-Schmidt Defense League soliciting support and funds, although he was later asked to take a more peripheral role because of his anarchist reputation. AB left Los Angeles in July on a tour to collect funds for the league and to establish local branches of the Caplan-Schmidt Defense League. He traveled through the country, collecting money in Denver, Kansas City, St. Louis, Chicago, Pittsburgh, Detroit, Buffalo, and New York, and he became the league's treasurer upon his arrival in New York. EG also collected money for the defense in San Francisco. In New York City a local branch of the league was formed by delegates from seventy-five labor organizations. On 16 May a meeting in New York was held for Caplan and Schmidt, at which Anton Johannsen of the Building Trades Council of San Francisco recounted the history of the case and worked to involve New York labor unions in the league's work. Carlo Tresca and Saul Yanovsky also spoke. EG often spoke in support of Caplan and Schmidt. While in Los Angeles, she spoke at a meeting for the two on 30 June 1915, and she hosted a fund-raising social the same evening. She spoke on their case on 23 August in Seattle and again on 16 September with AB in New York City, and she spoke again in New York on 4 October, the day Schmidt's trial began.

On 30 December 1915 Schmidt was found guilty of first-degree murder, and on 12 January 1916 he was sentenced to life imprisonment. On 15 December 1916 Caplan, whose first trial ended in a hung jury, was found guilty of voluntary manslaughter, and on 17 December he was sentenced to ten years in prison. The league had published the leaflet *Read and Get Wise; How Los Angeles Welched* (Los Angeles: Caplan-Schmidt Defense League, 1915), which included evidence that the Merchants and Manufacturers Association of Los Angeles and the prosecuting attorney had worked together to handpick a jury that was antilabor and pro–big business. A second leaflet, *A Message to Labor from David Caplan and M. A. Schmidt* (Los Angeles: Caplan-Schmidt Defense League, 1915), had sold as a fund-raiser for 10 cents and reiterated the accusation about the handpicked jury by the Merchants and Manufactures Association (evidence rejected by the judge in both Caplan's and Schmidt's trials). Their arrests and trials were publicized in both the socialist and anarchist presses, including the *International Socialist Review*, the *Western Comrade, Everyman,* the *Masses, Mother Earth,* and *The Blast.* The executive committee of the Caplan-Schmidt Defense League was criticized privately by EG, AB, C. E. S. Wood, and others for denying that any crimes had been committed in the *Los Angeles Times* bombing in an effort to preserve the reputations of labor leaders like Olaf Tvietmoe and Anton Johannsen, while ultimately sacrificing the freedom of Caplan and Schmidt.

**Francisco Ferrer Association** The Francisco Ferrer Association was formed 3 June 1910, a year after the execution of the Spanish anarchist and libertarian educator Francisco Ferrer, at a meeting hall of the Harlem Liberal Alliance. The meeting was suggested by EG and convened by

Leonard Abbott and William Van der Weyde. At the inaugural meeting, chaired by Harry Kelly and including speakers Leonard Abbott, Jaime Vidal, and AB, the association adopted two main goals: to perpetuate the work and memory of Francisco Ferrer and, also at EG's suggestion, to publish a volume dedicated to Ferrer's life and work.

EG had delivered lectures on Ferrer and the Modern School on her annual tours, and as Abbott wrote in *Mother Earth*, "EG has done more than anyone else to keep alive American interest in the martyred founder of the Modern Schools" (see "The Continuing Interest in Francisco Ferrer," Article in *Mother Earth,* June 1910). Also present at the inaugural meeting was school teacher Henrietta Rodman, whose affiliation was concealed because it could have jeopardized her public school position. The twenty-two charter members agreed to pay a yearly membership fee of $1.

In 1910 the Ferrer Association published *The Rational Education of Children, the Program of the International League for Rational Education of Children*; Voltairine de Cleyre's *The Modern School* (both of which were reprinted in *Mother Earth* the same year); and *Francisco Ferrer: His Life Work and Martyrdom,* edited by Leonard Abbott. The association was the subject of a lengthy article in the *New York Times Sunday Magazine* ("World-Wide Movement to Honor Memory of Ferrer," 31 July 1910). In 1911 the association published Bayard Boyesen's *The Modern School in New York* and William Durant's *The Ferrer Modern School.*

Within the first year Modern Schools and Ferrer Association chapters spread throughout the country. The first Modern School, though short-lived, was a Sunday school started by AB and other New York anarchists in 1910. Also organized in 1910 were a Modern School in Philadelphia, affiliated with the Radical Library and organized by Joseph Cohen; the Chicago Modern School organized by William Nathanson and Voltairine de Cleyre; a Modern School in Salt Lake City organized by William Thurston Brown; and the Seattle Modern School, organized by Bruce Rogers and Anna Falcoff.

The fall of 1910 marked the publication of the first issue of the *Monthly News Letter* of the Francisco Ferrer Association. Edited by Leonard Abbott and Stewart Kerr (a salesman for New York Telephone Company and politically close to EG, AB, and Abbott), it featured articles by Harry Kelly, Abbott, Hutchins Hapgood, Bayard Boyesen (then secretary of the association and teacher of the adult school), Jaime Vidal, and Rose Pastor Stokes.

In January 1911 the Ferrer Modern School in New York opened at 6 St. Marks Place. Directed by Bayard Boyesen and organized first as an adult center, it moved to 104 East 12th Street on 1 October 1911, expanding its mission into a day school for children with John and Abby Coryell as teachers. In 1911, a school was also opened in Portland, Oregon, by William Thurston Brown after the school in Salt Lake City folded. Modern Schools were also organized in San Francisco, Detroit, and elsewhere during this period.

The New York Ferrer Modern School, the flagship of the association, became a center for radicalism and activism in New York, bringing together revolutionary anarchists, syndicalists, socialists, and freethinkers. The Kōtoku Protest Defense Committee Fund was established there in 1910, and the Syndicalist Educational League, in 1912. The unemployed movement, and especially The Conference of the Unemployed, were based in the center. A Mexican revolutionary committee was established at the center in 1911, and the Anti-Militarist League was founded there in 1914. Speakers at the center included Elizabeth Gurley Flynn, who spoke on "Women and Syndicalism," and Margaret Sanger, who spoke on "Family Limitation" and organized a series of Mother Meetings to discuss birth control. The school also supported and raised funds for the

Lawrence strike (1912), the Paterson strike (1913), the Ludlow strike (1913–1914), and the New York unemployment movement (1913–1914).

The school also served as a center for art and creativity. Art classes were taught by Robert Henri and George Bellows, and a Free Theatre was organized by Moritz A. Jagendorf. Leonard Abbott often taught English and drama classes, and Adolf Wolff composed his first poems in one of his classes. In December 1912 the center held an art exhibit that included the work of Manuel Komroff, Helen West, Ben Benn, Gilbert Stodola, and Man Ray (Ray's illustrations became the covers for two issues of *Mother Earth* and were printed in the *Modern School*). In 1912 the *Monthly News Letter* of the association became the magazine the *Modern School*, edited by Lola Ridge, then by Leonard Abbott, Harry Kelly, William Thurston Brown, Carl Zigrosser, and Frank V. Anderson.

On 1 October 1912 the Ferrer Center moved to a larger and more central location at 63 East 107th Street, where it remained until 1918. In 1913 Joseph Cohen moved from Philadelphia to New York City. Working first as a janitor at the Ferrer Center, by December 1913 he was manager of the center. During this time the political groups based at the school proliferated, often overshadowing the children's school. After the Lexington Avenue explosion of 4 July 1914, which killed three Ferrer Center regulars, tensions mounted along with an influx of police spies and informers, newspaper reporters, and even tourists who had come to gawk at anarchists. The Ferrer Association, in an effort to distance the school and center from the explosion, issued a leaflet, *To the People*, shortly after the event in which it claimed (incorrectly) that those killed in the explosion were not members of the association and stated that the Ferrer Center was neither a bomb factory nor a place of militant anarchists but simply a center for libertarian education. Also in the wake of the explosion, Alden Freeman, fearful of any association with violence, withdrew his significant financial support of the association. Others who distanced themselves from the association included Upton Sinclair, J. G. Phelps Stokes, and Cora Bennett Stephenson, who resigned from her position as principal and teacher of the children's day school.

Although 1915 was essentially a successful year for the school, residual problems from the Lexington explosion continued to permeate the school and the center. In trouble financially, the association was unable to escape its reputation as a bomb factory. As early as the summer of 1914, Harry Kelly had considered moving the school away from New York and into the country. On 15 March 1915 the association took official possession of land in New Jersey and on 16 May 1915 the day school officially moved to Stelton, New Jersey.

A conference of radical delegates from New York, Philadelphia, Newark, Paterson, and New Brunswick, held at Stelton on 15 June 1916, founded the Modern School Association of North America to maintain and sustain the Stelton school. The Francisco Ferrer Association was somewhat weakened but continued to function as a minor association, maintaining its connections to the Ferrer Center in New York until the demise of the center in 1918. Harry Kelly served as first chairman of the Modern School Association, and Leonard Abbott, as secretary; Joseph Cohen, Mary Hansen, Stewart Kerr, and Dr. C. L. Andrews were members. From 1916 on, Stelton was the site of the annual convention of the Modern School Association of North America.

**Free Speech League** The Free Speech League, first organized on 1 May 1902, was formally incorporated on 7 April 1911 in New York. Its stated purpose was "to end, by all lawful means, to oppose every form of government censorship over any method for the expression, communication or transmission of ideas." Theodore Schroeder and Leonard Abbott led the movement to consolidate and incorporate the league, hoping to give it a more permanent status. At the time of incorporation Abbott served as president; Brand Whitlock, mayor of Toledo, Ohio, vice president; Dr. E. B. Foote Jr., secretary; and Gilbert Roe, treasurer. Schroeder served as author and lawyer, and Lincoln Steffens, Bolton Hall, Edwin Cox Walker, and Hutchins Hapgood were active members.

The league sponsored meetings and lectures, organized legal defenses of free speech, and, under Schroeder's direction, published and circulated literature. EG was closely connected to the Free Speech League; she often contributed the proceeds of her lectures to the league, used *Mother Earth* to solicit contributions, and worked to raise public awareness about the activities of the Free Speech League.

The league provided legal and financial support for political activists, sex radicals, and free-thinkers. It supported the free speech cases of Jay Fox in 1911–1915, Margaret Sanger in 1914–1916, Rebecca Edelsohn, the Tarrytown protesters in 1914 with Leonard Abbott a special advocate, and a host of other radicals (the league, and Leonard Abbott especially, was involved at all levels in the Tarrytown protests). Local and regional Free Speech League branches included the 1912 California Free Speech League, organized at the start of the San Diego IWW free speech fight, in the week following the 8 January 1912 passage of an anti-street-speaking ordinance within the city limits of San Diego. The executive committee of the league included members of the IWW, the Socialist Party, and labor unions and religious organizations; Wood Hubbard, an IWW member, was sec-retary; Casper Bauer, a Socialist Party member, treasurer; and E. E. Kirk, staff attorney. The New York Free Speech League offered financial assistance to the California league, publicized the San Diego case, and supplied the group with free speech literature. During a 1914 IWW free speech fight in which EG and BR were engaged, a Denver Free Speech League was formed with Ellen Kennan as president. The Free Speech League was a critical support for EG during her annual lecture tours, defending her from the frequent and erratic arbitrary barring of her talks by local government and police. See also vol. 2, *Making Speech Free*.

The Free Speech League's work can be measured by its remarkable array of publications. See the bibliography of its publications in Publications of the Free Speech League, 1910–1919.

**Industrial Workers of the World (IWW)** The IWW was a union based on the principles of organiza-tion by industry and of class struggle, rather than of craft unionization. Organized in 1905 by left-wing members of the Socialist Party, members of the Socialist Labor Party, anarchists, and militant unionists, by 1910 the IWW had changed its preamble to remove any reference to political action, and the Western Federation of Miners, one of the driving forces behind its creation, had withdrawn from the organization. During this period the IWW focused its organizing campaigns primarily on migrant workers in the West and unskilled industrial workers in the East.

Free speech fights, which began in 1909 and spread quickly throughout the West and Midwest, were fought when city authorities attempted to prevent Wobblies (IWW members) from holding street meetings. IWW newspapers called for members across the country to flood into identified towns and clog the jails. Locations of free speech fights included Missoula, Montana (1909); Spokane, Washington (1909–1910); Fresno, California (1910–1911); San Diego, California (1912); Denver, Colorado (1912–1913); Kansas City, Missouri (1914); and Everett, Washington (1916–1917). *Mother Earth* frequently covered news of IWW free speech fights, especially the 1912 fight in San Diego, as EG was prevented from speaking in the city and BR was abducted by vigilantes and severely beaten.

This was a particularly rich period of IWW activity: The union was organizing workers in the textile, agriculture, mine, lumber, construction, marine transport, and other industries. The IWW had branches in Australia, New Zealand, Canada, and England. The IWW's first significant labor victory was the Lawrence, Massachusetts, textile strike, which broke out in January 1912 and was primarily led by the Italian branch of the IWW local. Before the strike the unskilled, non-English-speaking immigrant men and women who were the majority of workers in Lawrence were not unionized. The AFL felt that it was impossible to organize in Lawrence because of its multi-ethnic population of Italians, Poles, Russians, Syrians, and Lithuanians. The strike was marked by clashes between strikers and the police and militia, but on 14 March strikers voted to return to work and accept the wage-increase settlement offered by the American Woolen Company. This success was followed by IWW victories in textile mills in Lowell, Massachusetts; New Bedford, Massachusetts; and Little Falls, New York.

In 1913 the IWW became involved in a strike in Paterson, New Jersey, another textile center. Discontent had been brewing for a year, and it erupted into a mass strike in late February. Although the strike gained much outside support, including that of the radical and liberal middle class in New York City, it was ultimately unsuccessful. This event, and the failure of strikes of rubber workers in Akron, Ohio, and auto workers in Detroit, Michigan, during the same year, contributed to the discussion in the IWW press over the effectiveness of the union in the industrial East. One correspondent in the 6 February 1914 edition of Solidarity remarked, "It is obvious from the present conditions of our locals that we have failed to hold organizations which were effected during strikes at McKees Rocks, Lawrence, Paterson, Akron, and other places. We enroll a large membership during a strike. . . . But in all this chain of revolutionary thinking there seems to be a weak link that gives way almost as soon as the last mass meeting is held and the strikers return to work."

One exception, however, was the Marine Transport Workers Union, which was strong in Philadelphia as well as New York. In April 1913 the Marine Firemen Oilers and Water Tenders' Union (MFOWTU) of the Atlantic and Gulf, with an estimated 25,000 members, voted to affiliate with the IWW. The local in New York City, which was Spanish dominated, had close ties with the anarchist movement. When the affiliation did not materialize, many anarchists in New York left the MFOWTU and helped organize the IWW Marine Transport Workers Industrial Union. Robert Lee Warwick, secretary-treasurer of the local Marine Transport Workers Union in 1913 and editor of the radical newspaper the Social War, was an anarchist. Jaime Vidal, a leading labor organizer and secretary of the New York City MFOWTU local before the proposed IWW affiliation, was a Spanish anarchist, co-founder of the Ferrer Association, and personal friend of Francisco Ferrer. Max Baginski published a German-language newspaper, Internationale Arbeiter Chronik (seven issues, 30 March–23 September 1914), in collaboration with the union. The Marine Transport Workers Industrial Union Local 8 controlled most of the Philadelphia waterfront. After a two-week strike in 1913 the longshoremen won a ten-hour workday, a pay increase, time and a half for overtime, and double-time on Sundays and holidays. IWW organizing would have equal successes in the western United States in subsequent years.

Until the foundation of the Agricultural Workers Organization (AWO) in April 1915 IWW efforts to organize agricultural workers had been ineffectual. The AWO organized the migrant farm workers of the grain belt and the fertile West. At the formation conference, held in Kansas City on 21 April 1915, delegates decided that organizers would employ the job delegate system, in which organizers worked on the job, recruiting members, collecting dues, and distributing literature, rather than street-speaking in town centers. At the 1916 convention, the delegate system was acknowledged as a recruiting tactic that brought in thousands of new members. The IWW published propaganda in multiple languages to reach the large immigrant-worker population. The AWO, which signed up nearly 20,000 members in its first years, proved so profitable financially that it helped nurture other sections of the IWW. The IWW also made significant gains in the southern and northwestern timber industries. In the South the IWW was affiliated with the Brotherhood of Timber Workers, an interracial union, which was responsible for the unsuccessful Merryville, Louisiana, strike of 1912–1913. In the lumber camps of the Northwest the Lumber Workers Industrial Union adopted the job delegate system from the AWO, which proved as effective among lumber workers as it had in agricultural work.

The IWW also made efforts to organize mine workers in the Midwest. It participated in the Mesabi Range strike in Minnesota in 1916, which eventually failed as strikers returned to work, but the companies did implement some of the strikers' demands. The strike also resulted in the arrest of IWW organizers as accessories to the murder of a deputy sheriff and an innocent bystander. The charges were later dropped. IWW members were frequently prosecuted by states on various charges and treated as martyrs of the class struggle by the IWW. IWW organizer and songwriter Joe Hill was executed by the state of Utah in 1915 for his murder conviction. Other cases of IWW members being prosecuted include Ettor and Giovannitti (Massachusetts, 1912), Little Falls defendants (New York, 1913), Ford and Suhr (California, 1913–1914), Rangel and Cline (Texas, 1913–1915), and the Everett defendants (Washington, 1916–1917).

Although the IWW was not an anarchist organization, some members were anarchists or sympathetic to various anarchist campaigns. English-language IWW newspapers, such as *Solidarity* and *Industrial Worker,* reported on EG, AB, Lucy Parsons, Francisco Ferrer, the Modern School movement, and the Kōtoku Shūsui Defense Fund. Every November the IWW press published articles in remembrance of the Haymarket anarchists. Many anarchists, including EG and AB, collected money for IWW strikes, free speech fights, and defense funds (see Fund Appeals Directory in *Mother Earth*). IWW members in the West closely worked with the anarchist Partido Liberal Mexicano (Mexican Liberal Party) and participated in the Baja Revolution in 1911. When the United States faced an economic crisis in 1913, the IWW helped organize unemployed workers in protest. In January 1914 Lucy Parsons and IWW members were arrested in San Francisco after she attempted to speak to a group of unemployed men and women. The IWW Unemployed Union of New York worked with the anarchist-organized Conference for the Unemployed in New York City from 1913 to 1915. Arthur Caron, an anarchist and IWW Unemployed Union member, was killed, along with Charles Berg and Carl Hanson, in the Lexington Avenue explosion on 4 July 1914, when a bomb intended for Rockefeller exploded in their tenement apartment in New York City.

Like EG and many other radicals during this period, the IWW was influenced by the ideas of European syndicalism. The IWW regularly presented the ideas of syndicalism, reported on the activities of the French syndicalist union Confédération Générale du Travail (CGT), sold syndicalist literature—including Andre Tridon's *The New Unionism* (New York, B. W. Huebsch, 1913) and Émile Pouget's *Sabotage* (Chicago: Charles H. Kerr, 1913)—and the *Industrial Worker* reprinted translated excerpts from the *Bulletin International du Mouvement Syndicaliste*. IWW men William Haywood and William Z. Foster separately visited Europe in 1910 and 1911 and met with syndicalists such as Tom Mann and leaders of the CGT. When Foster returned from Europe, convinced of the superiority of CGT tactics, he proposed that the IWW focus its energy on "boring from within" the AFL to radicalize American workers. Gaining little support, he and his sympathizers eventually left the IWW and formed the Syndicalist League of North America in 1912.

Despite the fact that the IWW removed any reference to political action from its constitution in 1908, many Wobblies retained their membership to the Socialist Party of America. At the 1912 national convention of the Socialist Party, right-wing leaders presented Article II, Section 6, an amendment to the party's constitution aimed at the IWW: "Any member of the party who opposes political action or advocates crime, sabotage, or other methods of violence as a weapon of the working class to aid in its emancipation, shall be expelled from membership in the party." The amendment was approved, and William D. Haywood, IWW organizer and Socialist Party national executive committee member, was recalled from his position in the party the following year. He later resigned. Thousands of other IWW supporters were expelled from the party for violating the anti-sabotage clause or withdrew because of their disgust over the recall.

"Sabotage" was a loose term for the IWW, used to describe any tactic employed by organized labor against the capitalist class, from striking on the job, to the slowing down of work, to property destruction. Graphics of the wooden shoe, borrowed from French syndicalists, and the "sab cat," used to represent sabotage, also entered IWW propaganda during this period. IWW members had always supported direct action and the methods of sabotage, but the IWW as an organization did not officially and directly advocate the use of "sabotage" until the 1914 annual convention, when a resolution was unanimously passed that instructed speakers to recommend using sabotage to workers. IWW literature on sabotage included *Sabotage: The Conscious Withdrawal of the Workers' Industrial Efficiency* (1915) by Elizabeth Gurley Flynn; *Sabotage: Its History, Philosophy and Function* (1913) by Walker C. Smith; and *Direct Action and Sabotage* (1912) by William E. Trautmann. The report of the 1912 annual convention, issued by the General Executive Board of the IWW, addressed the organization's position on violence. The report stated that if the capitalist class decided to use violence against workers the IWW would "cheerfully accept their decision and meet them to the best of our ability and we do not fear the result" ("Report of the General Executive Board of the Industrial Workers of the World," *Industrial Worker*, 14 October 1912, p. 4).

During this period the IWW was immersed in intense debate over the structure of the organization. Decentralists, mainly from the West, wanted greater local autonomy from the General Executive Board, which was centered in Chicago. B. H. Williams, editor of *Solidarity*, published the centralist "Constructive Program of the IWW" in the 7 June 1913 edition of the paper in an attempt to describe the union's ideal structural organization. Williams's description divided the one big union into six industry departments. These departments each presided over various national industrial unions, which were made up of the nation's IWW locals of a certain industry. Locals were also part of an industrial district council, which was a group of locals in a designated geographical area. In July 1913 tensions arose when the General Executive Board suspended decentralist Walker C. Smith as editor of the *Industrial Worker*, which was published in Spokane, Washington. Locals began boycotting the paper and refused to pay subscription fees. The *Industrial Worker* soon folded. The organization decided to discuss the issue at the eighth annual convention in September 1913. At the convention several western locals called for the abolition of the General Executive Board, a resolution that failed by a vote of 76 to 44. A resolution was passed that declared all publications of the IWW be under the supervision of the General Executive Board. At the tenth convention of the IWW, in November 1916, delegates made serious changes to the structure of the organization, as it was felt by many (particularly William D. Haywood) that the IWW must increase its work in practical union organization. The propaganda leagues were to be phased out, and any new members, unaffiliated with a local industrial union, were to become members of a "General Recruiting Union." In addition, much of the former autonomy of the national and local industrial unions was removed in favor of greater control by the central administration.

In 1916 the IWW formulated its official position on World War I. At the tenth convention a resolution was unanimously adopted that declared the IWW "determined opponents of all nationalistic sectionalism, or patriotism, and the militarism preached and supported by our one enemy, the capitalist class."

**International Association of Bridge and Structural Iron Workers** The International Association of Bridge and Structural Iron Workers (IABSIW) was the union for iron workers and builders of skyscrapers and bridges; it was affiliated with the American Federation of Labor. Formed in 1896 at a convention in Pittsburgh, the union had a reputation for aggressive tactics. The union had a strong and cordial relationship with the National Association of Manufacturers and Erectors of Structural Steel and Iron Work until 1905, when a strike was called against the American Bridge Company for its use of a nonunion subcontractor. In 1906 the manufacturers reorganized themselves as the National Erectors Association (NEA) and adopted a militantly open shop policy, in an effort to destroy the IABSIW. This led to a period of violent conflict between the union and the National Erectors Association. Between 1905 and 1910 the IABSIW dynamited about 150 NEA-affiliated buildings and bridges, without injury or loss of life, as part of an ongoing conflict over open and closed shops. Herbert Hockin, a member of the executive board of the union, became an informant for the private detectives of the National Erectors Association in late June of 1910.

In the spring of 1910 the conflict had shifted to California. California's Building Trades Council and other unions began a campaign to unionize Los Angeles, both to protect the sanctity of the closed shop in San Francisco and to extend the practice to Los Angeles. The steelworkers, whose strong union was known for its militancy, led the unionizing effort. On 1 June 1,500 metalworkers struck in Los Angeles. Other unions in the city were on strike for better wages and an eight-hour day. Then, on 1 October 1910, the building of the outspokenly anti-union *Los Angeles Times* was bombed. Dynamite was placed in the alley behind the building and ignited ink that was stored there, setting the building on fire and killing twenty-one people working inside. After an investigation by William J. Burns into the bombing, John J. McNamara, secretary-treasurer of the IABSIW, his brother, James B. McNamara, and Ortie McManigal were kidnapped by Burns detectives in Indianapolis and transported to Los Angeles, where they were arrested on charges of murder. McManigal confessed and agreed to testify against the McNamaras.

The McNamaras claimed innocence and were defended by labor leaders in Los Angeles and throughout the country, including Samuel Gompers and the American Federation of Labor. However, when the evidence against them seemed overwhelming, a deal was brokered between the McNamara brothers, their lawyer Clarence Darrow, and representatives of the Merchants and Manufactures Association in Los Angeles and their lawyers, with the help of Lincoln Steffens. Steffens, who had traveled to Los Angeles to cover the McNamara trial for the *New York Globe*, hoped to facilitate a compromise between labor and capital, both in the city and in the country at large by exposing the impetus for the dynamiting and the extent of responsibility on both sides, while promoting a shared desire for industrial peace. The deal mandated that in exchange for the McNamara brothers' guilty pleas, they would receive light sentences, no further charges would be brought against labor, and a truce in the ongoing war between labor and capital in Los Angeles would be called. On 1 December 1911 both brothers pleaded guilty, James McNamara to the *Los Angeles Times* bombing and John McNamara to complicity in dynamiting the Llewellyn Iron Works in Los Angeles on 25 December 1910. Their guilty pleas, three days before the city election, with one of their lawyers, socialist Job Harriman, the favorite for the office of mayor, resulted in a general upset among labor and Harriman's defeat. James McNamara was sentenced to life in prison and John McNamara to fifteen years of hard labor. Soon after, in Indianapolis in 1913, thirty-eight members and supporters of the IABSIW—including its president, Frank Ryan, and all but two members of the executive board, plus O. A. Tvietmoe and Anton Johannsen of the San Francisco Building Trades Council—were found guilty of transporting dynamite across state lines and sentenced to one to seven years in prison. (Charges against Tvietmoe and Johannsen were later dropped.) The next year David Caplan and Matthew Schmidt also were arrested and prosecuted for their alleged part in the *Los Angeles Times* bombing. EG defended the McNamara brothers and chastised other labor leaders, organizations, and especially Lincoln Steffens for his naïve sacrifice of them.

**International Workers' Defense League**  The International Workers' Defense League (IWDL) was formed in 1912 in San Francisco, the first of a loose network of workers' defense leagues organized by radical labor to defend their imprisoned members. The IWDL was officially composed of delegates from local trade unions, especially those with radical influence. The San Francisco branch was particularly strong: Thomas J. Mooney (who became secretary of the league after December 1913), Selig Schulberg, David Milder, Anton Johannsen, Eric B. Morton, and Edward D. Nolan were all active in the IWDL. The IWDL helped defend Mooney after his arrest for harboring dynamiting equipment and guns in a boat in Richmond, California, and Warren K. Billings after his arrest for transporting dynamite in Sacramento in 1913. The IWDL also helped to defend Joseph J. Ettor and Arturo Giovannitti, Joe Hill, Ricardo and Enrique Flores Magón, Mother Jones, the IWW defendants in the Calumet, Michigan, mine strike, the Wheatland Wobblies, and David Caplan and Matthew A. Schmidt. By 1916 the league had active locals in Chicago, Denver, Detroit, Kansas City, Los Angeles, New York, Pittsburgh, San Francisco, and St. Louis. In 1915 AB worked actively for the defense of Caplan and Schmidt, speaking in May under the auspices of the league in San Francisco with Lincoln Steffens, Nolan, and Schulberg, and later that year embarking on a lecture tour to establish local branches to aid Caplan and Schmidt. Following the San Francisco Preparedness Day bombing on 22 July 1916, the IWDL, having been inactive for a brief period, was revived by EG, AB, M. E. Fitzgerald, former IWDL members Schulberg and Milder, and Robert Minor, who became secretary and later treasurer of the league. Shortly after Billings's conviction in October 1916 AB left San Francisco for New York City to raise funds on behalf of the IWDL. By mid-November, a New York City publicity committee of the IWDL was working to publicize the case of Thomas and Rena Mooney, Warren Billings, Edward Nolan, and Israel Weinberg.

**Kōtoku Defense Committee**  The Kōtoku Defense Committee was formed after the arrest of three protesters, Benjamin Weinstein, Simon Frieman, and Victor Flasseur, in New York during the Kōtoku Protest Conference on 29 January 1911. The Kōtoku Protest Conference, called in response to the execution of Kōtoku and the eleven other Japanese anarchists convicted of high treason, was organized by the local New York Socialist Labor Party and attended by many socialists and anarchists. The meeting was chaired by Bayard Boyesen and included speeches by Louis C. Fraina, Simon P. Abbott, Carl Samenberg, Simon O. Pollack, James Schlossberg, S. Yanovsky, B. Rosson, and AB. The conference resolved to condemn the brutality of the Japanese government, to avenge the martyrs' deaths "by the abolition of class rule and despotism," and, in the spirit of Kōtoku and his comrades, to carry forward the struggle for freedom.

Upon conclusion of the meeting the audience decided to confront the Japanese consul and began marching down the street. The police stopped the procession and arrested Weinstein, Frieman, and Flasseur, charging them with unlawfully parading and inciting to riot. The Kōtoku Defense Committee sent out a circular shortly after the meeting, announcing the formation of the committee and calling for donations to the fund. Those listed on the Defense Committee of the Conference included L. C. Fraina, Carl Samenberg, Hippolyte Havel, AB, Jaime Vidal, BR, Edmondo Rossini, Antonio Crivello, S. Fine, EG, and Rose Strunsky. The committee's two objectives were to aid the arrested protesters and to send financial assistance to the families of the Tokyo martyrs. AB, the committee's treasurer, gathered contributions from Nunia Seldes, Rose Pastor Stokes, Dr. C. L. Andrews, Carl Schmidt, Emma Clausen, Leonard Abbott, W. E. Jackson, and C. T. Takahashi (SLP member and editor of the Japanese-language paper *Revolution* in Chicago), among others. The Kōtoku Defense Fund was first publicized in the February 1911 *Mother Earth*. Hippolyte Havel wrote several articles in *Mother Earth* praising Kōtoku's life and condemning the trial, as well as an article in the *New York Call*, "Facts Regarding Japanese Radicals" (28 November 1910). The Kōtoku protests began after an article, signed by EG, Hippolyte Havel, AB, BR, and Sadakichi Hartmann, was published in the 12 November 1910 issue of the *New York Call*. The first public meeting to protest the Japanese treason trial was held 12 December 1910 at Lloyd Hall. The chairman, Leonard Abbott, read telegrams from Jack London, Eugene Debs, and Hulda Potter Loomis. Speakers included EG and Bayard Boyesen, accompanied by Grace Potter, Arthur Bullard, Hippolyte Havel, Saul Yanovsky, Arturo Caroti, Jaime Vidal, Max Baginski, Michel Dumman, and Vaclar Rejesk.

**Liberal Club** The liberal movement, organized on the principles of freethought, was devoted primarily to countering and protesting the dominant role of organized religion in state affairs. The national movement cohered at the first Centennial Congress of Liberals, in Philadelphia on 4 July 1876, where members ratified a constitution that promoted the adoption of a religious freedom amendment to the federal Constitution, along with a platform that included advocacy of public control of railroads, cessation of the sale or grant of public land, and legislation giving workers the right to organize. In 1884 the National Liberal League split into two factions, divided by the conflict between those who favored further involvement in social and political initiatives and those who campaigned strictly for the secularization of the state. Following this split, one faction of the Liberal Club renamed itself the American Secular Union, with its own constitution and organizational structure, leaving those who favored a broader social agenda to work through regional and local branches of the Liberal Club.

The New York Liberal Club, also known as the Manhattan Liberal Club, was founded in 1869 as an open forum on politics. The club sold radical literature, including *Mother Earth*. Between 1910 and 1916, ideological differences, including the admission of African American members, issues of sexual morality, and fear of a "feminist takeover" by Henrietta Rodman, led to the resignation of the cabinet, including Reverend Grant (president), Mrs. James Wright (second vice president), Everett Hamilton (treasurer), and Edith Hamilton (secretary), eventually breaking up the club in October 1913. Edith Hamilton identified three factions: the Greenwich Villagers, the socialists, and the ascensionists (the more conservative faction named after Reverend Grant's Church of the Ascension). The radical branch of the club moved to Greenwich Village after 1913, settling at 137 MacDougall Street, above Polly Halladay's restaurant. Greenwich Village members included president Ernest Halcombe and his wife Grace Potter, John Reed, Max Eastman, AB, Hippolyte Havel, Hutchins Hapgood, Horace Traubel, Sinclair Lewis, Floyd Dell, Theodore Dreiser, Upton Sinclair, Lincoln Steffens, Harry Kemp, Edna St. Vincent Millay, Louise Bryant, Theodore Schroeder, Gilbert Roe, Rebecca Edelsohn, and E. B. Foote Jr. The club hosted a wide range of lecturers—including EG—who addressed the issues of anarchism and free love and protested against the arrest of Tannenbaum in 1914. Club activities included dances, socials, and plays produced and directed by Floyd Dell, with the Washington Square Players and the Provincetown Players.

Liberal clubs often provided EG with lecture venues. Other liberal organizations active at this time included the Harlem Liberal Alliance. Theodore Schroeder was an important member, and both EG and Voltairine de Cleyre lectured at the Harlem Liberal Alliance hall. The 1910 inaugural meeting of the Francisco Ferrer Association also took place at the Harlem hall. The Brooklyn Philosophical Association and the Sunrise Club (founded by individualist anarchist E. C. Walker), also hosted EG's lectures. The Los Angeles Liberal Club, an important West Coast liberal group, was presided over by both Charles Sprading and Claude Riddle. See also vols. 1 and 2.

**The Open Forum** The Open Forum was organized in San Diego in response to the free speech fight of 1912. It was founded by George Edwards, a local musician who had offered EG his hall during her 1912 visit, and A. Lyle de Jarnette, a Baptist minister. By 1915 de Jarnette was delivering lectures with titles that echoed those of the anarchists, including "No God No Master." According to Edwards, the membership of the San Diego Open Forum quickly grew to several hundred, and by 1915 when EG returned to San Diego, she delivered three undisturbed lectures there. Other halls and meeting places of the same name were relatively common at this time, such as an Open Forum Hall in St. Louis, and the Open Forum in Chicago, led by anarchist Hulda Potter Loomis. "Open forum" may have been a code for clubs or groups that promoted free speech.

**Partido Liberal Mexicano (PLM; Mexican Liberal Party)** The Partido Liberal Mexicano united as the most radical opposition to the dictatorship of Porfirio Díaz and was responsible for the coordination of the unsuccessful 1906 and 1908 uprisings in Mexico. The Junta Organizador del Partido Liberal Mexican (Organizing Board of the Mexican Liberal Party) was officially announced in *Regeneración* (which became the official organ of the PLM) on 25 September 1906. The board consisted of Rosalio Bustamante, Enrique and Ricardo Flores Magón, Librado Rivera (1864–1932), Juan (1882–1920) and Manuel Sarabia, and Antonio I. Villarreal (1879–1944).

When Francisco Madero, Mexican presidential candidate in exile in the United States, issued his Plan of San Luis Potosí, calling for revolution to begin on 20 November 1910, the PLM hoped to use this planned uprising to its advantage. Such hopes were to no avail. In a 16 November 1910 circular the PLM distanced itself from Madero's Anti-Reelectionst Party, anticipating the confusion that might ensue upon its own simultaneous armed uprisings with Madero's revolt. Praxedis G. Guerrero, a skilled PLM military leader, was killed early in the fighting in Chihuahua, on 30 December 1910. The PLM's inadequate leadership ultimately dispersed PLM groupings to join forces with other revolutionaries, leaving northern Baja California as the only territory controlled by the PLM.

Following Madero's arrest of PLM militants in Guadalupe, Chihuahua, *Regeneración* (25 February 1911) published a denunciation of Madero, proclaiming him "a traitor to the cause of liberty" and suggesting that they had not fought against Díaz in order to empower another dictator. Many United States socialists took issue with this stance, among them the editors of the *New York Call* (27 February 1911), who criticized the PLM for dividing the anti-Díaz forces.

On 3 April 1911 the PLM issued a Manifesto to the Workers of the World. The manifesto advocated direct action, expropriation, worker and peasant solidarity, and destruction of government. However, because the PLM did not want to lose socialist support, it continued to avoid describing itself as anarchist, sending appeal letters to Eugene V. Debs. Socialists, however, were beginning to be more critical of the PLM. Debs, in an article in *Appeal to Reason* (19 August 1911), while supporting the courage of the PLM, complained that it had insulted the Socialist Party, and he challenged the PLM to openly identify itself as anarchist.

On 13 June 1911 representatives of Madero, including Jesus Flores Magón (Enrique and Ricardo's older brother) and Juan Sarabia, met with the PLM junta in Los Angeles in an effort to form an alliance between the two forces. The PLM, however, refused to lay down its arms until the peasants and workers had seized the means of production. The next day, Ricardo and Enrique Flores Magón and several others were arrested for violation of the neutrality laws. Although briefly released on bail, Ricardo and Enrique Flores Magón, Librado Rivera, and Anselmo Figueroa were convicted, and imprisoned until 19 January 1914. During this time Teodoro Gaytán, Blas Lara, and William C. Owen continued intermittently to publish *Regeneración*.

The PLM finally issued a new manifesto on 23 September 1911 to replace the 1906 program. The manifesto called upon the Mexican people to take control of the land, factories, and means of transportation without waiting for legal sanctions. The document attacked the "somber trinity" of "Capital, Authority, and the Church," and was, in essence, anarchist. (The document was published in the March 1912 *Mother Earth*.)

Although the precise political identification of the PLM appeared vague, most United States anarchists, unlike the socialists, continued to support it. Voltairine de Cleyre, who found "more anarchism in *Regeneración* in a week's issue than the rest of our publications put together," actively supported the PLM by speaking, raising funds, selling pamphlets, and organizing the Chicago Mexican Liberal Defense League. Anarchists in New York organized a Mexican Revolution Conference in 1911, which held weekly meetings at the Ferrer Center and organized mass meetings with speakers, including anarchists Harry Kelly, Jaime Vidal, Max Baginski, Leonard Abbott, William Thurston Brown, AB, and EG. William C. Owen became editor of the English-language page of *Regeneración*, replacing Ethel Duffy Turner, in the 15 April 1911 issue, and the IWW *Industrial Worker* continued through 1911 to support the PLM as authentic Mexican revolutionaries, calling Madero a "fake."

EG's support for the PLM through this time was consistent and continuous. *Mother Earth* frequently carried news of events in Mexico as well, serving as an important English-language source of information on the subject. It published the above-mentioned manifesto, reports on the frequent arrests of members of the junta, articles by William C. Owen, and a report of the Chicago Mexican Liberal Defense League. It also supported the Flores Magón brothers during their 1916 imprisonment (see below). EG often spoke on behalf of the Mexican Revolution and donated the proceeds from her lectures to the PLM.

Although by this time the PLM was receiving support from anarchists and left-wing socialists in the United States, when the Flores Magón brothers were released, the organization had already lost much of its support in Mexico. Most PLM supporters had since aligned themselves with various opposition leaders in Mexico, not in exile. From abroad the PLM denounced the various men who came to power, although its influence was waning.

Still, the continued agitation of *Regeneración* worried the Mexican government, then headed by Venustiano Carranza. Mexican agents filed a complaint with the U.S. Postal Service, which led to the indictment of the Flores Magón brothers and William C. Owen on 18 February 1916, on three counts of mailing "indecent" material. Although Owen was in Washington State and escaped arrest by traveling to New York and then London, the Flores Magón brothers were arrested. Unable to raise their $8,000 bail, the brothers remained in jail. Although EG had sent money for their defense, it was not until her arrival in Los Angeles in June 1916 that she was able to raise the necessary funds at her lectures for their bail. In addition, throughout 1916 *Mother Earth* published frequent letters from Enrique Flores Magón, and EG continued collections at her lectures on the brothers' behalf. See also vol. 2, *Making Speech Free*.

**Provincetown Players** Provincetown, Massachusetts, situated on the tip of Cape Cod, was a summer gathering place for radical artists and writers, including the authors George Cram Cook and his wife Susan Glaspell. Cook and Glaspell were proponents of the new "little theater" movement, influenced by the Free Theatre at the Ferrer Modern School in New York, the Washington Square Players, and Maurice Browne's Little Theater in Chicago. In the summer of 1915 the couple—along with Neith Boyce and Hutchins Hapgood, John Reed, Louise Bryant, Mary Heaton Vorse and her husband Joe O'Brian, Bror Nordfeldt, Wilbur Daniel Steele, and Ida Rauh and her husband Max Eastman—met informally to write and produce their own work. Robert Edmond Jones designed the set for the performances of the plays, which were written by and for the amusement of the group of friends, and they changed their venue to a fish house at the end of a wharf that had been the studio of Joe O'Brian and Mary Heaton Vorse. George Cook introduced the idea of a public collective theater. The following summer (1916) many Greenwich Villagers flocked to Provincetown to participate in the new theater as writers, performers, and members of an eager audience. Founding members also included Stella Comyn Ballantine and her actor husband Teddy Ballantine, Grace Potter, and Harry Weinberger, who acted as the group's attorney. The Provincetown Players opened 13 July 1916 to a full house. After their initial success, the anarchist Terry Carlin suggested they perform the plays of his roommate, Eugene O'Neill.

In the fall of 1916 the Provincetown Players moved to a theater in Greenwich Village at 139 MacDougal Street, next door to the New York Liberal Club and Polly Holladay's restaurant, located at 137 MacDougal Street, and near the Washington Square Bookstore at 135 MacDougal Street. The first Greenwich Village performance by the Provincetown Players included three one-act plays, O'Neill's *Bound East of Cardiff*, Louise Bryant's *The Game*, and Floyd Dell's *King Arthur's Socks*. Both EG and M. Eleanor Fitzgerald attended the plays, and Fitzgerald would later become business manager of the group. The Provincetown Players was an innovative force in the history of American theater and one of the first successful noncommercial theater groups, fostering the early works of a number of Pulitzer Prize–winning playwrights.

**Radical Library** The Ladies Liberal League in Philadelphia joined the Radical Library around 1895, and, guided by Voltairine de Cleyre and her friends, worked to "repair a deficit in the public libraries by furnishing radical works upon all subjects at convenient hours for working men and accessible to all at only a slight expense." By 1905 the Ladies Liberal League had disbanded, and Philadelphia anarchist Natasha Notkin, who had been the caretaker of the library, passed the books on to Joseph Cohen, a former student of de Cleyre.

Cohen started a new group, which settled at 424 Pine Street. The newly reconfigured Radical Library, led by Cohen, became a center of Philadelphia anarchism. In 1906 the Radical Library and the Social Science Club sponsored a Paris Commune commemoration, at which Voltairine de Cleyre, George Brown, Frank Stephens, and Chaim Weinberg, as well as French and Italian anarchists, spoke. In 1910 Joseph Cohen and the Radical Library organized a Modern Sunday School and affiliated themselves with the Ferrer Association. That same year the Radical Library was the location of a Jewish anarchist conference from which the Anarchist Federation of America was formed. In 1911 the Radical Library became Branch 273 of the Arbeiter Ring in Philadelphia. During the 1912 Lawrence strike, members of the Radical Library offered temporary homes for the children of striking workers. The library organized a memorial meeting on the night of Voltairine de Cleyre's funeral; speakers included George Brown and Chaim Weinberg. In 1915 members of the library collected money to support AB's campaign for the Caplan-Schmidt Defense League. Into the 1960s the Radical Library maintained its historic roots as a branch of the Arbeiter Ring.

In other cities the name "Radical Library" was also used as a code as gathering places for anarchists. For a short time there was a Radical Progressive Library in New York, and in 1916 the International Radical Library of Chicago announced its formation under the guidance of secretary Max Charnick. The library included a reading room and circulating library with radical books and pamphlets, and it became the meeting place for a series of lectures on anarchism.

**Rangel-Cline Defense Fund** The Rangel-Cline Defense Fund was formed in Los Angeles in December 1913 to aid the defense of J. M. Rangel, Charles Cline, and twelve other members of the Partido Liberal Mexicano. The case brought together socialists, labor unions, IWW members, and anarchists to fight the prosecution of these revolutionists. Their case illustrates the conflict on both sides of the U.S.-Mexican border and the United States' active opposition to the Mexican Revolution. Rangel was a U.S. resident and a member of the Partido Liberal Mexicano (PLM) with a history of militant activity. In 1906 he had served two months in a Texas prison for violation of neutrality laws; in 1908 he had led a PLM attack on the town of Las Vacas that resulted in its temporary capture by the PLM and his subsequent arrest and sentence of eighteen months' imprisonment for violating neutrality laws; in January 1910 and in 1911 he was wounded in battle in Mexico and held as a prisoner of war for almost two years. Cline was an American IWW member and union organizer who had previously worked with lumber workers in Louisiana, as well as organized workers in Colorado, St. Louis, New York, and Boston. Cline joined a group of Mexican workingmen, including Rangel, who were PLM members and planned to cross the border to join the revolutionary activities in Mexico. The names of the other men were Miguel P. Martinez, Leonardo L. Vasquez, Jesus Gonzales, Jose Angel Serrato, Lino Gonzales, Jose Abraham Cisneros, Domingo R. Rosas, Bernardino Mendoza, Eugenio Alzalde, Luz Mendoza, Lucio R. Ortiz, Juan Rincon Jr., Jose Guerra, and Pedro Perales. They left Carriza Springs, Texas, on 11 September 1913. On 12 September the men were attacked by a sheriff and three deputies, and one of the Mexicans, Silvestre Lomas, was shot in the back of the head and killed. The PLM group counterattacked, taking two Texas deputies prisoner.

There are conflicting stories of what transpired next. In one account one of the prisoners,

Candelario Ortiz, attempted to escape and attacked one of the PLM members, Jose Guerra. Guerra, acting in self-defense, shot and killed Ortiz. Later that day PLM members agreed to hand over the other Texas deputy, Eugene Buck, in exchange for safe passage to the Mexican border. However, the following day, 13 September, an armed posse attacked the group, severely wounding two of its members and killing Juan Rincon Jr. and possibly Jose Guerra, who was missing. A second account asserts that Candelario Ortiz was killed in the shoot-out when the armed posse attacked.

In any case, the result was the arrest of all fourteen remaining PLM men, who were charged with the death of Ortiz; Rangel, Cline, Eugenio Alzalde, and Jose Abraham Cisneros faced the death penalty. *Mother Earth* made two appeals for the Rangel-Cline Defense Fund, and EG collected $12.50 at a lecture in Stockton, California, and $16.29 at a debate with Joseph Gilbert in Seattle, in 1914. She also participated in a benefit social for Rangel and Cline (and Ford and Suhr) in Portland in August 1914 at which $35 was raised. The Anti-Militarist League held a ball and bazaar on 24 October 1914, and part of the proceeds were sent to the Rangel-Cline Defense Fund.

The Rangel-Cline Defense Fund, which brought together trade unionists, socialists, IWW members, and anarchists, was organized by Charles Ashleigh, R. Wirth, Victor Cravello, P. Khan, M. Lerner, Frank Roney, Jaime Vidal, William C. Owen, M. Lerner, H. Stanley Calvert, M. Fasano, G. W. Stamm, Harry P. Alexander, B. Litoff, F. Baffa, W. B. Cook, Georgia Kotsch, and John Murray. Committee members included Victor Cravello, R. Wirth, Stanley M. Gue, Georgia Kotsch, Ricardo and Enrique Flores Magón, John Murray, and Frank Roney, while an advisory committee included Jack Zamford, A. J. Mooney, Arturo Giovannitti, Emanuel Julius, John Altman, Anton Johannsen, B. H. Williams, W. C. Owen, Cynthelia Kneefler, Eugene Debs, Leonard Abbott, and Margaret Sanger. All communications were to be sent to the committee's secretary, Victor Cravello. Another defense fund was started in April 1915 in San Antonio, closer to the prisoners, with contributions being sent to the secretary, Mrs. Vera Mayfield. Both groups worked to publicize the case and collect money for attorneys at the trials. The trial of Rangel and Cline, which began on 6 July 1914 in San Antonio, ended with J. M. Rangel receiving a ninety-nine-year sentence, which could not be appealed due to lack of funds. Cline was initially also given ninety-nine years, but his trial was appealed and a new trial ordered. Four men, alleged to have been minor offenders, were convicted and sentenced to terms ranging from twenty-five to ninety-nine years. In Cline's second trial he was sentenced to life imprisonment. In the end, four men were given ninety-nine-year sentences, three were given twenty-five-year sentences, two were given fifteen-year sentences, two were given ten-year sentences, and the remaining three were given sentences of six, five, and three years. In August 1926 all the men still alive, including Rangel and Cline, were released from prison on a full pardon from Governor Miriam "Ma" Ferguson.

**Single Tax** Single-tax doctrine is based on the idea that the private ownership of land is the fundamental source of social and economic injustice, evidenced by the fact that at that time the majority of wealth accrued to landlords rather than to those considered "the productive classes," encompassing both laborers and capitalists. Single-taxers advocated the elimination of the existing system of taxation in favor of a "single tax" on land, a strategy intended to end land speculation, create common land ownership, and abolish private property. Lifting the weight of taxation on productive industry would also increase wages, according to single-taxers. The single-tax movement achieved limited legislative success, although its theories retained a popular attraction for decades.

The single-tax movement emerged under the leadership of Henry George and Father McGlynn (who was expelled from the Catholic Church for his support of the single tax). Although the single-tax theory had taken root before, George proposed single tax as a solution to the land question and popularized the theory in *Our Land and Land Policy* (San Francisco: White and Bauer, 1871) and his landmark book *Progress and Poverty* (San Francisco: W. M. Hilton, 1879). Bolton Hall, G. Frank Stephens, A. C. Pleydell, and George Seldes linked the underlying principles of the single tax to anarchism. Supporters included mostly middle-class intellectuals and some populists and wealthy individuals.

The Great Adventure, a single-tax movement launched in 1915, was led by Luke North, editor of *Everyman*, and Herman Kuehn. The Great Adventure, which in 1916 was criticized by AB in *The Blast*, was a failed attempt during the 1918 election to amend the California constitution to incorporate the single tax. The Great Adventure was rooted in the 1913 Henning, Minnesota, proclamation by the Fellowship of Freedom, a group that included Kuehn and Joseph Labadie.

**Socialist Party of America (SPA)** The Socialist Party began to show more electoral strength in 1910, reaching its apex of power and influence from 1910 to 1912. This can in part be attributed to the tensions between the left and right wings of the party. Spurred on by the militancy and criticism of the left wing, the party took on new drive and activity. However, the right wing embraced reform as the official means of moving society toward socialism, and this appealed to many people who were attracted to the growing reform and progressive movements yet who seemed unsatisfied with the failure to provide any real economic or social change. Socialist Party members won various state and local elections, and in 1910 Victor Berger won a congressional seat for a Milwaukee district. Socialists won mayoral positions in cities such as Berkeley, California, and Butte, Montana, and party membership rose to its all-time high of nearly 150,000 by the May 1912 party convention. In his run for president that year Eugene V. Debs received 6 percent of the total vote.

The SPA during this time continued its involvement in the free speech fights. Socialist unions in Tacoma, Washington, helped prevent the passage of an ordinance curtailing free speech in 1911, and later that same year in Victoria, British Columbia, socialists helped the IWW crowd the jails and win the right to speak on the streets. However, amid the violence and bloodshed of the 1912 San Diego free speech fight many socialists such as John Spargo criticized free speech fighters as being vicious and criminal, and he questioned the benefit of these free speech battles to the labor movement. After debate within the party regarding the matter the national executive committee gave only $250 to the effort in San Diego.

SPA support of the Partido Liberal Mexicano (PLM) also waned. After initially being support-ive of the Magón brothers' cause, Debs and other socialists questioned their seemingly anarchist platform. *Appeal to Reason,* which initially devoted considerable space to the PLM's efforts, in 1911 began to criticize its refusal to openly announce its anarchism. The socialist *New York Call* criticized the PLM's break with Madero and argued, along with Debs, that they should maintain a united front to defeat Díaz. The July 1911 *Mother Earth* reprinted a statement from Victor Berger's secretary criticizing the PLM and its efforts in Baja California, calling the members anarchists and opposed to socialism. *Mother Earth* lambasted Berger and the socialists for working with Madero and not supporting the PLM. The Socialist Party was equally as unsupportive of the anarchist cause in America; as BR notes in the May 1911 *Mother Earth*, over the past three years EG was rarely allowed to speak in halls controlled by socialists.

Factionalism between the right and left in the party continued as William Haywood was criticized heavily by Morris Hillquit and others for advocating direct action and sabotage. Haywood was ultimately recalled from the party's national executive committee in January 1913 for remarks he made promoting direct action and sabotage. Haywood and many of his followers left the party, and membership dropped significantly. Also significant was the decline of socialist influence in labor unions, as well as the financial aid and support the party offered to unions. During the 1912 IWW-led Lawrence strike the SPA contributed notably to the strikers' relief fund and directed public attention to their cause, but the party's early support of the IWW-led Paterson strike in 1913 eventually turned to sharp criticism. The financial support given to similar strikes and labor defense cases had dropped by 1914 to nothing.

Following Haywood's recall, the party became even more electoral and reformist in nature and membership. Meyer London was elected to Congress in 1914 representing Manhattan's Lower East Side (New York's Twelfth District), which was an immigrant and working-class area. Debs refused to run for president in 1916, and the right wing nominated Allan Benson instead. Benson received only 3 percent of the total vote. Debs was clearly the party's best-known and most-popular leader. A member of the party's left wing, Debs had previously often tried to play the part of conciliator between the factions, calling for tolerance and understanding.

At the outbreak of the First World War the party initially maintained an official position of neutrality regarding the conflict, but in 1915 Hillquit drafted a series of proposals opposing the war. The major socialist publications during this period were *Appeal to Reason*, the *International Socialist Review*, and the *New York Call* (New York, 1909–1923, daily). All three took stands against the war and wanted the United States to stay out of the conflict. In 1917, however, *Appeal to Reason* supported the U.S. involvement in the war so as to avoid government repression and remain in business. The *Party Bulletin* (Chicago, 1912–1914, weekly) was a manifestation of the right wing's attempt at centralization of the party and was used mainly as an internal tool for the party to coordinate local activities.

**The Unemployed Movement** Beginning in winter 1913 and continuing through 1915 increasing numbers of people found themselves unemployed as a severe economic depression swept the United States. In New York demonstrations of the unemployed were common, with demands that the government aid their efforts to find work, shelter, and food. Organizers of the many demonstrations and rallies included Frank Strawn Hamilton, Charles Robert Plunkett, Arthur Caron, AB, and Frank Tannenbaum. In February 1914 Tannenbaum, an IWW member and Ferrer School supporter, led marches of unemployed workers to churches demanding food and shelter. The "church raids," as they became known, were initially successful, gaining food, shelter, and a cascade of publicity for the unemployed. On 4 March 1914 a crowd marched to St. Alphonsus Church, and the priest called the police. As the men dispersed, a newspaper photographer's flash bulb malfunctioned and was mistaken for gunfire, sparking chaos and fear. The police responded with force as men attempted to flee the scene. A minor riot ensued, and many were arrested, including Tannenbaum, who was fined for inciting to riot and sentenced to a year at Blackwell's Island. In response, and as the intensity of the unemployed movement grew, the number of protest demonstrations escalated. A Labor Defense Committee was founded by Elizabeth Gurley Flynn, Carlo Tresca, and William Haywood at Mary Heaton Vorse's apartment; the IWW Unemployed Union of New York was organized; and at the Ferrer Center the Conference of the Unemployed was formed, with Joseph Cohen as secretary. AB coordinated these groups and organized demonstrations (although in an article in the April 1914 *Mother Earth* he criticized prominent socialists and IWW leaders for refraining from joining Tannenbaum's defense or supporting the unemployed, singling out the *New York Call* for not printing a paid advertisement announcing the 21 May demonstration). On 21 March 1914, at AB's suggestion, the Conference of the Unemployed held a meeting addressed by EG and Carlo Tresca. The meeting ended with a peaceful march of 1,000 jobless up Fifth Avenue. On 4 April another meeting of the Conference of the Unemployed took place in Union Square, at which mounted police charged the protesters. Demonstrators, including Adolf Wolff, Arthur Caron, and IWW member Joe O'Carroll, were clubbed, beaten, and arrested. All those arrested were later released by a judge who was appalled at the amount of force used, especially on O'Carroll, who was beaten so badly that he spent a month in the hospital.

As the confrontational atmosphere increased, the slaughter of striking miners' families in Ludlow, Colorado, on 20 April 1914 at a mine owned by John D. Rockefeller Jr.'s Colorado Fuel and Iron Company escalated the level of militancy of the unemployed movement. The movement of the unemployed joined the Ludlow protest and the work of the Anti-Militarist League. Demonstrations focused on the sites of Rockefeller's business and property, prompting him to flee to his mansion near Tarrytown, New York, in fear of the many calls for revenge for the beaten unemployed and the murdered workers. Caron, AB, and others led demonstrations in May and June 1914 in Tarrytown, where protesters were repeatedly suppressed with force. In late June a plan by Ferrer Center affiliates to plant a bomb in Tarrytown was devised, intended to convey a threat to Rockefeller. The operation was organized, according to Charles Plunkett, by himself, Arthur Caron, Carl Hanson, Charles Berg, Louise Berger (Hanson's half sister), Becky Edelsohn, and AB (Paul Avrich, *Anarchist Voices: An Oral History of Anarchism in America* [Princeton, N.J.: Princeton University Press, p. 219]). The bomb exploded unexpectedly in the apartment of Louise Berger on 4 July, killing Caron, Hanson, Berg, and a nonparticipant, Marie Chavez. AB organized a mass memorial meeting on 11 July 1914 in Union Square, which brought together anarchists from New York and the surrounding area. At this meeting the suffering of the unemployed, the killings at Ludlow, the suppression of free speech, and the violence of the police were cited as the causes for the actions of those killed, who were dubbed as martyrs and heroes of the movement. EG was on the West Coast at the time, and she sent a telegram of support and condolence but was privately disturbed by the many overt calls to violence it sparked and by the overt confrontational attitude taken by AB and those at the memorial and later printed in the July *Mother Earth*. She also criticized the irresponsibility of Caron, Berg, and Hanson, who had stored the dynamite in a crowded tenement building where innocent people were subject to harm.

A less confrontational movement of the unemployed was under way in Chicago. The unemployed in that city had been organized since BR (who in 1908 had once been arrested and beaten by the police at an unemployed demonstration) founded a chapter of the International Brotherhood Welfare Association (IBWA) in 1907. The Brotherhood of the Unemployed, an IBWA offshoot, held weekly meetings at Hull House. As the number of unemployed workers continued to increase, the militancy of the movement also increased. On 17 January 1915 James Eads How, founder of the International Brotherhood Welfare Association, rented a hall at Hull House for a meeting and march of the Brotherhood of the Unemployed. After the speeches, 1,500 men, women, and children assembled on the streets. As they began to march, carrying banners that read "We Want Work; Not Charity," and "Give US This Day Our Daily Bread," police officers attempted to stop them, and a riot ensued. Twenty-one men and women were arrested, including the prominent Chicago socialist and priest Irwin St. John Tucker and Lucy Parsons. The next month (February 1915) *Mother Earth* published "Proclamation! To the City of Chicago," written by the Brotherhood of the Unemployed reaffirming its resolve. According to *Land and Liberty* (April 1915), the International Propaganda Group of Chicago issued an appeal to the American workingmen on the subject of unemployment, asking the workers not to trust organized labor but to demand that the "land, mines, mills, and factories shall be owned and controlled by the workers. What we want is an opportunity for every person—in return for a few hours of healthy and productive work—to enjoy a life worth living. This in no idle dream. By refusing to feed millionaires we can easily get rid of misery and poverty and live a wholesome life."

## Fund Appeals in *MOTHER EARTH*

**Aberdeen Free Speech Fund (December 1911)** On 2 August 1911 the city council in Aberdeen, Washington, passed an ordinance banning street speaking. Police arrested IWW members for violating the ban. On 24 November the city's mayor deputized several hundred local business-men. IWW members were arrested and escorted out of the city. The IWW called for men to go to Aberdeen to participate in the IWW free speech fight. The collection was used to feed men en route to Aberdeen. Funds were sent directly to Ed Gilbert in Tacoma, Washington. In January 1912 the free speech fight ended when the city council voted to set aside five streets for street speaking.

**Alexander Aldamas Defense Fund (October 1912 to January 1913)** Aldamas was a member of the Marine Firemen's Union in Brooklyn, New York. On 8 July 1912, during a strike against the Morgan steamship line, a brawl broke out; three police officers were shot, and Aldamas was arrested, charged with knifing a strikebreaker and shooting the three policemen. Allegedly tor-tured in jail, he maintained throughout his trial that he acted only in self-defense. All charges against him were dismissed except one, for which he was sentenced to one and a half years' impris-onment. Contributions were sent directly to Laureano Builes, treasurer of the Marine Firemen's Union, and later a defense committee was formed. AB and Harry Kelly served as the committee's co-secretaries, and Jaime Vidal was treasurer. Money was collected at EG's meetings: $50 from part of the proceeds of the Kropotkin jubilee meeting on 7 December 1912 in Carnegie Hall and almost $40 from a mass meeting for Aldamas organized by AB and sent to the defense committee. In a 1915 letter AB wrote, "Within two months of intense agitation, we changed the public mind on the matter that Aldamas was sentenced to one and half years instead of 40 years the District Attorney threatened us with, and instead even of the seven that the lawyers were quite ready to accept for him" (AB to Joe [illegible], 3 April 1915, Kate Sharpley Library).

**Anarchist Red Cross (October 1907 to 1916)** The Anarchist Red Cross of New York was created in 1907 to collect money and clothing to send to Russian political prisoners and exiles who were incarcerated after the 1905 revolution (see Directory of Organizations). The annual Prisoners' Balls were advertised regularly in *Mother Earth* (the first was in 1911). The organization was also funded by collections from EG's meetings.

**Anti-Conscription League (August 1915)** This appeal was sent out by *Freedom* (London). Mem-bership was open only to men who were eligible for conscription. Funds were collected by *Mother Earth* and forwarded to the league.

**Anti-Militarist League Fund (May to December 1914)** Initially listed in combination with the Unemployed Fund (see Unemployed and Anti-Militarist League Fund and Directory of Organizations). Collections financed the publication of literature and circulars and paid for advertisements for league events. The secretary-treasurer was AB. Leonard Abbott and Mary Heaton O'Brian were significant contributors. Collections were made by Rebecca Edelsohn, Louise Berger, and the Lettish Anarchist Red Cross. The Friends of Art and Education and the Brooklyn Anarchist Federation also contributed funds. Raffle tickets, general strike buttons, and pictures of the Adolf Wolff–designed urn with the ashes of the anarchists who died in the Lexington Avenue bomb were sold. The league held a fund-raising ball and bazaar on 24 October 1914; the event also included a one-act anti-militarist play by Adolf Wolff.

**Birth Control Defense Fund (May to October 1916)** In the May 1916 issue of *Mother Earth* BR recounted his arrest for discussing birth control methods and distributing pamphlets at a mass meeting in New York on 23 April. He made an appeal for funds to aid in the legal battles to defend the right to disseminate birth control information. Funds were collected at EG's meetings. Collections were sent to Leonard D. Abbott, secretary of the Birth Control Committee (see Directory of Organizations).

**The Blast Fund (September 1916)** *Mother Earth* called for contributions to be sent to AB in San Francisco after the *Blast* office was raided by police on 29 July. The funds were used to continue publication of the newspaper.

**Caminita Defense (January 1913)** Caminita Defense collected funds to aid the defense of Ludovico Caminita, an Italian anarchist who was arrested for displaying his satirical cartoon at the Social Library of Paterson, New Jersey. The cartoon depicted two wealthy Europeans, one sporting military medals, strolling past a row of hanged men in tattered robes. It was drawn in response to the atrocities the Italian government was allegedly committing against Arabs who, according to *Mother Earth*, "are guilty only of defending their firesides against robber invasion." Caminita's "crime" (he was arrested for "inciting to revolt against a friendly power") was punishable with a maximum sentence of fifteen years. He was released on $1,000 bail.

**Caplan-Schmidt Defense Fund/Caplan Defense Fund (July 1915 to December 1916)** The Caplan-Schmidt Defense Fund started when funds were requested by the Caplan-Schmidt Defense League (committee members included C. F. Grow, Edward D. Nolan, and Tom Barker). The fund's purpose was to defend David Caplan and Matthew Schmidt, who were arrested for conspiracy to blow up the *Los Angeles Times* building on 1 October 1910. Collections were made at AB's and EG's meetings, which garnered substantial trade union support, and by individuals, including Ellen Kennan, Gertrude Nafe, and John Spies. AB went on tour in summer 1915 specifically to raise funds for Caplan and Schmidt. Especially from September to December 1915 a groundswell of support materialized from individuals, organizations, and unions. Funds were also raised at mass meetings and from the Special Publicity Fund.

By March 1916 Schmidt had already been convicted, and the collection shifted exclusively to Caplan, becoming the Caplan Defense Fund. EG made special pleas in the March and April 1916 issues of *Mother Earth*, urging readers not to abandon Caplan after Schmidt's conviction. Luke North, editor of *Everyman*, collected funds for Caplan. In 1916 funds were raised at EG's and AB's meetings and at anarchists' socials in California and went directly to Caplan or to his legal aid.

**Collections [Flores] Magón Brothers (April to October 1916)** In the April 1916 issue of *Mother Earth*, Edgcumb Pinchon, the general secretary of the International Workers' Defense League of Los Angeles and member of the Partido Liberal Mexicano (PLM), announced the arrest of the Flores Magón brothers and requested funds for their defense. As editors of *Regeneración*, the Flores Magón brothers were indicted by a grand jury for using the mails to distribute material "tending to incite murder, arson, and treason." In June 1916 the men were convicted and sentenced to prison terms. Additional requests were published in the May and June issues. Collections were made at EG's meetings and forwarded to the Flores Magón brothers, who eventually were released on bail, raised by EG and AB.

**(Colorado) War Fund (May 1914)** The War Fund was formed to aid the Ludlow, Colorado, strikers in the "war between labor and capital," during the coal strike of 1913–1914. A series of violent conflicts had arisen between the strikers and hired strikebreakers, including the Colorado National Guard. On 20 April 1914 the National Guard opened fire on the strikers' tent colony at Ludlow, keeping up fire through the day and eventually setting the tents on fire. In what was known as the Ludlow Massacre several miners, twelve children, and two women were killed. A general state of labor insurrection followed until President Woodrow Wilson sent federal troops to Colorado on 30 April. By December 1914 the strike had been called off, with the union never gaining recognition and no indictments filed for the Ludlow deaths. The fund received a large contribution from the Russian Progressive Circle in America and from the Anti-Militarist League, which held daily collections to send "arms and ammunition" to the striking miners in Colorado.

**Contributions to Funeral Expenses of Those Killed in 4 July 1914 Bombing on Lexington Avenue (September 1914)** On 4 July 1914 an explosion on Lexington Avenue, New York, killed three young anarchists: Arthur Caron, Charles Berg, and Carl Hanson; Marie Chavez, who had attended occasional lectures at the Ferrer Center, was also killed. The men had been involved in a conspiracy to bomb Rockefeller's estate, and the dynamite in their tenement had been ignited accidentally. AB planned a public funeral and procession, which was prohibited by the police. Instead, the bodies were cremated and a small funeral was held in Queens. On 11 July a mass memorial took place in Union Square. The next day the urn holding their ashes was displayed at the *Mother Earth* office, where thousands of mourners filed through to view it; it was later displayed at the Ferrer Center. A huge number of contributions poured in from individuals and some groups. Many politically sympathetic groups and individuals contributed to the fund, including the Anarchist International Federation, Group Pietro Gori, Leonard Abbott, Jacob Margolis, John Rompapas, Annie and Jake Livshis, and William English Walling. The funds were recorded as totaling $624.37.

**Defense Committee for the Butte Mine Workers (January 1915)** On 13 June 1914 the annual Miners' Union Day celebration in Butte, Montana, turned into a riot. A mob of miners, frustrated by the inability of the Western Federation of Miners (WFM) to improve working conditions, attacked a parade of company-supported union miners and in the melee destroyed the union hall and threw Butte's acting mayor out of a second-story window. The local chapter of the WFM was dominated by company-influenced conservatives, who cooperated with company officials in using the rustling card system to blacklist workers. Miners were denied a rustling card if they did not keep their union dues current or opposed local union leaders, and therefore could not work. An independent union, the Butte Mine Workers' Union, was formed. Charles Moyer, president of the WFM, went to Butte to meet with both sides to try to mediate the conflict. At the meeting shots were fired, one man was killed, and the hall was destroyed by a dynamite explosion. The state militia was called in, martial law was established, and Butte Mine Workers' Union officials were arrested. They were later convicted in military court on rioting and kidnapping charges. The president and vice president of the union were sentenced to three and five years in prison, respectively. Collections were used to aid the defense of the workers and were to be sent directly to George R. Tompkins at the Butte Mine Workers' headquarters.

**Defense Fund San Francisco Labor Prisoners (September to October 1916)/ San Francisco Defense Fund (December 1916 to March 1917)** Thomas Mooney and his wife, Rena Mooney, Warren K. Billings, Israel Weinberg, and Edward Nolan were arrested after a bomb exploded at a Preparedness Day parade in San Francisco on 22 July 1916, killing ten people and injuring forty others. In the September 1916 issue of *Mother Earth* Robert Minor made an appeal for funds to be sent to the International Workers' Defense League in San Francisco, California. Funds were collected to raise money for the defense of labor leaders arrested. Collections garnered by EG and AB at EG's meetings were submitted to Minor, treasurer of the fund. The fund was later renamed the San Francisco Defense Fund.

**Edward F. Mylius Defense Fund (January 1913)** In 1911 Mylius, an English radical, was arrested and sentenced to one year in prison for publishing an article in the *Liberator: An International Journal Devoted to the Extension of the Republic* (Paris) that charged that King George V had a previous marriage while serving with the Mediterranean Fleet. After his release Mylius tried to settle in the United States but was held for deportation on Ellis Island. Immigration authorities tried to keep him from entering the United States because they considered him an anarchist who had served time in prison. He was eventually released and obtained work with the Ferrer Center in New York. Later, he edited the *Social War* (New York) and became advertising manager for the *Liberator* (New York). Contributions sent to *Mother Earth* were used to aid his legal defense while he was held on Ellis Island.

**Emma Goldman and Ben L. Reitman Defense Fund (June to December 1916)** The fund was initiated after EG and BR were arrested for convening a birth control meeting on 20 May 1916 in Union Square at which birth control information was distributed. It was followed by the Birth Control Collections and Defense Fund, earmarked for Ben Reitman's birth control trials.

**Emma Goldman Defense Committee (April 1916)** The Emma Goldman Defense Committee was a fund collected after EG was arrested on 8 February for lecturing about birth control in New York. On 20 April she was sentenced to fifteen days in Queens County Jail after refusing to pay a $100 fine.

**Errico Malatesta Fund (July 1912)** In May 1912 Malatesta was sentenced to three months in prison for libeling an ex-anarchist named Ballelli by charging that he was an Italian spy. Malatesta was recommended for deportation as an undesirable citizen from Great Britain. On 17 June 1912 Malatesta's deportation order was lifted by the British home secretary. Collections were made to cover the expenses of his appeal, of protest meetings, and of publications about his case. The appeal for funds in *Mother Earth* was made by T. H. Keell of the London anarchist newspaper *Freedom*.

**Ettor-Giovannitti Defense Fund (May 1912 to July 1912)** At a rally on 29 January 1912 held by textile strikers in Lawrence, Massachusetts, a confrontation between demonstrators and the police left one bystander dead and an officer stabbed. On 31 January IWW organizers Joseph Ettor and Arturo Giovannitti were charged with incitement to riot and murder and were jailed. After the Lawrence strike ended the Ettor-Giovannitti Defense League was founded, and collections were made to aid their legal defense. EG collected money through *Mother Earth* and at her lectures and forwarded it to the league. In November 1912 Ettor and Giovannitti were acquitted of all charges.

**Francisco Ferrer Association Fund (March 1915)** Secretary Joseph J. Cohen appealed for funds for the Ferrer Association to finance the day school and pay its debts. Contributions were sent directly to the association's headquarters in New York. The amounts collected were not recorded in later issues of *Mother Earth.*

**Francisco Ferrer Day School Fund (January 1911 to July 1911)** Secretary Bayard Boyesen appealed for $5,000 to open a Ferrer children's day school in New York. The organization issued $1 and $5 certificates to pay the tuition for any child. Funds were also collected to buy and publish textbooks for the school. At a dinner held on 30 June 1911 to celebrate the first anniversary of the Francisco Ferrer Association in New York, EG donated $100 on behalf of the Mother Earth Publishing Association.

**Francisco Ferrer Fund (June 1910)** The Francisco Ferrer Fund was announced for the purpose of funding a biography of Ferrer. The announcement coincided with the founding of the Ferrer Association. Substantial sums were collected at EG's Ferrer lectures. (The contributions listed in *Mother Earth* were raised exclusively at EG's meetings.) This fund eventually subsidized the publication of *Francisco Ferrer, His Life, Work, and Martyrdom*, ed. Leonard Abbott (New York: Francisco Ferrer Association, 1910).

**Free Speech Fight, Everett, Washington (December 1916)** On 30 October 1916 IWW members arrived by boat in Everett from Seattle to support striking shingle weavers in their conflict with company strikebreakers. Met at the dock by the local sheriff and his deputies, the IWW members were beaten by local vigilantes. The incident was known as the Everett massacre, foreshadowing a later, bloodier event by the same name. More than 250 IWW members returned to Everett on 5 November by boat and were met with gunfire at the dock. Five IWW members were killed, twenty-seven were wounded, and two deputies were killed and twenty others wounded. The origin of the first shot is still unknown. Upon the return of the boat to Seattle, the IWW members were arrested and charged with the first-degree murder of Deputy Jefferson Beard. In March 1917 IWW member Thomas Tracy was tried and acquitted. The other men facing trial were eventually released. The appeal was published in *Mother Earth,* and funds were collected at EG's meetings and sent directly to the IWW office in Seattle.

**(General) Free Speech Fund (November 1909 to May 1910)** The Free Speech Fund was the successor to the Free Speech Defense Fund. Major contributors included Joseph Fels ($100), Alice Stone Blackwell, Alden Freeman, Italian Labor Union, Carpenters and Joiners' Local 390 (N.Y.), and the Typographical Union, Local 7 (N.Y.). Many small individual contributions were also received. Large donations were collected by Leonard Abbott and at EG's meetings. Money was raised for legal fees, a free speech meeting, EG's and BR's expenses, Elizabeth Gurley Flynn's defense,

Buffalo and Chicago free speech work, plus free speech fights in Spokane (where the money was given to S. A. Stodel); Philadelphia (where the money was sent to Frank Stephens); Springfield, Illinois; Detroit; and Cheyenne.

**Gussie Winn Fund (September 1912 to January 1913)** Collections were raised from an appeal in *Freie Arbeiter Stimme,* from an appeal in *Mother Earth,* and from EG's meetings, as well as donations from individuals. Funds went to support the widow and family of longtime anarchist editor Ross Winn.

**Ingar Defense Committee (March 1916)** The fund was raised for the defense of David Ingar, who was arrested after a mill strike in East Youngstown, Ohio, where mill guards fired on peaceful protestors. Ingar was jailed with a bullet wound, though *Mother Earth* states that he was not even in East Youngstown during the riot.

**Ipswich Defense Fund (July 1913)** In April 1913 textile workers in Ipswich, Massachusetts, went on strike, demanding a 20 percent wage increase. Collections aided the defense of nineteen men and women, some of them IWW organizers, who were arrested for rioting outside of the Ipswich Hosiery Mill on 10 June. During the riot a confrontation with police ended with one woman dead and ten men and women wounded. Contributions were sent directly to the Ipswich Defense League.

**Italian Boys' Defense (May to June 1915)** The name was a reference to Frank Abarno and Carmine Carbone, two Italian anarchists who had been arrested in New York. Detective Amedeo Polignani, who was working undercover in the Italian anarchist movement, plotted with Abarno and Carbone to bomb St. Patrick's Cathedral. The bomb was made, and Abarno and Polignani went to the cathedral on 2 March 1915 to plant it. As Abarno was about to light the fuse, he was arrested. Carbone was arrested in his home shortly afterward. Abarno and Carbone were charged with conspiracy to bomb the cathedral, and despite an argument by the two men and their supporters that they were victims of an agent provocateur, the jury decided that Abarno and Carbone acted on their own initiative. They were sentenced to six to twelve years in prison. Collections were made at EG's meetings and sent to the defense fund.

**Italian Prisoners' Defense Fund (October 1908 to April 1910)** The fund was started as a result of an appeal from Voltairine de Cleyre on behalf of the Italian workers arrested at her 20 February 1908 meeting in Philadelphia. The Anarchist Federation donated $225, and *Freie Arbeiter Stimme,* $50.00. Voltairine de Cleyre was herself a large contributor. Funds were given to support the prisoners' wives and Michael Costello, a prisoner who had been freed but lost his job.

**Jay Fox Defense (October 1911 to January 1913)** In 1911 Jay Fox, editor of the *Agitator,* was arrested for publishing "The Nude and the Prudes," an article that endorsed nude bathing at Home Colony and criticized those who wanted the activity banned. Fox was charged with violating a Washington statute that prohibited the printing and circulation of matter that advocated or encouraged the commission of a crime or disrespect for the law. Fox claimed that the Washington statute was vague and unconstitutional in that it violated his rights of free expression and due process, and the Free Speech League sponsored his case. Found guilty and sentenced to two months in prison, he appealed, but his sentence was upheld in both the Washington State and United States supreme courts. The offending article was reprinted in the March 1912 edition of *Mother Earth* as an act of solidarity by EG and AB. The Kropotkin Jubilee meeting donated $25 to the fund in 1912. The fund financed Fox's legal defense.

**Kōtoku Protest Conference Defense Committee Fund (February to May 1911)** Kōtoku Shūsui was a Japanese anarchist who was executed in Tokyo for allegedly plotting to assassinate the Japanese emperor in January 1911. After his execution a mass meeting, the Kōtoku Protest Conference, was held at Webster Hall in New York. At the meeting resolutions were passed that condemned the Japanese government and praised Kōtoku. The February 1911 edition of *Mother Earth* contained an article on the meeting and published the resolutions. The Defense Committee of the Kōtoku Protest Conference made an appeal that asked people to contribute to a fund to defend "indicted comrades" still held in Japanese prisons and to send aid to their families. Funds were sent to treasurer AB. A long list of contributors appeared in the May 1911 issue. An evening of entertainment in the Tokyo martyrs' honor organized by Nunia Seldes in Pittsburgh raised $51.37. Funds were also collected at EG's meetings.

**Lawrence Strike Fund (February to May 1912)** This fund was organized by the IWW and established to help the striking textile workers in Lawrence, Massachusetts. A plea for funds appeared in the February 1912 edition of *Mother Earth*. A bystander, Anna Lapizzo, was killed during a skirmish between the strikers and the militia, and strike leaders and IWW organizers Joseph Ettor and Arturo Giovannitti were charged with incitement to murder. This case brought in thousands of dollars to the fund, money that was used to aid the men's defense as well as the strikers. Funds were submitted to Bill Haywood, Elizabeth Gurley Flynn, and Joseph Bedard. Collections were garnered mostly from EG's meetings and debates. In March 1912 the strike ended in victory for the workers as they secured their demands from the American Woolen Company. After the end of the strike funds were directed to aid the Ettor-Giovannitti case (see Ettor-Giovannitti Defense Fund).

**Little Falls Strike Fund (December 1912 to February 1913)** In October 1912 approximately 1,500 textile workers in Little Falls, New York, struck against company-mandated wage reductions. Supported by the IWW, the strike lasted for twelve weeks, winning wage increases of up to 12 per cent. Collections were used to aid the strike and included $75 raised from the Kropotkin seventieth-birthday jubilee, and $24.07 from an 11 November Haymarket commemorative meeting in New York.

**Lumber Strike, Lake Charles, Louisiana (January 1913)** At the Galloway Lumber Company in Lake Charles, Louisiana, fifty-eight men were arrested and charged with murder after a conflict erupted on 7 July 1912 between IWW-affiliated union members and the mill owner and his men. Sixty-five IWW men were indicted, four of whom under assumed names twice. One man died of injuries sustained during the conflict, one was killed during arrest, and another evaded capture. A $25 contribution from the Kropotkin jubilee of 7 December 1912 at Carnegie Hall was sent to the defense fund.

**Margaret Sanger Fund (January to March 1916)** On 25 August 1914 Margaret Sanger was indicted on three counts of obscenity for publishing the March, May, and July issues of the *Woman Rebel*, and one count of inciting to murder and assassination by publishing "In Defense of Assassination" by Herbert Thorpe in the July issue. She fled to England but returned to the United States in 1915 to face charges against her; the charges were eventually dropped. This fund aided her defense and was the successor to Sanger's Defense fund (collected for her husband William Sanger). Collections were made at several EG meetings; most contributions came from Jewish audiences. Money was sent to E. Byrne in New York.

**Marmol Fund (May 1915)** The fund assisted the wife and children of Fernando Tarrida Del Marmol, a Spanish anarchist who died on 15 March 1915 in Chingford, Essex (on the outskirts of London). In 1896 Tarrida was arrested after the Corpus Christi Day bombing in Barcelona, Spain. He was accused of instigating the bombing and was held at the Montjuich prison. After he was released, he was banished from Spain. His book *Les Inquisiteurs d'Espagne* (Paris, 1897) exposed prison conditions and tortures witnessed during his imprisonment. Tarrida went into exile, living in France and Belgium before settling in England. Through his writings and lectures he continued to support the Spanish working class. Signatories of the appeal included William Archer (author of *The Life, Trial, and Death of Francisco Ferrer* [London, 1911]), Errico Malatesta, W. Heaford, J. McCabe (a noted freethought writer), J. Ramsay MacDonald (of the International Labour Party), and G. H. B. Ward.

**Mesabi Iron Range Strikers Defense Committee (August to November 1916) and Minnesota Defense (December 1916)** The fund's secretary-treasurer, James Gilday, appealed to the *Mother Earth* readers for support for the strikers. The strike began on 2 June 1916 when miners walked out after their monthly paychecks were minus the increase they demanded. The IWW sent organizers Elizabeth Gurley Flynn, Joseph Ettor, Carlo Tresca, and others to the front line of the strike. After a violent altercation on 3 July, which resulted in two deaths, seven IWW organizers, including Carlo Tresca and James Gilday, were arrested and charged with being accessories to murder. *Mother Earth* labeled them "war prisoners." The charges were later dropped. By 17 September the Metal Mine Workers' Industrial Union called off the strike. Collections from EG's meetings went directly to William Haywood on behalf of the IWW.

**Mexican Liberal Party (PLM) Junta Fund (August 1911 to April 1915)** The fund helped to finance the publication of the PLM newspaper *Regeneración* and support the organization's members in prison. The September 1911 issue of *Mother Earth* reported that $95 was collected through the Brazilian journal *Laterna* by Neno Vasco and forwarded to *Mother Earth* by Edgard Leuenroth, an anarchist in Portugal. The money was sent by *Mother Earth* to the secretary of the PLM in Los Angeles.

**Mother Earth Sustaining Fund/Mother Earth Propaganda Fund (December 1906 to July 1917)** This appeal was the largest and longest-running in *Mother Earth*. EG announced a need for a sustaining fund in December 1906, and it was inaugurated with large contributions from the Carpenters' Union and H. Comarow. Major contributors included Gilbert Roe, Dr. M. A. Cohn, Dr. J. H. Greer, Paul Kutchan, Group Edelstadt, the Chicago Social Science League, and the New York Free Speech League; large collections were solicited by Rebecca Edelsohn and from collection appeals at EG's meetings (and some of AB's meetings). EG's article "What I Believe," published in the *New York World* in August 1908, brought in $250. In addition to helping to underwrite the publication of *Mother Earth* the fund paid for EG's and BR's travel expenses.

Contributions to the *Mother Earth* Sustaining Fund were listed in almost every issue through July 1907, and they appeared sporadically between 1909 and 1913, growing in length especially when the magazine was in dire need. Generally, the fund was replenished by collections at EG's meetings and socials. In June 1913 the fund was renamed the *Mother Earth* Propaganda Fund, with major contributions continuing to come from Dr. Michael Cohn, along with newer supporters like George Herron in Italy (including $10 from Jessie Ashley). From 1913 to 1917 lists of contributions were infrequent. The list of contributions was longest in May 1915, an issue that included acknowledgments of contributions for the *Mother Earth* tenth-anniversary souvenir edition.

**Paterson Strike Fund (June 1913)** On 23 January 1913 800 broad-silk weavers at the Doherty Company mill in Paterson, New Jersey, left work to protest the introduction of a multiple-loom system, leading to a drop in wages. IWW Local 152 voted to approve a general strike of all silk workers in Paterson, and by March more than 20,000 workers were on strike. In August the strike was officially called off after workers accepted individual shop settlements. Collections were made at EG's meetings in Los Angeles and San Francisco to aid striking silk workers.

**Prince Rupert, British Columbia, Strike Fund (September 1912 to January 1913)** Construction workers on the Grand Trunk Pacific Railway in British Columbia struck in response to the exploitative treatment of the workers and the neglect of the sick in hospitals. Following the railroad company's disregard of their demands for better working conditions, the workers walked out. A. O. Morse, the secretary of the strike committee, wrote a letter on 10 August 1912 to *Mother Earth,* published in the September 1912 issue, asking readers to support their cause and requesting contributions to aid the fight. From a twenty-fifth-anniversary Haymarket commemoration meeting in New York in 1912, at which EG spoke, $24.07 was sent to the strikers.

**Rangel-Cline Defense Fund (December 1913 to September 1914)** The fund was formed to aid IWW member Charles Cline and PLM member Jesus Rangel and twelve other PLM members who were arrested in Texas and charged with the murder of a deputy sheriff. Appeals for funds appeared in the December and February issues of *Mother Earth.* An article on the case appeared in the August 1914 issue with a renewed appeal for funds. All members of the group were eventually convicted; Rangel was sentenced to ninety-nine years, and Cline was sentenced to life imprisonment. Two of the men died in prison, and six served their full sentences. On 20 August 1926 Texas governor Miriam A. Ferguson granted a full pardon to the remaining six men in prison, including Rangel and Cline. A total of $140 was raised from EG's West Coast meetings, including debates and socials, in 1914. Defense funds were also raised by the Anti-Militarist League.

**Relief Society for the Political Exiles in Siberia (December 1913)** The appeal raised funds to send books and periodicals to exiles and Russian prisoners in Siberia. The committee was organized in Paris. Collections were sent to Z. Steeglis in Paris and Rose Baron in New York.

**San Diego Free Speech Fund (March 1912 to July 1912, January 1913)** The initial appeal was made in the March 1912 issue of *Mother Earth* by Jack Whyte, who was arrested in San Diego for violating the city's ordinance that banned street speaking. Thirty-eight men and three women were arrested on 8 February after the IWW called for people to defy the law. Over the following months hundreds of people were arrested. On 14 May BR was kidnapped from his hotel by vigilantes in San Diego. The California Free Speech League, an extension of the San Diego Free Speech Fund, was formed, composed of members of the IWW, AFL, Socialist Party, and a few church groups. Collections were made mostly at EG's meetings and disbursed to the California Free Speech League through Treasurer Kaspar Bauer and used for related expenses. In January 1913 *Mother Earth* reported that a collection was taken and sent directly to Jack Whyte in prison.

**San Francisco Joe Hill Defense Committee (September 1915)** The committee appealed for funds to aid IWW member Hill's defense. Funds were to be sent to George Childs, secretary of the Joe Hill Defense Committee in Salt Lake City. Hill was convicted of murder, and in November 1915 he was executed by a firing squad.

**Sanger's Defense (May 1915)** Leonard Abbott collected funds for William Sanger, who had been arrested in January 1915 for selling a copy of *Family Limitations* to a Comstock agent. On 10 September 1915 Sanger was convicted and began serving a thirty-day jail sentence, in lieu of paying a $150 fine. This fund eventually became the Margaret Sanger Fund.

**Savra Federenko Defense Fund (November 1910)** Federenko was a Russian sailor and revolutionary who had taken part in the *Potemkin* mutiny of 1905. He was arrested in Winnipeg, Canada. The Russian government charged him with the murder of a police officer and tried to extradite him back to Russia. Contributions were used to aid his defense. Federenko was later released on bail and fled to London.

**Spanish Fund (December 1909 to January 1910)** Funds supported anarchists imprisoned after "the Tragic Week" in Barcelona in July 1909. Contributions came from EG's meetings, the Ferrer memorial meetings, and others and were sent to Charles Malato in Paris. In *Mother Earth* an "Appeal for Solidarity" for the revolution in Spain from the Pro-Spanish Revolutionary Committee of New York included a request for political support and funds, with sixteen signatures, including that of Secretary Jaime Vidal. Contributions were not recorded in *Mother Earth*.

**Special Publicity Fund (October 1915)** Part of the Caplan-Schmidt Defense Fund, this fund was used to launch a publicity campaign to raise the consciousness of workers and others in California to the labor versus capital struggle in Caplan and Schmidt's *Los Angeles Times* bombing case. Some, including EG, AB, and C. E. S. Wood, argued that favorable publicity was more important than funds for lawyers. More than $1,700 was raised, augmenting the Caplan-Schmidt Defense Fund for the publicity work.

**Suhr and Ford Cases (August to September 1914)** Funds to defend these cases were collected at EG's meetings and at a Portland social in November 1914. Richard "Blackie" Ford and Herman D. Suhr were among approximately thirty IWW members who organized a hop pickers' protest against the poor working conditions at the Durst brothers' ranch in Wheatland, California. Ford and Suhr were elected to a committee to present ten workers' demands to the ranch owners, who refused to comply and in turn were threatened by the committee with a strike. Durst ordered Ford off the ranch at gunpoint, and when Ford returned to speak at a mass meeting, he was met by the district attorney and sheriff's deputies. The crowd surrounded the police, preventing them from arresting Ford and sparking a conflict in which two deputies and the district attorney were shot. Ford and Suhr were arrested and convicted of second-degree murder and sentenced to life imprisonment. Ford was granted parole on 11 September 1925, rearrested for the murder of a deputy sheriff during the Wheatland incident, and then acquitted in January 1926. Suhr was paroled and released on 25 October 1926.

**Tannenbaum Fund (May 1914)** During the depression in the winter of 1913–1914 Frank Tannenbaum led a group of unemployed and homeless men to various churches in New York to solicit Christian charity and shelter. On 4 March a Catholic priest not only refused to give them shelter but also called the police. Newspaper reporters accompanied the police to the Church of St. Alphonsus; a riot broke out after the burst of a camera flash bulb was mistaken for gunfire. Tannenbaum was arrested and convicted for "inciting to riot," and sentenced to a year's imprisonment. The Tannenbaum Fund was supported by collections made at EG's meetings in Chicago.

**Unemployed and Anti-Militarist League Fund (May to June 1914)** This combined fund was raised primarily by Rebecca Edelsohn and Louise Berger, and supplemented by the selling of political buttons. Proceeds were spent on general strike buttons and on expenses related to the Tarrytown free speech fight, including a disbursement by AB to prisoners Marie Ganz, Al Turner, and those arrested for the Tarrytown protests.

**Unemployed Fund (March to April 1914)** This was an informal collection at EG's meetings for "the unemployed activities" and preceded the official fund. Collections financed the publication of circulars and literature and paid for advertisements to publicize events. Continued collections from EG's meetings were combined with those of the Anti-Militarist League Fund in May 1914. (See Unemployed and Anti-Militarist League Fund.)

**Voltairine de Cleyre Publication Fund (July 1912 to August 1913)** Following the death of Voltairine de Cleyre, her friends and co-workers solicited funds in the July issue of *Mother Earth* for the publication of her collected works. Anarchists raised funds through special events in de Cleyre's honor in Los Angeles, San Francisco, New York, and Chicago. Her poem "The Hurricane" was set to music by San Diego musician George Edwards, and the arrangement was sold as a benefit. *Mother Earth* published the Chicago Voltairine de Cleyre Memorial Group's financial report in the August 1913 issue. The group collected money to pay for the expenses incurred at the time of de Cleyre's death. The remaining money was transferred to the publication fund. *Selected Works of Voltairine de Cleyre,* edited by AB with a biographical sketch by Hippolyte Havel, was published by the Mother Earth Publishing Association in 1914.

**Westinghouse Defense Committee (July 1916)** In April 1916 40,000 workers of the Westinghouse Electric and Manufacturing Company went on strike in Pittsburgh. Dozens of strikers were arrested for rioting on 2 May after a violent confrontation with police. Three strikers were killed, and three others were fatally wounded. The company issued an ultimatum, and the strikers went back to work. By July eleven men had been convicted and more than a dozen more were awaiting trial for charges of rioting during the strike. Funds were collected to aid the imprisoned strikers and were sent directly to the committee in Pittsburgh.

# SELECTED BIBLIOGRAPHY

Abad de Santillan, Diego. *Historia de la revolucion mexicana*. Mexico City: Frente de Afirmacion Hispanista, 1992.

Abrams, Edward. *The Lyrical Left: Randolph Bourne, Alfred Stieglitz, and the Origins of Cultural Radicalism in America*. Charlottesville: University Press of Virginia, 1986.

Adamic, Louis. *Dynamite: The Story of Class Violence in America*. Gloucester, Mass: Peter Smith, 1960.

Adams, Graham, Jr. *Age of Industrial Violence, 1910–1915*. New York: Columbia University Press, 1966.

Anderson, Carlotta R. *All-American Anarchist: Joseph A. Labadie and the Labor Movement*. Detroit: Wayne State University Press, 1998.

Anderson, Margaret. *My Thirty Years' War; An Autobiography by Margaret Anderson*. New York: Covici, Friede, 1930.

———. *The Little Review Anthology*. New York: Hermitage House, 1953.

Antliff, Allan. *Anarchist Modernism*. Chicago: University of Chicago Press, 2001.

Archer, William. *The Life, Trial, and Death of Francisco Ferrer*. London: Chapman and Hall, 1911.

Ashbaugh, Carolyn. *Lucy Parsons: American Revolutionary*. Chicago: Charles H. Kerr, 1976.

Avrich, Paul. *The Russian Anarchists*. Princeton, N.J.: Princeton University Press, 1967.

———. *An American Anarchist: The Life of Voltairine de Cleyre*. Princeton, N.J.: Princeton University Press, 1978.

———. *The Haymarket Tragedy*. Princeton, N.J.: Princeton University Press, 1984.

———. *The Modern School Movement: Anarchism and Education in the United States*. Princeton, N.J.: Princeton University Press, 1980.

———. *Anarchist Portraits*. Princeton, N.J.: Princeton University Press, 1988.

———. *Sacco and Vanzetti: The Anarchist Background*. Princeton, N.J.: Princeton University Press, 1991.

———. *Anarchist Voices: An Oral History of Anarchism in America*. Princeton, N.J.: Princeton University Press, 1995.

Bakunin, Michael. *God and the State*. Boston: Benjamin R. Tucker, 1883.

Balzer, Anitra. "Donald Vose: Home Grown Traitor" in *Communal Societies* 8 (1988): 90–103.

Barrett, James R. *William Z. Foster and the Tragedy of American Radicalism*. Urbana: University of Illinois Press, 1999.

Bergmann, Anna. *Everyday Life After Socialism.* Edited by Susan Gal and Gail Kilgman. Princeton, N.J.: Princeton University Press, 2000.

Berkman, Alexander. *Prison Memoirs of an Anarchist.* New York: Mother Earth Publishing Association, 1912.

Bettini, Leonardo. *Bibliographia dell' anarchismo. Vol. 1: Periodice e numeri unici anarchici in linguaq italiana.* 2 parts. Florence, Italy: CP Editrice, 1972.

Bingham, Edwin, and Tim Barnes, eds. *Wood Works: The Life and Writings of Charles Erskine Scott Wood.* Corvallis: Oregon State University Press, 1997.

Blackwell, Alice Stone, ed. *The Little Grandmother of the Russian Revolution: Reminiscences and Letters of Catherine Breshkovsky.* Boston: Little, Brown, 1917.

Blaisdell, Lowell L. *The Desert Revolution: Baja California, 1911.* Madison: University of Wisconsin Press, 1962.

Blatt, Martin Henry. *Free Love and Anarchism: The Biography of Ezra Heywood.* Urbana: University of Illinois Press, 1989.

Bloomfield, Maxwell H. *Alarms and Diversions: The American Mind Through American Magazines 1900–1914.* The Hague: Mouton, 1967.

Boyce, Neith. *The Modern World of Neith Boyce: Autobiography and Diaries.* Edited by Carol De Boeer-Langworthy. Albuquerque: University of New Mexico Press, 2003.

Boyce, Neith, and Hutchins Hapgood. *Intimate Warriors: Portraits of a Modern Marriage, 1899–1944: Selected Works by Neith Boyce and Hutchins Hapgood.* Edited by Ellen Kay Trimberger. New York: The Feminist Press at the City University of New York, 1991.

Boyd, Andrew. *The Rise of the Irish Trade Unions.* Tralee, Ireland: Anvil Books, 1985.

Boyer, Paul S. *Purity in Print: Book Censorship in America from the Gilded Age to the Computer.* 2nd ed. Madison: University of Wisconsin Press, 2002.

Brissenden, Paul F. *The IWW: A Study of American Syndicalism.* 1919. Reprint, New York: Russell and Russell, 1957.

Brommel, Bernard J. *Eugene V. Debs: Spokesman for Labor and Socialism.* Chicago: Charles H. Kerr, 1978.

Brooks, Van Wyck. *The Confident Years.* New York: E. P. Dutton, 1952.

Brown, Emily C. *Har Dayal: Hindu Revolutionary and Rationalist.* Tucson: University of Arizona Press, 1975.

Brown, Milton. *The Story of the Armory Show.* New York: Abbeville Press, 1988.

Bruns, Roger. *The Damndest Radical.* Urbana: University of Illinois Press, 1987.

———. *Preacher Billy Sunday and Big-Time American Evangelism.* New York: W. W. Norton, 1992.

Bullard, Arthur. *Comrade Yetta.* New York: Macmillan, 1913.

Bunko, Shakai, ed. *Zaibei Shakaishugish/Museifushugisha Enkaku.* Kashiwa-Shobo, 1964.

Burns, William J. *The Masked War.* New York: George H. Doran, 1913.

Camp, Helen C. *Iron in Her Soul: Elizabeth Gurley Flynn and the American Left.* Pullman: Washington State University Press, 1995.

Carpenter, Edward. *Prisons, Police, and Punishment.* London: Arthur C. Fifield, 1905.

———. "The Intermediate Sex." In *Love's Coming of Age.* London: Swann Sonnenschein, 1906.

Carpenter, Mecca Reitman. *No Regrets: Dr. Ben Reitman and the Women Who Loved Him.* Lexington: Southside Press, 1999.

Carroll, James. *Break-Out from the Crystal Palace: The Anarcho-Psychological Critique: Stirner, Nietzsche, Dostoevsky.* London: Routledge and Kegan Paul, 1974.

Chambers, John Whiteclay. *The Tyranny of Change: America in the Progressive Era, 1890–1920.* 2nd ed. Piscataway, N.J.: Rutgers University Press, 2000.

Chaplin, Ralph. *Wobbly: The Rough-and-Tumble Story of an American Radical.* Chicago: University of Chicago Press, 1948.

Chen, Constance M. *The Sex Side of Life: Mary Ware Dennett's Pioneering Battle for Birth Control and Sex Education.* New York: The New Press, 1996.

Cherny, Robert W. *American Politics in the Gilded Age, 1868–1900.* American History Series. Wheeling, Ill.: Harlan Davidson, 1997.

Chesler, Ellen. *Woman of Valor: Margaret Sanger and the Birth Control Movement in America.* New York: Simon and Schuster, 1992.

Cohen, Joseph. *Di yidish-anarkhistishe bavegung in Amerike: historisher iberblik un perzenlekhe iberlebungen (The Jewish Anarchist Movement in the United States: A Historical Review and Personal Reminiscenses).* Philadelphia: Workmen's Circle, 1945.

Cole, Peter. *Wobblies on the Waterfront.* Urbana: University of Illinois Press, 2007.

Conlin, Joseph R., ed. *The American Radical Press 1880–1960.* Westport, Conn.: Greenwood Press, 1974.

Conttrell, Robert C. *Roger Nash Baldwin and the American Civil Liberties Union.* New York: Columbia University Press, 2000.

Cott, Nancy. *Public Vows: A History of Marriage and the Nation.* Cambridge, Mass.: Harvard University Press, 2000.

Cowan, Geoffrey. *The People v. Clarence Darrow.* New York: Times Books, 1993.

Crump, John. *Hatta Shuzo and Pure Anarchism in Interwar Japan.* New York: St. Martin's Press, 1983.

———. *The Origins of Socialist Thought in Japan.* London: Croom Helm, 1983.

Curti, Merle. *Peace or War. The American Struggle 1636–1936.* New York: W. W. Norton, 1936.

Darsey, James. "Eugene Debs and American Class." In *A Rhetorical History of the United States.* Vol. 6, *Rhetoric and Reform in the Progressive Era.* Edited by J. Michael Hogan. Lansing: Michigan State University Press, 2003.

Davis, Oscar. *William Howard Taft, the Man of the Hour.* Philadelphia: P. W. Ziegler, 1908.

Davis, Sally, and Betty Baldwin. *Denver Dwellings and Descendants.* Denver: Sage Books, 1963.

De Cleyre, Voltairine. *Selected Works of Voltairine de Cleyre.* Edited by Alexander Berkman. New York: Mother Earth Publishing Association, 1914.

Debs, Eugene. *The Letters of Eugene V. Debs.* Edited by J. Robert Constantine. 3 vols. Urbana: University of Illinois Press, 1990.

Dell, Floyd. *Women as World Builders: Studies in Modern Feminism.* Chicago: Forbest, 1913.

———. *Love in Greenwich Village.* New York: George H. Doran, 1926.

———. *Homecoming: An Autobiography.* New York: Farrar and Rinehart, 1933

Dennett, Mary Ware. *Birth Control Laws: Shall We Keep Them Change Them or Abolish Them.* 1926. Reprint, New York: De Capo Press, 1970.

Dombrowski, James. *The Early Days of Christian Socialism in America.* New York: Columbia University Press, 1936.

Drinnon, Richard. *Rebel in Paradise: A Biography of Emma Goldman*. Chicago: University of Chicago Press, 1982.

———. "The Blast: An Introduction and an Appraisal." *Labor History* 11, no. 1 (1970): 82–88.

Drinnon, Richard, and Anna Drinnon, eds. *Nowhere at Home: Letters from Exile of Emma Goldman and Alexander Berkman*. New York: Schocken Books, 1975.

Dubofsky, Melvyn. *We Shall Be All: A History of the Industrial Workers of the World*. New York: Quadrangle/New York Times Book Company, 1969.

———. *"Big Bill" Haywood*. Manchester: Manchester University Press, 1987.

DuBois, Ellen C. *Feminism and Suffrage: The Emergence of an Independent Women's Movement in America, 1848–1869*. 2nd ed. Ithaca, N.Y.: Cornell University Press, 1999.

Duden, Arthur Power. *Joseph Fels and the Single Tax Movement*. Philadelphia: Temple University Press, 1971.

Ebner, Michael H. "The Passaic Strike of 1912 and the Two I.W.W.s." *Labor History* 11, no. 4 (Fall 1970): 452–66.

*Edward Bond Foote: Biographical Notes and Appreciatives*. New York: Free Speech League, 1913.

Egan, Leona Rust. *Provincetown as a Stage*. Orleans, Mass.: Parnassus Imprints, 1994.

Ellis, Havelock. *The Criminal*. New York: Charles Scribner's and Sons, 1890.

England, George Allan. *The Story of the Appeal*. Girard, Kans.: Appeal Publishing Company, 1917.

Esposito, Anthony V. *The Ideology of the Socialist Party of America, 1901–1917*. New York: Garland, 1997.

Falk, Candace. *Love, Anarchy and Emma Goldman*. New York: Holt, Rinehart and Winston, 1984. Rev. ed., New York: Rutgers University Press, 1990, 1999.

———. "Emma Goldman." In *Encyclopedia of U.S. Labor and Working Class History*. New York: Routledge, 2007.

———. "Emma Goldman—Jewish Spokeswoman for Freedom." In *Encyclopedia of Jewish History*, edited by S. Norwood and E. Pollack. Santa Barbara: ABC-CLIO, 2008.

———. "Let Icons Be Bygones! Emma Goldman, the Grand Expositor." In *Feminist Interpretations of Emma Goldman*, edited by Penny A. Weiss and Loretta Kensinger. University Park: Penn State University Press, 2008

Falk, Candace, Stephen Cole, and Sally Thomas, eds. *Emma Goldman: A Guide to Her Life and Documentary Sources*. Alexandria, Va.: Chadwyck-Healey, 1995.

Ferguson, Kathy. *Emma Goldman: Political Thinking in the Streets*. Lanham, Md.: Rowan and Littlefield, 2011.

Fink, Gary M., ed. *Biographical Dictionary of American Labor*. Westport, Conn.: Greenwood Press, 1984.

Fink, Leon. *Progressive Intellectuals and the Dilemmas of Democratic Commitment*. Cambridge: Harvard University Press, 1997.

Fishman, William J. *Jewish Radicals: From Czarist Stetl to London Ghetto*. New York: Pantheon Books, 1974.

Flanagan, Maureen. *America Reformed: Progressives and Progressivisms*. New York: Oxford University Press, 2007.

Flynn, Elizabeth Gurley. *I Speak My Own Piece: Autobiography of "The Rebel Girl."* New York: International Publishers, 1973.

———. *The Rebel Girl*. New York: International Publishers, 1976.

Foner, Eric. *The Story of American Freedom*. New York: W. W. Norton, 1999.

Foner, Philip S. *History of the Labor Movement in the United States*. 9 vols. New York: International Publishers: 1947–1991.

———. *The Case of Joe Hill*. New York: International Publishers, 1965.

———. *My Fellow Workers and Friends: I.W.W. Free-Speech Fights as Told by Participants*. Westport, Conn.: Greenwood Press, 1981.

Foner, Philip S., ed. *Helen Keller: Her Socialist Years*. New York: International Publishers, 1967.

Frazer, Winifred L. *E.G. and E.G.O.: Emma Goldman and the Iceman Cometh*. Gainesville: University Presses of Florida, 1974.

Freeberg, Ernst. *Democracy's Prisoner*. Cambridge, Mass.: Harvard University Press, 2008.

Freud, Sigmund. *Civilization and Its Discontents*. New York: J. Cape and H. Smith, 1930.

Frost, Richard H. *The Mooney Case*. Stanford, Calif.: Stanford University Press, 1968.

Gallagher, Dorothy. *All the Right Enemies*. New York: Penguin Books, 1989.

Galsworthy, John. *Justice*. New York: Charles Scribner and Sons, 1920.

Ganz, Marie, and Nat J. Ferber. *Rebels*. New York: Dodd, Mead, 1920.

Geifman, Anna. *Thou Shalt Kill: Revolutionary Terrorism in Russia, 1894–1917*. Princeton, N.J.: Princeton University Press, 1993.

Gentry, Curt. *Frame-Up: The Incredible Story of Tom Mooney and Warren K. Billings*. New York: W. W. Norton, 1987.

Girard, Frank, and Ben Perry. *The Socialist Labor Party, 1876–1991: A Short History*. Philadelphia: Livra Books, 1991.

Glassgold, Peter. *Anarchy: An Anthology of Emma Goldman's* Mother Earth. New York: Counterpoint, 2001.

Goldman, Emma. *Emma Goldman Papers: A Microfilm Edition*. 69 reels. Edited by Candace Falk, Ronald J. Zboray, and Daniel Conford. The Emma Goldman Papers Project. Alexandria, Va.: Chadwyck-Healey, 1995.

Golin, Steve. *The Fragile Bridge: Paterson Silk Strike, 1913*. Philadelphia: Temple University Press, 1988.

Gompers, Samuel. *The Samuel Gompers Papers*. Edited by Stuart Kaufman, Peter J. Alpert, and Grace Palladino, et al. 8 vols. Urbana: University of Illinois Press, 1986–2000.

Gordon, Linda. *Woman's Body, Woman's Right: A Social History of Birth Control in America*. New York: Penguin Books, 1974.

Goyens, Tom. *Beer and Revolution: The German Anarchist Movement in New York City, 1880–1914*. Urbana: University of Illinois Press, 2007.

Graham, Hugh Davis, and Ted Gurr, eds. *The History of Violence in America: Historical and Comparative Perspectives*. New York: Frederick A. Praeger, 1969.

Graham, John, ed. *Yours for the Revolution: The Appeal to Reason 1895–1922*. Lincoln: University of Nebraska Press, 1990.

Green, Martin. *New York 1913: The Armory Show and the Paterson Strike Pageant*. New York: Charles Scribner's Sons, 1988.

Guérin, Daniel, ed. *No Gods No Masters*. 2 vols. Translated by Paul Sharkey. San Francisco: AK Press, 1998

Halperin, Joan Ungersma. *Félix Fénéon Aesthete and Anarchist in Fin-de-Siécle Paris*. New Haven, Conn.: Yale University Press, 1988.

Hamburger, Robert. *Two Rooms: The Life of Charles Erskine Scott Wood*. Lincoln: University of Nebraska Press, 1998.

Hamon, Augustin. *The Technique of Bernard Shaw's Plays*. Translated by Frank Maurice. London: C. W. Daniel, 1912.

Hane, Mikiso, trans. and ed. *Reflections on the Way to the Gallows: Rebel Women in Prewar Japan*. Berkeley: University of California Press, 1988.

Hapgood, Hutchins. *A Victorian in the Modern World*. New York: Harcourt, Brace, 1939.

Harrison, Royden, Gillian B. Woolven, and Robert Duncan. *The Warwick Guide to British Labour Periodicals 1790–1970*. Hassocks, Sussex: The Harvester Press, 1977.

Hart, John. *Revolutionary Mexico*. Berkeley and Los Angeles: University of California Press, 1987.

Hays, Samuel P. "The New Organizational Society." In *Building the Organizational Society: Essays on Association Activities in Modern America*, edited by Jerry Israel. New York: Free Press, 1972.

Haywood, William D. *Bill Haywood's Book*. New York: International Publishers, 1929.

*The History of the San Diego Free Speech Fight, Republished from the* New York Call, *Sunday Issues Beginning March 15, 1914*. San Diego: Industrial Workers of the World, 1973.

Herrmann, Dorothy. *Helen Keller: A Life*. New York: Alfred A. Knopf, 1998.

Hildermeier, Manfred. *The Russian Socialist Revolutionary Party Before the First World War*. New York: St. Martin's Press, 2000.

Hoerder, Dirk, ed. *The Immigrant Labor Press in North America, 1840–1970*. New York: Greenwood Press, 1987.

Hoffman, Frederick J., Charles Allen, and Carolyn F. Ulrich. *The Little Magazine: A History and a Bibliography*. Princeton, N.J.: Princeton University Press, 1946.

Hofstadter, Richard. *Age of Reform*. New York: Knopf, 1955.

Hug, Heinz. *Peter Kropotkin (1842–1921): Bibliographie*. Grafenau, Germany: Edition Anares in Trotzdem-Verlag, 1994.

Huneker, J. G. *Iconoclasts: A Book of Dramatists: Ibsen, Strindberg, Becque, Hauptmann, Sudermann, Herviu, Gorky, Duse, and D'Annunzio, Maeterlinck and Bernard Shaw*. New York: Charles Scribner's Sons, 1905.

Hunsberger, Willard D. *Clarence Darrow: A Bibliography*. Metuchen, N.J.: The Scarecrow Press, 1981.

Hunt, William R. *Body Love: The Amazing Career of Bernarr Macfadden*. Bowling Green, Ohio: Bowling Green State University Press, 1989.

———. *William J Burns and the Detective Profession 1880–1930*. Bowling Green, Ohio: Bowling Green State University Press, 1990.

Hustvedt, Lloyd. "O. A. Tveitmoe: Labor Leader." *Norwegian-American Studies* 30 (1985): 3–54.

Hutchinson, E. P. *Legislative History of American Immigration Policy 1798–1965*. Philadelphia: University of Pennsylvania Press, 1981.

Jacoby, Russell. *The Last Intellectuals: American Culture in the Age of Academe*. New York: Basic Books, 1987.

Jensen, Joan M. *The Price of Vigilance*. Chicago: Rand McNally, 1968.

Johanningsmeier, Edward P. "William Z. Foster and the Syndicalist League of North America." *Labor History* 30, no. 3 (Summer 1989): 329–53.

———. *Forging American Communism: The Life of William Z. Foster*. Princeton, N.J.: Princeton University Press, 1994.

Jones, Mary. *The Autobiography of Mother Jones*. 2d ed. Chicago: Charles H. Kerr, 1972.

———. *Mother Jones Speaks, Collected Writings and Speeches*. Edited by Philip Foner. New York: Monad Press, 1983.

Kairys, David. "Freedom of Speech." In *The Politics of Law: A Progressive Critique*, edited by David Kairys. 3rd ed. New York: Basic Books, 1998.

Katayama, Sen. *The Labor Movement in Japan*. Chicago: Charles H. Kerr, 1918.

Katz, Jonathan. *Gay American History: Lesbians and Gay Men in the USA*. New York: Harper and Row, 1985.

Katz, Sherry Jeanne. "Dual Commitments: Feminism, Socialism, and Women's Political Activism in California, 1890–1920." PhD diss., University of California, 1991.

Kazin, Michael. *Barons of Labor: The San Francisco Building Trades and Union Power in the Progressive Era*. Urbana: University of Illinois Press, 1989.

Kennedy, David M. *Birth Control in America: The Career of Margaret Sanger*. New Haven, Conn.: Yale University Press, 1970.

Kershaw, Alex. *Jack London: A Life*. New York: St Martin's Press, 1997.

Kipling, Rudyard. *Rudyard Kipling's Verse*. Rev. ed. London: Hodder and Stoughton, 1933.

Kipnis, Ira. *The American Socialist Movement 1897–1912*. Westport, Conn.: Greenwood Press, 1968.

Kornbluh, Joyce. *Rebel Voices: An I.W.W. Anthology*. Ann Arbor: University of Michigan Press, 1965.

Lambert, Gavin. *Nazimova: A Biography*. New York: Alfred A. Knopf, 1997.

Lannon, Albert Vetere. *Fight or Be Slaves: The History of the Oakland-East Bay Labor Movement*. Lanham, Md.: University Press of America, 2000.

Ledbetter, Rosanna. *A History of the Malthusian League 1877–1927*. Columbus: Ohio State University Press, 1976.

Lehrer, Susan. *Origins of Protective Labor Legislation for Women 1905–1925*. Albany: State University of New York Press, 1987.

Leier, Mark. *Bakunin: The Creative Passion*. New York: Thomas Dunne Books, 2006.

Levine, Louis. *The Labor Movement in France*. New York: Columbia University Press, 1914.

LeWarne, Charles Pierce. *Utopias on Puget Sound, 1885–1915*. Seattle: University of Washington Press, 1975.

Livingston, James. *Origins of the Federal Reserve System: Money, Class, and Corporate Capitalism, 1890–1913*. Ithaca, N.Y.: Cornell University Press, 1986.

Lorwin, Val R. *The French Labor Movement*. Cambridge, Mass.: Harvard University Press, 1954.

Loughery, John. *John Sloan: Painter and Rebel*. New York: Henry Holt, 1995.

Lowith, Karl. *From Hegel to Nietzsche: The Revolution in Nineteenth-Century Thought*. New York: Holt, Rinehart, and Winston, 1964.

Luhan, Mabel Dodge. *Intimate Memories*. New York: Harcourt, Brace, 1936.

MacDonald, George E. *Fifty Years of Freethought*. 2 vols. New York: The Truth Seeker Company, 1929, 1931. Reprint, New York: Arno Press, 1972.

MacLachlan, Colin M. *Anarchism and the Mexican Revolution: The Political Trials of Ricardo Flores Magón in the United States*. Berkeley: University of California Press, 1991.

Madison, Charles A. *Jewish Publishing in America: The Impact of Jewish Writing on American Culture*. New York: Sanhedrin Press, 1976.

Maitron, Jean, ed. *1871–1914. De la Commune à la Grande Guerre*. Part 3, vols. 8–15 of *Dictionnaire biographique du mouvement ouvrier français*. Paris: Les Éditions Ouvrières, 1973–1977.

Mann, Thomas. *Tom Mann's Memoirs*. London: Labour Publishing Company, 1923.

Marsh, Margaret S. *Anarchist Women, 1870–1920*. Philadelphia: Temple University Press, 1981.

Martin, James J. *Men Against the State*. DeKalb, Ill.: Adrian Allen Associates, 1953.

Mathur, Sobhag. *Echoes of Indian National Movement in America*. Jodhpur, India: Kusumanjali Prakashan, 1996.

Mattson, Kevin. *Creating a Democratic Public: The Struggle for Urban Participatory Democracy During the Progressive Era*. University Park: Penn State University Press, 1998.

McLennan, Rebecca M. *The Crisis of Imprisonment: Protest, Politics, and the Making of the American Penal State, 1776–1941*. Cambridge History of American Law. Cambridge: Cambridge University Press, March 2008.

Miles, Dionne. *Something in Common: An IWW Bibliography*. Detroit: Wayne State University Press, 1986.

Miller, Martin A. *Kropotkin*. Chicago: University of Chicago Press, 1976.

Mitchell, Barbara. *The Practical Revolutionaries*. New York: Greenwood Press, 1987.

Moore, Gloria, and Ronald Moore. *Margaret Sanger and the Birth Control Movement: A Bibliography, 1911–1984*. Metuchen, N.J.: The Scarecrow Press, 1986.

Mott, Frank Luther. *A History of American Magazines, Vol. 5: Sketches of 21 Magazines 1905–1930*. Cambridge, Mass.: Belknap Press of Harvard University Press, 1968.

Munson-Williams-Proctor Institute. *The Armory Show—50th Anniversary Exhibition*. Utica, N.Y.: Munson-Williams-Proctor Institute, 1968.

Murphy, Paul. *World War I and the Origin of Civil Liberties in the United States*. New York: W. W. Norton, 1979.

Nacht, Siegfried. *The Social General Strike*. Translated from the German by F. K. Chicago: The Debating Club, 1905.

Naumann, Francis M., and Paul Avrich. "Adolf Wolff: 'Poet, Sculptor and Revolutionist, but Mostly Revolutionist.'" *Art Bulletin* 67, no. 3 (September 1985): 486–500.

Nettlau, Max. *A Short History of Anarchism*. Edited by Heiner M. Becker and translated by Ida Pilat Isca. London: Freedom Press, 1996.

Nietzsche, Friedrich. *Will to Power, An Attempted Transvaluation of All Values*. Translated by Anthony M. Ludovici. New York: Macmillan, 1914.

Notehelfer, F. G. *Kōtoku Shūsui: Portrait of a Japanese Radical*. London: Cambridge University Press, 1971.

Novkov, Julie. *Constituting Workers, Protecting Women: Gender, Law, and Labor in the Progressive Era and New Deal Years*. Ann Arbor: University of Michigan Press, 2001.

Ohara, Kaoru. "The Japanese Socialists and Anarchists in the San Francisco Bay Area, from 1900 to 1910." *Kokugakuin Journal* 40 (2002): 108–28.

Passet, Joanne. *Sex Radicals and the Quest for Women's Equality*. Urbana: University of Illinois Press, 2003.

Paterson, R. W. K. *The Nihilistic Egoist: Max Stirner*. London: Oxford University Press, 1971.

Patten, Jon, ed. *Yiddish Anarchist Bibliography*. London: Kate Sharpley Library, 1998.

Perlin, Terry M. "Anarchism in New Jersey: The Ferrer Colony at Stelton." *New Jersey History* (Fall 1971): 133–48.

Perlman, Bennard B. *Robert Henri: His Life and Art*. New York: Dover Publications, 1991.

Perry, Lewis, and Richard S. Perry. *A History of the Los Angeles Labor Movement, 1911–1941*. Berkeley and Los Angeles: University of California Press, 1963.

Plotkin, Ira L. *Anarchism in Japan: A Study of the Great Treason Affair, 1910–1911*. Lewiston, N.Y.: Edwin Mellen Press, 1990.

Poole, David, ed. *Land and Liberty: Anarchist Influences in the Mexican Revolution*. Sanday, Orkney: Cienfuegos Press, 1977.

Preston, William Jr. *Aliens and Dissenters. Federal Suppression of Radicals, 1903–1933*. Urbana: University of Illinois Press, 1963.

Putnam, Samuel P. *400 Years of Freethought*. New York: The TruthSeeker Company, 1894.

Raat, W. Dirk. *Revoltosos: Mexico's Rebels in the United States, 1903–1923*. College Station: Texas A&M University Press, 1981.

Rabban, David M. *Free Speech in Its Forgotten Years*. Cambridge: Cambridge University Press, 1997.

Radosh, Ron. *Debs*. Englewood Cliffs, N.J.: Prentice Hall, 1971.

Rafter, Nicole Hahn, and Debra L. Stanley. *Prisons in America: A Reference Handbook*. Santa Barbara: ABC-CLIO, 1999.

Reichart, William O. *Partisans of Freedom*. Bowling Green, Ohio: Bowling Green University Popular Press, 1976.

Reitman, Ben. "Following the Monkey." Unpublished manuscript, ca. 1925–1940.

Renshaw, Patrick. *The Wobblies: The Story of the IWW and Syndicalism in the United States*. Chicago: Ivan R. Dee, 1999.

Rich, Charlotte J. *Transcending the New Woman: Multi-ethnic Narratives in the Progressive Era*. Columbia: University of Missouri Press, 2009.

Ridley, F. F. *Revolutionary Syndicalism in France*. Cambridge: Cambridge University Press, 1970.

Ringenbach, Paul T. *Tramps and Reformers 1873–1916*. Westport, Conn.: Greenwood Press, 1973.

Robinson, William J., M.D. *Fewer and Better Babies or the Limitation of Offspring by the Prevention of Conception*. New York: The Critic and Guide Company, 1915.

Rocker, Rudolf. *Anarcho-Syndicalism*. London: Secker and Warburg, 1938.

Roediger, David. *Wages of Whiteness: Race and the Making of the American Working Class*. Rev. ed. London and New York: Verso, 1999.

Rogoff, Harry. *An East Side Epic: The Life and Work of Meyer London*. New York: The Vanguard Press, 1930.

Rosen, Ruth. *The Lost Sisterhood: Prostitution in America, 1900–1918*. Baltimore: John Hopkins University Press, 1982.

Rowbotham, Sheila. *Edward Carpenter: A Life of Liberty and Love*. London: Verso, 2008.

Rowbotham, Sheila, and Jeffrey Weeks. *Socialism and the New Life: The Personal and Sexual Politics of Edward Carpenter and Havelock Ellis*. London: Pluto Press, 1977.

Rudnick, Lois Palken. *Mabel Dodge Luhan: New Woman, New Worlds*. Albuquerque: University of New Mexico Press, 1984.

Sack, A. J. *The Birth of the Russian Democracy*. New York: Russian Information Bureau, 1918.

Salerno, Salvatore. *Red November, Black November: Culture and Community in the Industrial Workers of the World*. New York: State University of New York Press, 1989.

Salvatore, Nick. *Eugene V. Debs: Citizen and Socialist*. Urbana: University of Illinois Press, 1982.

Sanger, Margaret. *An Autobiography*. 1938. Reprint, New York: Dover Publications, 1971.

——. *Selected Papers of Margaret Sanger*, edited by Esther Katz. Vol. 1, *The Woman Rebel 1900–1928*. Urbana: University of Illinois Press, 2003.

Sarlós, Robert Károly. *Jig Cook and the Provincetown Players Theatre in Ferment*. Amherst: University of Massachusetts Press, 1982.

Schlissel, Lillian, ed. *Conscience in America: A Documentary History of Conscientious Objection in America, 1757–1967*. New York: E. P. Dutton, 1968.

Schneider, Dorothy, and Carl Schneider. "Black Women on the Move." In *American Women in the Progressive Era, 1900–1920*. New York: Facts on File, 1993.

Schroeder, Theodore. *Free Speech for Radicals*. New York: Free Speech League, 1916.

——. *Free Speech Bibliography*. New York: H. W. Wilson Company, 1922.

Schwarz, Judith. *Radical Feminists of Heterodoxy: Greenwich Village, 1912–1940*. Lebanon, N.H.: New Victoria Publishers, 1986.

Sears, Hal D. *The Sex Radicals: Free Love in High Victorian America*. Lawrence: Regents Press of Kansas, 1977.

Shannon, David A. *The Socialist Party of America*. Chicago: Quadrangle Books, 1967.

Shapiro, Herbert. "The McNamara Case: A Crisis of the Progressive Era." *Southern California Quarterly* 59, no. 3 (Fall 1977): 271–87.

Shore, Elliott. *Talking Socialism*. Lawrence: University Press of Kansas, 1988.

Sklar, Martin J. *The Corporate Reconstruction of American Capitalism, 1890–1916: The Market, the Law, and Politics*. Cambridge: Cambridge University Press, 1988.

Smith, Bernard. *Forces in American Criticism: A Study in the History of American Literary Thought*. New York: Harcourt, Brace, 1939.

Smith, Gibbs M. *Labor Martyr: Joe Hill*. New York: Grosset and Dunlap, 1969.

Sochen, June. *The New Woman: Feminism in Greenwich Village 1910–1920*. New York: Quadrangle Books, 1972.

Southern, David W. *The Progressive Era and Race: Reaction and Reform 1900–1917*. Wheeling, Ill.: Harlan Davidson, 2005.

Sprading, Charles T., ed. *Liberty and the Great Libertarians*. Los Angeles: Golden Press for the author, 1913.

Stansell, Christine. *American Moderns: Bohemian New York and the Creation of a New Century*. New York: Henry Holt, 2000.

Stearns, Peter. *Revolutionary Syndicalism and French Labor*. New Brunswick, N.J.: Rutgers University Press, 1971.

Stimson, Grace Heilman. *The Rise of the Labor Movement in Los Angeles*. Berkeley and Los Angeles: University of California Press, 1955.

Stirner, Max. *The Ego and Its Own*. Translated by Steven Byington. 1884, New York: Benjamin Tucker, 1907.

Stromquist, Shelton. *Reinventing "The People": The Progressive Movement, the Class Problem, and the Origins of Modern Liberalism*. Urbana: University of Illinois Press, 2006.

Sullivan, Larry E. *The Prison Reform Movement: Forlorn Hope*. Boston: Twayne Publishers, 1990.

Taft, Philip. "The I.W.W. in the Grain Belt." *Labor History* 1, no. 1 (Winter 1960): 53–67.

Thompson, Fred. *The I.W.W.: Its First Seventy Years (1905–1975)*. Chicago: Industrial Workers of the World, 1976.

Thorpe, Wayne. *"The Workers Themselves": Revolutionary Syndicalism and International Labour, 1913–1923*. Dordrecht, The Netherlands: Kluwer Academic Publishers/Amsterdam: International Institute of Social History, 1989.

Torres Parés, Juan. *La revolutión sin frontera*. Mexico City.: Ediciones y Distribuciones Hispánicas, 1990.

Townsend, John Clendenin. *Running the Gauntlet: Cultural Sources of Violence Against the IWW*. New York: Garland Publishing, 1986.

Traubel, Horace L., Richard Maurice Bucke, and Thomas B. Harned, eds. *In Re Walt Whitman: Edited by his Literary Executors*. Philadelphia: Published by the Editors through Davis McKay, 1893.

Tridon, André. *The New Unionism*. New York: B. W. Huebsch, 1913.

Tripp, Anne Huber. *The IWW and the Paterson Silk Strike of 1913*. Urbana: University of Illinois Press, 1987.

Turner, Ethel Duffy. *Revolution in Baja, California: Ricardo Flores Magon's High Noon*. Detroit: Blaine Etheridge, 1981.

Turner, John Kenneth. *Barbarous Mexico*. Chicago: Charles H. Kerr, 1911.

Van der Linden, Marcel Thorpe, and Wayne Thorpe. *Revolutionary Syndicalism: An International Perspective*. Scolar Press, 1990.

Vose, Mary Heaton. *A Footnote to Folly*. New York: Farrar and Rinehart, 1935.

Ward, Estolv E. *The Gentle Dynamiter: A Biography of Tom Mooney*. Palo Alto, Calif.: Ramparts Press, 1983.

Warren, Sidney. *American Freethought, 1860–1914*. New York: Columbia University Press, 1943.

Weinstein, James. *The Corporate Ideal and the Liberal State, 1900–1918*. Boston: Beacon Press, 1968.

Wells-Barnett, Ida B. *A Red Record: Tabulated Statistics and Alleged Causes of Lynching in the United States, 1892–1893–1894, Respectfully Submitted to the Nineteenth Century Civilization in the "Land of the Free and the Home of the Brave."* Chicago: Donohue and Henneberry, 1895.

Wexler, Alice. "Emma Goldman on Mary Wollstonecraft." *Feminist Studies* 7, no. 1 (Spring 1981): 113–33.

———. *Emma Goldman: An Intimate Life*. New York: Pantheon Books, 1984.

Whitman, Walt. *The Complete Poems*. Edited by Francis Murphy. New York: Penguin Books, 1996.

Wiebe, Robert H. *The Search for Order, 1877–1920*. New York: Hill and Wang, 1967.

Wilde, Oscar. *The Soul of Man Under Socialism*. London: privately printed, 1904.

Wood, Janice Ruth. *The Struggle for Free Speech in the United States, 1872–1915: Edward Bliss Foote, Edward Bond Foote, and Anti-Comstock Operations*. New York: Routledge, 2007.

Woodcock, George. *Anarchism: A History of Libertarian Ideas and Movements*. Cleveland: Meridian Books, 1962.

Woodcock, George, and Ivan Avakumovic. *The Anarchist Prince: A Biographical Study of Peter Kropotkin*. London: T. V. Boardman, 1950.

Young, Arthur Nichols. *The Single Tax Movement in the United States*. Princeton, N.J.: Princeton University Press, 1916.

Zinn, Howard. *The Politics of History*. Boston: Beacon Press, 1970.

———. *A Power Governments Cannot Suppress*. San Francisco: City Lights Books, 2007.

## PUBLICATIONS BY EMMA GOLDMAN, 1910–1916

### BOOKS

*Anarchism and Other Essays.* New York: Mother Earth Publishing Association, 1910; 2nd ed., 1911; 3rd ed., 1917. 277 pp.

*The Social Significance of the Modern Drama.* Boston: Richard G. Badger, 1914. 315 pp.

### PAMPHLETS

*The White Slave Traffic.* New York: Mother Earth Publishing Association, 1909. Published in *Mother Earth* 4, no. 11 (January 1910) with the name "Dr. Ploss" replaced by "Dr. Bloss"; published in *Anarchism and Other Essays* as "The Traffic in Women" with many changes.

*Anarchism: What It Really Stands For.* New York: Mother Earth Publishing Association, 1911; 2nd ed., 1916. 23 pp. Published originally in *Anarchism and Other Essays* with minor differences.

*Marriage and Love.* New York: Mother Earth Publishing Association, 1911; 2nd ed., 1916, with minor differences; 3rd ed., 1917. 15 pp.

*The Psychology of Political Violence.* New York: Mother Earth Publishing Association, 1911. 30 pp. First published in *Anarchism and Other Essays* (1910) with minor grammatical and typographical differences.

*Victims of Morality and the Failure of Christianity: Two Lectures.* New York: Mother Earth Publishing Association, 1913, 14 pp. An identical version of "Victims of Morality" was published in *Mother Earth* 8, no. 1 (March 1913); an identical version of "The Failure of Christianity" was first published in *Mother Earth* 8, no. 2 (April 1913).

*Syndicalism: The Modern Menace to Capitalism.* New York: Mother Earth Publishing Association, 1913. 14 pp. An identical version was first published in *Mother Earth* 7, nos. 11–12 (January 1913) as "Syndicalism: Its Theory and Practice"; an edited version was published as "Syndicalism," with many paragraphs omitted, in Charles Sprading, ed., *Liberty and Great Libertarians.* Los Angeles: Charles Sprading, 1913.

*Philosophy of Atheism and the Failure of Christianity: Two Lectures.* New York: Mother Earth Publishing Association, [1913?]; 2nd ed., 1916. 14 pp. An identical version of "Philosophy of Atheism" was published in *Mother Earth* 10, no. 12 (February 1916); an identical version of "The Failure of Christianity" was published in *Mother Earth* 8, no. 2 (April 1913).

*Preparedness: The Road to Universal Slaughter.* New York: Mother Earth Publishing Association, 1916. 9 pp. First published in *Mother Earth* 10, no. 10 (December 1915); the pamphlet had substantial revisions from the *Mother Earth* edition.

## PUBLICATIONS OF MOTHER EARTH PUBLISHING ASSOCIATION

### BOOKS

Berkman, Alexander. *Prison Memoirs of an Anarchist,* September 1912. 512 pp.

De Cleyre, Voltairine. *Selected Works of Voltairine de Cleyre.* 1914. Edited by Alexander Berkman, biographical sketch by Hippolyte Havel. 471 pp.

## PAMPHLETS

Bakunin, Michael. *God and the State.* 1916. With portrait and with preface by Élisée Reclus. 96 pp. Incorrectly identified as the first American edition.

Champney, Adeline. *What Is Worthwhile? A Study of Conduct from the Viewpoint of the Man Awake.* 1911. 16 pp. First identical version published in *Mother Earth* 5, nos. 9–11 (November 1910–January 1911).

De Cleyre, Voltairine. *The Dominant Idea.* 1910. 16 pp. First published in *Mother Earth* 5, nos. 3–4 (May–June 1910), with minor typographical differences.

———. *The Mexican Revolt.* 1911. 4 pp. First published in *Mother Earth* 6, no. 6 (August 1911), an identical version.

———. *Direct Action.* 1912. 19 pp.

James, C. L., *Anarchism and Malthus.* 1910. 30 pp. First published in *Mother Earth* 4, nos. 2–6 (April–August 1909), with minor grammatical differences.

Kuh, Edwin James. *The Right to Disbelieve.* 1910. 16 pp.

Light, C. D. *Crime and Punishment.* 1910. 12 pp.

Owen, William C. *Anarchy Versus Socialism.* 1910. 30 pp.

Schroeder, Theodore. *Liberal Opponents and Conservative Friends of Unabridged Free Speech: Being Notes of a Lecture Delivered March 13, 1910, Before the Brooklyn Philosophical Association.* 1910. 16 pp. First published in *Mother Earth* 5, no. 3 (June 1910), with two sentences that were omitted from this version.

*Workingmen, Don't Vote!* 1912. 2 pp. First published in *Mother Earth* 7, no. 8 (1912), an identical version.


## PUBLICATIONS OF THE FREE SPEECH LEAGUE, 1910–1916

### 1910

Schroeder, Theodore. *The Historical Interpretation of Unabridged Freedom of Speech.*
———. *A Lobby for Liberty.*

### 1911

Schroeder, Theodore. *Conflict Between Religious Morals and Ethical Science, Being a Study in the Uncertainty of the Moral Test of the Crime.*
———. *Protest of the Free Speech League Against the Passage of Senate Bill No. 1790, Assembly Bill No. 650, New York Legislature, 1911, Which Proposes to Penalize Certain Medical Advertising and Intelligence.*
———. *Table of Cases Involving Obscenity and Kindred Statutes.*

### 1912

Ellis, Havelock. *Witchcraft and Obscenity; Twin Superstitions.*
Hapgood, Hutchins. *Fire and Revolution.* Riverside, Conn.: Hillacre Press for the Free Speech League.
Schroeder, Theodore. *Concerning the Free Speech Anthology.*
———. *The Free Speech Case of Jay Fox.*

———. *Free Speech for Radicals: Seven Essays.*

———. *Obscene Literature and Constitutional Law: A Forensic Defense of Freedom of Press.*

## 1913

Mills, James. *On Liberty of the Press for Advocating Resistance to Government.* Edited by Theodore Schroeder.

*Partial Bibliography of the Writings of Theodore Schroeder.*

Schroeder, Theodore, ed. *Edward Bond Foote: Biographical Notes and Appreciatives.* Riverside, Conn.: Hillacre Press for the Free Speech League.

## 1914

Roe, Gilbert Ernstein. *Reasonable Restrictions upon the Freedom of Assemblage.*

Schroeder, Theodore. *Methods of Constitutional Construction. The Synthetic Method Illustrated on the Free Speech Cause of the Federal Constitution . . . With Three Supplements Bearing on the Rights of Revolutionists by James Mill, J. L. De Lolme and John Cartwright.*

Steffens, Lincoln. *Free Speech, With and Without.* Riverside, Conn.: Hillacre Press for the Free Speech League.

## 1915

Eastman, Max. *Is the Truth Obscene?*

Roe, Gilbert. *Reasonable Restrictions upon the Freedom of Assemblage.*

Schroeder, Theodore. *McNamaras: Martyrs or Criminals.*

———. *Our Prudish Censorship Unveiled.*

———. *Presumption and Burden of Proof as to Malice in Criminal Libel.*

## 1916

Schroeder, Theodore. *Free Speech and Industrial Unrest: From Final Report of U.S. Commission on Industrial Relations.*

———. *Free Speech for Radicals.* Riverside, Conn.: Hillacre Press for the Free Speech League.

Free Speech League. *Self-Evident Truths About It.*

## EMMA'S LIST

*The Emma Goldman Papers Project thanks our sustaining sponsors and the following additional donors, who have led Emma's List, for their vote of confidence and material support over the years.*

### IN REMEMBRANCE

BELLA ABZUG is remembered by Gloria Steinem.

LYDIA AND GEORGE ARONOWITZ, loved for their wit and passion. May their goodness and sparkle—like Emma's—live on. Remembered by Merrill, Andrew, Todd, and Adam Stone, and by Candace Falk.

PAUL AVRICH, esteemed historian of anarchism is remembered by Federico Arcos and by generations of researchers at the Emma Goldman Papers.

ROGER BALDWIN is remembered by his goddaughter, Katrina vanden Heuvel.

Dedicated to STELLA COMINSKY BALLANTINE Emma's "favorite niece" and aide, and her two sons, IAN BALLANTINE and DAVID BALLANTINE by their lifelong friend, Roy Kahn.

ANNA BARON is remembered by Prof. Millicent and the late Eugene Bell.

LEONARD BASKIN is remembered by Lisa Baskin.

THOMAS H. BEADLING is remembered by Patricia A. Thomas.

SARAH BELLUSH, who loved and taught him to admire Emma Goldman, is remembered by her son, Bernard Bellush.

SUSAN PORTER BENSON is remembered by Judith E. Smith & Family, and Sarah and Jonathan Malino.

WARREN K. BILLINGS, dignified friend and colleague of Alexander Berkman, sentenced to life imprisonment in association with the 1916 Preparedness Day bombing, is remembered by his niece, the late Marguerite Joseph.

SUSAN BLAKE is remembered by Leonard J. Lehrman and Helene R. Spierman for her assistance in performances of E.G.: A Musical Portrait of Emma Goldman.

BEN AND IDA CAPES, Emma's dear friends and comrades, are remembered by David and Bonnie Capes, their grandchildren; by Bonnie Capes Tabatznick, their daughter; and by Albert Chasson and Susan Chasson, their nephew and great niece.

ALICE CHECKOVITZ MAHONEY is remembered by her niece, Susan Wladaver-Morgan.

STEFANIE CHECKOVITZ WLADAVER is remembered by her daughter, Susan Wladaver-Morgan.

MARLENE CAROL CLEMENS is remembered by her parents, Mary and the late Alan Dietch.

SARAH T. CROME, who helped found the Emma Goldman Papers, is remembered by Andrea Sohn, her niece; the late Esther and the late Eugene Revitch, her sister and brother-in-law; and by her friends Victoria Brady, Dale Freeman, Ken Kann, Stephanie Pass, Lyn Reese, and Judy Shattuck, and by her ever grateful colleague and friend Candace Falk.

SOPHIE AND JOE DESSER, Emma's dear friends and comrades, are remembered by their daughter, Mildred Desser Grobstein.

CHANELE (ANNA) SCHILHAUS DIAMOND, Emma Goldman's seamstress, is remembered by her son, the late David Diamond.

MRS. RUTH DUBOW is remembered by Merrill, Andrew, Todd and Adam Stone.

FRANK AND EDITH EIVE are remembered by Gloria Eive.

ALICIA EINWOHNER'S BELOVED MOTHER is remembered by R. Bonnie Glaser.

WALTER AND LILLY ELSON are remembered by Eleanor Lee and Ronald Elson.

NATHAN FALKOWITZ is remembered by Neil Solomon, Paula Birnbaum, and his daughters Jane and Candace Falk.

REBECCA FEILER (1982–2004), spirited young member of the Emma Goldman Papers, is remembered by Debbie and Michael Fieler, the late Rabbi Arnold and Linda Levine, Emily and Bill Marthinsen, the late Cecelia (Aunt Seal) Polan, Miriam Polan, Ruth Polan and Fred Protopapas, Stephen Tobias and Alice Webber, Jan Schmuckler and Anna Martin, Ann Whitehead, and by Candace Falk and Barry Pateman of the Emma Goldman Papers.

JUDITH ANN FEINBERG is remembered by her mother, Sally Brown.

THE FERRER COLONY AND MODERN SCHOOL OF STELTON, NEW JERSEY are remembered by Sally Brown.

MARTHA FREEDMAN is remembered by Estelle Freedman.

RACHEL FRUCHTER is remembered by Susan Reverby.

EMMA GOLDMAN was remembered by the late Art Bortolotti with gratitude for fighting "her last battle with the authorities, a battle that lasted until her last breath," on his behalf.

EMMA GOLDMAN is also remembered by the late David Diamond with gratitude for encouraging him in his youth to pursue his love of music and the violin and "Kling in de ganze Velt" (play for the entire world).

SAMUEL GOMPERS is remembered by Grace Palladino, the co-editor of *The Samuel Gompers Papers*.

JOAN GRUEN is honored by Erich Gruen.

LOUIS R. HARLAN is remembered by Sadie Harlan.

DOROTHY R. HEALEY is remembered by Carol Jean and the late Edward F. Newman.

JOAN HORWICH is remembered by John and Kristene Scholefield.

AGNES INGLIS is remembered by Julie Herrada.

GABRIEL JAVSICAS, Emma's "young friend," is remembered by his daughter, Michele Childers.

LY KAUFMAN is remembered by Neil Goteiner and N. Joseph.

SYLVIA KAUFMAN is remembered by Linda K. Kerber.

JOAN KELLY is remembered by Donna Shulman.

PEG KERANEN is remembered by Sally Miller.

ISIDORE KIVIAT, a contemporary and fellow anarchist with Emma Goldman, is remembered by his grandson J. David Sackman.

SHIRLEY KRAVITZ is remembered by Susan Laine.

ESTHER LADDON, who gave Emma a home in Canada during her exile, is remembered by her daughter, the late Ora Laddon Robbins.

ORA LADDON ROBBINS, who shared her many stories with good humor and generosity, is fondly remembered by Candace Falk and by her granddaughter, Miranda Robbins.

DEBORAH LANGE is remembered by Judith Smith.

LAWRENCE W. LEVINE is remembered by Cornelia R. Levine and Ronald Grele.

AUNT FAYE LEVY—a great lady!—is remembered by Merrill Stone, by her nephew Neil Solomon and family, and by her niece Candace Falk, whom she counseled over the years to "let the woman (Emma Goldman) rest in peace, already."

RACHEL LIMA-JONES is lovingly remembered by Margy Wilkinson.

PETER LISKER is remembered by William and Rae Lisker.

RELLA LOSSY, who captured Emma's spirit in her plays, is remembered by Frank T. Lossy.

OSVALDO MARAVIGLIA is remembered by Louis Maraviglia.

HENRY MAYER is remembered by his wife, Elizabeth Anderson, and by his friend and fellow biographer, Candace Falk.

JANE MAVERICK WELSH and MAURY MAVERICK JR. are remembered by Beá Welsh Weicker (Vita Wells).

ESTHER MERER is remembered by Estelle and the late Howard Bern.

JESSICA MITFORD is remembered by her daughter, Constancia Romilly.

JESSICA MITFORD AND BOB TREUHAFT are remembered by Peter Stansky.

BEN NICHOLS is remembered by E. Wayles Browne.

RUTH ROSENBLATT NOVICK is remembered by Sheldon Novick and Carolyn Clinton.

TILLIE OLSEN is remembered by Nancy Hewitt and Steven Lawson.

UTAH PHILLIPS is remembered by Nancy Lenox and Barry Pateman.

CECELIA POLAN is remembered by Debbie and Michael Feiler.

CURTIS W. REESE, who delivered Emma's last eulogy at her gravesite, is remembered by his son, the late Curtis W. Reese, Jr.

JACQUELINE REINIER is remembered by Richard Walker.

BEN REITMAN, Emma's road manager and lover, is remembered by his daughter, Mecca Reitman Carpenter.

SOPHIA LEVITIN RODRIGUEZ is remembered by Catherine Pantsios.

MIGUEL ROSNER is remembered by Bella Rosner.

ARTHUR LEONARD ROSS, Emma's lawyer and friend, is remembered by his sons, the late Ralph and Edgar Ross.

MARSHALL ROSS is remembered by Matthew Ross and Gloria Lawrence.

MARICARMEN RUIZ-TORRES is remembered by Linda Gort.

IRENE SCHNEIDERMAN is remembered by her dear friend Hilda Rubin, Rosalind and Fred Scheiner, and by her daughters Josephine, Sarah, and Susan Schneiderman.

HELEN SEITZ is remembered by Beth Wilson.

IRMA SHERMAN, aunt, soul-mate and respected member of Emma's List, is remembered by her husband, Julius Sherman, her daugh-

ter, Valerie Broad, her friends Alfred Miller, her niece, Candace Falk, and an anonymous supporter.

JENNY SIDNEY, comrade and mother, is remembered by Barry and Paul Pateman.

JOHN Y. SIMON, Editor of The Papers of the Ulysses S. Grant, is remembered by Harriet Simon.

WINSOR SOULE is remembered by Marcia Tanner.

RUTH SPITZ is remembered by Judith Lorber.

RABBI DR. HARRY JOSHUA STERN is remembered by Stephanie Stern Glaymon.

MATTHEW STOLZ is remembered by Kathy Kahn.

"EMMA GEE" SULLIVAN is remembered by Mark Sullivan.

EMANUEL B. TISHMAN is remembered by his son, Donald Tishman.

DR. HAL J. TODD is remembered by Joan Todd.

CARLO TRESCA is remembered by the late Rudolph J. Vecoli.

OLGA TUGANOVA is remembered by Elena Danielson.

ZITHA ROSEN TURITZ is remembered by her niece, Nancy Chodorow.

NATHAN WALROD is remembered by his father, Stephen Walrod, and the Love Cultivating Assets Fund.

LEON WALTER, of the Stelton community, is remembered by his daughters, Linn Walter Solomon and Ruth Walter Croton.

NORMA WIKLER is remembered by her siblings, Marjorie Senechal and Daniel Wikler, and by her friend Candace Falk.

KATE WOLFSON is remembered by her daughter, the late Irene Schneiderman.

CARLOS WUPPERMANN is remembered by Valerie Yaros.

REGGIE ZELNIK, our "Prince Kropotkin," is remembered by his wife, Elaine Zelnik, Zelda Bronstein, and many members of the Emma Goldman Papers, who benefited from his wisdom and wit.

HOWARD ZINN and ANTHONY RUSSO are remembered by Rick Goldsmith.

## IN HONOR OF THOSE WHO CONTINUE TO KEEP EMMA'S SPIRIT ALIVE

ANTONIA, who embodies Emma's spirit, is honored by her father, David Madson.

LOIS BLUM FEINBLATT is honored by Carolyn Patty Blum and Harry Chotiner, the Malino family, Candace Falk, and the Emma Goldman Papers for her remarkable presence and generosity.

JANE M. BOUVIER is honored by her daughter, Virginia Bouvier.

TALIA ROSE BRAND is honored by Susan and Jeffrey Brand.

JUNE BRUMER is honored by Elaine and Lester Dropkin, and Mary Ann Frankel.

MARI JO BUHLE is honored by Judith E. Smith for her many contributions as a teacher and scholar of women's history.

MARY BURTON is honored for her 60th birthday by her son, James O'Neil.

DANIEL BURTON-ROSE is honored by his father Peter Rose.

RUTH BUTLER is honored by Judith Bank.

BONNIE CAPES TABATZNIK is honored by David and Judith Capes.

DAVID CAPLAN is honored by his father, Michael Caplan.

SUSAN CHASSON is honored by the late Sylvia F. Scholtz.

LINC COHEN is honored by Sandi Wisenberg.

OLIVIA CRAWFORD is honored by Robert Hillmann.

ELEANOR ENGSTRAND AND MARGE FRANTZ are honored by Carol Jean and the late Edward F. Newman.

CANDACE FALK is honored by Allida Black and Judy A. Beck, Carolyn Patty Blum and Harry Chotiner, Carol Brosgart, Yvette Chalom and Paul Fogel, Rabbi Ferenc Raj and Paula L. Raj, Allen and Hannah King, Lois Schiffer, Valerie Sherman and Richard Broad, Merrill Stone, Peter Stansky, the late Rudolph J. Vecoli, and the late Denyse Gross, among many others.

JANE FALK is honored by Neil Goteiner and N. Joseph, by Merrill, Andy, Todd and Adam Stone, her friend Annette Kolodny, and by her sister, Candace, who all wish her continued good health and happiness.

SARAH FINK is honored on her 16th Birthday by Sandi L. Wisenberg.

VICTOR FISCHER is honored by Cheryl Nichols Fischer.

JOSEPH FRIEDMAN is honored by his son, Larry Friedman.

R. BONNIE GLASER in honored by Rose Weilerstein, Hildegard Berliner, and Susan Thompson.

LEONARD GOLDSMITH and GEORGE SELDES are honored by Rick Goldsmith.

SARAH BARRINGER GORDON is honored in recognition of her work and support of the legacy of Emma Goldman.

MARION GREENE is honored by Marina Drummer.

ELSIE HILLMANN is honored by Robert Hillmann and Olivia Crawford.

LINDA HIRSCHORN is honored for her song, "Dance a Revolution," which carries on the spirit of Emma Goldman, by Nancy Shimmel and Claudia Morrow.

ERIC ALAN ISAACSON, mentor and friend, is honored by C. Benjamin Nutley.

DAVID KANDEL is honored by Betsy Krieger.

BEN AND GINNY KENDALL are honored by the late Sheldon Rovin.

J. HANNAH KRANZBERG is honored by Michael Goldhaber and Candace Falk.

CAROL LASSER is honored by Cathy Kornblith.

LYNN LERER LAUPHEIMER is honored by Angeleen Campra.

LEON LITWACK is honored by William M. Tuttle, Jr., Lisa Baskin and all the Emma Goldman Papers staff for his generous guiding hand and advocacy of the history of dissent.

LIVER ORGAN DONORS are honored by William C. Rosa.

EDITH LOBE is honored by Lori Marso.

LAUREN MCINTOSH is honored by Alice Hoffman.

ROSE VIVIAN MURPHY-JONES is honored by Renee Samelson.

BARRY PATEMAN is honored for his on-going support and research of the Emma Goldman Papers by Michael Caplan, among many others.

EERO D. and ESME PANKONIN is honored by Dan Wohlfeiler.

GAIL REIMER of the Jewish Women's Archive is honored by Shelly Tenenbaum, and Candace Falk.

LEAH REIS-DENNIS is honored by Elizabeth Reis and Matthew Dennis.

KIERSTEN AMANDA ROESEMANN is honored by her father and mother, Douglas N. Roesemann and Marla Erbin-Roesemann, and by her grandmother, the late Audrey Roesemann.

SYLVIA ALEXIS ROLLOFF is honored by Carol DeBoer-Langworthy and Russell Langworthy.

EMMA SAMELSON JONES'S graduation is honored by Renee Samelson.

JORDAN AND COREY SCHER are honored by Christine Sorensen for future choice and freedom of expression!

EMMA SHAW CRANE is honored by Susan Shaw and Thomas W. Crane.

EMMA AND ALEXANDER SIPE are honored by Gary Doebler.

SHARON H. STROM is honored by Judith E. Smith.

FRED THOMPSON is honored by David Roediger and Jean Allman.

TIM WARDEN-HERTZ is honored by David Hertz and Mary Ellen Warden.

ROSE WEILERSTEIN, HILDEGARD BERLINER, and SUSAN THOMPSON are honored by R. Bonnie Glaser.

EMMA ARIELLE WEINSTEIN, named after Emma Goldman, is honored by Jessica Litwak.

VERA WEISS is honored by Barbara and Arthur Bloch.

The late JEAN WILKINSON is honored by her friend, Lyn Reese.

ARI, ELLIE AND WILL WOHLFEILER are honored by Dan Wohlfeiler.

EMMA WOLF is honored by her parents, the late Dolores Neuman, and Louis Wolf.

ANTONIO F. YOON is honored by Eric Alan Isaacson and Susan Kay Weaver.

JOSEPH ZELNICK is honored by Carl N. Degler.

## INSTITUTIONAL DONORS

Action Democrats

American Council for Learned Societies

Albert and Pamela Bendich Charitable Trust

Millicent and Eugene Bell Foundation

California Council for the Humanities

Chadwyck-Healey, Inc.

The Catticus Corporation

The Commonwealth Fund

Congregration Beth El

The Emma Goldman Clinic

The Ford Foundation

The Funding Exchange

Furthermore: A Project of the J.M. Kaplan Foundation

George Gund Foundation

Hunt Alternatives Fund

Han Min Liu of the Kellogg Foundation

Herbert Anzon Mills Revocable Trust

Institute for Democratic Education and Culture

James Kimo Campbell of the Pohaku Fund

Lainey Feingold and Randy Shaw Justice Fund

The Irving and Lois Blum Foundation

The L.J. Skaggs and Mary C. Skaggs Foundation

The Lucius N. Littauer Foundation

The Los Angeles Educational Partnership

Max and Anna Levinson Foundation

Milken Family Foundation

Mills College Library

Eric Berg of Price Waterhouse Coopers, Ltd.

The Rockefeller Foundation

Samuel Rubin Foundation

The San Francisco Foundation: Love Cultivating Assets Fund

The Barbara Streisand Foundation

Ken Morrison of Sun Microsystems

Tides Foundation

The University of San Francisco *Peace Review*

The Vanguard Foundation

Earl Warren Chapter of the American Civil Liberties Union

H.W. Wilson Foundation

The Williams Bingham Foundation
Women's Studies Program at Middle
   Tennessee State University
Saul Zaentz Trust

## INDIVIDUAL DONORS

Anonymous
Mark Aaronson and Marjorie Gelb
Martha Ackelsberg
Andrew Jackson Adams and Marty Durling
Herb Adelman
The late Janet Adelman and Robert Osserman
Alice Merner Agogino
Harriet Alonso
Meryl Altman
Lisa D. Alvarez and Andrew Tonkovich
Carol Amyx
Ron Anastasia and Kim Anway-Anastasia
Elizabeth Anderson and the late Henry Mayer
William L. and Charron F. Andrews
Joyce Appleby
Jeffrey Travis Atwood
Lisa Aug
Bob Baldock and Kathleen Weaver
Judith Bank
Lisa Baskin
Rosalyn Baxandall
Alan Becker
Helen Becker
Jaime Becker
Jonathan Becker
Pessl Beckler-Semel-Stern
Prof. Millicent and the late Eugene Bell
Bernard Bellush
Marlou Belyea and William (Zach) Taylor
Lenni Benson
Eric Berg
Richard Berger and Judith Derman
Estelle and the late Howard Bern
Carmina Bernardo
Elizabeth Berry
Mary F. Berry
Hilton Bertalan and Michele Donnelly
Stephen Berzon
Sheila Biddle
Rebeccalyn Bilodeau
Nancy Bissell Segal and Robert Segal

Allida Black and Judy A. Beck
Katharine and Charles Blackman
Martin Blatt
Barbara and Arthur Bloch
Jack and Jean Block
Paul Bluestone
Carolyn Patty Blum and Harry Chotiner
Lois Blum Feinblatt
Stephen Blum and Lorraine T. Midanik
Herman and Margaret Blumenthal
Lynn A. Bonfield
Anne Borchardt
Danice Bordett
Eileen Boris and Nelson Lichtenstein
The late Art and Libera Bortolotti
Virginia Bouvier and James Lyons
Mary Katherine Bowen
The late Jo Ann Boydston
Victoria Brady
Betty Lou and the late Ted Bradshaw
Susan and Jeffrey Brand
Marion Brenner and Robert Shimshak
Carroll and the late Robert Brentano
Ramsay Bell Breslin
Valerie Sherman and Richard Broad
Bill Broderick and Bea Kumasaka
Addy and Merle Brodsky
Sunny and Philip Brodsky
Zelda Bronstein
Carol Brosgart and Joseph Gross
Michael Brown and Laura Malakoff
Sally Brown
E. Wayles Browne
Robert Pack Browning and Linda Maio
June and the late Abe Brumer
Dorothy Bryant
Paul Bundy
Michael Burawoy
Julianne Burton-Carvajal
Nancy Caldwell Sorel and Ed Sorel
Laurie Calhoun
James Kimo Campbell
Angeleen Campra
David and Judith Capes
Bonnie Capes Tabatznik
Jane Caplan
Michael and Marsha Caplan

The late Mortimer M. Caplin

Catalina Cariaga and Grant Nakamura

Scott Carpenter

Mecca Reitman Carpenter

Candace M. Carroll

Clayborne and Susan Carson

JoAnn Castagna

Joseph and Susan Cerny

Yvette Chalom and Paul Fogel

Mariam Chamberlain

Marlene and Albert Chasson

Susan Chasson

Nupur and Sam Chaudhuri

Robert Cherny

Marcia Chicca

Michele and Rory Childers

The late Leah and the late Marvin Chodorow

Nancy Chodorow

Noam and the late Aviva Chomsky

Joy Christenberry

Joy Ann Chuck

Eleanor C. Clarke and Alan Davis

The late Pat Cody

The late Ms. Natalie Cohen

The late Marcus and the late Harryette Cohn

Elizabeth Colton

William Connell

Charles and Beverly Connor (Harriette Austin Writers)

Scott and Jana Conover

J. Scott Corporon and Josie Porras

Margaret Corrigan and Larry Gibbs

Maureen Corrigan and Richard J. Yeselson

Robert E. Cotner

Nancy Cott

Patrick Coughlin

Carole M. Counihan and James M. Taggart

Victoria Crane and Matthew Engle

Matthew, Linda, and Ellen Creager

Fred Croton

Christina Crowley and Peter Hobe

Ken Cunkle

Naomi Dagen and Ronald L. Bloom

Suzanne K. Damarin

Pete Daniel

Elena and Ron Danielson

Tom Debley and Mary Jane Holmes

Carol DeBoer-Langworthy and Russell Langworthy

Carl N. Degler

Edward de Grazia

Anna de Leon

Michael Denneny, Andrew Miller, Robert Weil (formerly of St. Martin's Press)

Cleo Deras and Carlos Hernandez

Patchara and Arthur Devenport, III.

The late David Diamond

Mary and the late Alan Dietch

The late John P. Diggens

Christine Distefano

Barbara Dobkin

E.L. and Helen Doctorow

Jill and Martin Dodd

Sarah J. Dodder

Gary Doebler

Conrad and Sandra Donner

Shawn Donnille

Janet Drake and Kevin Lee

Elaine and Lester Dropkin

Marina Drummer

Martin Duberman

Thomas Dublin and Kitty Sklar

Robert Dunn

William Dunn

Jack and Dorothy Edelman

The late Samuel and Hope Efron

Diane Ehrensaft and Jim Hawley

Robin Einhorn

Laurel and Eugene Eisner

Gloria Eive

Robert Elias and Jennifer Turpin

Alan and Dianne Elms

Roslyn Elms Sutherland

Barbara Epstein

Edwin M. and Sandra Epstein

Shelly Errington and Leo Goodman

Marilyn Fabe

Jane Fajans and Terry Turner

Jane Falk

Deborah Farrell

Claire Feder

Debbie and Michael Feiler

Elaine Feingold and Randall M. Shaw

Jacob Feldman

Ovina Maria Feldman

Katy Fenn

Laura Fenster and Jon Rosenberg

Pietro and Franco Ferrua

Cheryl Nichols Fischer

Emily Filloy and David Weintraub

Joseph A. and Elizabeth Fisher

Barbara and Robert Fishman

Bruce Fodiman

Christopher B. and Shirley J. Forester

Steve Fortuna

Nancy Fox

Norman Francis and Beverly Dean Williams

Mary Ann Frankel

The late B. Franklin and the late Joan F. Kahn

Suzanne E. Franks

Marge Frantz and Eleanor Engstrand

Donald and Dava Freed

Estelle Freedman

Dale C. Freeman

The late Marilyn French

Bette Fried

Larry and Sharon Friedman

Mark Friedman and Marjorie Solomon
    Friedman

Robert and Ann Friedman

James and Dianne Fristrom

Lisa Fruchtman and Norman Postone

Donna Gabaccia

Beverly Gage

John Gage and Linda Schacht Gage

Lisa and Jeff Ganung

Judith Gardiner

Daniel Garrison

Rochelle Gatlin

Dan C. George and Erica L. Marks

Carl Djerassi and the late Diane Middlebrook

Robert and Nancy Gerber

Donald Gibson and Dai Sil Kim-Gibson

Patricia Gill

Christina and John Gillis

Abigail Ginzberg

R. Bonnie Glaser

Peter Glassgold and Suzanne Thibodeau

T. J. Glauthier and M. Brigid O'Farrell

Stephanie Stern Glaymon

Traci Gleason

Susan Glenn and James Gregory

Burton Gold

Neil Goldberg and Hagit Cohen

Sam and Maria Goldberger

Michael Goldhaber

Janet Goldner

Rick Goldsmith

Sherry L. Goodman and Jordan D. Luttrell

Nancy Gordon & Associates

Richard Gordon and Meredith Miller

Sarah Barringer Gordon

Ralph Gorin

Nancy and the late Mark Gorrell

Linda Gort

Neil Goteiner and N. Joseph

Hilda Gould

Janet Greenberg

Eleanor Greene

Ronald Grele

Susan Grigg

Mildred Desser Grobstein

Richard Grosboll

Rachael J. Grossman and John Doll

Susan Groves and Eric Anderson

Erich Gruen

Paul A. Gruskoff and Sondra J. Gruskoff

Gay Gullickson

Mary Gutzi

Roland Guyotte

Alice Hall and Michael Smith

Conn and Anne Hallinan

David and Joan Halperin

The late Alice Hamburg

Robert Hamburger

Joan F. Hamel

Larry Hannant

Karen Hansen and Andrew Bundy

Donna J. Haraway and Rusten Hogness

Sadie and the late Louis R. Harlan

James Harrell

Gillian P. Hart

Nina Hartley

Giles Haworth

Virginia G. and Mike Hazlewood (Hazlewood
    Family Fund)

Jean Hegland and Douglas Fisher

Martin O. and Professor Barbara S. Heisler

Stuart Hellman

Clare Hemmings

Linda J. Henry

Julie Herrada

Leroy J. Hertel

David Hertz and Mary Ellen Warden

Frederick Hertz and Randolph Langenbach

Nancy Hewitt and Steven Lawson

Barbara Hill

Ronald Hill

Robert Hillmann and Olivia Crawford

Sally Hindman

Adrienne Hirt and Jeff Rodman

Deborah Hirtz and Dan Waterman

Laura Hithcox-Gibertson

Barbara Hoffer

Alice Hoffman

Deborah Hoffmann and Francis Reid

Ronald W. Hogeland

Patricia Holland

Catherine W. Hollis

Lorraine and Victor Honig

Chris Hoofnagle

David A. Horowitz and Gloria E. Myers

Frank Hunter

Scott A. Ickes and Mary T.B. Currie

Isbel Ingham and Lorraine Kerwood

Eric Alan Isaacson and Susan Kay Weaver

Dorene Isenberg

Elizabeth Jameson

Susan Jarratt

Dr. Thomas E. and Pamela Jeffrey

Philip M. Jelley

Mary Jennings and Donald Sarason

Carole Joffe and Fred Block

Judy Johnson (Los Angeles Educational
  Partnership)

Val Marie Johnson

Erica Jong and Ken Burrows

The late Marguerite Joseph

Henry Kahn and Mickey Gillmor

Jane Kahn

Jean Kahn

Kathy Kahn

Lorraine Kahn

Peggy Kahn

Roy Kahn

Rabbi Yoel Kahn (Congregation Beth El)

The late Wu Ke Kang

Kenneth L. Kann and Stephanie Pass

Timothy Kantz and Simone Levine

Doris Kaplan

Susan Kaplan

Michael Katz

Deborah Sylvia Kaufman and Alan Snitow

Bruce Kayton

Meaghan Keegan

The late Frances Richardson Keller and the
  late William P. Rhetta

Kathleen Kennedy Townsend

Loretta Kensinger

Linda K. and Richard E. Kerber

Ilan and Marlene Keret

John L. Kessell

Shirley Kessler and Bill Jersey

Alice Kessler-Harris

Mha Atma Singh Khalsa

Kristina Kiehl and Bob Friedman

Allen and Hannah King

Kathleen King

Barbara Kingsolver and Stephen Hopp

Jessie and James Kingston

Betty and Bob Klausner

Harvey Klein

Heather and Scott Kleiner

Gerald M. Kline and Julie Florinkline

Maurice Knoepler

Brigitte Koenig and Mark Christopher
  Graman

Annette Kolodny

Cathy Kornblith (The People's Eye)

J. Hannah Kranzberg

Julia Rose Kraut

Betsy Krieger

Stephan Krug

Uldis and Ann Kruze

Jay Kugelman

Mark Kulikowski

Susan Laine

Vera La Farge

Robin Lakoff

Arthur Charles Leahy and Mary Kathryn
  Leahy

Madeleine Lee

Eleanor Lee and Ronald Elson

Elaine Leeder

John Leggett

Leonard J. Lehrman and Helene R. Spierman

Jesse Lemisch and Naomi Weisstein
Nancy Lenox
Gerda Lerner
Paula Goldman Leventman
Cornelia R. and the late Lawrence W. Levine
Simone Levine and Timothy Kantz
The late Linda Levine
The late Rabbi Arnold and Linda Levine
Rhonda Levine
Lynda and Carl Levinson
Rita Lewis and family
Jody LeWitter and Marc Van Der Hout
Doris H. Linder
Steven and Judith Lipson
Wendy Lichtman
Rae and William Lisker
Jessica Litwak
Leon and Rhoda Litwack
Judith Lorber
Frank T. Lossy
Kristin Luker and Jerome Karabel
Zella Luria
Joe Luttrell and Sherry Goodman
Dorothy Lyons
Nancy Mackay
David J. Madson
Sarah and Jonathon Malino
Peter Theodore Manicas
Louis Maraviglia
Maeva Marcus
Victor and Katalin Markowitz
Daniel Marschall
Lori Marso
Emily and Bill Marthinsen
Mary Ann Mason and Paul Ekman
Antje Mattheus and David Kairys
Anne Mattina
Lary and Elaine T. May
Tom Mayer
Judith McCombs and Ernst Benjamin
Pamela McCorduck and Joseph Traub
Mary Lynn McCree Bryan
Dennis McEnnerny and Bryant (Tip) Ragan, Jr.
Margaret H. McFadden
Blaine and Virginia McKinley
Gillies McKenna and Ruth Muschel
Peter A. McNamara

Jennifer Mei and Han Min Liu
(Kellogg Foundation)
Barbara Meislin
Russell and Karen Merritt
Muffie Meyer
Suzanne Meyer
The late Al Meyerhoff
Donna Migliaccio
Laurie and Michael Milken
Ruth Milkman
Alfred and the late Joan Miller
Fredrika V. Miller and Howard Millman
Jesse Miller
The late Maya Miller
Sally Miller and the late Peg Keranen
Sigrid Miller and Robert Pollin
Herbert Mills
The late Jessica Mitford and the late
Robert Treuhaft
Elissa Mondschein
Dominic Montagu and Diep Ngoc Doan
(Nepheli Foundation)
Marie Morgan
Kenneth Morrison and the late Denyse Gross
James Mullins
Carol Murphy
Laura X Murra
Michael Nagler
Victor Navasky
Marty Nesselbush Green
Dolores Neuman and Louis Wolf
The late Ed Newman and Carol Jean Newman
Dolores Newman
Jeffrey Nichols
William Nichols
Brian Norman and Greg Nicholl
Mary Beth Norton
Thom Nosewicz
Sheldon Novick and Carolyn Clinton
The late Morris Novik
Walter Nugent and Suellen Hoy
C. Benjamin Nutley
Robert O'Dell
Karen Offen
Kaoru Ohara
Philip O'Keefe, M.D.
James O'Neil
Nell Painter

Grace Palladino

Catherine Pantsios

Keith Park

Pamela Parker

Barry and Paul Pateman

Thomas Peabody

John Peck

Shana Penn

Mary Elizabeth and Ralph Perry, III.

Joan K. Peters and Peter Passell

The late Agnes F. Peterson

Margaret B. Phillips

Frances Pici

Janice Plotkin

The late Cecelia H. Polan

Miriam Polan

Ruth Polan and Fred Protopappas

Gerald Porter

Linda Post and Eugene Rosow

Tara Prairie

Ruth Price

Carl Prince and family

Jacoba Prins

The late Adele Proom

Leslie and Merle Rabine

The late Victor Rabinowitz and the late
Joanne Grant

Rabbi Ferenc Raj and Paula Wolk

Harold and Erica Ramis

Alan Ramo

Ellen Marie Ratcliffe

Charles H. and Carolyn J. Reese

The late Curtis W. Reese, Jr.

Joan, Robert, and Heather Reese

Michael Reich

Elizabeth Reis and Matthew Dennis

Marylin B.Reizbaum

Susan Reverby

The late Esther and the late Eugene Revitch

Hon. Jennie Rhine and Tom Meyer

Brenda Richardson

Leonard Rico

Thomas P. and Milla Riggio

The late Ora Laddon Robbins

Victor Roberge

Dennis Roberts

Morton S. and Josephine T. Roberts

Renée Robin and Scott McCreary

David Roediger and Jean Allman

Doug Roesemann, Marla Erbin-Roesemann,
Kiersten Amanda Roesemann, and the late
Audrey Roesemann

Florence Wagman Roisman

Rachel Eleah Roisman, M.D.

Coleman and Shelly Romalis

Constancia Romilly

Steve and Suzy Ronfeldt

William C. Rosa

Daniel and Joanna S. Rose

Peter Rose and Daniel Burton-Rose

Ruth Rosen and Wendel Brunner, M.D.

Shale Rosen

Carolyn Cavalier Rosenberg

Erica Rosenfeld and James Wilson

Susan Rosenfeld and Frederick Stielow

Florence Rosenstock and James van Luik

The late Roy Rosenzweig

Bella Rosner and Saul Schapiro

The late Marshall Ross

Matthew Ross and Gloria Lawrence

The late Ralph and Edgar Ross

Steve Rosswurm

Elizabeth Rotundo

Nancy and the late Sheldon Rovin

Sheila Rowbotham

Ronald Rowell

Lillian and the late Hank Rubin

Linda Gort and the late Maricarmen
Ruiz-Torrez

Marcia and the late Lucio Ruotolo

Janet Saalfeld

Paul Sack

J. David and Jerolyn Sackman

Harriet Sage

Samuel J. Salkin and Frankie Whitman

Renee Samelson and Richard Jones

Hendrika Samuels

Ethel Sanjines

Susan Sarandon

Camille Saviola

Jaymie Sawyer

The late Virginia Scardigli

William Schechner

Seth Schein and Sherry Crandon

Danny Scher

Lois Schiffer

Nancy Schimmel and Claudia Morrow
Lillian and Rebecca Schlissel
Ann and Richard Schmidt, Jr.
Walter J. Schmidt
Jan Schmuckler and Anna Martin
Ann M. Schneider
The late Irene Schneiderman
John and Kristene Scholefield
The late Syliva F. Scholtz
Herb Schreier
Frank and Irene Schubert
Donna L. Schulman
Ann Schultis
Constance Schulz
Jane and Jerome Schultz
Marilyn and Harvey Schwartz
John and Kathleen Scott
Nina Scott Frisch and Bjorn Gronnesby
The late Jules and the late Helen Seitz
Martin Selig
Mary Selkirk, Lee Ballance and Zoe
Veronica Selver and Catherine Coates
Marjorie Senechal and Daniel Wikler
Juliet Popper Shaffer
Judy Shattuck
Susan Shaw and Thomas W. Crane
Richard and Martha Sheldon
Julius and the late Irma Sherman
Valerie Sherman and Richard Broad
Michelle Shocked
Alan & Heidi Shonkoff
Hannah Shostack
Alix Kates Shulman
Elizabeth Sibley
Barbara Sicherman
Stephen M. Silberstein
Harriet F. Simon
Arlene and Jerome Skolnick
Janet Small
Deborah L. Smith and Lucas E. Guttentag
Gibbs M. Smith
Judith Smith and family
Yvon Soares
Carol Soc
Andrea Sohn
Margaret E. Sokolik
Daniel Solomon
Linn Walter Solomon

Mark Solomon
Naomi Solomon
Neil Solomon and Paula Birnbaum
Christine Sorensen
Claire Sotnick
Daniel Soyer and Jocelyn Cohen
Robert Grayson Spillers
John Spragens, Jr.
Judith Stacey
Christine Stansell and Sean Willentz
Peter Stansky
Nancy, Charles, David, and Judith Stanton
Randolph and Frances Starn
Brenda Start and Charlene Lofgren
David Steichen
Gloria Steinem
Pessl Beckler-Semel-Stern
The late Philip M. Stern
Joanne Sterricker
Laura Lee Stewart
Judith Stiehm
Eric Stone and Eva Eilenberg
The late Jean Stone
Merrill, Andrew, Todd, and Adam Stone
Landon Storrs
Susan Strasser
Carolyn Sutcher Schumaker and Maggie
Kimball
Craig Syverson and Christina Allen
Evelyn and Norman Tabachnick
Margery Tabankin
Suzanne Talmachoff
Nancy and Robert Taniguchi
Marcia Tanner
G. Thomas Tanselle
Reesa Tansey and Gary Greenfield
Miquel Tapies
Dickran L. Tashjian and Ann Hulting
Jill Taylor
Judith Taylor
Marcy Telles
Sydney Temple and Sarah Kupferberg
Shelly Tenenbaum
Nancy and Robert Terrebonne
Laurel Thatcher, Gael and Amy Ulrich
John S. Thiemeyer, III
Patricia Anne Thomas
Sally Thomas

Barrie Thorne and the late Peter Lyman
T.L. Thousand
Fern Tiger
Irene Tinker
Ted J. Tipton
Barbara Tischler
Donald Tishman
Stephen Tobias and Alice Webber
Joan Todd
Wortham Trainer
Joseph Traub and Pamela McCorduck
George L. Turin
William M. Tuttle, Jr.
Petra Uhrig and Rik Scarce
Carol and Steven Unger
Patricia Valva and Martin Smith
Shirley van Bourg
Katrina vanden Heuvel
Mark and Carol van der Hout
The late Rudolph Vecoli
Maria Vullo
Nora Wagner
Richard Walker
Judith and Daniel Walkowitz
Stephen and Lauren Walrod
Bridget Walsh and Louis Plachowski
Joan W. Scott
Susan Ware
Bruce Watson and Julie Kumble
Brenda Webster and Ira Lapidus
Jill Weed
Bonnie Lynn Weimer
Beá Welsh Weicker
Lila Weinberg
Lynn Weiner and Thomas Moher
Janet Corey Weiss and Jeffrey Conrad
Cora and Peter Weiss
Susan Wengraf and Mark Berger
Kirk M. White
Marcia Whitebook
Ann Whitehead

Myra and Neil Wiener
Blanche Weisen Cook
The late Norma Wikler
Margy Wilkinson
Margaret and Stanley Wilkerson
Carol Williams
John Alexander Williams
Beverly Dean Williams and Norman Francis
The late Victoria Williams
Brigitte and John Williams-Searle
Elsbeth Wilson
Victoria Wilson
Elizabeth Wingrove
Martha Winnacker
Barbara Winslow
Priscilla Winslow
Sandi L. Wisenberg
Susan Wladaver-Morgan
Leon and the late Roz Wofsy
Dan Wohlfeiler
Margery J. Wolf and Keith M. Marshall
Elizabeth A. Wood
Ann Wrixon
Yamaguchi Momoru
Yamaizumi Susumu
Valerie Yaros
Fay Zadeh
Naomi Zauderer
Rhonda Zangwill
Naomi Zauderer
Martin Zeilig
Elaine Zelnik and the late Reggie Zelnik
Natalie Zemon and Chandler Davis
Gundars Zentelis
Margaret Zierdt
Charlotte and the late Arthur Zilversmit
The late Howard and the late Rosalyn Zinn
Joan Zoloth
Carol Zulman and Eric Taub
Bennet Zurofsky and Susan Vercheak

---

*And special thanks to our many donors who chose to remain anonymous and to the literally thousands of others, whose contributions, large and small, have been absolutely critical to the survival of the Emma Goldman Papers Project. We mourn the recently deceased friends of the Project; among them is the beloved "people's historian," Howard Zinn, who devoted his life to sharing the stories of those who dared to speak up against injustice and who inspired others to do the same. We will remember his years of friendship, enthusiasm for Emma Goldman, and support for the ongoing work of the Emma Goldman Papers.*

## ACKNOWLEDGMENTS

Collaboration is the core component of the Emma Goldman Papers Project. For over thirty years, many hands have created what has become a secular cathedral to the remembrance of things past and almost forgotten. Every effort, large and small, built the structure, added complexity and nuance to the work, and confirmed the importance of situating the advocates of free expression into the historical record as a lasting tribute to courageous spirits.

Emma Goldman's amazing foresight and daring, her insistence that both political and personal freedom are realizable—no matter how difficult the struggle or intangible the outcome along the way—remain an inspiration. The work of preserving and publishing the written artifacts of Goldman's active life has elicited an almost unmatched outpouring of generosity and enthusiasm from those whose determination and vision resonate with her essential daring.

One hundred years ago, Goldman expressed her belief in the power of "the Ideal, sweeping across space and time, knitting people together into one great, sweet comradeship." Today, one can imagine her rallying support for the occupation of public spaces, spontaneous assemblies of free-flowing ideas, and global waves of rebellion against tyranny and greed as the paradigm shifts toward economic and social justice, cooperation, and social integration. To this new generation, we offer a glimpse into the past— accounts of Goldman's victories and defeats, her refusal to succumb to despair, and her unwavering faith in humanity.

The controversy surrounding Goldman—the anarchist deported from the United States, the woman who challenged sexual mores, involuntary conscription into the military, and government misuse of power—sometimes adds a political edge to our capacity to maintain a steady funding base. Although we remain a research project of the University of California (UC), Berkeley, the Emma Goldman Papers Project no longer receives direct financial support, thus necessitating outside funds for the research and editorial staff and students, as well as for the office rent and utilities. Our editorial and administrative staff has shrunk, and our office is downsized but not downtrodden; the Emma Goldman Papers' small dazzling archive now seems a bit like a vest pocket park.

ALTHOUGH WE HAVE WEATHERED LAPSES in financial support and editorial continuity, an individual or institution has always risen to the occasion and made an extraordinary effort on our behalf; and the project, like Emma Goldman herself, has survived. That her papers and these volumes, so full of scholarship and insight into a world whose tracings are rare and whose importance has often been obscured by political prejudice, are now an indelible part of the historical record is the shared accomplishment of literally hundreds of people over the years.

MANY OF OUR EXTENDED FAMILY of friends and colleagues can assert with great authority and confidence that their individual efforts helped bring the project to publication and made all the difference. Every bit of research over the years has added to the depth of our work—small details gradually linked to present a complex picture of Goldman's world. Others supported us by creating a foundation for our efforts, a frame for public history and meticulous research, providing archival sources and funding resources, cushioning us with kindness. In the mountain of words and ideas that comprise our work, none can express fully the depth of our appreciation for the devotion and selflessness showered upon us, sanctioning our perseverance, in spite of all odds, to preserve the written legacy of Emma Goldman.

It would be impossible to name all those associated with the Emma Goldman Papers Project over the years, whose remarkable solidarity and support have sustained us. I, who have facilitated the Emma Goldman Papers Project from the beginning, have been privileged to spend so much of my life poring through Emma Goldman's papers in the company of those, past and present, who were drawn to the many facets of her grand vision and remarkable life.

IT IS A GREAT PLEASURE TO THANK the extraordinary people and institutions without whom publication of this edition of Emma Goldman's Papers would have been impossible.

First and foremost, a great tribute is due to the Project's editorial staff, whose tireless and creative work gave life to a time and a movement otherwise hidden from history. Barry Pateman, a scholar and archivist of anarchist sources, in his thirteen years with the Project has transformed the raw coal of the thirty years of archival research into diamonds of scholarship. His association with the Emma Goldman Papers, which began in the Project's early years of searching through archives and private collections in England, came full circle with his arrival in California in 1999—when he became the fastest study in the West. As a colleague—every step of the way from daily administrative tasks to intellectual engagement in the writing of the introductory essays—and as an enthusiastic mentor to students and aficionado of anarchist history, Barry Pateman's efforts are unmatched. It is largely due to his herculean efforts that we owe the timely and accurate recording and contextualization of Goldman's American years.

The editorial group that has shepherded to completion the volumes covering Goldman's American years also stands out in the history of the Emma Goldman Papers Project as the very best. Each volume's editor laid the foundation for the next; many thanks, especially to Jessica Moran, assistant editor of the first two volumes. The editorial and research assistance of Nicole Waugh and Erik Hetzner carried the high standards forward into this third volume. Morgan Shahan and Susan Kahng, both incredibly talented young research editors, played an indispensable role in tying up the loose ends of years of work on the introductory essay, on almost every level. A virtual army of undergraduate research apprentices checked and rechecked sources, proofread, edited, chased obscure leads, and helped consolidate mounds of research for the volumes—and in the process experienced both the thrill of contact with primary sources and the frustrations of seeking and not finding.

The work of the Emma Goldman Papers Project evolved from the earliest days of searching for Goldman's correspondence, writings, newspaper reportage, legal and government surveillance reports, and photographic images for the comprehensive microfilm edition to the production of these volumes documenting Goldman's American years.

SUSAN WENGRAF'S IMPECCABLE VISUAL SENSIBILITY and fascination with Goldman and her time graced the Project with an ever-increasing photographic archive that allowed us to attend to the edition's artistic form as well as historical content. Wengraf created a parallel narrative composed of facsimiles of original documents from newspapers, magazines, government documents, and personal correspondence, gathered from a wide variety of sources—complementing and distilling the volumes' daunting abundance of historical texts. Wengraf began the search for Goldman-related images almost thirty years ago—building our visual archive and helping to create a sort of family album that evolved into a wonderful traveling exhibition. She created the Project's original slides (now a PowerPoint presentation) and continues to assist me by culling them for local color and historical context as I prepare public lectures on Goldman, her time, her circle, and the issues that continue to resonate with our own.

ROBERT COHEN, THE CONSULTING EDITOR, began his association with the Project when he was a graduate student studying the history of student movements. With his constant focus on free expression and education (as a teacher of teachers), he has followed the thread of his interests from the early years of the twentieth century with Emma Goldman, through the 1930s, continued with the new left of the free speech movement in the 1960s on UC Berkeley's campus, to a dazzling biography of the movement's most articulate advocate, Mario Savio. A generous and insightful colleague and friend, he collaborated on the selection of documents for the volumes and critiqued the introductory essays, encouraging me to take a longer view on Goldman, to face her limitations even as I celebrated her grand achievements. And when, midstream in the Project's work, I faced a life-threatening illness, he was among the most devoted to the work, and his unwavering kindness to me during that harrowing time created a shield of support—which continues on to this day, when emergencies are more in the realm of publishing deadlines.

AT A TIME WHEN THE PUBLISHING INDUSTRY WAS IN FLUX and university presses were struggling to stay afloat, the cuts in the state budget prompted the University of California Press to prune away many of its long-term costly editions. Because of the recent trend of transferring pre-publication costs to the authors, the Emma Goldman Papers' editors faced the problem of finding funds and a new publisher to complete the last two volumes of the American Years series. We are fortunate to have Stanford University Press as the publisher of volume 3 *Light and Shadows* and volume 4 *The War Years*. A subvention grant from the National Historical Publications and Records Commission covered one third of the expenses we incurred. As per our agreement with the press, we contracted with David Peattie —the hardworking supportive head of the publishing service BookMatters—who oversaw every detail of our volume prior to its printing and distribution. Mike Mollett, the copyeditor, did a noble, careful job in tackling the diverse styles of this mammoth documentary edition, and Tanya Grove's editorial touches enhanced the quality of our volume.

Building and expanding on the work, we thank our publishers, past and present: for our microfilm with Chadwyck-Healey, Inc. (now ProQuest); the University of California Press (hardback edition of volumes 1 and 2); the University of Illinois Press (paperback editions of volumes 1 and 2), with special thanks to its former editor-in-chief, Joan Catapano and to Laurie Matheson, the new editor-in-chief; and now Stanford University Press (hardback and paperback editions of volumes 3 and 4), with special thanks to the gracious and erudite director of scholarly publishing, Norris Pope, who welcomed us to the press and agreed to retain the original design and paper quality of our first two volumes; and historian Stephen Zipperstein, who brought our work to the attention of the press. They have all played important parts in inscribing Emma Goldman's life and work indelibly into the historical record.

AMONG THE HISTORIANS DEVOTED TO THE HISTORY OF DISSENT and to recording the violent underside of the nation's response to issues of race and labor unrest is the revered Leon Litwack, indefatigable and captivating Alexander F. and Mary T. Morrison Professor of American History at UC Berkeley and chair of the original Emma Goldman Papers Project's Faculty Advisory Board. Our designated "principal investigator"—his P.I. acronym could easily signify "prince of integrity"—continues to stand by the Emma Goldman Papers tirelessly and with compassion and enthusiasm. To have the camaraderie and respect of one who embodies the challenging spirit of Emma Goldman has been an honor. We thank him for his generosity and his willingness to go the extra mile even when his schedule was overflowing. Without his constancy, the Emma Goldman Papers Project could never have come this far; he has done so much for so many with his combination of modesty and force—qualities shared by his wife, Rhoda Litwack, who cheered us on through years of hard times, always trusting that we could make it through.

Professor Emeritus *Edwin M. Epstein*, also the consummate *mensch*, stood in for Professor Litwack during a short period of his convalescence. At the time, Professor Epstein was the Interim director of the Peace and Conflict Studies, a program that was initiated by the welcoming and forward-thinking Michael Nagler—under the auspices of the campus' International Area Studies (IAS). The Emma Goldman Papers were sheltered under the umbrella of its director, John Lie, Professor of Sociology, who hosted a Resilient Rebels event to celebrate the publication of volume 2 *Making Speech Free*—as well as to mark the culmination of the official censorship snafu we had braved on campus the year before. (See "Old Words on War Stirring a New Dispute at Berkeley" by Dean E. Murphy, *New York Times*, 14 January 2003 and "Now Berkeley Lets Words of Anarchist Stay in Letter," *New York Times*, 17 January 2003.) In the current period of draconian budget cuts, IAS and the EGP have been folded into the Institute for International Studies, headed by the cordial Professor Pradeep Chhibber.

A pattern of resilience, determination, and never turning back was set with the aid of two of our earliest research companions—practical political visionary, the late Sarah Crome; and multi-talented public librarian, Sally Thomas. Crome joined me upon her retirement from teaching and, although she initially cringed at the impracticality of Emma's politics, developed a fascination for the history of the anarchists, eventually becoming known among younger anarchist and anti-nuclear activists as "cosmic Sarah." Thomas worked with the Project in many different roles over a fourteen-year period; she gave the Emma Goldman Papers a presence on the Web and helped set a tone and direction that has remained our hallmark.

For over twenty-five years, the Project has been graced with the weekly presence of three remarkable Women for Peace—June Brumer, Rae Lisker, and Beth Wilson—our dedicated volunteers willing to do absolutely anything that needs to be done including editing, proofing, filtering through 20,000 documents for just the right quote, helping with outreach mailings, sorting, folding, and stamping, as they have done for so many other causes in their lifelong commitment to social justice. They continue to add ingenuity, warmth, and the gift of continuity that has bolstered the Project's ability to withstand the many challenges we've faced over the years.

The Emma Goldman Papers Project was conceived in an era of resurgence of interest in women's history. The initiator of the Emma Goldman Papers Project was the National Historical Publications and Records Commission of the National Archives. The NHPRC was mandated by Congress in 1934 to sponsor documentary editing projects to collect, organize, and publish the papers of the Founding Fathers. By the 1970s there was a groundswell of interest among historians in expanding the definition of the nation's finest leaders to include women, labor, and civil rights activists. The Emma Goldman Papers, sometimes labeled in jest as one of the "Destroying Mother" projects, began quietly in 1980. The NHPRC has been the Emma Goldman Papers Project's most consistent supporter—setting an unparalleled standard of excellence and respect for documentary editing and laying the foundation for the abundance of high-quality historical editions in American history published in the twentieth century. The irony of a federal agency becoming the deported Emma Goldman's primary source of support was not lost on the NHPRC's longtime officer, Roger Bruns, who often mused that perhaps Goldman was mistakenly identified on the commission's list of mandated subjects for projects. Bruns jested that they might have presumed they were funding a great *archivist*, rather than a feared *anarchist*. Piercing through such speculation was the NHPRC's genuine belief in free expression as a crucial element of the identity of America, which propelled the commission and its remarkably kind and engaged staff to value Goldman's contribution to American history and sustain the long scholarly quest to document her life and work.

In addition to the compassionate, modest, and erudite Roger Bruns, who guided the Emma Goldman Papers through the years, the Project was fortunate to have the support of the commission's staff, Tim Connelly, now director of publications, who impressively tended to the myriad of detail, proving that the best administrative work is done with kindness and intellectual engagement in the task at hand. Over the years, NHPRC staff members became our most consistently involved colleagues and friends. We thank the new crowd—Executive Director Kathleen Williams and Deputy Executive Director Lucy Barber, who have kept the NHPRC itself afloat in difficult times.

My appreciation extends to those who played an integral part in the history of the Emma Goldman Papers Project over the last thirty years—from staff members, volunteers, archivists, librarians, scholars in the United States and across the globe, students, grant administrators, and the many university and community facilitators of our work. Because the preparation for the volumes spread over many years, it is a challenge to recount all those who had a hand in its completion—those who assisted in checking and re-checking facts, writing and re-writing annotations, framing and re-framing the texts, and pushing themselves to the max with great equanimity and kindness to meet incredibly stringent deadlines; they clearly deserve the lion's share of appreciation. The volumes have benefited from the talents of each editorial group as they improved on the fine efforts of the one before it.

For a fuller account of the hundreds of people who worked with us over the years, especially as we collected material for the microfilm and guide, please see *Emma Goldman: A Guide to Her Life and Documentary Sources* (Alexandria, Va.: Chadwyck-Healey, 1995) for the lists of editors, administrative and program staff (especially the army of graduate students), research associates, production editors, editorial assistants, international search coordinators, international researchers, research assistants and translators, the hundreds of contributing library institutions, and donors—as well as acknowledgments in the earlier volumes to all those from near and far who came to work with us, even briefly. We extend our thanks and hope that you can see the imprint of your work in this documentary edition and recognize the many facts that you tracked down years ago, now integrated into the historical fabric of these volumes.

For a more extensive collection of the sources from which much of the documents in this edition were selected, researchers may consult *Emma Goldman: A Comprehensive Microfilm Collection* (Alexandria, Va.: Chadwyck-Healey, 1991–1993, now distributed by ProQuest). Though a remarkable number of new documents were found in the process of working on the annotations for the American years' edition, the material already in the Emma Goldman Papers Project microfilm collection, brought together from over a thousand archives and private collections, sets a broader documentary context (in raw form without the scholarly apparatus of annotations). The search for documents and their organization, identification, and publication in the microfilm archive of correspondence, writings, newspaper reports, and government surveillance and trial transcripts laid the foundation for the book edition and took almost fifteen years. I thank the many people who worked with the Project in its early years, when its mission seemed more ephemeral, its tasks somewhat more mundane—and for the result, an archive that is a quiet gift to scholars and political activists.

A very spirited and talented group of undergraduate research assistants helped us pull the final details together, provided a fact-checking safety net, and shared our enthusiasm for expanding the scope of our documentary history to include a history of the anarchist activity in America and Europe that motivated and informed Goldman's work. This task required remarkable detective work and tenacity. Primarily guided by Barry Pateman, the office has been buzzing with the excitement of discovery, the thrill of working with primary sources, and the sense that the time has come to fill this gap in the historical record: a mission the Emma Goldman Papers Project has been primed for and working toward for more than thirty years. Sadly, we mourn the death of the reflective Rebecca Feiler, whom we will always remember as the spunky young enthusiastic student who felt so at home with Emma. Among the many students who helped with background research for the annotations and appendices and performed critical fact checking for the volumes, we thank especially Christopher Cadena, Haylee Currier, Patrick Goldem, Susan Kahng, Connie Lee, Heather Nelson, David Priddy, as well as Morgan Shahan. The full list is long, the quality immeasurable: Natalie Avalos, Gabriel Berumen, Emily Busch, Seung Yeon Choi, Kathryn Cousineau, Sean da Costa, Manuel Escamilla, Rhawn Friedlander, Eric Garcia, Patrick Golden, Angelica Gonzalez, Brynn Holland, Stella Huynh, Anna Kallett, Ruby Kalson-Bremer, Emiliana Kissova, Caitlin Knowlton, Charles Li, Michelle Luneau, Anna Melyantsev, Anne Powers, Alaska Quiligi, Veronica Rodriguez, Polina Rubanova, Ben Taylor, Andrina Tran, Vikram Venkatesh, Kenosha Washington, and Stephanie Whelan.

The administrative coordination of such a research project is enormous. We thank especially Tessa Fischer, Xuan An Ti Ho, Tiffany Panganiban, Porsche Winston, Yara Alas, and more recently Winifred Chan. And in this age of rapidly aging computers and dwindling finances, we thank Erik Hetzner for years of frugal technical problem solving and for coming to our rescue so effectively over this past year of all-too-frequent computer crashes. The UC computer whiz Kim

Carl, along with Bill Gross, not only rescued us in times of need but also worked to update our original and ongoing website: http://ucblibrary3.berkeley.edu/Goldman/.

Stephen Silberstein also came to our rescue. He was a librarian and developer of computer systems who advanced the field of digitized access and catalogue information retrieval. Working with others, Silberstein ensured that the written and visual history of that dramatic time in the 1960s would be preserved and he established the Free Speech Movement Cafe in Moffitt Library—a visible point of pride on the Berkeley campus. We thank him for the value he placed in the documentation of Emma Goldman's early battles for free speech; his extraordinary one-time contribution to the Emma Goldman Papers Project, many years ago, allowed for the continuity of our work, proudly now part of the legacy of those who fought to uphold the right of free expression on college campuses across the nation.

Every writer and historian needs a sounding board, constructive criticism, and people on the outside of the work willing to jump in and pretend to be the average reader, especially in the final hours when clarity is of the essence. I thank my many friends who functioned as outside editors and personal advisers (including meetings of a remarkable group of psychoanalysts, psychologists, and biographers)—spending hours reading through drafts and re-drafts of the various configurations of this edition as well as the proposals, letters, and ancillary public history material. First and foremost among those who gave so generously of themselves and their talents is Lorraine Kahn—filmmaker, humorist, cultural theorist, wellspring of creative insight, 24/7 consultant, and last-minute enhancer of almost every aspect of our work. My remarkable friend, Ramsay Breslin, talented editor, art critic, and art maker, worked on the earlier introductions, graciously offered a serious glance at this one, and left her mark, once again. Remi Omodele, wise friend, neighbor, and scholar of the theater, shared her insights into the political history of the theater and Goldman's relationship to it, and prods all those in her radius to aspire to excellence. Harriet Sage, modest force, staunch friend, and appreciator of books and of people, shared her keen psychological insights into the inner Goldman, patiently, again and again, over decades of weekly walks. Ruth Butler, across the ocean, and Shirley Kessler, across the country, seem to pop in and out of Berkeley just when it matters most—I thank you both for your soulful friendship and years of thoughtful reflections about Emma, and about life itself.

A documentary editing project would be nowhere without the assistance of archivists and librarians, whose quiet, persistent, meticulous dedication makes all research possible. We thank you all. Fine anarchist collections are especially rare, and the Emma Goldman Papers Project has been fortunate to work—on an almost daily basis—with Julie Herrada, curator of the Labadie Collection at the University of Michigan; Herrada shared her material and her expertise with utmost generosity. The International Institute for Social History in Amsterdam, where Goldman placed both her own collection and Berkman's after his death, allowed much of their extensive Goldman archives to be integrated into our comprehensive microfilm collection, graciously filling in for previous omissions from her early political years. Fortunately for the Emma Goldman Papers, associate editor Barry Pateman is also the curator of the Kate Sharpley Library, the largest collection of English-language anarchist material in the U.K., including material on Goldman's early years and full-run copies of rare anarchist journals. It has been remarkable to have access to a breadth of material, literally at our fingertips, deepening the Project's understanding of the anarchist movement and refining the historical research for the books.

The Project is also privileged to be part of UC Berkeley, an institution with one of the most extensive research libraries in the nation. We borrowed over a thousand books, kept up a steady stream of interlibrary loan requests, constantly used the newspaper microfilm reading room, and made frequent trips to the Bancroft Library's archival collection. As kindred book people, we salute your work and thank you for your assistance over the years—we literally could not have completed our volumes without you.

We would particularly like to acknowledge the pioneering work of Richard Drinnon, who in 1961 (twenty-one years after Goldman's death) published *Rebel in Paradise*, the first biography of Emma Goldman; that book, along with *Nowhere at Home*—selected letters between Emma Goldman and Alexander Berkman, prepared with Anna Maria Drinnon—led the way for generations of "Emmasaries" everywhere. We thank him for his belief in the value of our work and the gift of his renewed friendship.

There are no books at the Project's office as worn as those written by the late Paul Avrich, the renowned scholar of multiple books on the history of anarchism, who generously helped us with innumerable questions over the years. For his careful reading of our texts, and for his camaraderie, he will forever occupy a place of profound respect and appreciation, and his dignity and fine work continue to be an inspiration and our guide.

The story of those who helped sustain the work of the Emma Goldman Papers deserves a book in itself. Like all good projects without a secure financial base, we have relied on the generosity of our friends and our kindred spirits to pull us through. Over time, our "Emma's List" (the counterpart to "Emily's List," a fund focused on electing women to public office) has evolved into a strong community bound together by a desire to preserve the courage of those who, like Emma Goldman, dared to challenge hypocrisy and to affirm what she considered everybody's right to a world of economic and social liberty. Our staunch Emma's List supporters at all levels have surrounded us with kindness, affirming the significance of our work and replenishing our resilience and perseverance. We thank you all, from the bottom of our hearts. (See Emma's List in volume, pp. 785–797.)

Like Goldman's own circle of political theorists, writers, journalists, and creative thinkers on the burning issues of her time, the wide array of professional and personal paths represented on Emma's List is a tribute to the all-encompassing hope and inspiration the story of her life continues to evoke. It is important to note, however, that Emma's List contributors by no means all agree on every aspect of Goldman's political trajectory. The unifying principle of their support is the belief that the history of the early battles for free expression and the story of courage of individuals like Emma Goldman deserve a permanent place in the nation's documentary record.

Among the most compassionate and generous of our sustaining contributors is Lois Blum Feinblatt, to whom we dedicate this volume. Her modest dignity and concern for every aspect of the Project's well-being has grounded us in love. Her commitment to the promotion of mentoring in the schools and her own work as a psychotherapist combined to bestow upon us all the wisdom, tolerance, and open-mindedness that characterize Emma's List. The matriarch of a remarkably generous and politically impressive family—whose members have all contributed to the Emma Goldman Papers—Lois Blum Feinblatt has been the sweet soul who at various times underwrote the cost of our office space. Her constancy and faith in the value of long-term research allowed us to push on when all else seemed lost. Her daughter, Carolyn Patty Blum, a dear friend and colleague, is a lawyer who has championed human rights and protected political exiles; her work—in the spirit of Emma—puts fear into the heart of torturers everywhere. She not only contributed to our material well-being but also was a brilliant reader for the introductory essays, especially on issues of human rights so integral to Goldman's work. Patty's husband Harry Chotiner, spirited historian and film buff, generously contributed much of his Goldman-related library to our Project. Lois's son, Larry Blum, is a philosopher of the intersection of race and class. His wife and colleague, Judith Smith, an insightful historian of gender and race, generously sent the Emma Goldman Papers Project the royalties from her book on urban history to promote our work; and her sister, Sarah Malino, also a women's historian, added her contribution as well. Lois's son, Jeff Blum, executive director of USAction, is a longtime activist who continues to carry his family values of dedication to social justice. And to add to the mix, Lois's cousin, Sunny Jo Brodsky, quilted beautiful wall hangings with photographic images of Emma to adorn the walls of our office and even designed a pot holder based on a previous year's holiday card of Goldman's lament— "Wishing you were here, for I am making blintzes."

Cora Weiss, an Emma Goldman in her own right, proclaimed, "You don't have to be an anarchist to want Emma Goldman resources readily available. Women need role models on how to be effective advocates, and how to make a perfect blintz." Weiss is one of the most consistent, persevering nongovernmental advocates for world peace and the rights of women and girls in the twentieth and twenty-first centuries—her accomplishments and force of character have had a remarkable impact on the movement against war and for global harmony and freedom. With her leadership, the Samuel Rubin Foundation, committed to the promotion of work for peace and justice, graciously stretched their guidelines for many years to honor the importance of the documentation of the lives and activities of those in our past whose courage and vision laid the groundwork for the well-being of present and future generations across the world.

Singularly devoted to books, the J.M. Kaplan Fund, through its project Furthermore, directed by Joan Davidson in association with Anne Brickmeyer, has also contributed generously to our work, helping us get closer to publication and sharing our commitment to the printed word (even as its distribution format changes), and to the documentary history of the long and arduous struggle for freedom.

The Lucius N. Littauer Foundation and its longtime director, the late William Frost, and more recently, his son Robert Frost, honored Emma Goldman and the Emma Goldman Papers as an integral part of their commitment to Jewish scholarship and education.

A large proportion of our supporters, though by no means *all*, are people I've known for a very long time who generously extended their friendship to the Emma Goldman Papers Project. The constant thread that ties this extended family of friends is our belief in the possibility of change— the ongoing quest for social and economic ethics, the blossoming of individual creativity, and the readiness to question authority in the name of social justice. Kernels of such values are evident in the myriad activities and life choices of many on Emma's List.

The generous contributions of Judith Taylor, elegant poet and loyal friend, include her finely honed literary sensibilities—and the willingness to make the judgment call at midnight for a sentence fix, to reign in excess, and to extend to the Project her compassion for the arduous process of years of small victories and minor setbacks. For her belief in the value of work outside conventional norms and her acceptance and tolerance for both "the good and bad Emma"—icon and complex political figure—we thank her.

Hannah Kranzberg, a soulful spirit and friend, who has helped give voice to the progressive Jewish community, to a vision of peace and justice, and to the arts, gave graciously of herself in my moments of despair—like Emma herself, Hannah is grounded in her culture and reaches beyond it, in the name of freedom.

My long-lost, energetic cousin Marjorie Solomon, cutting-edge research practitioner on teenage autism, and her husband Mark Friedman, Sacramento's urban revivalist, have contributed generously to our project. In fact most of the Solomon family have extended their family ties to our work—notably Neil Solomon, family historian and health advocate, and Paula Birnbaum, accomplished feminist art historian.

We thank also Eric Berg, Thomas Debley and Mary Jane Holmes, Ken Morrison, Robert Segal, and Nancy Bissell Segal—shining stars among our longtime friends and supporters.

AMONG THOSE FRIENDS whose contributions to the Project extended into the actual writing and research were the magnificent Marge Frantz, radical historian, and Eleanor Engstrand, veteran librarian, both women for peace and pillars of the community, who saw me through the very beginnings of the Emma Goldman Papers Project, spent endless hours discussing nuances of history and musing about whether or not the world had in fact moved forward. They and the modest Emma Goldman-like Sarah Crome, my closest early associate at the Project, invited me to join the Chamakome ranch, a cooperative retreat named after an earlier Native American village on the same ridge along the north coast of California. Surrounded by beauty and rare quiet, the Chamakome ranch has become for me a sacred space for finding the focus so vital to the writing and editing of the Goldman volumes. (I often wonder whether Goldman's ability to put her thoughts in writing could have been attributed in part to those who gave her "the farm," her country retreat up the Hudson River in Ossining, New York, and later, Bon Esprit in St. Tropez, France, where she wrote her autobiography. For the privilege of solitude and the solace of community, I thank my Chamakome-mates, many of whom have also generously extended the ranch spirit of mutual aid to Emma's List.

I have had the honor of being in the company of the very impressive group of fellows of the John Simon Guggenheim Foundation; the grant allowed for the gift of time to reflect upon the personal and political issues that have emerged over years of editorial engagement with Emma Goldman—a story told in my essay "Nearer My Subject to Thee," forthcoming in *Seeking Others, Finding Ourselves* (Oxford University Press).

One of the most gratifying aspects of Emma's List support has been the great privilege of receiving contributions in memory of those who lived in Emma's spirit and in honor of those who continue to keep her legacy alive. Most touching of all are the contributions from the families of Goldman's nearest and dearest friends—a gesture of continuity that has grounded our historical research across time, across generations. The first of such contributions came years before the volumes had even begun. The late Art Bortollotti, the Italian anarchist jailed in Canada under the repressive laws of the pre–World War II era, won his freedom largely due to what was Goldman's last political battle—arousing public opinion on his behalf. In homage and appreciation to his dear friend and comrade, Bortollotti sent his generous contribution of funds for the preservation of Goldman's papers and the documentation of her political work with a note written on the Goldman stationery that he had saved for over forty years.

Mecca Reitman Carpenter, the daughter of Goldman's wayward lover and road manager, Ben Reitman, embraced the Project with great ideas especially for our public outreach and funding, as her father had done for Emma for over a decade. Giving generously of her own resources, she weathered our struggles and celebrated our victories. Years ago when I wrote the very graphic, erotic story of Goldman's complex and passionate relationship with Mecca's father in *Love, Anarchy, and Emma Goldman,* I feared the censure of members of the Reitman family who might take offense at the sexual themes of the book. Instead, I found the compassionate Mecca, who had worked through her own relationship to her father in the unusually accepting biography of his many loves, *No Regrets: Dr. Ben Reitman and the Women Who Loved Him,* never shunning the raw complexity of the clash of love and anarchy between her father and Emma. Even when her own health failed her, Mecca Reitman Carpenter did not falter in her support of the Emma Goldman Papers.

The same devotion that propelled Goldman's dear friends Ida and Ben Capes to move close to her Missouri prison, thus minimizing her isolation with the comfort of visitors during those bleak eighteen months from 1917 to 1919, also propelled the Capes's children, grandchildren, nephews, and nieces to support the Emma Goldman Papers—one of the most moving outpourings of friendship across generations and across the continents. In a similar extension of camaraderie, we also have been honored with support from Michelle Childers, the daughter (and family) of Goldman's "young friend" Gabriel Javsicas; as well as from the sons of Goldman's witty lawyer, Arthur Leonard Ross; the daughter of Goldman's Canadian friends, Sophie and Joe Desser, who in her youth had also assisted Goldman with her secretarial work; the son of Curtis Reese, who delivered an oration at Goldman's funeral; the daughter of Esther Laddon, who provided Goldman a home base in Canada; and the daughter and extended family of friends of Goldman's friend Irene Scheiderman. David Diamond, composer and violinist, and son of Goldman's Rochester, New York, seamstress, Chanele (Anna) Schilhaus, sent his contribution with a remembrance of Goldman standing on a footstool with pins in her skirt as she cheered on his musical career as a violinist—*Kling in de ganze Velt* ("Play for the entire world")—as the smell of her rosewater perfume suffused the air. Warren Billings, a friend of Alexander Berkman, who was jailed in connection with the 1916 Preparedness Day bombing in San Francisco, was remembered by his niece, who also contributed many of Billings's books by Goldman to the Project. The Ferrer Colony in Stelton, New Jersey, was remembered by many of the children of its members, including the late Helen Seitz, who as a child sat on Emma's lap when she visited the colony. (Helen remembered being scared and repelled by the sweaty embrace of this anarchist celebrity.) She told us that her parents met at a soiree in New York City given in Goldman's honor. Don Tishman remembered his father and grandfather enthusiastically discussing Emma's talks on Sunday afternoons. We were fortunate to have befriended and recorded the stories of many of Goldman's friends, a touchstone to the past, reminders of the flesh-and-blood lives of those who we know only through their correspondence.

Another dear friend of the Project is Amy Olay Kaplan, whose grandfather Maximiliano Olay was one of Emma Goldman's Spanish translators; together we uncovered her grandparents' hidden past. Others who joined Emma's List grew up in anarchist circles in Chicago, Toronto, New York, and London. Wu Ke Kang (aka Woo Yang Hao), a member of the Chinese anarchist circle living in Paris and translator of Goldman's works, was one among many who sent his support and recollections of Goldman's influence on China's early revolution—especially of the revered author, Ba Jin. The late Arthur Weinberg, who attended Goldman's funeral services in Chicago, kindly corrected the reminiscences of others interviewed by the Project about the event. Many who grew up in the circle of Chicago anarchists, including Evelyn Tabachnik and her husband Norman, have carried the anarchist respect for the development and flourishing of the individual in their work in the field of psychology. Katrina vanden Heuvel, editor of the *Nation* magazine, remembered her godfather Roger Baldwin, the cofounder of the American Civil Liberties Union, tucking her into bed with exciting stories of Emma's courageous resolve and frequent run-ins with the police. One contributor found a chance notation in his mother's diary chronicling her attempt to mount the stairs with a baby buggy to a crowded hall in San Francisco, anxious to hear Goldman lecture. These and other stories add life to our work and the sweetness of friendship across time.

Contributors with personal contact to Goldman in her lifetime added their recollections to the Project's reminiscence file, which contains interviews with Goldman associates, now deceased, ranging from Roger Baldwin to Mollie Ackerman, one among many of Goldman's young secretaries and friends. Ahrne Thorne, editor of *Fraye Arbeter Stimme*, spent hours sharing his ideas and commiserating about the mammoth task I had taken on. Albert Meltzer, the London anarchist whom Goldman referred to as "a young hooligan," opened his heart to the Emma Goldman Papers Project, sharing his ideas and his books, widening his circle to include us and our work. Poet Federico Arcos and his late wife, Pura, inspired by Goldman in their youth in Spain, opened their home in Canada and displayed their collection of Goldman's books and suitcases, preserved and contributed some of their jewels to the Emma Goldman Papers, to the Labadie Collection at the University of Michigan, and to archives in Spain.

Most basic to the actual publication of Goldman's works has been the generosity and friendship bestowed upon us by Goldman's nephews and literary heirs—the late David and the late Ian Ballantine. I remember Ian Ballantine, the publisher of Bantam (and Ballantine) Books, sitting at his desk in a very tall office building in New York and proclaiming, "Aunt Emma never believed in restrictions of any kind, so why should I?" Over the years, David Ballantine, an author and collector of antique guns, shared with the Project various items his aunt had secreted away, including the ledger documenting those who contributed to her work, her legal fees, and the cost of incidentals for her magazine and lecture tours. Without their sanction, the written legacy of Emma Goldman could never have been as extensively preserved—and as accessible.

Among the most devoted of all "Emmasaries" was the late Howard Zinn, a historian who devoted his life to chronicling the quest for social justice, to bringing *People's History* to the people. Our longtime friendship and the camaraderie of our shared interest in Emma Goldman was a gift for which I will always remain grateful.

Parents, children, and friends—all have been honored on Emma's List. The group as a whole is a remarkable blend—joining together political thinkers including Noam Chomsky; pioneers of the women's movement, most notably Gloria Steinem, and of women's research, such as Mariam Chamberlain, Gerda Lerner, and Naomi Weisstein, among many others; and stellar literary figures including E.L. Doctorow, Barbara Kingsolver, Marilyn French, Erica Jong, Ken Burrows, the late Dianne Middlebrook, Peter Glassgold, Brenda Webster, and the late and witty muckraking author Jessica Mitford, who was completely in thrall to issues raised by Emma's life but thought it "deadly boring" to brave organizing anybody's papers, no matter how great they were.

Among the more theatrical figures on Emma's List drawn to Goldman's life are Susan Sarandon and Tim Robbins, Harold Ramis, and documentary filmmakers Bill Jersey and Shirley Kessler, Vivian Kleiman, Rick Goldsmith, Colemen Romalis (who honored the Emma Goldman Papers in his film). Others include Deborah Kauffman and Alan Snitow, and the many actresses who have played Emma in the theatrical adaptation of E.L. Doctorow's *Ragtime*. The spirited singer/ songwriter Michelle Shocked has been one of the Emma Goldman Papers' biggest fans, as we are hers. The political satirist and illustrator Ed Sorel once identified Emma in a cartoon as one of the "messy" characters with which a certain kind of political activist feels at home—a sentiment to which we all concur. One-time contributor, Nina Hartly, feminist and pornographic film actress, linked her work to Goldman's celebration of sexuality and campaign against Puritanism.

Among the contributors to Emma's List are many who have devoted their lives to the documentation of the struggle for freedom. Most generous and enthusiastic among women's historians is Nancy Hewitt, who believes that much of what has shaped America is "wisdom from the margins." In her article published in *Voices of Women Historians* (1999; edited by Eileen Boris and Nupur Chaudhuri), Hewitt has claimed us all as the keepers of "Emma's Thread" of communitarian values and global visions. In a touching gesture of solidarity, over the years Hewitt has made contributions to the Project in honor of many of her students; when they earn their doctorates, they receive an archival photograph of Emma Goldman writing at a desk adorned with lilies, to keep the inspiration flowing!

Kathy Ferguson's remarkable volume on the development of Goldman's intellectual and political ideas, *Political Thinking in the Streets* and Peter Glassgold's magnificent edited collection and comment, *Anarchy! Mother Earth Magazine,* are the two standouts of recent Goldman-related books. Other scholars continue to visit our office archive, comb through the files for gems of future works, to which we look forward. The volume on Goldman, (edited by Penny Weiss and Loretta Kensinger) *Feminist Interpretations of Emma Goldman* in the Re-Reading the Canon series presented an interesting array of essays written largely before the publication of the Emma Goldman Papers' volumes. In an attempt to summarize our discoveries in their collection (including evidence on who might have thrown the Haymarket bomb!), my essay "Let Icons be Bygones: Emma Goldman, the Grand Expositor" pulled me away from volume 3, but also consolidated many of the aspects of Goldman's seen and unseen activities that helped shape the next phase of our work on the volumes.

The Goldman Papers could not have continued without the financial support of so many, and the intellectual vote of confidence from historians across the nation: Martha Ackelsberg, Harriet Alonso, Eric Anderson, Elizabeth Berry, Eileen Boris, Virginia Bouvier, Robert Cherny, Harry Chotiner, Blanche Weisen Cook, Nancy Cott, Carol DeBoer-Langworthy, Carl N. Degler, the late John Diggens, Martin Duberman, Tom Dublin, Bob Dunn, Robin Einhorn, Robert Elias, Kathy Ferguson, Estelle Freedman, Susan Glenn, Jim Gregory, the late Louis Harlan, Elizabeth Jameson, Linda Kerber, Alice Kessler-Harris, Ira Lapidus, Jesse Lemisch, Cornelia and the late Lawrence Levine, Lori Marso (also an Emma Goldman scholar), Lary May, Sally Miller, Nell Painter, Carl Prince, David Roediger, Ruth Rosen, Carol Rosenberg, Florence Rosenstock and James Van Luik, the late Roy Rosenzweig, Sheila Rowbotham, the late Lucio Ruotolo, Lillian Schlissel, Harvey Schwartz, Joan Scott, Alix Shulman, Barbara Sicherman, Kitty Sklar, Daniel Soyer, Christine Stansell, Peter Stansky, Randolph Starn, G. Thomas Tanselle, Barbara Tischler, William Tuttle Jr., Elaine Tyler, Laurel Ulrich, Susan Vladmir-Morgan, Daniel and Judith Walkowitz, Yamaguchi Momoru, Yamaizumi Susumu, Bonnie Lynn Weiner Martin Zelig, and many others—and from our colleagues among scholarly documentary editors, especially the late Rudolph Vecoli of the Immigration History Research Center (now directed by Donna Gaboccia), Maeva Marcus of the First Federal Congress Papers, Harriet and the late John Simon of the Ulysses S. Grant and of the John Dewey Papers, respectively, and my dear friends Clayborne and Susan Carson of the Martin Luther King Jr. Papers—all of whose historical work resonates with Goldman's and makes a difference today. We are especially grateful for the research assistance and camaraderie of the early Consortium for Women's History: most notably Esther Katz and Cathy Moran Hajo of the Margaret Sanger Papers, Ann Gordon and Patricia Holland of the Elizabeth Cady Stanton and Susan B. Anthony Papers, and the soulful pioneer of women in documentary editions, Mary Lynn McCree Bryan of the Jane Addams Papers. And, three cheers for Allida Black for launching the Eleanor Roosevelt Papers. Members of the Emma Goldman Papers faculty advisory board answered our queries and validated our work among colleagues across scholarly disciplines. Led by Leon Litwack, they included, among others, Susan Schweik, as well as the late Lawrence Levine, the late Reginald Zelnik, and the late Michael Rogin, whose appreciation was familial and dated back to 1906, when his great aunt Rosie Rogin was arrested with Emma Goldman. The late Eli Katz, Yiddish scholar, shared delightful forays into the old world through his many translations of newspaper features about Goldman. (In his absence, we send a *sheinem danke* to Dov Faust for his overnight illustration translations and for those of Jack Adelman, both of whom helped us preserve the integrity of the Yiddish language.)

Emma's List has elicited an unusual gathering of supporters for whom Goldman's story taps into both their desire to promote the social good and their own streak of rebelliousness and daring. These desires are expressed in the way they live their lives and in the manner in which they choose and perform their work—and are the common denominator of this outstanding group. It has been an honor to be in their midst and to have their support. Members of Emma's List come from a wide range of occupations—from workers in methadone clinics, psychotherapists, and doctors, to retired women who send $18 each year to signify *chai* or "life" in Hebrew. Many are archivists and anarchists, students, teachers, librarians, social scientists, university administrators, community activists, labor leaders, publishers, editors, journalists, newscasters, radio personalities, economics analysts, philanthropists, foundation officials, professors from an amazing array of scholarly disciplines, anthropologists, secretaries, flight attendants, architects, designers, photographers, public health advocates, environmental activists, arborists, scientists, statisticians, engineers, tennis and soccer moms and dads, Pulitzer prize–winners, progressive religious leaders, gourmet cooks, computer whizzes, mathematicians, artists, progressive business executives, and a large contingent of progressive attorneys. Young anarchists who seek to occupy the world with social justice continue to add their spirit and support to the mix.

Among those who welcome our calls for help, we thank Richard Gordon, the impeccably thoughtful critical realist photographer, whose friendship includes ever-inventive ideas as well as masterful printings of an archival photograph of Emma Goldman at her desk with lilies for many of our Emma's List supporters. Graphic designer Andrea Sohn (the grandniece of the Project's cofounder Sarah Crome) has been the generous force behind the inspiring whimsy of the Project's artful holiday cards, year after year.

San Diego consumer-advocacy attorney Eric Isaacson, who found us through the Emma Goldman Papers website, single-handedly determined to change the bad reputation of his city in which Goldman's lover and manager Ben Reitman was driven into the desert—tarred, sagebrushed, and sexually attacked by a band of high-level city officials acting as vigilantes—as part of the incredibly brutal San Diego free speech fight of 1912. Eric Isaacson organized support for the Emma Goldman Papers Project, even rallying his partners and friends to come to our aid in a moment of deep financial crisis. There is a kind of ironic justice underlying this outpouring of support for the Emma Goldman Papers from advocates for consumer and stockholders' rights who have chosen to share a portion of the proceeds of their victories with those who are documenting the papers of one of the great foremothers of the battle against corporate greed.

Our research base has always been UC Berkeley. By far the most compassionate and forward-thinking members of the university's administrative team have been Joseph Cerny, the former vice chancellor for research, and his core staff Linda Fabbri and Susan Hirano—all of whom recognized the value of the kind of research that didn't fit neatly into the established categories of the university. These volumes are a tribute to their belief and early support, and to the quiet but critical efforts of others who add courage and vision to the mix of administrative duties. More recently, the administrator who did the most to ensure the continuity of the project was Joan Kask, Deputy Director of International Area Studies, who worked with the director John Lie at a critical time in the Project's history. Of the Research Enterprise staff, those who have been most helpful on every level are Charlene Nicholas, Susan Meyers, Mary Lewis, Annie Somthida, Sonia Garcia, Vicki Garcia, Laura Herrera, Linda Marmalejo, Kelly Fuller, and Clara Fieldler. We thank them all, especially for keeping their humanity intact while being tossed and turned out in these times of severe budget cuts.

We are grateful too for our recent grants from the National Endowment for the Humanities, and program officer Daniel Sack for bridging a gap in funding that allowed us to complete this volume while continuing to work on the next. We also appreciate our continued friendship and support of several grantors who no longer work with the foundations that had supported us, including Donald Gibson, formerly of the NEH, and Richard Sheldon, formerly of the NHPRC, among others—especially the extraordinary Sheila Biddle, formerly of the Ford Foundation.

There are anarchist archives across the globe, including centers in France and Switzerland, in which all the work of processing the material is voluntary and completely run as a cooperative. Their staffs, unlike ours, all share the same anarchist political perspective. The idea of applying for government grants and constantly jumping through administrative hoops would be abhorrent to them. We revere their tenacity, devotion, and ability to merge the form and content of their work. We have benefited from their sources and from their wisdom, and hope that they too value our efforts, recognize the validity of our struggles, and will reap the benefits of the Emma Goldman Papers' remarkable depth of research—now available to all. And we thank others, especially Dana Ward, professor at Pitzer College, who created a much-appreciated resource, Anarchy Archive, years before most books and essays were digitized—posting significant writings online. One day, with adequate funding, we would hope to do the same for the extensive correspondence, writings, news clippings, and government documents in our office and in the Emma Goldman Papers' microfilm.

Among the most far-reaching online evolving collection with which the Project has collaborated is the Jewish Women's Archive—directed by Gail Reimer who, like Emma Goldman and the women she and her staff document, is a true woman of valor.

To all our supporters, material and spiritual, the ever-generous members of Emma's List— and all who have carried us through our sparsest times—we wish to convey our sincere appreciation and respect and hope that you will take pride in contributing to a work intended for posterity. The most important grants are intangible—the gestures of support from friends, family, and community that affirm that this very long process is worth the effort.

To all those institutions, foundations, and individuals who have lent their names and generous spirit and talent to the Emma Goldman Papers, we thank you. Your contribution has laid the foundation for the comprehensive reach of the volumes. We appreciate your support but relieve you of responsibility for factual mistakes or errors of omission on our part. We are deeply grateful to our extended family of friends and colleagues, unnamed here but not forgotten, without whom this work would never have come this far.

Emma Goldman and the Emma Goldman Papers Project have been fixed constellations in my immediate family, looming over and around us with a constancy that has been both reassuring and disconcerting at times—a long-term relationship that has deepened with time. It has been more than thirty-five years since the day my husband-to-be and I browsed in a guitar store in Chicago's Hyde Park with my dog Emma—a rambunctious Irish setter–golden retriever who burst into the shop after us. From the moment my friend John Bowen, who worked at the shop, asked her name, my personal history was transformed forever. Scratching his head as he stroked the dog, Bowen remembered that he had seen back in the storeroom a box of letters that bore the large scrawl "E. Goldman" on the envelopes' return addresses. Within minutes, a boot box of old, yellowed letters appeared, and we were overtaken with the torrent of passion and torment between Emma Goldman, the great heroine of personal and political freedom, and the wayward and promiscuous Ben Reitman, her talented road manager and lover. It was not long before I embarked on the first of many challenging attempts to draw together and interpret the complexities of Goldman's all-encompassing spirit.

For me, a young student in my twenties and very much a part of the women's movement and counterculture/love generation, reading letters Goldman had written when she was thirty-eight years old seemed like prying into the surprising vulnerabilities of a very old woman. Many people helped me muster the confidence to write a respectful biography of her struggle to balance intimate life with her public proclamations. After more than twenty-five years of living with the papers of Emma Goldman, the perspective of age became an important overlay, and my concerns have shifted and broadened.

All through my intense engagement with the issues in and around Goldman's life, the love and constancy of my family and friends kept me from losing myself to the past, from losing track of my own trajectory and parallel entitlement to a full life. For this, and more, I especially thank my husband, Lowell Finley—there from the very first discovery of Emma's letters—master of titles, editorial sounding board, advocate of free speech and political justice, shield of caring and love; and to my daughter Mara and my son Jesse, whose creativity and strength of character have been gifts to behold. I so appreciate the patience, affection, and edgy humor with which they have allowed Emma to be a constant presence in the constellation of our lives—and for respecting the preemptive demands of work on the Emma Goldman Papers Project.

I thank my ever-supportive sister, Jane Falk, creative thinker and linguist, for our years of "conversational duets." And I am grateful for my many kind cousins, in-laws, and adopted family across the country—for their caring and love. Among those friends who have remained by my side I thank especially Yvette Chalom and Paul Fogel, Meredith Miller and Richard Gordon, Julianne Burton-Carvajal, Daniel Burton-Rose and Meghan Fidler, Ruth Butler and Arie Arnon, Tina Jencks, Remi Omodele and Ric Lucien, Joanne Sterricker and Edward Grassl; my University of Chicago friends, Deborah Hirtz-Waterman, David Moberg, Jo Patten, Noel Barker, Judith Gardiner, and Nancy Knight; and my old Brooklyn buddy, "Dr. B" Bernstein.

I have been graced with the Bay Area's remarkably forward-thinking restorers of health. When

I was pulled away abruptly by illness, my family, friends, colleagues, and talented healers rallied to my support. That my children's lives were cradled in kindness and the momentum of the work of the Emma Goldman Papers remained steady are tributes to an extraordinary community for whom the desire to repair the world extends to caring for each other. For keeping me on the planet, I am ever-grateful for my doctors Debu Tripathy, Laura Esserman, and Catherine Park, as well as Beth Crawford and Debbie Hamolsky, all of whom combine amazing compassion with cutting-edge research; for Michael Broffman (and his compassionate assistant Louise Estupinian), doctor of acupuncture and complementary medicine, as well as a research practitioner, whose creativity and willingness to step away from the dominant paradigm is in the spirit of Emma herself; for the genius nutritionist, Natalie Ledesma; innovative oncologist, Garrett Smith; and for Neil Kostick and the late Marion Rosen, whose intuitions about the intersection of the mind and the body gave me hope in my darkest hours. I extend my appreciation and respect to Philip O'Keefe, a doctor who cares for the body and soul of all who are fortunate enough to be in his care (and to his compassion-ate associates, Deborah Graves and Susan Sullivan); to doctors Risa Kagan and Charles Jenkins, whose attention to detail literally saved my life; and to my "bosom buddies" support group, Barbara Hoffer, the late Denyse Gross, the late Anja Hübener, and the late Jeannie McGregor.

Without a community of support, ultimately, the Emma Goldman Papers Project too could not have survived. We have been enlivened by scholars, donors, political activists, and ordinary people whose imaginations were sparked by Goldman's daring. The unique and intrepid City of Berkeley formally recognized and honored Emma Goldman "as a major figure in the history of American radicalism and feminism . . . early advocate of free speech, birth control, women's equal-ity and independence, union organization" and commended the Project for its "perseverance" and for inspiring the "collaboration of scholars, archivists, activists, students, and volunteers, both in Berkeley and around the world." Years ago, the city council proclaimed May 14—the day of Emma Goldman's death—as Emma Goldman Papers Project Day. With the hope that a new world is pos-sible, we present these volumes to mark a rebirth of interest in Goldman as "a voice crying out against injustice and oppression, wherever it has existed"—and we honor all those who helped make our work possible.

WITH APPRECIATION AND RESPECT,
CANDACE FALK

# INDEX

Page numbers in italics indicate illustrations; other abbreviations used include EG (Emma Goldman), BR (Ben Reitman), and AB (Alexander Berkman).

Agricultural Workers Organization (AWO), 744–45

*The Alarm* (Chicago), 725

Albee, Harry Russell (mayor of Portland), 527

Aldred, Guy, 93, 166, 221, 534, 623, 706, 713, 728

Alexander, George B. (mayor of Los Angeles), 689

Alexander, Harry P., 754

Alexander Aldamas Defense Committee, 721

Alexander Aldamas Defense Fund, 759

Allgra, Pietro, 736

Allison, Van K., 739

Altgeld, Governor, 253

Altman, John, 754

Alzalde, Eugenio, 753, 754

Amalgamated Association of Iron and Steel Workers, 256

American Federation of Labor (AFL): apprenticeships, 47; IABSIW and, 747; *Los Angeles Times* building bombing, 68, 109; organizing by, 73, 76; racism within, 9, 47

*American Journal of Eugenics* (Chicago), 725

American Secular Union, 749

Ames, Blanche Ames, 739

anarchism: action vs. theory debate within, 111; archism and, 332n3; avant-garde and, 32; BR on, 527; defined, 12, 54, 102–3, 209, 292–93; EG on, 123, 273–86; constructive vision of, 479–81; egalitarian vision of, 67; egoism and, 14; EG's conversion to, 110–11, 483; EG's lectures on, 620, 621, 625, 627, 628, 630, 633, 634, 636, 638, 639, 643, 646, 649, 650, 651, 653, 657, 668, 670, 671, 672, 674, 677, 678, 679, 681, 682; EG's stirring interest in, 110–11; EG, human nature and, 282; in every phase of life, 54; fears of betrayal among adherents, 112; IWW and, 745; Kōtoku and, 703–4; the morality of law vs., 37; as new vs. old, 102–4; opposition and objections to, 274; tactics, 133, 282–83; terminology for, 106–7; values and social transformation, 14, 84–85, 91, 192, 264–65, 414; variations of, 14

"Anarchism and Human Nature: Do They Harmonize?" (EG), 166

*Anarchism and Other Essays* (EG): BR and, 93, 100, 103; financing of, 321; frontpiece to, 247; introduction to, 100, 288; overview of, 19–23, 99–100; preface to, 85; preparation of, 48, 93, 99, 101–2; publication of, 245, 246; reviews and appraisals of, 22–23, 102, 111, 296, 318, 732

"Anarchism and Socialism," (EG), in *Herald of Revolt*, 103n368

"Anarchism and Vice" (EG), 125

"Anarchism vs. Socialism" (debate), *358*

"Anarchism: What It Really Means" (EG), 21, 86

"Anarchism: What It Really Stands For" (EG), 21, 207, 215, 221, 273–85, 318n6

anarchist egoism, 14

Anarchist Federation, 734–35

Anarchist Manifesto on the War. *See* "International Anarchist Manifesto on the War"

anarchist movement, internal debates within, 82, 136–37

Anarchist Red Cross (ARC), 735, 759

anarchist sectarianism, 136–37

anarchists: audiences for, 242–44; BR on, 203–4; code of ethics of, 79; creativity and critical inquiry and, 59–60; defined, 203, 209; "Down with the Anarchists," 609–12; EG as "queen of," 67, 439; internal conflict among, 82, 136–37; sexist attitudes of, 123; Socialists and, 14, 92, 105, 112, 289, 350, 358, U.S. as sanctuary for, 82. *See also specific topics*

"anarcho-communist," 106

anarchy, defined, 209, 292–93

*Anarchy Versus Socialism* (W.C. Owen), 289, 350

Anderson, Frank V., 730, 742

Anderson, Margaret Caroline: biographical summary on, 513n5, 683–84; on birth control, 160; admired by EG for courage to live openly as lesbian, 54, 134; as editor of

*Little Review,* 160, 730; on EG, 54, 56, 160, 134n428; EG and, 55, 56, 64, 151, 160, 513; EG on, 513, 521; house rented by, 521. *See also Little Review*

Andrews, Dr. Charles L., 734, 742, 749

Andrews, Mr. (chief research worker), 198

Andreyev, Leonid Nikolayevitch: *Anathema,* 648, 649, 653, 654, 656, 664; biographical summary on, 684; EG and, 731; EG on, 639, 640, 642, 645, 646, 648, 649, 653, 654, 656, 658, 661, 664, 679, 681; *King Hunger,* 639, 640, 648, 649, 661; lectures of, 639, 640; *The Life of Man,* 661; *Poet Lore* and, 731; *Savva,* 661; translations of the works of, 728

Angiolillo, Michele (alias José Santos), 261–62, 684

Anthony, Susan B., 667

Anti-Conscription League, 759

anti-militarism campaign, 163n484, 458, 599

Anti-Militarist League, 146, *458,* 496, 509, 655–57, 735–37

Anti-Militarist League Fund, 760, 769

anti-Semitism, 7, 115

*Appeal to Reason* (Kansas City, Mo.; Kansas City, Kans.; and Girard, Kans.), 107, 725–26

Appel, Theodore, 680, 711, 725

Arbeiter Ring, 737

ARC. *See* Anarchist Red Cross

Archer, William, 338, 766

archism and archists, 332

Armour & Company, 466

arrest(s) of EG: adeptness at averting, 44–45; for distribution of birth control literature, 44, 152, 156–57, 160–61, 165, 526–30, *531,* 583, 598, 600, 613–14, 668, 669; at lecture about Atheism, 561; for lecture on birth control, 571; strategy of deliberately courting, 315; for supporting cloakmakers' union strike, 317

art, EG interest in, 52–54; "Art and Revolution" (EG), 52; "social" artists and, 54–56. *See also* beauty

Artzibashev, Michael, 679, 681

Asch, Sholem, 660, 665, 675

Ashleigh, Charles, 726, 729, 754

Ashley, Jessie: arrested, 693, 698; biographical summary on, 684; birth control literature distributed by, 597, 693; EG's friendship with, 57; Haywood and, 700; *Mother Earth* and, 767; National Birth Control League and, 738

Ashley, William. *See* Sunday, Billy

assassins, 248–49. *See also* violence

atheism. *See* "The Philosophy of Atheism" (EG); religion

avant-garde, 32, 140, 192–200

Averbuch, Lazarus (Harry), 91, 193, 193n3, 201n1, 202–4, 255

Avrich, Paul, 141–42, 757

AWO (Agricultural Workers Organization), 744–45

"Babushka." *See* Breshkovskaya, Catherine

Bachofen, Johann Jakob, 287

Badger, Richard G. (publisher), 731

Baffa, F., 754

Baginski, Max: biographical summary on, 684–85; Champney and, 224; EG and, 125, 429, 442; finances, 392; Johann Most memorialized by, 709; on Kōtoku Incident, 624, 749; Mexican Revolution and, 630, 751; *Mother Earth* and, 60, 125, 731; speeches of, 624, 625, 630, 631, 749, 751; writings of, 349, 705

Baja California invasion, PLM and IWW participation in, 109. *See also* Flores Magón; Mexican Revolution

Bakunin, Michael: accused of being police spy, 112, 318–19; biographical summary on, 685; EG influenced by, 22; EG on, 112, 282–83, 318–20, 403, 552–53; Elisée Reclus and, 712; International Workingmen's Association and, 403; Kōtoku translation of the works of, 234; Marx and, 112; on religion, 552–53; writings of, 11n30, 275, 485, 552–53, 685, 726, 728

Speech League protest, 651; Gilbert Roe and, 715; "Goldman-Berkman group of anarchists" and, 483; Harry Weinberger as attorney for, 722; Haywood and, 700; Henry Clay Frick and, 256, 483; Homestead and, 101, 256; imprisonment of, 81, 660, 715 (see also *Prison Memoirs of an Anarchist*); IWDL and, 678, 748; IWW movement and, 474–75, 745; Jack London and, 116; Kelly and, 703; Kōtoku and, 703, 749; on Kōtoku Incident, 233–35, 624, 626, 704, 749; Leon Malmed and, 706; letter to Post Office Assistant Attorney General, *185*; letters from EG to, 117, 345, 566; letters from William Holmes to, 395–98; letters to EG, 147, 148, 502, 508–10; letters to Jack London, 633; Lexington Avenue bombing and, *503*, 761; Ludlow Massacre and, 655, 715, 757; manifestos signed by, 517, 663, 728, 734; in the media, 745; *Mother Earth* and, 60, 78, 105–6, 117, 125, 185, 619, 731, 760, 766; moved to San Francisco, 672; Paul Avrich on, 141–42; photographs of, *191, 396, 501, 503*; police and, 660; Preparedness Day Bombing and, 34–35, 163, 682, 708, 761; protesting the Magón brothers' arrest, 674; Provincetown Players and, 52; on publicity vs. funds, 768; renting space in EG's house, 442; at retreat in Ossining, 630; returns to New York, 35; Robert Reitzel and, 714; at Sanger trial, 87; on Saul Yanovsky, 724; speeches of, 480, *503*, 520n5, 626, 641, 646, 651, 653, 655–56, 657, 681, 724, 736, 740, 741, 748, 749, 751; Stewart Kerr and, 741; as strategist, 141–42; support for Caplan and Schmidt, 30, 151, 690, 724, 740; Tannenbaum and, 719, 757; in Tarrytown, *501*; "The Great Adventure," 603; Thomas Keell and, 702; Thomas Mooney and, 708; as translator, 60; uncle of (Mark Natanson), 126; unemployed movement and, 143, 756, 757, 769; at Union Square meeting, 478, 653; unionists and, 34–35, 164; violence and, 219–20; W. C. Owen and, 711; on war,

149, 703; Warren Knox Billings and, 687, 708; on World War I, 704; writings of, 163–64, 637, 727, 730, 749, 755, 763, 769 (see also *Prison Memoirs of an Anarchist*)

Berlin, Barney, 205

Bernard, G., 517

Bernardo, A., 517

Bernhardi, Friedrich von, 542

Bersani, L., 517

Berth, Edouard, 403

Bertoni, Luigi, 517, 517n4

Bierman, Francis, 370

Billings, Warren Knox: arrested in association with Preparedness Day Bombing, 678, 707, 708, 722, 761; biographical summary on, 687; *The Blast and*, 34, 726; Fitzgerald and, 695; fund-raising meeting for, 700, 723; IWDL and, 707, 748; Robert Minor and, 730; Thomas Mooney's first meeting with, 708; trial and sentencing of, 679, 680, 681

Bingham, Theodore A., 202

Birth Control Committee (New York City), 739

Birth Control Defense Fund, 760

Birth Control Leagues, 737–39

birth control literature, distribution of: arrests for, 44, 152, 156–57, 160–61, 165, 526–30, *531*, 583, 598, 600, 613–14, 668, 669 (*see also* Eastman, Ida Rauh; Queens County Jail; Reitman, Ben; Sanger, Margaret; Sanger, William); by EG with others, 597, 693; mocked by *The Blast, 563*; sexuality and, 86–90; support for those facing charges for, 162, 583. *See also* eugenics

birth control movement: access to, 143–44; arrests of activists, 33n125, 571; building support for, 162; Committee on Birth Control of New York, 739; Comstock's censorship and, 87–89, 95–96, 561, 737–38; EG on, 533, 578, 613; EG's lectures on, *381*, 526, 532, 633, 635, 637, 638, 640, 644, 649, 654, 655, 657, 658, 662, 664, 665, 666, 668, 670, 671, 672, 673, 674, 675, 676,

birth control movement *(continued)*
677, 678, 679, 681; EG's writings on,
560–562, 573–78; eugenics, 80, 86, 89,
418n11; first clinic in U.S., 88; meetings,
562, 564, 571, 572, 593, 600; obscenity laws
and, 156–59; pre-war progressive escalation
of, 83; reasons for, 17n54, 86, 118, 158

*Birth Control Review*, 88

bisexuality in women, 32n123, EG and,
124–25. *See also* Almeda Sperry; women;
homosexuality

Bjørnson, Bjørnstjerne: biographical
summary on, 688; EG and, 435, 658, 731;
Ibsen and, 701; writings of, 248–49, 648,
688

Black, Dr. and Mrs. Melville, 380

Black, Mrs. S. K., 529

black flag of anarchy and hunger, as symbol,
487

Black Hundred, 455

Blackstone, William, 280

Blackwell, Alice Stone, 763

Blaschko, Alfred, 183, 189

*The Blast: A Revolutionary Labor Weekly* (San
Francisco): Berkman and, 31, 34, 163–64,
672, 678, 726, 760; cover pages of, *563,
608, 615*; EG on, 549, 605, 606, 607; first
edition of, 31; Mooney and, 708; *Mother
Earth* compared with, 31–32; raid of offices
of, 678, 760; use of title, 612

The *Blast* group, 612

Bloody Sunday. *See* Everett (1916)

Blossom, Frederick, 739

Boccaccio, Giovanni, 229n7

Bohemian milieu, 56–58, 488

Bohm, Adolf, 726

Bohn, Frank, 700, 731, 732

Bohn, William E., 729, 731

Bonfils, Frederick Gilmer, 119, 359–61, 379

*Bookman*, 23, 50

Boris, Samuel, 630

Boston, free speech in, 205

Boudot, Edouard Eugène, 517, 518n6

Boyce, Neith, 58, 104, 752

Boyesen, Bayard: biographical summary on,
688; EG and, 237; Ferrer Schools and, 625,
741, 763; finances, 391; Kōtoku Incident
and, 624, 626, 749; speeches of, 624, 625,
626, 749; writings of, 731, 741

Boyesen, Hjalmar Hjorth, 688

Bread and Roses Strike, 1912 (Lawrence,
Mass.), 122, 374–75

Bresci, Gaetano, 262–63, 688

Breshkovskaya, Catherine ("Babushka"):
biographical summary on, 688–89; EG
on, 324, 469, 641, 643, 644; Eric Morton
and, 709; exile of, 97, 97n357; Kōtoku on,
703; treason charge against, 97n357, 240;
William Walling and, 722

Brevoort Hotel, EG honored at, 160

Brieux, Eugène: biographical summary on,
689; BR and, 289; *Damaged Goods*, 641,
643–45, 644, 649, 663, 669; distribution of
the plays of, 103, 289, 438; EG on, 469, 631,
634, 635, 641, 642, 643–45, 647, 649, 663,
669; *Maternity*, 631, 634, 635, 637, 647,
648; *Three Plays by Brieux*, 289; *Woman as
a Sex Commodity*, 645

Brisbane, Albert, 462

Brisbane, Arthur, 462–63

Brooklyn Philosophical Society, 237–38, 504

Brooks, Van Wyck, 28

Brotherhood of the Unemployed, 757–58

Browder, Earl R., 733

Brown, Bert, 498

Brown, George, 753

Brown, John, 16, 284, 719

Brown, William Thurston (Reverend):
biographical summary on, 689; courses
taught by, 363; EG and, 621; EG on,
334; Ferrer Schools and, 334, 694, 741;
speeches of, 630, 640, 676, 751; *The
Modern School* and, 730, 742; writings of,
688, 725, 732

Browne, Maurice, 27, 138n439, 491, 752

Bruno, Giordano, 425

*Bruno's Weekly* (New York), 726

Bryan, William Jennings, 286

censorship *(continued)*

> freedom of speech and of the press, 43–46; evading arrest and, 43–46; mail delivery and, 43–44, 95–96, 144, 185, 227, 228, 413, 619–20; countering repression, and, 117–18

CF&I (Colorado Fuel and Iron). *See* Ludlow Massacre

CGT. *See* Confédération Générale du Travail

Chaikovsky, Nikolai, 240n5, 429

Chaikovsky Circle, 126, 399n1

Champney, Adeline, 94, 95, 223–26, 731, 732

Chaplin, Ralph, 725, 729

Charnick, Max, 735, 753

Chase, Edith, 433, 461, 498, 520, 521

Chase, John, 456

Chautauqua, N.Y. (Chautauqua gatherings): EG considers rallying support for the Mexican Revolution at, 113, 328

Chattel slavery, 120. *See also* racism

Chavez, Marie, 657, 698, 757, 761

Chekhov, Anton: *The Cherry Orchard,* 647, 649, 656; EG on, 49, 642, 645, 646, 647, 648, 649, 658, 661, 664, 679, 680, 681; *The Swan Song,* 647, 648, 649, 653, 654, 664; *The Three Sisters,* 661

Chernyshevsky, Nikolay, 99, 135

Chicago, 195–97, 201–6, 337, 347

Chicago Anarchists, 193, 243, 255, 400, 475, 483

Chicago Anthropological Society, 201

Chicago Mexican Liberal Defense League, 751

*Chicago Tribune,* 205

Childs, George, 768

"child's right not to be born," 156, 672

Chirikov, Evgeny, 648, 649

Christianity: EG on, 124, 128, 129–30, 183, 420–26; Catholic Church and, 338. *See also* Jesus Christ

Church and State, separation of, 59

church raids, 77, 476, 477, 756. *See also* Tannenbaum, Frank

Ciancabilla, Giuseppe, 688

Ciofalo, Andrea, 660

Cisneros, Jose Abraham, 753, 754

civil libertarians, 88, 89, 167

Clark, John (Chief of Police, Portland), 527, 530, 669

Class, antagonisms, 149; EG bridging cultural divide and, 10–11; "respectables," 157; and race, 3; and struggle against injustice, 124; wage slavery, 120, 269. *See also* working class; labor

Clausen, Emma, 333, 749

Clavia, Ignacio, 694

Clay, Bertha M., 691

Clement II, Pope, 183

Cleveland (Ohio), 196–97

Cleveland Freethought Society, 223, 224, 225

Cline, Charles, 81, 650, 753–54, 767

cloakmakers strike (1910), 317

clothing, women's, 145, 488, 489

Cockran, W. Bourke, 34, 680

Cohen, Joseph J.: biographical summary on, 518n7; Conference of the Unemployed and, 756–57; de Cleyre and, 692, 753; Ferrer School and, 741, 742; Francisco Ferrer Association Fund and, 763; Modern School Association and, 742; Modern School in Philadelphia organized by, 741; Radical Library and, 753; residences and professions of, 742; writings of, 517, 692, 728, 729

Cohn, Michael A., 631, 640, 664, 766, 767

Colarossi, Umberto, 726

Colorado Fuel and Iron Company (CF&I), 71. *See also* Ludlow Massacre

Colorado mine strike. *See* Ludlow Massacre

(Colorado) War Fund, 761

Comarow, H., 766

Combes, Henry Emmanuel Jules, 517–18, 518n8

Cominsky, Isidore (Saxe Commins), 441

Cominsky, Miriam (EG's niece), 662

Cominsky, Stella. *See* Ballantine, Stella Comyn

Commins, Saxe (Isidore Cominsky) (EG's nephew), 441

Commons, John R., 198–99

family, EG critique of marriage and 4–5, 12; EG on divorce, 267; EG on motherhood and, 123. *See also* marriage; motherhood

*Family Limitation* (M. Sanger), 661, 662, 715, 716, 737

Fasano, M., 754

Faure, Sébastien, 59

Federation of Italian Bottle-Blowers, 412n3

Federenko, Savra, 768

Fels, Joseph, 90–91, 190, 763. *See also* single-taxers

feminism, 16, 25, 32, 118–19, 354. *See also* women

Fenians (Irish nationalist organization), 611

Ferdinand, Francis (Archduke of Austria), 657

Ferguson, Miriam Amanda Wallace "Ma" (governor of Texas), 754, 767

Ferm, Elizabeth, 731

Ferrari, Robert, 461, 521

Ferrer, Francisco Galcerán, 338

Ferrer Association. *See* Francisco Ferrer Association

Ferrer Center Modern School. *See* Francisco Ferrer Center Modern School

Ferrer y Guardia, Francisco: biographical summary on, 694; Champney on, 224; commemorations of the death of, 650, 659; de Cleyre and, 692; Dr. Hailmann and, 224; EG and, 631; EG on, 196–97, 215, 619, 620, 621, 622, 623, 624, 626, 627; execution of, 623, 631, 740; Ferrer case, 241, 338–39; *Industrial Worker* and, 728; James Vidal and, 721, 744; Jesus Christ contrasted with, 425; in the media, 745; Spanish Modern Schools, 59; writings of, 103, 692, 731

Fickert, Charles (San Francisco district attorney), 708

Field, Sara Bard: biographical summary on, 589n1; Charles Wood and, 724; letters from EG to, 589–90; writings of, 726, 730

Fielden, Alice, 397

Fielden, Harry, 397

Fielden, Samuel, 396–97

Fieldman, Sol, *358*, 632, 633

Fifth Avenue demonstration (New York), 474, 478–79

Figueroa, Anselmo, 639, 695, 751

Fine, S., 749

Fischer, Peter. *See* Berg, Charles

Fishman, William J., 513

Fitzgerald, Margaret Eleanor (Fitzi/the Lioness): Anti-Militarist League and, 146, 735; Becky Edelsohn's bond paid by, 694; Berkman and, 29, 30, 148, 672, 687, 694, 695; Berkman on, 508–9; biographical summary on, 694–95; *The Blast* and, 678, 726; BR and, 30, 60, 135, 453, 695; Conference of the Unemployed and, 735; EG and, 135, 164–65, 508–9, 607; EG on, 442–43, 605; at house on 74 West 119th Street, 650; IWDL and, 748; letter to Ellen Kennan, 607; letters from EG to, 165; *Mother Earth* and, 30, 32, 60, 650; moved to San Francisco, 672; Preparedness Day Bombing and, 163–65; as Provincetown Players' business manager, 752

Flasseur, Victor, 748, 749

Fleming, J. W., 733

Flores Magón, Enrique: biographical summary on, 695; charges against and imprisonment of, 81, 108–9, 162–63, 602, 639, 677; EG's support for, 162–63, 602; Mexican Revolution and, 81, 107, 108, 113, 751; PLM and, 107, 113, 634, 750, 751, 752; *Regeneración* and, *326*; trial of, 676, 695; writings of, 726, 752

Flores Magón, Jesus, 751

Flores Magón, Ricardo: anarchists and, 108; biographical summary on, 695–96; charges against and imprisonment of, 81, 108–9, 162–63, 325nn7–8, 602, 623, 639, 677; criticism of, 109; Debs and, 311; EG's support for, 162–63, 602, 627; Harry Weinberger as attorney for, 722; John Turner and, 721; letters between Debs and, 311; letters between EG and, 81, 107, 108, 109, 311–14; Madrero and, 623, 627; Mexican Revolution and, 81, 107, 108, 109,

113, 623, 627, 751; PLM and, 107, 113, 311nn1–2, 325nn7–8, *326*, 634, 695, 750, 751, 752; portrait of, *326*; *Regeneración* and, *326*, 623, 725, 732; Samuel Gompers and, 311; trial of, 638, 676; writings of, 311n1, 725, 727, 728

Flores Magón brothers (Enrique and Ricardo): arrests and indictments of, 673, 674, 732, 751, 752; conviction of, 109, 639, 677; Debs and, 311, 755; EG on, 602, 603; fund-raising and support for, 16, 109, 602, 677, 761; influence on EG, 107; IWDL and, 748; Jack London's support for, 705; *Land and Liberty* and, 729; *Mother Earth* and, 664, 751, 752; Rangel-Cline Defense Fund and, 754; Socialist Party of America and, 107–8; W. C. Owen and, 113, 711

Flynn, Elizabeth Gurley: *Anarchism and Other Essays* and, 100, 247; arrest of, 642, 763; biographical summary on, 696; Carlo Tresca and, 720; as described by Margaret Anderson 54–55; EG and, 54–55, 57, 100, 247; at Ferrer School, 479, 741; fund-raising by, 633; fund-raising for, 763; imprisonment of, 484; Joe Hill and, 669; labor advocacy of, 57, 64, 141, 696, 756, 765, 766; speeches of, 479, 625, 642, 657, 741; "The Nudes and The Prudes," 764–65; Thomas Mooney and, 708; at William Sanger trial, 87; writings of, 696, 729, 730, 733, 746

Foote, Dr. Edward Bond, Jr.: biographical summary on, 696–97; death of, 364; EG and, 120, 236, 364, 365; Ferrer Associations and, 694; in Free Speech League, 628, 743; in Liberal Club, 750; *Mother Earth* and, 120

Foote, Edward Bliss, Sr., 364n3, 696, 737

Forbes, Edwin Alexander, 456

Ford, Richard "Blackie," 454n3, 658, 745, 768

Forel, Auguste, 521, 560

Forman, Flora L., 530

Foster, William Z., 122, 639, 711, 725, 733, 745–46

Fox, Jay: *Agitator* and, 725; arrest and imprisonment of, 348, 764–65; biographi-

cal summary on, 697; Free Speech League and, 743; Lucy Parsons and, 711; at National Convention of Reform Clubs and Trade Unions, 723; nude swimming advocated by, 117, 764–65; Schroeder and, 717; Syndicalist League of North America, challenging IWW separatism, and, 122; writings of, 725, 727, 731, 733

Fraina, Louis C., 749, 752

Francis, John Oswald, 654, 656

"Francisco Ferrer" (EG), 626

"Francisco Ferrer and the Modern School" (EG), 215, 620, 621, 622, 623, 624

Francisco Ferrer Association: Berkman and, 630, 646, 694; founding of, 622–23, 740–41; historical summary of, 740–42; Kelly and, 622–23, 630, 646, 694, 741; Lexington Avenue bombing and, 657

Francisco Ferrer Association Fund, 763

Francisco Ferrer Center Modern School: Berkman and, 59, 741; Boyesen and, 625, 741, 763; branches of, 59; as center for radicalism, 58, 78, 476, 479–81, 741–42; Charles Thompson on, 142, 474; Frank Tannenbaum and, 476–77, 481, 756; instruction at, 16, 52, 58, 59–60, 479–80, 625; Kelly and, 59, 677, 683, 730, 742; Leonard Abbott and, 59, 476, 479, 481, 625, 741, 742; opening and pioneers of, 479, 652, 741; surveillance of, 58, 77; Upton Sinclair and, 59

Francisco Ferrer Day School Fund, 763

Francisco Ferrer Fund, 763

Franco-Prussian War, 257n22

Frank, Helena, 719

*Free Comrade* (Wellesley, Mass.), 727

free love: bisexuality in, 124–25; polyamory, 24, 152–53, 441; promiscuity vs., 24–25, 62–63, 93–94, 113, 152–53, 271; "Variety or Monogomy. Which?"(EG), 24

free motherhood movement, 159

"Free of Forced Motherhood—the Necessity for Birth Control" (EG), 162

*Free Press* (Pittsburgh Socialist newspaper), 132

Free Silence Movement. *See* Tarrytown silent vigil

free speech: advocacy for, 45, 67, 88–89; anarchists and, 6; arbitrary protection of, 43–46, 121; BR and, 91, 92, 146–47, 651, 655, 743; EG on, 131; as essential right, 90; George Shippy and, 201, 202, 205; liberal and middle-class affinity to issue of, 6; obscenity laws and birth control, 156–59; religious freedom vs., 96; renamed, 95–96; as right to organize in the workplace, 120; theater and, 133

Free Speech Committee, 92, 205

Free Speech Fight, 165–66, 360, 616, 680, 763

"Free Speech Fight" (EG), 91, 201–6

Free Speech League, 87, 120, 496n7, 696–97, 742–43

*Freedom* (London), 82, 727–28

*Freedom* (San Francisco), 82, 727

freedom of speech and of the press, discrepancies in laws governing, 43–46

Freeman, Alden: biographical summary on, 697; on EG, 630; Ferrer School and, 480, 742; Free Speech Fund and, 763; writings of, 697

*Freie Arbeiter Stimme* (Free Voice of Labor, New York), 82, 728

*Fresno Morning Republican,* 110

Freud, Sigmund, 118–19

Freytag-Loringhoven, Elsa von (Dada performance artist), 56

Frick, Henry Clay, 115, 256, 483

Frieman, Simon, 748, 749

Frigerio, Carl, 518

Funston, Frederick, 195


Gallart, George, 727

Galleani, Luigi (pseudonyms Grigi Galleani, Luigi Pimpino, Mentana, and Tramp), 692, 726

Galleanistas, 109

Galsworthy, John: biographical summary on, 697; EG on, 49, 50, 435, 450, 579, 620, 621, 622, 626, 627, 642, 646, 647, 648, 649, 652, 654, 656, 658, 660, 664, 675; *The Eldest Son,* 647, 648, 652, 654; *Escape,* 50; *The Fugitive,* 654; *Justice,* 579, 620, 626, 627; *The Mob,* 660, 675; *The Pigeon,* 656; *The Silver Box,* 652; *Strife,* 620, 621, 622, 664; *The Wheels of Justice Crush All,* 646, 649

Ganz, Marie, 714–15, 736, 769

Garcia, Vicente, 518

Garland, Hamlin, 676

Garner, A. H., 620

Garrison, Lindley Miller, 539

Garrison, William Lloyd, 41, 120, 367, 369

Gary, Joseph E., 253

Gatens, William (District Judge, Multnomah Co., Oreg.), 577, 669

Gaytán, Teodoro, 695, 751

Gegan, James J., 473

gender roles, 25–26, 86; New Man, 25. *See also* feminism; New Woman movement; women

General Confederation of Labour. *See* Confédération Générale du Travail

(General) Free Speech Fund, 364, 763–64

General Strike and syndicalism, 408–10

George, Henry, 755

Germany, 316, 539–40

Gershuni, Gregori, 429

Gerson, Harriet, 499

Gerson, Mrs. T. Perceval, 435, 506

Gerson, T. Perceval, 132, 147, 434–35, 504–6, 667

Gibson, Lydia, *563*

Giegerich, Leonard A. (Supreme Court Justice), 628

Gilbert, Joseph, 754

Gilday, James, 766

Gilman, Charlotte Perkins, 726, 731, 732

Giocosa, Giuseppe, 660, 664

Giovannitti, Arturo: Lawrence, Mass. strike and, 632, 633, 639, 640, 763, 765; *New Review* and, 731; support for accused in Preparedness Day bombing, 681

Gladys, Evelyn. *See* Kuehn, Herman

Glaspell, Susan, 752

699; speeches of, 624, 625, 630, 640, 646, 647, 749; Syndicalist Educational League and, 716; writings of, 354n7, 518, 637, 690, 699, 716, 726, 728, 749

Hawthorne, Nathaniel, 189

Hayes, Max, 729

Hayman, Miss, 447

Haymarket affair: anniversaries of, 77, 383–84, 400, 535, 606, 624; *New York Times* reporter retrospective commentary on, 473, 483–84; effect of hangings of accused, 105, 117, 341n11; EG and, 105, 483; as not reason for trial, 253; other events compared with, 96, 142, 163, 341, 425, 606; persons inspired to political action in response to, 35, 483–84. *See also* Chicago Anarchists

Haywood, William D. ("Big Bill"): arrests, 15, 644, 707, 709; biographical summary on, 699–700; Charles Thompson on, 478, 483–84; Debs and, 693; EG and, 408n25, 700; finances of, 32, 696; *International Socialist Review* and, 729; IWW and, 408n25, 474, 475, 696, 699, 700, 747, 766; Joe Hill and, 671; Labor Defense Committee founded by, 141, 756; Lawrence Strike Fund and, 765; miners and, 136; Mooney and, 708; Morris Hillquit's criticism of, 756; Patterson Strike and, 461, 644; personality of, 461; Socialist Party of America and, 127, 636, 640–41, 644, 699–700, 722, 746, 756; speeches of, 633, 640, 680, 711; Steunenberg and, 483–84; syndicalism and, 745; textile strikers and, 632; writings of, 700, 729, 732

Heaford, W., 766

Heap, Jane, 54, 730

Hearst, William Randolph, 16, 605, 609

Hearst family, 338

Hecht, Ben, 730

*Hedda Gabler* (Ibsen), 491, 647, 648, 652, 653

Heiminsha group/circle, 702

Heldge, Marx (Max Halbe), 659

Hemingway, Ernest, 730

Henri, Robert: art classes of, 480, 742; biographical summary on, 480n21, 700; Birth

Control Committee and, 674, 739; EG and, 160, 675; George Bellows and, 685; John Sloan and, 718; portrait of EG by, 52, 664

*Herald of Revolt: An Organ of the Coming Social Revolution* (London), 728

Herbert, Judge, 676

Herrick, Robert, 267

Herron, George D., 335

Hervé, Gustave, 697

Heslewood, Fred W., 728

Heterodoxy Club (Greenwich Village), 32, 57, 58, 135–36

Heywood, Ezra, 685, 725

High Treason Incident. *See* Kōtoku Incident

Hill, Joe (Joel Hägglund): arrest of, 652; Flynn and, 696; IWDL and, 748; sentencing and execution of, 122, 657, 668–71, 745, 768; writings of, 729

Hillquit, Morris, 467, 467n14, 700, 722, 756

Hinduism, 264

Hochstein, David (EG's nephew), 150, 514, 662

Hockin, Herbert, 747

Holmes, Lizzie, 725

Holmes, Mr. (hotel manager), 369, 370

Holmes, Sarah E., 685

Holmes, William T., 126, 395–98, 729

Homestead Lockout (Pa., 1892), 101, 256

homosexuality, 26, 150–52, 267, 520–21. See also "the intermediate sex"; bisexuality; lesbians

Horowitch, A., 498

Horr, Alexander, 722, 727

Houghton, Stanley, 646, 649, 652

Hourwich, Isaac, 664

How, James Eads, 757

Howe, Julia, 667

Howe, Marie Jennie, 667, 674, 739

Howell, Detective, 530

Hoyt, Helen, 676

Hubbard, Wood, 743

Hugo, Victor, 592

Hulburt, W., 658

Huneker, J. G., 50

hunger and black flag of anarchy, 487. *See* Black Flag of Anarchy

Hunt, George W. P., 397

Hunter, Robert, 722

Hurlbut, William, 652–53, 654, 656

Huxley, T. H., and evolution, 83

Hyndman, Henry Mayers, 335

IABSIW (International Association of Bridge and Structural Iron Workers), 434n2, 747–48

Ibsen, Henrik: biographical summary on, 701; Boyesen and, 688; *Brand*, 620, 647, 652; *The Comedy of Love*, 659; distribution of his works at EG's lectures, 438; *A Doll's House*, 5n8, 267, 647, 648; EG influenced by, 22; EG on, 49, 258, 334, 435, 448, 450, 463, 620, 637, 645, 646, 647, 648, 649, 652, 657, 658, 663, 697, 701; *An Enemy of the People*, 637, 638, 645, 666, 682, 701; Eric Morton and, 709; *Ghosts*, 138n438, 272, 301, 682, 710; *Hedda Gabler*, 491, 647, 648, 652, 653; marriage and, 267, 272, 286; *The Master Builder*, 647, 648, 652, 653; *Specter*, 659; spiritual and social revolt in the works of, 448–49; translations of the works of, 728

IBWA (International Brotherhood Welfare Association), 575

*The Iceman Cometh* (O'Neill), 151

ILGWU (International Ladies' Garment Workers' Union), 466n10

Illinois Central Railroad, 70

Imlay, Gilbert, 327

immigrant labor. *See* labor

immigrant life, EG diverges from common trajectory of, 7–8

imprisonment: of EG, 41–42, 160–62, 566, 579–80, 587, 593; EG on, 160–62, 579–80, 591, 594–95; EG's adeptness in averting, 44–45; intermittent, decentralized, fear-inducing, 40, 45; strategy of deliberately courting, 315. *See also* prison(s); *specific topics*

"In Defense of Assassination" (Thorpe), 87, 547n3, 658, 733, 765

individual will vs. groups/masses, EG on, 14. See also *Anarchism and Other Essays; Stirner*

individualism, 14, 85, 86, 415n7, 424

"individualist-anarchist," 106. *See also* anarchism

industrial sabotage, acts of, 170. *See also* IWW

*Industrial Worker* (Spokane, Wash.), 123, 124, 376–78, 728–29, 733, 746

Industrial Workers of the World (IWW): Adolph Wolff and, 477; AFL and, 127, 697; anarchists and, 147; Caroline Nelson and, 123; EG and, 122, 124, 127, 478–79; EG on, 372, 378, 402, 430, 468, 500; EG preaching anarchism to, 315–16; electoral engagement of, 131; "food, not politics," 481–83; free speech fights, 65, 76, 121–22, 146, 372, 496n7, 497; historical summary of, 743–47; history of, 474–76; "I. W. W. raids," 473–84; Jack White and, 506n9; membership of, 127, 153; New York local, 141; organizers and direct action, 121–22; PLM and, 109; Socialist Party of America and, 402, 430n5, 743, 746, 755, 756; *Solidarity* and, 732–33; strikes led by, 69–70, 122, 374–75, 461, 767; support for, 153; syndicalism and, 127; violence against, 120, 121, 165, 166; war industry and, 170

*Inferno* (Dante), 266

Ingar Defense Committee, 764

Ingersoll, Robert: biographical summary on, 701; mail censorship and, 228; religion and, 481; Walt Whitman and, 723

Inglis, Agnes Ann, 165, 166, 701

*Instead of a Magazine* (Minneapolis, Minn.), 729

"The Intellectual Proletarians" (EG), 51, 136, 444, 462–70

intellectuals: EG on, 75–76, 98, 139–40; interest in anarchism, 110; as proletarians, 140, 470n24, 476–77; Russian revolutionary vanguard, 76

"intermediate sex": "The Intermediate Sex" (EG), 152, 267n7, 520–21; *The Intermediate*

summary on, 703–4; conspiracy charge against, 239; EG on, 107, 239, 241; Kanno Suga and, 702; as Kropotkinist, 107; letters of, 731; photograph of, *232*; protest against trial of, 625; protests against the execution of, 97, 105, 233–35; role in Kōtoku Incident, 96–97; in San Francisco, 241; translations of Kropotkin's works, 308. *See also* Kōtoku Incident

Kōtoku Defense Committee, 306, 748–49

Kōtoku Incident (Japan), 105–7, 622, 702; Anna Walling on, 722; Berkman on, 233–35, 624, 626, 704, 749; Boyesen on, 624, 626, 749; BR and, 236, 624, 626, 749; compared with Ferrer, 241, 624; EG on, 236, 301–2, 624; end of trial for, 625; executions of defendants in, 626; Hapgood on, 234–35, 699; Hippolyte Havel and, 233–35, 624, 625, 699, 704, 749; international solidarity and, 81, 96–97; Jack London on, 624, 705, 749; Leonard Abbott on, 234–35, 624, 625, 749; Sadakichi Hartmann on, 233–35, 624, 749. *See also* Kanno Suga

Kōtoku Protest Conference Defense Committee Fund, 741, 765

Kōtoku protests, 306–10

Kōtoku Shusui Defense Fund, 728

Komroff, Manuel, 730, 742

Kotsch, Georgia, 739, 754

Kreymborg, Alfred, 676

Kropotkin, Peter: anarchism and, 126, 164, 399–401, 716; on *Anarchism and Other Essays*, 111, 318; biographical summary on, 704; BR and, 93, 623, 713; EG and, 22, 110, 112–13; EG on, 126, 130, 197, 219–20, 283, 324, 469; EG's letters to, 93, 111, 113, 130–31, 214, 317–20, 429–31; EG's tribute to, 399–401; George Seldes and, 718; Ida Eastman and, 693; imprisonment of, 126; on intellectuals, 110; Japanese and, 308; Kelly and, 703; Kōtoku and, 107, 703; on law, punishment, and government, 281; Max Nettlau and, 709–10; Octave Mirbeau and, 708; on PLM, 634; Russia and, 130; Saul

Yanovsky and, 724; seventieth birthday, 126, 384, 400, 641, 690, 722, 731, 759, 765; on sterilization and women's right to choose, 86; translations of the works of, 107, 308; violence and, 219–20; on wars, 82, 149, 533, 659, 663, 706, 715, 728–30; on workers, 111; writings in periodicals of, 149, 726, 727, 728, 731; writings of, 103, 288, 289, 704

Kropotkin, Sasha, 431

Kropotkin, Sophia, 431

Krupp family, 544, 545

Kucera, Joseph, 692, 733

Kuehn, Herman (pen names Evelyn Gladys and Willard Grosvenor): biographical summary on, 704; BR on, 350; EG and, 565; Great Adventure and, 755; *Instead of a Magazine* and, 729; writings of, 704, 726

Kutchan, Paul, 766

La Monte, Robert Rives, 729, 731

Labadie, Joseph Antoine: biographical summary on, 704; Carl Nold and, 710; criticism of EG, 114–15; Herman Kuehn and, 704; letters from EG to, 333–34; letters to EG, 331–32; Minneapolis Fellowship of Freedom and, 704, 755; writings of, 725, 733

labor: affinity to anarchist practice, 128; child, 3–4; closed- vs. open-shop workplaces, 68; EG's lectures on, 632, 635–36, 638, 655–56, 659, 662, 670; EG's position on issues of, 122; EG's relationship to, 47; immigrant, 9; lock-outs, 68; scab vs. union strikers, 68; "Self-Defense for Labor" (EG), 76, 454–57; skilled and unskilled, 47; as "the new slavery," 137–38; The Uprising of 20,000, 46n10; U.S. Commission on Industrial Relations findings, 69–74; violence, 2–3, 67–69, 165–66; war industry and, 46; working conditions of industrial workers, 3–4. *See also* American Federation of Labor; Industrial Workers of the World; McNamara brothers; Syndicalism; unions

on, 705; de Cleyre and, 692; EG on, 197, 215; Lexington Avenue bombing and, 761

Livshis, Jacob "Jake": biographical summary on, 705; de Cleyre and, 692; EG on, 197; Lexington Avenue bombing and, 761

Livshis, Peter, 215

Llewellyn Iron Works, 68. See also *Los Angeles Times* building bombing

Lloyd, J. William, 683, 725, 727

Loans, Grace, 535

Loans, Tom, 535

lockouts. *See* Homestead Strike

Lomas, Silvestre, 753

London, Charmian: biographical summary on, 321n1; EG and, 97, 336, 622; EG's letters to, 81, 111, 112, 241, 321–23; writings of, 115–16

London, Jack: anarchism and defense of EG by, 116; Anna Strunsky Walling and, 722; Berkman and, 116; biographical summary on, 705; EG and, 97, 112, 323, 335n1, 622; EG on, 111, 115–16, 322; EG's letters to, 81, 116, 241, 322n5, 335–36; Ferrer School and, 625; Kōtoku and, 241nn1–2, 624; on Kōtoku Incident, 624, 705, 749; MacMillan Company as publisher of, 336; speeches of, 624, 625, 749; writings of, 336, 631, 633, 722, 728, 729, 732, 733

London, Meyer, 737, 756

Loomis, Hulda L. Potter, 624, 630, 749, 750

Lorenzo, Anselmo, 694, 727

Lorwin, Lewis Levitzki. *See* Levine, Louis

Los Angeles (Calif.), 68, 132, 491

*Los Angeles Times*, 68, 132

*Los Angeles Times* building bombing (1910), 68–69, 109–10, 117, 342–44, 689–90, 706–7, 717, 739. *See also* Caplan and Schmidt case; McNamara brothers

Lott, August, 640

love, 24–25, 113–14, 134–35. *See also* free love; Reitman, Ben

"Love and Marriage" (EG), 7

Lowie, Robert H., 731

Lubbock, John, 287

Luccheni, Luigi, 401

Ludlow Massacre (Colo.): Berkman and, 655, 715, 757; John D. Rockefeller, Jr. and, 71–72, 147, 148; overview of, 136n435, 460n7, 495, 543; protesting the, 30, 78, 147, 458, 655, 757, 761; tent colony, U.S. militia and national guard, and, 70–72. *See also* Tarrytown silent vigil

Luhan, Mabel Dodge. *See* Dodge Luhan, Mabel

Lumber Strike, Lake Charles, La., 765

lynching, 12, 40, 43, 66n248, 117, 120, 486

Macario, Joseph, 583–84, 712

MacDonald, J. A., 729

MacDonald, J. Ramsay, 766

Mackay, John Henry, 273

Madero, Francisco: Anti-Reelectionist Party, 750; biographical summary on, 320n14; criticism of, 751; Debs and, 693; Díaz and, 108, 109; EG on, 320; Mexican Revolution and, 325, 623, 627, 750, 751; PLM and, 325n8, 629, 750, 751, 755; presidency and execution of, 108, 109, 631, 642; Ricardo Flores Magón and, 107, 623, 695; Socialist Party of America and, 107–8, 325n8, 630

Madison (Wis.), 198–200

*Madison Democrat* (Wis.), 199

Maeterlinck, Maurice, 642, 647, 648, 649, 652, 663

Magón brothers. *See* Flores Magón brothers

Mahan, Alfred Thayer, 715

Mahoney (Catholic socialist), 665

mail censorship. *See under* Comstock, Anthony. *See also* birth control literature; free speech

Maisel, Max N., 502n3, 705

"Majorities and Minorities" (EG), 19

Malatesta, Errico: arrest and imprisonment of, 702, 762; biographical summary on, 518n15, 706; BR and, 93, 623, 713; Errico Malatesta Fund, 762; on Ibsen, 701; "International Anarchist Manifesto on the War" signed by, 518, 663, 728; London anarchist movement and, 716; Marmol Fund and, 766; Max Nettlau and, 709–10

cause, 344; frame-up, trial defense fund, and plea bargain for, 69, 132, 151, 631–32, 696, 697, 707, 747–48; Gompers' support for, 696, 747; manifestos signed by, 734; Matthew Schmidt and, 77n288, 151–52, 343n4, 348n3, 492n3, 522n5, 533n3, 551n8, 585nn2–3, 632, 689, 690, 717, 724, 739–40, 748; in the media, 730; sentencing of, 632, 748; trial of, 116–17, 341–44, 348, 348n3, 631, 739–40, 747–48; Victor Berger and, 686; working class support for, 110. *See also* Caplan and Schmidt case; Darrow, Clarence Seward; *Los Angeles Times* building bombing

*ME. See Mother Earth*

Mella, Ricardo, 694

Mendoza, Bernardino, 753

Mendoza, Luz, 753

Merchants and Manufacturers Association, 68, 609. *See also Los Angeles Times* building bombing

Merlino, F. Saverio, 727

Mesabi Iron Range Strikers Defense Committee, 766

Mesabi Range, Minn., miners' strike (1916), 766

Metana, 692, 726

Metzkow, Max, 115

Meunier, Constantin, 448–49

Mexican farmers, 108

Mexican Liberal Party (PLM). *See* Partido Liberal Mexicano

Mexican Liberal Party (PLM) Junta Fund, 766

"The Mexican Revolution" (Turner), 320

Mexican Revolution of 1911, 81, 107–9, 112–13, 162–63, 315–16, 324–26; New York Mexican Revolutionary Conference, 324n1, 327–28. *See also* Flores Magón brothers; Madero, Francisco

Meyers, S., *458*, 736

MFOWTU (Marine Firemen Oilers and Water Tenders' Union), 744

Michaelis Strangeland, Katharina Marie (Karin Michaelis), 353, 354

Michel, Louise, 692, 707

Michigan: Detroit, 194, 331, 513; EG in, 300–301

Middleton, George, 450, 654, 656, 658, 660, 665

Midney, Frank, 633, 640

Mikhailovitch, Herman "Mickie," 216, 237, 649

Mikolasek, Joseph, 497n10, 636, 645

Milder, David, 748

militarism, 544

Millay, Edna St. Vincent, 58, 750

Miller, Jean-François, 448–49

Milwaukee (Wis.), 196, 200

mines in Colorado. *See* Ludlow Massacre

Minneapolis Fellowship of Freedom, 704

Minor, Robert: biographical summary on, 707; EG and, 52, 160, 627, 673; IWDL and, 748; Margaret Sanger and, 673; National Birth Control League and, 564; Preparedness Day Bombing and, 606, 762; *Revolt* and, 732; writings of, 52, *525, 608, 707, 726,* 730

"Minorities Versus Majorities" (EG), 85

Mirbeau, Octave Henri Marie, 469, 642, 663, 707–8, 728

Mob violence, "Are We Really Advancing?" (EG), 41; brutality of, 120; EG on psychology of, 582. *See also* San Diego; IWW; "outrage of San Diego"

*The Modern School* (New York; Ridgefield, N.J.; and Stelton, N.J.), 730–31

Modern School Association of North America, 677

Modern Schools. *See* Francisco Ferrer Center Modern School

Moisu, 508

Moloch (Old Testament), 576

Momento ("Memento"), Police Inspector, 253

Monatte, Pierre, 405

monogamy. *See* free love; polyamory

Monroe, Frank, 431, 498

Monroe, Lina, 498

*Monthly News Letter* (New York), 731

Mooney, A. J., 754

Mooney, Rena, 678, 681, 687, 708, 722, 748, 761. *See also* Preparedness Day Bombing

Mooney, Thomas J.: arrest of, 678, 681, 707, 761; biographical summary on, 708; *The Blast*, 34, 726; death of, 698; Fitzgerald and, 695; fund-raising meeting for, 700, 723; Harry Weinberger as attorney for, 722; Israel Weinberg and, 722; IWDL and, 707, 748; IWW, AFL, and, 122; labor forces and, 606; *The Masses*, 730; prosecution and trial of, 680, 722; protest and demonstration for, 681, 707; *Revolt: The Voice of the Militant Worker* and, 732; Robert Minor and, 730; Syndicalist League of North America and, 122; Warren Knox Billings and, 687; writings of, 726. *See also* Preparedness Day Bombing

Moore, Frances, 733

Moore, Fred, 634

Moore, Walter, 666–67

Morgan, Ed, 724

Morgan, J. P., 714

Morris, William, 134

Morrison, Arling, 651

Morrison, John G. (grocer), 651, 652

Morse, A. O., 767

Morton, Eric B. ("Eric the Red"): biographical summary on, 709; *The Blast* and, 726; Caplan-Schmidt Defense League and, 740; David Caplan and, 689; *Freedom* and, 727; IWDL and, 748

Morton, James F., Jr., 630, 641, 646, 694, 708, 711, 725, 729

Moses, books of, 183

Moss, Judge, 676

Most, Johann: biographical summary on, 709; EG on, 237, 244, 407; Livishes and, 705; memorialized by Baginski, 709; speeches and propaganda of, 244; writings of, 728

Moterman, 287

*Mother Earth: Monthly Magazine Devoted to Social Science and Literature* (*ME*, New York): Berkman and, 60, 77, 78, 105–6, 117, 125, 185, 619, 731, 760, 766; birth control and, 158–59, 571, 572, 584; covers of, 487, 494, 507, 525, 537; EG on, 192, 193, 549–50; EG's influence and, 8; EG's lectures and, 93, 173, 351; EG reports on lecture tours in, 41–62; finances of, 125, 158, 193, 392, 485, 572; goals of, 7, 60–62, 77, 122; influence of, 174; issue devoted to Kropotkin, 126; office and living quarters of, 93, 135, 511; office staff of, 60, 509–10; "San Diego outrage" and, 120, 121; sixth-year anniversary issue of, 105–7, 303–5; subscribers, circulation, and distribution of literature, pamphlets, and, 485, 572; W. S. Mayer and, 184

*Mother Earth* bookstore, 216

Mother Earth Publishing Association, 78, 103

*Mother Earth* Sustaining Fund/*Mother Earth* Propaganda Fund, 766–67

motherhood: EG on, 123, 354–55, 576; EG's rejection of the prospect of, 159; hypocrisy of the glorification of, 159; idealization of, 118; marriage and, 270–72. *See also* birth control

"Motherhood" (EG), 436

Moyer, Charles H. (president of Western Federation of Miners), 15, 456, 707, 709, 761–62

Muller, Roberto, 726–27

Murray, John, 721, 729, 754

Murray, Thomas Cornelius, 647, 648, 652, 654, 674

mutual aid, 128. *See also* Kropotkin; anarchism

Mylius, Edward F., 762

NAACP (National Association for the Advancement of Colored People), 722

Nafe, Gertrude E.: biographical summary on, 709; Caplan-Schmidt Defense Fund and, 760; EG and, 428, 433, 461, 498, 521; Ellen Kennan and, 703, 709

Nakata, Yoshiatsu, 241

Narodnaya Volya, 140; and Lenin, 99

Nathanson, William, 197, 741

Nation, Carry Amelia, as described by Margaret Anderson, 55, 393

National Birth Control League (NBCL), 157, 564, 738

National Convention of Reform Clubs and Trade Unions, 723

National Erectors Association (NEA), 747

National Liberal League, 749

National Security League (NSL), 33n124

National Women's Christian Temperance Union (WCTU), 414

NBCL (National Birth Control League), 157, 564, 738

NEA (National Erectors Association), 747

Neebe, Oscar, 676

Negri, Ada, 259

Nelson, Caroline (journalist for *Industrial Worker*): article on EG by, 123; biographical summary on, 376n2; birth control movement and, 738; EG on, 500; EG's critique of reformist socialist women and, 123; interviews with EG and/or BR, 139–40, 376–78, 729; periodicals contributed to by, 726, 729, 732, 733; support elicited for San Diego Free Speech Fight by, 124

Nelson, Reverend, 626

Neo-Malthusian League, 87, 89

Nettlau, Max, 709–10, 728

New Jersey, 229

*New Review* (New York), 731

New Woman movement of the 1890s, 16, 25, 32

New York Birth Control League, 739

*New York Call*, 109, 120

New York City, EG on, 561, 641, 651. *See also* Greenwich Village; Bohemian milieu

New York City Board of Education, 576

*New York Evening Telegram*, 613–14

New York Ferrer Center. *See* Francisco Ferrer Center Modern School

New York Ferrer Modern School. *See* Francisco Ferrer Center Modern School

New York Liberal Club, 57–58, 749–50

Newlander, Carl, 726

Nieman, Fred C. *See* Czolgosz, Leon F.

Nietzsche, Friedrich Wilhelm: anarchism and, 715; biographical summary on, 710; on Christianity, 420; concept of transvaluation, 14, 84–85, 91, 192, 414, 414n5; EG influenced by, 22, 84, 91, 420n1; EG on, 399, 427, 529; EG's course on, 130, 132; EG's identification with, 710; EG's lectures on, 645–49, 651, 656, 664–66, 668, 670, 671, 673, 675, 677; individualism of, 424; on slave morality, 420; on the "untimely," 463

"Nietzsche: The Intellectual Storm Center of Europe" (EG), 152

Nieuwenhuis, Ferdinand Domela, 407, 518, 518n16, 710

Nolan, Edward D., 760, 761. *See also* Preparedness Day Bombing

Nold, Carl: anti-Semitic attitudes of, 115; biographical summary on, 710; on EG, 115; EG on, 115, 331n2, 332, 333; Lucy Parsons and, 711

Nordau, Max, 660, 665

Nordfeldt, Bror, 752

North, Luke. *See* Griffes, James Hartness

Notkin, Natasha, 701, 753

NSL (National Security League), 33n124

"The Nude and the Prudes" (Fox), 764–65

Oatman, Mrs. M. T., 529

"Obedience, A Social Vice" (EG), 166

O'Brian, Joe, 752

O'Brien, Mary Heaton Vorse, 730, 752, 756, 760

obscenity laws and birth control, 156–59. *See also* birth control; Comstock Law

O'Carroll, Joseph, 143, 477, 653, 757

"October Twenty-Ninth, 1901" (EG), 337–40

O'Hare, Kate Richards, 726

O'Keefe, Judge, 584, 676

O'Kelly, Seamus, 656, 674, 675

Olarovsky, Alexandre Epitketovich, 322, 629

Olson, Culbert (governor of Calif.), 708, 717

Olson, Ruth S., 485

"On the Trail" (EG), 81

O'Neill, Eugene, 51–52, 58, 752

O'Neill, Joseph, 728

Fitzgerald and, 30, 60, 135, 453, 695; Frank
Walsh and, 73; free speech and, 91, 92,
146–47, 561, 655, 743; Harry Weinberger as
attorney for, 722; on Hauptmann's plays,
134; Hutchins Hapgood and, 32n123, 67,
297–99, 347; illustrations of, *203, 218,
381, 554, 595; Industrial Worker* and, 729;
interview of, 376–78; Joseph Fels and, 90–
91, 190; Kelly and, 703; Kōtoku Defense
Committee and, 749; Kōtoku Incident and,
233–36, 624, 626, 749; labor and, 62, 67,
146, 165–66, 497, 757; Leon Malmed and,
706; letters from EG to, 94–95, 97, 100,
114, 124, 149, 210–13, 215–22, 236–38, 246,
327–30, 379–82, 391–94, 441–43, 471–72,
511–13; letters to Berkman, 292–93; letters
to EG, 63, 103, 118, 140, 289–93, 347–50,
451, 452–53; Malatesta and, 93, 713; Max
Eastman and, 739; McNamara brothers
and, 734; meetings chaired by, 621, 627,
630, 631, 640, 680; Mexican Revolution
and, 630, 751; Minnie Rimer and, 616;
*Mother Earth* and, 60, 92, 103, 113, 120, 121,
125, 639; not allowed to speak in Detroit,
619; Nuna Seldes and, 388–89; organizing
skills, 146, 169, 214; personality of, 24, 63,
66–67, 104, 452–53, 497; as physician, 62;
police brutality and, 91, 119, 121; Portland
Birth Control League and, 738; preserving
anarchist history and, 103; Provincetown
Players and, 52; relations with women, 62,
63, 66, 94, 148; on repression, 117; reputation of, 90–91; sexuality of, 62, 63, 94, 103,
104, 113; Socialist Students' Club and, 200;
speeches of, *458, 595,* 623, 624, 629, 637,
651, 657, 665, 676, 680, 711; on Steffens,
348; struck by freight train in Spokane,
622; suspects harbored by, 67; talents, 92,
98; on target practice, 118; Thomas Keell
and, 702, 713; as tour and public outreach
manager of EG, 24, 30, 62, 103–4, 124–25,
130, 141, 169, 173, 291, 315, 328, 349, 379,
438, 472, 483, 526, 528, 529, 530; on
violence, 94–95, 148, 512; *Why and How*

*the Poor Should Not Have Children,* 17n54;
writings to periodicals by, 619, 728, 731,
732, 749, 755
Reitman, Ida (BR's mother), 125, 135, 140, 141,
148, 452, 650
Reitman, Lew (BR's brother), 442, 452
Reitzel, Robert: biographical summary on,
714; EG and, 194, 331n2; freedom and, 194;
portrait of, *554*; writings of, 685, 714
Rejsek, Vaclar, 624, 625, 749
Relief Society for the Political Exiles in
Siberia, 767
religion: concepts of heaven and hell, 129;
EG on, 9–12, *10*, 128, 155, 275–76; EG's
counters religious determinism, 83–86;
EG on Christian oppositional duality of the
body and soul, 128; fundamentalist revival
of, 83–84; *God and the State* (Bakunin),
11n30, 275, 552–53, 685; Marx on, 10; protest
meeting "against the growing Religious
Superstition," *339*; EG on Romans and
Jesus Christ, 129n417; separation of Church
and State, 59; "the gospel of non-resistance"
and, 128–30; theistic "tolerance," 554–55.
*See also* capitalism; Christianity; family;
government; Jesus Christ
Renan, Ernest, 421
*Reno Evening Gazette,* 136n434
reproductive rights and poverty. *See* poverty
and birth control
*Revolt* (New York), 732
*Revolt: The Voice of the Militant Worker* (San
Francisco), 732
Riddle, Claude, 750
Ridge, Lola, 730, 731, 742
Ries, W. F. (professor), 649
Rimer, Minnie Parkhurst, 165, 166, 616–17
Rincon, Juan, Jr., 753, 754
Rivera, Librado, 623, 639, 695, 732, 750, 751
Rjinders, G., 518
Robbins, Marcus, 634
Robinson, Boardman, 596, 675, 730
Robinson, Dudley W., 637
Robinson, Fred, 696

Schleis, P. R., 728

Schlossberg, James, 749

Schmidt, Carl, 332, 333, 749

Schmidt, Elizabeth Livermore, 717

Schmidt, Joseph, 677

Schmidt, Matthew A.: Belle Lavin and, 687; biographical summary on, 717; Boyesen and, 688; BR and, 67; Caplan and, 689–90, 717, 739–40; conviction of, 672, 675; Donald Vose and, 655, 659, 662; Jacob Margolis and, 151, 581, 586, 706; lawyers of, 581; McNamara brothers and, 77n288, 151–52, 343n4, 348n3, 492n3, 522n5, 533n3, 551n8, 585nn2–3, 632, 689, 690, 717, 724, 739–40, 748; trial of, 669. *See also* Caplan and Schmidt case; *Los Angeles Times* building bombing

Schnitzler, Arthur, 642

Schoonmaker, Edwin Davis, 653

Schopenhauer, Arthur, 388

Schroeder, Theodore Albert: advice to EG, 158; biographical summary on, 717–18; Birth Control League of Massachusetts and, 739; at birth control meetings, *593, 674;* Committee on Birth Control of New York and, 739; on EG, 630; Ferrer School and, 480; finances, 391; Free Speech League and, 120, 628, 670, 742–43; letters from EG to, 120, 158, 364–65, 568–69; Liberal Club and, 750; Margaret Sanger and, 547; speeches of, *593, 640, 674, 739;* writings of, 717–18, 731

Schulberg, Selig, 748

Schulder, Fred: biographical summary on, 194n8; Champney and, 223, 224; EG and, 194, 224, 619; letters to EG, 194–95; on Philosophic Anarchists, 307–8

Schwab, Justus, 58–59, 709

Scripps, E. W., 707

*Seattle Post-Intelligencer,* 133

Second International (Socialist): anarchist expulsion and, 82; EG's lectures on the war and, 659, 662, 667

Seldes, George S., 389, 718, 755

Seldes, Nunia Berman: Berkman and, 125; biographical summary on, 718; EG's friendship with, 104, 125; EG's letters to, 104–5, 300–302, 388–90; Kōtoku Defense Committee and, 749, 765

"Self-Defense for Labor" (EG), 76, 454–57

Seltzer, Thomas, 730

Sercombe, Parker, 631

Sernaker, Bernard, 630, 734

Serrato, Jose Angel, 753

settlement house movement, EG on, 133

Severance, Caroline M., 667

Severance, Juliet H., 734

"Sex, the Great Element of Creative Work" (EG), 355

sex enslavement, 36–40, 118, 287. *See also* prostitution

sex roles, 25–26, 86. *See also* feminism; gender; women

sexuality: codes used by EG and BR for body parts, 94; distribution of birth control and, 86–90; EG's coded letters, 124, 125; Freud vs. EG on, 118–19; Granville Stanley Hall on, 380. *See also* free love; homosexuality; polyamory; white slavery

Shakespeare, William, 710

Shatov (Shatoff), William, 519, 640, 660, 664, 687

Shaw, George Bernard: *Androcles and the Lion,* 675; Augustin Hamon on, 49; Benjamin Tucker and, 230n10; on birth control, 560; Comstock on censorship of the works of, 230; *The Devil's Disciple,* 656; distribution of the plays of, 103; *The Doctor's Dilemma,* 647, 664; EG on, 37, 230, 279–80, 435, 450, 560, 583, 591, 620, 642, 647, 648, 649, 652, 656, 658, 660, 664, 675; *Fanny's First Play,* 660, 675; "First Aid to Critics," 591; "The Impossibilities of Anarchism," 279–80; *Major Barbara,* 591, 620; *Misalliance,* 660; *Mrs. Warren's Profession,* 37, 182, 649; *The Shewing-Up of Blanco Posnet,* 647, 648, 652; translations of the works of, 728; *Widower's Houses,* 652, 656

shingle weavers' strike in Everett, Wash., 165–66

Shipley, Minot "Maynard" (professor), 648, 650

Shippey, Hartwell S., 728

Shippy, George: BR on, 201, 202, 205; EG and, 201, 202; free speech and, 201, 202, 205; Harry Averbuch and, 202; Lazarus Averbuch and, 91, 193n3, 201n1, 255; in the media, 201, 205; police brutality and, 201; son of, 202; unemployed parade and, 201

shirtwaist makers strike of 1909 (New York City), 466

Sigel, Tobias, 333

Silverstein, Selig, 193, 203

Simms, Judge, 674

Simons, Algie Martin, 195n12, 722

Simpson, Herman, 731

Sims, Robert B., 397

Sinclair, Upton, 58, 466–67, 625, 655, 690, 726, 742, 750

single tax, 107, 308, 310, 585n1, 603n6, 727, 754–55

single-taxers, and free speech, 90; Great Adventure movement, 755. *See also* Fels, Joseph

Sloan, Anna, 674, 739

Sloan, John: biographical summary on, 718; EG and, 160, 675; *Masses* and, 685

Smith, Abner S., 196

Smith, Rhoda ("Smithy"), 442, 509, 650

Smith, Walker C., 728, 729, 732, 733, 746

Snyder, Thomas F., 297, 298

"So-Called I. W. W. Raids Really Hatched by Schoolboys" (Thompson), 473–84

*Social and Revolutionary Significance of Modern Drama, The* (EG), 134

"The Social Aspects of Birth Control" (EG), 158–59, 573–78

social clubs, ethnic, racial, and political affiliations through, 59. *See also* Social Science Club

Social Science Club (Chicago), 197

*The Social Significance of the Modern Drama* (EG), 28, 49, 52, 448–50, 459, 490

socialism: EG on, 437–38; EG's lectures on, 632, 635–36, 638, 655–56, 659, 662, 670

"Socialism, Caught in the Political Trap" (EG), 103

Socialist Party of America (SPA): anarchism and, 755; constitution of, 636, 641; criticism of, 14, 755; EG's discussion of, 14; electoral engagement of, 131; first candidate elected to Congress, 624; Haywood and, 127, 636, 641, 644, 699–700, 722, 746, 756; leadership hierarchy of, 4; Madero and, 107; Magón brothers and, 107; on sabotage, 14, 127, 196, 430, 756

Socialist Revolutionary Party (PSR), 130–31, 429

Socialist Students' Club (Milwaukee, Wis.), 200

socialists: anarchists and, 14, 92, 103, 112, 289, 350, 358; BR on, 206; Champney on, 225; EG and, 45; EG barred from speaking in halls controlled by, 637, 755; EG on, 14, 103, 195–96, 219, 221, 322

Society for the Suppression of Vice, 87

Socrates, 129, 425

*Solidarity* (New Castle, Pa.), 732–33

Solotaroff, Dr. Hillel, 640, 641, 731

Sonnichsen, Albert, 731

Sorel, Georges, 403, 409–10

South, EG's relationship to the, 41, 45

Sowerby, Githa, 649

Soyer, Moses, 52

SPA. *See* Socialist Party of America

Spain, political violence in, 252, 261–62, 684

Spanish Fund, 768

Spanish Modern Schools, 59. *See also* Ferrer, education

Spargo, John, 755

Special Publicity Fund (Caplan and Schmidt), 768

Speed, George, 708

Spencer, Herbert, 728

Sperry, Almeda, 124–25, 132–33, 386–87

Spielman, Jean E., 733

Spies, John, 431, 498, 760

Spiridonova, Maria Aleksandrovna, 425–26

Spokane, Wash., 123, 622

*Spokane Chronicle,* 205

*Spokane Review,* 205

Sprading, Charles T., 637, 646, 750

Spreckels, John, 378

St. John, Vincent, 700, 708, 725, 729, 732

St. Louis (Mo.), 200, 245

*St. Louis Republican,* 110

St. Patrick's Cathedral (N.Y.), bombing
    attempt at, 77

Stadter, F. W. (acting municipal judge,
    Portland), 528, 530

Stahl, Mrs. George, 380

Stamm, G. W., 754

Starrett, Walter. *See* Van Valkenburgh,
    Warren Starr

Steeglis, Z., 767

steel workers. *See* Homestead Strike

Steele, Wilbur Daniel, 752

Steffens, Lincoln: BR on, 348; Clarence
    Darrow and, 69, 132, 631–32; EG on, 480,
    748; Free Speech League and, 628, 651,
    743; IWDL and, 748; Liberal Club and, 750;
    McNamara brothers and, 69, 132, 348, 522,
    631–32, 707, 747, 748; *The Modern School*
    and, 731; National Birth Control League
    and, 738; speeches of, 640, 651, 748

Steinlin, Théophile Alexandre, 469

Stephens, G. Frank, 753, 755, 764

Stephenson, Cora Bennett, 479, 646, 647,
    742

Stetzle, Charles, 227, 229, 230, 231

Steunenberg, Frank (governor of Idaho), 15,
    484n28, 709

Stewart, Dr., 221–22

Stieglitz, Alfred: biographical summary on,
    514n1; *Camera Work,* 699; EG and, 52–53,
    150; letter from EG to, 514

Stillman, Clara Gruening, 738

Stirner, Max: EG and, 14, 22, 84–85, 86,
    415n7, 420n11; EG on, 85, 674; *The Ego and
    Its Own,* 85, 415n7, 416, 674, 726; individu-
    alism of, 14, 85, 86, 415n7, 424; on morality,

415n7; rejection of universal concepts, 84,
    85; religion, atheism, and, 420; on revolu-
    tion vs. continuous state of rebellion, 85;
    toppling the "Holy Trinity of God, the State,
    and the Family," 11–12

Stodell, S. A., 764

Stodola, Gilbert, 742

Stokes, J. G. Phelps, 322, 625, 630, 718, 742

Stokes, Rose Pastor: arrested, 590; biographi-
    cal summary on, 718–19; birth control
    and, 160, 587, 588, 597, 676; on EG, 630;
    EG and, 57, 322, 675; EG on, 587, 590,
    597, 676; Ferrer School and, 625; Kōtoku
    Defense Committee and, 749; literature
    distributed by, 587, 588, 590, 597, 676;
    speeches of, 587, 593, 625, 676, 739; at Walt
    Whitman's birthday celebration, 676; as
    woman loyal to EG, 157; writings of, 719,
    732, 741

Strauss, David Friedrich, 421

Strauss, Richard, 231n11

streetcar operators on strike (Philadelphia),
    208n1

Streit, 223, 224

Strindberg, August: EG and, 22, 731; EG on,
    49, 435, 448–50, 463, 469, 639, 641, 646,
    647, 648, 649, 652, 663, 668, 669, 682;
    *Poet Lore* and, 731

Strunsky, Annie. *See* Walling, Anna Strunsky

Strunsky, Rose, 195, 335, 630, 731, 732, 749

Sudermann, Herman, 49, 647, 648, 652, 653,
    659

suffrage: direct action and, 284; reform and,
    136n434; universal, 284; limitations of/
    and women's, 5–6, 48–49; "and women of
    Titanic, 119, 356–57;

Sugako. *See* Kanno Suga

Suhr, Herman D., 658, 745, 768

Sullivan, John J. (San Francisco judge), 712

Summers, Pauline B. C., 529

Sunday, Billy (born William Ashley): on EG,
    84; EG on, 84, 665, 668, 669; *Mother Earth*
    cover of, 525; revivalism and, 83; revivalism
    and, 555, 555n8; war supporters and, 155

Tolstoy, Leo Nikolayevich *(continued)*
661, 664, 679, 680–82; *The Fruits of Enlightenment,* 647, 649; George Seldes and, 718; Hall on, 698; Kōtoku translation of the works of, 234, 703; *Kreutzer Sonata,* 691; Octave Mirbeau and, 708; *The Power of Darkness,* 647; *Resurrection,* 229; *The Slavery of Our Times,* 265n39; spiritual and social revolt in the works of, 448–49

Tompkins, George, 762

Tracy, Thomas, 763

"The Tragedy of Women's Emancipation" (EG), 5, 7, 301. *See also* suffrage

transvaluation, 14, 84–85, 91, 192, 414. *See also* Nietzsche

Traubel, Horace L.: biographical summary on, 720; New York Liberal Club and, 750; speech at Walt Whitman's birthday celebration, 676; writings of, 720, 726, 731, 733

Trautmann, William E., 729, 746

Travaglio, Eugene, 733

Treitschke, Heinrich von, 542

Tresca, Carlo: arrested for incitement to riot, 642, 681; biographical summary on, 720; Conference of the Unemployed and, 757; farewell dinner for EG hosted by, 665; Flynn and, 696; iron ore miners strike organized by, 676; IWW and, 766; Labor Defense Committee founded by, 141, 756; speeches of, 642, 653, 664, 724, 740; at Union Square meeting, 478, 653; writings of, 733

Tressols, Police Inspector/Chief, 252–53

Triangle Shirtwaist Factory fire (New York City, 1911), 2–3, 70, 454n1

Tridon, André, 479–80, 745

Trnka, Alois, 676

Trombetti, C., 519

"The Tsar and 'My Jews'" (EG), 11. *See also* Jews/Jewish culture and religion

Tucker, Benjamin R.: on anarchy and socialism, 306; biographical summary on, 720; George Bernard Shaw and, 230n10; on resisting oppression, 307; Tolstoy and, 719; Walt Whitman and, 723; works translated by, 708

Tucker, Irwin St. John, 758

Tucker, John Francis, 675

Tudarman, Ekman, 659

Turgenev, Ivan, 29; biographical summary on, 720; EG on, 679, 680; *Fathers and Sons,* 469; spiritual and social revolt in the works of, 448–49; translations of the works of, 728

Turner, Al, 769

Turner, Ethel Duffy, 625, 628, 721, 732, 751

Turner, George Kibbe, 181, 182, 467

Turner, John Kenneth: biographical summary on, 720–21; writings of, 313, 320, 729, 731

Tveitmoe, Olaf A., 523n9, 678, 689, 740, 748

Tynan, Thomas J., 397

UHT. *See* United Hebrew Trades

Ulrich, Henry, 352

Umberto I of Italy, 262, 263, 688

unemployed: Conference of the Unemployed, 477, 486n6, 735, 756–57; demonstrations of the, 141–43, 317, 474n3, 478–79; movement, 508, 756–58

Unemployed and Anti-Militarist League Fund, 760, 769

Unemployed Fund, 769

unemployment, 146

Union of Russian Workers, 164

Union Square meetings, 113, 165, 613

unions: abolitionists' relationship with trade, 120; EG on, 47, 127, 609; EG's relationship to, 8–9, 47; gradualists, 127, 128; labor movement failures, 127, 128; leadership hierarchies of, 4; militants, 76–79, 127; recruitment, 132; socialist party and, 8; syndicalism and, 127; tactics of, 46–47, 76–79, 122, 127, 136 *(see also* direct action; labor strikes); Tom Mann lectures about British and French, 136; treasury of, 128

United Hebrew Trades (UHT), 34–35, 477

United Mine Workers (UMW). *See* Ludlow Massacre

Untermann, Ernest, 726

The Uprising of 20, 000 (New York City), 46n10

"An Urgent Appeal to My Friends" (EG), 571–72

U.S. Commission on Industrial Relations, facts, analysis, and pro-labor findings on industrial violence, 69–74, 72–74

U.S. Grant Hotel (San Diego), 369, 377

Uthoff, H. C., 530, 738

Vaillant, Auguste, 249, 256–59, 260

Valdinoci, Carlo, 726

Van der Weyde, William, 222, 741

van Diepen, Nestor Ciele, 518

Van Valkenburgh, Warren Starr (pseudonym Walter Starrett): biographical summary on, 721; EG's letters to, 53, 157, 160, 161, 163, 564–65, 587–88, 602–4; writings of, 604, 726, 729

Van Zant-Spie, Nina, 725

Vanzetti, Bartolomeo, 726

"Variety or Monogamy, Which" (EG), 24

Vasco, Neno, 766

Vasquez, Leonardo L., 753

"Vice, Its Cause and Cure," 391

"Victims of Morality" (EG), 413–19, 555n10

Vidal, Jaime: Alexander Aldamas Defense Fund and, 759; Berkman and, 686; biographical summary on, 721; Ferrer School and, 625; Francisco Ferrer Association and, 741; Kōtoku Defense Committee and, 749; on Kōtoku Incident, 624, 749; Mexican Revolution and, 630, 751, 768; MFOWTU and, 744; Rangel-Cline Defense Fund and, 754; speeches of, 624, 625, 630, 749, 751; writings of, 727, 729, 741

vigilantes. *See* "outrage of San Diego"

Vignati, G., 519

Villa, Francisco "Pancho," 713

Villareal, Antonio I., 623, 695, 732, 750

violence: anarchism and, 19–20, 164, 207–9, 610; desperation and, 610–11; EG on, 19–20, 76, 121, 133, 134, 219–20, 341–44, 437, 508n4 (*see also* "The Psychology of Political Violence"); EG on Czolgosz and, 337–340; EG's concept of intelligent violence, 95; erosion of civil liberties in response to, 67; European acts of political, 256–63; government, 101; inciting, 67–69, 76, 341–44; industrial, 74–76, 101; against IWW, 120, 121, 165, 166; labor, 2–3, 67–69, 165–66; labor's right to respond to attacks with, 454–457; mob, 65–67; as retribution against tyranny in Africa, England, France, Germany, India, Spain, the U.S., 101; socialist vs. anarchist attitudes toward, 67. *See also* "In Defense of Assassination"; Lexington Avenue Bombing; McNamara brothers; "outrage of San Diego"; Preparedness Day Bombing

Vlag, Piet, 730

Vogl, A. (lawyer), 497

Vogle, Albert, 635

Volonta (Italian anarchist group), 163–64

Voltaire, François Marie Arouet de, 480, 701

Voltairine de Cleyre Publication Fund, 769

von Freytag-Loringhoven, Elsa, 56

Vorse, Mary Heaton. *See* O'Brien, Mary Heaton Vorse

Vose, Donald, 151, 535–36, 655, 662, 663, 689, 690, 717

Vose, Gertie, 151, 690, 717

voting, EG on, 131, 283. *See also* suffrage; elections

Wadham, James E. (mayor of San Diego), 368

Wald, Lillian, 81, 97, 239–40, 721

Walker, Edwin C., 630, 711, 750

Walkowitz, Abraham, 52

Walling, Anna Strunsky: biographical summary on, 722; EG and, 58, 195, 322; EG's letters to, 162, 600–601; New York Liberal Club and, 58; speeches of, 640, 641, 674

Williams, B. H., 732, 733, 746, 754

Wilson, James, 728

Wilson, Jefferson "Keno" (San Diego Chief of Police), 368, 370, 371, 377

Wilson, President Woodrow: on anarchists, 13; biographical summary on, 539n5; compared with Theodore Roosevelt, 540; EG on, 539–42, 603; elected president, 640, 715; Frank Walsh on, 73–74; freedom of expression and, 167; Joe Hill and, 669; Lilian Wald and, 721; Ludlow protest and, 655, 761; organized labor and, 33n124; preparedness campaign, 673; U.S. Commission on Industrial Relations and, 69; war, peace, and, 32–33, 73–74, 539–42, 603, 673

Winchevsky, Morris, 728

Winn, Gussie, 723n1

Winn, Ross: biographical summary on, 723; death of, 383, 639; Gussie Winn Fund and, 764; Joseph Labadie and, 331, 334; writings of, 725

Winslow, Horatio, 730

Wirth, R., 754

Wisconsin (University of), campus free speech conflicts and, 92

Witcop, Milly, 715

Witcop, Rose, 534, 728, 733

Wobblies (IWW members). See Industrial Workers of the World

Wolfe, Lilian, 702

Wolfe, M., 647, 648, 652

Wolff, Adolf, 700; Anti-Militarist League Fund and, 760; biographical summary on, 477n12, 723; Conference of the Unemployed and, 757; EG on, 541n14, 647; Leonard Abbott on, 477; *Modern School* and, 730; poetry of, 477, 742; *Revolt* and, 732; writings of, 723

Wolff, Regina, 736

Wollstonecraft, Mary, 113–14, 327, 353, 631

*The Woman Rebel* (W.R., New York): birth control and, 737; ceased publication, 87; EG on, 144, 492, 500; finances and distribution of, 492, 499, 691; first issue of, 652; legal problems and censorship of, 87, 143, 653, 658, 673, 683, 738; Margaret Sanger and, 87, 492, 499, 652, 653, 658, 673, 683, 737, 738; "No Gods, No Masters" subtitle of, 87; overview of, 733

"Woman Suffrage" (EG), 48, 49

women: bisexuality of, 32n123; EG on, 5–7, 15–17, 105, 113–14, 123–24, 156; EG's friendships with, 32n123, 57, 123, 125, 156; feminism and, 16, 25, 32, 118–19, 354; gender roles of, 25–26, 86; morality and, 416–19; prostitution of, 37, 39, 102, 187–88, 285–86; reformist socialist, 123; suffrage for, 5–6, 48–49; white slavery of, 37–38, 40, 120, 181n1. *See also* marriage

Women's Drama Club, 130

women's movement. *See* feminism

Women's Trade Union League (WTUL), 454n1, 466n10

Wood, Charles Erskine Scott: biographical summary on, 526, 723–24; Caplan and Schmidt case and, 522, 549n1, 550, 724, 740; EG and, 152, 526, 529, 590, 669; letters from EG to, 119–20, 362–63, 522–24, 549–51; meetings chaired by, 658, 668; on publicity vs. funds, 768; raised EG's bail, 527, 528, 529, 668; writings of, 549, 726, 730, 731, 732

Wood, Clement, 676

Woolf, Lillian Gertrude, 519, 519n24

Woolman, H. M., 734

working class: and industrial organization, 402–412; commonalities between intellectuals and, 136; EG on intermittent opposition to anarchism among, 110–11; EG on lack of radicalism among, 242–244; EG on race and class injustice in, 120; and sabotage, 408–409

World War I: anarchists and, 82, 515n1; EG on, 170, 658, 660, 661–71, 673, 675, 678; "International Anarchist Manifesto on the War," 149–50, 515–19; pre-war in the U.S., 32–35, 83, 137–38, 153–54, 170, 533, 537, 615; protesting against, 166